Pearson New International Edition

Financial Management
Principles and Applications
Titman Keown Martin
Twelfth Edition

PEARSON

Pearson Education Limited
Edinburgh Gate
Harlow
Essex CM20 2JE
England and Associated Companies throughout the world

Visit us on the World Wide Web at: www.pearsoned.co.uk

ISBN 10: 1-292-02306-6
ISBN 13: 978-1-292-02306-9

British Library Cataloguing-in-Publication Data
A catalogue record for this book is available from the British Library

Printed in the United States of America

Table of Contents

Glossary
Sheridan J Titman
1

1. Getting Started
Sheridan J Titman
9

2. Firms and the Financial Market
Sheridan J Titman
27

3. Understanding Financial Statements, Taxes, and Cash Flows
Sheridan J Titman
49

4. Financial Analysis
Sheridan J Titman
89

5. Time Value of Money – The Basics
Sheridan J Titman
141

6. Time Value of Money – Annuities and Other Topics
Sheridan J Titman
173

7. An Introduction to Risk and Return
Sheridan J Titman
209

8. Risk and Return
Sheridan J Titman
241

9. Debt Valuation and Interest Rates
Sheridan J Titman
275

10. Stock Valuation
Sheridan J Titman
323

11. Investment Decision Criteria
Sheridan J Titman
355

12. Analyzing Project Cash Flows
Sheridan J Titman
401

13. Risk Analysis and Project Evaluation
Sheridan J Titman   **439**

14. The Cost of Capital
Sheridan J Titman   **477**

15. Capital Structure Policy
Sheridan J Titman   **515**

16. Dividend Policy
Sheridan J Titman   **559**

17. Financial Forecasting and Planning
Sheridan J Titman   **587**

18. Working Capital Management
Sheridan J Titman   **611**

19. International Business Finance
Sheridan J Titman   **643**

20. Corporate Risk Management
Sheridan J Titman   **671**

Index   **707**

Glossary

Accounting break-even analysis A type of analysis to determine the level of sales necessary to cover total operating costs and produce a zero level of net operating income or EBIT.

Accounts payable deferral period The average period of time the firm uses to repay its trade creditors.

Accounts payable The credit suppliers extend to the firm when it purchases items for its inventories.

Accounts receivable Credit sales that have not yet been collected.

Accounts receivable turnover ratio The number of times that accounts receivable are rolled over each year.

Accredited investor Investor who is permitted to invest in certain types of higher-risk investments. These investors include wealthy individuals, corporations, endowments, and retirement plans.

Accumulated depreciation The sum of all depreciation expenses that have been deducted from the firm's income statement in previous periods for the plant and equipment the firm currently has on its balance sheet.

Acid-test (quick) ratio A measure of firm liquidity that has as its numerator current assets minus inventories, or "quick" assets, compared to current liabilities in the denominator.

Agency costs The costs incurred by a firm's common stockholders when the firm's management makes decisions that are not in the shareholders' best interest but instead further the interests of the management of the firm.

Agency problem Conflicts that arise out of the separation of management and ownership of the firm.

American option An option that may be exercised at any time up through the contract's expiration date.

American Stock Exchange (AMEX) The nation's second-largest floor-based exchange.

Amortized loan A loan that is paid off in equal periodic payments.

Amortizing bond Bonds that are paid off in equal periodic payments with those payments including part of the principal (par value) along with the interest payments.

Annual percentage rate (APR) The interest rate paid or earned in one year without compounding. It is calculated as the interest rate per period (for example, per month or week) multiplied by the number of periods during which compounding occurs during the year *(m)*.

Annuity A series of equal dollar payments for a specified period of time.

Annuity due An annuity in which the payments occur at the beginning of each period.

Annuity future value interest factor The value, $\left[\dfrac{(1 + i)^n - 1}{i}\right]$, used as a multiplier to calculate the future value of an annuity.

Annuity present value interest factor The value, $\left[\dfrac{1 - \dfrac{1}{(1 + i)^n}}{i}\right]$, used as a multiplier to calculate the present value of an annuity.

Arbitrage The process of buying and selling in more than one market to make riskless profits.

Arithmetic average return The sum of the set of returns divided by their number.

Asked rate The rate a bank or foreign exchange trader "asks" the customer to pay in home currency for foreign currency when the bank is selling and the customer is buying. Also known as the selling rate.

Average collection period The average number of days required to collect on the firm's credit sales.

Average tax rate The ratio of the tax liability divided by taxable income.

Balance sheet A financial statement that contains a summary of the firm's assets (everything of value the company owns), liabilities (the firm's debts), and shareholders' equity (the money invested by the company owners).

Bank transaction loan An unsecured short-term bank credit made for a specific purpose.

Basis point One percent equals 100 basis points.

Basis risk Risk associated with imperfect hedging that arises because the asset underlying the futures contract is not identical to the asset that underlies the firm's risk exposure.

Benchmarking Comparing the firm's current and proposed capital structures to those of a set of firms that are considered to be in similar lines of business and consequently subject to the same types of risk.

Beta coefficient A measure of the relationship between the returns of a security such as a share of common stock and the returns of the portfolio of all risky assets.

Bid rate The rate at which the bank buys the foreign currency from the customer by

paying in home currency. The bid rate is also known as the buying rate.

Bid-asked spread The difference between the bid quote and ask price quote.

Block holding The situation when one investor holds 10,000 shares or more of a single stock.

Block trade A transaction involving 10,000 shares or more by one holder.

Bond A long-term (10-year or more) promissory note issued by a borrower, promising to pay the owner of the security a predetermined amount of interest each year.

Bond indenture A written agreement between the bond issuer and bondholders specifying the terms of the bond.

Bond rating The credit rating given to a bond, providing an indication of the creditworthiness of the bond.

Book value per share Common equity divided by the number of outstanding shares of common stock.

Break-even analysis A type of analysis used to identify the level of sales needed to meet the costs associated with a project.

Buying rate The rate at which the bank buys the foreign currency from the customer by paying in its home currency. The buying rate is also known as the bid rate.

Call option A contract that gives its holder the right to purchase a given number of shares of stock or some other asset at a specified price over a given time period.

Call provision A provision that entitles the corporation to repurchase its preferred stock from its investors at stated prices over specified periods.

Capital Asset Pricing Model (CAPM) A model that describes the theoretical link between the expected rate of return on a risky security such as a share of stock and the security's risk as measured by its beta coefficient.

Capital budgeting The decision-making process used to analyze potential investments in fixed assets.

Capital market The market for long-term financial instruments.

Capital rationing A situation in which a firm's access to capital is limited such that it is unable to undertake all projects that have positive NPVs.

Capital structure The mix of debt and equity securities a firm uses to finance its assets.

Capital structure The mix of long-term sources of funds used by the firm.

Cash break-even point The level of sales that covers total cash operating costs (specifically excluding consideration for depreciation expense).

Cash budget A plan for a future period that details the sources of cash a firm anticipates receiving and the amounts and timing of cash it plans to spend.

Cash conversion cycle The operating cycle (average collection period plus the inventory conversion period or days of sales in inventories) less the accounts payable deferral period.

Cash dividend Cash paid directly to stockholders.

Cash flow from operations The portion of the firm's total cash flow resulting from its operating activities.

Cash flow statement A financial statement that reports cash received and cash spent by the firm over a period of time, usually one quarter of a year or a full year.

Cash return The monetary increase (decrease) in the value of an investment measured over a particular span of time.

Collateral A borrower's pledge of specific property to a lender, to secure repayment of a loan.

Commercial bank A financial institution that accepts demand deposits, makes loans, and provides other services to the public.

Commercial paper A money market security with a maturity of 1 to 270 days, issued (sold) by large banks and corporations, and that is backed by the issuing firm's promise to pay the face amount on the maturity date specified on the note.

Commodity futures A contract to buy or sell a stated commodity (such as wheat and corn as well as metals, wood products, or fibers) at a specified price and at a specified future date.

Common stock A form of equity security that represents the residual ownership of the firm.

Compound interest The situation in which interest paid on the investment during the first period is added to the principal and, during the second period, interest is earned on the original principal plus the interest earned during the first period.

Constant dividend growth rate model A common stock valuation model that assumes that dividends will grow at a constant rate forever.

Contribution margin The difference between the selling price per unit and the variable cost per unit.

Conversion feature A feature of some debt that allows the bondholder to convert the bond into a prescribed number of shares of the firm's common stock.

Convertible bond A debt security that can be converted into a firm's stock at a pre-specified price.

Corporate bond A bond issued by a corporation.

Corporation A business entity that legally functions separate and apart from its owners.

Correlation coefficient A measure of the degree to which the variation in one variable is related to the variation in another. The coefficient ranges from −1 for a perfectly negative relationship to 1 for perfectly positive dependence.

Cost of capital The discount rate that is used to calculate the firm's overall value.

Cost of common equity (k_{cs}) The rate of return the firm must earn in order to satisfy the requirements of its common stockholders.

Cost of debt The rate that has to be received from an investment in order to achieve the required rate of return for the creditors. This rate must be adjusted for the fact that an increase in interest payments will result in lower taxes. The cost is based on the debtholders' opportunity cost of debt in the capital markets.

Cost of goods sold The cost of producing or acquiring the products or services that the firm sold during the period covered by an income statement.

Cost of preferred equity The rate of return that must be earned on the preferred stockholders' investment in order to satisfy their required rate of return. The cost is based on the preferred stockholders' opportunity cost of preferred stock in the capital markets.

Coupon interest rate The percentage of the par value of the bond that will be paid out annually in the form of interest.

Coupon rate The amount of interest paid per year expressed as a percent of the face value of the bond.

Credit default swap An insurance contract that pays off in the event of a credit event such as default or bankruptcy.

Credit risk The risk of loss as a result of default on a financial obligation; also referred to as default risk.

Credit scoring A numerical evaluation of the creditworthiness of an individual borrower based on the borrower's current debts and history of making payments in a timely basis.

Credit spread The spread, or difference in interest rates (generally expressed in terms of basis points), of the corporate bond over a U.S. Treasury security of the same maturity.

Cross rate The exchange rate between two foreign currencies, neither of which is the currency of the domestic country.

Cumulative preferred stock Preferred stock that requires all past unpaid preferred stock dividends to be paid before any common stock dividends are declared.

Cumulative voting Voting in which each share of stock allows the shareholder a number of votes equal to the number of directors being elected. The shareholder can then cast all of his or her votes for a single candidate or split them among the various candidates.

Currency swap The exchange or trading of debt obligations whose payments are denominated in different currencies.

Current assets Cash plus other assets that the firm expects to convert into cash within 12 months or less.

Current liabilities The debts of the firm that must be repaid within a period of 12 months or less.

Current ratio A measure of firm liquidity equal to the ratio of current assets to current liabilities.

Current yield The ratio of the annual interest payment to the bond's market price.

Date of record The date on which the company looks at its records to see who receives dividends.

Days' sales in inventory Inventory divided by cost of goods sold per day (Cost of goods ÷ 365).

Debenture Any unsecured long-term debt.

Debt Money that has been borrowed and must be repaid. This includes such things as bank loans and bonds.

Debt ratio Total liabilities divided by total assets.

Debt securities Financial instruments that represent loans to corporations. Long-term debt securities are called bonds and can be bought and sold in the bond market.

Declaration date The date upon which a dividend is formally declared by the board of directors.

Default-risk premium A premium reflecting the default risk of the note or bond.

Defined benefit plans A company retirement plan, such as a pension plan, in which a retired employee receives a specific amount based on his or her salary history and years of service.

Defined contribution plans A company retirement plan, such as a 401(k) plan, in which the employee elects to contribute some amount of his or her salary to the plan and the employee takes responsibility for the investment decisions.

Degree of operating leverage (DOL) The percentage change in NOI caused by a percentage change in sales.

Delivery date   The future date on which the actual payment of one currency in exchange for another takes place in a foreign exchange transaction.

Depreciation expenses   The allocation of the cost of the firm's long-lived assets (such as its plant and equipment) in the income statement over the useful lives of the assets.

Derivative contract   A security whose value is *derived* from the value of another asset or security (which is referred to as the *underlying asset*).

Developed country   Sometimes referred to as an industrialized country, where the term is used to identify those countries such as the United States, Great Britain, France, and so forth that have highly sophisticated and well-developed economies.

Direct cost   Variable cost.

Direct foreign investment   When a company from one country makes a physical investment such as building a factory in another country.

Direct quote   The exchange rate that indicates the number of units of the home currency required to buy one unit of a foreign currency.

Discount bond   A bond that sells at a discount below par value.

Discount rate   The interest rate used in the discounting process.

Discounted payback period   The number of years required for a project's discounted cash flows to recover the initial cash outlay for an investment.

Discounting   The inverse of compounding. This process is used to determine the present value of a future cash flow.

Discretionary financing needs (DFN) The total amount of financing a firm estimates that it will need for a future period that will not be funded through the retention of earnings or by increases in the firm's accounts payable and accrued expenses.

Discretionary sources of financing Sources of financing that require explicit action by the firm's management. For example, the decision to borrow money from a bank is an example of discretionary financing, whereas the automatic financing of inventory purchases from an existing supplier that increases a firm's accounts payable is not a discretionary source of financing.

Diversifiable risk   Risk that can be eliminated through diversification.

Diversification   The reduction in risk that comes about by combining two or more risky assets into a portfolio where the individual assets are less than perfectly positively correlated.

Dividend clienteles   Groups of investors who prefer the firm's cash distribution policy.

Dividend payout ratio   The total dollar amount of dividends relative to the company's net income.

Dividend policy   The firm's policy that determines how much cash it will distribute to its shareholders and when these distributions will be made.

Dividends   The portion of corporation's earnings that are distributed to its shareholders.

Dividends per share   The per share cash distribution a firm pays for each share of stock.

Divisional WACC   The cost of capital for a specific business unit or division.

DuPont method   A method for decomposing the return on equity ratio into three components: net profit margin, total asset turnover, and an equity multiplier that reflects the use of debt financing.

Earnings before interest and taxes (EBIT) Revenues from sales minus the cost of goods sold and less operating expenses. Also referred to as net operating income.

Earnings per share   Net income divided by the number of common shares outstanding.

EBIT-EPS chart   Graphic representation of the relationship between EPS and the level of firm EBIT.

EBIT-EPS indifference point   The level of EBIT that produces the same level of EPS for two different capital structures.

EBITDA coverage ratio   The ratio of the sum of EBIT plus depreciation expense (EBITDA) divided by interest plus annual before-tax principal payments (principal divided by 1 minus the firm's tax rate).

Effective annual rate (EAR)   The annual compounded rate that produces the same return as the nominal, or stated, rate.

Efficient market   A market in which prices quickly respond to the announcement of new information.

Efficient markets hypothesis (EMH) This hypothesis states that securities prices accurately reflect future expected cash flows and are based on all information available to investors.

Emerging market   One located in an economy with low-to-middle per-capita income. These countries constitute roughly 80 percent of the world's population and represent about a fifth of the world's economies. China and India are perhaps the best known and largest of the emerging-market economies.

Enterprise value   The sum of the firm's market capitalization plus net debt.

Equity   The ownership interest in a corporation. It is the stockholders' investment in the firm and the cumulative profits retained in the business up to the date of the balance sheet.

Equity risk premium   The difference between returns of the riskier stock investments and the less risky investments in government securities.

Equity securities   Financial instruments that represent ownership claims on a business. Equity securities for corporations are called shares of stock and can be bought and sold in the stock market.

Equivalent annual cost (EAC)   The annuity cash flow amount that is equivalent to the present value of the project's costs.

Eurobond   A bond issued in a country different from the one in whose currency the bond is denominated; for example, a bond issued in Europe or Asia by an American company that pays interest and principal to the lender in U.S. dollars.

European option   An option that can only be exercised on its expiration date.

Ex-dividend date   The date upon which stock brokerage companies have uniformly decided to terminate the right of ownership to the dividend, which is two days prior to the date of record.

Exchange rate   The price of a foreign currency stated in terms of the domestic or home currency.

Exchange rate risk   The risk that tomorrow's exchange rate will differ from today's rate.

Exchange-traded fund (ETF)   An investment vehicle traded on stock exchanges much like a share of stock. The entity holds investments in assets that meet the investment objective of the entity (e.g., shares of stock of companies from emerging markets).

Exercise price   The price at which the stock or asset may be purchased from the option writer in the case of a call, or sold to the option writer in the case of a put; also called the strike or striking price.

Expansion project   An investment proposal that increases the scope of the firm's operations, including the addition of both revenues and costs, but does not replace any existing assets or operations.

Expected rate of return   The average of all possible rates of return, where each possible return is weighted by the probability that it might occur.

Expected value   A probability-weighted average of all possible outcomes.

Face, or par value   On the face of a bond, the stated amount that the firm is to repay on the maturity date.

Factor   A financial institution that purchases accounts receivable from firms.

Favorable financial leverage   When the firm's investments earn a rate of return (before taxes) that is greater than the cost of borrowing, this results in higher EPS and a higher rate of return on the firm's common equity.

Financial distress costs The costs incurred by a firm that cannot pay its bills (including principal and interest on debt) in a timely manner.

Financial futures A contract to buy or sell an underlying asset such as Treasury securities, certificates of deposit, Eurodollars, foreign currencies, or stock indices at a specified price at a specified future time.

Financial intermediaries Institutions whose business is to bring together individuals and institutions with money to invest or lend with other firms or individuals in need of money.

Financial leverage The magnifying effect of the use of debt financing on the rate of return earned on the equity invested in a firm.

Financial leverage effect The use of debt financing in a firm's capital structure, which increases firm EPS when leverage is favorable and reduces EPS when leverage is unfavorable.

Financial markets Mechanisms that allow people to easily buy and sell financial claims.

Financial ratios Restating the accounting data in relative terms to identify some of the financial strengths and weaknesses of a company.

Financial structure The mix of sources of financing used by the firm to finance its assets. Commonly described using the ratio of each source of financing on the right-hand side of the firm's balance sheet divided by the sum of the firm's total liabilities plus owners' equity.

Fisher effect The relationship between the nominal rate of interest, the anticipated rate of inflation, and the real rate of interest.

Fixed asset turnover ratio A measure of the efficiency of a firm's use of its fixed assets equal to the ratio of sales to net fixed assets.

Fixed assets Those assets that the firm does not expect to sell or otherwise convert to cash within one year.

Fixed cost Costs that do not vary with the level of sales or output, including both cash fixed costs (or fixed operating costs before depreciation) and depreciation.

Float The amount of the difference between the cash balance shown on a firm's books and the available balance at the firm's bank.

Floating rate An interest rate on a loan agreement, such as a bond, that adjusts up or down depending on the movements of an agreed-upon benchmark, such as LIBOR (the London Interbank Offered Rate).

Floating-rate bonds Bonds that have a floating rate of interest.

Flotation costs The transaction costs incurred when a firm raises funds by issuing a particular type of security.

Foreign exchange (FX) market The market in which the currencies of various countries are traded.

Forward contract A contract wherein a price is agreed upon today for an asset to be sold in the future. These contracts are privately negotiated between the buyer and seller.

Forward exchange contract A contract that requires delivery on a specified future date of one currency in return for a specified amount of another currency.

Forward exchange rate The exchange rate agreed upon today for the delivery of currency at a future date.

Forward-spot differential The difference (premium or discount) between the forward and spot currency exchange rates for a country's currency.

Future value What a cash flow will be worth in the future.

Future value interest factor The value $(1 + i)^n$ used as a multiplier to calculate an amount's future value.

Futures contract A contract to buy or sell a stated commodity (such as soybeans or corn) or financial claim (such as U.S. Treasury bonds) at a specified price at some future specified time.

Futures margin The amount of money or collateral that must be provided to control credit or default risk on a futures contract; this margin is required to prevent default.

General partner A member of a general partnership or a member of a limited partnership who actually runs the business and faces unlimited liability for the firm's debts.

General partnership A partnership in which all of the partners are fully liable for the indebtedness incurred by the partnership.

Geometric or compound average returns The rate of return earned on an investment that incorporates consideration for the effects of compound interest.

Gross plant and equipment The sum of the historical cost of the plant and equipment owned by the firm.

Gross profit margin The ratio of gross profit (sales less cost of goods sold) divided by sales.

Growing perpetuity A perpetuity in which the payments grow at a constant rate from period to period over time.

Hedge fund An investment fund that is open to a limited range of investors (accredited investors) and that can undertake a wider range of investment and trading activities than other types of investment funds that are open to the general public (e.g., mutual funds).

Hedging A strategy designed to minimize exposure to unwanted risk by taking a position in one market that offsets exposure to price fluctuations in an opposite position in another market.

Holding period return The rate of return earned by investing for a specific period of time, such as one year or one month.

Income statement The financial statement that includes the revenue the firm has earned over a specific period of time, usually a quarter of a year or a full year; the expenses it has incurred during the year to earn its revenues; and the profit the firm has earned.

Incremental cash flow The change in a firm's cash flows that is a direct consequence of its having undertaken a particular project.

Independent investment project An investment project whose acceptance will not affect the acceptance or rejection of any other project.

Indirect cost Fixed cost.

Indirect quote The exchange rate that expresses the number of units of foreign currency that can be bought for one unit of home currency.

Inflation premium A premium for the expected rate of increase in prices of goods and services in the economy over the term of the bond or note.

Initial public offering (IPO) The first time a company issues stock to the public. This occurs in the primary markets.

Insurance A contract that involves compensation for specific potential future losses in exchange for periodic payments and that provides for the transfer of the risk of a loss, from one entity to another, in exchange for a premium.

Interest rate parity (IRP) A theory that relates the interest rates in two countries to the exchange rates of their currencies.

Interest rate swap The swapping or trading between two companies of fixed interest payments for variable or floating-rate interest payments.

Interest tax savings The reduction in income tax resulting due to the tax deductibility of interest expense.

Interest-bearing debt ratio The ratio of interest-bearing debt (short and long term) to total assets.

Interest-rate risk The variability in a bond's value (risk) caused by changing interest rates.

Internal rate of return (IRR) The compound annual rate of return earned by an investment.

Internal sources of financing The retention and reinvestment of firm earnings (i.e., retained earnings) in the firm.

International Fisher Effect (IFE) A theory that states that real rates of return are the same across the world, with the difference in returns across the world resulting from different inflation rates.

Inventories Raw materials used to make the firm's products, goods in process, and finished goods that are ready for sale.

Inventory conversion period The number of days a firm uses to convert its inventory into cash or accounts receivable following a sale.

Inventory management The control of the firm's store of assets that are to be sold in the normal course of the firm's operations. The general categories of inventory include raw-materials inventory, work-in-process inventory, and finished-goods inventory.

Inventory turnover ratio A measure of the efficiency of a firm's use of its inventory equal to the ratio of cost of goods sold to inventory.

Investment bank A financial institution that raises capital, trades in securities, and manages corporate mergers and acquisitions.

Investment company A firm that invests the pooled funds of retail investors for a fee.

Junk (high-yield) bond Any bond rated BB or below.

Law of one price An economic principle that states that a good or service cannot sell for different prices in the same market. Applied to international markets this law states that the same goods should sell for the same price in different countries after making adjustment for the exchange rate between the two currencies.

Level perpetuity An annuity with a constant level of payments with an infinite life.

Leveraged buyout fund A private equity firm that raises capital from individual investors and uses these funds along with significant amounts of debt to acquire controlling interests in operating companies.

Limited liability company (LLC) A business organizational form that blends elements of the partnership and corporate forms.

Limited partner A member of a limited partnership who is only liable up to the amount invested by that member.

Limited partnership A partnership in which one or more of the partners has limited liability that is restricted to the amount of capital he or she invests in the partnership.

Line of credit An informal agreement or understanding between the borrower and the bank about the maximum amount of credit that the bank will provide the borrower at any one time.

Liquidity The speed with which the asset can be converted into cash without loss of value.

Liquidity ratios Measures of the ability of a firm to pay its bills in a timely manner when they come due.

Liquidity-risk premium A premium, required by investors for securities that cannot quickly be converted into cash at a reasonably predictable price.

Load fund A mutual fund that charges investors a sales commission called a "load."

Loan amortization schedule A breakdown of the interest and principal payments on an amortized loan.

London Interbank Offered Rate (LIBOR) LIBOR is a daily rate that is based on the interest rates at which banks offer to lend in the London wholesale or interbank market (the market where banks loan each other money).

Long position A term used to refer to the ownership of a security, contract, or commodity. When someone owns a security he or she is said to be "long" on the security, such that when the price of the security rises, the individual profits.

Long-term debt Loans from banks and other lenders that have maturities longer than one year as well as bonds sold by the firm in the public markets.

Long-term financial plan A detailed estimate of a firm's sources and uses of financing for a period that extends three to five years into the future.

Majority voting Each share of stock allows the shareholder one vote, and each position on the board of directors is voted on separately.

Marginal tax rate The tax rate that the company will pay on its next dollar of taxable income.

Market portfolio The portfolio of all risky and risk-free assets.

Market risk premium The difference in the expected rate of return on the market portfolio and the risk-free rate of return.

Market value The price that an asset would trade for in a competitive market.

Market value ratios Ratios used to compare the market value of a firm's shares to either the book value per share or earnings per share.

Market's required yield The rate of return on the preferred stock's contractually promised dividend. This market's required yield is analogous to the market's required yield to maturity on a bond.

Market-to-book ratio The ratio of the market value of a firm's equity (share price times the number of shares outstanding) to the book value of the firm's equity.

Marking to market Transferring daily gains or losses from a firm's futures contracts to or from its margin account.

Maturity The date when a debt must be repaid.

Maturity-risk premium A premium to reflect the added price volatility that accompanies bonds with longer terms to maturity.

Modified internal rate of return (MIRR) The compound annual rate of return earned by an investment whose cash flows have been moved through time so as to eliminate the problem of multiple IRRs. For example, all negative cash flows after Year 0 are discounted back to Year 0 using the firm's required rate of return and then the IRR is determined for this modified cash flow stream.

Money market The financial market for short-term debt securities (maturing in one year or less).

Money market securities Short-term, low-risk debt instruments that can be sold easily and with very low risk of loss.

Mortgage bond A bond secured by a lien on real property.

Multinational corporation (MNC) A company that has control over direct foreign investments in more than one country.

Mutual fund A professionally managed investment company that pools the investments of many individuals and invests it in stocks, bonds, and other types of securities.

Mutually exclusive projects Related or dependent investment proposals where the acceptance of one proposal means the rejection of the other.

Nasdaq An electronic stock exchange where OTC stocks are traded.

Net asset value (NAV) The difference between the current market value of an entity's (such as a mutual fund) assets and the value of its liabilities.

Net debt The book value of interest-bearing debt less excess cash.

Net income The income that a firm has after subtracting costs and expenses from total revenue.

Net operating income The firm's profits from its ongoing operations—before it makes interest payments and pays its taxes. Also referred to as earnings before interest and taxes (EBIT).

Net plant and equipment The cumulative historical cost of plant and equipment owned by the firm (gross plant and equipment) less accumulated depreciation expense that has been charged against those assets over their useful life.

Net present value (NPV) The difference in the present value of an investment proposal's future cash flows and the initial cash outlay. This difference is the expected increase in value of the firm due to the acceptance of the project.

Net profit margin   Net income divided by sales.

Net working capital   The difference between the firm's current assets and current liabilities.

New York Stock Exchange (NYSE)   The largest organized stock exchange.

No-load fund   A mutual fund that doesn't charge a commission.

Nominal (or quoted) interest rate   The stated rate of interest that is unadjusted for inflation.

Nominal cash flows   Cash flows that account for the effects of inflation.

Nominal or quoted (stated) interest rate The interest rate paid on debt securities without an adjustment for any loss in purchasing power.

Nominal rate of interest   The rate of interest that is observed in financial markets and that incorporates consideration for inflation.

Non-amortizing bond   A bond that only pays interest.

Non-diversifiable risk   Risk that cannot be eliminated through diversification.

Note   Another term used to refer to indebtedness. Notes generally have a maturity between 1 and 10 years when originally issued.

Notes payable   A loan contract reflecting the fact that a firm has borrowed money that it promises to repay according to the terms of the agreement.

Notes payable   Short-term notes or loans that must be repaid in one year or less.

Notional principal   The nominal or face amount on a swap agreement. This is the principal used to calculate payments for swap contracts, but because this principal does not change hands it is commonly referred to as the "notional" amount of the contract.

NPV break-even analysis   A type of analysis used to identify the level of sales necessary to produce a zero level of NPV.

NPV profile   A plot of multiple NPV estimates calculated using a succession of different discount rates. This profile illustrates when there are multiple IRRs, that is, where NPV is equal to zero for more than one discount rate.

Open market repurchase   A method of repurchasing the firm's stock whereby the firm acquires the stock on the market, often buying a relatively small number of shares every day, at the going market price.

Operating cycle   The period of time (usually measured in days) that elapses from the time the firm acquires an item of inventory until that item has been sold and cash has been collected.

Operating leverage   The inclusion of fixed operating costs in a firm's cost structure that magnify the effect of changes in revenues on the firm's net operating income.

Operating profit margin   The ratio of net operating income to sales.

Operating return on assets (OROA) ratio A measure of the return earned by a firm's operations divided by total assets.

Opportunity cost   The value of the next best alternative that is foregone as a result of making a decision.

Optimal capital structure   The mix of financing sources in the capital structure that maximizes shareholder value.

Option contract   The right, but not the obligation, to buy or sell something (e.g., 100 shares of stock for a stock option) at a specified price and within a specified period of time.

Option expiration date   The date on which the option contract expires.

Option premium   The price paid for an option.

Option writing   The process of *selling* puts and calls.

Ordinary annuity   A series of equal dollar payments for a specified number of periods with the payments occurring at the end of each period.

Organized security exchanges   Security exchanges that physically occupy space (such as a building or part of a building) and trade financial instruments on their premises.

Over-the-counter (OTC) market   A network of dealers who trade stocks that has no listing or membership requirements.

Over-the-counter markets   All security markets except the organized exchanges.

Paid-in capital   The money contributed to a corporation by its stockholders in addition to the par value of the firm's stock. Sometimes called *paid-in capital above par*.

Par or face value of a bond   On the face of a bond, the stated amount that the firm is to repay upon the maturity date.

Par value   The stated value of a bond or share of stock at the time of issue.

Partnership   An association of two or more individuals joining together as co-owners to operate a business for profit.

Payback period   The number of years of future cash flows needed to recover the initial investment in a proposed project.

Payment date   The date on which the company mails a dividend check to each investor of record.

Percent-of-sales method   A financial forecasting technique that uses the proportion of the item being forecast (e.g., accounts receivable)

to the level of firm sales as the basis for predicting the future level of the item.

Permanent investments   Investments in assets that the firm expects to hold for a period longer than one year. These include the firm's minimum level of current assets, such as accounts receivable and inventories, as well as fixed assets.

Permanent sources of financing   A source of financing that is expected to be used by the firm for an extended period of time, such as an intermediate-term loan, bonds, or common equity.

Perpetuity   An annuity with an infinite life.

Political risk   The potential for losses that can occur when investing in foreign countries where political decisions can result in losses of property.

Portfolio beta   The beta coefficient of a portfolio of different investments.

Preferred stock   An equity security that holds preference over common stock in terms of the right to the distribution of cash (dividends) and the right to the distribution of proceeds in the event of the liquidation and sale of the issuing firm.

Premium bond   A bond that is selling above its par value.

Present value interest factor   The value $[1/(1 + i)n]$ used as a multiplier to calculate a future payment's present value.

Present value   The value in today's dollars of a future payment discounted back to the present at the required rate of return.

Price-earnings (PE) ratio   The ratio of price per share of common stock divided by earnings per share.

Price/earnings ratio   The price the market places on $1 of a firm's earnings. For example, if a firm has an earnings per share of $2, and a stock price of $30, its price-to-earnings ratio is 15 ($30 ÷ $2).

Primary market   A part of the financial market where new security issues are initially bought and sold.

Principle of self-liquidating debt   A guiding rule of thumb for managing firm liquidity that calls for financing permanent investments in assets with permanent sources of financing, and temporary investments with temporary sources of financing.

Private equity firm   A financial intermediary that invests in equities that are not traded on the public capital markets.

Private market transaction   A loan that only involves the two parties.

Pro forma balance sheet   A forecast of each of the elements of a firm's balance sheet.

Pro forma financial statements   A forecast of financial statements for a future period.

Pro forma income statement A forecast of each of the elements of a firm's income statement.

Probability distribution For an investment's rate of return, a description of all possible rates of return from the investment along with the associated probabilities for each outcome.

Profitability index (PI) The ratio of the present value of the expected future cash flows for an investment proposal (discounted using the required rate of return for the project) divided by the initial investment in the project.

Profits Another term for income.

Proprietary trading Using the bank's capital to make speculative bets on derivatives and securities.

Proxy A means of voting in which a designated party is provided with the temporary power of attorney to vote for the signee at the corporation's annual meeting.

Purchasing-power parity (PPP) A theory that states that exchange rates adjust so that identical goods cost the same amount regardless of where in the world they are purchased.

Put option An option that gives its owner the right (but not the obligation) to sell a given number of shares of common stock or an asset at a specified price within a given period.

Quality of earnings ratio The ratio of cash flow from operations divided by net income.

Range of earnings chart Same as EBIT-EPS chart.

Rate of return See Holding period return.

Real cash flows Cash flows that would occur in the absence of any inflation.

Real options Opportunities that allow for the alteration of the project's cash flow stream while the project is being operated (e.g., changing the product mix, level or output, or the mix of inputs).

Real rate of interest The nominal rate of interest less any loss in purchasing power of the dollar during the time of the investment.

Recovery rate The percent of the principal and interest that is owed that a bondholder will end up receiving if the bond defaults.

Replacement investment An investment proposal that is a substitute for an existing investment.

Residual dividend payout policy A payout policy whereby the company's dividend payment should equal the cash left after financing all the investments that have positive net present values.

Retained earnings The accumulation of prior-year net income that was retained and reinvested in the firm (i.e., not paid in dividends).

Return on equity A measure of the rate of return earned on the common shareholders' investment in the firm equal to net income divided by common equity.

Revenues Sales recognized for the period and recorded in the firm's income statement.

Risk premium The amount by which the required rate of return exceeds the risk-free rate of interest.

Risk profile The concept of a firm's "appetite" for assuming risk.

Risk-free rate of return The rate of return earned by investing in a security that always pays the promised rate of return (without risk).

Rule of 72 A method for estimating the time it takes for an amount to double in value. To determine the approximate time it takes for an amount to double in value, 72 is divided by the annual interest rate.

Scenario analysis Analysis that allows the financial manager to simultaneously consider the effects of changes in the estimates of multiple value drivers on the investment opportunity's NPV.

Secondary market The financial market where previously issued securities such as stocks and bonds are bought and sold.

Secured bond A bond that is backed or secured by pledged assets or collateral to reduce the risk associated with lending.

Secured current liabilities Loans that involve the pledge of specific assets as collateral in the event the borrower defaults in payment of principal or interest.

Security A negotiable instrument that represents a financial claim that has value. Securities are broadly classified as debt securities (bonds) and equity securities (shares of common stock).

Security market line A graphical representation of the Capital Asset Pricing Model.

Self-insurance A risk management approach where the entity sets aside a sum of money as protection against potential future loss rather than purchasing an insurance policy.

Selling rate The rate a bank or foreign exchange trader "asks" the customer to pay in home currency for foreign currency when the bank is selling and the customer is buying, also known as the asked rate.

Semi-strong-form efficient market A market in which all publicly available information is quickly and accurately reflected in prices.

Sensitivity analysis The process of determining how the distribution of possible net present values or internal rates of return for a particular project is affected by a change in one particular value driver.

Share or stock repurchase Also called a stock buyback; the repurchase of common stock by the issuing firm for any of a variety of reasons, resulting in reduction of shares outstanding.

Shareholders The owners of the firm; those who own shares of stock in a corporation.

Shares Units of ownership.

Short position A term used to refer to the fact that you have sold a security, contract, or commodity. A short position is exactly the opposite of a long position, such that when the price of the security goes up, the holder of the short position loses money.

Short-term financial plan A forecast of a firm's sources of cash and planned uses of cash spanning the next 12 months.

Simple arbitrage Trading to eliminate exchange rate differentials across the markets for a single currency, for example, for the New York and London markets.

Simple interest The interest earned on the principal.

Simulation analysis The process of imitating the performance of a risky investment project through repeated evaluations, usually using a computer. This type of experimentation is designed to capture the critical realities of the decision-making situation.

Sole proprietorship A business owned by a single individual.

Source of cash Any activity that brings cash into the firm, such as when the firm sells goods and services or sells an old piece of equipment that it no longer needs.

Sources of spontaneous financing Sources of financing that arise automatically out of changes in the firm's sales. For example, as firm sales rise the firm may order new items of inventory that are automatically financed with accounts payable based on the terms and conditions negotiated earlier with the firm's suppliers.

Spontaneous sources of financing Financing sources that arise naturally out of the course of doing business and that do not call for an explicit financing decision each time the firm uses them.

Spot contract An exchange in which the buyer agrees to purchase something and the seller agrees to sell it for a specified price, and the exchange is completed at the same time.

Spot exchange rate The ratio of a home currency and foreign currency in which the transaction calls for immediate delivery.

Spread to Treasury bonds The spread, or difference in interest rates (generally expressed in terms of basis points), of the corporate bond over a U.S. Treasury security of the same maturity.

Standard deviation The square root of the variance.

Stock dividend The distribution of shares of up to 25 percent of the number of shares currently outstanding, issued on a pro rata basis to the current stockholders.

Stock split A stock dividend exceeding 25 percent of the number of shares currently outstanding.

Stockholders The owners of the corporation's stock. The corporation is legally owned by its current set of stockholders, or owners, who elect a board of directors.

Stockholders' equity The sum of the par value of common stock plus paid-in capital plus retained earnings. This quantity is sometimes referred to as the book value of the firm's equity.

Strategic plan A general description of the firm, its products and services, and how it plans to compete with other firms in order to sell those products and services.

Strike price The price at which the stock or asset may be purchased from the option writer in the case of a call, or sold to the option writer in the case of a put; also called the exercise price.

Strong-form efficient market A market in which even private information is fully and quickly reflected in market prices.

Subordinated debenture A debenture that is subordinated to other debentures in being paid in case of insolvency.

Sunk costs Costs that have already been incurred.

Swap contract An agreement in which two parties agree to exchange one set of payments for another. For example, the holder of a stream of fixed interest rate payments on a loan might exchange them for variable-rate payments on a like-size loan.

Syndicate A group of investment bankers that is invited to help buy and resell the issue.

Systematic risk See Non-diversifiable risk.

Taxable income Firm revenues for the period less all tax-deductible expenses (such as cost of goods sold, operating expenses, and interest expense for the period).

Temporary investments in assets Current assets that will be liquidated and not replaced within the current year, including cash and marketable securities, accounts receivable, and seasonal fluctuations in inventories. Also referred to simply as temporary assets.

Temporary sources of financing Typically these consist of current liabilities the firm incurs on a discretionary basis. Examples include unsecured bank loans and commercial paper (which is simply unsecured

promissory notes with maturities of 1 to 270 days that firms sell in the money market), as well as short-term loans that are secured by the firm's inventories or accounts receivable.

Tender offer A formal offer by the company to buy a specified number of shares at a predetermined and stated price. The tender price is set above the current market price in order to attract sellers.

Term structure of interest rates Also called the yield curve. The relationship between interest rates and the term to maturity, where the risk of default is held constant.

Terms of sale The time period until payment must be made, any discount for early payment, the quality of customer who is to receive credit, and the collection efforts put forth by the firm to collect its delinquent accounts.

Timeline A linear representation of the timing of cash flows.

Times interest earned ratio A measure of the ability of the firm to pay its interest expense equal to the ratio of net operating income divided by interest expense.

Total assets The sum total of current and long-term assets recorded in the firm's balance sheet.

Total asset turnover (TATO) ratio A measure of the efficiency of a firm's use of its total assets equal to the ratio of sales to total assets.

Total liabilities The total amount of money the firm owes its creditors (including the firm's banks and other creditors).

Total shareholders' equity Total assets less total liabilities.

Trade credit A type of account payable that arises when one firm provides goods or services to a customer with an agreement to bill the customer later.

Transaction loan A loan where the proceeds are designated for a specific purpose— for example, a bank loan used to finance the acquisition of a piece of equipment.

Treasury stock Stock that has been bought back by the issuing company.

Trend analysis The use of historical ratios compared to a firm's current-period ratios to indicate whether the firm's financial condition is improving or deteriorating.

Unfavorable financial leverage When the firm's investments earn a rate of return (before taxes) that is less than the cost of borrowing, this results in lower EPS and a lower rate of return on the firm's common equity.

Unsecured current liabilities Debts of the company that are due and payable within a

period of one year and that are secured only by the promise of the firm to repay the debt.

Unsubordinated debenture A debenture that is unsubordinated to other debentures in being paid in case of insolvency.

Unsystematic risk See Diversifiable risk.

Use of cash Any activity that causes cash to leave the firm, such as the payment of taxes or payments made to stockholders, creditors, and suppliers.

Value drivers The primary determinants of an investment's cash flows and its performance (e.g., number of units sold, cost per unit to produce, and so forth).

Variable costs Costs that change with the level of sales or output.

Variance The average of the squared difference in possible rates of return and the expected rate of return. As such, the variance is a measure of the average squared difference in possible and expected rates of return.

Venture capital firm An investment company that raises money from accredited investors and uses the proceeds to invest in new start-up companies.

Volatility Another term for the fluctuation in returns.

Weak-form efficient market A market in which current prices quickly and accurately reflect information that can be derived from patterns in past security prices and trading volumes.

Weighted average cost of capital (WACC) A composite of the individual costs of financing incurred by each capital source. A firm's weighted cost of capital is a function of (1) the individual costs of capital, (2) the capital structure mix, and (3) the level of financing necessary to make the investment.

Working capital management Management of day-to-day operations and decisions related to working capital and short-term financing.

Yield curve Also called the term structure of interest. The relationship between interest rates and the term to maturity, where the risk of default is held constant.

Yield to maturity The promised rate of return to an investor who holds the bond until maturity, assuming the bond does not default on any of the interest and principal payments.

Zero-coupon bond A bond that pays no interest to the lender but instead is issued at a substantial discount from its face value. The lender realizes its interest when the bond matures and repays the full face value to the holder.

Getting Started

From Chapter 1 of *Financial Management: Principles and Applications*, Twelfth Edition. Sheridan Titman, Arthur J. Keown, and John D. Martin.

Getting Started
Principles of Finance

Chapter **Outline**

1 Finance: An Overview ——————→ **Objective 1.** Understand the importance of finance in your personal and professional lives and identify the three primary business decisions that financial managers make.

2 Three Types of Business ——————→ **Objective 2.** Identify the key differences between the three major legal forms of business.
Organizations

3 The Goal of the Financial ——————→ **Objective 3.** Understand the role of the financial manager within the firm and the goal for making financial choices.
Manager

4 The Five Basic Principles of ——————→ **Objective 4.** Explain the five principles of finance that form the basis of financial management for both businesses and individuals.
Finance

Principles P1, P2, P3, P4, and P5 Applied

People make a wide range of financial decisions in their business lives as well as in their personal lives. In this chapter, we describe the boundaries of the study of finance, the different ways that businesses are organized, and the role that the financial manager plays within the firm. We also address some of the ethical dilemmas that the financial manager must face daily.

Finally, we take an in-depth look at the five principles of finance, P Principle 1: **Money Has a Time Value,** P Principle 2: **There Is a Risk-Return Tradeoff,** P Principle 3: **Cash Flows Are the Source of Value,** P Principle 4: **Market Prices Reflect Information,** and P Principle 5: **Individuals Respond to Incentives** that underlie all financial decisions.

On any given day, Apple, Inc. (AAPL), will sell thousands of iPhones, iPods, iPads, and personal computers. In addition to a myriad of production and pricing decisions, Apple must evaluate potential new products, make personnel choices, and consider new locations for Apple retail stores. Because each of these decisions affects the risk of, timing of, and amount of cash generated by Apple's operations, we can view all of them as financial decisions.

Like Apple, you also face financial decisions in your personal life. Whether evaluating the terms of credit card offers or weighing whether to go to graduate school right after graduation or to work full-time for a year or two, you will find that the same fundamental principles that guide business decisions are useful to you in making personal financial decisions.

Regardless of Your Major...

"Welcome to the World of Finance"

For the rest of your life, you will be both working and living in a world where you will be making choices that have financial consequences. Corporations make money by introducing new products, opening new sales outlets, hiring the best people, and improving their productivity. All of these actions involve investing or spending money today with the hope of generating more money in the future. Regardless of your major, after graduation you are likely to be working for an organization where your choices have uncertain costs and benefits, both now and in the future. This will be the case if you are working for a major corporation such as General Electric, starting your own firm, or working for a non-profit organization such as St. Jude Children's Research Hospital. Moreover, you will be faced with a variety of personal choices—whether you can afford a new car or a mortgage or how much to begin investing in a retirement fund—that also require you to evaluate alternatives that involve uncertain future payoffs. Regardless of your major, there is simply no getting around the fact that you will be making financial choices throughout your life.

Your Turn: See Study Question 1.

1   Finance: An Overview

To begin our study of business finance, we present an overview of the field and define the types of decisions addressed by the study of business finance. We also discuss the motivation for studying finance and briefly introduce the five principles of finance.

What Is Finance?

Finance is the study of how people and businesses evaluate investments and raise capital to fund them. Our interpretation of an investment is quite broad. When Google (GOOG) designed its first Android cell phone, it was clearly making a long-term investment. The firm had to devote considerable expense to designing, producing, and marketing the cell phone with the hope that it would eventually capture a sufficient amount of market share from the iPhone to make the investment worthwhile. But Google also makes an investment decision whenever it hires a fresh new graduate, knowing that it will be paying a salary for at least six months before the employee will have much to contribute.

Thus, three basic questions are addressed by the study of finance:

1. **What long-term investments should the firm undertake?** This area of finance is generally referred to as **capital budgeting**.

2. **How should the firm raise money to fund these investments?** The firm's funding choices are generally referred to as **capital structure** decisions.

3. **How can the firm best manage its cash flows as they arise in its day-to-day operations?** This area of finance is generally referred to as **working capital management**.

Why Study Finance?

Even if you are not planning a career in finance, a working knowledge of finance will take you far in both your personal and professional lives.

Those interested in management will need to study topics such as strategic planning, personnel, organizational behavior, and human relations, all of which involve spending money today in the hopes of generating more money in the future. For example, GM made a strategic decision to introduce an electric car and invest $740 million to produce the Chevy Volt, a decision designed to generate momentum for the company as it came out of bankruptcy reorganization in July of 2009. Similarly, marketing majors need to understand and decide how aggressively to price products and how much to spend on advertising those products. Because aggressive marketing costs money today but generates rewards in the future, it should be viewed as an investment that the firm needs to finance. Production and operations management majors need to understand how best to manage a firm's production and control its inventory and supply chain. These are all topics that involve risky choices that relate to the management of money over time, which is the central focus of finance.

Although finance is primarily about the management of money, a key component of finance is the management and interpretation of information. Indeed, if you pursue a career in management information systems or accounting, finance managers are likely to be your most important clients.

For the student with entrepreneurial aspirations, an understanding of finance is essential—after all, if you can't manage your finances, you won't be in business very long.

Finally, an understanding of finance is important to you as an individual. The fact that you are reading this chapter indicates that you understand the importance of investing in yourself. By obtaining a college degree, you are clearly making sacrifices in the hopes of making yourself more employable and improving your chances of having a rewarding and challenging career. Some of you are relying on your own earnings and the earnings of your parents to finance your education, whereas others are raising money or borrowing it from the **financial markets**, institutions that facilitate financial transactions.

Financial decisions are everywhere, both in your personal life and in your career. Although our primary focus is on developing the corporate finance tools and techniques that are used in the business world, you will find that much of the logic and many of the tools we develop and explore will also apply to decisions you will be making in your own personal life. In the future, both your business and personal lives will be spent in the world of finance. Because you're going to be living in that world, it's time to learn about its basic principles.

We will take an in-depth look at these principles at the end of this chapter. As you will see, you do not need an extensive knowledge of finance to understand these principles. When you are looking at more complex financial concepts, think of these principles as taking you back to the roots of finance.

Before you move on to 2

Concept Check | 1

1. What are the three basic types of issues that arise in business that are addressed by the study of business finance?
2. List three non-finance careers to which the study of finance applies.

 # Three Types of Business Organizations

Although numerous and diverse, the legal forms of business organization fall into three categories: the sole proprietorship, the partnership, and the corporation. Figure 1 provides a quick reference guide for organizational forms.

Sole Proprietorship

The **sole proprietorship** is a business owned by a single individual who is entitled to all of the firm's profits and who is also responsible for all of the firm's **debt**; that is, what the firm owes. In effect, there is no separation between the business and the owner when it comes to debts or being sued. If sole proprietors are sued, they can lose not only all they invested in the proprietorship, but also all of their personal assets. Sole proprietorships are often used in

Figure 1

Characteristics of Different Forms of Business

Business Form	Number of Owners	Are Owners Liable for the Firm's Debts?	Do Owners Manage the Firm?	Does an Ownership Change Dissolve the Firm?	Access to Capital	Taxation
Sole Proprietorship	One	Yes	Yes	Yes	Very limited	Personal Taxes
Partnership	Unlimited	Yes; each partner has unlimited liability	Yes	Yes	Very limited	Personal Taxes
Limited Partnership (with General Partners (GPs) and Limited Partners (LPs))	At least one GP, but no limit on LPs	GPs—unlimited liability LPs—limited liability	GPs—manage the firm LPs—no role in management	GPs—Yes LPs—No, can change[1]	Limited	Personal Taxes
Limited Liability Company	Unlimited	No	Yes	No	Dependent upon size	Personal Taxes
Corporation	Unlimited	No	No—although managers generally have an ownership stake[2]	No	Very easy access	Double Taxation: Earnings taxed at corporate level Dividends taxed at personal level

[1]It is common for LLCs to require approval from the other partners before a partner's ownership can be transferred.

[2]Owners are not prohibited from managing the corporation.

>> END FIGURE 1

the initial stages of a firm's life. This in part is because forming a sole proprietorship is very easy; there are no forms to file and no partners to consult—the founder of the business is the sole owner. However, these organizations typically have limited access to outside sources of financing. The owners of a sole proprietorship typically raise money by investing their own funds and by borrowing from a bank. However, because there is no difference between the sole proprietor and the business he or she runs, there is no difference between personal borrowing and business borrowing. The owner of the business is personally liable for the debts of that business. In addition to banks, personal loans from friends and family are important sources of financing for sole proprietorships.

Partnership

A **general partnership** is an association of two or more persons who come together as co-owners for the purpose of operating a business for profit. Just as with the sole proprietorship, there is no separation between the general partnership and its owners with respect to debts or being sued. Its primary point of distinction from a sole proprietorship is that the **partnership** has more than one owner. Just like with a proprietorship, the profits of the partnership are taxed as personal income. An important advantage of the partnership is that it provides access to **equity**, or ownership, as well as financing from multiple owners in return for partnership **shares**, or units of ownership.

In **limited partnerships**, there are two classes of partners: general and limited. The **general partner** actually runs the business and faces unlimited liability for the firm's debts, whereas the **limited partner** is only liable up to the amount the limited partner invested. The life of the partnership, like that of the sole proprietorship, is tied to the life of the general partner. In addition, it is difficult to transfer ownership of the general partner's interest in the business—this generally requires the formation of a new partnership. However, the limited partner's shares can be transferred to another owner without the need to dissolve the partnership, although finding a buyer may be difficult.

Corporation

If very large sums of money are needed to build a business, then the typical organizational form chosen is the **corporation**. As early as 1819, U.S. Supreme Court Chief Justice John Marshall set forth the legal definition of a corporation as "an artificial being, invisible, intangible, and existing only in the contemplation of law."[1] The corporation legally functions separately and apart from its owners (the **shareholders**, also referred to as the **stockholders**). As such, the corporation can individually sue and be sued, purchase, sell, or own property, and its personnel are subject to criminal punishment for crimes committed in the name of the corporation.

There are three primary advantages of this separate legal status. First, the owners' liability is confined to the amount of their investment in the company. In other words, if the corporation goes under, the owners can only lose their investment. This is an extremely important advantage of a corporation. After all, would you be willing to invest in US Airways if you would be held liable if one of its planes crashed? The second advantage of separate legal status for the corporation is that the life of the business is not tied to the status of the investors. The death or withdrawal of an investor does not affect the continuity of the corporation. The management continues to run the corporation when the ownership shares are sold or when they are passed on through inheritance. For example, the inventor Thomas Edison founded General Electric (GE) over a century ago. Edison died in 1931, but the corporation lives on. Finally, these two advantages result in a third advantage, the ease of raising capital. It is much easier to convince investors to put their money in a corporation knowing that the most they can lose is what they invest, and that they can easily sell their stock if they wish to do so.

The corporation is legally owned by its current set of stockholders, or owners, who elect a board of directors. The directors then appoint management who are responsible for determining the firm's direction and policies. Although even very small firms can be organized as corporations, most often larger firms that need to raise large sums of money for investment and expansion use this organizational form. As such, this is the legal form of business that we will be examining most frequently in this chapter.

One of the drawbacks of the corporate form is the double taxation of earnings that are paid out in the form of **dividends**. When a corporation earns a profit, it pays taxes on that profit (the first taxation of earnings) and pays some of that profit back to the shareholders in the form of dividends. Then the shareholders pay personal income taxes on those dividends (the second taxation of earnings). In contrast, the earnings of proprietorships and partnerships are not subject to double taxation. Needless to say, this is a major disadvantage of corporations.[2]

When entrepreneurs and small business owners want to expand, they face a tradeoff between the benefits of the corporate form and the potential loss of control and higher taxes that accompany it. For this reason, an attractive alternative to the corporation for such a small business is the **limited liability company (LLC)**, a cross between a partnership and a corporation. An LLC combines the tax benefits of a partnership (no double taxation of earnings) with the limited liability benefit of a corporation (the owners' liability is limited to what they invested).[3] Thus, unlike a proprietorship or partnership, there is a separation between the LLC and the owners with respect to debts or being sued. As a result, the most a limited partner can lose is what he

---

[1]*The Trustees of Dartmouth College v. Woodward*, 4 Wheaton 636 (1819).

[2]Before the 2003 tax law changes, you paid your regular tax rate on dividend income, which could be as high as 35 percent. However, since the 2003 tax law, qualified dividends from domestic corporations and qualified foreign corporations are taxed at a maximum rate of 15 percent. Moreover, if you're in the 10 percent or 15 percent rate brackets, your tax rate on these dividends drops to 0 percent. However, on January 2, 2013, President Obama signed into law the American Taxpayer Relief Act of 2012 which kept the reduced tax rate on dividend income for all but those in the highest tax bracket and raised the tax rate on qualified dividends from 15 to 20 percent for individuals with taxable income over $450,000 (married filing jointly) and $400,000 (individual filers).

[3]In addition, there is the S-type corporation, which provides limited liability while allowing the business owners to be taxed as if they were a partnership—that is, distributions back to the owners are not taxed twice as is the case with dividends in the standard corporate form. Unfortunately, a number of restrictions that accompany the S-type corporation detract from the desirability of this business form. As a result, the S-type corporation has been losing ground in recent years in favor of the limited liability company.

or she invested. Because LLCs operate under state laws, both the states and the Internal Revenue Service (IRS) have rules for what qualifies as an LLC, and different states have different rules. The bottom line is that if an LLC looks too much like a corporation, it will be taxed as one.

Figure 1 describes some major characteristics of the different forms of business. As you can see, the corporation is the business form that provides the easiest access to capital, and as such it is the most common choice for firms that are growing and need to raise money.

How Does Finance Fit into the Firm's Organizational Structure?

Finance is intimately woven into any aspect of the business that involves the payment or receipt of money in the future. For this reason it is important that everyone in a business have a good working knowledge of the basic principles of finance. However, within a large business organization, the responsibility for managing the firm's financial affairs falls to the firm's chief financial officer (CFO).

Figure 2 shows how the finance function fits into a firm's organizational chart. In the typical large corporation, the CFO serves under the corporation's chief executive officer (CEO) and is responsible for overseeing the firm's finance-related activities. Typically, both a treasurer and controller serve under the CFO, although in a small firm the same person may fulfill both roles. The treasurer generally handles the firm's financing activities. These include managing its cash and credit, exercising control over the firm's major spending decisions, raising money, developing financial plans, and managing any foreign currency the firm receives. The firm's controller is responsible for managing the firm's accounting duties, which include producing financial statements, paying taxes, and gathering and monitoring data that the firm's executives need to oversee its financial well-being.

Figure 2

How the Finance Area Fits into a Corporation
A firm's vice president of finance is many times called its chief financial officer, or CFO. This person oversees all of the firm's financial activities through the offices of the firm's treasurer and controller.

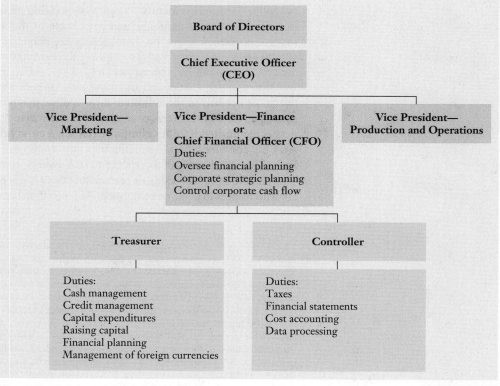

>> END FIGURE 2

Concept Check | 2

1. What are the primary differences between a sole proprietorship, a partnership, and a corporation?
2. Explain why large and growing firms tend to choose the corporate form of organization.
3. What are the duties of a corporate treasurer?
4. What are the duties of a corporate controller?

The Goal of the Financial Manager

In 2001 Tony Fadell turned to Apple, Inc., to develop his idea for a new MP3 player. Fadell's idea had already been rejected by his previous employer and another company, but the executives at Apple were enthusiastic about the new MP3 player idea. They hired Fadell, and the rest is history. The successful sales of the new iPod MP3 player, coupled with efficient uses of financing and day-to-day funding, raised the firm's stock price. This exemplifies how a management team appointed by a corporate board made an important investment decision that had a very positive effect on the firm's total value.

As previously mentioned, we can characterize the financial activities of a firm's management in terms of three important functions within a firm:

- Making investment decisions (capital budgeting decisions): The decision by Apple to introduce the iPod.
- Making decisions on how to finance these investments (capital structure decisions): How to finance the development and production of the iPod.
- Managing funding for the company's day-to-day operations (working capital management): Apple's decision regarding how much inventory to hold.

In carrying out these tasks, the financial managers must be aware that they are ultimately working for the firm's shareholders, who are the owners of the firm, and that the choices they make as financial managers will generally have a direct impact on their shareholders' wealth.

Maximizing Shareholder Wealth

The CEO of a publicly owned corporation such as Coca-Cola (KO) is selected by a board of directors; the members of the board of directors are elected by the shareholders who purchase stock in the company. The shareholders, ranging from individuals who purchase stock for a retirement fund to large financial institutions, have a vested interest in the company. Because the shareholders are their true owners, companies commonly have a principal goal described as *maximizing shareholder wealth*, which is achieved by maximizing the stock price.

We can get some insight into the goals companies have by looking at their annual reports or websites. Consider Coca-Cola's "vision" statement in a recent annual report:

Vision

To achieve sustainable growth, we have established a vision with clear goals.

- **Profit.** Maximizing return to shareowners while being mindful of our overall responsibilities.
- **People.** Being a great place to work where people are inspired to be the best they can be.
- **Portfolio.** Bringing to the world a portfolio of beverage brands that anticipate and satisfy people's desires and needs.
- **Partners.** Nurturing a winning network of partners and building mutual loyalty.
- **Planet.** Being a responsible global citizen that makes a difference.

Notice that only the first item in this list relates to the financial interests of the company's owners—the one that mentions "maximizing return" and "being mindful of our overall responsibilities."

Now let's examine Google, Inc. On the corporate portion of its website, Google states that its goal is "to develop services that significantly improve the lives of as many people as possible," and that its motto is simply, "Don't be evil." Does this mean Google doesn't care about money or the firm's owners (stockholders)? For the sake of all Google stockholders, we certainly hope not. After all, why do you buy stock in a company in the first place? You do it in the hopes of making money, right? It's nice to be altruistic and make the world a better place, but in reality, companies had better earn money if they expect banks to continue to loan them money and stockholders to continue to buy their shares. Google apparently believes both goals are possible: In addition to making the world a better place, the company says it "will optimize for the long-term rather than trying to produce smooth earnings for each quarter."

We believe in the same goal that Google does—that maximizing the wealth of your share-holders and doing the right thing can go hand in hand. Think of this goal not as moving *away* from creating wealth for shareholders, but moving *toward* what will truly increase the value of their shares in the long-term. We assume that businesses don't act out of greed to "get rich quick." Instead, we assume they try to maximize the wealth of their shareholders by making decisions that have long-term positive effects. Very simply, managers can't afford to ignore the fact that shareholders want to see the value of their investments rise—they will sell their shares if it doesn't. This, in turn, will cause the company's share price to fall, jeopardizing the managers' jobs, if they are seen to have an excessively short-term focus.

Ethical Considerations in Corporate Finance

Although ethics is not one of the five principles of finance, ethics is fundamental to the notion of trust and is therefore essential to doing business. The problem is that in order to cooperate, business participants have to rely on one another's willingness to treat them fairly. Although businesses frequently try to describe the rights and obligations of their dealings with others using contracts, it is impossible to write a perfect contract. Consequently, business dealings between people and firms ultimately depend on the willingness of the parties to trust one another.

Ethics, or a lack thereof, is a recurring theme in the news. Recently, finance has been home to an almost continuous series of ethical lapses. Financial scandals at companies such as Enron and WorldCom, Bernie Madoff's Ponzi scheme that cost investors billions of dollars, and the mishandling of depositor money by financial institutions such as Sanford Financial show that the business world does not forgive ethical lapses. Not only is acting in an ethical manner morally correct, it is also a necessary ingredient of long-term business and personal success.

You might ask yourself, "As long as I'm not breaking society's laws, why should I care about ethics?" The answer to this question lies in consequences. Everyone makes errors of judgment in business, which is to be expected in an uncertain world. But ethical errors are different. Even if they don't result in anyone going to jail, they tend to end careers and thereby terminate future opportunities. Why? Because unethical behavior destroys trust, and businesses cannot function without a certain degree of trust.

Regulation Aimed at Making the Goal of the Firm Work: The Sarbanes-Oxley Act

Because of growing concerns about both agency and ethical issues, in 2002 Congress passed the Sarbanes-Oxley Act, or "SOX" as it is commonly called. One of the primary inspirations for this new law was Enron, which failed financially in December 2001. Prior to bankruptcy, Enron's board of directors actually voted on two occasions to temporarily suspend its own "code of ethics" to permit its CFO to engage in risky financial ventures that benefited the CFO personally while exposing the corporation to substantial risk.

SOX holds corporate advisors who have access to or influence on company decisions (such as a firm's accountants, lawyers, company officers, and board of directors) legally accountable for any instances of misconduct. The act very simply and directly identifies its purpose as being "to protect investors by improving the accuracy and reliability of corporate disclosures made pursuant to the securities laws, and for other purposes," and it mandates that senior executives take individual responsibility for the accuracy and completeness of the firm's financial reports.

SOX safeguards the interests of the shareholders by providing greater protection against accounting fraud and financial misconduct. Unfortunately, all of this has not come without a price. Although SOX has received praise from the likes of the former Federal Reserve Chairman Alan Greenspan and has increased investor confidence in financial reporting, it has also been criticized. The demanding reporting requirements are quite costly and, as a result, may inhibit firms from listing on U.S. stock markets.

Before you move on to 4

Concept Check | 3

1. What is the goal of a firm?
2. Why is ethics relevant to the financial management of a firm?
3. What was the Sarbanes-Oxley Act of 2002? What did it accomplish?

 # The Five Basic Principles of Finance

At first glance, finance can seem like a collection of unrelated decision rules. Nothing could be further from the truth. The logic behind most financial concepts arises from five simple financial principles, each of which is described next.

Principle 1: Money Has a Time Value

A dollar received today is worth more than a dollar received in the future. Conversely, a dollar received in the future is worth less than a dollar received today.

Perhaps the most fundamental principle of finance is that money has a time value. A dollar received today is more valuable than a dollar received one year from now. That is, we can invest the dollar we have today to earn interest so that at the end of one year we will have more than one dollar.

Because we can earn interest on money received today, it is better to receive money sooner rather than later. For example, suppose you have a choice of receiving $1,000 either today or one year from now. If you decide to receive it a year from now, you will have passed up the opportunity to earn a year's interest on the money. Economists would say you suffered an "opportunity loss" or an **opportunity cost**.

Principle 2: There Is a Risk-Return Tradeoff

We won't take on additional risk unless we expect to be compensated with additional return.

Principle 2 is based on the idea that individuals are risk-averse, which means that they prefer to get a certain return on their investment rather than an uncertain return. However, the world is an inherently risky place, so at least some individuals will have to make investments that are risky. How are investors induced to hold these risky investments when there are safer alternative investments? By offering investors a higher *expected* rate of return on the riskier investments.

Notice that we refer to *expected* return rather than *actual* return. As investors, we have expectations about what returns our investments will earn; however, a higher expected rate of return is not always a higher realized rate of return. For example, you probably would not have been willing to invest in Eastman Kodak (EKDKQ) stock at the beginning of 2011 unless you expected the returns on Kodak to be very high. However, GM stock returns in 2011 were terrible; the stock lost more than 90 percent of its value as it headed toward bankruptcy.

Figure 3

There Is a Risk-Return Tradeoff

Investors demand a return for delaying their consumption. To convince them to take on added risk, they demand a higher expected return.

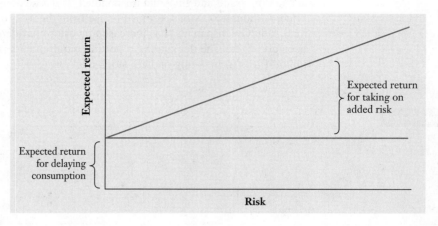

>> END FIGURE 3

The risk-return relationship is a key concept in valuing assets and proposed new investment projects. It is also involved in how investors measure risk. Interestingly, much of the work for which the 1990 Nobel Prize for economics was awarded centered on the graph shown in Figure 3 and how to measure risk.

Principle 3: Cash Flows Are the Source of Value

Profit is an accounting concept designed to measure a business's performance over an interval of time. Cash flow is the amount of cash that can actually be taken out of the business over this same interval.

You may recall from your accounting classes that a company's profits can differ dramatically from its cash flows. Cash flows represent actual money that can be spent and cash flows are what determine an investment's value.

Profits are different. To determine a company's accounting profit, its accountants have to make a judgment about how the business's costs and revenues are allocated to each time period. Consequently, different judgments result in different profit measurements. In fact, a firm can show a profit on paper even when it is generating no cash at all. This isn't to say that accounting profits are unimportant to investors. Investors see accounting profits as an important indicator of a firm's past—and perhaps its future—ability to produce cash flows for its investors. So, to the extent that profits affect investors' expectations, they are an important source of information.

There is another important point we need to make about cash flows. Recall from your economics classes that people make the best choices when they look at marginal, or *incremental,* cash flows. That's why we focus on the incremental cash flow to the company as a whole that is produced as a consequence of a decision. The incremental cash flow to the company as a whole is the difference between the cash flows the company will produce with the potential new investment it's thinking about making, and the cash flows it would produce without that investment. To understand this concept, let's think about the incremental cash flows of the *Pirates of the Caribbean* movies. Not only did Disney make money on the movies, but also the movies increased the number of people attracted to Disney theme parks to go on the "Pirates of the Caribbean" ride. So, if you were to evaluate a *Pirates of the Caribbean* movie, you'd want to include its impact on sales throughout the entire company.

Principle 4: Market Prices Reflect Information

Investors respond to new information by buying and selling their investments. The speed with which investors act and the way that prices respond to the information determine the efficiency of the market.

The prices of financial claims traded in the public financial markets respond rapidly to the release of new information. Thus, when earnings reports come out, prices adjust immediately to the new information, moving upward if the information is better than expected and downward if it is worse than expected. In efficient markets, such as those that exist in the United States and other developed countries, this process takes place *very* quickly. As a result, it's hard to profit from trading on publicly released information.

To illustrate how quickly stock prices can react to information, consider the following set of events: While Nike (NKE) CEO William Perez flew aboard the company's Gulfstream jet one day in November 2005, traders on the ground sold off a significant amount of Nike's stock. Why? Because the plane's landing gear was malfunctioning, and they were watching TV coverage of the event! While Perez was still in the air, Nike's stock dropped 1.4 percent. Once Perez's plane landed safely, Nike's stock price immediately bounced back. This example illustrates that in the financial markets there are ever-vigilant investors who are looking to act even *in anticipation of* the release of new information.

Consequently, managers can expect their company's share prices to respond quickly to the decisions they make. Good decisions will result in higher stock prices. Bad decisions will result in lower stock prices.

Principle 5: Individuals Respond to Incentives

The conflict of interest between the firm's managers and its stockholders is called a *principal-agent problem*, or **agency problem**, in which the firm's common stockholders, the owners of the firm, are the principals in the relationship, and the managers act as "agents" to these owners. If the managers have little or no ownership in the firm, they have less incentive to work energetically for the company's shareholders and may instead choose to enrich themselves with perks and other financial benefits—say, luxury corporate jets, expensive corporate apartments, or resort vacations. They will also have an incentive to turn down risky investments that may jeopardize their jobs—even though their shareholders would like the company to pursue these projects. The lost shareholder value that results from managerial actions that are inconsistent with the goal of maximizing shareholder value is called an *agency* cost.

Agency problems also arise when the firm's executives are considering how to raise money to finance the firm's investments. In some situations debt may be the cheapest source of financing, but managers may avoid debt financing because they fear the loss of their jobs if the firm is unable to pay its bills. Stockholders, on the other hand, might prefer that the firm use more debt financing because it puts pressure on management to perform at a high level.

Agency costs are typically difficult to measure, but occasionally their effect on the firm's stock price can be seen. For example, on the announcement of the death of Roy Farmer, the CEO of Farmer Brothers (FARM), a seller of coffee-related products, the firm's stock price rose about 28 percent. Many attributed the rise in price to the perceived benefits of removing a CEO who was not acting in accordance with general stockholder interests.

Fortunately, there are several measures that can be taken to help mitigate the agency problem:

- Compensation plans can be put in place that reward managers when they act to maximize shareholder wealth.
- The board of directors can actively monitor the actions of managers and keep pressure on them to act in the best interests of shareholders.

- The financial markets can (and do) play a role in monitoring management by having auditors, bankers, and credit agencies monitor the firm's performance, while security analysts provide and disseminate analysis on how well the firm is doing, thereby helping shareholders monitor the firm.
- Firms that underperform will see their stock prices fall and may be taken over and have their management teams replaced.

To see the power of incentives, consider the case of football player Edgerrin James. Mr. James was a running back for the Indianapolis Colts playing in a game against Detroit when he was told by his coach to get a first down and then fall down and run out the clock. That way the Colts wouldn't be accused of running up the score against a team they were already beating badly. However, because James's contract included incentive payments associated with rushing yards and touchdowns, he acted in his own self-interest and ran for a touchdown on the very next play. Following the play, he commented, "I heard the cash register ringing the whole way."

Before you begin end-of-chapter material

Concept Check | 4

1. What are the five principles of finance?
2. A fundamental guiding principle of investing is that higher risks require higher rewards or returns. Give two examples of the risk-return relationship.
3. What do we mean when we say that market prices reflect information?

Applying the Principles of Finance to This Chapter

[P] Principle 1: **Money Has a Time Value** A dollar received today is worth more than a dollar received in the future. Conversely, a dollar received in the future is worth less than a dollar received today.

[P] Principle 2: **There Is a Risk-Return Tradeoff** We won't take on additional risk unless we expect to be compensated with additional return.

[P] Principle 3: **Cash Flows Are the Source of Value** Cash flow measures the amount of cash that can actually be taken out of the business over an interval of time. As a result, it is the source of value.

[P] Principle 4: **Market Prices Reflect Information** Investors respond to new information by buying and selling. As a result, prices reflect what is known. The speed with which investors act and prices respond reflects the efficiency of the market.

[P] Principle 5: **Individuals Respond to Incentives** Large firms are often run by professional managers who own a small fraction of the firm's equity. The individual actions of these managers are often motivated by self-interest, which may result in managers not acting in the best interest of the firm's owners. When this happens, the firm's owners will lose value.

Chapter Summaries

Understand the importance of finance in your personal and professional lives and identify the three primary business decisions that financial managers make.

SUMMARY: Finance is the study of how individuals and businesses allocate money over time. We all face choices that involve spending or receiving money now versus sometime in the future. Knowledge of financial concepts will help you to better understand how to make those choices, both in your personal life and as a financial manager.

The decision-making process of planning and managing a firm's long-term investments is called capital budgeting. The mix of long-term sources of funds used by a firm to finance its operations is called its capital structure. Working capital management involves management of the firm's short-term investment in assets and liabilities and ensuring that the firm has sufficient resources to maintain its day-to-day business operations.

KEY TERMS

Capital budgeting The decision-making process used to analyze potential investments in fixed assets.

Capital structure The mix of long-term sources of funds used by the firm.

Financial markets Mechanisms that allow people to easily buy and sell financial claims.

Working capital management Management of day-to-day operations and decisions related to working capital and short-term financing.

Concept Check | **1**

1. What are the three basic types of issues that arise in business that are addressed by the study of business finance?
2. List three non-finance careers to which the study of finance applies.

Identify the key differences between the three major legal forms of business.

SUMMARY: The sole proprietorship is a business operation owned and managed by an individual. Initiating this form of business is simple and generally does not involve any substantial organizational costs. The proprietor has complete control of the firm but must be willing to assume full responsibility for its outcomes.

Similar to the sole proprietorship, a general partnership is simply a coming together of two or more individuals who face unlimited liability for their involvement in the partnership. The limited partnership is another form of partnership sanctioned by states to permit all but one of the partners to have limited liability if this is agreeable to all partners. The one partner with unlimited liability is the general partner.

The corporation form of organization is taken when a business has an increased need to raise capital from public investors. Although greater organizational costs and regulations are imposed on this legal entity, the corporation is more conducive to raising large amounts of capital. Limited liability, continuity of life, and ease of transfer in ownership, all of which increase the marketability of the investment, have greatly contributed to attracting large numbers of investors to the corporate environment. The formal control of the corporation is vested in the parties who own the greatest number of shares. However, day-to-day operations are managed by the corporate officers, who theoretically serve on behalf of the stockholders. An attractive alternative to the corporation for a small business is the limited liability company (LLC), a cross between a partnership and a corporation. An LLC combines the tax benefits of a partnership (no double taxation of earnings) and the limited liability benefit of corporations (the owners' liability is limited to what they invest).

KEY TERMS

Corporation A business entity that legally functions separate and apart from its owners.

Debt Money that has been borrowed and must be repaid. This includes such things as bank loans and bonds.

Dividends The portion of corporation's earnings that are distributed to its shareholders.

Equity The ownership interest in a corporation. It is the stockholders' investment in the firm and the cumulative profits retained in the business up to the date of the balance sheet.

General partner A member of a general partnership or a member of a limited partnership who actually runs the business and faces unlimited liability for the firm's debts.

General partnership A partnership in which all of the partners are fully liable for the indebtedness incurred by the partnership.

Limited liability company (LLC) A business organizational form that blends elements of the partnership and corporate forms.

Limited partner A member of a limited partnership who is only liable up to the amount invested by that member.

Limited partnership A partnership in which one or more of the partners has limited liability that is restricted to the amount of capital he or she invests in the partnership.

Partnership An association of two or more individuals joining together as co-owners to operate a business for profit.

Shareholders The owners of the firm; those who own shares of stock in a corporation.

Shares Units of ownership.

Sole proprietorship A business owned by a single individual.

Stockholders The owners of the corporation's stock. The corporation is legally owned by its current set of stockholders, or owners, who elect a board of directors.

Concept Check | 2

1. What are the primary differences between a sole proprietorship, a partnership, and a corporation?
2. Explain why large and growing firms tend to choose the corporate form of organization.
3. What are the duties of a corporate treasurer?
4. What are the duties of a corporate controller?

Understand the role of the financial manager within the firm and the goal for making financial choices.

SUMMARY: The finance function in most large firms is headed by a vice president of finance or chief financial officer (CFO). The CFO typically reports directly to the firm's chief executive officer (CEO). The CFO oversees the firm's financing decisions, including the management of the firm's cash position (in larger firms this responsibility is delegated to the company treasurer, who reports to the CFO) as well as corporate reporting and general accounting. (Once again, in large firms this task is delegated to the company controller, who also reports to the CFO.)

A critically important goal of finance is to design incentive compensation plans that better align the interests of managers with those of the firm's owners (stockholders).

Firms are in business to make their owners, or shareholders, wealthier. With this goal in mind, financial managers must make financial decisions regarding long-term investments, financing, and management of short-term cash needs. For very large firms whose shares of stock are publicly traded, this goal is commonly described as *maximizing the wealth of shareholders* (the business's owners).

In finance, ethics—or a lack thereof—is a recurring theme in the news. Ethics is fundamental to the notion of trust and is therefore essential to doing business. In order to cooperate, business participants have to rely on one another's willingness to treat them fairly.

Concept Check | 3

1. What is the goal of a firm?
2. Why is ethics relevant to the financial management of a firm?
3. What was the Sarbanes-Oxley Act of 2002? What did it accomplish?

Explain the five principles of finance that form the basis of financial management for both businesses and individuals.

SUMMARY:

P Principle 1: **Money Has a Time Value**

A dollar received today is worth more than a dollar received in the future. Conversely, a dollar received in the future is worth less than a dollar received today.

P Principle 2: **There Is a Risk-Return Tradeoff**

We won't take on additional risk unless we expect to be compensated with additional return.

P Principle 3: **Cash Flows Are the Source of Value**

Profit is an accounting concept designed to measure a business's performance over an interval of time. Cash flow is the amount of cash that can actually be taken out of the business over this same interval.

Concept Check | 4

1. What are the five principles of finance?

2. A fundamental guiding principle of investing is that higher risks require higher rewards or returns. Give two examples of the risk-return relationship.

3. What do we mean when we say that market prices reflect information?

P Principle 4: **Market Prices Reflect Information**

Investors respond to new information by buying and selling such that prices reflect what is known. The speed with which investors act and prices respond reflects the efficiency of the market.

P Principle 5: **Individuals Respond to Incentives**

Incentives motivate, and the actions of managers are often motivated by self-interest, which may result in managers not acting in the best interests of the firm's owners. When this happens the firm's owners will lose value.

KEY TERMS

Agency problem Conflicts that arise out of the separation of management and ownership of the firm.

Opportunity cost The value of the next best alternative that is foregone as a result of making a decision.

Study Questions

1. **(Related to Regardless of Your Major: Welcome to the World of Finance)** In the Regardless of Your Major feature box at the beginning of this chapter, we discussed how the topic of Principle 1, the time value of money, is relevant to both your personal and professional lives. Describe a decision you might face in the future that will require you to consider the future value of money received (or invested). For example, how might the time value of money enter into a decision to push back your graduation date by one year?

2. Explain the three types of business decisions that a financial manager faces.

3. According to Principle 2, how should investors decide where to invest their money?

4. In very basic terms, describe how profits and cash flow are different.

5. List the three main forms of business organization and describe their advantages and disadvantages. If you were to consider starting up a lawn-care business for the summer, what type of business organization might you use?

6. Who really owns a corporation, and how does that impact the goal of the firm?

7. What goal do the owners of a for-profit business generally strive for?

8. Why is maximizing a firm's accounting profits not an appropriate goal for the firm?

Photo Credits

Firms and the Financial Market

From Chapter 2 of *Financial Management: Principles and Applications*, Twelfth Edition. Sheridan Titman, Arthur J. Keown, and John D. Martin.

Firms and the Financial Market

Chapter **Outline**

1 The Basic Structure of the U.S. Financial Markets

→ **Objective 1.** Describe the structure and functions of financial markets.

2 The Financial Marketplace: Financial Institutions

→ **Objective 2.** Distinguish between commercial banks and other financial institutions in the financial marketplace.

3 The Financial Marketplace: Securities Markets

→ **Objective 3.** Describe the different securities markets for bonds and stocks.

Principles P2, P4, and P5 Applied

When reading this chapter, you should keep in mind three of the basic principles of finance: **P** Principle 2: **There Is a Risk-Return Tradeoff, P** Principle 4: **Market Prices Reflect Information,** and **P** Principle 5: **Individuals Respond to Incentives.** Financial markets are organized to offer investors a wide range of investment opportunities that have different risks and different expected rates of return that reflect those risks.

The goal of these markets is to provide investors with opportunities that best fit their risk and return objectives, while at the same time to provide businesses with opportunities to raise funds—to train employees, do research, and build new plants—at prices that appropriately reflect the prospects of the business.

If you have a student loan or a car loan, you have already been introduced to financial markets. You are spending more than you currently earn and have borrowed money through the financial markets to make ends meet. But once you graduate and enter the workforce, you may earn more than you spend and therefore be able to save. Once again, you will become involved in the financial markets, but this time as a saver rather than a borrower. This pattern of borrowing and saving also holds true for businesses, as they borrow money to finance their investments and as they invest their savings in the hopes of generating even more money in the future.

In this chapter we provide a preliminary overview of the U.S. financial markets. We first review some of the primary institutions that facilitate the transfer of money from investors to companies and individuals. Next, we discuss the securities markets in which different securities issued by businesses are bought and sold. The primary objective of this chapter is to provide a sense of the richness of the financial marketplace, the critical role that it plays in each of our lives, and how corporations use the financial markets to raise capital.

Regardless of Your Major...

"Defined Benefit vs. Defined Contribution Retirement Plans"

When you start your first job after graduating, your employer will probably give you the option of automatically investing part of your paycheck each pay period for your retirement. Learning about the financial markets will help you analyze your options and make good selections. Twenty years ago, retirement plans were typically **defined benefit plans**. You would work for only one company, and the company would reward your loyalty and hard work by paying you a pension during your retirement based on your years of employment and the level of pay that you earned. In other words, the company set aside money to pay your pension benefit and invested it for you. Today, people change jobs often, and pension plans like the one just described are very rare. Instead, most employers now offer their employees **defined contribution plans**, such as a 401(k) savings plan. With a defined contribution pension plan, you, the employee, and your employer make periodic cash contributions to your retirement fund that you must take responsibility for investing. So, it doesn't matter whether you're a doctor, lawyer, truck driver, or salesperson, you are going to be a pension fund manager.

Your Turn: See Study Question 1.

The Basic Structure of the U.S. Financial Markets

Businesses typically opt to take on the form of a corporation when they need to raise large amounts of capital. In this chapter, we will demonstrate how a corporation raises capital using the U.S. financial markets.

A financial market is any place where money and credit are exchanged. When you take out a car loan from your bank, you participate in the financial markets. Within the financial markets there are three principal sets of players that interact:

1. **Borrowers.** Those who need money to finance their purchases. This includes businesses that need money to finance their investments or to expand their inventories as well as individuals who borrow money to purchase a new automobile or a new home.

2. **Savers (Investors).** Those who have money to invest. These are principally individuals who save money for a variety of reasons, such as accumulating a down payment for a home or saving for a return to graduate school. Firms also save when they have excess cash.

3. **Financial Institutions (Intermediaries).** The financial institutions and markets that help bring borrowers and savers together. The financial institution you are probably most familiar with is the **commercial bank,** a financial institution that accepts deposits and makes loans, such as Bank of America or Citibank, where you might have a checking account. However, as we discuss in the next section, there are many other types of financial institutions that bring together borrowers and savers.

The Financial Marketplace: Financial Institutions

The financial markets facilitate the movement of money from savers, who tend to be individuals, to borrowers, who tend to be businesses. In return for the use of the savers' money, borrowers provide the savers with a return on their investment.

As shown in Figure 1, the institutions that make up the financial marketplace consist of commercial banks, finance companies, insurance companies, investment banks, and investment companies. We call these institutions that help bring together individuals and businesses

Figure 1

Financial Markets, Institutions, and the Circle of Money

Financial markets consist of institutions that facilitate the transfer of savings from individuals and firms with excess cash to borrowers who have less cash than they need.

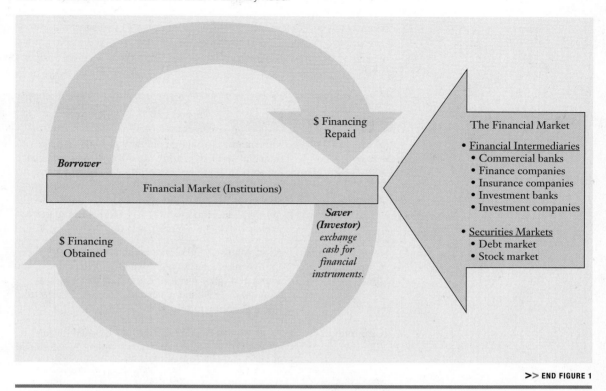

Borrower

Financial Market (Institutions)

$ Financing Repaid

$ Financing Obtained

Saver (Investor) exchange cash for financial instruments.

The Financial Market

- Financial Intermediaries
  - Commercial banks
  - Finance companies
  - Insurance companies
  - Investment banks
  - Investment companies

- Securities Markets
  - Debt market
  - Stock market

>> END FIGURE 1

financial intermediaries, because these institutions stand between those who have money to invest and those who need money. Financial markets are often described by the maturities of the securities traded in them. For example, the **money markets** are markets for short-term debt instruments, with "short-term" meaning maturities of one year or less. On the other hand, **capital markets** are markets for long-term financial instruments. "Long-term" here means having maturities that extend beyond one year.

There are no national boundaries on financial markets. A borrower in Brazil, for example, might borrow money from a bank in London to finance a plant expansion. Furthermore, it's not just individuals and companies that raise money and invest in the global financial markets. Governments can enter the financial markets when they are experiencing a deficit and need to raise money to finance their expenditures. Governments can also enter financial markets when they have more money than they plan to spend and want to invest the surplus. For example, the Chinese government invests huge sums of money in U.S. Treasury bonds, which are long-term debt securities issued by the U.S. government.

Commercial Banks: Everyone's Financial Marketplace

As previously mentioned, the commercial bank is probably the first financial intermediary each of us has dealt with in the financial marketplace. And, because they provide many firms with their initial funding, commercial banks also tend to be one of the first financial intermediaries that businesses deal with. Banks collect the savings of individuals as well as businesses and then lend these pooled savings to other individuals and businesses. They make money by charging a rate of interest to borrowers that exceeds the rate they pay to savers. They are also one of the major lenders to businesses.

In the United States, although banks can loan money to industrial corporations, banks are prohibited by law from owning them. This restriction prevents banks from loaning money to the industrial firms that they own; however, this restriction is not universal around the world.

Table 1	Four Largest Commercial Banks in the United States at the End of Third Quarter 2009

Commercial banks are ranked by the total dollar value of their deposits. Most large banks are owned by holding companies, which are companies that own other types of businesses in addition to the bank. However, the types of businesses that holding companies can own are restricted by federal law. Any firm that owns or controls 25 percent or more of a commercial bank is classified as a bank holding company and must register with the Federal Reserve System, which is the primary regulator of commercial banking in the United States. The financial crisis of 2008–2009 led to consolidations of weaker banks, most notably the acquisition of Wachovia by Wells Fargo.

Institution Name	Description	Total Deposits ($ in thousands)
JPMorgan Chase & Co. (JPM)	This financial holding company provides a range of financial services worldwide through six segments: Investment Banking, Retail Financial Services, Card Services, Commercial Banking, Treasury and Securities Services, and Asset Management. The company was founded in 1823 and is headquartered in New York, New York.	$1,162,998,000
Bank of America Corporation (BAC)	As of August 2, 2012, the company operated approximately 5,693 retail banking offices and 18,000 automated teller machines. Bank of America was founded in 1874 and is headquartered in Charlotte, North Carolina.	$1,062,273,625
Citigroup, Inc. (C)	As of August 3, 2012, Citigroup operated through a network of 1,036 offices. The company was founded in 1812 and is based in New York, New York.	$ 950,510,000
Wells Fargo Bank (WFC)	Wells Fargo & Company was founded in 1852 and is headquartered in San Francisco, California. The bank acquired Wachovia Corporation in 2008, resulting in 6,345 offices.	$ 921,071,000

Source: http://www.ibanknet.com/scripts/callreports/fiList.aspx?type=031

For instance, in countries such as Japan and Germany, banks are among the largest owners of industrial firms. Table 1 lists the four largest banks in the United States and their total deposits. It is very possible that you will recognize your personal bank among this list because the very largest banks operate throughout the entire United States, and the 25 largest banks hold more than 50 percent of total deposits.

Non-Bank Financial Intermediaries

In addition to commercial banks, there are a number of highly specialized financial intermediaries that also provide financial services to businesses. These include:

- financial services corporations, such as General Electric's (GE) GE Capital division and CIT Corporation (CIT);
- insurance companies, such as American International Group, Inc. (AIG), and Prudential (PRU);
- investment banks, such as Goldman Sachs (GS) and Morgan Stanley (MS); and
- investment companies, including mutual funds, hedge funds, and private equity firms.

Financial Services Corporations

Perhaps the best-known financial service corporation in the world is GE Capital, the finance unit of the General Electric Corporation. GE Capital provides commercial loans, financing programs, commercial insurance, equipment leasing of every kind, and other services, in over

35 countries around the world. GE provides credit services to more than 130 million customers, including consumers, retailers, auto dealers, and mortgage lenders, offering products and services ranging from credit cards to debt consolidation to home equity loans. CIT Group, Inc. is another commercial finance company that offers a wide range of financing services to businesses. The important thing to note here is that although financial services corporations are in the lending or financing business, they are not commercial banks.

Insurance Companies

Insurance companies are by definition in the business of selling insurance to individuals and businesses to protect their investments. This means that they collect premiums, hold the premiums in reserves until there is an insured loss, and then pay out claims to the holders of the insurance contracts. Note that in the course of collecting and holding premiums, the insurance companies build up huge pools of reserves to pay these claims. These reserves are then used in various types of investments, including loans to individuals and businesses. American International Group, Inc. (AIG) is now a household name because of the debt market crisis of 2008 and the ensuing government bailout. However, the company's business activities serve as an example of the degree to which insurance companies have become involved in business finance. AIG not only sells insurance products but also provides financial services, including aircraft and equipment leasing, consumer finance, insurance premium financing, and debt and loan insurance. Of particular note in this listing of services is debt and loan insurance, which includes selling guarantees to lenders that reimburse them should the loans they made go into default. This type of transaction is called a **credit default swap**.

Investment Banks

Investment banks are specialized financial intermediaries that help companies and governments raise money and provide advisory services to client firms when they enter into major transactions such as buying or merging with other firms. Prominent firms that provide investment banking services include Bank of America, Merrill Lynch, Barclays, Citigroup, Credit Suisse, Deutsche Bank, Goldman Sachs, HSBC, JPMorgan Chase, Morgan Stanley, and UBS AG.

Investment Companies

Investment companies are financial institutions that pool the savings of individual savers and invest the money, purely for investment purposes, in the securities issued by other companies.

Mutual Funds and Exchange-Traded Funds (ETFs)

Perhaps the most widely known type of investment company is the **mutual fund**, a special type of intermediary through which individuals can invest in virtually all of the securities offered in the financial markets.[1] When individuals invest in a mutual fund, they receive shares in a fund that is professionally managed according to a stated investment objective or goal—for example, investing only in international stocks. Shares in the mutual fund grant ownership claim to a proportion of the mutual fund's portfolio.

A share in a mutual fund is not really like a share of stock because you can only buy and sell shares in the mutual fund directly from the mutual fund itself. The price that you pay when you buy your shares and the price you receive when you sell your shares is called the mutual fund's **net asset value (NAV)**, which is calculated daily based on the total value of the fund divided by the number of mutual fund shares outstanding. In effect, as the value of the mutual fund investments goes up, so does the price of the mutual fund's shares.

Mutual funds can either be *load* or *no-load* funds. A **load fund** is a mutual fund that is sold through a broker, financial advisor, or financial planner who earns a commission in the form of the load fee when he or she sells shares of the mutual fund. The term *load* refers to the sales commission you pay when acquiring ownership shares. These commissions can be quite large, typically in the 3.0 to 6.0 percent range, but in some cases they can run as high as

---

[1]For a more in-depth discussion of mutual funds go to http://www.sec.gov/answers/mutfund.htm.

The Business of Life

Controlling Costs in Mutual Funds

In choosing the right mutual fund, one thing is clear—costs kill. You will want to pick your fund with an eye toward keeping expenses down. In fact, the Securities and Exchange Commission has put together a website (www.sec.gov/investor/tools/mfcc/mfcc-int .htm) to show you how much damage mutual fund expenses will do to your investment. If you start with $10,000 and invest it for 30 years, achieving gross returns (before expenses) of 10.2 percent (the market average for the last three-quarters of a century),

and assuming fund operating expenses of 1.4 percent (the average expense on a U.S. domestic stock fund), your $10,000 will grow to $120,713. That sounds pretty good until you notice that the cost of that 1.4 percent operating expense plus foregone earnings on your investment totals $63,554! That's over 34 percent of the gross earnings of the fund. If you knock expenses down to 0.18 percent, your investment grows to $174,572 and your expenses drop down to $9,695!

It is possible to cut your expenses down to as little as 0.10 percent by investing in an index fund (i.e., a fund that tries to track a market index, such as the S&P 500, by buying the stocks that make up that index). In general, index funds perform better than the actively managed funds. In fact, from 1985 to 2000, 84.5 percent of U.S. actively managed stock mutual funds (as opposed to index funds) underperformed the S&P 500 index, with 77.5 percent underperforming over the entire 10 years and 81.6 percent underperforming in the most recent 5 years. According to a study from Jeremy J. Siegel's book *Stocks for the Long Run*, between 1982 and 2003, there were only three years in which more than 50 percent of mutual funds beat the S&P 500.

Your Turn: See Study Question 9.

8.5 percent. A mutual fund that doesn't charge a commission is referred to as a **no-load fund**. When you purchase a no-load mutual fund, you generally don't deal with a broker or advisor. Instead, you deal directly with the mutual fund investment company via its website, by direct mail, or through an 800 telephone number.

An **exchange-traded fund** (or **ETF**) is very much like a mutual fund except for the fact that the ownership shares in the ETF can be bought and sold on the stock exchanges. Most ETFs track an index, such as the Dow Jones Industrial Average or the S&P 500, and generally have relatively low expenses.

Mutual funds and ETFs provide a cost-effective way to diversify, which reduces risk—a great benefit for the small investor. If you only have $10,000 to invest, it would be difficult to diversify by purchasing shares of individual companies, as you would have to pay a brokerage commission for each individual stock you purchase. For example, buying 50 different stocks is likely to cost you $500 or more in commissions, which would be 5 percent of the amount invested. By buying a mutual fund or ETF you can indirectly purchase a portfolio of 50 or more stocks with just one transaction.

Hedge Funds

A **hedge fund** is very much like a mutual fund, but hedge funds are less regulated and tend to take more risk. They also tend to more actively influence the managers of the corporations that they invest in. Because of the higher risk, hedge funds are open to a limited range of investors who are deemed to be sufficiently savvy. Only an **accredited investor**, which means an individual with a net worth that exceeds $1 million, can invest in a hedge fund.

Management fees are also quite a bit higher for hedge funds; they typically run at about 2 percent of the assets and include an incentive fee (typically 20 percent of profits) based on the fund's overall performance.

Private Equity Firms

A **private equity firm** is a financial intermediary that invests in equities that are not traded on the public capital markets. Two types of private equity firms dominate this group: venture capital (VC) firms and leveraged buyout (LBO) firms. **Venture capital firms** raise money from investors (wealthy people and other financial institutions), which they then use to provide financing for private start-up companies when they are first founded. For example, Sevin Rosen Funds, established in 1980, has provided venture financing to Cypress Semiconductor (CY) and Silicon Graphics (SGIC). Kleiner Perkins Caufield & Byers, or KPCB as it is commonly called, is a venture capital firm located in Silicon Valley. KPCB is perhaps best known today for its involvement in the initial financing of Google (GOOG). It has also partnered with Apple to found the iFund™, a $100 million investment initiative that will fund market-changing ideas and products that extend the iPhone and iPod Touch platform.

The second major category of private equity firms is the **leveraged buyout fund**. These funds acquire established firms that typically have not been performing very well with the objective of making them profitable again and then selling them. LBO funds have been the subject of a number of movies, including *Barbarians at the Gate, Other People's Money,* and *Wall Street.*

Prominent LBO private equity firms include Cerberus Capital Management, L.P., which purchased the Chrysler Corporation from Daimler Benz, and TPG (formerly Texas Pacific Group), which has invested in a number of prominent firms, including Continental Airlines (CAL), Ducati (DMH.BE), Neiman Marcus, Burger King (BKC), MGM (MGM), Harrah's (HAG.HM), and Freescale Semiconductor (FSL-B). A third well-known LBO private equity firm is KKR (Kohlberg, Kravis, and Roberts), whose investment in the likes of RJR Nabisco provided the storyline for the popular movie *Barbarians at the Gate.*

The amount of money managed by private equity firms has grown dramatically over the last three decades, with new funds raised surpassing $262 billion in 2011. Three-quarters of the total is raised in North America; the majority of the remainder is raised in Europe. Of the total amount of money managed by private equity firms, roughly two-thirds is invested in the buyout or LBO category. In fact, LBO transactions grew from $7.5 billion in 1991 to $500 billion in 2006! But as you might expect, the number of deals dropped dramatically in the fourth quarter of 2008 and 2009, and is still not up to the 2006 level. However, the dollar amount of capital invested by the private equity intermediaries understates their importance to the economy. Private equity funding is largely responsible for financing the birth of new businesses and underwriting the renovation of old and faltering businesses.

Before you move on to 3

Concept Check | 2

1. Explain how individuals and firms use financial intermediaries to raise money in the financial markets.
2. How do commercial banks differ from other non-bank financial intermediaries?
3. What are examples of investment companies?
4. What is a hedge fund, and how does it differ from a mutual fund?
5. What are the two principal types of private equity firms?

The Financial Marketplace: Securities Markets

A **security** is a negotiable instrument that represents a financial claim. It can take the form of ownership (stocks) or a debt agreement. The securities markets allow businesses and individual investors to trade the securities issued by public corporations. Public corporations are those whose debt and equity are traded in public markets. Securities markets are typically discussed in terms of the primary and secondary markets. A **primary market** is a market in which new, as opposed to previously issued, securities are bought and sold for the first time. In this market, firms issue new securities to raise money that they can then use to help finance their businesses. The key feature of the primary market is that the firms selling securities actually receive the money raised.

The **secondary market** is where all subsequent trading of previously issued securities takes place. In this market the issuing firm does not receive any new financing, as the securities it has sold are simply being transferred from one investor to another. The principal benefit of the secondary market for the shareholders of firms that sell their securities to the public is liquidity. That is, if you purchased some of the shares of Google when it went public, you could easily sell those shares in the secondary market if you decided you no longer wanted to hold them. This

Figure 2

Security Markets Provide a Link between the Corporation and Investors

Step 1: Initially, the corporation raises funds in the financial markets by selling securities (a primary market transaction). Step 2: The corporation then invests this cash in return-generating assets—new projects. Step 3: The cash flow from those assets is either reinvested in the corporation, given back to the investors, or paid to the government in the form of taxes. Step 4: Immediately after the securities have been issued, they are traded among investors in the secondary market, thereby setting their market price.

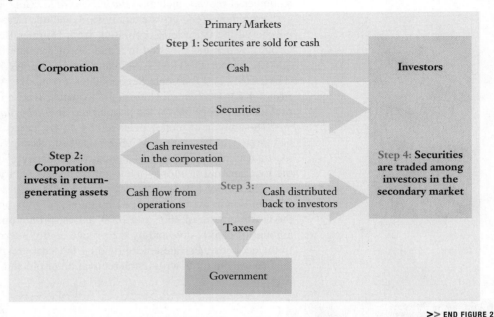

>> END FIGURE 2

ability to sell when you want to means that your Google stock is a very liquid investment. As a result, investors are more willing to invest in these securities, which benefits the issuing firm.

How Securities Markets Bring Corporations and Investors Together

Figure 2 describes the role of securities markets in bringing investors together with businesses looking for financing. In this regard, the securities markets are just another component of the financial marketplace. They are unique, however, in that investors in securities markets provide money directly to the firms that need it, as opposed to making deposits in commercial banks that then loan money to those firms.

We can think of the process of raising money in the securities markets in terms of the four-step process highlighted in Figure 2:

Step 1. **The firm sells securities to investors.** Corporations raise money in the securities markets by selling either debt or equity. When the firm initially sells the securities to the public, it is considered to take place in the primary markets. This is the only time the firm receives money in return for its securities.

Step 2. **The firm invests the funds it raises in its business.** The corporation invests the cash raised in the security market in hopes that it will generate cash flows—for example, it may invest in a new restaurant, a new hotel, a factory expansion, or a new product line.

Step 3. **The firm distributes the cash earned from its investments.** The cash flow from the firm's investments is reinvested in the corporation, paid to the government in taxes, or distributed to the investors who own the securities issued in Step 1. In the latter case, the cash is distributed to the investors who loaned the firm money (that is, bought the firm's debt securities) through the payment of interest and principal.

Cash is paid to the investors who bought equity (stock) through the payment of cash dividends or the repurchase of the shares of the firm's previously issued stock.

Step 4. Securities trading in the secondary market. Immediately after the securities are sold to the public, the investors who purchased them are free to resell them to other investors. These subsequent transactions take place in the secondary market.

Types of Securities

If you read the financial section of your newspaper or watch financial TV channels such as CNBC, you are already aware of the wide variety of investment alternatives to choose from. These choices fall into one of two basic categories: debt and equity.

Debt Securities

Firms borrow money by selling **debt securities** in the debt market. If the debt must be repaid in less than a year, these securities are sold in the short-term debt market, also called the money market. If the debt has a **maturity** (the length of time until the debt is due) between 1 and 10 years, it is often referred to as a **note**, and if longer than 10 years it is called a **bond** and is sold in the capital market. The capital market refers to the market for long-term financial instruments. The vast majority of these bonds pay a fixed interest rate, which means that the interest the owner of the bond receives never changes over its lifetime. Bonds are generally described using fairly exotic terminology. For example, we might say that a bond has a **face** or **par value** of $1,000 and that it pays an 8 percent **coupon rate** with two payments per year. What this means is that when the bond matures and the issuer (borrower) has to repay it, the owner of the bond (the lender) will receive a payment of $1,000. In the meantime, the holder will receive an interest payment every six months equal to $40, or $80 per year, which is 8 percent of $1,000.

Equity Securities

Equity securities represent ownership of the corporation. There are two major types of equity securities: *common stock* and *preferred stock*. When you buy equity security you are making an investment that you expect will generate a return. However, unlike a bond, which provides a promised set of interest payments and a schedule for the repayment of principal, the returns earned from an equity security are less certain. To further explore this topic, let's take a brief look at both types of equity securities.

Common Stock

Common stock is a security that represents equity ownership in a corporation, provides voting rights, and entitles the holder to a share of the company's success in the form of dividends and any capital appreciation in the value of the security. Investors who purchase common stock are the residual owners of the firm. This means that the common stockholder's return is earned only after all other security-holder claims (debt and preferred equity) have been satisfied in full.

If you were to purchase 100 shares of Disney's common stock, you would be a part-owner in the company. In essence, you would own an interest in the firm's studios, a piece of its movies, and a piece of its theme parks, including the new park in Shanghai. The more shares you buy, the bigger the portion of Disney you own. What do you get as an owner of Disney's stock? Don't count on free tickets to Disney World or a copy of the latest *Pirates of the Caribbean* movie. As an owner of the firm, you will have voting rights that entitle you to vote for the members of the firm's board of directors who oversee the selection of the management team. But as a small-time investor, you will have limited voting rights—your 100 shares of Disney's stock give you about 0.00000556 percent of Disney's shares. So, you aren't going to have much say about who gets elected to the Disney board of directors. Nonetheless, if Disney earns a profit, you will probably receive a portion of those profits in the form of a dividend payment. *It should be noted that unlike bond payments, firms don't have to pay dividends.* For example, if a company needs money to invest in a new product or project, it can choose to retain all of its earnings within the firm and pay no dividends.

Generally, firms that earn higher profits can pay higher dividends, and this often means that investors place a higher value on that firm's stock. For example, in 1999 the stock price of Qualcomm, a high-tech communications firm, went up 2,621 percent! However, when Qualcomm's profits and dividends, and people's expectations about its future prospects, deteriorated, its stock price fell by 50 percent in 2000, another 26 percent in 2001, and then by another drop of 30 percent in 2002. Since the end of 2002 there have been ups and downs, but by 2013 the price of Qualcomm rose almost three-fold from its 2003 level. This all goes to show that stock prices can fluctuate dramatically.

Preferred Stock

Preferred stock, like common stock, is an equity security. However, as the name implies, preferred stockholders take a "preferred" position relative to common shareholders. This means that preferred shareholders receive their dividends before any dividends are distributed to the common stockholders, who receive their dividends from whatever is left over. Note, however, that if the company does not earn enough to pay its interest expenses, neither preferred nor common stockholders will be paid a dividend. However, the dividends promised to the preferred stockholders will generally accrue and must be paid in full before common shareholders can receive any dividends. This feature is oftentimes referred to as a cumulative feature, and preferred stock with this feature is often referred to as cumulative preferred stock. In addition, preferred stockholders have a preferred claim on the distribution of assets of the firm in the event that the firm goes bankrupt and sells or liquidates its assets. Very simply, the firm's creditors (bondholders) get paid first, followed by the preferred stockholders, and anything left goes to the common stockholders. Of interest is that not all firms issue preferred stock.

Preferred stock is sometimes referred to as a hybrid security because it has many characteristics of both common stock and bonds. Preferred stock is similar to common stock in that (i) it has no fixed maturity date, (ii) the nonpayment of dividends does not bring on bankruptcy for the firm, and (iii) the dividends paid on these securities are not deductible for tax purposes. However, preferred stock is similar to corporate bonds in that (i) the dividends paid on the stock, like the interest payments made on bonds, are typically a fixed amount, and (ii) it does not come with any voting rights.

Stock Markets

A stock market is a public market in which the stock of companies is traded. Traditionally, the stock markets are classified as either organized security exchanges or the over-the-counter markets. **Organized security exchanges** are tangible entities; that is, they physically occupy space (such as a building or part of a building), and financial instruments are traded on their premises. The **over-the-counter markets** include all security markets except the organized exchanges. In the United States, the largest public market is the New York Stock Exchange (NYSE), whose history is traced back to 1792. Because it occupies a physical space (it is located at 11 Wall Street in Manhattan), it is considered an organized exchange. The common stock of more than 4,000 listed companies is traded on this exchange, which has monthly trading volume that exceeds 20 billion shares! In addition, the total value of the shares of stock listed on the NYSE at the beginning of 2013 reached just over $14.5 trillion. As you might expect, the dramatic stock market slide in 2008 took a toll on this figure; in fact, it was down from its peak of over $18 trillion in 2007.

Today, the NYSE is a hybrid market, having qualities of both an organized exchange and an over-the-counter market, allowing for face-to-face trading between individuals on the floor of the stock exchange in addition to automated electronic trading. As a result, during times of extreme flux in the market, at the opening or close of the market, or on large trades, human judgment can be called upon to make sure that the trade is properly executed.

NASDAQ, which stands for National Association of Securities Dealers Automated Quotations, is an over-the-counter market and describes itself as a "screen-based, floorless market." NASDAQ was formed in 1971 and is actually home to the securities of more companies than the NYSE. In 2013 some 3,200 companies were listed on NASDAQ, after reaching a peak of 5,556 in 1996. It has become highly popular as the trading mechanism of choice of several fast-growth sectors in the United States, including the high-technology sector. The common stock of computer chip maker Intel (INTC), for example, is traded via the NASDAQ, as is that of Dell (DELL), Starbucks (SBUX), Whole Foods Market (WFM), and Google (GOOG).

Reading Stock Price Quotes

Figure 3 illustrates how to read stock price quotes from www.google.com/finance. This is just a bit of the information available on Google Finance. You'll also find stock price charts, any news items, Internet discussions, information on related companies, and analyst estimates along with the firm's financial statements and key statistics and ratios. Similar information

Figure 3

Common Stock Price Quotes

The following is typical of what you would see if you looked at www.google.com/finance.

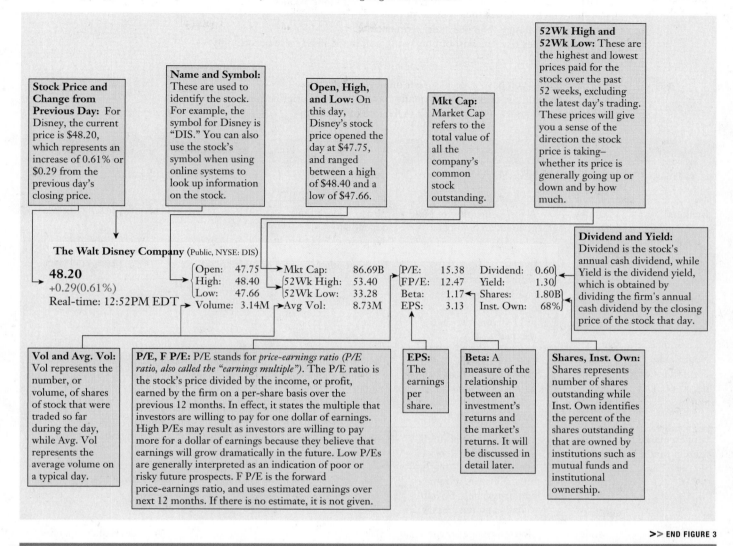

Stock Price and Change from Previous Day: For Disney, the current price is $48.20, which represents an increase of 0.61% or $0.29 from the previous day's closing price.

Name and Symbol: These are used to identify the stock. For example, the symbol for Disney is "DIS." You can also use the stock's symbol when using online systems to look up information on the stock.

Open, High, and Low: On this day, Disney's stock price opened the day at $47.75, and ranged between a high of $48.40 and a low of $47.66.

Mkt Cap: Market Cap refers to the total value of all the company's common stock outstanding.

52Wk High and 52Wk Low: These are the highest and lowest prices paid for the stock over the past 52 weeks, excluding the latest day's trading. These prices will give you a sense of the direction the stock price is taking– whether its price is generally going up or down and by how much.

The Walt Disney Company (Public, NYSE: DIS)

48.20
+0.29(0.61%)
Real-time: 12:52PM EDT

Open:	47.75	Mkt Cap:	86.69B	P/E:	15.38	Dividend:	0.60
High:	48.40	52Wk High:	53.40	FP/E:	12.47	Yield:	1.30
Low:	47.66	52Wk Low:	33.28	Beta:	1.17	Shares:	1.80B
Volume:	3.14M	Avg Vol:	8.73M	EPS:	3.13	Inst. Own:	68%

Dividend and Yield: Dividend is the stock's annual cash dividend, while Yield is the dividend yield, which is obtained by dividing the firm's annual cash dividend by the closing price of the stock that day.

Vol and Avg. Vol: Vol represents the number, or volume, of shares of stock that were traded so far during the day, while Avg. Vol represents the average volume on a typical day.

P/E, F P/E: P/E stands for *price-earnings ratio (P/E ratio, also called the "earnings multiple")*. The P/E ratio is the stock's price divided by the income, or profit, earned by the firm on a per-share basis over the previous 12 months. In effect, it states the multiple that investors are willing to pay for one dollar of earnings. High P/Es may result as investors are willing to pay more for a dollar of earnings because they believe that earnings will grow dramatically in the future. Low P/Es are generally interpreted as an indication of poor or risky future prospects. F P/E is the forward price-earnings ratio, and uses estimated earnings over next 12 months. If there is no estimate, it is not given.

EPS: The earnings per share.

Beta: A measure of the relationship between an investment's returns and the market's returns. It will be discussed in detail later.

Shares, Inst. Own: Shares represents number of shares outstanding while Inst. Own identifies the percent of the shares outstanding that are owned by institutions such as mutual funds and institutional ownership.

>> END FIGURE 3

is given at finance.yahoo.com and *Wall Street Journal Online* (*www.wsj.com*) in the "Market Data Center" under the "U.S. Stocks" link.

Other Financial Instruments

So far we have touched on only the tip of the iceberg in terms of the variety of different types of financial instruments that are available to investors and firms. Table 2 provides a listing of a number of different financial instruments used by firms to raise money, beginning with the shortest-maturity instruments that are traded in the money market and moving through the longest-maturity securities that are traded in the capital market.

Financial Markets and the Financial Crisis

Beginning in 2007 the United States experienced its most severe financial crisis since the Great Depression of the 1930s. As a result, some financial institutions collapsed while the government bailed others out, unemployment skyrocketed, the stock market plummeted, and the United States entered into a recession. Although the recession is now officially over, the economy still faces the lingering effects of the financial crisis that continue in the form of both a high rate of unemployment and a dramatic rise in our country's debt.

Table 2   Characteristics of Different Financial Instruments

Money Market Debt

For the Borrower:
- Good way of inexpensively raising money for short periods of time.
- Rates tend to be lower than long-term rates.
- Can borrow money to match short-term needs.
- If interest rates rise, the cost of borrowing will immediately rise accordingly.

For the Investor:
- Very liquid—you have access to your money when you need it.
- Safe—generally invested in high-quality investments for brief periods.
- Low returns—rates tend to be close to the rate of inflation.

Instrument	Market	Major Participants	Riskiness	Original Maturity	Interest Rates*
U.S. Treasury bills	Money—Debt	Issued by U.S. Treasury	Default-free	4 weeks to 1 year	0.09% to 0.14%
Bankers' acceptances	Money—Debt	A firm's promise to pay, guaranteed by a bank	Low risk of default, dependent on the risk of the guaranteeing bank	Up to 180 days	0.23% to 0.38%
Commercial paper	Money—Debt	Issued by financially secure firms to fund operating expenses or current assets (e.g., inventories and receivables)	Low default risk	Up to 270 days	0.14% to 0.25%
Negotiable certificates of deposit (CDs)	Money—Debt	Issued by major money-center commercial banks with a denomination of at least $100,000 to large investors	Default risk depends on the strength of the issuing bank	2 weeks to 1 year	National average 0.30%
Money market mutual funds	Money—Debt	Issued by mutual funds and invested in debt obligations such as Treasury bills, CDs, and commercial paper; held by individuals and businesses	Low degree of risk	No specific maturity date (can be redeemed any time)	0.02% to 0.19%
Consumer credit, including credit card debt	Money—Debt	Non-mortgage consumer debt issued by banks/credit unions/finance companies	Risk is variable	Varies	Variable depending upon the risk level

Long-Term Debt and Fixed Income Securities Market

For the Borrower:
- Interest rates are locked in over the entire life of the debt.
- Has a tax advantage over common stock in that interest payments are tax deductible, whereas dividend payments are not.

For the Investor:
- Can be used to generate dependable current income.
- Some bonds produce tax-free income.
- Long-term debt tends to produce higher returns than short-term debt.
- Less risky than common stock.
- Investor can lock in an interest rate and know the future returns (assuming the issuer does not default on its payments).

(TABLE 2 CONTINUED >> ON NEXT PAGE)

Table 2 Characteristics of Different Financial Instruments *continued*

Instrument	Market	Major Participants	Riskiness	Original Maturity	Interest Rates*
U.S. Treasury notes and bonds	Capital—Debt	Issued by the U.S. government to mutual funds, businesses, individuals, and foreign countries	No default risk but price will decline if interest rates rise	Notes have original maturities of 2, 5, and 10 years; bonds have original maturities greater than 10 years	0.17% to 2.31%
Federal agency debt	Capital—Debt	Issued by federal agencies (Fannie Mae, Ginnie Mae, and others) to businesses, individuals, and foreign countries	Close to Treasury debt, but not obligations of the federal government, still very low risk	Up to 30 years	0.14% to 2.74%
Mortgages	Capital—Debt	Borrowings from commercial banks and savings and loans (S&Ls) by individuals	Risk is variable, with subprime mortgages having a good deal of risk	Up to 30 years	2.83% (15-year fixed) to 3.41% (30-year fixed)
Municipal bonds (state and local government bonds)	Capital—Debt	Issued by state and local governments to individuals, institutional investors, and foreign countries	Riskier than U.S. government securities, with the level of risk dependent upon the issuer, but exempt from most taxes	Up to 30 years	3.41% (30-year, AAA-rated bonds)
Corporate bonds	Capital—Debt	Issued by corporations to individuals and institutional investors	Risk is dependent upon the financial strength of the issuer; riskier than U.S. government securities but less risky than preferred and common stocks	In general up to 40 years, however Walt Disney and Coca-Cola have issued 100-year bonds	2.11% (10-year, AAA bonds), 3.85% (20-year AAA bonds)

Preferred Stock

For the Insurer:
- Dividends can be omitted without the risk of bankruptcy.
- Has the disadvantage that dividends are not tax deductible for the issuer, whereas interest payments from debt are tax deductible.

For the Investor:
- To corporate investors, it has a tax advantage because at minimum, 70 percent of dividends received are tax free.

Instrument	Market	Major Participants	Riskiness	Original Maturity	Interest Rates*
Preferred stocks	Capital—Equity (Preferred Stock)	Issued by corporations to individuals, other corporations, and institutional investors	Riskier than corporate bonds, but less risky than common stock	No maturity date	Dependent upon risk, generally ranging from 4.03% to 8.47%

Common Stock

For the Issuer:
- The issuing firm is not legally obligated to make payments.
- Does not have a maturity date.
- Issuance of common stock increases creditworthiness because the firm has more investor money to cushion the firm in the case of a loss.
- Has a tax disadvantage relative to debt; whereas debt interest payments are deductible for tax purposes, common stock dividends are not.

For the Investor:
- Over the long run, common stock has outperformed debt-based financial assets.
- Along with the increased expected return comes increased risk.

Instrument	Market	Major Participants	Riskiness	Original Maturity	Interest Rates
Common stocks	Capital—Equity (Common Stock)	Issued by corporations to individuals, other corporations, and institutional investors	Risky, with dividends only paid when they are declared	No maturity date	Do not pay interest

* The yields were taken from http://online.wsj.com, http://www.bloomberg.com, http://research.stlouisfed.org, http://finance.yahoo.com, and http://www.bankrate.com, retrieved November 21, 2012.

Finance in a **Flat World**

Where's the Money around the World

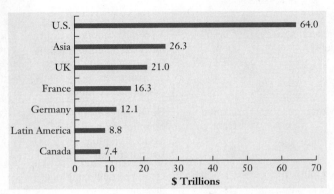

The figure above describes the total value of financial assets (bonds, equities, and bank assets) in the financial markets for each of the major regions of the world at the end of 2010. Although the totals change from year to year, these data provide some insight into the distribution of the value of financial assets around the world. When it comes to stock market capitalization—that is, the value of all equities—the United States clearly dominates, being the home for about one-third of equities.

Source: International Monetary Fund, Global Financial Stability Report Statistical Appendix, April 2012, http://www.imf.org/external/pubs/ft/gfsr/2012/01/pdf/statapp.pdf

Your Turn: See Study Question 10.

Although many factors contributed to the financial crisis, the most immediate cause has been attributed to the collapse of the real estate market and the resulting real estate loan (mortgage) defaults—in particular, what are commonly referred to as subprime mortgages. These were loans made to borrowers whose ability to repay them was highly doubtful. When the market for real estate began to falter in 2006, many of the homebuyers with subprime mortgages began to default. As the economy contracted during the recession, people lost their jobs and could no longer make their mortgage loan payments, resulting in even more defaults.

To complicate the problem, most real estate mortgages were packaged in portfolios and resold to investors around the world. This process of packaging mortgages is called securitization, because it takes loans that cannot be publicly traded and turns them into securities that can be freely bought and sold by financial institutions. Here's how mortgages are securitized:

1. First, homebuyers borrow money by taking out a mortgage to finance a home purchase.

2. Second, the lender, generally a bank, savings and loan institution, or mortgage broker that made the loan, then sells the mortgage to another firm or financial institution.

3. Third, that financial institution pools together a portfolio of many different mortgages, and the purchase of that pool of mortgages is financed through the sale of securities called mortgage-backed securities, or MBSs.

4. Fourth, these MBSs are sold to investors who can hold them as an investment or resell them to other investors.

This process allows the mortgage bank or other financial institution that made the original mortgage loan to get its money back out of the loan and lend it to someone else. Thus, securitization provides liquidity to the mortgage market and makes it possible for banks to loan more money to homebuyers.

Okay, so what's the catch? As long as lenders properly screen the mortgages to make sure the borrowers are willing and able to repay their home loans and real estate values remain higher than the amount owed, everything works fine. However, if the financial institution that originates the mortgage plans on selling it rather than holding it, it may have less incentive to properly screen the borrower. Why would lenders do this? It all goes back to **P** Principle 5: **Individuals**

Respond to Incentives; the lenders made their money by making the loans, and sold them almost immediately. As a result, some lenders were not concerned with whether or not the borrower could repay the loan; they were only concerned with making the loan—to them, repayment was someone else's problem.

As a result, starting around 2006, homeowners began to default on their mortgage loans. These defaults triggered losses at major banks, which in turn triggered a recession, causing people to lose their jobs and, correspondingly, the ability to make their mortgage payments. This was the scenario that played out at least through 2009. In essence, this was a perfect storm of bad loans, falling housing prices, and a contracting economy.

Unfortunately, these problems did not stay in the United States, as banks in Europe also held many of these mortgage-backed securities (MBSs), triggering a world-wide banking crisis. On top of this, European banks hold a lot of the European sovereign debt, so if countries such as Greece default on their debt, the European banking system will be in trouble. The recession that was originally sparked by the banking crisis revealed that the government budget situation in countries such as Greece was unsustainable, leading to the current European debt crisis. Many members of the European Union (EU) are experiencing severe budget problems, including Greece, Italy, Ireland, Portugal, and Spain. These nations are all unable to balance their budgets and face a very real prospect of defaulting on payments tied to government loans.

As a further result of the financial crisis, the stand-alone investment banking industry in the United States is no more. From the time of George Washington until the Great Depression in the 1930s, the U.S. economy experienced financial panics and banking crises about every 15 years. In response to the Great Depression and the failures of 4,004 banks in 1933, Congress enacted the National Banking Act of 1933, of which several sections are commonly referred to as the Glass–Steagall Act. An important component of the Glass–Steagall Act was the separation of commercial banking and the investment industry. Specifically, the act prohibited commercial banks from entering the investment industry in order to limit risks to banks. As a result, a "stand-alone" investment banking industry was created with firms like Lehman Brothers, Bear Stearns, Merrill Lynch, Goldman Sachs, and Morgan Stanley. However, in 1999 Glass–Steagall was repealed, and many commercial banks acquired investment banks, whereas others, such as JPMorgan Chase & Co. (JPM), entered the investment banking business. The advantage of this combination was that it gave investment banks access to stable funding through bank deposits along with the ability to borrow from the Federal Reserve in the case of an emergency, while the commercial bank gained access to the more lucrative, albeit more risky, investment industry.

In the wake of the 2008 financial crisis, the financial industry was again transformed. During the crisis, the major stand-alone investment banks either failed (Lehman Brothers), were acquired by commercial banks (Bear Stearns and Merrill Lynch), or were converted to commercial banks (Morgan Stanley and Goldman Sachs). Indeed, by the end of 2008, there were no major stand-alone investment banking firms left.

Then in 2010 the Dodd–Frank Wall Street Reform and Consumer Protection Act was passed. Under Dodd–Frank, banks as well as non-bank financial institutions are subject to considerably more oversight and are required to be more transparent. Another important feature of this legislation is what is known as the "Volker" rule, which prohibits banks that take deposits from **proprietary trading**, which is using the bank's capital to make speculative bets on derivatives and securities.

The hope is that these changes will increase the stability of the U.S. financial system and ensure that we will no longer be subject to financial crises that throw our economy into a severe recession. However, critics have argued that on one hand the recent legislation has not done enough to protect consumers as well as the safety of the financial system, and on the other hand that it adds unnecessary bureaucracy to our financial institutions.

Before you begin end of chapter material

Concept Check | 3

1. What are debt and equity securities, and how do they differ?

2. How is a primary market different from a secondary market?

3. How does common stock differ from preferred stock?

P Principle 2: **There Is a Risk-Return Tradeoff** Financial markets are organized to offer investors a wide range of investment opportunities that have different risks and different expected rates of return that reflect those risks.

P Principle 5: **Individuals Respond to Incentives** One of the reasons for the recent subprime mortgage crisis may have been in improper incentives to screen borrowers.

P Principle 4: **Market Prices Reflect Information** It is through the operations of the financial markets that new information is efficiently impounded in security prices.

Chapter Summaries

1 Describe the structure and functions of financial markets.

SUMMARY: Financial markets allocate the supply of savings in the economy to the individuals and companies that need the money. A primary market is a market in which new, as opposed to previously issued, securities are bought and sold for the first time. In this market firms issue new securities to raise money that they can then use to help finance their businesses. The key feature of the primary market is that the firms that raise money by selling securities actually receive the money.

The secondary market is where all subsequent trading of previously issued securities takes place. In this market the issuing firm does not receive any new financing, as the securities it has sold are simply being transferred from one investor to another. The principal benefit to investors of having a secondary market is the ease with which the investor can sell or liquidate investments.

KEY TERMS

Commercial bank A financial institution that accepts demand deposits, makes loans, and provides other services to the public.

Defined benefit plans A company retirement plan, such as a pension plan, in which a retired employee receives a specific amount based on his or her salary history and years of service.

Defined contribution plans A company retirement plan, such as a 401(k) plan, in which the employee elects to contribute some amount of his or her salary to the plan and the employee takes responsibility for the investment decisions.

2 Distinguish between commercial banks and other financial institutions in the financial marketplace.

SUMMARY: Financial institutions are intermediaries that stand in the middle between borrowers who need money and savers who have money to invest. Widely varying financial institutions have evolved over time to meet special needs for intermediation, including commercial banks that accept deposits from savers and lend to borrowers, investment banks that help companies sell their securities to investors in order to raise the money they need, and many other institutions. Of particular interest are mutual funds that collect the investments of many small investors and invest the pool of funds in stocks, bonds, and other types of securities that are issued by businesses. In recent years, two types of investment companies have captured the headlines: hedge funds and private equity funds. Both of these types of investment companies accept investments from other financial institutions or wealthy individuals and invest in speculative and risky ventures.

KEY TERMS

Accredited investor Investor who is permitted to invest in certain types of higher-risk investments. These investors include wealthy individuals, corporations, endowments, and retirement plans.

Capital market The market for long-term financial instruments.

Credit default swap An insurance contract that pays off in the event of a credit event such as default or bankruptcy.

Exchange-traded fund (ETF) An investment vehicle traded on stock exchanges much like a share of stock. The entity holds investments in assets that meet the investment objective of the entity (e.g., shares of stock of companies from emerging markets).

Financial intermediaries Institutions whose business is to bring together individuals and institutions with money to invest or lend with other firms or individuals in need of money.

Hedge fund An investment fund that is open to a limited range of investors (accredited investors) and that can undertake a wider range of investment and trading activities than other types of investment funds that are open to the general public (e.g., mutual funds).

Investment bank A financial institution that raises capital, trades in securities, and manages corporate mergers and acquisitions.

Investment company A firm that invests the pooled funds of retail investors for a fee.

Leveraged buyout fund A private equity firm that raises capital from individual investors and uses these funds along with significant amounts of debt to acquire controlling interests in operating companies.

Load fund A mutual fund that charges investors a sales commission called a "load."

Money market The financial market for short-term debt securities (maturing in one year or less).

Mutual fund A professionally managed investment company that pools the investments of many individuals and invests it in stocks, bonds, and other types of securities.

Net asset value (NAV) The difference between the current market value of an entity's (such as a mutual fund) assets and the value of its liabilities.

No-load fund A mutual fund that doesn't charge a commission.

Private equity firm A financial intermediary that invests in equities that are not traded on the public capital markets.

Venture capital firm An investment company that raises money from accredited investors and uses the proceeds to invest in new start-up companies.

Concept Check | **2**

1. Explain how individuals and firms use financial intermediaries to raise money in the financial markets.
2. How do commercial banks differ from other non-bank financial intermediaries?
3. What are examples of investment companies?
4. What is a hedge fund, and how does it differ from a mutual fund?
5. What are the two principal types of private equity firms?

Describe the different securities markets for bonds and stocks.

SUMMARY: When a corporation needs to raise large sums of money, it generally turns to the public market for bonds if it borrows or equity if it seeks funds from new owners. The buyers of these securities include individual investors and investment companies such as mutual funds. The U.S. stock and bond markets are the largest and most active in the world. In some instances these markets are physical locations where buyers and sellers interact, such as the New York Stock Exchange at 11 Wall Street, or they consist of an electronic market of interconnected computers, such as NASDAQ. Beginning in 2007, the United States experienced its most severe financial crisis since the Great Depression of the 1930s. Although there is not a single cause for the crisis, the collapse of the real estate market certainly contributed to this event.

KEY TERMS

Bond A long-term (10-year or more) promissory note issued by a borrower, promising to pay the owner of the security a predetermined amount of interest each year.

Common stock A form of equity security that represents the residual ownership of the firm.

Coupon rate The amount of interest paid per year expressed as a percent of the face value of the bond.

Debt securities Financial instruments that represent loans to corporations. Long-term debt securities are called bonds and can be bought and sold in the bond market.

Equity securities Financial instruments that represent ownership claims on a business. Equity securities for corporations are called shares of stock and can be bought and sold in the stock market.

Face, or par value On the face of a bond, the stated amount that the firm is to repay on the maturity date.

Maturity The date when a debt must be repaid.

Note Another term used to refer to indebtedness. Notes generally have a maturity between 1 and 10 years when originally issued.

Organized security exchanges Security exchanges that physically occupy space (such as a building or part of a building) and trade financial instruments on their premises.

Over-the-counter markets All security markets except the organized exchanges.

Proprietary trading Using the bank's capital to make speculative bets on derivatives and securities.

Concept Check | **3**

1. What are debt and equity securities, and how do they differ?

2. How is a primary market different from a secondary market?

3. How does common stock differ from preferred stock?

Preferred stock An equity security that holds preference over common stock in terms of the right to the distribution of cash (dividends) and the right to the distribution of proceeds in the event of the liquidation and sale of the issuing firm.

Primary market A part of the financial market where new security issues are initially bought and sold.

Secondary market The financial market where previously issued securities such as stocks and bonds are bought and sold.

Security A negotiable instrument that represents a financial claim that has value. Securities are broadly classified as debt securities (bonds) and equity securities (shares of common stock).

Study Questions

1. **(Related to Regardless of Your Major: Defined Benefit vs. Defined Contribution Retirement Plans)** In the *Regardless of Your Major* box feature, two types of pension plans are discussed. Describe each. Which type is now the dominant type in use?

2. What are the three principal sets of players that interact in the financial markets?

3. What is a financial intermediary? List and describe the principal types of financial intermediaries in the U.S. financial markets.

4. What do investment banks do in the financial markets?

5. Describe the difference between the primary market and the secondary market.

6. What is a mutual fund, and how does it differ from an exchange-traded fund (ETF)?

7. What is the difference between a debt security and an equity security?

8. What makes preferred stock "preferred"?

9. **(Related to The Business of Life: Controlling Costs in Mutual Funds)** In *The Business of Life: Controlling Costs in Mutual Funds* feature, the importance of keeping expenses down is discussed. The Financial Industry Regulatory Authority website provides an easy way to compare two mutual funds. Go to the website, http://apps.finra.org/fundanalyzer/1/fa.aspx, then enter Vanguard 500 Index Fund Investor Class (you will enter the ticker symbol VFINX), American Beacon Balanced Fund Class A (ABFAX), and Quantitative Futures Strategy Fund Class C Shares (QMFCX). Now, click on "show results." Set your investment at $10,000, your return at 8%, and your period at 10 years. What is your profit or loss? Why do you think there is such a big difference? (Think expenses and fees.)

10. **(Related to Finance in a Flat World: Where's the Money around the World)** The distribution of financial assets around the world is described in the *Finance in a "Flat" World* box feature. What country dominates in terms of the stock market and total financial assets? Of the UK, Germany, and France, which country has the most in the way of financial assets and which country has the least?

11. What is a hedge fund, and how is it different from a mutual fund?

12. What are the two types of private equity funds? What does each do with the money it raises from investors?

13. Go to Yahoo! Finance (http://finance.yahoo.com) and enter the symbol for Google (GOOG) in the "Enter Symbol(s)" box at the top of the page. What price did it last trade at? What is the last trade time, and how long ago was that? What is the day's price range for the stock? What is the closing change in the price of the stock, both in dollar and percentage terms? What is the stock's 52-week price range? Now check out some of the links on the left-hand side of the page. What kind of information listed there do you find interesting?

14. Go to the CNN-Money website (http://money.cnn.com) and visit the retirement section by clicking on "Personal Finance" on the top banner. From there, click on "Retirement." You'll find all kinds of interesting articles under this link. (But be forewarned: Some are a bit scary. Saving for retirement is not an easy task.) Write up a summary of any one of the articles listed there.

15. Go to the Market Watch website (www.marketwatch.com) Personal Finance section by clicking on "Personal Finance" on the top banner. This is a great website for information and help in managing your personal finances. Find an article you like, read it, and write a summary of it. Also, consider bookmarking this website—it's one you might want to start visiting on a regular basis.

16. Calculate the value of the total shareholder wealth for Google, Inc., using the number of common shares outstanding and the current price of the firm's shares. You can obtain the necessary information from the Yahoo! Finance website.

17. Go to the Smartmoney.com website (www.smartmoney.com) and select one of the listed stories for the day; read it and prepare a brief summary to share with the class.

18. Go to the Motley Fool website (www.fool.com) and select the Retirement tab. Describe the information available here for planning for your retirement.

Photo Credits

Understanding Financial Statements, Taxes, and Cash Flows

From Chapter 3 of *Financial Management: Principles and Applications*, Twelfth Edition. Sheridan Titman, Arthur J. Keown, and John D. Martin.

Understanding Financial Statements, Taxes, and Cash Flows

Chapter **Outline**

1 An Overview of the Firm's Financial Statements

→ **Objective 1.** Describe the content of the four basic financial statements and discuss the importance of financial statement analysis to the financial manager.

2 The Income Statement

→ **Objective 2.** Evaluate firm profitability using the income statement.

3 Corporate Taxes

→ **Objective 3.** Estimate a firm's tax liability using the corporate tax schedule and distinguish between the average and marginal tax rate.

4 The Balance Sheet

→ **Objective 4.** Use the balance sheet to describe a firm's investments in assets and the way it has financed them.

5 The Cash Flow Statement

→ **Objective 5.** Identify the sources and uses of cash for a firm using the firm's cash flow statement.

In this chapter we apply P Principle 1: **Money Has a Time Value,** P Principle 3: **Cash Flows Are the Source of Value,** P Principle 4: **Market Prices Reflect Information,** and P Principle 5: **Individuals Respond to Incentives.** Financial statements are prepared in accordance with a set of accounting principles that drives a wedge between reported statement figures, present values, and cash flows, but we can determine the cash flow implications for the firm from its reported financial statements. It is critical that we learn how to do this. Moreover, we learn that the firm's financial statements do contain information that can be important to the formation of investor expectations concerning the firm's future performance and, consequently, market prices.

In the summer of 1969, Don and Doris Fisher got so frustrated looking for a good pair of jeans in San Francisco that they decided to do something about it. They opened their own store called the Generation Gap, which sold Levi's jeans and record albums. The Generation Gap was an immediate hit, becoming a prime counterculture shopping spot. By 1976, The Gap, Inc. (GPS), as it is now known, had expanded to over 200 stores and its shares were trading on the New York Stock Exchange.

Until the late 1990s, it seemed that The Gap could do no wrong. The firm owned Old Navy and the Banana Republic. Sales just kept on climbing. But if we examine The Gap's financial statements, we can spot some alarming signs. Same-store sales were declining, and the number of Gap stores had been cut in half. The Gap's common stock price dropped from a high of $51 in 1999 to less than $10 a share in the spring of 2009 before recovering to more than $35 in 2012. The firm's financial statements contain information about the firm's past performance that is helpful in predicting future cash flows (remember P Principle 3: **Cash Flows Are the Source of Value**), and this information is helpful in estimating the value of the firm's common stock (remember P Principle 4: **Market Prices Reflect Information**).

This chapter focuses on accounting and, specifically, financial statements. You might be asking yourself (or your teacher), "Why we are spending so much time delving into financial statements?" The answer is simply that *accounting is the language of business*. When firms communicate with their stockholders and creditors, the principal form of communication is through the firm's financial statements. Moreover, when managers communicate with their fellow employees about the firm's performance, they often do so using benchmarks that are based on accounting profits.

In this chapter, we review the basic financial statements used by firms to report their financial performance. These financial statements can be viewed as a model or representation of the firm at a particular point in time. We first investigate why both a student of finance and a manager need to understand financial statements as well as the basic accounting principles that underlie their construction.

Regardless of Your Major...

"Accounting Is the Language of Business"

A firm's financial statements provide a visual representation of the firm that is used to describe the business to investors and others outside of the firm as well as to the firm's employees. Consequently, we can think of a firm's financial statements and the various terms used to describe the firm and its operations as the language of business. As such, everyone who becomes a manager, no matter what their area of expertise, needs to know how to "speak business," and this means knowing how to read and interpret financial statements. For example, when the firm communicates with its banker or the investment analysts who follow the firm's common stock, financial statement results provide the common language. When members of the firm's top management are determining the bonuses to pay at year-end, they look to the firm's financial performance as reflected in the financial statements. Moreover, progressing up the ranks of the firm's management team requires that you develop a broader understanding of the firm and how each of its components fits together. The firm's financial statements provide the key to gaining this knowledge.

1 An Overview of the Firm's Financial Statements

In this chapter, we look at the firm from the perspective of the financial analyst by reviewing the firm's financial statements, including the income statement, balance sheet, and cash flow statement. Understanding the financial health of a business by reviewing its financial statements is also important to the financial manager whose goal is to determine how to increase the value of the firm.

Basic Financial Statements

The accounting and financial regulatory authorities mandate the following four types of financial statements:

1. **Income statement**—includes the revenue the firm has earned *over a specific period of time,* usually a quarter of a year or a full year; the expenses it has incurred during the year to earn its revenues; and the profit the firm has earned.

2. **Balance sheet**—contains information as of the date of its preparation about the firm's assets (everything of value the company owns), liabilities (the firm's debts), and shareholders' equity (the money invested by the company owners). As such, the balance sheet is a snapshot of the firm's assets, liabilities, and owners' equity for a particular date.

3. **Cash flow statement**—reports cash received and cash spent by the firm *over a specified period of time,* usually a quarter of a year or a full year.

4. **Statement of shareholders' equity**—provides a detailed account of the firm's activities in the common and preferred stock accounts, the retained earnings account, and changes to owners' equity that do not appear in the income statement.

In this chapter we review the basic content and format of the income statement, balance sheet, and cash flow statement. We do not discuss the statement of shareholders' equity, as the information we need from this statement can be obtained from the income statement and balance sheet.

Why Study Financial Statements?

Analyzing a firm's financial statements can help managers carry out three important tasks: assess current performance, monitor and control operations, and plan and forecast future performance.

1. **Financial statement analysis.** The basic objective of financial statement analysis is to assess the financial condition of the firm being analyzed. In a sense, the analyst performs a financial analysis so he or she can see the firm's financial performance the same way an outside investor would see it.

2. **Financial control.** Managers use financial statements to monitor and control the firm's operations. The performance of the firm is reported using accounting measures that compare the prices of the firm's products and services with the estimated cost of providing them to buyers. Moreover, the board of directors uses these performance measures to determine executives' bonuses. The company's creditors also use performance measures based on the firm's financial statements to determine whether or not to extend the company's loans. For example, a common restriction included in loan agreements prohibits firms from borrowing more than a specific percentage of their total assets as reflected in the firms' financial statements.

3. **Financial forecasting and planning.** Financial statements provide a universally understood format for describing a firm's operations. Consequently, financial planning models are typically built using the financial statements as a prototype.

This chapter focuses on ▣ Principle 3: **Cash Flows Are the Source of Value**. A key issue that we will discuss is the distinction between the earnings numbers that the firm's accountants calculate and the amount of cash that a firm generates from its various lines of business. This difference is a primary source of differentiation between the study of finance and the study of accounting. For example, firms can earn positive accounting earnings while hemorrhaging cash, and can generate positive cash flow while reporting accounting losses. So, a key objective for the financial manager in this chapter involves developing a good understanding of accounting earnings and how they relate to cash flows.

What Are the Accounting Principles Used to Prepare Financial Statements?

Accountants use three fundamental principles when preparing a firm's financial statements: the revenue recognition principle, the matching principle, and the historical cost principle. Understanding these principles is critical to a full and complete understanding of what information is reported in a firm's financial statements and how that information is reported. Much of the accounting fraud that has occurred in the United States can be traced back to violations of one or more of these basic principles of accounting.

1. **The revenue recognition principle.** This principle provides the basis for deciding what **revenue**—the cumulative dollar amount of goods and services the firm sold to its customers during the period—should be reported in a particular income statement. The principle states that revenue should be included in the firm's income statement for the period in which (1) its goods and services were exchanged for either cash or **accounts receivable** (credit sales that have not yet been collected), or (2) the firm has completed what it must do to be entitled to the cash. As a general rule, a sale can be counted only when the goods sold leave the business's premises en route to the customer. The revenue recognition principle guides accountants when it is difficult to determine whether revenues should be reported in one period or another.

2. **The matching principle.** This principle determines what costs or expenses can be attributed to this period's revenues. Once the firm's revenues for the period have been determined, its accountants then determine the expenses for the period by letting the expenses "follow" the revenues, so to speak. For example, employees' wages aren't recognized when the wages are paid, or when their work is performed, but when the product produced as a result of that work is sold. Therefore, expenses are matched with the revenues they helped to produce.

3. **The historical cost principle.** This principle provides the basis for determining the dollar values the firm reports on the balance sheet. Most assets and liabilities are reported in the firm's financial statements on the basis of the price the firm paid to acquire them. This price is called the asset's historical cost. This may or may not equal the price the asset might bring if it were sold today. (Usually it does not.)[1]

Remembering these three principles will help you understand what you see in the firm's financial statements and why it is reported that way. Furthermore, having a basic understanding of accounting principles will make you a much more informed user of accounting information and a much better financial analyst.

 # The Income Statement

An **income statement**, also called a profit and loss statement, measures the amount of profits generated by a firm over a given time period (usually a year or a quarter). In its most basic form, the income statement can be expressed as follows:

$$\text{Revenues (or Sales)} - \text{Expenses} = \text{Profits} \tag{1}$$

Revenues represent the sales for the period. **Profits** are the difference between the firm's revenues and the expenses the firm incurred in order to generate those revenues for the period. Recall that revenues are determined in accordance with the revenue recognition principle and expenses are then matched to these revenues using the matching principle.

Income Statement of H. J. Boswell, Inc.

The typical format for the income statement is shown in Table 1 for H. J. Boswell, Inc., a fictitious firm we will use as an example throughout this chapter. Boswell is a well-known manufacturer of orthopedic devices and supplies. Its products include hip replacement supplies; knee, shoulder, and spinal implants; products used to fix bone fractures; and operating room products.

Reading and Interpreting Boswell's Income Statement

Recall from Equation (1) that the income statement contains three basic elements: revenues, expenses, and profits. We will use these elements to analyze each of the components of the income statement found in Table 1:

1. **Revenues**—Boswell's revenues totaled $2,700 million for the 12-month period ended December 31, 2013.
2. **Cost of Goods Sold**—Next we see that the various expenses the firm incurred in producing revenues are broken down into various subcategories. For example, the firm spent $2,025 million on **cost of goods sold**, the cost of producing or acquiring the products or services that the firm sold during the period.

---

[1]There are exceptions to the historical cost principle for recording asset values on the firm's balance sheet. A prime example involves the firm's cash and marketable securities portfolio. These assets are recorded on the balance sheet using the lesser of cost or their current market value. Changing the value of the firm's cash and marketable securities to reflect current market prices is commonly referred to as "marking to market." However, the historical cost principle is the guiding rule for determining the value to be recorded on the balance sheet in most cases.

Table 1   H. J. Boswell, Inc.

Income Statement (expressed in millions, except per share data)
for the Year Ended December 31, 2013

Sales		$ 2,700.00
Cost of goods sold		(2,025.00)
Gross profits		$ 675.00
Operating expenses:		
Selling expenses	$ (90.00)	
General and administrative expense	(67.50)	
Depreciation and amortization expense	(135.00)	
Total operating expense		(292.50)
Net operating income (EBIT, or earnings before interest and taxes)		$ 382.50
Interest expense		(67.50)
Earnings before taxes		$ 315.00
Income taxes		(110.25)
Net income		$ 204.75
Additional information:		
Dividends paid to stockholders during 2013		$ 45.00
Number of common shares outstanding		90.00
Earnings per share (EPS)		$ 2.28
Dividends per share		$ 0.50

Callout labels: Income from operating activities; Cost of debt financing; Cost of corporate income taxes; Net Income — Income resulting from operating and financing activities

3. **Gross Profit**—Subtracting cost of goods sold from revenues produces an estimate of the firm's gross profit of $675 million.

4. **Operating Expenses**—Next, we examine Boswell's operating expenses (this includes the salaries paid to the firm's administrative staff, the firm's electric bills, and so forth). One of the operating expense categories is depreciation expense ($135 million for Boswell in 2013). **Depreciation expense** is a non-cash expense used to allocate the cost of the firm's long-lived assets (such as its plant and equipment) over the useful lives of the assets. For example, suppose that, during 2013, Boswell was to build a new distribution facility in Temple, Texas, at a cost of $10 million. The firm would not expense the full $10 million against 2013 revenues, but instead would spread out the costs over many years to match the revenues the facility helped create.[2]

5. **Net Operating Income**—After deducting $292.50 million in operating expenses, Boswell's *net operating income* is $382.50 million. The firm's **net operating income** shows us the firm's ability to earn profits from its ongoing operations—before it makes interest payments and pays its taxes. For our purposes, net operating income will be synonymous with **earnings before interest and taxes (EBIT)**.

6. **Interest Expense**—To this point, we have calculated the profits resulting only from operating the business, without regard for any financing costs, such as the interest paid on money the firm might have borrowed. In this instance Boswell incurred interest expense equal to $67.50 million during 2013.

7. **Earnings before Taxes**—Now we can subtract Boswell's interest expense of $67.50 million from its operating income of $382.50 million to determine its earnings before taxes (also known as taxable income). Boswell's earnings before taxes are $315 million.

8. **Income Taxes**—Next, we determine the firm's income tax obligation. We will show how to calculate the tax obligation later in this chapter. For now, note that Boswell's income tax obligation is $110.25 million.

---

[2]Although there are many types of depreciation methods that can be used, we restrict our attention in this chapter to a simplified version of straight-line depreciation (e.g., we ignore the half-year convention). Using this method, the total cost of the asset minus any salvage value is divided by the number of years of useful life to calculate annual depreciation. For example, if a piece of equipment is purchased for $125,000 and has a $25,000 salvage value at the end of its five-year useful life, then the annual straight-line depreciation is calculated as follows: ($125,000 − $25,000) / 5 years = $20,000

9. **Net Income**—The income statement's bottom line is **net income,** which is calculated by subtracting the firm's tax liability of $110.25 million from its earnings before taxes of $315 million. This leaves net income of $204.75 million.

Evaluating Boswell's per Share Earnings and Dividends

At this point, we have completed the income statement. However, the firm's owners (common stockholders) will want to know how much income the firm made on a per share basis, or what is called **earnings per share**. We can calculate earnings per share by dividing the company's net income by the number of common shares it has outstanding. Because H. J. Boswell, Inc. had 90 million shares outstanding in 2013 (see Table 1), its earnings per share were $2.28 ($2.28 per share = $204.75 million net income ÷ 90 million shares).

Investors also want to know the amount of dividends a firm pays for each share outstanding, or the **dividends per share**. In Table 1 we see that H. J. Boswell, Inc. paid $45 million in dividends during 2013. You can then determine that the firm paid $0.50 in dividends per share ($0.50 = $45 million total dividends ÷ 90 million shares outstanding).

Connecting the Income Statement and Balance Sheet

If Boswell earned net income of $204.75 million (or $2.28 per share) and paid out only $45 million in dividends ($0.50 in dividends per share), what happened to the $204.75 million − 45 million = $159.75 million in earnings that were not paid out in dividends? The answer is that this amount was retained and reinvested in the firm. As we will later discuss, in the balance sheet Boswell's retained earnings rise by exactly this amount. Thus the income statement feeds directly into the balance sheet to record any profit or loss from the firm's operations for the period.

Interpreting Firm Profitability Using the Income Statement

The first conclusion we can draw from our quick survey of H. J. Boswell, Inc.'s income statement is that the firm was profitable because its revenues for 2013 exceeded the sum of all its expenses. Furthermore, as we move down the income statement beginning with the firm's revenues or sales, we can identify three different measures of profit or income. For example, the company's gross profit was $675 million, while its operating income—or earnings before interest and taxes—was just $382.5 million, and its net income was just $204.75 million. It is common practice to divide gross profit, operating income, and net income by the level of the firm's sales to calculate the firm's *gross profit margin, operating profit margin,* and the *net profit margin*, respectively. For H. J. Boswell, Inc., we calculate each of these profit margins as follows:

1. The *gross profit margin* is 25 percent ($675 million of gross profits ÷ $2,700 million of sales = 25%). Because the gross profit equals revenues minus the firm's cost of goods sold, the **gross profit margin** indicates the firm's "markup" on its cost of goods sold per dollar of sales. Note that the percent markup is generally expressed as a percentage of the firm's cost of goods sold. That is, the markup percentage equals gross profit divided by cost of goods sold, or $675 million ÷ $2,025 million = 33.3%. Because gross profit is 25 percent of sales and cost of goods is 75 percent of sales, we can also compute the markup percentage using these percentages; that is, 25% ÷ 75% = 33.3%.

2. The *operating profit margin* is only 14.2 percent ($382.5 million of net operating income ÷ $2,700 million of sales = 14.2%). The **operating profit margin** is equal to the ratio of net operating income or earnings before interest and taxes (EBIT) divided by firm sales.

3. The *net profit margin* is only 7.6 percent of firm revenues (7.6% = $204.75 million of net profits ÷ $2,700 million of sales). The **net profit margin** captures the effects of all of the firm's expenses and indicates the percentage of revenues left over after interest and taxes have been considered.

Notice that as we move down the income statement, calculating different profit margins after incorporating consideration for more categories of expenses, the successive profit margins naturally get smaller and smaller. By comparing these margins to those of similar businesses, we can dissect a firm's performance and identify expenses that are out of line. Because the firm's profit margins are an important indicator of how well the firm is doing financially, managers pay close attention to them, carefully watching for any changes either up or down. They also compare the firm's margins with those of its competitors.

GAAP and Earnings Management

In the United States, firms must adhere to a set of accounting principles commonly referred to as Generally Accepted Accounting Principles, or GAAP.[3] Even so, there is considerable room for a company's managers to actively influence the firm's reported earnings. Corporate executives have an incentive to manage the firm's earnings, both because their pay depends upon earnings and because investors pay close attention to the firm's quarterly earnings announcements. Executives sometimes "smooth out" reported earnings, by making choices that, for example, transfer earnings from years when they are abnormally high to future years when earnings would otherwise be low. The specifics of how this is done can be very complex and are beyond the scope of this chapter.[4] However, in extreme cases, earnings management can lead to fraudulent efforts to create earnings where none exist.

Companies hire accountants to maintain the firm's financial records and prepare the firm's quarterly and annual financial statements. **P** Principle 5: **Individuals Respond to Incentives** serves to remind us that managers may at times find themselves in situations where they would like to be less than forthcoming in describing the firm's financial condition to investors and may be tempted to stretch the rules of financial reporting to disguise the firm's current circumstances. Although the incentive to misreport the firm's financial condition is ever present (remember Enron?), investors (stockholders) in publicly held companies, whose bonds and/or stock can be bought and sold in the public markets, do not have to depend on the honesty of the firm's accountants for assurance that the firm has followed GAAP. The reason is that public firms are required to have their financial statements audited by an independent accounting firm. The audit of the financial statements provides a verification of the financial statements of the firm and an audit opinion. The audit opinion is intended to provide *reasonable assurance that the financial statements are presented fairly, in all material respects, and/or give a true and fair view in accordance with the financial reporting framework.* As such, the audit serves to enhance the degree of confidence that investors and others have when they use the financial statements. In essence, the audit by an independent accounting firm serves as a check and balance to control management's incentive to disguise the firm's true financial condition.

Checkpoint 1

Constructing an Income Statement

Use the following information to construct an income statement for Gap, Inc. (GPS). The Gap is a specialty retailing company that sells clothing, accessories, and personal-care products under the Gap, Old Navy, Banana Republic, Piperlime, and Athleta brand names. Use the scrambled information below to calculate the firm's gross profits, operating income, and net income for the year ended January 31, 2009. Calculate the firm's earnings per share and dividends per share.

Interest expense	$74,000,000	Revenues (sales)	$14,549,000,000
Cost of goods sold	$9,079,000,000	Common stock dividends	$243,000,000
Operating expenses	$3,836,000,000	Income taxes	$536,000,000
Shares outstanding	716,296,296	Other income or expense	$5,000,000

STEP 1: Picture the problem

The income statement can be visualized as a mathematical equation using Equation (1) as follows:

$$\text{Revenues} - \text{Expenses} = \text{Profits} \tag{1}$$

(1 CONTINUED >> ON NEXT PAGE)

---

[3]GAAP represents the compilation of a voluminous set of standards that guides the construction of the firm's financial statements. These standards are set by governmental entities such as the Securities and Exchange Commission and the Accounting Oversight Board, as well as by industry groups from the accounting profession, including the American Institute of Certified Public Accountants.

[4]If you want to learn more about this and other tools of earnings management (i.e., manipulation), see Howard M. Schilit, *Financial Shenanigans: How to Detect Accounting Gimmicks & Fraud in Financial Reports*, 2nd ed. (McGraw-Hill, 2002).

However, this equation belies the level of detail normally included in the income statement. That is, expenses are typically broken down into multiple categories, including cost of goods sold, operating expenses (including such things as selling expenses, administrative expenses, and depreciation expenses), finance charges or expenses (interest), and income taxes. After subtracting each of these general categories of expenses, a new profit number is calculated. The following template provides a useful guide for reviewing the format of the income statement:

Revenues

Less: Cost of Goods Sold

Equals: Gross Profit

Less: Operating Expenses

Equals: Net Operating Income

Less: Interest Expense

Equals: Earnings before Taxes

Less: Income Taxes

Equals: Net Income

STEP 2: Decide on a solution strategy

Given the account balances provided, constructing the income statement simply entails substituting the appropriate balances into the template found above.

STEP 3: Solve

Revenues = **$14,549,000,000**

Less: Cost of Goods Sold = $9,275,000,000

Equals: Gross Profit = $5,274,000,000

Less: Operating Expenses = $3,836,000,000

Equals: Net Operating Income = $1,438,000,000

Less: Interest Expense = $74,000,000

Equals: Earnings before Taxes = $1,364,000,000

Less: Income Taxes = $536,000,000

Equals: Net Income = $828,000,000

Earnings per share ($930,000,000 net income ÷ 716,296,296 shares) = **$1.16**
Dividends per share ($243,000,000 dividends ÷ 716,296,296 shares) = **$0.34**

STEP 4: Analyze

There are some important observations we can make about Gap's income statement. First, the firm is profitable because it earned net income of $828,000,000 over the year ended January 31, 2012. Second, the firm earned more net income than it distributed to its shareholders in dividends.

STEP 5: Check yourself

Reconstruct Gap's income statement assuming the firm is able to cut its cost of goods sold by 10 percent and that the firm pays taxes at a 40 percent rate. What is the firm's net income and earnings per share?

ANSWER: $1,374,900,000 and $1.92.

Your Turn: For more practice, do related **Study Problem** 1 at the end of this chapter.   **>> END Checkpoint 1**

Concept Check | 2

1. What information can we derive from a firm's income statement?
2. List the entries in the income statement.
3. What does the acronym GAAP stand for?

 # Corporate Taxes

In our discussion of the income statement, we simply listed the firm's income tax obligation without further explanation. It is important that the financial manager understand how taxes are computed, as taxes are a critical factor in determining cash flow (P Principle 3: **Cash Flows Are the Source of Value**) and consequently in making many financial decisions. The tax rules can be extremely complex, requiring specialized expertise to understand them, so for our purposes we will provide a simplified overview of how corporate income taxes are computed.

Computing Taxable Income

A corporation's **taxable income** is often referred to in its income statement as *earnings before taxes*. Earnings before taxes are equal to the firm's net operating income less interest expenses. Note that taxable income was item 7 in our earlier description of the firm's income statement. The firm's income tax liability is calculated using its taxable income and the tax rates on corporate income, which we will now discuss.

Federal Income Tax Rates for Corporate Income

For 2013, the corporate income tax rates in the United States were as follows:

Taxable Income	Marginal Tax Rate
$0–$50,000	15%
$50,001–$75,000	25%
$75,001–$100,000	34%
$100,001–$335,000	39%
$335,001–$10,000,000	34%
$10,000,001–$15,000,000	35%
$15,000,001–$18,333,333	38%
Over $18,333,333	35%

Notice that corporate tax rates increase for taxable income up to $335,000, then drop back and plateau at 35 percent for taxable income of $18,333,333 and higher. This means that large corporations pay taxes at the 35 percent tax rate, and smaller firms with before-tax income up to $100,000 per year face tax rates ranging from 15 percent up to 34 percent.

Note that to this point we have only discussed federal income taxes. Many states and even cities have their own income taxes that also are necessary to consider in computing a firm's after-tax net income. However, the possible tax consequences brought by these added tax jurisdictions are beyond the scope of this chapter.

Marginal and Average Tax Rates

When firms analyze the tax consequences of a new business venture, it is important that they use the proper tax rate in their analysis. The appropriate rate is the **marginal tax rate**, which is the tax rate that the company will pay on its next dollar of taxable income.

Consider the income tax liability of a firm with $100,000 in taxable income:

Taxable Income	Marginal Tax Rate	Tax Liability	Cumulative Tax Liability	Average Tax Rate
$ 50,000	15%	$7,500	$ 7,500	15.00%
75,000	25%	6,250	13,750	18.33%
100,000	34%	8,500	22,250	22.25%

The firm's $100,000 in earnings before taxes results in a total tax liability of $22,250. As a result, the firm's **average tax rate** on $100,000 in taxable income is $22,250 ÷ $100,000, or 22.25 percent. However, if the firm earns a dollar more than $100,000, then the marginal tax rate jumps from 34 to 39 percent. So the firm's marginal tax rate would be 39 percent.

The reason the marginal corporate tax rate jumps up to 39 percent for taxable income of $100,001 to $335,000, and then falls to 34 percent before eventually rising to 38 percent is to make sure that firms that have very high taxable income don't benefit from the lower rates on the initial dollars that they earn. As a result, if a firm earns between $335,001 and $10 million, both its marginal and average tax rates are 34 percent, whereas if a firm earns over $18 1/3 million, both its marginal and average tax rates are 35 percent. In order to simplify our tax calculations, throughout the balance of the chapter we will assume that firms pay a single tax rate of 35 percent, which is the rate for large corporations.

Dividend Exclusion for Corporate Stockholders

For corporate stockholders, the dividends received are at least partially exempt from taxation. The rationale behind the exclusion is to avoid double taxation (i.e., taxes are paid on corporate income before dividends are paid, and if these dividends were subjected to taxation as part of the taxable income of the receiving corporation, they would effectively be taxed twice at the corporate level). However, not all the dividends received by the corporation are excluded from taxes. A corporation that owns less than 20 percent of the stock in another company can exclude 70 percent of the dividends received from its taxable income. When between 20 and 79 percent of the stock of another company is owned, 75 percent of the dividends received from that firm can be excluded from taxation. When 80 percent or more of another company's stock is owned, then all of the dividends received from that firm can be excluded from taxation. Note that dividend exclusion is *not* applicable to individual investors.

To illustrate the dividend exclusion, consider a situation in which Firm A receives $100,000 in dividends from Firm B. The dividend exclusion and taxable income under each of the possible scenarios listed previously are as follows:

Ownership Interest	Dividend Exclusion	Dividend Income	Taxable Income
Less than 20%	70%	$100,000	$30,000
20% to 79%	75%	$100,000	$25,000
80% or more	100%	$100,000	$0

If Firm A owns less than 20 percent of Firm B's shares, then it pays tax on only 30 percent of the dividends it receives, as it gets a 70 percent dividend exclusion; whereas if Firm A owns 80 percent or more of Firm B's shares, then it gets a 100 percent dividend exclusion and pays no taxes on the $100,000 in dividend income.

Concept Check | 3

1. What is the difference between average and marginal tax rates?
2. What is the marginal tax rate for a firm that currently earns $75,000 in earnings before taxes and expects to earn $80,000 next year?
3. How are dividends received by corporations taxed?

The Balance Sheet

The income statement reports the cumulative results from operating the business over a period of time, such as one year. By contrast, the **balance sheet** is a snapshot of the firm's financial position on a specific date. In its simplest form, the balance sheet is defined by the following equation:

$$\text{Total Assets} = \text{Total Liabilities} + \text{Total Shareholders' Equity} \qquad \textbf{(2)}$$

Total liabilities represent the total amount of money the firm owes its creditors (including the firm's banks and suppliers). **Total shareholders' equity** refers to the difference in the value of the firm's total assets and the firm's total liabilities recorded in the firm's balance sheet. As such, total shareholders' equity refers to the book value of their investment in the firm, which includes both the money they invested in the firm to purchase its shares and the accumulation of past earnings from the firm's operations. The sum of total shareholders' equity and total liabilities is equal to the firm's **total assets**, which are the resources owned by the firm.

In general, GAAP requires that the firm report assets on its balance sheet using the historical cost of acquiring them. Cash and assets held for resale (such as marketable securities) are an exception to the historical cost principle. These assets are reported in the balance sheet using the lower of their cost or their current **market value**, which is the price that an asset would trade for in a competitive market. Assets whose value is expected to decline over time as they are used, such as plant and equipment, are adjusted downward periodically by depreciating the historical cost. Consequently, the amount recorded on the firm's balance sheet for **net plant and equipment** is equal to the historical cost incurred when the assets were purchased less the depreciation accumulated on them. Note that this book value is not intended to measure the market value of these assets. In fact, book and market values of plant and equipment can differ dramatically. It is important to note that depreciation expense, and consequently the recorded book value of the firm's net plant and equipment, does not account for **P** Principle 1: **Money Has a Time Value**.

In summary, the balance sheet contains the book value of the firm's assets. Generally, the book value is not equal to the current market value of the firm's assets; consequently, book value does not reflect the value of the company if it were to be sold to another owner or liquidated by selling off the individual assets it owns. This distinction between accounting (or book) value and market value is important for understanding the different perspectives taken with respect to a firm's financial statements by accountants and finance professionals. The accounting approach is to count or "account" for the firm's past actions, whereas the financial manager seeks to understand the implications of the financial statements for future cash flows and the value of the firm.

The Balance Sheet of H. J. Boswell, Inc.

Consider the 2012 and 2013 balance sheets for H. J. Boswell, Inc. found in Table 2. At the end of 2010, Boswell owned $1,971 million in total assets, had debts totaling $1,059.75 million, and had total common shareholders' equity of $911.25 million.

Assets: The Left-Hand Side of the Balance Sheet

The left-hand side of Boswell's balance sheet lists the firm's assets, which are categorized into current and fixed assets. The distinction between current and fixed assets is simply the time it takes for them to be converted to cash.

Table 2 H. J. Boswell, Inc.

Balance Sheet ($ millions)
December 31, 2012 and 2013

Assets			Liabilities and Owners' Equity		
	2012	**2013**		**2012**	**2013**
Cash	$ 94.50	$ 90.00	Accounts payable	$ 184.50	$ 189.00
Accounts receivable	139.50	162.00	Accrued expenses	45.00	45.00
Inventory	229.50	378.00	Short-term notes	63.00	54.00
Other current assets	13.50	13.50	Total current liabilities	$ 292.50	$ 288.00
Total current assets	$ 477.00	$ 643.50	Long-term debt	720.00	771.75
Gross plant and equipment	1,669.50	1,845.00	Total liabilities	$1,012.50	$1,059.75
Less accumulated depreciation	(382.50)	(517.50)	Common stockholders' equity		
Net plant and equipment	$1,287.00	$1,327.50	Common stock–par value	45.00	45.00
Total assets	$1,764.00	$1,971.00	Paid-in capital	324.00	324.00
			Retained earnings	382.50	542.25
			Total common stockholders' equity	$ 751.50	$ 911.25
			Total liabilities and stockholders' equity	$1,764.00	$1,971.00

Legend:

Assets: The Left-Hand Side of the Balance Sheet

Current Assets. Assets that the firm expects to convert into cash in 12 months or less. Examples include cash, accounts receivable, inventories, and other current assets.

- **Cash.** Every firm must have some cash on hand at all times because cash expenditures can sometimes exceed cash receipts.
- **Accounts receivable.** The amounts owed to the firm by its customers who purchased on credit.
- **Inventory.** Raw materials that the firm utilizes to build its products, partially completed items or work in process, and finished goods held by the firm for eventual sale.
- **Other current assets.** All current assets that do not fall into one of the named categories (cash, accounts receivable, and so forth). Prepaid expenses (prepayments for insurance premiums, for example) are a common example of an asset in this catch-all category.

Gross Plant and Equipment. The sum of the original acquisition prices of plant and equipment still owned by the firm.

Accumulated Depreciation. The sum of all the depreciation expenses charged against the prior year's revenues for fixed assets that the firm still owns.

Net Plant and Equipment. The undepreciated value of the firm's plant and equipment.

Liabilities and Stockholders' Equity: The Right-Hand Side of the Balance Sheet

Current Liabilities. Liabilities that are due and payable within a period of 12 months or less. Examples include the firm's accounts payable, accrued expenses, and short-term notes.

- **Accounts payable.** The credit suppliers extended to the firm when it purchased items for its inventories.
- **Accrued expenses.** Liabilities that were incurred in the firm's operations but not yet paid. For example, the company's employees might have done work for which they will not be paid until the following week or month. The wages owed by the firm to its employees are recorded as accrued wages.
- **Short-term notes.** Debts created by borrowing from a bank or other lending source that must be repaid in 12 months or less.

Long-Term Debt. All firm debts that are due and payable more than 12 months in the future. A 25-year mortgage loan used to purchase land or buildings is an example of long-term liability. If the firm has issued bonds, the portion of those bonds that is not due and payable in the coming 12 months is also included in long-term debt.

Common Stockholders' Equity. Common stockholders are the residual owners of a business. They receive whatever income is left over after the firm has paid all of its expenses. In the event the firm is liquidated, the common stockholders receive only what is left over—but never lose more than they invested—after the firm's other financial obligations have been paid.

Current Assets

Current assets consist of the firm's cash plus other assets the firm expects to convert to cash within 12 months or less. Boswell had current assets of $643.5 million at the end of 2013, comprised principally of its **inventories** of $378 million (including raw materials used to make the firm's products, goods in process, and finished goods that are ready for sale), and its accounts receivable of $162 million, which reflects the value of prior credit sales that have not been collected.

Fixed Assets

Fixed assets are assets that the firm does *not* expect to sell within one year. These include plant and equipment, land, and other investments that are expected to be held for an extended period of time and frequently cannot be easily converted to cash. Boswell has **gross plant and equipment** totaling $1,845 million at the end of 2013. This total represents the combined historical dollar amounts the firm has paid to acquire fixed assets. Net plant and equipment is equal to gross plant and equipment less **accumulated depreciation** expense. The latter is the sum of all depreciation expenses deducted in the firm's income statement in previous periods for the plant and equipment.

Gross plant and equipment changes over time as new assets are acquired and others are sold. When a firm purchases a new computer system, for example, it does not immediately report the cost as an expense in its income statement for the period. Instead, the computer system is considered to be an asset and is included on the balance sheet. Then the cost of the computer system is depreciated over time. Some assets, such as land, are not expected to depreciate; these assets are carried on the firm's balance sheet at their original cost until they are sold for a profit or a loss.

H. J. Boswell's gross fixed assets for 2012 and 2013 are shown in Table 2. In 2012, the firm had $1,669.50 million in gross plant and equipment. By the end of 2013, this amount had grown to $1,845 million. In other words, Boswell acquired an additional $175.5 million in fixed assets during the year (i.e., $1,845 million − $1,669.5 million = $175.5 million). In addition, during 2013, the firm's accumulated depreciation expense rose from $382.5 million to $517.5 million. This increase in accumulated depreciation is equal to the amount of depreciation expense for the year (or the $135 million reported in the firm's income statement found in Table 1). Thus, Boswell's net fixed assets rose by $40.5 million (the difference in the company's new fixed assets of $175.5 million and the depreciation expense recorded for 2013 of $135 million).

Liabilities and Stockholders' Equity: The Right-Hand Side of the Balance Sheet

We now turn to the right-hand side of the balance sheet in Table 2 labeled "Liabilities and Owner's Equity." This side of the balance sheet indicates how the firm finances its assets. H. J. Boswell, Inc. has borrowed a total of $1,059.75 million and raised $911.25 million in equity to finance its total investment in firm assets. Boswell's **current liabilities** represent the amount that the firm owes to creditors that must be repaid within a period of 12 months or less. Typically a firm's current liabilities will include **accounts payable**, which is what the firm owes its suppliers for items purchased for its inventories, and **notes payable**, which are short-term loans from banks and other creditors. Current liabilities totaled $288 million at the end of 2013. The firm also owed $771.75 million in **long-term debt** such as loans from banks and other lenders that have maturities longer than one year. This also includes bonds sold by the firm in the public markets.

To understand the stockholders' equity account, we need to know how accountants construct this account. Specifically, it is broken down into the following components:

1. **The amount the company received from selling stock to investors.** This amount may simply be shown as common stock in the balance sheet or it may be divided into two components: par value and additional paid-in capital above par.[5] **Par value** is the stated or face value a firm puts on each share of stock prior to it being offered for sale. The par value has no relationship to the market value of the shares. For example, Boswell's par value per share is $1.00 and the firm has 45 million shares outstanding, such that the par value of the firm's common equity is $45 million. The paid-in capital above par, or simply

---

[5]We assume that the firm has not issued any preferred stock.

paid-in capital, is the additional amount of capital the firm raised when buyers purchased Boswell's stock for more than its par value.[6] This amounts to $324 million for Boswell.

2. **The amount of the firm's retained earnings. Retained earnings** are the portion of net income that has been retained (i.e., not paid in dividends) from prior years' operations. Boswell has retained a total of $542.25 million over the course of its existence.

In effect, **stockholders' equity** is equal to the sum of the par value of common stock plus paid-in capital plus retained earnings.

$$\begin{array}{c}\text{Stockholders'} \\ \text{Equity}\end{array} = \begin{array}{c}\text{Par Value of} \\ \text{Common Stock}\end{array} + \begin{array}{c}\text{Paid-in} \\ \text{Capital}\end{array} + \begin{array}{c}\text{Retained} \\ \text{Earnings}\end{array} \tag{3}$$

Alternatively, shareholders' equity can be thought of as the difference between total assets and total liabilities. For example, if some of your company's assets included stocks or bonds that had declined in value over time, then the value of the company's assets would decline accordingly. Thus, in order for the balance sheet to balance, stockholders' equity must decline, and that is done through a reduction in common equity. In effect,

$$\left(\begin{array}{c}\text{Stockholders'} \\ \text{Equity}\end{array}\right) = \left(\begin{array}{c}\text{Total} \\ \text{Assets}\end{array}\right) - \left(\begin{array}{c}\text{Total} \\ \text{Liabilities}\end{array}\right) \tag{4}$$

Firm Liquidity and Net Working Capital

The **liquidity** of an asset refers to the speed with which the asset can be converted into cash without loss of value. Obviously, the firm's bank account is perfectly liquid because it consists of cash that can be readily spent. However, other types of assets are less liquid because they are more difficult to sell and convert into cash.

We can also think in terms of the liquidity of the firm as a whole, the firm's ability to regularly convert its current assets (principally accounts receivable and inventories) into cash so that it can pay its bills on time. This is a function of both the liquidity of the firm's current assets and the size of the bills the firm must pay. A common way to assess a firm's overall liquidity therefore involves comparing its current assets to its current liabilities. This simple measure of the firm's liquidity is its **net working capital**, the difference between the firm's current assets and current liabilities.

$$\begin{array}{c}\text{Net Working} \\ \text{Capital}\end{array} = \left(\begin{array}{c}\text{Current} \\ \text{Assets}\end{array}\right) - \left(\begin{array}{c}\text{Current} \\ \text{Liabilities}\end{array}\right) \tag{5}$$

Graphically, this is presented in Figure 1. Recall that current assets are those assets that the firm expects to be able to convert to cash within a period of one year or less, and current liabilities are those debts the firm owes that must be paid within one year. Consequently, a firm with current assets much larger than its current liabilities is in a good position to repay its debts on time and is consequently very liquid. Lenders frequently focus on the amount of net working capital as an important indicator of a firm's ability to repay its loans.

For H. J. Boswell, Inc., net working capital for year-end 2013 is computed as follows, using information from Table 2:

Current Assets	$643,500,000
Less: Current liabilities	288,000,000
Equals: Net working capital	$355,500,000

Debt and Equity Financing

The right-hand side of the firm's balance sheet reveals the sources of the money used to finance the purchase of the firm's assets listed on the left-hand side of the balance sheet. It shows how much was borrowed (debt financing) and how much was provided by the firm's

---

[6]The amount of common stock issued will be offset by any stock that has been repurchased by the company. The amount of the repurchases is listed as **Treasury stock**.

Figure 1

The Balance Sheet

The balance sheet represents a snapshot of the firm. Specifically, it lists the assets the firm has acquired, classified as current and long-term (or fixed) assets, as well as the sources of financing the firm has used to finance the acquisition of its assets. Net working capital is an important measure of a firm's ability to pay its bills on time and is equal to the difference in the dollar amount of current assets (assets the firm expects to convert to cash within the year) and current liabilities (debts the firm must repay within the year). Stockholders' equity is the total investment of the firm's owners in the firm and is equal to the difference in total assets and total liabilities.

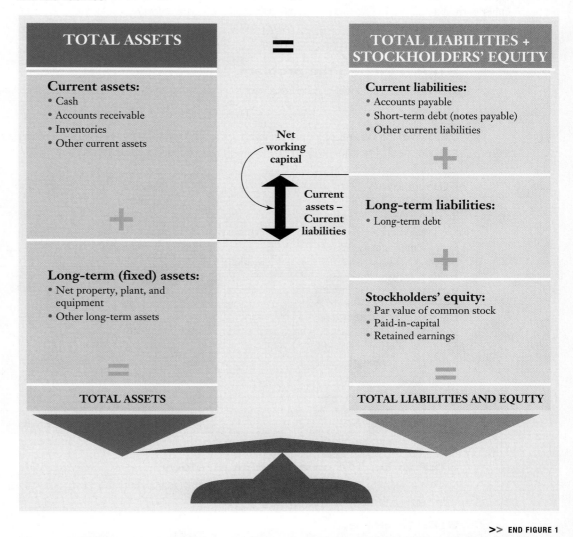

>> END FIGURE 1

owners (equity financing), either through the sale of equity to investors or through the retention of prior years' earnings.

Debt and equity differ with regard to how the holders of these types of securities get paid and the priority of their respective claims in the event the firm were to become bankrupt, because debt security holders or lenders get paid first. They typically receive periodic interest payments up until the maturity of the debt, at which time the principal must be repaid. Equity securities, on the other hand, do not mature, and although equity security holders may receive dividends, there is no contractual or predetermined dividend payment (for example, as late as 2010, Apple had not paid a dividend since 1995). Another key difference between debt and equity is the fact that debt holders are paid before equity holders in the event of bankruptcy.

Constructing a Balance Sheet

Construct a balance sheet for Gap, Inc. (GPS) using the following list of jumbled accounts for January 31, 2009. Identify the firm's total assets and net working capital.

Net property, plant, and equipment	$ 2,523,000,000	Accounts receivable	$ 0
Cash	1,885,000,000	Long-term liabilities	2,539,000,000
Current liabilities	2,128,000,000	Common equity	2,755,000,000
Other current assets	809,000,000	Inventories	1,615,000,000
Other long-term assets	590,000,000	Accounts payable	2,069,000,000

STEP 1: Picture the problem

The firm's balance sheet can be visualized as a mathematical equation using Equation (2) as follows:

$$\text{Total Assets} = \text{Total Liabilities} + \text{Total Shareholders' Equity} \qquad (2)$$

Just as with the income statement equation, this equation belies the level of detail normally included in the firm's balance sheet. The following template shows how to construct the balance sheet:

Current assets
Cash
Accounts receivable
Inventories
Other current assets
Total current assets

Current liabilities
Accounts payable
Short-term debt (notes payable)
Other current liabilities
Total current liabilities

Long-term liabilities
Long-term debt

Long-term (fixed) assets
Gross property, plant and equipment
Less: Accumulated depreciation
Net property, plant and equipment
Other long-term assets
Total long-term assets

Owners' equity
Par value of common stock
Paid in capital
Retained earnings
Total equity

Total assets

Total liabilities and owners' equity

STEP 2: Decide on a solution strategy

Given the account balances provided, constructing the balance sheet simply entails substituting the appropriate balances into the template found above.

STEP 3: Solve

Current Assets	$4,309,000,000	Current Liabilities	$2,128,000,000
Long-Term Assets	3,113,000,000	Long-Term Liabilities	2,539,000,000
Total Assets	$7,422,000,000	Common Equity	2,755,000,000
		Total Liabilities and Equity	$7,422,000,000

Total assets = Current assets + Long-term assets = $4,309,000,000 + $3,113,000,000 = $7,422,000,000

Net working capital = Current assets − Current liabilities = $4,309,000,000 − $2,128,000,000 = $2,181,000,000

STEP 4: Analyze

There are some important observations we can make about Gap's balance sheet. First, the firm has invested a total of $7.422 billion in assets that have been financed using current liabilities of $2.128 billion, $2.539 billion in long-term liabilities, and $2.755 billion in owner-supplied funds. Second, the firm has $4.309 billion tied up in current assets and $2.128 billion in current liabilities, leaving the firm with a net working capital position of $4.309 billion − 2.128 billion = $2.181 billion. The latter suggests that the value of the firm's current assets could shrink by as much as $2.181 billion and the firm could still pay its current liabilities.

STEP 5: Check yourself

Reconstruct Gap's balance sheet to reflect the repayment of $1 billion in short-term debt using a like amount of the firm's cash. What is the balance for total assets and net working capital?

ANSWER: $6.422 billion and $2.181 billion, respectively.

Your Turn: For more practice, do related **Study Problems** 11 and 12 at the end of this chapter.　　　>> **END Checkpoint 2**

It is often said that equity holders have the residual claim on income. This simply means that they have a claim on any income that is left over after paying the firm's obligations. This income is either paid to them in the form of dividends, used to buy back outstanding stock, or added to their investment in the firm when the firm reinvests the retained earnings.

Book Values, Historical Costs, and Market Values

The different objectives of the accountants who prepare financial statements and the financial managers who interpret those statements are perhaps nowhere more apparent than in the comparison of book values based on historical costs and market values. Moreover, the difference between an asset's book value and its current market value can be very significant. For example, the book values of current assets are generally very close to their market values. By contrast, the book and market values of fixed assets can differ substantially. For example, in January 2009 Home Depot (HD) had total assets (book value) of $44.2 billion; however, the market value of its liabilities plus equity totaled more than $65 billion. There are two reasons for book and market values to be different. First, over time, inflation greatly affects the cost of fixed assets. For example, when Boswell purchased land for one of its plant sites in 1998, the price of the parcel of land was $3.2 million. By 2009 the value of the land had risen to over $8 million; however, on Boswell's balance sheet the land continues to be valued at its historical cost.

The second reason for a difference in book and market values is that the firm adjusts the book value of its fixed assets (other than land) downward each year as it depreciates them. This depreciation expense represents the firm's acknowledgement of the fact that fixed assets wear out and the cost of the wear must be accounted for in determining the profits the firm earns. For example, if Boswell were to pay $25,000 for a new forklift truck in 2009 that it expected to depreciate over five years toward a zero salvage value, the truck would have a book value in 2009 equal to its cost, but this book value would decline by $5,000 every year until the end of 2014, when it would drop to zero (i.e., the truck would then be fully depreciated). However, the depreciation expense the firm uses reflects accounting and tax rules rather than actual changes in market values. As a consequence, the adjusted book values can sometimes bear little resemblance to market values.

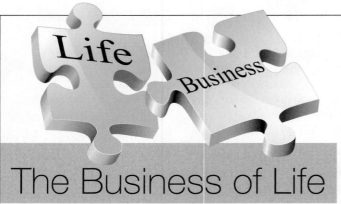

The Business of Life

Your Personal Balance Sheet and Income Statement

We can apply the concepts of financial statements to prepare a personal balance sheet and income statement. A personal balance sheet is a snapshot of your financial status at a particular point in time. It lists the assets you own and the debts, or liabilities, you owe. Your personal net worth is equal to the difference between your assets and your liabilities. A sample balance sheet worksheet is provided in Figure 2. As you can see, it looks a lot like H. J. Boswell's corporate balance sheet.

Once you've prepared your personal balance sheet and identified your net worth, the next step is to trace where your money comes from and how it is spent. To do this, we put together a personal income statement that looks at both the money you take in and the money you spend. What's left over (if anything) is, like a firm's profit, the amount you have available for savings or investment. If you're spending too much, your income statement will show you exactly where your money is going so that you can spot these problem areas quickly. With a good income statement, you'll never end another month wondering where your money went. A sample income statement is provided in Figure 3.

The income statement and balance sheet should be used together. The balance sheet lets you assess your financial standing by showing your net worth. The income statement tells you exactly how your spending and saving habits are affecting your net worth. If your balance sheet shows you that you're not building your net worth as quickly as you'd like, or if you're overspending and actually decreasing your net worth, your income statement can help you identify where your money is going.

Figure 2

Your Personal Balance Sheet

Assets (What You Own)

A. Monetary Assets (bank account, etc.)   _____

B. Investments   + _____

C. Retirement Plan Investments   + _____

D. Housing (market value)   + _____

E. Automobiles   + _____

F. Personal Property   + _____

G. Other Assets   + _____

H. Your Total Assets (add lines A–G)   = _____

Liabilities or Debt (What You Owe)

Current Debt

I. Current Bills   _____

J. Credit Card Debt   + _____

Long-Term Debt

K. Housing   _____

L. Automobile Loans   + _____

M. Other Debt   + _____

N. Your Total Debt (add lines I–M)   = _____

Your Net Worth

H. Total Assets   + _____

N. Less: Total Debt   – _____

O. Equals: Your Net Worth   = _____

>> END FIGURE 2

Figure 3

Your Personal Income Statement

Your Take-Home Pay

A. Total Income .... _____

B. Total Income Taxes .... − _____

C. After-Tax Income Available for Living Expenditures or
Take-Home Pay (line A minus line B) .... = _____

Your Living Expenses

D. Total Housing Expenditures .... _____

E. Total Food Expenditures .... + _____

F. Total Clothing and Personal Care Expenditures .... + _____

G. Total Transportation Expenditures .... + _____

H. Total Recreation Expenditures .... + _____

I. Total Medical Expenditures .... + _____

J. Total Insurance Expenditures .... + _____

K. Total Other Expenditures .... + _____

L. Total Living Expenditures (add lines D–K) .... = _____

Total Available for Savings and Investments

C. After-Tax Income Available for Living Expenditures or
Take-Home Pay .... _____

L. Total Living Expenditures .... − _____

M. Income Available for Savings and Investment
(line C minus line L) .... = _____

>> END FIGURE 3

Your Turn: See Study Question 9.

Tools of Financial Analysis—Financial Statement Relationships

Name of Tool	Formula	What It Tells You
Balance Sheet Equation	$\text{Total Assets} = \text{Total Liabilities} + \text{Owners' Equity}$	• The sum of the dollar cost of the firm's investment in assets • The sources of financing used to acquire the firm's assets
Stockholders' Equity Equation	$\text{Stockholders' Equity} = \text{Total Assets} - \text{Total Liabilities}$	• The amount of money invested in the firm by its common stockholders • Because most of the firm's assets are recorded in the balance sheet at their historical cost, stockholders' equity is not a measure of the market value of the equity.

Before you move on to 5

Concept Check | **4**

1. Describe the basic categories of assets and liabilities reported in a firm's balance sheet.

2. What does the term *net working capital* mean, and how is it computed?

 The Cash Flow Statement

We now move on to the third financial statement we want to review. The **cash flow statement** is a report, like the income statement and balance sheet, that firms use to explain changes in their cash balances over a period of time by identifying all of the sources and uses of cash for the period spanned by the statement. The focus of the cash flow statement is the change in the firm's cash balance for the period of time covered by the statement (i.e., one year or one quarter):

$$\text{Change in Cash Balance} = \text{Ending Cash Balance} - \text{Beginning Cash Balance} \quad \textbf{(6)}$$

Because the beginning cash balance for 2013 is the ending balance for 2012, we typically evaluate Equation (6) as follows:

$$\text{Change in Cash Balance for 2013} = \text{Ending Cash Balance for 2013} - \text{Ending Cash Balance for 2012} \quad \textbf{(7)}$$

Still another way to look at the change in cash balance for the period is to compare the sources and uses of cash for the period.

We can find the information needed to prepare the cash flow statement in the income statement for the period and the beginning and ending balance sheets for the period. So before we dig into the specific format of the cash flow statement, let us first identify a firm's sources and uses of cash by looking at its balance sheet changes from the beginning to the end of the year. These changes will tell the story of where the firm obtained cash and how it was spent.

Sources and Uses of Cash

A **source of cash** is any activity that brings cash into the firm, such as when the firm sells goods and services or sells an old piece of equipment that it no longer needs. A **use of cash** is any activity that causes cash to leave the firm, such as the payment of taxes, the purchase of a new piece of equipment, and so forth.

We can identify both sources and uses of cash by looking at the changes in balance sheet entries from the beginning to the end of the period. For example, we can use the 2012 and 2013 balance sheets found in Table 3 to see how Boswell's balance sheet entries for assets changed from 2012 to 2013. First, note that the cash balance declined by $4.5 million. This change is the object of the analysis, so let us move on to accounts receivable, which increased from $139.5 million to $162 million. Accounts receivable represents the sum total of all credit sales that have not been collected yet. Thus, the increase in receivables resulted because Boswell's sales are made on credit, and the firm's customers owed Boswell $22.5 million *more* at the end of 2013 than they did at the end of 2012. This means that Boswell *used* cash to invest in accounts receivable.[7] Similarly, inventories rose by $148.5 million, indicating the use of cash to invest in a higher level of inventory, which represents the firm's stockpile of products that are either ready for sale (finished goods) or in the process of being made ready for sale (work-in-progress inventory). *So, in general, we can think of increases in assets as an indication of the use of cash, whereas a decrease in an asset account is a source of cash.*

What about changes in the firm's liability accounts? Note that accounts payable, which includes the credit extended to the firm to acquire inventory, increased by $4.5 million in 2010. This indicates that Boswell obtained an additional $4.5 million from accounts payable, *so an increase in a liability account indicates a source, whereas a decrease in a liability is a use of cash.* For example, short-term notes decreased by $9 million, which means that Boswell paid down its short-term notes owed to banks and other creditors by this amount, which is a use of cash.

Note that Boswell's retained earnings, which represent the sum of all its past earnings that have been reinvested in the firm, increased by $159.75 million for the period. This increase

---

[7]It is easier to see how changes in accounts receivable affect cash when the account balance falls. For example, if a firm's accounts receivable balance fell by $10,000 during the period, this means that the firm's customers have paid the firm cash. So, a decrease in accounts receivable is actually a source of cash!

Table 3   H. J. Boswell, Inc., Balance Sheets and Balance Sheet Changes

Balance Sheets for the Years Ending December 31, 2012
and 2013 ($ millions)

	2012	2013	Change
Cash	$ 94.50	$ 90.00	$ (4.50)
Accounts receivable	139.50	162.00	22.50
Inventory	229.50	378.00	148.50
Other current assets	13.50	13.50	0.00
Total current assets	$ 477.00	$ 643.50	$166.50
Gross plant and equipment	1,669.50	1,845.00	175.50
Less accumulated depreciation	(382.50)	(517.50)	(135.00)
Net plant and equipment	$1,287.00	$1,327.50	$ 40.50
Total assets	$1,764.00	$1,971.00	$207.00

	2012	2013	Change
Accounts payable	$ 184.50	$ 189.00	$ 4.50
Accrued expenses	45.00	45.00	0.00
Short-term notes	63.00	54.00	(9.00)
Total current liabilities	$ 292.50	$ 288.00	$ (4.50)
Long-term debt	720.00	771.75	51.75
Total debt	$1,012.50	$1,059.75	$ 47.25
Common stockholders' equity			
Common stock—par value	45.00	45.00	0.00
Paid-in capital	324.00	324.00	0.00
Retained earnings	382.50	542.25	159.75
Total common stockholders' equity	$ 751.50	$ 911.25	$159.75
Total liabilities and equity	$1,764.00	$1,971.00	$207.00

represents a source of cash to the firm from the firm's operations. The increase in retained earnings is calculated from the income statement (Table 1) as follows:

Net income for 2013	$204.75 million
Less: Dividends paid in 2013	45.00 million
Equals: Change in retained earnings for 2013	$159.75 million

We can summarize all the sources and uses of cash for Boswell in 2010 using the following criteria for identifying sources and uses of cash:

Sources of Cash	Uses of Cash
Decrease in an asset account	Increase in an asset account
Increase in a liability account	Decrease in a liability account
Increase in an owners' equity account	Decrease in an owners' equity account

For Boswell, we summarize sources and uses of cash for 2013 as follows ($ millions):

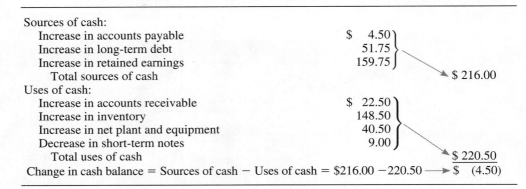

Sources of cash:		
Increase in accounts payable	$ 4.50	
Increase in long-term debt	51.75	
Increase in retained earnings	159.75	
Total sources of cash		$ 216.00
Uses of cash:		
Increase in accounts receivable	$ 22.50	
Increase in inventory	148.50	
Increase in net plant and equipment	40.50	
Decrease in short-term notes	9.00	
Total uses of cash		$ 220.50

Change in cash balance = Sources of cash − Uses of cash = $216.00 − 220.50 ⟶ $ (4.50)

So, here is what we have learned about H. J. Boswell's operations during 2013 from analyzing its sources and uses of cash:

- The firm used more cash than it generated; thus its cash balance declined by $4.5 million.
- Boswell's primary source of cash was from the retention of earnings from operations, although it did increase long-term debt by $51.75 million.
- The largest single use of cash involved the addition of $148.5 million in inventories.
- The firm paid down $9 million of short-term debt but on balance increased its borrowing substantially due to the increase in long-term borrowing just above.

By analyzing the firm's sources and uses of cash over the period, we begin to paint an overall picture of the firm's financial activities. By looking at changes in the firm's balance sheet accounts, we learn what actions the management took over the year, not just the end results of those actions.

H. J. Boswell's Cash Flow Statement

The format of the cash flow statement is a bit different than the simple sources and uses of cash analysis we just completed. However, it utilizes the same information. In the cash flow statement, we bring in information from the income statement directly and provide more details about the change in retained earnings. Moreover, sources and uses of cash are classified into one of three broad categories:

- **Operating activities** represent the company's core business, including sales and expenses (basically any cash activity that affects net income for the period).
- **Investment activities** include the cash flows that arise out of the purchase and sale of long-term assets such as plant and equipment.
- **Financing activities** represent changes in the firm's use of debt and equity. The latter include the sale of new shares of stock, the repurchase of outstanding shares, and the payment of dividends.

The basic format of the statement is the following:

> Beginning Cash Balance
> > Plus: Cash Flow from Operating Activities
> > Plus: Cash Flow from Investing Activities
> > Plus: Cash Flow from Financing Activities
>
> Equals: Ending Cash Balance

Evaluating the Cash Flow Statement

Table 4 contains the 2013 cash flow statement for Boswell. This statement explains why the firm's cash balance declined by $4.5 million during 2013. As such, the statement can be used to answer a number of important questions:

- **How much cash did the firm generate from its operations?** Boswell generated $173.25 million in cash from its operations based on net income of $204.75 million.

Finance in a **Flat World**

GAAP vs. IFRS

Accounting Principles, or GAAP for short. However, the increasing globalization of financial markets has led to the growing acceptance of many accountants that the new standards for financial reporting within the United States will look a lot more like the International Financial Reporting Standards (IFRS) used by many foreign companies. Although the two systems are similar, the IFRS system is typically characterized as being simpler while offering more reporting flexibility than GAAP rules. The transition to the IFRS began in April 2007 when President Bush announced that IFRS would be recognized in the United States within two years as part of an agreement with the European Union.

Financial reporting in the United States is governed by a collection of accounting principles referred to as Generally Accepted

Source: Sarah Johnson, "Goodbye GAAP," *CFO* (April 2008), 49–54.

Your Turn: See Study Question 10.

Table 4	H. J. Boswell, Inc.

Statement of Cash Flows for the Year Ending December 31, 2013
($ millions)

Ending cash balance for 2012 (beginning balance for 2013)			**$94.50**
Operating Activities			
Net income	$204.75		
Increase in accounts receivable	(22.50)		
No change in other current assets			
Depreciation expense	135.00		
Increase in accounts payable	4.50		
No change in accrued expenses			
Cash flow from operating activities		*$ 173.25*	
Investing activities			
Purchases of plant and equipment	(175.50)		
Cash flow from investing activities		*(175.50)*	
Financing activities			
Decrease in short-term notes	(9.00)		
Increase in long-term debt	51.75		
Cash dividends paid to shareholders	$ (45.00)		
Cash flow from financing activities		*(2.25)*	
Increase (decrease) in cash during the year			*$ (4.50)*
Ending cash balance for 2013			**$90.00**

- **How much did the firm invest in plant and equipment?** The firm purchased a total of $175.5 million in new capital equipment during 2013.
- **Did the firm raise additional funds during the period, and if so, how much and from what sources?** Boswell raised a net amount of new financing of $2.25 million. By *net amount* we refer to the sum of new short-term notes of $9 million that were repaid, $51.75 million in new long-term debt the firm issued, less the $45 million that was paid in common stock dividends.

In addition, the statement of cash flows provides a tool that can be used to analyze a wide variety of questions, such as the following:

- Is the firm able to generate positive cash flows?
- Was the firm able to meet its cash obligations, and did the firm need to raise added external sources of funds?
- Why was the firm's net income greater (less) than its cash flow from operations?

Quality of Earnings—Evaluating Cash Flow from Operations

A firm's net income or earnings is one of the most important pieces of information analysts use to analyze a firm's past performance and use to make an assessment of future performance. However, reported earnings can sometimes be a misleading indicator of firm performance in that earnings are comprised of the income earned from the firm's business operations as well as asset sales and other forms of non-operating revenues. To address this problem we can combine information from the firm's income statement and the statement of cash flows to evaluate the quality of a firm's reported earnings.

Consider the performance of two companies: Alpha and Beta. The companies operated in the same industry, reported the same earnings last year, and each realized a 10 percent rate of growth in earnings over the last five years. However, the two firms have generated their earnings in different ways, as follows:

- Alpha's earnings came solely from the successful operations of the firm's primary business.
- Beta's earnings from its operations have been flat for the last three years and its growth in earnings resulted from gains realized from the sale of company assets.

Which company do you feel has the most promising future? I think you will agree that because Beta is generating its earnings growth out of asset sales, Alpha's earnings are a much better indicator of the firm's performance potential.

Note that we did not suggest that Beta has done anything illegal or wrong. We simply observed that the firm's growth in income has come from selling off assets, which is probably not a sustainable way to generate future earnings. However, Beta might also have been engaged in accounting chicanery to prop up its earnings. We do not want to delve into the specifics of these practices. However, they can include anything from aggressive interpretation of the reporting rules (i.e., GAAP) up to using fraudulent reporting practices.[8] The point is simply that a financial analyst would be more confident about using Alpha's earnings as an indicator of firm performance going forward. Another way to say this is that Alpha's earnings are a higher-quality indicator of the firm's future performance than are Beta's.

So, how can financial analysts appraise the quality of a firm's reported earnings? One popular indicator of earnings quality is the **quality of earnings ratio**.[9] We compute the ratio as follows:

$$\text{Quality of Earnings} = \frac{\text{Cash Flow from Operations}}{\text{Net Income}} \qquad (8)$$

---

[8]Common types of fraudulent financial reporting arise out of reporting revenues before they are earned (i.e., inflating revenues) and/or delaying or failing to report expenses when they are incurred (i.e., underreporting expenses).

[9]An alternative formulation of the quality of earnings ratio is the following:

$$\text{Quality of Earnings} = \frac{\text{Net Income} - \text{Cash from Operations}}{\text{Total Assets}}$$

In this formulation, lower ratios indicate higher-quality earnings, as the difference in the firm's reported net income and cash from operations is smaller.

Net income is simply reported earnings for the period found in the income statement, and **cash flow from operations** is that portion of the firm's total cash flow resulting from its operating activities and is taken from the firm's statement of cash flows.

A quality of earnings ratio of 1.00 indicates very-high-quality earnings, as the firm's cash from operations is 100 percent of firm-reported net income. In effect, this ratio tells us whether or not the firm's operating cash flows and net income are in sync with each other. On the other hand, a ratio of, say, .20 or 20 percent would indicate that the firm's cash from operations is only 20 percent of reported net income, which raises a serious question as to the firm's ability to continue producing this level of net income because it is so dependent on non-operating sources of cash.

If the quality of earnings ratio is low for a single year, there could be a logical explanation. However, if the ratio is persistently low, this suggests the very real possibility that the firm is using aggressive reporting practices to inflate its reported earnings.

Example—H. J. Boswell, Inc. To illustrate the computation of the quality of earnings ratio found in Equation (8), we refer back to the cash flow statement found in Table 4. Substituting for cash flow from operations and net income for 2013, we get the following:

$$\text{Quality of Earnings} = \frac{\text{Cash Flow from Operations}}{\text{Net Income}} = \frac{\$173.25 \text{ million}}{\$204.75 \text{ million}} = .846, \text{ or } 84.6\%$$

Thus, in 2013 Boswell's cash flow from operations was 84.6 percent of the firm's reported net income. The reasons for the difference are outlined in the computation of cash flow from operations found in Table 4. Specifically, Boswell received less cash from its operations than it reported in earnings because it had more credit sales than it collected during the period (i.e., accounts receivable increased by $22.5 million), and the firm actually increased its inventories (i.e., bought more inventory items than it sold by $148.5 million). In addition, the firm realized non-cash depreciation expenses of $135 million that increased its cash flow from operations. Boswell also increased its reliance on accounts payable by $4.5 million.

So, what have we learned by evaluating Boswell's quality of earnings ratio? First, after reviewing the reasons for the difference in cash flow from operations and reported net income, we can see that firms that are growing will tend to report quality of earnings ratios less than 1. This is true because growing firms experience growing accounts receivable due to growing sales, and growing inventories that are built up in anticipation of higher sales in the future. Second, in order to say whether Boswell's quality of earnings ratio is good or bad, we need to know two things: How do Boswell's competitor firms compare, and how has the ratio been changing over time? For example, if Boswell operates in an industry where firm sales and profits are growing, then having a quality of earnings ratio less than 1 is to be expected. Moreover, if the quality of earnings ratio is fairly stable over time, this suggests that the firm's earnings and cash flows are in sync and that reported earnings provide a high-quality indicator of the firm's future performance potential. Dramatic deviations from the historical trend could, however, signal problems for Boswell in the future and would be a cause for concern.

Sustainable Capital Expenditures—Evaluating Investment Activities

In Table 4 we saw that H. J. Boswell, Inc. spent $175.5 million on plant and equipment during 2013, yet the firm only raised an additional $2.25 million in new financing during the period. The additional funds needed to finance the firm's capital expenditures came from the firm's operations.

Raising the funds needed to finance the firm's capital expenditures from operations means that a firm has less need for external financing, and would be less dependent on the whims of the capital markets. For this reason financial analysts have devised a capital acquisitions ratio that compares the firm's cash flow from operating activities to the cash paid for property, plant, and equipment. The capital acquisitions ratio is defined as follows:

$$\text{Capital Acquisitions Ratio} = \frac{\text{Cash Flow from Operations}}{\text{Cash Paid for Capital Expenditures (CAPEX)}} \qquad \textbf{(9)}$$

This ratio indicates whether there are sufficient operating cash flows to pay for capital expenditures. The higher the ratio, other things being equal, the less dependent is the firm on capital markets for financing the firm's expenditures on new capital equipment. Because a firm's capital expenditures can vary dramatically from year to year, it is common to calculate this ratio as an average of, say, three years. In addition, because capital expenditures can vary dramatically between different industries, this ratio should only be compared to the ratios of firms in the same industry as well as past capital acquisitions ratios for the same firm.

Example—H. J. Boswell, Inc.

Given the information from Table 4 along with the 2011 and 2013 information given below, the capital acquisitions ratio for H. J. Boswell, Inc. can be calculated as follows:

($ millions)	2011	2012	2013	3-Year Average
Cash Flow from Operations	$158.00	$142.00	$173.25	$157.75
Capital Expenditures (CAPEX)	$168.00	$135.00	$175.50	$159.50

$$\text{Capital Acquisitions Ratio} = \frac{\text{3-Year Average Cash Flow from Operations}}{\text{3-Year Average Cash Paid for Capital Expenditures (CAPEX)}} = \frac{\$157.75 \text{ million}}{\$159.5 \text{ million}} = .989, \text{ or } 98.9\%$$

Consequently, for the past three years, Boswell was on average able to finance 98.9 percent of its new expenditures for plant and equipment out of the firm's current-year operations.

Checkpoint 3

Interpreting the Statement of Cash Flows

It is the spring of 2013, and although the national economy is still suffering from the effects of a deep recession, the U.S. energy boom from the exploitation of shale gas reserves was booming. You are in your second rotation in the management training program at a regional brokerage firm, and your supervisor calls you into her office on Monday morning to discuss your next training rotation. When you enter her office you are surprised to learn that you will be responsible for compiling a financial analysis of Peatry Energy Inc. Peatry is one of the largest producers of natural gas in the United States and is headquartered in Dallas, TX. Your boss suggests that you begin your analysis by reviewing the firm's cash flow statements for 2009 through 2012 (as follows):

In Millions of U. S. Dollars	12 Months Ending December 31			
	2012	2011	2010	2009
Net income	1,451.00	2,003.32	948.30	515.15
Depreciation/depletion	1,971.00	1,449.44	935.97	605.59
Deferred taxes	835.00	1,251.74	544.89	289.53
Non-cash items	350.00	(659.40)	(3.43)	(7.76)
Changes in working capital	325.00	798.37	(18.84)	29.75
Cash from operating activities	**4,932.00**	**4,843.47**	**2,406.89**	**1,432.27**
Capital expenditures	(6,744.00)	(4,765.61)	(2,856.08)	(1,426.14)
Other investing cash flow items, total	(1,178.00)	(4,176.89)	(4,065.30)	(1,955.06)
Cash from investing activities	**(7,922.00)**	**(8,942.50)**	**(6,921.38)**	**(3,381.20)**
Financing cash flow items	(196.00)	52.51	39.05	77.40
Total cash dividends paid	(210.00)	(175.43)	(92.01)	(79.81)
Issuance (retirement) of stock, net	15.00	2,303.59	2,344.92	941.11
Issuance (retirement) of debt, net	3,379.00	1,860.85	2,275.65	976.54
Cash from financing activities	**2,988.00**	**4,041.52**	**4,567.62**	**1,915.24**
Net change in cash	**(2.00)**	**(57.51)**	**53.13**	**(33.69)**

She asked that you write out a narrative describing Peatry's operations over the last four years using just the cash flows of the firm. In the narrative, you should address some very basic questions: (i) How much cash has the firm generated from its operations? (ii) How much cash has the firm been investing? (iii) How has the firm financed its needs for cash?

STEP 1: Picture the problem

The cash flow statement uses information from the firm's balance sheet and income statement to identify the net sources and uses of cash for a specific period of time. Moreover, the sources and uses are organized into cash from operating activities, from investing activities, and from financing activities:

Beginning Cash Balance

Plus: Cash flow from operating activities

Plus: Cash flow from investing activities

Plus: Cash flow from financing activities

Equals: Ending Cash Balance

We can write an equation to represent the cash flow statement as follows:

$$\text{Beginning Cash Balance} + \text{Cash Flow from Operating Activities} + \text{Cash Flow from Investing Activities} + \text{Cash Flow from Financing Activities} = \text{Ending Cash Balance}$$

The cash flow statements for Peatry focus on the change in cash for the period or the difference between the beginning and ending balances. This can be expressed as an equation as follows:

$$\text{Net Change in Cash} = \left(\text{Ending Cash Balance} - \text{Beginning Cash Balance}\right) = \text{Cash Flow from Operating Activities} + \text{Cash Flow from Investing Activities} + \text{Cash Flow from Financing Activities}$$

STEP 2: Decide on a solution strategy

The basic format of the cash flow statements provides a useful guide to the analysis of a firm's cash flows for the period. For example, the cash flow from operating activities section describes how much cash the firm generated from operations, the investing cash flow section summarizes how much money the firm invested in new fixed assets, and the financing section summarizes the net results of the firm's financing decisions for the period. To analyze what the firm has done that affects its cash balance, we need only review the balances under each of these sections of the cash flow statement.

STEP 3: Solve

Cash flow from operating activities:
- Peatry has had positive and growing cash flows from operations every year during the entire period.
- The primary contributors to the operating cash flows were the firm's net income plus depreciation/depletion expense.[10]
- Working capital is a source of cash in three of the four years, indicating the net reduction in the firm's investment in working capital.

Cash flow from investing activities:
- Peatry has been a very aggressive investor in new fixed assets and acquisitions of new oil and gas properties.
- Total investments have been roughly two times the firm's operating cash flows, which meant that the firm had to raise a substantial amount of outside financing in the financial markets.

Cash flow from financing activities:
- Peatry has been a regular issuer of both equity and debt throughout the period.
- The firm's peak year for raising external financing was 2005, when it raised over $4.5 billion.
- The firm issued a total of $5.6 billion in equity and $8.5 billion in debt over the four-year period.
- The firm has paid a total of $557.25 million in dividends to its stockholders over the period.

(3 CONTINUED >> ON NEXT PAGE)

---

[10]Depletion expense represents the expensing of the cost of oil and gas properties as they are produced. It is similar in concept to depreciation, except the cost being expensed is the cost of acquiring and developing oil and gas properties.

Summary Comments:
- Peatry has made a lot of money over this four-year period.
- However, the firm has been investing in new properties at a much higher pace (it invested a total of $27.2 billion over the last four years) such that the firm has had to go to the financial market every year to raise the additional capital it required to finance its investments.
- The net result is that the cumulative change in cash over the four-year period is a negative $40.07 million.

STEP 4: Analyze

The cash flow statements portray a very profitable firm that has been investing at a pace that is roughly double the firm's operating cash flows. The net result was the ability to raise over $13.5 billion in new financing from the financial markets. Moreover, the firm has made relatively modest cash distributions to its shareholders and has, instead, reinvested the firm's substantial earnings back into the firm.

STEP 5: Check yourself

Go to http://finance.google.com/finance and get the cash flow statements for the most recent four-year period for Exco Resources (XCO). How does its cash from investing activities compare to its cash flow from operating activities in 2012?

ANSWER: Cash flow from operating activities = $577.83 million and cash flow from investing activities = ($2,396) million.

Your Turn: For more practice, do related **Study Problems** 14 at the end of this chapter.   >> **END Checkpoint 3**

Tools of Financial Analysis—Cash Flow Statement

Name of Tool	Formula	What It Tells You
Cash Flow Statement Equation	$\text{Change in Cash Balance} = \text{Ending Cash Balance} - \text{Beginning Cash Balance}$	• The net amount of cash that the firm collected or spent during the period. • Because accountants follow the accrual method of accounting, the change in cash balance for the period will not necessarily match up with reported net income.

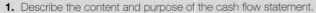

Before you begin end-of-chapter material

Concept Check | 5

1. Describe the content and purpose of the cash flow statement.
2. Is an increase in accounts receivable a source of cash or a use of cash? Explain.
3. Is a decrease in accounts payable a source of cash or use of cash? Explain.
4. When an asset balance increases, this indicates that the firm has more of that asset, so why is this a use of cash?

Applying the Principles of Finance to This Chapter

Chapter Summaries

Describe the content of the four basic financial statements and discuss the importance of financial statement analysis to the financial manager.

SUMMARY: The accounting and financial regulatory authorities have mandated that firms should report four different financial statements, with each having its own perspective and objective:

1. **Income statement**—includes the revenue the firm has earned over a specific period of time, usually a quarter of a year or a full year; the expenses it has incurred during the period to earn its revenues; and the profit the firm has earned during that period.
2. **Balance sheet**—contains information about the firm's assets (everything of value the company owns), liabilities (the firm's debts), and shareholders' equity (the money invested by the company owners).
3. **Cash flow statement**—reports cash received and cash spent by the firm over a period of time, usually a quarter of a year or a full year.
4. **Statement of shareholders' equity**—provides a detailed account of the firm's activities in the common and preferred stock accounts, the retained earnings account, and changes to owners' equity that do not appear in the income statement.

First, financial managers use the firm's financial statements to assess the firm's financial condition. Second, financial statements provide a tool for controlling the firm's operations. Finally, financial statements provide the model that managers use to develop forecasts and plans.

KEY TERMS

Accounts receivable Credit sales that have not yet been collected.

Revenues Sales recognized for the period and recorded in the firm's income statement.

Concept Check | 1

1. Name the four basic financial statements that make up the published financial reports of a firm and describe the basic function of each.
2. What are the three uses of a firm's financial statements for the firm's management?
3. Describe the revenue recognition, matching, and historical cost principles as they are applied in the construction of a firm's financial statements.

Evaluate firm profitability using the income statement.

SUMMARY: A firm's income statement reflects its sales (also called revenues) earned during a specific period of time (for example, for one year or one quarter) less the expenses the firm incurred in producing those revenues. The firm's income statement is typically analyzed by calculating profit margins based on gross profits (revenues less cost of goods sold), operating income (gross profits less operating expenses), and net income (operating profits less interest expenses and the firm's tax liability for the period).

KEY TERMS

Cost of goods sold The cost of producing or acquiring the products or services that the firm sold during the period covered by an income statement.

Depreciation expenses The allocation of the cost of the firm's long-lived assets (such as its plant and equipment) in the income statement over the useful lives of the assets.

Dividends per share The per share cash distribution a firm pays for each share of stock.

Earnings before interest and taxes (EBIT) Revenues from sales minus the cost of goods sold and less operating expenses. Also referred to as net operating income.

Earnings per share Net income divided by the number of common shares outstanding.

Gross profit margin The ratio of gross profit (sales less cost of goods sold) divided by sales.

Income statement The financial statement that includes the revenue the firm has earned over a specific period of time, usually a quarter of a year or a full year; the expenses it has incurred during the year to earn its revenues; and the profit the firm has earned.

Net income The income that a firm has after subtracting costs and expenses from total revenue.

Net operating income The firm's profits from its ongoing operations—before it makes interest

payments and pays its taxes. Also referred to as earnings before interest and taxes (EBIT).

Net profit margin Net income divided by sales.

Operating profit margin The ratio of net operating income to sales.

Profits Another term for income.

Concept Check | **2**

1. What information can we derive from a firm's income statement?
2. List the entries in the income statement.
3. What does the acronym GAAP stand for?

KEY EQUATION

$$\text{Revenues (or Sales)} - \text{Expenses} = \text{Profits} \tag{1}$$

Estimate a firm's tax liability using the corporate tax schedule and distinguish between the average and marginal tax rate.

SUMMARY: For the most part, taxable income for the corporation is equal to the firm's operating income less any interest expense. Rather than a single tax rate, the corporate tax is calculated using a schedule of rates applicable to various income brackets, where the maximum tax rate of 35 percent in 2010 applies to all taxable income in excess of $18,333,333. If a firm pays $10,000 in taxes on $40,000 in taxable income, then its average tax rate is 25 percent. However, with a progressive tax rate, the last dollar of income will be taxed at a higher rate than the first dollar of income. The tax rate applicable to the last dollar of taxable income is the marginal tax rate. Moreover, the marginal tax rate is the rate that impacts any new earnings and consequently is the appropriate rate for use when making financial decisions.

KEY TERMS

Concept Check | **3**

1. What is the difference between average and marginal tax rates?
2. What is the marginal tax rate for a firm that currently earns $75,000 in earnings before taxes and expects to earn $80,000 next year?
3. How are dividends received by corporations taxed?

Average tax rate The ratio of the tax liability divided by taxable income.

Marginal tax rate The tax rate that the company will pay on its next dollar of taxable income.

Taxable income Firm revenues for the period less all tax-deductible expenses (such as cost of goods sold, operating expenses, and interest expense for the period).

Use the balance sheet to describe a firm's investments in assets and the way it has financed them.

SUMMARY: The balance sheet presents a snapshot of the company's assets, liabilities, and equity on a specific date. The firm's total assets represent the historical cost of all the investments that have been made in the business. Total assets must equal the firm's total debt and equity because every dollar of investment made in assets has been financed by the firm's creditors and owners. Assets are categorized into one of two groupings: current assets, which are assets expected to be converted to cash within a period of 12 months or less, or fixed assets, which are expected to remain on the firm's books for a period longer than one year. The firm's debts, or liabilities, include both its short-term debt (payable in 12 months or less) and its long-term debt (payable in more than 12 months). The balance sheet also includes the owners' equity, which includes (1) common stock, which can be shown as par value plus additional paid-in capital (the additional amount of capital the firm raised when investors purchased its stock for more than its par value); and (2) the firm's retained earnings (the earnings that have been retained and reinvested in the business rather than being distributed to the company's shareholders).

KEY TERMS

Accounts payable The credit suppliers extend to the firm when it purchases items for its inventories.

Accumulated depreciation The sum of all depreciation expenses that have been deducted from the firm's income statement in previous periods for the plant and equipment the firm currently has on its balance sheet.

Balance sheet A financial statement that contains a summary of the firm's assets (everything of value the company owns), liabilities (the firm's debts), and shareholders' equity (the money invested by the company owners).

Current assets Cash plus other assets that the firm expects to convert into cash within 12 months or less.

Current liabilities The debts of the firm that must be repaid within a period of 12 months or less.

Fixed assets Those assets that the firm does not expect to sell or otherwise convert to cash within one year.

Gross plant and equipment The sum of the historical cost of the plant and equipment owned by the firm.

Inventories Raw materials used to make the firm's products, goods in process, and finished goods that are ready for sale.

Liquidity The speed with which the asset can be converted into cash without loss of value.

Long-term debt Loans from banks and other lenders that have maturities longer than one year as well as bonds sold by the firm in the public markets.

Market value The price that an asset would trade for in a competitive market.

Net plant and equipment The cumulative historical cost of plant and equipment owned by the firm (gross plant and equipment) less accumulated depreciation expense that has been charged against those assets over their useful life.

Net working capital The difference between the firm's current assets and current liabilities.

Notes payable A loan contract reflecting the fact that a firm has borrowed money that it promises to repay according to the terms of the agreement.

Paid-in capital The money contributed to a corporation by its stockholders in addition to the par value of the firm's stock. Sometimes called *paid-in capital above par*.

Par value The stated value of a bond or share of stock at the time of issue.

Retained earnings The accumulation of prior-year net income that was retained and reinvested in the firm (i.e., not paid in dividends).

Stockholders' equity The sum of the par value of common stock plus paid-in capital plus retained earnings. This quantity is sometimes referred to as the book value of the firm's equity.

Total assets The sum total of current and long-term assets recorded in the firm's balance sheet.

Total liabilities The total amount of money the firm owes its creditors (including the firm's banks and other creditors).

Total shareholders' equity Total assets less total liabilities.

Treasury stock Stock that has been bought back by the issuing company.

KEY EQUATIONS

$$\text{Total Assets} = \text{Total Liabilities} + \text{Total Shareholders' Equity} \qquad (2)$$

$$\text{Stockholders' Equity} = \text{Par Value of Common Stock} + \text{Paid-in Capital} + \text{Retained Earnings} \qquad (3)$$

$$\text{Stockholders' Equity} = \left(\text{Total Assets} \right) - \left(\text{Total Liabilities} \right) \qquad (4)$$

$$\text{Net Working Capital} = \left(\text{Current Assets} \right) - \left(\text{Current Liabilities} \right) \qquad (5)$$

Concept Check | **4**

1. Describe the basic categories of assets and liabilities reported in a firm's balance sheet.
2. What does the term *net working capital* mean, and how is it computed?

5 Identify the sources and uses of cash for a firm using the firm's cash flow statement.

SUMMARY: The cash flow statement explains the change in the firm's cash account, which equals the difference in the ending and beginning balance in the firm's cash account. The statement categorizes cash flows into one of three buckets: cash flow from operating activities, from investing activities, and from financing activities. This financial statement is widely used by financial analysts because it provides a very clear picture of what the firm did during the period to generate and spend cash.

KEY TERMS

Cash flow from operations The portion of the firm's total cash flow resulting from its operating activities.

Cash flow statement A financial statement that reports cash received and cash spent by the firm over a period of time, usually one quarter of a year or a full year.

Net income The income that a firm has after subtracting costs and expenses from total revenue.

Quality of earnings ratio The ratio of cash flow from operations divided by net income.

Concept Check | **5**

1. Describe the content and purpose of the cash flow statement.

2. Is an increase in accounts receivable a source of cash or a use of cash? Explain.

3. Is a decrease in accounts payable a source of cash or use of cash? Explain.

4. When an asset balance increases, this indicates that the firm has more of that asset, so why is this a use of cash?

Source of cash Any activity that brings cash into the firm, such as when the firm sells goods and services or sells an old piece of equipment that it no longer needs.

Use of cash Any activity that causes cash to leave the firm, such as the payment of taxes or payments made to stockholders, creditors, and suppliers.

KEY EQUATIONS

$$\frac{\text{Change in Cash}}{\text{Balance}} = \frac{\text{Ending Cash}}{\text{Balance}} - \frac{\text{Beginning Cash}}{\text{Balance}} \quad (6)$$

$$\frac{\text{Change in Cash}}{\text{Balance for 2013}} = \frac{\text{Ending Cash}}{\text{Balance for 2013}} - \frac{\text{Ending Cash}}{\text{Balance for 2012}} \quad (7)$$

$$\text{Quality of Earnings} = \frac{\text{Cash Flow from Operations}}{\text{Net Income}} \quad (8)$$

$$\text{Capital Acquisitions Ratio} = \frac{\text{Cash Flow from Operations}}{\text{Cash Paid for Capital Expenditures (CAPEX)}} \quad (9)$$

Study Questions

1. Describe the content of the balance sheet and the income statement.

2. How do gross profits, operating income, and net income differ?

3. From the firm's perspective, how are dividends different from interest payments?

4. What is a firm's net working capital, and what does it tell you about the liquidity of a firm?

5. When a firm's accounts receivable balance increases from one period to the next, the firm has experienced a use of cash. How is it that an increase in an asset such as accounts receivable represents a use of cash?

6. Appleby Southern Inc. had an accounts payable balance of $5 million at the end of 2012 and the balance rose to $7 million in 2013. What is the cash flow consequence of this change in accounts payable?

7. In 2013 RubKing Barbeque Sauce, Inc. purchased a new bottling machine at a cost of $1.5 million. The new machine is expected to last for 10 years and the firm plans to depreciate it using straight-line depreciation of $150,000 per year. What is the cash flow consequence of the purchase for 2013?

8. The cash flow statement is one of the four basic financial statements. Define the objective in preparing this statement and discuss some of the types of questions that can be addressed using its content.

9. **(Related to The Business of Life: Your Personal Balance Sheet and Income Statement)** In The Business of Life: Your Personal Balance Sheet and Income Statement box feature we learned that individuals have financial statements just like firms. Prepare your personal balance sheet using the following items: (i) you have a 2003 Corolla that you bought for $3,500 and still owe a note of $2,000; (ii) your checking account has a balance of $453.28 and you have a savings account with a $2,412.49 balance; (iii) you have an unpaid balance on your school loan of $12,591.22 (your tuition for last year). What is your current net worth?

10. **(Related to Finance in a Flat World: GAAP vs. IFRS)** In the Finance in a Flat World: GAAP vs. IFRS box feature, we learned that GAAP, the financial reporting system used in the United States, is not the same as that used throughout the rest of the world. However, the U.S. system is converging with the international system. Do a web search and write up a brief statement summarizing the current status of the convergence of the U.S. and international accounting systems.

Study Problems

The Income Statement

1. **(Related to Checkpoint 1)** (**Working with the income statement**) At the end of its third year of operations, the Sandifer Manufacturing Co. had $4,500,000 in revenues; $3,375,000 in cost of goods sold; $450,000 in operating expenses, which included depreciation expense of $150,000; and had a tax liability equal to 35 percent of the firm's taxable income. What is the net income of the firm for the year?

2. **(Working with the income statement)** Sandifer Manufacturing Co. (from the previous problem) plans to reinvest $50,000 of its earnings back in the firm. What does this plan leave for the payment of a cash dividend to Sandifer's stockholders?

3. **(Working with the income statement)** If the Marifield Steel Fabrication Company earned $500,000 in net income and paid a cash dividend of $300,000 to its stockholders, what are the firm's earnings per share if the firm has 100,000 shares of stock outstanding?

Corporate Taxes

4. **(Corporate income tax)** Barrington Enterprises earned $4 million in taxable income (earnings before taxes) during its most recent year of operations. Use the corporate tax rates found in the chapter to calculate the firm's tax liability for the year. What are the firm's average and marginal tax rates?

5. **(Corporate income tax)** Last year Sanderson, Inc. had sales of $3 million. The firm's cost of its goods sold came to $2 million, operating expenses excluding depreciation of $100,000 were $400,000, and the firm paid $150,000 in interest on its bank loans. Also, the corporation received $50,000 in dividend income (from a company in which it owned less than 20 percent of its shares) but paid $25,000 in the form of dividends to its own common stockholders. Calculate the corporation's tax liability. What are the firm's average and marginal tax rates?

6. **(Corporate income tax)** The Robbins Corporation is an oil wholesaler. The firm's sales last year were $1 million, with the cost of goods sold equal to $600,000. The firm paid interest of $200,000 and its cash operating expenses were $100,000. Also, the firm received $40,000 in dividend income from a firm in which the firm owned 22 percent of the shares, while paying only $10,000 in dividends to its stockholders. Depreciation expense was $50,000. Compute the firm's tax liability. Based on your answer, does management need to take any additional action? What are the firm's average and marginal tax rates?

7. **(Corporate income tax)** Sales for J. P. Hulett Inc. during the past year amounted to $4 million. Gross profits totaled $1 million, and operating and depreciation expenses were $500,000 and $350,000, respectively. Dividend income for the year was $12,000, which was paid by a firm in which Hulett owns 85 percent of the shares. Compute the corporation's tax liability. What are the firm's average and marginal tax rates?

8. **(Corporate income tax)** G. R. Edwin Inc. had sales of $6 million during the past year. The cost of goods sold amounted to $3 million. Operating expenses totaled $2.6 million, and interest expense was $30,000. Determine the firm's tax liability. What are the firm's average and marginal tax rates?

9. **(Corporate income tax)** Meyer Inc. has taxable income (earnings before taxes) of $300,000. Calculate Meyer's federal income tax liability using the tax table in this chapter. What are the firm's average and marginal tax rates?

10. **(Corporate income tax)** Boisjoly Productions had taxable income of $19 million.
    a. Calculate Boisjoly's federal income taxes.
    b. Now calculate Boisjoly's average and marginal tax rates.

The Balance Sheet

11. **(Related to Checkpoint 2) (Working with the balance sheet)** The Caraway Seed Company grows heirloom tomatoes and sells their seeds. The heirloom tomato plants are preferred by many growers for their superior flavor. At the end of the most recent year the firm had current assets of $50,000, net fixed assets of $250,000, current liabilities of $30,000, and long-term debt of $100,000.

a. Calculate Caraway's stockholders' equity.
b. What is the firm's net working capital?
c. If Caraway's current liabilities consist of $20,000 in accounts payable and $10,000 in short-term debt (notes payable), what is the firm's net working capital?

12. **(Related to Checkpoint 2) (Review of financial statements)** A scrambled list of accounts from the income statement and balance sheet of Belmond, Inc. is as follows:

Inventory	$ 6,500
Common stock	45,000
Cash	16,550
Operating expenses	1,350
Short-term notes payable	600
Interest expense	900
Depreciation expense	500
Sales	12,800
Accounts receivable	9,600
Accounts payable	4,800
Long-term debt	55,000
Cost of goods sold	5,750
Buildings and equipment	122,000
Accumulated depreciation	34,000
Taxes	1,440
General and administrative expense	850
Retained earnings	?

a. How much is the firm's net working capital?
b. Complete an income statement and a balance sheet for Belmond.
c. If you were asked to respond to complete parts a. and b. as part of a training exercise, what could you tell your boss about the company's financial condition based on your answers?

13. **(Review of financial statements)** Prepare a balance sheet and income statement for the Warner Company from the following scrambled list of items:

Depreciation expense	$ 66,000
Cash	225,000
Long-term debt	334,000
Sales	573,000
Accounts payable	102,000
General and administrative expense	79,000
Buildings and equipment	895,000
Notes payable	75,000
Accounts receivable	167,500
Interest expense	4,750
Accrued expenses	7,900
Common stock	289,000
Cost of goods sold	297,000
Inventory	99,300
Taxes	50,500
Accumulated depreciation	263,000
Taxes payable	53,000
Retained earnings	262,900

a. Prepare an income statement for the Warner Company.
b. Prepare a balance sheet for the Warner Company.
c. What can you say about the firm's financial condition based on these financial statements?

Cash Flow Statement

14. **(Related to Checkpoint 3) (Analyzing the cash flow statement)** Goggle, Inc. is an Internet firm that has experienced a period of very rapid growth in revenues over the period 2007–2010. The cash flow statements for Goggle, Inc. spanning the period are as follows:

In Millions of U.S. Dollars	12 Months Ending			
	12/31/2010	12/31/2009	12/31/2008	12/31/2007
Net income	$ 4,000	$ 3,000	$ 1,500	$ 400
Depreciation expense	1,000	600	300	150
Changes in working capital	600	50	50	(250)
Cash from operating activities	$ 5,600	$ 3,650	$ 1,850	$ 300
Capital expenditures	$(3,600)	$(7,000)	$(3,300)	$(2,000)
Cash from investing activities	$(3,600)	$(7,000)	$(3,300)	$(2,000)
Interest and financing cash flow items	$ 400	$ 600	$ 0	$ 5
Total cash dividends paid	0	0	0	0
Issuance (retirement) of stock	24	2,400	4,400	1,200
Issuance (retirement) of debt	0	0	(2)	(5)
Cash from financing activities	$ 424	$ 3,000	$ 4,398	$ 1,200
Net change in cash	$ 2,424	$ (350)	$ 2,948	$ (500)

Answer the following questions using the information found in these statements:
a. Is Goggle generating positive cash flow from its operations?
b. How much did Goggle invest in new capital expenditures over the last four years?
c. Describe Goggle's sources of financing in the financial markets over the last four years.
d. Based solely on the cash flow statements for 2007 through 2010, write a brief narrative that describes the major activities of Goggle's management team over the last four years.

15. **(Analyzing the cash flow statement)** The cash flow statements for retailing giant BigBox, Inc. spanning the period 2010–2013 are as follows:

In Millions of U.S. Dollars	12 Months Ending			
	12/31/2013	12/31/2012	12/31/2011	12/31/2010
Net income	$ 13,000	$ 12,000	$ 11,000	$ 10,000
Depreciation expense	6,500	6,300	5,000	4,000
Changes in working capital	1,200	2,300	2,400	1,000
Cash from operating activities	$ 20,700	$ 20,600	$ 18,400	$ 15,000
Capital expenditures	$ (16,000)	$ (14,500)	$ (14,000)	$ (12,300)
Cash from investing activities	$ (16,000)	$ (14,500)	$ (14,000)	$ (12,300)
Interest and financing cash flow items	$ (350)	$ (250)	$ (350)	$ 100
Total cash dividends paid	(3,600)	(2,800)	(2,500)	(2,200)
Issuance (retirement) of stock	(8,000)	(1,500)	(3,600)	(4,500)
Issuance (retirement) of debt	1,500	(100)	4,000	4,100
Cash from financing activities	$ (10,450)	$ (4,650)	$ (2,450)	$ (2,500)
Net change in cash	$ (5,750)	$ 1,450	$ 1,950	$ 200

Answer the following questions using the information found in these statements:

a. Does BigBox generate positive cash flow from its operations?
b. How much did BigBox invest in new capital expenditures over the last four years?
c. Describe BigBox's sources of financing in the financial markets over the last four years.
d. Based solely on the cash flow statement for 2010 through 2013, write a brief narrative that describes the major activities of BigBox's management team over the last four years.

16. **(Analyzing the Quality of Firm Earnings)** Kabutell, Inc. had net income of $750,000, cash flow from financing activities of $50,000, depreciation expenses of $50,000, and cash flow from operating activities of $575,000. Calculate the quality of earnings ratio. What does this ratio tell you?

a. Kabutell, Inc. reported the following in its annual reports for 2011–2013:

($ millions)	2011	2012	2013
Cash Flow from Operations	$478	$403	$470
Capital Expenditures (CAPEX)	$459	$447	$456

b. Calculate the average capital acquisitions ratio over the three-year period. How would you interpret these results?

17. **(Analyzing the quality of earnings and sustainability of capital expenditures)** Look up the statement of cash flows for both Home Depot and Lowes using Yahoo! Finance.

a. Compute the quality of earnings ratio for both firms and all three years of data provided.
b. Compare the quality of earnings ratio for the two firms. For which firm do you feel most comfortable about the reported earnings quality? Explain.
c. Compute the capital acquisitions ratios for the latest three years for both firms.
d. Compare Home Depot's and Lowes' abilities to use of operating cash flow to finance their capital expenditures. Which firm has relied more on the capital markets?

Mini-Case

In the introduction to this chapter, we describe the situation faced by Gap, Inc. (GPS). We learned that the retail clothing chain had grown dramatically over the first two decades of its existence but had fallen on difficult times in 2007. Assume that you were hired as a new management trainee by the corporate offices of Gap in the spring of 2009 and you report directly to the director of sales and marketing. Although your job is not specifically in finance, your boss is a major contributor to the firm's overall financial success and wants you to familiarize yourself with the firm's recent financial performance. Specifically, she has asked that you review the following income statements for years 2005–2008. You are to review the firm's revenues, gross profit, operating income, and net income trends over the past four years.

Gap, Inc.
Income Statements (2005–2008)

In Millions of USD (except for per share items)	2008	2007	2006	2005
Total revenue	$15,763	$15,923	$16,019	$16,267
Cost of goods sold	10,071	10,266	10,145	9,886
Gross profit	$ 5,692	$ 5,657	$ 5,874	$ 6,381
Total operating expense	4,377	4,432	4,099	4,402
Net operating income	$ 1,315	$ 1,225	$ 1,775	$ 1,979
Interest income (expense)	91	90	48	(108)
Income before tax	$ 1,406	$ 1,315	$ 1,823	$ 1,871
Income taxes	539	506	692	721
Net income	$ 867	$ 809	$ 1,131	$ 1,150

After contemplating the assignment, you decide to calculate the gross profit margin, operating profit margin, and net profit margin for each of these years. It is your hope that by evaluating these profit margins you will be able to pinpoint any problems that the firm may be experiencing.

Finally, your boss pointed out that the firm may need to raise additional capital in the near future and suggested that you review the firm's past financing decisions using both the firm's balance sheets and statements of cash flows. Specifically, she asked that you summarize your assessment of the firm's use of debt financing over the last four years.

Gap, Inc.
Balance Sheets (2005–2008)

In millions of USD (except for per share items)	2008	2007	2006	2005
Cash and short-term investments	1,901.00	2,600.00	2,987.00	3,062.00
Total inventory	1,575.00	1,796.00	1,696.00	1,814.00
Other current assets, total	610.00	633.00	556.00	1,428.00
Total current assets	4,086.00	5,029.00	5,239.00	6,304.00
Property/plant/equipment, total—gross	7,320.00	7,135.00	6,958.00	7,169.00
Other long-term assets, total	485.00	318.00	336.00	368.00
Total assets	7,838.00	8,544.00	8,821.00	10,048.00
Accounts payable	1,006.00	772.00	1,132.00	1,240.00
Accrued expenses	1,259.00	1,159.00	725.00	924.00
Notes payable/short-term debt	0.00	0.00	0.00	0.00
Current portion of long-term debt and leases	138.00	325.00	0.00	0.00
Other current liabilities	30.00	16.00	85.00	78.00
Total current liabilities	2,433.00	2,272.00	1,942.00	2,242.00
Long-term debt	50.00	188.00	513.00	1,886.00
Other liabilities, total	1,081.00	910.00	941.00	984.00
Total liabilities	3,564.00	3,370.00	3,396.00	5,112.00
Common stock	55.00	55.00	54.00	49.00
Additional paid-in capital	2,783.00	2,631.00	2,402.00	904.00
Retained earnings (accumulated deficit)	9,223.00	8,646.00	8,133.00	7,181.00
Treasury stock—common	(7,912.00)	(6,225.00)	(5,210.00)	(3,238.00)
Other equity	125.00	77.00	46.00	40.00
Total equity	4,274.00	5,174.00	5,425.00	4,936.00
Total liabilities and shareholders' equity	7,838.00	8,544.00	8,821.00	10,048.00

Legend:

Treasury stock—shares of a firm's common stock that had previously been issued to the public but that have been repurchased in the equity market by the firm.

Gap, Inc.
Statement of Cash Flows (2006–2008)

In Millions of USD (except for per share items)	2008	2007	2006
Net income	$ 833	$ 778	$ 1,113
Depreciation	547	530	625
Deferred taxes	(51)	(41)	(46)
Non-cash items	107	67	(28)
Changes in working capital	645	(84)	(113)
Cash from operating activities	**$ 2,081**	**$ 1,250**	**$ 1,551**
Capital expenditures	(682)	(572)	(600)
Other investing cash flow items, total	408	422	886
Cash from investing activities	**$ (274)**	**$ (150)**	**$ 286**
Financing cash flow items	132	213	0
Total cash dividends paid	(252)	(265)	(179)
Issuance (retirement) of stock, net	(1,700)	(1,050)	(1,861)
Issuance (retirement) of debt, net	(326)	0	0
Cash from financing activities	**$(2,146)**	**$(1,102)**	**$(2,040)**
Foreign exchange effects	33	(3)	(7)
Net change in cash	**$ (306)**	**$ (5)**	**(210)**

Legend:

Deferred taxes—A liability account that reflects the accumulated difference between the amount of income tax that the firm shows each year as an expense on its financial statements and the amount of income tax, usually lower, that the firm pays to the government.

Foreign exchange effects—the cash flow consequences of foreign exchange gains (losses) during the year.

Photo Credits

Financial Analysis

From Chapter 4 of *Financial Management: Principles and Applications*, Twelfth Edition. Sheridan Titman, Arthur J. Keown, and John D. Martin.

Financial Analysis
Sizing Up Firm Performance

Chapter **Outline**

1 Why Do We Analyze Financial Statements? ⟶ **Objective 1.** Explain what we can learn by analyzing a firm's financial statements.

2 Common Size Statements: Standardizing Financial Information ⟶ **Objective 2.** Use common-size financial statements as a tool of financial analysis.

3 Using Financial Ratios ⟶ **Objective 3.** Calculate and use a comprehensive set of financial ratios to evaluate a company's performance.

4 Selecting a Performance Benchmark ⟶ **Objective 4.** Select an appropriate benchmark for use in performing a financial ratio analysis.

5 Limitations of Ratio Analysis ⟶ **Objective 5.** Describe the limitations of financial ratio analysis.

Principles P3, P4, and P5 Applied

In this chapter we apply P Principle 3: **Cash Flows Are the Source of Value**. Accounting statements contain important information that can be used to calculate current cash flows as well as evaluate the potential of the firm to generate future cash flows. In addition, we apply P Principle 4: **Market Prices Reflect Information**. Specifically, we extract information from a firm's reported financial statements using financial ratios that are useful in discerning the financial health of the firm and consequently the value of the firm. Finally, we discuss P Principle 5: **Individuals Respond to Incentives**. Managers respond to incentives they are given in the workplace, and when their incentives are not properly aligned with those of the firm's stockholders, managers may not make decisions that are consistent with increasing shareholder value.

Chesapeake, Inc. (CHK), the largest producer of natural gas in the United States, frequently purchases oil and gas properties to develop and operate. Because the firm is a very active acquirer, it often needs to borrow money or sell new shares of common stock. In fact, during 2007 alone, the firm borrowed $3.379 billion. Chesapeake's ability to sell new shares and to borrow money hinges on the financial condition of the firm and its past performance, attributes that are apparent in the firm's financial statements. So, when Chesapeake approaches its bank with a loan request, it does so with its financial statements in hand. These statements help the banker determine how much money Chesapeake already owes, when that debt is due, the ability of the firm to repay its debt, and the capacity of Chesapeake to borrow even more money.

Now consider a very different business. Carla and Pete Morse own and operate a small independent coffee shop called the Trident Coffeehouse in Westlake, a suburb of Austin, Texas. The family started the business four years ago using their personal savings. Because the business has grown and prospered, they are now thinking about opening a second store. Although the first store is profitable, the owners have reinvested all the store profits back into the business, so they will need to borrow the majority of the $150,000 needed to open a second store. When applying for a business loan, the banker asked them to fill out a loan application that requires detailed financial information about the Morses' coffee shop and their personal finances. For example, the banker asked how much income their coffee shop earned in each of the last four years, how much money the business owed, and a host of questions that can be answered using financial statements.

The process of extracting information from a firm's financial statements is called financial statement analysis and is the subject of this chapter. A fundamental reason for engaging in financial statement analysis is to gather information about a firm's financial condition, which is important in the valuation of the firm (remember P Principle 4: **Market Prices Reflect Information**). We begin our discussion of financial statement analysis by discussing the various reasons for analyzing a firm's financial statements. From there we transition to an in-depth discussion of the basic tools of financial statement analysis, which consist of common-size financial statements and financial ratios. We next discuss the importance of identifying a proper benchmark for use in comparisons with a firm's financial ratios. We conclude the chapter by identifying some of the more important limitations of financial ratio analysis.

Regardless of Your Major...

"Financial Ratios and Business"

It is easy to imagine why a finance or accounting manager might be interested in using financial ratios; however, it may not be obvious that sales and marketing professionals would be interested in financial ratios as well. In fact, marketers use financial ratios to assess the creditworthiness of their customers. After all, there is something worse than missing a sales opportunity—making a sale that is uncollectible!

Managers in charge of firm operations also find financial ratios useful. For example, they monitor inventory levels using financial ratios to help make decisions regarding which products the firm should be producing. Financial ratios are used by everyone, regardless of their functional area, to help them identify and solve business problems.

You will also find that financial ratios are important to your personal financial planning. For example, financial ratios are used regularly by banks and lending institutions to determine whether you get a loan.

1 | Why Do We Analyze Financial Statements?

A firm's financial statements can be analyzed internally from within the firm or externally by bankers, investors, customers, and other interested parties. Internal financial analysis is performed by a firm's own employees. Non-employees from outside the firm perform external financial analysis.

There are several reasons an internal financial analysis might be done:

- To evaluate the performance of employees and determine their pay raises and bonuses
- To compare the financial performance of the firm's different divisions
- To prepare financial projections, such as those associated with the launch of a new product
- To evaluate the firm's financial performance in light of its competitors' performance and determine how the firm might improve its own operations

A variety of firms and individuals that have an economic interest in a firm's financial performance might undertake an external financial analysis:

- Banks and other lenders deciding whether to loan money to the firm
- Suppliers who are considering whether to grant credit to the firm
- Credit-rating agencies trying to determine the firm's creditworthiness
- Professional analysts who work for investment companies considering investing in the firm or advising others about investing
- Individual investors deciding whether to invest in the firm

Before you move on to 2

Concept Check | 1

1. What are some common reasons for analyzing a firm's financial statements?
2. What are some of the firms that engage in external financial statement analysis, and what are their motives?

2 Common-Size Statements: Standardizing Financial Information

It is meaningless to compare the individual entries in a firm's financial statements with those of firms that are not the same size. For example, the inventory balance for Walmart (WMT) would dwarf that of a small retail store. However, we can compare the ratios if we standardize the inventory balance by dividing it by the firm's total assets. One way to do this is by converting the statements to what are referred to as *common-size financial statements*.

A common-size financial statement is a standardized version of a financial statement in which all entries are presented in percentages. To create a common-size income statement, we simply divide each entry in the income statement by the company's sales. For a common-size balance sheet, we divide each entry in the balance sheet by the firm's total assets. Once these entries are converted to percentages, we can compare them with other firms that may have higher or lower sales and assets.

The Common-Size Income Statement: H. J. Boswell, Inc.

If we wanted to compare the financial statements for the fictional firm H. J. Boswell, Inc. against those of another firm, as potential investors in Boswell might do, we would produce common-size statements based on the balance sheets and income statements for Boswell. By dividing each entry in the income statement for Boswell by firm sales for 2010, we come up with the 2010 common-size statement for H. J. Boswell, Inc. shown in Table 1. For example, by dividing $90 million in selling expenses by firm sales of $2,700 million, we see that selling expenses are 3.3 percent of revenues. Note that each of the expenses appears in Table 1 as a negative percent because the expenses are subtracted in the process of calculating net income.

The common-size income statement allows us to quickly identify Boswell's largest expenses. For example, the firm's cost of goods sold makes up 75 percent of the firm's sales. By contrast, the firm's operating expenses make up only 10.8 percent of its sales. Finally, the company's net income constitutes 7.6 percent of each dollar of sales. The decline in gross profits to net income as a percent of sales is expected because as we move down the income statement, we deduct more types of expenses.

Table 1	H. J. Boswell, Inc.

Common-Size Income Statement for the Year Ending December 31, 2013

Sales		100.0%
Cost of goods sold		−75.0%
Gross profits		25.0%
Operating expenses:		
Selling expenses	−3.3%	
General and administrative expense	−2.5%	
Depreciation and amortization expense	−5.0%	
Total operating expense		−10.8%
Operating income (EBIT, or earnings before interest and taxes)		14.2%
Interest expense		−2.5%
Earnings before taxes		11.7%
Income taxes		−4.1%
Net income		7.6%

The Common-Size Balance Sheet: H. J. Boswell, Inc.

H. J. Boswell's common-size balance sheets for both 2012 and 2013 are found in Table 2. We construct these statements by dividing each entry in the balance sheet for Boswell by total assets for the year. The common-size balance sheets for both 2012 and 2013 makes it relatively easy to analyze what changed during the year. For example, you can tell that the firm increased its investment in current assets by 5.6 percent of its total assets (due to the sizeable increase in its inventories by 6.2 percent). Meanwhile, the firm's investment in its fixed assets actually declined. The firm's current liabilities fell by 2 percent of its total assets, and its long-term debt decreased by 1.7 percent of its total assets.

Although these changes are interesting and seem to indicate that the firm made some changes in either its strategy or operations, they don't tell us much about the company's financial condition. To learn more about whether the firm's financial position is improving or deteriorating, we will compare it to other firms as well as to itself over time. Financial ratios are a handy tool for doing this.

Table 2 H. J. Boswell, Inc.

Common-Size Balance Sheets for the Years Ending December 31, 2012 and 2013

	2012	2013	Change
Cash	5.4%	4.6%	−0.8%
Accounts receivable	7.9%	8.2%	0.3%
Inventory	13.0%	19.2%	6.2%
Other current assets	0.8%	0.7%	−0.1%
Total current assets	27.0%	32.6%	5.6%
Gross plant and equipment	94.6%	93.6%	−1.0%
Less accumulated depreciation	−21.7%	−26.3%	−4.6%
Net plant and equipment	73.0%	67.4%	−5.6%
Total assets	100.0%	100.0%	0.0%
	2012	**2013**	**Change**
Accounts payable	10.5%	9.6%	−0.9%
Accrued expenses	2.6%	2.3%	−0.3%
Short-term notes	3.6%	2.7%	−0.8%
Total current liabilities	16.6%	14.6%	−2.0%
Long-term debt	40.8%	39.2%	−1.7%
Total debt	57.4%	53.8%	−3.6%
Common stockholders' equity			
Common stock—par value	2.6%	2.3%	−0.3%
Paid in capital	18.4%	16.4%	−1.9%
Retained earnings	21.7%	27.5%	5.8%
Total common stockholders' equity	42.6%	46.2%	3.6%
Total liabilities and equity	100.0%	100.0%	0.0%

Before you move on to 3

Concept Check | 2

1. What is the reason for converting financial statements to common-size statements?
2. How are the common-size income statement and balance sheet constructed?

3 Using Financial Ratios

Financial ratios provide a second method for standardizing the financial information in the income statement and balance sheet. Ratios can help us answer the following questions about the firm's financial health:

Question	Category of Ratios Used to Address the Question
1. How liquid is the firm? Will it be able to pay its bills as they come due?	Liquidity ratios
2. How has the firm financed the purchase of its assets?	Capital structure ratios
3. How efficient has the firm's management been in utilizing its assets to generate sales?	Asset management efficiency ratios
4. Has the firm earned adequate returns on its investments?	Profitability ratios
5. Are the firm's managers creating value for shareholders?	Market value ratios

To address each question, there is a corresponding category of financial ratios that is commonly used.

We can answer these questions by performing two types of comparisons: first, comparing the firm's current financial ratios to its past ratios to see if they have been moving up or down over time; second, comparing the firm's ratios to the ratios of its competitors, or peer (or comparison) firms, to see if they are different. The ratio comparisons are seldom the end of the analysis. If the differences in the ratios are significant, more in-depth analysis must be done. Thus, financial ratios essentially provide the analyst with clues. The analyst then uses these clues the same way a detective uses clues generated by evidence—to find out exactly what to investigate more closely.

In the following ratio computations, we have color coded the numbers so that you can easily tell whether a particular number is coming from the income statement (these numbers are highlighted in red) or the balance sheet (these numbers are highlighted in blue). (Note: An Excel spreadsheet is available with this chapter at www.pearsonhighered.com/titman. We suggest you use this spreadsheet as you work through the different examples in the chapter.)

Liquidity Ratios

Liquidity ratios are used to address a very basic question about the firm's financial health: How liquid is the firm? A business is financially liquid if it is able to pay its bills on time. However, not all firms are equally liquid. That is, some firms have more than enough earning power to pay their bills even under very adverse market conditions, whereas others are just barely able to pay their bills in a timely fashion. How can we determine whether a firm is more liquid or less liquid than other firms?

This question can be answered by comparing the firm to other firms from two complementary perspectives: overall or general firm liquidity and liquidity of specific current asset accounts.

- **Analyzing measures of overall liquidity**—The first way to analyze a firm's liquidity is by comparing the firm's current assets, which can be converted quickly and easily into cash, to the firm's current liabilities. This is basically the same process as calculating the firm's net working capital. However, instead of just calculating net working capital by subtracting current liabilities from current assets, we express this quantity using a ratio. By standardizing the relationship between current assets and current liabilities using a ratio, we can compare the firm's liquidity to the liquidity of other firms.
- **Analyzing the liquidity of accounts receivable and inventories**—The second way to analyze firm liquidity is by examining the timeliness with which the firm's primary liquid assets—accounts receivable and inventories—are converted into cash. Remember Principle 3: **Cash Flows Are the Source of Value.**

Let's consider each of these two approaches.

Measuring the Overall Liquidity of a Firm

Current Ratio. We can assess a firm's overall liquidity by comparing its current (liquid) assets to its current (short-term) liabilities. The most commonly used measure of a firm's overall liquidity is the **current ratio**, which is defined as follows:

$$\text{Current Ratio} = \frac{\text{Currrent Assets}}{\text{Current Liabilities}} \tag{1}$$

Using the 2010 balance sheet for H. J. Boswell, Inc., we estimate the firm's current ratio as follows (remember that the blue numbers are taken from the balance sheet):

$$\text{Current Ratio} = \frac{\$643.5 \text{ million}}{\$288.0 \text{ million}} = 2.23 \text{ times}$$

Peer-group current ratio = 1.80 times

Based on its current ratio, H. J. Boswell, Inc. is more liquid than the peer group because its current ratio is higher. The firm had $2.23 in current assets for every $1 it owed in short-term debt, compared to a peer-group average ratio of 1.80, which indicates $1.80 in current assets to every $1 owed in short-term debt. Note that the peer-group ratio is an average of the ratios of the individual firms in the group.

Acid-Test (Quick) Ratio. When we use the current ratio to assess firm liquidity, we assume that the firm's accounts receivable will be collected and turned into cash on a timely basis and that its inventories can be sold without an extended delay. But the truth is that a company's inventory might not be very liquid at all. For example, a furniture maker's inventory might be in the form of partially finished chair legs—not an item that you could sell quickly or for very much. So, if we want a more stringent test of the firm's liquidity, we can exclude inventory from the firm's current assets in the numerator of our liquidity measure. This revised ratio is called the **acid-test ratio** (or **quick ratio**) and is calculated as follows:

$$\frac{\text{Acid-Test}}{\text{(or Quick) Ratio}} = \frac{\text{Current Assets} - \text{Inventory}}{\text{Current Liabilities}} \tag{2}$$

For H. J. Boswell, Inc. we calculate the acid-test ratio as follows:

$$\text{Acid-Test Ratio} = \frac{\$643.5 \text{ million} - \$378 \text{ million}}{\$288.0 \text{ million}} = 0.92 \text{ times}$$

Peer-group acid-test ratio = 0.94 times

Based on the acid-test ratio, H. J. Boswell, Inc. appears to be slightly less liquid than it did using the current ratio. Boswell has $0.92 in cash and accounts receivable per $1 in current liabilities, compared to $0.94 for the average company in the peer group. However, the difference is very modest and probably not significant. To address this problem, peer-group ratios are typically reported using quartiles.[1] For example, consider the following quartile values of the acid-test ratio for Boswell's peer group:

	Quartile 1	Quartile 2	Quartile 3	Quartile 4
Acid-test ratio	.50	.94	1.21	1.68

The quartile information tells us that one-fourth of the peer firms had an acid-test ratio equal to or less than .50, half had ratios equal to or less than .94, three-quarters had ratios equal to or less than 1.21, and the highest ratio of any of the peer group firms was 1.68. H. J. Boswell's acid-test ratio of .92 falls near the middle of the pack (quartile 2), so it is not out of line with the peer group.

Measuring the Liquidity of Individual Asset Categories

A second approach to measuring liquidity examines the liquidity of the firm's individual current asset accounts, including accounts receivable and inventories. For example, the firm's current ratio may be as high as the peer-group average, suggesting the company has sufficient liquidity to meet its financial obligations. However, if the firm has uncollectible accounts receivable or is carrying a great deal of obsolete inventory, the current ratio will not be a valid indication of its liquidity. To get a more complete understanding of the firm's liquidity we need to know something about the liquidity of the firm's accounts receivable and inventory. We can gauge the liquidity of both of these current asset accounts by measuring how long it takes the firm to convert its accounts receivable and inventories into cash.

How Long Does It Take to Turn the Firm's Accounts Receivable into Cash?

Average Collection Period. We can measure how many days it takes the firm to collect its receivables by computing its **average collection period** as follows:[2]

$$\text{Average Collection Period} = \frac{\text{Accounts Receivable}}{\text{Annual Credit Sales}/365 \text{ days}} = \frac{\text{Accounts Receivable}}{\text{Daily Credit Sales}} \qquad (3)$$

Assuming that all of H. J. Boswell's sales are made on credit, we can calculate the firm's average collection period for 2010 as follows (recall that red numbers come from the income statement):

$$\text{Average Collection Period} = \frac{\$162 \text{ million}}{\$2,700 \text{ million}/365 \text{ days}} = 21.9 \text{ days}$$

Peer-group average collection period = 25.00 days

H. J. Boswell, Inc. collects its accounts receivable in 21.9 days compared to 25 days for the peer group, indicating that Boswell's receivables are slightly more liquid than the peer group's receivables.

Accounts Receivable Turnover Ratio. We could have reached the same conclusion by measuring how many times accounts receivable are "rolled over" during a year, using the **accounts receivable turnover ratio**, which can also be calculated as follows:

$$\text{Accounts Receivable Turnover} = \frac{\text{Annual Credit Sales}}{\text{Accounts Receivable}} \qquad (4)$$

---

[1] If you ranked 100 numbers from lowest to highest, the one that ranked the 25th from the bottom would identify the first quartile; the one that ranked 50 is the second quartile, and so forth.

[2] When computing a given ratio that uses information from both the income statement and the balance sheet, we should remember that the income statement is for a given time period (e.g., 2013), whereas balance sheet data are at a point in time (e.g., December 31, 2013). If there has been a significant change in an asset from the beginning of the period to the end of the period, it would be better to use the average balance for the year. For example, if the accounts receivable for a company increased from $1,000 at the beginning of the year to $2,000 at the end of the year, it would be more appropriate to use the average accounts receivable of $1,500 in our computations. Nevertheless, in an effort to simplify, we will use year-end amounts from the balance sheet in our computations.

For H. J. Boswell, Inc.:

$$\text{Accounts Receivable Turnover} = \frac{\$2{,}700 \text{ million}}{\$162 \text{ million}} = 16.67 \text{ times}$$

$$\text{Peer-group accounts receivable turnover} = 14.60 \text{ times}$$

Note that H. J. Boswell collected its accounts receivable every 21.90 days in 2013, which means that the receivables were turning over at a rate of 16.67 times per year (365 days ÷ 21.90 days = 16.67 times per year). As you can see, we learn exactly the same thing from the accounts receivable turnover ratio as we did from the average collection period and would only use one of these ratios in our analysis, not both.

Regardless of whether we use the average collection period or the accounts receivable turnover ratio, the conclusion is the same: H. J. Boswell, Inc. collected its accounts receivable more quickly than competing firms. This suggests that H. J. Boswell, Inc.'s accounts receivable are at least as liquid as those of the peer group.

How Long Does It Take to Turn the Firm's Inventory into Cash?

Inventory Turnover Ratio. We now turn to an analysis of the quality of H. J. Boswell, Inc.'s inventories. A key indication of the quality of a firm's inventory is the length of time it is held before being sold. Shorter inventory cycles lead to greater liquidity because the items in inventory are converted to cash more quickly. This can be measured by looking at the inventory turnover ratio, which indicates how many times the company turns over its inventory during the year. The **inventory turnover ratio** is equal to cost of goods sold divided by the firm's investment in inventories and is calculated as follows:[3]

$$\text{Inventory Turnover} = \frac{\text{Cost of Goods Sold}}{\text{Inventories}} \qquad \textbf{(5)}$$

For H. J. Boswell, Inc.:

$$\text{Inventory Turnover} = \frac{\$2{,}025 \text{ million}}{\$378 \text{ million}} = 5.36 \text{ times}$$

$$\text{Peer-group inventory turnover} = 7.00 \text{ times}$$

We see that H. J. Boswell, Inc. turned over its inventory more slowly than the average peer-group firm—5.36 times per year at H. J. Boswell, Inc., compared with 7.0 times for the peer group. This suggests that the firm's inventory is less liquid than that of the peer group.

Days' Sales in Inventory. We can also express the inventory turnover in terms of the number of **days' sales in inventory**; that is, the number of days the inventory sits unsold on the firm's shelves (or elsewhere). Because H. J. Boswell, Inc. turns its inventory over 5.36 times per year, on average it is holding its inventory for 68 days (365 days ÷ 5.36 times per year), whereas the average peer firm carries its inventory only 52 days (365 days ÷ 7.0 times per year).

Because Boswell's inventory turnover ratio is lower than that of its peer group, Boswell's inventory is not as liquid as the peer-group inventory. Our next task is to see if there is an acceptable explanation for this difference. For example, Boswell might have increased its inventory because the firm's customers depend on it to not be out of stock and to be able to meet their inventory needs quickly. Again, the point here is that ratio comparisons provide the clues that lead us to further investigation and analysis.

Let's sum up our analysis of H. J. Boswell, Inc.'s liquidity. First, the current ratio indicates that H. J. Boswell, Inc. is more liquid than the competing firms on average; however, Boswell's inventory turnover was lower than that of the peer group, indicating that Boswell's inventory is less liquid than the peer-group inventory. The higher-than-average investment

---

[3]Note that cost of goods sold appears in the numerator of the inventory turnover ratio. This is because inventory (the denominator) is measured at cost, so we want to use the cost-based measure of sales in the numerator. Otherwise our answer will vary from one firm to the next solely because of the difference in how each firm marks up its sales over cost. However, some of the industry norms provided by financial reporting services are computed using sales in the numerator. In those cases, we will want to use sales in our computation of inventory turnover so that our computed ratio will be comparable to the industry norm.

in inventories, coupled with a higher-than-average current ratio, indicates that if we took inventory out of the current ratio (which is precisely what the acid-test ratio does), we would end up with an acid-test ratio that was close to average. That's exactly what we found with H. J. Boswell's acid-test ratio—Boswell was close to the industry average.

Evaluating Dell Computer Corporation's (DELL) Liquidity

You work for a small company that manufactures a new memory storage device. Computer giant Dell has offered to put the new device in its laptops if your firm will extend credit terms that allow the firm 90 days to pay. Because your company does not have many cash resources, your boss has asked that you look into Dell's liquidity and analyze its ability to pay its bills on time using the following accounting information for Dell and two other computer firms (Apple and Hewlett Packard; figures in thousands of dollars):

	Dell 2011	Apple 2011	Hewlett Packard 2011
Current assets	$29,448,000	57,653,000	$51,021,000
Accounts receivable	9,803,000	21,275,000	21,386,000
Cash	13,852,000	10,746,000	8,043,000
Inventories	1,404,000	791,000	7,490,000
Other current assets	3,423,000	6,458,000	14,102,000
Sales	62,071,000	156,508,000	127,245,000
Cost of goods sold	48,260,000	87,846,000	97,529,000
Total current liabilities	22,001,000	38,542,000	50,442,000

STEP 1: Picture the problem

The analysis of firm liquidity entails looking at overall measures of liquidity using the current and acid-test ratios, as well as measures of the liquidity of specific assets. Overall measures of liquidity compare the firm's current assets to its current liabilities.

Current Assets (assets that are to be converted to cash in a period of a year or less):		Current Liabilities (liabilities that must be paid within a period of a year or less):
• Cash	Compared to:	• Accounts Payable
• Accounts Receivable		• Notes Payable
• Inventories		• Current Portion of Long-term Debt

In addition to comparing current assets and liabilities, we also look at just how quickly the firm is able to convert both accounts receivable and inventories into cash. That is, the liquidity of the firm's assets is determined by the speed with which the firm collects its credit sales (as indicated by the firm's average collection period) and how quickly the firm is able to convert inventories to sales (as reflected in the inventory turnover ratio).

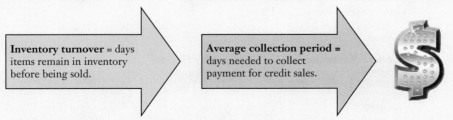

Inventory turnover = days items remain in inventory before being sold.

Average collection period = days needed to collect payment for credit sales.

Note that shorter cycles through inventories and accounts receivable mean greater liquidity.

STEP 2: Decide on a solution strategy

The approach we take in analyzing firm liquidity, using only the firm's financial statements, is very much like that of a detective who looks for clues that will help determine the answer to the question being researched. Here the question centers on Dell's liquidity, and the clues you use to solve it are ratios. These include the current ratio, acid-test ratio, inventory turnover ratio, and accounts receivable turnover ratio.

(1 CONTINUED >> ON NEXT PAGE)

STEP 3: Solve

The following information (expressed in millions of dollars) is taken from Dell Computer Corporation's 2011 financial statements along with the 2011 financial statements of two competitor firms (Apple and Hewlett Packard):

	Dell 2011	Apple 2011	Hewlett Packard 2011	Peer-Group Average
Current ratio	1.34	1.50	1.01	1.25
Acid-test ratio	1.27	1.48	0.86	1.17
Accounts receivable turnover	6.33	7.36	5.95	6.65
Inventory turnover	34.37	111.06	13.02	62.04

STEP 4: Analyze

Based on all four liquidity ratios, Dell looks very similar to both Apple and Hewlett Packard (HP). In fact, Dell's liquidity ratios place it below Apple and above HP in each ratio. For example, Dell turns over its accounts receivable 6.33 times per year, which is somewhat lower than the 7.36 times for Apple but higher than the 5.95 times for HP. Furthermore, both Dell and Apple manage their inventories more efficiently than HP, as indicated in Dell's inventory turnover of 34.37 and Apple's amazing 111.06 compared to only 13.02 for HP.

Earlier we said that analysts use ratios the same way a detective uses clues. So what would we find if we looked closer? First, we would find that Dell uses a just-in-time inventory system designed to keep inventories as low as possible by producing only what is needed, when it is needed. In addition, Dell's computers are "built-to-order"; that is, they are only assembled once they are ordered. Dell's suppliers make multiple shipments to Dell daily, supplying Dell with the parts it needs when, and only when, it requires them. In effect, Dell's suppliers, rather than Dell, hold Dell's inventory. As a result, Dell maintains a very small inventory, resulting in an inventory turnover ratio that is higher than HP but much lower than Apple.

STEP 5: Check yourself

Why do you think HP's inventory turnover ratio is so much lower than Dell's inventory turnover ratio?

ANSWER: Whereas Dell builds computers only when customers order them, HP holds an inventory of computers and sells out of that inventory. In addition, HP carries more parts inventory on hand than does Dell, which only builds a computer when it has received an order.

Your Turn: For more practice, do related **Study Problems** 4 and 18 at the end of this chapter.   >> END Checkpoint 1

Can a Firm Have Too Much Liquidity?

Because the liquidity of a firm is defined in terms of its ability to pay its bills on time, is it possible for a firm to have too much liquidity? The answer is yes. The reason is that holding lots of cash and other very liquid assets can be costly. For example, in 2012 Microsoft Corporation (MSFT) had more than $63 billion in cash and marketable securities. Does this mean that the firm is excessively liquid?

Tools of Financial Analysis—Liquidity Ratios

Name of Tool	Formula	What It Tells You
Current Ratio	$\dfrac{Current\ Assets}{Current\ Liabilities}$	• Measures a firm's liquidity in terms of the relationship between the dollar value of its current assets that are expected to be converted to cash within the year and its current liabilities that must be repaid within the year • A higher ratio means greater firm liquidity.

Name of Tool	Formula	What It Tells You
Acid-Test Ratio	$$\dfrac{Current\ Assets\ -\ Inventory}{Current\ Liabilities}$$	• A more stringent measure of liquidity than the current ratio, as it omits the least liquid current asset (inventory) • A higher ratio means greater liquidity.
Average Collection Period	$$\dfrac{Accounts\ Receivable}{Annual\ Credit\ Sales\ /\ 365\ days}$$	• An indicator of the number of days required for a firm to collect its accounts receivable • The lower the number, the shorter the time it takes for a firm to collect its credit sales, and therefore the greater is firm liquidity.
Accounts Receivable Turnover	$$\dfrac{Annual\ Credit\ Sales}{Accounts\ Receivable}$$	• An indicator of the time required for a firm to collect its accounts receivable • The higher the number of turnovers per year, the faster the collection of the firm's credit accounts and the more liquid is the firm.
Inventory Turnover	$$\dfrac{Cost\ of\ Goods\ Sold}{Inventory}$$	• An indicator of the size of the firm's investment in inventory • The higher the turnover, the lower is the firm's investment in inventory, and the more liquid is this investment.

Capital Structure Ratios

In finance we use the term **capital structure** to refer to the way a firm finances its assets using a combination of debt and equity. Thus, capital structure ratios are used to answer a very important question: How has the firm financed the purchase of its assets? To address this issue, we use two types of capital structure ratios: the **debt ratio**, a measure of the proportion of the firm's assets that were financed by borrowing or debt financing, and the times interest earned ratio, the firm's operating earnings divided by interest expense. The **times interest earned ratio** looks at the firm's ability to pay the interest expense on its debt.

Debt Ratio. The debt ratio measures the percentage of the firm's assets that were financed using current plus long-term liabilities.[4] We calculate the firm's debt ratio as total liabilities divided by total assets, that is,

$$\text{Debt Ratio} = \frac{\text{Total Liabilities}}{\text{Total Assets}} \qquad \textbf{(6)}$$

For H. J. Boswell, Inc.:

$$\text{Debt Ratio} = \frac{\$1{,}059.75\ \text{million}}{\$1{,}971\ \text{million}} = 53.8\%$$

Peer-group debt ratio $= 35\%$

H. J. Boswell, Inc. financed 53.8 percent of its assets with debt (taken from H. J. Boswell, Inc.'s balance sheet), compared with the peer-group average of 35 percent. Thus, H. J. Boswell, Inc. used significantly more debt than the average of the peer-group firms.

---

[4]This ratio is sometimes computed using only interest-bearing debt in the numerator such as **notes payable**, the current portion of long-term debt, and long-term debt. For our purposes, however, we include all the firm's liabilities, which is customary in most such applications.

Times Interest Earned Ratio. Another important dimension of a firm's capital structure is its ability to service its debt or pay the interest on the debt. Because interest expense is paid before a firm pays its taxes, we can get an indication of whether the firm can afford to pay interest by comparing its interest expense to its operating earnings, or earnings before interest and taxes (EBIT). The ratio of EBIT to interest expense is called the times interest earned ratio and it is calculated as follows:

$$\text{Times Interest Earned} = \frac{\text{Net Operating Income or EBIT}}{\text{Interest Expense}} \qquad (7)$$

For H. J. Boswell, Inc. we calculate the times interest earned ratio as follows:

$$\text{Times Interest Earned} = \frac{\$382.5 \text{ million}}{\$67.50 \text{ million}} = 5.67 \text{ times}$$

Peer-group times interest earned $= 7.0$ times

H. J. Boswell, Inc.'s interest expense was $67.50 million, compared to its net operating income of $382.5 million. This means that Boswell could have paid its total interest expense 5.67 times in 2010. Stated differently, the firm's interest consumed 1/5.67th or 17.7 percent of its net operating income, which means that its operating earnings could shrink by 82.3 percent (i.e., 100% − 17.7%) and it could still pay its interest expenses. The peer-group ratio is 7.0 times, which means that the peer-group operating earnings could shrink by 85.71 percent (i.e., 100% − 14.29%) before the peer-group average firm could not pay its interest expense.

Why would H. J. Boswell, Inc. have a lower times interest earned ratio than the peer group? An important reason is that Boswell has used significantly more debt in its capital structure (53.5 percent debt to assets) than the average company in the peer group (35 percent), so its interest expense is higher.

Tools of Financial Analysis—Capital Structure Ratios

Name of Tool	Formula	What It Tells You
Debt Ratio	$\dfrac{\textit{Total Debt}}{\textit{Total Assests}}$	• Measures the extent to which the firm has used non-owner financing (borrowed money) to finance its assets • Borrowed funds create financial leverage • A higher ratio indicates a greater reliance on non-owner financing or financial leverage.
Times Interest Earned Ratio	$\dfrac{\textit{Net Operating Income or EBIT}}{\textit{Interest Expense}}$	• Measures the firm's ability to pay its interest expense from the firm's operating income • A higher ratio indicates that the firm's ability to pay its interest in a timely manner is greater.

Asset Management Efficiency Ratios

We now consider how effective H. J. Boswell's management has been in utilizing its assets to generate sales. To measure this very important determinant of firm performance we use asset management efficiency ratios, which are commonly defined using ratios in which the numerator comes from the firm's income statement (firm sales or cost of goods sold) and the denominator comes from the balance sheet (e.g., total assets or fixed assets). These ratios are commonly referred to as turnover ratios, as they reflect the number of times a particular asset account balance turns over during the year.

The first asset management efficiency ratio we consider is the **total asset turnover (TATO) ratio**, which represents the amount of sales generated per dollar invested in the firm's assets. Thus, TATO is a measure of how well the firm's assets are managed. For example, suppose that Company A generates $3 in sales for every $1 invested in assets, whereas Company B generates the same $3 in sales but has invested $2 in assets. We can conclude that Company A is using its assets more efficiently to generate sales, which leads to a higher return on the firm's investment in assets.

Checkpoint 2

Comparing the Financing Decisions of Home Depot (HD) and Lowe's Corporation (LOW)

You inherited a small sum of money from your grandparents and currently have it in a savings account at your local bank. After enrolling in your first finance class in business school, you have decided that you would like to begin investing your money in the common stock of a few companies. The first investment you are considering is stock in either Home Depot or Lowes. Both firms operate chains of home improvement stores throughout the United States and other parts of the world.

In your finance class you learned that an important determinant of the risk of investing in a firm's stock is driven by the firm's capital structure, or how it has financed its assets. In particular, the more money the firm borrows, the greater is the risk that the firm may become insolvent and bankrupt. Consequently, the first thing you want to do before investing in either company's stock is to compare how they financed their investments. Just how much debt financing have the two firms used?

STEP 1: Picture the problem

The use of debt financing has two important dimensions that can be stated as questions: "How much debt has the firm used?" and "Can the firm afford to pay the interest on its debt?"

We can visualize the basis for answering the first question by looking at the relative importance of the components of the right-hand side of the firm's balance sheet; that is,

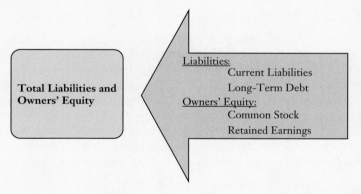

The second question we ask with respect to the use of debt financing can be addressed by looking at the firm's income statement. In this instance we are interested in comparing the amount of net operating income (or earnings before interest and taxes [EBIT]) the firm earned with the amount of interest expense the firm owes on its debt financing. So, envision the income statement as follows:

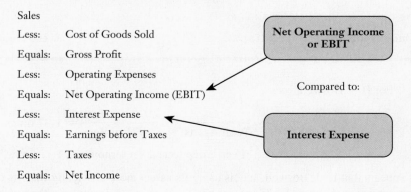

Sales		
Less:	Cost of Goods Sold	
Equals:	Gross Profit	
Less:	Operating Expenses	
Equals:	Net Operating Income (EBIT)	
Less:	Interest Expense	
Equals:	Earnings before Taxes	
Less:	Taxes	
Equals:	Net Income	

(2 CONTINUED >> ON NEXT PAGE)

STEP 2: Decide on a solution strategy

Our strategy for addressing this problem is to act like a financial detective. Here the question centers on determining how Home Depot and Lowes have chosen to finance their assets, and the clues you are going to use to solve it are ratios. Specifically, we will be using the debt ratio calculated from information contained in the firms' balance sheets, and the times interest earned ratio, which is calculated using information contained in the firms' income statements.

STEP 3: Solve

Using the following financial information from the Home Depot and Lowe's 2007 annual reports, the debt ratio and times interest earned ratio can be easily calculated (the figures below are in thousands of dollars).

	Home Depot 2012	Lowes 2012
Total Debt	$ 22,620,000	$ 17,026,000
Total Common Equity	17,898,000	16,533,000
Total Assets	40,518,000	33,559,000
Operating Profits	6,661,000	3,277,000
Interest Expense	606,000	371,000

As you can see from the calculations below, in 2012 Home Depot's debt ratio exceeds that of Lowe's by 5.10 percent, and its times interest earned ratio is 10.99 compared to 8.83 for Lowes.

	Home Depot 2012	Lowes 2012
Debt Ratio	55.83%	50.73%
Times Interest Earned	10.99	8.83

STEP 4: Analyze

Home Depot's debt ratio exceeds that of Lowe's by roughly 5 percent (55.83 percent compared to 50.73 percent); however, Home Depot's earnings are such that it appears to be able to afford the higher debt level (i.e., it has a higher times interest earned ratio). Although Home Depot uses slightly more financial leverage than Lowe's, we still do not know whether stockholders are benefiting from the higher leverage. Later when we evaluate firm profitability we will determine whether this use of debt financing has been beneficial or not. The key concern here is whether Home Depot is able to consistently earn a higher rate of return on its investments than it must pay to its creditors. For example, if you borrow money and pay 7 percent interest and then invest the money to earn 12 percent, you will get to keep the 5 percent difference. In this case debt financing is beneficial. If, on the other hand, you earn only 5 percent, then you will have to make up the 2 percent shortfall and debt financing is destructive.

STEP 5: Check yourself

As you can see from the earlier table, Home Depot's times interest earned ratio is 10.99. What would it be if interest payments remained the same, but net operating income dropped by 80 percent to only $1.332 billion? Similarly, if Lowe's net operating income dropped by 80 percent, what would its times interest earned ratio be?

ANSWER: The times interest earned ratio would drop to 2.20 and 1.77 for Home Depot and Lowes, respectively.

Your Turn: For more practice, do related **Study Problem** 6 at the end of this chapter.   **>> END Checkpoint 2**

For H. J. Boswell, Inc.:

$$\frac{\text{Total Asset}}{\text{Turnover}} = \frac{\text{Sales}}{\text{Total Assets}} = \frac{\$2,700 \text{ million}}{\$1,971 \text{ million}} = 1.37 \text{ times} \tag{8}$$

Peer-group total asset turnover = 1.15 times

It appears that H. J. Boswell, Inc. is using its assets more efficiently than its competitors because it generates about $1.37 in sales per dollar of assets. In contrast, the peer group produces only $1.15 in sales per dollar of assets.

However, we should not stop here with our analysis of the asset management efficiency of H. J. Boswell, Inc.'s management. We have learned that, on the whole, H. J. Boswell, Inc.'s managers used the firm's assets efficiently. But was this the case for each and every type of asset? How efficiently did the firm's management utilize the firm's investments in accounts receivable, inventories, and fixed assets, respectively?

To answer these questions, we can look at the turnover ratios for each of the firm's major asset subcategories—its accounts receivable, inventories, and fixed assets (net plant and equipment). Recall that we already calculated turnover ratios for the company's investments in accounts receivable and its inventories earlier when we analyzed firm liquidity. There we concluded that H. J. Boswell, Inc.'s managers were managing the firm's accounts receivable more efficiently than the peer group, but not its inventories. So, at this point, the only asset category we have not yet analyzed is fixed assets such as property, plant, and equipment. To analyze the efficiency with which the firm uses these assets we compute the **fixed asset turnover ratio** as follows:

$$\frac{\text{Fixed Asset}}{\text{Turnover}} = \frac{\text{Sales}}{\text{Net Plant and Equipment}} = \frac{\$2{,}700 \text{ million}}{\$1{,}327.5 \text{ million}} = 2.03 \text{ times} \qquad \textbf{(9)}$$

$$\text{Peer-group fixed asset turnover} = 1.75 \text{ times}$$

H. J. Boswell, Inc. appears to have managed the use of fixed assets more efficiently than the peer group.

The following grid summarizes our findings about the efficiency of Boswell's management in utilizing its assets to generate sales:

Asset Utilization Efficiency	Boswell	Peer Group	Assessment
Total asset turnover	1.37	1.15	Good
Fixed asset turnover	2.03	1.75	Good
Receivables turnover	16.67	14.60	Good
Inventory turnover	5.36	7.0	Poor

Overall, H. J. Boswell, Inc.'s managers utilized the firm's total investment in assets efficiently. The turnover of its total assets, fixed assets, and receivables were all better than those of the peer group. Only the firm's inventory turnover appears to have lagged behind the peer-group average.

Tools of Financial Analysis—Asset Management Efficiency Ratios

Name of Tool	Formula	What It Tells You
Total Asset Turnover Ratio	$\dfrac{Sales}{Total\ Assets}$	• Measures the firm's efficient use of its investment in total assets • A higher ratio means the firm is more efficiently using its assets to generate sales (i.e., more sales per dollar of assets).
Fixed Asset Turnover Ratio	$\dfrac{Sales}{Net\ Plant\ and\ Equipment}$	• Measures the firm's efficient use of its investment in fixed assets (specifically, net plant and equipment) • A higher ratio means the firm is using its fixed assets more efficiently.

Profitability Ratios

Profitability ratios are used to address a very fundamental question: Has the firm earned adequate returns on its investments? To answer this question, the analyst turns to two measures—the firm's profit margins, which predict the ability of the firm to control its expenses, and the firm's rates of return on investments. The fundamental determinants of firm profitability and returns on investment are the following:

- **Cost control**—How well has the firm controlled its costs of goods sold, operating expenses, financing costs, and other expenses relative to each dollar of firm sales?
- **Efficiency of asset utilization**—How effective is the firm's management at using the firm's assets to generate sales?

We consider both of these factors as we discuss profitability ratios.

Cost Control: Is the Firm Earning Reasonable Profit Margins?

The firm's gross profit margin, operating profit margin, and net profit margin ratios express various profit computations as a percent of firm sales, and indicate the fraction of firm sales that remain after deducting various categories of expenses. Therefore, we can use them as an indication of the firm's success or failure in managing each of these categories of expenses. To see how this is done we return to the Boswell example.

Gross Profit Margin. How well the firm's management controls its expenses determines the firm's profit margins. For example, in the common-size income statement found in Table 1 we saw that Boswell spends $0.75 for cost of goods sold for each dollar of sales. This leaves $0.25 out of each dollar of sales that goes to gross profits. The gross profit margin, then, is simply the ratio of gross profits divided by sales:

$$\frac{\text{Gross Profit}}{\text{Margin}} = \frac{\text{Gross Profits}}{\text{Sales}} \qquad (10)$$

Boswell's gross profit margin for 2010 was 25 percent; that is,

$$\frac{\text{Gross Profit}}{\text{Margin}} = \frac{\text{Gross Profits}}{\text{Sales}} = \frac{\$675 \text{ million}}{\$2,700 \text{ million}} = .25 \text{ or } 25\%$$

$$\text{Peer-group gross profit margin} = 28.2\%$$

Operating Profit Margin. The operating profit margin (OPM) is the firm's net operating income divided by its sales. OPM tells managers how much profit they generated from each dollar of sales after accounting for both costs of good sold and operating expenses. Because an objective of managing operations is to keep costs and expenses low relative to sales, we often say that the operating profit margin measures how well the firm is managing its income statement.

For H. J. Boswell, Inc.:

$$\frac{\text{Operating Profit}}{\text{Margin (OPM)}} = \frac{\text{Net Operating Income or EBIT}}{\text{Sales}} = \frac{\$382.5 \text{ million}}{\$2,700 \text{ million}} = 14.2\% \qquad (11)$$

$$\text{Peer-group operating profit margin} = 15.5\%$$

The lower operating profit margin suggests that H. J. Boswell, Inc.'s managers have not done as good a job of managing the firm's cost of goods sold and operating expenses as comparable firms' managers have. In this instance it appears that H. J. Boswell has a low-price strategy when compared to its peer firms, which have a gross profit margin of 28.2 percent compared to only 25 percent for Boswell—that is, Boswell earns a lower profit margin on every dollar of revenue it collects but tries to make up the difference by generating higher revenues overall. How can you tell if this low-price strategy is successful? You can tell by looking at the company's sales volume *relative* to its investment in assets, which we will discuss shortly.

Net Profit Margin. The final profit margin we consider is the net profit margin, which is calculated as the ratio of the firm's net income divided by sales; that is,

$$\frac{\text{Net Profit}}{\text{Margin}} = \frac{\text{Net Income}}{\text{Sales}} \qquad (12)$$

For H. J. Boswell, Inc. we calculate the net profit margin as follows:

$$\frac{\text{Net Profit}}{\text{Margin}} = \frac{\text{Net Income}}{\text{Sales}} = \frac{\$204.75 \text{ million}}{\$2,700 \text{ million}} = .076 \text{ or } 7.6\%$$

$$\text{Peer-group net profit margin} = 10.2\%$$

Thus, for every dollar of sales, Boswell keeps $0.076 in profits after paying all of the firm's expenses, whereas the peer-group firms earn $0.102. Clearly, Boswell has lower net income per dollar of sales revenue than the peer-group firms. However, profit margins, which reflect how well the firm has controlled its costs, are not the total story. The return earned on a firm's investments also depends on how much money the firm has invested in assets in order to generate those revenues and profits.

Return on Invested Capital

Our summary measure of operating profitability is the **operating return on assets (OROA) ratio**, which takes into account both management's success in controlling expenses (contributing to high profit margins) and its efficient use of assets to generate firm sales. The OROA ratio is defined as follows:

$$\frac{\text{Operating Return}}{\text{on Assets (OROA)}} = \frac{\text{Net Operating Income or EBIT}}{\text{Total Assets}} \qquad \textbf{(13)}$$

For H. J. Boswell, Inc.:

$$\frac{\text{Operating Return}}{\text{on Assets (OROA)}} = \frac{\$382.5 \text{ million}}{\$1,971 \text{ million}} = 19.4\%$$

$$\text{Peer-group operating return on assets} = 17.8\%$$

H. J. Boswell, Inc. generated $0.194 of operating profits for every $1 of its invested assets. That's better than the peer-group firms, which generated an average $0.178 for every $1 of their assets. The firm's higher-than-average OROA ratio suggests that the firm's managers have done a good job of controlling costs and generating sales. However, this interpretation is not always correct. For example, differences in OROA ratios may simply reflect the fact that the firm with the lower OROA spent more money on research and development than the other firm spent. So it is important that when analyzing the OROA ratio (or any financial ratio, for that matter) we look behind the ratio to determine why it differs from the peer-group norm. However, all else equal, a lower OROA ratio indicates that the firm's costs are higher per dollar of revenues than the firm with the higher OROA. The point here is that, once again, ratio comparisons are only clues indicating that further investigation and analysis are needed.

Decomposing the Operating Return on Assets Ratio

H. J. Boswell, Inc. generated a higher operating return on its assets than the average of the peer group. The analyst will want to know why this is so. To investigate this issue, we can further decompose the operating return on assets ratio into two other ratios that capture the firm's ability to control costs and its ability to utilize its investment in assets efficiently, as follows:

$$\frac{\text{Operating Return}}{\text{on Assets}} = \left(\overset{\textbf{Cost Control}}{\underset{}{\frac{\text{Operating Profit}}{\text{Margin (OPM)}}}}\right) \times \left(\overset{\textbf{Asset Utilization}}{\underset{}{\frac{\text{Total Asset}}{\text{Turnover (TATO)}}}}\right) \qquad \textbf{(13a)}$$

We calculate this as follows:

$$\frac{\text{Operating Return}}{\text{on Assets}} = \left(\frac{\text{Net Operating Income or EBIT}}{\text{Sales}}\right) \times \left(\frac{\text{Sales}}{\text{Total Assets}}\right) \qquad \textbf{(13b)}$$

$$= \left(\frac{\text{Net Operating Income or EBIT}}{\text{Total Assets}}\right)$$

Putting It All Together: Determinants of Operating Profitability

Figure 1 provides a summary of our analysis of H. J. Boswell, Inc.'s operating profitability. We can summarize our findings as follows:

- Boswell's operating return on assets (OROA) is higher than the average for the peer firms. This means that it earned more net operating income per dollar of investment in assets than the peer group did.

- Boswell's operating profit margin (OPM) is lower than that of the peer group. This means that the firm didn't retain as high a percentage of its sales in net operating income as did the peer group.

- Boswell's total asset turnover (TATO) ratio is higher than that of its peers, indicating that it utilizes its assets to generate sales more efficiently than the peer group; this more than offsets the firm's slightly lower operating profit margin. The result is a higher operating return on assets for Boswell than the peer group. However, not all of Boswell's assets are utilized as efficiently as those of its peers. Specifically, Boswell's inventory turnover ratio is lower than its peers, as shown in Panel B of Figure 1.

These observations suggest that the firm has two opportunities to improve its operating profitability:

- The first opportunity relates to cost control: H. J. Boswell's managers might investigate both the firm's cost of goods sold and its operating expenses, both of which directly affect EBIT (recall, EBIT = sales – cost of goods sold – operating expenses), to see if they are out of line with those of other firms. If they are, perhaps there are opportunities to reduce these costs.

- The second opportunity relates to H. J. Boswell's inventories. The firm carries a larger investment in inventories than the peer group. There may be opportunities for the firm to reduce the size of this investment.

Figure 1

Analyzing H. J. Boswell, Inc.'s Operating Return on Assets (OROA)

Description: The operating return on assets ratio can be easily separated into the product of two other ratios: (i) the operating profit margin and (ii) the total asset turnover ratio. You can then dig deeper and investigate the underlying factors affecting the two individual ratios.

Panel A. Decomposing the Operating Return on Assets Ratio

	Operating Return on Assets	=	Operating Profit Margin	×	Total Asset Turnover
Equation	$\left(\dfrac{\text{Net Operating Income or EBIT}}{\text{Total Assets}}\right)$	=	$\left(\dfrac{\text{Net Operating Income or EBIT}}{\text{Sales}}\right)$	×	$\left(\dfrac{\text{Sales}}{\text{Total Assets}}\right)$
H. J. Boswell	19.4%	=	14.2%	×	1.37
Peer Group	17.8%	=	15.5%	×	1.15

Panel B. Analyzing the Determinants of the Total Asset Turnover Ratio

	Accounts Receivable Turnover	Inventory Turnover	Fixed Asset Turnover
Equation	$\left(\dfrac{\text{Annual Credit Sales}}{\text{Accounts Receivable}}\right)$	$\left(\dfrac{\text{Cost of Goods Sold}}{\text{Inventories}}\right)$	$\left(\dfrac{\text{Sales}}{\text{Net Plant and Equipment}}\right)$
H. J. Boswell	16.67	5.8	2.03
Peer Group	14.60	7.0	1.75

>> END FIGURE 1

Evaluating the Operating Return on Assets (OROA) for Home Depot (HD) and Lowe's (LOW)

In Checkpoint 2 we evaluated how much debt financing Home Depot and Lowe's used. We continue our analysis by evaluating the operating return on assets (OROA) earned by the two firms. Calculate the net operating income each firm earned during 2012 relative to the total assets of each firm using the information found below:

	Home Depot 2012	Lowe's 2012
Accounts receivable	$ 1,245,000	$ 183,000
Inventories	10,325,000	8,355,000
Sales	70,395,000	50,208,000
Operating profits	6,661,000	3,277,000
Cost of goods sold	46,133,000	32,858,000
Net fixed assets	24,448,000	21,970,000
Total assets	40,518,000	35,559,000

STEP 1: Picture the problem

The operating return on assets ratio for a firm is determined by two factors: cost control and the efficiency of asset utilization. We can visualize this relationship in terms of Equation (13a):

$$\text{Operating Return on Assets} = \underbrace{\left(\begin{array}{c}\text{Operating Profit}\\\text{Margin (OPM)}\end{array}\right)}_{\text{Cost Control}} \times \underbrace{\left(\begin{array}{c}\text{Total Asset}\\\text{Turnover (TATO)}\end{array}\right)}_{\text{Asset Utilization}} \quad \text{(13a)}$$

Substituting for the operating profit margin and total asset turnover ratio:

$$\text{Operating Return on Assets} = \left(\frac{\text{Net Operating Income or EBIT}}{\text{Sales}}\right) \times \left(\frac{\text{Sales}}{\text{Total Assets}}\right) = \left(\frac{\text{Net Operating Income or EBIT}}{\text{Total Assets}}\right)$$

Moreover, we can dig deeper into the total asset turnover ratio's determinants by considering the efficiency with which the various components of total assets are managed, including accounts receivable (accounts receivable turnover ratio), inventory (inventory turnover ratio), and fixed assets (fixed asset turnover ratio).

STEP 2: Decide on a solution strategy

We will analyze the determinants of the operating return on assets by decomposing the determinants of this rate of return measure into its basic component parts, as detailed in Equation (13a).

STEP 3: Solve

Using the following financial information from the 2012 annual reports of Home Depot and Lowe's, we first calculate the operating return on assets for Home Depot and Lowe's to be 16.44 percent and 9.22 percent, respectively. So, we can make a very important observation right away that Home Depot earned a substantially higher return on its total assets. Our objective from this point forward, then, is to explore the source of this difference, and to look for anything that is unusual and that we might want to explore further.

Next, we break down the operating return on assets ratio into the product of the operating profit margin (OPM) and the total asset turnover ratio (TATO). We learn that the firms share very similar operating profit margins of 9.46 percent compared to only 6.53 percent for Lowes. Also, Lowe's total asset turnover ratio is slightly lower than Home Depot's. The combination of a higher OPM and TATO ratio for Home Depot results in its higher OROA.

	Home Depot 2012	Lowe's 2012
Operating return on assets (OROA)	16.44%	9.22%
Operating profit margin (OPM)	9.46%	6.53%
Total asset turnover (TATO)	1.74	1.41
Accounts receivable turnover	56.54	274.36
Inventory turnover	4.47	3.93
Fixed assets turnover	2.88	2.29

(3 CONTINUED >> ON NEXT PAGE)

From there, we can look closer at the total asset turnover ratio and determine the turnover ratios for the major asset subcategories that make up total assets—receivables, inventories, and fixed assets. In this analysis we are struck by the dramatic difference in the accounts receivable turnover ratios of the two firms. Home Depot turns its accounts receivable over every 56.54 days or 6.46 times per year. Lowe's, in contrast, collects its receivables every 1.33 days, which indicates it turns over its accounts receivable 274.36 times a year. Why this dramatic difference? Looking at the determinants of these two ratios, we see that Lowe's has a very low accounts receivable balance compared to Home Depot. It would appear that the two firms follow very different policies with respect to offering credit with Home Depot offering lengthy credit terms and Lowe's offering virtually no credit terms at all.

STEP 4: Analyze

In 2012 Home Depot's operating profit per dollar of total assets (i.e., its OROA) was significantly higher than that of competitor Lowe's. The reason for the difference relates to both a higher OPM and TATO for Home Depot. A real difference we observe relates to the accounts receivable turnover ratio, which is dramatically lower for Home Depot than for Lowe's.

STEP 5: Check yourself

If Home Depot were able to raise its total asset turnover ratio to 2.5 while maintaining its current operating profit margin, what would happen to its operating return on assets?

ANSWER: The operating return on assets would rise to 23.66 percent.

Your Turn: For more practice, do related **Study Problems** 8 and 11 at the end of this chapter.   >> **END Checkpoint 3**

Once again, remember that financial ratios won't give you rock-solid answers—just clues that you need to keep digging.

Is the Firm Providing a Reasonable Return on the Owners' Investment?

Having analyzed the firm's operating profitability, we now move further down the income statement to the firm's net income. A firm's net income consists of the earnings it has left over after its interest expense has been paid. These are the earnings available for distribution to the firm's shareholders. When net income is divided by the dollar amount of equity, we get the accounting return on the common stockholders' investment, or the **return on equity** (frequently shortened to ROE), expressed as follows:

$$\text{Return on Equity} = \frac{\text{Net Income}}{\text{Common Equity}} \tag{14}$$

For H. J. Boswell, Inc.:

$$\text{Return on Equity} = \frac{\$204.75 \text{ million}}{\$911.25 \text{ million}} = 22.5\%$$

$$\text{Peer-group return on equity} = 18.0\%$$

In the preceding computation, note that common equity includes both common stock (par value and paid-in capital) plus the firm's retained earnings—that is, the company's prior year's profits that weren't paid out in dividends.

The return on equity for H. J. Boswell, Inc. and the peer group is 22.5 percent and 18 percent, respectively. Hence, the owners of H. J. Boswell, Inc. receive a higher return on their equity than the shareholders in the peer-group firms, on average. Why did this happen?

Using the DuPont Method for Decomposing the Return on Equity Ratio

Many years ago a finance executive at the E. I. du Pont de Nemours Company created what has come to be known as the **DuPont method** for analyzing the return on equity ratio. This decomposition method has proven to be a very useful tool for analyzing a firm's return on equity ratio. Let's see how Boswell was able to earn a higher return on equity than the peer group even though its net profit margin was much lower (7.6 percent versus 10.2 percent).

In the previous section, we used ratio analysis to assess a firm's return on equity. The DuPont method provides an alternative approach to evaluating a firm's return on equity by breaking down the return on equity equation into three component parts: profitability, efficiency, and an equity multiplier. The equity multiplier captures the effect of the firm's use of debt financing on its return on equity. This effect is commonly referred to as **financial leverage**, because debt financing can magnify the rate of return earned on a firm's common equity much like a lever magnifies the power of the person that uses it to lift an object.[5]

$$\frac{\text{Return on}}{\text{Equity}} = \text{Profitability} \times \text{Efficiency} \times \frac{\text{Equity}}{\text{Multiplier}}$$

$$= \frac{\text{Net Profit}}{\text{Margin}} \times \frac{\text{Total Asset}}{\text{Turnover}} \times \frac{\text{Equity}}{\text{Multiplier}}$$

$$= \frac{\text{Net Income}}{\text{Sales}} \times \frac{\text{Sales}}{\text{Total Assets}} \times \frac{1}{1 - \text{Debt Ratio}} \qquad \textbf{(14a)}$$

The final term in Equation (14a) is an equity multiplier that increases in value as the firm uses more debt to finance its assets. For example, a firm that has no debt financing has a multiplier of 1, whereas a firm that uses 50 percent debt to assets has an equity multiplier of 2.

To see why Boswell's return on equity ratio was 22.5 percent compared to an industry peer ratio of only 18 percent, we need to do a side-by-side comparison of each of the three ratios found in Equation (14a):

	Return on Equity	=	Net Profit Margin	×	Total Asset Turnover	×	Financial Leverage or Equity Multiplier
Equation	$\dfrac{\text{Net Income}}{\text{Common Equity}}$	=	$\dfrac{\text{Net Income}}{\text{Sales}}$	×	$\dfrac{\text{Sales}}{\text{Total Assets}}$	×	$\dfrac{1}{1 - \text{Debt Ratio}}$
H. J. Boswell, Inc.	**22.5%**		7.6%		**1.37**		**2.16**
Peer-Group Averages	18.0%		**10.2%**		1.15		1.54

This analysis provides the answer to our earlier question about the return on equity. That is, Boswell's superior return on equity may be due to its efficient use of assets to generate sales (total asset turnover) and the fact that Boswell benefitted from its use of more debt financing or financial leverage (Boswell financed 53.8 percent of its assets using debt, whereas the peer group used only 35 percent).

Boswell's higher use of debt financing was beneficial in this instance, but this will not always be the case. Financial leverage results from the use of debt financing, which helps the firm earn higher rates of return on the common stockholder's investment only if the firm is able to earn a higher rate of return on the borrowed money than it costs in interest to borrow it.

Figure 2 provides a more detailed analysis of the determinants of the return on equity ratio. In Equation (14a) we decompose the return on equity earned by the firm into three determinants (the net profit margin, total asset turnover, and equity multiplier). Figure 2 expands this analysis even further by looking at the determinants of each of these three ratios.

---

[5]The product of the net profit margin and total asset turnover ratio is the return on investment (or ROI) ratio.

Figure 2

Expanded DuPont Analysis for H. J. Boswell, Inc.

Equation (14a) decomposes the firm's Return on Equity into three basic determinants related to profitability, asset management efficiency, and the use of financial leverage (an equity multiplier) as follows:

$$\frac{\text{Return on}}{\text{Equity}} = \frac{\text{Net Profit}}{\text{Margin}} \times \frac{\text{Total Asset}}{\text{Turnover}} \times \frac{\text{Equity}}{\text{Multiplier}}$$

$$= \frac{\text{Net Income}}{\text{Sales}} \times \frac{\text{Sales}}{\text{Total Assets}} \times \frac{1}{1-\text{Debt Ratio}}$$

(14a)

We can further analyze the return on equity equation by looking at the determinants of each of these three components. For example, the net profit margin is determined by net income and sales; net income reflects the difference in the firm's sales and its total costs which, in turn, consist of cost of goods sold, operating expenses, interest expense, and taxes. Similarly, the firm's sales and total assets (where total assets can be broken down into current and fixed assets, and so forth) determine the total asset turnover ratio. By looking at the determinants of each of the component ratios in Equation (14a) we can learn more about why H. J. Boswell's return on equity is equal to 22.5%.

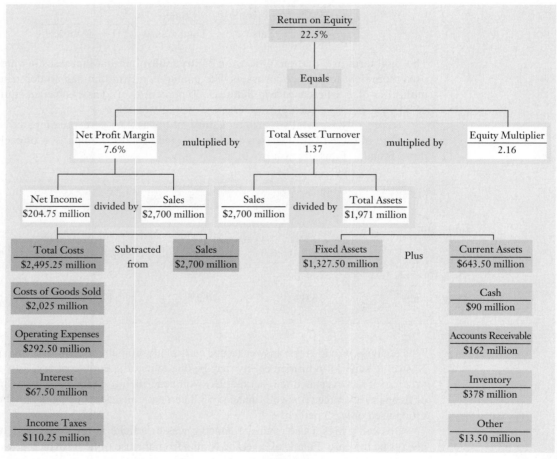

>> END FIGURE 2

Tools of Financial Analysis—Profitability Ratios

Name of Tool	Formula	What It Tells You
Gross Profit Margin	$$\frac{Gross\ Profit}{Sales}$$	• Measures profitability after considering the firm's cost of goods sold; this indicates the firm's "markup" on its cost of goods sold • A higher ratio means greater profitability and better control of costs of goods sold expenses by the firm's management.
Operating Profit Margin (OPM)	$$\frac{Net\ Operating\ Income\ or\ EBIT}{Sales}$$	• Measures profitability after considering both cost of goods sold and operating expenses • A higher ratio means greater profitability and better control of costs of goods sold and operating expenses.
Net Profit Margin (NPM)	$$\frac{Net\ Income}{Sales}$$	• Measures profitability after considering all expenses incurred by the firm during the period • A higher ratio means greater profitability and better control of the firm's expenses.
Operating Return on Assets (OROA)	$$\frac{Net\ Operating\ Income\ or\ EBIT}{Total\ Assets}$$	• Measures the rate of return earned on the total asset investment in the firm that results from operating income (before interest and taxes) • The higher the number, the greater is the return earned from the firm's operations.
Return on Equity	$$\frac{Net\ Income}{Common\ Equity}$$	• Measures the rate of return earned on the stockholders' equity investment in the firm • The higher the number, the greater is the return earned for the firm's stockholders.

Market Value Ratios

Market value ratios are used to address the basic question: How are the firm's shares valued in the stock market? To this point, we have relied exclusively on accounting data to assess the performance of a firm's managers. We now want to look at their performance in terms of how the stock market values the firm's equity. To do this, we examine two market value ratios that indicate what investors think of both the managers' past performance and the firm's future prospects.

Price-Earnings Ratio

A firm's **price-earnings (PE) ratio** is its stock price divided by the net income earned by the firm on a per-share basis. The PE ratio indicates how much investors have been willing to pay for $1 of reported earnings. H. J. Boswell, Inc. had net income in 2013 of $204.75 million and 90 million shares of common stock outstanding. Accordingly, its earnings per share are $2.28 ($2.28 = $204.75 million net income ÷ 90 million shares). The firm's stock is selling for $32 per share. Thus, the price-earnings ratio was 14.07 times, calculated as follows:

$$\text{Price-Earning Ratio} = \frac{\text{Market Price per Share}}{\text{Earnings per Share}} \tag{15}$$

$$\text{Price-Earning Ratio} = \frac{\$32.00}{\$2.28} = 14.07 \text{ times}$$

Peer-group average price-earnings ratio = 12.0 times

H. J. Boswell, Inc.'s PE ratio tells us that the investors were willing to pay $14.07 for every dollar of earnings per share that H. J. Boswell, Inc. produced, compared to an average price-earnings ratio of 12 times for the firms making up the peer group. Thus, investors are willing to pay more for H. J. Boswell, Inc.'s earnings than investors are willing to pay for the average earnings of the peer-group firms. Why might that be? The PE ratio will be higher for companies expected to have better earnings growth prospects and less risk. Thus, investors must perceive H. J. Boswell, Inc. to have more growth potential and/or less risk than the peer group.

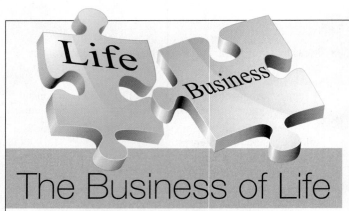

The Business of Life

Your Cash Budget and Personal Savings Ratio

In this chapter, you learned that ratios can be used to assess the financial health of a company. The same is true for your personal financial health. For example, you can calculate your savings ratio, which is the ratio of your income available for savings divided by your after-tax income:

$$\text{Personal Savings Ratio} = \frac{\text{Personal savings}}{\text{Income available for living expenses}}$$

For example, if your personal annual savings were $3,000 and your after-tax income was $30,000, your savings ratio would be 10 percent. Just calculating this ratio can be a sobering experience. According to the Hoover Institute, the average saving rate in the United States was close to 10 percent between 1970 and the mid-1980s; then it steadily declined during the 1990s. Between 1999 and 2004, it averaged around 2 percent before turning negative for a short while in 2005. Between 2005 and 2008 it dropped to less than 1 percent before it jumped to around 4 percent as the stock market plummeted and the economy collapsed.

When you graduate and start a full-time job, you can use the following three-step procedure to estimate your savings ratio:

STEP 1. Estimate your income for next year. Examine the income you earned last year and make any adjustments you expect for the coming year. You can now estimate your after-tax income available to pay your living expenses.

STEP 2. Estimate your living expenses for next year. Look first at your fixed expenses, which generally include such things as expenditures for housing, food, clothing, utilities, and transportation. Then determine your variable expenses, which are the expenses that you can control. These include entertainment expenses and other non-essential expenditures. This is the category where you can start looking for ways to reduce spending and increase your savings.

STEP 3. Finally, subtract your anticipated living expenses from your anticipated take-home pay to determine your income available for savings and investment. Compare your anticipated monthly savings with your target savings level. If it doesn't look as if you'll be able to fund all your goals, then you must earn more, spend less, or downsize your goals.

Your Turn: See Study Question 11.

Market-to-Book Ratio

A second frequently used indicator of investors' assessment of the firm is its **market-to-book ratio**, which is simply the ratio of the market value of a share of the firm's stock divided by the book value per share of the firm's equity as reported in its balance sheet. We already know that the market price of H. J. Boswell, Inc.'s common stock is $32. To determine the **book value per share**, we divide the book value of the firm's common equity by the number of shares of stock it has outstanding. From H. J. Boswell, Inc.'s balance sheet, we see that the book value was $911.25 million (including both common stock and retained earnings). Given that H. J. Boswell, Inc. had 90 million shares outstanding, the book value per share was $10.13 ($10.13 = $911.25 million book equity value ÷ 90 million shares). With this information, we calculate the market-to-book ratio as follows:

$$\frac{\text{Market-to-}}{\text{Book Ratio}} = \frac{\text{Market Price per Share}}{\text{Book Value per Share}} = \frac{\text{Market Price per Share}}{\dfrac{\text{Common Shareholders'}}{\text{Equity}} \Big/ \dfrac{\text{Common Shares}}{\text{Outstanding}}} \qquad (16)$$

$$\frac{\text{Market-to-}}{\text{Book Ratio}} = \frac{\$32.00}{\$911.25 \text{ million}/90 \text{ million}} = \frac{\$32.00}{\$10.13} = 3.16$$

$$\text{Peer-firm market-to-book ratio} = 2.7X$$

Because the book value per share is an accounting number that reflects historical costs, we can think of it roughly as the amount shareholders have invested in the business over its lifetime.[6] So, a market-to-book ratio greater than 1 indicates that the market value of the firm's shares is greater than the book value or the accumulated investment in the firm's equity. Conversely, a ratio less than 1 suggests that the stock is worth less than the accumulated investment made by the shareholders in the firm. Clearly, investors believe the stock of H. J. Boswell, Inc. is worth more than the accumulated investment, because they are now paying $3.16 for each dollar of book value. In comparison, the average firm in the peer group was selling for $2.70 for every $1 in book value. One interpretation is that investors believe that H. J. Boswell, Inc. has better growth prospects than the average of the peer firms.

Tools of Financial Analysis—Market Value Ratios

Name of Tool	Formula	What It Tells You
Price-Earnings Ratio	$\dfrac{Market\ Price\ per\ Share}{Earnings\ per\ Share}$	• Indicates the valuation of the firm's shares relative to earnings • A higher ratio indicates that investors place a higher dollar value on each dollar of firm earnings.
Market-to-Book Ratio	$\dfrac{Market\ Price\ per\ Share}{Book\ Value\ per\ Share}$	• Indicates the valuation of the firm's shares relative to the investment made by the shareholders in the firm • A higher ratio indicates that investors place a higher dollar value on each dollar of investment made in the firm by its common shareholders.

Checkpoint 4

Comparing the Valuation of Dell (DELL) to Apple (APPL) Using Market Value Ratios

The following information on Dell and Apple was gathered on April 9, 2012:

Financial Statement as of (millions of dollars except per share figures)	9/28/2012 Dell	2/2/2012 Apple
Net income ($ millions)	$3,492	$ 41,733
Shares outstanding (millions)	1,740	940.69
Earnings per share ($)	$ 2.01	$ 44.36
Price per share (11/26/12)	$ 9.70	$ 586.29
Book value of common equity ($ millions)	$8,917	$118,210
Book value per share	5.12	125.66

Suppose that you are considering whether to invest in the stock of Dell or Apple and want to first learn something about how the two firms' stock is currently being priced. You know that simply comparing the prices of the two firms' shares is meaningless because each has a different number of shares outstanding and the two firms are not the same in many other dimensions. So, you decide to standardize the market prices of the firms' shares by comparing them to accounting information from their financial statements. Use earnings per share from each firm's income statement to calculate the price-to-earnings ratio and use book value per share from the firm's balance sheet to calculate the market-to-book ratio.

(4 CONTINUED >> ON NEXT PAGE)

---

[6]We use the qualifier "roughly" here because the firm's assets do not reflect two very important investments made by the firm's owners in the firm: research and development (R&D) expenditures and advertising. Both of these expenditures are made in the hopes of producing long-term benefits to the firm, just like acquisitions of plant and equipment. However, generally accepted accounting principles calls for R&D and advertising expenditures to be fully expensed (i.e., run through the current period's income statement), and they do not appear as assets in the firm's balance sheet. Consequently, for firms that make very large investments in R&D or advertising, the firm's book value assets will understate the total invested capital in the firm.

STEP 1: Picture the problem

We can visualize the problem of comparing stock prices as one of first standardizing the prices and then making ratio comparisons:

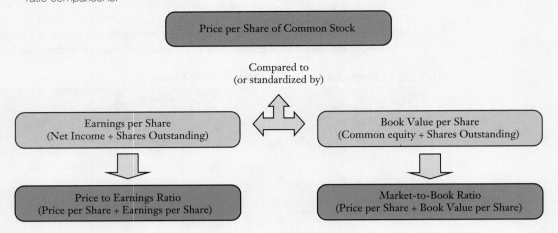

STEP 2: Decide on a solution strategy

Calculating the price-earnings ratio and the market-to-book value ratio for Dell and Apple will tell us how much investors are willing to pay for one dollar of earnings and one dollar of its book value of equity, respectively.

STEP 3: Solve

We can now calculate the price-to-earnings ratio and market-to-book value for both Dell and Apple as follows:

	Dell	Apple
Price-to-Earnings Ratio (PE ratio)	4.83	13.22
Market-to-Book Ratio	1.89	4.67

STEP 4: Analyze

Dell's share price of $9.70 is dramatically less than the Apple share price of $586.29, but this tells us very little about how investors are valuing the shares of the two companies. To learn more, we standardize the market price by dividing it first by earnings per share to calculate the price-to-earnings ratio and then by book value per share to calculate the market-to-book ratio. We are now prepared to compare the prices of the two company's shares because the share prices have now been standardized. It appears that Apple enjoys a higher price per share when compared to its 2012 earnings as well as a higher book-to-market value ratio.

STEP 5: Check yourself

What price per share for Dell would it take to increase the firm's price-to-earnings ratio to the level of Apple?

Answer: Dell's stock price would have to increase to $26.52 per share.

Your Turn: For more practice, do related **Study Problem** 20 at the end of this chapter.

>> **END Checkpoint 4**

Summing Up the Financial Analysis of H. J. Boswell, Inc.

We conclude our discussion of financial ratios by reviewing all of the financial ratios we have applied to the analysis of H. J. Boswell, Inc. in Table 3. In the right-hand column of the table, we show how the ratios stack up to the peer-group ratios—whether they are better, worse, or on par.

Our analysis revealed the following clues about H. J. Boswell's financial performance:

- **Liquidity**—With the exception of the inventory turnover ratio, H. J. Boswell's liquidity ratios were adequate to good. The next step then would be to look into the firm's inventory management practices to see if there are problems that can be addressed. For example, has the firm accumulated inventories of older and less saleable products or is the firm simply overstocked with inventory?

Finance in a **Flat World**

Ratios and International Accounting Standards

Financial statement analysis can be challenging even if the companies being compared are all domestic firms that follow the same set of accounting standards (in the United States, these standards are referred to as Generally Accepted Accounting Principles, or GAAP). However, when comparing firms from different countries with different accounting rules, the task can become extremely difficult.

For example, when comparing the price-earnings ratios of companies from the United States and Hong Kong, we must be aware of differences in how earnings are calculated in the different countries and the impact of these differences on reported earnings. U.S. firms amortize the goodwill created by the acquisition of another firm over time if the value of the acquisition appears to have fallen. However, in Hong Kong, firms write off goodwill immediately in the year of the acquisition. This difference can have a significant impact on the reported earnings per share of two otherwise similar firms. Consequently, the price-earnings ratios would differ simply because of the difference in accounting conventions.

Two factors limit the severity of the problem of international comparisons: First, if the foreign firm's shares are listed on a U.S. exchange, the foreign firm's financial statements must comply with GAAP. Second, companies in the largest economies throughout the world appear to be converging on a set of reporting rules along the lines of the International Financial Reporting Standards, or IFRS. In fact, the U.S. Securities and Exchange Commission has laid out a road map for the adoption of IFRS by U.S. issuers in the next decade.

Your Turn: See Study Question 12.

- **Financial leverage**—H. J. Boswell used more debt to finance investments than the peer group, which we saw in Boswell's higher-than-average debt ratio and below-average times interest earned ratio. This suggests that the firm is exposing itself to a higher degree of financial risk than is the norm for firms in its industry. In other words, there's a greater risk it might not be able to meet its debt obligations.

- **Profitability**—H. J. Boswell's net operating income (before interest expense is considered) compared very favorably with its peer firms. This is because the firm's asset turnover rate (the efficiency with which it utilizes its investment in assets to produce sales) more than offsets the firm's lower profit margins. But the firm's management of its inventory may present a problem and should be investigated further, as we noted earlier. H. J. Boswell's return on the stockholders' investment (i.e., its return on equity) was much higher than that of the peer group due to its higher-than-average use of financial leverage.

- **Market value ratios**—When we compare H. J. Boswell's market value ratios to the peer group's ratios, it is obvious that investors appreciate what the firm is doing and have rewarded it with an above-average market price relative to both the firm's earnings per share and book value.

Before you move on to 4

Concept Check | 3

1. Why are ratios helpful in financial statement analysis?
2. What are the five basic questions that we address with financial statement analysis?
3. What is the DuPont system of financial analysis, and why is it a useful tool for analyzing financial performance?

Table 3 H. J. Boswell, Inc.

Financial Ratio Analysis

Category of Financial Ratios	H. J. Boswell, Inc.	Compared to the Industry Ratio	
1. Liquidity Ratios			
$\text{Current Ratio} = \dfrac{\text{Current Assets}}{\text{Current Liabilities}}$	$\dfrac{\$643.5 \text{ million}}{\$288.0 \text{ million}} = 2.23$	1.8 times	Better
$\text{Acid-Test Ratio} = \dfrac{\text{Current Assets} - \text{Inventory}}{\text{Current Liabilities}}$	$\dfrac{\$643.5 \text{ million} - \$378 \text{ million}}{\$288.0 \text{ million}} = 0.92$	0.94 times	On Par
$\dfrac{\text{Average Collection}}{\text{Period}} = \dfrac{\text{Accounts Receivable}}{\text{Annual Credit Sales/365 days}}$	$\dfrac{\$162 \text{ million}}{\$2,700 \text{ million/365 days}} = 21.9 \text{ days}$	25 days	Better
$\dfrac{\text{Accounts Receivable}}{\text{Turnover}} = \dfrac{\text{Accounts Credit Sales}}{\text{Accounts Receivable}}$	$\dfrac{\$2,700 \text{ million}}{\$162 \text{ million}} = 16.67 \text{ times}$	14.6 times	Better
$\text{Inventory Turnover} = \dfrac{\text{Cost of Goods Sold}}{\text{Inventories}}$	$\dfrac{\$2,025 \text{ million}}{\$378 \text{ million}} = 5.36 \text{ times}$	7 times	Worse
2. Capital Structure Ratios			
$\text{Debt Ratio} = \dfrac{\text{Total Liabilities}}{\text{Total Assets}}$	$\dfrac{\$1,059.75 \text{ million}}{\$1,971 \text{ million}} = 53.8\%$	35%	Worse
$\dfrac{\text{Times Interest}}{\text{Earned}} = \dfrac{\text{Net Operating Income or EBIT}}{\text{Interest Expense}}$	$\dfrac{\$382.5 \text{ million}}{\$67.5 \text{ million}} = 56.7 \text{ times}$	7 times	Worse
3. Asset Management Efficiency Ratios			
$\text{Total Asset Turnover} = \dfrac{\text{Sales}}{\text{Total Assets}}$	$\dfrac{\$2,700 \text{ million}}{\$1,971 \text{ million}} = 1.37$	1.15 times	Better
$\text{Fixed Asset Turnover} = \dfrac{\text{Sales}}{\text{Net Plant and Equipment}}$	$\dfrac{\$2,700 \text{ million}}{\$1,327.5 \text{ million}} = 2.03$	1.75 times	Better
4. Profitability Ratios			
$\text{Gross Profit Margin} = \dfrac{\text{Gross Profits}}{\text{Sales}}$	$\dfrac{\$675 \text{ million}}{\$2,700 \text{ million}} = .25 \text{ or } 25\%$	28.2%	Worse
$\dfrac{\text{Operating Profit}}{\text{Margin (OPM)}} = \dfrac{\text{Net Operating Income or EBIT}}{\text{Sales}}$	$\dfrac{\$382.5 \text{ million}}{\$2,700 \text{ million}} = 14.2\%$	15.5%	Worse
$\text{Net Profit Margin (NPM)} = \dfrac{\text{Net Income}}{\text{Sales}}$	$\dfrac{\$204.75 \text{ million}}{\$2,700 \text{ million}} = 7.6\%$	10.2%	Worse
$\dfrac{\text{Operating Return}}{\text{on Assets (OROA)}} = \dfrac{\text{Net Operating Income or EBIT}}{\text{Total Assets}}$	$\dfrac{\$382.5 \text{ million}}{\$1,971 \text{ million}} = 19.4\%$	17.8%	Better
$\text{Return on Equity} = \dfrac{\text{Net Income}}{\text{Common Equity}}$	$\dfrac{\$204.75 \text{ million}}{\$911.25 \text{ million}} = 22.5\%$	18%	Better
5. Market Value Ratios			
$\text{Price-Earnings Ratio} = \dfrac{\text{Market Price per Share}}{\text{Earnings per Share}}$	$\dfrac{\$32.00}{\$2.28} = 14.07 \text{ times}$	12 times	Better
$\text{Market-to-Book Ratio} = \dfrac{\text{Market Price per Share}}{\text{Book Value per Share}}$	$\dfrac{\$32.00}{\$10.13} = 3.16$	2.7 times	Better

Selecting a Performance Benchmark

There are two types of benchmarks that we use when we analyze a firm's financial performance using its financial statements:

- **Trend analysis**—comparing the firm's financial statements over time (time-series comparisons).
- **Peer-group comparisons**—comparing the subject firm's financial statements with those of similar, or "peer," firms.

Throughout this chapter we have been using the second of these methods as we benchmarked H. J. Boswell's performance against a peer group. However, it also makes sense to look at H. J. Boswell in terms of its historical ratios by doing a time-series (trend) analysis, which we will consider next.

Trend Analysis

As we explained at the outset of the chapter, comparing a firm's recent financial ratios with its past financial ratios provides insight into whether the firm is improving or deteriorating over time. This type of financial analysis is referred to as **trend analysis**. Figure 3 shows a trend analysis of the inventory turnover ratios for Dell (Dell) relative to Hewlett Packard (HP) spanning the period 1995–2011.

Notice how dramatically Dell's inventory turnover ratio improved beginning in 1996. The inventory management practices Dell implemented during this period have been widely mimicked by other firms. Among other things, Dell had its suppliers back their trucks up to Dell's assembly plant in Round Rock, Texas, for off-loading just as the plant needed the items. But until the items left the trucks, they were not considered part of Dell's inventories. The practice dramatically reduced the time it took suppliers to deliver merchandise to Dell.

Figure 3

A Time-Series (Trend) Analysis: Dell's Inventory Turnover Ratio Versus Hewlett Packard's: 1995–2011

Description: The inventory turnover ratio is defined as follows:

$$\frac{\text{Cost of Goods Sold}}{\text{Inventory}}$$

For example, Hewlett Packard Corporation's inventory turnover ratio is used as a benchmark for comparison purposes.

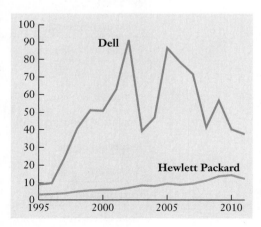

>> END FIGURE 3

But what Dell gained in terms of reduced inventories was lost by the firm's suppliers, who instead had to carry the inventories themselves.

Peer-Firm Comparisons

A peer firm is simply one that the analyst believes will provide a relevant benchmark for the analysis at hand. This can vary depending upon whether the analysis is conducted internally or carried out by an external analyst. For example, when Dell was a startup firm in the late 1980s, much of its internal analysis focused on the then-industry leader, Compaq. However, when Dell approached a bank to borrow money during this period, the banker would probably not have used Compaq as a peer firm for Dell, because Compaq was much larger and better established at the time.

Industry Average Financial Ratios

In practice, peer groups often consist of firms from the same industry. Moreover, industry-average financial ratios can be obtained from a number of sources. A very popular source of financial data is Compustat, a database of accounting and financial information owned by Standard & Poor's Corporation. Today, these financial ratios can also be found on the Internet at www.google.com/finance and finance.yahoo.com. For example, Figure 4 contains a set of financial ratios for the Gap, Inc., along with the industry average for those ratios. As you see, the Gap's price-earnings ratio was lower than the average for the industry. We could make similar comparisons for the remaining ratios. Although this figure only contains an average of the ratios for firms in the Gap's industry, industry-average ratios are frequently supplemented with more descriptive information about the distribution of ratios within an industry. For example, we might also have the first quartile (25 percent of the firms in the industry have a lower ratio) and third quartile (only 25 percent of the firms in the industry have a higher ratio than this quartile).

Figure 4

Financial Analysis of the Gap, Inc., June 2009

Industry average financial ratios are often used to benchmark the ratios of firms that are being analyzed. When this is done we look for deviations from the average that may indicate either a problem or a strength of the subject firm.

Financial Ratios	Gap, Inc.	Industry Average
Price-earnings ratio	14.10	15.51
Market-to-book ratio	2.99	4.71
Gross margin	40.91%	36.14%
Net profit margin	6.88%	3.51%
Operating profit margin	10.64%	7.68%
Return on equity	21.36%	28.24%
Debt ratio	1.39%	17.31%
Current ratio	1.80	1.57
Total assets turnover ratio	1.86	1.81
Inventory turnover ratio	4.94	4.31

>> END FIGURE 4

Before moving on to 5

Concept Check | 4

1. Describe how time-series comparisons of a firm's ratios provide a benchmark for performing financial statement analysis.
2. Why is the selection of a proper set of peer firms so important when using these firms as a benchmark of performance?

 # Limitations of Ratio Analysis

The financial ratios discussed in this chapter are a very useful tool for assessing a firm's financial condition. That said, those who work with financial ratios need to be aware of their limitations. Some of the more noteworthy problems are as follows:

1. **Picking an industry benchmark can sometimes be difficult.** It is sometimes difficult to determine the industry to which a firm belongs when the firm engages in multiple lines of business. This problem is particularly difficult if the firm you are analyzing operates in multiple lines of business and consequently in multiple industries. In this case, you must select your own set of peer firms and construct your own norms. For example, General Electric Company (GE) operates as a technology, media, and financial services company worldwide.

2. **Published peer-group or industry averages are not always representative of the firm being analyzed.** The published data provide the user with general guidelines rather than scientifically determined averages of the ratios for all, or even a representative sample, of the firms within an industry. For example, some sources of peer-group financial ratios report averages of the firms that report to a particular industry trade group (e.g., companies that apply to banks for loans).

3. **An industry average is not necessarily a desirable target ratio or norm.** There is nothing magical about an industry norm. At best, an industry average provides an indication of the financial position of the average firm within the industry. It does not mean it is the ideal or best value for the ratio. For various reasons, a well-managed company might be above the average, whereas another equally good firm might choose to be below the average. For example, one firm might use a just-in-time inventory approach, and as a result might have a very high inventory turnover ratio. By contrast, another firm in the same industry might be a supplier to companies like Dell that employ just-in-time inventory approaches. If this is the case, the firm will have to keep a large amount of inventory on hand and will have a lower inventory turnover ratio. Both firms might be successful companies but approach inventory differently.

4. **Accounting practices differ widely among firms.** For example, different firms choose different methods to depreciate their fixed assets. Differences such as these can make the computed ratios of different firms difficult to compare.

5. **Many firms experience seasonal changes in their operations.** As a result, their balance sheet entries and their corresponding ratios will vary with the time of year the statements were prepared. To avoid this problem, financial analysts should use average account balances calculated on the basis of several months or quarters during the year rather than simply year-end account balances. For example, an average of the firm's month-end inventory balances might be used to compute its inventory turnover ratio versus a year-end inventory balance.

6. **Understanding the numbers.** Financial ratios are simply clues that can suggest the need for further investigation. For example, consider two firms that each have annual credit sales of $1.2 million. One has $200,000 in accounts receivable, and thus an accounts receivable turnover ratio of 6 times, whereas the other has a $100,000 accounts receivable balance and thus a 12 times receivable turnover ratio. This difference suggests the need

to look into the receivables management practices of the first firm, which reveals that it offers credit terms that allow customers 60 days to pay, whereas the latter company only allows 30 days. Based on this investigation, we find the difference in receivables turnover ratios to be reasonable.

7. **The results of a ratio analysis are no better than the quality of the financial statements.** If the financial statements were not prepared in accordance with GAAP or are fraudulent, then no amount of ratio analysis will reveal the firm's problems. There are many degrees to which a firm might manipulate data when reporting its financial results, ranging from minor exaggerations to fraudulent reporting. Outright fraud is generally less prevalent. However, as we learned with the scandals of Enron, WorldCom, and a multitude of other firms, we must always be wary of the potential for fraud.

Before you begin end-of-chapter material

Concept Check | 5

1. Why is picking a peer group a limitation of financial ratio analysis?
2. How are financial ratio comparisons like clues in solving a puzzle?

Applying the Principles of Finance to This Chapter

 Principle 3: **Cash Flows Are the Source of Value** Accounting statements contain important information that can be used to calculate current cash flows as well as evaluate the potential of the firm to generate future cash flows.

 Principle 4: **Market Prices Reflect Information** The information gleaned from studying a firm's financial statements ultimately helps the analyst make decisions. For investors this analysis may lead to a decision to buy or sell the firm's stock, for a lender the analysis might lead to the approval or denial of a loan request, and for a financial manager working at the firm the analysis could lead to decisions to improve the firm's operations.

 Principle 5: **Individuals Respond to Incentives** Because managers respond to incentives they are given in the workplace, when their incentives are not properly aligned with those of the firm's stockholders, they may not make decisions that are consistent with increasing shareholder value.

Chapter Summaries

Concept Check | 1

1. What are some common reasons for analyzing a firm's financial statements?
2. What are some of the firms that engage in external financial statement analysis, and what are their motives?

 Explain what we can learn by analyzing a firm's financial statements.

SUMMARY: Financial statements provide information useful both to the management of the firm being analyzed and to outsiders who are concerned about the firm's financial performance. Consequently, financial statement analysis is useful for both internal analysis directed at such things as assessing employee performance, analyzing business unit or divisional performance, preparing financial forecasts, determining the creditworthiness of a potential new credit customer, and applying for bank loans. External analysis of a firm's financial statements is frequently performed by lenders who are considering the extension of credit to the firm, and by investors who are considering whether to purchase the firm's stock.

Concept Check | 2

1. What is the reason for converting financial statements to common-size statements?
2. How are the common-size income statement and balance sheet constructed?

 Use common-size financial statements as a tool of financial analysis.

SUMMARY: Common-size financial statements are simply financial statements that have been converted to a percent measure. For example, each entry in the income statement is divided by firm sales, and each entry in the balance sheet is divided by total assets. By standardizing the financial statement information in the income statement and balance sheet, we can easily compare one firm's statements to those of another firm.

 Calculate and use a comprehensive set of financial ratios to evaluate a company's performance.

SUMMARY: Financial ratios are the principal tool of financial analysis. They standardize the financial information so that comparisons can be made across firms of varying sizes.

Financial ratios can be used to answer at least five questions: (1) How liquid is the company? (2) Are the company's managers effectively generating profits from the firm's assets? (3) How is the firm financed? (4) Are the firm's managers providing a good return on the capital the shareholders have provided the firm? (5) Are the firm's managers creating or destroying shareholder value?

Two methods can be used to analyze a firm's financial ratios: (1) We can examine the firm's ratios across time (say, for the last five years) to compare its current performance with its past performance; and (2) we can compare the firm's ratios with the ratios of peer firms.

KEY TERMS

Accounts receivable turnover ratio The number of times that accounts receivable are rolled over each year.

Acid-test (quick) ratio A measure of firm liquidity that has as its numerator current assets minus inventories, or "quick" assets, compared to current liabilities in the denominator.

Average collection period The average number of days required to collect on the firm's credit sales.

Book value per share Common equity divided by the number of outstanding shares of common stock.

Capital structure The mix of debt and equity securities a firm uses to finance its assets.

Current ratio A measure of firm liquidity equal to the ratio of current assets to current liabilities.

Days' sales in inventory Inventory divided by cost of goods sold per day (Cost of goods ÷ 365).

Debt ratio Total liabilities divided by total assets.

DuPont method A method for decomposing the return on equity ratio into three components: net profit margin, total asset turnover, and an equity multiplier that reflects the use of debt financing.

Financial leverage The magnifying effect of the use of debt financing on the rate of return earned on the equity invested in a firm.

Financial ratios Restating the accounting data in relative terms to identify some of the financial strengths and weaknesses of a company.

Fixed asset turnover ratio A measure of the efficiency of a firm's use of its fixed assets equal to the ratio of sales to net fixed assets.

Inventory turnover ratio A measure of the efficiency of a firm's use of its inventory equal to the ratio of cost of goods sold to inventory.

Liquidity ratios Measures of the ability of a firm to pay its bills in a timely manner when they come due.

Market-to-book ratio The ratio of the market value of a firm's equity (share price times the number of shares outstanding) to the book value of the firm's equity.

Market value ratios Ratios used to compare the market value of a firm's shares to either the book value per share or earnings per share.

Notes payable Short-term notes or loans that must be repaid in one year or less.

Operating return on assets (OROA) ratio A measure of the return earned by a firm's operations divided by total assets.

Price-earnings (PE) ratio The ratio of price per share of common stock divided by earnings per share.

Return on equity A measure of the rate of return earned on the common shareholders' investment in the firm equal to net income divided by common equity.

Times interest earned ratio A measure of the ability of the firm to pay its interest expense equal to the ratio of net operating income divided by interest expense.

Total asset turnover (TATO) ratio A measure of the efficiency of a firm's use of its total assets equal to the ratio of sales to total assets.

KEY EQUATIONS

$$\text{Current Ratio} = \frac{\text{Currrent Assets}}{\text{Current Liabilities}} \tag{1}$$

$$\text{Acid-Test (or Quick) Ratio} = \frac{\text{Current Assets} - \text{Inventory}}{\text{Current Liabilities}} \tag{2}$$

$$\text{Average Collection Period} = \frac{\text{Accounts Receivable}}{\text{Annual Credit Sales/365 days}} = \frac{\text{Accounts Receivable}}{\text{Daily Credit Sales}} \tag{3}$$

$$\text{Accounts Receivable Turnover} = \frac{\text{Annual Credit Sales}}{\text{Accounts Receivable}} \tag{4}$$

$$\text{Inventory Turnover} = \frac{\text{Cost of Goods Sold}}{\text{Inventories}} \tag{5}$$

$$\text{Debt Ratio} = \frac{\text{Total Liabilities}}{\text{Total Assets}} \tag{6}$$

$$\text{Times Interest Earned} = \frac{\text{Net Operating Income or EBIT}}{\text{Interest Expense}} \tag{7}$$

$$\text{Total Asset Turnover} = \frac{\text{Sales}}{\text{Total Assets}} \tag{8}$$

$$\text{Fixed Asset Turnover} = \frac{\text{Sales}}{\text{Net Plant and Equipment}} \tag{9}$$

$$\text{Gross Profit Margin} = \frac{\text{Gross Profits}}{\text{Sales}} \tag{10}$$

$$\text{Operating Profit} \atop \text{Margin (OPM)} = \frac{\text{Net Operating Income or EBIT}}{\text{Sales}} \qquad \text{(11)}$$

$$\text{Net Profit} \atop \text{Margin} = \frac{\text{Net Income}}{\text{Sales}} \qquad \text{(12)}$$

$$\text{Operating Return} \atop \text{on Assets (OROA)} = \frac{\text{Net Operating Income or EBIT}}{\text{Total Assets}} \qquad \text{(13)}$$

$$\text{Operating Return} \atop \text{on Assets} = \left(\text{Operating Profit} \atop \text{Margin (OPM)}\right) \times \left(\text{Total Asset} \atop \text{Turnover (TATO)}\right) \qquad \text{(13a)}$$

$$\text{Operating Return} \atop \text{on Assets} = \left(\frac{\text{Net Operating Income or EBIT}}{\text{Sales}}\right) \times \left(\frac{\text{Sales}}{\text{Total Assets}}\right)$$
$$= \left(\frac{\text{Net Operating Income or EBIT}}{\text{Total Assets}}\right) \qquad \text{(13b)}$$

$$\text{Return on} \atop \text{Equity} = \frac{\text{Net Income}}{\text{Equity}} = \frac{\text{Net Income}}{\text{Sales}} \times \frac{\text{Sales}}{\text{Total Assets}} \times \frac{1}{1 - \text{Debt Ratio}} \qquad \text{(14a)}$$

$$\text{Price Earnings Ratio} = \frac{\text{Market Price per Share}}{\text{Earnings per Share}} \qquad \text{(15)}$$

$$\text{Market-to-} \atop \text{Book Ratio} = \frac{\text{Market Price per Share}}{\text{Book Value per Share}} = \frac{\text{Market Price per Share}}{\text{Common Shareholders' Equity} \big/ \text{Common Shares Outstanding}} \qquad \text{(16)}$$

Concept Check | **3**

1. Why are ratios helpful in financial statement analysis?
2. What are the five basic questions that we address with financial statement analysis?
3. What is the DuPont system of financial analysis, and why is it a useful tool for analyzing financial performance?

Concept Check | **4**

1. Describe how time-series comparisons of a firm's ratios provide a benchmark for performing financial statement analysis.
2. Why is the selection of a proper set of peer firms so important when using these firms as a benchmark of performance?

4. Select an appropriate benchmark for use in performing a financial ratio analysis.

SUMMARY: Financial ratios are useful in analyzing a firm's financial condition only where they are compared to a meaningful standard or benchmark. Two general types of benchmarks are typically used: historical ratios for the same firm (trend analysis) and average ratios for similar firms. In the latter case, industry classifications are often used to select comparable firms. However, firms often identify their own target set of firms when analyzing their own performance.

KEY TERM

Trend analysis The use of historical ratios compared to a firm's current-period ratios to indicate whether the firm's financial condition is improving or deteriorating.

Concept Check | **5**

1. Why is picking a peer group a limitation of financial ratio analysis?
2. How are financial ratio comparisons like clues in solving a puzzle?

5. Describe the limitations of financial ratio analysis.

SUMMARY: The following are some of the limitations that you will encounter as you compute and interpret financial ratios:

1. It is sometimes difficult to determine the appropriate industry within which to place the firm.
2. Published industry averages are only approximations rather than scientifically determined averages.
3. Accounting practices differ widely among firms and can lead to differences in computed ratios.
4. An industry average may not be a desirable target ratio or norm.
5. Many firms experience seasonal business conditions. As a result, the ratios calculated for them will vary with the time of year during which the statements are prepared.

Study Questions

1. Why do financial analysts engage in the analysis of a firm's financial statements?

2. What are common-size financial statements and how are they constructed?

3. List and describe the five basic questions used to discuss financial statement analysis.

4. What does the term *liquidity* mean in the context of a firm's financial condition, and what financial ratios can the analyst use to assess liquidity?

5. What two ratios are typically used to measure how a firm has financed its assets (i.e., its capital structure)?

6. What are the differences among gross profit margin, operating profit margin, and net profit margin?

7. What are the two determinants of a firm's operating return on assets?

8. What is the DuPont system of financial statement analysis, and how is it applied to the analysis of a company's return on equity?

9. What can we learn about a firm from its price-to-earnings ratio and market-to-book ratio?

10. What are the limitations of industry-average ratios as a source of benchmarks for firm financial condition? Discuss briefly.

11. **(Related to The Business of Life: Your Cash Budget and Personal Savings Ratio)** In *The Business of Life: Your Cash Budget and Personal Savings Ratio* box feature, we defined something called your personal savings ratio. What is this ratio and how can it be used when thinking about gaining control over your personal finances?

12. **(Related to Finance in a Flat World)** In the *Finance in a Flat World box,* we note that differences in accounting standards around the world can influence financial ratios. Describe how differences in the way that goodwill is treated in the United States versus Hong Kong might influence financial ratio comparisons between companies in each country.

Study Problems

MyFinanceLab

Go to **www.myfinancelab.com** to complete these exercises online and get instant feedback.

Common-Size Statements

1. **(Preparing common-size financial statements)** The balance sheet and income statement for Carver Enterprises, Inc. are as follows:

Balance Sheet	2013
Cash and marketable securities	$ 500
Accounts receivable	6,000
Inventories	9,500
Current assets	$16,000
Net property, plant, and equipment	17,000
Total	$33,000
Accounts payable	$ 7,200
Short-term debt	6,800
Current liabilities	$14,000
Long-term liabilities	7,000
Total liabilities	$21,000
Total owners' equity	12,000
Total liabilities and owners' equity	$33,000

Income Statement	2013
Revenues	$30,000
Cost of goods sold	(20,000)
Gross profit	$10,000
Operating expenses	(8,000)
Net operating income	$ 2,000
Interest expense	(900)
Earnings before taxes	$ 1,100
Taxes	(400)
Net income	$ 700

    a. Prepare a common-size balance sheet for Carver Enterprises.
    b. Prepare a common-size income statement for Carver Enterprises.

2.   (**Analyzing common-size financial statements**) Use the common-size financial statements prepared for Study Problem 1 to respond to your boss's request that you write up your assessment of the firm's financial condition. Specifically, write up a brief narrative that responds to the following questions:

    How much cash does Carver have on hand relative to its total assets?

    a. What proportion of Carver's assets has the firm financed using short-term debt? Long-term debt?
    b. What percent of Carver's revenues does the firm have left over after paying all of its expenses (including taxes)?
    c. Describe the relative importance of Carver's major expense categories, including cost of goods sold, operating expenses, and interest expenses.

3.   (**Using common-size financial statements**) The S&H Construction Company expects to have total sales next year totaling $15,000,000. In addition, the firm pays taxes at 35 percent and will owe $300,000 in interest expense. Based on last year's operations, the firm's management predicts that its cost of goods sold will be 60 percent of sales and operating expenses will total 30 percent. What is your estimate of the firm's net income (after taxes) for the coming year?

Using Financial Ratios

4.   (**Related to Checkpoint 1**) (**Liquidity analysis**) Airspot Motors, Inc. has $2,145,000 in current assets and $858,000 in current liabilities. The company's managers want to increase the firm's inventory, which will be financed using short-term debt. How can the firm increase its inventory without its current ratio falling below 2.0 (assuming all other current assets and current liabilities remain constant)?

5.   (**Liquidity analysis**) The King Carpet Company has $3,000,000 in cash and a total of $12,000,000 in current assets. The firm's current liabilities equal $6,000,000 such that the firm's current ratio equals 2. The company's managers want to reduce the firm's cash holdings down to $1,000,000 by paying $500,000 in cash to expand the firm's truck fleet and using $1,500,000 in cash to retire a short-term note. If they carry this plan through, what will happen to the firm's current ratio?

6. **(Related to Checkpoint 2) (Capital structure analysis)** The liabilities and owners' equity for Campbell Industries is as follows:

Accounts payable	$ 500,000
Notes payable	250,000
Current liabilities	$ 750,000
Long-term debt	$1,200,000
Common equity	$5,000,000
Total liabilities and equity	$6,950,000

a. What fraction of the firm's assets does the firm finance using debt (liabilities)?

b. If Campbell were to purchase a new warehouse for $1 million and finance it all using long-term debt, what would happen to the firm's debt ratio?

7. **(Capital structure analysis)** The Karson Transport Company currently has net operating income of $500,000 and pays interest expense of $200,000. The company plans to borrow $1 million on which the firm will pay 10 percent interest. The borrowed money will be used to finance an investment that is expected to increase the firm's net operating income by $400,000 a year.

a. What is Karson's times interest earned ratio before the loan is taken out and the investment is made?

b. What effect will the loan and the investment have on the firm's times interest earned ratio?

8. **(Related to Checkpoint 3) (Profitability analysis)** The Allen Corporation had sales in 2013 of $65 million, total assets of $42 million, and total liabilities of $20 million. The interest rate on the company's debt is 6 percent, and its tax rate is 35 percent. The operating profit margin is 12 percent.

a. Compute the firm's 2013 net operating income and net income.

b. Calculate the firm's operating return on assets and return on equity. (Hint: You can assume that interest must be paid on all of the firm's liabilities.)

9. **(Efficiency analysis)** Baryla Inc. manufactures high-quality decorator lamps in a plant located in eastern Tennessee. Last year the firm had sales of $100 million and a gross profit margin of 40 percent.

a. How much inventory can Baryla hold and still maintain an inventory turnover ratio of at least 6.0 times?

b. Currently, some of Baryla's inventory includes $2 million of outdated and damaged goods that simply remain in inventory and are not salable. What inventory turnover ratio must the good inventory maintain in order to achieve an overall turnover ratio of at least 6.0 (including the unsalable items)?

10. **(Efficiency analysis)** ALei Industries has credit sales of $150 million a year. ALei's management reviewed its credit policy and decided that it wants to maintain an average collection period of 40 days.

a. What is the maximum level of accounts receivable that ALei can carry and have a 40-day average collection period?

b. If ALei's current accounts receivable collection period is 50 days, by how much would it have to reduce its level of accounts receivable in order to achieve its goal of 40 days?

11. **(Related to Checkpoint 3) (Profitability analysis)** Last year the P. M. Postem Corporation had sales of $400,000, with a cost of goods sold of $112,000. The firm's operating expenses were $130,000, and its increase in retained earnings was $58,000. There are currently 22,000 shares of common stock outstanding, the firm pays a $1.60 dividend per share, and the firm has no interest-bearing debt.

a. Assuming the firm's earnings are taxed at 35 percent, construct the firm's income statement.

b. Compute the firm's operating profit margin.

12. **(Profitability and capital structure analysis)** In the year just ended, Callaway Lighting had sales of $5,000,000 and incurred a cost of goods sold equal to

$4,500,000. The firm's operating expenses were $130,000 and its increase in retained earnings was $40,000 for the year. There are currently 100,000 common-stock shares outstanding and the firm pays a $1.485 dividend per share. The firm has $1,000,000 in interest-bearing debt on which it pays 8 percent interest.

a. Assuming the firm's earnings are taxed at 35 percent, construct the firm's income statement.

b. Calculate the firm's operating profit margin and net profit margin.

c. Compute the times interest earned ratio. What does this ratio tell you about Callaway's ability to pay its interest expense?

d. What is the firm's return on equity?

13. **(DuPont analysis)** Garwryk, Inc., which is financed with debt and equity, presently has a debt ratio of 80 percent. What is the firm's equity multiplier? How is the equity multiplier related to the firm's use of debt financing (i.e., if the firm increased its use of debt financing, would this increase or decrease its equity multiplier)? Explain.

14. **(DuPont analysis)** Triangular Chemicals has total assets of $100 million, a return on equity of 40 percent, a net profit margin of 5 percent, and an equity multiplier of 2.5. How much are the firm's sales?

15. **(DuPont analysis)** Dearborn Supplies has total sales of $200 million, assets of $100 million, a return on equity of 30 percent, and a net profit margin of 7.5 percent. What is the firm's debt ratio?

16. **(DuPont analysis)** Bryley, Inc. earned a net profit margin of 5 percent last year and had an equity multiplier of 3.0. If its total assets are $100 million and its sales are $150 million, what is the firm's return on equity?

17. **(Capital structure analysis)** Last year the Rondoelea Products Company had $140 million in annual sales and a net profit margin of 10 percent. In addition, Rondoelea's average tax rate was 30 percent. If Rondoelea had $40 million of debt outstanding with an average interest rate of 10 percent, what is the firm's times interest earned ratio?

18. **(Related to Checkpoint 1)** **(Liquidity analysis)** The most recent balance sheet of Raconteurs, Inc. (in millions) is as follows:

Current assets	
Cash and marketable securities	$ 10
Accounts receivable	40
Inventory	60
Total	$110
Current liabilities	
Accrued wages and taxes	$ 5
Accounts payable	35
Notes payable	30
Total	$ 70

a. Calculate Raconteurs' current ratio and acid-test (quick) ratio.

b. Benchmark ratios for the current and acid-test (quick) ratio are 1.50 and 1.20, respectively. What can you say about the liquidity of Raconteur's operations based on these two ratios?

19. **(Profitability analysis)** Last year Triangular Resources earned $5 million in net operating income and had an operating profit margin of 20 percent. If the firm's total asset turnover ratio was 1.5, what was the firm's investment in total assets?

20. **(Related to Checkpoint 4)** **(Market value analysis)** Greene, Inc.'s balance sheet indicates that the book value of stockholders' equity (book value per share × total shares outstanding) is $750,500. The firm's earnings per share are $3, which produces a price-earnings ratio of 12.25. If there are 50,000 shares of common stock outstanding, what is the firm's market-to-book ratio (i.e., the ratio of price per share to book value per share)? What does the market-to-book ratio tell us?

21.   **(Market value analysis)** The balance sheet for Larry Underwood Motors shows a book value of stockholders' equity (book value per share × total shares outstanding) of $1,300,000. Furthermore, the firm's income statement for the year just ended has a net income of $500,000, which is $0.25 per share of common stock outstanding. The price-earnings ratio for firms similar to Underwood Motors is 20.

   a. What price would you expect Underwood Motors shares to sell for?
   b. What is the book value per share for Underwood's shares?

22.   **(Market value analysis)** Lei Materials' balance sheet lists total assets of $1 billion, $100 million in current liabilities, $400 million in long-term debt, $500 million in common equity, and 50 million shares of common stock. If Lei's current stock price is $50, what is the firm's market-to-book ratio?

23.   **(Liquidity analysis)** The Mitchem Marble Company has a target current ratio of 2.0 but has experienced some difficulties financing its expanding sales in the past few months. At present, the firm has a current ratio of 2.5 and current assets of $2.5 million. If Mitchem expands its receivables and inventories using its short-term line of credit, how much additional short-term funding can it borrow before its current ratio standard is reached?

24.   **(Liquidity analysis)** When firms enter into loan agreements with their banks, it is very common for the agreement to have a restriction on the minimum current ratio the firm has to maintain. So, it is important that the firm be aware of the effects of its decisions on the current ratio. Consider the situation of Advanced Autoparts (AAP) in 2009. The firm had total current assets of $1,807,626,000 and current liabilities of $1,364,994,000.

   a. What is the firm's current ratio?
   b. If the firm were to expand its investment in inventory and finance the expansion by increasing accounts payable, how much could it increase its inventory without reducing the current ratio below 1.2?
   c. If the company needed to raise its current ratio to 1.5 by reducing its investment in current assets and simultaneously reducing accounts payable and short-term debt, how much would it have to reduce current assets to accomplish this goal?

25.   **(Calculating financial ratios)** The balance sheet and income statement for the J. P. Robard Mfg. Company are as follows:

J. P. Robard Mfg., Inc. Balance Sheet ($000)	
Cash	$ 500
Accounts receivable	2,000
Inventories	1,000
Current assets	3,500
Net fixed assets	4,500
Total assets	$8,000
Accounts payable	$1,100
Accrued expenses	600
Short-term notes payable	300
Current liabilities	$2,000
Long-term debt	2,000
Owners' equity	4,000
Total liabilities and owners' equity	$8,000

J. P. Robard Mfg., Inc. Income Statement ($000)	
Net sales (all credit)	$8,000
Cost of goods sold	(3,300)
Gross profit	$4,700
Operating expenses (includes $500 depreciation)	(3,000)
Net operating income	$1,700
Interest expense	(367)
Earnings before taxes	$1,333
Income taxes (40%)	(533)
Net income	$ 800

Calculate the following ratios:

Current ratio	Operating return on assets
Times interest earned	Debt ratio
Inventory turnover	Average collection period
Total asset turnover	Fixed asset turnover
Operating profit margin	Return on equity

26. **(Financial statement analysis)** Carson Electronics' management has long viewed BGT Electronics as an industry leader and uses this firm as a model firm for analyzing its own performance. The balance sheets and income statements for the two firms are as follows:

	Carson Electronics, Inc. Balance Sheet ($000)	BGT Electronics, Inc. Balance Sheet ($000)
Cash	$ 2,000	$ 1,500
Accounts receivable	4,500	6,000
Inventories	1,500	2,500
Current assets	$ 8,000	$10,000
Net fixed assets	16,000	25,000
Total assets	$24,000	$35,000
Accounts payable	$ 2,500	$ 5,000
Accrued expenses	1,000	1,500
Short-term notes payable	3,500	1,500
Current liabilities	$ 7,000	$ 8,000
Long-term debt	8,000	4,000
Owners' equity	9,000	23,000
Total liabilities and owners' equity	$24,000	$35,000

	Carson Electronics, Inc. Income Statement ($000)	BGT Electronics, Inc. Income Statement ($000)
Net sales (all credit)	$48,000	$70,000
Cost of goods sold	(36,000)	(42,000)
Gross profit	$12,000	$28,000
Operating expenses	(8,000)	(12,000)
Net operating income	$ 4,000	$16,000
Interest expense	(1,150)	(550)
Earnings before taxes	2,850	15,450
Income taxes (40%)	(1,140)	(6,180)
Net income	$ 1,710	$ 9,270

a. Calculate the following ratios for both Carson and BGT:

Current ratio   Operating return on assets

Times interest earned   Debt ratio

Inventory turnover   Average collection period

Total asset turnover   Fixed asset turnover

Operating profit margin   Return on equity

b. Analyze the differences you observe between the two firms. Comment on what you view as weaknesses in the performance of Carson as compared to BGT that Carson's management might focus on to improve its operations.

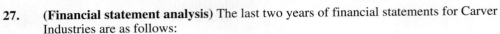

27. **(Financial statement analysis)** The last two years of financial statements for Carver Industries are as follows:

Carver Industries
Balance Sheets for December 31, 2012 and 2013

	2012	2013
Cash	$ 11,250	$ 650
Accounts receivable	15,625	20,800
Inventories	36,250	59,150
Total current assets	$ 63,125	$ 80,600
Land	$ 25,000	$ 33,800
Buildings and equipment	87,500	130,000
Less: Accumulated depreciation	$ (35,000)	$ (49,400)
Total fixed assets	77,500	114,400
Total assets	$140,625	$195,000
Accounts payable	$ 13,125	$ 28,600
Short-term bank notes	21,250	61,100
Total current liabilities	$ 34,375	$ 89,700
Long-term debt	$ 35,938	$ 29,835
Common stock	39,375	40,950
Retained earnings	30,938	34,515
Common equity	$ 70,313	$ 75,465
Total debt and equity	$140,625	$195,000

Carver Industries
Income Statements
Years Ending December 31, 2012 and 2013

	2012	2013
Sales (all credit)	$187,500	$ 400,000
Cost of goods sold	(112,500)	(240,000)
Gross profit	$ 75,000	$ 160,000
Operating expenses		
Fixed cash operating expenses	$ (31,500)	$ (52,500)
Variable operating expenses	(18,750)	(40,000)
Depreciation expense	(6,750)	(25,000)
Total operating expenses	$ (57,000)	$ (117,500)
Earnings before interest and taxes	$ 18,000	$ 42,500
Interest expense	(5,719)	(9,094)
Earnings before taxes	$ 12,281	$ 33,407
Taxes	(6,141)	(16,703)
Net income	$ 6,141	$ 16,703

a. Calculate the following financial ratios for 2012 and 2013:

	Industry Averages	2012	2013
Current ratio	2.00		
Acid-test ratio	0.80		
Average collection period	37 days		
Inventory turnover	2.50		
Debt ratio	58.00%		
Times interest earned	3.80		
Operating profit margin	10.00%		
Total asset turnover	1.14		
Fixed asset turnover	1.40		
Operating return on assets	11.40%		
Return on equity	9.50%		

b. Evaluate the firm's financial position at the end of 2012 in terms of its liquidity, capital structure, asset management efficiency, and profitability.

c. At the end of 2013 the firm has 5,000 shares of common stock outstanding, selling for $15 each. What were the firm's (i) earnings per share, (ii) price-earnings ratio, and (iii) market-to-book ratio?

d. What observations can you make about the financial condition and performance of the firm from your answers to parts a through c?

28. **(Profitability analysis)** The R. M. Smithers Corporation earned an operating profit margin of 10 percent based on sales of $10 million and total assets of $5 million last year.

a. What was Smithers' total asset turnover ratio?

b. During the coming year, the company's president has set a goal of attaining a total asset turnover of 3.5. How much must firm sales increase, other things being the same, for the goal to be achieved? (State your answer in both dollars and the corresponding percent increase in sales.)

c. What was Smithers' operating return on assets last year? Assuming the firm's operating profit margin remains the same, what will the operating return on assets be next year if the total asset turnover goal is achieved?

29. **(Efficiency analysis)** The Brenmar Sales Company had a gross profit margin (gross profits ÷ sales) of 30 percent and sales of $9 million last year. Seventy-five percent of the firm's sales are on credit, and the remainder is cash sales. Brenmar's current assets equal $1.5 million, its current liabilities equal $300,000, and it has $100,000 in cash plus marketable securities.

a. If Brenmar's accounts receivable equal $562,500, what is its average collection period?

b. If Brenmar reduces its average collection period to 20 days, what will be its new level of accounts receivable?

c. Brenmar's inventory turnover ratio is 9 times. What is the level of Brenmar's inventories?

30. **(Financial statement analysis)** Using the following financial statements for Pamplin, Inc:

a. Compute the following ratios for both 2012 and 2013 using the financial statements that follow.

	Industry Norm
Current ratio	5.00
Acid-test (quick) ratio	3.00
Inventory turnover	2.20
Average collection period	90 days
Debt ratio	0.33
Times interest earned	7.00
Total asset turnover	0.75
Fixed asset turnover	1.00
Operating profit margin	20%
Return on equity	9%

b. Compare Pamplin's financial ratios to the industry norms listed above and assess each of the following attributes of the firm's financial condition: liquidity, capital structure, asset management efficiency, and profitability.

Pamplin, Inc.
Balance Sheets

Assets	2012	2013
Cash	$ 200	$ 150
Accounts receivable	450	425
Inventory	550	625
Current assets	$ 1,200	$ 1,200
Plant and equipment	$ 2,200	$ 2,600
Less: Accumulated depreciation	(1,000)	(1,200)
Net plant and equipment	$ 1,200	$ 1,400
Total assets	$ 2,400	$ 2,600

Liabilities and Owners' Equity	2012	2013
Accounts payable	$ 200	$ 150
Notes payable—current (9% interest)	0	150
Current liabilities	$ 200	$ 300
Bonds (8.33% interest)	$ 600	$ 600
Owners' equity		
Common stock	$ 300	$ 300
Paid-in capital	600	600
Retained earnings	700	800
Total owners' equity	$1,600	$1,700
Total liabilities and owners' equity	$2,400	$2,600

Pamplin, Inc.

Income Statements	2012	2013
Sales (all credit)	$1,200	$1,450
Cost of goods sold	700	850
Gross profit	$ 500	$ 600
Operating expenses (cash)	$ 30	$ 40
Depreciation expense	220	200
Total operating expenses	$ 250	$ 240
Net operating income	$ 250	$ 360
Interest expense	50	64
Earnings before taxes	$ 200	$ 296
Taxes (40%)	80	118
Net income	$ 120	$ 178

31. **(Financial statement analysis)** The annual sales for Salco, Inc. were $4.5 million last year. The firm's end-of-year balance sheet was as follows:

Current assets	$500,000	Liabilities	$1,000,000
Net fixed assets	1,500,000	Owners' equity	1,000,000
Total	$2,000,000	Total	$2,000,000

Salco's income statement for the year was as follows:

Sales	$ 4,500,000
Less: Cost of goods sold	(3,500,000)
Gross profit	$ 1,000,000
Less: Operating expenses	(500,000)
Net operating income	$ 500,000
Less: Interest expense	(100,000)
Earnings before taxes	$ 400,000
Less: Taxes (35%)	(140,000)
Net income	$ 260,000

a. Calculate Salco's total asset turnover, operating profit margin, and operating return on assets.

b. Salco plans to renovate one of its plants and the renovation will require an added investment in plant and equipment of $1 million. The firm will maintain its present debt ratio of 50 percent when financing the new investment and expects sales to remain constant. The operating profit margin will rise to 13 percent. What will be the new operating return on assets ratio (i.e., net operating income/total assets) for Salco after the plant's renovation?

c. Given that the plant renovation in part b occurs and Salco's interest expense rises by $50,000 per year, what will be the return earned on the common stockholders' investment? Compare this rate of return with that earned before the renovation. Based on this comparison, did the renovation have a favorable effect on the profitability of the firm?

32. **(Financial statement analysis)** The T. P. Jarmon Company manufactures and sells a line of exclusive sportswear. The firm's sales were $600,000 for the year just ended, and its total assets exceeded $400,000. The company was started by Mr. Jarmon just 10 years ago and has been profitable every year since its inception. The chief financial officer for the firm, Brent Vehlim, has decided to seek a line of credit from the firm's bank totaling $80,000. In the past, the company has relied on its suppliers to finance a large part of its needs for inventory. However, in recent months tight money conditions have led the firm's suppliers to offer sizable cash discounts to speed up payments for purchases. Mr. Vehlim wants to use the line of credit to supplant a large portion of the firm's payables during the summer, which is the firm's peak seasonal sales period.

The firm's two most recent balance sheets were presented to the bank in support of its loan request. In addition, the firm's income statement for the year just ended was provided. These statements are found in the following tables:

T. P. Jarmon Company Balance Sheets

	2012	2013
Cash	$115,000	$114,000
Marketable securities	6,000	6,200
Accounts receivable	42,000	33,000
Inventory	51,000	84,000
Prepaid rent	1,200	1,100
Total current assets	$115,200	$138,300
Net plant and equipment	286,000	270,000
Total assets	$401,200	$408,300

	2012	2013
Accounts payable	$ 48,000	$ 57,000
Notes payable	15,000	13,000
Accruals	6,000	5,000
Total current liabilities	$ 69,000	$ 75,000
Long-term debt	$160,000	$150,000
Common stockholders' equity	$172,200	$183,300
Total liabilities and equity	$401,200	$408,300

T. P. Jarmon Company
Income Statement for 2013

Sales (all credit)		$600,000
Less: Cost of goods sold		460,000
Gross profit		$140,000
Less: Operating and interest expenses		
General and administrative	$30,000	
Interest	10,000	
Depreciation	30,000	
Total		$ 70,000
Earnings before taxes		$ 70,000
Less: Taxes		27,100
Net income available to common stockholders		$ 42,900
Less: Cash dividends		31,800
Change in retained earnings		$ 11,100

Jan Fama, associate credit analyst for the Merchants National Bank of Midland, Michigan, was assigned the task of analyzing Jarmon's loan request.

a. Calculate the following financial ratios for 2013:

	Ratio Norms
Current ratio	1.8
Acid-test ratio	0.9
Debt ratio	0.5
Times interest earned	10.0
Average collection period	20.0
Inventory turnover (based on cost of goods sold)	7.0
Return on equity	12.0%
Operating return on assets	16.8%
Operating profit margin	14.0%
Total asset turnover	1.2
Fixed asset turnover	1.8

b. Which of the ratios calculated in part a do you think should be most crucial in determining whether the bank should extend the line of credit?

c. Use the information provided by the financial ratios and industry-norm ratios to decide if you would support making the loan. Discuss the basis for your recommendation.

33. **(Analyzing market values using financial ratios)** On August 1, 2007, Dell Computer Corporation's stock closed trading at $27.76 per share, whereas Apple Corporation's shares closed at $133.64. Does this mean that because Apple's stock price is roughly four times that of Dell's, Apple is the more valuable company? Interpret the prices for these two firms using the following information:

(Most recent 12 months)	Dell 2007	Apple 2007
Net income ($ millions)	$3,572	$ 3,130
Shares outstanding (millions)	2,300	869.16
Earnings per share ($)	$ 1.55	$ 3.60
Price per share (8/1/07)	$27.76	$133.64
Price-to-earnings ratio (PE ratio)	**17.91**	**37.11**
Book value of common equity ($ millions)	$4,129	$ 9,984
Book value per share ($)	$ 1.80	$ 11.49
Market-to-book ratio	**15.42**	**11.63**

34. **(Analyzing market values using financial ratios)** On May 25, 2009, the stock of Emerson Electric (EMR) was trading for $32.18 per share, whereas the stock of its larger rival, the General Electric Corporation (GE), was trading for only $13.11. Interpret the relative pricing of the two firm's shares using the following information:

(Most recent 12 months)	Emerson Electric (EMR) 2009	General Electric (GE) 2009
Net income ($ millions)	$ 2,170	$ 16,420
Shares outstanding	787,658,802	10,662,337,662
Earnings per share ($)	$ 2.76	$ 1.54
Price per share (5/25/09)	$ 32.18	$ 13.11
Price-to-earnings ratio (PE ratio)	11.68	8.51
Book value of common equity ($ millions)	$ 8,608	$101,708
Book value per share ($)	$10.929	$ 9.539
Market-to-book ratio	2.94	1.37

Selecting a Performance Benchmark

35. **(Selecting a benchmark company)** The National Semiconductor Corporation (NSM) develops and manufactures semiconductors for electronic systems. The firm's products are used in a variety of applications, including LED lighting, high-speed communications, renewable energy, and security and surveillance. The company's chief financial officer (CFO) has a report prepared annually that compares the firm's performance to that of several key competitors. The CFO has identified Analog Devices Inc. (ADI) and Texas Instruments (TXN) as key competitors. Selected information for all three companies follows for the 12-month period ended June 2009. Based on this information, which of the two companies appears to be the best match for a performance benchmark, and why?

	National Semiconductor (NSM)	Analog Devices Inc. (ADI)	Texas Instruments (TXN)
Revenue (billions)	$ 1.64	$ 2.27	$11.32
Gross margin	64.41%	58.83%	46.80%
Operating margin	25.35%	20.09%	17.67%
Net income	220.20M	349.78M	1.28B
Earnings per share	$0.924	$1.225	$0.978
Price-to-earnings ratio	15.56	20.48	21.31

36. **(Selecting a benchmark company)** Following you will find the income statements and balance sheets for Sears Holdings (SHLD) and Target Corp (TGT). Assume that you are a financial manager at Sears and want to compare your firm's situation with Target. Calculate representative ratios for liquidity, asset management efficiency, financial leverage (capital structure), and profitability for both Sears and Target. How would you summarize the financial performance of Sears compared to Target (its benchmark firm)?

Period Ended	Sears Holdings (SHLD) 31-Jan-09	Target Corp (TGT) 31-Jan-09
Total revenue	$46,770,000	$64,948,000
Cost of revenue	34,118,000	44,157,000
Gross profit	$12,652,000	$20,791,000
Operating expenses	12,050,000	16,389,000
Operating income or loss	$ 302,000	$ 4,402,000
Interest expense	272,000	894,000
Net income	$ 53,000	$ 2,214,000

	Sears Holdings (SHLD)	Target Corp (TGT)
PERIOD ENDING	31-Jan-09	31-Jan-09
Cash and cash equivalents	$ 864,000	$ 1,297,000
Accounts receivable	9,446,000	866,000
Inventory	6,705,000	8,795,000
Other current assets	473,000	458,000
Total current assets	$17,488,000	$11,416,000
Long-term investments	163,000	
Property, plant, and equipment	25,756,000	8,091,000
Other assets	699,000	5,835,000
Total assets	$44,106,000	$25,342,000
Liabilities		
Accounts payable	$ 7,366,000	$ 3,430,000
Short-/current long-term debt	1,262,000	787,000
Other current liabilities	1,884,000	4,295,000
Total current liabilities	$10,512,000	$ 8,512,000
Long-term debt	17,490,000	2,132,000
Other long-term liabilities	12,904,000	13,830,000
Total liabilities	$30,394,000	$15,962,000
Total stockholders' equity	13,712,000	9,380,000
Total liabilities and owners' equity	$44,106,000	$25,342,000

Mini-Case

Go to http://finance.yahoo.com/ and locate current financial information for Starbucks Corp. (SBUX) and McDonald's Corp. (MCD), both in terms of each company's current financial statements and stock market prices. With this information:

a. Compute the financial ratios for both firms for the most recent year, and evaluate the relative performance of the two firms in the following areas:
1. Liquidity
2. Asset-management efficiency
3. Financing practices (capital structure)
4. Profitability

b. What is each firm's current price-to-earnings ratio and market-to-book ratio? What do these ratios tell you about how investors value these two firms' future prospects?

c. Based on your analysis, what is your personal assessment of the two firms' past performance?

Photo Credits

Time Value of Money-
The Basics

From Chapter 5 of *Financial Management: Principles and Applications*, Twelfth Edition. Sheridan Titman, Arthur J. Keown, and John D. Martin.

Time Value of Money
The Basics

Chapter **Outline**

1 Using Timelines to Visualize Cash Flows

→ **Objective 1.** Construct cash flow timelines to organize your analysis of problems involving the time value of money.

2 Compounding and Future Value

→ **Objective 2.** Understand compounding and calculate the future value of cash flows using mathematical formulas, a financial calculator, and an Excel spreadsheet.

3 Discounting and Present Value

→ **Objective 3.** Understand discounting and calculate the present value of cash flows using mathematical formulas, a financial calculator, and an Excel spreadsheet.

4 Making Interest Rates Comparable

→ **Objective 4.** Understand how interest rates are quoted and know how to make them comparable.

Principle **P1** **Applied**

This chapter is dedicated to P Principle 1: **Money Has a Time Value**. This basic idea—a dollar received today, other things being the same, is worth more than a dollar received a year from now—underlies many financial decisions faced in business. In this chapter, we learn how to calculate the value today of money you will receive in the future, as well as the future value of money you have today.

Payday Loans

Sometimes marketed to college students as quick relief for urgent expenses, a payday loan is a short-term loan to cover expenses until the next payday. As some borrowers turn to these loans during times of financial desperation, lenders can charge them extremely high rates of interest. For example, in 2012, one payday lender advertised that you could borrow $500 and repay $626.37 in eight days. This might not sound like a bad deal on the surface, but if we apply some basic rules of finance to analyze this loan, we see quite a different story. The annual interest rate for this payday loan is a whopping 2,916,780 percent! (We will examine this later in the chapter .)

The very high rates of interest charged by these lenders have led some states to impose limits on the interest rates payday lenders can charge. Even so, the cost of this type of loan can be extremely high. Understanding the time value of money is an essential tool to analyzing the cost of this and other types of financing.

Regardless of Your Major...

"A Dollar Saved Is Two Dollars Earned"

Suppose that you and your classmate each receive a gift of $10,000 from grandparents, but choose different ways to invest the newfound money. You immediately invest your gift until retirement, whereas your classmate carries around his gift in his wallet in the form of 100 crisp $100 bills. Then, after 15 years of carrying around a fat wallet, your classmate decides to invest his $10,000 for retirement.

If you invest your $10,000 for 46 years and earn 10 percent per year until you retire, you'll end up with over $800,000. If your classmate invests his $10,000 for 31 years (remember that he carried his money around for 15 years in his wallet) and earns the same 10 percent per year, he'll only end up with about $192,000. Knowing about the power of the time value of money provided you with an additional $600,000 at retirement. In this chapter we'll learn more about these kinds of valuation problems. For now, keep in mind that the time value of money is a concept you will want to understand, regardless of your major.

Your Turn: See Study Question 7 and 8.

 # Using Timelines to Visualize Cash Flows

To evaluate a new project, a financial manager must be able to compare benefits and costs that occur at different times. We will use the time-value-of-money tools we develop in this chapter to make the benefits and costs comparable, allowing us to make logical decisions. We begin our study of time value analysis by introducing some basic tools. As a first step, we can construct a **timeline**, a linear representation of the timing of cash flows. A timeline identifies the timing and amount of a stream of payments—both cash received and cash spent—along with the interest rate earned. Timelines are a critical first step that financial analysts use to solve financial problems.

To learn how to construct a timeline, consider the following example, where we have annual cash inflows and outflows over the course of four years. The following timeline illustrates these cash inflows and outflows from time Period 0 (the present) until the end of Year 4:

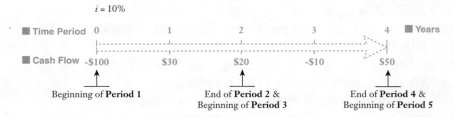

For our purposes, time periods are identified on the top of the timeline. In this example, the time periods are measured in years, indicated on the far right of the timeline. For example, time Period 0 in this example is the current year. The dollar amount of the cash flow received or spent during each time period is shown below the timeline. Positive values represent *cash inflows*. Negative values represent *cash outflows*. For example, in the timeline shown, a $100 cash outflow occurs at the beginning of the first year (at Time 0), followed by cash inflows of $30 and $20 in Years 1 and 2, a cash outflow (a negative cash flow) of $10 in Year 3, and finally a cash inflow of $50 in Year 4.

Timelines are typically expressed in years, but could be expressed in months, days, or, for that matter, any unit of time. For now, let's assume we're looking at cash flows that occur annually, so the distance between 0 and 1 represents the time period between today and the end of the first year. The interest rate, 10 percent in this example, is listed above the timeline.

Checkpoint 1

Creating a Timeline

Suppose you lend a friend $10,000 today to help him finance a new Jimmy John's Sub Shop franchise and in return he promises to give you $12,155 at the end of the fourth year. How can one represent this as a timeline? Note that the interest rate is 5%.

STEP 1: Picture the problem

A timeline provides a tool for visualizing cash flows and time:

STEP 2: Decide on a solution strategy

To complete the timeline we simply record the cash flows onto the template.

STEP 3: Solve

We can input the cash flows for this investment on the timeline as shown below. Time period zero (the present) is shown at the left end of the timeline, and future time periods are shown above the timeline, moving from left to right, with the year that each cash flow occurs shown above the timeline.

Keep in mind that Year 1 represents the end of the first year as well as the beginning of the second year.

STEP 4: Analyze

Using timelines to visualize cash flows is useful in financial problem solving. From analyzing the timeline, we can see that there are two cash flows, an initial $10,000 cash outflow, and a $12,155 cash inflow at the end of Year 4.

STEP 5: Check yourself

Draw a timeline for an investment of $40,000 today that returns nothing in one year, $20,000 at the end of Year 2, nothing in Year 3, and $40,000 at the end of Year 4, where the interest rate is 13.17 percent.

ANSWER:

>> **END Checkpoint 1**

Before you move on to 2

Concept Check | 1

1. What is a timeline, and how does it help you solve problems involving the time value of money?
2. Does Year 5 represent the end of the fifth year, the beginning of the sixth year, or both?

145

2 Compounding and Future Value

If we assume that an investment will only earn interest on the original principal, we call this **simple interest**. Suppose that you put $100 in a savings account earning 6 percent interest annually. How much will your savings grow after one year? If you invest for one year at an interest rate of 6 percent, you will earn 6 percent simple interest on your initial deposit of $100, giving you a total of $106 in your account. What if you left your $100 in the bank for two years? In this case, you will earn interest not only on your original $100 deposit but also on the $6 in interest you earned during the first year. This process of accumulating interest on an investment over multiple time periods is called **compounding**. And, when interest is earned on both the initial principal and the reinvested interest during prior periods, the result is called **compound interest**.

Time-value-of-money calculations are essentially comparisons between what we will refer to as **present value**, what a cash flow would be worth to you today, and **future value**, what a cash flow will be worth in the future. The following is a mathematical formula that shows how these concepts relate to each other when the future value is in one year:

$$\text{Future Value in 1 Year} = \text{Present Value} \times (1 + \text{Interest Rate}) \qquad \textbf{(1)}$$

In the earlier example, you began with a $100 investment, so the present value is $100. The future value in one year is then given by the equation

$$\$100 \times (1 + .06) = \$106.00$$

To see how to calculate the future value in two years, let's do a timeline and a few calculations:

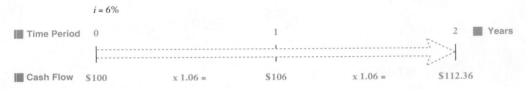

During the first year, your $100 deposit earns $6 in interest. Summing the interest and the original deposit gives you a balance of $106 at the end of the first year. In the second year, you earn $6.36 in interest, giving you a future value of $112.36. Why do you earn $0.36 more in interest during the second year than during the first? Because in the second year, you earn an additional 6 percent on the $6 in interest you earned in the first year. This amounts to $0.36 (or $6 × .06). Again, this result is an example of compound interest. Anyone who has ever had a savings account or purchased a government savings bond has received compound interest.

What happens to the value of your investment at the end of the third year, assuming the same interest rate of 6 percent? We can follow the same approach to calculate the future value in three years.

Using a timeline, we can calculate the future value of your $100 as follows:

Note that every time we extend the analysis for one more period, we just multiply the previous balance by *(1 + Interest Rate)*. Consequently, the future value of any amount of money for any number of periods can be expressed with the following equation, where *n* = the number of periods during which the compounding occurs:

$$\text{Future Value}_{\text{Period } n} = \text{Present Value (Deposit)} \times \left(1 + \text{Interest Rate } (i)\right)^{n}$$

or

$$FV_n = PV\left(1 + i\right)^{n} \qquad \text{(1a)}$$

where FV_n is the Future Value in Year n, PV is the Present Value, i is the Annual Interest Rate, and n is the Number of Years.

Important Definitions and Concepts:

- FV_n = the future value of the investment at the end of n periods.
- i = the interest (or growth) rate per period.
- PV = the present value, or original amount invested at the beginning of the first period.

We also refer to $(1 + i)^n$ as the **future value interest factor**. To find the future value of a dollar amount, simply multiply that dollar amount by the appropriate future value interest factor,

$$FV_n = PV(1 + i)^n$$

$$FV_n = PV \times \text{Future Value Interest Factor}$$

$$\text{where, Future Value Interest Factor} = (1 + i)^n$$

Panel A in Figure 1 shows what your investment of $100 would grow to in four years if it continues to earn an annual compound interest rate of 6 percent. Notice how the amount of interest earned increases each year. In the first year, you earn only $6, but by Year 4, you earn $7.15 in interest.

Prior to the introduction of inexpensive financial calculators and Excel, future values were commonly calculated using time-value-of-money tables containing future value interest factors for different combinations of i and n. Table 1 provides an abbreviated future value interest factor table. So, to find the value of $100 invested for four years at 6 percent, we would simply look at the intersection of the $n = 4$ row and the 6% column, finding a future value interest factor of 1.262. We would then multiply this value by $100 to find that our investment of $100 at 6 percent for four years would grow to $126.20.

Compound Interest and Time

As Panel C of Figure 1 shows, the future value of an investment grows with the number of periods we let it compound. For example, after five years, the future value of $100 earning 10 percent interest each year will be $161.05. However, after 25 years, the future value of that investment will be $1,083.47. Note that although we increased the number of years threefold, the future value increases by more than sixfold ($1,083.47/$161.05 = 6.7 fold). This illustrates an important point: Future value is not directly proportional to time. Instead, future value grows exponentially. This means it grows by a fixed percentage each year, which means that the dollar value grows by an increasing amount each year.

Compound Interest and the Interest Rate

Panel C of Figure 1 illustrates that future value increases dramatically with the level of the rate of interest. For example, the future value of $100 in 25 years, given a 10 percent interest rate, compounded annually, is $1,083.47. However, if we double the rate of interest to 20 percent, the future value increases almost ninefold in 25 years to equal $9,539.62. This illustrates another important point: The increase in future value is not directly proportional to the increase in the rate of interest. We doubled the rate of interest, and the future value of the investment increased by 8.80 times. Why did the future value jump by so much? Because there is a lot of time over 25 years for the higher interest rate to result in more interest being earned on interest.

Figure 1

Future Value and Compound Interest Illustrated

(Panel A) Calculating Compound Interest

This panel shows how interest compounds annually. During the first year, $100 invested at a 6% interest rate earns only $6. Because we earn 6% on the ending value for Year 1 (or $106), in Year 2 we earn $6.36 in interest. This increase in the amount of interest results from interest being earned on both the initial deposit of $100 plus the $6.00 in interest earned during Year 1. The fact that we earn interest on both principal and interest is why we refer to this as compound interest. Simple interest, on the other hand, would be earning only $6.00 in interest each and every year.

$$\boxed{\text{Interest Earned} = \text{Beginning Value} \times \text{Interest Rate}}$$

Year	Beginning Value	Interest Earned	Ending Value
1	$ 100.00	$ 6.00	$ 106.00
2	$ 106.00	$ 6.36	$ 112.36
3	$ 112.36	$ 6.74	$ 119.10
4	$ 119.10	$ 7.15	$ 126.25

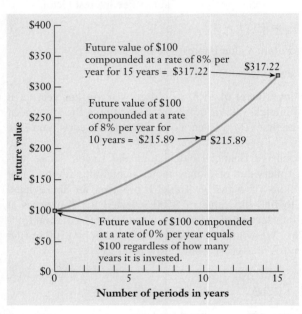

Future value of $100 compounded at a rate of 8% per year for 15 years = $317.22

Future value of $100 compounded at a rate of 8% per year for 10 years = $215.89

Future value of $100 compounded at a rate of 0% per year equals $100 regardless of how many years it is invested.

(Panel B) The Power of Time

This figure illustrates the importance of time when it comes to compounding. Because interest is earned on past interest, the future value of $100 deposited in an account that earns 8% compounded annually grows over threefold in 15 years. If we were to expand this figure to 45 years (which is about how long you have until you retire, assuming you're around 20 years old right now), it would grow to over 31 times its initial value.

(Panel C) The Power of the Rate of Interest

This figure illustrates the importance of the interest rate in the power of compounding. As the interest rate climbs, so does the future value. In fact, when we change the interest rate from 10% to 20%, the future value in 25 years increases by over 8 times, jumping from $1,083.47 to $9,539.62.

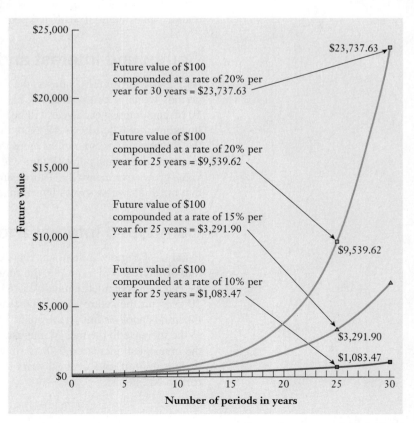

Future value of $100 compounded at a rate of 20% per year for 30 years = $23,737.63

Future value of $100 compounded at a rate of 20% per year for 25 years = $9,539.62

Future value of $100 compounded at a rate of 15% per year for 25 years = $3,291.90

Future value of $100 compounded at a rate of 10% per year for 25 years = $1,083.47

>> END FIGURE 1

Table 1	Future Value Interest Factors			
Number of Periods (*n*)	***i* = 3%**	***i* = 6%**	***i* = 9%**	***i* = 12%**
1	1.030	1.060	1.090	1.120
2	1.061	1.124	1.188	1.254
3	1.093	1.191	1.295	1.405
4	1.126	1.262	1.412	1.574

Techniques for Moving Money through Time

In this chapter, we will refer to three methods for solving problems involving the time value of money: mathematical formulas, financial calculators, and spreadsheets.

- **Do the math.** You can use the mathematical formulas just as we have done in this chapter. You simply substitute the values that you know into the appropriate time-value-of-money equation to find the answer.
- **Use financial calculators.** Financial calculators have preprogrammed functions that make time-value-of-money calculations simple.
- **Use a spreadsheet on your personal computer.** Spreadsheet software such as Excel has preprogrammed functions built into it. The same inputs that are used with a financial calculator are also used as inputs to Excel. As a result, if you can correctly set a problem up to solve on your financial calculator, you can easily set it up to solve using Excel. In the business world, Excel is the spreadsheet of choice and is the most common way of moving money through time.

Because the authors of this chapter believe that spending enough time solving problems the old-fashioned way—by doing the math—leads to a deeper understanding and better retention of the concepts, we will first demonstrate how to solve problems using the formulas; but we will also demonstrate, whenever possible, how to derive the solution using a financial calculator and Excel.

Applying Compounding to Things Other Than Money

Although this chapter focuses on moving money through time at a given interest rate, the concept of compounding applies to almost anything that grows. For example, let's suppose we're interested in knowing how big the market for wireless printers will be in five years, and assume the demand for them is expected to grow at a rate of 25 percent per year over the next five years. We can calculate the future value of the market for printers using the same formula we used to calculate the future value for a sum of money. If the market is currently 25,000 printers per year, then 25,000 would be *PV*, *n* would be 5, and *i* would be 25 percent. Substituting into Equation (1a) we would solve for *FV*,

$$\begin{matrix} \text{Future Value} \\ \text{in Year } n \\ (FV_n) \end{matrix} = \begin{matrix} \text{Present} \\ \text{Value } (PV) \end{matrix} \left(1 + \begin{matrix} \text{Annual} \\ \text{Interest Rate } (i) \end{matrix} \right)^{\begin{matrix} \text{Number of} \\ \text{Years } (n) \end{matrix}} = 25{,}000 \, (1 + .25)^5 = 76{,}293$$

The power of compounding can also be illustrated through the story of a peasant who wins a chess tournament sponsored by the king. The king then asks him what he would like as his prize. The peasant answers that, for his village, he would like one grain of wheat to be placed on the first square of his chessboard, two pieces on the second square, four on the third square, eight on the fourth square, and so forth, until the board is filled up. The king, thinking he was getting off easy, pledged his word of honor that this would be done. Unfortunately for the king, by the time all 64 squares on the chessboard were filled, there were 18.5 million trillion grains of wheat on the board, because the kernels were compounding at a rate of 100 percent over the 64 squares of the chessboard. In fact, if the kernels were one-quarter inch long, they would have stretched, if laid end to end, to the sun and back 391,320 times! Needless to say, no one in the village ever went hungry. What can we conclude from this story? There is incredible power in compounding.

Compound Interest with Shorter Compounding Periods

So far, we have assumed that the compounding period is always a year in length. However, this isn't always the case. For example, banks often offer savings accounts that compound

---

Checkpoint 2

Calculating the Future Value of a Cash Flow

You are put in charge of managing your firm's working capital. Your firm has $100,000 in extra cash on hand and decides to put it in a savings account paying 7 percent interest compounded annually. How much will you have in your account in 10 years?

STEP 1: Picture the problem

We can set up a timeline to identify the cash flows from the investment as follows:

i = 7%

| Time Period | 0 | 1 | 2 | 3 | 4 | 5 | 6 | 7 | 8 | 9 | 10 | Years |

Cash Flow -$100,000   Future Value = ?

STEP 2: Decide on a solution strategy

This is a simple future value problem. We can find the future value using Equation (1a).

STEP 3: Solve

Using the Mathematical Formulas. Substituting PV = $100,000, i = 7%, and n = 10 years into Equation (1a), we get

$$\text{Future Value in Year } n \ (FV_n) = \text{Present Value } (PV) \left(1 + \frac{\text{Annual Interest Rate } (i)}{}\right)^{\text{Number of Years } (n)} \tag{1a}$$

$$FV_n = \$100,000(1 + .07)^{10}$$
$$= \$100,000(1.96715)$$
$$= \$196,715$$

At the end of 10 years, you will have $196,715 in the savings account.

Using a Financial Calculator.

Enter	10	7.0	−100,000	0	
	N	I/Y	PV	PMT	FV
Solve for					196,715

Using an Excel Spreadsheet.

= FV(rate,nper,pmt,pv) or with values entered = FV(0.07,10,0,−100000)

STEP 4: Analyze

Notice that you input the present value with a negative sign because present value represents a cash outflow. In effect, the money leaves your firm when it's first invested. In this problem your firm invested $100,000 at 7 percent and found that it will grow to $196,715 after 10 years. Put another way, given a 7 percent compound rate, your $100,000 today will be worth $196,715 in 10 years.

STEP 5: Check yourself

What is the future value of $10,000 compounded at 12 percent annually for 20 years?

ANSWER: $96,462.93.

Your Turn: For more practice, do related **Study Problems** 1, 2, 4, 6, and 8 through 11 at the end of this chapter.

>> END Checkpoint 2

interest every day, month, or quarter. Savers prefer more frequent compounding because they earn interest on their interest sooner and more frequently. Fortunately, it's easy to adjust for different compounding periods, and later in the chapter we will examine how to compare two loans with different compounding periods in more detail.

Consider the following example: You invest $100 for five years to earn a rate of 8 percent, and the investment is compounded semiannually (twice a year). This means that interest is calculated every six months. Essentially, you are investing your money for 10 six-month periods, and in each period, you will receive 4 percent interest. In effect, we divide the annual interest rate (i) by the number of compounding periods per year (m), and we multiply the number of years (n) times the number of compounding periods per year (m) to convert the number of years into the number of periods. So, our future value formula found in Equation (1a) must be adjusted as follows:

$$\text{Future Value in Year } n\ (FV_n) = \text{Present Value } (PV) \left(1 + \frac{\text{Annual Interest Rate } (i)}{\text{Compounding Periods per Year } (m)}\right)^{m \times (\text{Number of Years } (n))} \quad \textbf{(1b)}$$

Substituting into Equation (1b) gives us the following estimate of the future value in five years:

$$FV_n = \$100\ (1 + .08/2)^{2 \times 5}$$
$$= \$100(1.4802)$$
$$= \$148.02$$

But if the compounding had been annual rather than semiannual, the future value of the investment would have been only $146.93. Although the difference here seems modest, it can be significant when large sums of money are involved and the number of years and the number of compounding periods within those years are both large. For example, for your $100 investment, the difference is only $1.09. But if the amount were $50 million (not an unusually large bank balance for a major company), the difference would be $545,810.41.

Table 2 shows how shorter compounding periods lead to higher future values. For example, if you invested $100 at 15 percent for one year, and the investment was compounded

Table 2 The Value of $100 Compounded at Various Non-Annual Periods and Various Rates

Notice that the impact of shorter compounding periods is heightened by both higher interest rates and compounding over longer time periods.

For 1 Year at *i* Percent	*i* = 2%	5%	10%	15%	
Compounded annually	$102.00	$105.00	$110.00	**$115.00**	
Compounded semiannually	102.01	105.06	110.25	115.56	
Compounded quarterly	102.02	105.09	110.38	115.87	$1.18
Compounded monthly	102.02	105.12	110.47	116.08	
Compounded weekly (52)	102.02	105.12	110.51	116.16	
Compounded daily (365)	102.02	105.13	110.52	**116.18**	
For 10 Years at *i* Percent	*i* = 2%	5%	10%	15%	
Compounded annually	$121.90	$162.89	$259.37	**$404.56**	
Compounded semiannually	122.02	163.86	265.33	424.79	
Compounded quarterly	122.08	164.36	268.51	436.04	$43.47
Compounded monthly	122.12	164.70	270.70	444.02	
Compounded weekly (52)	122.14	164.83	271.57	447.20	
Compounded daily (365)	122.14	164.87	271.79	**448.03**	

Calculating Future Values Using Non-Annual Compounding Periods

You have been put in charge of managing your firm's cash position and noticed that the Plaza National Bank of Portland, Oregon, has recently decided to begin paying interest compounded semiannually instead of annually. If you deposit $1,000 with Plaza National Bank at an interest rate of 12 percent, what will your account balance be in five years?

STEP 1: Picture the problem

If you earn a 12 percent annual rate compounded semiannually for five years, you really earn 6 percent every six months for 10 six-month periods. Expressed as a timeline, this problem would look like the following:

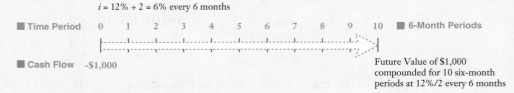

$i = 12\% \div 2 = 6\%$ every 6 months

| ■ Time Period | 0 | 1 | 2 | 3 | 4 | 5 | 6 | 7 | 8 | 9 | 10 | ■ 6-Month Periods |

■ Cash Flow   -$1,000

Future Value of $1,000 compounded for 10 six-month periods at 12%/2 every 6 months

STEP 2: Decide on a solution strategy

In this instance we are simply solving for the future value of $1,000. The only twist is that interest is calculated on a semiannual basis. Thus, if you earn 12 percent compounded semiannually for five years, you really earn 6 percent every six months for 10 six-month periods. We can calculate the future value of the $1,000 investment using Equation (1b).

STEP 3: Solve

Using the Mathematical Formulas. Substituting number of years (n) = 5, number of compounding periods per year (m) = 2, annual interest rate (i) = 12%, and PV = $1,000 into Equation (1b):

$$\text{Future Value in Year } n \, (FV_n) = \text{Present Value } (PV) \left(1 + \frac{\text{Annual Interest Rate } (i)}{\text{Compounding Periods per Year } (m)}\right)^{m \times (\text{Number of Years } (n))}$$

$$\text{Future Value in Year } n \, (FV_n) = \$1,000 \left(1 + \frac{.12}{2}\right)^{2 \times 5} = \$1,000 \times 1.79085 = \$1,790.85$$

Using a Financial Calculator.

Enter	10	6.0	-1,000	0	
	N	I/Y	PV	PMT	FV
Solve for					1,790.85

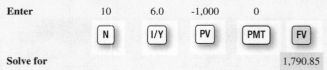

You will have $1,790.85 at the end of five years.

Using an Excel Spreadsheet.

= FV(rate,nper,pmt,pv) or with values entered = FV(0.06,10,0,−1000)

STEP 4: Analyze

The more often interest is compounded per year—that is, the larger m is, resulting in a larger value of nper—the larger the future value will be. That's because you are earning interest more often on the interest you've previously earned.

STEP 5: Check yourself

If you deposit $50,000 in an account that pays an annual interest rate of 10 percent compounded monthly, what will your account balance be in 10 years?

ANSWER: $135,352.07.

Your Turn: For more practice, do related **Study Problems** 5 and 7 at the end of this chapter.

>> END Checkpoint 3

The Business of Life

Saving for Your First House

There was a time in the early and mid-2000s when you didn't need to worry about a down payment when you bought a new house. But that all changed as the housing bubble burst and home prices fell. Today you may be able to get away with only putting down around 10 percent, but the rate on your mortgage will be lower if you can come up with 20 percent. To buy a median-priced home, which was just over $180,000 at the beginning of 2013, you'd have to come up with a 10 percent down payment of $18,000 or a 20 percent down payment of $36,000. On top of that, you'll need to furnish your new home, and that costs money too.

Putting into practice what you have learned in this chapter, you know that the sooner you start to save for your first home, the easier it will be. Once you estimate how much you'll need for that new house, you can easily calculate how much you'll need to save annually to reach your goal. All you need to do is look at two variables: *n* (the number of years you'll be saving the money) and *i* (the interest rate at which the savings will grow). You can start saving earlier, which gives you a larger value for *n*. Or, you can earn more on your investments—that is, invest at a higher value for *i*. Of course, you always prefer getting a higher *i* on your savings, but this is not something you can control.

First, let's take a look at a higher value for *i*, which translates into a higher return. For example, let's say you've just inherited $10,000, and you invest it at 6 percent annually for 10 years—after which you want to buy your first house. The calculation is easy. At the end of 10 years, you will have accumulated $17,908 on this investment. But suppose you are able to earn 12 percent annually for 10 years. What would the value of your investment be then? In this case, your investment would be worth $31,058. Needless to say, the rate of interest that you earn plays a major role in determining how quickly your investment will grow.

Now consider what happens if you wait five years before investing your $10,000. The value of *n* drops from 10 to 5, and, as a result, the amount you've saved also drops. In fact, if you invested your $10,000 for five years at 6 percent, you'd end up with $13,382, and even at 12 percent you'd end up with only $17,623.

The bottom line is the earlier you begin saving, the more impact every dollar you save will have.

Your Turn: See Study Problem 3.

daily rather than annually, you would end up with $1.18 ($116.18 − $115.00) more. However, if the period were extended to 10 years, then the difference grows to $43.47 ($448.03 − $404.56).

Before you move on to 3

Concept Check | 2

1. What is compound interest, and how is it calculated?
2. Describe the three basic approaches that can be used to move money through time.
3. How does increasing the number of compounding periods affect the future value of a cash sum?

3 Discounting and Present Value

So far we have only been moving money forward in time; that is, we have taken a known present value of money and determined how much it will be worth at some point in the future. Financial decisions often require calculating the future value of an investment made today. However, there are many instances where we want to look at the reverse question: What is the value today of a sum of money to be received in the future? To answer this question, we now turn our attention to the analysis of a present value—the value today of a future cash flow—and the process of **discounting**, determining the present value of an expected future cash flow.

The Mechanics of Discounting Future Cash Flows

Discounting is actually the reverse of compounding. We can demonstrate the similarity between compounding and discounting by referring back to the future value formula found in Equation (1a):

$$\underset{(FV_n)}{\text{Future Value in Year } n} = \underset{\text{Value } (PV)}{\text{Present}} \left(1 + \underset{\text{Interest Rate } (i)}{\text{Annual}}\right)^{\text{Number of Years } (n)} \tag{1a}$$

To determine the present value of a known future cash flow, we simply take Equation (1a) and solve for PV:

$$\underset{\text{Value } (PV)}{\text{Present}} = \underset{(FV_n)}{\text{Future Value in Year } n} \left[\frac{1}{\left(1 + \dfrac{\text{Annual}}{\text{Interest Rate } (i)}\right)^{\text{Number of Years } (n)}}\right] \tag{2}$$

We also refer to the term in the brackets as the **present value interest factor**, which is the value that multiples the future value to calculate the present value. Thus, to find the present value of a future cash flow, we multiply the future cash flow by the present value interest factor.

$$\underset{\text{Value } (PV)}{\text{Present}} = \underset{(FV_n)}{\text{Future Value in year } n} \times \left(\underset{(PVIF)}{\text{Present Value Interest Factor}}\right)$$

$$\text{where Present Value Interest Factor } (PVIF) = \frac{1}{(1+i)^n}$$

Note that the present value of a future sum of money decreases as we increase the number of periods, n, until the payment is received, or as we increase the interest rate, i. That, of course, only makes sense because the present value interest factor is the *inverse* of the future value interest factor. Graphically, this relationship can be seen in Figure 2. Thus, given a **discount rate**, or interest rate at which money is being brought back to present, of 10 percent, $100 received in 10 years would be worth only $38.55 today. By contrast, if the discount rate is 5 percent, the present value would be $61.39. If the discount rate is 10 percent, but the

---

Figure 2

The Present Value of $100 Compounded at Different Rates and for Different Time Periods

The present value of $100 to be received in the future becomes smaller as both the interest rate and number of years rise. At $i = 10\%$, notice that when the number of years goes up from 5 to 10, the present value drops from $62.09 to $38.55.

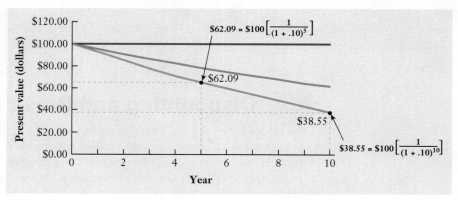

>> END FIGURE 2

Solving for the Present Value of a Future Cash Flow

Your firm has just sold a piece of property for $500,000, but under the sales agreement, it won't receive the $500,000 until 10 years from today. What is the present value of $500,000 to be received 10 years from today if the discount rate is 6 percent annually?

STEP 1: Picture the problem

Expressed as a timeline, this problem would look like the following:

$i = 6\%$

| ■ Time Period | 0 | 1 | 2 | 3 | 4 | 5 | 6 | 7 | 8 | 9 | 10 | ■ Years |

■ Cash Flow   Present Value = ? $500,000

STEP 2: Decide on a solution strategy

In this instance we are simply solving for the present value of $500,000 to be received at the end of 10 years. We can calculate the present value of the $500,000 using Equation (2).

STEP 3: Solve

Using the Mathematical Formulas. Substituting FV_{10} = $500,000, n = 10, and i = 6% into Equation (2), we find

$$PV = \$500,000 \left[\frac{1}{(1 + .06)^{10}} \right]$$

$$= \$500,000 \left[\frac{1}{1.79085} \right]$$

$$= \$500,000 \left[.558394 \right]$$

$$= \$279,197$$

The present value of the $500,000 to be received in 10 years is $279,197. Earlier we noted that discounting is the reverse of compounding. We can easily test this calculation by considering this problem in reverse: What is the future value in 10 years of $279,197 today if the rate of interest is 6 percent? Using our *FV* Equation (1a), we can see that the answer is $500,000.

Using a Financial Calculator.

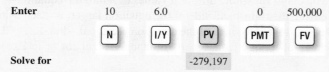

Enter	10	6.0		0	500,000
	N	I/Y	PV	PMT	FV
Solve for			-279,197		

Using an Excel Spreadsheet.

= PV(rate,nper,pmt,fv) or with values entered = PV(0.06,10,0,500000)

STEP 4: Analyze

Once you've found the present value of any future cash flow, that present value is in today's dollars and can be compared to other present values. The underlying point of this exercise is to make cash flows that occur in different time periods comparable so that we can make good decisions. Also notice that regardless of which method we use to calculate the future value—computing the formula by hand, with a calculator, or with Excel—we always arrive at the same answer.

STEP 5: Check yourself

What is the present value of $100,000 to be received at the end of 25 years given a 5 percent discount rate?

ANSWER: $29,530.

Your Turn: For more practice, do related **Study Problems** 12, 15, 19, and 28 at the end of this chapter.   >> END Checkpoint 4

$100 is received in 5 years instead of 10 years, the present value would be $62.09. This concept of present value plays a central role in the valuation of stocks, bonds, and new proposals. You can easily verify this calculation using any of the discounting methods we describe next.

Two Additional Types of Discounting Problems

Time-value-of-money problems do not always involve calculating either the present value or future value of a series of cash flows. There are a number problems that require that you solve for either the number of periods in the future, n, or the rate of interest, i. For example, to answer the following questions you will need to calculate the value for n:

- How many years will it be before the money I have saved will be enough to buy a second home?

- How long will it take to accumulate enough money for a down payment on a new retail outlet?

And to answer the following questions you must solve for the interest rate, i:

- What rate do I need to earn on my investment to have enough money for my newborn child's college education ($n = 18$ years)?

- If our firm introduces a new product line, what interest rate will this investment earn?

Fortunately, with the help of the mathematical formulas, a financial calculator, or an Excel spreadsheet, you can easily solve for i or n in any of these or similar situations.

Solving for the Number of Periods

Suppose you want to know how many years it will take for an investment of $9,330 to grow to $20,000 if it's invested at 10 percent annually. Let's take a look at how to solve this using the mathematical formulas, a financial calculator, and an Excel spreadsheet.

Using Mathematical Formulas. Substituting for FV, PV, and i in Equation (1a),

$$\begin{matrix} \text{Future Value} \\ \text{in Year } n \\ (FV_n) \end{matrix} = \begin{matrix} \text{Present} \\ \text{Value } (PV) \end{matrix} \left(1 + \begin{matrix} \text{Annual} \\ \text{Interest Rate } (i) \end{matrix}\right)^{\begin{matrix}\text{Number of}\\\text{Years }(n)\end{matrix}} \qquad \textbf{(1a)}$$

$$\$20,000 = \$9,330(1.10)^n$$

Solving for n mathematically is tough. One way is to solve for n using a trial-and-error approach. That is, you could substitute different values of n into the equation—either increasing the value of n to make the right-hand side of the equation larger, or decreasing the value of n to make it smaller, until the two sides of the equation are equal—but that will be a bit tedious. Using the time-value-of-money features on a financial calculator or in Excel is much easier and faster.

Using a Financial Calculator. Using a financial calculator or an Excel spreadsheet, this problem becomes much easier. With a financial calculator, all you do is substitute in the values for i, PV, and FV, and solve for n:

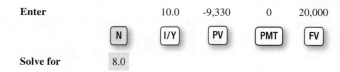

You'll notice that PV is input with a negative sign. In effect the financial calculator is programmed to assume that the $9,330 is a cash outflow (the money leaving your hands), whereas the $20,000 is money that you will receive. If you don't give one of these values a negative sign, you can't solve the problem.

Using an Excel Spreadsheet. With Excel, solving for n is straightforward. You simply use the =NPER(rate,pmt,pv,fv) or with variables entered, =NPER(0.10,0,–9330,20000).

Solving for the Number of Periods, *n*

Let's assume that the Toyota Corporation has guaranteed that the price of a new Prius will always be $20,000, and you'd like to buy one but currently have only $7,752. How many years will it take for your initial investment of $7,752 to grow to $20,000 if it is invested so that it earns 9 percent compounded annually?

STEP 1: Picture the problem

In this case we are solving for the number of periods:

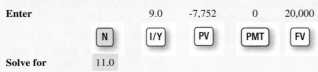

STEP 2: Decide on a solution strategy

In this problem we know the interest rate, the present value, and the future value, and we want to know how many years it will take for $7,752 to grow to $20,000 at 9 percent per year. We are solving for *n*, and we can calculate it using Equation (1a).

STEP 3: Solve

Using a Financial Calculator.

Enter		9.0	-7,752	0	20,000
	N	I/Y	PV	PMT	FV
Solve for	11.0				

Using an Excel Spreadsheet.

= NPER(rate,pmt,pv,fv) or with values entered = NPER(0.09,0,−7752,20000)

STEP 4: Analyze

It will take about 11 years for $7,752 to grow to $20,000 at 9 percent compound interest. This is the kind of calculation that both individuals and business make in trying to plan for major expenditures.

STEP 5: Check yourself

How many years will it take for $10,000 to grow to $200,000 given a 15 percent compound growth rate?

ANSWER: 21.4 years.

Your Turn: For more practice, do related **Study Problems** 13 and 18 at the end of this chapter.   >> END Checkpoint 5

The Rule of 72

Now you know how to determine the future value of any investment. What if all you want to know is how long it will take to double your money in that investment? One simple way to approximate how long it will take for a given sum to double in value is called the **Rule of 72**. This "rule" states that you can determine how many years it will take for a given sum to double by dividing the investment's annual growth or interest rate into 72. For example, if an investment grows at an annual rate of 9 percent per year, according to the Rule of 72 it should take $72/9 = 8$ years for that sum to double.

Keep in mind that this is not a hard-and-fast rule, just an approximation—but it's a pretty good approximation. For example, the *future value interest factor* of $(1 + i)^n$ for 8 years ($n = 8$) at 9 percent ($i = 9\%$) is 1.993, which is pretty close to the Rule of 72's approximation of 2.0.

Solving for the Rate of Interest

You have just inherited $34,946 and want to use it to fund your retirement in 30 years. If you have estimated that you will need $800,000 to fund your retirement, what rate of interest would you have to earn on your $34,946 investment? Let's take a look at solving this using the mathematical formulas, a financial calculator, and an Excel spreadsheet to calculate i.

Using Mathematical Formulas. If you write this problem using our time value of money formula you get,

$$\underset{(FV_n)}{\substack{\text{Future Value} \\ \text{in Year } n}} = \underset{\text{Value } (PV)}{\text{Present}} \left(1 + \underset{\text{Interest Rate } (i)}{\text{Annual}}\right)^{\substack{\text{Number of} \\ \text{Years } (n)}} \tag{1a}$$

$$\$800,000 = \$34,946(1+i)^{30}$$

Once again, you could resort to a trial-and-error approach by substituting different values of i into the equation and calculating the value on the right-hand side of the equation to see if it is equal to $800,000. However, again, this would be quite cumbersome and unnecessary. Alternatively, you can solve for i directly by dividing both sides of the equation above by $34,946,

$$(1+i)^{30} = \$800,000/\$34,946 = 22.8925$$

and then taking the 30th root of this equation to find the value of $(1 + i)$. Because taking the 30th root of something is the same as taking something to the 1/30 (or 0.033333) power, this is a relatively easy process if you have a financial calculator with a "y^n" key. In this case, you (1) enter 22.8925, (2) press the "y^n" key, (3) enter 0.033333, and (4) press the "=" key. The answer should be 1.109999, indicating that $(1 + i) = 1.109999$, and $i = 10.9999\%$ or 11%. As you might expect, it's faster and easier to use the time-value-of-money functions on a financial calculator or in Excel.

Using a Financial Calculator. Using a financial calculator or an Excel spreadsheet, this problem becomes much easier. With a financial calculator, all you do is substitute in the values for n, PV, and FV, and solve for i:

Enter	30		-34,946	0	800,000
	N	I/Y	PV	PMT	FV
Solve for		11.0			

Using an Excel Spreadsheet.

$= \text{RATE(nper,pmt,pv,fv)}$ or with values entered $= \text{RATE}(30,0,-34946,800000)$

Concept Check | 3

1. What does the term *discounting* mean with respect to the time value of money?
2. How is discounting related to compounding?

Checkpoint 6

Solving for the Interest Rate, *i*

Let's go back to that Prius example in Checkpoint 5. Recall that the Prius always costs $20,000. In 10 years, you'd re-ally like to have $20,000 to buy a new Prius, but you only have $11,167 now. At what rate must your $11,167 be com-pounded annually for it to grow to $20,000 in 10 years?

STEP 1: Picture the problem

We can visualize the problem using a timeline as follows:

$i = ?\%$

| ■ Time Period | 0 | 1 | 2 | 3 | 4 | 5 | 6 | 7 | 8 | 9 | 10 | ■ Years |

| ■ Cash Flow | -$11,167 | | | | | | | | | | $20,000 | |

STEP 2: Decide on a solution strategy

Here we know the number of years, the present value, and the future value, and we are solving for the interest rate. We'll use Equation (1a) to solve this problem.

STEP 3: Solve

Using the Mathematical Formulas.

$20,000 = $11,167 $(1 + i)^{10}$,
or $1.7910 = (1 + i)^{10}$

We then take the 10th root of this equation to find the value of $(1 + i)$. Because taking the 10th root of something is the same as taking something to the 1/10 (or 0.10) power, this can be done if you have a financial calculator with a "y^n" key. In this case, you (1) enter 1.7910, (2) press the "y^n" key, (3) enter 0.10, and (4) press the "=" key. The answer should be 1.06, indicating that $(1 + i) = 1.06$, and $i = 6\%$.

Using a Financial Calculator.

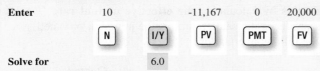

Enter	10		-11,167	0	20,000
	N	I/Y	PV	PMT	FV
Solve for		6.0			

Using an Excel Spreadsheet.

= RATE(nper,pmt,pv,fv) or with values entered = RATE(10,0,−11167,20000)

STEP 4: Analyze

You can increase your future value by growing your money at a higher interest rate or by letting your money grow for a longer period of time. For most of you, when it comes to planning for your retirement, a large *n* is a real positive for you. Also, if you can earn a slightly higher return on your retirement savings, or any savings for that matter, it can make a big difference.

STEP 5: Check yourself

At what rate will $50,000 have to grow to reach $1,000,000 in 30 years?

ANSWER: 10.5 percent.

Your Turn: For more practice, do related **Study Problems** 14, 16, 17, 20 to 22, 26, and 27 at the end of this chapter.

>> **END Checkpoint 6**

Making Interest Rates Comparable

Sometimes it's difficult to determine exactly how much you are paying or earning on a loan. That's because the loan might not be quoted as compounding annually, but rather as compounding quarterly or daily. To illustrate, let's look at two loans, one that is quoted as 8.084 percent compounded annually and another quoted as 7.85 percent compounded quarterly. Unfortunately, because on one the interest is compounded annually (you pay interest just once a year) but on the other, interest is compounded quarterly (you pay interest four times a year), they are difficult to compare. To allow borrowers to compare rates between different lenders, the U.S. Truth-in-Lending Act requires what is known as the annual percentage rate (APR) to be displayed on all consumer loan documents. The **annual percentage rate (APR)** indicates the interest rate paid or earned in one year without compounding. We can calculate APR as the interest rate per period (for example, per month or week) multiplied by the number of periods during which compounding occurs during the year (m):

$$\begin{matrix} \text{Annual Percentage} \\ \text{Rate } (APR) \\ \text{or Simple Interest} \end{matrix} = \begin{pmatrix} \text{Interest Rate per} \\ \text{Period (for example} \\ \text{per month or week)} \end{pmatrix} \times \begin{matrix} \text{Compounding} \\ \text{Periods per} \\ \text{Year } (m) \end{matrix} \qquad \textbf{(3)}$$

Thus, if you are paying 2 percent per month, m, the number of compounding periods per year, would be 12, and the *APR* would be:

$$APR = 2\%/\text{month} \times 12 \text{ months/year} = 24\%$$

Unfortunately, the APR does not help much when the rates being compared are not compounded for the same number of periods per year. In fact, the APR is also called the **nominal or quoted (stated) interest rate** because it is the rate that the lender states you are paying. In our example, both 8.084 percent and 7.85 percent are the annual percentage rates (APRs), but they aren't comparable because the loans have different compounding periods.

To make them comparable, we calculate their equivalent rate using an annual compounding period. We do this by calculating the **effective annual rate (EAR)**, the annual compounded rate that produces the same return as the nominal, or stated, rate. The EAR can be calculated using the following equation:

$$\text{Effective Annual Rate } (EAR) = \left(1 + \frac{\begin{matrix}\text{Quoted} \\ \text{Annual Rate}\end{matrix}}{\begin{matrix}\text{Compounding Periods} \\ \text{per Year } (m)\end{matrix}} \right)^{m} - 1 \qquad \textbf{(4)}$$

We calculate the *EAR* for the loan that has a 7.85 percent quoted annual rate of interest compounded quarterly (i.e., $m = 4$ times per year) using Equation (4) as follows:

$$EAR = \left[1 + \frac{0.0785}{4} \right]^{4} - 1 = .08084 \text{ or } 8.084\%$$

So if your banker offers you a loan with a 7.85 percent rate that is compounded quarterly or an 8.084 percent rate with annual compounding, which should you prefer? If you didn't know how the time value of money is affected by compounding, you would have chosen the 7.85 percent rate because, on the surface, it looked like the loan with the lower cost. However, you should be indifferent because these two offers have the same cost to you—that is to say, they have the same EAR. The key point here is that to compare the two loan terms you need to convert them to the same number of compounding periods (annual in this case). Given the wide variety of compounding periods used by businesses and banks, it is important to know how to make these rates comparable so you can make logical decisions.

Now let's return to that payday loan we introduced at the chapter opening. What is its EAR? In that example, we looked at a payday lender that advertised that you could borrow $500 and repay $626.37 eight days later. On the surface, that looks like you are paying 25.274 percent ($626.37/$500 = 1.25274), but that's really what you are paying every eight days. To find the quoted annual rate we multiply the eight-day rate of 25.274 percent times the

Calculating an Effective Annual Rate or EAR

Assume that you just received your first credit card statement and the APR, or annual percentage rate, listed on the statement is 21.7 percent. When you look closer you notice that the interest is compounded daily. What is the EAR, or effective annual rate, on your credit card?

STEP 1: Picture the problem

We can visualize the problem using a timeline as follows:

If i = an annual rate of 21.7% which is compounded on a daily basis, what is the EAR?

■ Time Period   0   1   2   3   4   5   6   7   8   9   10   ■ Daily Periods

■ Cash Flow   -$ Amount

STEP 2: Decide on a solution strategy

We'll use Equation (4) to solve this problem:

$$\text{Effective Annual Rate } (EAR) = \left(1 + \frac{\text{Quoted Annual Rate}}{\text{Compounding Periods per year } (m)}\right)^m - 1 \qquad \textbf{(4)}$$

STEP 3: Solve

To calculate the EAR we can use Equation (4), where the quoted annual rate is 21.7 percent, or 0.217, and m is 365. Substituting in these values, we get

$$EAR = \left[1 + \frac{0.217}{365}\right]^{365} - 1$$

$$EAR = 1.242264 - 1 = 0.242264 \text{ or } 24.2264\%$$

You were right in thinking that the amount of interest you owed seemed high. In reality, the EAR, or effective annual rate, is actually 24.2264 percent. Recall that whenever interest is compounded more frequently, it accumulates faster.

STEP 4: Analyze

When you invest in a certificate of deposit, or CD, at a bank, the rate the bank will quote you is the EAR—that's because it actually is the rate that you will earn on your money—and it's also higher than the simple APR. It's important to make sure when you compare different interest rates that they are truly comparable, and the EAR allows you to make them comparable. For example, if you're talking about borrowing money at 9 percent compounded daily, although the APR is 9 percent, the EAR is actually 9.426 percent. That's a pretty big difference when you're paying the interest.

STEP 5: Check yourself

What is the EAR on a quoted or stated rate of 13 percent that is compounded monthly?

ANSWER: 13.80 percent.

Your Turn: For more practice, do related **Study Problems** 35 through 38 at the end of this chapter.   **>> END Checkpoint 7**

number of eight-day periods in a year (in effect, you are paying 25.274 percent every eight days, or 25.274% × 45.625 = 1,153.13%). In this case m is 45.625 because there are 45.625 eight-day periods in a year (365 days), and the annual rate is 0.25274 × 45.625 = 11.5313 (the eight-day rate times the number of eight-day periods in a year). Substituting into Equation (4), we get

$$EAR = \left[1 + \frac{11.5315}{45.625}\right]^{45.625} - 1$$

$$EAR = 29{,}168.80 - 1 = 29{,}167.80, \text{ or } 2{,}916{,}780\%$$

Needless to say, you'll want to stay away from payday loans.

Calculating the Interest Rate and Converting It to an EAR

When you have non-annual compounding and you calculate a value for *i* using your financial calculator or Excel, you're calculating the rate per non-annual compounding period, which is referred to as the periodic rate:

$$\text{Periodic Rate} = \frac{\text{Quoted Annual Rate}}{\text{Compounding Periods per Year}\,(m)}$$

You can easily convert the periodic rate into an APR by multiplying it by the number of times that compounding occurs per year (*m*). However, if you're interested in the EAR, you'll have to subsequently convert the value you just calculated into an EAR. Let's look at an example.

Suppose that you've just taken out a two-year, $100,000 loan with monthly compounding and that at the end of two years you will pay $126,973 to pay the loan off. How can we find the quoted interest rate on this loan and convert it to an EAR? This problem can be solved using either a financial calculator or Excel.[1] Because the problem involves monthly compounding, *m*, the number of compounding periods per year is 12; *n*, the number of periods, becomes 24 (number of years times *m*, or 2 times 12); and the solution, *i*, will be expressed as the *monthly rate*.

Financial Calculator. Substituting in a financial calculator we find

Enter	24		-100,000	0	126,973
	N	I/Y	PV	PMT	FV
Solve for		1.0			

To determine the APR you're paying on this loan, you need to multiply the value you just calculated for *i* times 12—thus the APR on this loan is 12 percent—but that is *not* the loan's EAR. It's merely the APR. To convert the APR to an EAR, we can use Equation (4):

$$\text{Effective Annual Rate }(EAR) = \left(1 + \frac{\text{Quoted Annual Rate}}{\text{Compounding Periods per Year }(m)}\right)^m - 1 \tag{4}$$

where the quoted annual rate is 0.12, and *m* is 12. Substituting these values into the above equation we get

$$EAR = \left[1 + \frac{0.12}{12}\right]^{12} - 1$$

$$EAR = 1.1268 - 1 = 0.126825, \text{ or } 12.6825\,\%$$

In reality, the EAR, or effective annual rate, is actually 12.6825 percent. In effect, if you took out a two-year loan for $100,000 at 12.6825 percent compounded annually, your payment at the end of two years would be $126,973, the same payment you had when you borrowed $100,000 at 12 percent compounded monthly.

To the Extreme: Continuous Compounding

As *m* (the number of compounding periods per year) increases, so does the EAR. That only makes sense because the greater the number of compounding periods, the more often interest is earned on interest. As you just saw, we can easily compute the EAR when interest is compounded daily (*m* = 365). We can just as easily calculate EAR if the interest, *i*, is compounded hourly (*m* = 8,760), compounded every minute (*m* = 525,600), or every second

[1] Using either a TI BAII-Plus or an HP 10BII calculator, there is a shortcut key that allows you to enter the number of compounding periods and the nominal rate to calculate the EAR.

($m = 31{,}536{,}000$). We can even calculate the EAR when interest is continuously compounded; that is, when the time intervals between interest payments are infinitely small, as

$$EAR = \left(e^{quoted\ annual\ rate}\right) - 1 \qquad \textbf{(5)}$$

where e is the number 2.71828, with the corresponding calculator key generally appearing as "e^x." This number e is an irrational number that is used in applications that involve things that grow continuously over time. It is similar to the number $\prod$ in geometry.[2]

Let's take another look at the credit card example we looked at in Checkpoint 7, but with continuous compounding. Again, the APR, or annual percentage rate, is listed at 21.7 percent. With continuous compounding, what's the EAR, or effective annual rate, on your credit card?

$$EAR = e^{.217} - 1 = 1.2423 - 1 = 0.2423, \text{ or } 24.23\%$$

Finance in a **Flat World**

Financial Access at Birth

Approximately half the world's population has no access to financial services such as savings, credit, and insurance. Inspired by the One-Laptop-Per-Child campaign, UCLA finance professor Bhagwan Chowdhry has a plan to take this number to zero by 2030, called the Financial Access at Birth (FAB) Campaign.

This is how FAB could work. Each child would have an on-line bank account opened at birth with an initial deposit of $100. The bank account would be opened together with the child's birth registration, and the deposit plus interest could be withdrawn when the child reaches 16 years of age. If the program were launched in 2011, in just 20 short years every child and young adult in the world would have access to financial services. Assuming a 5 percent annual rate of interest on the deposit, the $100 deposit would grow to about $218 when the child reaches 16. If we wait until the child reaches 21 before turning over the account, it will have grown to about $279. In many parts of the world this would be a princely sum of money. Moreover, the recipient would have a bank account!

So what's the cost of implementing FAB? Currently there are about 134 million children born annually, and assuming that a quarter of these children would not need the service, this leaves 100 million children that otherwise would not have access to a bank account. The cost of the program would then be just $10 billion per year, which is less than the amount spent per week on military expenditures around the world. If 100 million individuals would contribute just $100 per year the dream of the FAB could become a reality. Every person in the world would have access to financial services in just 20 years!

Want to learn more? Go to http://tr.im/fabcam.

Before you begin end-of-chapter material

Concept Check | 4

1. How does an EAR differ from an APR?

2. What is the effect of having multiple compounding periods within a year on future values?

---

[2] Like the number $\prod$, it goes on forever. In fact, if you're interested, you can find the first 5 million digits of e at http://antwrp.gsfc.nasa.gov/htmltest/gifcity/e.5mil

Principle 1: **Money Has a Time Value** This chapter begins our study of the time value of money—a dollar received today, other things being the same, is worth more than a dollar received a year from now. The concept of time value of money underlies many financial decisions faced in business. In this chapter, we learn how to calculate the value today of a sum of money received in the future and the future value of a present sum.

Chapter Summaries

Construct cash flow timelines to organize your analysis of problems involving time value of money.

SUMMARY: Timelines can help you visualize and then solve time-value-of-money problems. Time periods—with 0 representing today, 1 the end of Period 1, and so forth—are listed on top of the timeline. Note that Period 1 represents the end of Period 1 and the beginning of Period 2. The periods can consist of years, months, days, or any unit of time. However, in general, when people analyze cash flows, they are looking at yearly periods. The cash flows appear below the timeline. Cash inflows are labeled with positive signs. Cash outflows are labeled with negative signs.

KEY TERM

Timeline A linear representation of the timing of cash flows.

Understand compounding and calculate the future value of cash flows using mathematical formulas, a financial calculator, and an Excel spreadsheet.

SUMMARY: Compounding begins when the interest earned on an investment during a past period begins earning interest in the current period. Financial managers must compare the costs and benefits of alternatives that do not occur during the same time period. Calculating the time value of money makes all dollar values comparable; because money has a time value, it moves all dollar flows either back to the present or out to a common future date. All time value formulas presented in this chapter actually stem from the single compounding formula $FV_n = PV(1 + i)^n$. The formulas are used to deal simply with common financial situations, for example, discounting single flows or moving single flows out into the future.

Financial calculators are a handy and inexpensive alternative to doing the math. However, most professionals today use spreadsheet software, such as Excel.

KEY TERMS

Compounding The process of determining the future value of a payment or series of payments when applying the concept of compound interest.

Compound interest The situation in which interest paid on the investment during the first period is added to the principal and, during the second period, interest is earned on the original principal plus the interest earned during the first period.

Future value What a cash flow will be worth in the future.

Future value interest factor The value $(1 + i)^n$ used as a multiplier to calculate an amount's future value.

Present value The value in today's dollars of a future payment discounted back to the present at the required rate of return.

Simple interest The interest earned on the principal.

KEY EQUATIONS

$$\underset{(FV_n)}{\text{Future Value in Year } n} = \underset{(PV)}{\text{Present Value}} \left(1 + \underset{\text{Interest Rate } (i)}{\text{Annual}}\right)^{\text{Number of Years } (n)} \tag{1a}$$

$$\underset{(FV_n)}{\text{Future Value in Year } n} = \underset{(PV)}{\text{Present Value}} \left(1 + \dfrac{\underset{}{\text{Annual Interest Rate } (i)}}{\underset{}{\text{Compounding Periods per Year } (m)}}\right)^{m \times (\text{Number of Years } (n))} \tag{1b}$$

where m is the number of compounding periods per year.

---

3 **Understand discounting and calculate the present value of cash flows using mathematical formulas, a financial calculator, and an Excel spreadsheet.**

SUMMARY: Previously we were solving for the future value (FV_n) of the present value (PV) of a sum of money. When we are solving for the present value, we are simply doing the reverse of solving for the future value. We can find the present value by solving for PV,

$$PV = FV_n \left[\dfrac{1}{(1 + i)^n}\right]$$

In addition, increasing the number of compounding periods within the year, while holding the rate of interest constant, will magnify the effects of compounding. That is, even though the rate of interest does not change, increasing the number of compounding periods means that interest gets compounded sooner than it would otherwise. This magnifies the effects of compounding.

KEY TERMS

Discount rate The interest rate used in the discounting process.

Discounting The inverse of compounding. This process is used to determine the present value of a future cash flow.

Present value interest factor The value $[1/(1 + i)^n]$ used as a multiplier to calculate a future payment's present value.

Rule of 72 A method for estimating the time it takes for an amount to double in value. To determine the approximate time it takes for an amount to double in value, 72 is divided by the annual interest rate.

KEY EQUATIONS

$$\underset{\text{Value } (PV)}{\text{Present}} = \dfrac{\underset{}{\text{Future Value in Year } n \ (FV_n)}}{\left(1 + \underset{\text{Interest Rate } (i)}{\text{Annual}}\right)^{\text{Number of Years } (n)}}$$

$$\underset{\text{Value } (PV)}{\text{Present}} = \underset{(FV_n)}{\text{Future Value in Year } n} \left[\dfrac{1}{\left(1 + \dfrac{\text{Annual Interest Rate } (i)}{\text{Compounding Periods per Year } (m)}\right)^{m \times (\text{Number of Years } (n))}}\right] \tag{2}$$

where m is the number of compounding periods per year.

4 Understand how interest rates are quoted and know how to make them comparable.

SUMMARY: One way to compare different interest rates is to use the annual percentage rate (APR), which indicates the amount of interest earned in one year without compounding. The APR is the simple interest rate and is calculated as the interest rate per period multiplied by the number of periods in the year:

$$APR = \text{Interest Rate per Period} \times \text{Periods per Year} \qquad (3)$$

The problem with the APR is that if compounding occurs more than once a year—for example, if the interest you owe is calculated every month, then in the second month, and from then on, you will end up paying interest from the first month. The end result of this is that the actual interest rate you are paying is greater than the APR. To find out the actual amount of interest we would pay over the course of one time period, we must convert the quoted APR rate to an effective annual rate (EAR). The EAR is the annual compounded rate that produces the same cash flow as the nominal interest rate:

$$EAR = \left(1 + \frac{\text{Quoted Annual Rate}}{m}\right)^m - 1 \qquad (4)$$

where EAR is the effective annual rate, and m is the number of compounding periods within a year.

KEY TERMS

Annual percentage rate (APR) The interest rate paid or earned in one year without compounding. It is calculated as the interest rate per period (for example, per month or week) multiplied by the number of periods during which compounding occurs during the year (m).

Effective annual rate (EAR) The annual compounded rate that produces the same return as the nominal, or stated, rate.

Nominal or **quoted (stated) interest rate** The interest rate paid on debt securities without an adjustment for any loss in purchasing power.

KEY EQUATIONS

$$\begin{array}{c} \text{Annual Percentage} \\ \text{Rate } (APR) \\ \text{or simple interest} \end{array} = \left(\begin{array}{c} \text{Interest} \\ \text{Rate per} \\ \text{Period} \end{array}\right) \times \begin{array}{c} \text{Compounding} \\ \text{Periods per} \\ \text{Year} \end{array} \qquad (3)$$

$$\text{Effective Annual Rate } (EAR) = \left(1 + \frac{\text{Quoted Annual Rate}}{\begin{array}{c}\text{Compounding Periods} \\ \text{per Year } (m)\end{array}}\right)^m - 1 \qquad (4)$$

where EAR = the effective annual rate.

Concept Check | **4**

1. How does an EAR differ from an APR?

2. What is the effect of having multiple compounding periods within a year on future values?

Study Questions

1. What is the time value of money? Give three examples of how the time value of money might take on importance in business decisions.

2. The processes of discounting and compounding are related. Explain this relationship.

3. What is the relationship between the number of times interest is compounded per year on an investment and the future value of that investment? What is the relationship between the number of times compounding occurs per year and the EAR?

4. How would an increase in the interest rate (i) or a decrease in the number of periods (n) affect the future value (FV_n) of a sum of money?

5. How would an increase in the interest rate (i) or a decrease in the number of periods until the payment is received (n) affect the present value (PV) of a sum of money?

6. Compare some of the different financial calculators that are available on the Internet. Look at Kiplinger Online calculators (www.kiplinger.com/tools/index .html), which include saving and investing, mutual funds, bonds, stocks, home, auto, credit cards, and budgeting online calculators. Also go to www.dinkytown.net, www.bankrate.com/calculators.aspx, and www.interest.com and click on the "Calculators" links. Which financial calculators do you find to be the most useful? Why?

7. **(Related to Chapter Introduction: Payday Loans)** The introduction to this chapter examined payday loans. Recently, Congress passed legislation limiting the interest rate charged to active military to 36 percent. Go to the Predatory Lending Association website at www.predatorylendingassociation.com and find the military base closest to you and identify the payday lenders that surround that base. Also, identify any payday lenders near you.

8. **(Related to Chapter Introduction: Payday Loans)** In the introduction to this chapter, payday loans were examined. Go to the Responsible Lending Organization website at www.responsiblelending.org/payday-lending/. How does the "debt trap" (www .responsiblelending.org/payday-lending/tools-resources/debttrap.html) associated with payday loans work?

Study Problems

MyFinanceLab

Go to **www.myfinancelab.com** to complete these exercises online and get instant feedback.

Compound Interest

1. **(Related to Checkpoint 2)** **(Future value)** To what amount will the following investments accumulate?
   a. $5,000 invested for 10 years at 10 percent compounded annually
   b. $8,000 invested for 7 years at 8 percent compounded annually
   c. $775 invested for 12 years at 12 percent compounded annually
   d. $21,000 invested for 5 years at 5 percent compounded annually

2. **(Related to Checkpoint 2)** **(Future value)** Leslie Mosallam, who recently sold her Porsche, placed $10,000 in a savings account paying annual compound interest of 6 percent.
   a. Calculate the amount of money that will accumulate if Leslie leaves the money in the bank for 1, 5, and 15 years.
   b. Suppose Leslie moves her money into an account that pays 8 percent or one that pays 10 percent. Rework part (a) using 8 percent and 10 percent.
   c. What conclusions can you draw about the relationship between interest rates, time, and future sums from the calculations you just did?

3. **(Related to The Business of Life: Saving for Your First House)** **(Future value)** You are hoping to buy a house in the future and recently received an inheritance of $20,000. You intend to use your inheritance as a down payment on your house.
   a. If you put your inheritance in an account that earns a 7 percent interest rate compounded annually, how many years will it be before your inheritance grows to $30,000?
   b. If you let your money grow for 10.25 years at 7 percent, how much will you have?
   c. How long will it take your money to grow to $30,000 if you move it into an account that pays 3 percent compounded annually? How long will it take your money to grow to $30,000 if you move it into an account that pays 11 percent?
   d. What does all of this tell you about the relationship among interest rates, time, and future sums?

4. **(Related to Checkpoint 2)** **(Future value)** Bob Terwilliger received $12,345 for his services as financial consultant to the mayor's office of his hometown of Springfield. Bob says that his consulting work was his civic duty and that he should not receive any compensation. So, he has invested his paycheck into an account paying 3.98 percent annual interest and left the account in his will to the city of Springfield on the condition that the city could not collect any money from

the account for 200 years. How much money will the city receive from Bob's generosity in 200 years?

5. **(Related to Checkpoint 3) (Compound interest with non-annual periods)** Calculate the amount of money that will be in each of the following accounts at the end of the given deposit period:

Account Holder	Amount Deposited	Annual Interest Rate	Compounding Periods per Year (M)	Compounding Periods (Years)
Theodore Logan III	$ 1,000	10%	1	10
Vernell Coles	95,000	12	12	1
Tina Elliott	8,000	12	6	2
Wayne Robinson	120,000	8	4	2
Eunice Chung	30,000	10	2	4
Kelly Cravens	15,000	12	3	3

6. **(Related to Checkpoint 2) (Compound interest with non-annual periods)** You just received a $5,000 bonus.

   a. Calculate the future value of $5,000, given that it will be held in the bank for five years and earn an annual interest rate of 6 percent.
   b. Recalculate part (a) using a compounding period that is (1) semiannual and (2) bimonthly.
   c. Recalculate parts (a) and (b) using a 12 percent annual interest rate.
   d. Recalculate part (a) using a time horizon of 12 years at a 6 percent interest rate.
   e. What conclusions can you draw when you compare the answers in parts (c) and (d) with the answers in parts (a) and (b)?

7. **(Related to Checkpoint 3) (Compound interest with non-annual periods)** Your grandmother just gave you $6,000. You'd like to see what it might grow to if you invest it.

   a. Calculate the future value of $6,000, given that it will be invested for five years at an annual interest rate of 6 percent.
   b. Recalculate part (a) using a compounding period that is (1) semiannual and (2) bimonthly.
   c. Now let's look at what might happen if you can invest the money at a 12 percent rate rather than 6 percent rate; recalculate parts (a) and (b) for a 12 percent annual interest rate.
   d. Now let's see what might happen if you invest the money for 12 years rather than 5 years; recalculate part (a) using a time horizon of 12 years (annual interest rate is still 6 percent).
   e. With respect to the changes in the stated interest rate and length of time the money is invested in parts (c) and (d), what conclusions can you draw?

8. **(Related to Checkpoint 2) (Future value)** A new finance book sold 15,000 copies following the first year of its release, and was expected to increase by 20 percent per year. What sales are expected during Years 2, 3, and 4? Graph this sales trend and explain.

9. **(Related to Checkpoint 2) (Future value)** You have just introduced "must-have" headphones for the iPod. Sales of the new product are expected to be 10,000 units this year and are expected to increase by 15 percent per year in the future. What are expected sales during each of the next three years? Graph this sales trend and explain why the number of additional units sold increases every year.

10. **(Related to Checkpoint 2) (Future value)** If you deposit $3,500 today into an account earning an 11 percent annual rate of return, what would your account be worth in 35 years (assuming no further deposits)? In 40 years?

11. **(Related to Checkpoint 2) (Future value) (Simple and compound interest)** If you deposit $10,000 today into an account earning an 11 percent annual rate of return, in the third year how much interest would be earned? How much of the total is simple interest and how much results from compounding of interest?

Discounting and Present Value

12. **(Related to Checkpoint 4) (Present value)** Sarah Wiggum would like to make a single investment and have $2 million at the time of her retirement in 35 years. She has found a mutual fund that will earn 4 percent annually. How much will Sarah have to invest today? What if Sarah were a finance major and learned how to earn a 14 percent annual return? How soon could she then retire?

13. **(Related to Checkpoint 5) (Solving for *n*)** How many years will the following take?
   a. $500 to grow to $1,039.50 if it's invested at 5 percent compounded annually
   b. $35 to grow to $53.87 if it's invested at 9 percent compounded annually
   c. $100 to grow to $298.60 if it's invested at 20 percent compounded annually
   d. $53 to grow to $78.76 if it's invested at 2 percent compounded annually

14. **(Related to Checkpoint 6) (Solving for *i*)** At what annual interest rate would the following have to be invested?
   a. $500 to grow to $1,948.00 in 12 years
   b. $300 to grow to $422.10 in 7 years
   c. $50 to grow to $280.20 in 20 years
   d. $200 to grow to $497.60 in 5 years

15. **(Related to Checkpoint 4) (Present value)** What is the present value of the following future amounts?
   a. $800 to be received 10 years from now discounted back to the present at 10 percent
   b. $300 to be received 5 years from now discounted back to the present at 5 percent
   c. $1,000 to be received 8 years from now discounted back to the present at 3 percent
   d. $1,000 to be received 8 years from now discounted back to the present at 20 percent

16. **(Related to Checkpoint 6) (Solving for *i*)** Kirk Van Houten, who has been married for 23 years, would like to buy his wife an expensive diamond ring with a platinum setting on their 30-year wedding anniversary. Assume that the cost of the ring will be $12,000 in seven years. Kirk currently has $4,510 to invest. What annual rate of return must Kirk earn on his investment to accumulate enough money to pay for the ring?

17. **(Related to Checkpoint 6) (Solving for *i*)** You are considering investing in a security that will pay you $1,000 in 30 years.
   a. If the appropriate discount rate is 10 percent, what is the present value of this investment?
   b. Assume these investments sell for $365, in return for which you receive $1,000 in 30 years; what is the rate of return investors earn on this investment if they buy it for $365?

18. **(Related to Checkpoint 5) (Solving for *n*)** Jack asked Jill to marry him, and she has accepted under one condition: Jack must buy her a new $330,000 Rolls-Royce Phantom. Jack currently has $45,530 that he may invest. He has found a mutual fund that pays 4.5 percent annual interest in which he will place the money. How long will it take Jack to win Jill's hand in marriage?

19. **(Related to Checkpoint 4) (Present value)** Ronen Consulting has just realized an accounting error that has resulted in an unfunded liability of $398,930 due in 28 years. In other words, the company will need $398,930 in 28 years. Toni Flanders, the company's CEO, is scrambling to discount the liability to the present to assist in valuing the firm's stock. If the appropriate discount rate is 7 percent, what is the present value of the liability?

20. **(Related to Checkpoint 6) (Solving for *i*)** Seven years ago, Lance Murdock purchased a wooden statue of a Conquistador for $7,600 to put in his home office. Lance has recently married, and his home office is being converted into a sewing room. His new wife, who has far better taste than Lance, thinks the Conquistador is hideous and must go immediately. Lance decided to sell it on e-Bay and only received $5,200 for it, and so he took a loss on the investment. What was his rate of return, that is, the value of *i*?

21. **(Related to Checkpoint 6) (Solving for *i*)** Springfield Learning sold zero-coupon bonds (bonds that don't pay any interest—instead the bondholder gets just one payment, coming when the bond matures, from the issuer) and received $900 for each bond that will pay $20,000 when it matures in 30 years.

    a. At what rate is Springfield Learning borrowing the money from investors?

    b. If Nancy Muntz purchased a bond at the offering for $900 and sold it 10 years later for the market price of $3,500, what annual rate of return did she earn?

    c. If Barney Gumble purchased Muntz's bond at the market price of $3,500 and held it 20 years until maturity, what annual rate of return would he have earned?

22. **(Related to Checkpoint 6) (Solving for *i*)** If you were offered $1,079.50 ten years from now in return for an investment of $500 currently, what annual rate of interest would you earn if you took the offer?

23. **(Solving for *i*)** An insurance agent just offered you a new insurance product that will provide you with $2,376.50 ten years from now if you invest $700 today. What annual rate of interest would you earn if you invested in this product?

24. **(Solving for *n* with non-annual periods)** Approximately how many years would it take for an investment to grow fourfold if it were invested at 16 percent compounded semiannually?

25. **(Solving for *n* with non-annual periods)** Approximately how many years would it take for an investment to grow by sevenfold if it were invested at 10 percent compounded semiannually?

26. **(Related to Checkpoint 6) (Solving for *i*)** You lend a friend $10,000, for which your friend will repay you $27,027 at the end of five years. What interest rate are you charging your "friend"?

27. **(Related to Checkpoint 6) (Solving for *i*)** You've run out of money for college, and your college roommate has an idea for you. He offers to lend you $15,000, for which you will repay him $37,313 at the end of five years. If you took this loan, what interest rate would you be paying on it?

28. **(Related to Checkpoint 4) (Present-value comparison)** You are offered $100,000 today or $300,000 in 13 years. Assuming that you can earn 11 percent on your money, which should you choose?

29. **(Present-value comparison)** Much to your surprise, you were selected to appear on the TV show "The Price Is Right." As a result of your prowess in identifying how many rolls of toilet paper a typical American family keeps on hand, you win the opportunity to choose one of the following: $1,000 today, $10,000 in 12 years, or $25,000 in 25 years. Assuming that you can earn 11 percent on your money, which should you choose?

30. **(Related to Checkpoint 6) (Solving for *i*)** In September 1963, the first issue of the comic book *X-MEN* was issued. The original price for the issue was 12 cents. By September 2013, 50 years later, the value of this comic book had risen to $9,500. What annual rate of interest would you have earned if you had bought the comic in 1963 and sold it in 2013?

31. **(Solving for *i*)** In March 1963, Ironman was first introduced in issue number 39 of the comic book *Tales of Suspense*. The original price for that issue was 12 cents. By March of 2013, 50 years later, the value of this comic book had risen to $9,000. What annual rate of interest would you have earned if you had bought the comic in 1963 and sold it in 2013?

32. **(Solving for *i*)** A financial planner just offered you a new investment product that would require an initial investment on your part of $35,000, and then 25 years from now will be worth $250,000. What annual rate of interest would you earn if you invested in this product?

33. **(Spreadsheet problem)** If you invest $900 in a bank where it will earn 8 percent compounded annually, how much will it be worth at the end of seven years? Use a spreadsheet to calculate your answer.

34. **(Spreadsheet problem)** In 20 years, you would like to have $250,000 to buy a vacation home. If you have only $30,000, at what rate must it be compounded annually for it to grow to $250,000 in 20 years? Use a spreadsheet to calculate your answer.

Making Interest Rates Comparable

35. **(Related to Checkpoint 7) (Calculating an EAR)** After examining the various personal loan rates available to you, you find that you can borrow funds from a finance company at 12 percent compounded monthly or from a bank at 13 percent compounded annually. Which alternative is the most attractive?

36. **(Related to Checkpoint 7) (Calculating an EAR)** You have a choice of borrowing money from a finance company at 24 percent compounded monthly or borrowing money from a bank at 26 percent compounded annually. Which alternative is the most attractive?

37. **(Related to Checkpoint 7) (Calculating an EAR)** Your grandmother asks for your help in choosing a certificate of deposit (CD) from a bank with a one-year maturity and a fixed interest rate. The first certificate of deposit, CD #1, pays 4.95 percent APR compounded daily, and the second certificate of deposit, CD #2, pays 5.0 percent APR compounded monthly. What is the effective annual rate (the EAR) of each CD, and which CD do you recommend to your grandmother?

38. **(Related to Checkpoint 7) (Calculating an EAR)** Based on effective interest rates, would you prefer to deposit your money into Springfield National Bank, which pays 8.0 percent interest compounded annually, or into Burns National Bank, which pays 7.8 percent compounded monthly? (Hint: Calculate the EAR on each account.)

39. **(Calculating an EAR)** Payday loans issued by banks are often referred to as "direct deposit advances." In early 2013, the average direct deposit advance charged $10 for a $100 advance and was due in 10 days. What is the effective annual rate on this type of loan?

40. **(Calculating an EAR)** In early 2013, typical terms on a payday loan involved a $15 charge for a two-week payday loan of $100. Assuming there are twenty-six 14-day periods in a year, what is the effective annual rate on such a loan?

Mini-Case

Emily Dao, 27, just received a promotion at work that increased her annual salary to $37,000. She is eligible to participate in her employer's 401(k) retirement plan to which the employer matches, dollar for dollar, workers' contributions up to 5 percent of salary. However, Emily wants to buy a new $25,000 car in three years, and she wants to have enough money to make a $7,000 down payment on the car and finance the balance. Fortunately, she expects a sizable bonus this year that she hopes will cover that down payment in three years.

A wedding is also in her plans. Emily and her boyfriend, Paul, have set a wedding date two years in the future, after he finishes medical school. In addition, Emily and Paul want to buy a home of their own as soon as possible. This might be possible because at age 30, Emily will be eligible to access a $50,000 trust fund left to her as an inheritance by her late grandfather. Her trust fund is invested in 7 percent government bonds.

Questions

1. Justify Emily's participation in her employer's 401(k) plan using the time-value-of-money concepts by explaining how much an investment of $10,000 will grow to in 40 years if it earns 10 percent.

2. Calculate the amount of money that Emily needs to set aside from her bonus this year to cover the down payment on a new car, assuming she can earn 6 percent on her savings. What if she could earn 10 percent on her savings?

3. What will be the value of Emily's trust fund at age 60, assuming she takes possession of half of the money ($25,000 of the $50,000 trust fund) at age 30 for a house down payment, and leaves the other half of the money untouched where it is currently invested?

4. What is the relationship between discounting and compounding?

5. List at least two actions that Emily and Paul could take to accumulate more for their retirement (think about i and n).

Photo Credits

Time Value of Money-Annuities and Other Topics

From Chapter 6 of *Financial Management: Principles and Applications*, Twelfth Edition. Sheridan Titman, Arthur J. Keown, and John D. Martin.

The Time Value of Money
Annuities and Other Topics

Chapter **Outline**

1 Annuities   ⟶   **Objective 1.** Distinguish between an ordinary annuity and an annuity due, and calculate the present and future values of each.

2 Perpetuities   ⟶   **Objective 2.** Calculate the present value of a level perpetuity and a growing perpetuity.

3 Complex Cash Flow Streams ⟶   **Objective 3.** Calculate the present and future values of complex cash flow streams.

In this chapter we provide tools that allow you to determine the value of a stream of cash flows, both with a limited life as well as those that continue forever and have no maturity date. Once you've mastered these tools, you can apply them to the valuation of stocks, bonds, and other investment opportunities, in addition to using them to determine your mortgage and car loan payments. In doing so, we will continue our examination of the first principle of finance—**P** Principle 1: **Money Has a Time Value**. In moving money through time, we will focus on cash flows because as we learned in **P** Principle 3: **Cash Flows Are the Source of Value**.

Many of you have bought a car that was financed by a bank. To repay such a loan, you make payments to the bank of a certain fixed amount each month for 48 or 60 months. Similarly, if you buy a house that you finance with a conventional mortgage, you will again face a schedule of payments due over a fixed period of time. Just like individuals, firms make loan payments that are due at regular intervals. In addition, they pay a fixed amount over a set period of time to lease equipment. And they often have investments that generate regular payments of cash. These examples all have one thing in common—they each require a fixed cash flow stream over a set period of time. As we'll see in this chapter, we call this type of cash flow stream an *annuity*.

Regardless of Your Major...

"Annuities We All Know"

We encounter annuities often in our day-to-day lives. An annuity, as defined in this chapter, is simply a series of equal payments, each payable at the end of each period (month or year) and over multiple periods. For example, if you're paying off a student loan, you're paying off an annuity. In this case, the annuity represents the payment of principal and interest on your student loan. So if you have $30,000 in student loans outstanding at a 6.8 percent interest rate that you plan to repay in 10 years, you'll be making monthly payments of $345.24 over the next 10 years. We sometimes encounter annuities in which the payments are made to us. For example, if your grandparents leave you $30,000 to help pay your college expenses, you might purchase a 6 percent annuity that provides you with monthly payments of $704.55 over the next four years.

1 Annuities

To move single cash flows through time, we must calculate their future and present values. We must extend these formulas to find the future and present values of a constant stream of cash flows. The material in this chapter provides the tools to implement Principle 1: **Money Has a Time Value**. This principle, along with Principle 3: **Cash Flows Are the Source of Value**, provides the logic behind the valuation of stocks, bonds, and other investment opportunities.

Ordinary Annuities

We define an **annuity** as a series of *equal* dollar payments that are made at the end of equidistant points in time, such as monthly, quarterly, or annually, over a finite period of time, such as three years. Payments for an annuity can be made at either the beginning or the end of each period. If payments are made at the end of each period, the annuity is often referred to as an **ordinary annuity**. An ordinary annuity is the most common form of annuity and is oftentimes referred to simply as an annuity, without the term *ordinary* preceding it. However, some annuities have payments that are made at the beginning of each period, such as apartment rent. We'll discuss this type of annuity later in this chapter. For now, when we refer to an annuity, you should assume we are referring to an ordinary annuity where the payments are made:

- at the end of each period,
- at equidistant periods of time, such as monthly or annually, and
- for a finite period of time, such as three years.

The present and future values of an ordinary annuity can be computed using the methods described illustrated in Figure 1. However, this process can be time consuming, especially for longer annuities, so next we will discuss some simple time-value-of-money formulas for easily calculating the present value and future value of an annuity.

The Future Value of an Ordinary Annuity

Let's assume that you are saving money to go to graduate school. You've taken your first job and you plan to save $5,000 each year for the next five years for your grad school fund. How much money will you accumulate by the end of Year 5?

This scenario presents a common annuity valuation problem, one we can solve by finding the future value. To answer this question, we first need to know two things: first, the rate of interest you earn on your savings, and second, for how long each of your savings deposits (the annuity payments) will earn interest. For our purposes, let's assume you save $5,000 each year for five years and that you deposit that amount in an account that earns 6 percent interest

Figure 1

Future Value of a Five-Year Annuity—Saving for Grad School

The five annual annuity payments consist of $5,000 in savings that are placed in an account that earns 6% interest. This is a five-year ordinary annuity such that the first cash flow occurs at the *end* of the first year. This, in turn, means that this payment is only compounded until the end of year five (or for four years).

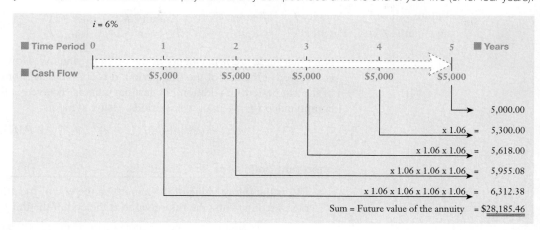

>> END FIGURE 1

per year. A timeline depicting this is shown in Figure 1. We can use the following equation to find the future value of each of the deposits:

$$\underset{(FV_n)}{\overset{\text{Future Value}}{\text{in year } n}} = \underset{\text{Value } (PV)}{\text{Present}}\left(1 + \underset{\text{Interest Rate } (i)}{\text{Annual}}\right)^{\text{Number of Years } (n)}$$

The future value at the end of Year *5* of the deposit made at the end of Year *1* (growing for four years) can be calculated as follows:

$$FV_n = PV(1 + i)^n$$

$$FV_{year\,4} = \$5,000(1 + .06)^4 = \$6,312.38$$

Note that the deposit made at the end of Year 1 has only four years to earn interest until the end of Year 5. Similarly, the deposit made at the end of Year 2 will have only three years to earn interest, and so forth. The future value of the first- through fifth-year deposits is as follows:

Interest Rate = 6%
Annuity Payment = $5,000

Year	Payment	Future Value at the End of Year 5
1	$5,000	$ 6,312.38
2	$5,000	$ 5,955.08
3	$5,000	$ 5,618.00
4	$5,000	$ 5,300.00
5	$5,000	$ 5,000.00
Sum = Future Value of Annuity =		$28,185.46

What this calculation tells us is that by the end of five years you should, if all goes as planned, have saved a total of $28,185.47 to help fund graduate school.

Figure 1 illustrates the computation of a future value of an annuity using a timeline. It's important to note that the future value of an annuity is simply the sum of the future values of each of the annuity payments compounded out to the end of the annuity's life—in this case the end of Year 5.

The Formula for the Future Value of an Ordinary Annuity

We can solve for the future value of an ordinary annuity using the following equation:

Future value of an annuity = The sum of the future value of the individual cash flows that make up the annuity

$$\text{Future value of an annuity, } FV_n = \text{Annuity Payment}\left(1 + \frac{\text{Interest}}{\text{Rate}}\right)^{n-1} + \text{Annuity Payment}\left(1 + \frac{\text{Interest}}{\text{Rate}}\right)^{n-2} + \cdots + \text{Annuity Payment}\left(1 + \frac{\text{Interest}}{\text{Rate}}\right)^{0}$$

Note that there are n payments in the ordinary annuity. However, because the first payment is received at the end of the first period, it is compounded for only $n-1$ periods until the end of the nth period. In addition, the last payment is received at the end of the nth period so it is compounded for $n-n$, or zero periods. Using symbols:

$$FV_n = PMT(1 + i)^{n-1} + PMT(1 + i)^{n-2} + \cdots + PMT(1 + i)^{1} + PMT(1 + i)^{0} \quad \textbf{(1)}$$

Important Definitions and Concepts:

- FV_n is the future value of the annuity at the end of the nth period. Thus if periods were measured in years, the future value at the end of the third year would be FV_3.
- PMT is the annuity payment deposited or received at the end of each period.
- i is the interest (or compound) rate per period. Thus, if the periods were measured in years, it would be the annual interest rate.
- n is the number of periods for which the annuity will last.

If we just factor out the PMT term in Equation (1) we get the following expression:

$$FV_n = PMT\left[(1 + i)^{n-1} + (1 + i)^{n-2} + \cdots (1 + i)^{1} + (1 + i)^{0}\right] \quad \textbf{(1a)}$$

The sum found in brackets is commonly referred to as the **annuity future value interest factor**. This sum can be reduced to the following expression:

$$\text{Annuity Future Value Factor} = \left[\frac{(1 + i)^{n} - 1}{i}\right] \quad \textbf{(1b)}$$

So to calculate the future value of an ordinary annuity of n years where the individual payments are compounded at a rate i, we simply multiply the payment by the annuity future value interest factor:

$$FV_n = PMT\left[\frac{(1 + i)^{n} - 1}{i}\right] \quad \textbf{(1c)}$$

Using Mathematical Formulas. Continuing with our saving-for-grad-school example, we note that PMT is $5,000 per year, the rate of interest, i, is 6 percent annually, and n is five years. Thus,

$$FV_n = PMT\left[\frac{(1 + i)^{n} - 1}{i}\right] = \$5,000\left[\frac{(1 + .06)^{5} - 1}{.06}\right] = \$5,000(5.63709296) = \$28,185.46$$

By simply substituting the values given above for PMT, n, and i into Equation (1c), we compute the future value of the level payment annuity with one computation rather than five separate future value computations that must then be summed.

Using a Financial Calculator.

Enter	5	6.0	0	-5,000	
	N	I/Y	PV	PMT	FV
Solve for					28,185.46

Using an Excel Spreadsheet.

$= FV$(rate,nper,pmt,pv) or with values entered $= FV$(.06,5,−5000,0)

Solving for the PMT in an Ordinary Annuity

Instead of figuring out how much money you will accumulate if you deposit a steady amount of money in a savings account each year, perhaps you would like to know how much money you *need to save* each year to accumulate a certain amount by the end of n years. In this case, we know the values of n, i, and FVn in Equation (1c); what we do not know is the value of *PMT*, the annuity payment deposited each period.

Let's look at an example where you are trying to find out how much you must deposit annually in an account in order to reach a set goal. Suppose that you would like to have $50,000 saved 10 years from now to finance your goal of getting an MBA. If you are going to make equal annual end-of-year payments to an investment account that pays 8 percent, how big do these annual payments need to be?

Here, using Equation (1c), we know that $n = 10$, $i = 8$, and $FV_{10} = \$50,000$, but what we do not know is the value of *PMT*, the annuity payment deposited each year. Substituting into Equation (1c), we get

$$FV_n = PMT\left[\frac{(1 + i)^n - 1}{i}\right] \tag{1c}$$

$$\$50,000 = PMT\left[\frac{(1 + .08)^{10} - 1}{.08}\right]$$

$$\$50,000 = PMT(14.4866)$$

$$\frac{\$50,000}{14.4866} = PMT = \$3,451$$

Checkpoint 1 demonstrates the calculation of an annuity payment using the mathematical formulas, a financial calculator, and Excel.

Solving for the Interest Rate in an Ordinary Annuity

You may also want to calculate the *interest rate* you must earn on your investment that will allow your savings to grow to a certain amount of money by a certain future date. In this case, you will be solving for i. Consider the following example: In 15 years you hope to have $30,000 saved to buy a sports car. You are able to save $1,022 at the end of each year for the next 15 years. What rate of return must you earn on your investments in order to achieve your goal?

It is easy to solve this problem with either a financial calculator or with Excel; but, as we describe next, solving it with the mathematical formula can be somewhat difficult.

Using the Mathematical Formula. Substituting the numbers into Equation (1c) we get

$$FV_n = PMT\left[\frac{(1 + i)^n - 1}{i}\right] \tag{1c}$$

$$\$30,000 = \$1,022\left[\frac{(1 + i)^{15} - 1}{i}\right]$$

$$\frac{\$30,000}{\$1,022} = \left[\frac{(1 + i)^{15} - 1}{i}\right]$$

$$29.354 = \left[\frac{(1 + i)^{15} - 1}{i}\right]$$

The only way to solve for the interest rate at this point is by trial and error. Specifically, we substitute different numbers for i until we find the value of i that makes the right-hand side of the expression equal to 29.354.

Using a Financial Calculator. We can use a financial calculator to solve for i directly as follows:

Enter	15		0	-1,022	30,000
	N	I/Y	PV	PMT	FV
Solve for		9.0			

Checkpoint 1

Solving for an Ordinary Annuity Payment

How much must you deposit at the end of each year in a savings account earning 8 percent annual interest in order to accumulate $5,000 at the end of 10 years? Let's solve this problem using the mathematical formulas, a financial calculator, and an Excel spreadsheet.

STEP 1: Picture the problem

We can use a timeline to identify the annual payments earning 8 percent that must be made in order to accumulate $5,000 at the end of 10 years as follows:

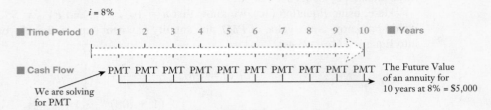

STEP 2: Decide on a solution strategy

This is a future-value-of-an-annuity problem where we know the values for n, i, and FV; and we are solving for PMT (PV is zero because there is no cash flow at time period 0). We'll use Equation (1c) to solve the problem.

STEP 3: Solution

Using the Mathematical Formulas. Substituting these example values in Equation (1c), we find

$$\$5,000 = PMT\left[\frac{(1 + .08)^{10} - 1}{.08}\right]$$

$$\$5,000 = PMT(14.4866)$$

$$PMT = \$5,000 \div 14.4866 = \$345.15$$

Thus, you must deposit $345.15 in the bank at the end of each year for 10 years at 8 percent interest to accumulate $5,000.

Using a Financial Calculator.

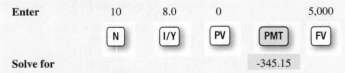

Enter	10	8.0	0		5,000
	N	I/Y	PV	PMT	FV
Solve for				-345.15	

Using an Excel Spreadsheet.

= PMT(rate,nper,pv,fv) or with values entered = PMT(.08,10,0,5000)

STEP 4: Analyze

Notice that in a problem involving the future value of an ordinary annuity, the last payment actually occurs at the time the future value occurs. In this case, the last payment occurs at the end of Year 10, and the end of Year 10 is when you want the future value of the annuity to equal $5,000. In effect, the final payment does not have a chance to earn any interest.

STEP 5: Check yourself

If you can earn 12 percent on your investments, and you would like to accumulate $100,000 for your newborn child's education at the end of 18 years, how much must you invest annually to reach your goal?

ANSWER: $1,793.73 at the end of each year.

Your Turn: For more practice, do related **Study Problems** 5, 17, 19, and 34 at the end of this chapter.   **>> END Checkpoint 1**

Using an Excel Spreadsheet.

= RATE(nper,pmt,pv,fv) or with values entered = RATE(15,−1022,0,30000).

Solving for the Number of Periods in an Ordinary Annuity

You may also want to calculate the *number of periods* it will take for an annuity to reach a certain future value. Just as with the calculation of the interest rate in an ordinary annuity, the easiest way to do this is with a financial calculator or with a spreadsheet. For example, suppose you are investing $5,000 at the end of each year in an account that pays 7 percent. How long will it be before your account is worth $51,300?

Using a Financial Calculator. We can use a financial calculator to solve for *n* directly as follows:

			7.0	0	-5,000	51,300
Enter						
	N	I/Y	PV	PMT	FV	
Solve for	8.0					

Thus, it will take eight years for end-of-year deposits of $5,000 every year to grow to $51,300.

Using an Excel Spreadsheet.

= NPER(rate,pmt,pv,fv) or with values entered = NPER(7%,−5000,0,51300).

The Present Value of an Ordinary Annuity

Let's say you just won a radio contest, and the prize is $2,500. The only catch is that you are to receive the $2,500 in the form of five $500 payments at the end of each of the next five years. Alternatively, the radio station has offered to pay you a total of $2,000 today. Which alternative should you choose?

To make this decision, you will need to calculate the present value of the $500 annuity and compare it to the $2,000 lump sum. You can do this by discounting each of the individual future cash flows back to the present and then adding all the present values together. This can be a time-consuming task, particularly when the annuity lasts for several years. Nonetheless, it can be done. If you want to know what $500 received at the end of each of the next five years is worth today, assuming you can earn 6 percent interest on your investment, you simply substitute the appropriate values into Equation (5–2), such that

$$PV = \$500\left[\frac{1}{(1 + .06)^1}\right] + \$500\left[\frac{1}{(1 + .06)^2}\right] + \$500\left[\frac{1}{(1 + .06)^3}\right] + \$500\left[\frac{1}{(1 + .06)^4}\right] + \$500\left[\frac{1}{(1 + .06)^5}\right]$$

$$= \$500(0.94340) + \$500(0.89000) + \$500(0.83962) + \$500(0.79209) + \$500(0.74726)$$

$$= \$2,106.18$$

Thus, the present value of this annuity is $2,106.18. As a result, you'd be better off taking the annuity rather than the $2,000 immediately. By examining the math and the timeline presented in Figure 2, you can see that the present values of each cash flow are simply summed. However, many times we will be faced with a situation where *n*, the number of cash flows in the annuity, is very large. For example, a 15-year mortgage involves 180 equal monthly payments, and a 30-year mortgage involves 360 equal monthly payments—that's just too many individual cash flows to work with. For this reason, we will want to use a financial calculator, Excel, or a mathematical shortcut. Let's examine a mathematical shortcut for valuing the present value of an annuity.

In this method for finding the present value of an annuity, we discount each cash flow separately and then add them up, as represented by the following equation:

$$PV = PMT\left[\left(\frac{1}{(1 + i)^1}\right) + \left(\frac{1}{(1 + i)^2}\right) + \cdots + \left(\frac{1}{(1 + i)^n}\right)\right] \tag{2}$$

Timeline of a Five-Year, $500 Annuity Discounted Back to the Present at 6 Percent
To find the present value of an annuity, discount each cash flow back to the present separately and then add them. In this example, we simply add up the present value of five future cash flows of $500 each to find a present value of $2,106.18.

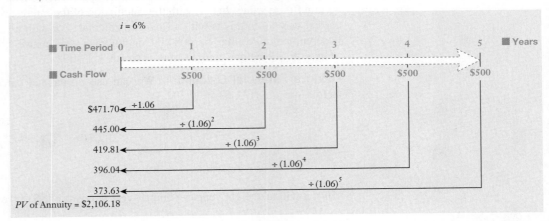

PV of Annuity = $2,106.18

The term in brackets is commonly referred to as the **annuity present value interest factor**. We can simplify the present value interest factor for an annuity formula as follows:

$$\text{Annuity Present Value Interest Factor} = \frac{1 - \dfrac{1}{(1 + i)^n}}{i} \tag{2a}$$

Thus, we can rewrite Equation (2) as follows:

$$\text{Present Value} = PMT \left[\frac{1 - \dfrac{1}{(1 + i)^n}}{i} \right] \tag{2b}$$

Important Definitions and Concepts:

- PV is the present value of the annuity.
- PMT is the annuity payment deposited or received at the end of each period.
- i is the discount (or interest) rate on a per-period basis. For example, if annuity payments were received annually, i would be expressed as an annual rate; if the payments were received monthly, it would be the monthly rate.
- n is the number of periods for which the annuity will last. If the annuity payments were received annually, n would be the number of years; if the payments were received monthly, it would be the number of months.

Notice that the frequency of the payment, that is, whether payments are made on an annual, semiannual, or monthly basis, will play a role in determining the values of n and i. Moreover, it is important that n and i match; that is, if periods are expressed in terms of number of monthly payments, the interest rate must be expressed in terms of the interest rate per month. To find the present value of an annuity, all we need to do is multiply the annuity payment by the annuity present value interest factor. Checkpoint 2 demonstrates the use of this formula along with the other techniques for calculating the present value of an annuity.

---

[2]in MyFinanceLab

Checkpoint 2

The Present Value of an Ordinary Annuity

Your grandmother has offered to give you $1,000 per year for the next 10 years. What is the present value of this 10-year, $1,000 annuity discounted back to the present at 5 percent? Let's solve this using the mathematical formula, a financial calculator, and an Excel spreadsheet.

STEP 1: Picture the problem

We can use a timeline to identify the cash flows from the investment as follows:

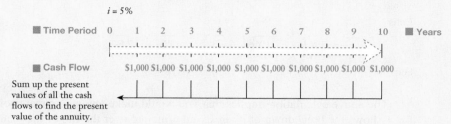

Sum up the present values of all the cash flows to find the present value of the annuity.

STEP 2: Decide on a solution strategy

In this case we are trying to determine the present value of an annuity, and we know the dollar value that is received at the end of each year, and the number of years the annuity lasts. We also know that the discount rate is 5 percent. We can use Equation (2b) to solve this problem.

STEP 3: Solution

Using the Mathematical Formulas. Substituting these example values in Equation (2b), we find that

$$PV = \$1,000 \left[\frac{1 - \dfrac{1}{(1 + .05)^{10}}}{.05} \right] = \$1,000[(1 - .6139)/.05] = \$1,000(7.722) = \$7,721.73$$

Using a Financial Calculator.

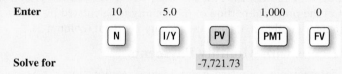

Enter	10	5.0		1,000	0
	N	I/Y	PV	PMT	FV

Solve for   -7,721.73

Using an Excel Spreadsheet.

= PV(rate,nper,pmt,fv) or with values entered = PV(0.05,10,1000,0)

STEP 4: Analyze

We will see this formula at work a bit later when we look at the value of a bond. When you buy a bond, you get the same amount of interest every year on either an annual or semiannual basis, and then at maturity you get the repayment of the bond's principal. Part of calculating the value of a bond involves calculating the present value of the bond's interest payments, which is an annuity.

STEP 5: Check yourself

What is the present value of an annuity of $10,000 to be received at the end of each year for 10 years given a 10 percent discount rate?

ANSWER: $61,446.

Your Turn: For more practice, do related **Study Problems** 2, 4, 28, and 35 at the end of this chapter.   **>> END** Checkpoint 2

Amortized Loans

An **amortized loan** is a loan paid off in equal payments—consequently, the loan payments are an annuity. The present value can be thought of as the amount that has been borrowed, n is the number of periods the loan lasts, i is the interest rate per period, *future value* takes on a value of zero because the loan will be paid off after n periods, and *payment* is the loan payment that is made. Generally, the payments are made monthly, but sometimes they are made yearly. Most mortgages are amortized loans, as are almost all car loans. Suppose you plan to get a $6,000 car loan at 15 percent annual interest with annual payments that you will pay off over four years. What will your annual payments be on this loan? Let's solve this using a financial calculator.

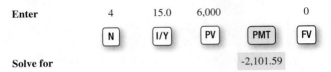

The above calculation implies that you would make annual payments of $2,101.59. Table 1 shows the breakdown of interest and principal over the life of the loan, which is commonly referred to as a **loan amortization schedule**.

As you can see, the interest payment declines each year as the amount owed declines and more of the principal is repaid. This is because a loan payment is made up of two parts: interest and principal. With each payment that goes toward the principal, the size of the outstanding balance goes down. And as the size of the outstanding balance goes down, the amount of interest that is due in the next period declines. Because the size of each payment remains the same and the amount of the next payment that goes toward interest declines, the amount of the next payment that goes toward principal must increase. You can see this clearly in Table 1. Also, if you look at Table 1, you'll see that the interest portion of the annuity (column 3) is calculated by multiplying the outstanding loan balance at the beginning of the year (column 1) by the interest rate of 15 percent. Thus, for the first year, the interest portion of the first year's payment is $6,000.00 \times .15 = $900.00; for Year 2 it is $4,798.41 \times .15 = $719.76, and so on. Of course, the amount that isn't the interest portion must be the principal portion. Thus, the repayment of the principal portion of the annuity is calculated by subtracting the interest portion of the annuity (column 3) from the annuity payment (column 2).

Amortized Loans with Monthly Payments

Many loans—for example, auto and home loans—require monthly payments. As we saw before, dealing with monthly, as opposed to yearly, payments is easy. All we do is multiply the number of years by m, the number of times compounding occurs during the year, to determine n, the number of periods. Then we divide the annual interest rate, or APR, by m to find the interest rate per period.

Let's look at an example. You've just found the perfect home. However, in order to buy it, you'll need to take out a $150,000, 30-year mortgage with monthly payments at an annual rate of 6 percent. What will your monthly mortgage payments be?

Table 1	The Loan Amortization Schedule for a $6,000 Loan at 15% to Be Repaid in Four Years				
Year	Amount Owed on the Principal at the Beginning of the Year (1)	Annuity Payment (2)	Interest Portion of the Annuity = (1) × 15% = (3)	Repayment of the Principal Portion of the Annuity = (2) − (3) = (4)	Outstanding Loan Balance at Year End, after the Annuity Payment = (1) − (4) = (5)
1	$6,000.00	$2,101.59	$900.00	$1,201.59	$4,798.41
2	4,798.41	2,101.59	719.76	1,381.83	3,416.58
3	3,416.58	2,101.59	512.49	1,589.10	1,827.48
4	1,827.48	2,101.59	274.12	1,827.48	0.00

Mathematical Formulas. In order to determine n, the number of periods, we multiply the number of years by m, where m is the number of times compounding occurs each year. To determine the interest rate per period, we divide the annual interest rate by m, where m is the number of times compounding occurs per year. Modifying this equation for non-annual compounding, we find

$$PV = PMT \left[\frac{1 - \dfrac{1}{(1 + \text{annual interest rate}/m)^{\#\,\text{years} \times m}}}{\text{annual interest rate}/m} \right] \qquad \textbf{(2c)}$$

Substituting *annual interest rate* = .06, *number of years* = 30, m = 12, and PV = $150,000 into Equation (2c), we get

$$\$150,000 = PMT \left[\frac{1 - \dfrac{1}{(1 + .06/12)^{30 \times 12}}}{.06/12} \right]$$

Notice that when you convert the annual rate of 6 percent to a monthly rate (by dividing it by 12), the monthly rate drops to 0.005, or 0.5 percent.

$$\$150,000 = PMT \left[\frac{1 - \dfrac{1}{(1 + .005)^{360}}}{.005} \right]$$

$$\$150,000 = PMT(166.7916144)$$

$$PMT = \$150,000/166.7916144 = \$899.33$$

Using a Financial Calculator. Because there are 360 monthly periods in 30 years, 360 is entered for ⃞N , and ⃞I/Y becomes 0.5 (annual interest rate of 6% divided by m, which is 12).

Enter	360	0.5	150,000		0
	N	I/Y	PV	PMT	FV
Solve for				-899.33	

Using an Excel Spreadsheet.

$= \text{PMT(rate,nper,pv,fv)}$ or with values entered $= \text{PMT}(0.005,360,150000,0)$

Computing Your Outstanding Balance. Let's take a look at how you might use your understanding of annuities to calculate the outstanding balance on a home mortgage loan, which is equal to the present value of your future loan payments. Remember, when you solve for your payment, the final future value of the loan is zero because after your last payment is made, the loan is paid off. The present value of the loan represents how much you originally borrowed—that is, it is the initial outstanding loan balance. What all that means is that the *remaining outstanding balance on a loan must be equal to the present value of the remaining payments on that loan.* An example of this calculation is provided in Checkpoint 3.

Annuities Due

Thus far, we have looked only at ordinary annuities, annuities in which payments are made at equidistant points in time at the end of a period. Now we turn our attention to valuing an **annuity due**, an annuity in which all the cash flows occur at the beginning of each period. For example, rent payments on apartments are typically annuities due because the payment for the month's rent occurs at the beginning of the month. Fortunately, compounding annuities due and determining their future and present value is actually quite simple. Let's look at how this affects our compounding calculations.

Determining the Outstanding Balance of a Loan

Let's say that exactly 10 years ago you took out a $200,000, 30-year mortgage with an annual interest rate of 9 percent and monthly payments of $1,609.25. But since you took out that loan, interest rates have dropped. You now have the opportunity to refinance your loan at an annual rate of 7 percent over 20 years. You need to know what the outstanding balance on your current loan is so you can take out a lower-interest-rate loan and pay it off. If you just made the 120th payment and have 240 payments remaining, what's your current loan balance?

STEP 1: Picture the problem

Because we are trying to determine how much you still owe on your loan, we need to determine the present value of your remaining payments. In this case, because we are dealing with a 30-year loan, with 240 remaining monthly payments, it's a bit difficult to draw a timeline that shows all the monthly cash flows. Still, we can mentally visualize the problem, which involves calculating the present value of 240 payments of $1,609.25 using a discount rate of 9%/12.

STEP 2: Decide on a solution strategy

Initially you took out a $200,000, 30-year mortgage with an interest rate of 9 percent, and monthly payments of $1,609.25. Because you have made 10 years worth of payments—that's 120 monthly payments—there are only 240 payments left before your mortgage will be totally paid off. We know that the outstanding balance is the present value of all the future monthly payments. To find the present value of these future monthly payments, we'll use Equation (2c).

STEP 3: Solve

Using the Mathematical Formulas.

Using Equation (2c), we'll solve for the present value of the remaining monthly payment. To find n, we multiply the number of years left until the mortgage is paid off (20) times the number of months in a year (12). Thus n becomes 240. The future value will be equal to zero because the loan will be fully paid off in 20 years. The payment will be $1,609.25, as given above. In effect, the present value of the payments you still need to make is how much you still owe.

$$PV = PMT\left[\frac{1 - \dfrac{1}{(1 + \text{annual rate of interest}/m)^{\#\ \text{years}\times m}}}{\text{annual rate of interest}/m}\right] \qquad \text{(2c)}$$

where m = number of times compounding occurs per year and # years is the number of years.

Substituting annual interest rate = .09, number of years = 20, m = 12, and PMT = $1,609.25 into Equation (2c), we get,

$$PV = \$1,609.25\left[\frac{1 - \dfrac{1}{(1 + .09/12)^{20\times12}}}{.09/12}\right]$$

$$PV = \$1,609.25(111.145)$$

$$PV = \$178,860.02$$

Using a Financial Calculator.

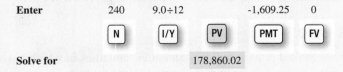

Enter	240	9.0÷12		-1,609.25	0
	N	I/Y	PV	PMT	FV
Solve for			178,860.02		

Using an Excel Spreadsheet.

= PV(rate,nper,pmt,fv) or with values entered = PV((9/12)%, 240,-1609.25,0)

STEP 4: Analyze

To solve this problem, we began with our monthly payments. Then we determined what the present value was of the remaining payments—this is how much you still owe. Thus, after making 10 years of monthly payments on your $200,000 mortgage that originally had a maturity of 30 years and carries a 9 percent annual rate of interest with monthly payments of $1,609.25, you still owe $178,860.02.

The logic behind what was done here is that the amount you owe on a loan should be equal to the present value of the remaining loan payments. However, if interest rates dropped and you decided to refinance your mortgage, you'd find that there are some real costs associated with refinancing that we haven't touched on here. For example, there is an application fee, an appraisal fee, legal and title search fees, an origination fee for processing the loan, and a prepayment penalty, all adding to the cost of refinancing. Once you decide on a mortgage refinancing lender, make sure that you get all of your mortgage refinancing terms written down on paper.

STEP 5: Check yourself

Let's assume you took out a $300,000, 30-year mortgage with an annual interest rate of 8 percent and monthly payments of $2,201.29. Because you have made 15 years worth of payments (that's 180 monthly payments), there are another 180 payments left before your mortgage will be totally paid off. How much do you still owe on your mortgage?

ANSWER: $230,345.

Your Turn: For more practice, do related **Study Problem** 38 at the end of this chapter.

>> **END Checkpoint 3**

Because an annuity due merely shifts the payments from the end of the period to the beginning of the period, we can calculate its future value by compounding the cash flows for one additional period. Specifically, the compound sum, or future value, of an annuity due is simply

$$FV_n(\text{annuity due}) = PMT\left[\frac{(1 + i)^n - 1}{i}\right](1 + i) \tag{3}$$

Recall that earlier we calculated the future value of a five-year ordinary annuity of $5,000 earning 6 percent interest to be $28,185.46. If we now assume this is a five-year annuity due, its future value increases from $28,185.46 to $29,876.59:

$$= \$5,000\left[\frac{(1 + .06)^5 - 1}{.06}\right](1 + .06) = \$28,185.46(1 + .06) = \$29,876.59$$

Because each cash flow is received one year earlier with an annuity due, its present value will be discounted back for one less period. To determine the present value of the annuity due, we merely figure out what its present value would be if it were an ordinary annuity and multiply that value by $(1 + i)$. This, in effect, cancels out one year's discounting.[1]

$$PV(\text{annuity due}) = PMT\left[\frac{1 - \dfrac{1}{(1 + i)^n}}{i}\right](1 + i) \tag{4}$$

Let's go back to our radio contest example. Suppose the radio station offered you a five-year annuity due instead of an ordinary annuity. If you were given $500 at the beginning of each

---

[3]Within each of the Excel functions you are given the option of identifying any cash flow as being at the beginning of a period. To solve for an annuity due in Excel, you simply change the value for "type" from 0 to 1. Recall that 0 is the default setting—the setting used to calculate an ordinary annuity. Consequently, if you don't designate a value for the variable "type," Excel will default to 0, or end-of-year payments. If you look at any of the Excel problems we have done so far, you'll notice that we have omitted entering a variable for "type," thus indicating that the cash flows occur at the end of each time period.

of those five years and were able to invest it at an interest rate of 6 percent, its value would increase from $2,106.18 (the value of the ordinary annuity) to $2,232.55:

$$= \$500\left[\frac{1 - \dfrac{1}{(1 + .06)^5}}{.06}\right](1 + .06)$$

$$= \$2,106.18(1 + .06) = \$2,232.55$$

The result of all this is that both the future value and the present value of an annuity due are larger than that of an ordinary annuity because, in each case, all payments are received or paid earlier. Thus, when *compounding* an annuity due, the cash flows come at the beginning of the period rather than the end of the period. They are, in effect, invested one period earlier, and as a result, grow to a larger future value. By contrast, when we *discount* an annuity due, the cash flows come at the beginning of each period, in effect coming one period earlier, so their

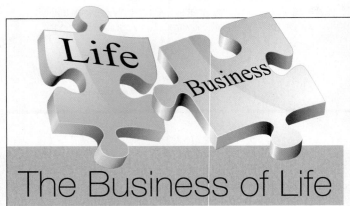

The Business of Life

Saving for Retirement

If you understand **P** Principle 1: **Money Has a Time Value**, you will have a better idea of why it's so important to begin saving for retirement as soon as possible. Putting off saving for just one year can have a big impact on the amount of money you have when you retire—in fact, it may reduce your retirement funds by over $250,000.

Individual retirement accounts, or IRAs, are personal retirement savings plans that have certain tax advantages. With a regular IRA, contributions are made on a before-tax basis. However, Roth IRA contributions are paid from earnings that have already been taxed. The difference is that after you retire and begin withdrawing money from a regular IRA, you have to pay taxes on your withdrawals. With a Roth, you don't.

Figure 3 assumes that at a certain age, you contribute $5,000 at the beginning of each year to a Roth IRA earning 8 percent interest per year, and you continue making contributions until age 70. For example, if at age 20 you start contributing $5,000 at the beginning of each year, you will have made 51 contributions by age 70, and you will end up with the following:

$$FV_n(\text{annuity due}) = PMT\left[\frac{(1 + i)^n - 1}{i}\right](1 + i) \quad \textbf{(3)}$$

$$= \$5,000\left[\frac{(1 + .08)^{51} - 1}{.08}\right](1 + .08)$$

$$= \$3,103,359(1 + .08) = \$3,351,628$$

Your Turn: See Study Problem 3.

Figure 3

Skipping Just One Year Can Cost You Over a Quarter of a Million Dollars

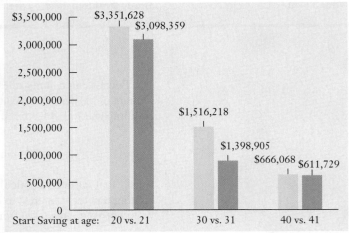

>> END FIGURE 3

But what if you wait until you're 21 to start contributing? How much money would you end up with then? By waiting just one year longer to begin investing, you end up with $253,269 less in the account:

$$= \$5,000\left[\frac{(1 + .08)^{50} - 1}{.08}\right](1 + .08)$$

$$= \$2,868,850(1 + .08) = \$3,098,359$$

As you can see, instead of accumulating $3,351,628, you would accumulate only $3,098,359.

In this example, you put $5,000 into a Roth IRA each year, but if you had only put in $2,500 each year, your total accumulation would only be half of what is listed in Figure 3. At present the maximum you can put into your Roth IRA per year is $5,000; and, if you're over 50, you can even put more into it. Study Problem 3 looks at Roth IRAs.

present value is larger. Although annuities due are used with some frequency in accounting, their usage is less frequent in finance. Nonetheless, an understanding of annuities due can be powerful, as you can see in the box feature *Business of Life: Saving for Retirement*.

Before you move on to 2

Concept Check | 1

1. Define the term *annuity* as it relates to cash flows.
2. Distinguish between an ordinary annuity and an annuity due.
3. Describe the adjustments necessary when annuity payments occur on a monthly basis.
4. How would you determine how much you currently owe on an outstanding loan?

 # Perpetuities

A **perpetuity** is simply an annuity that continues forever or has no maturity. It is difficult to conceptualize such a cash flow stream that goes on forever. One such example, however, is the dividend stream on a share of preferred stock. In theory, this dividend stream will go on as long as the firm continues to pay dividends, so technically the dividends on a share of preferred stock form an infinite annuity, or perpetuity.

There are two basic types of perpetuities that we will encounter in our study of finance. The first is a **level perpetuity** in which the payments are constant over time. The second is a **growing perpetuity** in which the payments grow at a constant rate from period to period over time. Let's consider each in turn.

Calculating the Present Value of a Level Perpetuity

Determining the present value of a perpetuity is simple—you merely divide the constant flow, or payment, by the discount rate. For example, the present value of a $100 perpetuity discounted back to the present at 5 percent is $100/.05 = $2,000. The equation representing the present value of a level perpetuity is as follows:

$$PV = \frac{PMT}{i}$$ (5)

Important Definitions and Concepts:

- PV = the present value of a level perpetuity.
- PMT = the constant dollar amount provided by the perpetuity.
- i = the interest (or discount) rate per period.

Calculating the Present Value of a Growing Perpetuity

Not all perpetuities have equal cash payments. One type of growing perpetuity provides for the periodic cash flows to grow at a constant rate each period. For example, if the first payment at the end of Year 1 is $100 and the payments are assumed to grow at a rate of 5 percent per year, then the payment for Year 2 will be $100(1.05) = $105, and the payment for Year 3 will be $100(1.05)(1.05) = $110.25, and so forth.

We can calculate the present value of a growing perpetuity as follows:

$$PV = \frac{PMT_{period1}}{i-g}$$ (6)

Checkpoint 4

The Present Value of a Level Perpetuity

What is the present value of a perpetuity of $500 paid annually discounted back to the present at 8 percent?

STEP 1: Picture the problem

With a perpetuity, a timeline doesn't have an ending point but goes on forever, with the same cash flow occurring period after period, or in this case, year after year:

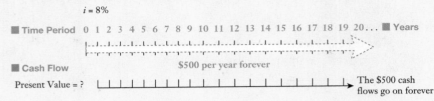

STEP 2: Decide on a solution strategy

Because calculating the present value of a perpetuity only involves simple division, we don't need to look at an Excel solution or any unique keystrokes with a financial calculator; instead, using Equation (5), we just divide the amount you received at the end of each period (forever) by the interest rate.

STEP 3: Solve

Substituting *PMT* = $500 and *i* = .08 into Equation (5), we find

$$PV = \frac{\$500}{.08} = \$6,250$$

Thus, the present value of this perpetuity is $6,250.

STEP 4: Analyze

Notice there is no symbol for the future value of a perpetuity. This is because there isn't a future time period when things end because a perpetuity goes on indefinitely. So, how much will this perpetuity be worth at the end of 2 years or 100 years? The answer is $6,250. That is because this perpetuity will always return $500—regardless of what the time period is, the present value of a perpetuity paying $500 at 8 percent is always $6,250.

STEP 5: Check yourself

What is the present value of stream of payments equal to $90,000 paid annually and discounted back to the present at 9 percent?

ANSWER: $1,000,000

Your Turn: For more practice, do related **Study Problem** 42 at the end of this chapter.   >> END Checkpoint 4

Important Definitions and Concepts:

- *PV* = the present value of a growing perpetuity.
- *PMT*_{period 1} = the amount of the payment made at the end of the first period (e.g., this was $100 in the example used above).
- *i* = the rate of interest used to discount the growing perpetuity's cash flows.
- *g* = the rate of growth in the payment cash flows from period to period.

The growth rate, *g*, must be less than the rate of interest used to discount the cash flows, *i*. If *g* is greater than *i*, then the present value becomes infinitely large because the cash flows are growing at a faster rate than they are being discounted.

Checkpoint 5

The Present Value of a Growing Perpetuity

What is the present value of a perpetuity stream of cash flows that pays $500 at the end of Year 1 but grows at a rate of 4 percent per year indefinitely? The rate of interest used to discount the cash flows is 8 percent.

STEP 1: Picture the problem

With a growing perpetuity, a timeline doesn't have an ending point, but goes on forever, with the cash flow growing at a constant rate period after period, or in this case, year after year:

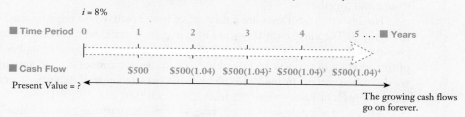

The growing cash flows go on forever.

STEP 2: Decide on a solution strategy

Because calculating the present value of a growing perpetuity only involves substituting into Equation (6), we don't need to look at an Excel solution or any unique keystrokes with a financial calculator. Instead, we just divide the amount receive at the end of each period (forever) by the interest rate minus the growth rate.

STEP 3: Solve

Substituting $PMT_{period\ 1}$ = $500, g = .04, and i = .08 into Equation (6), we find

$$PV = \frac{PMT_{period\ 1}}{i - g} = \frac{\$500}{.08 - .04} = \$12{,}500$$

Thus, the present value of the growing perpetuity is $12,500.

STEP 4: Analyze

Comparing the value of the $500 level perpetuity in Checkpoint 5 to the $500 perpetuity that grows at 4 percent per year, we see that adding growth to the cash flows has a dramatic effect on value. To see why this occurs, consider the Year 50 payment under both the level perpetuity and growing perpetuity. For the level perpetuity, this payment is still $500; however, for the growing perpetuity, the payment for Year 50 is the following:

$$PMT_{year\ 50} = \$500(1 + .04)^{50} = \$3{,}553.34$$

STEP 5: Check yourself

 What is the present value of a stream of payments where the Year 1 payment is $90,000 and the future payments grow at a rate of 5 percent per year? The interest rate used to discount the payments is 9 percent.

ANSWER: $2,250,000

Your Turn: For more practice, do related **Study Problem** 44 at the end of this chapter.

>> **END Checkpoint 5**

Before you move on to 3

Concept Check | 2

1. Define the term *perpetuity* as it relates to cash flows.
2. What is a growing perpetuity, and how is it calculated?

Complex Cash Flow Streams

Actual investment cash flows are often more complicated than the examples we have considered thus far. They often consist of multiple sets of annuities or different cash flow amounts mixed in with annuities. In general they will involve spending money today in the hopes of receiving more in the future, and once we bring all the future cash flows back to the present, they can be compared. For example, Marriott recently decided to build timeshare resorts in Dubai, United Arab Emirates. The resorts are close to Dubailand, a giant entertainment complex that, when finished, will be twice the size of the entire Disneyland and Disney World resorts put together.

The resorts' cash flows are a mixture of both positive and negative cash flows, as shown in Figure 4. The early cash flows are negative as Marriott begins construction on the various phases of the project and later become positive as the development makes money. Because of this mixture of positive and negative cash flows, we cannot use the annuities formulas that we described earlier. Instead, we calculate the present value of the investment project by summing the present values of all the individual cash flows.

Assuming a 6 percent discount rate, we can calculate the present value of all 10 years of cash flows by discounting each back to the present and adding the positive flows and subtracting the negative ones. Note that the cash flows for Years 1 through 3 are different, so we will have to find their present values by discounting each cash flow back to the present. The present values of the payments (in millions of $) received in Years 1 through 3 are $471.70 = $500/(1 + .06), $178.00 = $200/(1 + .06)^2, and –$335.85 = –$400/(1 + .06)^3.

Next, we see that in Years 4 through 10 the cash flows correspond to an ordinary annuity of $500 per year. Because these cash flows are all equal and are received annually, they are a seven-year annuity. The unique feature of the annuity is that the first cash flow comes at the end of Year 4. To find the present value of the seven-year annuity, we follow a two-step process:

- First, we consolidate the seven-year annuity into a single cash flow that is equal to its present value. In effect, we are consolidating the $500 million payments that occur at the end of Years 4 through 10 into an equivalent single cash flow at the beginning of Year 4 (or the end of Period 3). Recall that we can find the present value of the annuity by multiplying the annual payment of $500 by the annuity present value interest factor:

$$\frac{1 - \dfrac{1}{(1 + i)^n}}{i}.$$ In Figure 4 we see that the present value of this annuity at the end of Year 3 is $2,791 million.

Present Value of Single Cash Flows and an Annuity ($ value in millions)

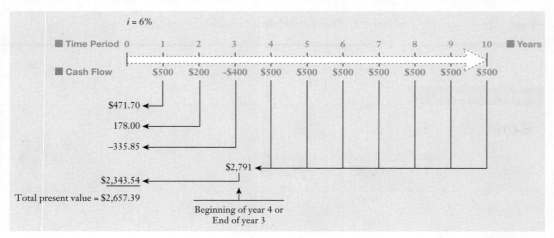

>> END FIGURE 4

Checkpoint 6

The Present Value of a Complex Cash Flow Stream

What is the present value of cash flows of $500 at the end of Years 1 through 3, a cash flow of a negative $800 at the end of Year 4, and cash flows of $800 at the end of Years 5 through 10 if the appropriate discount rate is 5 percent?

STEP 1: Picture the problem

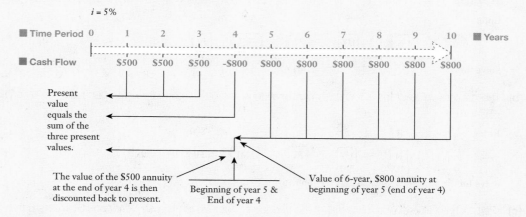

$i = 5\%$

| Time Period | 0 | 1 | 2 | 3 | 4 | 5 | 6 | 7 | 8 | 9 | 10 | Years |

Cash Flow: $500 $500 $500 -$800 $800 $800 $800 $800 $800 $800

Present value equals the sum of the three present values.

The value of the $500 annuity at the end of year 4 is then discounted back to present.

Beginning of year 5 & End of year 4

Value of 6-year, $800 annuity at beginning of year 5 (end of year 4)

STEP 2: Decide on a solution strategy

This problem involves two annuities and the single (negative) cash flow. Once their present value is determined they will be added together. The $500 annuity over Years 1 through 3 can be discounted directly to the present using Equation (2b), and the $800 cash outflow at the end of Year 4 can be discounted back to present using the equation from earlier in the chapter. Because it is an outflow, it will carry a negative sign and be subtracted from the present value of the inflows. To determine the present value of the six-year, $800 annuity over Years 5 through 10, we must first consolidate the six-year annuity that runs from Years 5 through 10 into an equivalent single cash flow at the beginning of Year 5, which is the same as the end of Year 4, using Equation (2b). We now have an equivalent single cash flow at the end of Year 4 that we can bring directly back to the present using the equation from earlier in the chapter. Once everything is in today's dollars, we simply add the values together.

STEP 3: Solve

Using the Mathematical Formulas.

Here we have two annuities. One of them, an annuity of $500 over Years 1 through 3, can be discounted directly back to the present by multiplying it by the annuity present value interest factor, or

$$\left[\frac{1 - \dfrac{1}{(1 + .05)^3}}{.05} \right]$$

for a value of $1,361.62. The second annuity, which is a six-year annuity of $800 per year over Years 5 through 10, must be discounted twice—once to find the value of the annuity at the beginning of Year 5, which is also the end of Year 4, and then again to bring that value back to the present. The value of the second annuity at the end of Year 4 is found by multiplying it ($800) by the annuity present value interest factor, or

$$\left[\frac{1 - \dfrac{1}{(1 + .05)^6}}{.05} \right]$$

resulting in a value $4,060.55. In effect, we have now consolidated the annuity into an equivalent single cash flow at the end of Year 4. This equivalent single cash flow is then discounted back to the present by multiplying it by the value of $1/(1.05)^4$, for a value of $3,340.62. Because cash flows in the same time period can be added and subtracted from each other, to arrive at the total present value of this investment, we subtract the present

(6 CONTINUED >> ON NEXT PAGE)

value of the $800 cash outflow at the end of Year 4 (which is $658.16) from the sum of the present value of the two annuities ($1,361.62 and $3,340.62). Thus, the present value of this series of cash flows is $4,044.08. Remember, once the cash flows from an investment have been brought back to the present, they can be combined by adding and subtracting to determine the project's total present value.

Using a Financial Calculator. Using a financial calculator, we can arrive at the same answer:

(a) The present value of the first annuity, Years 1 through 3 (give it a positive sign because it is an inflow) = **$1,361.62**.

Enter	3	5		500	0
	N	I/Y	PV	PMT	FV
Solve for			-1,361.62		

(b) The present value of the $800 cash **outflow** (thus it is given a negative sign because it is an outflow) = **−$658.16**.

Enter	4	5		0	-800
	N	I/Y	PV	PMT	FV
Solve for			658.16		

(c) (Part 1) The value at end of Year 4 of the second annuity (which is a six-year annuity), Years 5 through 10 (give it a positive sign because it is an inflow) = $4,060.55,

Enter	6	5		800	0
	N	I/Y	PV	PMT	FV
Solve for			-4,060.55		

and then,

(Part 2) The present value (give it a positive sign because it is an inflow) of the $4,060.55 (which was calculated in c: part 1 and is received at the end of Year 4) = **$3,340.62**.

Enter	4	5		0	4,060.55
	N	I/Y	PV	PMT	FV
Solve for			-3,340.62		

(d) Summing the present values together, the total present value = **$4,044.08**.

Using an Excel Spreadsheet. Using Excel, the cash flows are brought back to the present using the =PV function, keeping in mind that inflows will take on positive signs and outflows negative signs.

STEP 4: Analyze

When cash flows from different time periods are expressed in the same time period's dollars, they can be added in the case of an inflow or subtracted in the case of an outflow to come up with a total value at some point in time. In fact, we can combine ▣ Principle 1: **Money Has a Time Value** with ▣ Principle 3: **Cash Flows Are the Source of Value** to value stocks, bonds, and investment proposals. The bottom line is that understanding the time value of money is a key to making good decisions.

STEP 5: Check yourself

What is the present value of cash flows of $300 at the end of Years 1 through 5, a cash flow of negative $600 at the end of Year 6, and cash flows of $800 at the end of Years 7 through 10 if the appropriate discount rate is 10 percent?

ANSWER: $2,230.

Your Turn: For more practice, do related **Study Problem** 48 at the end of this chapter.   >> **END** Checkpoint 6

- Second, we discount the $2,791 million present value of the annuity cash flows back three years to the present, which is the beginning of Year 1. The present value of this sum (in millions), then, is $2,343.54 = $2,791/(1 + .06)^3$.

Finally, we can calculate the present value of the complex set of future cash flows by adding up the individual present values of each of the future cash flows. The result is a present value of $2,657.39 million. We would then compare the present value of all the future cash flows with what the project costs. It should now be apparent that drawing out a timeline is a critical first step when trying to solve any complex problem involving the time value of money.

Before you begin end-of-chapter material

Concept Check | 3

1. When are cash flows comparable—that is, when can they be added together or subtracted from each other?

2. Why would you want to be able to compare cash flows that occur in different time periods with each other?

P Principle 1: **Money Has a Time Value** This chapter discusses the time value of money—a dollar received today, other things being the same, is worth more than a dollar received a year from now. In this chapter, we apply the time value of money to annuities, perpetuities, and complex cash flows.

P Principle 3: **Cash Flows Are the Source of Value** In this chapter we introduced the idea that we can use **Principle 1** in combination with **Principle 3** to value stocks, bonds, and investment proposals.

Chapter Summaries

 Distinguish between an ordinary annuity and an annuity due, and calculate the present and future values of each.

SUMMARY: An annuity is a series of equal dollar payments, where the periods between the payments are of equal length, such as monthly or annually. An ordinary annuity involves cash payments made at the end of each period, whereas an annuity due involves payments at the beginning of each period.

KEY TERMS

Amortized loan A loan that is paid off in equal periodic payments.

Annuity A series of equal dollar payments for a specified period of time.

Annuity due An annuity in which the payments occur at the beginning of each period.

Annuity future value interest factor The value, $\left[\dfrac{(1 + i)^n - 1}{i}\right]$, used as a multiplier to calculate the future value of an annuity.

Annuity present value interest factor The value, $\left[\dfrac{1 - \dfrac{1}{(1 + i)^n}}{i}\right]$, used as a multiplier to calculate the present value of an annuity.

Loan amortization schedule A breakdown of the interest and principal payments on an amortized loan.

Ordinary annuity A series of equal dollar payments for a specified number of periods with the payments occurring at the end of each period.

KEY EQUATIONS

Concept Check | 1

1. Define the term *annuity* as it relates to cash flows.
2. Distinguish between an ordinary annuity and an annuity due.
3. Describe the adjustments necessary when annuity payments occur on a monthly basis.
4. How would you determine how much you currently owe on an outstanding loan?

$$FV_n = PMT\left[\frac{(1 + i)^n - 1}{i}\right] \tag{1c}$$

$$PV = PMT\left[\frac{1 - \dfrac{1}{(1 + i)^n}}{i}\right] \tag{2b}$$

$$PV = PMT\left[\frac{1 - \dfrac{1}{(1 + \text{annual interest rate}/m)^{\#\,years\times m}}}{\text{annual interest rate}/m}\right] \tag{2c}$$

$$FV_n = PMT\left[\frac{(1 + \text{annual interest rate}/m)^{\#\,years\times m} - 1}{\text{annual interest rate}/m}\right]$$

$$FV_n(\text{annuity due}) = PMT\left[\frac{(1 + i)^n - 1}{i}\right](1 + i) \tag{3}$$

$$PV(\text{annuity due}) = PMT \left[\frac{1 - \dfrac{1}{(1 + i)^n}}{i} \right] (1 + i) \qquad \textbf{(4)}$$

2   Calculate the present value of a level perpetuity and a growing perpetuity.

SUMMARY: A perpetuity is an annuity that continues forever. That is, every period it pays the same dollar amount. With a growing perpetuity, rather than receiving the same amount each period, the periodic payment increases at a constant rate every period.

KEY TERMS

Growing perpetuity A perpetuity in which the payments grow at a constant rate from period to period over time.

Perpetuity An annuity with an infinite life.

Level perpetuity An annuity with a constant level of payments with an infinite life.

KEY EQUATIONS

Concept Check | **2**

1. Define the term *perpetuity* as it relates to cash flows.
2. What is a growing perpetuity, and how is it calculated?

$$PV = \frac{PMT}{i} \qquad \textbf{(5)}$$

$$PV = \frac{PMT_{period\,1}}{i - g} \qquad \textbf{(6)}$$

3   Calculate the present and future values of complex cash flow streams.

Concept Check | **3**

1. When are cash flows comparable—that is, when can they be added together or subtracted from each other?
2. Why would you want to be able to compare cash flows that occur in different time periods with each other?

SUMMARY: Understanding how to make cash flows that occur in different time periods comparable is essential to understanding finance. All time value formulas presented in this chapter stem from the single compounding formula $FV_n = PV(1 + i)^n$. The formulas are used to deal simply with common financial situations, such as, for example, discounting single flows, compounding annuities, and discounting annuities.

Study Questions

1. What is an annuity? Give some examples of annuities.

2. How do you calculate the future value of an annuity?

3. What is the relationship between the present value interest factor and the annuity present value interest factor (from Equation [2])?

4. Assume you bought a home and took out a 30-year mortgage on it 10 years ago. How would you determine how much principal on your mortgage you still have to pay off?

5. Distinguish between an ordinary annuity and an annuity due.

6. What is a level perpetuity? A growing perpetuity?

7. How do you calculate the present value of an annuity? A perpetuity? A growing perpetuity?

8. With an uneven stream of future cash flows, the present value is determined by discounting all of the cash flows back to the present and then adding the present values up. Is there ever a time when you can treat some of the cash flows as annuities and apply the annuity techniques you learned in this chapter?

Study Problems

MyFinanceLab

Go to **www.myfinancelab.com** to complete these exercises online and get instant feedback.

Annuities

1. **(Future value of an ordinary annuity)**

   What is the future value of each of the following streams of payments?

   a. $500 a year for 10 years compounded annually at 5 percent
   b. $100 a year for 5 years compounded annually at 10 percent
   c. $35 a year for 7 years compounded annually at 7 percent
   d. $25 a year for 3 years compounded annually at 2 percent

2. **(Related to Checkpoint 2) (Present value of an ordinary annuity)**

   What is the present value of the following annuities?

   a. $2,500 a year for 10 years discounted back to the present at 7 percent
   b. $70 a year for 3 years discounted back to the present at 3 percent
   c. $280 a year for 7 years discounted back to the present at 6 percent
   d. $500 a year for 10 years discounted back to the present at 10 percent

3. **(Related to The Business of Life: Saving for Retirement) (Future value of an ordinary annuity)** You are graduating from college at the end of this semester and after reading the *The Business of Life* box in this chapter, you have decided to invest $5,000 at the end of each year into a Roth IRA for the next 45 years. If you earn 8 percent compounded annually on your investment, how much will you have when you retire in 45 years? How much will you have if you wait 10 years before beginning to save and only make 35 payments into your retirement account?

4. **(Related to Checkpoint 2) (Present value of an ordinary annuity)** Nicki Johnson, a sophomore mechanical engineering student, received a call from an insurance agent who believes that Nicki is an older woman who is ready to retire from teaching. He talks to her about several annuities that she could buy that would guarantee her a fixed annual income. The annuities are as follows:

Annuity	Purchase Price of the Annuity	Amount of Money Received Per Year	Duration of the Annuity (Years)
A	$50,000	$8,500	12
B	$60,000	$7,000	25
C	$70,000	$8,000	20

   Nicki could earn 11 percent on her money by placing it in a savings account. Alternatively, she could place it in any of the above annuities. Which annuities in the table above, if any, will earn Nicki a higher return than investing in the savings account earning 11 percent?

5. **(Related to Checkpoint 1) (Annuity payments)** Mr. Bill S. Preston, Esq., purchased a new house for $80,000. He paid $20,000 up front on the down payment and agreed to pay the rest over the next 25 years in 25 equal annual payments that include principal payments plus 9 percent compound interest on the unpaid balance. What will these equal payments be?

6. **(Annuity payments)** Emily Morrison purchased a new house for $150,000. She paid $30,000 up front and agreed to pay the rest over the next 25 years in 25 equal annual payments that include principal payments plus 10 percent compound interest on the unpaid balance. What will these equal payments be?

7. **(Annuity payments)** To pay for your education, you've taken out $25,000 in student loans. If you make monthly payments over 15 years at 7 percent compounded monthly, how much are your monthly student loan payments?

8. **(Annuity payments)** To pay for your child's education, you wish to have accumulated $15,000 at the end of 15 years. To do this, you plan to deposit an equal amount into the bank at the end of each year. If the bank is willing to pay 6 percent compounded annually, how much must you deposit each year to obtain your goal?

9. **(Annuity payments)** You plan to retire in 10 years and buy a house in Oviedo, Florida. The house you are looking at currently costs $100,000 and is expected to increase in value each year at a rate of 5 percent. Assuming you can earn 10 percent annually on your investments, how much must you invest at the end of each of the next 10 years to be able to buy your dream home when you retire?

10. **(Annuity payments)** The Aggarwal Corporation needs to save $10 million to retire a $10 million mortgage that matures in 10 years. To retire this mortgage, the company plans to put a fixed amount into an account at the end of each year for 10 years. The Aggarwal Corporation expects to earn 9 percent annually on the money in this account. What equal annual contribution must the firm make to this account to accumulate the $10 million by the end of 10 years?

11. **(Annuity payments)** The Knutson Corporation needs to save $15 million to retire a $15 million mortgage that matures in 10 years. To retire this mortgage, the company plans to put a fixed amount into an account at the end of each year for 10 years. The Knutson Corporation expects to earn 10 percent annually on the money in this account. What equal annual contribution must the firm make to this account to accumulate the $15 million by the end of 10 years?

12. **(Future value of an annuity)** Upon graduating from college 35 years ago, Dr. Nick Riviera was already planning for his retirement. Since then, he has made deposits into a retirement fund on a quarterly basis in the amount of $300. Nick has just completed his final payment and is at last ready to retire. His retirement fund has earned 9 percent compounded quarterly.

   a. How much has Nick accumulated in his retirement account?
   b. In addition to this, 15 years ago Nick received an inheritance check for $20,000 from his beloved uncle. He decided to deposit the entire amount into his retirement fund. What is his current balance in the fund?

13. **(Annuity number of periods)** How long will it take to pay off a loan of $50,000 at an annual rate of 10 percent compounded monthly if you make monthly payments of $600?

14. **(Annuity number of periods)** Alex Karev has taken out a $200,000 loan with an annual rate of 8 percent compounded monthly to pay off hospital bills from his wife Izzy's illness. If the most Alex can afford to pay is $1,500 per month, how long will it take to pay the loan off? How long will it take for him to pay off the loan if he can pay $2,000 per month?

15. **(Present value of an annuity)** What is the present value of a 10-year annuity that pays $1,000 annually, given a 10 percent discount rate?

16. **(Annuity interest rate)** Your folks just called and would like some advice from you. An insurance agent just called them and offered them the opportunity to purchase an annuity for $21,074.25 that will pay them $3,000 per year for 20 years. They don't have the slightest idea what return they would be making on their investment of $21,074.25. What rate of return would they be earning?

17. **(Related to Checkpoint 1) (Annuity payments)** On December 31, Beth Klemkosky bought a yacht for $50,000. She paid $10,000 down and agreed to pay the balance in 10 equal annual installments that include both the principal and 10 percent interest on the declining balance. How big will the annual payments be?

18. **(Annuity interest rate)** You've been offered a loan of $30,000, which you will have to repay in five equal annual payments of $10,000, with the first payment to be received one year from now. What interest rate would you be paying on that loan?

19. **(Related to Checkpoint 1)** **(Annuity payments)** A firm borrows $25,000 from the bank at 12 percent compounded annually to purchase some new machinery. This loan is to be repaid in equal annual installments at the end of each year over the next five years. How much will each annual payment be?

20. **(Annuity payments)** You plan to buy some property in Florida five years from to-day. To do this, you estimate that you will need $20,000 at that time. You would like to accumulate these funds by making equal annual deposits in your savings account, which pays 12 percent annually. If you make your first deposit at the end of this year, and you would like your account to reach $20,000 when the final deposit is made, how much will you have to deposit in the account annually?

21. **(Annuity number of periods)** You've just bought a new flat-screen TV for $3,000 and the store you bought it from offers to let you finance the entire purchase at an annual rate of 14 percent compounded monthly. If you take the financing and make monthly payments of $100, how long will it take to pay the loan off? How much will you pay in interest over the life of the loan?

22. **(Comprehensive problem)** You would like to have $75,000 in 15 years. To accu-mulate this amount, you plan to deposit an equal sum in the bank each year that will earn 8 percent interest compounded annually. Your first payment will be made at the end of the year.

a. How much must you deposit annually to accumulate this amount?
b. If you decide to make a large lump-sum deposit today instead of the annual de-posits, how large should the lump-sum deposit be? (Assume you can earn 8 per-cent on this deposit.)
c. At the end of five years, you will receive $20,000 and deposit it in the bank in an effort to reach your goal of $75,000 at the end of 15 years. In addition to the deposit, how much must you deposit in equal annual deposits to reach your goal? (Again, assume you can earn 8 percent on this deposit.)

23. **(Annuity payments)** You plan to buy property in Florida five years from today. To do this, you estimate that you will need $30,000 at that time for the purchase. You would like to accumulate these funds by making equal annual deposits in your sav-ings account, which pays 10 percent annually. If you make your first deposit at the end of this year, and you would like your account to reach $30,000 when the final deposit is made, what amount do you need to deposit annually?

24. **(Future value of an annuity and annuity payments)** You are trying to plan for retirement in 10 years and currently you have $150,000 in a savings account and $250,000 in stocks. In addition, you plan to deposit $8,000 per year into your savings account at the end of each of the next five years, and then $10,000 per year at the end of each year for the final five years until you retire.

a. Assuming your savings account returns 8 percent compounded annually, and your investment in stocks will return 12 percent compounded annually, how much will you have at the end of 10 years?
b. If you expect to live for 20 years after you retire, and at retirement you deposit all of your savings in a bank account paying 11 percent, how much can you withdraw each year after you retire (making 20 equal withdrawals beginning one year after you retire) so that you end up with a zero balance at death?

25. **(Annuity payments)** On December 31, Son-Nan Chen borrowed $100,000, agreeing to repay this sum in 20 equal annual installments that include both principal and 15 percent interest on the declining balance. How large will the annual payments be?

26. **(Annuity payments)** To buy a new house, you must borrow $150,000. To do this, you take out a $150,000, 30-year, 10 percent mortgage. Your mortgage payments, which are made at the end of each year (one payment each year), include both prin-cipal and 10 percent interest on the declining balance. How large will your annual payments be?

27. **(Components of annuity payments)** You've just taken on a 20-year, $150,000 mortgage with a quoted interest rate of 6 percent calling for payments semiannually. How much of your first year's loan payments (the initial two payments, with the first coming after six months have passed, and the second one coming at the end of the first year) goes toward paying *interest*, rather than principal?

28. **(Related to Checkpoint 2)** **(Present value of annuity payments)** The state lottery's million-dollar payout provides for $1 million to be paid over the course of 19 years in amounts of $50,000. The first $50,000 payment is made immediately, and the 19 remaining $50,000 payments occur at the end of each of the next 19 years. If 10 percent is the discount rate, what is the present value of this stream of cash flows? If 20 percent is the discount rate, what is the present value of the cash flows?

29. **(Future value of an annuity)** Find the future value at the end of Year 10 of an annuity that pays $1,000 per year for 10 years compounded annually at 10 percent. What would be the future value of this annuity if it were compounded annually at 15 percent?

30. **(Present value of an annuity due)** Determine the present value of an annuity due of $1,000 per year for 10 years discounted back to the present at an annual rate of 10 percent. What would be the present value of this annuity due if it were discounted at an annual rate of 15 percent?

31. **(Present value of an annuity)** Determine the present value of an ordinary annuity of $1,000 per year for 10 years, assuming it earns 10 percent. Assume that the first cash flow from the annuity comes at the end of Year 8 and the final payment at the end of Year 17. That is, no payments are made on the annuity at the end of Years 1 through 7. Instead, annual payments are made at the end of Years 8 through 17.

32. **(Components of an annuity payment)** You take out a 25-year mortgage for $300,000 to buy a new house. What will your monthly payments be if the interest rate on your mortgage is 8 percent? Use a spreadsheet to calculate your answer. Now, calculate the portion of the 48th monthly payment that goes toward interest and principal.

33. **(Comprehensive problem)** Over the past few years, Microsoft founder Bill Gates's net worth has fluctuated between $20 and $130 billion. In early 2006, it was about $26 billion—after he reduced his stake in Microsoft from 21 percent to around 14 percent by moving billions into his charitable foundation. Let's see what Bill Gates can do with his money in the following problems.

   a. Manhattan's native tribe sold Manhattan Island to Peter Minuit for $24 in 1626. Now, 387 years later in 2013, Bill Gates wants to buy the island from the "current natives." How much would Bill have to pay for Manhattan if the "current natives" want a 6 percent annual return on the original $24 purchase price?

   b. Bill Gates decides to pass on Manhattan and instead plans to buy the city of Seattle, Washington, for $50 billion in 10 years. How much would Bill have to invest today at 10 percent compounded annually in order to purchase Seattle in 10 years?

   c. Now assume Bill Gates only wants to invest half his net worth today, $13 billion, in order to buy Seattle for $50 billion in 10 years. What annual rate of return would he have to earn in order to complete his purchase in 10 years?

   d. Instead of buying and running large cities, Bill Gates is considering quitting the rigors of the business world and retiring to work on his golf game. To fund his retirement, Bill would invest his $20 billion fortune in safe investments with an expected annual rate of return of 7 percent. He also wants to make 40 equal annual withdrawals from this retirement fund beginning a year from today, running his retirement fund to $0 at the end of 40 years. How much can his annual withdrawal be in this case?

34. **(Related to Checkpoint 1)** **(Annuity payments)** Lisa Simpson wants to have $1,000,000 in 45 years by making equal annual end-of-the-year deposits into a tax-deferred account paying 8.75 percent annually. What must Lisa's annual deposit be?

35. **(Related to Checkpoint 2)** **(Present value of an annuity)** Imagine that Homer Simpson actually invested the $100,000 he earned providing Mr. Burns entertainment five years ago at 7.5 percent annual interest and that he starts investing an additional $1,500 a year today and at the beginning of each year for 20 years at the same 7.5 percent annual rate. How much money will Homer have 20 years from today?

36. **(Annuity payments)** Prof. Finance is thinking about trading cars. She estimates she will still have to borrow $25,000 to pay for her new car. How large will Prof. Finance's monthly car loan payment be if she can get a five-year (60 equal monthly payments) car loan from the VTech Credit Union at 6.2 percent APR?

37. **(Annuity payments)** Ford Motor Company's current incentives include 4.9 percent APR financing for 60 months or $1,000 cash back on a Mustang. Let's assume Suzie Student wants to buy the premium Mustang convertible, which costs $25,000, and she has no down payment other than the cash back from Ford. If she chooses the $1,000 cash back, Suzie can borrow from the VTech Credit Union at 6.9 percent APR for 60 months (Suzie's credit isn't as good as that of Prof. Finance). What will Suzie Student's monthly payment be under each option? Which option should she choose?

38. **(Related to Checkpoint 3) (Determining the outstanding balance of a loan)** Five years ago you took out a $300,000, 25-year mortgage with an annual interest rate of 7 percent and monthly payments of $2,120.34. What is the outstanding balance on your current loan if you just made the 60th payment?

39. **(Annuity payments)** Calvin Johnson has a $5,000 debt balance on his Visa card that charges 12.9 percent APR compounded monthly. In 2005, Calvin's minimum monthly payment is 3 percent of his debt balance, which is $150. How many months (round up) will it take Calvin Johnson to pay off his credit card if he pays the current minimum payment of $150 at the end of each month? In 2006, as the result of a federal mandate, the minimum monthly payment on credit cards rose to 4 percent. If Calvin made monthly payments of $200 at the end of each month, how long would it take to pay off his credit card?

40. **(Future value of an annuity)** Let's say you deposited $160,000 in a 529 plan (a tax-advantaged college savings plan) hoping to have $420,000 available 12 years later when your first child starts college. However, you didn't invest very well, and two years later the account's balance dropped to $140,000. Let's look at what you need to do to get the college savings plan back on track.

a. What was the original annual rate of return needed to reach your goal when you started the fund two years ago?

b. With only $140,000 in the fund and 10 years remaining until your first child starts college, what annual rate of return would the fund have to make to reach your $420,000 goal if you add nothing to the account?

c. Shocked by your experience of the past two years, you feel the college fund has invested too much in stocks, and you want a low-risk fund in order to ensure you have the necessary $420,000 in 10 years. You are willing to make end-of-the-month deposits to the fund as well. You find you can get a fund that promises to pay a guaranteed annual return of 6 percent that is compounded monthly. You decide to transfer the $140,000 to this new fund and make the necessary monthly deposits. How large of a monthly deposit must you make into this new fund each month?

d. After seeing how large the monthly deposit would be (in part c of this problem), you decide to invest the $140,000 today and $500 at the end of each month for the next 10 years into a fund consisting of 50 percent stock and 50 percent bonds and hope for the best. What APR would the fund have to earn in order to reach your $420,000 goal?

41. **(Saving for retirement—future value of an annuity)** Selma and Patty Bouvier are twins and both work at the Springfield DMV. Selma and Patty Bouvier decide to save for retirement, which is 35 years away. They'll both receive an 8 percent annual return on their investment over the next 35 years. Selma invests $2,000 per year at the end of each year *only* for the first 10 years of the 35-year period—for a total of $20,000 saved. Patty doesn't start saving for 10 years and then saves $2,000 per year at the end of each year for the remaining 25 years—for a total of $50,000 saved. How much will each of them have when they retire?

Perpetuities

42. **(Related to Checkpoint 4) (Present value of a perpetuity)**
What is the present value of the following?

a. A $300 perpetuity discounted back to the present at 8 percent
b. A $1,000 perpetuity discounted back to the present at 12 percent
c. A $100 perpetuity discounted back to the present at 9 percent
d. A $95 perpetuity discounted back to the present at 5 percent

43. **(Present value of a perpetuity)** At a discount rate of 8.5 percent, find the present value of a perpetual payment of $1,000 per year. If the discount rate were lowered to half the size (4.25 percent), what would be the value of the perpetuity?

44. **(Related to Checkpoint 5) (Present value of a growing perpetuity)** What is the present value of a perpetuity stream of cash flows that pays $1,000 at the end of Year 1, and the annual cash flows grow at a rate of 4 percent per year indefinitely, if the appropriate discount rate is 8 percent? What if the appropriate discount rate is 6 percent?

45. **(Present value of a growing perpetuity)** What is the present value of a perpetuity stream of cash flows that pays $50,000 at the end of Year 1 and then grows at a rate of 6 percent per year indefinitely? The rate of interest used to discount the cash flows is 10 percent.

46. **(Present value of a growing perpetuity)** As a result of winning the Gates Energy Innovation Award, you are awarded a growing perpetuity. The first payment will occur in a year and will be for $20,000. You will continue receiving monetary awards annually, with each award increasing by 5 percent over the previous award, and these monetary awards will continue forever. If the appropriate interest rate is 10 percent, what is the present value of this award?

47. **(Present value of a growing perpetuity)** Your firm has taken on cost-saving measures that will provide a benefit of $10,000 in the first year. These cost savings will decrease each year at a rate of 3 percent forever. If the appropriate interest rate is 6 percent, what is the present value of these savings?

Complex Cash Flow Streams

48. **(Related to Checkpoint 6) (Present value of annuities and complex cash flows)** You are given three investment alternatives to analyze. The cash flows from these three investments are as follows:

Investment Alternatives

End of Year	A	B	C
1	$10,000		$10,000
2	10,000		
3	10,000		
4	10,000		
5	10,000	$10,000	
6		10,000	50,000
7		10,000	
8		10,000	
9		10,000	
10		10,000	10,000

Assuming a 20 percent discount rate, find the present value of each investment.

49. **(Present value of annuities and complex cash flows)** You are given three investment alternatives to analyze. The cash flows from these three investments are as follows:

End of Year	Investment A	B	C
1	$15,000		$20,000
2	15,000		
3	15,000		
4	15,000		
5	15,000	$15,000	
6		15,000	60,000
7		15,000	
8		15,000	
9		15,000	
10		15,000	20,000

Assuming a 20 percent interest rate, find the present value of each investment.

50. **(Present value of an uneven stream of payments)** You are given three investment alternatives to analyze. The cash flows from these three investments are as follows:

End of Year	Investment A	B	C
1	$2,000	$2,000	$ 5,000
2	3,000	2,000	5,000
3	4,000	2,000	(5,000)
4	(5,000)	2,000	(5,000)
5	5,000	5,000	15,000

What is the present value of each of these three investments if the appropriate discount rate is 10 percent?

51. **(Present value of complex cash flows)** You have an opportunity to make an investment that will pay $100 at the end of the first year, $400 at the end of the second year, $400 at the end of the third year, $400 at the end of the fourth year, and $300 at the end of the fifth year.

a. Find the present value if the interest rate is 8 percent. (Hint: You can simply bring each cash flow back to the present and then add them up. Another way to work this problem is to either use the $=$NPV function in Excel or to use the CF key on your financial calculator—but you'll want to check your calculator's manual before you use this key. Keep in mind that with the $=$NPV function in Excel, there is no initial outlay. That is, all this function does is bring all of the future cash flows back to the present. With a financial calculator, you should keep in mind that CF_0 is the initial outlay or cash flow at time 0, and, because there is no cash flow at time 0, $CF_0 = 0$.)

b. What would happen to the present value of this stream of cash flows if the interest rate were 0 percent?

52. **(Present value of complex cash flows)** How much do you have to deposit today so that beginning 11 years from now you can withdraw $10,000 a year for the next five years (Periods 11 through 15) plus an *additional* amount of $20,000 in the last year (Period 15)? Assume an interest rate of 6 percent.

53. **(Comprehensive problem)** You would like to have $50,000 in 15 years. To accumulate this amount, you plan to deposit an equal sum in the bank each year that will earn 7 percent interest compounded annually. Your first payment will be made at the end of the year.

a. How much must you deposit annually to accumulate this amount?

b. If you decide to make a large lump-sum deposit today instead of the annual deposits, how large should this lump-sum deposit be? (Assume you can earn 7 percent on this deposit.)

c. At the end of five years, you will receive $10,000 and deposit this in the bank toward your goal of $50,000 at the end of 15 years. In addition to this deposit, how much must you deposit in equal annual deposits to reach your goal? (Again, assume you can earn 7 percent on this deposit.)

54. **(Complex annuity payments)** Milhouse, 22, is about to begin his career as a rocket scientist for a NASA contractor. Being a rocket scientist, Milhouse knows that he should begin saving for retirement immediately. Part of his inspiration came from reading an article on Social Security in *Time*. The article indicated that the ratio of workers paying taxes to retirees collecting checks will drop dramatically in the future. In fact, the number will drop to two workers for every retiree in 2040. Milhouse's retirement plan allows him to make equal yearly contributions, and it pays 9 percent interest annually. Upon retirement, Milhouse plans to buy a new boat, which he estimates will cost him $300,000 in 43 years, which is when he plans to retire (at age 65). He also estimates that in order to live comfortably he will require a yearly income of $80,000 for each year after he retires. Based on his family history, Milhouse expects to live until age 80 (that is, he would like to receive 15 payments of $80,000 at the end of each year). When he retires, Milhouse will purchase his boat in one lump sum and place the remaining balance into an account that pays 6 percent interest, from which he will withdraw his $80,000 per year. If Milhouse's first contribution is made one year from today, and his last is made the day he retires, how much money must he contribute each year to his retirement fund?

55. **(Comprehensive problem)** Having just inherited a large sum of money, you are trying to determine how much you should save for retirement and how much you can spend now. For retirement, you will deposit today (January 1, 2013) a lump sum in a bank account paying 10 percent compounded annually. You don't plan on touching this deposit until you retire in five years (January 1, 2018), and you plan on living for 20 additional years. During your retirement, you would like to receive income of $50,000 per year to be received the first day of each year, with the first payment on January 1, 2018, and the last payment on January 1, 2037. Complicating this objective is your desire to have one final three-year fling during which time you'd like to track down all the original members of *Hey Dude* and *Saved by the Bell* and get their autographs. To finance this, you want to receive $250,000 on January 1, 2033, and *nothing* on January 1, 2034, and January 1, 2035, because you will be on the road. In addition, after you pass on (January 1, 2038), you would like to have a total of $100,000 to leave to your children.

a. How much must you deposit in the bank at 10 percent interest on January 1, 2013, to achieve your goal? (Use a timeline to answer this question. Keep in mind that the last second of December 31st is equivalent to the first second of January 1st.)

b. What kinds of problems are associated with this analysis and its assumptions?

56. **(Future value of a complex annuity)** Springfield mogul Montgomery Burns, age 80, wants to retire at age 100 so he can steal candy from babies full time. Once Mr. Burns retires, he wants to withdraw $1 billion at the beginning of each year for 10 years from a special offshore account that will pay 20 percent annually. In order to fund his retirement, Mr. Burns will make 20 equal end-of-the-year deposits in this same special account that will pay 20 percent annually. How much money will Mr. Burns need at age 100, and how large of an annual deposit must he make to fund this retirement amount?

57. **(Comprehensive problem)** Suppose that you are in the fall of your senior year and are faced with the choice of either getting a job when you graduate or going to law school. Of course, your choice is not purely financial. However, to make an informed decision you would like to know the financial implications of the two alternatives. Let's assume that your opportunities are as follows:

If you take the "get a job" route you expect to start off with a salary of $40,000 per year. There is no way to predict what will happen in the future, your best guess is that your salary will grow at 5 percent per year until you retire in 40 years. As a law student, you will be paying $25,000 per year tuition for each of the three years you are in graduate school. However, you can then expect a job with a starting salary of $70,000 per year. Moreover, you expect your salary to grow by 7 percent per year until you retire 35 years later.

Clearly, your total expected lifetime salary will be higher if you become a lawyer. However, the additional future salary is not free. You will be paying $25,000 in tuition at the beginning of each of the three years of law school. In addition, you will be giving up a little more than $126,000 in lost income over the three years of law school: $40,000 the first year, $42,000 the second year, and $44,100 the third year.

a. To start your analysis of whether to go to law school, calculate the present value of the future earnings that you will realize by going directly to work, assuming a 3 percent discount rate.

b. What is the present value today of your future earnings if you decide to attend law school, assuming a 3 percent discount rate? Remember that you will be in law school for three years before you start to work as a lawyer. (Hint: Assume that you are paid at the end of each year so that your first salary payment if you decide to go to law school occurs four years from now.)

c. If you pay your law school tuition at the beginning of each year, what is the present value of your tuition, assuming a 3 percent discount rate?

58. **(Present value of a complex stream)** Don Draper has signed a contract that will pay him $80,000 at the end of each year for the next six years, plus an additional $100,000 at the end of Year 6. If 8 percent is the appropriate discount rate, what is the present value of this contract?

59. **(Present value of a complex stream)** Don Draper has signed a contract that will pay him $80,000 at the *beginning* of each year for the next six years, plus an additional $100,000 at the end of Year 6. If 8 percent is the appropriate discount rate, what is the present value of this contract?

60. **(Complex stream of cash flows)** Roger Sterling has decided to buy an ad agency and is going to finance the purchase with seller financing—that is, a loan from the current owners of the agency. The loan will be for $2,000,000 financed at a 7 percent nominal annual interest rate. This loan will be paid off over five years with end-of-month payments along with a $500,000 lump-sum payment at the end of Year 5. That is, the $2 million loan will be paid off with monthly payments and there will also be a final payment of $500,000 at the end of the final month. How much will the monthly payments be?

Mini-Case

Bill Petty, 56, just retired after 31 years of teaching. He is a husband and father of two children who are still dependent. He received a $150,000 lump-sum retirement bonus and will receive $2,800 per month from his retirement annuity. He has saved $150,000 in a 403(b) retirement plan and another $100,000 in other accounts. His 403(b) plan is invested in mutual funds, but most of his other investments are in bank accounts earning 2 or 3 percent annually. Bill has asked your advice in deciding where to invest his lump-sum bonus and other accounts now that he has retired. He also wants to know how much he can withdraw per month, considering he has two children and a nonworking spouse. Because he has children, his current monthly expenses total $5,800. He is not eligible for Social Security until age 62, when he will draw approximately $1,200 per month; however, he would rather defer drawing on Social Security until age 67 to increase his monthly benefit amount to $1,550.

Questions

1. Bill has an emergency fund already set aside, so he can use his $400,000 of savings for retirement. How much can he withdraw on a monthly basis to supplement his retirement annuity if his investments return 5 percent annually and he expects to live 30 more years?

2. Ignoring his Social Security benefit, is the amount determined in question 1 sufficient to meet his current monthly expenses (keep in mind that he will receive a pension of $2,800 per month)? If not, how long will his retirement last if his current expenses remain the same? What if his expenses are reduced to $4,500 per month?

3. Considering the information obtained in question 2, should Bill wait until age 67 for his Social Security benefits? If he waits until age 67, how will his monthly Social Security benefit change the answers to question 2? (*Hint:* Calculate his portfolio value as of age 67 and then calculate how long that amount will last if it earns 5 percent annually.)

4. If the inflation rate averages 3.5 percent during Bill's retirement, how old will he be when prices have doubled from current levels? How much will a soda cost when Bill dies, if he lives the full 30 years and the soda costs $1 today?

Photo Credits

An Introduction
to Risk and Return

From Chapter 7 of *Financial Management: Principles and Applications*, Twelfth Edition. Sheridan Titman, Arthur J. Keown, and John D. Martin.

An Introduction to Risk and Return
History of Financial Market Returns

Chapter **Outline**

1 Realized and Expected Rates of Return and Risk ——————▶ **Objective 1.** Calculate realized and expected rates of return and risk.

2 A Brief History of Financial Market Returns ——————▶ **Objective 2.** Describe the historical pattern of financial market returns.

3 Geometric vs. Arithmetic Average Rates of Return ——————▶ **Objective 3.** Compute geometric (or compound) and arithmetic average rates of return.

4 What Determines Stock Prices? ——————▶ **Objective 4.** Explain the efficient market hypothesis and why it is important to stock prices.

To develop an understanding of why different investments earn different returns, we will focus much of our attention on **P** Principle 2: **There Is a Risk–Return Tradeoff**. Specifically, although investing in higher-risk investments does not always result in higher realized rates of return (that's why they call it risk), higher-risk investments are expected to realize higher returns, on average. So, as we review historical rates of return realized on securities with different risks, we will be looking to see whether or not the riskier investments are indeed rewarded with higher returns. In addition, **P** Principle 4: **Market Prices Reflect Information** will help us understand the wisdom of markets and how investor purchases and sales of a security drive its price to fully reflect all the relevant information about the securities future cash flows.

Trust Fund Baby

Suppose that in January of 1926, your great-grandfather set up a trust for you, his unknown heir, with an investment of $100. If your great-grandfather was very conservative and invested the trust fund in long-term bonds issued by the U.S. government, the trust fund would have grown at a rate of 5.7 percent from January 1926 through December 2011 (a period of 86 years) to be worth about $11,761. This is quite a nice windfall that will help with your books and spending money at college. If, however, the money had been invested in a portfolio of large U.S. stocks, it would have grown at a rate of 9.8 percent and would be worth about $310,314, enough to pay for all of your tuition, and then some. But if your great-grandfather was willing to really gamble with your future and invested the money in the common stock of a portfolio of the smallest publicly traded firms, the investment would have grown at a compound annual rate of return of 11.9 percent and would now be worth more than $1.58 million, enough to pay for your tuition and living expenses and then buy a pretty nice house and car for your graduation present.

In this chapter, we answer three important questions that help us understand why each investment just described yielded very different returns. First, how do we measure the risk and return for an individual investment? Second, what is the history of financial market returns on various classes of financial assets, including domestic and international debt and equity securities as well as real estate and commodities? Finally, what returns should investors expect from investing in risky financial assets? In answering these questions, our introduction to the history of financial market returns will focus primarily on securities such as bonds and shares of common stock, as most corporations use these securities to finance their investments. As we discuss later, the expected rates of return on these securities provide the basis for determining the rate of return that firms require when they invest in new plant and equipment, sales outlets, and the development of new products.

Regardless of Your Major...

"Using Statistics"

Statistics permeate almost all areas of business. Because financial markets provide rich sources of data, it is no surprise that the tools used by statisticians are so widely used in finance. In this chapter, we use the basic tools of descriptive statistics, such as the mean and measures of dispersion, to analyze the riskiness of potential investments. These tools, which are essential for the study of finance, are widely used in all business disciplines as well as in the social sciences. A good understanding of statistics is extremely useful, regardless of your major.

Your Turn: See Study Question 1.

1 Realized and Expected Rates of Return and Risk

We begin our discussion of risk and return by defining some key terms that are critical to developing an understanding of the risk and return inherent in risky investments. We will focus our examples on the risk and return encountered when investing in various types of securities in the financial markets—but the methods we use to measure risk and return are equally applicable to any type of risky investment, such as the introduction of a new product line. Specifically, we provide a detailed definition of both realized and expected rates of return. In addition, we begin our analysis of risk by showing how to calculate the variance and the standard deviation of historical, or realized, rates of return.

Calculating the Realized Return from an Investment

If you bought a share of stock and sold it one year later, the return you would earn on your stock investment would equal the ending price of the share (plus any cash distributions such as dividends) minus the beginning price of the share. This gain or loss on an investment is called a **cash return**, which is summarized in Equation (1) as follows:

$$\text{Cash Return} = \text{Ending Price} + \text{Cash Distribution (Dividend)} - \text{Beginning Price} \tag{1}$$

Consider what you would have earned by investing in one share of Dick's Sporting Goods (DKS) stock at the end of May 2008 and then selling that share one year later at the beginning of June 2009. Substituting into Equation (1), you would calculate the cash return as follows:

$$\text{Cash Return} = \text{Ending Price} + \text{Cash Distribution (Dividend)} - \text{Beginning Price} = \$17.80 + 0.00 - 23.15 = -\$5.35$$

In this instance, you would have realized a loss of $5.35 on your investment, because the firm's stock price dropped over the year from $23.15 down to $17.80 and the firm did not make any cash distributions to its stockholders.

The method we have just used to compute the return on Dick's Sporting Goods stock provides the gain or loss we experienced during a period. We call this the cash return for the period.

In addition to calculating a cash return, we can calculate the rate of return as a percentage. As a general rule, we summarize the return on an investment in terms of a percentage return, because we can compare these percentage rates of return across different investments. The **rate of return** (sometimes referred to as a **holding period return**) is simply the cash return divided by the beginning stock price, as defined in Equation (2):

$$\frac{\text{Rate of}}{\text{Return}} = \frac{\text{Cash Return}}{\text{Beginning Price}} = \frac{\overset{\text{Ending}}{\text{Price}} + \overset{\text{Cash Distribution}}{\text{(Dividend)}} - \overset{\text{Beginning}}{\text{Price}}}{\overset{\text{Beginning}}{\text{Price}}} \qquad (2)$$

Table 1 contains beginning prices, dividends (cash distributions), and ending prices spanning a one-year holding period for five public firms. We use this data to compute the realized rates of return for a one-year period of time beginning on October 8, 2008, and ending with October 9, 2009. To illustrate, we calculate the rate of return earned from the investment in Dick's Sporting Goods stock as the ratio of the cash return (found in Column D of Table 1) to your investment in the stock at the beginning of the period (found in Column A). For this investment, your rate of return is a whopping 45% = $7.37/15.32. Even though Dick's paid no cash dividends, its stock price rose from $15.32 at the beginning of the period to $22.69, or by $7.37 over the year—you would have earned a 45 percent rate of return on the stock if you had bought and sold on these dates.

Notice that all the realized rates of return found in Table 1 are positive except for Walmart (WMT), which experienced a negative rate of return. Does this mean that if we purchase shares of Walmart stock today we should expect to realize a negative rate of return over the next year? The answer is an emphatic no. The fact that Walmart's stock earned a negative rate of return in the past is evidence that investing in stock is risky. So, the fact that we realized a negative rate of return does not mean we should expect negative rates of return in the future. Future returns are risky and they may be negative or they may be positive; however, **P** Principle 2: **There Is a Risk–Return Tradeoff** tells us that we will expect to receive higher returns for assuming more risk (even though there is no guarantee we will get what we expect).

Calculating the Expected Return from an Investment

We call the gain or loss we actually experienced on a stock during a period the realized rate of return for that period. However, the risk–return tradeoff that investors face is *not* based on realized rates of return; it is instead based on what the investor *expects* to earn on an investment

Table 1	Measuring an Investor's Realized Rate of Return from Investing in Common Stock					
	Stock Prices		**Cash Distribution (Dividend)**	**Return**		
	Beginning (Oct. 8, 2008)	**Ending (Oct. 9, 2009)**		**Cash**	**Rate**
Company	A	B	C	D = C + B − A	E = D/A
Dick's Sporting Goods (DKS)	$15.32	$22.69	$0.00	$ 7.37	45.0%
Duke Energy (DUK)	16.38	15.82	1.16	$ 0.60	1.8%
Emerson Electric (EMR)	32.73	37.75	1.32	$ 6.34	19.4%
Sears Holdings (SHLD)	57.74	67.86	0.00	$10.12	17.5%
Walmart (WMT)	55.81	49.68	1.06	(5.07)	−9.1%

Legend:

We formalize the return calculations found in Columns D and E using Equations (1) and (2):

Column D (Cash or Dollar Return)

$$\frac{\text{Cash}}{\text{Return}} = \frac{\text{Ending}}{\text{Price}} + \frac{\text{Cash Distribution}}{\text{(Dividend)}} - \frac{\text{Beginning}}{\text{Price}} = P_{End} + \text{Div} - P_{Beginning} \qquad (1)$$

Column E (Rate of Return)

$$\frac{\text{Rate of}}{\text{Return}, r} = \frac{\text{Cash Return}}{\text{Beginning Price}} = \frac{P_{End} + \text{Div} - P_{Beginning}}{P_{Beginning}} \qquad (2)$$

in the future. We can think of the rate of return that will ultimately be realized from making a risky investment in terms of a range of possible return outcomes, much like the distribution of grades for a class at the end of the term. The **expected rate of return** is the weighted average of the possible returns, where the weights are determined by the probability that it occurs.

To illustrate the calculation of an expected rate of return, consider an investment of $10,000 in shares of common stock that you plan to sell at the end of one year. To simplify the computations we will assume that the stock will not pay any dividends during the year, so that your total cash return comes from the difference between the beginning-of-year and end-of-year prices of the shares of stock, which will depend on the state of the overall economy. In Table 2 we see that there is a 20 percent probability that the economy will be in recession at year's end and that the value of your $10,000 investment will be worth only $9,000, providing you with a loss on your investment of $1,000 (a −10 percent rate of return). Similarly, there is a 30 percent probability the economy will experience moderate growth, in which case you will realize a $1,200 gain and a 12 percent rate of return on your investment by year's end. Finally, there is a 50 percent chance that the economy will experience strong growth, in which case your investment will realize a 22 percent gain.

Column G of Table 2 contains the products of the probability of each state of the economy (recession, moderate growth, or strong growth) found in Column B and the rate of return earned if that state occurs (Column F). By adding up these probability-weighted rates of return for the three states of the economy, we calculate an expected rate of return for the investment of 12.6 percent.

Equation (3) summarizes the calculation in Column G of Table 2, where there are n possible outcomes.

$$\begin{pmatrix} \text{Expected Rate} \\ \text{of Return} \\ [E(r)] \end{pmatrix} = \begin{pmatrix} \text{Rate of} & \text{Probability} \\ \text{Return 1} \times \text{of Return 1} \\ (r_1) & (Pb_1) \end{pmatrix} + \begin{pmatrix} \text{Rate of} & \text{Probability} \\ \text{Return 2} \times \text{of Return 2} \\ (r_2) & (Pb_2) \end{pmatrix} + \cdots + \begin{pmatrix} \text{Rate of} & \text{Probability} \\ \text{Return } n \times \text{of Return } n \\ (r_n) & (Pb_n) \end{pmatrix} \quad \textbf{(3)}$$

We can use Equation (3) to calculate the expected rate of return for the investment in Table 2, where there are three possible outcomes, as follows:

$$E(r) = (-10\% \times .2) + (12\% \times .3) + (22\% \times .5) = 12.6\%$$

Measuring Risk

In the example we just examined, we *expect* to realize a 12.6 percent return on our investment; however, the return could be as little as −10 percent or as high as 22 percent. There are two methods financial analysts can use to quantify the variability of an investment's returns. The

Table 2   Calculating the Expected Rate of Return for an Investment in Common Stock

State of the Economy	Probability of the State of the Economy[a] (Pb_i)	End-of-Year Selling Price for the Stock	Beginning Price of the Stock	Cash Return from Your Investment	Percentage Rate of Return = Cash Return/Beginning Price of the Stock	Product = Rate of Return × Probability of State of the Economy
Column A	Column B	Column C	Column D	Column E = C − D	Column F = E ÷ D	Column G = B × F
Recession	20%	$ 9,000	$10,000	$(1,000)	−10% = − $1,000 ÷ $10,000	−2.0%
Moderate growth	30%	11,200	10,000	1,200	12% = $1,200 ÷ $10,000	3.6%
Strong growth	50%	12,200	10,000	2,200	22% = $2,200 ÷ $10,000	11%
Sum	100%					12.6%

[a]The probabilities assigned to the three possible economic conditions have to be determined subjectively, which requires management to have a thorough understanding of both the investment cash flows and the general economy.

first is the **variance** of the investment returns and the second is the **standard deviation**, which is the square root of the variance. Recall that the variance is the average squared difference between the individual realized returns and the expected return. To better understand this we will examine both the variance and the standard deviation of an investment's rate of return.

Calculating the Variance and Standard Deviation of the Rate of Return on an Investment

Let's compare two possible investment alternatives:

1. **U.S. Treasury Bill.** A short-term (maturity of one year or less) debt obligation of the U.S. government. The particular Treasury bill that we consider matures in one year and promises to pay an annual return of 5 percent. This security has a **risk-free rate of return**, which means that if we purchase and hold this security for one year, we can be confident of receiving no more and no less than a 5 percent return. The term *risk-free security* specifically refers to a security for which there is no risk of default on the promised payments.

2. **Common Stock of the Ace Publishing Company.** A risky investment in the common stock of a company we will call Ace Publishing Company.

The **probability distribution** of an investment's returns contains all the possible rates of return from the investment that might occur, along with the associated probabilities for each outcome. Figure 1 contains a probability distribution of the possible rates of return that we might realize on these two investments. The probability distribution for a risk-free investment in Treasury bills is illustrated as a single spike at a 5 percent rate of return. This spike indicates that if you purchase a Treasury bill, there is a 100 percent chance that you will earn a 5 percent annual rate of return. The probability distribution for the common stock investment, however, includes returns as low as −10 percent and as high as 40 percent. Thus, the common stock investment is risky, whereas the Treasury bill is not.

Figure 1

Probability Distribution of Returns for a Treasury Bill and the Common Stock of the Ace Publishing Company

A probability distribution provides a tool for describing the possible outcomes or rates of return from an investment and the associated probabilities for each possible outcome. Technically, the following probability distribution is a discrete distribution because there are only five possible returns that the Ace Publishing Company stock can earn. The Treasury bill investment offers only one possible rate of return (5%) because this investment is risk-free.

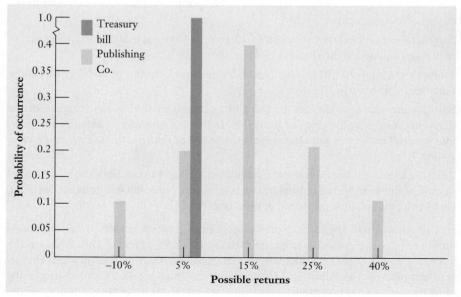

Chance or Probability of Occurrence	Rate of Return on Investment
1 chance in 10 (10%)	−10%
2 chances in 10 (20%)	5%
4 chances in 10 (40%)	15%
2 chances in 10 (20%)	25%
1 chance in 10 (10%)	40%

>> END FIGURE 1

Using Equation (3), we calculate the expected rate of return for the stock investment as follows:

$$E(r) = (.10)(-10\%) + (.20)(5\%) + (.40)(15\%) + (.20)(25\%) + (.10)(40\%) = 15\%$$

Thus, the common stock investment in Ace Publishing Company gives us an expected rate of return of 15 percent. As we saw earlier, the Treasury bill investment offers an expected rate of return of only 5 percent. Does this mean that the common stock is a better investment than the Treasury bill because it offers a higher expected rate of return? The answer is no, because the two investments have very different risks. The common stock might earn a negative 10 percent rate of return or a positive 40 percent, whereas the Treasury bill offers only one positive rate of 5 percent.

One way to measure the risk of an investment is to calculate the variance of the possible rates of return, which is the average of the squared deviations from the expected rate of return. Specifically, the formula for the return variance of an investment with n possible future returns can be calculated using Equation (4) as follows:

$$
\begin{aligned}
\begin{matrix} \text{Variance in} \\ \text{Rates of Return} \\ (\sigma^2) \end{matrix} = &\left[\left(\begin{matrix} \text{Rate of} \\ \text{Return 1} \\ (r_1) \end{matrix} - \begin{matrix} \text{Expected Rate} \\ \text{of Return} \\ E(r) \end{matrix} \right)^2 \times \begin{matrix} \text{Probability} \\ \text{of Return 1} \\ (Pb_1) \end{matrix} \right] \\[2ex]
+ &\left[\left(\begin{matrix} \text{Rate of} \\ \text{Return 2} \\ (r_2) \end{matrix} - \begin{matrix} \text{Expected Rate} \\ \text{of Return} \\ E(r) \end{matrix} \right)^2 \times \begin{matrix} \text{Probability} \\ \text{of Return 2} \\ (Pb_2) \end{matrix} \right] \\[2ex]
+ \cdots + &\left[\left(\begin{matrix} \text{Rate of} \\ \text{Return 3} \\ (r_n) \end{matrix} - \begin{matrix} \text{Expected Rate} \\ \text{of Return} \\ E(r) \end{matrix} \right)^2 \times \begin{matrix} \text{Probability} \\ \text{of Return } n \\ (Pb_n) \end{matrix} \right]
\end{aligned}
\tag{4}
$$

Note that the variance is measured using squared deviations of each possible return from the mean or expected return. Thus, the variance is a measure of the average "squared" deviation around the mean. For this reason it is customary to measure risk as the square root of the variance—which, as we learned in our statistics class, is called the standard deviation.

For Ace Publishing Company's common stock, we calculate the variance and standard deviation using the following five-step procedure:

Step 1. Calculate the expected rate of return using Equation (3). This was calculated previously to be 15 percent.

Step 2. Subtract the expected rate of return of 15 percent from each of the possible rates of return and square the difference.

Step 3. Multiply the squared differences calculated in Step 2 by the probability that those outcomes will occur.

Step 4. Sum all the values calculated in Step 3 together. The sum is the variance of the distribution of possible rates of return. Note that the variance is actually the *average squared difference between the possible rates of return and the expected rate of return.*

Step 5. Take the square root of the variance calculated in Step 4 to calculate the standard deviation of the distribution of possible rates of return. Note that the standard deviation (unlike the variance) is measured in rates of return.

Table 3 illustrates the application of this procedure, which results in an estimated standard deviation for the common stock investment of 12.85 percent. This standard deviation compares to the 0 percent standard deviation of a risk-free Treasury bill investment. The investment in Ace Publishing Company carries higher risk than investing in the Treasury bill because it can potentially result in a return of 40 percent or possibly a loss of 10 percent. The standard deviation measure captures this difference in the risks of the two investments.

Table 3	Measuring the Variance and Standard Deviation of an Investment in Ace Publishing's Common Stock

Computing the variance and standard deviation in the rate of return earned from a stock investment can be carried out using the following five-step process:

Step 1. Calculate the expected rate of return.

Step 2. Subtract the expected rate of return from each of the possible rates of return and square the difference.

Step 3. Multiply the squared differences calculated in Step 2 by the probability that those outcomes will occur.

Step 4. Sum all the values calculated in Step 3 together to calculate the variance of the possible rates of return.

Step 5. Take the square root of the variance calculated in Step 4 to calculate the standard deviation of the distribution of possible rates of return.

State of the World	Rate of Return	Chance or Probability		Step 2	Step 3
a	b	c	$d = b \times c$	$e = [b - E(r)]^2$	$f = e \times c$
1	−0.10	0.10	−0.01	0.0625	0.00625
3	0.05	0.20	0.01	0.0100	0.00200
4	0.15	0.40	0.06	0.0000	0.00000
4	0.25	0.20	0.05	0.0100	0.00200
5	0.40	0.10	0.04	0.0625	0.00625

Step 1: Expected Return (E(r)) = ⟶ 0.15
Step 4: Variance = ⟶ 0.0165
Step 5: Standard Deviation = ⟶ 0.1285

Alternatively, we can formalize the five-step procedure above for the calculation of the standard deviation as follows:

$$\text{Standard Deviation, } \sigma = \sqrt{\text{Variance}}$$

$$\sigma = \sqrt{([r_1 - E(r)]^2 \, Pb_1) + ([r_2 - E(r)]^2 \, Pb_2) + \cdots + ([r_n - E(r)]^2 \, Pb_n)} \qquad \textbf{(5)}$$

where	
$\sigma =$	standard deviation
$r_i =$	possible return i
$E(r) =$	the expected return
$Pb_i =$	the probability of return i

Using Equation (5) to calculate the standard deviation we find:

$$\sigma = \left[\begin{array}{l} ((-.10 - .15)^2 \times .10) + ((.05 - .15)^2 \times .20) \\ +((.15 - .15)^2 \times .40) + ((.25 - .15)^2 \times .20) \\ +((.40 - .15)^2 \times .10) \end{array} \right]^{1/2} = \sqrt{.0165} = .1285 \text{ or } 12.85\%$$

Now, let's suppose that you are considering putting all of your wealth in either the Ace Publishing Company or in a quick-oil-change franchise. The quick-oil-change franchise provides a high expected rate of return of 24 percent, but the standard deviation is estimated to be 18 percent.

Which investment would you prefer? The oil-change franchise has a higher expected rate of return, but it also has more risk, as is evidenced by its larger standard deviation. So your choice will be determined by your attitude toward risk. You might select the publishing company, whereas another investor might choose the oil-change investment, and neither would be wrong. You would each simply be expressing your tastes and preferences about risk and return.

Checkpoint 1

Evaluating an Investment's Return and Risk

Clarion Investment Advisors is evaluating the distribution of returns for a new stock investment and has come up with five possible rates of return for the coming year. Their associated probabilities are as follows:

Chance (Probability) of Occurrence	Rate of Return on Investment
1 chance in 10 (10%)	−20%
2 chances in 10 (20%)	0%
4 chances in 10 (40%)	15%
2 chances in 10 (20%)	30%
1 chance in 10 (10%)	50%

a. What expected rate of return might they expect to realize from the investment?
b. What is the risk of the investment as measured using the standard deviation of possible future rates of return?

STEP 1: Picture the problem

The distribution of possible rates of return for the investment, along with the probabilities of each, can be depicted in a probability distribution as follows:

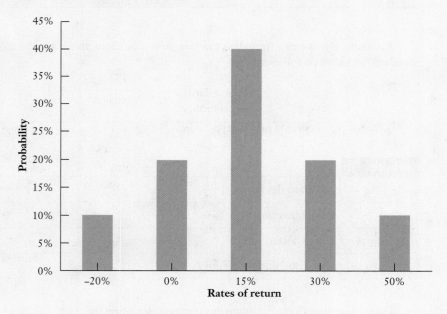

The probabilities of each of the potential rates of return are read off the vertical axis and the returns are found on the horizontal axis.

STEP 2: Decide on a solution strategy

We use the expected value of the rate of return to measure Clarion's expected return from the investment and the standard deviation to evaluate its risk. We can use Equations (3) and (5) for these tasks.

STEP 3: Solve

Calculating the Expected Return.

We use Equation (3) to calculate the expected rate of return for the investment as follows:

$$E(r) = r_1 Pb_1 + r_2 Pb_2 + \cdots + r_n Pb_n \tag{3}$$

$$E(r) = (-20\% \times .10) + (0\% \times .20) + (15\% \times .40) + (30\% \times .20) + (50\% \times .10) = 15\%$$

Calculating the Standard Deviation.

Next, we calculate the standard deviation using Equation (5) as follows:

$$\sigma = \sqrt{([r_1 - E(r)]^2 Pb_1) + ([r_2 - E(r)]^2 Pb_2) + \cdots + ([r_n - E(r)]^2 Pb_n)} \tag{5}$$

$$\sigma = \sqrt{([-.20 - .15]^2 .10) + ([.00 - .15]^2 .20) + ([.15 - .15]^2 .40) + ([.30 - .15]^2 .20) + ([.50 - .15]^2 .10)}$$

$$\sigma = \sqrt{.0335} = .183 \text{ or } 18.3\%$$

STEP 4: Analyze

The expected rate of return for the investment is 15 percent; however, because there is a 10 percent chance that the actual return may be 50 percent and a 10 percent chance that the actual return may be −20 percent, it is obvious that this is a *risky* investment. In this example, the standard deviation, which is a measure of the average or expected dispersion of the investment returns, is equal to 18.3 percent. Because the distribution of returns is described in terms of five discrete return possibilities, we can make probability statements about the possible outcomes from the investment such as the following: There is a 10 percent probability of a realized rate of return of 50 percent, and a 20 percent probability of a return of 30 percent, and so forth.

STEP 5: Check yourself

Compute the expected return and standard deviation for an investment with the same rates of return as in the previous example but with probabilities for each possible return equal to: .2, .2, .3, .2, and .1.

ANSWER: Expected return = 11.5 percent and standard deviation = 21.10 percent.

Your Turn: For more practice, do related **Study Problems** 1 and 6 at the end of this chapter.   **>> END Checkpoint1**

Tools of Financial Analysis—Measuring Investment Returns

Name of Tool	Formula	What It Tells You
Cash (Dollar) Return	$= \dfrac{Ending}{Price, P_{End}} + \dfrac{Cash\ Distribution}{(Dividend, Div)} - \dfrac{Beginning}{Price, P_{Beginning}}$	• Measures the return from investing in a security in dollars • The higher the cash return, the greater the return earned by the investment (measured in dollars).
Rate of Return, r =	$\dfrac{Cash\ (Dollar)\ Return}{Beginning\ Price} = \dfrac{P_{End} + Div - P_{Beginning}}{P_{Beginning}}$	• Measures the return from investing in a security as a percent of the dollars invested • A higher rate of return means a greater return earned by the investment (measured as a percent of the initial investment).
Expected Rate of Return, E(r)	$\left(\begin{array}{c} Rate\ of \\ Return\ 1\ (r_1) \end{array} \times \begin{array}{c} Probability\ that \\ Return\ 1\ will\ occur\ (Pb_1) \end{array}\right) +$ $\left(\begin{array}{c} Rate\ of \\ Return\ 2\ (r_2) \end{array} \times \begin{array}{c} Probability\ that \\ Return\ 2\ will\ occur\ (Pb_2) \end{array}\right) +$ $\left(\begin{array}{c} Rate\ of \\ Return\ 3\ (r_3) \end{array} \times \begin{array}{c} Probability\ that \\ Return\ 3\ will\ occur\ (Pb_3) \end{array}\right)$	• The probability weighted average rate of return anticipated for an investment • The higher the expected rate of return, the greater its impact on the wealth of the investor.

Name of Tool	Formula	What It Tells You
Variance in the Rate of Return, σ^2	$$\left(\begin{array}{c}\text{Rate of} \\ \text{Return } 1(r_1)\end{array} - \begin{array}{c}\text{Expected Rate} \\ \text{of Return, } E(r)\end{array}\right)^2$$ $$\times \begin{array}{c}\text{Probability that} \\ \text{Return 1 will Occur }(Pb_1)\end{array}$$ $$+\left(\begin{array}{c}\text{Rate of} \\ \text{Return } 2(r_2)\end{array} - \begin{array}{c}\text{Expected Rate} \\ \text{of Return, } E(r)\end{array}\right)^2$$ $$\times \begin{array}{c}\text{Probability that} \\ \text{Return 1 will Occur }(Pb_2)\end{array} + \cdots$$ $$+\left(\begin{array}{c}\text{Rate of} \\ \text{Return } n(r_n)\end{array} - \begin{array}{c}\text{Expected Rate} \\ \text{of Return, } E(r)\end{array}\right)^2$$ $$\times \begin{array}{c}\text{Probability that} \\ \text{Return } n \text{ will Occur }(Pb_n)\end{array}$$	• The average variability of the rate of return • The higher the variability, in general, the greater the total riskiness of the security.

Before you move on to 2

Concept Check | 1

1. If you invested $100 one year ago that is worth $110 today, what rate of return did you earn on your investment?
2. What is the expected rate of return, and how is it different than the realized rate of return?
3. What is the variance in the rate of return of an investment?
4. Why is variance used to measure risk?

2 A Brief History of Financial Market Returns

Now that we have learned how to measure the risk and return of an investment, we can use these measurement tools to analyze how securities have performed in the past. This is useful when an investor wants to assess whether or not to invest in a security. Let's look at the historical returns earned on a wide variety of domestic and international investments. As we might expect from **P** Principle 2: **There Is a Risk-Return Tradeoff**, investors have historically earned higher rates of return on riskier investments.

Note, however, that having a higher expected rate of return simply means that you expect to realize a higher rate of return, not that you will always receive a higher return. In fact, the very definition of risk suggests that there will be times when you are not rewarded for assuming more risk. Think back to Table 1 where we looked at the realized rates of return for five different companies' stock for the year that ended in June 2009. In all five example companies, the realized rates of return were negative, suggesting that, at least for this time period, risk was not rewarded. This is what we mean by risk—you face the prospect of not realizing your expected return!

U.S. Financial Markets: Domestic Investment Returns

In the introduction to this chapter we talked about a $100 investment made by a benevolent great-grandfather that grew over a period of 84 years. In this example, we saw how different investment options with different levels of risk can result in very different returns. Let's take a look at how different investments have performed. Figure 2 shows the historical returns earned on four types of investments over the period 1926–2009:

- **Small stocks.** Shares of the smallest 20 percent of all companies whose stock is traded on the public exchanges. (Firm size is measured using the market capitalization of the company's equity, which is equal to the share price multiplied by the number of shares outstanding.)

- **Large stocks.** The Standard & Poor's (S&P) 500 stock index, which is a portfolio that consists mainly of large company stocks such as Walmart (WMT), Intel (INTC), and Microsoft (MSFT).

- **Government bonds.** 20-year bonds issued by the federal government. These bonds are typically considered to be free of the risk of default or non-payment because the government is the most credit-worthy borrower in the country.

- **Treasury bills.** Short-term securities issued by the federal government that have maturities of one year or less.

P Principle 2: **There Is a Risk-Return Tradeoff** tells us that higher-risk investments should expect to receive higher rates of return. Let's see what would have happened if your great-grandfather invested $1 in each of these investment alternatives.

The graph in Figure 2 shows the value of a $1 investment made in each of these asset categories in 1926 and held until the end of 2011. Large and small stocks have provided the

---

Figure 2

Historical Rates of Return for U.S. Financial Securities: 1926–2011

The following graph provides historical insight into the performance characteristics of various asset classes over an 86-year period of time. This graph illustrates the hypothetical growth of inflation and a $1 investment in four traditional asset classes over the time period January 1, 1926, through December 31, 2011.

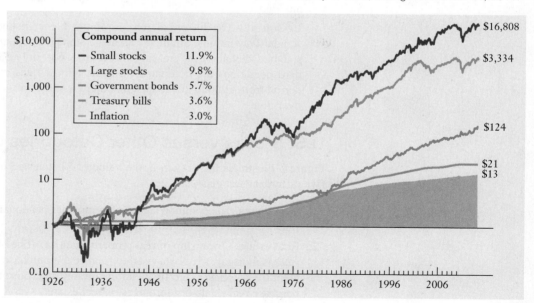

Legend:

Small stocks in this example are represented by the fifth capitalization quintile of stocks on the NYSE for 1926–1981 and the performance of the Dimensional Fund Advisors, Inc. (DFA) U.S. Micro Cap Portfolio thereafter. Large stocks are represented by the Standard & Poor's 90 index from 1926 through February 1957 and the S&P 500® index thereafter, which is an unmanaged group of securities and considered to be representative of the U.S. stock market in general. Government bonds are represented by the 20-year U.S. government bond, Treasury bills by the 30-day U.S. Treasury bill, and inflation by the Consumer Price Index. Underlying data is from the *Stocks, Bonds, Bills, and Inflation® (SBBI®) Yearbook*, by Roger G. Ibbotson and Rex Sinquefield, updated annually. An investment cannot be made directly in an index.

Source: © 2012 Morningstar. All rights reserved. Used with permission.

>> **END FIGURE 2**

highest returns and largest increase in wealth over the past 86 years. Fixed-income investments provided only a fraction of the growth provided by stocks. However, the higher returns achieved by stocks are associated with much greater risk, which can be identified by the fluctuation of the graph lines. Moreover, in the following table we see that the standard deviations of the annual rates of return for the four investment alternatives are highest for small company stocks and lowest for the risk-free Treasury bills.

	Small Stocks	Large Stocks	Government Bonds	Treasury Bills
Compound annual return	11.9%	9.8%	5.7%	3.6%
Standard deviation	32.8%	20.5%	9.6%	3.1%

Lessons Learned

A review of the historical returns in the U.S. financial markets reveals two important lessons:

- **Lesson #1.** The riskier investments have historically realized higher returns. The riskiest investment class is comprised of the stocks of the smallest set of firms followed by the stocks of large companies, then corporate bonds, long-term U.S. government bonds, and finally Treasury bills. The difference between the returns of the riskier stock investments and the less risky investments in government securities is called the **equity risk premium**. For example, referring to the previous compound annual return table, the premium of large company common stocks over long-term government bonds averages 9.8% − 5.4% = 4.4%. A similar comparison to short-term Treasury bills reveals an average risk premium of 9.8% − 3.7% = 6.1%. The risk premiums for small company stocks are even higher because the average returns earned by the smaller and riskier firms are higher.

- **Lesson #2.** The historical returns of the higher-risk investment classes have higher standard deviations. Small stocks had a standard deviation of 32.8 percent, whereas the standard deviation of Treasury bill returns was only 3.1 percent. Note that these standard deviations are computed from the annual rates of return realized over the entire period from 1926 to 2011, such that there is some variation even in the Treasury bill rate over time.

U.S. Stocks versus Other Categories of Investments

Figure 3 illustrates the growth in the value of $1 invested in 1980 until the end of 2009 for five different asset classes:

1. **U.S. stocks.** The common shares of companies headquartered in the United States whose shares are traded in the U.S. stock market.
2. **Real estate.** Ownership of real property such as office buildings, land, and apartments as well as mortgages or loans used to finance the purchase of real estate. Real estate investment trusts (REITs) are financial institutions that raise money from investors and either purchase real estate or mortgages on real estate.
3. **International stocks.** The common shares of companies headquartered outside of the United States.
4. **Commodities.** Basic resources such as iron ore, crude oil, coal, ethanol, salt, sugar, coffee beans, soybeans, aluminum, copper, rice, wheat, gold, silver, and platinum.
5. **Gold.** This particular commodity has historically been used as a store of value by many investors. Its value tends to rise with inflation such that investors often purchase gold as a means of preserving the value of their savings during times of rising prices or inflation.

Figure 3

Stocks, Bonds, Commodities, and Real Estate

This image illustrates the hypothetical growth of a $1 investment in domestic stocks, international stocks, commodities such as copper, REITs (real estate investment trusts that invest in commercial real estate and real estate mortgage loans), and commodities over the time period January 1, 1980, to December 31, 2011.

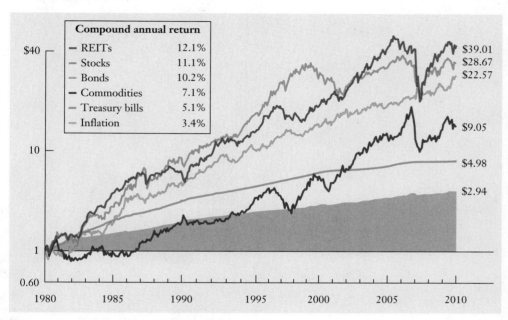

Legend:

Stocks in this example are represented by the Standard & Poor's 500®, which is an unmanaged group of securities and considered to be representative of the U.S. stock market in general. Bonds in this example are represented by the 20-year U.S. government bond, Treasury bills by the 30-day U.S. Treasury bill, and inflation by the Consumer Price Index. Commodities are represented by the Morningstar Long-Only Commodity Index and REITs by the FTSE NAREIT All Equity REITs Index®. An investment cannot be made directly in an index.

Source: © 2012 Morningstar. All rights reserved. Used with permission.

>> END FIGURE 3

Global Financial Markets: International Investing

Figure 4 compares the historical returns from investing in U.S. stocks and bonds to the returns on international stocks and bonds. These annual ranges of returns provide an indication of the historical risk experienced by investments in various global markets. This fluctuation in rates of return earned over a period of time is called the investment's **volatility**. We measure investment return volatility using the standard deviation as we discussed earlier. For example, an investment in Pacific stocks generated annual rates of return as high as 107.5 percent—or as low as −36.2 percent. In contrast, U.S. stocks had the narrowest range of returns, which implies that U.S. stocks experienced less volatility than an investment in other regions of the world.

Figure 5 compares the average rates of return earned from investing in developed countries, such as the U.S., Europe, and some parts of Asia, to the returns from investing in the equities of companies located in emerging markets. An **emerging market** is one located in an economy with low-to-middle per capita income. These countries constitute roughly 80 percent of the world's population and represent about a fifth of the world's economies.

Figure 4

Historical Rates of Return in Global Markets: 1970–2011

This figure reports the ranges of annual returns for domestic and international composites, as well as the Europe and Pacific regional composites, over the period 1970 through 2011.

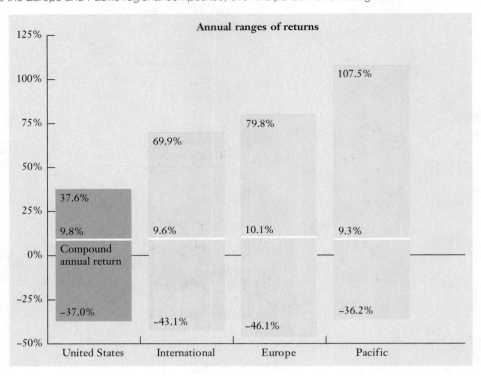

Legend:

U.S. stocks in this example are represented by the Standard & Poor's 500® index, which is an unmanaged group of securities and considered to be representative of the U.S. stock market in general. International stocks are represented by the Morgan Stanley Capital International Europe, Australasia, and Far East (EAFE®) Index, European stocks by the Morgan Stanley Capital International Europe Index, and Pacific stocks by the Morgan Stanley Capital International Pacific Index. An investment cannot be made directly in an index. The data assumes reinvestment of income and does not account for taxes or transaction costs.

Source: © 2012 Morningstar. All rights reserved. Used with permission.

>> END FIGURE 4

China and India are perhaps the best known and largest of the emerging market economies. A **developed country** is sometimes referred to as an industrialized country, where the term is used to identify those countries such as the U.S., Great Britain, France, and so forth that have highly sophisticated and well-developed economies. The average rates of return from investing in developed countries were generally lower than those earned in the emerging market group. However, the most apparent difference in the two relates to risk as reflected in the range of annual rates of return. The top of the bar chart indicates the maximum rate of return realized over the period covered by the chart and the bottom reflects the minimum, so the span of the bar reflects the variability of past rates of return. Note that the emerging market rates of return were much more volatile over the period 1988–2011.

If investing in the stock of companies from emerging markets is so much more risky than investing in domestic equities or equities of companies from developed countries, why do it? The answer may well come from a consideration of the risk-reduction benefits that come about when you invest in both types of securities.

Figure 5

Investing in Emerging Markets: 1988–2011

The following graph illustrates the range of returns as well as the compound annual return of selected developed and emerging countries. Although both sets experienced growth, emerging markets experienced a much greater upside and often deeper downside.

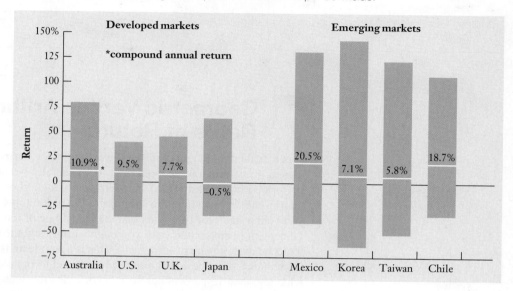

Legend:

Equities for the U.K., Australia, Japan, Taiwan, and Mexico are represented by the Morgan Stanley Capital International country indexes. Equities for Korea and Chile are represented by the Morgan Stanley Capital International Emerging Market country indexes. United States equities are represented by the Standard & Poor's 500®, which is an unmanaged group of securities and considered to be representative of the U.S. stock market in general. An investment cannot be made directly in an index. Keep in mind that the countries illustrated do not represent investment advice. The developed countries illustrated are a common range of investment options. Emerging-market countries were chosen based on availability of historical data; those with the longest stream of data were selected.

*Compounded annual return

Source: © 2012 Morningstar. All rights reserved. Used with permission.

>> END FIGURE 5

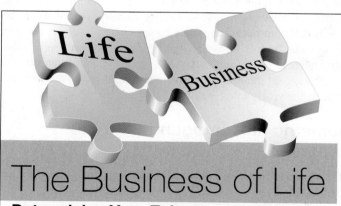

The Business of Life

Determining Your Tolerance for Risk

An important factor affecting individuals' decisions as to how to invest their savings is their personal tolerance for risk. Consider the following scenario:

You have just finished saving up for a "once-in-a-lifetime" vacation. Three weeks before you plan to leave, you lose your job. How would you handle this situation? Specifically, choose the one response from the following list that best describes what you would do:

- Cancel the vacation.
- Take a much more modest vacation.
- Go as scheduled, reasoning that you need the time to prepare for a job search.
- Extend your vacation because this might be your last chance to go first-class.[1]

As you might guess, the alternative that you select suggests something about your personal tolerance for risk. If you want to learn more about your risk tolerance, take a look at the Rutgers' RCE website: (www.rce.rutgers.edu/money/riskquiz).

Your Turn: See Study Question 14.

[1]Risk Tolerance Quiz Source: Grable, J. E., & Lytton, R. H. (1999). Financial risk tolerance revisited: The development of a risk assessment instrument. *Financial Services Review, 8,* 163–181. Ruth Lytton and John Grable, Investment Risk Tolerance Quiz, www.rce.rutgers.edu/money/riskquiz/

Before you move on to 3

Concept Check | 2

1. How well does the risk–return principle hold up in light of historical rates of return? Explain.
2. What is the equity risk premium, and how is it measured?
3. Does the historical evidence suggest that investing in emerging markets is more or less risky than investing in developed markets?

Geometric Versus Arithmetic Average Rates of Return

When evaluating the possibility of investing in a security or financial asset such as those discussed in the previous section, investors generally begin by looking at how that investment performed in the past. This often entails looking at how the investment has performed over many years. It is common to summarize the past returns as a yearly average. For example, if you held a stock for two years that realized a rate of return of 10 percent in the first year and 20 percent in the second year, you might simply add the two rates together and divide by two to get an average rate of 15 percent. This is a simple **arithmetic average return**. However, as we will describe, the actual return you realized from holding the stock for two years is somewhat less than 15 percent per year. To describe the actual two-year return you would need to know the **geometric** or **compound average return**.

Let's look at an example. Suppose you invest $100 in a particular stock. After one year, your investment rises to $150. But unfortunately, in the second year it falls to $75. What was the average return on this investment? In this first year, the stock realized a rate of return of 50 percent and in the second year, it realized a rate of return of −50 percent. If we took the simple average of these two rates, we get 0 percent, indicating that the average yearly investment return over the two-year period is 0 percent. However, this does not mean that you earned a 0 percent rate of return, because you began with $100 and ended two years later with only $75! In actuality, over the two-year investment period, the $100 investment lost the equivalent of −13.4 percent.

In the above example, the 0 percent rate is referred to as the arithmetic average rate of return, whereas the −13.4 percent rate is referred to as the geometric or compound average rate. The arithmetic average is the simple average we have already learned to calculate in this chapter. The geometric average is different because it takes compounding into account. For example, a 50 percent increase in value from $100 is $50, but a 50 percent decrease in value from $150 is $75. The geometric average rate of return answers the question, "What was the growth rate of your investment?" whereas the arithmetic average rate of return answers the question, "What was the average of the yearly rates of return?"

Computing the Geometric or Compound Average Rate of Return

The geometric average rate of return for a multiyear investment spanning n years is calculated as follows:

$$\text{Geometric Average Return} = \left[\left(1 + \frac{\text{Rate of Return}}{\text{for Year 1, } r_{Year\,1}}\right) \times \left(1 + \frac{\text{Rate of Return}}{\text{for Year 2, } r_{Year\,2}}\right) \times \cdots \times \left(1 + \frac{\text{Rate of Return}}{\text{for Year } n, r_{Year\,n}}\right)\right]^{1/n} - 1 \quad \textbf{(6)}$$

Note that we multiply together 1 plus the annual rate of return for each of the n years, and then take the nth root of the product to get the geometric average of (1 + annual rate of return), and then subtract 1 to get the geometric average rate of return.

To illustrate the calculation of the geometric average rate of return, consider the return earned by the $100 investment that grew in value by 50 percent to $150 in Year 1 and dropped by 50 percent to $75 in Year 2. The arithmetic average rate of return is 0 percent.

We can calculate the geometric annual rate of return for this investment using Equation (6) as follows:

$$\begin{array}{c}\text{Geometric}\\ \text{Average Return}\end{array} = \left[\left(1 + r_{Year\,1}\right) \times \left(1 + r_{Year\,2}\right) \right]^{1/2} - 1$$

$$= \left[(1 + .50) \times (1 + (-.50))\right]^{1/2} - 1 = .866025 - 1 = -13.40\%$$

So, over the two-year investment period, the $100 investment lost the equivalent of −13.40 percent per year.

We could also solve for the geometric mean or compound rate of return using a financial calculator, taking the initial investment and final value and solving for i:

Enter	2		-100	0	75
	N	I/Y	PV	PMT	FV
Solve for		-13.4			

Using either approach we find the geometric mean or compound average rate of return to be −13.4 percent.

Choosing the Right "Average"

Which average should we be using? The answer is that they both are important and, depending on what you are trying to measure, correct. The following grid provides some guidance as to which average is appropriate and when:

Question Being Addressed:	Appropriate Average Calculation:
What annual rate of return can we expect for next year?	The arithmetic average rate of return calculated using annual rates of return.
What annual rate of return can we expect over a multiyear horizon?	The geometric, or compound, average rate of return calculated over a similar past period.

It's important to note that arithmetic average rates of return are only appropriate for thinking about future periods that are equal in duration to the period over which the historical returns were calculated. For example, if we want to evaluate the expected rate of return for a period of one year and our data corresponds to quarters, we would want to convert these quarterly returns to annual returns using a geometric average, and then use the arithmetic mean of these annual rates of return (not four times the quarterly rate of return, as some might assume).

Computing the Arithmetic and Geometric Average Rates of Return

Five years ago Mary's grandmother gave her $10,000 worth of stock in the shares of a publicly traded company founded by Mary's grandfather. Mary is now considering whether she should continue to hold the shares, or perhaps sell some of them. Her first step in analyzing the investment is to evaluate the rate of return she has earned over the past five years.

The following table contains the beginning value of Mary's stock five years ago as well as the values at the end of each year up until today (the end of Year 5):

(2 CONTINUED >> ON NEXT PAGE)

Year	Annual Rate of Return	Value of the Stock
0		$10,000.00
1	10.0%	11,000.00
2	15.0%	12,650.00
3	−15.0%	10,752.50
4	20.0%	12,903.00
5	10.0%	14,193.30

What rate of return did Mary earn on her investment in the stock given to her by her grandmother?

STEP 1: Picture the problem

The value of Mary's stock investment over the past five years looks like the following:

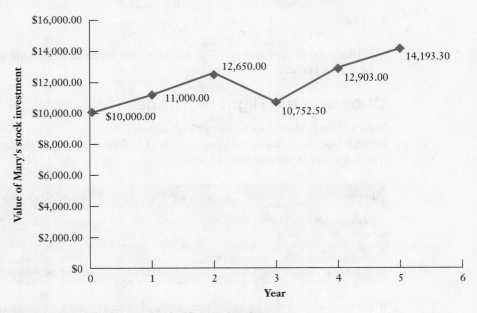

STEP 2: Decide on a solution strategy

Our first thought might be to just calculate an average of the five annual rates of return earned by the stock investment. However, this arithmetic average fails to capture the effect of compound interest. Thus, to estimate the compound annual rate of return we calculate the geometric mean using Equation (6) or a financial calculator.

STEP 3: Solve

Calculate the Arithmetic Average Rate of Return for the Stock Investment.

The arithmetic average annual rate of return is calculated by summing the annual rates of return over the past five years and dividing the sum by 5. Thus the arithmetic average annual rate of return equals 8.00 percent.

Note that the sum of the annual rates of return is equal to 40 percent and when we divide by five years we get an arithmetic average rate of return of 8.00 percent. Thus, based on the past performance of the stock, Mary should expect that it would earn 8 percent next year.

Calculate the Geometric Average Rate of Return for the Stock Investment.

We calculate the geometric average rate of return using Equation (6):

$$\text{Geometric Average Return} = [(1 + .1)(1 + .15)(1 + (-.15))(1 + .20)(1 + .10)]^{1/5} - 1 = (1.4193)^{1/5} - 1 = .0725 \text{ or } 7.25\%$$

Alternatively, using a financial calculator and solving for *i* we get:

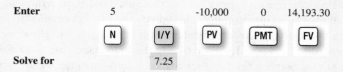

Enter 5   -10,000   0   14,193.30

N   I/Y   PV   PMT   FV

Solve for   7.25

STEP 4: Analyze

The arithmetic average rate of return Mary has earned on her stock investment is 8 percent, whereas the geometric, or compound, average is 7.25 percent. The reason for the lower geometric, or compound, rate of return is that it incorporates consideration for compounding of interest; it takes a lower rate of interest with annual compounding to get a particular future value. The important thing to recognize here is that both of these averages are useful and meaningful, but they answer two very different questions. The arithmetic mean return of 8 percent answers the question, *What rate of return should Mary expect to earn from the stock investment over the next year, assuming all else remains the same as in the past*? However, if the question is *What rate of return should Mary expect over a five-year period*? (during which the effect of compounding must be taken into account), the answer is 7.25 percent, or the geometric average.

STEP 5: Check yourself

Mary has decided to keep the stock given to her by her grandmother. However, she now wants to consider the prospect of selling another gift made to her five years ago by her other grandmother. What are the arithmetic and geometric average rates of return for the following stock investment?

Year	Annual Rate of Return	Value of the Stock
0		$10,000.00
1	−15.0%	8,500.00
2	15.0%	9,775.00
3	25.0%	12,218.75
4	30.0%	15,884.38
5	−10.0%	14,295.94

ANSWER: 9 percent and 7.41 percent.

Your Turn: For more practice, do related **Study Problem** 8 at the end of this chapter.

>> **END** Checkpoint 2

Tools of Financial Analysis—Geometric Mean Rate of Return

Name of Tool	Formula	What It Tells You
Geometric Average Return	$$\left[\left(1 + \frac{Rate\ of\ Return}{for\ Year\ 1,\ r_{Year\ 1}}\right) \times \left(1 + \frac{Rate\ of\ Return}{for\ Year\ 1,\ r_{Year\ 2}}\right) \times \cdots \times \left(\frac{Rate\ of\ Return}{for\ Year\ 1,\ r_{Year\ n}}\right)\right]^{1/n} - 1$$	• Measures the compound rate of return earned from an investment using multiple annual rates of return • The higher the estimated rate of return, the higher is the value of the investment at the end of the holding period in *n* years.

Before you move on to 4

Concept Check | 3

1. How is a simple arithmetic average computed? For example, what is the arithmetic average of the following annual rates of return: 10 percent, −10 percent, and 5 percent?

2. How is a geometric average rate of return computed? For example, what is the geometric average of the following annual rates of return: 10 percent, −10 percent, and 5 percent?

3. Why is the geometric average different from the arithmetic average?

What Determines Stock Prices?

Our review of financial market history tells us that stock and bond returns are subject to substantial fluctuations. As an investor, how should you use this information to form your portfolio? Should you invest all of your retirement account in stocks, because historically stocks have performed very well? Or, should you be timing the market, buying stocks when the returns look good and buying bonds when the stock market is looking rather weak? Note that this is exactly the question the great-grandfather faced in the example we used to introduce this chapter.

To answer these questions, we must first understand what causes stock prices to move from month to month. In short, stock prices tend to go up when there is good news about future profits, and they go down when there is bad news about future profits. This, in part, explains the favorable returns of stocks in the United States over the past 80 years, and it also explains the very bad returns of 2008 through early 2009. Although the country certainly has gone through some challenging times, for the most part the last century was quite good for American businesses and, as a result, stock prices did quite well.

One might be tempted to use this logic and invest more in stocks when the economy is doing well and less in stocks when the economy is doing poorly. Indeed, one might think that it is possible to do even better by picking the individual stocks of companies whose profits are likely to increase. For example, one might want to buy oil stocks when oil prices are increasing and at the same time sell airline stocks, as the profits of these firms will be hurt by the increased cost of jet fuel.

Unfortunately, according to the *efficient markets hypothesis*, a strategy of shifting one's portfolio in response to public information, such as changes in oil prices, will not result in higher expected returns. This is because in an efficient market, stock prices are forward looking and reflect all available public information about future profitability. Strategies that are based on such information can generate higher expected returns only if they expose the investor to higher risk. This theory underlies much of the study of financial markets and is the foundation for the rest of this chapter.

The Efficient Markets Hypothesis

The concept that *all* trading opportunities are fairly priced is referred to as the **efficient markets hypothesis (EMH)**, which is the basis of P Principle 4: **Market Prices Reflect Information**. The efficient markets hypothesis states that securities prices accurately reflect future expected cash flows and are based on all information available to investors.

An **efficient market** is a market in which all the available information is *fully* incorporated into securities prices, and the returns investors will earn on their investments cannot be predicted. Taking this concept a step further, we can distinguish between **weak-form efficient markets**, **semi-strong-form efficient markets**, and **strong-form efficient markets**, depending on the degree of efficiency:

1. The *weak-form efficient market hypothesis* asserts that all past security market information is fully reflected in securities prices. This means that all price and volume information is already reflected in a security's price.

2. The *semi-strong-form efficient market hypothesis* asserts that all publicly available information is fully reflected in securities prices. This is a stronger statement because it isn't limited to price and volume information, but includes all public information. Thus, the firm's financial statements; news and announcements about the economy, industry, or company; analysts' estimates on future earnings; or any other publicly available information is already reflected in the security's price. As a result, taking an investments class won't be of any value to you in picking a winner.

3. The *strong-form efficient market hypothesis* asserts that all information, regardless of whether this information is public or private, is fully reflected in securities prices. This form of the efficient market hypothesis encompasses both the weak-form and semi-strong-form efficient market hypotheses. It asserts that there isn't any information that isn't already embedded into the prices of all securities. In other words, even insider information—that is, material information that isn't available to any other investor—is of no use.

Do We Expect Financial Markets to Be Perfectly Efficient?

A famous quote from Milton Friedman says that "there is no such thing as a free lunch." In other words, everything that has benefits also has costs. The efficient markets hypothesis can be viewed as a special case of Milton Friedman's notion of "no free lunch." The basic idea is that if someone is offering free lunches, the demand for those lunches will explode, and will be impossible to satisfy.

Similarly, if there were a simple trading strategy that made money without subjecting investors to risk, then every investor would want to invest with that strategy. However, this is clearly impossible, because for every stock that is bought, there must be someone selling. In other words, the stock market can offer you a free lunch (in this case, an underpriced stock) only when other investors exist who are willing to provide millions of free lunches—to both you and all the other investors who would be very pleased to buy underpriced stocks and sell overpriced stocks. Individuals generally like to think that when they buy and sell stock they are trading with an impersonal "market." In reality, when you buy or sell a stock, in most cases you are trading with professional investors representing institutions such as Goldman Sachs, Fidelity, and Merrill Lynch. What this means is that when you buy a stock because you think it is underpriced, you are likely to be buying it from someone who thinks the same stock is overpriced!

This argument suggests that one should not expect to find profitable investment strategies based on publicly available information. In other words, markets should be at least weak-form and semi-strong-form efficient. If there did exist simple profitable strategies, then they would attract the attention of investors who, by implementing those strategies, would compete away their profits. For example, suppose that it became known that the stocks of well-managed firms tended to realize higher rates of return. This would encourage investors to increase their holdings of well-managed companies, thereby increasing the stock prices of these firms to the point where their stocks would be no better or worse long-term investments than the stocks of poorly managed firms.

What about investment strategies that require private information, or that are complicated and require quite a bit of work to figure out? If the market were so efficient that investment strategies, no matter how complex, earned no profits, then no one would bother to take the time and effort to understand the intricacies of security pricing. Indeed, it is hard to imagine how security markets could be efficient if no one put in the time and effort to study them. For this reason, we would not expect financial markets to be strong-form efficient. We expect the market will partially, but not perfectly, reflect information that is privately collected.

To understand this concept, let's think about how biotech stock prices are likely to respond when a promising new drug receives Food and Drug Administration (FDA) approval. If almost all market investors ignored information about drug approvals, the market might respond very little. This would allow those investors who collected and interpreted information about new drugs to be able to exploit the information to earn significant trading profits. However, if those profits are very high, then we might expect more investors to become interested in collecting information of this type, which would in turn make the market more efficiently incorporate this type of information into market prices. However, if there were absolutely no profits to be made from collecting this type of information, then the incentive to collect the information would be eliminated. For this reason, we expect markets to be just inefficient enough to provide some investors with an opportunity to recoup their costs of obtaining information, but not so inefficient that there is easy money to be made in the stock market.

The Behavioral View

Milton Friedman's "no free lunch" view of markets assumes that investors, as a group, are pretty rational. This was the view taken by most economists until very recently. Financial economists have started to study the implications of the fact that individuals are not strictly rational. This new approach to the study of finance has gained a strong following and even resulted in a Nobel Prize for Princeton psychologist Daniel Kahneman in 2002.

If we believe that investors do not rationally process information, then market prices may not accurately reflect even public information. As an example, economists have suggested that overconfident investors tend to underreact when a company's management announces earnings or makes other statements that are relevant to the value of the firm's stock. This is because investors have too much confidence in their own views of the company's true value and tend to place

Table 4	Summarizing the Evidence of Anomalies to the Efficient Market Hypothesis	
Anomaly	**Description**	
#1. Value stocks outperform growth stocks	*Value stocks, which are stocks with tangible assets that generate current earnings, have tended to outperform growth stocks, which are stocks with low current earnings that are expected to grow in the future.* More specifically, stocks with low price-to-earnings ratios, low price-to-cash-flow ratios, and low price-to-book-value ratios tend to outperform the market.	
#2. Momentum in stock returns	Stocks that have performed well in the past 6 to 12 months tend to continue to outperform other stocks.	
#3. Over- and underreaction to corporate announcements	*The market has tended to underreact to many corporate events.* For example, stock prices react favorably on dates when firms announce favorable earnings news, which is exactly what we would expect in an efficient market. However, on the days after favorable earnings news, stock returns continue to be positive on average. This is known as post-earnings announcement drift. Similarly, there is evidence of some degree of predictability in stock returns following other major announcements, such as the issuance of stock or bonds.	

too little weight on new information provided by management. As a result, this new information, even though it is publicly and freely available, is not completely reflected in stock prices.

Market Efficiency: What Does the Evidence Show?

The extent to which financial markets are efficient is an important question with broad implications. As a result, this question has generated thousands of empirical studies. Although this is a topic that has generated considerable debate and disagreement, our interpretation of the matter is that, historically, there has been some evidence of inefficiencies in the financial markets. Most of the evidence of market inefficiency can be summarized by three observations found in Table 4. Note that evidence that the equity market is inefficient is tantamount to saying that investors can earn returns—greater than their investment's risks would warrant—by engaging in a trading strategy designed to take advantage of the mispricing.

We should stress that although the evidence relating to the return patterns described in Table 4 is quite strong for studies that examine returns prior to 2000, more recent evidence suggests that strategies that exploit these patterns have been quite risky and have not been successful after 2000. Indeed, the quantitative hedge funds that exploited those patterns lost considerable amounts of money during the 2007 to 2009 financial crisis period. What do we learn from the initial success and demise of strategies using these patterns? The first lesson is that there may be information that predicts returns that are not well known. However, when the information becomes widely known, which was the case after the publication of academic research that documented these return patterns, we expect institutional investors to trade aggressively on the patterns, and thereby eliminate the inefficiencies. This suggests that, looking forward, one should probably assume that the financial markets are pretty efficient, at least in the semi-strong form. In particular, we do not expect the simple momentum and value strategies that worked so well prior to 2000 to work well going forward. However, we cannot rule out the possibility that one of our clever readers will develop an innovative and successful strategy.

Before you begin end-of-chapter material

Concept Check | 4

1. What is an "efficient market"?
2. What are the three categories of information that are commonly used to categorize tests of the efficient market hypothesis?
3. How do behavioral biases affect the efficiency of market prices?

Applying the Principles of Finance to This Chapter

P Principle 2: **There Is a Risk-Return Tradeoff** In examining historical rates of return realized on securities with different risks, we see that Principle 2 does indeed hold true—riskier investments are indeed rewarded with higher expected returns. However, it should be pointed out that although investors expect to receive higher returns for assuming more risk, there is no guarantee that they will get what they expect.

P Principle 4: **Market Prices Reflect Information** This helps us understand the wisdom of markets and how investor purchases and sales of a security drive its price to reflect everything that is known about that security's risk and expected return and provides the basis for the efficient markets hypothesis.

Chapter Summaries

 1

Calculate realized and expected rates of return and risk.

SUMMARY: We refer to the actual rate of return earned on an investment as the *realized rate of return*. This can be expressed as a percentage or as a cash amount gained or lost on the investment. But because investment returns are uncertain, we must speak in terms of expected returns. The *expected rate of return* is the rate we anticipate earning on an investment and is the rate relied on when evaluating a particular investment opportunity. We can calculate the expected rate of return using Equation (3):

$$
\begin{aligned}
\begin{matrix} \text{Expected Rate} \\ \text{of Return} \\ [E(r)] \end{matrix}
&= \left(\begin{matrix} \text{Rate of} \\ \text{Return 1} \\ (r_1) \end{matrix} \times \begin{matrix} \text{Probability} \\ \text{of Return 1} \\ (Pb_1) \end{matrix} \right) + \left(\begin{matrix} \text{Rate of} \\ \text{Return 2} \\ (r_2) \end{matrix} \times \begin{matrix} \text{Probability} \\ \text{of Return 2} \\ (Pb_2) \end{matrix} \right) + \cdots \\
&+ \left(\begin{matrix} \text{Rate of} \\ \text{Return } n \\ (r_n) \end{matrix} \times \begin{matrix} \text{Probability} \\ \text{of Return } n \\ (Pb_n) \end{matrix} \right)
\end{aligned}
\tag{3}
$$

The risk of an individual asset can be measured by the dispersion in possible return outcomes from an investment in that asset. We measure dispersion using the *variance*, which is calculated using Equation (4):

$$
\begin{aligned}
\begin{matrix} \text{Variance in} \\ \text{Rates of Return} \\ (\sigma^2) \end{matrix}
&= \left[\left(\begin{matrix} \text{Rate of} \\ \text{Return 1} \\ (r_1) \end{matrix} - \begin{matrix} \text{Expected Rate} \\ \text{of Return} \\ E(r) \end{matrix} \right)^2 \times \begin{matrix} \text{Probability} \\ \text{of Return 1} \\ (Pb_1) \end{matrix} \right] \\
&+ \left[\left(\begin{matrix} \text{Rate of} \\ \text{Return 2} \\ (r_2) \end{matrix} - \begin{matrix} \text{Expected Rate} \\ \text{of Return} \\ E(r) \end{matrix} \right)^2 \times \begin{matrix} \text{Probability} \\ \text{of Return 2} \\ (Pb_2) \end{matrix} \right] \\
&+ \cdots + \left[\left(\begin{matrix} \text{Rate of} \\ \text{Return } n \\ (r_n) \end{matrix} - \begin{matrix} \text{Expected Rate} \\ \text{of Return} \\ E(r) \end{matrix} \right)^2 \times \begin{matrix} \text{Probability} \\ \text{of Return } n \\ (Pb_n) \end{matrix} \right]
\end{aligned}
\tag{4}
$$

Risk is also measured using the square root of the variance or the *standard deviation*. The latter provides the same indication of investment risk but is stated in terms of percent returns, so it is sometimes preferred because of its easier interpretation.

KEY TERMS

Cash return The monetary increase (decrease) in the value of an investment measured over a particular span of time.

Expected rate of return The average of all possible rates of return, where each possible return is weighted by the probability that it might occur.

Holding period return The rate of return earned by investing for a specific period of time, such as one year or one month.

Probability distribution For an investment's rate of return, a description of all possible rates of return from the investment along with the associated probabilities for each outcome.

Rate of return See Holding period return.

Risk-free rate of return The rate of return earned by investing in a security that always pays the promised rate of return (without risk).

Standard deviation The square root of the variance.

Variance The average of the squared difference in possible rates of return and the expected rate of return. As such, the variance is a measure of the average squared difference in possible and expected rates of return.

KEY EQUATIONS

$$\frac{\text{Cash}}{\text{Return}} = \frac{\text{Ending}}{\text{Price}} + \frac{\text{Cash Distribution}}{\text{(Dividend)}} - \frac{\text{Beginning}}{\text{Price}} \qquad (1)$$

$$\frac{\text{Rate of}}{\text{Return}} = \frac{\text{Cash Return}}{\text{Beginning Price}} = \frac{\dfrac{\text{Ending}}{\text{Price}} + \dfrac{\text{Cash Distribution}}{\text{(Dividend)}} - \dfrac{\text{Beginning}}{\text{Price}}}{\dfrac{\text{Beginning}}{\text{Price}}} \qquad (2)$$

$$
\begin{aligned}
\begin{array}{c}\text{Expected Rate}\\ \text{of Return}\\ [E(r)]\end{array} =
&\left(\begin{array}{ccc}\text{Rate of} & & \text{Probability}\\ \text{Return 1} & \times & \text{of Return 1}\\ (r_1) & & (Pb_1)\end{array}\right) +
\left(\begin{array}{ccc}\text{Rate of} & & \text{Probability}\\ \text{Return 2} & \times & \text{of Return 2}\\ (r_2) & & (Pb_2)\end{array}\right)\\[2em]
&+\cdots+ \left(\begin{array}{ccc}\text{Rate of} & & \text{Probability}\\ \text{Return } n & \times & \text{of Return } n\\ (r_n) & & (Pb_n)\end{array}\right)
\end{aligned} \qquad (3)
$$

$$
\begin{aligned}
\begin{array}{c}\text{Variance in}\\ \text{Rates of Return}\\ (\sigma^2)\end{array} =
&\left[\left(\begin{array}{ccc}\text{Rate of} & & \text{Expected Rate}\\ \text{Return 1} & - & \text{of Return}\\ (r_1) & & E(r)\end{array}\right)^2 \begin{array}{c}\text{Probability}\\ \times\ \text{of Return 1}\\ (Pb_1)\end{array}\right]\\[2em]
&+\left[\left(\begin{array}{ccc}\text{Rate of} & & \text{Expected Rate}\\ \text{Return 2} & - & \text{of Return}\\ (r_2) & & E(r)\end{array}\right)^2 \begin{array}{c}\text{Probability}\\ \times\ \text{of Return 2}\\ (Pb_2)\end{array}\right]\\[2em]
&+\cdots+\left[\left(\begin{array}{ccc}\text{Rate of} & & \text{Expected Rate}\\ \text{Return } n & - & \text{of Return}\\ (r_n) & & E(r)\end{array}\right)^2 \begin{array}{c}\text{Probability}\\ \times\ \text{of Return } n\\ (Pb_n)\end{array}\right]
\end{aligned} \qquad (4)
$$

$$\begin{array}{c}\text{Standard}\\ \text{Deviation, } \sigma\end{array} = \sqrt{\text{Variance}} \text{ or}$$

$$\sigma = \sqrt{([r_1 - E(r)]^2 Pb_1) + ([r_2 - E(r)]^2 Pb_2) + \cdots + ([r_n - E(r)]^2 Pb_n)} \qquad (5)$$

Concept Check | **1**

1. If you invested $100 one year ago that is worth $110 today, what rate of return did you earn on your investment?

2. What is the expected rate of return, and how is it different than the realized rate of return?

3. What is the variance in the rate of return of an investment?

4. Why is variance used to measure risk?

---

2 | ## Describe the historical pattern of financial market returns.

SUMMARY: Perhaps the most important observation we can make about the historical returns of different types of investments is that the average rates of return earned on more risky investments have been higher than the average rates of return earned on investments that have less risk. Specifically, equity securities have earned higher returns than debt securities, corporate debt securities have earned higher returns than government debt securities, and long-term debt securities have earned higher returns than short-term debt securities.

KEY TERMS

Developed country Sometimes referred to as an industrialized country, where the term is used to identify those countries such as the United States, Great Britain, France, and so forth that have highly sophisticated and well-developed economies.

Emerging market One located in an economy with low-to-middle per-capita income. These countries constitute roughly 80 percent of the world's population and represent about a fifth of the world's economies. China and India are perhaps the best known and largest of the emerging-market economies.

Equity risk premium The difference between returns of the riskier stock investments and the less risky investments in government securities.

Volatility Another term for the fluctuation in returns.

Concept Check | **2**

1. How well does the risk–return principle hold up in light of historical rates of return? Explain.

2. What is the equity risk premium, and how is it measured?

3. Does the historical evidence suggest that investing in emerging markets is more or less risky than investing in developed markets?

Compute geometric (or compound) and arithmetic average rates of return.

SUMMARY: When analyzing how a particular investment has performed in the past, we typically begin by calculating the rates of return earned over several years. These annual rates of return are then averaged to calculate the arithmetic average in an effort to understand how the investment has performed in comparison with other investments. The geometric mean is the preferred type of average for use when analyzing compound average rates of return, because it provides the rate at which the investment's value has grown.

KEY TERMS

Arithmetic average return
The sum of the set of returns divided by their number.

Geometric or **compound average returns** The rate of return earned on an investment that incorporates consideration for the effects of compound interest.

KEY EQUATIONS

$$\begin{aligned} \text{Geometric} \atop \text{Average Return} = \Bigg[\left(1 + \frac{\text{Rate of Return}}{\text{for Year 1}} \right) \times \left(1 + \frac{\text{Rate of Return}}{\text{for Year 2}} \right) \\ \times \cdots \times \left(1 + \frac{\text{Rate of Return}}{\text{for Year } n} \right) \Bigg]^{1/n} - 1 \end{aligned} \qquad (6)$$

Concept Check | 3

1. How is a simple arithmetic average computed? For example, what is the arithmetic average of the following annual rates of return: 10 percent, −10 percent, and 5 percent?

2. How is a geometric average rate of return computed? For example, what is the geometric average of the following annual rates of return: 10 percent, −10 percent, and 5 percent?

3. Why is the geometric average different from the arithmetic average?

Explain the efficient market hypothesis and why it is important to stock prices.

SUMMARY: The concept of efficient markets describes the extent to which information is incorporated into security prices. In an efficient market, security prices reflect *all* available information at *all* times; and, because of this, it is impossible for an investor to consistently earn high rates of return without taking substantial risk.

Market efficiency is a relative concept. We do not expect financial markets to reflect 100 percent of the available information, but we also do not expect to see very many easy profit opportunities. In general, we expect financial markets to be *weak-form efficient*, which means that information about past prices and volumes of trading are fully reflected in current prices. For the most part we also expect financial markets to be *semi-strong-form efficient*, which means that market prices fully reflect all publicly available information (that is, information from the firm's publicly released financial statements, information revealed in the financial press, and so forth). Finally, to a lesser extent, finance markets are *strong-form efficient,* meaning that prices fully reflect privately held information that has not been released to the general public.

KEY TERMS

Efficient market A market in which prices quickly respond to the announcement of new information.

Efficient markets hypothesis (EMH) This hypothesis states that securities prices accurately reflect future expected cash flows and are based on all information available to investors.

Semi-strong-form efficient market A market in which all publicly available information is quickly and accurately reflected in prices.

Strong-form efficient market
A market in which even private information is fully and quickly reflected in market prices.

Weak-form efficient market
A market in which current prices quickly and accurately reflect information that can be derived from patterns in past security prices and trading volumes.

Concept Check | 4

1. What is an "efficient market"?

2. What are the three categories of information that are commonly used to categorize tests of the efficient market hypothesis?

3. How do behavioral biases affect the efficiency of market prices?

Study Questions

1. **(Related to Regardless of Your Major: Using Statistics)** In the *Regardless of Your Major feature,* we note that statisticians analyze data. Moreover, in your statistics class you learned about how to describe random outcomes using statistical measures such as expected values and the variance. How does our knowledge of basic statistics help us evaluate investment opportunities?

2. Describe in words the concept of a realized rate of return. Assume that you are trying to describe the concept to your grandfather, who has never had a finance class!

3. How do cash dividends affect the realized rate of return from investing in shares of common stock?

4. How does the expected rate of return concept differ from that of the realized rate of return?

5. Describe the concept of an expected rate of return as if you were explaining it to your 10-year-old niece.

6. Why is the volatility or variance in an investment's rate of return a reasonable indication of the risk of the investment?

7. Describe the five-step process used to calculate the variance in the rate of return for an investment.

8. Describe the information contained in Figure 2 identifying which securities have performed the best over long periods of time. Some investors with long investment time horizons invest exclusively in bonds. Why do you think that is so?

9. What is the equity risk premium, and how is it calculated?

10. What does Figure 3 tell us about how the U.S. stock market has performed when compared to all the alternatives included in the figure over the period 1980–2011?

11. What can you conclude about the relative risk of investing in the United States versus the Pacific region from Figure 3?

12. What is the relationship between the geometric average rate of return and compound interest?

13. Under what circumstances would you prefer to use the geometric average rate of return as opposed to the arithmetic average?

14. **(Related to The Business of Life: Determining Your Tolerance for Risk)** What is your tolerance for risk? Take the risk tolerance quiz referenced in *The Business of Life: Determining Your Tolerance for Risk* feature and found at the website www.rce.rutgers.edu/money/riskquiz.

15. What is the efficient markets hypothesis? Explain this concept in your own words.

16. Compare and contrast the notions of weak-form, semi-strong-form, and strong-form market efficiency.

17. Do you think that the capital markets are completely efficient, efficient most of the time, or completely inefficient? Support your position as if you were talking to your favorite nephew who is only 10 years old.

18. What is the "behavioral view" of market efficiency?

Study Problems

MyFinanceLab

Go to www.myfinancelab.com to complete these exercises online and get instant feedback.

Realized and Expected Rates of Return and Risk

1. **(Related to Checkpoint 1)** **(Calculating rates of return)** On December 24, 2007, the common stock of Google Inc. (GOOG) was trading for $700.73. One year later the shares sold for only $298.02. Google has never paid

a common stock dividend. What rate of return would you have earned on your investment had you purchased the shares on December 24, 2007?

2. **(Calculating rates of return)** The S&P stock index represents a portfolio comprised of 500 large publicly traded companies. On December 24, 2007, the index had a value of 1,410 and on December 23, 2008, the index was approximately 890. If the average dividend paid on the stocks in the index is approximately 4 percent of the value of the index at the beginning of the year, what is the rate of return earned on the S&P index? What is your assessment of the relative riskiness of the Google investment (analyzed in the previous problem) compared to investing in the S&P index?

3. **(Calculating rates of return)** The common stock of Placo Enterprises had a market price of $12 on the day you purchased it just one year ago. During the past year the stock had paid a $1 dividend and closed at a price of $14. What rate of return did you earn on your investment in Placo's stock?

4. **(Calculating rates of return)** Blaxo Balloons manufactures and distributes birthday balloons. At the beginning of the year Blaxo's common stock was selling for $20 but by year end it was only $18. If the firm paid a total cash dividend of $2 during the year, what rate of return would you have earned if you had purchased the stock exactly one year ago? What would your rate of return have been if the firm had paid no cash dividend?

5. **(Computing rates of return)** From the following price data, compute the annual rates of return for Asman and Salinas.

Time	Asman	Salinas
1	$10	$30
2	12	28
3	11	32
4	13	35

How would you interpret the meaning of the annual rates of return?

6. **(Related to Checkpoint 1) (Expected rate of return and risk)**
B. J. Gautney Enterprises is evaluating a security. One-year Treasury bills are currently paying 2.9 percent. Calculate the following investment's expected return and its standard deviation. Should Gautney invest in this security?

Probability	Return
.15	−3%
.30	2%
.40	4%
.15	6%

7. **(Expected rate of return and risk)** Syntex, Inc. is considering an investment in one of two common stocks. Given the information that follows, which investment is better, based on risk (as measured by the standard deviation) and return?

Common Stock A		Common Stock B	
Probability	Return	Probability	Return
.30	11%	.20	−5%
.40	15%	.30	6%
.30	19%	.30	14%
		.20	22%

Geometric vs. Arithmetic Average Rates of Return

8. **(Related to Checkpoint 2) (Calculating the geometric and arithmetic average rate of return)** Caswell Enterprises had the following end-of-year stock prices over the last five years and paid no cash dividends:

Time	Caswell
1	$10
2	15
3	12
4	9
5	10

a. Calculate the annual rate returns for each year from this information.
b. What is the arithmetic average rate of return earned by investing in Caswell's stock over this period?
c. What is the geometric average rate of return earned by investing in Caswell's stock over this period?
d. Considering that the beginning and ending stock prices for the five-year period are the same, which type of average rate of return best describes the average annual rate of return earned over the period (the arithmetic or geometric)?

9. **(Calculating the geometric and arithmetic average rate of return)** The common stock of the Brangus Cattle Company had the following end-of-year stock prices over the last five years and paid no cash dividends:

Time	Brangus Cattle Company
1	$15
2	10
3	12
4	23
5	25

a. Calculate the annual rate of return for each year from this information.
b. What is the arithmetic average rate of return earned by investing in the company's stock over this period?
c. What is the geometric average rate of return earned by investing in the company's stock over this period?
d. Which type of average rate of return best describes the average annual rate of return earned over the period (the arithmetic or geometric)? Why?

10. **(Comprehensive problem)** Use the following end-of-year price data to answer the following questions for the Barris and Carson Companies.

Time	Barris	Carson
1	$10	$20
2	12	28
3	8	32
4	15	27

a. Compute the annual rates of return for each time period and for both firms.
b. Calculate both the arithmetic and geometric mean rates of return for the entire three-year period using your annual rates of return from part a. Note: You may assume that neither firm pays any dividends.
c. Compute a three-year rate of return spanning the entire period (i.e., using the beginning price for Period 1 and ending price for Period 4).
d. Because the rate of return calculated in part c is a three-year rate of return, convert it to an annual rate of return by using the following equation:

$$\left(1 + \frac{\text{Three-Year}}{\text{Rate of Return}}\right) = \left(1 + \frac{\text{Annual Rate}}{\text{of Return}}\right)^3$$

e. How is the annual rate of return calculated in part d related to the geometric rate of return? When you are evaluating the performance of an investment that has been held for several years, what type of average rate of return should you use (arithmetic or geometric)? Why?

Mini-Case

After graduating from college last spring with a major in accounting and finance, Jim Hale took a job as an analyst trainee for an investment company in Chicago. His first few weeks were filled with a series of rotations throughout the firm's various operating units, but this week he was assigned to one of the firm's traders as an analyst. On his first day Jim's boss called him in and told him that he wanted to do some rudimentary analysis of the investment returns of a semiconductor manufacturer called Advanced Micro Devices, Inc. (Ticker: AMD). Specifically, Jim was given the following month-end closing prices for the company spanning the November 1, 2011, through November 1, 2012:

Date	Closing Price	Date	Closing Price
1-Nov-11	5.69	1-Jun-12	5.73
1-Dec-11	5.4	2-Jul-12	4.06
3-Jan-12	6.71	1-Aug-12	3.72
1-Feb-12	7.35	4-Sep-12	3.37
1-Mar-12	8.02	1-Oct-12	2.05
2-Apr-12	7.36	1-Nov-12	1.88
1-May-12	6.08		

He was then instructed by his boss to complete the following tasks using the AMD price data (note that AMD paid no dividend during 2008).

Questions

1. Compute the monthly realized rates of return earned by AMD for the entire year.

2. Calculate the average monthly rate of return for AMD using both the arithmetic and geometric averages.

3. Calculate the year-end price for AMD, computing the compound value of the beginning-of-year price of $5.69 per share for 12 months at the monthly geometric average rate of return calculated earlier:

$$\frac{\text{End-of-Year}}{\text{Stock Price}} = \frac{\text{Beginning-of-Year}}{\text{Stock Price}} \left(1 + \frac{\text{Geometric Average}}{\text{Monthly Rate of Return}}\right)^{12}$$

4. Compute the annual rate of return for AMD using the beginning stock price for the period and the ending price (i.e., $5.69 and $1.88).

5. Now calculate the annual rate of return using the geometric average monthly rate of return using the following relationship:

$$\frac{\text{Compound Annual}}{\text{Rate of Return}} = \left(1 + \frac{\text{Geometric Average}}{\text{Monthly Rate of Return}}\right)^{12} - 1$$

6. If you were given annual rate of return data for AMD or any other company's stock and you were asked to estimate the average annual rate of return an investor would have earned over the sample period by holding the stock, would you use an arithmetic or geometric average of the historical rates of return? Explain your response as if you were talking to a client who has had no formal training in finance or investments.

Photo Credits

Risk and Return

From Chapter 8 of *Financial Management: Principles and Applications*, Twelfth Edition. Sheridan Titman, Arthur J. Keown, and John D. Martin.

Risk and Return
Capital Market Theory

Chapter **Outline**

1 Portfolio Returns and
Portfolio Risk

→ **Objective 1.** Calculate the expected rate of return and volatility for a portfolio of investments and describe how diversification affects the returns to a portfolio of investments.

2 Systematic Risk and the
Market Portfolio

→ **Objective 2.** Understand the concept of systematic risk for an individual investment and calculate portfolio systematic risk (beta).

3 The Security Market Line
and the CAPM

→ **Objective 3.** Estimate the investor's expected rate of return using the Capital Asset Pricing Model.

In this chapter we will discuss **P** Principle 2: **There Is a Risk–Return Tradeoff**. In particular, we will extend our analysis of risk and return to consider portfolios of risky investments and the beneficial effects of portfolio diversification on risk. In addition, we will learn more about what types of risk are associated with both higher and lower expected rates of return. To do this we first develop the tools needed to calculate both the expected rate of return and the variance of the return of a portfolio consisting of many investments. Having developed these tools, we then investigate the concept of diversification and define what is meant by an investment's diversifiable and non-diversifiable risks. Finally, we describe the Capital Asset Pricing Model (CAPM), which helps us understand how the risk of an individual investment should be measured. In addition, as **P** Principle 4: **Market Prices Reflect Information** states, as new information arrives and changes investors' risk and return expectations, prices will change.

Good News Plus Bad News Equals No News

On Monday, April 28, 2008, Veeco Instruments Inc. (VECO) reported quarterly earnings that exceeded analysts' expectations for the quarter by 200 percent. The surprise earnings performance was greeted by a 6 percent rise in the company's share price for the day. On the same day, Travelzoo Inc. (TZOO) reported quarterly earnings that were dramatically below the level that was expected, and the company's stock price declined by more than 7 percent. Taken individually, Veeco's shareholders would be very happy at the end of the day, but Travelzoo's stockholders would not. Yet if you held a portfolio that included both company's shares, its value may not have changed much at all.

This example illustrates how diversification can reduce risk. **Diversification** is simply "not putting all your eggs in one basket." For example, if your portfolio consists only of stocks of oil companies such as ExxonMobil (XOM) and ConocoPhillips (COP), you would lose a substantial amount of money if the price of oil fell. Similarly, if your portfolio consists entirely of banking stocks such as that of Bank of America (BAC) and JPMorgan Chase (JPM), you are likely to lose a lot of money when the default rate on loans increases. On the other hand, if you were to invest half your money in oil stocks and the other half in banking stocks, the ups and downs of these investments would tend to offset one another, which would reduce the extreme returns on the downside as well as the upside. This is diversification.

Regardless of Your Major...

"Risk and Your Personal Investment Plan"

Vanguard, one of the leading mutual fund families, identifies four key guidelines you should consider when making personal investment decisions:

1. Select investment products suited to your objective.

2. Find a comfortable balance between risk and return.

3. Diversify wisely to help manage risks.

4. Evaluate your portfolio periodically.

Notice that two of these four common-sense suggestions deal with risk. When you set up your own personal investment plan, which you might create for a variety of reasons—a rainy day fund, a down payment on a home, an education fund for your children, or simply retirement—you will need to determine your comfort level with risk and adjust your investments accordingly.

Some people can live with the substantial ups and downs of very risky investments. Others reach for the antacid when the value of their investments takes a plunge.

Your Turn: See Study Question 1.

Portfolio Returns and Portfolio Risk

The most important thing that we learn in this chapter is that with appropriate diversification, you can lower the risk of your portfolio without lowering the portfolio's expected rate of return. How does this concept of diversification relate to Principle 2: **There Is a Risk–Return Tradeoff**? What we learn in this chapter is that some risk can be eliminated by diversification, and that those risks that can be eliminated are not necessarily rewarded in the financial marketplace. To understand this, we must delve into the computation of portfolio expected return and portfolio risk.

Calculating the Expected Return of a Portfolio

The expected rate of return for a portfolio of investments is simply a weighted average of the expected rates of return of the individual investments in that portfolio. To calculate a portfolio's expected rate of return we *weight* each individual investment's expected rate of return using the fraction of the portfolio invested in that particular investment. For instance, if you put half your money in the stock of ExxonMobil, with an expected rate of return of 12 percent, and the other half in General Electric (GE) stock, with an expected rate of return of 8 percent, then we can calculate the expected rate of return of the portfolio as follows: $(1/2 \times 12\%) + (1/2 \times 8\%) = 10\%$.

In general, we calculate the expected rate of return of a portfolio that includes n different assets as follows:

$$
\begin{aligned}
\text{Expected Portfolio Return} &= \left(\begin{array}{c}\text{Fraction of Portfolio}\\\text{Invested in Asset 1}\end{array} \times \begin{array}{c}\text{Expected Rate of}\\\text{Return on Asset 1}\end{array}\right)\\[6pt]
&+ \left(\begin{array}{c}\text{Fraction of Portfolio}\\\text{Invested in Asset 2}\end{array} \times \begin{array}{c}\text{Expected Rate of}\\\text{Return on Asset 2}\end{array}\right)\\[6pt]
&+ \left(\begin{array}{c}\text{Fraction of Portfolio}\\\text{Invested in Asset 3}\end{array} \times \begin{array}{c}\text{Expected Rate of}\\\text{Return on Asset 3}\end{array}\right)\\[6pt]
&+ \cdots + \left(\begin{array}{c}\text{Fraction of Portfolio}\\\text{Invested in Asset } n\end{array} \times \begin{array}{c}\text{Expected Rate of}\\\text{Return on Asset } n\end{array}\right)
\end{aligned}
$$

Because the number of elements used to calculate the portfolio expected return is somewhat lengthy, we generally abbreviate the formula using symbols as follows:

Portfolio Expected Rate of Return

$$E(r_{portfolio}) = [W_1 \times E(r_1)] + [W_2 \times E(r_2)] + [W_3 \times E(r_3)] + \cdots + [W_n \times E(r_n)] \qquad \textbf{(1)}$$

Important Definitions and Concepts:

- $E(r_{portfolio})$ = the expected rate of return on a portfolio of n assets.
- W_i = the portfolio weight for asset i.
- $E(r_i)$ = the expected rate of return earned by asset i. We can estimate the expected rate of return for a risky asset using the following equation: In this chapter we will assume that this calculation has already been made and that the expected rate of return for risky assets is known.
- $[W_1 \times E(r_1)]$ = the contribution of asset 1 to the portfolio expected return.
- Note that the expected rate of return on a portfolio of n assets is simply a weighted average of the expected rates of return on each of the n assets.

Evaluating Portfolio Risk

In the last section we showed that the expected rate of return of a portfolio is simply the weighted average of the expected rates of returns of the individual investments that make up the portfolio. Next we calculate the risk of a portfolio using the standard deviation of portfolio returns. However, as we will illustrate in this section, the standard deviation of a portfolio's return is generally *not* equal to the weighted average of the standard deviations of the returns of the individual investments held in the portfolio. To understand why this is the case, we must look deeper into the concept of diversification.

Portfolio Diversification

In most cases, combining investments in a portfolio leads to risk reduction. This effect of reducing risks by including a large number of investments in a portfolio is called diversification. As a consequence of diversification, the standard deviation of a portfolio's return is typically less than the average of the standard deviations of the returns of each of the portfolio's individual investments.

To illustrate this, suppose you open a shop to cater to the tourist trade on a beautiful Caribbean island. The two products that you consider selling are sunglasses and umbrellas. Sunglasses generate a 20 percent rate of return during the sunny season and a 0 percent return during the rainy season. In contrast, umbrellas generate a 0 percent rate of return during the sunny season, but during the rainy season the umbrella business will generate a 20 percent return. So if the probability of a rainy year is 50 percent and the probability of a mostly sunny year is 50 percent, then the expected rate of return from each of these items is 10 percent. The problem comes into play when rainy and sunny seasons vary in length. For example, if you only sold sunglasses and the sunny season only lasted for 2 months, you wouldn't do very well at all; likewise, if you only invested in umbrellas and the sunny season lasted for 10 months, you would likewise do poorly.

In this example the revenues from both products, when viewed in isolation, are quite risky. However, if you invest half of your money in sunglasses and the other half in umbrellas, you will earn 10 percent on your total investment regardless of how long the sunny season lasts because at all times one of your products will be returning 20 percent while the other will be returning 0 percent. In effect, when you combine sunglasses and umbrellas, you completely eliminate risk.

Do you always get this diversification benefit when two investments are combined? Not necessarily. For example, if you were currently selling sunglasses and added sunscreen, which also returns 20 percent in the sunny season and 0 percent in the rainy season, there would be no benefit to diversification because the returns of the sunscreen and sunglasses investments are perfectly *correlated*. As a result, if the rainy season lasted for three-quarters of the year, you would only earn 5 percent that year. Moreover, your return would be the same whether you only invested in sunglasses or you invested half your money in sunglasses and half in sunscreen. In effect, you will achieve no diversification gains when investments are perfectly correlated.

The concept of correlation is critical to our understanding of portfolio diversification. We measure the degree to which the returns on two investments are correlated using the **correlation coefficient**, a measure of the relationship of the return earned by one investment to another. The correlation coefficient can range from −1.0 (perfect negative correlation), meaning that two variables move in perfectly opposite directions (e.g., the sales of umbrellas and sunglasses), to +1.0 (perfect positive correlation), meaning that two assets move exactly together (e.g., the sales of sunglasses and sunscreen increase and decrease simultaneously). A correlation coefficient of 0.0 means that there is no relationship between the returns earned by the two assets.

Checkpoint 1

Calculating a Portfolio's Expected Rate of Return

Penny Simpson has her first full-time job and is considering how to invest her savings. Her dad suggested she invest no more than 25 percent of her savings in the stock of her employer, Emerson Electric (EMR), so she is considering investing the remaining 75 percent in a combination of a risk-free investment in U.S. Treasury bills, currently paying 4 percent, and Starbucks (SBUX) common stock. Penny's father has invested in the stock market for many years and suggested that Penny might expect to earn 8 percent on the Emerson shares and 12 percent from the Starbucks shares. Penny decides to put 25 percent in Emerson, 25 percent in Starbucks, and the remaining 50 percent in Treasury bills. Given Penny's portfolio allocation, what rate of return should she expect to receive on her investment?

STEP 1: Picture the problem

The following figure shows the expected rates of return for each investment in Penny's portfolio.

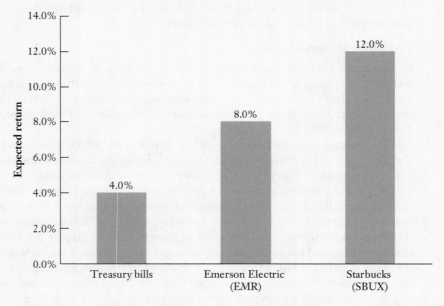

The expected rate of return for Penny's portfolio can be calculated as a weighted average of these expected rates of return, where the weights are the proportions of each investment.

STEP 2: Decide on a solution strategy

The portfolio expected rate of return is simply a weighted average of the expected rates of return of the investments in the portfolio. So we use Equation (1) to calculate the expected rate of return for Penny's portfolio. Fill in the *shaded cells* under the "Product" column in the following table to calculate a weighted average.

	E(Return) ×	Weight =	Product
U.S. Treasury bills	4.0%	0.50	
Emerson Electric (EMR)	8.0%	0.25	
Starbucks (SBUX)	12.0%	0.25	
Portfolio E(Return) = Sum of product column			

STEP 3: Solve

We can use Equation (8–1) to calculate the expected rate of return for the portfolio as follows:

$$E(r_{portfolio}) = W_{Treasury\ Bills}E(r_{Treasury\ Bills}) + W_{EMR}E(r_{EMR}) + W_{SBUX}E(r_{SBUX})$$

$$= (1/2 \times .04) + (1/4 \times .08) + (1/4 \times .12) = .07 \text{ or } 7\%$$

Alternatively, by filling out the table described above we get the same result.

	E(Return)	Weight	Product
Treasury bills	4.0%	0.50	2.0%
Emerson Electric (EMR)	8.0%	0.25	2.0%
Starbucks (SBUX)	12.0%	0.25	3.0%
	Portfolio E(Return) =		7.0%

STEP 4: Analyze

The expected rate of return for the portfolio composed of 50 percent invested in Treasury bills, 25 percent in Emerson Electric stock, and the remaining 25 percent in Starbucks stock is 7 percent. Note that we have referred to the Treasury bill rate as its expected rate of return. This is technically accurate because this return is assumed to be risk-free. That is, if you purchase a Treasury bill that promises to pay you 4 percent, because this security is risk-free, this is the only possible outcome. This is not the case for either of the other investment alternatives. We can calculate the expected rate of return for the portfolio in exactly the same way regardless of the risk of the investments contained in the portfolio. However, as we learn next, the risk of the portfolio is affected by the riskiness of the returns of the individual investments contained in the portfolio.

STEP 5: Check yourself

Evaluate the expected return for Penny's portfolio in which she places a quarter of her money in Treasury bills, half in Starbucks stock, and the remainder in Emerson Electric stock.

ANSWER: 9 percent.

Your Turn: For more practice, do related **Study Problems** 1 and 5 at the end of this chapter. >> END Checkpoint 1

In the previous example, sunglasses and sunscreen sales are perfectly *positively* correlated with one another. This means that their returns move up and down exactly in unison. The sale of umbrellas, on the other hand, goes up when sunscreen and sunglass sales fall, and vice versa. So umbrella sales are perfectly *negatively* correlated with sunscreen and sunglass sales. In most cases, the returns of two different investments will neither be perfectly correlated positively nor perfectly correlated negatively. However, there will be a tendency for most investment returns to move together, that is, in positive correlation. As long as the investment returns are not perfectly positively correlated, there will be diversification benefits. However, the diversification benefits will be greater when the correlations are low or negative.

Diversification Lessons

We can take away two key lessons from this initial look at portfolio risk and diversification:

- First, a portfolio can be less risky than the average risk of its individual investments in the portfolio.
- Second, the key to reducing risk through diversification is to combine investments whose returns do not move together and thus are not perfectly positively correlated (such as the sales of sunglasses and umbrellas).

Calculating the Standard Deviation of a Portfolio's Returns

Consider the problem faced by Patty. Patty just received $20,000 from her Aunt Gladys, who suggests she invest the money in the stock market. Patty told her aunt that she is considering the possibility of investing the money in the common stock of either Apple (AAPL) or Coca-Cola (KO). When she hears this, Aunt Gladys advises Patty to put half the money in Apple stock and half in Coca-Cola stock.

To analyze Aunt Gladys's suggested investment strategy, let's calculate the expected return and standard deviation of a portfolio that includes both Apple and Coca-Cola stocks. We saw from Equation (1) that the expected return is simply the weighted average of the expected returns of the individual securities in the portfolio. So if we assume that individually, Apple and Coca-Cola stocks have the same expected rate of return of 14 percent, and Patty invests in each equally, then the portfolio consisting of both stocks will have the same expected rate of return as the individual stocks, or 14 percent:

$$E(r_{portfolio}) = W_{Apple}E(r_{Apple}) + W_{CocaCola}E(r_{CocaCola}) = (1/2 \times .14) + (1/2 \times .14) = .14 \text{ or } 14\%$$

Now let's consider the riskiness of Patty's portfolio. To measure the portfolio's risk, we use the standard deviation of the portfolio. As we noted earlier, the standard deviation of the portfolio is *not* simply a weighted average of the respective standard deviations of the two stock investments. Indeed, if the returns on investing in Apple stock are less than perfectly correlated with the returns on Coca-Cola stock, the standard deviation of the portfolio that combines the two firms' shares will be less than this simple weighted average of the two firms' standard deviations. This reduction in portfolio standard deviation is due to the effects of diversification. The magnitude of the reduction in the portfolio's standard deviation resulting from diversification will depend on the extent to which the returns are correlated. This can be understood by looking at the mathematics for calculating the standard deviation of a portfolio with two stocks. The mathematics may look forbidding at first, but it offers a useful key to understanding how diversification works.

The standard deviation is the square root of the variance, so we first calculate the variance and then take the square root of the result. In the following formula, we will substitute Apple stock for asset 1 and Coca-Cola stock for asset 2. To illustrate, consider the following formula for the variance of a two-asset portfolio comprised of asset 1 and asset 2:

$$\sigma_{portfolio} = \sqrt{W_1^2\sigma_1^2 + W_2^2\sigma_2^2 + 2W_1W_2\rho_{1,2}\sigma_1\sigma_2} \tag{2}$$

Important Definitions and Concepts:

- $\sigma_{portfolio}$ = the standard deviation in portfolio returns,
- W_i = the proportion of the portfolio that is invested in asset i,
- σ_i = the standard deviation in the rate of return earned by asset i, and
- $\rho_{i,j}$ = correlation between the rates of return earned by assets i and j. The symbol $\rho_{i,j}$ (pronounced "rho") represents correlation between the rates of return for asset 1 and asset 2.

Once again, correlation tells us the strength of the linear relationship between two assets. It can take on a value that ranges from 1.0, meaning these two assets move in a perfectly opposite linear manner as in the sunglasses and umbrellas example, to $+1.0$, which means that these two assets move in a perfectly linear manner together as in the sunglasses and sunscreen example. A value of 0.0 would mean that there is no linear relationship between the movements of the two assets. The amount of risk reduction that takes place as a result of diversification is a function of correlation. The higher correlation between two assets, the less benefit, or risk reduction, there is from diversification.[1]

---

[1]The correlation coefficient is actually a standardized covariance. The covariance provides an absolute measure of how two securities move over time; however, because it depends upon the volatility of the two series of returns, it can be hard to interpret. For this reason we generally standardize the covariance by the variability of the two series of returns, and that way it varies between 1.0 and $+1.0$.

Now, let's look at the calculation of the standard deviation of this two-asset portfolio and let the correlation coefficient vary between −1.0 and +1.0. Let's also assume the following:

- Patty invests half of her money in each of the two company's shares.
- The standard deviation for both Apple and Coca-Cola's individual stock returns is .20.
- Correlation between the stock returns of Apple and Coca-Cola is .75.

Substituting into Equation (8–2) we get the following result:

$$\sigma_{portfolio} = \sqrt{W_{Apple}^2 \sigma_{Apple}^2 + W_{Coke}^2 \sigma_{Coke}^2 + 2W_{Apple}W_{Coke}\rho_{Apple,Coke}\sigma_{Apple}\sigma_{Coke}}$$

$$= \sqrt{(.5^2 \times .20^2) + (.5^2 \times .20^2) + (2 \times .5 \times .5 \times .75 \times .20 \times .20)}$$

$$= \sqrt{.035} = .187$$

> Correlation coefficient of +0.75 indicates the stock returns of the two firms move together but not in perfect unison.

Because the standard deviation of each of the stocks is equal to .20, a simple weighted average of the standard deviations of the Apple and Coca-Cola stock returns would produce a portfolio standard deviation of .20. However, a correlation coefficient of .75 indicates that the stocks are not perfectly correlated and produces a portfolio standard deviation of 0.187. To see how the correlation between the investments influences the portfolio standard deviation, let's look at what happens when we substitute a correlation coefficient of 1.0 into Equation (2):

$$\sigma_{portfolio} = \sqrt{W_{Apple}^2 \sigma_{Apple}^2 + W_{Coke}^2 \sigma_{Coke}^2 + 2W_{Apple}W_{Coke}\rho_{Apple,Coke}\sigma_{Apple}\sigma_{Coke}}$$

$$= \sqrt{(.5^2 \times .20^2) + (.5^2 \times .20^2) + (2 \times .5 \times .5 \times 1.00 \times .20 \times .20)}$$

$$= \sqrt{.040} = .20$$

> Correlation coefficient of +1.0 indicates the stock returns of the two firms move in exact unison.

When the two stocks' rates of return are perfectly positively correlated (move in unison), the standard deviation of the portfolio is simply the weighted average of their individual standard deviations. When this is the case, there is no benefit to diversification. However, when the correlation coefficient is less than +1.0, the standard deviation of the portfolio is less than the weighted average of the individual stock standard deviations, indicating a benefit from diversification.

Figure 1 illustrates the importance of the correlation coefficient as a determinant of the portfolio standard deviation. Note that the lower the correlation between the returns of the investments in the portfolio, the greater the benefit of diversification. For example, consider the diversification benefits derived from combining two investments whose returns are perfectly positively correlated (+1), uncorrelated (0), and perfectly negatively correlated (−1):

Correlation between Investment Returns	Diversification Benefits
+1	None. No risk has been eliminated because there is no diversification realized by combining the investments because they move together perfectly. This is exactly the case we saw earlier in this chapter when we combined the sunglasses product line with the sunscreen lotion—no elimination of risk.
0.0	There is substantial value to diversification.
−1	Diversification is extremely effective in reducing portfolio risk. In fact, it is possible to select the portfolio weights for two investments whose returns are perfectly negatively correlated, such that all variability is eliminated from the portfolio return and the portfolio standard deviation is zero. Earlier, we encountered a correlation of −1.0 when we considered the sunglasses and umbrellas example.

Figure 1

Diversification and the Correlation Coefficient—Apple and Coca-Cola

The effects of diversification on the risk of the portfolio are contingent on the degree of correlation between the assets included in the portfolio. If the correlation is +1 (meaning the two assets are perfectly correlated and move together in lockstep, as was the case with sunglasses and sunscreen), then there is no benefit to diversification. However, if the correlation is −1 (meaning the two assets move in lockstep in opposite directions, as was the case with sunglasses and umbrellas), it will be possible to construct a portfolio that completely eliminates risk.

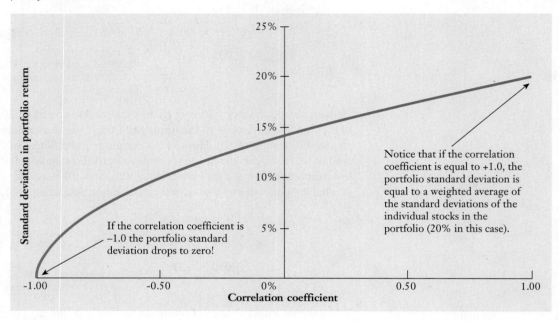

Legend:

Correlation	E(Return)	Standard Deviation
−1.00	0.14	0%
−0.80	0.14	6%
−0.60	0.14	9%
−0.40	0.14	11%
−0.20	0.14	13%
0.0	0.14	14%
0.20	0.14	15%
0.40	0.14	17%
0.60	0.14	18%
0.80	0.14	19%
1.00	0.14	20%

All portfolios are comprised of equal investments in Apple and Coca-Cola shares.

>> END FIGURE 1

Finance in a **Flat World**

International Diversification

One of the great things about diversification is that it reduces risk without reducing expected return. That is, whereas returns are simply the weighted average of the returns on the investments that make up your portfolio, the portfolio's risk, as measured by its standard deviation, is less than the weighted average of the standard deviations of these investments. In effect, the less closely the returns of the investments move together over time, the greater the benefit of diversification. The key, then, is to include stocks in your portfolio that are not too highly correlated with each other.

One way to do this is to include more international stocks in your portfolio. International and domestic securities tend to react differently to the same economic or market information. For example, historically, when the price of oil rises, the prices of U.S. auto companies react differently than those of their Japanese counterparts because Japanese consumers prefer fuel-efficient economy cars to gas-guzzling SUVs that are a mainstay of the U.S. automakers. Thus, the price increase for oil may be bad for the economy in general, but it is worse news for domestic automakers than for Toyota and Nissan. Because of this, a portfolio that includes Japanese as well as U.S. auto stocks will be less risky than a portfolio that includes only U.S. auto stocks.

Unfortunately, international diversification appears to be less effective than it used to be. Over the past 20 years, the returns of U.S. stocks and foreign stocks have become more highly correlated. This is one of the side effects of economic globalization. Only time will tell the full extent of this trend, but it still makes sense to invest beyond the U.S. borders as part of an effort to effectively diversify.

Checkpoint 2

Evaluating a Portfolio's Risk and Return

Sarah Marshall Tipton is considering her 401(k) retirement portfolio and wonders if she should move some of her money into international investments. To this point in her short working life (she graduated just four years ago), she has simply put her retirement savings into a mutual fund with an investment strategy that mimicked the returns of the S&P 500 stock index (large company stocks). This fund has historically earned a return averaging 12 percent over the last 80 or so years, but recently the returns were depressed somewhat, as the economy was languishing in a mild recession. Sarah is considering an international mutual fund that diversifies its holdings around the industrialized economies of the world and has averaged a 14 percent annual rate of return. The international fund's higher average return is offset by the fact that the standard deviation in its returns is 30 percent compared to only 20 percent for the domestic index fund. Upon closer investigation, Sarah learned that the domestic and international funds tend to earn high returns and low returns at about the same times in the business cycle, such that correlation is .75. Suppose Sarah moves half her money into the international fund and leaves the remainder in the domestic fund. What is the expected return and standard deviation of the combined portfolio?

STEP 1: Picture the problem

We can visualize the expected rates of return and corresponding standard deviations as follows:

Investment Fund	Expected Return	Standard Deviation	Investment Proportion
S&P 500 Fund	12%	20%	50%
International Fund	14%	30%	50%
Portfolio			100%

(2 CONTINUED >> ON NEXT PAGE)

The challenge Sarah faces is estimating the portfolio's expected return and standard deviation when she places half her money in each of the two mutual funds. She needs answers to place in the shaded squares in the grid.

STEP 2: Decide on a solution strategy

The portfolio expected rate of return is simply a weighted average of the expected rates of return of the investments in the portfolio. However, the standard deviation is a bit more complicated, as diversification can lead to a reduction in the standard deviation below the weighted average of the standard deviations of the investments in the portfolio. We use Equations (1) and (2) to calculate the expected rate of return and standard deviation for the portfolio.

STEP 3: Solve

Calculating the Expected Return for the Portfolio.

We use Equation (1) to calculate the expected rate of return for the portfolio as follows:

$$E(r_{portfolio}) = W_{S\&P\ 500}E(r_{S\&P\ 500}) + W_{International}E(r_{International})$$

$$= (1/2 \times .12) + (1/2 \times .14) = .13\ or\ 13\%$$

Calculating the Standard Deviation for the Portfolio.

The standard deviation can be calculated using Equation (2) as follows:

$$\sigma_{portfolio} = \sqrt{W_1^2\sigma_1^2 + W_2^2\sigma_2^2 + 2W_1W_2\rho_{1,2}\sigma_1\sigma_2}$$

$$= \sqrt{(.5^2 \times .20^2) + (.5^2 \times .30^2) + (2 \times .5 \times .5 \times .75 \times .20 \times .30)}$$

$$= .235\ or\ 23.5\%$$

STEP 4: Analyze

The expected rate of return for the portfolio comprised of 50 percent in the S&P 500 fund and 50 percent in the international fund is 13 percent, which plots exactly halfway between the two investments' expected returns on the following graph:

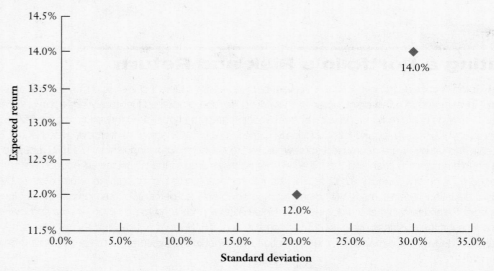

However, the standard deviation of the portfolio is not equal to 25 percent, the midpoint between the standard deviations of 20 percent and 30 percent (i.e., the weighted average of the two investments' standard deviations). It is, instead, equal to only 23.5 percent, which shows that we gain something from diversifying between the international and domestic markets. The returns in these two markets are not perfectly positively correlated, so there is some reduction in the standard deviation of the portfolio that is gained by putting the two investment alternatives together.

STEP 5: Check yourself

Evaluate the expected return and standard deviation of the portfolio of the S&P 500 and international fund where correlation is estimated to be .20 and Sarah still places half of her money in each of the funds.

ANSWER: Expected return = 13 percent and standard deviation = 19.6 percent.

Your Turn: For more practice, do related **Study Problem** 2 at the end of this chapter.

>> END Checkpoint 2

Tools of Financial Analysis—Portfolio Mean and Variance

Name of Tool	Formula	What It Tells You
Expected Portfolio Return, $E(r_{portfolio})$	$[W_1 \times E(r_1)] + [W_2 \times E(r_2)] + \ldots + [W_n \times E(r_n)]$ • $E(r_{portfolio})$ = the expected rate of return for a portfolio of n assets. • W_i = the proportion of the portfolio that is invested in asset i. • $E(r_i)$ = the expected rate of return earned by asset i.	• Measures the expected rate of return from investing in a portfolio of n different assets or securities • The portfolio return is simply an average of the rates of return expected from each security in the portfolio, where the weights reflect the relative amount of funds invested in each security.
Portfolio Variance, $\sigma_{Portfolio}$	$\sqrt{W_1\sigma_2^2 + W_2\sigma_2^2 + 2W_1\sigma_2^2 + 2W_1W_2\rho_{1,2}\sigma_1\sigma_1}$ • $\sigma_{portfolio}$ = the standard deviation in portfolio returns, • W_i = the proportion of the portfolio that is invested in asset i, • σ_i = the standard deviation in the rate of return earned by asset i, and • $\rho_{i,j}$ = correlation between the rate of return earned by assets i and j. The symbol $\rho_{i,j}$ (pronounced "rho") represents correlation between the rates of return for asset 1 and asset 2.	• Measures the return from investing in a security as a percent of the dollars invested • A higher rate of return means a greater return earned by the investment (measured as a percent of the initial investment).

Before you move on to 2

Concept Check | 1

1. How is the expected rate of return on a portfolio related to the expected rates of return of the individual assets contained in the portfolio?
2. When the returns of two risky investments are perfectly negatively correlated, how does combining them in a portfolio affect the overall riskiness of the portfolio?
3. When the returns of two risky investments are perfectly positively correlated, how does combining them in a portfolio affect the overall riskiness of the portfolio?

2 Systematic Risk and the Market Portfolio

In the last section, we showed that the correlation between the returns of two stocks in a portfolio plays a key role in determining the overall risk of the portfolio. The intuition that combining imperfectly correlated investments into a portfolio reduces risk also applies to portfolios that include many different investments. In particular, those investments whose returns have low correlations with other investments in the portfolio contribute less to the overall riskiness of a diversified portfolio than those investments whose returns are highly correlated with the other investments in the portfolio.

This logic implies that we cannot simply say that the standard deviation of an individual investment is the relevant measure of the investment's risk. The standard deviation ignores how the investment's returns are correlated with the returns of other investments, and thus cannot tell us how the investment would contribute to the overall risk of an investor's portfolio. However, because there are thousands of possible investments, it is impractical to calculate all of the correlations of each investment's returns with all other investments, so coming up with a simple measure of the riskiness of an investment is clearly a challenge.

Fortunately, we have a theory, known as the **Capital Asset Pricing Model (CAPM)**, that provides a relatively simple measure of risk. This theory, which was recognized in 1990 in the Nobel Memorial Prize in Economics for Harry Markowitz and William Sharpe, assumes that investors choose to hold the optimally diversified portfolio that includes *all* risky investments. This optimally diversified portfolio that includes all of the economy's assets is generally referred to as the **market portfolio**. According to the CAPM, the relevant risk of an investment relates to how the investment contributes to the risk of this market portfolio.

To understand how an investment contributes to the risk of the market portfolio, it is useful to categorize the risks of the individual investments into two categories—*systematic* and *unsystematic*. The **systematic risk** component measures the contribution of the investment to the risk of the market portfolio. In contrast, the **unsystematic risk** component is the element of risk that does not contribute to the risk of the market portfolio. This component is effectively diversified away when the investment is combined with other investments. In summary, we can think of the total risk of an investment as follows:

$$\text{Total risk} = \text{Systematic risk} + \text{Unsystematic risk} \qquad \textbf{(3)}$$

Intuitively, systematic risk refers to those risks that affect the returns of almost all investments. This is the common element of investment returns that causes the returns to be correlated. For example, if the economy were to slip into a recession, virtually all investments would experience negative returns. Alternatively, if all wars in the world were suddenly ended, it is likely that all stocks (with the exception of the firms that supply armaments and weapons of war) would experience positive returns.

The returns of some investments are more sensitive to systematic (or market-wide) risk than those of other investments. The returns of these investments will tend to be more highly correlated with the returns of most of the other stocks in a portfolio, and will thus make a substantial contribution to the portfolio's overall risk. Unsystematic risk is simply the variability in the returns of an investment that is due to events that are specific to the investment. For example, variation in the stock returns of a particular company can result from the death of the firm's CEO, a product recall, a major fire at a manufacturing plant, or perhaps an event that helps one industry at the expense of other industries. If the risk of an investment comes mainly from unsystematic risk, the investment will tend to have a low correlation with the returns of most of the other stocks in the portfolio, and will thus make only a minor contribution to the portfolio's overall risk. Thus, an investment's systematic risk is far more important than its unsystematic risk.

Diversification and Unsystematic Risk

A more descriptive term for systematic risk is **non-diversifiable risk**. Likewise, unsystematic risk is **diversifiable risk**. The idea here is that large diversified portfolios are still subject to systematic risk—in other words, systematic risk is non-diversifiable. However, unsystematic risk contributes almost nothing to the standard deviation of large diversified portfolios—in other words, unsystematic risk can be diversified away. We illustrate in Figure 2 that as

---

Figure 2

Portfolio Risk and the Number of Investments in the Portfolio
Adding more investments to a portfolio that are not highly correlated with the other assets in the portfolio can dramatically reduce the portfolio's risk. In fact, for randomly selected shares of common stock, the benefits of diversification can be virtually fully achieved with a portfolio of about 50 stocks (assuming equal investment in each stock).

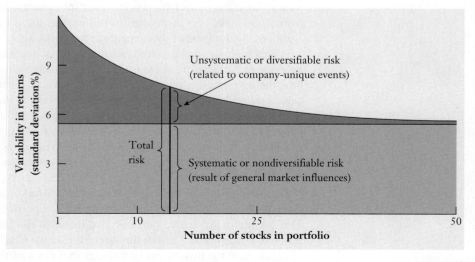

>> END FIGURE 2

the number of securities in a portfolio increases, the contribution of unsystematic risk to the standard deviation of the portfolio declines. This happens because the unsystematic risk of the individual stocks is uncorrelated, so the unsystematic components of the individual stock returns tend to offset one another. If a portfolio consists of stocks in different industries with very different characteristics, then as the number of stocks gets large, virtually all of the variation of the portfolio will come from systematic risk, and virtually none will come from unsystematic risk. The unsystematic component of risk has been diversified away and portfolio risk is comprised almost entirely of the systematic risk of the portfolio stocks.

Diversification and Systematic Risk

Diversification leads to the reduction and eventual elimination of unsystematic risk (the dark green area in Figure 2), but this does not hold true for systematic risk. Because systematic risk is common to most investments, it is a source of correlation between the returns. Indeed, by definition, the systematic sources of risk are perfectly correlated. As we learned earlier, when the returns of two investments are perfectly positively correlated, there is no risk reduction benefit to be gained by diversifying. This means that very large and diversified portfolios are likely to be influenced by the risks associated with interest rates, inflation, wars, and all other factors that affect all companies' stock returns.

Systematic Risk and Beta

Up to this point, we have examined the basic intuition behind systematic risk and why it is important to any investor. In this section, we will describe how systematic risk is measured. Recall that we have defined systematic risk as that portion of an asset's return variation that is shared with many other investments. Because investments with a high level of systematic risk tend to be highly correlated with the returns of many other investments, they are also highly correlated with the returns of a broad market portfolio that includes all investments. This suggests that we can measure the systematic risk of an investment using the extent to which the returns of the investment correlate with the returns on the overall market portfolio.

To measure the systematic risk of an investment, we estimate what is referred to as the investment's **beta coefficient**, often simply called beta. The beta of an investment, which is referenced using the Greek letter β, measures the extent to which a particular investment's returns vary with the returns of the market portfolio. Specifically, our measure of systematic risk is referred to as the investment's beta because in practice it is estimated as the slope of a straight line such as the one found in Figure 3. Note that the figure contains historical monthly rates of return earned by Home Depot (HD) and a market index (the S&P 500) for the period November 2010 through October 2012. The beta for Home Depot is simply the slope of the straight line that best fits the market and Home Depot stock return pattern. In this case the slope is .67, which means that if the market increases by 10 percent over the year, Home Depot would only increase by 6.7 percent. In other words, the systematic risk of Home Depot's shares is less than the average for all stocks (the index, which has a beta of 1.00). This may seem a bit odd, but remember that we are talking about only that portion of Home Depot's return volatility that is shared with the market portfolio, or its systematic risk. The rest of the volatility in Home Depot's stock returns is unsystematic and can be diversified away by simply investing in a diversified portfolio.

Although we could estimate betas ourselves, this is generally not necessary because these estimates are readily available from a wide variety of sources. Table 1 contains beta estimates for several well-known companies. Note that the beta estimates vary between Yahoo Finance and MoneyCentral.com. The difference reflects differences in the time intervals of data used in the estimate. To get some perspective on the size of these beta coefficients, we can compare them to the beta of a risk-free bond, which is zero, and the beta of the overall market portfolio, which is 1. Moreover, it appears that the beta coefficients of the computer and software companies are much higher than those of the utilities companies. For example, a 10 percent rise or fall in the overall market would lead to a smaller than 10 percent change in the utility stock returns, whereas the change would be much larger for the computer and software companies. In fact, for Apple the increase or decrease would be almost 30 percent.

Figure 3

Estimating Home Depot's (HD) Beta Coefficient

A firm's beta coefficient is the slope of a straight line that fits the relationship between the firm's stock returns and those of a broad market index. In the following graph, the market index used is the Standard and Poor's (S&P) 500 index.

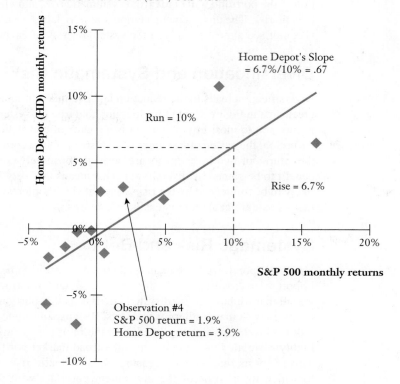

Calculating beta:

1. Visual—the slope of a straight line can be estimated visually by drawing a straight line that best "fits" the scatter of Home Depot's stock returns and those of the market index. The beta coefficient then is the "rise over the run." The blue dots on the graph correspond to values indicated on the chart.

2. Financial calculator—financial calculators have built-in functions for computing the beta coefficient. However, because the procedure varies from one calculator to another we do not present it here.

3. Excel—Excel's Slope function can be used to calculate the slope as follows: =slope(C2:C12,B2:B12)

4. Internet—there are a number of resources that can be used to obtain beta estimates on the Internet, including Yahoo! Finance and Google finance. The estimates can differ depending on the time period used to make the estimate.

Observation	Date	S&P 500 Returns	Home Depot Stock Returns
1	Nov-10	−0.23%	−1.47%
2	Dec-10	6.53%	16.05%
3	Jan-11	2.26%	4.88%
4	Feb-11	3.90%	1.90%
5	Mar-11	−0.10%	−0.43%
6	Apr-11	2.85%	0.24%
7	May-12	−1.35%	−2.34%
8	Jun-12	−1.83%	0.52%
9	Jul-12	−2.15%	−3.56%
10	Aug-12	−5.68%	−3.72%
11	Sep-12	−7.18%	−1.53%
12	Oct-12	10.77%	8.91%

>> END FIGURE 3

Calculating Portfolio Beta

The **portfolio beta** measures the systematic risk of the portfolio, just like a beta for an individual stock measures its systematic risk. The portfolio beta is straightforward to calculate because it is simply a weighted average of the betas for the individual investments contained in the portfolio. Therefore, for a portfolio that contains n different risky assets, the portfolio beta can be calculated as follows:

Portfolio Beta

$$\text{Portfolio Beta} = \left(\begin{array}{c} \text{Proportion of} \\ \text{Portfolio Invested} \\ \text{in Asset 1 } (W_1) \end{array} \times \begin{array}{c} \text{Beta for} \\ \text{Asset 1} \\ (\beta_1) \end{array} \right) + \left(\begin{array}{c} \text{Proportion of} \\ \text{Portfolio Invested} \\ \text{in Asset 2 } (W_2) \end{array} \times \begin{array}{c} \text{Beta for} \\ \text{Asset 2} \\ (\beta_2) \end{array} \right) + \cdots + \left(\begin{array}{c} \text{Proportion of} \\ \text{Portfolio Invested} \\ \text{in Asset } n \, (W_n) \end{array} \times \begin{array}{c} \text{Beta for} \\ \text{Asset } n \\ (\beta_n) \end{array} \right) \quad \textbf{(4)}$$

Or, written using symbols, the beta for a portfolio is simply the weighted average of the betas of individual assets that are held in the portfolio, that is,

$$\beta_{portfolio} = W_1\beta_1 + W_2\beta_2 + \cdots + W_n\beta_n$$

Important Definitions and Concepts:

- W_i = the proportion of the portfolio that is invested in asset i,
- β_i = the beta coefficient for asset i, and
- $\beta_{portfolio}$ = the portfolio beta, which is a weighted average of the betas for the individual assets contained in the portfolio.

For example, consider the following portfolio that is comprised of three investments with betas equal to 1.20, .70, and .25. If half of the portfolio is invested in the first investment and one-fourth in each of the remaining investments, we can calculate the portfolio beta using Equation (8–4) as follows:

$$\beta_{portfolio} = W_1\beta_1 + W_2\beta_2 + W_3\beta_3$$
$$= (.50 \times 1.20) + (.25 \times .70) + (.25 \times .25) = .8375$$

The beta for the three-investment portfolio is therefore .8375.

Table 1	Beta Coefficients for Selected Companies

This table contains two sources of beta estimates (Yahoo.com and MSN.com). These estimates were accessed on the same day and can vary over time because historical stock and market returns are used to calculate the beta estimates.

Company	Yahoo Finance (Yahoo.com)	Microsoft Money Central (MSN.com)
Computers and Software		
Apple Inc. (AAPL)	2.90	2.58
Dell Inc. (DELL)	1.81	1.37
Hewlett Packard (HPQ)	1.27	1.47
Utilities		
American Electric Power Co. (AEP)	0.74	0.73
Duke Energy Corp. (DUK)	0.40	0.56
Centerpoint Energy (CNP)	0.82	0.91

What if the first asset in the preceding example is a risk-free Treasury bond, which by definition has a zero beta? In this case, the portfolio beta calculation would be as follows:

$$\beta_{portfolio} = W_1\beta_1 + W_2\beta_2 + W_3\beta_3$$
$$= (.50 \times 0.00) + (.25 \times .70) + (.25 \times .25) = .2375$$

Tools of Financial Analysis—Portfolio Beta

Name of Tool	Formula	What It Tells You
Portfolio Beta, $\beta_{portfolio}$	$(W_1 \times \beta_1) + (W_2 \times \beta_2) + \cdots + (W_n \times \beta_n)$ • $\beta_{portfolio}$ = the weighted average beta for the portfolio. • W_i = the weight of the *i*th security's beta, which reflects the proportion of the portfolio invested in that security.	• Measures the systematic risk of a portfolio of securities • The average is weighted by the fraction of the portfolio invested in each security.

Before you move on to 3

Concept Check | 2

1. What are some factors that influence the returns of a company such as Home Depot that would constitute a source of systematic risk? Unsystematic risk?
2. How many different stocks are required to essentially diversify away unsystematic risk?

The Security Market Line and the CAPM

In addition to suggesting that an investment's beta is the appropriate measure of its risk, the Capital Asset Pricing Model (or the CAPM) describes how these betas relate to the expected rates of return that investors require on their investments. *The key insights of the CAPM are that investments with the same beta have the same expected rate of return and that investors will require a higher rate of return on investments with higher betas.*

To understand the CAPM expected return equation that comes from this theory, recall that the beta of a portfolio equals the average beta of the investments in the portfolio, and the expected return of a portfolio equals the average expected return of the investments in the portfolio. For example, let's consider the relation between the beta and expected return of a portfolio invested 80 percent in the market portfolio, W_M equals 80 percent, and 20 percent in a risk-free security. The market portfolio has a beta of 1.0 and, for purposes of this example, we will assume that the expected return for the market portfolio, $E(r_M)$ is 11 percent. The risk-free security has a beta of 0, and we will assume it offers a 6 percent risk-free return, r_f equals 6 percent. The expected rate of return using Equation 1) for this two-investment portfolio is then:

$$E(r_{portfolio}) = \begin{pmatrix} \text{Percent of} \\ \text{Funds Invested} \\ \text{in the Market} \\ \text{Portfolio } (W_M) \end{pmatrix} \begin{pmatrix} \text{Expected Return} \\ \text{on the Market} \\ \text{Portfolio } [E(r_m)] \end{pmatrix} + \left[1 - \begin{pmatrix} \text{Percent of} \\ \text{Funds Invested} \\ \text{in the Market} \\ \text{Portfolio } (W_M) \end{pmatrix} \right] \begin{pmatrix} \text{Risk-free} \\ \text{Rate } (r_f) \end{pmatrix}$$

> Because all money is invested in either the market portfolio or the risk-free security, the proportion invested in the risk-free security is equal to $(1 - W_M)$.

$$E(r_{portfolio}) = W_M[E(r_M)] + (1 - W_M)r_f = 0.8 \times 11\% + (1 - 0.8) \times 6\% = 9.3\%$$

If we rearrange the terms in this equation slightly we have,

$$E(r_{portfolio}) = r_f + W_M[E(r_M) - r_f] \qquad \textbf{(5)}$$

Similarly, we can calculate the portfolio beta using Equation (4), which says that a portfolio beta should be equal to the weighted average of the individual assets' betas that make up the portfolio. For this two-investment portfolio:

The beta coefficient for the risk-free security, β_{rf}, is equal to 0.0 because it has zero systematic risk.

$$\beta_{portfolio} = W_M \times \beta_M + (1 - W_M)\beta_f = 0.8 \times 1.0 + (1 - 0.8) \times 0.0 = 0.80$$

Figure 4 provides the expected returns and betas for a variety of portfolios comprised of the market portfolio and the risk-free asset. However, because the CAPM specifies that all investments with the same betas have the same expected returns, the expected return and beta combinations illustrated in this figure apply to all investments, not just to portfolios consisting of the market and the risk-free rate.

The straight-line relationship between the betas and expected returns in Figure 4 is called the **security market line**, and its slope is often referred to as the reward-to-risk ratio. Note that the security market line is simply a graphical representation of the Capital Asset Pricing Model. We can measure the slope of the security market line by computing the ratio of the change in expected rate of return measured along the vertical axis divided by the corresponding change in the beta for the portfolios with these two expected returns. To illustrate how this is done we compare the expected rates of return for a portfolio with zero beta (the risk-free security, which earns 6 percent) and a portfolio that has an expected rate of return of 9 percent and has a beta of 0.60. The slope then is calculated as follows:

$$\text{Slope} = \frac{\text{Rise}}{\text{Run}} = \frac{.09 - .06}{0.60 - 0.0} = \frac{.03}{.60} = 0.05 \text{ or } 5\%$$

The security market line can be expressed as the following equation, which is often referred to as the CAPM pricing equation:

$$\begin{array}{c}\text{Expected Return on} \\ \text{Risky Asset } j\end{array} = \begin{array}{c}\text{Risk-free} \\ \text{Rate of Return}\end{array} + \begin{array}{c}\text{Beta for} \\ \text{Asset } j\end{array} \times \left(\begin{array}{c}\text{Expected Return} \\ \text{on the Market Portfolio}\end{array} - \begin{array}{c}\text{Risk-free} \\ \text{Rate of Return}\end{array}\right)$$

$$E(r_{Asset\,j}) = r_f + \beta_{Asset\,j}[E(r_{Market}) - r_f] \qquad \textbf{(6)}$$

Note that Equation (6) looks very much like Equation (5). The weight associated with the market portfolio, W_M, in Equation (5) is equal to the portfolio beta in Equation (6). In other words, if we substitute beta for W_M in Equation (5), we get Equation (6). Hence, according to the CAPM, low-beta investments are equivalent to portfolios that are mostly invested in the risk-free investment and just slightly invested in the market portfolio. These portfolios are less risky and thus require lower rates of return. In contrast, higher-beta investments are equivalent to portfolios that are more heavily invested in the market portfolio, and hence require a higher expected rate of return. Of course, most investments cannot be viewed as simply a combination of the market and the risk-free investment. They also contain unsystematic risk. However, because unsystematic risk can be eliminated in a diversified portfolio, it is does not affect the investment's expected rate of return.

A critically important learning point here is that because systematic risk cannot be eliminated through diversification and must be borne by the investor, this is the source of risk that is reflected in expected returns. The higher the systematic risk of an investment, other things remaining the same, the higher will be the expected rate of return an investor would require to invest in the asset. This is a simple restatement of ▣ Principle 2: **There Is a Risk–Return Tradeoff**.

Using the CAPM to Estimate Expected Rates of Return

The CAPM provides a theory of how risk and expected return are connected or traded off in the capital markets. For example, earlier we estimated the beta for Home Depot to be .92. If the risk-free rate of interest in the economy is currently about 3 percent, and if the **market risk premium**, which is the difference between the expected return on the market portfolio

Figure 4

Risk and Return for Portfolios Containing the Market and the Risk-Free Security

The following graph depicts the systematic risk and expected rate of return for portfolios comprised of the risk-free security (with beta of zero) plus the market portfolio of all risky assets (with a beta of 1). In the most extreme case, we invest 120 percent in the market portfolio by borrowing 20 percent of the funds and paying the risk-free rate. The risk-free rate is assumed to be 6 percent, and the market risk premium (difference in the expected rate of return on the market portfolio and the risk-free rate) is 5 percent.

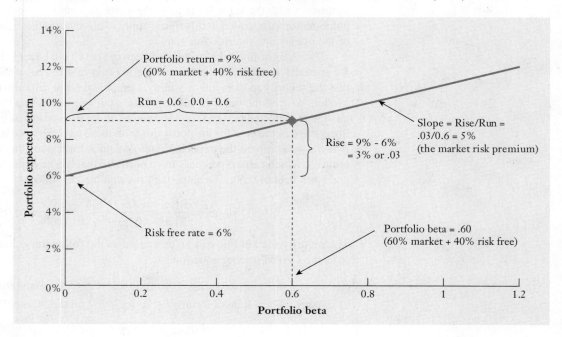

Legend:

% Market Portfolio, W_{Market}	% Risk-Free Asset, $W_{Risk\text{-}free}$	Portfolio Beta, $\beta_{Portfolio}$	Expected Portfolio Return, $E(r_{Portfolio})$
0%	100%	0.0	6.0%
20%	80%	0.2	7.0%
40%	60%	0.4	8.0%
60%	**40%**	**0.6**	**9.0%**
80%	20%	0.8	10.0%
100%	0%	1.0	11.0%
120%	−20%	1.2	12.0%

>> END FIGURE 4

and the risk-free rate of return, is estimated to be 5 percent, we can estimate the expected rate of return on Home Depot's common stock using the CAPM from Equation (8–6) as follows:

$$E(r_{Home\ Depot}) = r_{risk\text{-}free} + \beta_{Home\ Depot}[E(r_{market}) - r_{risk\text{-}free}]$$
$$E(r_{Home\ Depot}) = .03 + .92[.05] = .076\ or\ 7.6\%$$

The systematic risk of Home Depot's shares is reflected in the beta, which was only .92, suggesting that the shares have very nearly the same systematic risk as the market portfolio which has a beta of 1.0.

Checkpoint 3

Estimating the Expected Rate of Return Using the CAPM

Jerry Allen graduated from the University of Texas with a finance degree in the spring of 2013 and took a job with a Houston-based investment banking firm as a financial analyst. One of his first assignments is to investigate the investor-expected rates of return for three technology firms: Apple (APPL), Dell (DELL), and Hewlett Packard (HPQ). Jerry's supervisor suggests that he make his estimates using the CAPM, where the risk-free rate is 4.5 percent, the expected return on the market is 10.5 percent, and the risk premium for the market as a whole (the difference between the expected return on the market and the risk-free rate) is 6 percent. Use the two estimates of beta provided for these firms in Table 1 to calculate two estimates of the investor-expected rates of return for the sample firms.

STEP 1: Picture the problem

Calculating the expected rates of return using the CAPM can be viewed graphically using the security market line, where the intercept of the line equals the risk-free rate (4.5 percent in this case) and the slope is equal to the market risk premium (6 percent in this case):

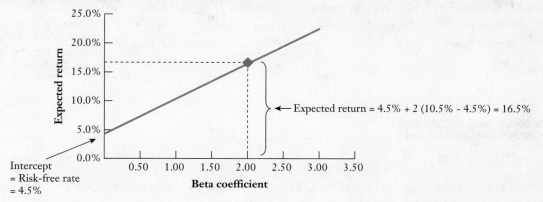

Thus, using Equation (6) and a beta coefficient of 2.00, the investor's expected rate of return is 16.5 percent.

STEP 2: Decide on a solution strategy

Although the expected rates of return plot along the security market line, we can solve for them directly by substituting into the CAPM formula found in Equation (6):

$$E(r_j) = r_f + \beta[E(r_{Market}) - r_f]$$

STEP 3: Solve

Solving for the expected return for Apple using the beta from Yahoo, the beta from MSN, a risk-free rate of 4.5 percent, and a market risk premium of 6 percent yields the following:

- Apple expected return assuming a beta of 2.90 (the Yahoo estimate of beta): 4.5% + 2.90(6.0%) = 4.5% + 17.4% = 21.9%
- Apple expected return assuming a beta of 2.58 (the MSN estimate of beta): 4.5% + 2.58(6.0%) = 4.5% + 15.48% = 19.98%

Calculating the expected return with the CAPM equation using each of the beta estimates found in Table 1 for the three technology firms yields the following results:

	Beta		E(return)	
	Yahoo	MSN	Yahoo	MSN
Apple Inc. (APPL)	2.90	2.58	21.90%	19.98%
Dell Inc. (DELL)	1.81	1.37	15.36%	12.72%
Hewlett Packard (HPQ)	1.27	1.47	12.12%	13.32%

(3 CONTINUED >> ON NEXT PAGE)

STEP 4: Analyze

The expected rate of return for the individual stocks varies somewhat depending upon the source of the beta estimate. This raises a question as to whether it makes sense to carry our estimates out to multiple decimal places.

STEP 5: Check yourself

Estimate the expected rates of return for the three utility companies found in Table 1, using the 4.5 percent risk-free rate and market risk premium of 6 percent.

ANSWER: American Electric Power (AEP) estimates are 8.94 percent and 8.88 percent for the Yahoo! and MSN beta estimates, respectively.

Your Turn: For more practice, do related **Study Problems** 8 and 10 at the end of this chapter.   **>> END Checkpoint 3**

Tools of Financial Analysis—Capital Asset Pricing Model

Name of Tool	Formula		What It Tells You
Capital Asset Pricing Model	$\dfrac{Risk\text{-}free}{Rate\ of\ Return}$ + $\dfrac{Beta\ for}{Asset\ j}$ ×	$\left(\dfrac{Expected\ Return}{on\ the\ Market\ Portfolio} - \dfrac{Risk\text{-}free}{Rate\ of\ Return}\right)$	• Measures the expected rate of return for a risky security, where risk is measured by its systematic (or non-diversifiable) risk.

Before you begin end-of-chapter material

Concept Check │ 3

1. Who are Harry Markowitz and William Sharpe, and what did they do that was so important in finance?
2. How is the portfolio beta related to the betas of the individual investments in the portfolio?
3. Explain the concept of the security market line.
4. What is the market risk premium, and how is it related to the Capital Asset Pricing Model?

Principle 2: The Risk–Return Tradeoff The Capital Asset Pricing Model provides a model that links the risk of an investment as measured by its beta coefficient to its expected rate of return.

Principle 4: Market Prices Reflect Information Market prices reflect the risk and return expectations of investors.

Chapter Summaries

1 **Calculate the expected rate of return and volatility for a portfolio of investments and describe how diversification affects the returns to a portfolio of investments.**

SUMMARY: A portfolio is a combination of several individual investments. The expected rate of return for a portfolio is calculated as a weighted average of the expected rates of return of the individual investments. However, the calculation of the risk of a portfolio (which is reflected in the volatility of the portfolio returns) is more complicated because diversification can influence the overall volatility of the portfolio returns. Consequently, when we compute the portfolio variance or its square root, the standard deviation, we must consider the correlation of the returns of the various individual investments in the portfolio.

KEY TERMS

Correlation coefficient A measure of the degree to which the variation in one variable is related to the variation in another. The coefficient ranges from –1 for a perfectly negative relationship to +1 for perfectly positive dependence.

Diversification The reduction in risk that comes about by combining two or more risky assets into a portfolio where the individual assets are less than perfectly positively correlated.

KEY EQUATIONS

$$E(r_{portfolio}) = [W_1 \times E(r_1)] + [W_2 \times E(r_2)] + [W_3 \times E(r_3)] + \cdots + [W_n \times E(r_n)] \tag{1}$$

$$\sigma_{portfolio} = \sqrt{W_1^2\sigma_1^2 + W_2^2\sigma_2^2 + 2W_1W_2\rho_{1,2}\sigma_1\sigma_2} \tag{2}$$

where	
$\sigma_{portfolio} =$	the standard deviation in portfolio returns,
$W_i =$	the proportion of the portfolio that is invested in asset i,
$\sigma_i =$	the standard deviation in the rate of return earned by asset i, and
ρ_{ij} (pronounced "rho") $=$	correlation between the rates of return earned by assets i and j.
$E(r_{portfolio}) =$	the expected rate of return on a portfolio of n assets.
$E(r_i) =$	the expected rate of return earned by asset i.

Concept Check | **1**

1. How is the expected rate of return on a portfolio related to the expected rates of return of the individual assets contained in the portfolio?

2. When the returns of two risky investments are perfectly negatively correlated, how does combining them in a portfolio affect the overall riskiness of the portfolio?

3. When the returns of two risky investments are perfectly positively correlated, how does combining them in a portfolio affect the overall riskiness of the portfolio?

Understand the concept of systematic risk for an individual investment and calculate portfolio systematic risk (beta).

SUMMARY: We have made an important distinction between systematic and non-systematic risk. The distinction is important because non-systematic risk can be eliminated in large diversified portfolios. Because this risk can be diversified away in large portfolios, investors do not require a premium for holding diversifiable risk. Beta measures the average sensitivity of a security's returns to the movement of the general market, such as the S&P 500. If beta is 1, the security's returns move on average 1 percent for each 1 percent change in the market returns; if beta is 1.5, the security's returns will on average move up and down 1.5 percent for every 1 percent change in the market's returns, and so forth.

KEY TERMS

Beta coefficient A measure of the relationship between the returns of a security such as a share of common stock and the returns of the portfolio of all risky assets.

Capital Asset Pricing Model (CAPM) A model that describes the theoretical link between the expected rate of return on a risky security such as a share of stock and the security's risk as measured by its beta coefficient.

Diversifiable risk Risk that can be eliminated through diversification.

Market portfolio The portfolio of all risky and risk-free assets.

Non-diversifiable risk Risk that cannot be eliminated through diversification.

Portfolio beta The beta coefficient of a portfolio of different investments.

Systematic risk See Non-diversifiable risk.

Unsystematic risk See Diversifiable risk.

KEY EQUATIONS

$$\text{Total risk} = \text{Systematic risk} + \text{Unsystematic risk} \tag{3}$$

$$\begin{aligned}\text{Portfolio} \atop \text{Beta} = &\left(\begin{array}{c}\text{Proportion of} \\ \text{Portfolio Invested} \\ \text{in Asset 1 } (W_1)\end{array} \times \begin{array}{c}\text{Beta for} \\ \text{Asset 1} \\ (\beta_1)\end{array}\right) + \left(\begin{array}{c}\text{Proportion of} \\ \text{Portfolio Invested} \\ \text{in Asset 2 } (W_2)\end{array} \times \begin{array}{c}\text{Beta for} \\ \text{Asset 2} \\ (\beta_2)\end{array}\right) \\ &+ \cdots + \left(\begin{array}{c}\text{Proportion of} \\ \text{Portfolio Invested} \\ \text{in Asset } n \ (W_n)\end{array} \times \begin{array}{c}\text{Beta for} \\ \text{Asset } n \\ (\beta_n)\end{array}\right)\end{aligned} \tag{4}$$

Estimate an investor's expected rate of return using the Capital Asset Pricing Model.

SUMMARY: The Capital Asset Pricing Model (CAPM) provides an intuitive framework for understanding the risk–return relationship. The CAPM suggests that the expected rate of return on an investment is determined by the investment's systematic risk. The model can be stated as follows:

$$\begin{array}{c}\text{Expected Return on} \\ \text{Risky Asset } j\end{array} = \begin{array}{c}\text{Risk-free} \\ \text{Rate of Return}\end{array} + \begin{array}{c}\text{Beta for} \\ \text{Asset } j\end{array} \times \left(\begin{array}{c}\text{Expected Return} \\ \text{on the Market Portfolio}\end{array} - \begin{array}{c}\text{Risk-free} \\ \text{Rate of Return}\end{array}\right)$$

Note that the expected rate of return on risky asset j is equal to the risk-free rate of interest plus a risk premium that is specifically tailored to asset j by the systematic risk of the asset as measured by its beta coefficient. If the beta is equal to 1, then the expected return for the risky asset is simply the expected rate of return for the market portfolio of all risky assets.

KEY TERMS

Market risk premium The difference in the expected rate of return on the market portfolio and the risk-free rate of return.

Security market line A graphical representation of the Capital Asset Pricing Model.

KEY EQUATIONS

$$\begin{array}{c}\text{Expected Return on} \\ \text{Risky Asset } j\end{array} = \begin{array}{c}\text{Risk-free} \\ \text{Rate of Return}\end{array} + \begin{array}{c}\text{Beta for} \\ \text{Asset } j\end{array} \times \left(\begin{array}{c}\text{Expected Return} \\ \text{on the Market Portfolio}\end{array} - \begin{array}{c}\text{Risk-free} \\ \text{Rate of Return}\end{array}\right) \tag{6}$$

Concept Check | 2

1. What are some factors that influence the returns of a company such as Home Depot that would constitute a source of systematic risk? Unsystematic risk?

2. How many different stocks are required to essentially diversify away unsystematic risk?

Concept Check | 3

1. Who are Harry Markowitz and William Sharpe, and what did they do that was so important in finance?

2. How is the portfolio beta related to the betas of the individual investments in the portfolio?

3. Explain the concept of the security market line.

4. What is the market risk premium, and how is it related to the Capital Asset Pricing Model?

Study Questions

1. **(Related to Regardless of Your Major: Risk and Your Personal Investment Plan)** In the *Regardless of Your Major* feature box, what are the four guidelines suggested for analyzing your personal investment decisions?

2. What did Depression-era humorist Will Rogers mean when he said "People tell me about the great return I'm going to get *on* my investment, but I'm more concerned about the return *of* my investment"?

3. Describe the relationship between the expected rate of return for an individual investment and the expected rate of return for a portfolio of several investments.

4. On a recent trip home for fall break, your grandfather tells you that he has purchased the stock of two firms in the automobile industry: Toyota and Ford. He goes on to discuss the merits of his decision and one of the points he makes is that he has avoided the risk of purchasing only one company's stock by diversifying his holdings across two stocks. What do you think of his argument? Be specific and describe to your grandfather what you have learned about portfolio diversification.

5. True or false: Portfolio diversification is affected by the volatility of the returns of the individual investments in the portfolio as well as the correlation among the returns. Explain this statement.

6. Describe what is meant by systematic and unsystematic risk. How is this distinction related to an investment's beta?

7. How is the beta of a portfolio related to the betas of the individual investments in the portfolio?

8. What is the security market line? What do the slope and intercept of this line represent?

9. Describe what the Capital Asset Pricing Model tells you to your father, who has never had a course in finance. What is the key insight we gain from this model?

10. Why would we expect the reward-to-risk ratio (slope of the security market line) to be the same across all risky investments? Assume that you are able to earn 5 percent per unit of risk for investing in the stock of Company A and 7 percent for investing in Company B. How would you expect investors to act in light of this difference in reward-to-risk ratio? (Hint: Which stock do you think investors would want to buy?)

11. Presently you own shares of stock in Company A and are considering adding some shares in either Company B or Company C. The standard deviations of all three firms are exactly the same but the correlation between the common stock returns for Company A and Company B is .5, whereas it is –.5 between the common stock of Company A and Company C. How will the risk or standard deviation of your investment returns change if you decide to invest in A and B's common stock? How will the risk or standard deviation of your portfolio returns change if you decide to invest in A and C's common stock? If the expected return on the stock of all three companies is the same, how will your portfolio's expected return be impacted by your decision to invest in either B or C along with A?

12. True or false: If the standard deviation of Company A's stock returns is greater than the standard deviation of Company B's stock returns, then the beta of Stock A *must* be greater than the beta of Stock B. Explain your answer.

13. If a company's beta jumped from 1.5 to 4.5, would its expected rate of return triple? Explain why or why not. (Hint: Assume the risk-free rate is 4 percent and the market risk premium is 5 percent.)

Study Problems

MyFinanceLab

Go to www.myfinancelab.com
to complete these exercises online
and get instant feedback.

Portfolio Returns and Portfolio Risk

1. **(Related to Checkpoint 1) (Expected rate of return)** James Fromholtz is considering whether to invest in a newly formed investment fund. The fund's investment objective is to acquire home mortgage securities at what it hopes will be bargain prices. The fund sponsor has suggested to James that the fund's performance will hinge on how the national economy performs in the coming year. Specifically, he suggested the following possible outcomes:

State of the Economy	Probability	Fund Return
Rapid expansion and recovery	5%	100%
Modest growth	45%	35%
Continued recession	45%	5%
Falls into depression	5%	−100%

   a. Based on these potential outcomes, what is your estimate of the expected rate of return from this investment opportunity?

   b. Would you be interested in making such an investment? Note that you lose all your money in one year if the economy collapses into the worst state or you double your money if the economy enters into a rapid expansion.

2. **(Related to Checkpoint 2) (Computing the standard deviation for an individual investment)** Calculate the standard deviation in the anticipated returns found in Problem 1.

3. **(Computing the standard deviation for a portfolio of two risky investments)** Mary Guilott recently graduated from college and is evaluating an investment in two companies' common stock. She has collected the following information about the common stock of Firm A and Firm B:

	Expected Return	Standard Deviation
Firm A's common stock	0.15	0.12
Firm B's common stock	0.1	0.06
Correlation coefficient	0.4	

   a. If Mary invests half her money in each of the two common shares, what is the expected rate of return and standard deviation in portfolio return?

   b. Answer question a, where correlation between the two common stock investments is equal to zero.

   c. Answer question a, where correlation between the two common stock investments is equal to +1.

   d. Answer question a, where correlation between the two common stock investments is equal to −1.

   e. Using your responses to questions a–d, describe the relationship between correlation and the risk and return of the portfolio.

4. **(Computing the standard deviation for a portfolio of two risky investments)** Answer the following questions using the information provided in Problem 3:

   a. Answer question a of Problem 3, where Mary decides to invest 10 percent of her money in Firm A's common stock and 90 percent in Firm B's common stock.

   b. Answer question a of Problem 3, where Mary decides to invest 90 percent of her money in Firm A's common stock and 10 percent in Firm B's common stock.

c. Recompute your responses to both questions a and b, where the correlation between the two firms' stock returns is −4.

d. Summarize what your analysis tells you about portfolio risk when combining risky assets in a portfolio.

5. **(Related to Checkpoint 1)** **(Portfolio expected rate of return)** Penny Francis inherited a $100,000 portfolio of investments from her grandparents when she turned 21 years of age. The portfolio is comprised of the following three investments:

	Expected Return	$ Value
Treasury bills	4.5%	40,000
Ford (F)	8.0%	30,000
Harley Davidson (HOG)	12.0%	30,000

a. Based on the current portfolio composition and the expected rates of return, what is the expected rate of return for Penny's portfolio?

b. If Penny wants to increase her expected portfolio rate of return, she could increase the allocated weight of the portfolio she has invested in stock (Ford and Harley Davidson) and decrease her holdings of Treasury bills. If Penny moves all her money out of Treasury bills and splits it evenly between the two stocks, what will be her expected rate of return?

c. If Penny does move money out of Treasury bills and into the two stocks she will reap a higher expected portfolio return, so why would anyone want to hold Treasury bills in their portfolio?

6. **(Portfolio expected rate of return)** Barry Swifter is 60 years of age and considering retirement. Barry's retirement portfolio currently is valued at $750,000 and is allocated in Treasury bills, an S&P 500 index fund, and an emerging-market fund as follows:

	Expected Return	$ Value
Treasury bills	4.5%	75,000
S&P 500 Index Fund	8.0%	450,000
Emerging Market Fund	12.0%	225,000

a. Based on the current portfolio composition and the expected rates of return, what is the expected rate of return for Barry's portfolio?

b. Barry is considering a reallocation of his investments to include more Treasury bills and less exposure to emerging markets. If Barry moves all of his money from the emerging market fund and puts it in Treasury bills, what will be the expected rate of return on the resulting portfolio?

7. **(Expected rate of return and risk)** Kelly B. Stites, Inc., is considering an investment in one of two portfolios. Given the information that follows, which investment is better, based on risk (as measured by the standard deviation) and the expected rate of return?

Portfolio A		Portfolio B	
Probability	Return	Probability	Return
.20	−2%	.10	5%
.50	19%	.30	7%
.30	25%	.40	12%
		.20	14%

Systematic Risk and the Market Portfolio

8. **(Related to Checkpoint 3) (Systematic risk and expected rates of return)** Table 1 contains beta coefficient estimates for six firms and from two different sources. Calculate the expected increase in the value of each firm's shares if the market portfolio were to increase by 10 percent (use either the Yahoo Finance or Microsoft Money Central beta estimates). Perform the same calculation where the market drops by 10 percent. Which set of firms has the most variable or volatile stock returns?

9. **(Estimating betas)** Consider the following stock returns for B&A Trucking, Inc. and the market index:

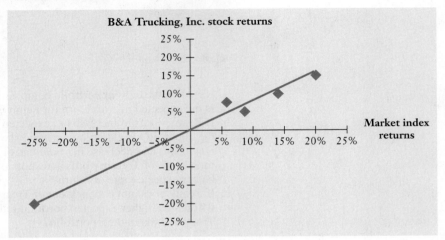

B&A Trucking, Inc. stock returns

Use the visual method described in Figure 3 to estimate the beta for B&A. Is the firm more or less risky than the market portfolio? Explain.

The Security Market Line and the CAPM

10. **(Related to Checkpoint 3) (CAPM and expected returns)**

a. Given the following holding-period returns, compute the average returns and the standard deviations for the Sugita Corporation and for the market.

Month	Sugita Corp.	Market
1	1.8%	1.5%
2	−0.5	1.0
3	2.0	0.0
4	−2.0	−2.0
5	5.0	4.0
6	5.0	3.0

b. If Sugita's beta is 1.18 and the risk-free rate is 4 percent, what would be an expected return for an investor owning Sugita? (Note: Because the preceding returns are based on monthly data, you will need to annualize the returns to make them comparable with the risk-free rate. For simplicity, you can convert from monthly to yearly returns by multiplying the average monthly returns by 12.)

c. How does Sugita's historical average return compare with the return you should expect based on the Capital Asset Pricing Model and the firm's systematic risk?

11. **(CAPM and expected returns)**
    a. Given the following holding-period returns, compute the average returns and the standard deviations for the Zemin Corporation and for the market.

Month	Zemin Corp.	Market
1	6%	4%
2	3	2
3	1	−1
4	−3	−2
5	5	2
6	0	2

    b. If Zemin's beta is 1.54 and the risk-free rate is 4 percent, what would be an expected return for an investor owning Zemin? (Note: Because the preceding returns are based on monthly data, you will need to annualize the returns to make them comparable with the risk-free rate. For simplicity, you can convert from monthly to yearly returns by multiplying the average monthly returns by 12.)
    c. How does Zemin's historical average return compare with the return you believe you should expect based on the capital asset pricing model and the firm's systematic risk?

12. **(Security market line)** James Fromholtz from Problem 1 is evaluating the investment posed in that problem and wants to apply his recently acquired understanding of the security market line concept to his analysis.

    a. If the risk-free rate of interest is currently 2.5 percent, and the beta for the investment is 2, what is the slope of the security market line for the real estate mortgage security investment?
    b. James is also considering the investment of his money in a market index fund that has an expected rate of return of 10 percent. What is the slope of the security market line (i.e., the reward-to-risk ratio) for this investment opportunity?
    c. Based on your analysis of parts a and b, which investment should James take? Why?

13. **(Expected rate of return using CAPM)**

    a. Compute the expected rate of return for Intel common stock, which has a 1.2 beta. The risk-free rate is 3.5 percent and the market portfolio (composed of New York Stock Exchange stocks) has an expected return of 16 percent.
    b. Why is the rate you computed the expected rate?

14. **(Expected rate of return using CAPM)**

    a. Compute the expected rate of return for Acer common stock, which has a 1.5 beta. The risk-free rate is 4.5 percent and the market portfolio (composed of New York Stock Exchange stocks) has an expected return of 10 percent.
    b. Why is the rate you computed the expected rate?

15. **(Capital Asset Pricing Model)** Johnson Manufacturing, Inc., is considering several investments. The rate on Treasury bills is currently 4 percent, and the expected return for the market is 10 percent. What should be the the expected rates of return for each investment (using the CAPM)?

Security	Beta
A	1.50
B	.82
C	.60
D	1.15

16. **(Capital Asset Pricing Model)** Bobbi Manufacturing, Inc., is considering several investments. The rate on Treasury bills is currently 3.75 percent, and the expected return for the market is 10 percent. What should be the expected rates of return for each investment (using the CAPM)?

Security	Beta
A	1.40
B	.75
C	.80
D	1.20

17. **(Capital Asset Pricing Model)** Breckenridge, Inc., has a beta of .85. If the expected market return is 10.5 percent and the risk-free rate is 3.5 percent, what is the appropriate expected return of Breckenridge (using the CAPM)?

18. **(Capital Asset Pricing Model)** CSB, Inc. has a beta of .765. If the expected market return is 10.5 percent and the risk-free rate is 3.5 percent, what is the appropriate expected rate of return of CSB (using the CAPM)?

19. **(Capital Asset Pricing Model)** The expected return for the general market is 10.3 percent, and the risk premium in the market is 5.3 percent. Tasaco, LBM, and Exxos have betas of .864, .693, and .575, respectively. What are the appropriate expected rates of return for the three securities?

20. **(Portfolio beta and security market line)** You own a portfolio consisting of the following stocks:

Stock	Percentage of Portfolio	Beta	Expected Return
1	20%	1.00	16%
2	30%	0.85	14%
3	15%	1.20	20%
4	25%	0.60	12%
5	10%	1.60	24%

The risk-free rate is 3 percent. Also, the expected return on the market portfolio is 10.5 percent.

a. Calculate the expected return of your portfolio. (Hint: The expected return of a portfolio equals the weighted average of the individual stock's expected return, where the weights are the percentage invested in each stock.)

b. Calculate the portfolio beta.

c. Given the preceding information, plot the security market line on paper. Plot the stocks from your portfolio on your graph.

d. From your plot in part c, which stocks appear to be your winners and which ones appear to be losers?

e. Why should you consider your conclusion in part d to be less than certain?

21. **(Security market line)** Your father just learned from his financial advisor that his retirement portfolio has a beta of 1.80. He has turned to you to explain to him what this means. Specifically, describe what you would expect to happen to the value of his retirement fund if the following were to occur:

a. The value of the market portfolio rises by 7 percent.

b. The value of the market portfolio drops by 7 percent.

c. Is your father's retirement portfolio more or less risky than the market portfolio? Explain.

22. **(Security market line)** You are considering the construction of a portfolio comprised of equal investments in each of four different stocks. The betas for each stock on next page:

Security	Beta
A	2.5
B	1.0
C	0.5
D	−1.5

a. What is the portfolio beta for your proposed investment portfolio?

b. How would a 25 percent increase in the expected return on the market impact the expected return of your portfolio?

c. How would a 25 percent decrease in the expected return on the market impact the expected return on each asset?

d. If you are interested in decreasing the beta of your portfolio by changing your portfolio allocation to two stocks, which stock would you decrease and which would you increase? Why?

23. **(Portfolio beta and CAPM)** You are putting together a portfolio made up of four different stocks. However, you are considering two possible weightings:

		Portfolio Weightings	
Asset	Beta	First Portfolio	Second Portfolio
A	2.5	10%	40%
B	1.0	10%	40%
C	0.5	40%	10%
D	−1.5	40%	10%

a. What is the beta on each portfolio?

b. Which portfolio is riskier?

c. If the risk-free rate of interest were 4 percent and the market risk premium were 5 percent, what rate of return would you expect to earn from each of the portfolios?

24. **(Security market line)** If the risk-free rate of return is 4 percent and the expected rate of return on the market portfolio is 10 percent.

a. Graph the security market line (SML). Also, calculate and label the market risk premium on the graph.

b. Using your graph from question a, identify the expected rates of return on a portfolio with beta of .4 and a beta of 1.8, respectively.

c. Now assume that because of a financial crisis the economy slows down and anticipated inflation drops. As a result, the risk-free rate of return drops to 2 percent and the expected rate of return on the market portfolio drops to 8 percent. Draw the resulting security market line.

d. Now assume that because of economic fears, investors have become more risk averse, demanding a higher return on all assets that have any risk. This results in an increase in the expected rate of return on the market portfolio to 12 percent (with the risk-free rate equal to 4 percent). Draw the resulting SML. What can you conclude about the effect of a financial crisis on expected rates of return?

25. **(Portfolio beta and security market line)** You own a portfolio consisting of the following stocks:

Stock	Percentage of Portfolio	Beta	Return Expected
1	10%	1.00	12%
2	25	0.75	11
3	15	1.30	15
4	30	0.60	9
5	20	1.20	14

The risk-free rate is 4 percent. Also, the expected return on the market portfolio is 10 percent.

a. Calculate the expected return of your portfolio. (Hint: The expected return of a portfolio equals the weighted average of the individual stock's expected return, where the weights are the percentage invested in each stock.)

b. Calculate the portfolio beta.

c. Given the preceding information, plot the security market line on paper. Plot the stocks from your portfolio on your graph.

d. From your plot in part c, which stocks appear to be your winners and which ones appear to be losers?

e. Why should you consider your conclusion in part d to be less than certain?

26. **(Capital Asset Pricing Model)** Anita, Inc. is considering the following investments. The current rate on Treasury bills is 4.5 percent, and the expected return for the market is 11 percent. Using the CAPM, what rates of return should Anita require for each individual security?

Stock	Beta
H	0.75
T	1.4
P	0.95
W	1.25

27. **(Capital Asset Pricing Model)** Grace Corporation is considering the following investments. The current rate on Treasury bills is 2.5 percent and the expected return for the market is 9 percent.

Stock	Beta
K	1.12
G	1.3
B	0.75
U	1.02

a. Using the CAPM, what rates of return should Grace require for each individual security?

b. How would your evaluation of the expected rates of return for Grace change if the risk-free rate were to rise to 4.5 percent and the market risk premium were to be only 5 percent?

c. Which market risk premium scenario (from part a or b) best fits a recessionary environment? A period of economic expansion? Explain your response.

Mini-Case

Larry Lynch has been working for a year as an analyst for an investment company that specializes in serving very wealthy clients. These clients often purchase shares in closely held investment funds with very limited numbers of stockholders. In the fall of 2008, the market for certain types of securities based on real estate loans simply collapsed as the subprime mortgage scandal unfolded. Larry's firm, however, sees this market collapse as an opportunity to put together a fund that purchases some of these mortgage-backed securities that investors have shunned by acquiring them at bargain prices and holding them until the underlying mortgages are repaid or the market for these securities recovers.

The investment company began putting together sales information concerning the possible performance of the new fund and has made the following predictions regarding the possible performance of the new fund over the coming year as a function of how well the economy does:

State of the Economy	Probability	Fund Return
Rapid expansion	10%	50%
Modest growth	50%	35%
No growth	40%	5%
Recession	5%	−100%

Larry's boss has asked him to perform a preliminary analysis of the new fund's performance potential for the coming year. Specifically, he has asked that Larry address each of the following issues:

1. What are the expected rate of return and standard deviation?

2. What is the reward-to-risk ratio for the fund based on the fund's standard deviation as a measure of risk?

3. What is the expected rate of return for the fund based on the Capital Asset Pricing Model?

In addition to the information provided above, Larry has observed that the risk-free rate of interest for the coming year is 4.5 percent, the market risk premium is 5.5 percent, and the beta for the new investment is 3.55.

Based on your analysis, do you think that the proposed fund offers a fair return given its risk? Explain.

Photo Credits

Debt Valuation and Interest Rates

From Chapter 9 of *Financial Management: Principles and Applications*, Twelfth Edition. Sheridan Titman, Arthur J. Keown, and John D. Martin.

Debt Valuation and Interest Rates

Chapter **Outline**

1 Overview of Corporate Debt ⟶ **Objective 1.** Identify the key features of bonds and describe the difference between private and public debt markets.

2 Valuing Corporate Debt ⟶ **Objective 2.** Calculate the value of a bond and relate it to the yield to maturity on the bond.

3 Bond Valuation: Four Key Relationships ⟶ **Objective 3.** Describe the four key bond valuation relationships.

4 Types of Bonds ⟶ **Objective 4.** Identify the major types of corporate bonds.

5 Determinants of Interest Rates ⟶ **Objective 5.** Explain the effects of inflation on interest rates and describe the term *structure of interest rates*.

As you will see, the valuation of bonds, or for that matter any financial asset, relies on the first three basic principles of finance: **P** Principle 1: **Money Has a Time Value**—debt securities require that the borrower repay the lender over time, so the value of the security must incorporate consideration for when the debt is to be repaid; **P** Principle 2: **There Is a Risk–Return** **Tradeoff**—the risk of default by the borrower is considered when determining the rate to use when discounting future cash flows; and **P** Principle 3: **Cash Flows Are the Source of Value**—debt securities provide value to the lender through the interest payments on the outstanding loan amount and the repayment of the loan balance itself.

Using Debt to Finance Assets

Debt

Assets

Businesses take on debt to finance their operations. Just like individuals, they borrow from commercial banks and they also borrow when they sell their debt in the public bond market. Some firms finance their operations with substantial amounts of debt. For example, in 2012 the General Electric Corporation (GE) had short-term and long-term debt totaling over $600 billion. Other firms use much less debt. For example, Microsoft Corporation (MSFT) has virtually no debt.

To many investors, bonds are viewed as a low-risk investment alternative. This is not always the case. In 2008, when large U.S. stocks earned an average return of negative 37.0 percent, long-term government bonds produced a positive 25.9 percent return. However, just one year later in 2009, long-term government bonds returned only 3.0 percent while large U.S. stocks earned 26.5 percent. Then in 2011, long-term government bonds once again outperformed large U.S. stocks, earning 18.0 percent while stocks only returned 2.1 percent. Clearly bonds can be risky and their prices don't always increase and decrease with stocks. This chapter will give you an understanding of what determines the value of bonds and consequently why bond prices move up and down over time.

This chapter is organized around the discussion of two related topics: the valuation of bonds and other debt instruments, and the determinants of interest rates. We begin our study of debt valuation with a look at some basic features and terminology. Then we'll learn how to value a bond and its associated cash flows using the discounted cash flow valuation principles—**P** Principle 1: **Money Has a Time Value, P** Principle 2: **There Is a Risk–Return Tradeoff,** and **P** Principle 3: **Cash Flows Are the Source of Value**. Finally, because interest rates affect bond values, we'll look at the determinants of interest rates.

Regardless of Your Major…

"Borrow Now, Pay Later"

In 2012, the total amount of consumer debt (excluding mortgages and home equity lines of credit) exceeded $2.64 trillion or about $8,500 for every man, woman, and child living in the United States—and these figures don't even include mortgage debt on housing.

That's a lot of borrowing, but borrowing is necessary, and most of us borrow money from time to time. Borrowing money makes it possible for us to make purchases today in return for assuming a debt obligation that we will repay at a later date. We borrow money to pay for college tuition and books, we borrow when we buy homes, and we borrow when we buy new cars. In your personal life, you will have the opportunity to choose between many varieties of debt. Should you get a car loan that is repaid over four years or five years? Should you get a mortgage with fixed monthly payments or one where your monthly payments change if interest rates change? The only real difference between how individuals and how corporations operate in the debt markets is that corporations can issue bonds, whereas individuals cannot.

Your Turn: **See Study Question** 1.

1 Overview of Corporate Debt

When a corporation borrows money to finance its operations it can choose to either take out a loan from a financial institution, such as a bank or insurance company, or sell bonds. When debt is incurred through a loan from a financial institution, it is often referred to as private debt, because the debt is not publicly traded. In contrast, bonds are referred to as public debt because they can be traded in the public financial markets.

Because of the costs associated with issuing bonds, smaller firms raise debt capital almost exclusively by borrowing from banks. Large firms also borrow from banks and, in addition, they raise debt capital by issuing bonds. These firms generally borrow from banks when they need capital for a relatively short period of time and prefer raising capital in the bond markets when they need to borrow for a long period of time and prefer to lock in a fixed rate of interest.

This chapter will focus primarily on bonds, but because all companies take out loans from time to time, let's first examine the loan alternative.

Borrowing Money in the Private Financial Market

When most of us think about borrowing money, we probably think about going down to our local bank and filling out a loan application. Likewise, securing loans from financial institutions is also an important source of capital for business firms.

For example, to raise debt capital in the private financial market, the borrowing firm approaches a financial institution, such as a commercial bank like Bank of America (BAC) or GE Capital, General Electric's (GE) financing division, with a loan request. The loan might be used to finance the firm's day-to-day operations or it might be for the purchase of equipment or property. Such a loan is considered a **private market transaction** because it only involves the two parties to the loan. In contrast, when a firm borrows in the public financial market, anyone with money to invest can choose to participate. We will return to this possibility in a moment.

Private Debt Placements

Firms can raise money by selling debt securities to investors indirectly through a public offering that involves the sale of securities to an investment bank that acts as an intermediary who then resells the securities to investors, or directly to an investor through a private placement. The major investors in private placements are large financial institutions, with the three most important investor groups being (1) life insurance companies such as Metlife, (2) state and local retirement funds such as the California Public Employees Retirement System, and (3) private pension funds such as the AFL-CIO Pension Fund.

Well over half of all debt issuance involves private placements, and in 2012, record low interest rates resulted in the issuance of more than a half a trillion dollars of privately placed debt. Much of this new debt was used to retire outstanding debt that carried a higher rate of interest.

When a firm privately places debt, it may or may not use the services of an investment banker. Investment bankers provide valuable advice in the private placement process and are in frequent contact with major institutional investors who are the potential buyers for the issue. Moreover, their continuous involvement in the capital market means they can provide timely advice concerning the best terms for the new issue.

Private placements have advantages and disadvantages compared with public offerings, with the advantages being:

1. **Speed.** The firm usually obtains funds more quickly through a private placement than a public offering. The major reason is that registration of the issue with the Securities and Exchange Commission (SEC) is not required.

2. **Reduced Costs.** These savings result because the lengthy registration statement for the SEC does not have to be prepared, and the investment-banking underwriting and distribution costs do not have to be absorbed.

3. **Financing Flexibility.** In a private placement, the firm deals on a face-to-face basis with a small number of investors. This means that the terms of the issue can be tailored to meet the specific needs of the company. For example, if the investors agree to loan $50 million to a firm, the management does not have to take the full $50 million at one time. Managers may instead borrow as they need it, and thereby pay interest only on the amount actually borrowed. However, the company may have to pay a commitment fee of, say, 1 percent on the unused portion of the loan. That is, if the company only borrows $35 million, it will have to pay interest on that amount, and pay a commitment fee of 1 percent or so on the remaining $15 million. This provides some insurance against capital market uncertainties, and the firm does not have to borrow the funds if the need does not arise. There is also the possibility of renegotiation. The terms of the debt issue can be altered. The term to maturity, the interest rate, or any restrictive covenants can be discussed among the affected parties.

The following disadvantages of private placements must also be considered:

1. **Interest Costs.** It is generally conceded that interest costs on private placements exceed those of public issues. Whether this disadvantage is enough to offset the reduced costs associated with a private placement is a determination the financial manager must make. There is some evidence that on smaller issues, say, $500,000 as opposed to $30 million, the private placement alternative would be preferable.

2. **Restrictive Covenants.** A firm's dividend policy, working-capital levels, and the raising of additional debt capital may all be affected by provisions in the private-placement debt contract. This is not to say that such restrictions are always absent in public debt contracts. Rather, the firm's financial officer must be alert to the tendency for these covenants to be especially burdensome in private contracts.

3. **The Possibility of Future SEC Registration.** If the lender (investor) should decide to sell the issue to a public buyer before maturity, the issue must be registered with the SEC. Some lenders, then, require that the issuing firm agree to a future registration at their option.

Floating-Rate Loans

Loans made in the private financial market are typically **floating-rate** loans, which means that either every month or every quarter the rate of interest charged by the lender adjusts up or down depending on the movements of an agreed-upon benchmark rate of interest. There also exist fixed-rate loans, where the interest rate is set and does not vary. Perhaps the most popular benchmark rate of interest for floating-rate loans is the **London Interbank Offered Rate (LIBOR)**. This is a daily rate that is based on the interest rates at which banks offer to lend in the London wholesale or interbank market (the market where banks loan each other

Table 1	Types of Bank Debt

Bank loans are typically classified in one of two ways: (i) by the intended use of the loan, for example, working capital or transaction loans, and (ii) by whether the loan is secured by collateral or not.

(Panel A) Types of Bank Loans—Classified by Intended Use	
Working capital loans	Typically, these loans set up a line of credit based on an open-ended credit agreement whereby the firm has prior approval to borrow up to a set limit. This type of credit agreement is similar to that of a personal credit card that provides a line of credit up to an agreed-upon limit. The credit is then used to provide cash needed to support the firm's day-to-day business needs.
Transaction loans	Firms use this type of loan to finance a specific asset. These loans typically call for installment payments designed to repay the principal amount of the loan, plus interest, with fixed monthly or annual payments. Home mortgage and automobile loans are examples of transaction loans that require installment payments.

(Panel B) Types of Bank Loans—Classified by the Collateral Used to Secure the Loan	
Secured debt	This type of debt acts as a promise to pay that is backed by granting the lender an interest in a specific piece of property, known as collateral. The property used to secure the loan can include virtually any tangible business asset and could include accounts receivable, inventory, plant and equipment, and real estate.
Unsecured debt	A promise to pay that is not supported by collateral so that the lender relies upon the creditworthiness and reputation of the borrower to repay the debt when due.

money). As such, it is common to see interest rates quoted as the LIBOR rate plus a fixed percent. Typically, a floating-rate loan will specify the following:

- The spread or margin between the loan rate and the benchmark rate, expressed as **basis points**, where 100 basis points equals 1 percent.
- A maximum and a minimum annual rate, to which the rate can adjust, referred to as the ceiling and floor, respectively.
- A maturity date when the loan must be repaid.
- Collateral, which can be seized by the lender in the event that the loan is not paid back.

For example, a company may get a loan with a rate of 2.5 percent or 250 basis points over LIBOR, with a ceiling of 8 percent and a floor of 4 percent. Table 1 classifies bank loans by their intended use—either for working capital or a **transaction loan** used to finance a specific asset—and also by the presence or absence of any **collateral**; that is, assets pledged by the borrower that might be used to secure the debt, with secured loans having collateral and unsecured loans not having collateral. Later in the chapter we will examine secured and unsecured bonds.

Borrowing Money in the Public Financial Market

Firms also raise debt capital by selling debt securities to individual investors as well as to financial institutions such as mutual funds. A key distinction between public and private financial markets is that to sell a debt security to the public, the issuing firm has to meet the legal requirements for doing so as specified by the securities laws.

When funds are raised in the public financial market, the investment banker takes on an important role. Because most corporations do not raise long-term capital frequently and because the sums involved can be huge, this process is of great importance to financial managers. Because most managers are unfamiliar with the subtleties of raising long-term funds, they enlist the help of an expert, an investment banker. It is with the help of an investment banker serving as the underwriter that both stocks and bonds are generally sold in the primary markets. The underwriting process involves the purchase and subsequent resale of a new security issue with the risk of selling the new issue at a satisfactory price being assumed by the investment banker.

Actually, we use the term "investment banker" to describe both the firm itself and the individuals who work for it in that capacity. Just what does this intermediary role involve? The easiest way to understand it is to look at the basic investment-banking functions. Keep in mind that these functions apply to issues of both debt and equity. The investment banker performs three basic functions: (1) underwriting, (2) distributing, and (3) advising.

Underwriting. The term *underwriting* is borrowed from the field of insurance. It means assuming a risk. The investment banker assumes the risk of selling a security issued at a satisfactory price. A satisfactory price is one that generates a profit for the investment-banking house. The procedure goes like this. The managing investment banker and its syndicate will buy the security issue from the corporation in need of funds. The **syndicate** is a group of other investment bankers that is invited to help buy and resell the issue. The managing house is the investment-banking firm that originated the business because its corporate client decided to raise external funds. On a specific day, the client that is raising capital is presented with a check from the managing house in exchange for the securities being issued. At this point the investment-banking syndicate owns the securities. The client has its cash, so it is immune from the possibility that the security markets might turn sour. That is, if the price of the newly issued security falls below that paid to the firm by the syndicate, the syndicate will suffer a loss. The syndicate, of course, hopes that the opposite situation will result. Its objective is to sell the new issue to the investing public at a price per security greater than its cost.

Distributing. Once the syndicate owns the new securities, it must get them into the hands of the ultimate investors. This is the distribution or selling function of investment banking. The investment banker may have branch offices across the United States, or it may have an informal arrangement with several security dealers who regularly buy a portion of each new offering for final sale. It is not unusual to have 300 to 400 dealers involved in the selling effort. The syndicate can properly be viewed as the security wholesaler, and the dealer organization can be viewed as the security retailer.

Advising. The investment banker is an expert in the issuance and marketing of securities. A sound investment-banking house will be aware of prevailing market conditions and can relate those conditions to the particular type of security and the price at which it should be sold at a given time. For example, business conditions may be pointing to a future increase in interest rates, so the investment banker might advise the firm to issue its bonds in a timely fashion to avoid the higher interest rates that are forthcoming. The banker can analyze the firm's capital structure and make recommendations about what general source of capital should be issued. In many instances the firm will invite its investment banker to sit on the board of directors. This permits the banker to observe corporate activity and make recommendations on a regular basis.

Corporate Bonds

Bonds that are issued by corporations are often referred to as corporate bonds. Thus, a **corporate bond** is a security sold by corporations that has promised future payments and a maturity date. The promised payment of a bond should be contrasted to the dividend on a firm's stock, which is paid at the discretion of the issuing firm. If the firm fails to make its promised interest and principal payments, then the bond trustee (who looks over the bondholders' interests) can classify the firm as insolvent and force it into bankruptcy.

Calculating the Rate of Interest on a Floating-Rate Loan

The Slinger Metal Fabricating Company entered into a loan agreement with its bank to finance the firm's working capital. The loan called for a floating rate that was 25 basis points (.25 percent) over an index based on LIBOR. In addition, the loan is adjusted weekly based on the closing value of the index for the previous week within the bounds of a maximum annual rate of 2.5 percent and a minimum of 1.75 percent. Calculate the rate of interest for the weeks 2 through 10.

Week (t)	LIBOR (t)
Week 1	1.98%
Week 2	1.66%
Week 3	1.52%
Week 4	1.35%
Week 5	1.60%
Week 6	1.63%
Week 7	1.67%
Week 8	1.88%
Week 9	1.93%

STEP 1: Picture the problem

We can envision the problem solution by looking at a graph of the ceiling rate, the floor rate, and LIBOR plus the spread of 25 basis points. The rate of interest on the floating-rate loan is based on LIBOR plus the spread but can never exceed the ceiling rate of 2.5 percent, nor can it ever drop below the floor rate of 1.75 percent.

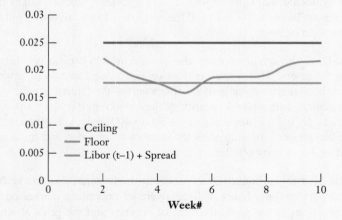

STEP 2: Decide on a solution strategy

To solve this problem we will calculate the floating rate of interest and then see if it exceeds the ceiling or falls below the floor. The floating rate of interest on the loan for any given week is equal to the LIBOR rate for the previous week (in the figure above) plus the spread of 25 basis points (bp) as long as the resulting rate does not exceed the ceiling rate of 2.5 percent or fall below the floor rate of 1.75 percent. If LIBOR $(t-1)$ (that is, the LIBOR on the previous week) plus the 25-bp spread should rise above the ceiling, then the rate will remain equal to the ceiling rate until the index falls back below the ceiling. Similarly, should LIBOR $(t-1)$ plus 25 bp fall below the floor rate, then the loan rate will be set equal to the floor until the index rises back above the floor.

STEP 3: Solve

The maximum rate of 2.5 percent is never reached; however, the minimum rate of 1.75 percent was a limiting factor for Week 5. Without the floor rate, the loan rate would have fallen to 1.6 percent for this week because LIBOR fell to 1.35 percent for Week 4. Note that the loan rate is set based on the observed LIBOR rate for the prior week.

Week (t)	LIBOR (t)	LIBOR (t − 1) + Spread	Loan Rate
Week 1	1.98%		
Week 2	1.66%	2.23%	2.23%
Week 3	1.52%	1.91%	1.91%
Week 4	1.35%	1.77%	1.77%
Week 5	1.60%	1.60%	1.75%
Week 6	1.63%	1.85%	1.85%
Week 7	1.67%	1.88%	1.88%
Week 8	1.88%	1.92%	1.92%
Week 9	1.93%	2.13%	2.13%
Week 10		2.18%	2.18%

STEP 4: Analyze

The cap or maximum rate is never reached, but the floor or minimum rate was a limit on the rate charged on the loan. In fact, without the floor rate, the loan rate would have fallen to 1.6 percent because LIBOR fell to 1.35 percent for Week 4. Floating-rate loans typically carry lower initial rates than their fixed-rate counterparts because the borrower assumes the risk of fluctuating interest rates.

STEP 5: Check yourself

Consider the same loan period as previously but change the spread over LIBOR from .25 percent to .75 percent. Is the ceiling rate violated during the loan period? The floor rate? Answer: Yes, the ceiling rate is violated during the first week and in the last two weeks of the loan period. The floor is never violated.

Your Turn: For more practice, do related **Study Problem** 1 at the end of this chapter. >> **END Checkpoint 1**

Basic Bond Features

In order to value a bond we first need to know some terminology. Table 2 contains a detailed set of definitions of bond terminology. The essential terms we need to value a bond include the following:

- Bond indenture
- Claims on assets and income
- Par or face value
- Coupon interest rate
- Maturity and repayment of principal
- Call provision and conversion features

Bond Indenture

The **bond indenture** is the legal agreement between the firm issuing the bonds and the bond trustee who represents the bondholders. It lists the specific terms of the loan agreement, including a description of the bonds and the rights of the bondholders and the issuing firm. This legal document may run 100 pages or more in length, with the majority of it devoted to defining protective provisions for the bondholder. A bond trustee, usually a banking institution or trust company, is then assigned the task of overseeing the relationship between the bondholder and the issuing firm, protecting the bondholder, and seeing that the terms of the indenture are carried out.

Claims on Assets and Income

If the borrowing firm is unable to repay the debt in accordance with the bond indenture, the claims of the debt holders must be honored before those of the firm's stockholders. In general,

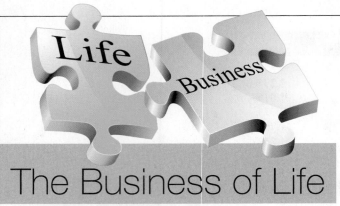

The Business of Life

Adjustable-Rate Mortgages

When you buy a house, you have a choice of borrowing money with a fixed-rate mortgage or an adjustable-rate mortgage. With a fixed-rate mortgage, your monthly payments will stay the same over the entire life of the mortgage. In contrast, with an adjustable-rate mortgage (ARM) loan, the interest rate fluctuates according to the level of current market interest rates within certain limits and at specific intervals. This is essentially the same as the floating-rate loans that are used by businesses.

ARMs can be attractive to banks because they reduce their risk by matching the rates they must pay on the savings accounts they use to raise the money for the mortgage to the interest rates that they receive from the mortgages. ARMs can also be attractive to borrowers, because the initial interest rates and monthly payments are generally lower for ARMs than for fixed-rate mortgages. However, ARMs are riskier for the borrower, because if interest rates increase, the monthly payments on an ARM will also increase. In contrast, with a fixed-rate loan, your monthly payments will be locked in for the life of the loan.

During the housing boom of the early and mid-2000s, lenders created new types of mortgages that helped people buy homes that they wouldn't normally be able to finance. These were often financed with ARMs with an initial "teaser" rate that was deceptively low and fixed for only a short period, generally between 3 and 24 months. Once the rate was allowed to move up and down, or float, it generally rose—and many times it rose to a level where the borrower could no longer afford to pay the new higher mortgage payments. Compounding the problem was the fact that some of these mortgages allowed for 100 percent financing, meaning the homebuyers borrowed the entire amount of the purchase price of the homes. Then, when housing prices dropped, these homeowners ended up owing more on their mortgages than their houses were worth. The result was an epidemic of defaults on home mortgages.

So what should you learn from all this? For the homebuyer, the primary advantage of an adjustable-rate mortgage is that the initial rate charged is lower than that on fixed-rate loans. Initial ARM rates are lower because the borrower assumes the risk that interest rates will go up. Thus, the rate gap between 1-year adjustable-rate mortgages (that is, mortgages that adjust every year) and 30-year fixed-rate mortgages is generally above 1 to 2 percent. Because of this low initial rate, you may qualify for a larger loan because your initial monthly payment is lower. However, beware—if interest rates rise, pushing your monthly ARM payment upward—you may find yourself overcommitted.

Don't choose an ARM in the hope that interest rates will fall and your payments will be lower. Doing this is tantamount to gambling your house and financial future on your prediction that future interest rates will not rise. That's what happened to quite a few people in the recent housing crash as they saw the interest rates on their ARMs climb to a level that they couldn't afford. If you can't afford the higher mortgage payments you would have to pay if interest rates rise, you probably shouldn't take out an adjustable-rate mortgage.

Your Turn: See Study Question 5.

---

if the interest on bonds is not paid, the bond trustees can classify the firm as insolvent and force it into bankruptcy.

Par or Face Value

The **par** or **face value of a bond** is the amount that must be repaid to the bondholder at maturity. In general, corporate bonds are issued in denominations of $1,000, although there are some exceptions to this rule. Also, when bond prices are quoted, either by financial managers or in the financial press, prices are generally expressed as a percentage of the bond's par value. For example, General Electric has a bond issue outstanding that was recently quoted as selling for 100.65. That does not mean you can buy the bond for $100.65. It means that this bond is selling for 100.65 percent of its par value of $1,000. Hence, the market price of this bond is actually $1,006.50. Finally, when the bond matures, the bondholder will receive the par value of the bond, which is $1,000.

Coupon Interest Rate

The **coupon interest rate** on a bond indicates the percentage of the par value of the bond that will be paid out annually in the form of interest. Typically, corporate bonds have a fixed coupon interest rate that must be paid on the principal amount, or par value, of the

| **Table 2** | **Bond Terminology** |

Understanding the terminology used to describe bonds is essential to gaining a full understanding of the world of corporate bonds.

Indenture	The legal agreement between the firm issuing the bonds and the bond trustee who represents the bondholders. It lists the specific terms of the loan agreement, including a description of the bonds, the rights of the bondholders, the rights of the issuing firm, and the responsibilities of the trustee.
Priority of claim on assets and income	In the case of insolvency, claims of debt in general, including bonds, are honored before those of both common stock and preferred stock. In addition, interest payments hold priority over dividend payments for common and preferred stock.
Par value	The par value of a bond, also known as its face value, is the principal that must be repaid to the bondholder at maturity. In general, corporate bonds are issued with par values in increments of $1,000. Also, when bond prices are quoted in the financial press, prices are generally expressed as a percentage of the bond's par value.
Maturity and repayment of principal	The maturity date refers to the date on which the bond issuer must repay the principal or par value to the bondholder.
Coupon interest rate	The coupon rate on a bond indicates the percentage of the par value of the bond that will be paid out annually in the form of interest.
Current yield	The current yield on a bond refers to the ratio of the annual interest payment to the bond's current market price. If, for example, we have a bond with an 8% coupon interest rate, a par value of $1,000, and a market price of $700, it would have a current yield of 11.4%, calculated as follows: $$\text{Current Yield} = \frac{\text{Annual Interest Payment}}{\text{Current Market Price of the Bond}} = \frac{0.08 \times \$1,000}{\$700}$$ $$= \frac{\$80}{\$700} = 0.114 \text{ or } 11.4\% \qquad (1)$$
Call provision	The call provision provides the issuer of the bond with the right to redeem or retire a bond before it matures.
Conversion feature	In addition, some bonds have a conversion feature that allows bondholders to convert their bonds into a set number of shares of common stock.

debt; and this rate does not change over the life of the bond. For example, the General Electric Capital Corporation bond just mentioned has a 4.625 percent coupon rate of interest and a $1,000 par value, such that it pays $46.25 each year in interest. However, as we will observe later, the interest may be paid semiannually, perhaps in June and December. In the General Electric example, the semiannual interest payment would be $23.125.

The coupon interest also determines the bond's **current yield**, the ratio of the annual interest payment to the bond's current market price. In effect, the current yield is the return that an investor would receive if the investor purchased the bond at its current price and simply received interest payments with no capital gains or losses (i.e., the bond's price did not change). **Floating-rate bonds**, however, have a floating rate of interest just like bank loans, which means that the rate adjusts up and down in response to changes in the market rate of interest.

Maturity and Repayment of Principal

The maturity of a bond indicates the length of time until the bond issuer returns the par value to the bondholder and terminates or redeems the bond. However, it is common for bonds to be repaid and retired in part or in entirety before they mature.

Call Provision and Conversion Feature

A **call provision** is most valuable when the bond is sold during a period of abnormally high rates of interest, such that there is a reasonable expectation that rates will fall in the future before the bond matures. Having the call feature allows the bond issuer to issue new bonds should rates decline and then use the proceeds to retire the higher-cost bonds. With a call protection period, the firm cannot call the bond for a pre-specified time period. Some bonds have a **conversion feature** that allows the bondholder to convert the bond into a prescribed number of shares of the firm's common stock. These bonds typically carry a lower rate of interest than straight bonds (which do not have the conversion feature), which reflects the value of the conversion option to the bondholder should the value of the firm's common stock rise in the future and make conversion beneficial.

Bond Ratings and Default Risk

John Moody first began to rate bonds in 1909 to help investors determine the riskiness of various bonds. Since that time, three rating agencies—Moody's, Standard & Poor's, and Fitch Investor Services—have provided **bond ratings** on corporate bonds, based on an evaluation of the probability that the bond issuer will make the bond's promised payments. Rating agencies come up with their ratings by analyzing the borrower's financial statements, looking at the firm's reliance on debt versus equity financing, and looking at the issuer's profitability and the variability of its past profits. They also make judgments about the quality of the firm's management and business strategies because all of these are indicators of the likelihood that the bonds will be repaid in a timely manner.

Bond ratings are extremely important to the financial manager. They provide an indicator of default risk and affect the rate of return that lenders require and the firm's cost of borrowing. In keeping with **P** Principle 2: **There Is a Risk–Return Tradeoff**, the rating a bond receives affects the rate of return demanded on the bond by the investors. The lower the bond rating, the higher the risk of default and the higher is the rate of return demanded in the capital markets. Table 3 provides a summary description of bond ratings.

Table 3   Interpreting Bond Ratings

Ratings are intended to reflect the likelihood of default by the issuing firm in the future.

Bond Rating Category	Standard & Poor's	Moody's	Description
Investment Grade:			
Prime or highest strong	AAA	Aaa	Highest quality; extremely strong capacity to pay
High quality	AA	Aa	Very strong capacity to pay
Upper medium	A	A-1, A	Upper medium quality; strong capacity to pay
Medium	BBB	Baa-1, Baa	Lower medium quality; changing circumstances could impact the firm's ability to pay
Not Investment Grade:			
Speculative	BB	Ba	Speculative elements; faces uncertainties
Highly speculative	B, CCC, CC	B, Caa, Ca	Extremely speculative and highly vulnerable to nonpayment
Default	D	C	Income bond; doesn't pay interest

Before you move on to 2

Concept Check | 1

1. What is a bond indenture?
2. What are the key features of a bond? Which of these features determines the cash flows paid to the bondholder?
3. What is the difference between an Aaa and a Ba bond in terms of risks to the bondholder? What are the principal bond rating agencies?

2 Valuing Corporate Debt

The value of corporate debt is equal to the present value of the contractually promised principal and interest payments (the cash flows) discounted back to the present using the market's required yield to maturity on similar risk. In effect, the valuation of corporate debt relies on the first three basic principles of finance: **Principle 1: Money Has a Time Value**, **Principle 2: There Is a Risk–Return Tradeoff**, and **Principle 3: Cash Flows Are the Source of Value**. Keep these principles in mind as we examine the process of valuation outlined in the following section. We focus here on the valuation of a corporate bond; however, the procedure we use can be used to value any debt security.

Valuing Bonds by Discounting Future Cash Flows

Step 1. Determine bondholder cash flows, which are the amount and timing of the bond's promised interest and principal payments to the bondholders. The interest payments for a bond are typically paid semiannually; however, for now we will assume annual payments to simplify the computations. The annual interest payment is equal to the product of the coupon rate and the par value of the bond, which is typically $1,000. That is, for a bond with a coupon interest rate of 8.5 percent and a par value of $1,000, $85 = .085 × $1,000.

Step 2. Estimate the appropriate discount rate on a bond *of similar risk*, where the discount rate is the return the bond will yield if it is held to maturity and all bond payments are made. The difficulty we face when valuing a bond is that although we know the contractual interest and principal payments, these are promised cash flows, not expected cash flows, because the issuer of the bond could default and be unable to make the payments at some point in the future. Thus, to value a bond we discount the promised interest and principal using the market's required yield to maturity on a bond of comparable risk. We can either calculate the discount rate ourselves or use market data for bonds of a similar default risk. For example, Yahoo! Finance reports average yields to maturity on corporate bonds of various maturities.

Step 3. Calculate the present value of the bond's interest and principal payments from Step 1 using the discount rate estimated in Step 2. The present value of an interest-only bond's interest and principal payments is computed as follows:

$$\text{Bond Value} = \left(\begin{array}{c} \text{Present Value of the} \\ \text{Bond's Coupon Interest} \\ \text{Payments} \end{array} \right) + \left(\begin{array}{c} \text{Present Value of the} \\ \text{Principal Amount (par Value)} \\ \text{of the Bond Issue} \end{array} \right) \quad \textbf{(2)}$$

Step 1: Determine Bondholder Cash Flows

Defining the contractually promised bondholder cash flows is straightforward and can be done by reviewing the bond indenture. For example, examining a bond indenture for Ford Motor Company (F), issued on September 5, 2007, shows us that the bond has a $1,000 par value, pays a coupon rate of 6.5 percent per year with interest paid semiannually, and matures in 2018. This means that Ford must pay .065 × $1,000/2 = $32.50 per bond every six months until 2018, at which time the $1,000 principal per bond will be due.

Step 2: Estimate the Appropriate Discount Rate

We find the present value of the bond's contractual interest and principal payments by using the *market's required yield to maturity* as our discount rate. We estimate the market's required yield to maturity by finding a bond of similar risk and maturity, that is, with the same default risk classification. In general, the **yield to maturity** (YTM) on any bond is the discount rate that equates the present value of the bond's contractual or promised cash flows (interest and principal at maturity) with the current market price of the bond. *This is also the return the investor will earn on the bond if the investor is paid everything that is contractually promised by the issuing firm and the bond is held until maturity.*

Calculating a Bond's Yield to Maturity

We calculate the yield to maturity (YTM) for a bond with annual interest payments and n years to maturity by solving Equation (2a) for YTM. You'll notice that in the final year this bond pays the bondholder both the interest and principal.

$$\text{Bond Price} = \frac{\text{Interest}_{\text{year 1}}}{(1 + YTM)^1} + \frac{\text{Interest}_{\text{year 2}}}{(1 + YTM)^2} + \frac{\text{Interest}_{\text{year 3}}}{(1 + YTM)^3} + \cdots + \frac{\text{Interest}_{\text{year } n}}{(1 + YTM)^n} + \frac{\text{Principal}}{(1 + YTM)^n} \qquad \textbf{(2a)}$$

This is similar to solving for the rate of return on an investment with multiple future cash flows.[1] In essence, we can think of YTM as the discount rate that makes the present value of the bond's promised interest and principal equal to the bond's observed market price. We review the process in the following exercise.

Checkpoint 2

Calculating the Yield to Maturity on a Corporate Bond

Calculate the yield to maturity for the following bond issued by Ford Motor Company (F) with a price of $744.80, where we assume that interest payments are made annually at the end of each year and the bond has a maturity of exactly 11 years.

STEP 1: Picture the problem

The cash flows for the Ford bond consist of the purchase price for the bond today of $744.80, annual interest payments for Years 1 through 10 of $65, and a final interest payment of $65 plus the principal payment of $1,000, both at the end of Year 11.

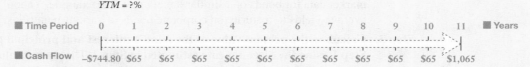

YTM = ?%

■ Time Period	0	1	2	3	4	5	6	7	8	9	10	11	■ Years
■ Cash Flow	–$744.80	$65	$65	$65	$65	$65	$65	$65	$65	$65	$65	$1,065	

STEP 2: Decide on a solution strategy

To solve for the bond's yield to maturity we must use Equation (2a), which is the rate of interest used to discount the cash flows paid to the bondholder in Years 1 through 11 that makes the present value equal to the current market price of $744.80. We can solve this mathematically, using a calculator, and using a spreadsheet.

---

[1]The YTM is technically the compound rate of interest that equates the present value of the future cash flows (interest and principal for the bond) with the bond's current market price.

STEP 3: Solve

Using the Mathematical Formulas.

It is cumbersome to solve for the yield to maturity by hand using a mathematical formula. For example, substituting the numbers for Ford's bonds into Equation (2a) where the term to maturity is 11 years we get the following result:

$$Bond\ Price = \frac{Interest_{year\ 1}}{(1+YTM)^1} + \frac{Interest_{year\ 2}}{(1+YTM)^2} + \frac{Interest_{year\ 3}}{(1+YTM)^3} + \cdots + \frac{Interest_{year\ 11}}{(1+YTM)^{11}} + \frac{Principal}{(1+YTM)^{11}} \quad \text{(2a)}$$

$$\$744.80 = \frac{\$65}{(1+YTM)^1} + \frac{\$65}{(1+YTM)^2} + \frac{\$65}{(1+YTM)^3} + \cdots + \frac{\$65}{(1+YTM)^{11}} + \frac{\$1,000}{(1+YTM)^{11}}$$

Note that to keep from having to write out all 11 years of interest payments, we have simply added ". . ." to reflect the omitted terms for Years 4 through 10. This would be a tough equation to solve mathematically because the variable we are solving for, *YTM*, is raised to powers ranging from 1 to 11. For this reason, investors and financial managers use either a financial calculator or Excel to calculate the yield to maturity.

Using a Financial Calculator.

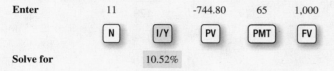

Enter	11		-744.80	65	1,000
	N	I/Y	PV	PMT	FV
Solve for		10.52%			

Using an Excel Spreadsheet.

=RATE (per,npmt,pv,fv) or with values entered =RATE (11,65,−744.80,1000)

Thus, the yield to maturity on this bond is 10.52 percent. Notice that the value of the bond, *PV*, is input with a negative sign because the purchase price of the bond is seen by both the financial calculator and Excel as a cash outflow.

STEP 4: Analyze

The yield to maturity on the bond is 10.52 percent, considerably higher than the coupon rate of interest of 6.5 percent that the bond promises to pay. The fact that the yield to maturity is higher than the coupon rate is also consistent with the fact that the current market price of the bond is considerably less than the bond's par value of $1,000. In fact, if the bond price were equal to the bond's par value, then the yield to maturity and coupon rate of interest would be the same.

STEP 5: Check yourself

Calculate the yield to maturity on the Ford bond where the bond price rises to $900 (holding all other things equal).

ANSWER: 7.89 percent.

Your Turn: For more practice, do related **Study Problems** 7 and 12 through 17 at the end of this chapter.   **>> END Checkpoint 2**

Using Market-Yield-to-Maturity Data

Market-yield-to-maturity data is regularly reported by a number of investor services and is often quoted in terms of **credit spreads** or **spreads to Treasury bonds**. Table 4 contains some example yield spreads. The spread values reported in the table represent basis points (i.e., 100 basis points equals 1 percent) over a U.S. Treasury security of the same maturity as the corporate bond. For example a 30-year Aa2/AA-rated corporate bond offers the bond-holder 1.28 basis points over the 2.76 percent yield earned on a similar 30-year U.S. Treasury bond. That is to say, a 30-year Aa2/AA-rated corporate bond should yield the credit spread (1.28 percent) plus the yield on a Treasury security of similar maturity (2.76 percent on 30-year Treasury bonds) for a total yield of 4.04 percent. Armed with this yield spread data,

| Table 4 | Corporate Bond Spread Tables |

Corporate bonds offer different yields to maturity for different maturities and different default risks. The following data reports the variation in yields to maturity for bonds across a wide range of default rating categories and terms to maturity. The body of the table is reported in basis points, or 1/100th of 1 percent. To get the yield to maturity for a particular bond rating and term to maturity, simply add the basis points in the spread table to the U.S. Treasury security with similar maturity. The data found below is not actual spread data but is representative of the spreads observed in early 2013. Spread data can be obtained from a number of sources including Bondsonline.com. Spreads fluctuate daily.

Rating	\multicolumn{7}{Maturity}
	1 yr	2 yr	3 yr	5 yr	7 yr	10 yr	30 yr
Aaa/AAA	5	7	12	19	31	49	78
Aa1/AA+	10	22	31	43	55	70	103
Aa2/AA	13	36	50	67	79	91	128
Aa3/AA−	16	40	54	72	84	96	134
A1/A+	17	42	58	76	88	101	140
A2/A	44	66	79	96	107	118	152
A3/A2−	53	84	103	127	143	160	210
Baa1/BBB+	78	113	132	157	174	191	245
Baa2/BBB	98	137	160	188	208	227	289
Baa3/BBB−	157	194	215	242	259	278	336
Ba1/BB+	251	287	310	337	358	379	433
Ba2/BB	343	379	403	433	455	479	532
Ba3/BB−	437	472	498	528	553	580	629
B1/B+	530	564	592	623	650	680	727
B2/B	624	656	686	719	749	781	824
B3/B−	716	749	780	814	847	881	923
Caa/CCC+	810	841	875	908	944	982	1020
U.S. Treasury Yield	0.18%	0.25%	0.32%	0.60%	1.00%	1.59%	2.76%

Callout (Aa2/AA, 30 yr):
$$\text{YTM}_{30 \text{ yr. Aa2/AA}} = \text{Spread} + \text{YTM}_{\text{Treas of like maturity}} = 1.28\% + 2.76\% = 4.04\%$$

Callout (Ba1/BB+, 30 yr):
$$\text{YTM}_{30 \text{ yr. Ba1/BB+}} = \text{Spread} + \text{YTM}_{\text{Treas of like maturity}} = 4.33\% + 2.76\% = 7.09\%$$

http://www.bondsonline.com/Todays_Market/Corporate_Bond_Spreads.php

we can estimate the yield to maturity that a Ba1/BB+-rated 30-year bond should earn. Specifically, this corporate bond should earn 433 basis points or 4.33 percent over the 2.76 percent yield earned on a U.S. Treasury bond, or 7.09 percent.

Promised versus Expected Yield to Maturity

The yield to maturity calculation *assumes* that the bond performs according to the terms in the bond contract or indenture. Thus, the yield to maturity that we calculated previously is actually the *promised* YTM for the bond. Because corporate bonds are subject to the risk of default, the promised yield to maturity can be an optimistic estimate of the yield that the bondholder will actually earn.

To illustrate the difference between the promised and expected YTM, consider a one-year bond that promises a coupon rate of 10 percent and has a principal amount (par value) of $1,000. Let's also assume that the bond has a current market price of $800. The promised yield to maturity on this bond can be calculated from the basic discounted cash flow valuation equation.

$$\text{Bond Price (for a bond with one year to maturity)} = \frac{\text{Interest}_{\text{year 1}} + \text{Principal}}{(1 + YTM)}$$

or

$$YTM = \frac{\text{Interest}_{\text{year 1}} + \text{Principal}}{\text{Bond Price}} - 1 = \frac{\$100 + \$1{,}000}{\$800} - 1 = .375 \text{ or } 37.5\%$$

This looks like a fantastic investment with a 37.5 percent rate of return. However, remember that this is the "promised rate" and not the "expected rate" for the bond. In fact, we would only earn this high rate of return if the promised cash flows are all paid to the bondholders when they come due. To calculate the expected return, let's assume that the probability of default on this bond is 50 percent; and, if the bond does default, the bondholder will end up receiving only 70 percent of the principal and interest that is owed. This 70 percent is known as the **recovery rate** on the defaulted bond.

To calculate the expected YTM we first calculate the YTM for both the default and non-default outcomes and then average these two possible YTM outcomes using the probability of default. The YTM for the non-default outcome is the promised YTM of 37.5 percent we first calculated. The YTM for the default outcome uses the recovered interest and principal from the bond in the event of default, which in this case is equal to 70 percent of the promised amounts. Let's plug these numbers into our valuation formula:

$$YTM_{Default} = \frac{(\text{Interest}_{\text{year 1}} + \text{Principal}) \times .70}{\text{Bond Price}} - 1 = \frac{\$70 + \$700}{\$800} - 1 = -0.0375 \text{ or } -3.75\%$$

Next, we calculate the expected YTM or E(YTM) as a weighted average of the YTM calculated in the default outcome and in the no-default outcome where the weights are based on the probability of default:

$$E(YTM) = YTM_{No\ Default} \times (1 - \text{Probability of Default}) + YTM_{Default} \times (\text{Probability of Default})$$

$$= [37.5\% \times (1 - .50)] + [-3.75\% \times (1 - .50)] = 16.9\% \quad \textbf{(3)}$$

Although the expected yield to maturity of 16.9 percent is still very high in light of typical bond yields, it now looks more reasonable than the 37.5 percent YTM we calculated under the assumption that the bond would not default.

Quoted Yields to Maturity for Corporate Bonds

The financial press quotes yields to maturity using contractual interest and principal payments so they are in fact promised yields and not expected rates of return. Nevertheless, we can use the yields to maturity of bonds we observe trading in the financial markets to estimate the values of other bonds. The procedure we use involves the application of discounted cash flow analysis, so we will refer to this bond valuation technique by that name.

Step 3: Use Discounted Cash Flow to Value Corporate Bonds

The valuation of a bond takes into account the time value of money by discounting the contractual or promised interest and principal payments back to the present by using the market's required yield to maturity, which is the promised rate of return for a comparable-risk bond. We refer to this rate as YTM_{Market}.

Because the bond interest payments are a level annuity payment stream (corresponding to *PMT* on your financial calculator) that stretches over the next *n* years, we can apply the level annuity discounting factor to calculate its present value as follows:

$$\text{Present Value of} \atop \text{Interest Payments} = \frac{\text{Interest}}{(1 + YTM_{\text{Market}})^1} + \frac{\text{Interest}}{(1 + YTM_{\text{Market}})^2} + \cdots + \frac{\text{Interest}}{(1 + YTM_{\text{Market}})^n}$$

$$= \text{Interest} \left[\frac{1 - \dfrac{1}{(1 + YTM_{\text{Market}})^n}}{YTM_{\text{Market}}} \right]$$

Recall that the *YTM* used here to discount the interest payments is the market's yield to maturity for a bond of similar risk and not the *YTM* of the bond being valued. To remind us of this important distinction, we have subscripted YTM_{Market}. The present value of the principal payment (par value) received at the maturity of the bond (corresponding to FV on your financial calculator) is calculated as follows:

$$\text{Present Value of} \atop \text{Principal} = \text{Principal} \left[\frac{1}{(1 + YTM_{\text{Market}})^n} \right]$$

Thus, Equation (2) can be restated as follows:

$$\text{Bond} \atop \text{Value} = \text{Interest} \left[\frac{1 - \dfrac{1}{(1 + YTM_{\text{Market}})^n}}{YTM_{\text{Market}}} \right] + \text{Principal} \left[\frac{1}{(1 + YTM_{\text{Market}})^n} \right] \qquad \textbf{(2b)}$$

Semiannual Interest Payments

In the preceding AT&T illustration, we assumed the interest payments were paid annually. However, corporate bonds typically pay interest to bondholders semiannually. For example, Time Warner (TWX) issues bonds that mature in 11 years and pay $91.25 per year

---

Checkpoint 3

Valuing a Bond Issue

Consider a $1,000 par value bond issued by AT&T (T) with a maturity date of 2032 and a stated coupon rate of 8.5 percent. On January 1, 2013, the bond had 20 years left to maturity, and the market's required yield to maturity for similar rated debt was 7.5 percent. What is the value of the bond?

STEP 1: Picture the problem

The cash flows for the AT&T bond consist of the value of the bond today, which we are trying to estimate, the annual interest payments for Years 1 through 20 of $85 each, and principal payment at the end of Year 20 equal to $1,085 (this is in addition to the $85 interest payment also at the end of Year 20).

$i = 7.5\%$

| ■ Time Period | 0 1 2 3 4 5 6 7 8 9 10 11 12 13 14 15 16 17 18 19 20 | ■ Years |

| ■ Cash Flow | $85 per year | $1,085 |

Present Value = ?

The $85 interest payment at the end of each year.

The $85 interest payment plus the $1,000 return of principal at the end of year 20.

STEP 2: Decide on a solution strategy

For this problem, we already know the market's required yield to maturity is 7.5 percent, but we do not know the value of the bond, which we will find using Equation (2b). We know the annual interest and principal payments to the bondholder (stated in the bond indenture). The discount rate is equal to yield to maturity on a comparable-risk bond, which we know to be 7.5 percent, so all we need to do to value the bond is discount the future interest and principal payments back to the present.

STEP 3: Solve

Estimation of the bond value requires that we substitute the appropriate values for the AT&T bond into the following equation and then solve it for bond value:

Using the Mathematical Formulas.

$$\text{Bond Value} = \text{Interest}\left[\frac{1 - \dfrac{1}{(1 + YTM_{Market})^n}}{YTM_{Market}}\right] + \text{Principal}\left[\frac{1}{(1 + YTM_{Market})^n}\right] \tag{2b}$$

$$\text{Bond Value} = \$85\left[\frac{1 - \dfrac{1}{(1 + .075)^{20}}}{.075}\right] + \text{Principal}\left[\frac{1}{(1 + .075)^{20}}\right]$$

$$\text{Bond Value} = \$866.53 + \$235.41 = \$1,101.94$$

Using a Financial Calculator.

Enter	20	7.50%		85	1,000
	N	I/Y	PV	PMT	FV
Solve for			-1,101.94		

Using an Excel Spreadsheet.

=PV(rate,nper,pmt,fv) or with values entered =PV(0.075,20,85,1000)

Thus, the present value of the interest-plus-principal payments to the bondholder is $1,101.94.

STEP 4: Analyze

The value we calculated for the AT&T bond is $1,101.94, which exceeds the $1,000 par value of the bond. This reflects the fact that the market's required yield to maturity on a comparable-risk bond is less than the coupon rate of interest paid on the bond of 8.5 percent. In all likelihood, when the AT&T bonds were originally issued, they were issued at par because the market's required yield to maturity on comparable-risk bonds was at or very near to the 8.5 percent coupon rate. Since the time of issue, however, market rates of interest have declined such that the bonds now sell at a premium. Thus if the bonds are sold for $1,101.94, they will yield a return of only 7.5 percent.

STEP 5: Check yourself

Calculate the present value of the AT&T bond should the market's required yield to maturity for comparable-risk bonds rise to 9 percent (holding all other things equal).

ANSWER: $954.36.

Your Turn: For more practice, do related **Study Problems** 3, 6, 10, 15, and 18 at the end of this chapter.

>> **END Checkpoint 3**

($91.25 = the bond's coupon interest rate of 9.125 percent times the par value of $1,000), but these bonds pay interest semiannually, with $45.625 paid each January 15 and July 15.

We can adapt Equation (2a) from annual to semiannual interest payments as follows:[2]

$$\begin{array}{l}\text{Bond Value} \\ \text{(semiannual payments)}\end{array} = (\text{Interest}/2)\left[\frac{1 - \dfrac{1}{\left(1 + \dfrac{YTM_{Market}}{2}\right)^{2n}}}{\dfrac{YTM_{Market}}{2}}\right] + \text{Principal}\left[\frac{1}{\left(1 + \dfrac{YTM_{Market}}{2}\right)^{2n}}\right] \tag{2c}$$

---

[2]The logic for calculating the value of a bond that pays interest semiannually is similar that for computing compound interest with non-annual periods.

Note that we halve the annual interest payments and the market's required YTM used to discount the payments, and we double the number of payments.

We can summarize the process for valuing bonds with the following financial decision tools.

Tools of Financial Analysis—Bond Valuation

Name of Tool	Formula	What It Tells You
Bond Value	$$= \begin{bmatrix} Present\ Value\ of \\ the\ Bond's\ Coupon \\ Interest\ Payments \end{bmatrix} + \begin{bmatrix} Present\ Value\ of\ the \\ Principal\ Amount\ (par \\ value)\ of\ the\ Bond \\ Issue \end{bmatrix}$$	• The value of a bond is equal to the present value of all the future cash flows the bondholder receives from the bond • The bond's value will rise when the discount rate declines and fall when the discount rate goes up.
Bond Value for a Bond with Semiannual Interest Payments	$$= (Interest/2) \left[\frac{1 - \dfrac{1}{\left(1 + \dfrac{YTM_{Market}}{2}\right)^{2n}}}{\dfrac{YTM_{Market}}{2}} \right]$$ $$+ Principal \left[\dfrac{1}{\left(1 + \dfrac{YTM_{Market}}{2}\right)^{2n}} \right]$$	• The value of a bond when interest payments are made on a semiannual basis • The YTM_{Market} is the discount rate on a bond of similar risk. It is common to use market data on bonds of a similar default risk as the appropriate discount rate for a bond.
Expected YTM or E(YTM)	$$Expected\ YTM = YTM_{No\ Default} \times (1 - Probability\ of\ Default)$$ $$+ YTM_{Default} \times (Probability\ of\ Default)$$	• The YTM is only equal to the E(YTM) if there is no probability of default. If there is a chance of default, the expected YTM will be less than the YTM • The YTM is the "promised rate," not the "expected rate" for the bond. So, when you hear about a high YTM on a junk bond, it is not the expected rate, but only the rate if the firm does not default.

Valuing a Bond Issue That Pays Semiannual Interest

Reconsider the bond issued by AT&T (T) with a maturity date of 2032 and a stated coupon rate of 8.5 percent. AT&T pays interest to bondholders on a semiannual basis on January 15 and July 15. On January 1, 2013, the bond had 20 years left to maturity. The market's required yield to maturity for a similarly rated debt was 7.5 percent per year or 3.75 percent for six months. What is the value of the bond?

STEP 1: Picture the problem

The cash flows for the AT&T bond consist of the value of the bond today, which we are trying to estimate, the semiannual interest payments for Periods 1 through 39 of $42.50 each, and a final interest-plus-principal payment at the end of Year 20 or Period 40 equal to $1,042.50.

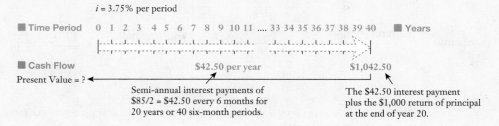

$i = 3.75\%$ per period

| Time Period | 0 1 2 3 4 5 6 7 8 9 10 11 .... 33 34 35 36 37 38 39 40 | Years |

Cash Flow $42.50 per year $1,042.50

Present Value = ?

Semi-annual interest payments of
$85/2 = $42.50 every 6 months for
20 years or 40 six-month periods.

The $42.50 interest payment
plus the $1,000 return of principal
at the end of year 20.

STEP 2: Decide on a solution strategy

For this problem, we know the market's required yield to maturity on a comparable-risk bond is 7.5 percent per year, or 3.75 percent for a six-month period, and we will use Equation (2b) to find the value of the bond. Thus, we know the annual interest and principal payments to the bondholder (stated in the bond indenture) and that the discount rate is equal to 3.75 percent, so all we need to do to value the bond is discount the future interest and principal payments back to the present.

STEP 3: Solve

Estimation of the bond value requires that we substitute the appropriate values for the AT&T bond into Equation (2c) and then solve for bond value:

Using the Mathematical Formulas.

$$\text{Bond Value (semiannual payments)} = (\text{Interest}/2)\left[\dfrac{1 - \dfrac{1}{\left(1 + \dfrac{YTM_{Market}}{2}\right)^{2n}}}{\dfrac{YTM_{Market}}{2}}\right] + \text{Principal}\left[\dfrac{1}{\left(1 + \dfrac{YTM_{Market}}{2}\right)^{2n}}\right]$$

$$\text{Bond Value (semiannual payments)} = (\$85/2)\left[\dfrac{1 - \dfrac{1}{(1 + .0375)^{40}}}{.0375}\right] + \text{Principal}\left[\dfrac{1}{(1 + .0375)^{40}}\right]$$

$$\text{Bond Value (semiannual payments)} = (\$873.42) + \$229.34 = \$1,102.75$$

Using a Financial Calculator.

Enter	40	3.75%		42.5	1,000
	N	I/Y	PV	PMT	FV
Solve for			-1,102.75		

Using an Excel Spreadsheet.

=PV(rate,nper,pmt,fv) or with values entered =PV(0.0375,40,42.5,1000)

Thus, the present value of the interest-plus-principal payments to the bondholder is $1,102.75.

STEP 4: Analyze

Using semiannual compounding, we calculate a value of $1,102.75 for the AT&T bond compared to the $1,101.94 we calculated using annual compounding—this value is not vastly different, but for a large investor buying thousands of bonds, this can certainly add up over time.

STEP 5: Check yourself

Calculate the present value of the AT&T bond should the yield to maturity on comparable-risk bonds rise to 9 percent (holding all other things equal).

ANSWER: $954.00.

Your Turn: For more practice, do related **Study Problem** 4 at the end of this chapter. **>> END Checkpoint 4**

Before you move on to 3

Concept Check | 2

1. How do you calculate the value of a bond?
2. How do you estimate the appropriate discount rate?
3. Why might the expected returns be different from the yield to maturity?
4. How do semiannual interest payments affect the asset valuation equation?

Bond Valuation: Four Key Relationships

We can now calculate the value of a bond using the discounted cash flow method. To do this, we need to know (1) the bond's interest payments, (2) its par value, (3) the term to maturity, and (4) the appropriate discount rate.

As we discuss next, bond values react in predictable ways to changes in market conditions. We summarize four bond valuation phenomena in terms of four very important relationships.

First Relationship

The value of a bond is inversely related to changes in the market's required yield to maturity.

When market interest rates increase, the value of the bond decreases, and vice versa. When the market rate of interest goes up, the market's required yield to maturity of the bonds must also go up. However, because the interest payments on a bond are fixed, the only way for the market's required yield to maturity to increase is if the bond's value declines.

To illustrate, assume that the market's required yield on a given bond is 12 percent. The bond has a par value of $1,000 and annual interest payments of $120, indicating a 12 percent coupon interest rate ($120 \div $1,000 = 12\%$). Assuming a five-year maturity date, the bond would be worth $1,000, computed as follows using Equation (2b):

$$\text{Bond Value} = \text{Interest}\left[\frac{1 - \frac{1}{(1 + YTM_{\text{Market}})^n}}{YTM_{\text{Market}}}\right] + \text{Principal}\left[\frac{1}{(1 + YTM_{\text{Market}})^n}\right] \quad \textbf{(2b)}$$

$$\text{Bond Value} = \$120\left[\frac{1 - \frac{1}{(1 + .12)^5}}{.12}\right] + \$1,000\left[\frac{1}{(1 + .12)^5}\right]$$

$$= (\$120 \times 3.6048) + (\$1,000 \times 0.567427)$$

$$= \$432.576 + \$567.427$$

$$= \$1,000.003 \approx \$1,000.00$$

If, however, the market's required yield increases from 12 percent to 15 percent as it would if the market rate of interest were to rise, the value of the bond would decrease to $899.44, computed as follows:

$$\text{Bond Value} = \$120\left[\frac{1 - \frac{1}{(1 + .15)^5}}{.15}\right] + \$1,000\left[\frac{1}{(1 + .15)^5}\right]$$

$$= (\$120 \times 3.3522) + (\$1,000 \times 0.497177)$$

$$= \$402.264 + \$497.177 = 899.441 \approx \$899.44$$

In contrast, if the market rate of interest declines and the required yield decreases to 9 percent, the bond's value would increase to $1,116.69:

$$\text{Bond Value} = \$120\left[\frac{1 - \frac{1}{(1 + .09)^5}}{.09}\right] + \$1,000\left[\frac{1}{(1 + .09)^5}\right]$$

$$= (\$120 \times 3.88965) + (\$1,000 \times 0.649931)$$

$$= \$466.7580 + \$1,116.689 = \$1,116.69$$

Figure 1 shows this inverse relationship between required yields and the value of a bond.

Changes in bond prices present an element of uncertainty for the bond investor as well as the financial manager. If the current interest rate changes, the price of the bond also fluctuates. An increase in interest rates causes the bondholder to incur a loss in market value. Because

Figure 1

Bond Value and the Market's Required Yield to Maturity (5-Year Bond, 12% Coupon Rate)

Bond prices and yields to maturity vary inversely. Because principal and interest payments are fixed, the price of the bond must adjust such that the bond yields the market's current yield to maturity. For example, if the market yield to maturity were to increase from 12% to 15%, the price of the bond would have to fall from $1,000 to $899 in order for an investor who bought the bond today to earn 15%.

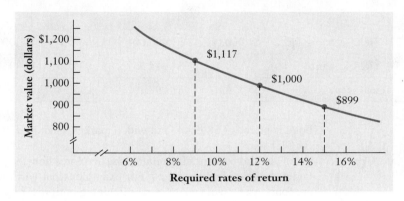

>> END FIGURE 1

future interest rates and the resulting bond value cannot be predicted with certainty, a bond investor is exposed to the risk of changing values as interest rates vary. This risk to an investor that the value of his or her investment will change is known as **interest-rate risk**.

Second Relationship

The market value of a bond will be less than the par value if the market's required yield to maturity is above the coupon interest rate and will be valued above par value if the market's required yield to maturity is below the coupon interest rate.

When you buy a bond, you can earn a return from your investment in two ways. First you receive interest payments, and second, you receive capital gains or losses equal to the difference in the price paid for the bond and the amount you receive when the bond matures.

For example, if you purchase a $1,000 par value bond at a discount for $850 and the full principal amount of the bond is repaid at maturity, you will realize a $150 capital gain ($1,000 − $850). Such a bond that is bought at less than its par value is called a **discount bond**. In contrast, if you purchase a bond at a premium for $1,150, and it repays $1,000 at maturity, then you suffer a $150 loss.[3] The latter case describes a **premium bond**, a bond that sells at a higher price than the bond's par value.

Bonds sell for less than their par value when the market's required yield to maturity on the bond exceeds the coupon rate. For example, if market rates of interest are such that the bonds of Capstar, Inc. have a market's required yield to maturity of 10 percent but the bonds pay interest based on a coupon rate of only 8 percent, then the bonds will sell for a discount or at less than par value. Likewise, if the market rate of interest is such that the bond is priced to yield a 6 percent rate of return and the bond has an 8 percent coupon rate of interest, then the bond will sell for more than its par value.

Third Relationship

As the maturity date approaches, the market value of a bond approaches its par value.

Let's continue to draw from the previous example of a bond with five years remaining until the maturity date that pays a 12 percent coupon rate. With a promised yield of 15 percent, the

---

[3]Note that the terms *premium* and *discount*, when referring to the purchase of a bond, refer to whether you paid more (premium) or less (discount) than the par value of the bond.

| Table 5 | Bond Prices Relative to Maturity Date |

Regardless of whether a bond is selling at a premium or discount, its price will approach its par value as the bond nears maturity. Bond prices are calculated for a $1,000 par value bond that pays a 12% coupon that spans the five years up to the time the bond matures. Three interest rate or yield scenarios are considered: a par scenario in which the market's required yield to maturity and coupon rate of the bond are equal, a discount bond scenario in which the market's required yield to maturity is 15% but the bond pays a coupon of only 12%, and, finally, a premium bond scenario in which the market's required yield to maturity is only 9% but the bond pays a coupon of 12%.

		Years to Maturity					
	12% Coupon Bond	**5**	**4**	**3**	**2**	**1**	**0**
	12% Yield scenario	$1,000.00	$1,000.00	$1,000.00	$1,000.00	$1,000.00	$1,000.00
Discount bond	15% Yield scenario	$ 899.44	$ 914.35	$ 931.50	$ 951.23	$ 973.91	$1,000.00
Premium bond	9% Yield scenario	$1,116.69	$1,097.19	$1,075.94	$1,052.77	$1,027.52	$1,000.00

bond is priced at $899.44, and with a market's required yield to maturity of 9 percent, it sells for $1,116.69.

The third bond pricing relationship explores how the price of this bond changes over time under the two yield scenarios. For example, what will the value of the bond be when there are four, three, two, and one year remaining until maturity? Table 5 shows (1) the values with five years remaining to maturity, (2) the values as recomputed with only two years left until the bonds mature, and (3) the changes in values between the five-year bonds and the two-year bonds. The following conclusions can be drawn from these results:

1. The premium bond sells for less as maturity approaches. Over the three years, the price decreases from $1,116.69 to $1,052.77.

2. The discount bond sells for more as maturity approaches. Over the three years, the price increases from $899.44 to $951.23.

The change in prices over the entire life of the bond is shown in Figure 2. The graph clearly demonstrates that the value of a bond, either a premium or a discount bond, approaches its par value as the maturity date becomes closer in time. That's because at maturity the bond will be taken away and the investor will receive the par value of the bond.

Fourth Relationship

Long-term bonds have greater interest-rate risk than short-term bonds.

In the first relationship, changes in interest rates lead to changes in bond prices. Our final bond pricing relationship states that longer-maturity bonds experience greater price changes in response to changes in interest rates as reflected in the market's required yield to maturity than do shorter-term bonds. This means that the prices of longer-term bonds fluctuate more when interest rates change than do the prices of shorter-term bonds.

Table 6 examines the changes in bond values for the bond in our previous example (12 percent coupon and $1,000 par value) for the cases where the market's required yield to maturity increases to 15 percent or declines to 9 percent. We examine the changes in prices for bonds with years to maturity ranging from 5 to 30. For example, assume first that the market's required yield to maturity is currently 12 percent and that interest rates rise to 15 percent. Note that the price of the bond must fall (relationship one), but notice that it falls the most for the bond with 30 years to maturity. That is, the bond price drops from $1,000 to $803.02, which represents a 19.7 percent decline in price. The five-year bond, on the other hand, suffers only a 10.1 percent price drop [($899.44 − $1,000)/$1,000]. Similarly, if we compare the price increase that results from a decline in rates from 12 percent down to 9 percent, we see that the 30-year bond price rises by 30.8 percent to $1,308.21, whereas the 5-year bond only rises by 11.7 percent to $1,116.69.

The reason long-term bond prices fluctuate more than short-term bond prices in response to interest-rate changes can be explained as follows. If an investor bought a 10-year bond yielding a 12 percent interest rate, and then the current interest rate for bonds of similar risk

Figure 2

Value of a 12% Coupon Bond during the Life of the Bond

As a bond approaches its maturity, the price of the bond approaches the principal or par value of the bond.

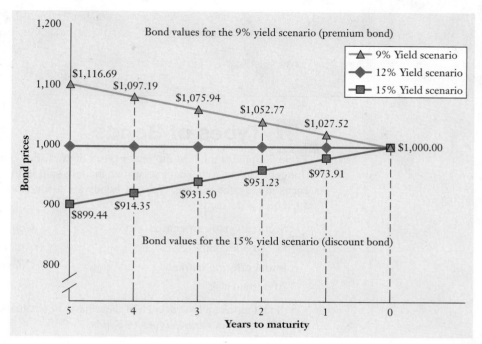

>> END FIGURE 2

increased to 15 percent, the investor would be receiving a below-market coupon for 10 years. If, however, a shorter-term bond had been purchased—say, one maturing in one month—the investor would have to accept the below-market rate for only one month. At the end of one month, the investor would get paid his or her original investment, which could then be invested at the new market rates. Thus, interest-rate risk is determined, at least in part, by the length of time an investor is required to commit to an investment.[4]

Table 6   Bond Price Fluctuations for Bonds with Different Maturities

The longer the term to maturity, the greater will be the changes in bond prices in response to a given change in the market rate of interest.

	Years to Maturity					
	5	10	15	20	25	30
15% (Increased yield)	$899.44	$849.44	$824.58	$812.22	$806.08	$803.02
% Price decrease	−10.1%	−15.1%	−17.5%	−18.8%	−19.4%	−19.7%
12% (Base case)	**$1,000.00**	**$1,000.00**	**$1,000.00**	**$1,000.00**	**$1,000.00**	**$1,000.00**
% Price increase	11.7%	19.3%	24.2%	27.4%	29.5%	30.8%
9% (Decreased yield)	$1,116.69	$1,192.53	$1,241.82	$1,273.86	$1,294.68	$1,308.21

---

[4]However, the holder of a long-term bond may take some comfort from the fact that long-term interest rates are usually not as volatile as short-term rates. If the short-term rate changed 1 percentage point, for example, it would not be unusual for the long-term rate to change only 0.3 percentage points.

Types of Bonds

Table 7 contains a list of the major types of corporate bonds. In all cases these are long-term (longer than one year) debt securities that are sold in the public financial market. The differences among the various types of bonds are a function of how each of the following bond attributes is defined:

Secured versus unsecured	Coupon level
Priority of claim	Amortizing or non-amortizing
Initial offering market	Convertibility
Abnormal risk	

So let us take a look at each of these basic bond attributes so that we can better understand the differences in various types of bonds.

Secured versus Unsecured

A basic distinction between types of bonds is whether the bond issue is secured by collateral or not. A **secured bond** has specific assets pledged to support repayment of the bond. The term **debenture** applies to any unsecured long-term debt, whereas a **mortgage bond** is a bond secured by a lien on real property.

Priority of Claims

The priority of claims refers to the place in line where the bondholders stand in securing repayment out of the dissolution of the firm's assets. For example, the claims of secured bonds are honored first, followed by debentures, but not all debentures are treated alike. **Subordinated debentures** have a lower priority than secured debt and **unsubordinated debentures**. Because of this increased risk, the interest rate paid on them is more than that on secured debt. For example, GE recently had subordinated debentures outstanding and the interest rate on them was about 1.8 percent higher than the rate on GE's secured debt. This is a direct illustration of **P** Principle 2: **There Is a Risk–Return Tradeoff**.

Initial Offering Market

Bonds are also classified by where they were originally issued (in the domestic bond market or elsewhere). For example, **Eurobonds** are bonds issued in a country different from the one in which the currency of the bond is denominated.

Abnormal Risk

Junk, or **high-yield, bonds** have a below-investment-grade bond rating. Originally, the term *junk bonds* was used to describe bonds issued by "fallen angels," that is, firms with sound financial histories that were facing severe financial problems and suffering from poor credit ratings.

Coupon Level

Bonds with a zero or very low coupon are called **zero-coupon bonds**. The firm issues these bonds at a substantial discount from their $1,000 par value and promises to pay a zero or very

Table 7   Types of Corporate Bonds

Corporations issue a variety of types of bonds that differ with respect to how principal and interest are to be repaid, where the bonds were initially issued or sold, and the type of collateral that is used to secure the bond.

Debentures	Any form of unsecured long-term debt. Because they are unsecured, the earning ability of the issuing corporation is of great concern to the bondholder. They are riskier than secured bonds and as a result must provide investors with a higher yield than secured bonds provide. Often, the issuing firm attempts to provide some protection to the holder of the bond by prohibiting the firm from issuing more secured long-term debt that would further tie up the firm's assets and leave the bondholders less protected. To the issuing firm, the major advantage of debentures is that no property has to be secured by them. This allows the firm to issue debt and still preserve some future borrowing power.
Subordinated debentures	The claims of the subordinated debentures are honored only after the claims of secured debt and unsubordinated debentures have been satisfied.
Mortgage bonds	Bonds secured by a lien on real property. Typically, the value of the real property is greater than the amount of the bonds issued. This provides the mortgage bondholders with a margin of safety in the event the market value of the secured property declines. In the case of foreclosure, the bondholders get the proceeds from the sale of the secured property. If the proceeds from this sale do not cover the bonds, the bondholders become general creditors, similar to debenture bondholders, for the unpaid portion of the debt.
Eurobonds	Bonds issued in a country different from the one in whose currency the bond is denominated. For example, a bond that is issued in Europe or in Asia by an American company and that pays interest and principal to the lender in U.S. dollars would be considered a Eurobond. Thus, even if the bond is not issued in Europe, it merely needs to be sold in a country different from the one in whose currency it is denominated to be considered a Eurobond.
Zero-coupon and very-low-coupon bonds	These bonds require either no coupon interest payments (these are called *zeroes*) or very low interest payments. Consequently, the bondholder receives all or most of their return at maturity. Because these bonds pay little or no interest they must sell at a deep discount. For the investor, a zero-coupon bond is like a U.S. savings bond. The obvious appeal of zero-coupon bonds is to those investors who need a lump sum of money at some future date but don't want to be concerned about reinvesting interest payments. Today, zero-coupon bonds are infrequently issued by corporations. The dominant player in this market is the U.S. government, with the government's zero-coupon bonds called STRIPS.
Junk (high-yield) bonds	High-risk debt that has a below-investment-grade bond rating (see the earlier discussion of bond ratings). Junk bonds are also called high-yield bonds because they pay interest rates that are 3 to 5% higher than those of the highest rated bonds.
Floating-rate bonds	A floating- or variable-rate bond is simply one whose coupon rate fluctuates according to the level of current market interest rates. These bonds are quite popular with municipalities and foreign governments, but are far less common among corporations.
Convertible bonds	Convertible bonds are debt securities that can be converted into a firm's stock at a pre-specified price.

low coupon rate of interest each year the bonds are outstanding. With these bonds the investor receives most (or with zero-coupon bonds, all) of their return from the appreciation of the bonds.

Amortizing or Non-Amortizing

The payments from **amortizing bonds**, such as a home mortgage loan, include both the interest and a portion of the principal. On the other hand, the payments to the bondholder from a **non-amortizing bond** only include interest. Then at maturity, the bondholder of a non-amortizing bond receives the full principal amount or par value of the bond regardless of how much was paid for the bond.

Convertibility

Convertible bonds are debt securities that can be converted into a firm's stock at a pre-specified price. For instance, you might have a convertible bond with a face (or par) value of $1,000 that pays 6 percent interest, or $60, each year. The bond matures in five years,

Finance in a **Flat World**

International Bonds

Not only can you buy bonds issued by the U.S. government and by U.S. companies, but you can also buy bonds issued by foreign governments and foreign companies. One benefit from buying foreign bonds is diversification. Because interest-rate movements differ from country to country, adding international bonds to your portfolio may provide added diversification. On the other hand, financial information used to analyze the foreign company may be less reliable, and is often more difficult to obtain. In addition, it is difficult to assess exposure to default risk in many foreign countries. Also, international investing exposes you to currency risk. Currency risk arises from changes in the exchange rate between the U.S. dollar and the currency in which the bond is denominated. For example, if you buy a Japanese bond, your coupons will be denominated in yen, which means that even if the coupons are fixed in yen they will fluctuate when you convert them to U.S. dollars. There are some international bonds that pay interest and are bought and sold in U.S. dollars. These are called Yankee bonds. They are generally issued by foreign governments, international banks, and on occasion by corporations and are generally highly rated. For example, in 2012, Heineken, the Dutch beer-maker, sold $3.25 billion worth of Yankee bonds.

Your Turn: See Study Question 14.

---

at which time the company must pay the $1,000 par value to the bondholder. However, at the time the bond was issued, the firm gave the bondholder the option of either collecting the $1,000 or receiving shares of the firm's stock at a conversion price of $50. In other words, the bondholder would receive 20 shares (20 = $1,000 par value ÷ $50 conversion price). What would you do if you were the bondholder? If the stock were selling for more than $50, then you would want to give up the $1,000 par value and take the stock. Thus, it's the investor's choice either to take the $1,000 promised when the bond was issued or to convert the bond into the firm's stock.

Before you move on to 5

Concept Check | 4

1. What is the difference between debentures, subordinated debentures, and mortgage bonds?
2. How does an investor receive a return from a zero- or very-low-coupon bond?
3. What are junk bonds, and why do they typically have a higher interest rate than other types of bonds?

 Determinants of Interest Rates

Bond prices vary inversely with interest rates; therefore, we need to understand what determines interest rates if we want to understand how bond prices fluctuate.

Although we often speak in terms of the rate of interest as a single rate, there are actually many rates of interest that correspond to different types of debt securities. In particular, some interest rates are adjusted for inflation, whereas others aren't. In addition, there are different interest rates for different terms of maturity. For example, the interest rate on a bond that matures in 2 years will have a different rate, or yield to maturity, than the interest rate or yield to maturity on a bond that matures in 10 years. This section also takes a look at the relationship between interest rates, or yields to maturity, and the number of years to maturity for bonds of similar risk.

Inflation and Real versus Nomimal Interest Rates

Rates of interest that we see quoted in the financial press are commonly referred to as **nominal (or quoted) interest rates** and are the interest rates unadjusted for inflation. Contrasted with the nominal rate, the **real rate of interest** adjusts for the expected effects of inflation. Thus, although the nominal interest rate or return tells us the actual dollar return that we receive, it says nothing about the purchasing power of that return. On the other hand, the real interest rate or return measures the purchasing power that we gain as a result of our investment—in effect, it is an inflation-adjusted interest rate or return.

For example, let's say you have a soft spot for Java Chip Frappuccinos and they cost $5.00 and you have $500. That means at today's price, you could purchase 100 Java Chip Frappuccinos. However, you decide to invest your money for one year at 10 percent, and during that year the inflation rate is 5 percent. That means at the end of one year you'll have $550, and the price of a Java Chip Frappuccino will climb to $5.25. As a result, you can now buy $550/$5.25 = 104.76 drinks. Although your nominal return was 10 percent, your real return—that is, the increase in your purchasing power—is only 4.76 percent.

Fisher Effect: The Nominal and Real Rate of Interest

The relationship between the nominal rate of interest, $r_{nominal}$, the anticipated rate of inflation, $r_{inflation}$, and the real rate of interest, r_{real}, is known as the **Fisher effect**. As we discuss the Fisher effect, keep in mind that the real rate of interest is not a risk-free rate. The Fisher effect is captured in Equation (4):

$$(1 + r_{nominal}) = (1 + r_{real})(1 + r_{inflation}) \qquad \textbf{(4)}$$

or, rearranging the terms of the equation, we can solve for the nominal rate of interest, $r_{nominal}$, as follows:

$$r_{nominal} = (1 + r_{real})(1 + r_{inflation}) - 1$$
$$= r_{real} + r_{inflation} + (r_{real} \times r_{inflation}) \qquad \textbf{(4a)}$$

Important Definitions and Concepts:

- $r_{nominal}$ = the nominal or observed rate of interest, which has not been adjusted for the effects of inflation.
- r_{real} = the rate of increase in purchasing power from an investment, which is calculated by netting out the anticipated increase in the price of goods and services (inflation) from the nominal rate of interest on the investment.
- $r_{inflation}$ = the rate of inflation in the economy, which reflects the anticipated rate at which the general level of prices for goods and services will rise annually.

Let's return to our latte example, for which we know that the nominal rate of interest is 10.0 percent and the anticipated rate of inflation is 5 percent. We can solve for the real rate of interest found in Equation (4b), r_{real}, as follows:

$$r_{real} = \frac{(1 + r_{nominal})}{(1 + r_{inflation})} - 1 \qquad \textbf{(4b)}$$

Substituting what we know into Equation (4b), we calculate the real rate of interest to be 4.76 percent, as follows:

$$r_{real} = \frac{(1 + .10)}{(1 + .05)} - 1 = .0476 \; or \; 4.76\%$$

Thinking back to Equation (4a), the nominal rate of interest is equal to the sum of the real rate of interest (r_{real}), the expected rate of inflation ($r_{inflation}$), and the product of the real rate and the rate of inflation.

Note that if the expected rate of inflation is low, then the cross-product ($r_{real} \times r_{inflation}$) will be very small. As a consequence, it is customary to ignore this cross-product term and estimate the real rate of interest simply by subtracting the anticipated rate of inflation (the inflation premium) from the nominal rate of interest. Using this approximation, we can approximate the real rate of interest as follows:

$$\text{Approximate Real Rate of Interest} = \text{Nominal Interest Rate} - \text{Inflation Premium}$$

Checkpoint 5

Solving for the Real Rate of Interest

You have managed to build up your savings over the three years following your graduation from college to a respectable $10,000 and are wondering how to invest it. Your banker says the bank could pay you 5 percent on your account for the next year. However, you recently saw on the news that the expected rate of inflation for next year is 3.5 percent. If you are earning a 5 percent annual rate of return but the prices of goods and services are rising at a rate of 3.5 percent, just how much additional buying power would you gain each year? Stated somewhat differently, what real rate of interest would you earn if you made the investment?

STEP 1: Picture the problem

To visualize the problem, let's assume that the price of goods and services cost you $1.00 per unit and that at the end of one year those same goods and services will cost you $1.035, which reflects the expected rate of inflation of 3.5 percent. You want to know how much the $10,500 = $10,000(1 + .05) that you expect to have in your savings account will buy you at the end of the year.

	Year 0	Year 1
Savings account balance	$10,000.00	$10,500.00
Price index (3.5% inflation)	$ 1.000	$ 1.035

STEP 2: Decide on a solution strategy

The Fisher effect found in Equation (4b) provides the basis for estimating the real rate of interest directly.

STEP 3: Solve

$$r_{real} = (1 + r_{nominal})/(1 + r_{inflation}) - 1 \qquad \textbf{(4b)}$$
$$r_{real} = (1 + .05)/(1 + .035) - 1$$
$$r_{real} = 1.014493 - 1 = .014493 \text{ or } 1.4493\%$$

STEP 4: Analyze

The real rate of interest of 1.4493 percent represents the percent increase in purchasing power you realize from investing your savings to earn 5 percent when the rate of inflation is expected to be 3.5 percent. Note that the purchasing power in units found in Step 1 increased by 144.93 units (remember, the units are priced at $1.00 per unit), or by 1.4493 percent.

STEP 5: Check yourself

Assume now that you expect that inflation will be 5 percent over the coming year and want to analyze how much better off you will be if you place your savings in an account that also earns just 5 percent. What is the real rate of interest in this circumstance?

ANSWER: 0.00 percent.

>> **END Checkpoint 5**

Solving for the Nominal Rate of Interest

After considering a number of investment opportunities, you have decided that you should be able to earn a real return of 2 percent on your $10,000 in savings over the coming year. If the rate of inflation is expected to be 3.5 percent over the coming year, what nominal rate of return must you anticipate in order to earn the 2 percent real rate of return?

STEP 1: Picture the problem

If we assume that the price of goods and services today is $1 per unit and we want to be able to purchase 2 percent more in one year when prices have risen by 3.5 percent, then we will need to earn a nominal rate of interest that provides a sufficient end-of-year balance to buy 10,200 units at a price of $1.035 each!

	Year 0	Year 1
Price index (3.5% inflation)	$ 1.000	$ 1.035
Purchasing power (units)	10,000.00	10,200.00
Desired real rate (% increase in purchasing power)		2.0000%

STEP 2: Decide on a solution strategy

The Fisher effect found in Equation (4a) provides a direct way of estimating the nominal rate of interest when we know the real rate and have an estimate of the anticipated rate of inflation.

STEP 3: Solve

$$r_{nominal} = (1 + r_{real})(1 + r_{inflation}) - 1 = r_{real} + r_{inflation} + (r_{real} \times r_{inflation}) \qquad \text{(4a)}$$

$$r_{nominal} = .02 + .035 + (.02 \times .035)$$

$$r_{nominal} = 0.557 = 5.57\%$$

STEP 4: Analyze

In order to achieve a 2 percent increase in purchasing power in the face of a 3.5 percent rate of inflation, you must earn a 5.57 percent return on your savings. Note that this total is greater than the sum of the real rate and the rate of inflation (i.e., 5.5 percent) because the price per unit rises over the year and you need a higher rate than 5.5 percent if you are to be able to increase your real purchasing power by the full 2 percent.

STEP 5: Check yourself

If you anticipate that the rate of inflation will now be 4 percent next year, holding all else the same, what rate of return will you need to earn on your savings in order to achieve the 2 percent increase in purchasing power?

ANSWER: 6.08 percent.

Your Turn: For more practice, do related **Study Problem** 23 at the end of this chapter.   **>> END Checkpoint 6**

Interest-Rate Determinants—Breaking It Down

Another way to help gain an understanding of why interest rates on different bond issues are different is to break the interest rate down into several components. Keep in mind that in this richer interest-rate model we are ignoring the effects of compounding of the various risk premium components in an effort to simplify the discussion. In so doing, we can think of the interest rate for a particular note or bond as being composed of five basic components: (1) the real risk-free rate of interest (the risk-free return in a period of zero inflation), (2) an **inflation premium** (which is a premium for the expected rate of inflation), (3) the **default-risk premium** (which is a premium reflecting the default risk of the note or bond), (4) a **maturity-risk premium** (to reflect the added price volatility that accompanies bonds with longer terms to maturity), and (5) a **liquidity-risk premium** (which compensates for the fact that some bonds cannot be converted or sold at reasonably predictable prices). Thus, the nominal interest rate for a long-term bond can be thought of in terms of Equation (5):

$$
\begin{array}{l}
\text{Nominal Rate} \\
\text{of Interest, } r_{nominal}
\end{array}
=
\begin{array}{l}
\text{Real Risk-free Rate} \\
\text{of Interest, } r_{real\ risk\text{-}free}
\end{array}
+
\begin{array}{l}
\text{Inflation} \\
\text{Premium}
\end{array}
+
\begin{array}{l}
\text{Default-risk} \\
\text{Premium}
\end{array}
+
\begin{array}{l}
\text{Maturity-risk} \\
\text{Premium}
\end{array}
+
\begin{array}{l}
\text{Liquidity-risk} \\
\text{Premium}
\end{array}
\qquad (5)
$$

Important Definitions and Concepts:

- **Nominal rate of interest or yield to maturity** = the rate of interest that will be earned from holding a bond until maturity where the bond pays the holder the promised interest and principal in accordance with what is promised. This rate is *not* adjusted for the loss of purchasing power resulting from inflation.

- **Real risk-free rate of interest** = the interest rate on a fixed-income security that has no risk in an environment of zero inflation. It could also be stated as the nominal interest rate less the inflation, default-risk, maturity-risk, and liquidity-risk premiums.

- **Inflation premium** = a premium for the expected rate of increase in prices of goods and services in the economy over the term of the bond or note.

- **Default-risk premium** = a premium to reflect the risk of default by the borrower. It is calculated as the difference in rates between a U.S. Treasury bond and a corporate bond of the same maturity and marketability (that is, there is no liquidity risk).

- **Maturity-risk premium** = a premium that reflects the additional return required by investors in longer-term securities to compensate them for the greater risk of price fluctuation on those securities caused by interest-rate changes.

- **Liquidity-risk premium** = a premium required by investors for securities that cannot quickly be converted into cash at a reasonably predictable price.

By using knowledge of various risk premiums as contained in Equation (5), the financial manager can generate useful information for the firm's financial planning process. For instance, if the firm is about to offer a new issue of corporate bonds to the investing marketplace, it is possible for the financial manager or analyst to estimate and better understand what interest rate (yield) would satisfy the market to help ensure that the bonds are actually bought by investors. To make sense out of the different interest-rate terminology—nominal, risk-free, and real—let's take a closer look at the difference between them.

Real Risk-Free Interest Rate and the Risk-Free Interest Rate

What's the difference between the real risk-free interest rate and the risk-free interest rate? The answer is that although both are risk-free measures, the risk-free interest rate, $r_{risk\text{-}free}$, includes compensation for inflation, whereas the real risk-free interest rate, $r_{real\ risk\text{-}free}$, is the risk-free rate after inflation. As a result,

$$r_{risk\text{-}free} = r_{real\ risk\text{-}free} + \text{Inflation premium}$$

or

$$r_{real\ risk\text{-}free} = r_{risk\text{-}free} - \text{Inflation premium}$$

In effect, when you see the term "real" in front of an interest rate, that interest rate is referring to an "after-inflation-adjusted" return—that is, the impact of inflation has been subtracted from the interest rate. Furthermore, the term "risk-free" indicates there is no compensation for default risk, maturity risk, or liquidity risk. As a result, when we put the concepts of "real" and "risk-free" together, we get the term "real risk-free," which indicates that (1) the interest rate does not include compensation for the inflation and, in addition to that, (2) it does not include compensation for default-risk, maturity-risk, and liquidity-risk premiums. That is, it is the return if there were no risk and no inflation. Thus, although it may change over time, given the fact that those changes are not easily predicted, a reasonable estimation of the real risk-free rate of interest would be the difference between the calculated average yield on three-month Treasury bills and the inflation rate.

Inflation Premium

The inflation premium compensates for the fact that inflation erodes the real value of the dollars that will be returned in the future. To compensate for the loss, investors demand a higher return. Thus the inflation premium could be estimated as the rate of inflation expected to occur over the life of the bond under consideration.

Default-Risk Premium

In addition to accounting for the time value of money and inflation, the interest rate that a firm's bonds must pay must account for the risk of default. The risk of default is the possibility that the bond issuer (the borrower) will fail to repay principal and interest in a timely manner. As we saw in Table 3, bond ratings are typically used to indicate default risk, with the lowest risk of default carrying the highest rating (AAA) and the highest risk of default carrying the lowest rating (C). For any given maturity, bonds with higher probabilities of default will require a higher promised yield. Thus, assuming there is no liquidity risk, the default-risk premium for a 10-year A2/A-rated corporate bond could be estimated as the difference between the average yield on a 10-year A2/A-rated corporate bond and 10-year Treasury notes, which is the same as the credit spreads or spread to Treasury bonds.

Maturity-Risk Premium

As we learned earlier in this chapter in the discussion of the fourth bond valuation relationship, long-term bonds have greater interest-rate risk than do short-term bonds. The maturity-risk premium compensates for the fact that longer-term bonds fluctuate more when interest rates change than do the prices of shorter-term bonds.

Liquidity-Risk Premium

Although many Treasury bonds trade on a regular basis, many bonds do not trade very often. Moreover, there is little demand for some bonds issued by smaller corporations. Thus, they are not particularly liquid, and as a result, the price an investor might receive for an infrequently traded bond might be less than that received for a bond of similar risk that is traded frequently. Thus, a liquidity-risk premium is demanded by investors on securities that cannot quickly be converted into cash at a reasonably predictable price.

The Maturity-Risk Premium and the Term Structure of Interest Rates

The longer the bond's maturity, the more the bond price fluctuates when interest rates change. Thus, long-term bonds have greater interest-rate risk than do short-term bonds. The maturity-risk premium is the compensation that investors demand for bearing interest-rate risk on longer-term bonds. The maturity-risk premium for a particular bond can be estimated as the difference between the calculated yield on a Treasury bond of similar maturity and the yield on a three-month Treasury bill.

The relationship between interest rates and time to maturity with default risk held constant is known as the **term structure of interest rates** or the **yield curve**. Figure 3 illustrates a hypothetical term structure of U.S. Treasury bonds. We have highlighted two different points on the yield curve: the 5-year maturity and 20-year maturity. The rate of interest on a 5-year note or bond is 11.5 percent, and the comparable rate on a 20-year bond is 13 percent. Generally, the yield curve rises for longer maturities, although there are times when it is flat, humpshaped, and even negative in slope.

The Shape of the Yield Curve

By looking back to Equation (5) we can gain an understanding of why a yield curve takes on one shape or another. To do this, let's look at the yield curve for Treasury securities. Thinking back to Equation (5), the default-risk premium and the liquidity-risk premium would both be zero because the Treasury doesn't have any default risk because in the worst case, it can print more money, and the Treasury debt market is the most liquid of all security markets. Taking the default-risk premium and the liquidity-risk premium out of the equation, we get

$$\frac{\text{Treasury}}{\text{Debt Yield}} = \frac{\text{Real Risk-Free Rate}}{\text{of Interest, } r_{real\ risk\text{-}free}} + \frac{\text{Inflation}}{\text{Premium}} + \frac{\text{Maturity-Risk}}{\text{Premium}}$$

The Term Structure of Interest Rates or Yield Curve

The yield curve shows the relationship between yield to maturity and maturity dates for a set of similar bonds (typically U.S. government or Treasury securities). In this example the 20-year bond has a yield to maturity of 13%, whereas the 5-year security yields only 11.5%. Thus, the yield curve is said to be upward sloping. The upward-sloping yield curve is the most typical; however, flat and inverted (downward-sloping) yield curves are sometimes observed.

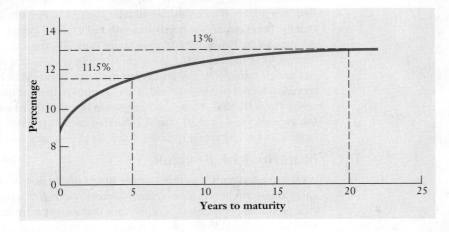

>> END FIGURE 3

Because there is no reason to believe that the real risk-free rate of interest will change over time, the shape of the yield curve must be determined by the inflation premium and the maturity-risk premium. Although the maturity-risk premium should increase over longer maturities, that is not always the case for the inflation premium. In periods when inflation is expected to increase over time, the inflation premium should increase accordingly for longer maturities. This is illustrated in Figure 4. During time periods when inflation is expected to subside, the inflation premium should decrease over longer maturities, resulting in a downward-sloping Treasury yield curve as shown in Figure 5.

For corporate debt, both the default-risk premium and the liquidity-risk premium come into play. In fact, the corporate bond credit spread, or spreads to Treasury bonds, discussed earlier can be viewed as being made up of the default-risk and liquidity-risk premiums:

$$\frac{\text{Bond Credit Spread or}}{\text{Spreads to Treasury Bonds}} = \frac{\text{Default-Risk}}{\text{Premium}} + \frac{\text{Liquidity-Risk}}{\text{Premium}}$$

For example, in Table 4, the yield spread between 30-year Treasury bonds and Aa2/AA-rated corporate bonds is shown to be 1.07 percent, and this spread represents the default-risk and the liquidity-risk premiums. Although the default-risk premium depends upon the risk level and bond rating of the particular bond, it tends to increase for longer maturities regardless of the bond rating. That is because the longer the maturity, the more likely it is that the firm issuing the debt will incur some type of financial problem that might lead to bankruptcy. As such, the default-risk premium is larger for longer maturities. With respect to the liquidity-risk premium, the degree of liquidity that a particular bond issue has varies from one bond issue to another. However, there are vast numbers of different bond issues outstanding, many of which do not trade on a regular basis. As a result, when they trade, they do not necessarily fetch their true intrinsic value.

Figure 4

Treasury Yield Curve during Period of Increasing Inflation

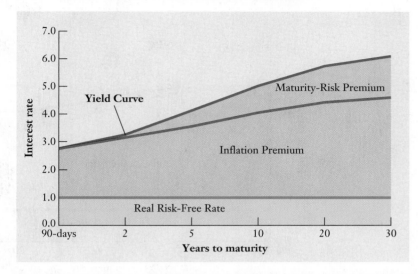

Maturity	Real Risk-Free Rate	Inflation Premium	Maturity-Risk Premium	Yield
90 days	1.00%	1.75%	0.01%	2.76%
2 years	1.00%	2.15%	0.11%	3.26%
5 years	1.00%	2.56%	0.57%	4.13%
10 years	1.00%	3.05%	0.97%	5.02%
20 years	1.00%	3.42%	1.32%	5.74%
30 years	1.00%	3.60%	1.50%	6.10%

>> END FIGURE 4

Shifts in the Yield Curve

The term structure of interest rates, or the yield curve, changes over time as expectations regarding each of the four factors that underlie interest rates change. Consequently, the yield curve observed today may be quite different from what it was a month earlier. For example, note what happened to the yield curve around the September 11, 2001, attack on the World Trade Center and the Pentagon. Figure 6 shows the yield curve one day before the attack and again just two weeks later. The change is noticeable, particularly for short-term interest rates. Investors quickly developed fears about the future following the attacks of 9/11 and moved their investments to very short-term Treasury securities that pushed up prices and pushed down yields on the short-term securities relative to long-term securities.

Although the yield curve is most often upward sloping, Figure 7 illustrates that at different times the yield curve can assume several shapes. For example, on September 7, 2000, the yield curve was slightly downward sloping, sharply upward sloping on September 28, 2001, and relatively flat on December 28, 2000.

Figure 5

Treasury Yield Curve during Period of Decreasing Inflation

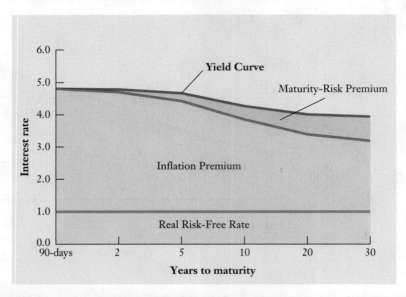

Maturity	Real Risk-Free Rate	Inflation Premium	Maturity-Risk Premium	Yield
90 days	1.00%	3.80%	0.01%	4.81%
2 years	1.00%	3.71%	0.08%	4.79%
5 years	1.00%	3.42%	0.25%	4.67%
10 years	1.00%	2.85%	0.42%	4.27%
20 years	1.00%	2.38%	0.63%	4.01%
30 years	1.00%	2.19%	0.75%	3.94%

>> END FIGURE 5

Before you begin end-of-chapter material

Concept Check | **5**

1. What is the yield curve?

2. What is the typical shape of the yield curve for U.S. Treasury securities?

Figure 6

Changes in the Term Structure of Interest Rates around September 11, 2001

Important economic events often lead to shifts in the shape and location of the term structure of interest rates as investors rebalance their portfolios to reduce risk. Such an event occurred on September 11, 2001.

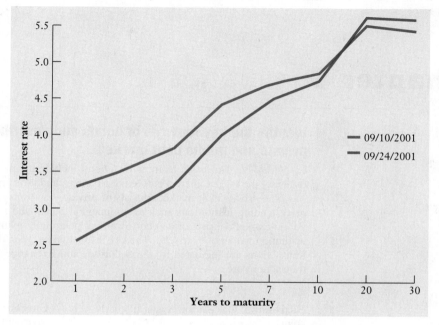

>> END FIGURE 6

Figure 7

Historical Term Structure of Interest Rates for Government Securities

The term structure of interest rates is not fixed and can change dramatically in a brief period of time in response to changing expectations and economic conditions. The three term structures plotted here capture upward-sloping, flat, and downward-sloping (inverted) term structures observed within a span of only 13 months.

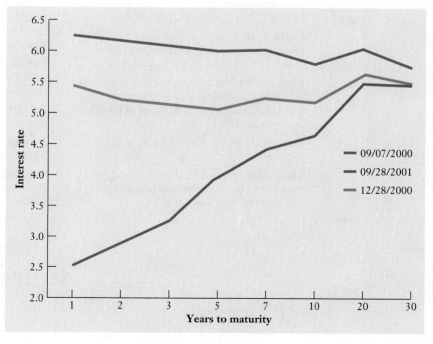

>> END FIGURE 7

Applying the Principles of Finance to This Chapter

P Principle 1: **Money Has a Time Value** The value of debt is equal to the present value of the contractually promised principal and interest payments (the cash flows) discounted back to the present using the market's required yield. As a result, Principle 1 plays a pivotal role in determining the value of debt.

P Principle 2: **There Is a Risk–Return Tradeoff** Different types of debt have different levels of risk associated with them, with more risk resulting in more expected return.

P Principle 3: **Cash Flows Are the Source of Value** It is the cash flows that are discounted back to present that determine the value of a bond.

Chapter Summaries

1 Identify the key features of bonds and describe the difference between private and public debt markets.

SUMMARY: The basic features of a bond include its maturity, how the interest is determined (whether the rate of interest is fixed or floating), and how principal is repaid.

The private debt market consists of private loan transactions between a borrower and one or more lending institutions such as commercial banks and finance companies. Debt raised in the public market consists of one borrower and potentially many lenders, including any individual or institution with money to lend. The key distinction between these two markets is that public market transactions are regulated by the Securities and Exchange Commission, whereas private market transactions are not.

KEY TERMS

Basis point One percent equals 100 basis points.

Bond indenture A written agreement between the bond issuer and bondholders specifying the terms of the bond.

Bond rating The credit rating given to a bond, providing an indication of the creditworthiness of the bond.

Call provision A provision that entitles the corporation to repurchase its preferred stock from its investors at stated prices over specified periods.

Collateral A borrower's pledge of specific property to a lender, to secure repayment of a loan.

Conversion feature A feature of some debt that allows the bondholder to convert the bond into a prescribed number of shares of the firm's common stock.

Corporate bond A bond issued by a corporation.

Coupon interest rate The percentage of the par value of the bond that will be paid out annually in the form of interest.

Current yield The ratio of the annual interest payment to the bond's market price.

Floating rate An interest rate on a loan agreement, such as a bond, that adjusts up or down depending on the movements of an agreed-upon benchmark, such as LIBOR (the London Interbank Offered Rate).

Floating-rate bonds Bonds that have a floating rate of interest.

London Interbank Offered Rate (LIBOR) LIBOR is a daily rate that is based on the interest rates at which banks offer to lend in the London wholesale or interbank market (the market where banks loan each other money).

Par or **face value of a bond** On the face of a bond, the stated amount that the firm is to repay upon the maturity date.

Private market transaction A loan that only involves the two parties.

Syndicate A group of investment bankers that is invited to help buy and resell the issue.

Transaction loan A loan where the proceeds are designated for a specific purpose—for example, a bank loan used to finance the acquisition of a piece of equipment.

Concept Check | 1

1. What is a bond indenture?

2. What are the key features of a bond? Which of these features determines the cash flows paid to the bondholder?

3. What is the difference between an Aaa and a Ba bond in terms of risks to the bondholder? What are the principal bond rating agencies?

KEY EQUATION

$$\text{Current Yield} = \frac{\text{Annual Interest Payment}}{\text{Current Market Price of the Bond}} \tag{1}$$

Calculate the value of a bond and relate it to the yield to maturity on the bond.

SUMMARY: Two basic factors determine the value of a bond: (1) the amount and timing of the bond's future cash flows and (2) the risk of the bond's cash flows. Incorporating these factors into the bond valuation process, we calculate the value of a bond as the present value of both future interest and principal to be received by the bondholder. The discount rate we use to do so is the market's required yield to maturity on a comparable-risk bond.

The yield to maturity is the promised rate of return to an investor who holds the bond until maturity, assuming the bond does not default on any of the interest and principal payments. To calculate a bond's yield to maturity, we find the discount rate that equates the present value of the future cash flows (interest and principal) with the current market price of the bond. The expected yield to maturity is generally less than the promised yield because it takes into account the possibility that the bond may default, which reduces the expected cash flows from holding the bond to below the promised interest and principal payment. This distinction is particularly important for bonds with low credit ratings (BB and below) because they face significant risk of default.

KEY TERMS

Credit spread The spread, or difference in interest rates (generally expressed in terms of basis points), of the corporate bond over a U.S. Treasury security of the same maturity.

Recovery rate The percent of the principal and interest that is owed that a bondholder will end up receiving if the bond defaults.

Spread to Treasury bonds The spread, or difference in interest rates (generally expressed in terms of basis points), of the corporate bond over a U.S. Treasury security of the same maturity.

Yield to maturity The promised rate of return to an investor who holds the bond until maturity, assuming the bond does not default on any of the interest and principal payments.

KEY EQUATIONS

$$\begin{matrix}\text{Bond}\\\text{Value}\end{matrix} = \left(\begin{matrix}\text{Present Value of the}\\\text{Bond's Coupon Interest}\\\text{Payments}\end{matrix}\right) + \left(\begin{matrix}\text{Present Value of the}\\\text{Principal Amount (par Value)}\\\text{of the Bond Issue}\end{matrix}\right) \qquad (2)$$

$$\text{Bond Price} = \frac{\text{Interest}_{\text{year 1}}}{(1 + YTM)^1} + \frac{\text{Interest}_{\text{year 2}}}{(1 + YTM)^2} + \frac{\text{Interest}_{\text{year 3}}}{(1 + YTM)^3} \qquad (2a)$$
$$+ \cdots + \frac{\text{Interest}_{\text{year } n}}{(1 + YTM)^n} + \frac{\text{Principal}}{(1 + YTM)^n}$$

$$\begin{matrix}\text{Bond}\\\text{Value}\end{matrix} = \text{Interest}\left[\frac{1 - \dfrac{1}{(1 + YTM_{\text{Market}})^n}}{YTM_{\text{Market}}}\right] + \text{Principal}\left[\frac{1}{(1 + YTM_{\text{Market}})^n}\right] \qquad (2b)$$

$$\begin{matrix}\text{Bond Value}\\\text{(semiannual payments)}\end{matrix} = (\text{Interest}/2)\left[\frac{1 - \dfrac{1}{\left(1 + \dfrac{YTM_{\text{Market}}}{2}\right)^{2n}}}{\dfrac{YTM_{\text{Market}}}{2}}\right] + \text{Principal}\left[\frac{1}{\left(1 + \dfrac{YTM_{\text{Market}}}{2}\right)^{2n}}\right] \qquad (2c)$$

$$E(YTM) = YTM_{\text{No Default}} \times (1 - \text{Probability of Default}) + YTM_{\text{Default}} \times (\text{Probability of Default}) \qquad (3)$$

Concept Check | **2**

1. How do you calculate the value of a bond?

2. How do you estimate the appropriate discount rate?

3. Why might the expected returns be different from the yield to maturity?

4. How do semiannual interest payments affect the asset valuation equation?

Describe the four key bond valuation relationships.

SUMMARY: There are four key relationships that underlie the valuation of bonds. These relationships characterize the behavior of bond prices as follows:

Relationship #1: A decrease in interest rates (and consequently the market's required yield to maturity for bonds) will cause the value of a bond to increase; an interest rate increase will cause a decrease in value. The change in value caused by changing interest rates is called interest-rate risk.

Relationship #2: The market value of a bond will be less than its par value if the market's required yield to maturity is higher than the coupon rate of interest paid by the bond, and the market value of the bond will be greater than the bond's par value if the market's required yield to maturity is less than the coupon interest rate of interest paid by the bond.

Relationship #3: As the maturity date approaches, the market value of a bond approaches its par value.

Relationship #4: Long-term bonds have greater interest-rate risk than short-term bonds. This translates into higher bond price volatility in response to changing interest rates.

KEY TERMS

Discount bond A bond that sells at a discount below par value.

Interest-rate risk The variability in a bond's value (risk) caused by changing interest rates.

Premium bond A bond that is selling above its par value.

Identify the major types of corporate bonds.

SUMMARY: All corporate bonds represent debt to the issuing corporation. However, the specific features of bonds can be quite different. For example, some bonds have specific assets pledged to the bondholders in the event that the firm should default in its payments, whereas other bonds have no collateral. Other key features that give rise to different types of bonds include the priority of claim against the firm's assets should it default on a principal or interest payment, and where the bonds are first issued.

KEY TERMS

Amortizing bond Bonds that are paid off in equal periodic payments with those payments including part of the principal (par value) along with the interest payments.

Convertible bond A debt security that can be converted into a firm's stock at a pre-specified price.

Debenture Any unsecured long-term debt.

Eurobond A bond issued in a country different from the one in whose currency the bond is denominated; for example, a bond issued in Europe or Asia by an American company that pays interest and principal to the lender in U.S. dollars.

Junk (high-yield) bond Any bond rated BB or below.

Mortgage bond A bond secured by a lien on real property.

Non-amortizing bond A bond that only pays interest.

Secured bond A bond that is backed or secured by pledged assets or collateral to reduce the risk associated with lending.

Subordinated debenture A debenture that is subordinated to other debentures in being paid in case of insolvency.

Unsubordinated debenture A debenture that is unsubordinated to other debentures in being paid in case of insolvency.

Zero-coupon bond A bond that pays no interest to the lender but instead is issued at a substantial discount from its face value. The lender realizes its interest when the bond matures and repays the full face value to the holder.

Explain the effects of inflation on interest rates and describe the term structure of interest rates.

SUMMARY: When lenders loan money, they must take into account the anticipated loss in purchasing power that results during a period of price inflation. Consequently, nominal or observed rates of interest incorporate an inflation premium that reflects the anticipated rate of inflation over the period of the loan.

The term structure of interest rates (also called the yield curve) defines the relationship between rates of return for similar securities that differ only with respect to their time to maturity. For instance, if long-term government bonds offer a higher rate of return than do U.S. Treasury bills, then the yield curve is upward sloping. But if the Treasury bill is paying a higher rate of interest than its long-term counterparts, then the yield curve is downward sloping.

KEY TERMS

Default-risk premium A premium reflecting the default risk of the note or bond.

Fisher effect The relationship between the nominal rate of interest, the anticipated rate of inflation, and the real rate of interest.

Inflation premium A premium for the expected rate of increase in prices of goods and services in the economy over the term of the bond or note.

Liquidity-risk premium A premium, required by investors for securities that cannot quickly be converted into cash at a reasonably predictable price.

Maturity-risk premium A premium to reflect the added price volatility that accompanies bonds with longer terms to maturity.

Nominal (or quoted) interest rate The stated rate of interest that is unadjusted for inflation.

Real rate of interest The nominal rate of interest less any loss in purchasing power of the dollar during the time of the investment.

Term structure of interest rates Also called the yield curve. The relationship between interest rates and the term to maturity, where the risk of default is held constant.

Yield curve Also called the term structure of interest. The relationship between interest rates and the term to maturity, where the risk of default is held constant.

KEY EQUATIONS

$$(1 + r_{nominal}) = (1 + r_{real})(1 + r_{inflation}) \tag{4}$$

$$r_{nominal} = (1 + r_{real})(1 + r_{inflation}) - 1$$
$$= r_{real} + r_{inflation} + (r_{real} \times r_{inflation}) \tag{4a}$$

$$\begin{array}{l} \text{Nominal Rate} \\ \text{of Interest, } r_{nominal} \end{array} = \begin{array}{l} \text{Real Risk-Free Rate} \\ \text{of Interest, } r_{real\ risk\text{-}free} \end{array} + \begin{array}{l} \text{Inflation} \\ \text{Premium} \end{array} + \begin{array}{l} \text{Default-Risk} \\ \text{Premium} \end{array}$$

$$+ \begin{array}{l} \text{Maturity-Risk} \\ \text{Premium} \end{array} + \begin{array}{l} \text{Liquidity-Risk} \\ \text{Premium} \end{array} \tag{5}$$

Concept Check | **5**

1. What is the yield curve?
2. What is the typical shape of the yield curve for U.S. Treasury securities?

Study Questions

1. **(Related to Regardless of Your Major: Borrow Now, Pay Later)** In the *Regardless of Your Major* feature, the suggestion is made that you may already be involved in the debt markets. List your current involvement in the debt markets. Do you have credit cards, a car loan, or a college tuition loan? How do you expect to be involved in the debt markets after you graduate?

2. Distinguish between public and private corporate debt.

3. What is a floating-rate bond?

4. Describe the relationship between yield to maturity and the value of a bond.

5. **(Related to The Business of Life: Adjustable-Rate Mortgages)** In *The Business of Life: Adjustable-Rate Mortgages* feature, we learn the difference between fixed- and adjustable-rate mortgages. Why would you ever want to use an adjustable-rate mortgage (ARM)?

6. Why does a bond's par or face value differ from its market value?

7. Distinguish between a bond's coupon interest rate, current yield, and yield to maturity.

8. What is the difference between the expected and promised yield to maturity on a bond?

9. What does a bond rating reflect? Why is the rating important to the firm's management?

10. Distinguish between the following:
    a. Debentures and mortgage bonds.
    b. Eurobonds, zero-coupon bonds, and junk bonds.
    c. Premium and discount bonds.

11. Why does the market value of a bond differ from its par value when the coupon interest rate does not equal the market yield to maturity on a comparable-risk bond?

12. Is the price of a long-term (longer-maturity) bond more or less sensitive to changes in interest rates than that of a short-term bond? Why?

13. How does inflation impact the rate of interest observed in financial markets?

14. **(Related to Finance in a Flat World: International Bonds)** In the *Finance in a Flat World: International Bonds* feature, we learn about the bonds issued in financial markets outside of the United States. What are the potential benefits and costs of investing in foreign-issue bonds?

Study Problems

Overview of Corporate Debt

1. **(Related to Checkpoint 1) (Floating-rate loans)** The Bensington Glass Company entered into a loan agreement with the firm's bank to finance the firm's working capital. The loan called for a floating rate that was 30 basis points (.30 percent) over an index based on LIBOR. In addition, the loan adjusted weekly based on the closing value of the index for the previous week and had a maximum annual rate of 2.2 percent and a minimum of 1.75 percent. Calculate the rate of interest for Weeks 2 through 10.

Date	LIBOR
Week 1	1.98%
Week 2	1.66%
Week 3	1.52%
Week 4	1.35%
Week 5	1.60%
Week 6	1.63%
Week 7	1.67%
Week 8	1.88%
Week 9	1.93%

2. **(Floating-rate loans)** After looking at a fixed-rate loan, Ace-Campbell Mfg. entered into a floating-rate loan agreement. This loan is set at 40 basis points (or .40 percent) over an index based on LIBOR. Ace-Campbell is concerned that the LIBOR index may go up, causing the loan to climb. That concern comes from the fact that the rate on the loan adjusts weekly based on the closing value of the LIBOR index for the previous week. Fortunately for Ace-Campbell, this loan has a maximum annual rate of 2.2 percent. It also has a minimum annual rate of 1.50 percent. Given the following information, calculate the interest rate that Ace-Campbell would pay during Weeks 2 through 10.

Date	LIBOR
Week 1	1.98%
Week 2	1.66%
Week 3	1.52%
Week 4	1.35%
Week 5	1.60%
Week 6	1.63%
Week 7	1.67%
Week 8	1.88%
Week 9	1.93%

Valuing Corporate Debt

3. **(Related to Checkpoint 3) (Bond valuation)** Calculate the value of a bond that matures in 12 years and has a $1,000 par value. The coupon interest rate is 8 percent and the market's required yield to maturity on a comparable-risk bond is 12 percent.

4. **(Related to Checkpoint 4) (Bond valuation)** Calculate the value of a bond that matures in 10 years and has a $1,000 par value. The annual coupon interest rate is 9 percent and the market's required yield to maturity on a comparable-risk bond is 15 percent. What would be the value of this bond if it paid interest semiannually?

5. **(Bond valuation)** Enterprise, Inc. bonds have a 9 percent annual coupon rate. The interest is paid semiannually and the bonds mature in eight years. Their par value is $1,000. If the market's required yield to maturity on a comparable-risk bond is 8 percent, what is the value of the bond? What is its value if the interest is paid annually?

6. **(Related to Checkpoint 3) (Bond valuation)** Pybus, Inc. is considering issuing bonds that will mature in 20 years with an 8 percent annual coupon rate. Their par value will be $1,000, and the interest will be paid semiannually. Pybus is hoping to get an AA rating on its bonds and, if it does, the yield to maturity on similar AA bonds is 7.5 percent. However, Pybus is not sure whether the new bonds will receive an AA rating. If they receive an A rating, the yield to maturity on similar A bonds is 8.5 percent. What will be the price of these bonds if they receive either an A or an AA rating?

7. **(Related to Checkpoint 2) (Yield to maturity)** The market price is $900 for a 10-year bond ($1,000 par value) that pays 8 percent annual interest, but makes interest payments on a semiannual basis (4 percent semiannually). What is the bond's yield to maturity?

8. **(Yield to maturity)** A bond's market price is $750. It has a $1,000 par value, will mature in eight years, and has a coupon interest rate of 9 percent annual interest, but makes its interest payments semiannually. What is the bond's yield to maturity? What happens to the bond's yield to maturity if the bond matures in 16 years? What if it matures in four years?

9. **(Yield to maturity)** A 20-year Fitzgerald bond pays 9 percent interest annually on a $1,000 par value. If the bond sells at $945, what is the bond's yield to maturity? What would be the yield to maturity if the bond paid interest semiannually? Explain the difference.

10. **(Related to Checkpoint 3) (Bond valuation)** Doisneau 20-year bonds have a 10 percent annual coupon interest, make interest payments on a semiannual basis, and have a $1,000 par value. If the bonds are trading with a 12 percent market's required yield to maturity, are these premium or discount bonds? Explain your answer. What is the price of the bonds?

11. **(Bond valuation)** Five years ago, XYZ International issued some 30-year zero-coupon bonds that were priced with a market's required yield to maturity of 8 percent. What did these bonds sell for when they were issued? Now that five years have passed and the market's required yield to maturity on these bonds has climbed to 10 percent, what are they selling for? If the market's required yield to maturity had fallen to 6 percent, what would they have been selling for?

12. **(Related to Checkpoint 2) (Yield to maturity)** Hoyden Co.'s bonds mature in 15 years and pay 8 percent interest annually. If you purchase the bonds for $1,175, what is their yield to maturity?

13. **(Related to Checkpoint 2 and Checkpoint 3) (Bond valuation)** A 14-year, $1,000 par value Fingen bond pays 9 percent interest annually. The market price of the bond is $1,100 and the market's required yield to maturity on a comparable-risk bond is 10 percent.

    a. Compute the bond's yield to maturity.
    b. Determine the value of the bond to you, given your required rate of return.
    c. Should you purchase the bond?

14. **(Related to Checkpoint 2) (Yield to maturity)** Abner Corporation's bonds mature in 15 years and pay 9 percent interest annually. If you purchase the bonds for $1,250, what is your yield to maturity?

15. **(Related to Checkpoint 2 and Checkpoint 3) (Bond valuation)** The seven-year $1,000 par bonds of Vail Inc. pay 9 percent interest. The market's required yield to maturity on a comparable-risk bond is 7 percent. The current market price for the bond is $1,100.

  a. Determine the yield to maturity.
  b. What is the value of the bond to you given the yield to maturity on a comparable-risk bond?
  c. Should you purchase the bond at the current market price?

16. **(Related to Checkpoint 2) (Yield to maturity)** The Saleemi Corporation's $1,000 bonds pay 5 percent interest annually and have 12 years until maturity. You can purchase a bond for $915.

  a. What is the yield to maturity on this bond?
  b. Should you purchase the bond if the yield to maturity on a comparable-risk bond is 9 percent?

Bond Valuation: Four Key Relationships

17. **(Related to Checkpoint 2) (Bond valuation relationships)** The 15-year, $1,000 par value bonds of Waco Industries pay 8 percent interest annually. The market price of the bond is $1,085, and the market's required yield to maturity on a comparable-risk bond is 10 percent.

  a. Compute the bond's yield to maturity.
  b. Determine the value of the bond to you given the market's required yield to maturity on a comparable-risk bond.
  c. Should you purchase the bond?

18. **(Related to Checkpoint 3) (Bond valuation relationships)** You own a bond that pays $100 in annual interest, with a $1,000 par value. It matures in 15 years. The market's required yield to maturity on a comparable-risk bond is 12 percent.

  a. Calculate the value of the bond.
  b. How does the value change if the yield to maturity on a comparable-risk bond (i) increases to 15 percent or (ii) decreases to 8 percent?
  c. Explain the implications of your answers in part b as they relate to interest-rate risk, premium bonds, and discount bonds.
  d. Assume that the bond matures in 5 years instead of 15 years and recalculate your answers in part b.
  e. Explain the implications of your answers in part d as they relate to interest-rate risk, premium bonds, and discount bonds.

19. **(Bond valuation relationships)** Arizona Public Utilities issued a bond that pays $80 in interest, with a $1,000 par value. It matures in 20 years. The market's required yield to maturity on a comparable-risk bond is 7 percent.

  a. Calculate the value of the bond.
  b. How does the value change if the market's required yield to maturity on a comparable-risk bond (i) increases to 10 percent or (ii) decreases to 6 percent?
  c. Explain the implications of your answers in part b as they relate to interest-rate risk, premium bonds, and discount bonds.
  d. Assume that the bond matures in 10 years instead of 20 years. Recompute your answers in part b.
  e. Explain the implications of your answers in part d as they relate to interest-rate risk, premium bonds, and discount bonds.

20. **(Bond valuation relationships)** A bond of the Telink Corporation pays $110 in annual interest, with a $1,000 par value. The bond matures in 20 years. The market's required yield to maturity on a comparable-risk bond is 9 percent.

  a. Calculate the value of the bond.
  b. How does the value change if (i) the market's required yield to maturity on a comparable-risk bond (i) increases to 12 percent or (ii) decreases to 6 percent?
  c. Interpret your findings in parts a and b.

21. **(Bond valuation relationships)** A bond of the Visador Corporation pays $70 in annual interest, with a $1,000 par value. The bond matures in 17 years. The market's required yield to maturity on a comparable-risk bond is 8.5 percent.

  a. Calculate the value of the bond.
  b. How does the value change if the market's required yield to maturity on a comparable-risk bond (i) increases to 11 percent or (ii) decreases to 6 percent?
  c. Interpret your finding in parts a and b.

22. **(Bond valuation relationships)** Stanley, Inc. issues a 15-year $1,000 bond that pays $85 annually. The market price for the bond is $960. The market's required yield to maturity on a comparable-risk bond is 9 percent.

  a. What is the value of the bond to you?
  b. What happens to the value if the market's required yield to maturity on a comparable-risk bond (i) increases to 11 percent or (ii) decreases to 7 percent?
  c. Under which of the circumstances in part b should you purchase the bond?

Determinants of Interest Rates

23. **(Related to Checkpoint 6) (Inflation and interest rates)** What would you expect the nominal rate of interest to be if the real rate is 4.5 percent and the expected inflation rate is 7.3 percent?

24. **(Inflation and interest rates)** Assume the expected inflation rate is 3.8 percent. If the current real rate of interest is 6.4 percent, what should the nominal rate of interest be?

25. **(Inflation and interest rates)** What would you expect the nominal rate of interest to be if the real rate is 5 percent and the expected inflation rate is 3 percent?

Mini-Case

Your grandfather is retired and living on his Social Security benefits and the interest he gets from savings. However, the interest income he receives has dwindled to only 2 percent a year on his $200,000 in savings as interest rates in the economy have dropped. You have been thinking about recommending that he purchase some corporate bonds with at least part of his savings as a way of increasing his interest income.

Specifically, you have identified three corporate bond issues for your grandfather to consider. The first is an issue from the Young Corporation that pays annual interest based on a 7.8 percent coupon rate and has 10 years before it matures. The second bond was issued by Thomas Resorts and it pays 7.5 percent annual interest and has 17 years until it matures. The final bond issue was sold by Entertainment, Inc., pays an annual coupon interest payment based on a rate of 7.975 percent, and has only 4 years until it matures. All three bond issues have a $1,000 par value. After looking at the bonds' default risks and credit ratings, you have very different yields to maturity in mind for the three bond issues, as noted below.

Before recommending any of these bond issues to your grandfather you perform a number of analyses. Specifically, you want to address each of the following issues:

1. Estimate an appropriate market's required yield to maturity for each of the bond issues using the table of credit spreads reported in Table 4.

	Young Corp.	Thomas Resorts, Inc.	Entertainment, Inc.
Coupon interest rates	7.8%	7.5%	7.975%
Years to maturity	10	17	4
Current market price	$1,030	$973	$1,035
Par value	$1,000	$1,000	$1,000
Bond rating	AA	B	BBB

2. The bond issues are currently selling for the following amounts:

Young Corp	$1,030
Thomas Resorts	$ 973
Entertainment, Inc.	$1,035

What is the yield to maturity for each bond?

3. Given your estimate of the proper discount rate, what is your estimate of the value of each of the bonds? In light of the prices recorded above, which issue do you think is most attractively priced?

4. How would the values of the bonds change if (i) the market's required yield to maturity on a comparable-risk bond increases 3 percentage points or (ii) decreases 3 percentage points? Which of the bond issues is the most sensitive to changes in the rate of interest?

5. What are some of the things you can conclude from these computations?

6. Which one(s) of the bonds (if any) would you recommend to your grandfather? Explain.

Photo Credits

Credits are listed in order of appearance.

Hudyma Natallia/Shutterstock; Monart Design/Fotolia

Stock Valuation

From Chapter 10 of *Financial Management: Principles and Applications*, Twelfth Edition. Sheridan Titman, Arthur J. Keown, and John D. Martin.

Stock Valuation

Chapter **Outline**

1 Common Stock ——————————→ **Objective 1.** Identify the basic characteristics and features of common stock and use the discounted cash flow model to value common shares.

2 The Comparables Approach ——————→ **Objective 2.** Use the price-to-earnings (P/E) ratio to value common stock.
to Valuing Common Stock

3 Preferred Stock ——————————→ **Objective 3.** Identify the basic characteristics and features of preferred stock and value preferred shares.

4 The Stock Market ——————————→ **Objective 4.** List the secondary markets for common stock.

The determinants of stock valuation reflect the first three principles of finance: P Principle 1: **Money Has a Time Value;** P Principle 2: **There Is a Risk–Reward Tradeoff;** P Principle 3: **Cash Flows Are the Source of Value.** We apply these principles to the valuation of a firm's common and preferred stock in this chapter. And because stock is typically sold in public markets where many investors are actively looking for under- and overpriced stock to purchase or sell, the fourth basic principle of finance comes into play. The fundamental implication of P Principle 4: **Market Prices Reflect Information** is that market prices are usually pretty good reflections of the value of the underlying shares of stock. In addition, P Principle 5: **Individuals Respond to Incentives** takes on importance because managers respond to incentives in their contracts, and if these incentives are not properly aligned with those of the firm's shareholders, they may not make decisions consistent with increasing shareholder value.

If success is having your firm's name become a verb, then the founders of Google, Inc. (GOOG), Sergey Brin and Larry Page, have reached the very pinnacle of success. If you don't know something and want to learn about it, what do you do? Go to an encyclopedia? No, you *google* it. If you're writing a paper for a class, you *google* the topic; if you're buying a product, you *google* it to find which brand is best; and, if you're considering a new doctor, you may even *google* him or her. By almost any criteria, Google is a phenomenal success story. But Google's early years were actually much like the early years of any start-up company.

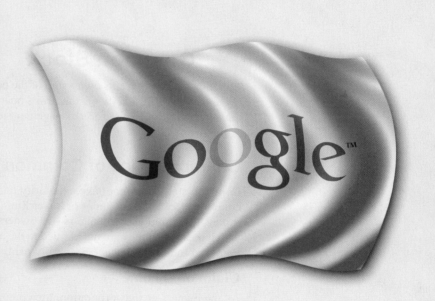

In early 2004, Google's board of directors deliberated over how to translate their firm's success into money. The answer came with their decision to sell some of Google's stock to the public. They decided to auction off about 20 million shares of Google's common stock for between $108 and $135 per share. The offering was a great success; the stock price doubled within the next year and then doubled again the following year.

The value of Google's stock has fluctuated substantially. For example, in late 2007 it reached a high of over $700 per share and then fell to less than half of that amount within a year, and by 2013 it had recovered and set a new all-time high closing above $800. As an investor considering the purchase of shares of Google (or any other company), one would want to understand the fundamental determinants of its value. As we will discuss in this chapter, that value is determined by the time value of money, the risk–reward tradeoff, and the value of expected cash flows.

We begin with an examination of the characteristics of common stock followed by a look at its valuation. Here we not only consider the discounted cash flow method to value a firm's stock but also look at some common market-based ratios, such as the price-to-earnings ratio, used to value common stock. We then move on to an examination of the characteristics and valuation of preferred stock. Finally, we conclude with a discussion of the various stock markets, where the shares of stock are traded after they are issued.

Regardless of Your Major...

"Getting Your Fair Share"

Are you interested in starting your own business? If you are, then you are probably aware that you share this dream with millions of college students who are majoring in almost every conceivable major. If you start a company that becomes a success, at some point, you will want to know the value of your ownership interest. When this occurs, you will need to know how equity securities are valued in the financial markets. For example, when Larry and Sergey were just getting started, they needed money to expand. Fortunately one of their professors linked them up with one of the founders of Sun Microsystems, Andy Bechtolsheim. After a short demonstration in Larry's dorm room, Andy was impressed with the potential and handed them a check for $100,000—after which Larry and Sergey immediately filed incorporation papers so they could cash the check made out to Google. But how did Larry and Sergey decide how much of Google an investment of $100,000 would buy? Should $100,000 buy 10 percent of the business? Is this is a fair price? To answer this question, you need to know the value of Google, and to do that you need to know something about finance and equity valuation.

Your Turn: See Study Question 1.

1   Common Stock

Common stock represents ownership of the corporation. So, the common stockholders are the owners of the firm. They elect the firm's board of directors, who in turn appoint the firm's top management team. The firm's management team then carries out the day-to-day management of the firm.

Characteristics of Common Stock

Common stock does not have a maturity date, but exists as long as the firm does. Nor does common stock have an upper or lower limit on its dividend payments. In the event of bankruptcy, the common stockholders—as owners of the corporation—have the most junior claim, which means that they are not entitled to the assets of the firm until the firm's debt holders and preferred shareholders have been fully paid.

Claim on Income

As the owners of the corporation, the common shareholders have the right to the firm's income that remains after bondholders and preferred stockholders have been paid. The common shareholders either receive cash payments in the form of dividends or, if the firm's management reinvests its earnings back into the firm, the shareholders will reap any increase in value that results from the reinvested earnings.

The right to residual income has both advantages and disadvantages for the common stockholder. The main advantage is that the potential return is unlimited. Once the claims of the more senior securities (bonds and preferred stock) have been satisfied, all the earnings that remain belong to common stockholders. The disadvantage, of course, is that there may be little or nothing left after paying the bondholders their principal and interest and paying the preferred dividends to the preferred shareholders.

Claim on Assets

Just as common stock has a residual claim on income, it also has a residual claim on assets in the case of liquidation. However, the claims of common shareholders get paid only after the claims of debt holders and preferred stockholders have been satisfied. Unfortunately, when bankruptcy does occur, the claims of the common shareholders generally go unsatisfied. This residual claim on assets adds to the risk of common stock. Thus, although common stock has historically provided a higher return than other securities, averaging 9.8 percent compounded annually from 1926 through 2011, the returns are also much riskier.

The Business of Life

Does a Stock by Any Other Name Smell as Sweet?

When you look up the price of a stock on such sites as The Wall Street Journal Online (*www.wsj.com*), Smart Money (*www.smartmoney.com*), Yahoo! Finance (*finance.yahoo.com*), or Market Watch (*www.marketwatch.com*), you'll notice that stocks are identified by ticker symbols, abbreviations that can be used to identify each company's stock. In 2013, the investor relations people at Interface, Inc., a worldwide carpet tile company decided their ticker symbol didn't fit their company, so they changed from "IFSIA" to "TILE." Why? Because it seemed to fit the company well.

Interestingly, recent research shows that companies who have chosen clever ticker symbols have outperformed the market. But any suggestion of a cause-and-effect relationship is likely to be nonsense. But there is no question, tickers symbols can make

investors chuckle or simply make them think of the underlying stock—think Dynamic Materials, an explosives-related company's use of BOOM, Sealy with ZZ, National Beverage's use of FIZZ, Advanced Medical Optics, Inc.'s use of EYE, Harley-Davidson's use of HOG, or PORK, the ticker for Premium Standard Farms, Inc. Other symbols may be a bit more cerebral, for example, AngloGold Ashanti, which specializes in exploration and production of gold uses AU as its symbol which is also the atomic symbol for gold. In one study, researchers at Princeton University found that companies with pronounceable symbols performed better after they first go public than companies with symbols that can't be said as a word. In another study, a portfolio of stocks with the cleverest symbols returned 23.6% compounded annually, compared with 12.3% for a hypothetical index of all NYSE and Nasdaq stocks. The clever stocks included such well-known stocks as Anheuser Busch Cos. (BUD) and Southwest Airlines Co. (LUV), along with companies eventually delisted or acquired, such as Grand Havana Enterprises, Inc. (PUFF) and Lion Country Safari (GRRR).

Source: Alex Head, Gary Smith, and Julia Wilson, "Would a Stock By Any Other Ticker Smell as Sweet?" Pamona College, Clairmont, CA 91711, http://economics-files.pomona.edu/GarySmith/Econ190/tickers.pdf; "46 Amusing ETF Ticker Symbols" by Daniela Pylypczak, Jul 17, 2012, http://finance.yahoo.com/news/46-amusing-etf-ticker-symbols-110013597.html; Selena Maranjian, "What's In a Ticker Symbol? More Than You Might Think," The Motley Fool, October 13, 2012, http://www.dailyfinance.com/2012/10/13/funny-ticker-symbols-companies/; Selena Maranjian, "Wall Street Actually Does Have a Sense of Humor," October 20, 2011 The Motley Fool, http://www.dailyfinance.com/2011/09/20/wall-street-actually-does-have-a-sense-of-humor/; and Jennifer Valentino, "Does Stock by Any Other Name Smell as Sweet?" *Wall Street Journal*, September 28, 2006, p. C1.

Your Turn: See Study Question 5.

Voting Rights

The common shareholders elect the board of directors and are in general the only security holders given a vote. Early in the twentieth century, it was not uncommon for a firm to issue two classes of common stock that were identical, except that only one carried voting rights. For example, the Great Atlantic and Pacific Tea Co. (GAP) had two such classes of common stock. This practice was virtually eliminated by three developments: (1) the Public Utility Holding Company Act of 1935, which gave the Securities and Exchange Commission the power to require that newly issued common stock carry voting rights; (2) the New York Stock Exchange's refusal to list common stock without voting privileges; and (3) investor demand for the inclusion of voting rights. However, with the merger boom of the 1980s, dual classes of common stock with different voting rights again emerged, this time as a defensive tactic used to prevent takeovers. Today, for example, Google, Inc. (GOOG) has two classes of common stock, which gives majority control to the firm's top three executives.[1] Likewise with Facebook (FB), just before Facebook went public in 2012, it created two classes of shares, and those owned by founder Mark Zuckerberg had far more voting power than the ones sold to outside shareholders. In fact, at the time of Facebook's initial public offering, Zuckerberg only owned 18 percent of the company but had control of 57 percent of the voting power.

Common shareholders not only have the right to elect the board of directors, but they also must approve any change in the corporate charter. A typical charter change might involve the authorization to issue new stock or perhaps engage in a merger.

---

[1] Google's Class A stock has one vote per share and its Class B stock, owned only by Chief Executive Eric Schmidt and founders Larry Page and Sergey Brin, has 10 votes per share. In late 2011, Zynga, the producer of FarmVille and Words With Friends did the same thing, issuing one class to the founder with 70 votes per share and another to the public with one vote per share.

Voting for directors and charter changes occurs at the corporation's annual meeting. Whereas shareholders may vote in person, the majority generally votes by proxy. A **proxy** gives a designated party the temporary power of attorney to vote for the signee at the corporation's annual meeting. The firm's management generally solicits proxy votes, and if the shareholders are satisfied with their performance, managers have little problem securing them. However, in times of financial distress or when management takeovers are being attempted, battles between rival groups for proxy votes often occur.

Although each share of stock generally carries the same number of votes, the voting procedure is not always the same from company to company. The two procedures commonly used are majority and cumulative voting. With **majority voting**, each share of stock allows the shareholder one vote, and each position on the board of directors is voted on separately. Because each member of the board of directors is elected by a simple majority, a majority of shares has the power to elect the entire board of directors.

With **cumulative voting**, each share of stock allows the shareholder a number of votes equal to the number of directors being elected. The shareholder can then cast all of his or her votes for a single candidate or split them among the various candidates. The advantage of a cumulative voting procedure is that it gives minority shareholders the power to elect a director.

Agency Costs and Common Stock

In theory, the common stockholders elect the corporation's board of directors and the board of directors picks the management team. As a result, shareholders effectively control the firm through their representatives on the board of directors. In reality, the system frequently works the other way around. Shareholders are offered a slate of nominees selected by management from which to choose a board of directors. The end result is that management effectively selects the directors, who then may have more allegiance to the managers than to the shareholders. This in turn sets up the potential for agency problems.

Recall from our discussion of ▣ Principle 5: **Individuals Respond to Incentives** that even though managers are employees and as such owe their loyalty to the firm's stockholders (its owners), if their incentives are not properly aligned with those of the firm's shareholders, they may put their personal interests ahead of those of the firm's owners. This is referred to as the *agency problem* and is particularly important in very large corporations that are run by professional managers who own only a small percentage of the firm's shares. When this is the case, managers are likely to avoid unpleasant tasks, such as reducing the number of employees; they may take less profitable projects that they personally like while avoiding very risky projects that may jeopardize their jobs.

The costs associated with the manager-stockholder (owner) agency problem are difficult to quantify, but occasionally we see indirect evidence of its importance. For instance, if investors feel that the management of a firm has been damaging shareholder value, we would observe a positive stock price response to the removal of that management team. For example, in 2005, on the day following the death of Roy E. Farmer, who had been chairman and president of the coffee roaster Farmers Brothers (FARM), the firm's stock price rose about 27 percent. Many investors felt that Farmer was not an effective CEO and that his decision to hold a huge cash reserve rather than using the cash to either expand the business or distribute the cash to the firm's stockholders had been harming the shareholders. So with his demise, investors perceived the chance to change the direction of the firm in ways that would increase its value.

Valuing Common Stock Using the Discounted Dividend Model

As with bonds, a common stock's value is equal to the present value of all future cash flows that the stockholder expects to receive from owning the share of stock. However, in contrast to bonds, common stock does *not* offer its owners a promised interest payment, maturity payment, or dividend. For common stock, the dividend is based on (1) the profitability of the firm, and (2) management's decision as to whether it will pay dividends or retain the firm's earnings in order to grow the firm.

Thus, dividends will vary with a firm's profitability and its stage of growth. In a company's early years, little if any dividends are typically paid because all of the firm's cash flow is reinvested to finance the firm's growth. As the company matures, additional investment opportunities become less attractive, and the financial manager will typically begin paying more and more dividends to the common stockholders.

Because there is no promised dividend, common stock is valued by discounting the dividend stream that the firm is *expected* to pay to its shareholders. These expected dividends are discounted back to the present using the investor's required or expected rate of return, which is the rate of return that investors expect to receive from an investment of equal risk. We will refer to this expected rate of return as the *investor's required rate of return*.

Three-Step Procedure for Valuing Common Stock

To value common stock, we will use a three-step procedure.

Step 1. Estimate the amount and timing of the receipt of the future cash flows the common stock is *expected* to provide.

Step 2. Evaluate the riskiness of the common stock's future dividends, and determine the rate of return an investor would expect to receive from a comparable-risk investment. The expected return of a comparable investment is the stock's required rate of return.

Step 3. Calculate the present value of the expected dividends by discounting them back to the present at the stock's required rate of return.

Let's take a look at these three steps. Each of these three steps relies on one of our basic principles: Step 1 relies on P Principle 3: **Cash Flows Are the Source of Value**, Step 2 relies on P Principle 2: **There Is a Risk–Return Tradeoff**, and Step 3 relies on P Principle 1: **Money Has a Time Value.** In Step 1, we estimate the amount and timing of future cash flows. If you bought a share of common stock and never sold it, the only cash flow you would ever receive would be the dividends that the firm paid. Step 2 involves an estimate of the required rate of return, whereas Step 3 involves calculating the present value of the future cash flows, discounted at the required rate of return. What this all means is that *the value of a common stock is equal to the present value of all future dividends.*

Not only do the first three principles come into play in determining the value of a share of common stock, because stock is typically sold in public markets where many investors are actively looking for under- and overpriced stock to purchase or sell, the fourth basic principle of finance also comes into play. The fundamental implication of P Principle 4: **Market Prices Reflect Information** is that market prices are usually pretty good reflections of the value of the underlying shares of stock.

Basic Concept of the Stock Valuation Model

To illustrate the basic concept of stock valuation, consider a situation in which we are valuing a share of common stock that we plan to hold for only one year. The stock pays a $1.75 dividend at the end of the year and is expected to have a price of $50.00 in one year when we plan to sell it. If the investor requires a 15 percent rate of return from investing in the stock, the value of the stock today is simply the present value of the dividend plus the selling price of the stock, discounted back one year using a 15 percent rate of return:

$$\frac{\text{Value of Common}}{\text{Stock Today}} = \frac{\$1.75 + 50.00}{(1 + .15)^1} = \$45.00$$

In this instance, the share of stock is worth $45.00 today. Now, let's assume that we decide to hold the stock for two years such that we receive two annual dividends of $1.75 and then sell the share of stock for $55.75. What value should we assign to the stock today if we plan on holding it for two years? We find the answer as follows:

$$\frac{\text{Value of Common}}{\text{Stock Today}} = \frac{\$1.75}{(1 + .15)^1} + \frac{\$1.75 + 55.75}{(1 + .15)^2} = \$45.00$$

In both examples the value of the share of stock today is equal to the present value of future dividends, plus the selling price of the stock at the end of the holding period. This selling price is simply the present value of the dividends for all subsequent periods. For example, based on what we know about this stock, what should the price of the firm's stock be at the end of Year 1?

The answer is found by discounting the dividend for Year 2 and the price at the end of Year 2 back one period to the end of Year 1:

$$\frac{\text{Value of Common}}{\text{Stock at Year 1}} = \frac{\$1.75 + 55.75}{(1 + .15)^1} = \$50.00$$

The important learning point is that the value of a share of common stock can be thought of as the present value of future dividends where there are an infinite number of years (∞) over which dividends are received.

$$\frac{\text{Value of}}{\text{Common Stock}} = \frac{\text{Dividend for Year 1}}{\left(1 + \dfrac{\text{Stockholder's}}{\text{Required Rate of Return}}\right)^1} + \frac{\text{Dividend for Year 2}}{\left(1 + \dfrac{\text{Stockholder's}}{\text{Required Rate of Return}}\right)^2}$$

$$+ \frac{\text{Dividend for Year 3}}{\left(1 + \dfrac{\text{Stockholder's}}{\text{Required Rate of Return}}\right)^3} + \cdots + \frac{\text{Dividend for Year } \infty}{\left(1 + \dfrac{\text{Stockholder's}}{\text{Required Rate of Return}}\right)^\infty}$$

Valuing a share of common stock using this general discounted cash flow model is made difficult by virtue of the fact that the analyst has to forecast each of the future dividends. However, the forecasting problem is greatly simplified if the future dividends are expected to grow at a fixed or constant rate each year.

The Constant Dividend Growth Rate Model

If the firm's cash dividends grow by a constant rate each year, then the discounted value of these growing dividends forms the basis for a common stock valuation model that can be defined as follows:

$$\frac{\text{Value of Common}}{\text{Stock in Year 0}} = \frac{\text{Dividend Paid in Year 0}\left(1 + \dfrac{\text{Dividend}}{\text{Growth Rate}}\right)^1}{\left(1 + \dfrac{\text{Stockholder's}}{\text{Required Rate of Return}}\right)^1} + \frac{\text{Dividend Paid in Year 0}\left(1 + \dfrac{\text{Dividend}}{\text{Growth Rate}}\right)^2}{\left(1 + \dfrac{\text{Stockholder's}}{\text{Required Rate of Return}}\right)^2}$$

$$+ \frac{\text{Dividend Paid in Year 0}\left(1 + \dfrac{\text{Dividend}}{\text{Growth Rate}}\right)^3}{\left(1 + \dfrac{\text{Stockholder's}}{\text{Required Rate of Return}}\right)^3} + \cdots + \frac{\text{Dividend Paid in Year 0}\left(1 + \dfrac{\text{Dividend}}{\text{Growth Rate}}\right)^\infty}{\left(1 + \dfrac{\text{Stockholder's}}{\text{Required Rate of Return}}\right)^\infty} \qquad \textbf{(1)}$$

Fortunately, Equation (1) can be simplified greatly using the present value of a growing perpetuity if dividends grow each year at a constant rate, g.

This **constant dividend growth rate model** of common stock valuation is defined in Equation (2) as follows:

$$V_{cs} = \frac{\text{Dividend in Year 0}\left(1 + \dfrac{\text{Dividend}}{\text{Growth Rate}}\right)}{\dfrac{\text{Stockholder's Required}}{\text{Rate of Return}} - \dfrac{\text{Dividend}}{\text{Growth Rate}}} = \frac{\text{Dividend in Year 1}}{\dfrac{\text{Stockholder's Required}}{\text{Rate of Return}} - \dfrac{\text{Dividend}}{\text{Growth Rate}}} \qquad \textbf{(2)}$$

Figure 1 provides a quick reference guide to Equation (2).

Although we do not expect a firm's dividends to grow forever at a constant rate, this model has value and is used in the real world. A commonly used variant of this model is known as a three-stage growth model. With a three-stage growth model, rather than assuming a constant rate forever, a constant rate is assumed for a number of years, perhaps 5 years, after which the growth rate changes, continuing on for a specified number of years, perhaps

Figure 1

A Quick Reference Guide for the Constant Dividend Growth Rate Valuation Model

If the rate of growth in common stock dividends is expected to be constant into the indefinite future and this rate of growth is less than the common stockholders' required rate of return, the discounted cash flow valuation model for common stock reduces to the following simple formula:

$$V_{cs} = \frac{D_0(1 + g)}{r_{cs} - g} = \frac{D_1}{r_{cs} - g} \qquad (2)$$

Definitions and Assumptions:

- V_{cs} = the value of a share of common stock, which is equal to the present value of all future expected dividends.
- D_0 = the most recent annual cash dividend received by the common stockholder that was paid in the year the valuation is being done (Year 0).
- g = the expected annual rate of growth in the cash dividend payment, which is assumed to be constant forever.
- $D_1 = D_0(1 + g)$ = the expected dividend for the end of Year 1.
- r_{cs} = the common stockholder's required rate of return for the shares of common stock. Note that this is not a market's required yield or promised rate of return but is the rate of return the investor expects to earn from investing in the firm's stock. This expected rate of return reflects the riskiness of the stock's future dividends.

>> END FIGURE 1

10 more years, after which it changes again and stays at that final rate forever. The implications of this more complicated model are the same as those of the simple constant growth model—that is, the level of dividends, the annual dividend rate of growth, and the common stockholder's required rate of return determine the value of the firm's common stock.

What Causes Stock Prices to Go Up and Down?

We can use the constant dividend growth rate model of stock valuation in Equation (2) to develop a better understanding of what causes stock prices to move up and down.

$$V_{cs} = \frac{D_0(1 + g)}{r_{cs} - g} = \frac{\text{Dividend in Year 1}}{\text{Stockholder's Required} - \text{Growth}} \qquad (2)$$
$$\text{Rate of Return} \quad \text{Rate}$$

There are three variables on the right-hand side of the above stock valuation model that drive share value, V_{cs}. These are the most recent dividend (D_0), the investor's required rate of return (r_{cs}), and the expected rate of growth in future dividends (g). Note that the most recent dividend has already been paid so it can't change, and thus this variable is not a source of variation or changes in the stock price. This leaves two variables, r_{cs} and g, that can vary and lead to changes in stock prices. Thus, to understand what causes stock prices to go up and down, we need to consider changes in the stockholder's required rate of return, r_{cs}, and the growth rate in future dividend payments, g.

Determinants of the Investor's Required Rate of Return

The investor's required rate of return is determined by two key factors—the level of interest rates in the economy and the risk of the firm's stock. The Capital Asset Pricing Model (CAPM) can be used to describe the determinants of investor-required rates of return. The expected or required rate of return of an investment using the CAPM is expressed as follows:

$$\frac{\text{Expected Rate}}{\text{of Return}} = \frac{\text{Risk-Free Rate}}{\text{of Interest}} + \frac{\text{Common Stock}}{\text{Beta Coefficient}}\left(\frac{\text{Expected Rate of Return}}{\text{on the Market Portfolio}} - \frac{\text{Risk-Free Rate}}{\text{of Interest}}\right)$$

Valuing Common Stock

Consider the valuation of a share of common stock that paid a $2 dividend at the end of last year and is expected to pay a cash dividend every year from now to infinity. Each year, the dividends are expected to grow at a rate of 10 percent. Based on an assessment of the riskiness of the common stock, the investor's required rate of return is 15 percent. What is the value of this common stock?

STEP 1: Picture the problem

With a growing perpetuity, a timeline doesn't have an ending point but goes on forever, with the cash flows growing at a constant rate period after period, or in this case, year after year:

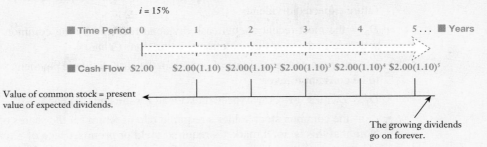

The growing dividends go on forever.

STEP 2: Decide on a solution strategy

Because a share of stock can be viewed as the present value of a growing perpetuity, the equation for the value of a share of stock, which is presented in Equation (2), looks exactly like the equation for a growing perpetuity. Because this equation only involves division, there is no need to look at an Excel solution or any unique keystrokes with a financial calculator.

STEP 3: Solve

In this problem we must first determine D_1, the dividend next period. We know they paid a $2 dividend at the end of last year and dividends are expected to grow at a rate of 10 percent forever. Because the $2 dividend was paid last period, $2 is D_0, and we are looking for D_1. Thus,

$$D_1 = D_0(1 + g) = \$2(1.10) = 2.20$$

Substituting $D_1 = \$2.20$, $g = .10$, and $r_{cs} = .15$ into Equation (2), we get the following result:

$$V_{cs} = \frac{\$2.20}{.15 - .10} = \$44$$

Thus, the value of the common stock is $44.

STEP 4: Analyze

As you can see, once we assume that dividends will grow at a constant rate forever, the equation for the value of a share of stock boils down to just three variables, and one of them, D_1, is simply the dividend that already took place times $(1 + g)$. That means that changes in the dividend growth rate, g, and the required rate of return, r_{cs}, will push the stock price up and down. Certainly, this is not a perfect formula—after all, we've assumed that dividends will grow at a constant rate forever and that simply isn't realistic. But it does allow us to take an unmanageable formula and boil it down to something pretty simple and as a result see what factors move stock prices up and down.

STEP 5: Check yourself

What is the value of a share of common stock that paid a $6 dividend at the end of last year and is expected to pay a cash dividend every year from now to infinity, with that dividend growing at a rate of 5 percent per year, if the investors' required rate of return is 12 percent on that stock?

ANSWER: $90.

Your Turn: For more practice, do related **Study Problem** 3 at the end of this chapter.   >> END Checkpoint 1

A Quick Reference Guide for the Capital Asset Pricing Model

The Capital Asset Pricing Model, CAPM, is deceptively simple. It states that the expected rate of return on any risky investment can be thought of as the sum of the risk-free rate of interest and a risk premium. The risk premium, in turn, is determined by the market risk premium for the market portfolio and the beta coefficient for the investment.

$$r_{cs} = r_f + \beta_{cs}[E(r_m) - r_f]$$

Important Definitions and Concepts:

- r_{cs} = the investor's required rate of return on a firm's common stock.
- r_f = the risk-free rate of interest.
- β_{cs} = the beta of the stock.
- $E(r_m) - r_f$ = the market risk premium or the difference in the expected rate of return on the market portfolio, $E(r_m)$, and the risk-free rate of interest, r_f.

>> END FIGURE 2

Figure 2 contains a quick reference guide to the CAPM, including definitions for each of the key terms.

If the risk-free rate rises, perhaps reacting to an increase in anticipated inflation, other things remaining the same, the investor's required rate of return will rise and the stock price will fall. Similarly, if the systematic risk of a stock increases, then the investor's required rate of return will rise accordingly and, all else remaining the same, the share price will fall.

Determinants of the Growth Rate of Future Dividends

The growth rate of expected future dividends can also change and lead to a change in the stock price. For example, if Merck (MRK), the large pharmaceutical firm, were to get approval to market a revolutionary cancer-fighting drug, this would certainly raise investor expectations regarding the future growth rate in its earnings and dividends, which would in turn lead to a higher price for Merck's stock.

The key determinants of a firm's growth opportunities relate to the rates of return the firm expects to earn when it reinvests earnings (the return on equity or ROE), and the proportion of firm's earnings that it reinvests (retains or does not pay out in cash dividends), which is known as the retention ratio, b. To better understand this, consider the case where the ROE the firm expects to earn on reinvested earnings and the proportion of firm earnings that is retained and reinvested, b, are both assumed to be constant in the future. The growth rate in the firm's dividends, g, can then be thought of as simply the product of the firm's ROE and the ratio of the earnings it retains (the retention ratio, b). Because we will find this formula useful later, it is worthwhile defining the growth rate formally as follows:

$$\frac{\text{Rate of Growth}}{\text{in Dividends } (g)} = \frac{\text{Retention}}{\text{Ratio } (b)} \times \frac{\text{Rate of Return}}{\text{on Equity } (ROE)}$$

where the retention ratio, b, is equal to one minus the dividend payout ratio (D_1/E_1):

$$\frac{\text{Rate of Growth}}{\text{in Dividends } (g)} = \left(1 - \frac{\text{Dividend}}{\text{Payout Ratio}}\right) \times \frac{\text{Rate of Return}}{\text{on Equity } (ROE)} \tag{3}$$

Figure 3 contains a quick reference guide to Equation (3).

A Quick Reference Guide for the Growth Rate in Earnings and Dividends
The rate of growth a firm can expect in its future dividends is a function of how much of the firm's earnings are reinvested in the firm (i.e., the dividend retention ratio, b), and the rate of return the firm is expected to earn on the reinvested earnings (ROE).

$$g = (1 - D_1/E_1) \times ROE \qquad (3)$$

Important Definitions and Concepts:

- g = the expected annual rate of growth in dividends.
- D_1/E_1 = the dividend payout ratio reflecting the ratio of cash dividends to be paid next period divided by the firm's earnings.
- $b = (1 - D_1/E_1)$, which is the proportion of firm earnings or net income that is retained and reinvested in the firm.
- ROE = the return on equity earned when the firm reinvests a portion of its earnings back into the firm.
- Equation (3) requires that the retention ratio, b, and ROE remain constant for all future periods.

>> END FIGURE 3

We now have the tools of financial analysis to value common stock assuming that the dividends grow at a constant rate in perpetuity, which are shown as follows:

Tools of Financial Analysis—Common Stock Valuation

Name of Tool	Formula	What It Tells You
Common stock valuation	$V_{cs} = \dfrac{D_1}{(1+r_{cs})^1} + \dfrac{D_2}{(1+r_{cs})^2} + \cdots + \dfrac{D_n}{(1+r_{cs})^n} + \cdots + \dfrac{D_\infty}{(1+r_{cs})^\infty}$	• The value of a share of stock is the present value of the expected dividends discounted using the investor's required or expected rate of return.
Common stock valuation assuming constant dividend growth	$V_{cs} = \dfrac{\text{Dividend in Year 1}}{\text{Required Rate of Return} - \text{Dividend Growth Rate}}$ $V_{cs} = \dfrac{D_1}{r_{cs} - g}$	• What the value of a share of stock would be if dividends grow at a constant rate in perpetuity • All else held constant: • If the required rate of return, r_{cs}, goes up, the value of the stock goes down. • If the growth rate, g, goes up, the value of the stock climbs.
Investor's required rate of return using the CAPM	$r_{cs} = r_f + \beta[E(r_m) - r_f]$	• A stock's required rate of return is a function of the risk-free rate and a return to compensate for the risk of the firm's stock.
Dividend growth rate	$\text{Rate of Growth in Dividends }(g) = \left(\dfrac{\text{Retention}}{\text{Ratio}(b)}\right) \times \dfrac{\text{Rate of Return}}{\text{on Equity }(ROE)}$ $g = (1 - D_1/E_1) \times ROE$	• Estimation of a company's growth rate to be used in valuing the stock • The growth rate of future dividends is dependent upon (1) the proportion of the firm's earnings that are reinvested, and (2) the rate of return the firm earns on earnings that it reinvests.

Concept Check | 1

1. What are the attributes of common stock that distinguish it from bonds and preferred stock?
2. What does agency cost mean with respect to the owners of a firm's common stock?
3. Describe the three-step process for valuing common stock using the discounted dividend model.

 # The Comparables Approach to Valuing Common Stock

The discounted dividend valuation model provides a good framework for estimating the value of common stock and for understanding what drives stock prices up and down. However, this approach requires a number of inputs, such as the rate of growth and the discount rate, that are difficult to estimate, especially for companies like Google (GOOG), eBay (EBAY), and Amazon.com (AMZN) that do not yet pay cash dividends. For this reason, analysts often use market comparables or "comps" to estimate firm values. This method estimates the value of the firm's stock as a multiple of some measure of firm performance, such as the firm's earnings per share, book value per share, sales per share, or cash flow per share, where the multiple is determined by the multiples observed from comparable companies. By far the most common performance metric is earnings per share, which means that the values are determined from the price-to-earnings ratio, or the earnings multiplier, of comparable firms.

Defining the P/E Ratio Valuation Model

Investors regularly use the **price/earnings ratio** (sometimes referred to as the *P/E ratio* or *P/E multiple*) as a measure of a stock's relative value. The price/earnings ratio, or earnings multiplier, is simply the price per share divided by the company's earnings per share. In effect, it is a relative value model because it tells the investor how many dollars investors are willing to pay for each dollar of the company's earnings. The earnings per share in the denominator will be either the earnings per share for the most recent four quarters or the expected earnings per share over the next four quarters.

We write it as:

$$\underset{V_{cs}}{\text{Value of Common Stock,}} = \left(\begin{array}{c} \text{Appropriate} \\ \text{Price/Earnings Ratio} \end{array} \right) \times \left(\begin{array}{c} \text{Estimated Earnings} \\ \text{per Share for Year 1} \end{array} \right) = \frac{P}{E_1} \times E_1 \qquad \textbf{(4)}$$

Figure 4 contains a quick reference guide to Equation (4).

P/E ratios allow us to express the price of stocks in relative terms—that is, the price per dollar of earnings—which makes it easier to compare one stock to another. The investor can decide what an appropriate P/E ratio is for the stock being valued by looking at the P/E ratio of other stocks, and then, based on the anticipated earnings, determine what the price of the stock should be. As a result, it takes the emphasis off determining the price per share and puts it on determining a fair P/E ratio.

What Determines the P/E Ratio for a Stock?

How do you determine an appropriate P/E ratio for a specific stock? One obvious answer would be to look at the P/E ratio of similar stocks.

As a first step we should look at the P/E ratio for the entire market—the P/E ratio of U.S. stock market indexes such as the S&P 500 is typically between 15 and 25, depending on the strength of the economy, the level of interest rates, the size of the federal deficit, and the inflation rate; however, recently, it has been lower. This overall market P/E ratio can then be adjusted depending on the specific prospects for the individual stock. For example, if the growth potential is above average, we would adjust the P/E ratio upward—but how much higher is the real question. Looking at the P/E ratios of firms of similar size in the same industry probably provides the most useful information.

| Figure 4 |

A Quick Reference Guide for the Price/Earnings Stock Valuation Model

The price/earnings stock valuation model is sometimes referred to as a relative valuation model that is based on comparable-firm valuations. This reflects the fact that the price/earnings ratio used to value the stock measures value relative to firm earnings and is chosen by looking at comparable firms.

$$V_{CS} = \frac{P}{E_1} \times E_1 \qquad (4)$$

Important Definitions and Concepts:

- V_{CS} = the value of the common stock of the firm.
- P/E_1 = the price/earnings ratio for the firm based on the current price per share divided by earnings for the end of Year 1.[2]
- E_1 = estimated earnings per share of common stock for the end of Year 1.

>> END FIGURE 4

P/E ratios can vary widely from stock to stock. For example, at the same time IBM (IBM) had a P/E ratio of 14, E-Trade (ETFC) had a P/E ratio of 37, Coca-Cola's (COKE) was 22, and Ford's (F) was 2.6—all in all a pretty wide range of P/E ratios! The question you might ask now is why anyone would pay $37 for every $1 of earnings that E-Trade made, but only $2.60 for every dollar of earnings that Ford made. As we now illustrate, different P/E ratios arise from differences in the risk and earnings growth expectations of the firms being compared.

To open our discussion of the determinants of a firm's P/E ratio, let's first review the constant dividend growth model of stock value presented earlier in Equation (2):

$$V_{cs} = \frac{D_0(1 + g)}{r_{cs} - g} = \frac{\text{Dividend in Year 1}}{\text{Stockholder's Required}\ -\ \text{Growth}} \qquad (2)$$
$$\text{Rate of Return} \qquad \text{Rate}$$

Recall that D_1 is the dividend expected at the end of the year, r_{cs} is the investor's required rate of return, and g is the expected rate of growth in dividends. If we assume that the current market price of the firm's shares (P) is equal to the value of the firm's shares, V_{cs} (i.e., the present value of expected future dividends), we can rewrite Equation (2) as follows:

$$P = \frac{D_1}{r_{cs} - g}$$

We now have a formula for the price of the firm's common stock. Let's divide both sides of this equation by our estimated earnings per share for next year, E_1, to find the P/E ratio, as follows:

$$\frac{P}{E_1} = \frac{D_1/E_1}{r_{cs} - g} \qquad (5)$$

To better understand the determinants of the P/E ratio, we expand Equation (5) by substituting in for g. Recall from Equation (3) that $g = (1 - D_1/E_1) \times ROE$, and now substitute $g = (1 - D_1/E_1) \times ROE$ into Equation (5):

$$\frac{P}{E_1} = \frac{D_1/E_1}{r_{cs} - g} = \frac{D_1/E_1}{r_{cs} - [(1 - D_1/E_1) \times ROE]} \qquad (5a)$$

[2]Technically this definition of the P/E ratio is the "forward P/E" ratio because it uses predicted earnings one year hence. The P/E ratio could be calculated using the most recent 12-month period's earnings, or trailing twelve months (TTM), E_{TTM}. However, for our purposes we will follow the convention of using the end-of-period earnings; that is, trailing twelve months.

Valuing Common Stock Using the P/E Ratio

The Heels Shoe Company sells a line of athletic shoes for children and young adults, including cleats and other specialty footwear used for various types of sports. The company is privately owned and is considering the sale of a portion of its shares to the public. The company owners are currently in discussions with an investment banker who has offered to manage the sale of shares to the public. The critical point of their discussion is the price that Heels might expect to receive upon the sale of its shares. The investment banker has suggested that this price can be estimated by looking at the P/E multiples of other publicly traded firms that are in the same general business as the Heels Shoe Company and multiplying their average P/E ratio by Heels' expected earnings per share (EPS) for the coming year. Last year the Heels Shoe Company had earnings of $1.65 per share for the 12-month period ended in March, 2013. Heels' CFO estimates that company earnings for 2014 will be $1.83 a share.

The investment banker suggested that estimation of an appropriate P/E ratio involves looking at the P/E multiples for similar companies. As a preliminary step the banker suggested that Heels' management team consider the P/E multiples of three companies: Wolverine World Wide (WWW), Nike (NKE), and Steve Madden (SHOO). The current P/E ratios for these firms are as follows:

	P/E Ratio
Wolverine	18.52
Nike	19.75
Steve Madden	16.32
Average	18.20

What is your estimate of the price of Heels' shares based on the above comparable P/E ratios?

STEP 1: Picture the problem

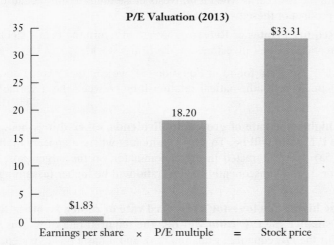

P/E Valuation (2013)

STEP 2: Decide on a solution strategy

The P/E valuation method is deceptively simple in that the analytics are simple. The estimated price per share is simply the product of the firm's estimated earnings per share for the coming year multiplied by what the analyst estimates to be an appropriate P/E ratio. That is, substitute into Equation (4):

$$V_{cs} = P/E_1 \times E_1 \qquad \text{(4)}$$

STEP 3: Solve

Substituting into Equation (4), we estimate that Heels' share price to be $33.31:

$$V_{cs} = P/E_1 \times E_1 = 18.20 \times \$1.83 = \$33.31$$

(2 CONTINUED >> ON NEXT PAGE)

STEP 4: Analyze

Based on the P/E ratios of these three comparable firms we estimate the offering price of Heels' shares to be $33.31. However, this estimate is contingent on the appropriateness of the comparable set of companies to the Heels Shoe Company. Also, because the sale of a privately held company's shares to the public can take several months, this estimate is contingent on no significant changes in the market. For example, if inflation worsens and the country slips into a recession, the P/E multiples of all public companies may fall. For this reason the final offering price for a firm's shares that are being sold to the public is typically set the night before the offering and reflects the most recent P/E ratios of comparable firms.

STEP 5: Check yourself

After some careful analysis and reflection on the valuation of the Heels' shares, the company CFO suggested that the earnings projections are too conservative and earnings for the coming year could easily jump to $2.00. What does this do to your estimate of the value of Heels' shares?

ANSWER: $36.40.

Your Turn: For more practice, do related **Study Problem** 12 at the end of this chapter.　　　　　　　>> END Checkpoint 2

Now we are ready to investigate the determinants of the P/E ratio. Specifically, looking at Equations (5) and (5a) we see that there are two fundamental determinants of a firm's P/E ratio:

1. **Growth Rate in Dividends.** The rate of growth in firm dividends is itself determined by how much of the firm's earnings are retained and reinvested (i.e., $1 - D_1/E_1$) and the rate of return the firm earns when it reinvests those funds (ROE) because the growth rate equals the product of these two variables.

2. **Investor-Required Rates of Return.** The rate of return the firm's stockholders require that the firm earn on their investment in the firm's stock, r_{cs}.

Looking at the P/E equation found in Equation (5), we can make some quick observations about the mechanical or mathematical relationships between these variables and the P/E ratio:

- **First, the higher the rate of growth in dividends, other things being the same, the higher the P/E ratio will be.** To see why, look at where g appears in the P/E equation, Equation (5a). It is subtracted in the denominator, so the larger g is, the smaller the denominator is, and consequently the P/E ratio will be higher (assuming all else is held constant).

- **Second, the higher the investor's required rate of return is, other things being the same, the smaller the P/E ratio will be.** The required rate of return, r_{cs}, is in the denominator of the P/E equation, Equation (5a), and it has a positive sign. As a result, the higher the required rate of return, r_{cs}, holding all else constant, the smaller will be the P/E ratio.

But what causes the growth rate in dividends (and earnings) and the investor's required rate of return to go up and down? These are the real determinants of the P/E ratio:

- **Firm factors impacting the investor's required rate of return, r_{cs}.** *The higher the investor's required rate of return, the lower the P/E ratio.* If the firm becomes more risky, r_{cs} will rise and, as a result, the P/E ratio will fall. Likewise, if the firm becomes less risky, r_{cs} will decline and, as a result, the P/E ratio will rise.

- **Economic or macro factors impacting the investor's required rate of return, r_{cs}.** All P/E ratios are affected by market interest rates and the general level of risk or uncertainty in the stock market. *Higher interest rates and greater uncertainty will increase the investor's required rate of return, whereas lower interest rates and less uncertainty will lower the investor's required rate of return.* As a result, when interest rates and uncertainty decline, r_{cs} will decline for all stocks and, as a result, the P/E ratios on all stocks will rise.

- **Firm factors impacting the growth rate.** The growth rate in firm dividends is itself determined by two variables—dividend policy and the profitability of the firm's investment opportunities.

  - **Dividend policy.** Firms that retain and reinvest their earnings put themselves in a position where future earnings might grow, whereas firms that pay out all their earnings in dividends cannot grow.
  - **Firm investment opportunities.** Firm earnings and future dividends can only grow if the firm's investment opportunities are good enough to offer growth opportunities. This occurs when ROE exceeds the investor's required rate of return, r_{cs}; if that's the case, the higher the return on new investments (ROE), the higher the growth rate.

An Aside on Managing for Shareholder Value

If the ROE on a firm's new investment is exactly equal to the firm's required rate of return, the new investment doesn't add any value. This is really a commonsense notion. If a company's investors require a 20 percent return on their stock, and the firm makes new investments with the same risk as its stock but that earn only 15 percent, the company's equity investors will not be pleased and the stock price will decline. The lesson here is that shareholder value is created only when the reinvested earnings generate a rate of return higher than the required risk-adjusted rate of return. This may not sound like rocket science, but you would probably be surprised to learn just how many managers lose sight of this fundamental fact of business life.

A Word of Caution about P/E Ratios

The P/E ratio is not always calculated using a consistent definition of firm earnings. Although you would expect that the measure of earnings would be based on net income calculated using Generally Accepted Accounting Principles (GAAP), this is not always the case. P/E ratios are often reported using operating earnings, economic earnings, core earnings, or ongoing earnings. These earnings numbers tend to be higher than reported net income because they add back non-recurring expenses that are labeled "one-time, exceptional, or non-cash." The rationale for using these alternative earnings numbers is that they provide a clearer picture of the firm's long-term earnings potential. The problem is that there isn't any standard approach for determining what expenses should be omitted to provide a clearer picture of the firm's performance and the performance we might be able to expect to continue in the future.

Before you move on to 3

Concept Check | 2

1. If a corporation decides to retain its earnings and reinvest them in the firm, does the market value of the firm's shares always increase? Why or why not?
2. What is the price/earnings model of equity valuation?
3. How does a firm's dividend policy affect the firm's P/E ratio?

 # Preferred Stock

Preferred stock is a hybrid security that shares some of the features of bonds and common stock. For example, like bonds that pay a contractually set interest payment, preferred stock has a contractually stated cash dividend that is paid to the preferred stockholder. Like common stock, and unlike bonds, there is no maturity for a preferred stock issue. Let's consider some of the key features of preferred stock that make it unique.

Features of Preferred Stock

In general, the size of the preferred stock dividend is fixed, and it is either stated as a dollar amount or as a percentage of the preferred stock's par value. For example, DuPont (DD.PB)

Table 1	Examples of Different Pacific Gas & Electric (PCG) Preferred Stock Issues Outstanding, February 2013					
Name	**Symbol**	**Par Value**	**Price**	**Dividend**	**Dividend Yield**
Pacific Gas & Electric 5% PF	PCG.PD	$25.00	$25.00	$1.25	5.00%
Pacific Gas & Electric 6% PF	PCG.PA	$30.00	$30.19	$1.50	4.97%
Pacific Gas & Electric 5.5% PF I	PCGprI	$25.00	$27.54	$1.375	4.99%

issued $4.50 preferred stock, meaning that the preferred stock pays $4.50 per year in dividends. On the other hand, Bank of America (BAC.PH) has 8.20 percent preferred stock outstanding with a par value of $25.00 per share. The annual dividend on the Bank of America preferred stock is $2.05, or 8.20% × $25. Keep in mind that preferred stock dividends are fixed; that is, regardless of how well the firm does, they still only pay their stated dividend. In effect, preferred stockholders do not share in any improvement in the earnings of the firm.

Multiple Classes

If a company desires, it can issue more than one class of preferred stock, and each class can have different characteristics. In fact, it is quite common for firms that issue preferred stock to issue more than one class. For example, Public Storage (PSA) has 14 different issues of preferred stock outstanding. These issues can be further differentiated in that some are convertible into common stock and others are not, and some have more seniority—that is, they get paid earlier, in the event of the issuing firm's bankruptcy. You'll notice in Table 1 that there are three listings of three different issues of preferred stock issued by Pacific Gas & Electric (PCG), each one with a different dividend and each one selling for a different price, but all with approximately the same dividend yield.

Claim on Assets and Income

In the event of bankruptcy, the claims of preferred stockholders have priority over those of common stockholders, which means that they must be paid in full before common stockholders are paid. However, they have lower priority than the claims of the firm's debt holders. In addition, the firm must pay its preferred stock dividends before it pays common stock dividends, and most preferred stocks carry a cumulative feature. **Cumulative preferred stock** requires all past unpaid preferred stock dividends to be paid before any common stock dividends are declared. Thus, in terms of risk, preferred stock is safer than common stock, but is riskier than the firm's debt.

Preferred Stock as a Hybrid Security

As we noted earlier, preferred stock has characteristics of both common stock and bonds. First, like common stock, preferred stock has no fixed maturity date. Also like common stock, the non-payment of dividends does not bring on bankruptcy, and dividends are not deductible for tax purposes. On the other hand, like debt, preferred stock dividends are fixed in amount similar to interest payments. In addition, although in theory preferred stock does not have a set maturity associated with it, many issues of preferred stock require that money be set aside regularly to retire the preferred stock issue, in effect resulting in a maturity date.

Valuing Preferred Stock

The owner of preferred stock generally receives a fixed dividend from the investment in each period. Because preferred stocks are perpetuities (non-maturing), and because the cash dividend is the same every period, the dividend stream is a level perpetuity that can be valued by calculating the present value of a level perpetuity. In effect, the value of a share of preferred stock is dependent upon P Principle 1: **Money Has a Time Value**; P Principle 2: **There Is a Risk–Return Tradeoff**; and P Principle 3: **Cash Flows Are the Source of Value.**

Figure 5

Quick Reference Guide for the Preferred Stock Valuation Model

The value of a share of preferred stock, like that of any security, is defined by the present value of the cash flows it is expected to produce to the owner of the stock. Because the preferred shares typically pay a fixed dividend, this cash flow stream is a level perpetuity, which makes discounting the future dividends simple. We divide the dividend by the required rate of return on the preferred stock:

$$\text{Value of Preferred Stock } (V_{ps}) = \frac{\text{Annual Preferred Stock Dividend}}{\text{Market's Required Yield on Preferred Stock}} = \frac{D_{ps}}{r_{ps}} \quad \text{(6)}$$

Important Definitions and Concepts:

- V_{ps} = the value of a share of preferred stock.

- D_{ps} = the annual preferred stock dividend. This dividend is the contractually *promised* dividend. Remember that preferred dividends are only paid if the firm has the cash to pay them, and they must be paid *before* common stockholders get any dividends. The critical point here is that the preferred stock dividend may be skipped in some years if the company is unable to pay it, such that the annual dividend is a *promised* dividend (not the expected dividend). The amount of the dividend is computed as the product of the promised dividend rate and the par or face value of the preferred stock and is prescribed in the security contract.

- r_{ps} = the *market's required yield* or promised rate of return on the preferred stock's contractually promised dividend. This market's required yield is analogous to the market's required yield to maturity on a bond discussed. Note that because this market yield is based on the promised dividend, we can also think of it as a *promised rate of return* to the preferred stock investor that will be realized only if preferred stock dividends are always paid in a timely manner.

- $\dfrac{D_{ps}}{r_{ps}}$ = the present value of a level perpetuity, which equals the promised dividend on preferred stock discounted using the market's required yield or promised rate of return to the preferred stockholders.

>> END FIGURE 5

Thus, the value of a share of preferred stock can be written as follows:

$$\text{Value of Preferred Stock} = \frac{\text{Annual Preferred Stock Dividend}}{\text{Market's Required Yield on Preferred Stock}} \quad \text{(6)}$$

Figure 5 contains a quick reference resource for this valuation model along with definitions of each of the symbols typically used. In addition, the figure contains other details concerning the valuation of preferred stock that you will find useful.

Dealing with Reality: Promised versus Expected Return for Preferred Stock

The market's required yield to maturity (YTM_{Market}) used to value a bond is not the same thing as the expected rate of return on the bond. The reason for this is that the bond interest and principal payments used to value the bond are *promised* payments that are received *only* if the borrowing firm makes all the interest and principal payments on time (i.e., the firm does not default). The same idea is applied to the valuation of preferred stock. Preferred stock dividends are *promised dividends* that are only paid if the firm earns sufficient income to pay them. This causes no problem for valuing the preferred stock because we simply discount the promised dividends back to the present using the market's required yield or promised rate of return for similar shares of preferred stock in the financial marketplace. *In other words, we value preferred shares by discounting the contractually promised dividend payments using a promised rate of return to the preferred shareholders.*

Estimating the Market's Required Yield. The **market's required yield** on a share of preferred stock is typically estimated using the market prices of similar shares of preferred stock that can be observed in the financial market. For example, let's assume that the electric utility Pacific Gas & Electric (PCG) is considering the sale of an issue of preferred stock. The preferred issue would pay a 5.00 percent annual dividend based on a par value of $50, for a dividend of $2.50. To determine the price that this issue might sell for, we must look at the market yields on other issues of preferred stock issued by PCG, or issues of preferred stock by similar companies. Let's for a moment assume that PCG does not have any other issues of preferred stock outstanding. In that case we would look for a company of similar risk with preferred stock outstanding. After a careful analysis of comparable firms, we will choose American Electric Power (AEP) because we deem the firm to be of very similar risk as PCG and it has an issue of preferred stock outstanding. The American Electric Power preferred has a promised annual dividend of $1.25 per share and each share is currently selling for $25.46. We can use Equation (6) to solve for the market's required yield, r_{ps}, as follows:

$$V_{ps} = \frac{D_{ps}}{r_{ps}}$$

$$V_{ps} = \frac{D_{ps}}{V_{ps}} = \frac{\$1.25}{\$25.46} = .0491 \text{ or } 4.91\%$$

We can now use the 4.91 percent market's required yield for the American Electric Power preferred issue to estimate the value of the preferred stock of Pacific Gas & Electric (PCG). First we calculate the annual dividend to reflect a 5.00 percent dividend yield and a par value of $50 per share. The resulting dividend is $2.50 = $50 × .05 a share. Substituting this dividend and the promised rate of return estimated using American Electric Power into Equation (6), we estimate the value of Pacific Gas & Electric's preferred stock to be $50.92, as follows:

$$V_{ps} = \frac{D_{ps}}{r_{ps}} = \frac{\$2.50}{.0491} = \$50.92$$

Note that we have valued the new issue of preferred using the contractual or promised dividend for the issue and estimated the market's required yield using a current market price and dividend for a comparable-risk preferred issue. Recall that this is very similar to the way that we value a corporate bond.

In summary, the value of a preferred stock is the present value of all future dividends. Because most preferred stocks are perpetuities and non-maturing, with the dividends continuing to infinity, we simply use our formula for the present value of a perpetuity to value them.

We now have the tools of financial analysis to value preferred stock assuming that the dividends grow at a constant rate in perpetuity, which are shown as follows:

Tools of financial analysis—Preferred Stock Valuation

Name of Tool	Formula	What It Tells You
Preferred stock valuation	$V_{ps} = \dfrac{\text{Annual Preferred Stock Dividend}}{\text{Market's Required Yield or Promised Rate of Return}}$ $$V_{ps} = \frac{D_{ps}}{r_{ps}}$$	• The value of preferred stock is equal to the present value of all the future dividends in perpetuity • As investors' required yield or return go up, perhaps as a result of the firm becoming riskier or market interest rates climbing, the value of a share of preferred stock falls.

A Quick Review: Valuing Bonds, Preferred Stock, and Common Stock

Bonds can be valued by discounting their contractually promised interest and principal payments back to the present. In this chapter, we used the same

Checkpoint 3

Valuing Preferred Stock

Consider Con Edison's (ED) preferred stock issue, which pays an annual dividend of $5.00 per share, does not have a maturity date, and on which the market's required yield or promised rate of return (r_{ps}) for similar shares of preferred stock is 6.02 percent. What is the value of the Con Edison preferred stock?

STEP 1: Picture the problem

Because preferred stock dividends are constant for all future years, they form a level perpetuity. In effect, a perpetuity can be visualized as a timeline that doesn't have an ending point, with the same cash flow occurring period after period, or in this case, year after year:

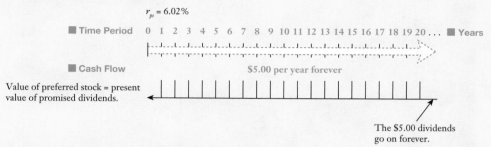

$r_{ps} = 6.02\%$

■ Time Period   0 1 2 3 4 5 6 7 8 9 10 11 12 13 14 15 16 17 18 19 20 . . .   ■ Years

■ Cash Flow $5.00 per year forever

Value of preferred stock = present value of promised dividends.

The $5.00 dividends go on forever.

STEP 2: Decide on a solution strategy

Because preferred stock dividends are constant and have no maturity or end date, these dividends are a level perpetuity. Consequently, calculating the present value of a share of preferred stock using Equation (6) only involves simple division and there is no need for an Excel solution, or any unique keystrokes with a financial calculator. We just divide the amount you receive at the end of each period forever by the market's required yield.

STEP 3: Solve

Substituting into Equation (6) a value of $5.00 for D_{ps}, and 0.0602 for r_{ps}, we can determine the value of the Con Edison preferred stock as follows:

$$V_{ps} = \frac{D_{ps}}{r_{ps}} = \frac{\$5.00}{0.0602} = \$83.06$$

Thus, the present value of this preferred stock is $83.06.

STEP 4: Analyze

Because preferred stock is a level perpetuity, its value on any future date will be the same as its present value today. That is, the value of the preferred stock is $83.06 today, and if all else remains the same, the preferred shares will be worth $83.06 five years from now, 10 years from now, and 100 years from now as long as the promised rate of return on the shares remains the same.

STEP 5: Check yourself

What is the present value of a share of preferred stock that pays a dividend of $12.00 per share if the market's required yield on similar issues of preferred stock is 8 percent?

ANSWER: $150.00.

Your Turn: For more practice, do related **Study Problem** 15 at the end of this chapter.   >> END Checkpoint 3

discounted cash flow procedure to value both preferred and common stock. However, there is a subtle but important difference between how bonds and preferred stock are valued and how common stock is valued using the discounted cash flow method.

Bonds and preferred stock are valued using *promised yields* and *promised cash flows*. However, because common stock does not have a promised cash flow and we must estimate the expected dividends for each future period, we discount these *expected dividends* using an *expected rate of return* for investing the company's shares. Table 2 summarizes the application of discounted cash flow in valuing all three types of securities.

Table 2   Summary of Discounted Cash Flow Valuation of Bonds, Preferred Stock, and Common Stock

Bonds and preferred stock state a promised cash payment to the security holder. In the case of a bond, interest and principal must be paid in accordance with the terms of the bond contract (indenture). Preferred shares have stated dividend yields, which when multiplied by the face or par value of the preferred stock, equal the promised preferred dividend. Both bonds and preferred stock are valued by discounting these promised cash flows back to the present. However, because these are promised (and not expected) cash flows, we discount the cash flows using promised rate of return as reflected in current market prices of similar securities. Common stock, on the other hand, does not have a contractual promised dividend payment, so we apply the discounted cash flow model in this instance by estimating expected future dividends and then discounting them back to the present using the expected rate of return that an investor would require if investing in a stock with the risk attributes of the shares being valued.

Type of Security	Cash Flow	Discount Rate	Valuation Model
Bond	**Promised interest and principal payments.** These payments are set forth in the contract between the bond-issuing company and the owner of the bond.	**Market's required yield to maturity (YTM market).** Typically the YTM on a similar bond is used to value a bond. This YTM is the realized rate of return to the bondholder *only* if all promised payments are made on time. Consequently, the yield to maturity calculated for a bond is a promised yield and not the expected yield.	$$\text{Bond Value} = \text{Interest}\left[\dfrac{1 - \dfrac{1}{(1 + YTM_{\text{Market}})^n}}{YTM_{\text{Market}}}\right] + \text{Principal}\left[\dfrac{1}{(1 + YTM)^n}\right]$$
Preferred stock	**Promised dividends.** Dividends are defined using a contractually set dividend yield that is multiplied by the par or face value of the preferred stock to get the preferred stock dividend.	**Market or promised yield on preferred stock.** We typically calculate this yield using market prices and promised dividends for similar shares of preferred stock. This yield is a promised yield that will only be earned if the preferred stock dividends are fully paid every period as promised.	$$\text{Value of Preferred Stock}(V_{ps}) = \dfrac{\text{Annual Preferred Stock Dividend}}{\text{Market's Required Yield on Preferred Stock}}$$ $$= \dfrac{D_{ps}}{r_{ps}}$$
Common Stock	**Expected future dividends.** No dividend is prescribed for common stock. Instead dividends must be estimated, so we value common stock using expected rather than promised future cash flows. In the constant dividend growth rate model, dividends are estimated using a constant rate of growth from year to year.	**Investor's expected rate of return, which is the investor's required rate of return.** Because common stock dividends are risky, we used expected future dividends and discount them using a risk-adjusted or expected rate of return for investing in shares of stock of firms with similar risk to the common stock being valued. We can estimate this expected rate of return using the CAPM.	$$\text{Value of Common Stock}(V_{cs}) = \dfrac{D_0(1 + g)}{r_{cs} - g}$$

Concept Check | 3

1. What are three common features of preferred stock?
2. What is the market's required yield on a preferred stock?
3. Explain the meaning of the following statement: The market yield is a promised rate of return rather than an expected rate of return.

4 The Stock Market

Now that we know how different securities are valued, let's take a look at where they are traded. New, as opposed to previously issued, securities trade in the primary market, whereas currently outstanding securities trade in the secondary market. In other words, if you bought 100 shares of Google stock during its **initial public offering (IPO)**, that is, the first time a company issues stock to the public, you'd have to sell them on the secondary market. When you sold them, the proceeds would go to you, the seller of the stock, not to Google. In fact, the only time Google ever receives money from the sale of one of its securities is when it is sold in the primary market.

There are two types of secondary markets: organized exchanges where trading occurs at a physical location, and over-the-counter market transactions where trading occurs over the telephone or through computer networks. Larger and more frequently traded securities such as GM, IBM, General Electric, and Disney, which meet the listing requirements, trade on organized exchanges. Those stocks that are less frequently traded, along with many new and high-tech stocks, trade in the over-the-counter markets.

Organized Exchanges

The **New York Stock Exchange (NYSE)**, also called the "Big Board," is the oldest of all the organized exchanges and is without question the big player. It began in 1792 when 24 traders signed the Buttonwood Agreement, a pact named after the tree under which traders gathered, obligating them to "give preference" to each other in security trading. When winter came, the 24 traders moved to the back of Wall Street's Tontine Coffee House, leaving the other traders out in the cold.

Although the NYSE is considered an organized exchange because of its physical location, the majority of its trades are done electronically without a face-to-face meeting of traders. To be listed on the NYSE, a firm must meet strict requirements dealing with profitability and market value, and be widely owned. If a listed company fails to meet the requirements, the exchange will delist it and it will no longer be traded on the NYSE.

The NYSE is the largest organized securities exchange in the world. Included among the NYSE-listed stocks are PepsiCo (PEP), AT&T (T), Walmart (WMT), and Coca-Cola (COKE). Much of the trading on the NYSE is made up of block trades. A **block trade** is a transaction involving 10,000 shares or more by one holder. In a similar vein, a **block holding** is a block of 10,000 shares or more held by a single individual or institution. In recent years, block trades have accounted for between a quarter and a third of the reported Big Board volume. This tells us that large, institutional investors play a major role in the workings of the NYSE.

The **American Stock Exchange (AMEX)** is the nation's second largest, floor-based exchange. Its listings generally include firms somewhat smaller than those listed on the NYSE. In addition to common stocks, the AMEX also has a significant presence in ETFs and options (which we will discuss later). The AMEX operates in a manner similar to the NYSE, has only 807 regular members, and has 57 members limited to option business.

When it comes to trading volume, the AMEX is a distant number two. Its trading volume is 3 percent of that on the NYSE. Although the AMEX merged with Nasdaq in 1998, it continues to operate as a separate entity.

Over-the-Counter (OTC) Market

The **over-the-counter (OTC) market** is a network of dealers that has no listing or membership requirements (although there are listing requirements on Nasdaq, which we will discuss shortly). It draws its name from the fact that, historically, banks acted as the primary dealer for many individuals, and they sold smaller securities and bonds right "over the counter" from inventory they kept on hand. Today, the OTC market is electronic rather than personal, with Nasdaq leading the way. It is also the primary market for bond trading.

OTC listings usually are companies too new or too small to be eligible for listing on a major exchange. These companies also often have fewer shares available. As a result, in some cases small amounts of buying or selling may have a significant impact on the price of those OTC-listed stocks.

Nasdaq handles the OTC stocks that are traded more frequently. Nasdaq, known more formally as the National Association of Security Dealers Automated Quotations system, debuted in 1971 and was the world's first electronic stock market. It was set up to allow dealers to post bid and ask prices, as well as how many shares the dealers were willing to buy or sell at that price. Although Nasdaq lists more companies than the NYSE, with the exception of a few large high-tech firms, they tend to be smaller companies.

The Nasdaq stock market has two tiers of listed companies: Nasdaq National Markets, made up of around 4,000 companies such as Dell (D), Microsoft (MSFT), eBay (EBAY), Intel (INTC), and Oracle (ORCL), and the Nasdaq Capital Market, which includes over 1,000 smaller emerging-growth companies. There are about 1,000 market participants, in general trading firms that are linked electronically, with price and trading information broadcast to over 350,000 terminals worldwide.

Before you begin end-of-chapter material

Concept Check 4

1. What are the largest organized exchanges on which shares of common stock are bought and sold?
2. What is the difference between an organized exchange and the over-the-counter market?

Principle 1: Money Has a Time Value The value of common stock is equal to the present value of the future cash flows, discounted at the required rate of return. As a result, Principle 1 plays a pivotal role in determining the value of debt.

Principle 2: There Is a Risk–Return Tradeoff Different common stocks have different levels of risk associated with them, with more risk resulting in a higher required rate of return.

Principle 3: Cash Flows Are the Source of Value The calculation of the value of a share of stock begins with an estimation of the amount and timing of future cash flows. If you bought a share of common stock and

never sold it, the only cash flow you would ever receive would be the dividends that the firm paid. It is the cash flows that are discounted back to present to determine the value of a share of stock.

Principle 4: Market Prices Reflect Information Principle 4 implies that market prices are a pretty good reflection of the value of the underlying shares of stock.

Principle 5: Individuals Respond to Incentives takes on importance because managers respond to incentives in their contracts, and if these incentives are not properly aligned with those of the firm's shareholders, they may not make decisions consistent with increasing shareholder value.

Chapter Summaries

 Identify the basic characteristics and features of common stock and use the discounted cash flow model to value common shares.

SUMMARY: Common stock does not have a maturity date, and has a life that is limited only by the life of the issuing firm. Common dividends have no minimums or maximums. In the event of bankruptcy, the common stockholders cannot exercise claims on assets until the firm's creditors, including the bondholders and preferred shareholders, have been satisfied.

The common stockholders are the owners of the firm, and are in general the only security holders given a vote. Common shareholders have the right to elect the board of directors and to approve any change in the corporate charter. Although each share of stock carries the same number of votes, the voting procedure is not always the same from company to company.

A popular model used to calculate the present value of the future dividends to a firm's common stock is the constant dividend growth rate model. This model can be stated as follows:

$$\frac{\text{Value of}}{\text{Common Stock}} = \frac{\text{Dividend for Year 1}}{\left(\begin{array}{c}\text{Investor's Required}\\\text{Rate of Return}\end{array}\right) - \left(\begin{array}{c}\text{Dividend Growth}\\\text{Rate}\end{array}\right)} \tag{2}$$

The valuation of common stock differs from the valuation of preferred stock (and bonds) because common stock has no promised dividends. As a result, we use expected future dividends to estimate the cash flows to the common stockholders. Because we are discounting expected future cash flows, we discount them using the expected rate of return the investor anticipates from an investment with the risk of the common stock being valued.

KEY TERMS

Constant dividend growth rate model A common stock valuation model that assumes that dividends will grow at a constant rate forever.

Cumulative voting Voting in which each share of stock allows the shareholder a number of votes equal to the number of directors being elected. The shareholder can then cast all of his or her votes for a single candidate or split them among the various candidates.

Majority voting Each share of stock allows the shareholder one vote, and each position on the board of directors is voted on separately.

Proxy A means of voting in which a designated party is provided with the temporary power of attorney to vote for the signee at the corporation's annual meeting.

KEY EQUATIONS

$$\begin{aligned}\frac{\text{Value of Common}}{\text{Stock in Year 0}} &= \frac{\text{Dividend}\\\text{Paid in Year 0}\left(1 + \frac{\text{Dividend}}{\text{Growth Rate}}\right)^1}{\left(1 + \frac{\text{Stockholder's}}{\text{Required Rate of Return}}\right)^1} + \frac{\text{Dividend}\\\text{Paid in Year 0}\left(1 + \frac{\text{Dividend}}{\text{Growth Rate}}\right)^2}{\left(1 + \frac{\text{Stockholder's}}{\text{Required Rate of Return}}\right)^2}\\[2em] &+ \frac{\text{Dividend}\\\text{Paid in Year 0}\left(1 + \frac{\text{Dividend}}{\text{Growth Rate}}\right)^3}{\left(1 + \frac{\text{Stockholder's}}{\text{Required Rate of Return}}\right)^3} + \cdots + \frac{\text{Dividend}\\\text{Paid in Year 0}\left(1 + \frac{\text{Dividend}}{\text{Growth Rate}}\right)^\infty}{\left(1 + \frac{\text{Stockholder's}}{\text{Required Rate of Return}}\right)^\infty} \tag{1}\end{aligned}$$

Concept Check | 1

1. What are the attributes of common stock that distinguish it from bonds and preferred stock?

2. What does agency cost mean with respect to the owners of a firm's common stock?

3. Describe the three-step process for valuing common stock using the discounted dividend model.

$$V_{cs} = \frac{\text{Dividend in Year } 0 \left(1 + \dfrac{\text{Dividend}}{\text{Growth Rate}} \right)}{\dfrac{\text{Stockholder's Required}}{\text{Rate of Return}} - \dfrac{\text{Dividend}}{\text{Growth Rate}}} = \frac{\text{Dividend in Year } 1}{\dfrac{\text{Stockholder's Required}}{\text{Rate of Return}} - \dfrac{\text{Dividend}}{\text{Growth Rate}}} \quad (2)$$

$$\frac{\text{Rate of Growth}}{\text{in Dividends } (g)} = \left(1 - \frac{\text{Dividend}}{\text{Payout Ratio}} \right) \times \frac{\text{Rate of Return}}{\text{on Equity } (ROE)} \quad (3)$$

2 Use the price-to-earnings (P/E) ratio to value common stock.

SUMMARY: The price/earnings valuation model for stock valuation is commonly referred to as a "relative valuation" approach. The reason is that we define value "relative" to firm earnings and "relative" to how similar firm earnings are valued. The P/E valuation model is defined as follows:

$$\frac{\text{Value of}}{\text{Common Stock}} = \left(\frac{\text{Price/Earnings}}{\text{Ratio}} \right) \times \left(\frac{\text{Firm}}{\text{Earnings Per Share}} \right) \quad (4)$$

The P/E valuation method is generally used in association with the comparables approach. Specifically, the P/E multiple is generally determined by examining the P/E ratios of comparable firms. We learned that the price/earnings ratio is determined by the profitability of the firm's investment opportunities, the fraction of the firm's earnings that it reinvests in the firm, and the riskiness of the firm's common stock.

KEY TERM

Price/earnings ratio The price the market places on $1 of a firm's earnings. For example, if a firm has an earnings per share of $2, and a stock price of $30, its price-to-earnings ratio is 15 ($30 ÷ $2).

KEY EQUATIONS

$$\frac{\text{Value of}}{\text{Common Stock}}, V_{cs} = \left(\frac{\text{Appropriate}}{\text{Price/Earnings Ratio}} \right) \times \left(\frac{\text{Estimated Earnings}}{\text{per Share for Year 1}} \right) = \frac{P}{E_1} \times E_1 \quad (4)$$

$$\frac{P}{E_1} = \frac{D_1/E_1}{r_{cs} - g} \quad (5)$$

3 Identify the basic characteristics and features of preferred stock and value preferred shares.

SUMMARY: Preferred stock has several characteristics that make it unique. Specifically, unlike bonds, preferred stock does not have a fixed maturity date. Moreover, preferred stock dividends are typically fixed, unlike common stock that may not pay any dividend. The following are some of the more common characteristics of preferred stock:

- There are multiple classes of preferred stock.
- Preferred stock has a priority claim over common stock with respect to the proceeds from the sale of assets and the distribution of income.
- Preferred stock dividends must be paid as promised, before any common stock dividends can be paid.
- Protective provisions are often included in the contract for the preferred shareholder in order to reduce the investor's risk.

The value of a share of preferred stock is equal to the present value of the stream of contractually promised future dividends discounted using the market's required yield on shares of preferred stock of similar risk. Because the preferred dividend is typically the same for all future years and there is no maturity date, the present value of these dividends can be solved as the present value of a level perpetuity. That is, the value of a preferred stock is simply the ratio of the promised preferred dividend divided by the promised yield of a preferred stock with similar risk.

$$\frac{\text{Value of}}{\text{Preferred Stock}} = \frac{\text{Annual Preferred Stock Dividend}}{\text{Market's Required Yield on Preferred Stock}} \quad (6)$$

Concept Check | 3

1. What are three common features of preferred stock?
2. What is the market's required yield on a preferred stock?
3. Explain the meaning of the following statement: The market yield is a promised rate of return rather than an expected rate of return.

KEY TERMS

Cumulative preferred stock Preferred stock that requires all past unpaid preferred stock dividends to be paid before any common stock dividends are declared.

Market's required yield The rate of return on the preferred stock's contractually promised dividend. This market's required yield is analogous to the market's required yield to maturity on a bond.

KEY EQUATION

$$\text{Value of Preferred Stock } (V_{ps}) = \frac{\text{Annual Preferred Stock Dividend}}{\text{Market's Required Yield on Preferred Stock}} = \frac{D_{ps}}{r_{ps}} \quad \textbf{(6)}$$

 List the secondary markets for common stock.

SUMMARY: The big player in the secondary market for common stock is the New York Stock Exchange (NYSE). The over-the-counter market is simply a linkup of dealers, with no listing or membership requirements. Today, the over-the-counter market is electronic rather than personal, with Nasdaq leading the way.

KEY TERMS

American Stock Exchange (AMEX) The nation's second largest floor-based exchange.

Block holding The situation when one investor holds 10,000 shares or more of a single stock.

Block trade A transaction involving 10,000 shares or more by one holder.

Initial public offering (IPO) The first time a company issues stock to the public. This occurs in the primary markets.

Nasdaq An electronic stock exchange where OTC stocks are traded.

New York Stock Exchange (NYSE) The largest organized stock exchange.

Over-the-counter (OTC) market A network of dealers who trade stocks that has no listing or membership requirements.

Concept Check | 4

1. What are the largest organized exchanges on which shares of common stock are bought and sold?
2. What is the difference between an organized exchange and the over-the-counter market?

Study Questions

1. **(Related to Regardless of Your Major: Getting Your Fair Share)** The *Regardless of Your Major* feature focuses on the valuation of a new business venture. If you were faced with the need to value this business, what would you want to know about the business?

2. Why is preferred stock referred to as a hybrid security?

3. Because preferred stock dividends must be paid before common stock dividends, should preferred stock be considered a liability and appear on the right side of the balance sheet alongside of the firm's long-term debt?

4. Why would a preferred stockholder want to have the cumulative dividend feature?

5. **(Related to The Business of Life: Does a Stock by Any Other Name Smell as Sweet?)** In *The Business of Life: Does a Stock by Any Other Name Smell as Sweet?* feature, we learn that ticker symbols for shares of stock are sometimes chosen with great care. Guess what you think the ticker symbols might be for Apple Computers, Ford Motor Company, and Exco Resources. Now look up the ticker symbol using one of the websites mentioned in the feature. How close did you get?

6. Compare the methods for valuing preferred stock and common stock.

7. The market's required yield on preferred stock is actually a "promised" rate of return. Explain this statement.

8. Common stockholders receive two types of return from their investment. What are they?

9. Is the NYSE considered part of the primary or secondary market?

10. What are over-the-counter markets, and how do they differ from organized exchanges?

11. **(Related to the chapter's opening vignette)** The opening vignette described Google first going public in 2004. Prior to going public, did Google's stock have a market price? What principles would go into determining the value of a company that hadn't gone public yet?

Study Problems

Common Stock

1. **(Measuring growth)** If Pepperdine, Inc.'s return on equity is 16 percent and the management plans to retain 60 percent of earnings for investment purposes, what will be the firm's growth rate?

2. **(Measuring growth)** If the Stanford Corporation's net income is $200 million, its common equity is $833 million, and management plans to retain 70 percent of the firm's earnings to finance new investments, what will be the firm's growth rate?

3. **(Related to Checkpoint 1) (Common stock valuation)** Header Motor, Inc., paid a $3.50 dividend last year. At a constant growth rate of 5 percent, what is the value of the common stock if the investors require a 20 percent rate of return?

4. **(Common stock valuation)** Gilliland Motor, Inc., paid a $3.75 dividend last year. If Gilliland's return on equity is 24 percent, and its retention rate is 25 percent, what is the value of the common stock if the investors require a 20 percent rate of return?

5. **(Common stock valuation)** The common stock of NCP paid $1.32 in dividends last year. Dividends are expected to grow at an 8 percent annual rate for an indefinite number of years.

   a. If your required rate of return is 10.5 percent, what is the value of the stock for you?
   b. Should you make the investment?

6. **(Measuring growth)** Given that a firm's return on equity is 18 percent and management plans to retain 40 percent of earnings for investment purposes, what will be the firm's growth rate? If the firm decides to increase its retention rate, what will happen to the value of its common stock?

7. **(Common stock valuation)** Wayne, Inc.'s outstanding common stock is currently selling in the market for $33. Dividends of $2.30 per share were paid last year, return on equity is 20 percent, and its retention rate is 25 percent.

   a. What is the value of the stock to you, given a 15 percent required rate of return?
   b. Should you purchase this stock?

8. **(Measuring growth)** Thomas, Inc.'s return on equity is 13 percent and management has plans to retain 20 percent of earnings for investment in the company.

   a. What will be the company's growth rate?
   b. How would the growth rate change if management (i) increased retained earnings to 35 percent or (ii) decreased retention to 13 percent?

9. **(Measuring growth)** Solarpower Systems expects to earn $20 per share this year and intends to pay out $8 in dividends to shareholders and retain $12 to invest in new projects with an expected return on equity of 20 percent. In the future, Solarpower expects to retain the same dividend payout ratio, expects to earn 20 percent return on its equity invested in new projects, and will not be changing the number of shares of common stock outstanding.

   a. Calculate the future growth rate for Solarpower's earnings.
   b. If the investor's required rate of return for Solarpower's stock is 15 percent, what would be the price of Solarpower's common stock?

    c. What would happen to the price of Solarpower's common stock if it raised its dividends to $12 this year and then continued with that same dividend payout ratio permanently? Should Solarpower make this change? (Assume that the investor's required rate of return remains at 15 percent.)

    d. What would happen to the price of Solarpower's common stock if it lowered its dividends to $4 this year and then continued with that same dividend payout ratio permanently? Does the constant dividend growth rate model work in this case? Why or why not? (Assume that the investor's required rate of return remains at 15 percent and that all future new projects will earn 20 percent.)

10. **(Measuring growth)** Green Gadgets Inc. is trying to decide whether to cut its expected dividends for next year from $8 per share to $5 per share in order to have more money to invest in new projects. If it does not cut the dividend, Green Gadgets' expected rate of growth in dividends is 5 percent per year and the price of its common stock will be $100 per share. However, if they cut their dividend, the dividend growth rate is expected to rise to 8 percent in the future. Assuming that the investor's required rate of return for Green Gadgets' stock does not change, what would you expect to happen to the price of its common stock if it cuts the dividend to $5? Should Green Gadgets' cut its dividend? Support your answer as best as you can.

11. **(Common stock valuation)** Dubai Metro's stock price was at $100 per share when it announced that it will cut its dividends for next year from $10 per share to $6 per share, with additional funds used for expansion. Prior to the dividend cut, Dubai Metro expected its dividends to grow at a 4 percent rate, but with the expansion, dividends are now expected to grow at 7 percent. How do you think the announcement will affect Dubai Metro's stock price?

Comparables Approach to Valuing Common Stock

12. **(Related to Checkpoint 2) (Relative valuation of common stock)**
Using the P/E ratio approach to valuation, calculate the value of a share of stock under the following conditions:

- the investor's required rate of return is 12 percent,
- the expected level of earnings at the end of this year (E_1) is $4.00,
- the firm follows a policy of retaining 30 percent of its earnings,
- the return on equity (ROE) is 15 percent, and
- similar shares of stock sell at multiples of 13.3325 times earnings per share.

Now show that you get the same answer using the discounted dividend model.

13. **(Common stock valuation)** Assume the following:

- the investor's required rate of return is 13.5 percent,
- the expected level of earnings at the end of this year (E_1) is $6.00,
- the retention ratio is 50 percent,
- the return on equity (ROE) is 15 percent (that is, it can earn 15 percent on reinvested earnings), and
- similar shares of stock sell at multiples of 16.667 times earnings per share.

Questions:

a. Determine the expected growth rate for dividends.
b. Determine the price/earnings ratio (P/E_1) using Equation (5a).
c. What is the stock price using the P/E ratio valuation method?
d. What is the stock price using the dividend discount model?
e. What would happen to the P/E ratio (P/E_1) and stock price if the company increased its retention rate to 60 percent (holding all else constant)? What would happen to the P/E ratio (P/E_1) and stock price if the company paid out all its earnings in the form of dividends?
f. What have you learned about the relationship between the retention rate and P/E ratios?

14. **(Common Stock Valuation)** Assume the following:

- the investor's required rate of return is 15 percent,
- the expected level of earnings at the end of this year (E_1) is $5.00,
- the retention ratio is 50 percent,
- the return on equity (ROE) is 20 percent (that is, it can earn 20 percent on reinvested earnings), and
- similar shares of stock sell at multiples of 10 times earnings per share.

Questions:

a. Determine the expected growth rate for dividends.
b. Determine the price/earnings ratio (P/E_1) using Equation (5a).
c. What is the stock price using the P/E ratio valuation method?
d. What is the stock price using the dividend discount model?
e. What would happen to the P/E ratio (P/E_1) and stock price if the firm could earn 25 percent on reinvested earnings (ROE)?
f. What does this tell you about the relationship between the rate the firm can earn on reinvested earnings and P/E ratios?

Preferred Stock

15. **(Related to Checkpoint 3) (Preferred stock valuation)** Calculate the value of a preferred stock that pays a dividend of $6 per share when the market's required yield on similar shares is 12 percent.

16. **(Preferred stock valuation)** Pioneer's preferred stock is selling for $33 in the market and pays a $3.60 annual dividend.

a. If the market's required yield is 10 percent, what is the value of the stock for that investor?
b. Should the investor acquire the stock?

17. **(Preferred stock valuation)** What is the value of a preferred stock where the dividend rate is 14 percent on a $100 par value, and the market's required yield on similar shares is 12 percent?

18. **(Preferred stock valuation)** You own 200 shares of Somner Resources' preferred stock, which currently sells for $40 per share and pays annual dividends of $3.40 per share. If the market's required yield on similar shares is 10 percent, should you sell your shares or buy more?

19. **(Preferred stock valuation)** Kendra Corporation's preferred shares are trading for $25 in the market and pay a $4.50 annual dividend. Assume that the market's required yield is 14 percent.

a. What is the stock's value to you, the investor?
b. Should you purchase the stock?

Mini-Case

You have finally saved $10,000 and are ready to make your first investment. You have the three following alternatives for investing that money:

- Capital Cities ABC, Inc. bonds with a par value of $1,000 and a coupon interest rate of 8.75 percent, are selling for $1,314 and mature in 12 years.
- Southwest Bancorp preferred stock is paying a dividend of $2.50 and selling for $25.50.
- Emerson Electric common stock is selling for $36.75. The stock recently paid a $1.32 dividend and the firm's earnings per share has increased from $1.49 to $3.06 in the past five years. The firm expects to grow at the same rate for the foreseeable future.

Your required rates of return for these investments are 6 percent for the bond, 7 percent for the preferred stock, and 15 percent for the common stock. Using this information, answer the following questions.

a. Calculate the value of each investment based on your required rate of return.

b. Which investment would you select? Why?

c. Assume Emerson Electric's managers expect an earnings downturn and a resulting decrease in growth of 3 percent. How does this affect your answers to parts a and b?

d. What required rates of return would make you indifferent to all three options?

Photo Credits

Investment Decision Criteria

From Chapter 11 of *Financial Management: Principles and Applications*, Twelfth Edition. Sheridan Titman, Arthur J. Keown, and John D. Martin.

Investment Decision Criteria

Chapter **Outline**

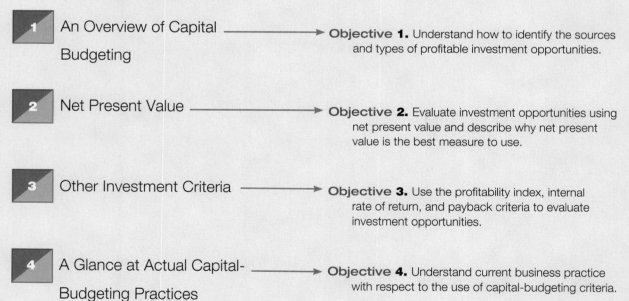

1 An Overview of Capital Budgeting → **Objective 1.** Understand how to identify the sources and types of profitable investment opportunities.

2 Net Present Value → **Objective 2.** Evaluate investment opportunities using net present value and describe why net present value is the best measure to use.

3 Other Investment Criteria → **Objective 3.** Use the profitability index, internal rate of return, and payback criteria to evaluate investment opportunities.

4 A Glance at Actual Capital-Budgeting Practices → **Objective 4.** Understand current business practice with respect to the use of capital-budgeting criteria.

Just as when we value stocks and bonds, the valuation of investment opportunities relies on the first three basic principles of finance, along with the final principle: P Principle 1: **Money Has a Time Value**—the cash inflows and outflows from an investment opportunity are generally spread out over a number of years; thus, we need the tools of the time value of money to make these cash flows that occur in different time periods comparable; P Principle 2: **There Is a Risk–Return Tradeoff**—different investment opportunities have different levels of risk,

and as a result, the risk–return tradeoff becomes important when determining the rate to use when discounting future cash flows; P Principle 3: **Cash Flows Are the Source of Value**—when evaluating investment opportunities we will rely on free cash flows rather than accounting profits; and P Principle 5: **Individuals Respond to Incentives**—Managers respond to incentives, and when their incentives are not properly aligned with those of the firm's stockholders, they may not make decisions that are consistent with increasing shareholder value.

Real Estate Investing

Suppose that you and your roommates rent a condo near campus and, at the end of your senior year, your landlord offers to sell you the condo for $90,000. If you buy the condo, you would make some minor repairs and sell it right away. Your father has agreed to loan you the money for the purchase and repairs. How would you decide whether to take your landlord up on the offer?

You estimate that it will cost $2,000 to get the condo repainted and ready for sale. Given the demand for student housing in the area, you think that you will be able to sell it in a few days for $100,000, which represents a profit of $8,000. By completing this analysis, you've just determined the *net present value* of this project, which is the $8,000 increase in your wealth that results from the purchase and sale of the condo.

This scenario is not unlike many investment problems in the world of corporate finance. A firm's manager considering a new investment, such as the launch of a new product, first analyzes the costs involved. Next, the manager forecasts the future cash inflows expected throughout the life of the product. Finally, unlike the condo investment, which took only two weeks from purchase to sale, the manager must account for the time value of money. The future cash flows of the investment must be discounted back to the present and then compared to the initial cash outlay to determine whether the investment is likely to create value. If the present value of the cash inflows exceeds the initial cash outlay, then the manager expects the new product to create value.

With the exception of the necessity of adjusting future cash flows for the time value of money, the analysis carried out by the manager is exactly what you would have done in analyzing the condo investment. Very simply, *a good investment is one that is worth more than it costs to make.* This observation is a good one to file away and come back to over and over as we go through the rest of this chapter. Throughout the chapter we will be talking about the analysis of investment opportunities; the commonsense approach we will use is to compare the benefits we derive from the investment with the costs we incur in making it.

Capital budgeting is the term we use to refer to the process used to evaluate a firm's long-term investment opportunities. As part of this process, managers rely on the five basic principles of finance:

- First, we value an investment opportunity by evaluating its expected cash flows, following P Principle 3: **Cash Flows Are the Source of Value**.
- Second, we discount all cash flows back to the present, taking into account P Principle 1: **Money Has a Time Value**.

- Next, we incorporate risk into the analysis by increasing the discount rate to calculate the present value of the project's future cash flows, bearing in mind ▣ Principle 2: **There Is a Risk–Reward Tradeoff**. The term *risk* means that more things can happen than will happen. So the reward for assuming more risk is not a sure thing but is simply a higher *expected* return.
- Finally, we must take into account ▣ Principle 5: **Individuals Respond to Incentives**. Managers respond to incentives, and when their incentives are not properly aligned with those of the firm's stockholders, they may not make decisions that are consistent with increasing shareholder value.

We begin this chapter with a look at the criteria managers use to determine if investment opportunities—such as the condo investment or the product introduction—are good investments. Our primary focus is on net present value, a measure of the value created by the investment. However, we also review other popular measures used in practice.

Regardless of Your Major...

"Making Personal Investment Decisions"

Over your career you will be faced with investment opportunities that require some type of evaluation and analysis. Whether the decision is to purchase a piece of property that you hope to develop and resell or to start and run a business, capital-budgeting analysis will help you make the right decision. In the introduction we described a very simple real estate investment opportunity. More typically, such an investment would require substantial investments to improve the property, with renovations over an extended period of time (perhaps as much as a year). Having completed the renovation, you might consider at least two alternatives: selling the property to someone else to rent and manage, or keeping the property and managing the rentals yourself. The tools we develop in this chapter will help you evaluate the initial property investment as well as the decision of whether or not to keep and manage the property.

Your Turn: See Study Question 1.

1   An Overview of Capital Budgeting

In 1955 the Walt Disney Company was largely a movie studio, but that all changed when Disney decided to invest $17.5 million to build Disneyland Park in Anaheim, California. The decision to build the park was a major capital-budgeting decision for Disney and was so successful that Disney later decided to open theme parks in Orlando, Tokyo, Paris, and Hong Kong. In retrospect, how important was this investment? Today, parks and resorts account for over 30 percent of Disney's revenue. There are three important lessons from the Disney theme park story:

Lesson #1: Capital-budgeting decisions are critical in defining a company's business. Had Disney not embarked on its theme park strategy, it would be a very different company today.

Lesson #2: Very large investments frequently consist of many smaller investment decisions that define a business strategy. Disney did not launch its theme parks in 1955 with a plan to invest $3.5 billion some 50 years later to build the Hong Kong site. Rather, the $3.5 billion investment in the Hong Kong Disneyland was the result of a series of smaller investments that led to the eventual decision to expand the franchise in Asia.

Lesson #3: Successful investment choices lead to the development of managerial expertise and capabilities that influence the firm's choice of future investments. Disney's early success with its theme park in California provided its managers with the expertise and confidence to replicate the theme park in Orlando and then internationally. This storehouse of talent and experience gives Disney a competitive edge on would-be competitors who might seek to enter the theme park business.

The Typical Capital-Budgeting Process

Although the capital-budgeting process can be long and complicated at many major corporations, we can sum up the typical capital-budgeting process at any firm in terms of two basic phases:

Phase I: **The firm's management identifies promising investment opportunities.** These opportunities generally arise from ideas generated by the management and employees of the firm. Employees who work closely with the firm's customers (generally, the marketing department), or who run the firm's operations (the production management department), are often the idea generators.

Phase II: **Once an investment opportunity has been identified, its value-creating potential, what some refer to as its "value proposition," *is thoroughly evaluated.*** In very simple terms, a project's value proposition answers the following question: "How do we plan to make money?" It is at this stage that financial analysts enter the picture.

The logic of the two-phase process is very simple: identify promising investment opportunities and select those that offer an opportunity to create value for the firm's common stockholders.

What Are the Sources of Good Investment Projects?

Finding good investment projects can be a daunting task, particularly when the firm faces substantial competition from other firms that are also looking for similar investment opportunities. Recall from your introductory economics class that firms tend to be more profitable when they operate in markets that have less competition. So, the search for good investments is largely a search for opportunities where the firm can exploit some competitive advantage over its competitors. For example, the firm may have a proprietary production process that uses fewer inputs and results in a lower cost of production.

As a general rule, good investments are most likely to be found in markets that are less competitive. These are markets where barriers to new entrants are sufficiently high to keep out would-be competitors. For example, the strong brand reputation of the Frito-Lay products that results from an ongoing barrage of advertising makes it difficult for competing brands to enter the salty snack food category, and at the same time makes it easier for Frito-Lay to introduce new products.

Types of Capital Investment Projects

Capital investment projects can be classified into one of three broad categories:

(i) Revenue-enhancing investments.

(ii) Cost-reduction investments.

(iii) Mandatory investments that are a result of government mandates.

Let's consider each of these briefly.

Revenue-Enhancing Investments

Investments that lead to higher revenues often involve the expansion of existing businesses, such as Apple's (APPL) decision to add the smaller Nano iPods. Alternatively, when Apple originally decided to begin selling MP3 players with its iPod line of products, it created an entirely new line of business.

Larger firms have research and development (R&D) departments that search for ways to improve existing products and create new ones. These ideas may come from within the R&D

department or be based on ideas from executives, sales personnel, or customers. The most common new investment projects might involve taking an existing product and selling it to a new market. That was the case when Kimberly-Clark (KMB), the manufacturer of Huggies, made its disposable diapers more waterproof and began marketing them as disposable swim pants called Little Swimmers. Similarly, the Sara Lee Corporation's (SLE) hosiery unit appealed to more customers when it introduced Sheer Energy pantyhose for support, including the Just My Size pantyhose aimed at larger-size customers.

Cost-Reduction Investments

The majority of a firm's capital expenditure proposals are aimed at reducing the cost of doing business. For example, Walmart (WMT) did not locate a regional distribution center in San Marcos, Texas, to expand firm revenues; the region was already populated with Walmart stores. Instead, the primary benefit of the distribution center came from lowering the costs of supporting stores within the region.

Other types of cost-reducing investments arise when equipment either wears out or becomes obsolete due to the development of new and improved equipment. For example, Intel's (INTC) semiconductor manufacturing plants (called "fabs") utilize equipment called handlers that move microprocessors from one processing station to another and test their functionality. Because the technology involved in the manufacture of these processors is always evolving, the handlers also change and evolve. This means that Intel is continually evaluating the replacement of existing equipment.

Mandated Investments

Companies frequently find that they must make capital investments to meet safety and environmental regulations. These investments are not revenue producing or cost reducing but are required for the company to continue doing business. An example would be the scrubbers that are installed on the smokestacks of coal-fired power plants. The scrubbers reduce airborne emissions in order to meet government pollution guidelines.

Not all investments have sufficient potential for value creation to be undertaken, and we need some analytical tools or criteria to help us ferret out the most promising investments. In the pages that follow, we consider the most commonly used criteria for determining the desirability of alternative investment proposals. These include net present value (NPV), a closely related metric called the equivalent annual cost (EAC), the profitability index (PI), the internal rate of return (IRR), the modified internal rate of return (MIRR), the payback period, and the discounted payback period.

Before you move on to 2

Concept Check | 1

1. What does the term *capital budgeting* mean?
2. Describe the two-phase process typically involved in carrying out a capital-budgeting analysis.
3. What makes a capital-budgeting project a good one?
4. What are the three basic types of capital investment projects?

 ## Net Present Value

In the introduction to this chapter, we described a simple investment opportunity involving the purchase and sale of a condo. The $8,000 difference between the $100,000 cash inflow from the sale of the condo and the $92,000 investment outlay (the $90,000 cost of buying the condo from your landlord plus $2,000 in painting and repair expenses) is the incremental effect of the investment on your personal wealth. Because both the inflow from the sale and outflows related to buying and fixing up the condo were only two weeks apart, we ignored the time value of money and compared the inflows to the outflows directly. We determined that the investment is a sound undertaking because it could be sold for more than it cost.

The analysis of most investments also requires a consideration of the time value of money. In other words, instead of simply calculating the profits of the investment, we must calculate the investment's *net present value*. The **net present value (NPV)** is the difference between the present value of the cash inflows and the cash outflows. As such, the NPV estimates the amount of wealth that the project creates. The NPV criterion simply states that investment projects should be accepted if the NPV of the project is positive and should be rejected if the NPV of the project is negative.[1]

Why Is NPV the Right Criterion?

One of the primary goals of a corporation is to improve the wealth of its shareholders. Because the NPV of an investment is an estimate of the impact of the investment opportunity on the value of the firm, NPV is the gold standard of criteria for evaluating new investment opportunities. However, it is not the only investment criterion that is used. In the pages that follow, we will describe other criteria that are used in practice and compare each of them to the NPV criterion.

We will first describe in more detail how NPV is used to evaluate investment projects. We will look at what happens when a firm is interested in choosing just one of many projects. We will then describe other criteria that are used in practice and compare each of them to the NPV criterion.

Calculating an Investment's NPV

Most investments that firms make are more complicated than the condo purchase and sale described previously. Firms typically make investments that involve spending cash today with the expectation of receiving cash over a period of several years. We may have a pretty good idea as to how much the investment will cost; however, the expected future cash flows are uncertain and must be discounted back to the present in order to estimate their value. Determining the appropriate discount rate is not easy; however, it can be thought of as the required rate of return or cost of capital.

The NPV of an investment proposal can be defined as follows:

$$\underset{\text{Value or } NPV}{\text{Net Present}} = \underset{\text{for Year 0 } (CF_0)}{\text{Cash Flow}} + \frac{\text{Cash Flow for Year 1 } (CF_1)}{\left(1 + \dfrac{\text{Discount}}{\text{Rate } (k)}\right)^1} + \frac{\text{Cash Flow for Year 2 } (CF_2)}{\left(1 + \dfrac{\text{Discount}}{\text{Rate } (k)}\right)^2} + \cdots + \frac{\text{Cash Flow for Year } n \ (CF_n)}{\left(1 + \dfrac{\text{Discount}}{\text{Rate } (k)}\right)^n} \tag{1}$$

Cost of making the investment = Initial cash flow, this is typically a cash outflow taking on a negative value.

Present value of the investment's cash inflows = Present value of the project's future cash inflows.

Once we calculate the NPV, we can make an informed decision about whether to accept or reject the project. Reflecting back on our first three principles, you can see that they are all reflected in the NPV: the project's cash flows are used to measure the benefits the project provides (P Principle 3: **Cash Flows Are the Source of Value**); the cash flows are discounted back to present (P Principle 1: **Money Has a Time Value**); and the discount rate used to discount the cash flows back to present reflects risk in future cash flows (P Principle 2: **There Is a Risk–Reward Tradeoff**).

> **NPV Decision Criterion:** *If the NPV is greater than zero, the project will add value and should be accepted, but if the NPV is negative, the project should be rejected. If the project's NPV is exactly zero (which is highly unlikely) the project will neither create nor destroy value.*

[1]Note that projects that have a zero NPV earn the required rate of return used to discount the project cash flows and technically are acceptable investments. However, given that we are estimating future cash flows, it is not uncommon for firms to require an "NPV cushion" or a positive NPV. They accomplish this by adding a premium to the discount rate.

Tools of Financial Analysis—Net Present Value

Name of Tool	Formula	What It Tells You
Net Present Value	$$Cash\ Flow\ for\ Year\ 0\ (CF_0) + \frac{Cash\ Flow\ for\ Year\ 1\ (CF_1)}{\left(1 + \frac{Discount}{Rate\ (k)}\right)^1} + \frac{Cash\ Flow\ for\ Year\ 2\ (CF_2)}{\left(1 + \frac{Discount}{Rate\ (k)}\right)^2}$$ $$+ \cdots + \frac{Cash\ Flow\ for\ Year\ n\ (CF_n)}{\left(1 + \frac{Discount}{Rate\ (k)}\right)^n}$$	• An estimate of the value added to shareholder wealth if an investment is undertaken • In simple terms, NPV represents the amount by which the value of the investment cash flows exceeds (or falls short of) the cost of making an investment • Thus, a good project is one that costs less than the value of its future cash flows, that is, one with a positive NPV.

Independent versus Mutually Exclusive Investment Projects

The settings in which capital-budgeting analysis is carried out can vary. For example, there are times when the firm is considering whether or not to make a single investment and other times when there are multiple investment opportunities that need to be analyzed simultaneously. In the first case, the firm is evaluating what is referred to as an independent investment project. An **independent investment project** is one that stands alone and can be undertaken without influencing the acceptance or rejection of any other project. For example, a firm may be considering whether or not to construct a shipping and handling warehouse in central Kentucky. In the second case, the firm is considering a group of mutually exclusive projects. Accepting a **mutually exclusive project** prevents another project from being accepted. For example, a firm may be interested in investing in an accounting software system and has two viable choices. If the firm decides to take the first system, it cannot take the second system.

Evaluating an Independent Investment Opportunity

Project Long, evaluated in Checkpoint 1, demonstrates the use of NPV to analyze an independent investment opportunity. Because the project is an independent investment opportunity, its analysis entails calculating its NPV to see if it is positive or not. If the NPV is positive, the investment opportunity adds value to the firm and should be undertaken.

Evaluating Mutually Exclusive Investment Opportunities

There are times when firms cannot undertake all positive-NPV projects. When this happens the firm must choose the best project or set of projects from the set of positive-NPV investment opportunities it has before it. Because the firm cannot undertake all of the positive NPV projects, they must be viewed as mutually exclusive. We will consider two such circumstances in which the firm is faced with choosing from among a set of mutually exclusive projects:

1. **Substitutes.** When a firm is analyzing two or more alternative investments, and each performs the same function, the mutually exclusive alternatives are substitutes. For example, a new pizza restaurant needs to buy a pizza oven. The managers consider a number of alternatives, each of which when viewed in isolation has a positive NPV. However, they need only one oven. Therefore, when analyzing which particular oven to buy, the pizza restaurant's management is choosing between mutually exclusive alternatives.

2. **Firm Constraints.** The second reason for mutually exclusive investment opportunities arises when the firm faces constraints that limit its ability to take every project that has a positive NPV. Here are some situations where such constraints arise:

   • **Limited managerial time.** Managers may have three projects that look attractive. Although it might be possible to take all three, the managers are very busy and feel that only one project can be properly implemented at any given time.
   • **Limited financial capital.** The managers may be reluctant to issue new equity or to borrow substantial amounts of money from their bank and, as a result, they may need to ration the capital that is readily available. If available investment funds are

Checkpoint 1

Calculating the NPV for Project Long

Project Long requires an initial investment of $100,000 and is expected to generate a cash flow of $70,000 in Year 1, $30,000 per year in Years 2 and 3, $25,000 in Year 4, and $10,000 in Year 5.

The discount rate (k) appropriate for calculating the NPV of Project Long is 17 percent. Is Project Long a good investment opportunity?

STEP 1: Picture the problem

Project Long requires an initial investment of $100,000 and is expected to produce the following cash flows over the next five years:

	$k = 17\%$					
■ Time Period	0	1	2	3	4	5 ■ Years
■ Cash Flow	−$100,000	$70,000	$30,000	$30,000	$25,000	$10,000

STEP 2: Decide on a solution strategy

Our strategy for analyzing whether this is a good investment opportunity involves first calculating the present value of the cash inflows and then comparing them to the amount of money invested, the initial cash outflow, to see if the difference or NPV is positive. The NPV for Project Long is equal to the present value of the project's expected cash flows for Years 1 through 5 minus the initial cash outlay (CF_0). We can use Equation (1) to solve this problem. Thus, the first step in the solution is to calculate the present value of the future cash flows by discounting the cash flows using $k = 17\%$. Then, from this quantity we subtract the initial cash outlay of $100,000.

We can calculate this present value using the mathematics of discounted cash flow, a financial calculator, or a spreadsheet. We demonstrate all three methods here.

STEP 3: Solve

Using the Mathematical Formulas.

Using Equation (1),

$$NPV = -\$100,000 + \frac{\$70,000}{(1 + .17)^1} + \frac{\$30,000}{(1 + .17)^2} + \frac{\$30,000}{(1 + .17)^3} + \frac{\$25,000}{(1 + .17)^4} + \frac{\$10,000}{(1 + .17)^5}$$

Solving the equation, we get

$$NPV = -\$100,000 + \$59,829 + \$21,915 + \$18,731 + \$13,341 + \$4,561$$

$$= -\$100,000 + \$118,378$$

$$NPV = \$18,378$$

Using a Financial Calculator.

Before using the CF button, make sure you clear your calculator by inputting CF; 2nd; CE/C.

Data and Key Input	Display
CF; −100,000; ENTER	CF0 = −100,000.00
↓; 70,000; ENTER	C01 = 70,000.00
↓; 1; ENTER	F01 = 1.00
↓; 30,000; ENTER	C02 = 30,000.00
↓; 2; ENTER	F02 = 2.00
↓; 25,000; ENTER	C03 = 25,000.00
↓; 1; ENTER	F03 = 1.00
↓; 10,000; ENTER	C04 = 10,000.00
↓; 1; ENTER	F04 = 1.00
NPV; 17; ENTER	I = 17
↓; CPT	NPV = 18,378

(1 CONTINUED >> ON NEXT PAGE)

Using an Excel Spreadsheet.

It should be noted that the NPV function in Excel does *not* compute the net present value that we want to calculate. Instead, the NPV function calculates the present value of a sequence of cash flows using a single discount rate. In addition, the function assumes that the first cash flow argument is for one period in the future (i.e., Period 1) so you *do not* want to incorporate the initial cash flow (CF_0) in the NPV function—instead, use the NPV function to calculate the present value of the cash flows, then adjust for the initial cash flow (CF_0), which is generally a negative number. Specifically, the inputs of the NPV function are the following for Project Long:

$$\text{Net Present Value} = NPV(\text{discount rate}, CF_1, CF_2, CF_3, CF_4, CF_5) + CF_0$$

$$\text{Net Present Value} = NPV(0.17, 70000, 30000, 30000, 25000, 10000) - 100000 = \$18,378$$

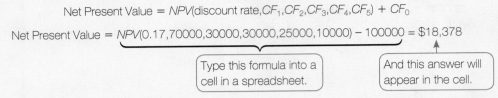

Type this formula into a cell in a spreadsheet.

And this answer will appear in the cell.

Thus, using the NPV function we calculate the Net Present Value of the investment to be $18,378.

STEP 4: Analyze

Project Long requires an initial investment of $100,000 and provides future cash flows that have a present value of $118,378. Consequently, the project cash flows are $18,378 more than the required investment. Because the project's future cash flows are worth more than the initial cash outlay required to make the investment, the project is an acceptable project.

STEP 5: Check yourself

Saber Electronics provides specialty manufacturing services to defense contractors located in the Seattle, Washington, area. The initial outlay is $3 million and management estimates that the firm might generate cash flows for Years 1 through 5 equal to $500,000; $750,000; $1,500,000; $2,000,000; and $2,000,000. Saber uses a 20 percent discount rate for projects of this type. Is this a good investment opportunity?

ANSWER: NPV = $573,817.

Your Turn: For more practice, do the NPV calculations for **Study Problems** 1, 6, 8, 12, 19, and 26 at the end of this chapter.

>> END Checkpoint 1

limited to a fixed dollar amount that is less than the total amount of money required to fund all positive-NPV projects, the firm will engage in **capital rationing**. This means that managers will need to choose between alternative investments that all have positive NPVs.

In either of the above situations, one might think that the investment opportunity with the highest NPV should be chosen. This intuition is often correct, but there are some important exceptions. In particular, it is sometimes better to choose a project with a lower NPV if the life of the project is shorter. With a shorter payback, the firm ties up its capital for less time. Intuitively, one might think in terms of the NPV created per year as a metric for evaluating a project. One might also want to choose projects that require less managerial time and less capital.

Later in this chapter we will describe popular alternative methods for evaluating investment projects in situations where firms must choose between mutually exclusive projects because capital is rationed. In the Appendices in MyFinanceLab, we consider an example of a firm that must choose between two alternative investments that serve the same purpose.

Choosing between Mutually Exclusive Investments

This section is relatively complex and can be skipped without loss of continuity. In fact, many students find the material to be somewhat easier if they return to it after finishing the chapter.

When comparing mutually exclusive investments that have the same useful life, we simply calculate the NPVs of the alternatives and choose the one with the higher NPV. However, it is often the case that mutually exclusive investments have different useful lives. For example, one alternative might last for 10 years while the other only lasts 6 years. This often occurs when the firm is considering the replacement of a piece of equipment where the alternatives have different initial costs to purchase, have different useful lives, and have different annual costs of operations. The decision the firm must make is to determine which alternative is most cost effective.

Before we can answer the question as to which alternative to select, we must determine whether we will need this piece of equipment forever—that is, at the end of its useful life, will we buy another one? If not, we can simply compare alternatives with different lives by calculating the NPV of each alternative and choosing the piece of equipment with the higher NPV. However, if we expect this new piece of equipment to be replaced over and over again with a similar piece of equipment with the same NPV for each replication of the investment, then we must calculate the **equivalent annual cost (EAC)**. The EAC is sometimes referred to as the equivalent annual annuity (EAA). The EAC capital budgeting technique provides an estimate of the annual cost of owning and operating the investment over its lifetime. We can then compare the EAC of two or more alternatives and select the most cost-effective alternative. The power of EAC is that it considers the time value of money, the initial cash outlay, and the productive life of the investment all in a single number that can be compared across alternative investments.

The EAC of the machine can be calculated as follows:

- First we calculate the sum of the present value of the project's costs, including the project's initial cost and the costs the firm will incur to operate the machine over its projected lifespan. Remember, in this case the revenues are the same for both of the alternatives we are considering, so the free cash flows for the alternative investments are all negative (thus the name *equivalent annual cost*).

- Next, we convert the present value of the costs into its annual equivalent, which is the EAC of the investment.

The EAC is simply the cost per year, and this is what we will use to compare the two alternatives because the revenues are the same regardless of which alternative is chosen. You will notice that the calculations are the same as those used in calculating the installment payment on a loan (PMT). In this case the EAC is the payment (PMT) for an installment loan with the loan value amount (PV) equal to the present value of the project's costs. Thus, EAC can be calculated as follows:

$$\begin{matrix} Equivalent \\ Annual\ Cost\ (EAC) \end{matrix} = \frac{PV\ of\ Costs}{\begin{matrix} Annuity\ Present\ Value \\ Interest\ Factor \end{matrix}} = \frac{CF_0 + \dfrac{CF_1}{(1+k)^1} + \dfrac{CF_2}{(1+k)^2} + \cdots + \dfrac{CF_n}{(1+k)^n}}{\left(\dfrac{1}{k} - \dfrac{1}{k(1+k)^n}\right)} = \frac{NPV}{\left(\dfrac{1}{k} - \dfrac{1}{k(1+k)^n}\right)} \quad (2)$$

We can also solve for EAC using a financial calculator as follows:

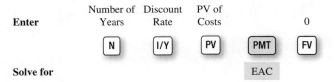

Step 1. Calculate the present value the annual operating costs for the machine over one life cycle of the project and add this sum to the initial cost of the machine.

Step 2. Divide the present value of the costs (calculated in Step 1) by the annuity present value interest factor (note the abbreviated formula for this present value interest factor found in Equation (2). You can think of the numerator of Equation (2) as an amount of money that you might borrow to purchase a new car and the EAC as your annual car payment.

Calculating the Equivalent Annual Cost (EAC)

Suppose your bottling plant is in need of a new bottle capper. You are considering two different capping machines that will perform equally well, but have different expected lives. The more expensive one costs $30,000 to buy, requires a payment of $3,000 per year for maintenance and operation expenses, and will last for five years. The cheaper model costs only $22,000, requires operating and maintenance costs of $4,000 per year, and lasts for only three years. Regardless of which machine you select, you intend to replace it at the end of its life with an identical machine with identical costs and operating performance characteristics. Because there is not a market for used cappers, there will be no salvage value associated with either machine. Let's also assume that the discount rate on both of these machines is 8 percent.

STEP 1: Picture the problem

You are considering two alternative pieces of equipment, one with a five-year life and one with a three-year life:

Project Long (Five-Year Life):

$k = 8\%$

| ■ Time Period | 0 | 1 | 2 | 3 | 4 | 5 | ■ Years |

| ■ Cash Flow | –$30,000 | –$3,000 | –$3,000 | –$3,000 | –$3,000 | –$3,000 |

Project Short (Three-Year Life):

$k = 8\%$

| ■ Time Period | 0 | 1 | 2 | 3 | ■ Years |

| ■ Cash Flow | –$22,000 | –$4,000 | –$4,000 | –$4,000 |

STEP 2: Decide on a solution strategy

The question we need to answer is which capping machine offers the lowest cost per year of operation. We can use a calculator to determine the equivalent annual cost (EAC) for each piece of equipment, which will tell us the cost per year for each alternative, and then choose the one with the lowest cost.

STEP 3: Solve

Using the Mathematical Formulas.

The present value of the costs of the five-year project can be calculated using a slightly modified (solving for PV of costs instead of NPV) version of Equation (1) as follows:

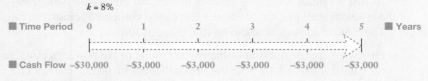

$$PV\ of\ Costs = CF_0 + \frac{CF_1}{(1+k)^1} + \frac{CF_2}{(1+k)^2} + \frac{CF_3}{(1+k)^3} + \frac{CF_4}{(1+k)^4} + \frac{CF_5}{(1+k)^5}$$

$$= -\$30,000 + \frac{-\$3,000}{(1+.08)^1} + \frac{-\$3,000}{(1+.08)^2} + \frac{-\$3,000}{(1+.08)^3} + \frac{-\$3,000}{(1+.08)^4} + \frac{-\$3,000}{(1+.08)^5}$$

$$= -\$41,978$$

Similarly, for the three-year project we calculate the present value of the costs as follows:

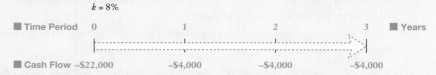

$$PV\ of\ Costs = CF_0 + \frac{CF_1}{(1+k)^1} + \frac{CF_2}{(1+k)^2} + \frac{CF_3}{(1+k)^3}$$

$$= -\$22,000 + \frac{-\$4,000}{(1+.08)^1} + \frac{-\$4,000}{(1+.08)^2} + \frac{-\$4,000}{(1+.08)^3}$$

$$= -\$32,308$$

Now that we have the present value of the costs we can compute the EAC for each, which is the annual cash flow that is equivalent to the present value of the costs. For the five-year project, the EAC is:

$$EAC_{long\ project} = \frac{PV\ of\ Costs}{Annuity\ Present\ Value\ Interest\ Factor} = \frac{-\$41,978}{\frac{1}{.08}\left(1 - \frac{1}{1+.08)^5}\right)} = -\$10,514$$

The three-year project's EAC can be computed in the same way, that is,

$$EAC_{short\ project} = \frac{PV\ of\ Costs}{Annuity\ Present\ Value\ Interest\ Factor} = \frac{-\$32,308}{\frac{1}{.08}\left(1 - \frac{1}{(1 + .08)^3}\right)} = -\$12,537$$

We are not going to go through the steps used to solve for EAC here because a financial calculator can be used to solve the problem quite easily.

Using a Financial Calculator.

First, after clearing your calculator, calculate the present value of the costs for one life cycle of each project.

Project Long:

Data and Key Input	Display
CF; −30,000; ENTER	CF0 = −30,000.00
↓; −3,000; ENTER	C01 = −3,000.00
↓; 5; ENTER	F01 = 5.00
NPV; 8; ENTER	I = 8
↓ CPT	NPV = −41,978

Project Short:

Data and Key Input	Display
CF; −22,000; ENTER	CF0 = −22,000.00
↓; −4,000; ENTER	C01 = −2,000.00
↓; 3; ENTER	F01 = 3.00
NPV; 8; ENTER	I = 8
↓ CPT	NPV = −32,308

Note that the present value of the costs of both pieces of equipment are negative because we are calculating the present value of the costs. Second, we calculate the value of the annuity payments over the project's life that would produce the same present value of the costs that you just calculated.

Project Long:

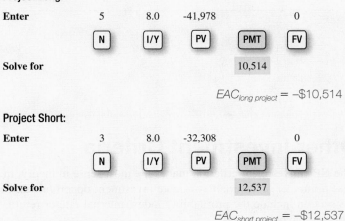

Enter	5	8.0	-41,978		0
	N	I/Y	PV	PMT	FV
Solve for				10,514	

$$EAC_{long\ project} = -\$10,514$$

Project Short:

Enter	3	8.0	-32,308		0
	N	I/Y	PV	PMT	FV
Solve for				12,537	

$$EAC_{short\ project} = -\$12,537$$

STEP 4: Analyze

We can see that the EAC associated with the longer-life project, −$10,514, is less than the EAC for the shorter-life project, −$12,537; thus, we should accept the longer project. In effect, it is the least expensive alternative even though it costs the most to purchase originally. The reason this works out is that by spending the extra money required to buy the longer-lived machine, we do not have to repeat the purchase for five years; in contrast, the shorter-life machine, although cheaper to purchase, must be replaced every three years. This is not always the case, however, as it depends on the cost of acquiring the longer-life machine and the annual operating costs.

(2 CONTINUED >> ON NEXT PAGE)

The EAC decision criteria is generally applied to mutually exclusive projects where the only difference is in length of life and costs. Thus, with the EAC we ignore cash inflows, because they are identical. However, if the mutually exclusive projects produce different cash inflows, we can still use this technique, but rather than calculate the present value of the costs (which would have a negative value), we would calculate the project's NPV (which would have a positive value) and select the project with the highest EAC.

STEP 5: Check yourself

What is the EAC for a machine that costs $50,000, requires payment of $6,000 per year for maintenance and operation expense, and lasts for six years? You may assume that the discount rate is 9 percent and there will be no salvage value associated with the machine. In addition, you intend to replace this machine at the end of its life with an identical machine with identical costs.

ANSWER: EAC = –$17,146.

Your Turn: For more practice, do related **Study Problem** 4 at the end of this chapter. >> **END Checkpoint 2**

Tools of Financial Analysis—Equivalent Annual Cost (or Equivalent Annual Annuity)

Name of Tool	Formula		What It Tells You
Equivalent Annual Cost (EAC) or Equivalent Annual Annuity (EAA)	$$\dfrac{PV\ of\ All\ Cash\ Flows}{Annuity\ Present\ Value\ Interest\ Factor} = \dfrac{CF_0 + \dfrac{CF_1}{(1+k)^1} + \dfrac{CF_2}{(1+k)^2} + \cdots + \dfrac{CF_n}{(1+k)^n}}{\left(\dfrac{1}{k} - \dfrac{1}{k(1+k)^n}\right)}$$ $$= \dfrac{NPV}{\left(\dfrac{1}{k} - \dfrac{1}{k(1+k)^n}\right)}$$		• An estimate of the annualized present value of a project's cash flows • Where all project cash flows are negative, then the lower the EAC, the less costly is the investment to operate per year • For a normal project with positive future cash flows, the EAC is the annualized NPV of the project. This metric is sometimes used to compare projects that have different initial costs and different useful lives.

Before you move on to 3

Concept Check | 2

1. Describe what the NPV tells the analyst about a new investment opportunity.
2. What is the equivalent annual cost (EAC) and when should it be used?
3. What is capital rationing?

---

3 | Other Investment Criteria

Although the NPV investment criterion makes the most sense in theory, in practice financial managers use a number of criteria to evaluate investment opportunities. Criteria that we explore in this section include the profitability index, internal rate of return, modified internal rate of return, and payback period.

Profitability Index

The **profitability index (PI)** is a cost-benefit ratio equal to the present value of an investment's future cash flows divided by its initial cost[3]:

$$\text{Profitability Index } (PI) = \left(\begin{array}{c}\text{Present Value of}\\\text{Future Cash Flows}\end{array}\right) \div \left(\begin{array}{c}\text{Initial Cash}\\\text{Outlay}\end{array}\right)$$

---

[3]While the initial outlay is a negative value because it is an outflow, we do not give it a negative sign in calculating the PI. Instead, the initial outlay is entered as a positive value since we are only interested in the ratio of benefits to costs.

or

$$\text{Profitability Index } (PI) = \cfrac{\cfrac{\text{Cash Flow for Year 1 } (CF_1)}{\left(1 + \cfrac{\text{Discount}}{\text{Rate } (k)}\right)^1} + \cfrac{\text{Cash Flow for Year 2 } (CF_2)}{\left(1 + \cfrac{\text{Discount}}{\text{Rate } (k)}\right)^2} + \cdots + \cfrac{\text{Cash Flow for Year } n \ (CF_n)}{\left(1 + \cfrac{\text{Discount}}{\text{Rate } (k)}\right)^n}}{\text{Initial Cash Outlay } (CF_0)} \tag{3}$$

A PI greater than 1 indicates that the present value of the investment's future cash flows exceeds the cost of making the investment and the investment should be accepted. So for the condo investment we discussed in the introduction, the PI is equal to $1.087 = \$100,000/\$92,000$.

Note that when computing the PI we use a positive value for the initial cash outlay (CF_0). This is done so that the PI is a positive ratio. Technically, because the initial outlay for most investments is a cash outflow, the sign on this number is negative.

The PI is closely related to NPV because it uses the same inputs: the present value of the project's future cash flows and the initial cash outlay. The PI is a ratio of these two quantities, and NPV is the difference between them, that is,

$$\text{Profitability Index } (PI) = \text{Present Value of Future Cash Flows} \div \text{Initial Cash Outlay}$$

And

$$\text{Net Present Value} = \text{Present Value of Future Cash Flows} - \text{Initial Cash Outlay}$$

> **PI Decision Criterion:** When the PI is greater than 1, the NPV will be positive, so the project should be accepted. When the PI is less than 1, which indicates a bad investment, NPV will be negative and the project should be rejected.

The PI of an investment is always greater than 1 for all positive-NPV projects and is always less than 1 for all negative-NPV projects. Thus, for independent projects the NPV criterion and the PI criterion are exactly the same. However, for mutually exclusive projects that have different costs, the criteria may provide different rankings. For example, suppose that Project 1 costs $200,000 and has future cash flows with a present value of $250,000, and Project 2 costs $500,000 and has future cash flows with a present value of $600,000. Project 2 has the higher NPV: $100,000 versus $50,000 for Project 1. But Project 1 has the higher PI: 1.25 versus 1.20 for Project 2.

Firms with easy access to capital prefer the NPV criterion, because it measures the amount of wealth created by the investment. However, if the firm's management is faced with a capital-rationing situation and cannot undertake all of its positive-NPV investments, the PI offers a useful way to rank order investment opportunities to determine which ones to accept. The PI is useful in this setting because, unlike NPV, it measures the amount of wealth created per dollar invested.

Tools of Financial Analysis— Profitability Index

Name of Tool	Formula	What It Tells You
Profitability Index (PI)	$\dfrac{\text{Present Value of Future Cash Flows}}{\text{Initial Cash Outlay } (CF_0)} =$ $\dfrac{\dfrac{\text{Cash Flow for Year 1 } (CF_1)}{\left(1 + \dfrac{\text{Discount}}{\text{Rate } (k)}\right)^1} + \dfrac{\text{Cash Flow for Year 2 } (CF_2)}{\left(1 + \dfrac{\text{Discount}}{\text{Rate } (k)}\right)^2} + \cdots + \dfrac{\text{Cash Flow for Year } n \ (CF_n)}{\left(1 + \dfrac{\text{Discount}}{\text{Rate } (k)}\right)^n}}{\text{Initial Cash Outlay } (CF_0)}$	• Sometimes referred to as the cost-benefit ratio, the PI is a "relative" valuation measure • A PI ratio greater than 1 indicates that the project's cash flows are more valuable than the cost of making the investment • If the PI is greater than 1, then the NPV is greater than 0, such that NPV and PI provide the same signal as to whether a project creates shareholder value.

Internal Rate of Return

The **internal rate of return (IRR)** of an investment is analogous to the yield to maturity (YTM) on a bond. Specifically, the IRR is the discount rate that results in a zero NPV for the project. For example, if you invest $100 today in a project expected to return $120 in one year, the IRR for the investment is 20 percent. We can show that this is correct by discounting the $120 cash flow one year at 20 percent, which results in a present value equal to the initial cash outlay of $100 ($CF_0 = -100$). The result, then, is an NPV of zero.

$$\text{Net Present Value} = \text{Cash Flow for Year 0 } (CF_0) + \frac{\text{Cash Flow for Year 1 } (CF_1)}{\left(1 + \frac{\text{Internal Rate}}{\text{of Return } (IRR)}\right)^1} = 0$$

$$0 = -\$100 + \frac{\$120}{(1 + IRR)}$$

Checkpoint 3

Calculating the Profitability Index for Project Long

Project Long is expected to provide five years of cash inflows and to require an initial investment of $100,000. The discount rate that is appropriate for calculating the PI of Project Long is 17 percent. Is Project Long a good investment opportunity? (See Checkpoint 1 for cash flow details.)

STEP 1: Picture the problem

Project Long requires an initial investment of $100,000, and is expected to produce the following cash flows over the next five years.

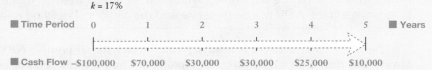

	$k = 17\%$					
■ Time Period	0	1	2	3	4	5 ■ Years
■ Cash Flow	–$100,000	$70,000	$30,000	$30,000	$25,000	$10,000

STEP 2: Decide on a solution strategy

The PI for Project Long is equal to the present value of the project's expected cash flows for Years 1 through 5 divided by minus (or the negative value of) the initial cash outlay ($-CF_0$). Thus, the first step in the solution is to calculate the present value of the future cash flows, discounting those cash flows using $k = 17\%$. We then divide this quantity by $100,000. Note that although the initial cash outlay is a negative number, we make it positive when we divide through so that the PI comes out positive.

STEP 3: Solve

In Checkpoint 1 we demonstrated how to calculate the present value of Project Long's future cash flows using the time-value-of-money formulas, a financial calculator, and a spreadsheet. Thus, we only summarize the results of these calculations below:

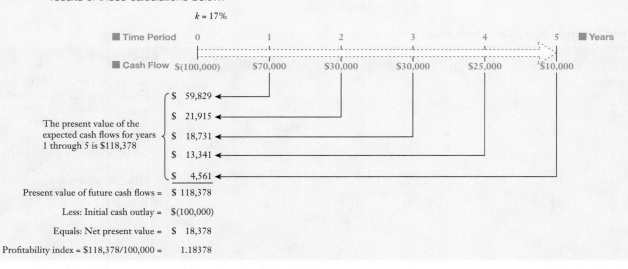

		$k = 17\%$					
■ Time Period	0	1	2	3	4	5 ■ Years
■ Cash Flow	$(100,000)	$70,000	$30,000	$30,000	$25,000	$10,000

The present value of the expected cash flows for years 1 through 5 is $118,378

$ 59,829
$ 21,915
$ 18,731
$ 13,341
$ 4,561

Present value of future cash flows = $ 118,378
Less: Initial cash outlay = $(100,000)
Equals: Net present value = $ 18,378
Profitability index = $118,378/100,000 = 1.18378

STEP 4: Analyze

Project Long requires an initial investment of $100,000 and provides future cash flows that have a present value of $118,378. Consequently, the project's future cash flows are worth 1.18378 times the initial investment. Because the project's future cash flows are worth more than the initial cash outlay required to create the investment, this is an acceptable project.

STEP 5: Check yourself

PNG Pharmaceuticals, Inc. is considering an investment in a new automated materials handling system that is expected to reduce its drug manufacturing costs by eliminating much of the waste currently involved in its specialty drug division. The new system will require an initial investment of $50,000 and is expected to provide cash savings over the next six-year period as follows:

Year	Expected Cash Flow	Year	Expected Cash Flow
Initial outlay (Year 0)	$(50,000)	Year 4	$12,000
Year 1	15,000	Year 5	14,000
Year 2	8,000	Year 6	16,000
Year 3	10,000		

PNG uses a 10 percent discount rate to evaluate investments of this type. Should PNG go forward with the investment? Use the PI to evaluate the project.

ANSWER: PI = 1.0733.

Your Turn: For more practice, do related **Study Problem** 26 at the end of this chapter.   **>> END Checkpoint 3**

For investments that offer more than one year of expected cash flows, the calculation is a bit more tedious. Mathematically, we solve for the internal rate of return for a multiple-period investment by solving for IRR, which is the unknown discount rate in the following equation, which makes the present value of the investment cash flows (the initial outlay and future cash flows) equal to zero. In other words, using the IRR as the discount rate would make the NPV equal to zero, that is,

$$
\begin{aligned}
\text{Net Present Value} = {} & \text{Cash Flow for Year 0 }(CF_0) + \frac{\text{Cash Flow for Year 1 }(CF_1)}{\left(1 + \dfrac{\text{Internal Rate of Return }(IRR)}{}\right)^1} + \frac{\text{Cash Flow for Year 2 }(CF_2)}{\left(1 + \dfrac{\text{Internal Rate of Return }(IRR)}{}\right)^2} \\
& + \cdots + \frac{\text{Cash Flow for Year } n \ (CF_n)}{\left(1 + \dfrac{\text{Internal Rate of Return }(IRR)}{}\right)^n} = 0
\end{aligned}
\tag{4}
$$

Solving for IRR when there are multiple future periods can be done in several ways, which we demonstrate in Checkpoint 4.

> **IRR Decision Criterion:** Accept the project if the IRR is greater than the required rate of return or discount rate used to calculate the net present value of the project, and reject it otherwise.

Checkpoint 4

Calculating the IRR for Project Long

Project Long is expected to provide five years of cash inflows and to require an initial investment of $100,000. The required rate of return or discount rate that is appropriate for valuing the cash flows of Project Long is 17 percent. What is Project Long's IRR, and is it a good investment opportunity?

STEP 1: Picture the problem

Project Long requires an initial investment of $100,000 and is expected to produce the following cash flows over the next five years.

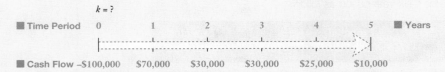

	$k = ?$					
■ Time Period	0	1	2	3	4	5 ■ Years
■ Cash Flow	–$100,000	$70,000	$30,000	$30,000	$25,000	$10,000

STEP 2: Decide on a solution strategy

With projects that provide multiple cash flows received over many years, calculating a single rate of return requires that we estimate the project's IRR. Specifically, the IRR for Project Long is the discount rate that makes the present value of Project Long's future cash flows equal, in absolute terms, to the initial cash outflow of $100,000. We could solve for this discount rate by trial and error—that is, by experimenting with different discount rates to find the one that satisfies our definition of NPV. However, as we demonstrate here, this can be very time consuming. Luckily, we can use either a financial calculator or a spreadsheet program such as Microsoft Excel to solve for the IRR. We illustrate both of these methods here.

STEP 3: Solve

Before we demonstrate the two solution methods, let's first take a look at the solution, which we will find to be 27.68 percent. Discounting the project cash flows for Years 1 through 5 back to the present using the IRR, which is 27.68 percent, we see that the resulting NPV is 0.

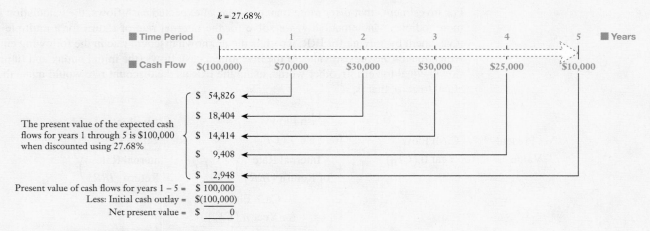

Using the Mathematical Formulas.

To solve for the IRR by hand, we follow a trial-and-error approach. Using this method, we must calculate NPV using many different discount rates until we find the discount rate that produces a zero NPV. For example, if we were to calculate the NPV for discount rates starting with 0 percent and increasing in increments of 4 percent up to 68 percent, we would get the following set of results (note that we have cheated here and used an Excel spreadsheet to reduce the tedium of making all these NPV calculations).

Discount Rates	Computed NPVs
0%	$ 65,000
4%	$ 51,304
8%	$ 39,532
12%	$ 29,331
16%	$ 20,428
20%	$ 12,603
24%	**$ 5,683**
28%	**$ (473)**
32%	$ (5,978)
36%	$ (10,926)
40%	$ (15,394)
44%	$ (19,445)
48%	$ (23,133)
52%	$ (26,504)
56%	$ (29,595)
60%	$ (32,439)
64%	$ (35,063)
68%	$ (37,492)

NPV = 0

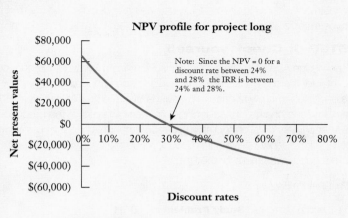

NPV profile for project long

Note: Since the NPV = 0 for a discount rate between 24% and 28% the IRR is between 24% and 28%.

Net present values — Discount rates

Notice that the computed NPV approaches a value of zero where we use a discount rate between 24 and 28 percent. This graph of NPVs and different discount rates is called the NPV profile of the project (we will have more to say about this profile later). We can calculate the IRR directly using either a financial calculator or spreadsheet, as we now demonstrate.

Using a Financial Calculator.

Data and Key Input	Display
CF; −100,000; ENTER	CF0 = −100,000.00
↓; 70,000; ENTER	C01 = 70,000.00
↓; 1; ENTER	F01 = 1.00
↓; 30,000; ENTER	C02 = 30,000.00
↓; 2; ENTER	F02 = 2.00
↓; 25,000; ENTER	C03 = 25,000.00
↓; 1; ENTER	F03 = 1.00
↓; 10,000; ENTER	C04 = 10,000.00
↓; 1; ENTER	F04 = 1.00
IRR; CPT	IRR = 27.68%

Using an Excel Spreadsheet.

Cell B10 contains the Excel formula for the IRR calculation, which appears as follows: "=IRR(B3:B8)". The only inputs to the IRR function in Excel are the project cash flows.[4]

	A	B
1		Annual
2	Year	Cash Flows
3	0	$(100,000)
4	1	70,000
5	2	30,000
6	3	30,000
7	4	25,000
8	5	10,000
9		
10	IRR =	27.68%

Entered equation in Cell B10: = IRR (B3:B8)

What appears in the spreadsheet, then, is the IRR of 27.68 percent.

(4 CONTINUED >> ON NEXT PAGE)

---

[4]Actually, the IRR function will appear with a final input option for [guess], which allows you to enter a guess as to what the IRR may be. However, this is typically not needed for Excel to calculate the IRR.

STEP 4: Analyze

Project Long requires an initial investment of $100,000 and provides future cash flows that offer a return on this investment of 27.68 percent. Because we have decided that the minimum rate of return we need to earn on this investment is 17 percent, it appears that Project Long is an acceptable investment opportunity.

STEP 5: Check yourself

Knowledge Associates is a small consulting firm in Portland, Oregon, considering the purchase of a new copying center for the office that can copy, fax, and scan documents. The new machine costs $10,010 to purchase and is expected to provide cash flow savings over the next four years of $1,000, $3,000, $6,000, and $7,000. The employee in charge of performing a financial analysis of the proposed investment has decided to use the IRR as her primary criterion for making a recommendation to the managing partner of the firm. If the required rate of return or discount rate the firm uses to value the cash flows from office equipment purchases is 15 percent, is this a good investment for the firm?

ANSWER: IRR = 19 percent.

Your Turn: For more practice, do related **Study Problems** 9, 10, 11, 12, 13, 16, 19, and 26 at the end of this chapter.

>> **END Checkpoint 4**

Complications with IRR: Unconventional Cash Flows

For a typical investment, money is spent in the early years to get the investment up and running and the initial outlay is followed by a period of cash inflows. For projects with this pattern of cash flows, the NPV will always be positive if the IRR is greater than the required rate of return or discount rate. Firms are also sometimes faced with opportunities where they initially receive cash inflows that require future cash expenditures. In the latter situation, an NPV greater than zero signifies that the IRR is less than the discount rate used to calculate the NPV.

To illustrate, consider the following project cash flows for Project Conventional and Project Unconventional using a 10 percent discount rate:

Projects

	Conventional	Unconventional
0	$(100,000)	$100,000
1	30,000	(30,000)
2	30,000	(30,000)
3	30,000	(30,000)
4	30,000	(30,000)
5	30,000	(30,000)
NPV	$13,724	$ (13,724)
IRR	15.24%	15.24%

Note that the IRR for both projects is 15.24 percent because each project's future cash flows are discounted to the present using this rate, and have a present value exactly equal to the cash flow realized in year zero. However, with a 10 percent discount rate, Project Conventional has a positive NPV and Project Unconventional has a negative NPV. Why is this? The answer becomes obvious when we consider that Project Conventional looks very much like the cash flow to a lender, such as a bank, that loans $100,000 in return for a series of five payments of $30,000 per year. The rate of return earned on the loan is the IRR of 15.24 percent. Because the lender's discount rate is 10 percent and it earns a return of 15.24 percent, this is a good investment. Project Unconventional cash flows are the mirror image of Project Conventional cash flows and can be interpreted as the cash flows for the borrower. In this instance, the borrower is paying a 15.24 percent rate of return when the appropriate discount rate is only 10 percent, so this is clearly not a good deal for the borrower. The borrower is effectively paying 15.24 percent for a loan when the borrower could raise funds at the opportunity cost, which is only 10 percent. Consequently, the borrower realizes a negative NPV equal to the positive NPV realized by the lender.

For conventional cash flow patterns, an IRR greater than the required rate of return or discount rate used to value the project cash flows implies a positive-NPV project, whereas for unconventional cash flows the opposite is true. Note, however, that the NPV of the two projects gives the correct indication as to the value of the investment being considered. Therefore, the prudent thing to do when evaluating any investment opportunity is to use the NPV criterion.

Complications with IRR: Multiple Rates of Return

Although any project can have only one NPV, a single project can, under certain circumstances, have more than one IRR. We can trace the reasons for this to the calculations involved in determining the IRR. In Equation (4) we defined the IRR as the discount rate that results in an NPV calculation of zero:

$$NPV = CF_0 + \frac{CF_1}{(1 + IRR)^1} + \frac{CF_2}{(1 + IRR)^2} + \frac{CF_3}{(1 + IRR)^3} + \cdots + \frac{CF_n}{(1 + IRR)^n} = 0 \qquad \textbf{(4)}$$

When the first cash flow is negative (the initial investment) and the subsequent cash flows are positive, there is one unique IRR. However, there can be multiple values for IRR that solve Equation (4) when some of the later cash flows are negative.[5] Consider, for example, the following project:

■ Time Period	0	1	2	■ Years

| ■ Cash Flow | −$235,000 | $540,500 | −$310,200 | |

In Checkpoint 5, we calculate the IRR for this project and find that both 10 and 20 percent solve this problem.

Which solution is correct? The answer is that neither solution is valid. Although each fits the definition of IRR, neither provides the true project returns. In summary, when there is more than one sign reversal in the cash flow stream, the possibility of multiple IRRs exists; and where there are multiple IRRs, we can no longer use this investment criterion to evaluate the project. Fortunately, NPV is not subject to this problem.

Using the IRR with Mutually Exclusive Investments

IRRs are often used by managers to select among mutually exclusive investments. A complication often arises because there can be ranking conflicts between the NPV and the IRR of the evaluated projects. That is, although both mutually exclusive projects may have positive NPVs and IRRs greater than their required rates of return, one project may have a higher NPV whereas the other has a higher IRR. When this is the case, which criterion should we go with, the higher NPV or higher IRR?

For example, Apex Engineering is considering the purchase of an automated accounting system. Two software systems are being considered that will perform the same functions, Automated Accounting Plus (AA+) and Business Basics Reporting (BBR). The cash flows

---

[5]To be specific, there can be as many IRRs as there are changes in the sign of the cash flows over the n-year project life. Technically, the multiple IRR problem arises out of the fact that the IRR we calculate is actually the solution to an nth degree polynomial equation, where n is the number of years over which cash flows are produced by the project (and, consequently, the highest exponent in the equation). The seventeenth-century philosopher René Descartes gave us something called Descartes' Rule of Signs that can be used to tell us the maximum number of IRRs that a given project can produce. Here's how it works: there can exist a different IRR for each sign change in a project's cash flows over its n-year life. For example, Project Long only has one sign change; in Year 0 the project has a negative $100,000 cash outlay, followed in Year 1 by a positive $70,000. The project can therefore have a maximum of one IRR. Note that the Rule of Signs says a project can have a *maximum* number of IRRs equal to the number of sign changes, but the actual number of IRRs may be fewer.

from the AA+ system grow over time because this system offers the user the opportunity to expand functionality. The cash flows for the BBR system, on the other hand, decline over time as the initial cost savings are captured in the early years of implementation. The expected cash flows of the two systems are found in Panel A of Figure 1.

Note that both accounting systems provide positive NPVs using the firm's 15 percent discount rate or required rate of return. This suggests that one of the two systems should indeed be purchased. However, the AA+ system, which offers an NPV of $412,730 compared to $370,241 for the BBR alternative, has the lower IRR (38 percent compared to 52 percent). Why do the two criteria provide different answers? It is because the larger cash flows come earlier for the BBR system. The BBR system earns a very high return, but over a shorter period of time. The fact that the BBR system uses the firm's capital over a shorter time period may be relevant if there are constraints on the firm's ability to raise capital (that is, if capital is being rationed). However, if the firm has access to external capital markets, the project with the higher NPV should be chosen.

To examine this more closely we will look at each project's **NPV profile**, a graph of the NPV of the AA+ and BBR alternatives using required rates of return ranging from 0 percent to 65 percent. As shown in Panel B of Figure 1, for discount rates below 19.5 percent, the AA+ system offers the higher NPV, and for higher discount rates the BBR system has higher NPVs. This implies that if the appropriate required rate of return for the projects is less than 19.5 percent, and the firm is not capital constrained, the AA+ system should be taken. However, if the firm is capital constrained and is likely to have opportunities with IRRs greater than 19.5 percent in the near future, it may want to take the BBR system, which allows it to recover its capital sooner.

Checkpoint 5

The Problem of Multiple IRRs for Projects

Descartes' Rule of Signs tells us that there can be as many IRRs for an investment project as there are changes in the sign of the cash flows over its n-year life. To illustrate the problem, consider a project that has three cash flows: a –$235,000 outlay in Year 0, a $540,500 inflow in Year 1, and a $310,200 outflow at the end of Year 2. Calculate the IRR for the investment.

STEP 1: Picture the problem

$k = ?$

■ Time Period   0   1   2   ■ Years

■ Cash Flow   –$235,000 $540,500   –$310,200

STEP 2: Decide on a solution strategy

To solve the problem, we determine the discount rate that makes the NPV = 0 by constructing an NPV profile for the project. In this instance we use discount rates in increments of 2 percent ranging from 0 percent to 30 percent.

STEP 3: Solve

We calculate the discount rate that makes the NPV = 0 for of the investment using discount rates ranging from 0 percent to 30 percent. For example, the NPV for a 10 percent discount rate is calculated using Equation (1) as follows:

$$NPV = CF_0 + \frac{CF_1}{(1 + k)^1} + \frac{CF_2}{(1 + k)^2} \tag{1}$$

$$= -\$235{,}000 + \frac{\$540{,}500}{(1 + .10)^1} + \frac{-\$310{,}200}{(1 + .10)^2} = 0$$

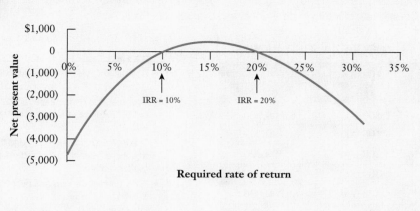

Discount Rates	Net Present Value
0%	$(4,700)
2%	$(3,253)
4%	$(2,086)
6%	$(1,171)
8%	$ (484)
10%	**$ 0**
12%	$ 300
14%	$ 434
16%	$ 419
18%	$ 270
20%	**$ 0**
22%	$ (379)
24%	$ (856)
26%	$(1,421)
28%	$(2,065)
30%	$(2,781)

STEP 4: Analyze

There are two IRRs for this project: 10 percent and 20 percent. This results from the fact that there are two sign changes in the project cash flows. Thus, if the risk-appropriate discount rate for the project is between 10 percent and 20 percent, the project creates value and should be undertaken; otherwise, it should be rejected.

STEP 5: Check yourself

McClary Custom Printers is considering whether to purchase a printer. The printer costs $200,000 to purchase, and McClary expects it can earn an additional $1.2 million in cash flows in the printer's first year of use. However, there is a problem with purchasing the printer today, because it will require a very large expenditure in Year 2, such that Year 2's cash flow is expected to be −$2.2 million. Finally, in Year 3 the printer investment is expected to produce a cash flow of $1.2 million. Use the IRR to evaluate whether the printer purchase would be worthwhile.

ANSWER: IRR = 100% and 200%.

>> END Checkpoint 5

Tools of Financial Analysis—Internal Rate of Return

Name of Tool	Formula	What It Tells You
Internal Rate of Return (IRR)	$$\left(\begin{array}{c} \textit{Present Value} \\ \textit{of Future Cash Flows} \\ \textit{Discounted Using IRR} \end{array} \right) = 0$$ Note that the IRR is the discount rate that makes the NPV equal to zero.	• The compound annual rate of return earned on an investment • An IRR greater than the required rate of return for the investment signals a good investment • The IRR is analogous to the yield to maturity (YTM) on a bond.

Modified Internal Rate of Return

As we discovered earlier, in cases where there is more than one IRR for a particular project, the IRR criterion is not particularly useful. In order to eliminate the problem of multiple IRRs, the **modified internal rate of return (MIRR)** was developed. *The idea behind the MIRR is to rearrange the project cash flows such that there is only one change in the sign of the cash flows over the life of the project.* This can be accomplished by discounting all the negative cash flows after the initial cash outflow back to Year 0 and adding them to the initial cash outflow. This process is described as follows:

Step 1. **Modify the project cash flow stream by discounting the negative future cash flows back to the present using the required rate of return (that is, the discount rate that is used to calculate the project's NPV).** The present value of these future negative cash flows is then added to the initial outlay to form a modified project cash flow stream in which all the cash outflows have been moved back to Year 0.

Figure 1

Ranking Mutually Exclusive Investments: NPV vs. IRR

Apex Engineering is considering the purchase of an automated accounting system and is trying to decide between the AA+ and BBR systems. Both systems have the same cost but because of functionality differences, the patterns of cash flows are quite different. Apex uses a 15 percent required rate of return or discount rate to evaluate its investments.

(Panel A) Expected Cash Flows

Cash Flows		
Year	AA+	BBR
0	$(500,000)	$(500,000)
1	100,000	400,000
2	200,000	300,000
3	300,000	200,000
4	400,000	200,000
5	500,000	100,000
NPV	$412,730	$370,241
IRR	38%	52%

- Both alternatives have positive NPVs and IRRs that exceed Apex's 15% required rate of return.
- However, the projects are ranked differently using NPV or IRR: AA+ has the higher NPV while BBR has a higher IRR.
- The ranking difference is due to the effect of discounting and the difference in the patterns of the cash flows for the two projects.
- AA+ cash flows increase over time while BBR's decrease.
- Higher discount rates have a disproportionate effect on present values as we see in Panel B.

(Panel B) NPV Profiles

NPV Profiles		
Discount Rate	AA+	BBR
0%	$1,000,000	$700,000
5%	$ 756,639	$568,722
10%	$ 565,259	$460,528
15%	$ 412,730	$370,241
20%	$ 289,673	$294,046
25%	$ 189,280	$229,088
30%	$ 106,532	$173,199
35%	$ 37,680	$124,709
40%	$ (20,111)	$ 82,317
45%	$ (69,011)	$ 44,998
50%	$ (110,700)	$ 11,934
55%	$ (146,489)	$ (17,531)
60%	$ (177,414)	$ (43,930)
65%	$ (204,298)	$ (67,701)

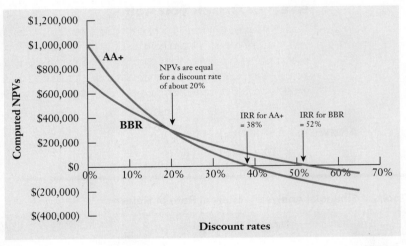

(Panel C) Estimating the Break-Even Discount Rate

Cash Flows			Differential Cash Flows
Year	AA+	BBR	BBR − AA+
0	$(500,000)	$(500,000)	$ 0
1	100,000	400,000	$ 300,000
2	200,000	300,000	$ 100,000
3	300,000	200,000	$(100,000)
4	400,000	200,000	$(200,000)
5	500,000	100,000	$(400,000)

IRR of the Differential Cash Flows = 19.5%

- Using a 19.5% discount rate the two projects have exactly the same NPV.
- For discount rates lower than this break-even 19.5% rate, AA+ has the higher NPV whereas for higher discount rates BBR has the higher NPV.
- Trust NPV. Given the discount rate appropriate for valuing project cash flows, NPV gives the correct ranking of projects!

>> END FIGURE 1

Step 2. Calculate the MIRR as the IRR of the modified cash flow stream. We add the "modified" to IRR because the MIRR is based on a *modified* set of cash flows.

Let's reconsider Checkpoint 5 where there were two sign changes. Checkpoint 6 illustrates how we can eliminate the sign changes by discounting the negative cash flow in Year 2 back to the present and combining it with the Year 0 initial cash outlay. The IRR of the modified cash flows, or MIRR, of 12.07 percent exceeds the 12 percent required rate of return or discount rate used to value the project cash flows, which indicates the project is a good one.

To close our discussion of MIRR, here are some summary points and caveats concerning its use:

- **There is more than one way to compute the MIRR, and each method can potentially result in a different value for the MIRR.** We used what we consider to be the simplest and least invasive approach to computing the MIRR. Specifically, we discounted the project's negative cash flows back to the present using the project's required rate of return and then computed the MIRR from the modified cash flows. Some analysts compute a MIRR by discounting negative cash flows back to the present using the project's required rate of return, as we do, and also compound the positive cash flows forward to the end of the project's life at an assumed "reinvestment rate" before computing the MIRR. We prefer our method as it uses only one modification to project cash flows.

- **Although doing either of the above modifications to the amount and timing of project cash flows will resolve the issue of multiple IRRs, the resulting MIRR is now a function of the discount rate.** Here's why. The internal rate of return is computed using only the project cash flows such that the rate we compute is "internal" or "intrinsic" to the project cash flows and does not depend on an external "discount" or "reinvestment" rate. This is not the case for the MIRR (regardless of how we compute it). After all, a project's value does not rise or fall if the project's cash flows are reinvested in an incredibly profitable project, used to pay bonuses, or invested in a safety project mandated by government.

- **Finally, NPV is our capital-budgeting method of choice because NPV is an estimate of the dollar value created by investing in the project.** This is true regardless of whether a unique estimate of IRR can be calculated or not.

Why do firms use the MIRR if it is not a perfect measure of the rate of return earned on the project? The answer probably comes out of a managerial preference for using a rate-of-return measure as a decision criterion, as opposed to a dollar measure such as NPV. Thus, if your firm asks for a MIRR and you compute one, make sure the NPV is positive before passing on a recommendation for the acceptance of the project based on the MIRR!

Checkpoint 6

Calculating the Modified Internal Rate of Return (MIRR)

Reconsider the investment project in Checkpoint 5. The project we analyzed has three cash flows: a –$235,000 outlay in Year 0, a $540,500 cash inflow in Year 1, and a $310,200 outflow at the end of Year 2. Our analysis in Checkpoint 5 indicated that this investment has two IRRs, 10 percent and 20 percent. One way to reduce the number of IRRs to only one is to use the MIRR method, which moves negative cash flows backward, discounting them using the required rate of return or discount rate for the project, which is 12 percent.

STEP 1: Picture the problem

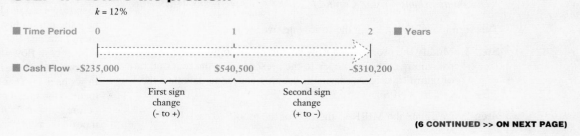

(6 CONTINUED >> ON NEXT PAGE)

STEP 2: Decide on a solution strategy

There are two sign changes in this cash flow stream. To implement the MIRR method we can discount the Year 2 negative cash flow back to Year 0 using the 12 percent discount rate used to calculate NPV, and then calculate the MIRR of the resulting cash flows for Years 0 and 1.

STEP 3: Solve

Discount the Year 2 negative cash flow back to Year 0:

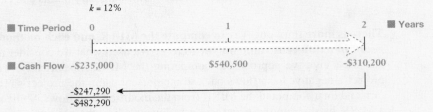

such that the modified cash flows of the investment are as follows:

Calculating the IRR for these modified cash flows produces the MIRR equal to 12.07 percent.

STEP 4: Analyze

By eliminating the second sign change, the computation of an IRR using the modified cash flow stream yields a single IRR we refer to as the MIRR. The MIRR is not the same as the IRR because it is based on modified cash flows that have been moved around in time using the discount rate used to both value project cash flows and calculate the NPV (which is not used in the IRR). Consequently, although the MIRR does produce a single rate-of-return estimate for the project, the MIRR depends on the discount rate used to move the cash flows from period to period and is no longer intrinsic to the project. For example, if the required rate of return had been 14 percent in the previous example, the MIRR would have been 14.10 percent (not 12.07 percent). The NPV, on the other hand, does not suffer from the multiple IRR problem and yields consistent results even in the face of multiple sign changes.

STEP 5: Check yourself

Analyze the MIRR for the preceding problem where the required rate of return used to discount the cash flows is 8 percent. What is the MIRR?

ANSWER: MIRR = 7.90%. Note that the project has a negative NPV of −$483.54 for this lower required rate of return. Can you explain why the NPV goes negative when the discount rate is lowered? (Hint: Reducing the discount rate from 12 percent to 8 percent makes the present value of the negative cash flow in Year 2 much larger.)

Your Turn: For more practice, do related **Study Problems** 14, 15, 17, and 18 at the end of this chapter.

>> **END** Checkpoint 6

Tools of Financial Analysis—Modified Internal Rate of Return

Name of Tool	Formula		What It Tells You
Modified Internal Rate of Return (MIRR)	$$\left(\begin{array}{c} \textit{Present Value} \\ \textit{of Negative Cash Flows} \\ \textit{Discounted Using Cost of Capital} \end{array} \right) + \left(\begin{array}{c} \textit{Present Value} \\ \textit{of Positive Cash Flows} \\ \textit{Discounted Using MIRR} \end{array} \right) = 0$$ This formula is solved using the following two steps: **Step 1.** Modify the project cash flow stream by discounting the negative future cash flows back to the present using the required rate of return (that is, the discount rate that is used to calculate the project's NPV). **Step 2.** Calculate the MIRR as the IRR of the modified cash flow stream.		• The compound annual rate of return earned on the "modified" cash flows for a project, where cash flows are modified to eliminate the possibility of getting more than one IRR • Project cash flows are modified by discounting all the negative cash flows back to Year 0 and adding them to the initial cash outflow before computing the IRR of the modified cash flows or MIRR.

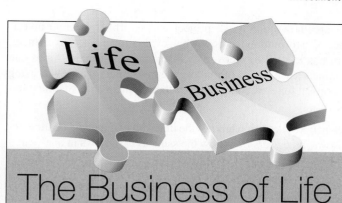

The Business of Life

Higher Education as an Investment in Yourself

Your decision to pursue a college education, and specifically a business degree, can be viewed as an investment decision. After all, to go to college you must delay entering the workforce for four to six years (or sometimes longer) and spend an average of $15,605 per year.[*] Financially speaking, is it worth it? We should hasten to point out that having a college education can (and should) enrich your life in ways that are not reflected in the amount of money you earn. However, for our purposes, let's concentrate on the financial implications of getting a college degree.

According to the U.S. Census Bureau of Labor Statistics, the average annual earnings for workers ranged from only $24,492 per year for workers with no high school diploma to $90,120 for those with professional degrees. Simply having a high school diploma increased earnings by over $9,000 a year, and the bachelor's degree almost doubled earnings for high school grads.

The salaries reported in the diagram are for all degrees and across the complete spectrum of years of experience (new hires to those close to retirement). What about business degrees and starting salaries in particular? For undergraduate business majors in the class of 2012, the average starting salary was $53,900. This would suggest that down the road, after some experience,

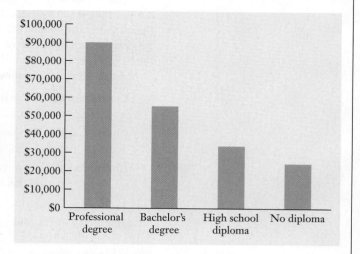

Average Earnings by Education Level: 2012

Source: U.S. Department of Labor, Bureau of Labor Statistics, Employment Projection (2012).

having a business degree would produce much higher average earnings than the $53,900 reported starting salary for all majors.

We do not have to do a lot of calculations to figure out that education pays. For example, the average differential of $21,530 between the holder of a bachelor's degree and a high school diploma $55,432 − $33,902, spread over a 45-year working life and discounted using a 5 percent discount rate, produces a present value at the end of college of $382,676. Looking at this as an NPV problem, if the cost of college is $15,605 a year for 4 years, and after that, the benefit of a degree is $21,530 per year for the following 45 years, using a 5% discount rate to discount these flows to the beginning of college, the NPV would be almost $260,000! Comparing this differential value of the extra income earned by having a bachelor's degree to the average cost of getting the education makes this decision look like a no-brainer!

Your Turn: See Study Question 11.

[*]This is the average cost of attending a public four-year college. The average cost of attending a private university was $31,395 in 2010.
Source: http://nces.ed.gov/fastfacts/display.asp?id=76 accessed 8th March 2013.

Payback Period

The **payback period** for an investment opportunity is the number of years needed to recover the initial cash outlay required to make the investment. For example, suppose Exec Corp. was deciding whether to spend $8 million for a new software system that would allow it to monitor the daily production from its thousands of operating oil and gas wells. If the new automated system were to reduce the costs of monitoring production by $4 million a year, the payback period for the investment would be only two years. Similarly, if the savings were only $2 million per year, the payback would be four years. If the savings are not the same each year, we simply cumulate the savings over time until we have accumulated the total investment outlay of $8 million. In this case the payback is often not an even number of years. For example, if the savings for the first three years of the investment were $4 million, $3 million, and $2 million, the payback period would equal 2.5 years. The first two years recover $7 million of the investment and the remaining $1 million is one-half the third year's savings, and thus a 2.5-year payback.

> **Payback Decision Criterion:** Accept the project if the payback period is less than a prespecified maximum number of years.

The payback criterion measures how quickly the project will return its original investment, which is a very useful piece of information to know when evaluating a risky investment. Specifically, the longer the firm has to wait to recover its investment, the more things can happen that might reduce or eliminate the benefits of making the investment. However, using the payback period as the sole criterion for evaluating whether to undertake an investment has three fundamental limitations:

Limitation #1: The payback period calculation ignores the time value of money, treating, for example, cash flows three years from now the same as cash flows in one year.

Limitation #2: The payback period ignores cash flows that are generated by the project beyond the end of the payback period.

Limitation #3: There is no clear-cut way to define the cutoff criterion for the payback period that is tied to the value creation potential of the investment.

To illustrate these limitations of the payback period, consider the cash flows for Project Long and Project Short found in Table 1. Both projects require an initial cash outlay of $100,000, and we assume that the payback criterion being used to evaluate the projects is three (3) years. Note that although both projects have the same payback of two years, which is shorter than the cutoff criteria of three years, we would clearly prefer Project Long to Project Short for the following reasons:

- First, regardless of what happens after the payback period, Project Long returns the initial investment earlier within the payback period (i.e., $70,000 in Year 1 as compared to only $50,000 for Project Short).
- Second, Project Long generates $65,000 in cash flows during Years 3 through 5, whereas Project Short provides no cash flows after the payback period.

Discounted Payback Period

To deal with the criticism that the payback period ignores the time value of money, some firms use the **discounted payback period** approach. The discounted payback period approach is similar to that of the traditional payback period except that it uses discounted cash flows (using the same discount rate used in calculating the NPV) to calculate the payback period. Thus, the discounted payback period is defined as the number of years needed to recover the initial cash outlay from the discounted cash flows.

> **Discounted Payback Decision Criterion:** Accept the project if its discounted payback period is less than the prespecified number of years.

If we assume that the discount rate for Projects Long and Short is 17 percent, the discounted cash flows from these projects are calculated in Table 2. After two years, Project Long still needs $18,256 in present value dollars to achieve payback. Therefore, payback occurs when approximately 97 percent of Year 3's discounted cash flow is received (i.e., $18,256/$18,731). Thus, Project Long has a discounted payback period of 2.97 years. Project Short, on the other hand, never achieves discounted payback, as the cumulative present value of its cash flows falls $20,739 short of the initial investment at the end of its life in Year 2. Clearly, the discounted payback is an improvement over the straight payback method.

Although the deficiencies of the payback criterion do limit the usefulness of the payback period and discounted payback period as tools for investment evaluation, these methods have several positive features as supplemental tools for evaluating investment opportunities in conjunction with net present value:

- First, for many individuals, both payback and discounted payback are more intuitive and easier to understand than other decision criteria such as NPV.
- Second, the payback period is often used as a crude indicator of project risk because payback favors projects that produce significant cash flows in the early years of a project's life, which, in general, are less risky than more distant cash flows.

Table 1   Limitations of the Payback Period Criterion

Limitations of the payback period as an investment criteria include:

a. Does not account for the time value of money.
b. Does not consider cash flows beyond the payback period.
c. Utilizes an arbitrary cutoff criterion.

	Project Long		Project Short	
	Cash Flows		Cash Flows	
	Annual	Cumulative	Annual	Cumulative
Initial cash outlay	$(100,000)	$(100,000)	$(100,000)	$(100,000)
Year 1	70,000	(30,000)	50,000	(50,000)
Year 2	**30,000**	**0**	**50,000**	**0**
Year 3	30,000	30,000	0	0
Year 4	25,000	55,000	0	0
Year 5	10,000	65,000	0	0

Payback equals two years for both projects because it takes two years to recover the cost of the initial outlay from the cash inflows. However, Project Long looks a lot better because it continues to provide cash inflows after the payback year!

Table 2   Discounted Payback Period Example (Discount Rate = 17 percent)

The standard payback period does not account for the time value of money, so the discounted payback period discounts investment cash flows back to the present before cumulating them to calculate payback.

Project Long

	Annual Cash Flows	Cumulative Cash Flows	Discounted Cash Flows	Cumulative Discounted Cash Flows
Initial cash outlay	$(100,000)	$(100,000)	$(100,000)	$(100,000)
Year 1	70,000	(30,000)	59,829	(40,171)
Year 2	**30,000**	**0**	**21,915**	**(18,256)**
Year 3	30,000	30,000	18,731	476
Year 4	25,000	55,000	13,341	13,817
Year 5	10,000	65,000	4,561	18,378

Discounted Payback equals 2.97 years for Project Long! Three years of discounted cash flows sum to a positive $476. However, since we need to sum to 0 we do not need a full three years of discounted cash flows (we need $18,256/$18,731 = .97 of Year 3's cash inflow).

Project Short

	Annual Cash Flows	Cumulative Cash Flows	Discounted Cash Flows	Cumulative Discounted Cash Flows
Initial cash outlay	$(100,000)	$(100,000)	$(100,000)	$(100,000)
Year 1	50,000	(50,000)	42,735	(57,265)
Year 2	**50,000**	**0**	**36,526**	**(20,739)**
Year 3	–	–	–	(20,739)
Year 4	–	–	–	(20,739)
Year 5	–	–	–	(20,739)

Discounted payback is *never* achieved for Project Short! The discounted cash flows never cumulate to equal zero.

383

- Third, the discounted payback is used as a supplemental analytical tool in instances where obsolescence is a risk, in attempt to provide insight as to whether we get our money back in today's dollars before the market disappears or the product is obsolete.
- Fourth, managers often find payback useful when capital is being rationed and they want to know how long the company's capital will be tied up in the project.

Tools of Financial Analysis—Payback Measures

Name of Tool	Formula	What It Tells You
Payback Period	The number of years of project cash flows that are required to recover the initial cash investment in the project	• The number of years needed to recover the initial cash outlay for the investment • Project cash flows are summed but not discounted to determine the payback period • There is no hard-and-fast rule for determining the minimum payback period, however.
Discounted Payback Period	The number of years of "discounted" project cash flows that are required to recover the initial cash investment in the project. Future cash flows are discounted using the cost of capital for the investment	• Discounted payback sums the present value of future cash flows to determine payback • There is no hard-and-fast rule for determining the minimum discounted payback period, however.

Summing Up the Alternative Decision Rules

We have reviewed six different decision rules that are used by businesses to evaluate new investment alternatives. NPV reflects the expected impact of an investment alternative on shareholder value; for this reason, NPV is the preferred standard for making investment decisions. However, as we have discussed, there are a number of other techniques that enjoy widespread use. Table 3 summarizes each of these methods, including a definition of the method, a description of the investment decision rule, and some brief comments concerning the pros and cons of each methodology.

Before you move on to 4

Concept Check | 3

1. Describe what the IRR metric tells the analyst about a new investment opportunity.
2. Describe the situations in which the NPV and IRR metrics can provide conflicting signals.
3. What is the modified internal rate of return metric, and why is it sometimes used?
4. What is the payback method, and what is the source of its appeal?
5. What is discounted payback, and how does it improve on the payback measure?

4 A Glance at Actual Capital-Budgeting Practices

During the past 50 years, the popularity of each of the capital-budgeting methods we have discussed here has shifted rather dramatically. In the 1950s and 1960s, the payback method dominated all other capital-budgeting metrics; however, in recent years the internal rate of return and the net present value techniques have gained in popularity and today are used by virtually all major corporations.

Table 3	Basic Capital-Budgeting Techniques

These are the primary capital-budgeting techniques or criteria that are used in industry practice. Of these techniques, net present value or NPV offers the best single indicator of the investment alternative's potential contribution to the value of the firm.

Investment Criterion	Definition	Decision Rule	Advantages	Disadvantages
Net Present Value (NPV)	Present value of expected cash inflows minus the present value of cash outflows.	Accept investments that have a positive NPV.	Theoretically correct in that it measures directly the increase in value that the project is expected to produce. Measures the increase in shareholder wealth expected from undertaking the project being analyzed.	Somewhat complicated to compute (requires an understanding of the time value of money). Not familiar to managers without formal business education.
Equivalent Annual Cost (EAC) or Equivalent Annual Annuity (EAA)	The annual cost that is equivalent in present value to the initial cost and annual cash flows of an investment.	Select the investment alternative that has the lowest annual cost.	Provides a tool that can be used to account for differences in initial cost of purchase, different annual costs of operations, and different productive lives.	Should only be used where the investments being compared are expected to be used indefinitely. For single-use investments, NPV is appropriate.
Profitability Index (PI)	Present value of expected future cash flows divided by the initial cash investment.	When the PI is greater than 1, the NPV will be positive, so the project should be accepted. When PI is less than 1, which indicates a bad investment, NPV will be negative and the project should be rejected.	Theoretically correct in that it measures directly the increase in value that the project is expected to produce. Useful when rank ordering positive-NPV projects where capital is being rationed.	Not as familiar to managers as NPV and does not add any additional information.
Internal Rate of Return (IRR)	The discount rate that makes NPV equal to zero.	Accept the project if the IRR is greater than the required rate of return or discount rate used to calculate the net present value of the project, and reject it otherwise.	Provides a rate-of-return metric, which many managers prefer.	Cannot always be estimated. Sometimes provides multiple rates of return for projects with multiple changes in the sign of their cash flows over time. Can provide conflicting indications to NPV for mutually exclusive projects.
Modified Internal Rate of Return (MIRR)	The discount rate that makes the NPV of the modified cash flow stream equal to zero.	Accept the project if the MIRR is greater than the required rate of return or discount rate used to calculate the net present value of the project, and reject it otherwise.	Always produces a single rate-of-return estimate.	The rate of return produced by the MIRR is not unique to the project because it is influenced by the discount rate used to discount the negative cash flows.
Payback	Time until the initial cash outlay has been recovered.	If the project payback is less than the maximum the firm will accept, the project is acceptable.	Easy to understand and calculate. An indication of risk (how long it takes to recover the investment).	Ignores time value of money. Ignores cash flows beyond the payback period. No rational way to determine the cutoff value for payback.
Discounted Payback	The number of years required to recover the initial investment out of project *discounted* future cash flows.	If the discounted project payback is less than the maximum the firm will accept, the project is acceptable.	Same as payback. Plus, by discounting the cash flows, this measure takes into account the time value of money.	Same as the last two items above. Also, because cash inflows must be discounted, discounted payback is more complicated to compute than payback.

Figure 2

Survey of the Popularity of Capital-Budgeting Methods

These survey results are based on the survey responses of 392 chief financial officers of large U.S. firms. CFOs were asked if they used any of the following standard techniques. Specifically, they were asked how frequently they used different capital-budgeting techniques on a scale of 0 to 4 (with 0 meaning "never," 1 "almost never," 2 "sometimes," 3 "almost always," and 4 "always"). The results below are the percentage of the CFOs who said they always or almost always used a particular method.

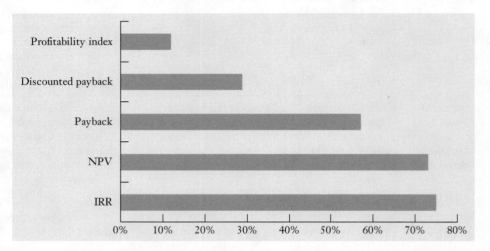

Source: John Graham and Campbell Harvey, "How Do CFOs Make Capital Budgeting and Capital Structure Decisions?" *Journal of Applied Corporate Finance*, Vol. 15, No. 1 (Spring 2002), 8–23.

>> END FIGURE 2

Figure 2 provides the results of a survey of the chief financial officers (CFOs) of large U.S. firms, showing the popularity of the payback, discounted payback, NPV, PI, and IRR methods for evaluating capital investment opportunities. The results show that IRR and NPV are by far the most widely used methods, although more than half the firms surveyed did use the payback method. The survey reported that larger firms tended to use NPV and IRR more frequently than their smaller counterparts and that the smaller firms tended to rely more on payback.

The popularity of the payback period may derive from its simplicity; however, an alternate explanation is that it is used in combination with NPV or IRR as a secondary method to control for project risk. The logic behind this is that the payback period dramatically emphasizes early period cash inflows, which are generally more certain—have less risk—than cash flows occurring later in a project's life. Managers believe its use will lead to projects with more certain cash flows.

Concept Check | 4

1. What is the most widely used measure of capital budgeting in business practice?
2. How does the payback method provide an indication of the risk of an investment proposal?

Applying the Principles of Finance to This Chapter

P Principle 1: **Money Has a Time Value** The value of an asset or an investment proposal is equal to the present value of the future cash flows, discounted at the required rate of return. As a result, Principle 1 plays a pivotal role in making investment decisions.

P Principle 2: **There Is a Risk–Return Tradeoff** Different projects have different levels of risk associated with them, and we deal with this by increasing the discount rate when calculating the present value of the project's future cash flows.

P Principle 3: **Cash Flows Are the Source of Value** The calculation of the value of an asset or an investment proposal begins with an estimation of the amount and timing of expected future cash flows. These free cash flows are then discounted back to present at the required rate of return.

P Principle 5: **Individuals Respond to Incentives** Managers respond to the incentives, and when their incentives are not properly aligned with those of the firm's stockholders, they may not make decisions that are consistent with increasing shareholder value.

Chapter Summaries

Understand how to identify the sources and types of profitable investment opportunities.

Concept Check | **1**

1. What does the term *capital budgeting* mean?
2. Describe the two-phase process typically involved in carrying out a capital-budgeting analysis.
3. What makes a capital-budgeting project a good one?
4. What are the three basic types of capital investment projects?

SUMMARY: Before a profitable project can be adopted, it must be identified. In general, the best source of ideas for potentially profitable investments is found within the firm. Specifically, the firm's marketing and operations employees are rich sources of investment ideas.

Evaluate investment opportunities using net present value and describe why net present value is the best measure to use.

SUMMARY: The net present value (NPV) of an investment proposal is equal to the present value of its cash flows (including the initial cash outlay in Year 0, CF_0),

$$NPV = CF_0 + \frac{CF_1}{(1 + k)^1} + \frac{CF_2}{(1 + k)^2} + \cdots + \frac{CF_n}{(1 + k)^n} \tag{1}$$

where CF_t is the *expected* cash flow for periods t equal to 0, 1, 2, and so forth; k is the required rate of return or discount rate used in calculating the present value of the project's expected future cash flows; and n is the last cash flow used to value the investment opportunity. If the computed NPV is greater than zero, this indicates that the project is expected to create value for the firm and its shareholders and therefore is an acceptable investment opportunity.

KEY TERMS

Capital rationing A situation in which a firm's access to capital is limited such that it is unable to undertake all projects that have positive NPVs.

Equivalent annual cost (EAC) The annuity cash flow amount that is equivalent to the present value of the project's costs.

Independent investment project An investment project whose acceptance will not affect the acceptance or rejection of any other project.

Mutually exclusive projects Related or dependent investment proposals where the acceptance of one proposal means the rejection of the other.

Net present value (NPV) The difference in the present value of an investment proposal's future cash flows and the initial cash outlay. This difference is the expected increase in value of the firm due to the acceptance of the project.

Concept Check | **2**

1. Describe what the NPV tells the analyst about a new investment opportunity.
2. What is the equivalent annual cost (EAC) measure, and when should it be used?
3. What is capital rationing?

KEY EQUATIONS

$$\underset{\substack{\text{Net Present} \\ \text{Value or } NPV}}{} = \underset{\substack{\text{Cash Flow} \\ \text{for Year 0 } (CF_0)}}{} + \cfrac{\underset{\substack{\text{Cash Flow} \\ \text{for Year 1 } (CF_1)}}{}}{\left(1 + \cfrac{\text{Discount}}{\text{Rate } (k)}\right)^1} + \cfrac{\underset{\substack{\text{Cash Flow} \\ \text{for Year 2 } (CF_2)}}{}}{\left(1 + \cfrac{\text{Discount}}{\text{Rate } (k)}\right)^2} + \cdots + \cfrac{\underset{\substack{\text{Cash Flow} \\ \text{for Year } n \ (CF_n)}}{}}{\left(1 + \cfrac{\text{Discount}}{\text{Rate } (k)}\right)^n} \quad \textbf{(1)}$$

Cost of making the investment = Initial cash flow, this is typically a cash outflow taking on a negative value.

Present value of the investment's cash inflows = Present value of the project's future cash inflows.

$$\underset{\substack{\text{Equivalent} \\ \text{Annual Cost } (EAC)}}{} = \cfrac{NPV}{(1 + k)^1 + (1 + k)^2 + \cdots + (1 + k)^n} = \cfrac{NPV}{\underset{\substack{\text{Present Value of an Annuity} \\ \text{Discount Factor}}}{}} \quad \textbf{(2)}$$

$$= \cfrac{NPV}{\left(\cfrac{1}{k} - \cfrac{1}{k(1 + k)^n}\right)}$$

3

Use the profitability index, internal rate of return, and payback criteria to evaluate investment opportunities.

SUMMARY: The profitability index (PI) is closely related to NPV. Specifically, instead of subtracting the initial cash outlay from the present value of future cash flows, the PI *divides* the present value of the future cash flows by the negative of the initial outlay, CF_0. The profitability index can be expressed as follows:

$$\text{Profibility Index (PI)} = \cfrac{\text{Present value of the project's expected cash flows}}{-\text{ Initial outlay or } CF_0}$$

Using the symbols we used earlier to define NPV, we define the PI as follows:

$$PI = \cfrac{\cfrac{CF_1}{(1 + k)^1} + \cfrac{CF_2}{(1 + k)^2} + \cfrac{CF_3}{(1 + k)^3} + \cdots + \cfrac{CF_n}{(1 + k)^n}}{-CF_0} \quad \textbf{(3)}$$

The decision criterion is this: Accept the project if the PI is greater than 1.00, and reject the project if the PI is less than 1.00.

The internal rate of return (IRR) attempts to answer this question: "What rate of return is an investment expected to earn?" For computational purposes, the internal rate of return is defined as the discount rate that results in an NPV of zero, that is,

$$NPV = 0 = CF_0 + \cfrac{CF_1}{(1 + IRR)^1} + \cfrac{CF_2}{(1 + IRR)^2} + \cfrac{CF_3}{(1 + IRR)^3} + \cdots + \cfrac{CF_n}{(1 + IRR)^n} \quad \textbf{(4)}$$

Note that in this formulation of NPV we use IRR to discount project cash flows. Specifically, IRR is that particular discount rate that makes the computed NPV equal to zero.

The decision rule for using IRR is the following: Accept the project if the IRR is greater than the required rate of return, which is equal to the discount rate used to value (discount) the project's future cash flows, and reject the project if the IRR is less than this discount rate.

There are circumstances, however, where IRR either cannot be calculated or where there are multiple discount rates that satisfy the definition of IRR in Equation (4). In either case IRR is no longer useful as a decision criterion. The problem of multiple estimates of IRR arises when project cash flows change sign multiple times over the life of the project. Some firms that want to use a rate-of-return criterion have adopted the use of something called the modified internal rate of return (MIRR) as a means to avoid the problem of multiple IRRs. The MIRR addresses this problem by combining cash flows until there is only one sign change. Specifically, negative cash flows are discounted back to Year 0 using the discount rate used in calculating the NPV before calculating the MIRR of the altered cash flow pattern.

The payback criterion measures how quickly the project will return its original investment, and this is a very useful piece of information because it indicates something about the risk of the investment. The longer the firm has to wait to recover its investment, the more things can happen that might reduce or eliminate the benefits of making the investment. However, using the payback period as the sole criterion for evaluating whether to undertake an investment has three fundamental limitations. First, the payback period calculation ignores the time value of money, as it does not require that the future cash flows be discounted back to the present. Second, the payback period does not take into account how much cash flow is expected to be generated by the project beyond the end of the payback period. Finally, there is no clear-cut way to define the cutoff criterion for the payback period that is tied to the value-creation potential of the investment.

To deal with the criticism that the payback period ignores the time value of money, some firms use the discounted payback period approach. The discounted payback period method is similar to that of the traditional payback period except that it uses discounted cash flows to calculate the payback period. Thus, the discounted payback period is defined as the number of years needed to recover the initial cash outlay from the discounted cash flows. However, discounted payback still ignores cash flows beyond the payback period, and there is still no clear-cut way to define the cutoff criterion for discounted payback.

KEY TERMS

Discounted payback period The number of years required for a project's discounted cash flows to recover the initial cash outlay for an investment.

Internal rate of return (IRR) The compound annual rate of return earned by an investment.

Modified internal rate of return (MIRR) The compound annual rate of return earned by an investment whose cash flows have been moved through time so as to eliminate the problem of multiple IRRs. For example, all negative cash flows after Year 0 are discounted back to Year 0 using the firm's required rate of return and then the IRR is determined for this modified cash flow stream.

NPV profile A plot of multiple NPV estimates calculated using a succession of different discount rates. This profile illustrates when there are multiple IRRs, that is, where NPV is equal to zero for more than one discount rate.

Payback period The number of years of future cash flows needed to recover the initial investment in a proposed project.

Profitability index (PI) The ratio of the present value of the expected future cash flows for an investment proposal (discounted using the required rate of return for the project) divided by the initial investment in the project.

KEY EQUATIONS

Concept Check | 3

1. Describe what the IRR metric tells the analyst about a new investment opportunity.

2. Describe the situations in which the NPV and IRR metrics can provide conflicting signals.

3. What is the modified internal rate of return metric, and why is it sometimes used?

4. What is the payback method, and what is the source of its appeal?

5. What is discounted payback, and how does it improve on the payback measure?

$$\text{Profitability Index } (PI) = \frac{\dfrac{\text{Cash Flow for Year 1 }(CF_1)}{\left(1 + \dfrac{\text{Discount}}{\text{Rate }(k)}\right)^1} + \dfrac{\text{Cash Flow for Year 2 }(CF_2)}{\left(1 + \dfrac{\text{Discount}}{\text{Rate }(k)}\right)^2} + \cdots + \dfrac{\text{Cash Flow for Year } n \,(CF_n)}{\left(1 + \dfrac{\text{Discount}}{\text{Rate }(k)}\right)^n}}{\text{Initial Cash Outlay }(CF_0)} \tag{3}$$

$$\begin{aligned}\text{Net Present Value} = 0 = {} & \text{Cash Flow for Year 0 }(CF_0) + \frac{\text{Cash Flow for Year 1 }(CF_1)}{\left(1 + \dfrac{\text{Internal Rate of Return }(IRR)}\right)^1} + \frac{\text{Cash Flow for Year 2 }(CF_2)}{\left(1 + \dfrac{\text{Internal Rate of Return }(IRR)}\right)^2} \\ & + \cdots + \frac{\text{Cash Flow for Year } n \,(CF_n)}{\left(1 + \dfrac{\text{Internal Rate of Return }(IRR)}\right)^n}\end{aligned} \tag{4}$$

4

Understand current business practice with respect to the use of capital-budgeting criteria.

Concept Check | 4

1. What is the most widely used measure of capital budgeting in business practice?

2. How does the payback method provide an indication of the risk of an investment proposal?

SUMMARY: Recent survey evidence from large U.S. firms on the popularity of the standard methods for evaluating capital investment opportunities showed that IRR and NPV are by far the most widely used. However, more than half the firms surveyed use the payback method. Larger firms use NPV and IRR more frequently than their smaller counterparts, and smaller firms tend to rely more on payback. Finally, most firms use multiple investment criteria and often use payback as a secondary measure to reflect project risk considerations.

Study Questions

1. **(Related to Regardless of Your Major: Making Personal Investment Decisions)** In the *Regardless of Your Major* feature box, what types of personal decisions that individuals make that can be addressed using capital-budgeting analyses are discussed?

2. Where do firms learn about new investment ideas, and what is the role of the financial analyst in determining what projects the firm should undertake?

3. Some firms categorize projects as revenue-enhancing, cost-reducing, and mandatory. Describe what this means.

4. How is the presence or absence of competition related to NPV? What are the types of barriers to competition (market entry) that tend to preserve positive NPVs?

5. Why is the NPV considered to be the best method for capital budgeting? What does the NPV tell you?

6. What does it mean to say that two or more investment projects are mutually exclusive?

7. What are the limitations of the payback period as an investment decision criterion? What are its advantages? Why do you think it is used so frequently?

8. Briefly compare and contrast the NPV, PI, and IRR criteria. What are the advantages and disadvantages of using each of these methods?

9. If a project's payback period is less than the maximum payback period that the firm will accept, does this mean that the project's NPV will also be positive?

10. What is the rationale for using the MIRR as opposed to the IRR decision criteria? Describe the fundamental shortcoming of the MIRR method.

11. **(Related to The Business of Life: Higher Education as an Investment in Yourself)** In *The Business of Life* feature box, the decision to get a college education is discussed in the context of an investment decision. Discuss the analogy in more detail by identifying the initial cash outlay(s) and the future benefits of your investment in higher education.

12. Under what conditions would the payback and discounted payback methods produce identical results?

13. What are the most widely used methods for evaluating capital expenditure projects in practice?

14. What is the logic behind using the payback method as a reflection of project risk?

Study Problems

MyFinanceLab

Go to www.myfinancelab.com to complete these exercises online and get instant feedback.

Net Present Value

1. **(Related to Checkpoint 1) (Net present value calculation)** Dowling Sportswear is considering building a new factory to produce aluminum baseball bats. This project would require an initial cash outlay of $5,000,000 and would generate annual net cash inflows of $1,000,000 per year for eight years. Calculate the project's NPV for each of the following discount rates:
   a. 9 percent
   b. 11 percent
   c. 13 percent
   d. 15 percent

2. **(Net present value calculation)** Carson Trucking is considering whether to expand its regional service center in Moab, Utah. The expansion requires the expenditure of $10,000,000 on new service equipment and would generate annual net cash inflows from reduced costs of operations equal to $2,500,000 per year for each of the next eight years. In Year 8 the firm will also get back a cash flow equal to the salvage value of the equipment, which is valued at $1 million. Thus, in Year 8 the investment cash inflow totals $3,500,000. Calculate the project's NPV using each of the following discount rates:

    a. 9 percent
    b. 11 percent
    c. 13 percent
    d. 15 percent

3. **(Net present value calculation)** Big Steve's, makers of swizzle sticks, is considering the purchase of a new plastic stamping machine. This investment requires an initial outlay of $100,000 and will generate net cash inflows of $18,000 per year for 10 years.

    a. What is the project's NPV using a discount rate of 10 percent? Should the project be accepted? Why or why not?
    b. What is the project's NPV using a discount rate of 15 percent? Should the project be accepted? Why or why not?
    c. What is this project's internal rate of return? Should the project be accepted? Why or why not?

4. **(Related to Checkpoint 2) (Equivalent annual cost calculation)** Barry Boswell is a financial analyst for Dossman Metal Works, Inc. and he is analyzing two alternative configurations for the firm's new plasma cutter shop. The two alternatives that are denoted A and B below perform the same task and although they both cost $80,000 to purchase and install they offer very different cash flows. Alternative A has a useful life of seven years whereas Alternative B will only last for three years. The after-tax costs for the two projects are as follows:

Year	Alternative A	Alternative B
0	$(80,000)	$(80,000)
1	(20,000)	(6,000)
2	(20,000)	(6,000)
3	(20,000)	(6,000)
4	(20,000)	
5	(20,000)	
6	(20,000)	
7	(20,000)	

    a. Calculate each project's equivalent annual cost (EAC) given a 10 percent discount rate.
    b. Which of the alternatives do you think Barry should select? Why?

5. **(Equivalent annual cost calculation)** The Templeton Manufacturing and Distribution Company of Tacoma, Washington, is contemplating the purchase of a new conveyor belt system for one of its regional distribution facilities. Both alternatives will accomplish the same task but the Eclipse Model is substantially more expensive than the Sabre Model and will not have to be replaced for 10 years, whereas the cheaper model will

need to be replaced in just 5 years. The costs of purchasing the two systems and the costs of operating them annually over their expected lives are as follows:

Year	Eclipse	Sabre
0	(1,400,000)	(800,000)
1	(25,000)	(50,000)
2	(30,000)	(50,000)
3	(30,000)	(60,000)
4	(30,000)	(60,000)
5	(40,000)	(80,000)
6	(40,000)	
7	(40,000)	
8	(40,000)	
9	(40,000)	
10	(40,000)	

a. Templeton typically evaluates investments in plant improvements using a 12 percent required rate of return. What are the NPVs for the two systems?
b. Calculate the equivalent annual costs for the two systems.
c. Based on your analysis of the two systems using both their NPV and EAC, which system do you recommend the company pick? Why?

Other Investment Criteria

6. **(Related to Checkpoint 1)** **(IRR calculation)** What are the internal rates of return for the following projects?

   a. An initial outlay of $10,000 resulting in a single cash inflow of $17,182 in 8 years
   b. An initial outlay of $10,000 resulting in a single cash inflow of $48,077 in 10 years
   c. An initial outlay of $10,000 resulting in a single cash inflow of $115,231 in 20 years
   d. An initial outlay of $10,000 resulting in a single cash inflow of $13,680 in 3 years

7. **(IRR calculation)** Determine the internal rate of return on the following projects:

   a. An initial outlay of $10,000 resulting in a cash inflow of $1,993 at the end of each year for the next 10 years
   b. An initial outlay of $10,000 resulting in a cash inflow of $2,054 at the end of each year for the next 20 years
   c. An initial outlay of $10,000 resulting in a cash inflow of $1,193 at the end of each year for the next 12 years
   d. An initial outlay of $10,000 resulting in a cash inflow of $2,843 at the end of each year for the next 5 years

8. **(Related to Checkpoint 1 and Checkpoint 4)** **(NPV and IRR calculation)** East Coast Television is considering a project with an initial outlay of $X (you will have to determine this amount). It is expected that the project will produce a positive cash flow of $50,000 a year at the end of each year for the next 15 years. The appropriate discount rate for this project is 10 percent. If the project has a 14 percent internal rate of return, what is the project's net present value?

9. **(Related to Checkpoint 4)** **(IRR calculation)** Determine the internal rate of return to the nearest percent on the following projects:

   a. An initial outlay of $10,000 resulting in a cash inflow of $2,000 at the end of Year 1, $5,000 at the end of Year 2, and $8,000 at the end of Year 3
   b. An initial outlay of $10,000 resulting in a cash inflow of $8,000 at the end of Year 1, $5,000 at the end of Year 2, and $2,000 at the end of Year 3
   c. An initial outlay of $10,000 resulting in a cash inflow of $2,000 at the end of Years 1 through 5 and $5,000 at the end of Year 6

10. **(IRR calculation)** Jella Cosmetics is considering a project that costs $800,000 and is expected to last for 10 years and produce future cash flows of $175,000 per year. If the appropriate discount rate for this project is 12 percent, what is the project's IRR?

11. **(IRR calculation)** Your investment advisor has offered you an investment that will provide you with a single cash flow of $10,000 at the end of 20 years if you pay premiums of $200 per year in the interim period. Specifically, the annual premiums begin immediately and extend through the end of Year 19. You then receive the $10,000 at the end of Year 20. Find the internal rate of return on this investment.

12. **(Related to Checkpoint 1 and Checkpoint 4) (IRR and NPV calculation)** The cash flows for three independent projects are as follows:

	Project A	Project B	Project C
Year 0 (Initial investment)	$(50,000)	$(100,000)	$(450,000)
Year 1	$ 10,000	$ 25,000	$ 200,000
Year 2	15,000	25,000	200,000
Year 3	20,000	25,000	200,000
Year 4	25,000	25,000	—
Year 5	30,000	25,000	—

a. Calculate the IRR for each of the projects.
b. If the discount rate for all three projects is 10 percent, which project or projects would you want to undertake?
c. What is the net present value of each of the projects where the appropriate discount rate is 10 percent? 20 percent?

13. **(IRR, payback, and calculating a missing cash flow)** Mode Publishing is considering a new printing facility that will involve a large initial outlay and then result in a series of positive cash flows for four years. The estimated cash flows associated with this project are as follows:

Year	Project Cash Flow
0	?
1	$800 million
2	400 million
3	300 million
4	500 million

If you know that the project has a regular payback of 2.5 years, what is the project's internal rate of return?

14. **(Related to Checkpoint 6) (MIRR calculation)** Emily's Soccer Mania is considering building a new plant. This project would require an initial cash outlay of $10 million and would generate annual cash inflows of $3 million per year for Years 1 through 4. In Year 5 the project will require an investment outlay of $5,000,000. During Years 6 through 10 the project will provide cash inflows of $5 million per year. Calculate the project's MIRR, given:

a. A discount rate of 10 percent
b. A discount rate of 12 percent
c. A discount rate of 14 percent

15. **(MIRR calculation)** Carraway Trucking Company runs a fleet of long-haul trucks and has recently expanded into the Midwest, where it has decided to build a maintenance facility. This project would require an initial cash outlay of $20 million and would generate annual cash inflows of $4 million per year for Years 1 through 3. In Year 4 the project will require an investment outlay of $5,000,000. During Years 5 through 10 the project will provide cash inflows of $2 million per year.

a. Calculate the project's NPV and IRR where the discount rate is 12 percent. Is the project a worthwhile investment based on these two measures? Why or why not?
b. Calculate the project's MIRR. Is the project a worthwhile investment based on this measure? Why or why not?

16. **(IRR of an uneven cash flow stream)** Microwave Oven Programming, Inc. is considering the construction of a new plant. The plant will have an initial cash outlay of $7 million ($CF_0 = -\$7$ million), and will produce cash flows of $3 million at the end of Year 1, $4 million at the end of Year 2, and $2 million at the end of Years 3 through 5. What is the internal rate of return on this new plant?

17. **(Related to Checkpoint 6) (MIRR)** The Dunder Muffin Paper Company is considering purchasing a new stamping machine that costs $400,000. This new machine will produce cash inflows of $150,000 each year at the end of Years 1 through 10. In addition to the cash inflows, at the end of Year 5, there will be a cash outflow of $200,000. The company has a required rate of return of 12 percent. What is the MIRR of the investment?

18. **(MIRR)** Star Industries owns and operates landfills for several municipalities throughout the U.S. Midwest. Star typically contracts with the municipality to provide landfill services for a period of 20 years. The firm then constructs a lined landfill (required by federal law) that has capacity for five years. The $10 million expenditure required to construct the new landfill results in negative cash flows at the end of Years 0, 5, 10, and 15. This change in sign on the stream of cash flows over the 20-year contract period introduces the potential for multiple IRRs, so Star's management has decided to use the MIRR to evaluate new landfill investment contracts. The annual cash inflows to Star begin in Year 1 and extend through Year 20 and are estimated to equal $3 million (this does not reflect the cost of constructing the landfills every five years). Star uses a 10 percent discount rate to evaluate its new projects, so it plans to discount all the construction costs every five years back to Year 0 using this rate before calculating the MIRR.

    a. What are the project's NPV, IRR, and MIRR?
    b. Is this a good investment opportunity for Star Industries? Why or why not?

19. **(Related to Checkpoint 1 and Checkpoint 4) (NPV, PI, and IRR calculations)** Fijisawa, Inc. is considering a major expansion of its product line and has estimated the following cash flows associated with such an expansion. The initial outlay would be $1,950,000, and the project would generate cash flows of $450,000 per year for six years. The appropriate discount rate is 9 percent.

    a. Calculate the net present value.
    b. Calculate the profitability index.
    c. Calculate the internal rate of return.
    d. Should this project be accepted? Why or why not?

20. **(Discounted payback period)** Gio's Restaurants is considering a project with the following expected cash flows:

Year	Project Cash Flow
0	$(150 million)
1	90 million
2	70 million
3	90 million
4	100 million

    If the project's appropriate discount is 12 percent, what is the project's discounted payback?

21. **(Discounted payback period)** The Callaway Cattle Company is considering the construction of a new feed handling system for its feed lot in Abilene, Kansas. The new system will provide annual labor savings and reduced waste totaling $200,000, and the initial investment is only $500,000. Callaway's management has used a simple payback method for evaluating new investments in the past but plans to calculate the discounted payback to analyze the investment. Where the appropriate discount rate for this type of project is 10 percent, what is the project's discounted payback period?

22. **(Payback and discounted payback period calculations)** The Bar-None Manufacturing Co. manufactures fence panels used in cattle feed lots throughout the Midwest. Bar-None's management is considering three investment projects for next year but doesn't want to make any investment that requires more than three years to recover the firm's initial investment. The cash flows for the three projects (Project A, Project B, and Project C) are as follows:

Year	Project A	Project B	Project C
0	$(1,000)	$(10,000)	$(5,000)
1	600	5,000	1,000
2	300	3,000	1,000
3	200	3,000	2,000
4	100	3,000	2,000
5	500	3,000	2,000

a. Given Bar-None's three-year payback period, which of the projects will qualify for acceptance?

b. Rank the three projects using their payback periods. Which project looks the best using this criterion? Do you agree with this ranking? Why or why not?

c. If Bar-None uses a 10 percent discount rate to analyze projects, what is the discounted payback period for each of the three projects? If the firm still maintains its three-year payback policy for the discounted payback, which projects should the firm undertake?

23. **(Payback period and NPV calculations)** Plato Energy is an oil and gas exploration and development company located in Farmington, New Mexico. The company drills shallow wells in hopes of finding significant oil and gas deposits. The firm is considering two different drilling opportunities that have very different production potentials. The first is in the Barnett Shale region of central Texas and the other is in the Gulf Coast. The Barnett Shale project requires a much larger initial investment but provides cash flows (if successful) over a much longer period of time than the Gulf Coast opportunity. In addition, the longer life of the Barnett Shale project also results in additional expenditures in Year 3 of the project to enhance production throughout the project's 10-year expected life. This expenditure involves pumping either water or CO_2 down into the wells in order to increase the flow of oil and gas from the structure. The expected cash flows for the two projects are as follows:

Year	Barnett Shale	Gulf Coast
0	$(5,000,000)	$ (1,500,000)
1	2,000,000	800,000
2	2,000,000	800,000
3	(1,000,000)	400,000
4	2,000,000	100,000
5	1,500,000	
6	1,500,000	
7	1,500,000	
8	800,000	
9	500,000	
10	100,000	

a. What is the payback period for each of the two projects?

b. Based on the calculated payback periods, which of the two projects appears to be the best alternative? What are the limitations of the payback period ranking? That is, what does the payback period not consider that is important in determining the value-creation potential of these two projects?

c. If Plato's management uses a 20 percent discount rate to evaluate the present values of its energy investment projects, what is the NPV of the two proposed investments?

d. What is your estimate of the value that will be created for Plato by the acceptance of each of these two investments?

24. **(Payback period, net present value, profitability index, and internal rate of return calculations)** You are considering a project with an initial cash outlay of $80,000 and expected cash flows of $20,000 at the end of each year for six years. The discount rate for this project is 10 percent.

   a. What are the project's payback and discounted payback periods?
   b. What is the project's NPV?
   c. What is the project's PI?
   d. What is the project's IRR?

25. **(Mutually exclusive projects and NPV)** You have been assigned the task of evaluating two mutually exclusive projects with the following projected cash flows:

Year	Project A Cash Flow	Project B Cash Flow
0	$(100,000)	$(100,000)
1	33,000	0
2	33,000	0
3	33,000	0
4	33,000	0
5	33,000	220,000

   If the appropriate discount rate on these projects is 10 percent, which would be chosen and why?

26. **(Related to Checkpoint 1, Checkpoint 3, and Checkpoint 4) (Net present value, profitability index, and internal rate of return calculations)** You are considering two independent projects, Project A and Project B. The initial cash outlay associated with Project A is $50,000 and the initial cash outlay associated with Project B is $70,000. The discount rate on both projects is 12 percent. The expected annual cash flows from each project are as follows:

Year	Project A	Project B
0	$(50,000)	$(70,000)
1	12,000	13,000
2	12,000	13,000
3	12,000	13,000
4	12,000	13,000
5	12,000	13,000
6	12,000	13,000

   Calculate the NPV, PI, and IRR for each project and indicate if the project should be accepted or not.

27. **(Comprehensive problem)** Garmen Technologies Inc. operates a small chain of specialty retail stores throughout the U.S. Southwest. The company markets technology-based consumer products both in its stores and over the Internet, with sales split roughly equally between the two channels of distribution. The company's products range from radar detection devices and GPS mapping systems used in automobiles to home-based weather monitoring stations. The company recently began investigating the possible acquisition of a regional warehousing facility that could be used both to stock its retail shops and to make direct shipments to the firm's online customers. The warehouse facility would require an expenditure of $250,000 for a rented space in Oklahoma City, Oklahoma, and would provide a source of cash flow spanning the next 10 years. The estimated cash flows are as follows:

Year	Cash Flow	Year	Cash Flow
0	$(250,000)	6	$65,000
1	60,000	7	65,000
2	60,000	8	65,000
3	60,000	9	65,000
4	60,000	10	90,000
5	(45,000)		

The negative cash flow in Year 5 reflects the cost of a planned renovation and expansion of the facility. Finally, in Year 10 Garmen estimates some recovery of its investment at the close of the lease, and consequently a higher-than-usual cash flow. Garmen uses a 12 percent discount rate in evaluating its investments.

a. As a preliminary step in analyzing the new investment, Garmen's management has decided to evaluate the project's anticipated payback period. What is the project's expected payback period? Jim Garmen, CEO, questioned the analyst performing the analysis about the meaning of the payback period because it seems to ignore the fact that the project will provide cash flows over many years beyond the end of the payback period. Specifically, he wanted to know what useful information the payback provides. If you were the analyst, how would you respond to Mr. Garmen?

b. In the past, Garmen's management has relied almost exclusively on the IRR to make its investment choices. However, in this instance the lead financial analyst on the project suggested that there may be a problem with the IRR because the sign on the cash flows changes three times over its life. Calculate the IRR for the project. Evaluate the NPV profile of the project for discount rates of 0 percent, 20 percent, 50 percent, and 100 percent. Does there appear to be a problem of multiple IRRs in this range of discount rates?

c. Calculate the project's NPV. What does the NPV indicate about the potential value created by the project? Describe to Mr. Garmen what NPV means, recognizing that he was trained as an engineer and has no formal business education.

Mini-Cases

RWE Enterprises: Expansion Project Analysis

RWE Enterprises, Inc. (RWE) is a small manufacturing firm located in the hills just outside of Nashville, Tennessee. The firm is engaged in the manufacture and sale of feed supplements used by cattle raisers. The product has a molasses base but is supplemented with minerals and vitamins that are generally thought to be essential to the health and growth of beef cattle. The final product is put in 125-pound or 200-pound tubs that are then made available for the cattle to lick as desired. The material in the tub becomes very hard, which limits the animals' consumption.

The firm has been running a single production line for the past five years and is considering the addition of a new line. The addition would expand the firm's capacity by almost 120 percent because the newer equipment requires a shorter downtime between batches. After each production run, the boiler used to prepare the molasses for the addition of minerals and vitamins must be heated to 180 degrees Fahrenheit and then must be cooled down before beginning the next batch. The total production run entails about four hours and the cool-down period is two hours (during which time the whole process comes to a halt). Using two production lines increases the overall efficiency of the operation because workers from the line that is cooling down can be moved to the other line to support the "canning" process involved in filling the feed tubs.

The second production line equipment will cost $3 million to purchase and install and will have an estimated life of 10 years, at which time it can be sold for an estimated after-tax scrap value of $200,000. Furthermore, at the end of five years the production line will have to be refurbished at an estimated

cost of $2 million. RWE's management estimates that the new production line will add $700,000 per year in after-tax cash flow to the firm, such that the full 10-year cash flows for the line are as follows:

Year	After-tax Cash Flow
0	$(3,000,000)
1	700,000
2	700,000
3	700,000
4	700,000
5	(1,300,000)
6	700,000
7	700,000
8	700,000
9	700,000
10	900,000

a. If RWE uses a 10 percent discount rate to evaluate investments of this type, what is the net present value of the project? What does this NPV indicate about the potential value RWE might create by purchasing the new production line?

b. Calculate the internal rate of return and profitability index for the proposed investment. What do these two measures tell you about the project's viability?

c. Calculate the payback and discounted payback for the proposed investment. Interpret your findings.

Jamie Dermott: Mutually Exclusive Project Analysis

Jamie Dermott graduated from Midland State University in June and has been working for about a month as a junior financial analyst at Caledonia Products. When Jamie arrived at work on Friday morning he found the following memo in his e-mail:

TO: Jamie Dermott

FROM: V. Morrison, CFO, Caledonia Products

RE: Capital-Budgeting Analysis

Provide an evaluation of two proposed projects with the following cash flow forecasts:

	Project A	Project B
Initial Outlay	$(110,000)	$(110,000)
Year 1	20,000	40,000
Year 2	30,000	40,000
Year 3	40,000	40,000
Year 4	50,000	40,000
Year 5	70,000	40,000

Because these projects involve additions to Caledonia's highly successful Avalon product line, the company requires a rate of return on both projects equal to 12 percent. As you are no doubt aware, Caledonia relies on a number of criteria when evaluating new investment opportunities. In particular, we require that projects that are accepted have a payback of no more than three years, provide a positive NPV, and have an IRR that exceeds the firm's discount rate.

Give me your thoughts on these two projects by 9 a.m. Monday morning.

Jamie was not surprised by the memo, for he had been expecting something like this for some time. Caledonia followed a practice of testing each new financial analyst with some type of project evaluation exercise after the new hire had been on the job for a few months.

After re-reading the memo, Jamie decided on his plan of attack. Specifically, he would first do the obligatory calculations of payback, NPV, and IRR for both projects. Jamie knew that the CFO would grill him thoroughly on Monday morning about his analysis, so he wanted to prepare well for the experience. One of the things that occurred to Jamie was that the memo did not indicate whether the two projects were independent or mutually exclusive. So, just to be safe, he thought he had better rank the two projects in case he was asked to do so on Monday morning. Jamie sat down and made up the following "to do" list:

1. Compute payback, NPV, and IRR for both projects.

2. Evaluate the two projects' acceptability using all three decision criteria (listed above) and based on the assumption that the projects are independent. That is, both could be accepted if both are acceptable.

3. Rank the two projects and make a recommendation as to which (if either) should be accepted under the assumption that the projects are mutually exclusive.

Assignment—Prepare Jamie's evaluation for his Monday meeting with the CFO by filling out your responses to the "to do" list.

Ethics Case: Ford's Pinto and the Value of Life

In 1968, Ford Motor Company executives decided to produce a subcompact car called the Pinto in response to the onslaught of Japanese economy cars. Known inside the company as "Lee's car," after Ford president Lee Iacocca, the Pinto was to weigh no more than 2,000 pounds and cost no more than $2,000.

Eager to have its subcompact ready for the 1971 model year, Ford decided to compress the normal drafting-board-to-showroom time from three-and-a-half down to only two years. The compressed schedule meant that design changes typically made before production-line tooling would have to be made during it.

Before producing the Pinto, Ford crash-tested 11 cars, in part to learn if they met the National Highway Traffic Safety Administration's (NHTSA) proposed safety standard that all autos be able to withstand a fixed-barrier impact of 20 miles per hour without fuel loss. Eight standard-design Pintos failed these tests. The three cars that passed the test all had some kind of gas-tank modification. One had a plastic baffle between the front of the tank and the differential housing; the second had a piece of steel between the tank and the rear bumper; and the third had a rubber-lined gas tank.

Ford officials faced a tough decision. Should they go ahead with the standard design, thereby meeting the production timetable but possibly jeopardizing consumer safety? Or should they delay production of the Pinto and redesign the gas tank to make it safer? If they chose the latter course of action, they would effectively concede another year of subcompact dominance to foreign companies.

To determine whether to proceed with the original design of the Pinto fuel tank, Ford compared the expected costs and benefits of making the change. Would the benefits of a new tank design outweigh design costs, or not? To find the answer, Ford estimated the costs of the design improvement to be $11 per vehicle. The benefit to Ford of having a safer gas tank relates to the avoidance of the potential costs Ford might incur in the event of a fatality resulting from a fuel tank rupture if the auto was involved in an accident. To analyze this benefit, Ford's analysts did an analysis of the dollar value of the average loss resulting from a traffic fatality. The NHTSA estimated the cost of a traffic fatality to be $200,725 for every time a person is killed in an auto accident. The costs were broken down as follows:

Future productivity losses	
Direct	$132,000
Indirect	41,300
Medical Costs	
Hospital	700
Other	425
Property damage	1,500
Insurance administration	4,700
Legal and court expenses	3,000
Employer losses	1,000
Victim's pain and suffering	10,000
Funeral	900
Assets (lost consumption)	5,000
Miscellaneous accident costs	200
Total per fatality	$200,725[a]

[a]Ralph Drayton, "One Manufacturer's Approach to Automobile Safety Standards," *CTLA News 8* (February 1968), p. 11.

Benefits	Losses avoided by re-designing the fuel tank in the Pinto
Savings:	180 burn deaths; 180 serious burn injuries; 2,100 burned vehicles
Unit cost:	$200,000 per death; $67,000 per injury; and $700 per vehicle
Total benefit:	$(180 \times \$200,000) + (180 \times \$67,000) + (2,100 \times \$700) = \$49.5$ million
Costs	Losses incurred by the re-design of the fuel tank in the Pinto
Sales:	11 million cars; 1.5 million light trucks
Unit cost:	$11 per car and $11 per truck
Total cost:	12.5 million $\times \$11 = \$137.5$ million[a]

[a]Mark Dowie, "Pinto Madness," *Mother Jones* (September–October 1977), p. 20. See also Russell Mokhiber, *Corporate Crime and Violence* (San Francisco: Sierra Club Books, 1988), pp. 373–82, and Francis T. Cullen, William J. Maakestad, and Gary Cavender, *Corporate Crime Under Attack: The Ford Pinto Case and Beyond* (Cincinnati: Anderson Publishing, 1987).

Ford used NHTSA's estimates and other statistical studies in its cost-benefit analysis, which yielded the following estimates:

Because the $137.5 million cost of the safety improvement outweighed the $49.5 million benefit of the redesign, Ford decided to push ahead with the original design.

Questions

1. Do you think Ford analyzed the problem of redesigning the Pinto fuel tank safety in a reasonable way?

2. Should questions involving the risk of loss of human life be analyzed in a cost-benefit analysis? After all, don't life insurance companies do this all the time in pricing life insurance policies to older versus younger customers?

Source: This case is based on William Shaw and Vincent Barry, "Ford's Pinto," *Moral Issues in Business*, 9th ed. (New York: Wadsworth, 2004), 84–86. © by Wadsworth, Inc.

Photo Credits

Analyzing Project Cash Flows

From Chapter 12 of *Financial Management: Principles and Applications*, Twelfth Edition. Sheridan Titman, Arthur J. Keown, and John D. Martin.

Analyzing Project Cash Flows

Chapter **Outline**

1 Identifying Incremental Cash Flows   → **Objective 1.** Identify incremental cash flows that are relevant to project valuation.

2 Forecasting Project Cash Flows   → **Objective 2.** Calculate and forecast project cash flows for expansion-type investments.

3 Inflation and Capital Budgeting   → **Objective 3.** Evaluate the effect of inflation on project cash flows.

4 Replacement Project Cash Flows   → **Objective 4.** Calculate the incremental cash flows for replacement-type investments.

In this chapter, we calculate investment cash flows and discuss methods that can be used to develop cash flow forecasts. Calculating the appropriate cash flows in a valuation exercise is not always obvious, and we offer some guidelines that are designed to avoid some of the more common mistakes. In particular, we will stress **P** Principle 3: **Cash Flows Are the Source of Value**. In addition, we will be reminded that managers are often incentivized to do things that are not in the best interest of the firm's shareholders, which is **P** Principle 5: **Individuals Respond to Incentives**. Specifically, when managers forecast cash flows for a project in their department, they may be tempted to paint a rosy picture for the project in the hopes of winning the funding from headquarters.

Forecasting Sales of Hybrid Automobiles

In 2001, when Toyota introduced the first-generation model of its gas-electric-powered hybrid car, the Prius, it seemed more like a science experiment than real competition for auto industry market share. Toyota's decision to introduce the Prius and enter the hybrid car market was particularly difficult to evaluate because the cash flows were so difficult to forecast. Revenues from the Prius would depend largely upon how many buyers the newly designed hybrids drew away from traditionally powered cars—a number that would be strongly influenced by the future price of gasoline. Moreover, some of the hybrid sales would come from customers who would have otherwise bought another Toyota model. These are difficult issues for any firm to face; however, they are issues a financial manager must address to make an informed decision about the introduction of an innovative new product.

Regardless of Your Major...

"The Internet on Airline Flights— Making It Happen"

Cash flow forecasting frequently involves more than just the finance specialists in the firm. In practice, teams of technical, marketing, accounting, and other specialists often work together to develop cash flow forecasts for large investments. For example, major airlines are now beginning to provide Internet access on their flights. The idea is that for a fee of, say, $10 per flight, a customer can buy wireless access to the Internet while in-flight. However, the airline must overcome a number of hurdles to offer this service. There are technical issues related to both the hardware that must be installed on the aircraft and the infrastructure required to support access to the Internet—and all of this costs money. Then there is the question of how much revenue the airline would receive from this service. Consequently, for the airline to analyze the decision to include in-flight Internet access, it needs a team that includes technical staff, such as engineers to address the cost of installing and maintaining the service, marketing personnel to estimate customer acceptance rates and revenues, and a financial analyst to combine the various cost and revenue estimates into a project evaluation.

Your Turn: See Study Question 1.

1 Identifying Incremental Cash Flows

When a firm takes on a new investment, it does so anticipating that the investment will increase the firm's future cash flows. So when we are evaluating whether to undertake the investment, as we learned from Principle 3**: Cash Flows Are the Source of Value**, we consider what we will refer to as the **incremental cash flow** associated with the investment— that is, the additional cash flow a firm receives from taking on a new project.

To understand this concept of incremental cash flows, suppose that you recently opened a small convenience store. The store is a big success and you are offered the opportunity to rent space in a strip mall six blocks away to open a second convenience store. To evaluate this opportunity, you begin by calculating the costs of the initial investment and the cash flows from the investment in exactly the same way you evaluated the initial site. However, before calculating the net present value (NPV) of this new opportunity, you start to think about how adding a second location will affect your sales in the initial location. To what extent will you generate business by simply stealing business from your initial location? Cash flows that are generated by stealing customers from your initial location are clearly worth less to you than cash flows generated by stealing customers from your competitors.

This example serves to emphasize that the proper way to look at the cash flows from the second convenience store involves calculating the incremental cash flows generated by the new store. That is, the cash flows for the second store should be calculated by comparing the total cash flows from two stores less the total cash flows without the second store. More generally, we define incremental project cash flows as follows:

$$\begin{matrix} \text{Incremental Project} \\ \text{Cash Flows} \end{matrix} = \begin{pmatrix} \text{Firm Cash Flows} \\ \text{with the Project} \end{pmatrix} - \begin{pmatrix} \text{Firm Cash Flows} \\ \text{without the Project} \end{pmatrix} \qquad \textbf{(1)}$$

Thus, to find the incremental cash flow for a project, we take the difference between the firm's cash flows if the new investment is, and is not, undertaken. This may sound simple enough, but there are a number of circumstances in which estimating this incremental cash flow can be very challenging, requiring the analyst to carefully consider each potential source of cash flow.

Guidelines for Forecasting Incremental Cash Flows

In this section we focus on some simple guidelines for proper identification of incremental cash flows for a project. As we will see, this is not always easy to do, so it is helpful to have a set of basic guidelines to help us avoid some common mistakes.

Sunk Costs Are Not Incremental Cash Flows

Sunk costs are those costs that have already been incurred or are going to be incurred regardless of whether or not the investment is undertaken. An example would be the cost of a market research study or a pilot program. These costs are not incremental cash flows resulting from the acceptance of the investment because they will be incurred in any case. For example, in the convenience store example just discussed, if last year you spent $1,000 getting an appraisal of the prospective site for the second store, this expenditure is not relevant to the decision we have to make today, because you already spent that money. The cost of the appraisal is a sunk cost because the money has already been spent and cannot be recovered whether or not you build the second convenience store.

Overhead Costs Are Generally Not Incremental Cash Flows

Overhead expenses such as the cost of heat, light, and rent often occur regardless of whether we accept or reject a particular project. In these instances, overhead expenses are not a relevant consideration when evaluating project cash flows.

To illustrate, consider the decision as to whether the university bookstore should open a sub shop in an underutilized portion of the bookstore. The bookstore manager estimates that the sub shop will take up one-tenth of the bookstore's floor space. If the store's monthly heat and light bill is $10,000, should the manager allocate $1,000 of this cost to the sub shop proposal? Assuming the space will be heated and lighted regardless of whether or not it is converted into a sub shop, the answer is no.

Look for Synergistic Effects

Oftentimes the acceptance of a new project will have an effect on the cash flows of the firm's other projects or investments. These effects can be either positive or negative, and if these synergistic effects can be anticipated, their costs and benefits are relevant to the project analysis.

Don't Overlook Positive Synergies

In 2000, GM's Pontiac division introduced the Aztek, a boldly designed sport-utility vehicle aimed at young buyers. The idea was to sell Azteks, of course, but also to help lure younger customers back into Pontiac's showrooms. Thus, in evaluating the Aztek, if Pontiac's analysts were to have focused only on the expected revenues from new Aztek sales, they would have missed the incremental cash flow from new customers who came in to see the Aztek but instead purchased another Pontiac automobile.

Another example of a synergistic effect is that of Harley-Davidson's introduction of the Buell Blast and the Lightning Low XB95—two smaller, lighter motorcycles targeted at younger riders and female riders not yet ready for heavier and more expensive Harley-Davidson bikes. The company had two goals in mind when it introduced the Buell Blast and Lightning Low bikes. First, it was trying to expand its customer base into a new market made up of Generation Xers. Second, it wanted to expand the market for existing products by introducing more people to motorcycling. That is, the Buell Blast and Lightning Low models were offered not only to produce their own sales, but also to ultimately increase the sales of Harley's heavier cruiser and touring bikes.

Beware of Cash Flows Diverted from Existing Products

An important type of negative synergistic effect comes in the form of revenue cannibalization. This occurs when the offering of a new product draws sales away from an existing product. This is a very real concern, for example, when a firm such as Frito-Lay considers offering a new flavor of Dorito® chips. A supermarket allocates limited shelf space to Frito-Lay's snack products. So, if a new flavor is offered, it must take space away from existing products. If the new flavor is expected to produce $10 million per year in cash flows, perhaps as much as $6 million of this cash flow may be at the expense of existing flavors of Doritos®.

Consequently, we take the resulting $4 million dollars, our incremental cash flow, as the relevant cash flow in evaluating whether or not to introduce the new flavor.

Account for Opportunity Costs

In calculating the cash flows of an investment, it is important to account for what economists refer to as opportunity cost, the cost of passing up the next best choice when making a decision. To illustrate, consider the convenience store example we introduced earlier. Remember that we were considering whether to open a second location just a few blocks from our first very successful store. Let's now assume that you have purchased the building in which the second store is to be located and it has space for two businesses. One of the spaces is occupied by a tanning salon and you are considering opening a second convenience store in the unoccupied space. Because you already own the building and the space needed for the convenience store is currently unused, should you charge the second convenience store business for use of the open space? The answer is no if you have no other foreseeable use for the space. However, what if a local restaurant owner approaches you with a proposal to rent the space for $2,000 a month? If you open the second convenience store, you will then forego the $2,000 per month in rent, and this becomes a very relevant incremental expense because it represents an opportunity cost of putting in the convenience store.

Work in Working Capital Requirements

Many times a new project involves an additional investment in working capital. Additional working capital arises out of the fact that cash inflows and outflows from the operations of an investment are often mismatched. That is, inventory is purchased and paid for before it is sold. For example, this may take the form of new inventory to stock a sales outlet or an additional investment in accounts receivable resulting from additional credit sales. Some of the funds needed to finance the increase in inventory and accounts receivable may come from an increase in accounts payable that arises when the firm buys goods on credit. As a result, the actual amount of new investment required by the project is determined by the difference in the sum of the increase in accounts receivables plus inventories less the increase in accounts payable. We will refer to this quantity as net operating working capital. Net working capital is defined as the difference in current assets and current liabilities. Net operating working capital is very similar but it focuses on the firm's accounts receivable and inventories compared to accounts payable.

Ignore Interest Payments and Other Financing Costs

Although interest payments are incremental to the investments that are partly financed by borrowing, we do not include the interest payments in the computation of project cash flows. The reason is that the cost of capital for the project takes into account how the project is financed, including the after-tax cost of any debt that is used in financing the investment. Consequently, when we discount the incremental cash flows back to the present using the cost of capital, we are implicitly accounting for the cost of raising funds to finance the new project (including the after-tax interest expense). Including interest expense in both the computation of the project's cash flows and in the discount rate would amount to counting interest twice.

Before you move on to 2

Concept Check | 1

1. What makes an investment cash flow relevant to the evaluation of an investment proposal?
2. What are sunk costs?
3. What are some examples of synergistic effects that affect a project's cash flows?
4. When borrowing the money needed to make an investment, is the interest expense incurred relevant to the analysis of the project? Explain.

Forecasting Project Cash Flows

To analyze an investment and determine whether it adds value to the firm, following **P** Principle 3: **Cash Flows Are the Source of Value**, we use the project's free cash flow. A free cash flow is the total amount of cash available for distribution to the creditors who have loaned money to finance the project and to the owners who have invested in the equity of the project. In practice this cash flow information is compiled from pro forma financial statements. **Pro forma financial statements** are forecasts of future financial statements. We can calculate free cash flow using Equation (2) as follows:

$$
\underbrace{\text{Free Cash Flow}}_{} = \underbrace{\overbrace{\underbrace{\text{Net Operating Income (Profit)} - \text{Taxes}}_{\text{Net Operating Profit after Taxes or NOPAT}} + \text{Depreciation Expense}}^{\text{Operating Cash Flow}}} - \underset{(CAPEX)}{\text{Increase in Capital Expenditures}} - \underset{\text{Capital } (NOWC)}{\text{Increase in Net Operating Working}} \quad \textbf{(2)}
$$

Dealing with Depreciation Expense, Taxes, and Cash Flow

When accountants calculate a firm's taxable income, one of the expenses they subtract out is depreciation. In fact, depreciation has already been deducted from revenues before we calculate net operating income. However, depreciation is a non–cash flow expense. If you think about it, depreciation occurs because you bought a fixed asset (for example, you built a plant) in an earlier period, and now, by depreciating the asset, you're effectively allocating the expense of acquiring the asset over time. However, depreciation is not a cash expense because the actual cash expense occurred when the asset was acquired. As a result, the firm's net operating income understates cash flows by the amount of the depreciation expense that is deducted for the period. Therefore, we'll want to compensate for this by adding depreciation back into net operating income when calculating cash flows.

For our purposes in this chapter, depreciation is calculated using a simplified version of the straight-line method. Specifically, we calculate annual depreciation for a piece of plant or equipment by taking its initial cost (including the cost of any equipment plus shipping costs and other costs incurred when installing the equipment) and dividing this total by the depreciable life of the equipment. If the equipment has an expected salvage value at the end of its useful life, this is deducted from the initial cost before determining the annual depreciation expense. For example, if a firm were to purchase a piece of equipment for $100,000 and paid an additional $20,000 in shipping and installation expenses, the initial outlay for the equipment and its depreciable cost would be $120,000. If the equipment is expected to last five years, at which time it will have a salvage value of $40,000, then the annual depreciation expense would be $16,000 = ($100,000 + 20,000 − 40,000) ÷ 5 years.

In the Appendix to this chapter we discuss the modified accelerated cost recovery system (MACRS), which is used for most tangible depreciable property. This method is typically used by firms to compute their tax liability, but the straight-line method is used for financial reporting to the public.

Four-Step Procedure for Calculating Project Cash Flows

Our objective is to identify incremental cash flows for the project, or changes to the firm's cash flows as a result of taking the project. To do this, we forecast cash flows for future periods and then estimate the value of the project using the investment criteria. As we introduce these calculations, keep in mind the guidelines introduced in the previous section dealing with sunk costs, synergistic effects, and opportunity costs. In order to estimate project cash flows for future periods, we use the following four-step procedure:

Step 1. Estimating a Project's Operating Cash Flows

Step 2. Calculating a Project's Working Capital Requirements

Step 3. Calculating a Project's Capital Expenditure Requirements

Step 4. Calculating a Project's Free Cash Flow

In the pages that follow we will discuss each of these steps in detail.

Step 1: Estimating a Project's Operating Cash Flows

Operating cash flow is simply the sum of the first three terms found in Equation (2). Specifically, operating cash flow for year t is defined in Equation (3):

$$\text{Operating Cash Flow}_t = \underbrace{\text{Net Operating Income (or Profit)}_t - \text{Taxes}_t}_{\text{NOPAT}_t} + \text{Depreciation Expense}_t \qquad (3)$$

There are two observations we should make regarding the computation of operating cash flow:

- **First, our estimate of cash flows from operations begins with an estimate of net operating income.** However, when calculating net operating income, we subtract out depreciation expense because it is a tax-deductible expense. Thus to estimate the cash flow the firm has earned from its operations, we first calculate the firm's tax liability based on net operating income and then add back depreciation expense.

- **Second, when we calculate the increase in taxes, we ignore interest expenses.** Even if the project is financed with debt, we do not subtract out the increased interest payments. Certainly there is a cost to money, but we are accounting for this cost when we

---

Checkpoint 1

Forecasting a Project's Operating Cash Flow

The Crockett Clothing Company, located in El Paso, Texas, owns and operates a clothing factory across the Mexican border in Juarez. The Juarez factory imports materials into Mexico for assembly and then exports the assembled products back to the United States without having to pay duties or tariffs. This type of factory is commonly referred to as a *maquiladora*.

Crockett is considering the purchase of an automated sewing machine that will cost $200,000 and is expected to operate for five years, after which time it is not expected to have any value. The investment is expected to generate $360,000 in additional revenues for the firm during each of the five years of the project's life. Due to the expanded sales, Crockett expects to have to expand its investment in accounts receivable by $60,000 and inventories by $36,000. These investments in working capital will be partially offset by an increase in the firm's accounts payable of $18,000, which makes the increase in net operating working capital equal to $78,000 in Year 0. Note that this investment will be returned at the end of Year 5 as inventories are sold, receivables are collected, and payables are repaid.

The project will also result in cost of goods sold equal to 60 percent of revenues while incurring other annual cash operating expenses of $5,000 per year. In addition, the depreciation expense for the machine is $40,000 per year. This depreciation expense is one-fifth of the initial investment of $200,000, where the estimated salvage value is zero at the end of its five-year life. Profits from the investment will be taxed at a 30 percent tax rate and the firm uses a 20 percent required rate of return. Calculate the operating cash flow.

STEP 1: Picture the problem

Operating cash flows only encompass the revenues and operating expenses (after taxes) corresponding to the operation of the asset. Therefore, they only begin with the end of the first year of operations (Year 1). The operating cash flow then is determined by the revenues less operating expenses for Years 1 through 5.

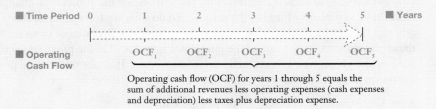

Operating cash flow (OCF) for years 1 through 5 equals the sum of additional revenues less operating expenses (cash expenses and depreciation) less taxes plus depreciation expense.

The following list summarizes what we know about the investment opportunity:

Equipment cost or CAPEX (today)	$(200,000)
Project life	5 years
Salvage value	0
Depreciation expense	$ 40,000 per year
Cash operating expenses	$ (5,000) per year
Revenues (Year 1)	$ 360,000 per year
Growth rate for revenues	0% per year
Cost of goods sold/revenues	60%
Investment in net operating working capital (Year 0)	$ (78,000)
Required rate of return	20%
Tax rate	30%

STEP 2: Decide on a solution strategy

Using Equation (3), we calculate operating cash flow as the sum of NOPAT and depreciation expense as follows:

$$\text{Operating Cash Flow} = \underbrace{\text{Net Operating Income (or Profit)} - \text{Taxes}}_{\text{NOPAT}} + \text{Depreciation Expense} \qquad (3)$$

STEP 3: Solve

The project produces $360,000 in revenues annually and cost of goods sold equals 60 percent of revenues or $(216,000), leaving gross profits of $144,000. Subtracting cash operating expenses of $5,000 per year and depreciation expenses of $40,000 per year, we get a net operating income of $99,000. Subtracting taxes of $29,700 leaves a net operating profit of $69,300. Finally, adding back depreciation expense, this gives us an operating cash flow of $109,300 per year for Years 1 through 5:

	Year 1	Year 2	Year 3	Year 4	Year 5
Project Revenues (**growing at 0% per year**)	$360,000	$360,000	$360,000	$360,000	$360,000
− Cost of Goods Sold (**60% of revenues**)	(216,000)	(216,000)	(216,000)	(216,000)	(216,000)
= Gross Profit	$144,000	$144,000	$144,000	$144,000	$144,000
− Cash Operating Expenses (**fixed at $5,000 per year**)	(5,000)	(5,000)	(5,000)	(5,000)	(5,000)
− Depreciation (**$200,000/5 years**)	(40,000)	(40,000)	(40,000)	(40,000)	(40,000)
= Net Operating Income	$ 99,000	$ 99,000	$ 99,000	$ 99,000	$ 99,000
− Taxes (**30%**)	(29,700)	(29,700)	(29,700)	(29,700)	(29,700)
= Net Operating Profit after Taxes (NOPAT)	$ 69,300	$ 69,300	$ 69,300	$ 69,300	$ 69,300
+ Depreciation	40,000	40,000	40,000	40,000	40,000
= Operating Cash Flow	$109,300	$109,300	$109,300	$109,300	$109,300

STEP 4: Analyze

The project contributes $99,000 to the firm's net operating income (before taxes), and if the project operates exactly as forecast here, this will be the observed impact of the project on the net operating income on the firm's income statement. Of course, in a world where the future is uncertain, this will not be the outcome. As such, we might want to analyze the consequences of lower revenues and higher costs. For example, if project revenues were to drop to $300,000, the operating cash flow would drop to only $92,500.

STEP 5: Check yourself

Crockett Clothing Company is reconsidering its sewing machine investment in light of a change in its expectations regarding project revenues. The firm's management wants to know the impact of a decrease in expected revenues from $360,000 to $240,000 per year. What would be the project's operating cash flows under the revised revenue estimate?

ANSWER: Operating cash flow = $75,700.

Your Turn: For more practice, do related **Study Problems** 8, 12, 14, and 22 at the end of this chapter.

>> **END Checkpoint 1**

discount the free cash flows back to present. If we were to subtract out any increase in interest expenses and then discount those cash flows back to the present, we would be double counting the interest expense—once when we subtracted it out, and once again when we discounted the cash flows back to the present. In addition, when we calculate the increased taxes from taking on the new project, we calculate those taxes from the change in net operating income so as not to allow any increase in interest expense to impact our tax calculations. The important point to remember here is that *no interest or other costs of financing* are deducted in determining the project's free cash flow.

The format we use in calculating a project's operating cash flow looks a lot like a typical income statement. The left-hand column below depicts the calculation of operating cash flow, whereas the right-hand column depicts the calculation of net income using a traditional income statement:

Note: Operating Expenses include both cash expenses and depreciation expense.

Differences

Operating Cash Flow Calculation	Income Statement Calculation
Revenues	Revenues
Less: Cost of Goods Sold	Less: Cost of Goods Sold
Equals: Gross Profit	Equals: Gross Profit
Less: Operating Expenses (including depreciation)	Less: Operating Expenses (including depreciation)
Equals: Net Operating Income (Profit or EBIT)*	Equals: Net Operating Income (Profit)
Less: Taxes (based on Net Operating Income or EBIT)	Less: Interest Expense
Equals: Net Operating Profit after Taxes (NOPAT)	Earnings before Taxes (EBT)
Plus: Depreciation Expense	Less: Taxes (based on EBT)
Operating Cash Flow	Net Income

*(Recall that NOI is the same as EBIT if there is no non-operating income or expense)

To compute operating cash flow in the left-hand column, we begin with Revenues (just like the income statement). Next, we subtract Cost of Goods Sold and Operating Expenses to calculate Net Operating Income (Profit). To this point, the calculation of operating cash flow looks just like the income statement in the right-hand column. From this point forward, the calculation of operating cash flow deviates from the standard form of the income statement. Specifically, to calculate operating cash flow, we estimate taxes based on the firm's net operating profit. Deducting taxes from net operating profit gives us an estimate of Net Operating Profit after Taxes, or NOPAT. Finally, because depreciation expense is a non-cash operating expense and was subtracted before the tax calculation, we add back the annual depreciation expense to NOPAT to estimate Operating Cash Flow.

Step 2: Calculating a Project's Working Capital Requirements

When a firm invests in a new project, it often leads to an increase in sales that requires the firm to extend credit, which means that the firm's accounts receivable balance will grow. In addition, new projects often lead to a need to increase the firm's investment in inventories. Both the increase in accounts receivable and the increase in inventories mean that the firm must invest more cash in the business. This is a cash outflow. However, if the firm is able to finance some or all of its inventories using trade credit, this offsets the effects of the increased investment in receivables and inventories. The difference in the increased accounts receivable plus inventories, less the increase in accounts payable (trade credit), indicates just how much cash the firm must come up with to cover the project's additional working capital requirements.

To calculate the increase in net operating working capital, we examine the levels of accounts receivable, inventory, and accounts payable with and without the project. For the Crockett Clothing Company, let's assume that the purchase of an automated sewing machine described in Checkpoint 1 would cause the following changes:

	Without the Project (A)	With the Project (B)	Difference (B − A)
Accounts receivable	$600,000	$660,000	$60,000
Inventory	390,000	426,000	36,000
Accounts payable	180,000	198,000	18,000

We can now use Equation (4) to calculate Crockett's additional investment in working capital as follows:

$$\begin{matrix} \text{Investment in} \\ \text{Net Operating} \\ \text{Working Capital} \end{matrix} = \begin{pmatrix} \text{Increase in} \\ \text{Accounts Receivable} \end{pmatrix} + \begin{pmatrix} \text{Increase in} \\ \text{Inventories} \end{pmatrix} - \begin{pmatrix} \text{Increase in} \\ \text{Accounts Payable} \end{pmatrix} \quad \textbf{(4)}$$

$$= \$60,000 + 36,000 - 18,000 = \$78,000$$

So to meet the needs of the firm for working capital in Year 1, Crockett must invest $78,000. Although this investment will be made throughout the year, to be conservative we assume that the full $78,000 is invested immediately in Year 0. In this particular example, sales do not grow or decline over the five-year life of the investment, so there are no additional investments in working capital in Years 1 through 5. However, at the end of Year 5, Crockett will collect outstanding receivables, sell down its remaining inventory, and pay off the outstanding balance of its accounts payable, thereby realizing a $78,000 cash inflow at the end of Year 5 from its initial investment of $78,000 in net operating working capital made in Year 0. In summary, Crockett expects to have a cash *outflow* of $78,000 for working capital in Year 0 and receive a cash *inflow* of $78,000 in Year 5 when the project is shut down.

Step 3: Calculating a Project's Capital Expenditure Requirements

Capital expenditures, or CAPEX, is the term we use to refer to the cash the firm spends to purchase fixed assets. As we discussed earlier, for accounting purposes, the cost of a firm's purchases of long-term assets is not recognized immediately, but is allocated or expensed over the life of the asset by depreciating the investment. Specifically, the difference between the purchase price and the expected salvage value of the investment is calculated as a depreciation expense over the life of the asset.

We incorporate depreciation into our computation of project cash flow by deducting it from taxable income and then adding it back after taxes have been computed. In this way, the effect of depreciation is simply to reduce the tax liability created by the investment. When the project life is over, the book value of the asset is expected to equal the salvage value. Because the book value and salvage value are equal, there is no taxable gain or loss on the sale, and we simply add the salvage value to the final year's free cash flow along with the recovery of any net operating working capital.

Step 4: Calculating a Project's Free Cash Flow

Using Equation (2), we calculate Crockett Clothing Company's free cash flows for the five-year life of its investment opportunity in the new automated sewing machine. These cash flows are as follows:

	Year 0	Year 1	Year 2	Year 3	Year 4	Year 5
Project Revenues (**growing at 0% per year**)		$ 360,000	$ 360,000	$ 360,000	$ 360,000	$ 360,000
− Cost of Goods Sold (**60% of revenues**)		(216,000)	(216,000)	(216,000)	(216,000)	(216,000)
= Gross Profit		$ 144,000	$ 144,000	$ 144,000	$ 144,000	$ 144,000
− Cash Operating Expenses (**fixed at $5,000 per year**)		(5,000)	(5,000)	(5,000)	(5,000)	(5,000)
− Depreciation (**$200,000 / 5 years**)		(40,000)	(40,000)	(40,000)	(40,000)	(40,000)
= Net Operating Income		$ 99,000	$ 99,000	$ 99,000	$ 99,000	$ 99,000
− Taxes (**30%**)		(29,700)	(29,700)	(29,700)	(29,700)	(29,700)
= Net Operating Profit after Taxes (NOPAT)		$ 69,300	$ 69,300	$ 69,300	$ 69,300	$ 69,300
+ Depreciation		40,000	40,000	40,000	40,000	40,000
= Operating Cash Flow		$ 109,300	$ 109,300	$ 109,300	$ 109,300	$ 109,300
Less: Increase in CAPEX	$(200,000)	—	—	—	—	—
Less: Increase in Net Operating Working Capital	(78,000)	—	—	—	—	78,000
Free Cash Flow	**(278,000)**	**$ 109,300**	**$ 109,300**	**$ 109,300**	**$ 109,300**	**$ 187,300**

Note that in Year 0, the free cash flow is simply the sum of the capital expenditure of $200,000 and the investment in net operating working capital of $78,000. The operating cash flows for Years 1 through 5 are $109,300, and in Year 5 we add back the $78,000 investment in net operating working capital, which produces a total free cash flow in this year of $187,300. Finally, note that because the equipment is not expected to have a salvage value, none is added back in Year 5.

Computing Project NPV

We can now evaluate the investment opportunity. If Crockett applies a 20 percent discount rate or required rate of return to evaluate the sewing machine investment, we can calculate the net present value (NPV) of the investment using the following equation:

$$NPV = CF_0 + \frac{CF_1}{(1 + k)^1} + \frac{CF_2}{(1 + k)^2} + \frac{CF_3}{(1 + k)^3} + \frac{CF_4}{(1 + k)^4} + \frac{CF_5}{(1 + k)^5} \qquad \textbf{(1)}$$

CF_0 is the −$278,000 initial cash outlay, k is the required rate of return (20 percent) used to discount the project's future cash flows, and CF_1 through CF_5 are the investment's free cash flows for Years 1 through 5. Substituting for each of these terms in the NPV equation above we get the following:

$$NPV = -\$278,000 + \frac{\$109,300}{(1 + .20)^1} + \frac{\$109,300}{(1 + .20)^2} + \frac{\$109,300}{(1 + .20)^3} + \frac{\$109,300}{(1 + .20)^4} + \frac{\$187,300}{(1 + .20)^5}$$

$$NPV = \$80,220$$

Based on our estimates of the investment's cash flows, it appears that Crockett should go ahead and purchase the new automated machine because it offers an expected NPV of $80,220.

Tools of Financial Analysis—Free Cash Flow

Name of Tool	Formula	What It Tells You
Free Cash Flow (FCF)	$$\frac{\text{Net Operating}}{\text{Income (Profit)}} - \text{Taxes} + \frac{\text{Depreciation}}{\text{Expense}} -$$ $$\frac{\text{Capital}}{\text{Expenditures}} - \frac{\text{Change in Net}}{\text{Operating Working}}$$ $$\text{(CAPEX)} \qquad \text{Capital (NOWC)}$$ *Net operating income* is the profit after deducting the cost of goods sold and all operating expenses (including depreciation expense). Net operating income or net operating profit is also equal to earnings before interest and taxes (EBIT) for capital investment projects because projects do not have other (non-operating) sources of income or expense. For firms that have both operating and non-operating income and expenses, EBIT differs from net operating income by the amount of these non-operating sources of income and expenses. *Net operating profit after taxes (NOPAT)* is equal to the firm's net operating profit times 1 minus the corporate tax rate, or simply net operating profit minus income taxes calculated using operating profit as taxable income. Note that we do not deduct interest expense before computing the corporate income taxes owed because the tax deductibility of interest is accounted for in the computation of the discount rate or the weighted average cost of capital. *Depreciation expense* is the allocation of the cost of fixed assets to the period when the assets are used. *Capital expenditures (CAPEX)* is the periodic expenditure of money for new capital equipment that generally occurs at the time the investment is undertaken (i.e., in Year 0). However, many investments require periodic expenditures over the life of the investment to repair or replace worn-out capital equipment. Finally, if the equipment has a salvage value, this becomes a cash inflow in the final year of the project's life. *Change in net operating working capital (NOWC)* represents changes in the balance of accounts receivable plus inventories less accounts payable. Any changes in this quantity represent either the need to invest more cash or an opportunity to extract cash from the project.	• Free cash flow (FCF) is the cash the firm has left over from its operations for the year that it can use to retire debt early and give to its stockholders through the payment of cash dividends or the repurchase of some of the firm's outstanding shares of stock • FCF is a key measure of firm performance during a particular period of time that is used both to value new investments and also by creditors (lenders) in determining whether to lend the firm money.

Before you move on to 3

Concept Check | 2

1. What does the term *free cash flow* mean?
2. What are the four steps used to forecast a project's future cash flows?
3. What is net operating working capital, and how does it affect a project's cash flows?
4. What is CAPEX, and how does it affect a project's cash flows?

3 | Inflation and Capital Budgeting

Because investments are expected to provide cash flows over many years, we cannot overlook the issue of price inflation. Fortunately, we can adjust project revenues and expenses for the anticipated effects of inflation. Cash flows that account for future inflation are generally referred to as **nominal cash flows**. Sometimes analysts calculate what is referred to as **real cash flows**, which are the cash flows that would occur in the absence of inflation.

When nominal cash flows are used, they should be discounted at the nominal interest rate, which is as the rate that we observe in the financial markets. In most cases, firms do use nominal rates of return for the discount rates that are used to evaluate a project, so it is appropriate to also calculate nominal cash flows. However, when firms calculate the real cash flows that are generated by a project, the cash flows should be discounted at the **real rate of interest**, which is the **nominal rate of interest** adjusted for inflation.

Typically, firms calculate project values by discounting nominal cash flows at nominal rates of interest. Let's see how nominal cash flows are estimated.

Estimating Nominal Cash Flows

Although not stated explicitly, the cash flows that we have looked at up to now have been nominal cash flows. To illustrate how we can directly incorporate the effects of inflation into our cash flow forecasts, consider the situation faced by the Plantation Chemical Company. The firm purchases HDPE (high-density polyethylene) pellets manufactured by oil refineries and uses them to manufacture the plastic containers used to package milk, fruit juice, and soft drinks. The firm is considering the expansion of one of its milk bottle plants, which will allow it to produce 5 million additional plastic bottles a year. The bottles currently sell for $0.20 each and cost $0.10 each to produce. The price of the bottles is expected to rise at a rate of 3 percent a year and the HDPE is expected to increase by 8 percent per year due to restrictions on world crude oil production. We can forecast the gross profit for the proposed investment for each of the next three years as follows:[1]

$.2060 = .20(1.03)$

	1	2	3
Units sold	5,000,000	5,000,000	5,000,000
Price per unit (inflation rate = 3%)	$0.2060	$0.2122	$0.2185
Cost per unit (inflation rate = 8%)	$0.1080	$0.1166	$0.1260
Revenues	$1,030,000.00	$1,060,900.00	$1,092,727.00
Cost of goods sold	(540,000.00)	(583,200.00)	(629,856.00)
Gross profit	$ 490,000.00	$ 477,700.00	$ 462,871.00

$.2185 = .2122(1.03)$

$.1260 = .1166(1.08)$

$.1080 = .10(1.08)$

Note that gross profit actually declines over time as the cost of raw materials is inflating more rapidly than the price of the end product.

Before you move on to 4

Concept Check | 3

1. What is the distinction between nominal and real interest rates?
2. If you forecast nominal cash flows, should you use the nominal or the real discount rate? Why?

[1]Although the numbers listed for price and cost per unit have been rounded to four decimal places in this table, the calculations for revenue and cost of goods sold have been made without rounding.

Replacement Project Cash Flows

To this point, we have been evaluating project cash flows for an expansion project. An **expansion project** increases the scope of the firm's operations, but does not replace any existing assets or operations. In this section, we consider a **replacement investment**, an acquisition of a new productive asset that replaces an older, less productive asset. A distinctive feature of many replacement investments is that the principal source of investment cash flows comes from cost savings, not new revenues, because the firm already operates an existing asset to generate revenues.

The objective of our analysis of investment cash flows is the same for a replacement project as it was for the expansion projects considered earlier. Specifically, project or investment free cash flow is still defined by Equation (3). However, with a replacement project, we must explicitly compare what the firm's cash flows would be without making a change to the firm's cash flows with the replacement assets. To perform this analysis, it is helpful to categorize investment cash flows as an initial outlay of CF_0 and future cash flows as CF_1, CF_2, CF_3, and so forth.

Category 1: Initial Outlay, CF_0

For an expansion project, the initial cash outlay typically includes the immediate cash outflow (CAPEX) necessary to purchase fixed assets and put them in operating order, plus the cost of any increased investment in net operating working capital (NOWC) required by the project. However, when the investment proposal involves the replacement of an existing asset, the computation of the initial cash outlay is a bit more complicated because disposing of the existing asset can involve immediate expenses. If the old asset is sold for more than the book value of the asset, this gives rise to a taxable gain on the sale. On the other hand, if the old asset is sold for less than its book value, then a tax-deductible loss occurs.

When an existing asset is sold, there are three possible tax scenarios:

- **The old asset is sold for a price above the depreciated value.** Here the difference between the selling price of the old machine and its depreciated book value is a taxable gain, taxed at the marginal corporate tax rate and subtracted from the CAPEX. For example, assume the old machine was originally purchased for $350,000, had a depreciated book value of $100,000 today, and could be sold for $150,000, and assume that the firm's marginal corporate tax rate is 30 percent. The taxes due from the gain would then be ($150,000 − $100,000) × (.30), or $15,000.

- **The old asset is sold for its depreciated value.** In this case, no taxes result, as there is neither a gain nor a loss from the asset's sale.

- **The old asset is sold for less than its depreciated value.** In this case, the difference between the depreciated book value and the salvage value of the asset is a taxable loss and may be used to offset capital gains. Thus, it results in tax savings and we add it to the CAPEX. For example, if the depreciated book value of the asset is $100,000 and it is sold for $70,000, we have a $30,000 loss. Assuming the firm's marginal corporate tax rate is 30 percent, the cash inflow from tax savings is ($100,000 − $70,000) × (.30), or $9,000.

Category 2: Annual Cash Flows

Annual cash flows for a replacement decision differ from a simple asset acquisition because we must now consider the differential operating cash flow of the new versus the old (replaced) asset.

Changes in Depreciation and Taxes

Once again, we are only interested in any change in taxes that the change in depreciation might bring about—after all, depreciation is not a cash flow expense, but because it is tax deductible it impacts taxes, which *are* a cash flow item. We want to look at the incremental change in taxes—that is, what the taxes would be if the asset were replaced versus what they would be if the asset were not replaced.

For a replacement project, the firm's depreciation expense increases by the amount of depreciation on the new asset but decreases by the amount of the depreciation on the replaced asset. Because our concern is with incremental changes, we take the new depreciation less the lost depreciation, and that difference would be our incremental change in depreciation. That is what we would use in our cash flow calculations to determine the change in taxes.

Changes in Working Capital

Many replacement projects require an increased investment in working capital. For example, if the new asset has greater capacity than the one it replaces and generates more sales, these new sales, if they are credit sales, will result in an increased investment in accounts receivable. Also, in order to produce and sell the product, the firm may have to increase its investment in inventory, which also requires additional financing. On the other hand, some of this increased investment in inventory is financed by an increase in accounts payable, which offsets the outlay for new investment in inventories.

Changes in Capital Spending

The replacement asset will require an outlay at the time of its acquisition but may also require additional capital over its life. We must be careful, however, to net out any additional capital spending requirements of the older, replaced asset when computing project free cash flows. Finally, at the end of the project's life, there will be a cash inflow equal to the after-tax salvage value of the new asset, if it is expected to have one. Once again, we need to be careful to net out any salvage value that the older asset might have had to get the net cash effect of salvage value.

Replacement Example

Checkpoint 2 describes an asset replacement problem faced by the Leggett Scrap Metal Company. The company operates a large scrap metal yard that buys junk automobiles, strips them of their valuable parts, and then crushes them in a large press. Leggett is considering the replacement of its largest press with a newer and more efficient model.

Checkpoint 2

Calculating Free Cash Flows for a Replacement Investment

Leggett Scrap Metal, Inc. operates an auto salvage business in Salem, Oregon. The firm is considering the replacement of one of the presses it uses to crush scrapped automobiles. The following information summarizes the new versus old machine costs:

	Machine	
	New	**Old**
Annual cost of defects	$ 20,000	$ 70,000
Net operating income	$580,000	$580,000
Book value of equipment	350,000	100,000
Salvage value (today)	NA	150,000
Salvage value (Year 5)	50,000	—
Shipping cost	$ 20,000	NA
Installation cost	30,000	NA
Remaining project life (years)	5	5
Net operating working capital	$ 60,000	$ 60,000
Salaries	100,000	200,000
Fringe benefits	10,000	20,000
Maintenance	60,000	20,000

Leggett faces a 30 percent marginal tax rate and uses a 15 percent discount rate to evaluate equipment purchases for its automobile scrap operation.

The appeal of the new press is that it is more automated (requires two fewer employees to operate the machine). The older machine requires four employees with salaries totaling $200,000 and fringe benefits costing $20,000. The new machine cuts this total in half. In addition, the new machine is able to separate out the glass and rubber components of the crushed automobiles, which reduces the annual cost of defects, which are $20,000 with the new machine compared to $70,000 for the older model. However, the added automation feature comes at the cost of higher annual maintenance fees of $60,000 compared to only $20,000 for the older press.

Should Leggett replace the older machine with the newer one?

STEP 1: Picture the problem

The automated scrap press machine requires an initial investment to purchase the equipment, which is partially offset by the after-tax proceeds realized from the sale of the older press. In addition, the newer press provides net cash savings to Leggett in Years 1 through 5 based on the predicted difference in the costs of operating the two machines. Finally, in Year 5 the new press can be sold for an amount equal to its book value of $50,000. The relevant cash flow for analyzing the replacement decision equals the difference in cash flow between the new and old machine, illustrated as follows:

$k = 15\%$

Time Period	0	1	2	3	4	5	Years

| Cash Flow (New) | $CF(New)_0$ | $CF(New)_1$ | $CF(New)_2$ | $CF(New)_3$ | $CF(New)_4$ | $CF(New)_5$ |

Minus

| Cash Flow (Old) | $CF(Old)_0$ | $CF(Old)_1$ | $CF(Old)_2$ | $CF(Old)_3$ | $CF(Old)_4$ | $CF(Old)_5$ |

Equals

| Difference (New – Old) | ΔCF_0 | ΔCF_1 | ΔCF_2 | ΔCF_3 | ΔCF_4 | ΔCF_5 |

where the cash flows to be used in analyzing the replacement decision equal the difference in cash flows of the new and old assets, that is,

$$\text{Replacement Cash Flows } (\Delta CF)_{\text{Year } t} = \begin{pmatrix} \text{Cash Flow for} \\ \text{the New Asset} \\ CF\,(New)_{\text{Year } t} \end{pmatrix} - \begin{pmatrix} \text{Cash Flow for} \\ \text{the Old Asset} \\ CF\,(Old)_{\text{Year } t} \end{pmatrix} \qquad (5)$$

STEP 2: Decide on a solution strategy

The cash flows of the replacement decision are still calculated using Equation (3), which requires that we identify operating cash flows after taxes, capital expenditure (CAPEX) requirements, and required investments in net operating working capital, that is,

$$\text{Free Cash Flow} = \begin{pmatrix} \text{Net Operating} \\ \text{Profit after} \\ \text{Taxes } (NOPAT) \end{pmatrix} + \begin{pmatrix} \text{Depreciation} \\ \text{Expense} \end{pmatrix} - \begin{pmatrix} \text{Increase in Capital} \\ \text{Expenditures} \\ (CAPEX) \end{pmatrix} - \begin{pmatrix} \text{Increase in Net} \\ \text{Operating Working} \\ \text{Capital } (NOWC) \end{pmatrix} \qquad (3)$$

However, for a replacement decision we focus on the difference in costs and benefits with the new machine versus the old. For this type of problem, it is helpful to focus on the initial cash outflow (CF_0) and then the annual cash flows, including any terminal cash flow resulting from the difference in the salvage values of the two machines in Year 5—in this case $50,000 for the new machine compared to $0 for the older machine.

(2 CONTINUED >> ON NEXT PAGE)

STEP 3: Solve

The initial cash outlay for Year 0 reflects the difference in the cost of acquiring the new machine (including shipping and installation costs) and the after-tax proceeds Leggett realizes from the sale of the old press, that is,

Analysis of the Initial Outlay	Year 0
New Machine	
Purchase price	$(350,000)
Shipping cost	(20,000)
Installation cost	(30,000)
Total installed cost of purchasing the new press	$(400,000)
Old Machine	
Sale price	$ 150,000
Less: Tax on gain = [($150,000 − 100,000) × .30]	(15,000)
After-tax proceeds from the sale of the old press	$ 135,000
Operating working capital	$ 0
Initial cash flow	(265,000)

The new press costs $400,000 to purchase and install. This cost is partially offset by the after-tax proceeds from the sale of the older press, which equal $135,000, such that the initial cash outlay is $265,000 = $400,000 − $135,000.

Next we estimate the annual cash flows for Years 1 through 5 assuming that the new press is purchased and the older one is sold.

Analysis of the Annual Cash Flows	Years 1–4	Year 5
Cash inflows		
Increase in operating income	$ 0	
Reduced salaries	$100,000	
Reduced defects	50,000	
Reduced fringe benefits	10,000	
	$ 160,000	$160,000
Cash outflows		
Increased maintenance	$ (40,000)	
Increased depreciation	(50,000)	
	(90,000)	$ (90,000)
Net operating income	$ 70,000	$ 70,000
less: Taxes	(21,000)	(21,000)
Net operating profit after taxes (NOPAT)	$ 49,000	$ 49,000
plus: Depreciation	50,000	50,000
Operating cash flow	$ 99,000	$ 99,000
less: Increase in net operating working capital	0	0
less: Increase in CAPEX	0	50,000
Free cash flows	$ 99,000	$149,000

Note: Capital expenditures (CAPEX) are generally outflows, and hence subtracted out. However, when a project has a salvage value at the end of its useful life, the CAPEX takes on a positive value and is added to the free cash flows in the project's final year.

The new press will reduce costs (totaling $160,000 per year) compared to the older press; however, the new press requires an additional $40,000 in maintenance expenses and has $50,000 more depreciation expense. For Years 1 through 4, this results in increased after-tax free cash flow of $99,000 per year. In Year 5 the new press is salvaged for an estimated $50,000 (recall that this is also the book value of the machine, so there is no gain on the sale, and consequently there is no tax to be paid).

STEP 4: Analyze

Free cash flows for replacement projects require us to explicitly consider the changes that occur when one asset is used to replace an existing asset. The replacement decision in this example resulted only in cost savings because it did not add to the firm's capacity to generate revenues. However, this will not always be the case. The new or replacement asset might have greater capacity, in which case additional revenues might be generated in addition to cost savings. Note, too, that where new revenues are produced, there will likely be an increase in the firm's investment in net operating working capital.

STEP 5: Check yourself

Forecast the project cash flows for the replacement press for Leggett where the new press results in net operating income per year of $600,000 compared to $580,000 for the old machine. This increase in revenues also means that the firm will also have to increase its net operating working capital by $20,000. The information for the replacement opportunity is summarized as follows:

	Machine	
	New	Old
Annual cost of defects	$ 20,000	$ 70,000
Net operating income	$600,000	$580,000
Book value of equipment	350,000	100,000
Salvage value (today)	NA	150,000
Salvage value (Year 5)	50,000	—
Shipping cost	$ 20,000	NA
Installation cost	30,000	NA
Remaining project life (years)	5	5
Net operating working capital	$ 80,000	$ 60,000
Salaries	100,000	200,000
Fringe benefits	10,000	20,000
Maintenance	60,000	20,000

Estimate the initial cash outlay required to replace the old machine with the new one and estimate the annual cash flows for Years 1 through 5.

ANSWER: Initial cash outflow = −$285,000; cash flows for Years 1–4 = $113,000; and cash flow for Year 5 = $183,000.

Your Turn: For more practice, do related **Study Problem** 30 at the end of this chapter.   **>> END Checkpoint 2**

Cash flows for the replacement decision are forecast in Checkpoint 2 and indicate that Leggett will have to invest an additional $265,000 to purchase the new press. This figure captures the deduction of the $150,000 the firm will receive from the sale of the older model. In addition, Leggett expects to generate additional free cash flows in Years 1 through 5 equal to $99,000 from the savings in personnel costs and reduced defects. Finally, in Year 5 the sale of the replacement press is expected to generate an additional $50,000 in after-tax cash flows for a total free cash flow of $149,000 = $99,000 + 50,000.

We are now prepared to estimate the NPV of the replacement proposal as follows:

$$NPV = -\$265,000 + \frac{\$99,000}{(1 + .15)^1} + \frac{\$99,000}{(1 + .15)^2} + \frac{\$99,000}{(1 + .15)^3} + \frac{\$99,000}{(1 + .15)^4} + \frac{\$149,000}{(1 + .15)^5}$$

$$= \$91,722$$

Thus, we estimate that the NPV of the replacement opportunity is $91,722, which suggests that the added cost savings from the newer press more than offset the cost of making the replacement.

Finance in a **Flat World**

Entering New Markets

When measuring free cash flow, it is important to think globally. We should consider threats from foreign competition as well as opportunities to sell internationally. To illustrate the threat from foreign competition, we need only look at how the U.S. auto industry has evolved over the past 30 years. When foreign car makers first started making inroads into the U.S. market during the 1970s, no one would have thought that firms like Toyota, Honda, and Nissan could challenge the likes of Ford and GM. On the other hand, the opportunities that come from selling in foreign markets can also be huge. For example, more than half of the revenues from Hollywood movies now come from abroad.

There are also other intangible benefits from investing in countries such as Germany and Japan, where cutting-edge technology is making its way into the marketplace. Here, investment abroad provides a chance to observe the introduction of new innovations on a first-hand basis. This allows firms such as IBM, GE, and 3Com to react more quickly to any technological advances and product innovations that might come out of such countries as Germany or Japan.

Finally, if a product is well received at home, international markets can be viewed as an opportunity to expand. For example, McDonald's was much more of a hit at home than anyone ever expected 40 years ago. Once it conquered the United States, it moved abroad—but it hasn't always been a smooth move. McDonald's faces cultural challenges whenever it opens in a new country. However, what McDonald's learns in the first store that it opens in a new country can be used to modify the firm's plans for opening subsequent stores in that country. McDonald's also learns what works in different countries, and maintains the flexibility to adapt to different tastes. As a result, you'll find McLaks, a sandwich made of grilled salmon and dill sauce in Norway, Koroke Burgers (mashed potato, cabbage, and katsu sauce, all in a sandwich), as well as green-tea-flavored milkshakes in Japan, and McHuevos (which are regular hamburgers topped with a poached egg) in Uruguay. In effect, taking a product that has been successful in the United States to a new country requires flexibility and the success of the venture is much less predictable.

Your Turn: See Study Question 14.

Before you begin end-of-chapter material

Concept Check | 4

1. What is a replacement investment?

2. What is the relevant depreciation expense when you are analyzing a replacement decision?

Principle 3: **Cash Flows Are the Source of Value** The process of deciding whether or not to accept an investment proposal begins with an estimation of the amount and timing of the relevant future free cash flows. These cash flows are discounted back to present at the project's required rate of return to determine the present value of the investment proposal.

Principle 5: **Individuals Respond to Incentives** When managers forecast cash flows for a project in their department, they may be tempted to paint a rosy picture for the project in the hopes of winning the funding from headquarters.

Chapter Summaries

1 Identify incremental cash flows that are relevant to project valuation.

SUMMARY: The cash flows that are relevant to the valuation of an investment project are those that are *incremental* to the firm. Although this seems straightforward, identifying incremental cash flows can be very challenging; therefore, we offered the following guidelines and words of caution:

- **Sunk costs are not incremental cash flows.** Sunk costs are one particular category of expenditures that frequently give rise to difficulty when evaluating an investment opportunity; they are expenditures that have already been made and cannot be undone if the project is not undertaken. By definition, such costs are not incremental to the decision to undertake a new investment.
- **Overhead costs are generally not incremental cash flows.** Overhead costs include such things as the utilities required to heat and cool a business. If the utility bills of the firm will not change whether the investment is undertaken or not, then the allocated costs of utilities are irrelevant to the analysis of the investment proposal.
- **Beware of cash flows diverted from existing products.** Oftentimes a new product will get some portion of its revenues from reduced demand for another product produced by the same firm. For example, you might purchase lime-flavored Dorito chips rather than Nacho Cheese Doritos. When this happens, the analyst must be careful not to count the cannibalized sales taken away from an existing product as incremental sales.
- **Account for opportunity costs.** Sometimes there are important cash flow consequences of undertaking an investment that do not actually happen but that are foregone as a result of the investment. For example, if you rent out a part of your floor space, you obviously cannot use it in your business. Similarly, if you decide to use the space yourself, you forego the rent that would otherwise be received. The latter is an opportunity cost of using the space.
- **Work in working capital requirements.** If an investment requires that the firm increase its investment in working capital (e.g., accounts receivable and inventories net of any corresponding increase in funding provided in the form of accounts payable), this investment is no different than capital expenditures and results in a cash outflow.
- **Ignore interest payments and other financing costs.** Interest expense associated with new debt financing used to finance an investment is not included as part of incremental cash flows. The interest expenses are considered part of the firm's cost of capital.

KEY TERMS

Incremental cash flow The change in a firm's cash flows that is a direct consequence of its having undertaken a particular project.

Sunk costs Costs that have already been incurred.

KEY EQUATION

$$\frac{\text{Incremental Project}}{\text{Cash Flows}} = \left(\begin{array}{c}\text{Firm Cash Flows}\\\text{with the Project}\end{array}\right) - \left(\begin{array}{c}\text{Firm Cash Flows}\\\text{without the Project}\end{array}\right) \tag{1}$$

Concept Check | **1**

1. What makes an investment cash flow relevant to the evaluation of an investment proposal?
2. What are sunk costs?
3. What are some examples of synergistic effects that affect a project's cash flows?
4. When borrowing the money needed to make an investment, is the interest expense incurred relevant to the analysis of the project? Explain.

Calculate and forecast project cash flows for expansion-type investments.

SUMMARY: An expansion project expands or increases the scope of the firm's operations, including the addition of both revenues and costs, but does not replace any existing assets or operations. Project cash flow is equal to the sum of operating cash flow less capital expenditures and any change needed in the firm's investment in working capital, that is,

$$\underbrace{\text{Free Cash Flow} = \overbrace{\underbrace{\begin{array}{c}\text{Net Operating} \\ \text{Income (Profit)}\end{array} - \text{Taxes} + \begin{array}{c}\text{Depreciation} \\ \text{Expense}\end{array}}_{\text{Net Operating Profit after Taxes or NOPAT}}}^{\text{Operating Cash Flow}} - \begin{array}{c}\text{Increase in Capital} \\ \text{Expenditures} \\ (CAPEX)\end{array} - \begin{array}{c}\text{Increase in Net} \\ \text{Operating Working} \\ \text{Capital } (NOWC)\end{array}} \quad \text{(2)}$$

Estimating a project's free cash flow involves a four-step process:

Step 1. **Measure the effect of the proposed investment on the firm's operating cash flows, or cash flows from operations.** This includes the estimated incremental revenues and operating expenses resulting from the project's acceptance.

Step 2. **Calculate the project's requirements for working capital and the resulting cash flows.** Here we consider the incremental investment that the project may require in accounts receivable plus inventories less any increase in accounts payable or trade credit.

Step 3. **Calculate the project's cash requirements for capital expenditures.** Capital expenditures include expenditures for property and plant and equipment that are expected to last for longer than one year. The biggest capital expenditure for most investments occurs when the investment is made. However, additional capital expenditures may have to be made periodically over the life of the project as older equipment wears out or new capacity needs to be added to meet the needs of growth over time.

Step 4. **Combine the project's operating cash flow with any investments made in net operating working capital and capital expenditures to calculate the project's free cash flow.** In the initial year the free cash flow will generally include only the required investment outlays for capital equipment and working capital. In subsequent years both operating revenues and expenses determine the project's cash flows, and in the final year of the project additional cash inflows from salvage value and the return of working capital may be present.

KEY TERM

Pro forma financial statements
A forecast of financial statements for a future period.

KEY EQUATIONS

$$\underbrace{\text{Free Cash Flow} = \overbrace{\underbrace{\begin{array}{c}\text{Net Operating} \\ \text{Income (Profit)}\end{array} - \text{Taxes} + \begin{array}{c}\text{Depreciation} \\ \text{Expense}\end{array}}_{\text{Net Operating Profit after Taxes or NOPAT}}}^{\text{Operating Cash Flow}} - \begin{array}{c}\text{Increase in Capital} \\ \text{Expenditures} \\ (CAPEX)\end{array} - \begin{array}{c}\text{Increase in Net} \\ \text{Operating Working} \\ \text{Capital } (NOWC)\end{array}} \quad \text{(2)}$$

$$\begin{array}{c}\text{Operating Cash} \\ \text{Flow}_t\end{array} = \underbrace{\begin{array}{c}\text{Net Operating} \\ \text{Income (or Profit)}_t\end{array} - \text{Taxes}_t + \begin{array}{c}\text{Depreciation} \\ \text{Expense}_t\end{array}}_{\text{NOPAT}} \quad \text{(3)}$$

$$\begin{array}{c}\text{Investment in} \\ \text{Net Operating} \\ \text{Working Capital}\end{array} = \left(\begin{array}{c}\text{Increase in} \\ \text{Accounts Receivable}\end{array}\right) + \left(\begin{array}{c}\text{Increase in} \\ \text{Inventories}\end{array}\right) - \left(\begin{array}{c}\text{Increase in} \\ \text{Accounts Payable}\end{array}\right) \quad \text{(4)}$$

Concept Check | **2**

1. What does the term *free cash flow* mean?

2. What are the four steps used to forecast a project's future cash flows?

3. What is net operating working capital, and how does it affect a project's cash flows?

4. What is CAPEX, and how does it affect a project's cash flows?

Evaluate the effect of inflation on project cash flows.

SUMMARY: Inflation can have a very significant effect on project cash flows and consequently the value of an investment opportunity. The consequences of inflation can be felt in both revenues and costs and the effect is often quite different, so project cash flows may increase as a result of inflation (revenues rise faster than costs) or fall (costs rise faster than revenues). The important thing is that the analysts carefully consider the potential effects of inflationary expectations and incorporate them into the cash flow forecast. These inflation-adjusted cash flows are referred to as nominal cash flows (as contrasted with real cash flows, which do not incorporate the effects of inflation). Because we forecast nominal cash flows, we should use nominal rates of interest as the basis for determining the discount rate for the project.

KEY TERMS

Nominal cash flows Cash flows that account for the effects of inflation.

Real cash flows Cash flows that would occur in the absence of any inflation.

Nominal rate of interest The rate of interest that is observed in financial markets and that incorporates consideration for inflation.

Real rate of interest The rate of interest that would occur in the absence of any inflation.

 Calculate the incremental cash flows for replacement-type investments.

SUMMARY: A replacement project is one in which an existing asset is taken out of service and another is added in its place. Thus, a distinctive feature of many replacement investments is that the principal source of investment cash flows comes from cost savings, not new revenues. Because the firm already operates an existing asset to generate revenues, the primary benefit of acquiring the new asset comes from the cost savings it offers.

The cash flows for a replacement project are calculated using Equation (1) just like those for an expansion project. The only difference is that with a replacement project, we are continually asking how cash flows with the new asset differ from those generated by the older asset. For this reason, computing project cash flows for replacement asset investments is a bit more complicated. However, the principles are exactly the same.

KEY TERMS

Expansion project An investment proposal that increases the scope of the firm's operations, including the addition of both revenues and costs, but does not replace any existing assets or operations.

Replacement investment An investment proposal that is a substitute for an existing investment.

Concept Check | 3

1. What is the distinction between nominal and real interest rates?
2. If you forecast nominal cash flows, should you use the nominal or the real discount rate? Why?

Concept Check | 4

1. What is a replacement investment?
2. What is the relevant depreciation expense when you are analyzing a replacement decision?

Study Questions

1. As you saw in the introduction, the Toyota Prius took some of its sales away from other Toyota products. Toyota has also licensed its hybrid technology to Ford Motor Company, which has allowed Ford to introduce a Ford Fusion Hybrid in 2010 with 39 miles per gallon (mpg), almost doubling the city efficiency of the non-hybrid Fusion. Obviously this new Ford product will compete directly with Toyota's hybrids. Why do you think Toyota licensed its technology to Ford?

2. **(Related to Regardless of Your Major: The Internet on Airline Flights—Making It Happen)** In the *Regardless of Your Major* feature, we describe an investment proposal involving the sale of Internet services on airlines. How would you approach the problem of calculating the cash flows for such a venture? What costs would you include in the initial cash outlay, the annual operating cash flows, capital expenditures, and working capital?

3. Corporate overhead expenses related to utilities and other corporate expenses are generally not relevant to the analysis of new investment opportunities. Why?

4. New investments often require that the firm invest additional money in working capital. Give some examples of what this means.

5. When a firm finances a new investment, it often borrows part of the money, so the interest and principal payments this creates are incremental to the project's acceptance. Why are these expenditures not included in the project's cash flow computation?

6. Discuss how free cash flow differs from a firm's operating cash flow.

7. If depreciation is not a cash flow item, why does it affect the level of cash flows from a project?

8. Describe net operating working capital, and explain how changes in this quantity affect an investment proposal's cash flows.

9. What are sunk costs, and how should they be considered when evaluating an investment's cash flows?

10. Should overhead expense ever be considered when evaluating investment cash flows?

11. What are opportunity costs, and how should they affect an investment's cash flows? Give an example.

12. Should anticipated inflation be incorporated into project cash flow forecasts? If so, how?

13. When McDonald's (MCD) moved into India, it faced a particularly difficult task. The major religion in India is the Hindu religion, and Hindus don't eat beef—in fact, most of the 1 billion people living in India are vegetarians. Still, McDonald's ventured into India and has been enormously successful. Why do you think the restaurant has been so successful, and what kinds of products do you think it sells in India?

14. **(Related to Finance in a Flat World: Entering New Markets)** In the *Finance in a Flat World: Entering New Markets* feature, we described the importance of thinking globally when making investments. Pick a new product that you have just learned about that is being sold domestically and describe how the product might benefit from international markets.

15. For years GM treated each car brand as if it were a separate company, considering all new car sales as incremental sales. Critically evaluate this position.

16. Throughout the examples in this chapter, we have assumed that the initial investment in working capital is later recaptured when the project ends. Is this a realistic assumption? Do firms always recover 100 percent of their investment in accounts receivable and inventories?

Study Problems

MyFinanceLab

Go to **www.myfinancelab.com** to complete these exercises online and get instant feedback.

Forecasting Project Cash Flows

1. **(Identifying incremental revenues from new product innovations)** Morten Food Products, Inc. is a regional manufacturer of salty food snacks. The firm competes directly with the national brands including Frito-Lay, but only in the U.S. Southeast. Last year Morten sold $300 million of its various chip products and hopes to increase its sales in the coming year by offering a new line of baked chips. The new product line is expected to generate $40 million in sales next year. However, the firm's analysts estimate that about 60 percent of these revenues will come from existing customers who switch their purchases from one of the firm's existing products to the new healthier baked chips.

   a. What level of incremental sales should the company analyst attribute to the new line of baked chips?

   b. Assume that 20 percent of Morten's existing customers are actively looking for a healthier snack alternative and will move to another company's baked chip offering if Morten does not introduce the new product. What level of incremental sales would you attribute to the new line of baked chips in this circumstance?

2. **(Determining relevant cash flows)** Landcruisers Plus (LP) has operated an online retail store selling off-road truck parts. As the name implies, the firm specializes in parts for the venerable Toyota FJ40 that is known throughout the world for its durability and off-road prowess. The fact that Toyota stopped building and exporting the FJ40 to the U.S. market in 1982 meant that FJ40 owners depended more and more on re-manufactured parts to keep their beloved off-road vehicles running. More and more FJ40 owners are replacing the original inline six-cylinder engines with a modern American-built engine. The engine replacement requires mating the new engine with the Toyota drive train.

LP's owners had been offering engine adaptor kits for some time but have recently decided to begin building their own units. To make the adaptor kits the firm would need to invest in a variety of machine tools costing a total of $700,000.

LP's management estimates that they will be able to borrow $400,000 from the firm's bank and pay 8 percent interest. The remaining funds would have to be supplied by LP's owners.

The firm estimates that they will be able to sell 1,000 units a year for $1,300 each. The units would cost $1,000 each in cash expenses to produce (this does not include depreciation expense of $70,000 per year or interest expense of $32,000). After all expenses, the firm expects earnings before interest and taxes of $198,000. The firm pays taxes equal to 30 percent, which results in net income of $138,600 per year over the 10-year expected life of the equipment.

a. What is the annual free cash flow LP should expect to receive from the investment in Year 1 assuming that it does not require any other investments in either capital equipment or working capital and the equipment is depreciated over a 10-year life to a zero salvage and book value? How should the financing cost associated with the $400,000 loan be incorporated into the analysis of cash flow?

b. If the firm's required rate of return for its investments is 10 percent and the investment has a 10-year expected life, what is the anticipated NPV of the investment?

3. **(Incremental earnings from advertising synergies)** Bangers, Inc. is a start-up manufacturer of Australian-style frozen veggie pies located in San Antonio, Texas. The company is five years old and recently installed the manufacturing capacity to quadruple its unit sales. To jump start the demand for its products, the company founders have hired a local advertising firm to create a series of ads for its new line of meat pies. The ads will cost the firm $400,000 to run for one year. Boomerang's management hopes that the advertising will produce annual sales of $2 million for its meat pies. Moreover, the firm's management expects that sales of its veggie pies will increase by $200,000 next year as a result of the company name recognition derived from the meat pie ad campaign. If Boomerang's operating profits per dollar of new sales revenue are 40 percent and the firm faces a 30 percent tax bracket, what is the incremental operating profit the firm can expect to earn from the ad campaign? Does the decision to place the ad look good from the perspective of the anticipated profits?

4. **(Incremental earnings from lowering product prices)** Apple's (AAPL) iPad jump started the touchscreen computer market to levels few analysts had ever dreamed possible. Moreover, the popularity of the iPad pushed Apple's competitors to offer similar touchscreen computers. Hewlett Packard offered its Slate product and others soon followed suit. One such manufacturer was Soko Industries. The Soko product, the sPad, had a number of appealing features but the relative obscurity of the company did not help product sales. In fact, the sPad was initially sold for $600, and disappointing sales led Soko Industries management to consider taking a 25 percent price break on its sPad, which costs $400 to manufacture and sell.

a. If Soko goes through with the price adjustment and it leads to total sales of 400,000 sPads, what are the incremental revenues attributable to the new pricing strategy?

b. Now suppose that for each new sPad it sells, the firm also sells an average of $100 worth of applications on which the firm has 75 percent operating profit margins (i.e., the firm earns $75 in additional operating profits for each $100 in application sales). What is the incremental impact on firm operating profits of the new lower-price strategy under these conditions?

5. **(Incremental costs and pilot studies)** In 2010 the Cameron Manufacturing Company began working on a new version of its tried-and-true wind-powered water pump. For 15 years the firm had manufactured replacement parts for older-style windmills used on farms and ranches throughout the U.S. Southwest. However, the old-style pumps required the use of rods and leather seals that would wear out over time and require servicing. When Cameron's owners initiated the design of a new pumping process in 2013, they explored a number of possible designs and spent over $150,000 in fabrication and testing the new design before perfecting the system that they are now ready to place into production and begin marketing. To manufacture the new pumps Cameron will have to spend $750,000 on new equipment plus

$300,000 in advertising and promotion for the launch of the new product. These expenditures will take place during 2013.

a. What is the relevant initial cost of the new pump product investment?

b. Cameron's management expects to sell 1,500 of the new units per year for the next 15 years and these units will produce free cash flow for Cameron of $150,000 per year. Furthermore, the firm's management estimates that the equipment purchased initially will last for the full 15 years, at which time it will have no salvage value. If Cameron uses a 10 percent rate of return to evaluate its investments, what is the NPV of the new pump investment?

c. Just as Cameron's management was about to launch the new investment, the firm's owner got a call from the A1 Windmill Company from Cross-Plains, Nebraska, inquiring about the possible purchase of the product design patent. The caller suggested that his company would be interested in paying as much as $110,000 for the exclusive rights to the new technology. Cameron would have to sign over all of its rights to the new design in return for the payment. How should this offer influence Cameron's decision to initiate manufacturing the new windmill design?

6. **(Determining relevant cash flows)** Captain's Cereal is considering introducing a variation of its current breakfast cereal, Crunch Stuff. This new cereal will be similar to the old, with the exception that it will contain sugar-coated marshmallows shaped in the form of stars. The new cereal will be called Crunch Stuff n' Stars. It is estimated that the sales for the new cereal will be $25 million; however, 20 percent of those sales will draw from former Crunch Stuff customers who have switched to Crunch Stuff n' Stars and who would not have switched if the new product had not been introduced. What is the relevant sales level to consider when deciding whether or not to introduce Crunch Stuff n' Stars?

7. **(Determining relevant cash flows)** Fruity Stones is considering introducing a variation of its current breakfast cereal, Jolt 'n Stones. This new cereal will be similar to the old with the exception that it will contain more sugar in the form of small pebbles. The new cereal will be called Stones 'n Stuff. It is estimated that the sales for the new cereal will be $100 million; however, 40 percent of those sales will be from former Fruity Stones customers who have switched to Stones 'n Stuff. These former customers will be lost regardless of whether the new product is offered because this is the amount of sales the firm expects to lose to a competitor product that is going to be introduced at about the same time. What is the relevant sales level to consider when deciding whether or not to introduce Stones 'n Stuff?

8. **(Related to Checkpoint1) (Calculating changes in net operating working capital)** Tetious Dimensions is introducing a new product that is expected to increase its net operating income by $775,000. Tetious Dimensions has a 34 percent marginal tax rate. This project will also produce $200,000 of depreciation per year. In addition, this project will cause the following changes:

	Without the Project	With the Project
Accounts receivable	$ 55,000	$ 89,000
Inventory	100,000	180,000
Accounts payable	70,000	120,000

What is the project's free cash flow for Year 1?

9. **(Calculating changes in net operating working capital)** Duncan Motors is introducing a new product that it expects will increase its net operating income by $300,000. Duncan Motors has a 34 percent marginal tax rate. This project will also produce $50,000 of depreciation per year. In addition, this project will cause the following changes:

	Without the Project	With the Project
Accounts receivable	$33,000	$23,000
Inventory	25,000	40,000
Accounts payable	50,000	86,000

What is the project's free cash flow for Year 1?

10. **(Calculating changes in net operating working capital)** Racin' Scooters is introducing a new product and has an expected change in net operating income of $475,000. Racin' Scooters has a 34 percent marginal tax rate. This project will also produce $100,000 of depreciation per year. In addition, this project will cause the following changes:

	Without the Project	With the Project
Accounts receivable	$45,000	$63,000
Inventory	65,000	80,000
Accounts payable	70,000	94,000

What is the project's free cash flow for Year 1?

11. **(Calculating changes in net operating working capital)** Visible Fences is introducing a new product and has an expected change in net operating income of $900,000. Visible Fences has a 34 percent marginal tax rate. This project will also produce $300,000 of depreciation per year. In addition, this project will cause the following changes:

	Without the Project	With the Project
Accounts receivable	$55,000	$ 63,000
Inventory	55,000	70,000
Accounts payable	90,000	106,000

What is the project's free cash flow for Year 1?

12. **(Related to Checkpoint 1) (Calculating operating cash flows)** Assume that a new project will annually generate revenues of $2,000,000 and cash expenses (including both fixed and variable costs) of $800,000, while increasing depreciation by $200,000 per year. In addition, the firm's tax rate is 34 percent. Calculate the operating cash flows for the new project.

13. **(Calculating operating cash flows)** The Heritage Farm Implement Company is considering an investment that is expected to generate revenues of $3 million per year. The project will also involve annual cash expenses (including both fixed and variable costs) of $900,000, while increasing depreciation by $400,000 per year. If the firm's tax rate is 34 percent, what is the project's estimated net operating profit after taxes? What are the project's annual operating cash flows?

14. **(Related to Checkpoint 1) (Calculating project cash flows and NPV)** You are considering expanding your product line that currently consists of skateboards to include gas-powered skateboards, and you feel you can sell 10,000 of these per year for 10 years (after which time this project is expected to shut down, with solar-powered skateboards taking over). The gas skateboards would sell for $100 each with variable costs of $40 for each one produced, and annual fixed costs associated with production would be $160,000. In addition, there would be a $1,000,000 initial expenditure associated with the purchase of new production equipment. It is assumed that this initial expenditure will be depreciated using the simplified straight-line method down to zero over 10 years. The project will also require a one-time initial investment of $50,000 in net working capital associated with inventory, and this working capital investment will be recovered when the project is shut down. Finally, assume that the firm's marginal tax rate is 34 percent.

 a. What is the initial cash outlay associated with this project?

 b. What are the annual net cash flows associated with this project for Years 1 through 9?

 c. What is the terminal cash flow in Year 10 (that is, what is the free cash flow in Year 10 plus any additional cash flows associated with termination of the project)?

 d. What is the project's NPV given a 10 percent required rate of return?

15. **(Calculating project cash flows and NPV)** You are considering new elliptical trainers and you feel you can sell 5,000 of these per year for five years (after which time this project is expected to shut down when it is learned that being fit is unhealthy). The elliptical trainers would sell for $1,000 each with variable costs of $500 for each one produced, and annual fixed costs associated with production would be $1,000,000. In addition, there would be a $5,000,000 initial expenditure associated with the purchase of new production equipment. It is assumed that this initial expenditure will be depreciated using the simplified straight-line method down to zero over five years. This project will also require a one-time initial investment of $1,000,000 in net working capital associated with inventory, and it is assumed that this working capital investment will be recovered when the project is shut down. Finally, assume that the firm's tax rate is 34 percent.

    a. What is the initial outlay associated with this project?

    b. What are the annual net cash flows associated with this project for Years 1 through 9?

    c. What is the terminal cash flow in Year 5 (that is, what is the free cash flow in Year 10 plus any additional cash flows associated with termination of the project)?

    d. What is the project's NPV given a 10 percent required rate of return?

16. **(Calculating project cash flows and NPV)** The Guo Chemical Corporation is considering the purchase of a chemical analysis machine. The purchase of this machine will result in an increase in earnings before interest and taxes of $70,000 per year. The machine has a purchase price of $250,000, and it would cost an additional $10,000 after tax to install this machine correctly. In addition, to operate this machine properly, inventory must be increased by $15,000. This machine has an expected life of 10 years, after which time it will have no salvage value. Also, assume simplified straight-line depreciation, that this machine is being depreciated down to zero, a 34 percent marginal tax rate, and a required rate of return of 15 percent.

    a. What is the initial outlay associated with this project?

    b. What are the annual after-tax cash flows associated with this project for Years 1 through 9?

    c. What is the terminal cash flow in Year 10 (i.e., what is the annual after-tax cash flow in Year 10 plus any additional cash flow associated with termination of the project)?

    d. Should this machine be purchased?

17. **(Calculating project cash flows and NPV)** El Gato's Motors is considering the purchase of a new production machine for $1 million. The purchase of this machine will result in an increase in earnings before interest and taxes of $400,000 per year. It would cost $50,000 after tax to install this machine; in addition, to operate this machine properly, workers would have to go through a brief training session that would cost $100,000 after tax. Also, because this machine is extremely efficient, its purchase would necessitate an increase in inventory of $150,000. This machine has an expected life of 10 years, after which time it will have no salvage value. Assume simplified straight-line depreciation, that this machine is being depreciated down to zero, a 34 percent marginal tax rate, and a required rate of return of 12 percent.

    a. What is the initial outlay associated with this project?

    b. What are the annual after-tax cash flows associated with this project for Years 1 through 9?

    c. What is the terminal cash flow in Year 10 (what is the annual after-tax cash flow in Year 10 plus any additional cash flows associated with termination of the project)?

    d. Should this machine be purchased?

18. **(Calculating project cash flows and NPV)** Weir's Trucking, Inc. is considering the purchase of a new production machine for $100,000. The purchase of this new machine will result in an increase in earnings before interest and taxes of $25,000 per year. To operate this machine properly, workers would have to go through a brief training session that would cost $5,000 after tax. In addition, it would cost $5,000 after tax to install this machine correctly. Also, because this machine is extremely efficient, its purchase would necessitate an increase in inventory of $25,000. This machine has an expected life of 10 years, after which it will have no salvage value. Finally, to purchase the new machine, it appears that the firm would have to borrow $80,000 at 10 percent interest from its local bank, resulting in additional interest payments of $8,000 per year. Assume simplified straight-line depreciation, that this machine is being depreciated down to zero, a 34 percent marginal tax rate, and a required rate of return of 12 percent.

    a. What is the initial outlay associated with this project?

    b. What are the annual after-tax cash flows associated with this project for Years 1 through 9?

    c. What is the terminal cash flow in Year 10 (what is the annual after-tax cash flow in Year 10 plus any additional cash flows associated with termination of the project)?

    d. Should this machine be purchased?

19. **(Calculating project cash flows and NPV)** The Chung Chemical Corporation is considering the purchase of a chemical analysis machine. Although the machine being considered will result in an increase in earnings before interest and taxes of $35,000 per year, it has a purchase price of $100,000, and it would cost an additional $5,000 after tax to correctly install this machine. In addition, to properly operate this machine, inventory must be increased by $5,000. This machine has an expected life of 10 years, after which it will have no salvage value. Also, assume simplified straight-line depreciation, that this machine is being depreciated down to zero, a 34 percent marginal tax rate, and a required rate of return of 15 percent.

    a. What is the initial outlay associated with this project?

    b. What are the annual after-tax cash flows associated with this project for Years 1 through 9?

    c. What is the terminal cash flow in Year 10 (what is the annual after-tax cash flow in Year 10 plus any additional cash flows associated with termination of the project)?

    d. Should this machine be purchased?

20. **(Calculating project cash flows and NPV)** Raymobile Motors is considering the purchase of a new production machine for $500,000. The purchase of this machine will result in an increase in earnings before interest and taxes of $150,000 per year. To operate this machine properly, workers would have to go through a brief training session that would cost $25,000 after tax. In addition, it would cost $5,000 after tax to install this machine correctly. Also, because this machine is extremely efficient, its purchase would necessitate an increase in inventory of $30,000. This machine has an expected life of 10 years, after which it will have no salvage value. Assume simplified straight-line depreciation, that this machine is being depreciated down to zero, a 34 percent marginal tax rate, and a required rate of return of 15 percent.

    a. What is the initial outlay associated with this project?

    b. What are the annual after-tax cash flows associated with this project for Years 1 through 9?

    c. What is the terminal cash flow in Year 10 (what is the annual after-tax cash flow in Year 10 plus any additional cash flows associated with termination of the project)?

    d. Should this machine be purchased?

21. **(Calculating project cash flows and NPV)** Garcia's Truckin', Inc. is considering the purchase of a new production machine for $200,000. The purchase of this machine will result in an increase in earnings before interest and taxes of $50,000 per year. To operate this machine properly, workers would have to go through a brief training session that would cost $5,000 after tax. In addition, it would cost $5,000 after tax to install this machine correctly. Also, because this machine is extremely efficient, its purchase would necessitate an increase in inventory of $20,000. This machine has an expected life of 10 years, after which it will have no salvage value. Finally, to purchase the new machine, it appears that the firm would have to borrow $100,000 at 8 percent interest from its local bank, resulting in additional interest payments of $8,000 per year. Assume simplified straight-line depreciation, that this machine is being depreciated down to zero, a 34 percent tax rate, and a required rate of return of 10 percent.

    a. What is the initial outlay associated with this project?

    b. What are the annual after-tax cash flows associated with this project for Years 1 through 9?

    c. What is the terminal cash flow in Year 10 (what is the annual after-tax cash flow in Year 10 plus any additional cash flows associated with termination of the project)?

    d. Should this machine be purchased?

22.	**(Related to Checkpoint 1) (Comprehensive problem—calculating project cash flows, NPV, PI, and IRR)** Traid Winds Corporation, a firm in the 34 percent marginal tax bracket with a 15 percent required rate of return or discount rate, is considering a new project. This project involves the introduction of a new product. This project is expected to last five years and then, because this is somewhat of a fad project, it will be terminated. Given the following information, determine the net cash flows associated with the project, the project's net present value, the profitability index, and the internal rate of return. Apply the appropriate decision criteria.

Cost of new plant and equipment: $14,800,000

Shipping and installation costs: $ 200,000

Unit sales:

Year	Units Sold
1	70,000
2	120,000
3	120,000
4	80,000
5	70,000

Sales price per unit: $300/unit in Years 1–4, $250/unit in Year 5

Variable cost per unit: $140/unit

Annual fixed costs: $700,000

Working capital requirements: There will be an initial working capital requirement of $200,000 to get production started. For each year, the total investment in net working capital will be equal to 10 percent of the dollar value of sales for that year. Thus, the investment in working capital will increase during Years 1 through 3, then decrease in Year 4. Finally, all working capital is liquidated at the termination of the project at the end of Year 5.

The depreciation method: Use the simplified straight-line method over five years. It is assumed that the plant and equipment will have no salvage value after five years.

23.	**(Calculating cash flows—comprehensive problem)** The Kumar Corporation, a firm in the 34 percent marginal tax bracket with a 15 percent required rate of return or discount rate, is considering a new project. This project involves the introduction of a new product. This project is expected to last five years and then, because this is somewhat of a fad product, it will be terminated. Given the following information, determine the net cash flows associated with the project, the project's net present value, the profitability index, and the internal rate of return. Apply the appropriate decision criteria.

Cost of new plant and equipment: $ 9,900,000

Shipping and installation costs: $ 100,000

Unit sales:

Year	Units Sold
1	70,000
2	100,000
3	140,000
4	70,000
5	60,000

Sales price per unit: $280/unit in Years 1–4, $180/unit in Year 5

Variable cost per unit: $140/unit

Annual fixed costs: $300,000

Working capital requirements: There will be an initial working capital requirement of $100,000 just to get production started. For each year, the total investment in net working capital will equal 10 percent of the dollar value of sales for that year. Thus, the investment in working capital will increase during Years 1 through 3, then decrease in Year 4. Finally, all working capital is liquidated at the termination of the project at the end of Year 5.

The depreciation method: Use the simplified straight-line method over five years. It is assumed that the plant and equipment will have no salvage value after five years.

24. **(Calculating cash flows—comprehensive problem)** The Shome Corporation, a firm in the 34 percent marginal tax bracket with a 15 percent required rate of return or discount rate, is considering a new project. This project involves the introduction of a new product. This project is expected to last five years and then, because this is somewhat of a fad project, it will be terminated. Given the following information, determine the net cash flows associated with the project, the project's net present value, the profitability index, and the internal rate of return. Apply the appropriate decision criteria.

Cost of new plant and equipment: $6,900,000

Shipping and installation costs: $ 100,000

Unit sales:

Year	Units Sold
1	80,000
2	100,000
3	120,000
4	70,000
5	70,000

Sales price per unit: $250/unit in Years 1–4, $200/unit in Year 5

Variable cost per unit: $130/unit

Annual fixed costs: $300,000

Working capital requirements: There will be an initial working capital requirement of $100,000 just to get production started. For each year, the total investment in net working capital will be equal to 10 percent of the dollar value of sales for that year. Thus, the investment in working capital will increase during Years 1 through 3, then decrease in Year 4. Finally, all working capital is liquidated at the termination of the project at the end of Year 5.

The depreciation method: Use the simplified straight-line method over five years. It is assumed that the plant and equipment will have no salvage value after five years.

25. **(Calculating cash flows—comprehensive problem)** The C Corporation, a firm in the 34 percent marginal tax bracket with a 15 percent required rate of return or discount rate, is considering a new project. This project involves the introduction of a new product. This project is expected to last five years and then, because this is somewhat of a fad product, it will be terminated. Given the following information, determine the net cash flows associated with the project, the project's net present value, the profitability index, and the internal rate of return. Apply the appropriate decision criteria.

Cost of new plant and equipment: $198,000,000

Shipping and installation costs: $ 2,000,000

Unit sales:

Year	Units Sold
1	1,000,000
2	1,800,000
3	1,800,000
4	1,200,000
5	700,000

Sales price per unit: $800/unit in Years 1–4, $600/unit in Year 5

Variable cost per unit: $400/unit

Annual fixed costs: $10,000,000

Working capital requirements: There will be an initial working capital requirement of $2,000,000 just to get production started. For each year, the total investment in net working capital will equal 10 percent of the dollar value of sales for that year. Thus, the investment in working capital will increase during Years 1 through 3, then decrease in Year 4. Finally, all working capital is liquidated at the termination of the project at the end of Year 5.

The depreciation method: Use the simplified straight-line method over five years. It is assumed that the plant and equipment will have no salvage value after five years.

Inflation and Capital Budgeting

26. **(Inflation and project cash flows)** If the price of a gallon of regular gasoline is $2.49 and the anticipated rate of inflation in energy prices is such that this cost of gasoline is expected to rise by 5 percent per year, what is the expected price per gallon in 10 years?

27. **(Inflation and project cash flows)** On June 1, 2003, the average price of a gallon of gasoline in San Francisco, California, was $1.80. Just three years later the price of that same gallon of gas was $3.20. What was the rate of inflation in the price of a gallon of gas over the period?

28. **(Inflation and project cash flows)** Carlyle Chemicals is evaluating a new chemical compound used in the manufacture of a wide range of consumer products. The firm is concerned that inflation in the cost of raw materials will have an adverse effect on the project cash flows. Specifically, the firm expects the cost per unit (which is currently $0.80) will rise at a 10 percent rate over the next three years. The per-unit selling price is currently $1.00 and this price is expected to rise at a meager 2 percent rate over the next three years. If Carlyle expects to sell 5, 7, and 9 million units for the next three years, respectively, what is your estimate of the gross profits to the firm? Based on these estimates, what recommendation would you offer to the firm's management with regard to this product?

29. **(Inflation and project cash flows)** After reporting your findings to the company management (Study Problem 29), the company CFO suggested that they could purchase raw materials in advance for future delivery. This would involve paying for the raw materials today and taking delivery as the materials are needed. Through the advance purchase plan the cost of raw materials would be $0.90 per unit. How does this new plan affect your cash flow estimates? How should the advance payment for the raw materials enter into your analysis of project cash flows?

Replacement Project Cash Flows

30. **(Related to Checkpoint 2) (Replacement project cash flows)** Madrano's Wholesale Fruit Company located in McAllen, Texas, is considering the purchase of a new fleet of tractors to be used in the delivery of fruits and vegetables grown in the Rio Grand Valley of Texas. If it goes through with the purchase, it will spend $400,000 on eight rigs. The new trucks will be kept for five years, during which time they will be depreciated toward a $40,000 salvage value using straight-line depreciation. The rigs are expected to have a market value in five years equal to their salvage value. The new tractors will be used to replace the company's older fleet of eight trucks, which are fully depreciated but can be sold for an estimated $20,000 (because the tractors have a current book value of zero, the selling price is fully taxable at the firm's 30 percent tax rate). The existing tractor fleet is expected to be useable for five more years, after which time they will have no salvage value. The existing fleet of tractors uses $200,000 per year in diesel fuel, whereas the new, more efficient fleet will use only $150,000. In addition, the new fleet will be covered under warranty, so the maintenance costs per year are expected to be only $12,000 compared to $35,000 for the existing fleet.

   a. What are the differential operating cash flow savings per year during Years 1 through 5 for the new fleet?

   b. What is the initial cash outlay required to replace the existing fleet with the newer tractors?

   c. Sketch a timeline for the replacement project cash flows for Years 0 through 5.

   d. If Madrano requires a 15 percent discount rate for new investments, should the fleet be replaced?

31. **(Replacement project cash flows)** The Minot Kit Aircraft Company of Minot, North Dakota, uses a plasma cutter to fabricate metal aircraft parts for its plane kits. The company currently is using a cutter that it purchased used four years ago that has an $80,000 book value and is being depreciated $20,000 per year over the next four years. If the old cutter were to be sold today, the company estimates that it would bring in an amount equal to the book value of the equipment.

The company is considering the purchase of a new automated plasma cutter that would cost $400,000 to install and that would be depreciated over the next four years toward a $40,000 salvage value using straight-line depreciation. The primary advantage of the new cutter is the fact that it is fully automated and can be run by one operator rather than the three employees currently required. The labor savings would be $100,000 per year. The firm faces a marginal tax rate of 30 percent.

    a. What are the differential operating cash flow savings per year during Years 1 through 4 for the new plasma cutter?

    b. What is the initial cash outlay required to replace the existing plasma cutter with the newer model?

    c. Sketch a timeline for the replacement project cash flows for Years 0 through 5.

    d. If the company requires a 15 percent discount rate for new investments, should the fleet be replaced?

32. **(Replacement project cash flows)** The Louisiana Land and Cattle Company (LL&CC) is one of the largest cattle buyers in the country. It has buyers at all the major cattle auctions throughout the U.S. Southeast who buy on the company's behalf and then have the cattle shipped to Sulpher Springs, Louisiana, where they are sorted by weight and type before shipping off to feed lots in the Midwest. The company has been considering the replacement of its tractor-trailer rigs with a newer, more fuel-efficient fleet for some time, and a local Peterbilt dealer has approached the company with a proposal. The proposal would call for the purchase of 10 new rigs at a cost of $100,000 each. Each rig would be depreciated toward a salvage value of $40,000 over a period of five years. If LL&CC purchases the rigs, it will sell its existing fleet of 10 rigs to the Peterbilt dealer for their current book value of $25,000 per unit. The existing fleet will be fully depreciated in one more year but is expected to be serviceable for five more years, at which time they would be worth only $5,000 per unit as scrap.

The new fleet of trucks is much more fuel-efficient and will require only $200,000 in fuel costs compared to $300,000 for the existing fleet. In addition, the new fleet of trucks will require minimal maintenance over the next five years, equal to an estimated $150,000 compared to the almost $400,000 that is currently being spent to keep the older fleet running.

    a. What are the differential operating cash flow savings per year during Years 1 through 5 for the new fleet? The firm pays taxes at a 30 percent marginal tax rate.

    b. What is the initial cash outlay required to replace the existing fleet with new rigs?

    c. Sketch a timeline for the replacement project cash flows for Years 0 through 5.

    d. If LL&CC requires a 15 percent discount rate for new investments, should the fleet be replaced?

Mini-Cases

Danforth & Donnalley Laundry Products Company

Determining Relevant Cash Flows

At 3:00 p.m. on April 14, 2010, James Danforth, president of Danforth & Donnalley (D&D) Laundry Products Company, called to order a meeting of the financial directors. The purpose of the meeting was to make a capital-budgeting decision with respect to the introduction and production of a new product, a liquid detergent called Blast.

D&D was formed in 1993 with the merger of Danforth Chemical Company (producer of Lift-Off detergent, the leading laundry detergent on the West Coast) and Donnalley Home Products Company (maker of Wave detergent, a major laundry product in the Midwest). As a result of the merger, D&D was producing and marketing two major product lines. Although these products were in direct competition, they were not without product differentiation: Lift-Off was a low-suds, concentrated powder, and Wave was a more traditional powder detergent. Each line brought with it considerable brand loyalty; and, by 2010, sales from the two detergent lines had increased ten-fold from 1993 levels, with both products now being sold nationally.

In the face of increased competition and technological innovation, D&D spent large amounts of time and money over the past four years researching and developing a new highly concentrated liquid laundry detergent. D&D's new detergent, which it called Blast, had many obvious advantages over the conventional powdered products. The company felt that Blast offered the consumer benefits in three major areas. Blast was so highly concentrated that only 2 ounces were needed to do an average load of laundry, as compared with 8 to 12 ounces of powdered detergent. Moreover, being a liquid, it was possible to pour Blast directly on stains and hard-to-wash spots, eliminating the need for a pre-soak and giving it cleaning abilities that powders could not possibly match. And, finally, it would be packaged in a lightweight, unbreakable plastic bottle with a sure-grip handle, making it much easier to use and more convenient to store than the bulky boxes of powdered detergents with which it would compete.

The meeting participants included James Danforth, president of D&D; Jim Donnalley, director of the board; Guy Rainey, vice-president in charge of new products; Urban McDonald, controller; and Steve Gasper, a newcomer to the D&D financial staff who was invited by McDonald to sit in on the meeting. Danforth called the meeting to order, gave a brief statement of its purpose, and immediately gave the floor to Guy Rainey.

Rainey opened with a presentation of the cost and cash flow analysis for the new product. To keep things clear, he passed out copies of the projected cash flows to those present (see Exhibits 1 and 2). In support of this information, he provided some insights as to how these calculations were determined. Rainey proposed that the initial cost for Blast include $500,000 for the test marketing, which was conducted in the Detroit area and completed in June of the previous year, and $2 million for new specialized equipment and packaging facilities. The estimated life for the facilities was 15 years, after which they would have no salvage value. This 15-year estimated life assumption coincides with company policy set by Donnalley not to consider cash flows occurring more than 15 years into the future, as estimates that far ahead "tend to become little more than blind guesses."

Rainey cautioned against taking the annual cash flows (as shown in Exhibit 1) at face value because portions of these cash flows actually would be a result of sales that had been diverted from Lift-Off and Wave. For this reason, Rainey also produced the estimated annual cash flows that had been adjusted to include only those cash flows incremental to the company as a whole (as shown in Exhibit 2).

At this point, discussion opened between Donnalley and McDonald, and it was concluded that the opportunity cost on funds was 10 percent. Gasper then questioned the fact that no

costs were included in the proposed cash budget for plant facilities that would be needed to produce the new product.

Rainey replied that at the present time, Lift-Off's production facilities were being used at only 55 percent of capacity, and because these facilities were suitable for use in the production of Blast, no new plant facilities would need to be acquired for the production of the new product line. It was estimated that full production of Blast would only require 10 percent of the plant capacity.

McDonald then asked if there had been any consideration of increased working capital needs to operate the investment project. Rainey answered that there had, and that this project would require $200,000 of additional working capital; however, as this money would never leave the firm and would always be in liquid form, it was not considered an outflow and hence not included in the calculations.

Donnalley argued that this project should be charged something for its use of current excess plant facilities. His reasoning was that if another firm had space like this and was willing to rent it out, it could charge somewhere in the neighborhood of $2 million. However, he went on to acknowledge that D&D had a strict policy that prohibits renting or leasing any of its production facilities to any party from outside the firm. If they didn't charge for facilities, he concluded, the firm might end up accepting projects that under normal circumstances would be rejected.

From here the discussion continued, centering on the question of what to do about the lost contribution from other projects, the test marketing costs, and the working capital.

Exhibit 1: D&D Laundry Products Company Forecast of Annual Cash Flows from the Blast Product (Including cash flows resulting from sales diverted from the existing product lines)

Year	Cash flows	Year	Cash flows
1	$280,000	9	$350,000
2	280,000	10	350,000
3	280,000	11	250,000
4	280,000	12	250,000
5	280,000	13	250,000
6	350,000	14	250,000
7	350,000	15	250,000
8	350,000		

Exhibit 2: D&D Laundry Products Company Forecast of Annual Cash Flows from the Blast Product (Excluding cash flows resulting from sales diverted from the existing product lines)

Year	Cash flows	Year	Cash flows
1	$250,000	9	$315,000
2	250,000	10	315,000
3	250,000	11	225,000
4	250,000	12	225,000
5	250,000	13	225,000
6	315,000	14	225,000
7	315,000	15	225,000
8	315,000		

Questions

1. If you were put in the place of Steve Gasper, would you argue for the cost from market testing to be included in a cash outflow?

2. What would your opinion be as to how to deal with the question of working capital?

3. Would you suggest that the product be charged for the use of excess production facilities and building space?

4. Would you suggest that the cash flows resulting from erosion of sales from current laundry detergent products be included as a cash inflow? If there was a chance of competitors introducing a similar product if you did not introduce Blast, would this affect your answer?

5. If debt were used to finance this project, should the interest payments associated with this new debt be considered cash flows?

6. What are the NPV, IRR, and PI of this project, both including cash flows resulting from sales diverted from the existing product lines (Exhibit 1) and excluding cash flows resulting from sales diverted from the existing product lines (Exhibit 2)? Under the assumption that there is a good chance that competition will introduce a similar product if you don't, would you accept or reject this project?

Caledonia Products

Calculating Free Cash Flow and Project Valuation

It's been two months since you took a position as an assistant financial analyst at Caledonia Products. Although your boss has been pleased with your work, he is still a bit hesitant about unleashing you without supervision. Your next assignment involves both the calculation of the cash flows associated with a new investment under consideration and the evaluation of several mutually exclusive projects. Given your lack of tenure at Caledonia, you have been asked not only to provide a recommendation, but also to respond to a number of questions aimed at judging your understanding of the capital-budgeting process. The memorandum you received outlining your assignment follows:

To: The Assistant Financial Analyst

From: Mr. V. Morrison, CEO, Caledonia Products

Re: Cash Flow Analysis and Capital Rationing

We are considering the introduction of a new product. Currently we are in the 34 percent tax bracket with a 15 percent discount rate. This project is expected to last five years and then, because this is somewhat of a fad project, it will be terminated. The following information describes the new project:

Cost of new plant and equipment: $ 7,900,000

Shipping and installation costs: $ 100,000

Unit sales:

Year	Units Sold
1	70,000
2	120,000
3	140,000
4	80,000
5	60,000

Sales price per unit: $300/unit in Years 1–4 and $260/unit in Year 5

Variable cost per unit: $180/unit

Annual fixed costs: $200,000 per year

Working capital requirements: There will be an initial working capital requirement of $100,000 just to get production started. For each year, the total investment in net working capital will be equal to 10 percent of the dollar value of sales for that year. Thus, the investment in working capital will increase during Years 1 through 3, then decrease in Year 4. Finally, all working capital is liquidated at the termination of the project at the end of Year 5.

Depreciation method: Straight-line over five years assuming the plant and equipment have no salvage value after five years.

Questions

1. Why should Caledonia focus on project free cash flows as opposed to the accounting profits earned by the project when analyzing whether to undertake the project?

2. What are the incremental cash flows for the project in Years 1 through 5, and how do these cash flows differ from accounting profits or earnings?

3. What is the project's initial outlay?

4. Sketch out a cash flow diagram for this project.

5. What is the project's net present value?

6. What is its internal rate of return?

7. Should the project be accepted? Why or why not?

Appendix: The Modified Accelerated Cost Recovery System

To simplify our computations we have used straight-line depreciation throughout this chapter. However, firms use accelerated depreciation for calculating their taxable income. In fact, since 1987 the **modified accelerated cost recovery system (MACRS)** has been used. Under the MACRS, the depreciation period is based on the **asset depreciation range (ADR)** system, which groups assets into classes by asset type and industry, and then determines the actual number of years to be used in depreciating the asset. In addition, the MACRS restricts the amount of depreciation that may be taken in the year an asset is acquired or sold. These limitations have been called **averaging conventions**. The two primary conventions, or limitations, may be stated as follows:

1. **Half-Year Convention:** Personal property, such as machinery, is treated as having been placed in service or disposed of at the midpoint of the taxable year. Thus, a half-year of depreciation generally is allowed for the taxable year in which property is placed in service and in the final taxable year. As a result, a three-year property class asset has a depreciation calculation that spans four years, with only a half a year's depreciation in the

Table A.1	Percentages for Property Classes					
Recovery Year	**3-Year**	**5-Year**	**7-Year**	**10-Year**	**15-Year**	**20-Year**
1	33.3%	20.0%	14.3%	10.0%	5.0%	3.8%
2	44.5	32.0	24.5	18.0	9.5	7.2
3	14.8	19.2	17.5	14.4	8.6	6.7
4	7.4	11.5	12.5	11.5	7.7	6.2
5		11.5	8.9	9.2	6.9	5.7
6		5.8	8.9	7.4	6.2	5.3
7			8.9	6.6	5.9	4.9
8			4.5	6.6	5.9	4.5
9				6.5	5.9	4.5
10				6.5	5.9	4.5
11				3.3	5.9	4.5
12					5.9	4.5
13					5.9	4.5
14					5.9	4.5
15					5.9	4.5
16					3.0	4.5
17						4.5
18						4.5
19						4.5
20						4.5
21						1.7
Total	100.0	100.0	100.0	100.0	100.0	100.0

first and fourth years. In effect, it is assumed that the asset is in service for six months during both the first and last years.

2. **Mid-Month Convention:** Real property, such as buildings, is treated as being placed in service or disposed of in the middle of the month. Accordingly, a half-month of depreciation is allowed for the month the property is placed in service and also for the final month of service.

Using the MACRS results in a different percentage of the asset being depreciated each year; these percentages are shown in Table A.1.

To demonstrate the use of the MACRS, assume that a piece of equipment costs $12,000 and has been assigned to a five-year class. Using the percentages in Table A.1 for a five-year class asset, the depreciation deductions would be calculated as shown in Table A.2.

Note that the averaging convention that allows for the half-year of depreciation in the first year results in a half-year of depreciation beyond the fifth year, or in Year 6.

WHAT DOES ALL OF THIS MEAN?

Depreciation, although an expense, is not a cash flow item. However, depreciation expense lowers the firm's taxable income, which in turn reduces the firm's tax liability and increases its cash flow. Throughout our calculations in this chapter, we used a simplified straight-line depreciation method to keep the calculations simple, but in reality you would use the MACRS method. The advantage of accelerated depreciation is that you end up with more depreciation expense (a non-cash item) in the earlier years and less depreciation expense in the later years. As a result, you have less taxable profits in the early years and more taxable profits in the later years. This reduces taxes in the earlier years when the present values are greatest, while increasing taxes in the later years when present values are smaller. In effect, the MACRS allows you to postpone paying taxes. Regardless of whether you use straight-line or accelerated depreciation (MACRS), the total depreciation is the same, it is just the timing of when the deprecation is expensed that changes.

Most corporations prepare two sets of books, one for calculating taxes for the Internal Revenue Service (IRS) in which they use the MACRS, and one for their stockholders in which they use straight-line depreciation. For capital-budgeting purposes, only the set of books used to calculate taxes is relevant.

Table A.2	MACRS Demonstrated	
Year	**Depreciation Percentage**	**Annual Depreciation**
1	20.0%	$ 2,400
2	32.0%	3,840
3	19.2%	2,304
4	11.5%	1,380
5	11.5%	1,380
6	5.8%	696
	100.0%	$12,000

Study Problems

A–1.   **(Depreciation)** Compute the annual depreciation for an asset that costs $250,000 and is in the five-year property class. Use the MACRS in your calculation.

A–2.   **(Depreciation)** The Mason Falls Mfg. Company just acquired a depreciable asset this year, costing $500,000. Furthermore, the asset falls into the seven-year property class using the MACRS.

a. Using the MACRS, compute the annual depreciation.

b. What assumption is being made about when you bought the asset within the year?

Photo Credits

Risk Analysis and Project Evaluation

From Chapter 13 of *Financial Management: Principles and Applications*, Twelfth Edition. Sheridan Titman, Arthur J. Keown, and John D. Martin.

Risk Analysis and Project Evaluation

Chapter **Outline**

1 The Importance of Risk Analysis

Objective 1. Explain the importance of risk analysis in the capital-budgeting decision-making process.

2 Tools for Analyzing the Risk of Project Cash Flows

Objective 2. Use sensitivity, scenario, and simulation analyses to investigate the determinants of project cash flows.

3 Break-Even Analysis

Objective 3. Use break-even analysis to evaluate project risk.

4 Real Options in Capital Budgeting

Objective 4. Describe the types of real options.

440

Principles P1, P2, and P3 Applied

How does a firm estimate the potential worst-case scenarios from taking on an investment project? What other "what-if" scenarios should the analyst consider? These are the types of issues that we address in this chapter. The focus of this chapter is on evaluating risk, which is central to **P** Principle 2: **There Is a Risk–Return Tradeoff**. To pose a more practical issue, we cannot hope to know how much reward to look for if we do not understand the nature of the risks we assume. In this chapter, we explore techniques that we can implement to understand the risk inherent in project cash flows, which, according to **P** Principle 3: **Cash Flows Are the Source of Value**, is the source of value. Finally, the timing of future cash flows is another source of project risk, and because money has a time value, **P** Principle 1: **Money Has a Time Value**, we need to incorporate this factor into our analysis of project risk.

Risk Analysis of a Condo Investment

Let's consider the role that risk can have in carrying out a project analysis with the example of a condo investment opportunity. Your landlord has offered to sell the condo that you and your college roommates have been renting for $90,000. You estimate that after spending $2,000 to paint and fix up the condo, you can turn around and sell it for $100,000.

In this example, the only certain cash flow is the purchase price of $90,000. The $2,000 painting and fix-up expenses as well as the eventual selling price are what we expect, but these numbers are just estimates that may turn out to be either too high or too low. For example, in the process of having the place painted, you may discover structural damage to the ceiling from a water leak that was not discovered at the time of the sale inspection. More important, the $100,000 estimated selling price is far from a sure thing. It may take several months to get an offer, and then it may be for substantially less than the $100,000 asking price.

Regardless of Your Major...

"Project Risk for Entrepreneurs"

Some day you may want to start your own business. But starting a new business is a very risky investment. About 40 percent of new businesses shut their doors during their first year, and only about one in five make it longer than five years. In part, this is because, as a group, entrepreneurs tend to be very optimistic and tend to put too little emphasis on evaluating the risks of their new ventures.

But a budding entrepreneur can avoid this mistake by drawing on the principles of finance. As we see in this chapter, there are several ways to predict and analyze possible outcomes for a new project under consideration. Assessing risk is so important to the entrepreneur that there's even a whole field dedicated to it: specialists, called decision analysts, study decision making under conditions of uncertainty by modelling the possible outcomes. Decision analysis is taught both in management departments of business schools and in operations research departments in schools of engineering.

Clearly, both marketing and economics also play a crucial role in the evaluation of a new business venture because the entrepreneur will need to forecast sales under a variety of scenarios that describe possible future states of the economy. Also, knowledge of cost accounting and operations is important for risk analysis because the entrepreneur will need to carefully calculate the cost of production under various circumstances.

Your Turn: See Study Question 1.

The Importance of Risk Analysis

Different projects have different levels of risk and, as a result, financial managers need to evaluate the risk of the proposed investment project.

There are two fundamental reasons to perform a project risk analysis before making the final accept/reject decision:

- **Project cash flows are risky.** The net present value (NPV) calculation is based on estimates of future cash flows, but the future cash flows that actually occur will almost certainly not be equal to our estimates. So, it is very helpful to explore the nature of the risks the project entails so that we can be better prepared to manage the project if it is accepted.

- **Forecasts are made by humans who can be either too optimistic or too pessimistic when making their cash flow forecasts.** The fact that the analyst may not be totally objective about the analysis injects a source of bias into the investment decision-making process. Overly optimistic biases can result in the acceptance of investments that fail to produce the optimistic forecasts, whereas a pessimistic bias can lead to the firm passing up worthwhile projects. Both types of bias are costly to the firm's shareholders, and a careful risk analysis of projects can minimize these biases.

Before you move on to 2

Concept Check | 1

1. What are the reasons for performing a project risk analysis?
2. How does the optimism or pessimism of the manager doing a cash flow forecast influence the cash flow estimates?

Tools for Analyzing the Risk of Project Cash Flows

We can assume that the actual cash flows an investment produces will almost never equal the expected cash flows we used to estimate the investment's NPV. There are many possible cash flow outcomes for any risky project, and simply specifying a single expected cash flow can provide a misleading characterization of the investment. Although it is generally impossible to specify all the ways in which an investment can perform, an analyst uses some basic tools to better understand the uncertain nature of future cash flows and, consequently, the reliability of the NPV estimate.

The first tool we will consider is *sensitivity analysis*, which is designed to identify the most important forces that ultimately determine the success or failure of an investment. The second tool we will consider is *scenario analysis*, which allows the analyst to consider alternative scenarios in which a number of possible value drivers differ. Finally, we consider the use of *simulation*, which allows the analyst to consider very large numbers of possible scenarios.

Key Concepts: Expected Values and Value Drivers

Before we launch into an investigation of the tools of risk analysis, we need to define two key concepts: expected values and value drivers. Both concepts will be used frequently throughout our discussion.

Expected Values

The cash flows used in the calculation of project NPV are actually the **expected values** of the investment's risky cash flows. The expected value of a future cash flow is simply a probability-weighted average of all the possible cash flows that might occur. For example, if there are only two possible cash flows, $0 and $100, and the probability of each is 50 percent, then the expected cash flow is $50 = (.5 × $0) + (.5 × $100). Because it is generally not possible to specify all the possible cash flows that might occur and their associated probabilities, it is customary to forecast cash flows for specific states of the economy—recession, normal, and expansion.

To illustrate how a firm might approach the problem of estimating the expected cash flow from an investment, consider the following hypothetical problem faced by one of the country's largest homebuilders. The firm is attempting to forecast the cash flows for a new subdivision in Kern County, California. Its management might estimate that if the homebuilding slump continues, cash flow will be –$2 million; if a recovery begins during the year, cash flow will climb to $1 million; and, if the turnaround in the economy is so dramatic that growth rates equal the high rates experienced before the recession began, cash flow will reach $6 million.

To complete this analysis of the expected cash flow, management must also make an estimate of the probabilities attached to each potential state of Kern County's homebuilding economy. Estimates of these probabilities, like the estimates of cash flows for each of the three states of the economy, are based on managerial judgment and are highly subjective. Suppose the homebuilders' management estimates that there is a .50 probability of a continued housing slump that will result in the recession cash flow, a .40 probability of the beginning of a turnaround, and only a .10 probability of a return to the dramatic growth rate experienced before the onset of the recession. Given these estimates, the expected cash flow for 2014 is:

$$\text{Expected Cash Flow for 2014} = (-\$2 \text{ million} × .50) + (\$1 \text{ million} × .40) + (\$6 \text{ million} × .10)$$
$$= \$0$$

In this example the homebuilder estimates that in 2014, it will get a zero cash flow out of the Kern County development. In actuality there are many possible cash flow outcomes, but the expected outcome in this example is estimated to be zero. In the pages that follow, we will learn how to use three types of tools for digging deeper into the determinants of each expected cash flow outcome and, in the process, learn more about the value of the investment.

Forecasting Revenues Using Expected Values

Marshall Homes is a Texas homebuilder that specializes in the construction of high-end homes costing $1.5 million to $10 million each. To estimate its revenues for 2014 following the economic downturn that began with the recession of 2007–2009, it divided its home sales into three categories based on selling price (high, medium, and low) and estimated the number of units it expects to sell under three different economic scenarios for 2014. These scenarios include a deep recession (Scenario I), a continuation of current conditions in which the economy is in a mild recession (Scenario II), and finally a turnaround in the economy and return to the economic conditions of 2004–2006 (Scenario III) before the housing bubble burst. What are Marshall's expected revenues for 2014?

STEP 1: Picture the problem

The following spreadsheet lays out the number of units the firm's managers estimate they will sell in each of the three home categories for each of the three possible states of the economy:

	Scenario I (Deep Recession)	Scenario II (Mild Recession)	Scenario III (Turn-around)
Probability	20%	60%	20%
High-Priced Home Category			
Unit sales	0	5	10
Average price per unit	$ 8,000,000	$ 8,000,000	$ 8,000,000
Total revenues	$ 0	$ 40,000,000	$ 80,000,000
Medium-Priced Home Category			
Unit sales	5	15	30
Average price per unit	$ 4,000,000	$ 4,000,000	$ 4,000,000
Total revenues	$20,000,000	$ 60,000,000	$120,000,000
Low-Priced Home Category			
Unit sales	10	20	60
Average price per unit	$ 2,000,000	$ 2,000,000	$ 2,000,000
Total revenues	$20,000,000	$ 40,000,000	$120,000,000
Total revenues for each scenario	$40,000,000	$140,000,000	$320,000,000

STEP 2: Decide on a solution strategy

The expected or forecast revenue for Marshall Homes is a probability-weighted average of the revenues the firm projects it will generate from building and selling homes in each of the three price categories. Solving for the expected total revenue for the company in 2014 therefore entails following a three-step procedure:

STEP 1: Estimate the probability of each state of the economy.

STEP 2: Calculate the total revenues from each category of homes for each of the three states of the economy.

STEP 3: Calculate a probability-weighted average of total revenues that is equal to the expected revenue for the firm in 2014.

STEP 3: Solve

The expected total revenue for Marshall Homes in 2014 is thus estimated to be $156 million by summing the product of the total revenues estimated for each scenario multiplied by the probabilities of each scenario:

	Scenario I (Deep Recession)	Scenario II (Mild Recession)	Scenario III (Turn-around)	
Probability	20%	60%	20%	Step 1
Total revenues for each scenario	$40,000,000	$140,000,000	$320,000,000	Step 2
Probability × total revenues	$ 8,000,000	$ 84,000,000	$ 64,000,000	
Expected Revenues = $ 156,000,000				Step 3

STEP 4: Analyze

The expected revenue for the coming year is quite sizeable; however, remember that this is neither the firm's profits nor the cash flow produced by the firm's operations. To calculate these quantities would require that we estimate the firm's expenses of operations under each economic scenario. It is important to note that these expenses are not likely to be the same percent of revenues in each scenario, as the firm is likely to tighten its belt (financially speaking) if conditions worsen such that its operating costs per home might actually decline.

STEP 5: Check yourself

Consider your forecast of Marshall Homes' expected revenues for 2014 where the probability of entering a deep recession increases to 40 percent, the probability of a mild recession drops to 50 percent, and the probability of a turnaround declines to only 10 percent. You may assume that the estimates of the number of units sold and the selling price of each remain unchanged. What is the new total expected revenue?

ANSWER: Expected total revenue for the firm declines to $118,000,000.

Your Turn: For more practice, do related **Study Problems** 1 and 2 at the end of this chapter. **>> END Checkpoint 1**

Value Drivers

Financial managers sometimes refer to the basic determinants of an investment's cash flows, and consequently its performance, by using the term **value drivers**. For example, a key value driver for a manufacturing firm would be its inventory turnover because high inventory turnover ratios indicate the efficient use of the firm's investment in inventories.

Identification of an investment's value drivers is crucial to the success of an investment project because it allows the financial manager to:

- Allocate more time and money toward refining forecasts of these key variables.
- Monitor the key value drivers throughout the life of the project, so that corrective action can be taken quickly in the event that the project does not function as planned.

Value drivers for investment cash flows consist of the fundamental determinants of project revenues (e.g., market size, market share, and unit price) and costs (e.g., variable costs and cash fixed costs, which are fixed costs other than depreciation).

Sensitivity Analysis

Sensitivity analysis occurs when a financial manager evaluates the effect of each value driver on the investment's NPV. To illustrate the use of sensitivity analysis as a tool of risk analysis, consider the investment opportunity faced by Longhorn Enterprises, Inc. Longhorn has the opportunity to manufacture and sell a novelty "third brake light" for automobiles. The light is mounted in the rear window of an automobile to replace the factory-installed third brake light. The replacement light can be shaped into the logo of your favorite university mascot or other preferred symbol. Producing the light requires an initial investment of $500,000 in manufacturing equipment, which depreciates over a five-year time period toward a $50,000 salvage value, plus an investment of $20,000 in net operating working capital (increase in receivables and inventory less increase in accounts payable). The discount rate used to analyze the project cash flows is 10 percent. This rate is the opportunity cost of investing in the proposed investment and should reflect the risk of the investment. Other pertinent information describing the investment opportunity is summarized as follows:

Initial cost of equipment	$(500,000)
Project and equipment life	5 years
Salvage value of equipment	$ 50,000
Working capital requirement	$ 20,000
Depreciation method	Straight line
Depreciation expense	$ (90,000)
Discount	10%
Tax rate	30%

Longhorn's management estimates that it can sell 15,000 units per year for the next five years and expects to sell them for $200 each. Longhorn's management team has identified four key value drivers for the project: unit sales, price per unit, variable cost per unit, and cash fixed costs (that is, fixed costs other than depreciation) per year. The expected values for the value drivers, along with corresponding estimates for best- and worst-case scenarios, are summarized as follows:

	Expected or Base Case	Worst Case	Best Case
Unit sales	15,000	12,500	18,000
Price per unit	$ 200	190	220
Variable cost per unit	(150)	(160)	(130)
Fixed cash cost per year	(285,000)	(285,000)	(285,000)
Depreciation expense	$ (90,000)	$ (90,000)	$ (90,000)

Using the expected or base-case values for each of the value drivers, we calculate the investment cash flows for the expected or base case as follows:

Calculating Net Operating Profit after Taxes (NOPAT).

Note: This calculation looks a lot like an income statement. But there is a subtle difference. We do not deduct interest expense when calculating the income tax liability.

Recapture of working capital in year 5.

Note: Because this is a recovery of the original investment in working capital, there is no profit; thus no taxes are owed on the $20,000.

Recovery of salvage value in year 5.

Note: Because the book value of the machinery and equipment is equal to the salvage value, there is no taxable gain or loss from the $50,000 salvage value received in Year 5.

	Year 0	Year 1	Year 2	Year 3	Year 4	Year 5
Revenues (15,000 units × $200)		$ 3,000,000	$ 3,000,000	$ 3,000,000	$ 3,000,000	$ 3,000,000
less: Variable cost ($150 per unit)		(2,250,000)	(2,250,000)	(2,250,000)	(2,250,000)	(2,250,000)
less: Depreciation expense		$ (90,000)	$ (90,000)	$ (90,000)	$ (90,000)	$ (90,000)
less: Fixed cash cost	NOPAT	(285,000)	(285,000)	(285,000)	(285,000)	(285,000)
Net operating income		375,000	375,000	375,000	375,000	375,000
less: Taxes		(112,500)	(112,500)	(112,500)	(112,500)	(112,500)
Net operating profit after tax (NOPAT)		$ 262,500	$ 262,500	$ 262,500	$ 262,500	$ 262,500
plus: Depreciation expense		90,000	90,000	90,000	90,000	90,000
less: Increase in CAPEX	$ (500,000)	—	—	—	—	50,000
less: Increase in working capital	(20,000)	—	—	—	—	20,000
Free cash flow (FCF)	$ (520,000)	$ 352,500	$ 352,500	$ 352,500	$ 352,500	$ 422,500

Note that the total initial cash outlay for Year 0 is −$520,000, which includes both the cost of acquiring machinery and equipment and the initial investment in net operating working capital required to get the business up and running.

Unit sales and price per unit are forecast to be the same for Years 1 through 5, so revenues are equal to $3,000,000 per year = 15,000 units × $200 per unit. Variable cost per unit of $150 multiplied by 15,000 units produces a total annual variable cost of $2,250,000. The firm has depreciation expense of $90,000 plus cash fixed costs (such as salaries and utilities, which are cash expenses) of $285,000 per year. Net operating income is estimated to be $375,000 per year, and taxes are 30 percent of this total ($112,500), such that net operating profit after tax (NOPAT) is $262,500 = $375,000(1 − .30) per year. Adding back depreciation expense (which is not a cash expense) of $90,000 produces a free cash flow estimate for Years 1 through 4 equal to $352,500. In Year 5 the company receives the salvage value of $50,000 for the equipment (note that because this amount equals the book value of the equipment in that year, there are no taxable gains from the sale) plus the return of the $20,000 investment in working capital to produce a free cash flow of $422,500.

We calculate the expected NPV using the expected or base-case cash flows, which are the expected future cash flows, as $859,717 as follows:

$$NPV = -\$520,000 + \frac{\$352,500}{(1 + .10)^1} + \frac{352,500}{(1 + .10)^2} + \frac{352,500}{(1 + .10)^3} + \frac{352,500}{(1 + .10)^4} + \frac{\$422,500}{(1 + .10)^5}$$

$$NPV = -\$520,000 + \$1,379,717 = \$859,717$$

Therefore, the investment looks like a good one. Note that when we calculate NPV for a project, we do so using expected future cash flows, and hence the NPV we estimate is the *expected* NPV. In this case the project has an *expected* NPV greater than zero, indicating that, based on the expected (base-case) forecasts of the project's value drivers, the company expects to create value by undertaking the project.

Although this analysis is based on the expected values of the key value drivers, it is very likely that the actual realizations of these value drivers will turn out to be very different than our estimate. For some value drivers, these inevitable deviations from expectations may not be crucial to the project's success, but for others, the deviations can be quite important. Clearly, managers would like to know which value drivers are the most critical to project success. Knowing this allows them to focus their attention on the most important ones, both when they are preparing forecasts as well as when they are monitoring the success of the project.

In this instance, the analyst can perform a sensitivity analysis to evaluate the project's risk. The analyst would do so by changing one variable at a time to determine its impact on the overall project NPV. For example, consider the effect of a 10 percent decrease in unit sales on the project's NPV. In this case, unit sales would drop to 13,500 and the resulting NPV (holding everything else constant) would drop to $660,700. This is a drop of 23 percent in NPV caused by a 10 percent drop in unit sales. Next, consider a 10 percent increase in variable cost per unit ($165), which results in an NPV of $262,668 or a drop of 69 percent. Finally, consider a 10 percent increase in annual cash fixed costs from ($285,000) to ($313,500). The resulting NPV is $784,091, which is only 9 percent less than the base-case NPV.

Value Driver	Expected NPV	Revised NPV	% Change in NPV
Unit sales (−10%)	$859,717	$660,700	−23%
Variable cost per unit (+10%)	$859,717	$262,668	−69%
Cash fixed cost per year (+10%)	$859,717	$784,091	−9%

Clearly, the most critical value driver we have considered here is variable cost per unit. This tells the analyst that having a very good grasp on the variable cost per unit is absolutely critical to the project's success. This, in turn, might lead the analyst to go back to the engineering staff that provided the basis for the variable cost estimate to better understand their confidence in their estimate. Longhorn's management might ask them how confident they are in their worst-case scenario estimate of variable costs equal to $160 per unit. Moreover, what are the factors that determine this cost, and what, if anything, might the company do if these costs are higher than anticipated? Answers to such questions might lead to a more in-depth analysis of the determinants of the variable cost per unit and a better understanding of the possible success or failure of the investment.

Checkpoint 2

Project Risk Analysis: Sensitivity Analysis

Crainium, Inc. is considering an investment in a new plasma cutting tool to be used in cutting out steel silhouettes that will be sold through the firm's catalog sales operations. The silhouettes can be cut into any two-dimensional shape such as a state, a university mascot or logo, and so forth. The products are expected to sell for an average price of $25 per unit, and the company analysts expect the firm can sell 200,000 units per year at this price for a period of five years. Launching this service will require the purchase of a $1.5 million plasma cutter and materials-handling system that has a residual or salvage value in five years of $250,000. In addition, the firm expects to have to invest an additional $500,000 in working capital to support the new business. Other pertinent information concerning the business venture is as follows:

Initial cost of equipment	$ (1,500,000)
Project and equipment life	5 years
Salvage value of equipment	$ 250,000
Working capital requirement	$ 500,000
Depreciation method	Straight line
Depreciation expense	$ (250,000) per year
Variable cost per unit	(20)
Cash fixed cost per year	(400,000)
Discount rate	12%
Tax rate	30%

(2 CONTINUED >> ON NEXT PAGE)

Crainium's analysts have estimated the project's expected or base-case cash flows as well as the NPV and internal rate of return (IRR) to be the following:

	Year 0	Year 1	Year 2	Year 3	Year 4	Year 5
Revenues		$ 5,000,000	$ 5,000,000	$ 5,000,000	$ 5,000,000	$ 5,000,000
less: Variable cost		(4,000,000)	(4,000,000)	(4,000,000)	(4,000,000)	(4,000,000)
less: Depreciation expense		$ (250,000)	$ (250,000)	$ (250,000)	$ (250,000)	$ (250,000)
less: Fixed cost		(400,000)	(400,000)	(400,000)	(400,000)	(400,000)
Net Operating Income		350,000	350,000	350,000	350,000	350,000
less: Taxes		(105,000)	(105,000)	(105,000)	(105,000)	(105,000)
Net Operating Profit after Tax (NOPAT)		$ 245,000	$ 245,000	$ 245,000	$ 245,000	$ 245,000
plus: Depreciation expense		250,000	250,000	250,000	250,000	250,000
less: Increase in CAPEX	$(1,500,000)	—	—	—	—	250,000
less: Increase in working capital	(500,000)	—	—	—	—	500,000
Free Cash Flow (FCF)	$(2,000,000)	$ 495,000	$ 495,000	$ 495,000	$ 495,000	$ 1,245,000
NPV	$ 209,934					
IRR	15.59%					

Although the project is expected to have a $209,934 NPV and a 15.59 percent IRR (which exceeds the project's 10 percent discount rate), it is risky, so the firm's analysts want to explore the importance of uncertainty in the project cash flows. Perform a sensitivity analysis on this proposed investment.

STEP 1: Picture the problem

To evaluate the sensitivity of the project's NPV and IRR to uncertainty surrounding the project's value drivers, we analyze the effects of changes in the value drivers (unit sales, price per unit, variable cost per unit, and annual fixed operating cost other than depreciation). Specifically, we consider each of the following changes:

Value Driver
Unit sales (−10%)
Price per unit (−10%)
Variable cost per unit (+10%)
Cash fixed cost per year (+10%)

STEP 2: Decide on a solution strategy

The objective of this analysis is to explore the effects of the prescribed changes in the value drivers on the project's NPV. In this instance, we estimate the project's NPV for estimates of each of the value drivers that deviate 10 percent from their expected or base-case value. The deviations we consider are each in an adverse direction (i.e., they lead to a reduction in NPV). The resulting NPVs are then compared to the base-case NPV (calculated using the expected values for all the value drivers) in order to determine which value driver has the greatest influence on NPV.

STEP 3: Solve

Recalculating project NPV by changing each value driver by 10 percent, we get the following results:

Value Driver	Expected NPV	Revised NPV	% Change in NPV
Unit sales (−10%)	$ 209,934	$ (42,400)	−120%
Price per unit (−10%)	$ 209,934	(1,051,737)	−601%
Variable cost per unit (+10%)	$ 209,934	$ (799,402)	−481%
Cash fixed cost per year (+10%)	$ 209,934	$ 109,001	−48%

STEP 4: Analyze

The first thing we observe is that a 10 percent adverse change from the estimated values of the first three value drivers results in a negative NPV for the project and that the 10 percent increase in annual fixed operating cost other than depreciation reduced the NPV by almost half. Moreover, the most critical value driver is price per unit followed closely by the variable cost per unit.

The results of this analysis suggest two courses of action. First, Crainium's management should make sure that they are as comfortable as possible with their price-per-unit forecast as well as their estimate of the variable cost per unit. This might entail using additional market research to explore the pricing issue and a careful cost-accounting study of unit production costs. Second, should the project be implemented, it is imperative that management monitor these two critical value drivers (price per unit and variable cost per unit) very closely so that they can react quickly should an adverse change in either variable occur.

STEP 5: Check yourself

After a careful analysis of the costs for making the silhouettes, Crainium's management has determined that it will be possible to reduce the variable cost per unit down to $18 per unit by purchasing an additional option for the equipment that will raise its initial cost to $1.8 million (the residual or salvage value for this configuration is estimated to be $300,000). All other information remains the same as before. For this new machinery configuration, analyze the sensitivity of the project NPV to the same percent changes analyzed above.

ANSWER: *NPV = $1,001,714 and IRR = 26.65%.*

Your Turn: For more practice, do related **Study Problem** 7 at the end of this chapter.   **>> END Checkpoint 2**

Scenario Analysis

Our sensitivity analysis of Longhorn Enterprises, Inc., involved changing only one value driver at a time and analyzing its effect on the investment NPV. This is very useful when attempting to determine the most critical value drivers, but it ignores the fact that some of the value drivers may move in unison or be correlated. For example, when unit sales are less than expected, it is probably the case that the unit selling price will be less than expected.

To consider the effects of multiple changes in value drivers, analysts often resort to something we will refer to as **scenario analysis**, which allows the financial manager to simultaneously consider the effects of changes in the estimates of multiple value drivers on the investment opportunity's NPV. Each scenario consists of a different set of estimates for the project value drivers. One possible scenario consists of value drivers all equal to Longhorn management's worst-case estimates presented earlier. To evaluate this possibility, we analyze the project cash flows and NPV using the worst-case estimates of the value drivers as follows:

	Year 0	Year 1	Year 2	Year 3	Year 4	Year 5
Revenues (12,500 units × $190 each)		$ 2,375,000	$ 2,375,000	$ 2,375,000	$ 2,375,000	$ 2,375,000
less: Variable cost ($160 per unit)		(2,000,000)	(2,000,000)	(2,000,000)	(2,000,000)	(2,000,000)
less: Depreciation expense		(90,000)	(90,000)	(90,000)	(90,000)	(90,000)
less: Fixed cash costs per year		(285,000)	(285,000)	(285,000)	(285,000)	(285,000)
Net Operating Income		$ —	$ —	$ —	$ —	$ —
less: Taxes (Tax rate = 30%)		—	—	—	—	—
Net Operating Profit after Tax (NOPAT)		$ —	$ —	$ —	$ —	$ —
plus: Depreciation expense		90,000	90,000	90,000	90,000	90,000
less: Increase in CAPEX	$(500,000)	—	—	—	—	50,000
less: Increase in working capital	(20,000)	—	—	—	—	20,000
Free Cash Flow (FCF)	$(520,000)	$ 90,000	$ 90,000	$ 90,000	$ 90,000	$ 160,000
NPV	$(135,365)					
IRR	0.00%					

Because the worst-case scenario has much lower estimates of revenues due to the lower selling price and number of units sold, the resulting cash flow estimates are much lower. Indeed, when we analyze the investment's NPV, we get a worst-case estimate of $135,365, which means that in this case the project reduces shareholder wealth. But what is the likelihood that this worst-case scenario will occur? We will leave this question unanswered for the moment, but will return to it shortly when we discuss the use of simulation analysis.

What about the best-case scenario? If this rosy outcome were to occur, then the following cash flows would result:

	Year 0	Year 1	Year 2	Year 3	Year 4	Year 5
Revenues (18,000 units × $220)		$ 3,960,000	$ 3,960,000	$ 3,960,000	$ 3,960,000	$ 3,960,000
less: Variable cost ($130 per unit)		(2,340,000)	(2,340,000)	(2,340,000)	(2,340,000)	(2,340,000)
less: Depreciation expense		$ (90,000)	(90,000)	(90,000)	(90,000)	(90,000)
less: Fixed cash cost		(285,000)	(285,000)	(285,000)	(285,000)	(285,000)
Net Operating Income		1,245,000	$ 1,245,000	$ 1,245,000	$ 1,245,000	$ 1,245,000
less: Taxes		(373,500)	(373,500)	(373,500)	(373,500)	(373,500)
Net Operating Profit after Tax (NOPAT)		$ 871,500	$ 871,500	$ 871,500	$ 871,500	$ 871,500
plus: Depreciation expense		90,000	90,000	90,000	90,000	90,000
less: Increase in CAPEX	$ (500,000)	—	—	—	—	50,000.00
less: Increase in working capital	(20,000)	—	—	—	—	20,000.00
Free Cash Flow (FCF)	$ (520,000)	$ 961,500	$ 961,500	$ 961,500	$ 961,500	$ 1,031,500
NPV	$3,168,306					
IRR	184.04%					

In this case the NPV of the project is a whopping $3,168,306 and the IRR is 184.04 percent!

Combining our analysis of the expected or base-case, worst-case, and best-case scenarios indicates a wide range of possible NPVs for the project:

Scenario	NOPAT	Free Cash Flow (Years 1–4)	NPV
Expected or Base Case	$262,500	$352,500	$ 859,717
Worst Case	$ 0	$ 90,000	($135,365)
Best Case	$871,500	$961,500	$3,168,306

In fact, we have learned that the investment is expected to create value for Longhorn with an expected NPV equal to $859,717. However, this estimate is based on Longhorn's forecast of the expected values for the key value drivers (unit sales, unit price, variable cost per unit, and cash fixed costs). After evaluating what Longhorn's management feels are worst- and best-case estimates of these value drivers, we discovered a wide range of possible NPVs depending on what actually happens. What we do not know is the likelihood or probability that the worst-case or best-case scenario will occur. Moreover, we do not know the probability that the project will lose money (i.e., have a negative NPV). Simulation offers the analyst a useful tool for risk analysis that provides us not only with estimates of NPV for many scenarios but also with probabilities for those scenarios.[1]

Simulation Analysis

Scenario analysis provides the analyst with a discrete number of estimates of project NPVs for a limited number of cases or scenarios. **Simulation analysis**, on the other hand, provides the analyst with a very powerful tool for generating thousands of estimates of NPV that are built upon thousands of values for each of the investment's value drivers. These different values arise out of each value driver's individual probability distribution. This may sound confusing if you have not heard the term *probability distribution* in a while, so here is a simple example. Let's say that the unit selling price for Longhorn's third brake light product can be either $180 or $220 with equal probability of 50 percent. The expected price then is $200 = (.50 × $180) + (.50 × $220). The probability distribution for unit price in this instance is fully described by the two possible values for price and their corresponding probabilities.[2]

---

[1] The number of scenarios in a simulation is equal to the number of iterations of the simulation. This can be tens if not hundreds or thousands as each of the iterations represents a different scenario with a probability equal to 1 divided by the total number of iterations.

[2] The distribution of unit price in this example is discrete because price can only take on one of two discrete values. If the price could be anything between $180 and $200, then the distribution would be continuous. The bell-shaped normal distribution, for example, is an example of a continuous probability distribution.

Let's consider how Longhorn might use simulation analysis to evaluate the NPV of its proposed brake light project. The simulation process is summarized in the following five-step process:

Step 1. Estimate probability distributions for each of the investment's key value drivers (i.e., the variables or factors that determine the project's cash flows). In the Longhorn example, the value drivers are the factors that determine project revenues, which include the number of units that are sold and the price per unit they command, as well as the factors underlying the cost of manufacturing and selling the brake lights (variable and fixed costs).

Step 2. Randomly select one value for each of the value drivers from their respective probability distributions.

Step 3. Combine the values selected for each of the value drivers to estimate project cash flows for each year of the project's life and calculate the project's NPV.

Step 4. Store or save the calculated value of the NPV and repeat Steps 2 and 3. Simulations are easily carried out using readily available computer software that allows one to easily repeat Steps 2 and 3 thousands of times.

Step 5. Use the stored values of the project NPV to construct a histogram or probability distribution of NPV.

Checkpoint 3

Project Risk Analysis: Scenario Analysis

The analysts performing the risk analysis on the plasma cutting tool being considered by Crainium, Inc. (described in Checkpoint 2) now want to evaluate the project risk using scenario analysis. Specifically, they now want to evaluate the project's risk using scenario analysis aimed at evaluating the project's NPV under worst- and best-case scenarios for the project's value drivers.

STEP 1: Picture the problem

The values for the expected or base-case along with the worst- and best-case scenarios are as follows:

	Expected or Base-Case	Worst Case	Best Case
Unit sales	200,000	150,000	250,000
Price per unit	$ 25	$ 23	$ 28
Variable cost per unit	(20)	(21)	(18)
Cash fixed cost per year	$(400,000)	$(450,000)	$(350,000)
Depreciation expense	$(250,000)	$(250,000)	$(250,000)

STEP 2: Decide on a solution strategy

The objective of scenario analysis is to explore the sensitivity of the project's NPV to different scenarios that are defined in terms of the estimated values for each of the project's value drivers. In this instance we have two scenarios corresponding to the worst- and best-case outcomes for the project.

STEP 3: Solve

Recalculating project NPV for both sets of value drivers results in the following estimates of project NPV:

Scenario	NOPAT	Free Cash Flow (Years 1–4)	NPV
Expected or Base-Case	$ 245,000	$ 495,000	$ 209,934
Worst Case	$ (280,000)	$ (30,000)	$(1,682,573)
Best Case	$1,330,000	$1,580,000	$ 4,121,117

STEP 4: Analyze

Examination of the worst- and best-case scenarios for the project indicates that although the project is expected to produce an NPV of $209,934, the NPV might be as high as $4,121,117 or as low as –$1,682,573. Clearly, this is a risky investment opportunity. Had the worst-case scenario produced an NPV close to zero, then Crainium's management could have been much more confident that the project would be a good one. If the very low NPV of the worst-case scenario is particularly troublesome to the firm's management, they might consider an alternative course of action that reduces the likelihood of this worst-case result.

(3 CONTINUED >> ON NEXT PAGE)

STEP 5: Check yourself

A recent economic downturn caused Crainium's management to reconsider the base-case scenario for the project by lowering their unit sales estimate to 175,000 at a revised price per unit of $24.50. Based on these revised projections, is the project still viable? What if Longhorn followed a higher price strategy of $35 per unit but only sold 100,000 units? What would you recommend Longhorn do?

ANSWER: NPV = ($326,276) and NPV = $1,471,606.

Your Turn: For more practice, do related **Study Problems** 4, 6, and 7 at the end of this chapter.   >> END Checkpoint 3

Once we have finished running the simulation, it is time to sit down and interpret the results. Note that in Step 5 we summarize the final set of simulation results in a probability distribution of possible NPVs like the one found in Figure 1. So, we can now analyze the distribution of *possible* NPVs to determine the probability for a negative NPV. In Figure 1, we see that the probability of achieving an NPV greater than zero is 85 percent, indicating a 15 percent probability that the project will produce an NPV that is less than zero. What a simulation does is allow us to analyze all sources of uncertainty simultaneously, and get some idea as to what might happen, before we actually commit to the investment.

Figure 1

Probability Distribution of NPVs for the Marketing of Longhorn's Brake Lights

The final output of the simulation is a probability distribution of the project's NPVs. Having set up and run the simulation experiment, the analyst not only knows the expected NPV but can also make probability statements about the likelihood of achieving any particular value of NPV. For example, in the results that follow, the probability of achieving a positive NPV is 85 percent.

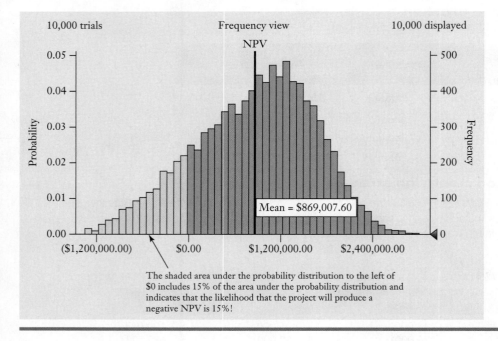

>> END FIGURE 1

Before you move on to 3

Concept Check | 2

1. What are value drivers, and how are they important in the analysis of project risk?
2. What is sensitivity analysis, and how is it used to evaluate the risk of project cash flows?
3. Describe scenario analysis and contrast it with sensitivity analysis.
4. Describe the five-step process used to carry out simulation analysis. How is simulation analysis similar to scenario analysis?

Finance in a **Flat World**

Currency Risk

When multinational firms do their risk analyses, a very important variable that they consider is uncertainty about exchange rates. For example, in 2010 Boeing began deliveries of its 787 Dreamliner aircraft, which competes directly with models made by European manufacturer Airbus. Boeing produces these planes in the United States, paying workers and suppliers in U.S. dollars. Airbus, on the other hand, has costs that are more closely tied to the euro. What this means is that when the dollar is very strong relative to the euro, Airbus has a competitive advantage over Boeing. However, when the euro is strong relative to the dollar, Boeing has a competitive advantage over Airbus. As a result, the exchange rate between the euro and the U.S. dollar plays a particularly important role in the sensitivity and scenario analysis of Boeing investment projects, and it can fluctuate dramatically. In fact, at the beginning of December in 2009 it took $1.51 to buy one euro, and the end of February 2010 that had dropped to $1.35, about an 11 percent drop in only three months. These exchange rate changes made Boeing's Dreamliner more expensive for those buying it with euros, and made the Airbus less expensive for those buying it with U.S. dollars.

Your Turn: See Study Question 4.

 # Break-Even Analysis

Although the tools of risk analysis discussed in the previous section provide us with an understanding of the different possible outcomes, it is also useful for a firm to know the least favorable scenarios in which the project still breaks even. Because the increase in sales that can be generated by an investment is one of the most critical value drivers, managers typically do a **break-even analysis** to determine the minimum level of output or sales that the firm must achieve in order to avoid losing money—that is, to break even. In most cases, the break-even sales estimate is defined as the level of sales for which net operating income equals zero.

To illustrate break-even analysis, we refer back to the Longhorn Enterprises example introduced in the previous section. The worst-case scenario results are repeated below for the novelty brake light investment proposal:

	Year 0	Year 1	Year 2	Year 3	Year 4	Year 5
Revenues (12,500 units × $190 each)		$ 2,375,000	$ 2,375,000	$ 2,375,000	$ 2,375,000	$ 2,375,000
less: Variable cost ($160 per unit)		(2,000,000)	(2,000,000)	(2,000,000)	(2,000,000)	(2,000,000)
less: Depreciation expense		(90,000)	(90,000)	(90,000)	(90,000)	(90,000)
less: Fixed cash costs per year		(285,000)	(285,000)	(285,000)	(285,000)	(285,000)
Net Operating Income		$ —	$ —	$ —	$ —	$ —
less: Taxes (Tax rate = 30%)		—	—	—	—	—
Net Operating Profit after Tax (NOPAT)		$ —	$ —	$ —	$ —	$ —
plus: Depreciation expense		90,000	90,000	90,000	90,000	90,000
less: Increase in CAPEX	$(500,000)	—	—	—	—	50,000
less: Increase in working capital	(20,000)	—	—	—	—	20,000
Free Cash Flow (FCF)	$(520,000)	$ 90,000	$ 90,000	$ 90,000	$ 90,000	$ 160,000

Notice that Net Operating Income is equal to zero for a sales level of $2,375,000, which illustrates the sale of 12,500 units at a price of $190 per unit, with variable cost per unit equal to $160. Let's now consider how we could calculate the break-even level of sales.

Accounting Break-Even Analysis

Accounting break-even analysis involves determining the level of sales necessary to cover total fixed costs, that is, both cash fixed costs (or fixed operating costs before depreciation) and depreciation. We use the term *accounting break-even* to refer to the fact that we are using accounting costs, which include non–cash flow items, specifically, depreciation.

Performing an accounting break-even analysis requires that we decompose production costs into two components: fixed costs and variable costs. This decomposition depends upon whether the costs being analyzed vary with firm sales (variable costs) or not (fixed costs).

Fixed Costs

Fixed costs do not vary directly with sales revenues, but instead remain constant despite any change to the business; they can be divided into fixed operating costs before depreciation and depreciation itself. Examples of fixed operating costs before depreciation include administrative salaries, insurance premiums, intermittent advertising program costs, property taxes, and rent. Because fixed costs do not vary directly with sales revenues, accountants often refer to them as **indirect costs**. As the number of units sold increases, the fixed cost *per unit* of product decreases, because the fixed costs are spread over larger and larger quantities of output.

Variable Costs

Variable costs are those costs that vary with firm sales. In fact, variable costs are sometimes referred to as **direct costs** because variable expenses vary *directly* with sales. Although it is a simplification, it is customary to assume that the variable cost per unit of sales is fixed. For example, in the Longhorn Enterprises' worst-case scenario, the variable cost per unit was $160. Consequently, when 10,000 units are sold, the total variable costs for the project are $1,600,000; and when 20,000 units are sold, the total variable costs double to $3,200,000. For a manufacturing operation, some examples of variable costs include sales commissions paid to the firm's sales personnel, hourly wages paid to manufacturing personnel, the cost of materials used, energy costs (fuel, electricity, natural gas), freight costs, and packaging costs. Thus it is important to remember that total variable costs depend on the quantity of product sold. Notice that if Longhorn makes zero units of the product, it incurs zero variable costs.

Figure 2 depicts Longhorn Enterprises' fixed, variable, and total costs of producing novelty brake lights for output levels ranging from 0 to 20,000 units. Panel A illustrates the behavior of fixed and variable costs as the number of units produced and sold increases. For example, at 20,000 units produced and sold, Longhorn will incur fixed costs of $375,000 plus $3,200,000 ($160 per unit × 20,000 units) of variable costs, for a total cost of $3,575,000.

Total Revenue or Volume of Output

The last element used in accounting break-even analysis is total revenue. Total revenue is equal to the unit selling price multiplied by the number of units sold. Panel B of Figure 2 contains a graphical depiction of the total revenues for Longhorn Enterprises' investment opportunity. Total revenues are equal to the product of the selling price of $190 per unit and the number of units produced and sold.

Calculating the Accounting Break-Even Point

The accounting break-even point is the level of sales or output that is necessary to cover both variable and total fixed costs, where total fixed costs equal cash fixed costs plus depreciation, such that the net operating income is equal to zero:

$$\text{Net Operating Income } (NOI) = \text{Total Revenues} - \text{Total Costs} = 0$$

or

$$\text{Net Operating Income } (NOI) = \text{Total Revenues} - \left(\text{Total Variable Cost} + \text{Total Fixed Cost}\right) = 0 \qquad \textbf{(1)}$$

In Panel B of Figure 2, Net Operating Income is equal to zero—and, consequently, Longhorn Enterprises experiences accounting break-even—when the firm produces and sells 12,500 units.

We do not have to graph total costs and revenues to determine break-even. In fact, we can solve for the break-even number of units mathematically. To do this, we need to define the determinants of each of the terms in Equation (1). The firm's total dollar revenues or sales is equal to the price per unit (P) multiplied by the number of units sold (Q); and total costs are

Figure 2

Accounting Break-Even Analysis

Longhorn Enterprises Inc. is evaluating the accounting break-even level of sales units for its novelty brake light investment opportunity. The firm is using its worst-case scenario estimates of selling price ($190 per unit) and variable cost ($160 per unit), and also its fixed cost estimate of $375,000, in its analysis. Variable costs include all the costs incurred in the manufacturing process that vary with the number of units produced. Fixed costs do not vary with the number of units produced.

(Panel A) Fixed and Variable Costs

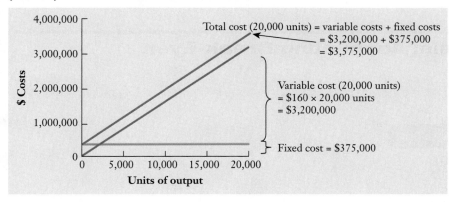

(Panel B) Accounting Break-Even

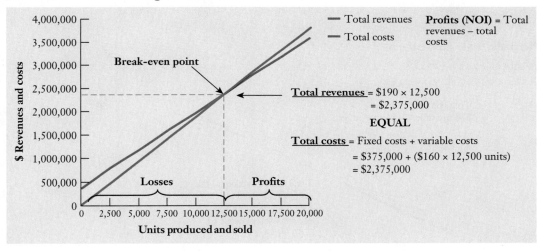

>> END FIGURE 2

equal to the total fixed costs (F) added to the product of the number of units sold (Q) times the variable cost per unit (V), that is,

$$\text{Net Operating Income } (NOI) = \underbrace{\left(\frac{\text{Price per}}{\text{Unit } (P)} \times \frac{\text{Units}}{\text{Sold } (Q)} \right)}_{\text{Total Revenues}} - \underbrace{\left[\left(\frac{\text{Variable Cost}}{\text{per Unit } (V)} \times \frac{\text{Units}}{\text{Sold } (Q)} \right) + \frac{\text{Total Fixed}}{\text{Cost } (F)} \right]}_{\text{Total Costs}} = 0 \qquad \textbf{(1a)}$$

We can find the accounting break-even level of units produced and sold ($Q_{Break\text{-}Even}$) by solving Equation (1a) for the value of Q that satisfies the requirement that $NOI = 0$ ($Q_{Break\text{-}Even}$):

$$Q_{Accounting\ Break\text{-}Even} = \frac{\text{Total Fixed Costs } (F)}{\dfrac{\text{Price per}}{\text{Unit } (P)} - \dfrac{\text{Variable Cost}}{\text{per Unit } (V)}} = \frac{\text{Total Fixed Costs } (F)}{\dfrac{\text{Contribution Margin}}{\text{per Unit}}} \qquad \textbf{(2)}$$

We call the denominator in Equation (2) the **contribution margin**, which is the difference between the selling price (P) per unit and the variable cost (V) per unit. That is, $P - V$ represents the dollar amount from each unit sold that goes toward covering total fixed costs, which, once fixed costs are covered, goes toward profits. Returning to our Longhorn break-even example, we substitute total fixed costs of \$375,000 and a contribution margin of \$30 = \$190 − \$160 into Equation (2) to calculate the firm's break-even 12,500 units:

$$Q_{Accounting\ Break\text{-}Even} = \frac{\text{Total Fixed Costs } (F)}{\text{Price per Unit } (P) - \text{Variable Cost per Unit } (V)} = \frac{375{,}000}{\$190 - \$160} = 12{,}500 \text{ units}$$

Checkpoint 4

Project Risk Analysis: Accounting Break-Even Analysis

The new plasma cutting tool that Crainium, Inc. is considering investing in as described in Checkpoint 2 has the following value driver estimates of fixed and variable costs:

	Expected or Base-Case
Unit sales	200,000
Price per unit	\$ 25
Variable cost per unit	(20)
Cash fixed cost per year	\$(400,000)
Depreciation expense	\$(250,000)

Company analysts are evaluating the project's risks and want to estimate the accounting break-even for the project's annual revenues and expenses. What is the break-even level of units?

STEP 1: Picture the problem

The annual cost structure for the proposed investment is comprised of total fixed costs plus variable costs, which are different for each possible level of output:

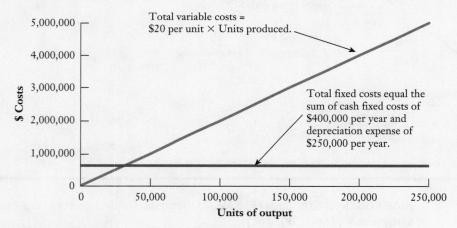

STEP 2: Decide on a solution strategy

To find the accounting break-even quantity of units produced and sold, we solve for a zero-level of net operating income, that is,

$$(P \times Q) - [(V \times Q) + F] = NOI = 0 \tag{1a}$$

Or we solve for the accounting break-even quantity, $Q_{Accounting\ Break\text{-}Even}$:

$$Q_{Break\text{-}Even} = \frac{F}{P - V} \tag{2}$$

STEP 3: Solve

Using Equation (2), we can solve for the accounting break-even quantity as follows:

$$Q_{Accounting\ Break\text{-}Even} = \frac{F}{P - V} = \frac{\$650{,}000}{\$25 - \$20} = 130{,}000 \text{ Units}$$

Graphically, we can locate the accounting break-even output level as follows:

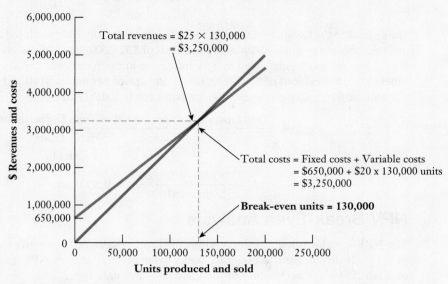

Total revenues = $25 × 130,000
= $3,250,000

Total costs = Fixed costs + Variable costs
= $650,000 + $20 x 130,000 units
= $3,250,000

Break-even units = 130,000

$ Revenues and costs

Units produced and sold

STEP 4: Analyze

Break-even analysis provides us with an understanding of what level of sales we need to break even in an accounting sense—that is, what level of sales we need in order to cover our total fixed and variable costs resulting in NOI equaling zero. Often managers are concerned with whether a project contributes to a firm's accounting earnings; accounting break-even analysis tells us if it does. A project that does not break even reduces the firm's earnings, whereas a project that breaks even will add to a firm's earnings. Still, we must keep in mind that just breaking even does not mean that shareholders will benefit. In fact, projects that merely break even in an accounting sense have negative NPVs and result in a loss of shareholder value. That's because we do include opportunity costs. In effect, the money spent on a project that merely breaks even simply covers the project's costs, but it does not provide investors with their required rate of return. In effect, it ignores the opportunity cost of money. Still, break-even analysis provides managers with excellent insights into what might happen if the projected level of sales is not reached.

STEP 5: Check yourself

Crainium, Inc.'s analysts have estimated the accounting break-even for the project to be 130,000 units and now want to consider how the worst-case scenario value driver values would affect the accounting break-even. Specifically, consider a unit price of $23, variable cost per unit of $21, and total fixed costs of $700,000.

ANSWER: $Q_{Accounting\ Break-Even}$ = 350,000 Units.

Your Turn: For more practice, do related **Study Problems** 8, 9, and 10 at the end of this chapter.   **>> END Checkpoint 4**

Calculating the Cash Break-Even Point

In addition to calculating the accounting break-even point, it is also common to calculate the cash break-even point. This certainly makes sense when we think back to P Principle 3: **Cash Flows Are the Source of Value**. The accounting break-even point tells us the level of sales necessary to cover our total fixed and variable operating costs, where total fixed costs include both cash fixed costs and depreciation expense (which is not a cash expense for the period). The **cash break-even point** tells us the level of sales where we have covered our cash fixed costs (ignoring depreciation) and as a result our cash flow is zero. To calculate the cash break-even point, we consider only those fixed costs that entail a cash payment by the firm (specifically, we exclude depreciation expense), that is,

$$Q_{Cash\ Break-Even} = \frac{\text{Fixed Operating Costs Other Than Depreciation per Year}}{\text{Price per Unit } (P) - \text{Variable Cost per Unit } (V)}$$

$$= \frac{\text{Total Fixed Costs } (F) - \text{Depreciation}}{\text{Contribution Margin per Unit}} \qquad \textbf{(2a)}$$

Going back to the Longhorn example, recall that the company had cash fixed costs of $285,000 and depreciation expense of $90,000, for a total of $375,000 in total fixed costs. In calculating the cash break-even point, we are only interested in the fixed cash expenses (or fixed costs other than depreciation) of $285,000. Longhorn's price per unit is $190 and its variable costs per unit are $160, so the cash break-even point can be calculated as

$$Q_{Cash\ Break\text{-}Even} = \frac{\text{Fixed Operating Expenses Other Than Depreciation per Year}}{\dfrac{\text{Price per}}{\text{Unit } (P)} - \dfrac{\text{Variable Cost}}{\text{per Unit } (V)}}$$

$$= \frac{\$375,000 - \$90,000}{\$190 - \$160} = 9,500 \text{ units}$$

NPV Break-Even Analysis

The **NPV break-even analysis** identifies the level of sales necessary to produce a zero level of NPV. It differs from accounting break-even analysis in that NPV break-even focuses on cash flows, not accounting profits, and also accounts for ▣ Principle 1: **Money Has a Time Value.** Let's return to the worst-case scenario for Longhorn Enterprises' novelty brake light investment to see just how NPV break-even differs from accounting break-even. The worst-case cash flows are presented below, along with the estimated NPV and IRR for this scenario:

	Year 0	Year 1	Year 2	Year 3	Year 4	Year 5
Revenues (12,500 units × $190 each)		$ 2,375,000	$ 2,375,000	$ 2,375,000	$ 2,375,000	$ 2,375,000
less: Variable cost ($160 per unit)		(2,000,000)	(2,000,000)	(2,000,000)	(2,000,000)	(2,000,000)
less: Depreciation expense		(90,000)	(90,000)	(90,000)	(90,000)	(90,000)
less: Fixed cash costs per year		(285,000)	(285,000)	(285,000)	(285,000)	(285,000)
Net Operating Income	$ —	$ —	$ —	$ —	$ —	$ —
less: Taxes (Tax rate = 30%)		—	—	—	—	—
Net Operating Profit after Tax (NOPAT)	$ —	$ —	$ —	$ —	$ —	$ —
plus: Depreciation expense		90,000	90,000	90,000	90,000	90,000
less: Increase in CAPEX	$(500,000)	—	—	—	—	50,000
less: Increase in working capital	(20,000)	—	—	—	—	20,000
Free Cash Flow (FCF)	$(520,000)	$ 90,000	$ 90,000	$ 90,000	$ 90,000	$ 160,000
NPV	$(135,365)					
IRR	0.00%					

Note that the Net Operating Income is zero, so this is the accounting break-even sales level. However, the annual free cash flows are equal to the depreciation expense, except for Year 5 when they also include the salvage value on the equipment plus the return of working capital. When we calculate the NPV for these cash flows, we find that it is negative and the IRR is equal to zero. The zero IRR indicates that if we discounted the future cash flows of the project using a 0 percent rate (that is, simply adding up the cash flows of $90,000 for years one through four plus $160,000 in Year 5), we would get our money back. However, if we require a rate of return greater than zero, the project does not produce enough cash flow to break even. This difference in results between break-even analysis and the NPV shouldn't come as much of a surprise; after all, break-even analysis does not look at cash flows and ignores the time value of money. Moreover, accounting break-even analysis only looks at one period, trying to determine the level of sales that will produce zero net operating income.

Solving for the break-even NPV is a bit more complicated than solving for accounting break-even, and it is very helpful to have a spreadsheet model to do the calculations. However, you can also do it using trial and error by simply trying different output levels until the calculated NPV equals zero. In this example, the sales units that lead to a zero NPV are 14,200, as the following set of cash flows shows:

	Year 0	Year 1	Year 2	Year 3	Year 4	Year 5
Revenues (14,200 units × $190 each)		$ 2,698,000	$ 2,698,000	$ 2,698,000	$ 2,698,000	$ 2,698,000
less: Variable cost ($160 per unit)		(2,272,000)	(2,272,000)	(2,272,000)	(2,272,000)	(2,272,000)
less: Depreciation expense		(90,000)	(90,000)	(90,000)	(90,000)	(90,000)
less: Fixed cash costs per year		(285,000)	(285,000)	(285,000)	(285,000)	(285,000)
Net Operating Income		$ 51,000	$ 51,000	$ 51,000	$ 51,000	$ 51,000
less: Taxes (Tax rate = 30%)		(15,300)	(15,300)	(15,300)	(15,300)	(15,300)
Net Operating Profit after Tax (NOPAT)		$ 35,700	$ 35,700	$ 35,700	$ 35,700	$ 35,700
plus: Depreciation expense		90,000	90,000	90,000	90,000	90,000
less: Increase in CAPEX	$(500,000)	—	—	—	—	50,000
less: Increase in working capital	(20,000)	—	—	—	—	20,000
Free Cash Flow (FCF)	$(520,000)	$ 125,700	$ 125,700	$ 125,700	$ 125,700	$ 195,700
NPV	$ 0					
IRR		10.00%				

Figure 3 contains NPV calculations for 7,500 to 17,500 units. The NPV calculations lie along a straight line that crosses the horizontal axis where NPV = 0 or at the break-even NPV of 14,200 units. This is much easier, of course, if you let the spreadsheet do the re-calculations of NPV. However, we leave this analysis to later finance classes because it is beyond the scope of this chapter.[3]

Figure 3

NPV Break-Even

Longhorn Enterprises is considering an investment that involves producing novelty brake lights for automobiles. The analysis of NPV break-even presented here corresponds to the assumptions underlying the worst-case scenario for the investment, that is,

	Worst-Case Scenario
Price per unit	$ 190
Variable cost per unit	(160)
Cash fixed costs per year	(285,000)

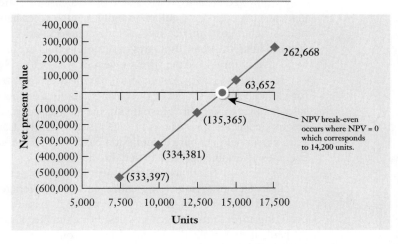

>> END FIGURE 3

---

[3]For those who would like to do this analysis, you will find the "Goal Seek" function in Excel very helpful. Also, note that because units produced must be a whole number, we have a break-even of 14,200. The solution we find using Goal Seek is 14,200.42 units.

Tools of Financial Analysis—Break-Even Concepts

Name of Tool	Formula	What It Tells You
Accounting Break-Even Units ($Q_{Accounting\ Break-Even}$)	$\dfrac{Total\ Fixed\ Costs\ (F)}{Price\ per\ Unit\ (P) - Variable\ Cost\ per\ Unit\ (V)} = \dfrac{Total\ Fixed\ Costs\ (F)}{Contribution\ Margin\ per\ Unit}$	• Measures the number of units a firm must sell in order to cover all its fixed and variable costs • Note that fixed costs include both out-of-pocket expenses for the period as well as depreciation expense.
Cash Break-Even Units ($Q_{Cash\ Break-Even}$)	$\dfrac{Fixed\ Operating\ Expenses\ Other\ Than\ Depreciation\ per\ Year}{Price\ per\ Unit\ (P) - Variable\ Cost\ per\ Unit\ (V)}$	• Measures the number of units a firm must sell in order to cover all its cash fixed costs and variable costs • The difference in accounting and cash break-even is driven by the inclusion of depreciation expense (which is a non-cash expense) in the former but not the latter.
Net Present Value Break-Even	Units produced and sold that produce a NPV = 0	• Measures the number of units the firm must sell annually in order to cover the present value of all its expenses (fixed and variable) over the life of an investment.

Operating Leverage and the Volatility of Project Cash Flows

In Equation (2) we learned that a project's accounting break-even point is determined by the project's total fixed costs and the difference between the price per unit and the variable costs per unit. In general this mixture of fixed and variable operating costs is determined by the nature of the business. For example, companies that manufacture semiconductors will have very high fixed costs associated with the expense of building and maintaining large factories that can cost billions of dollars to build. On the other hand, a law firm would have relatively modest fixed costs (office rent, administrative salaries, and utilities) but high variable costs (in particular, the bonuses it pays its attorneys) that are driven by the firm's attorneys' billable hours that in turn drive the firm's revenues.

Most businesses have some flexibility in their cost structure and can substitute fixed costs for variable costs to some degree. For example, Longhorn Enterprises may decide to pay its sales personnel for their "brake light project" with salaries, which are a fixed cost (i.e., salaries are not dependent on the level of sales). Alternatively, Longhorn's management might pay its sales personnel on a pure commission basis, in which case the cost of paying sales personnel becomes a variable cost that is tied directly to sales.

The mix of fixed and variable operating costs not only impacts the break-even output but also determines something called operating leverage. **Operating leverage** results from the use of fixed costs in the operations of the firm and measures the sensitivity of changes in operating income to changes in sales. For example, if Longhorn's sales were to increase by 20 percent, the project's operating costs would not increase proportionately because some of them are fixed. As a result, net operating income (NOI) may rise by 30 percent or more depending on how much operating leverage the firm has used. The greater the operating leverage, the greater is the sensitivity of the firm's operating income to changes in sales. We can measure the firm's operating leverage for a particular level of sales using the **degree of**

operating leverage (DOL), where the DOL tells us, when there is a percent change in sales, how that is reflected in a percent change in NOI, as follows:

$$DOL = \frac{\% \text{ change in net operating profits } (NOI)}{\% \text{ change in sales}} \qquad (3)$$

Thus, if the DOL is 4.0 and there is a 10 percent change in sales, NOI would increase by 40 percent (or 4.0 × 10%). To illustrate how this works, consider the Longhorn example found in Table 1. The firm's base case sales are $3,000,000 and the fixed costs are $375,000. To keep things simple, let's also assume that Longhorn's variable costs remain constant at $150 per unit. If Longhorn's sales increase 20 percent, up to $3,600,000, we calculate that the firm's NOI (or EBIT) will rise by 40 percent, from $375,000 to $525,000. Note that in the last column of Table 1 we calculate the percent change in both sales and NOI. Therefore, the DOL for Longhorn can be calculated using Equation (3) to equal 2.0 = 40%/20%. The reason that NOI rose by 40 percent while sales rose by only 20 percent is that some of Longhorn's costs are fixed and consequently do not increase with sales. If Longhorn had no operating leverage (that is, if all of its operating costs were variable), then the 20 percent increase in sales would have led to a 20 percent increase in NOI and a DOL equal to 1. Note also that if Longhorn had experienced a 20 percent decline in revenues, it would have experienced a 40 percent decline in NOI, as the numbers in Table 2 illustrate. Clearly, a higher operating leverage means higher volatility in operating profit or NOI!

Calculating the DOL using Equation (3) requires that we compute NOI for two sales levels. However, there is a simpler way to do this calculation using Equation (4) as follows:

$$DOL_{Sales=\$3,000,000} = 1 + \frac{\text{Fixed Costs}}{NOI_{Sales=\$3,000,000}} = 1 + \frac{\$375,000}{\$375,000} = 1 + 1 = 2 \qquad (4)$$

Interestingly, a firm's DOL is not only a function of its mix of fixed and variable costs but also depends on the level of firm sales in relation to its break-even sales level. Recall that the break-even sales level is where NOI equals zero. Thus, looking at Equation (4) we can

Table 1	How Operating Leverage Affects NOI for a 20% Increase in Longhorn's Sales		
	Base Sales Level for Year t	**Forecast Sales Level for Year $t+1$**	**Percentage Change in Sales and NOI**
Unit sales	15,000	18,000	
Sales	$3,000,000	$3,600,000	**+20%** = $3.6 million/$3.0 million − 1
Less: Total variable costs	2,250,000	2,700,000	
Revenue before fixed costs	$ 750,000	$ 900,000	
Less: Total fixed costs	375,000	375,000	
NOI (or EBIT)	$ 375,000	$ 525,000	**+40%** = $525,000/$375,000 − 1

Table 2	How Operating Leverage Affects NOI for a 20% Decrease in Longhorn's Sales		
	Base Sales Level for Year t	**Forecast Sales Level for Year $t+1$**	**Percentage Change in Sales and NOI**
Unit sales	15,000	12,000	
Sales	$3,000,000	$2,400,000	**−20%** = $2.4 million/$3.0 million − 1
Less: Total variable costs	2,250,000	1,800,000	
Revenue before fixed costs	$ 750,000	$ 600,000	
Less: Total fixed costs	375,000	375,000	
NOI or (EBIT)	$ 375,000	$ 225,000	**−40%** = $225,000/$375,000 − 1

see that because NOI is in the denominator, as NOI approaches 0, $\frac{\text{Fixed Costs}}{NOI_{Sales}}$ becomes very large. As a result, the DOL is most negative for sales levels just below the accounting break-even level and most positive for sales just over the break-even level. That only makes sense because DOL measures the *percent change* in NOI that results from a percent change in sales, and when NOI is near zero, a small dollar change in NOI will result in a large percent change in NOI. Thus when firms are operating near their break-even level of sales, we would expect that small changes in sales would have the greatest impact on their NOIs.

We can summarize what have we learned about operating leverage as follows:

- Operating leverage results from the substitution of fixed operating costs for variable operating costs.

- The effect of operating leverage is to increase the effect of changes in sales on operating income.

- The degree of operating leverage (DOL) is an indication of the firm's use of operating leverage and can be calculated as the ratio of the percent change in NOI divided by the corresponding percent change in sales. The DOL is not a constant but decreases as the level of sales increases beyond the break-even point.

- Finally, operating leverage is a double-edged sword, magnifying both profits and losses, helping in the good times and causing pain in the bad times.

Tools of Financial Analysis—Degree of Operating Leverage

Name of Tool	Formula	What It Tells You
Degree of Operating Leverage (DOL$_{Sales}$)	$$\frac{\%\ \textit{Change in Net Operating Profits (NOI)}}{\%\ \textit{Change in Sales}}$$	<ul><li>Measures the responsiveness of firm operating profits to a change in firm revenues or sales</li><li>The higher the DOL, the greater is the volatility of NOI in response to a given change in firm sales</li><li>The DOL changes for different levels of firm revenues, so it is not fixed across all revenues for a firm.</li></ul>

Before you move on to 4

Concept Check | 3

1. Explain the concepts of fixed and variable costs. Which is an indirect cost, and which is a direct cost?
2. What is accounting break-even analysis?
3. What is NPV break-even analysis, and why does it differ from accounting break-even analysis?
4. What is operating leverage?

4 Real Options in Capital Budgeting

NPV provides the proper tool for evaluating whether a project is expected to add value to the firm. However, NPV is generally calculated using a static set of expected future cash flows that do not reflect the fact that managers are likely to make changes to the operation of the investment over its life in response to changing circumstances that alter the profitability of the investment. For example, if a project that had an expected life of 10 years generates better-than-expected cash flows, its life may be extended, perhaps to 20 years. However, if its cash flows do not meet expectations, it may be scaled back or shut down earlier than anticipated.

Having the flexibility to alter an investment's scale, scope, and timing enhances the value of an investment. All else equal, we would surely prefer an investment that allows managers substantial flexibility in how it is implemented over an investment with no flexibility. However, traditional estimates of investment NPVs often ignore the implications of this flexibility, and so they tend to understate project values.

Opportunities to alter the project's cash flow stream after the project has begun are commonly referred to as **real options**. For example, if you own land that can be developed at your discretion, we would say the ownership of the land includes an option to build. Although there are a number of different categories of real options, the most common sources of flexibility or real options that can add value to an investment opportunity include:

1. **Timing Options.** The option to delay a project until estimated future cash flows are more favorable;

2. **Expansion Options.** The option to increase the scale and scope of an investment in response to realized demand; and

3. **Contract, Shut-Down, and Abandonment Options.** The options to slow down production, halt production temporarily, or stop production permanently (abandonment).

The Option to Delay the Launch of a Project

There is no question that the estimated cash flows associated with a project can change over time. Let's consider Go-Power Batteries, a company that developed a high-voltage nickel-metal hydride battery that can be used to power a hybrid automobile. It is still relatively expensive to manufacture the nickel-metal hydride battery, and the market for a hybrid car is still relatively small. As a result, gearing up to manufacture the batteries at the present time provides cash flows that are quite uncertain. However, owning the technology to produce the batteries may be quite valuable, because it is quite possible that, in the future, the technology may improve and the demand for hybrid automobiles will increase if gasoline prices continue to rise. Hence, having the option to delay manufacturing the hydride battery until a time when the profitability of the venture is more certain is extremely valuable.

Before leaving our discussion of the timing option, let's consider its source. Do all projects have this option? Not at all! In some cases the opportunity to make an investment is short-lived, and if one firm passes it up, another will take it. In the battery example, the option to delay probably rests on patent protection, which gives the owner the right to develop the new technology over the life of the patent. However, even here there are limits in that a competitor may develop a superior technology that makes the hydride battery obsolete.

The Option to Expand a Project

Just as we saw with the option to delay a project, the estimated cash flows associated with a project can change over time, making it valuable to expand its scale and scope. For example, if the new hydride battery project were launched and gasoline prices were to rise, the demand for the battery might increase dramatically. If this indeed happens, having the ability to expand the scale of production of the battery is quite valuable. Because this expansion option can have significant value, firms try to design their production facilities in ways that allow them to easily expand capacity in response to realized increases in demand.

The Option to Reduce the Scale and Scope of a Project

The option to reduce the scale and scope of an investment is the mirror image of the option to expand. In the face of worse-than-expected performance, it is very valuable to have the option to slow down or contract production, shut it down temporarily until prospects for the investment improve, or abandon the investment altogether.

The existence of this type of flexibility or optionality can greatly reduce the risks associated with the investment and thereby increases the project's value. To illustrate, let's go back to our example of the new hydride battery used in hybrid automobiles and, this time, examine the option to abandon that project. Assume that after a few years of production of the new batteries the cost of gasoline falls dramatically while the cost of producing the batteries remains

Analyzing Real Options: Option to Expand

You are considering introducing a new drive-in restaurant called Smooth-Thru, featuring high-protein and vitamin-laced smoothies along with other organic foods. The initial outlay on this new restaurant is $2.4 million and the present value of the free cash flows (excluding the initial outlay) is $2 million, such that the project has a negative expected NPV of –$400,000. Looking closer, you find that there is a 50 percent chance that this new restaurant will be well received and will produce annual cash flows of $320,000 per year forever (a perpetuity), and there is a 50 percent chance of it producing a cash flow of only $80,000 per year forever (a perpetuity) if it isn't received well. The required rate of return you use to discount the project cash flows is 10 percent. However, if the new restaurant is successful, you will be able to build four more of them and they will have costs and cash flows similar to those of the successful restaurant's cash flows. If your new restaurant is not received favorably, you will not expand. Ignoring the fact that there would be a time delay in building additional new restaurants if the project is favorably received, determine the project's NPV.

STEP 1: Picture the problem

Graphically, this can be viewed as:

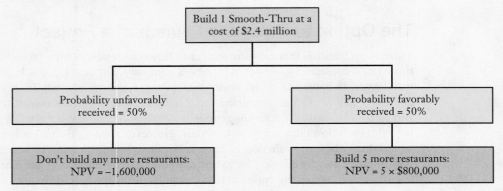

STEP 2: Decide on a solution strategy

Determine an NPV for this project, assuming you will build five identical Smooth-Thru restaurants if the project is favorably received, and assuming you will not build any additional restaurants if it is not favorably received.

STEP 3: Solve

In this problem we have an initial outlay of $2,400,000, a discount rate of 10 percent, and a 50 percent chance the new restaurant concept will be favorably received and a 50 percent chance it will be unfavorably received. If it is favorably received, it will produce a perpetuity of $320,000 per year, whereas if it is unfavorably received it will produce a perpetuity of $80,000 per year. Thus,

$$\text{NPV if favorably received} = (\$320,000 \div .10) - \$2,400,000 = \$800,000$$

$$\text{NPV if unfavorably received} = (\$80,000 \div .10) - \$2,400,000 = -\$1,600,000$$

Assuming we will open five Smooth-Thru restaurants if it is favorably received and only one if it is unfavorably received, and each of these outcomes has a 50 percent probability, the expected NPV is as follows:

$$\text{Expected NPV} = (5 \times .50 \times \$800,000) + (1 \times .50 \times -\$1,600,000) = \$1,200,000$$

STEP 4: Analyze

Without the option to expand, this project would have a NPV of –$400,000.

$$\text{NPV} = (\$800,000 \times .5) + (-\$1,600,000 \times .5) = -\$400,000$$

However, adding the option to expand allows the firm to take advantage of the increased certainty that the project will be received favorably and expand on it. This partially explains why many large restaurant chains introduce new theme restaurants in the hopes that they succeed. If they do, the chain can open additional new restaurants or franchise them.

STEP 5: Check yourself

If you thought there was a 40 percent chance that this project would be favorably received and a 60 percent chance that the project would be unfavorably received, what would be the NPV of the project if you were to introduce 10 restaurants if it was well received?

ANSWER: $2,240,000.

Your Turn: For more practice, do related **Study Problem** 15 at the end of this chapter.

>> **END Checkpoint 5**

high. Under these circumstances the manufacturer may decide first to scale back production and then, ultimately, to abandon the project and sell the technology, including all the patent rights it has developed. To the extent that the technology has value in applications other than hybrid automobiles, and to the extent that the manufacturer can realize value from the sale of the technology and patent rights, the original investment risk is minimized.

Before you begin end-of-chapter material

Concept Check | 4

1. What are real options, and how do they relate to the notion of managerial flexibility?
2. Define *timing options*, and describe how they add value to investments.
3. What is an expansion option?
4. What is an option to contract an investment? When would you expect this type of option to be most valuable?

Applying the Principles of Finance to This Chapter

 Principle 1: Money Has a Time Value Project risk can result in the delay of cash flows, which decreases the present value of those cash flows.

 Principle 2: There Is a Risk–Return Tradeoff Different investment projects have different levels of risk associated with them, and these differences must be recognized when evaluating the project. In order to effectively deal with risk, we use sensitivity, scenario, and break-even analyses to evaluate project risk.

 Principle 3: Cash Flows Are the Source of Value Project risk can cause cash flows to be smaller than expected, which results in a decrease in the value of the project.

Chapter Summaries

1 Explain the importance of risk analysis in the capital-budgeting decision-making process.

SUMMARY: The project's NPV estimate is simply that—an estimate. We perform a project risk analysis of NPV before making the final accept/reject decision because:

- **Project cash flows are risky.** Our NPV calculation is based on estimates of future cash flows, and the future probably will not look like our estimate. So, it is very helpful to explore the nature of the risks the project entails so that we can be better prepared to manage the project if it is accepted.
- **Forecasts are made by humans and they can be either too optimistic or too pessimistic.** The fact that the analyst may not be totally objective about the analysis injects a source of bias into the investment decision-making process. Overly optimistic behavior can result in the acceptance of investments that fail to produce the optimistic forecasts, and pessimistic bias can result in the firm's passing up worthwhile projects. Both types of bias are costly to the firm's shareholders, and a careful risk analysis of projects is one way to guard against such bias.

Concept Check | **1**

1. What are the reasons for performing a project risk analysis?
2. How does the optimism or pessimism of the manager doing a cash flow forecast influence the cash flow estimates?

2 Use sensitivity, scenario, and simulation analyses to investigate the determinants of project cash flows.

SUMMARY: We learned to use two common sense approaches to the evaluation of risky project cash flows—sensitivity analysis and scenario analysis. Both methods begin with an identification of the investment's value drivers, which are the key variables that determine project cash flows. For a new product offering, these drivers might include total market size, the estimated share of the market the new product can capture, product price, unit variable and fixed costs, and so forth.

With sensitivity analysis the analyst changes one value driver at a time in an attempt to identify the most critical determinants of investment success or failure. With scenario analysis the analyst develops alternative sets of estimates for each of the value drivers that correspond to sets of circumstances that the analyst thinks might occur in order to see how the investment might perform in those circumstances.

Simulation analysis provides the analyst with an even more powerful and sophisticated tool for exploring possible investment outcomes. Whereas sensitivity and scenario analysis involve the analysis of a limited number of possible outcomes, computer-based simulations can examine hundreds of thousands of possible outcomes. Because this analysis requires repeated recalculation of project NPV or IRR, it is best carried out with the use of computer software that is now readily available for your personal computer.

KEY TERMS

Concept Check | **2**

1. What are value drivers, and how are they important in the analysis of project risk?
2. What is sensitivity analysis, and how is it used to evaluate the risk of project cash flows?
3. Describe scenario analysis and contrast it with sensitivity analysis.
4. Describe the five-step process used to carry out simulation analysis. How is simulation analysis similar to scenario analysis?

Expected value A probability-weighted average of all possible outcomes.

Scenario analysis Analysis that allows the financial manager to simultaneously consider the effects of changes in the estimates of multiple value drivers on the investment opportunity's NPV.

Sensitivity analysis The process of determining how the distribution of possible net present values or internal rates of return for a particular project is affected by a change in one particular value driver.

Simulation analysis The process of imitating the performance of a risky investment project through repeated evaluations, usually using a computer. This type of experimentation is designed to capture the critical realities of the decision-making situation.

Value drivers The primary determinants of an investment's cash flows and its performance (e.g., number of units sold, cost per unit to produce, and so forth).

3 | Use break-even analysis to evaluate project risk.

SUMMARY: Accounting break-even analysis is a tool used by analysts to determine the level of sales that will result in a zero net operating income. Using the basic break-even model, the analyst can then investigate the effect of changes in unit prices, cost structure, and levels of output or sales on project profitability. However, accounting break-even is not the same thing as break-even NPV because accounting expenses do not include an opportunity cost for the capital invested in the project (i.e., buildings and equipment as well as working capital). Both break-even and NPV break-even analysis provide valuable tools for the analyst's quest to learn more about the determinants of investment risk and the prospects for success.

KEY TERMS

Accounting break-even analysis A type of analysis to determine the level of sales necessary to cover total operating costs and produce a zero level of net operating income or EBIT.

Break-even analysis A type of analysis used to identify the level of sales needed to meet the costs associated with a project.

Cash break-even point The level of sales that covers total cash operating costs (specifically excluding consideration for depreciation expense).

Contribution margin The difference between the selling price per unit and the variable cost per unit.

Degree of operating leverage (DOL) The percentage change in NOI caused by a percentage change in sales.

Direct cost Variable cost.

Fixed cost Costs that do not vary with the level of sales or output, including both cash fixed costs (or fixed operating costs before depreciation) and depreciation.

Indirect cost Fixed cost.

NPV break-even analysis A type of analysis used to identify the level of sales necessary to produce a zero level of NPV.

Operating leverage The inclusion of fixed operating costs in a firm's cost structure that magnify the effect of changes in revenues on the firm's net operating income.

Variable costs Costs that change with the level of sales or output.

KEY EQUATIONS

$$
\begin{aligned}
\text{Net Operating} \atop \text{Income } (NOI) &= \text{Total} \atop \text{Revenues} - \left(\text{Total Variable} \atop \text{Cost} + \text{Total Fixed} \atop \text{Cost} \right) = 0 \quad \textbf{(1)}
\end{aligned}
$$

$$
\text{Net Operating} \atop \text{Income } (NOI) = \underbrace{\left(\text{Price per} \atop \text{Unit } (P) \times \text{Units} \atop \text{Sold } (Q) \right)}_{\text{Total Revenues}} - \underbrace{\left[\left(\text{Variable Cost} \atop \text{per Unit } (V) \times \text{Units} \atop \text{Sold } (Q) \right) + \text{Total Fixed} \atop \text{Cost } (F) \right]}_{\text{Total Costs}} = 0 \quad \textbf{(1a)}
$$

$$
Q_{Accounting\ Break\text{-}Even} = \frac{\text{Total Fixed Costs } (F)}{\text{Price per} \atop \text{Unit } (P) - \text{Variable Cost} \atop \text{per Unit } (V)} = \frac{\text{Total Fixed Costs } (F)}{\text{Contribution Margin} \atop \text{per Unit}} \quad \textbf{(2)}
$$

$$
Q_{Cash\ Break\text{-}Even} = \frac{\text{Fixed Operating Costs Other Than Depreciation per Year}}{\text{Price per} \atop \text{Unit } (P) - \text{Variable Cost} \atop \text{per Unit } (V)}
$$

$$
= \frac{\text{Total Fixed Costs } (F) - \text{Depreciation}}{\text{Contribution Margin} \atop \text{per Unit}} \quad \textbf{(2a)}
$$

$$
DOL = \frac{\% \text{ change in net operating profits } (NOI)}{\% \text{ change in sales}} \quad \textbf{(3)}
$$

Concept Check | 3

1. Explain the concepts of fixed and variable costs. Which is an indirect cost, and which is a direct cost?

2. What is accounting break-even analysis?

3. What is NPV break-even analysis, and why does it differ from accounting break-even analysis?

4. What is operating leverage?

$$DOL = 1 + \frac{\text{Fixed Costs}}{NOI} \qquad (4)$$

 Describe the types of real options.

SUMMARY: Opportunities to alter the project's cash flow stream after the project has begun are commonly referred to as real options and include the flexibility to alter an investment's scale, scope, and timing. Three of the most common types of options that can add value to a capital-budgeting project are: (1) the option to delay a project until the future cash flows are more favorable—an option that is common when the firm has exclusive rights, perhaps a patent, to a product or technology; (2) the option to expand a project, perhaps in size or even to include new products that would not have otherwise been feasible; and (3) the option to abandon a project if the future cash flows fall short of expectations.

KEY TERM

Real options Opportunities that allow for the alteration of the project's cash flow stream while the project is being operated (e.g., changing the product mix, level or output, or the mix of inputs).

Study Questions

1. **(Related to Regardless of Your Major: Project Risk for Entrepreneurs)** The *Regardless of Your Major* feature discusses the risks that entrepreneurs face, with about 40 percent of new businesses shutting their doors during their first year.
   If you had to pick a business to start, what would it be and what type of risks might you face?

2. What is the objective of project risk analysis, and why is it critical to the investment decision-making process?

3. How do you perform a sensitivity analysis, and what is its purpose? Contrast the use of scenario analysis with that of simulation analysis.

4. **(Related to Finance in a Flat World: Currency Risk)** The *Finance in a Flat World* feature discusses the currency risk that multinational firms face. Between July 2008 and December 2009, the value of the yen relative to the U.S. dollar went up by about 17 percent, and as a result when companies traded dollars for yen, they got fewer dollars back. Did this hurt Japanese firms more that produced goods in Japan and sold them in the United States, or did it hurt U.S. firms more that produced goods in the United States and sold them in Japan?

5. Explain the five-step process used to carry out a simulation analysis of project risk.

6. What is the difference between accounting break-even and NPV break-even? Which will offer the higher break-even level of output and why?

7. List and describe the types of real options often encountered in investment opportunities. Why is it important that real options be identified as part of the risk analysis of new investments?

Study Problems

MyFinanceLab

Go to www.myfinancelab.com to complete these exercises online and get instant feedback.

Tools for Analyzing the Risk of Project Cash Flows

1. **(Related to Checkpoint 1) (Calculating expected revenues)** The owner of the Crusik Distribution Company is evaluating the expected annual sales for a new line of facial care products and estimates that there is a 50 percent chance that the product line will be extremely successful, in which case it will generate sales next year of $5 million. However, because the new product line has a unique appeal that will require substantial advertising by its manufacturer to gain consumer acceptance, there is a 50 percent chance that revenues for next year will be a modest $1 million. What is the expected level of revenues for the new product line?

2. **(Related to Checkpoint 1) (Forecasting cash flows using the expected value)** Peterson Trucking is contemplating the acquisition of Armour Transport, a competing trucking firm, and estimates that during the next year Armour Transport's flows from the acquisition will vary depending upon the state of the local economy:

	Scenario I	Scenario II	Scenario III
(State of the Economy)	(Recession)	(Normal)	(Expansion)
Probability	30%	50%	20%
Cash flow for each scenario	$(50,000)	$150,000	$250,000

    a. Calculate the expected cash flow for next year using the estimates provided above.
    b. Assume the probability of a recession increases to 40 percent, the normal scenario probability remains at 50 percent, and the expansion probability drops to only 10 percent. What is your estimate of the expected cash flow for next year under this circumstance?
    c. Your analysis of the acquisition suggests that for the investment to have at least a zero NPV, it must produce an annual expected cash flow of $100,000 per year over the next five years. Assuming that the cash flow you estimated in part a is the expected cash flow for Years 1 through 5, what would you like to know about the project cash flows to make you more comfortable with the idea that you can indeed generate the requisite $100,000 per year cash flow? (No computations required.)

3. **(Forecasting cash flows using the expected value)** Simpkins Trucking of Stillwater, Oklahoma, is also considering the acquisition of Armour Transport (see Problem 2). Simpkins has analyzed the annual cash flows for Armour Transport and come up with these estimates for each of the three states of the economy shown below:

	Scenario I	Scenario II	Scenario III
(State of the Economy)	(Recession)	(Normal)	(Expansion)
Probability	20%	50%	30%
Cash flow for each scenario	$(50,000)	$150,000	$250,000

    Simpkins' management is much more optimistic about the economy than the management at Peterson (Problem 2). In fact, they estimate the probability of a recession next year at only 10 percent, the probability of a normal state of the economy at 50 percent, and the probability of expansion at 30 percent.

    a. Based on Simpkins' estimated probabilities for each state of the economy, what is your estimate of expected cash flows for the Armour Trucking company?
    b. How do you think that Simpkins' optimism about the state of the economy will impact the outcome of acquisition? Which company is more likely to complete the acquisition deal, other things being equal?

4. **(Related to Checkpoint 3) (Forecasting revenues using scenario analysis)** Floating Homes, Inc. is a manufacturer of luxury pontoon and house boats that sell for $40,000 to $100,000. To estimate its revenues for the following year, Floating Homes divides its boat sales into three categories based on selling price (high, medium, and low) and estimates the number of units it expects to sell under three different economic scenarios.

These scenarios include a recession (Scenario I), a continuation of current conditions in which the economy is level (Scenario II), and a strong economy (Scenario III). These estimates are as follows:

	Scenario I (Recession)	Scenario II (Level Economy)	Scenario III (Strong Economy)
Probability	25%	50%	25%
High-Priced Boats Category			
Unit sales	50	400	1,000
Average price per unit	$90,000	$90,000	$90,000
Medium-Priced Boats Category			
Unit sales	100	800	3,000
Average price per unit	$70,000	$70,000	$70,000
Low-Priced Boats Category			
Unit sales	200	1,500	5,000
Average price per unit	$50,000	$50,000	$50,000

Using these estimates, calculate the expected revenue for Floating Homes, Inc. for the following year.

5. **(Calculating the expected NPV of a project)** Management at the Doctors Bone and Joint Clinic is considering whether to purchase a newly developed MRI machine that they feel will provide the basis for better diagnoses of foot and knee problems. The new machine is quite expensive and will be used for a number of years. The clinic's CFO asked an analyst to work up estimates of the NPV of the investment under three different assumptions about the level of demand for its use (high, medium, and low). The CFO assigned a 50 percent probability to the medium-demand state, a 30 percent probability to the high state, and the remaining 20 percent to the low state. After making forecasts of the demand for the machine based on the CFO's judgment and past utilization rates for MRI scans, the following NPV estimates were made:

Demand State	Probability of State	NPV Estimate
Low	20%	$(300,000)
Medium	50%	$200,000
High	30%	$400,000

a. What is the expected NPV for the MRI machine based on the above estimates? How would you interpret the meaning of the expected NPV? Does this look like a good investment to you?

b. Assuming that the probability of the medium-demand state remains 50 percent, calculate the maximum probability you can assign to the low-demand state and still have an expected NPV of zero or higher. (Hint: The sum of the probabilities assigned to all three states must be 100 percent.) How does knowing the maximum probability of realizing the low-demand state help you assess the project (no calculations required)?

6. **(Related to Checkpoint 3) (Scenario analysis)** Family Security is considering introducing tiny GPS trackers that can be inserted in the sole of a child's shoe, which would then allow for the tracking of that child if he or she was ever lost or abducted. The estimates, which might be off by 10 percent (either above or below), associated with this new product are as follows:

Unit price:	$125
Variable costs:	$75
Fixed costs:	$250,000 per year
Expected sales:	10,000 per year

Because this is a new product line, you are not confident in your estimates and would like to know how well you will fare if your estimates on the items listed above are 10 percent higher or 10 percent lower than expected. Assume that this new product line will require an initial outlay of $1 million, with no working capital investment, and will last for 10 years, being depreciated down to zero using straight-line depreciation. In addition, the firm's required rate of return or cost of capital is 10 percent, and the firm's marginal tax rate is 34 percent. Calculate the project's NPV under the "best-case scenario" (that is, use the high estimates—unit price 10 percent above expected, variable costs 10 percent less than expected, fixed costs 10 percent less than expected, and expected sales 10 percent more than expected). Calculate the project's NPV under the "worst-case scenario."

 7. **(Related to Checkpoint 2 and Checkpoint 3) (Comprehensive risk analysis)** Blinkeria is considering introducing a new line of hand scanners that can be used to copy material and then download it into a personal computer. These scanners are expected to sell for an average price of $100 each, and the company analysts performing the analysis expect that the firm can sell 100,000 units per year at this price for a period of five years, after which time they expect demand for the product to end as a result of new technology. In addition, variable costs are expected to be $20 per unit, and fixed costs, not including depreciation, are forecast to be $1,000,000 per year. To manufacture this product, Blinkeria will need to buy a computerized production machine for $10 million that has no residual or salvage value, and will have an expected life of five years. In addition, the firm expects it will have to invest an additional $300,000 in working capital to support the new business. Other pertinent information concerning the business venture is as follows:

Initial cost of the machine	$10,000,000
Expected life	5 years
Salvage value of the machine	$0
Working capital requirement	$300,000
Depreciation method	straight line
Depreciation expense	$2,000,000 per year
Cash fixed costs—excluding depreciation	$1,000,000 per year
Variable costs per unit	$20
Required rate of return or cost of capital	10%
Tax rate	34%

a. Calculate the project's NPV.
b. Determine the sensitivity of the project's NPV to a 10 percent decrease in the number of units sold.
c. Determine the sensitivity of the project's NPV to a 10 percent decrease in the cost per unit.
d. Determine the sensitivity of the project's NPV to a 10 percent increase in the variable cost per unit.
e. Determine the sensitivity of the project's NPV to a 10 percent increase in the annual fixed operating costs.
f. Use scenario analysis to evaluate the project's NPV under worst- and best-case scenarios for the project's value drivers. The values for the expected or base-case along with the worst- and best-case scenarios are as follows:

	Expected or Base Case	Worst Case	Best Case
Unit sales	100,000	70,000	130,000
Price per unit	$ 100	$ 90	$ 120
Variable cost per unit	$ (20)	$ (22)	$ (18)
Cash fixed costs per year	$(1,000,000)	$(1,200,000)	$ (900,000)
Depreciation expense	$(2,000,000)	$(2,000,000)	$(2,000,000)

Break-Even Analysis

8. **(Related to Checkpoint 4) (Break-even analysis)** The Marvel Mfg. Company is considering whether or not to construct a new robotic production facility. The cost of this new facility is $600,000 and it is expected to have a six-year life with annual depreciation expense of $100,000 and no salvage value. Annual sales from the new facility are expected to be 2,000 units with a price of $1,000 per unit. Variable production costs are $600 per unit, and fixed cash expenses are $80,000 per year.

   a. Find the accounting and the cash break-even units of production.
   b. Will the plant make a profit based on its current expected level of operations?
   c. Will the plant contribute cash flow to the firm at the expected level of operations?

9. **(Related to Checkpoint 4) (Break-even analysis)**

Project	Accounting Break-Even Point (in units)	Price per Unit	Variable Cost per Unit	Fixed Costs	Depreciation
A	6,250	☐	$55	$100,000	$ 25,000
B	750	$1,000	☐	$500,000	$100,000
C	2,000	$ 20	$15	$ 5,000	☐
D	2,000	$ 20	$ 5	☐	$ 15,000

   a. Calculate the missing information for each of the above projects.
   b. Note that Projects C and D share the same accounting break-even. If sales are above the break-even point, which project would you prefer? Explain why.
   c. Calculate the cash break-even for each of the above projects. What do the differences in accounting and cash break-even tell you about the four projects?

10. **(Related to Checkpoint 4) (Break-even analysis)** Farrington Enterprises runs a number of sporting goods businesses and is currently analyzing a new T-shirt printing business. Specifically, the company is evaluating the feasibility of this business based on its estimates of unit sales, the price per unit, variable cost per unit, and fixed costs. The company's initial estimates of annual sales and other critical variables are as follows:

	Base Case
Unit sales	5,000
Price per unit	$12.00
Variable cost per unit	8.00
Fixed cash expense per year	10,000
Depreciation expense	5,000

   a. Calculate the accounting and cash break-even annual sales volume in units.
   b. Bill Farrington is the grandson of the founder of the company and is currently enrolled in his junior year at the local state university. After reviewing the accounting break-even calculation done in part a, Bill wondered if the depreciation expense should be included in the calculation. Bill had just completed his first finance class and was well aware that depreciation is not an actual out-of-pocket expense but an allocation of the cost of the printing equipment used in the business over its useful life. What do you think? What do the cash and accounting break-even points tell you?

11. **(Break-even analysis)** Niece Equipment Rentals of Del Valle, Texas, has recently been approached about the prospect of purchasing a large construction crane. The crane rents for $500 an hour but operator, fuel, insurance, and miscellaneous expenses run $200 an hour when the crane is in use. The company owner estimates that it will cost $1,000 a month to store and maintain the crane and the annual depreciation expense is $50,000.

    a. Calculate the accounting break-even number of annual rental hours needed to produce zero operating earnings from the crane (before taxes).

    b. Calculate the cash break-even point. If we ignore non-cash expenses such as depreciation in the break-even calculation, for how many hours must the crane be rented in order to break even on a cash basis?

    c. Why do we have two different break-even points? What does each one tell you?

12. **(Degree of operating leverage)** Drewery Inc. has fixed costs of $50,000 and net operating income of $17,000. If sales increase by 18 percent, by how much will NOI increase? What would happen to NOI if sales decreased by 20 percent?

13. **(Degree of operating leverage)** Brackets, Inc. currently anticipates that if it had a 10 percent increase in sales, net operating profits would increase by 60 percent. If Brackets' NOI is $14 million, what level of fixed costs does it have?

Options in Capital Budgeting

14. **(Real options)** Hurricane Katrina brought unprecedented destruction to New Orleans and the Mississippi Gulf Coast in 2005. Notably, the burgeoning casino gambling industry along the Mississippi coast was virtually wiped out overnight. CGC Corporation owns one of the oldest casinos in the Biloxi, Missouri, area, and its casino was damaged but not destroyed by the tidal surge from the storm. However, because the competitor casinos were completely destroyed and will have to be rebuilt from scratch, CGC is considering the possibility of engaging in a major renovation of the casino to transform it from a second-tier operation into one of the top gambling operations in the area. Alternatively, CGC's owners are considering a relatively modest renovation of the property and building a newer casino in Gulf Shores, Alabama, which was also devastated by the storm. Of course, CGC could just shut down the operations of the casino and move to another area of the country that allows casinos but that is less prone to hurricane damage. Identify the real options inherent in the situation faced by CGC.

15. **(Related to Checkpoint 5) (Real options and capital budgeting)** You are considering introducing a new Tex-Mex–Thai fusion restaurant. The initial outlay on this new restaurant is $6 million and the present value of the free cash flows (excluding the initial outlay) is $5 million, such that the project has a negative expected NPV of $1 million. Looking closer, you find that there is a 50 percent chance that this new restaurant will be well received and will produce annual cash flows of $800,000 per year forever (a perpetuity), whereas there is a 50 percent chance of it producing a cash flow of only $200,000 per year forever (a perpetuity) if it isn't received well. The required rate of return you use to discount the project cash flows is 10 percent. However, if the new restaurant is successful, you will be able to build 10 more of them and they will have costs and cash flows similar to the successful restaurant's costs and cash flows.

    a. In spite of the fact that the first restaurant has a negative NPV, should you build it anyway? Why or why not?

    b. What is the expected NPV for this project if only one restaurant is built but isn't well received? What is the expected NPV for this project if 10 more are built after one year and are well received?

16. **(Real options and capital budgeting)** Go-Power Batteries has developed a high-voltage nickel-metal hydride battery that can be used to power a hybrid automobile and it can sell the technology immediately to Toyota for $10 million. Alternatively, Go-Power Batteries can invest $50 million in a plant and produce the batteries for itself and sell them. Unfortunately, the present value of the cash flows from such a plant would only be $40 million, such that the plant has a negative expected NPV of –$10 million. The problem, Go-Power executives recognize, is the small size of the market for a hybrid car today. Under what assumptions might Go-Power Batteries decide not to sell the technology to Toyota and delay investment in the new plant?

Mini-Case

It's been four months since you took a position as an assistant financial analyst at Caledonia Products. During that time, you've had a promotion and you are now working as a special assistant for capital budgeting, reporting directly to the CEO. Your latest assignment involves the analysis of several risky projects. Because this is your first assignment dealing with risk analysis, you have been asked not only to provide a recommendation on the projects in question, but also to respond to a number of questions aimed at judging your understanding of risk analysis and capital budgeting. The memorandum you received outlining your assignment follows:

TO: The Special Assistant for Capital Budgeting

FROM: Mr. V. Morrison, CEO, Caledonia Products

RE: Capital Budgeting and Risk Analysis

Provide a written response to the following questions:

1. Explain how sensitivity analysis and scenario analysis are useful tools for evaluating project risk.
2. What are real options? How does the presence of optionality in the investments that firms make cause the traditionally calculated NPV of a project to be underestimated?
3. Explain how simulation works. What is the value of using a simulation approach?
4. How can break-even analysis be helpful in evaluating project risk?
5. What is sensitivity analysis, and what is its purpose?

6. Now that management is comfortable with your skills, your boss would like you to look at a new project. This new project involves the purchase of a new plasma cutting tool that can be used in its metal works division. The products manufactured using the new technology are expected to sell for an average price of $300 per unit, and the company analyst performing the analysis expects the firm can sell 20,000 units per year at this price for a period of five years. To get into this business will require the purchase of a $2 million piece of equipment that has a residual or salvage value in five years of $200,000. In addition, the firm expects to have to invest an additional $300,000 in working capital to support the new business. Other pertinent information concerning the business venture is as follows:

Initial cost of equipment	$2,000,000
Project and equipment life	5 years
Salvage value of equipment	$200,000
Working capital requirement	$300,000
Depreciation method	Straight line
Depreciation expense	$360,000
Discount rate or required rate of return	12%
Tax rate	30%

In addition, estimates for unit sales, selling price, variable cost per unit, and fixed cash operating expenses for the base-case, worst-case, and best-case scenarios are as follows:

	Expected or Base-Case	Worst-Case	Best-Case
Unit sales	20,000	15,000	25,000
Price per unit	$300	250	330
Variable cost per unit	(200)	(210)	(180)
Cash fixed costs per year	(500,000)	(450,000)	(350,000)
Depreciation expense	$360,000	$360,000	360,000

a. Estimate the cash flows for the investment under the listed base-case or expected value assumptions. Calculate the project NPV for these cash flows.

b. Evaluate the NPV of the investment under the worst-case assumptions.

c. Evaluate the NPV of the investment under the best-case assumptions.

Photo Credits

Credits are listed in order of appearance.

Monart Design/Fotolia; Andy Dean Photography/Shutterstock; Alx/Fotolia;

The Cost of Capital

The Cost of Capital

Chapter **Outline**

1 The Cost of Capital: An Overview

→ **Objective 1.** Understand the concepts underlying the firm's overall cost of capital and the purpose for its calculation.

2 Determining the Firm's Capital Structure Weights

→ **Objective 2.** Evaluate a firm's capital structure, and determine the relative importance (weight) of each source of financing.

3 Estimating the Cost of Individual Sources of Capital

→ **Objective 3.** Calculate the after-tax cost of debt, preferred stock, and common equity.

4 Summing Up: Calculating the Firm's WACC

→ **Objective 4.** Calculate a firm's weighted average cost of capital.

5 Estimating Project Costs of Capital

→ **Objective 5.** Discuss the pros and cons of using multiple, risk-adjusted discount rates. Describe the divisional cost of capital as a viable alternative for firms with multiple divisions.

6 Flotation Costs and Project NPV

→ **Objective 6.** Adjust NPV for the costs of issuing new securities when analyzing new investment opportunities.

Principles P1, P2, P3, P4, and P5 Applied

The analysis of the cost of capital that should be used in evaluating the NPV of an investment opportunity relies on all five of the fundamental principles of finance:

- The costs of individual sources of capital are estimated using observed market prices for a firm's financial claims (debt or equity securities). We use these prices because they provide the best estimates of the underlying intrinsic value of the securities—**P** Principle 4: **Market Prices Reflect Information.**

- To extract investor-required rates of return from observed market prices, we use techniques that are based on **P** Principle 1: **Money Has a Time Value** and **P** Principle 3: **Cash Flows Are the Source of Value.**

- Investors who purchase a firm's common stock require a higher expected rate of return than investors who loan money to the firm because of the risk differences between these two types of investments, which reflects **P** Principle 2: **There Is a Risk–Return Tradeoff.**

- Managers respond to the incentives, and when their incentives are not properly aligned with those of the firm's stockholders, they may make decisions that are not consistent with increasing shareholder value. For example, it is in the best interest of the manager of a company division to argue for a low cost of capital for his or her division (compared to other divisions) when it may be in the company's best interest to have a higher cost of capital. This conflict of interest reflects **P** Principle 5: **Individuals Respond to Incentives.**

Acquiring Seattle's Best Coffee Company

In the spring of 2003, Starbucks Corporation (SBUX) was analyzing the acquisition of Seattle's Best Coffee Company. At the time, the acquisition suited Starbucks' long-term strategy of expanding and building upon its leadership position in the super-premium coffee segment of the foodservice and grocery businesses. However, was Seattle's Best worth the $72 million price tag? To answer this question, Starbucks' management needed to estimate the value of Seattle's Best. This required the company to forecast future cash flows for the acquisition and calculate its net present value. But what discount rate did Starbucks use to perform this analysis of Seattle's Best Coffee Company?

The discount rate that is appropriate for the valuation of a company is known as the firm's **cost of capital**. The firm's cost of capital is the discount rate that is used to calculate the firm's overall value, and in some situations it can be used to evaluate individual investments made by the company. One way to think about the cost of capital is as an opportunity cost. Starbucks can come up with lots of ways to invest $72 million. The company can make other acquisitions, repurchase its own stock, or repay some of its debt. The return that is likely to be generated by acquiring Seattle's Best needs to be evaluated relative to these other opportunities. The opportunities that are the most relevant for determining the cost of capital for Seattle's Best are those opportunities that have the same risk as Seattle's Best.

Regardless of Your Major...

"Understanding the Role of the Cost of Capital"

Imagine for a moment that your best friend comes to you with the news that he has just inherited $300,000 and is considering the purchase of a McDonald's fast-food restaurant. Because you are both taking your first finance class and have just studied capital budgeting, you are aware of the need to forecast the relevant cash flows for the franchise, discount them back to the present, and compare their discounted sum to the initial $300,000 investment to find the project's net present value (NPV). If the NPV is positive, you would advise your friend to buy the franchise.

The discount rate used to calculate the NPV, the investment's cost of capital, can be thought of as the cost of raising the capital needed to finance the investment. This cost is actually the opportunity cost of the money invested in the project. For example, your friend who just inherited $300,000 has lots of opportunities for investing the money, so the returns that are likely to be generated by a McDonald's franchise need to be evaluated relative to those other opportunities. For example, he could buy a government-insured bank certificate of deposit and earn a 5 percent rate of return without taking any risk, or he could make a risky investment such as buying shares of the common stock of the McDonald's Corporation (MCD) and get an *expected* rate of return that is much higher than the 5 percent CD. Which of these investments would you use as the appropriate cost of capital for discounting the cash flows of the McDonald's franchise? Quite obviously the risk of the McDonald's franchise is greater than that of the insured CD, so of these two alternatives, the expected rate of return from the McDonald's stock investment is a better alternative. However, the risk of the McDonald's shares of stock will also reflect how the corporation has financed its investments, which may not be the same as how your friend will finance the McDonald's franchise; so we need to think about the mix of financing sources used when evaluating the opportunity cost of capital or the discount rate for use in calculating the NPV.

Your Turn: See Study Question 4.

1 The Cost of Capital: An Overview

In this chapter, we will examine the relationship between a security's risk and its expected return from the perspective of the firm. Indeed, we can view the returns that investors expect to receive on the firm's stocks and bonds as the cost to the firm for attracting capital.

We can also think of the **cost of capital** for a firm as a weighted average of the required returns of the securities that are used to finance the firm. We refer to this as the firm's **weighted average cost of capital**, or **WACC**. WACC not only incorporates the required rates of return of the firm's lenders and investors but also accounts for the particular mix of financing sources that the firm uses. Most firms raise capital to fund investments with a combination of debt, equity, and hybrid securities that have attributes of both debt and equity. The firm's WACC is simply a weighted average of the cost of these sources of capital to the firm. As such, a firm's WACC is a blend of the costs of borrowing money (after taxes) and the cost of raising capital from common stockholders.

The riskiness of a firm affects its WACC in two ways. The first is that the required rate of return on the debt and equity securities the firm issues will be higher if the firm is riskier. The second is that risk influences how the firm chooses the extent to which it is financed with debt and equity securities. As we will discuss in this chapter, debt interest payments are tax deductible, whereas dividend payments are not—and this tax advantage lowers the cost of debt financing relative to equity financing. For now, we will take the firm's financing mix of debt and equity securities as given.

We should point out that the firm's WACC is useful in a number of settings:

- In particular, the WACC is used to value the entire firm. When Starbucks was considering the acquisition of Seattle's Best, the first step would have been to value Seattle's Best as a stand-alone company. To do this it would want to estimate the WACC for Seattle's Best to use in discounting its estimates of the future cash flows for Seattle's Best.

- Second, the firm's WACC is often used as the starting point for determining the discount rate for investment projects the firm might undertake. For example, if Cisco Systems were evaluating a new plant location, it might begin its analysis of the appropriate discount rate with the calculation of Cisco's WACC.

- Finally, the firm's WACC is the appropriate rate to use when evaluating firm performance, specifically whether or not the firm has created value for its shareholders.

Investor's Required Return and the Firm's Cost of Capital

We often use the terms *cost of capital* and *required rate of return* interchangeably. However, we need to be a bit more careful. The cost of capital refers to the cost to the firm of a financing source. For example, if the firm borrows $100,000 from its bank and promises to pay 8 percent interest annually for the loan, then the cost of capital to the firm (before tax considerations) for that loan is 8 percent. If the bank is confident that the firm can repay the loan plus interest in accordance with the terms of the loan, then it expects to earn a return of 8 percent, and consequently the expected rate of return is also the bank's required rate of return. Similarly, we can call the return a firm's shareholders expect to earn the firm's **cost of common equity** (k_{cs}), often referred to as the cost of common stock.

When we account for the effect of taxes, however, we see a very important difference between an investor's required rate of return and the firm's cost of debt. *Specifically, the cost of debt is less than the lender's required rate of return because of the tax deductibility of interest.* This point bears repeating, for it is very important: *The after-tax cost of debt to the firm is less than the investor's required rate of return because of the tax savings that the firm receives from deducting interest expense from the firm's taxable income.* Each dollar paid in interest can be deducted from the firm's taxable income, and this reduces the firm's taxes by an amount equal to the product of the interest expense times the corporate tax rate. Consequently, the after-tax cost of capital for the firm's debt is equal to the investor's required rate of return multiplied by 1 minus the tax rate. In contrast to interest payments, dividends are not tax deductible, which means that the costs of capital associated with preferred and common stock are equal to the investors' required rates of return on these sources of financing.

WACC Equation

Equation (1) defines the WACC as the weighted average of the estimated after-tax costs of the firm's debt and equity capital:

$$
\begin{pmatrix} \text{Weighted} \\ \text{Average Cost} \\ \text{of Capital } (WACC) \end{pmatrix} = \left[\begin{pmatrix} \text{After-tax Cost} \\ \text{of Debt } (k_d) \end{pmatrix} \times \begin{pmatrix} \text{Proportion of} \\ \text{Capital Raised} \\ \text{by Debt } (w_d) \end{pmatrix} \right]
$$

$$
+ \left[\begin{pmatrix} \text{Cost of Common} \\ \text{Stock } (k_{cs}) \end{pmatrix} \times \begin{pmatrix} \text{Proportion of} \\ \text{Capital Raised} \\ \text{by Common Stock } (w_{cs}) \end{pmatrix} \right] \quad \textbf{(1)}
$$

Note that only the cost of debt is adjusted for the effects of taxes. The reason for this is that only interest is tax deductible. That is, interest expense is deducted from operating earnings before income taxes are calculated, whereas preferred and common stock dividends are paid out of the firm's net income after taxes have been paid.

The following table contains a quick reference guide to an expanded version of Equation (1). We will use this formula to evaluate a firm's WACC. You will find this listing helpful as we work through the calculation of WACC.

Tools of Financial Analysis—Weighted Average Cost of Capital

Name of Tool	Formula	What It Tells You
Weighted Average Cost of Capital (k_{WACC})	$k_d \times (1 - T) \times w_d + k_{ps} \times w_{ps} + k_{cs} \times w_{cs}$ Definitions: • k_d is the required rate of return on the firm's debt. Correspondingly, the after-tax cost of debt to the firm is $k_d (1 - T)$. • T is the firm's marginal tax rate. • k_{ps} is the required rate of return of the firm's preferred stockholders and the cost of preferred equity capital to the firm. • k_{cs} is the required rate of return of the firm's common stockholders and the cost of common equity capital to the firm. • w_d is the fraction of the firm's total financing that is comprised of debt financing. • w_{ps} is the proportion of the firm's total financing that is comprised of preferred stock. • w_{cs} is the proportion of the firm's total financing that is comprised of common stock. Key Assumptions: • Required rates of return reflect current market rates of return. • The weights used to determine the relative importance of each of the firm's sources of capital reflect the current market values (not historical book values) of each source of capital. • The firm's capital structure and the costs of each source of capital do not change over time, so the WACC remains constant.	• The after-tax rate of return the firm pays for its invested capital • Investments in the firm's long-term assets (capital expenditures) must earn at least this rate of return in order to increase shareholder value.

Three-Step Procedure for Estimating the Firm's WACC

We can summarize the mechanics of calculating the firm's WACC using Equation (1) in the three-step procedure illustrated in Figure 1. The steps are as follows:

Step 1. **Define the firm's capital structure.** Evaluate the firm's mix of debt and equity financing (commonly referred to as its capital structure) and determine the relative importance of each component in the mix listed in column (1) of Figure 1. In column (2), we can see the importance (weight) of each source of capital, which is based on the current market value of each source of capital.

Step 2. **Estimate the opportunity cost of each of the sources of financing.** These costs are equal to the investor's required rates of return after adjusting the cost of debt for the effects of taxes, as shown in column (3). To estimate these costs, we'll use the current market value of each source of capital based on its current, not historical, costs.

Step 3. **Calculate a weighted average of the costs of each source of financing.** Finally, in column (4) we calculate the product of the after-tax cost of each capital source used by the firm and the weight associated with each source. The sum of these products is the weighted average cost of capital at the bottom of column (4). Consequently, the firm's WACC is nothing but a weighted average of the costs of each source of capital used by the firm, where the weights capture the relative importance of each source of capital to the firm's capital structure.

Here is a helpful tip for checking your calculation of the WACC. Because we are calculating a weighted average of the individual required rates of return, a useful "check" of your calculation is to make sure that the average you calculate falls between the after-tax cost of debt (the cheapest source of financing) and the required rate of return from the common stockholders (the most expensive source of financing).

Figure 1

A Template for Calculating WACC

A firm's WACC is a weighted average of the after-tax costs of each source of capital used by the firm in its capital structure. The following template demonstrates how to carry out the calculation of the WACC from Equation (1):

(1) Source of Capital (Note a)	(2) Market Value Weights (Note b)		(3) After-tax Cost of Financing (Note c)		(4) Product of (2) and (3) (Note d)
Debt	w_d	$\times$	$k_d(1-T)$	$=$	$w_d \times k_d(1-T)$
Preferred stock	w_{ps}	$\times$	k_{ps}	$=$	$w_{ps} \times k_{ps}$
Common equity	w_{cs}	$\times$	k_{cs}	$=$	$w_{cs} \times k_{cs}$
Sum =	100%				$WACC$

Notes:

Note a—The sources of capital included in the WACC calculation include all interest-bearing debt (short- and long-term) but exclude non-interest-bearing debt such as accounts payable and accrued expenses. In addition, preferred stock and common equity are included. The total of all the market values of all the capital sources included in the WACC computation is generally referred to as the firm's *enterprise value,* and the mix of debt and equity defines the firm's capital structure.

Note b—The weights used to average the costs of each source of capital should reflect the relative importance of each source of capital to the firm's value on the date of the analysis. This means that the proper weights are based on the market values of each source of capital as a percent of the sum of the market values of all sources.

Note c—The investor's required rate of return is the basis for estimating the cost of capital for each source of financing to the firm. However, because interest on the firm's debt is tax deductible to the firm, we must adjust the lender's required rate of return to an after-tax basis. The required rates of return for each source of financing, like the weights used to average them, should reflect current estimates based on current market conditions.

Note d—The weighted average of the individual costs of each source of capital is found by summing the product of the weights and costs of each source.

>> END FIGURE 1

Before you move on to 2

Concept Check | 1

1. How is an investor's required rate of return related to the firm's cost of capital?
2. Why is the firm's cost of capital calculated as a weighted average?
3. List the three-step procedure used to estimate a firm's weighted average cost of capital.

2 Determining the Firm's Capital Structure Weights

We illustrate how to calculate the WACC using the example of Templeton Extended Care Facilities, Inc. Templeton Extended Care owns and operates a chain of over 100 long-term care residences designed to meet the needs of the aging U.S. population. Each of these facilities provides a range of housing and support services designed for retirees who are capable of living with varying degrees of independence, ranging from apartments for those still able to care for all their needs to a full nursing home facility for those needing 24-hour care. In the spring of 2013, Templeton's debt had a market value of $100 million. In addition, the firm had $50 million outstanding in a preferred stock issue (2 million shares with a current market price of $25 per share), and the firm's common equity had a total market value of $250 million (20 million shares with a current market price of $12.50 per share).

Templeton is considering the acquisition of a small chain of similar facilities run by a competitor and wants to evaluate whether the investment opportunity has a positive NPV. As an initial step in making the analysis, Templeton's CFO wants to determine his firm's WACC.

The first step in our analysis of WACC is the determination of the weights placed on each of the sources of capital. In the case of Templeton Extended Care, these sources of capital include the firm's debt, preferred stock, and common equity.

We need to be a bit careful here when talking about invested capital, for it does not include everything on the right-hand side of the firm's balance sheet. A firm's capital structure includes the firm's interest-bearing debt (both short-term and long-term), preferred equity, and common equity. Interest-bearing debt includes things like bank loans (short- and long-term) as well as any bonds the firm has issued. To see the difference between a firm's balance sheet and the capital structure used to calculate the firm's WACC, consider the right-hand side of Templeton Extended Care's balance sheet:

($ millions)	Balance Sheet (Book Values)	Capital Structure (Market Values)
Accounts Payable	$ 20	
Accrued Expenses	30	
Short-Term Debt	25	$ 25
Long-Term Debt	75	75
Preferred Stock	50	50
Common Stock	100	250
Total	$300	$400

Note that the firm has total financing equal to $300 million based on book values of all the sources of financing found on the right-hand side of the firm's balance sheet. However, the market value of the firm's capital structure totals $400 million even though we exclude both accounts payable and accrued expenses.

Accounts payable and accrued expenses that are excluded from the capital structure components *do* have a cost; however, their costs are included in the prices the firm pays for the goods and services that give rise to the creation of the accounts payable and accrued expenses. So to include the cost of accounts payable and accrued expenses in the calculation of the WACC and also include them in the calculation of the firm's cash flow would effectively count them twice.

In theory, we should determine the weights used to calculate WACC based on observed market prices for each of the firm's securities (be they debt or equity) multiplied by the number of outstanding securities. In practice, however, capital structure weights are often calculated using market values for equity securities (preferred and common stock) and book values for debt securities. The market prices of equity securities are readily available, so an analyst can simply multiply the current market prices of the securities by the number of shares outstanding to calculate total market values. For debt securities, book values are often substituted for market values, because market prices for corporate debt are often difficult to obtain. However, when market values of debt are available, they should be used in place of book values.

Checkpoint 1 demonstrates the three-step procedure for the calculation of a firm's WACC in further detail.

Checkpoint 1

Calculating the WACC for Templeton Extended Care Facilities, Inc.

In the spring of 2013, Templeton was considering the acquisition of a chain of extended care facilities and wanted to estimate its own WACC as a guide to the cost of capital for the acquisition. Templeton's capital structure consists of the following:

	Market Values
Debt	$100 million
Preferred stock	50 million
Common stock	250 million
	$400 million

Templeton contacted the firm's investment banker to get estimates of the firm's current cost of financing and was told that if the firm were to borrow the same amount of money today, it would have to pay lenders 8 percent; however, given the firm's 25 percent tax rate, the after-tax cost of borrowing would only be 6% = 8%(1 − .25). Preferred stockholders currently demand a 10 percent rate of return, and common stockholders demand 15 percent.

Templeton's CFO knew that the WACC would be somewhere between 6 percent and 15 percent because the firm's capital structure is a blend of the three sources of capital whose costs are bounded by this range.

STEP 1: Picture the problem

The weighted average cost of capital combines the after-tax cost of financing for each of the firm's sources of capital in a weighted average, where the weights are proportionate to the relative importance of each source of financing in the firm's capital structure (note that these are market—not book—values) as follows:

	Capital Structure	Calculation	Weights
Debt (short- and long-term)	$100	$100/$400 =	0.250
Preferred stock	50	$ 50/$400 =	0.125
Common stock	250	$250/$400 =	0.625
Total	$400		1.000

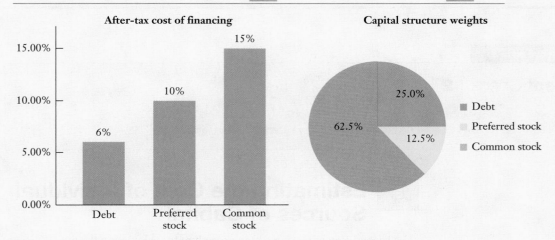

STEP 2: Decide on a solution strategy

To calculate the weighted average, we sum the products of the after-tax cost of each source of financing multiplied by its corresponding capital structure weight as defined in Equation (1), that is,

$$WACC = (k_d \times (1 - T) \times w_d) + (k_{ps} \times w_{ps}) + (k_{cs} \times w_{cs}) \tag{1}$$

where k_d is the required rate of return on the firm's debt; k_{ps} is the rate of return required by the firm's preferred stockholders; k_{cs} is the rate of return required by the firm's common stockholders; T is the firm's marginal tax rate on corporate income; w_d is the proportion of the firm's total financing that has been raised by borrowing; w_{ps} is the proportion of the firm's total financing consisting of preferred stock; and w_{cs} is the proportion of the firm's total financing consisting of common stock.

STEP 3: Solve

Using the template found in Figure 1, we calculate Templeton's WACC as follows:

Source	Weights ×	After-tax Cost of Financing =	Product
Debt	0.250	0.060	0.015
Preferred Stock	0.125	0.100	0.0125
Common Stock	0.625	0.150	0.09375
	100.0%	WACC =	0.12125 or 12.125%

(1 CONTINUED >> ON NEXT PAGE)

STEP 4: Analyze

Templeton's CFO estimated that the firm's WACC is 12.125 percent, which lies within the range between the highest cost source of capital (common stock at 15 percent) and the lowest (debt at 6 percent). The weighted average is much closer to the cost of common equity than to the cost of debt, because 62.5 percent of the firm's financing has been raised from common stock. We have carried the WACC calculation out to three decimal places, which suggests that we are able to measure the WACC with a great deal of precision.

STEP 5: Check yourself

After completing her estimate of Templeton's WACC, the CFO decided to explore the possibility of adding more low-cost debt to the capital structure. With the help of the firm's investment banker, the CFO learned that Templeton could probably push its use of debt to 37.5 percent of the firm's capital structure by issuing more debt and retiring (repurchasing) the firm's preferred shares. This could be done without increasing the firm's costs of borrowing or the required rate of return demanded by the firm's common stockholders. What is your estimate of the WACC for Templeton under this new capital structure proposal?

ANSWER: WACC = 11.625%.

Your Turn: For more practice, do related **Study Problem** 22 at the end of this chapter.   >> **END Checkpoint 1**

Before you move on to 3

Concept Check | 2

1. Should book or market values be used to determine the weights used in calculating the WACC? Explain.
2. Why are accounts payable not included in the capital structure used to estimate a firm's WACC?

---

3 | Estimating the Cost of Individual Sources of Capital

The second step in our three-step procedure for calculating the overall cost of capital calls for us to estimate the opportunity cost for each of the sources of financing, including both debt and equity. Before returning to our Templeton Extended Care example, let's look at how a company measures its costs of debt, preferred equity, and common equity. As you will notice, in extracting investor-required rates of return from observed market prices, we use techniques that have their roots in ⓟ Principle 1: **Money Has a Time Value** and ⓟ Principle 3: **Cash Flows Are the Source of Value**.

The Cost of Debt

Because we infer the cost of debt using its current market price, the key to estimating the cost of any source of capital is based on the application of ⓟ Principle 4: **Market Prices Reflect Information**. The **cost of debt** is the rate of return the firm's lenders demand when they loan money to the firm.

Do not confuse the cost of new debt with the coupon rate on a firm's outstanding debt. The coupon rate is the contractual rate of interest the firm must pay on the outstanding principal amount of the new debt, a rate set in the bond indenture when the debt was first issued.

We estimate the market's required rate of return on a firm's debt by using its yield to maturity. The yield to maturity is a reasonable estimate of the bondholder's required rate of return for bonds with a low risk of default. However, for bonds with a higher risk of default, the calculated yield to maturity *overstates* the bondholder's required rate of return. Thus, using the yield to maturity to estimate required rates of return for bonds with high default risk will result in a slightly higher estimated cost of capital. When this cost of capital is used to evaluate new investment projects it will result in the rejection of some marginal projects. Even so, the yield to maturity is commonly used as an estimate of the cost of debt.

To illustrate, consider the $1,000 par (face) value bond issued by Brainmo, Inc. The bond has a coupon interest rate of 7 percent and pays interest annually. The bond's current price is $945 and it matures in 20 years. The yield to maturity on this bond is calculated to be 7.54 percent,

Enter	20		-945	70	1,000
	N	I/Y	PV	PMT	FV
Solve for		7.54%			

But keep in mind that this is the *before-tax cost of debt*, and the *after-tax cost of debt* to the firm is $k_d(1 - T)$. Thus, if the firm's marginal tax rate is 40 percent, then the after-tax cost of Brainmo's debt is $7.54\%(1 - .4) = 4.52\%$.

Calculating the required rate of return for a firm's debt is straightforward when we have all the requisite information. Unfortunately, the majority of corporate bonds do not trade in public markets so we cannot observe their current market price and therefore cannot calculate their yields to maturity. Because of this, it is standard practice to estimate the cost of debt using the yield to maturity on a portfolio of bonds with a similar credit rating and maturity as the firm's outstanding debt.

Figure 2 provides a description of the corporate bond rating systems used by the three primary credit rating agencies. The highest ratings (Aaa or AAA) go to those firms with the

---

Figure 2

A Guide to Corporate Bond Ratings

Three firms are the primary sources of default ratings on corporate debt: Moody's, S&P, and Fitch. Investment grade debt is rated Baa3 and BBB– or higher.

Moody's	S&P	Fitch	Definitions
Aaa	AAA	AAA	Prime. Maximum Safety
Aa1	AA+	AA+	High Grade High Quality
Aa2	AA	AA	
Aa3	AA–	AA–	
A1	A+	A+	Upper Medium Grade
A2	A	A	
A3	A–	A–	
Baa1	BBB+	BBB+	Lower Medium Grade
Baa2	BBB	BBB	
Baa3	BBB–	BBB–	
Ba1	BB+	BB+	Non-Investment Grade
Ba2	BB	BB	Speculative
Ba3	BB–	BB–	
B1	B+	B+	Highly Speculative
B2	B	B	
B3	B–	B–	
Caa1	CCC+	CCC	Substantial Risk
Caa2	CCC	–	In Poor Standing
Caa3	CCC–	–	
Ca	–	–	Extremely Speculative
C	–	–	May be in Default
–	–	DDD	Default
–	–	DD	
–	D	D	

>> END FIGURE 2

Figure 3

Corporate Bond Yields: Default Ratings and Term to Maturity

Yield to maturity for corporate bonds, arrayed by default rating and term to maturity. These data are representative of first quarter 2013, and are typical for this time period. However, you would want to use the most recent data available when analyzing the cost of debt financing. Note that as the credit rating falls, the yield to maturity rises. Also, the yield to maturity typically increases for longer-maturity bonds.

Rating	1 yr	2 yr	3 yr	5 yr	7 yr	10 yr	30 yr
Aaa/AAA	0.22	0.31	0.42	0.76	1.26	2.00	3.41
Aa1/AA+	0.26	0.43	0.58	0.96	1.46	2.17	3.62
Aa2/AA	0.29	0.55	0.74	1.16	1.66	2.35	3.83
Aa3/AA−	0.31	0.58	0.77	1.20	1.70	2.39	3.88
A1/A+	0.32	0.60	0.80	1.23	1.73	2.43	3.93
A2/A	0.55	0.80	0.98	1.40	1.89	2.57	4.03
A3/A−	0.62	0.95	1.18	1.66	2.19	2.92	4.51
Baa1/BBB+	0.83	1.19	1.42	1.91	2.45	3.18	4.80
Baa2/BBB	1.00	1.39	1.65	2.17	2.73	3.48	5.17
Baa3/BBB−	1.49	1.87	2.11	2.62	3.16	3.91	5.56
Ba1/BB+	2.27	2.64	2.90	3.41	3.98	4.75	6.37
Ba2/BB	3.04	3.41	3.68	4.21	4.79	5.58	7.19
Ba3/BB−	3.82	4.18	4.47	5.00	5.61	6.42	8.00
B1/B+	4.60	4.95	5.25	5.79	6.42	7.26	8.82
B2/B	5.38	5.72	6.04	6.59	7.24	8.10	9.63
B3/B−	6.15	6.49	6.82	7.38	8.06	8.93	10.45
Caa/CCC+	6.93	7.26	7.61	8.17	8.87	9.77	11.26
U.S. Treasury Yield	0.18	0.25	0.32	0.60	1.00	1.59	2.76

Legend:
These data are actually reported as "spread to Treasury yields," so for a 30-year Baa1/BBB+ corporate bond the yield would be reported as 204 basis points over the 30-year Treasury yield of 2.76%. A basis point is 1/100th of a percent, so 204 basis points correspond to 2.04%.

>> END FIGURE 3

very lowest probability of default. Consequently, these bonds will offer the lowest yield to maturity to investors who purchase them. Figure 3 contains sample bond yields to maturity for corporate bonds with maturities ranging from 1 to 30 years and for all rating groups. So, for example, if your firm has Baa/BBB+ default rating, the yield to maturity on new 30-year bonds would have been about 6.26 percent on December 6, 2012.

Although yields on corporate bonds vary over time, and the data found in Figure 3 provides only a snapshot of a particular day, we can make some important observations from the data:

- First, higher-rated bonds such as AAA bonds are observed to have lower yields than the lower-rated bonds. This observation reflects **P** Principle 2: **There Is a Risk–Return Tradeoff.**
- Second, yields tend to be higher for longer-maturity bonds. This pattern of yields and terms to maturity is called the *term structure* of corporate bond yields. Although this upward sloping term structure is generally the pattern we see in yields, the term structure sometimes slopes downward or peaks in intermediate terms to maturity.

The Cost of Preferred Equity

The **cost of preferred equity** is the rate of return investors require of the firm when they purchase its preferred stock. Note that because the dividends paid to preferred stockholders come out of after-tax income, we do not adjust the cost of preferred stock for taxes as we did the cost of debt.

Estimating the cost of preferred stock is straightforward, because it typically pays the holder a fixed dividend each period, forever. We can find the present value of a constant stream of dividends as follows:

$$\text{Preferred Stock Price } (P_{ps}) = \frac{\text{Preferred Dividend } (Div_{ps})}{\text{Preferred Stockholder's Required Rate of Return } (k_{ps})} \qquad (2)$$

Because we know the amount of the preferred dividend and can observe the price of the preferred stock, we can calculate the preferred stockholder's required rate of return (k_{ps}) by solving Equation (2) for k_{ps}, as follows:

$$k_{ps} = \frac{Div_{ps}}{P_{ps}} \qquad (2a)$$

where: k_{ps} = the required rate of return of the firm's preferred stockholders and the cost of preferred equity capital to the firm.

$$Div_{ps} = \text{the preferred stock dividend}$$

Because preferred stock dividends are paid from the firm's after-tax earnings and are not tax deductible (unlike interest on the firm's debt), the investor's required rate of return is also the company's after-tax cost of capital for preferred stock.[1]

Consider the preferred shares issued by Alabama Power Company (ALP-PP), which pay a 5.3 percent annual dividend on a $25.00 par value, or $1.25 per share. On May 24, 2006, these preferred shares were selling for $23.35 per share. Consequently, investors required a 5.67 percent return on these shares, calculated as follows:

$$k_{ps} = \frac{\$1.325}{\$23.35} = .0567 \text{ or } 5.67\%$$

Tools of Financial Analysis—Cost of Preferred Stock

Name of Tool	Formula	What It Tells You
Cost of Preferred Stock (k_{ps})	$\dfrac{\text{Preferred Dividend } (Div_{ps})}{\text{Price of Preferred Stock}(P_{ps})}$	• The rate of return that the firm's preferred shareholders expect to receive from investing in the firm • Preferred stock generally calls for a fixed cash dividend payment • The cost of capital to the firm raised by the issuance of preferred stock.

The Cost of Common Equity

The cost of common equity capital (k_{cs}) is the cost of common equity financing to the firm, and is the rate of return investors *expect* to receive from investing in the firm's stock, which in turn reflects the risk of investing in the equity of the firm. This return comes in the form of cash distributions (dividends and cash proceeds from the sale of the stock).

---

[1] The cost of preferred stock calculated using Equation (2a) somewhat overstates the expected cost of preferred equity. The reason for this is that the contractually promised preferred dividend is the maximum dividend the preferred shareholders will receive, and because there is some chance that the dividend may not be paid, the expected dividend will be less than the contractually promised dividend. Even so, it is common practice to use this yield calculation to estimate the required rate of return for preferred stock. This is the same issue that we mentioned with respect to very risky debt financing where the promised interest and principal of the debt is used to estimate the investor's required rate of return.

Unfortunately, this cost is the most difficult estimate we have to make in evaluating a firm's cost of capital. The difficulty arises because the common shareholders do not have a contractually defined return like the interest on a bond or a preferred dividend rate for preferred stock. Instead, the common stockholders are the residual claimants of the firm's earnings. This means that they receive their return out of what is *left over* after the bondholders and preferred stockholders have been paid.

In estimating the cost of common equity, we will review two different approaches that are both widely used. The first relies on the discounted cash flow valuation of the firm's shares of stock, called the dividend growth model. The second uses the Capital Asset Pricing Model (CAPM). Because we are estimating the stockholder's required rate of return, it is generally considered good practice to use both approaches to better calibrate our estimate.

The Dividend Growth Model: Discounted Cash Flow Approach

The first approach to estimating a firm's cost of common equity is often referred to as the *dividend growth model approach*. Using this approach, we first estimate the expected stream of dividends that the common stock is expected to provide to the stockholder. With these dividend estimates as the estimated cash flows from the stock, along with the firm's current stock price, we can calculate the internal rate of return on the stock investment. This internal rate of return is then used as an estimate of the rate of return an investor expects to receive from holding the stock.

In theory, the dividend growth model approach requires that we have estimates for the dividends that will be paid in each year in the foreseeable future. In practice, however, analysts tend to use Gordon's Growth Model. This model assumes that dividends are expected to grow forever at a constant rate of g, and this rate g is less than the investor's required rate of return, k_{cs}. Under these assumptions, the value of a share of common stock, P_{cs}, can be written as follows:

$$\frac{\text{Market Price}}{\text{of Common Stock } (P_{cs})} = \frac{\text{Common Stock Dividend for Year 1 } (D_1)}{\left(\begin{array}{c}\text{Common Equity Required}\\\text{Rate of Return } (k_{cs})\end{array}\right) - \left(\begin{array}{c}\text{Growth Rate in}\\\text{Dividends } (g)\end{array}\right)} \tag{3}$$

Solving Equation (3) for the investor's required rate of return, we get an equation we can use to estimate the cost of common equity capital, that is,

$$k_{cs} = \frac{D_1}{P_{cs}} + g \tag{3a}$$

To illustrate the use of the dividend growth model in estimating the cost of common equity, we present the Pearson case described in Checkpoint 2. Pearson plc is a London-based publishing company that publishes textbooks and business information and also owns and operates the *Financial Times* newspaper.

Estimating the Rate of Growth, *g*

The key factor required to implement an estimate of the cost of common equity using the dividend growth model in Equation (3a) is the constant rate of growth in dividends. Remember that this growth rate is assumed to characterize the growth in the firm's dividends into the indefinite future (forever). Analysts typically estimate and publish earnings growth rates for the coming year and the next five years, available on such sources as Yahoo! Finance. These growth rates may provide a useful starting point in our estimation of the constant rate of growth in dividends over a much longer period of time.

Tools of Financial Analysis—Cost of Equity (Dividend Growth Model)

Name of Tool	Formula	What It Tells You
Cost of Common Equity (Dividend Growth Model) (k_{cs})	$\dfrac{D_1}{P_{cs}} + g$ Definitions: • $D_1 = D_0(1+g)$ is the dividend expected to be received by the firm's common shareholders one year in the future. That is, the most recent dividend paid to the common shareholders, D_0, multiplied by 1 plus the expected rate of growth in dividends, g. • g = the expected rate of growth in dividends each year, forever. This growth rate is expected to be constant for all future years such that the expected dividend in Year 1 is equal to the most recent dividend paid (D_0) multiplied by 1 plus the annual rate of growth in dividends. • k_{cs} = the investor's required rate of return for investing in the firm's shares of common stock. Key Assumptions: • The rate of growth in common stock dividends, g, is the same for all future years. • The rate of growth in dividends must be less than the rate of return the stockholder requires to invest in the firm's shares. The latter assumption may seem a bit odd, but it is critical and very reasonable once you think about it. For example, how much would you be willing to pay for an investment where the rate of increase in the cash flow you receive each year is greater than the rate of return you want, given the risk of the investment?	• The rate of return that the firm's common shareholders expect to receive from investing in the firm • The cost of equity capital to the firm before considering the cost of raising new equity capital.

In addition to observing analysts' estimates of earnings growth rates, we can also estimate our own growth rates using historical dividend data. Consider the following set of dividend payments:

Year	Dividend	$ Change	% Change
2009	$0.800		
2010	0.825	$0.025	3.1%
2011	0.840	0.015	1.8%
2012	0.875	0.035	4.2%
2013	0.900	0.025	2.9%
	Arithmetic Average		3.0%
	Geometric Average		2.99%

Note first that the dividends in this example always increase (although the amount of the dollar change from year to year varies). This is fairly typical of most firms. The percent change, or growth, in dividends from year to year ranges from a low of 1.8 percent to a high of 4.2 percent. If we take a simple average of the "% Change" column, we get an average annual percent change in dividends of 3 percent. Although we could use 3 percent as our estimate of the growth rate in dividends over the 2009–2013 period, this approach can prove to be misleading in some instances. Specifically, the compound rate of growth is the geometric mean of the annual growth rates, and because the geometric average rate of growth captures the effects of compounding, this mean is lower than the arithmetic mean. However, in most cases the difference between the arithmetic and geometric means will be slight and we can use the simpler arithmetic mean as our estimated rate of growth.

Pros and Cons of the Dividend Growth Model Approach

The primary appeal of the dividend growth model is its simplicity. To estimate an investor's required rate of return, the analyst only needs to observe the current dividend and stock price and then estimate the rate of growth in future dividends.

Estimating the Cost of Common Equity for Pearson plc Using the Dividend Growth Model

Pearson plc (PSO) is an international media company that operates three business groups: Pearson Education, the *Financial Times,* and Penguin. In the fall of 2012, Pearson's CFO called for an update of the firm's cost of capital. The first phase of the estimation focused on the firm's cost of common equity. How would the CFO determine the cost of the company's equity, using the dividend growth model?

STEP 1: Picture the problem

The financial analyst who got the assignment decided to first look at the dividend growth model to get an initial estimate of the cost of common equity. The equation for the cost of common equity using the dividend growth model describes the cost of common equity as the sum of two components: the expected dividend yield for the coming year (D_1/P_{cs}) plus the expected rate of growth in dividends, g.

$$k_{cs} = \frac{D_1}{P_{cs}} + g \tag{3a}$$

We need three numbers to carry out the estimate of the cost of common equity. Two of the numbers can be observed: the firm's stock price, which closed at $19.39 on December 4, 2012, and Pearson's 2011 common stock dividend of $0.49 per share. The remaining number needed to solve Equation (3a) is the growth rate in future dividends, which stock analysts estimate to be 6.25 percent.

STEP 2: Decide on a solution strategy

To estimate the dividend for 2012, which has not taken place yet, we multiply Pearson's $0.49 dividend for 2011 by 1 plus the estimated rate of growth in dividends of 6.25 percent. Although we could attempt an estimate of this growth rate, it is standard practice to rely on outside equity analysts whose estimates of growth in earnings (and, consequently, dividends) are published regularly in analyst reports found on the Internet (e.g., at Yahoo! Finance). All that is required now is to substitute these values into Equation (3a).

STEP 3: Solve

Substituting into Equation (3a), we calculate our estimate of the cost of common equity for Pearson as

$$k_{cs} = \frac{D_1}{P_{cs}} + g \text{ or substituting for } D_1 = D_0(1 + g)$$

$$k_{cs} = \frac{D_0(1 + g)}{P_{cs}} + g = \frac{\$0.49(1 + .0625)}{\$19.39} + .0625 = .0269 + .0625 = .0894 \text{ or } 8.94\%$$

STEP 4: Analyze

Pearson's cost of common equity is estimated to be 11.2 percent. The key driver of this estimate is the growth rate in Pearson's dividends, which Pearson's analyst established at 6.25 percent. This is a very difficult estimate to make, and the number we choose has a dramatic impact on the estimated cost of common equity.

Of course, forecasting the growth rate of a firm's dividends is likely to be difficult and subject to errors. Indeed, the examples we have presented here assume that dividends are expected to grow at a constant rate, *g,* forever, which is clearly an oversimplification. In practice, analysts often use more complex valuation models in which dividends are expected to grow for, say, five years at one rate and then grow at a lower rate from Year 6 forward. Consequently, these models require that the analyst estimate the period of initial growth as well as two different growth rates.

The Capital Asset Pricing Model

The Capital Asset Pricing Model (CAPM) was designed to determine the expected or required rate of return for risky investments. As Equation (4) illustrates, the expected return on common stock is determined by three key ingredients—the risk-free rate of interest, the beta or systematic risk of the common stock's returns, and the market risk premium. The product of the beta coefficient and the market risk premium defines the risk premium for the common equity. Thus, we determine the risk premium for a particular firm's common equity by its systematic risk (or beta) and the market risk premium.

$$\underset{\text{Equity } (k_{cs})}{\text{Cost of Common}} = \underset{\text{Rate } (r_f)}{\text{Risk-Free}} + \overbrace{\underset{\text{Coefficient } (\beta_{cs})}{\text{Equity Beta}} \underbrace{\left(\underset{\text{the Market Portfolio } (r_m)}{\text{Expected Return on}} - \underset{\text{Rate } (r_f)}{\text{Risk-Free}} \right)}_{\text{Market Risk Premium}}}^{\substack{\text{Risk Premium for Common Equity} \\ (= \text{Equity Beta} \times \text{Market Risk Premium})}} \qquad (4)$$

Important Definitions and Concepts:

- **Risk-free rate (r_f).** The rate of return an investor could expect to earn where there is no risk that the return on the investment or the money invested will not be received. Typically, the rate of return on U.S. Treasury securities is used as an estimate of this rate.
- **Common stock beta coefficient (β_{cs}).** Beta is a measure of the systematic risk of the common stock's returns. Systematic risk reflects how the returns earned by a risky investment co-vary with the returns earned by the market portfolio of all risky investments.
- **Market risk premium ($r_m - r_f$).** The difference in the rate of return that an investor expects to earn from investing in the market portfolio, comprised of all risky investments, and the risk-free rate.

Advantages of the CAPM Approach

The CAPM approach has two important advantages over the dividend growth rate model approach:

- First, the model is simple and easy to understand and calculate because it is simply the sum of two components: the risk-free rate of interest and the firm's risk premium.
- Second, because the model does not rely on dividends or any assumption about the growth rate in dividends, it can be applied to companies that do not currently pay dividends or are not expected to experience a constant rate of growth in dividends.

Disadvantages of the CAPM Approach

The CAPM approach suffers from some important disadvantages that arise because of difficulties in estimating the three variables that determine the cost of common equity (the risk-free rate, the beta coefficient, and the market risk premium).

- **Specifying the Risk-Free Rate.** The analyst has a wide range of U.S. government securities that can be used as the risk-free rate. Treasury securities with maturities from 30 days to 30 years are readily available, but the CAPM offers no guidance as to the appropriate choice. For applications of the cost of capital for long-term capital expenditure decisions, it seems reasonable to select a risk-free rate of comparable maturity. It is now customary to use the 10-year Treasury bond rate as the measure of the risk-free rate of return.

- **Estimating Beta.** Analysts can obtain estimates of beta coefficients from a wide variety of investment advisory services, such as Merrill Lynch and Value Line. Alternatively, they can use historical stock market returns for the company of interest and a general market index (such as the Standard and Poor's 500) to estimate the stock's beta. There are slight differences in the methodologies and time periods used to estimate beta, which is why beta estimates from various sources generally differ. For example, ExxonMobil's (XOM) beta estimates from Merrill Lynch, Value Line, and Yahoo! Finance ranged from 0.60 to 1.14; Lockheed Martin's (LMT) beta ranged from –0.30 to .70; and Starbucks' beta ranged from 0.62 to 1.21.

- **Estimating the Market's Risk Premium.** Finally, the analyst can estimate the market risk premium by looking at the history of stock returns and the premium earned over the risk-free rate of interest. Since 1926, common stocks have earned an average annual return of 9.8 percent, a premium of roughly 4.4 percent over long-term government bonds and 6.1 percent over short-term Treasury Bills.[2]

Estimates of the market's risk premium (even based on a single risk-free rate such as the 10-year U.S. Treasury bond) vary widely and have drifted downward over recent years. For our purposes we will use an estimate of 5 percent for the market's risk premium.

Checkpoint 3

Estimating the Cost of Common Equity for Pearson plc using the CAPM

A review of current market conditions on December 4, 2012, reveals that the 30-year U.S. Treasury bond yield that we will use to measure the risk-free rate was 2.78 percent, the estimated market risk premium is 6.5 percent, and the beta for Pearson's common stock is .99.

Determine Pearson's cost of common equity using the CAPM, as of December 4, 2012.

STEP 1: Picture the problem

The CAPM describes the relationship between the expected rates of return on risky assets in terms of their systematic risk. That is,

$$k_{cs} = r_f + \beta_{cs}(r_m - r_f) \tag{4}$$

The **risk premium** for a common stock issue is estimated as the risky common stock's beta, β_{cs}, multiplied by the market risk premium for the portfolio of all risky assets $(r_m - r_f)$. If the market risk premium for all risky assets is

---

[2]Analysts not only "look backward" at history to estimate the market risk premium but also "look forward" to infer the market risk premium using the Gordon Growth model with observed security prices and analyst-estimated earnings growth. These forward-looking risk premium estimates tend to be approximately 5 percent, which is somewhat lower than those observed from historical data.

6.5 percent, and the common stock's beta is .99, then the market risk premium for the common stock is equal to .999 times 6.5 percent, or 6.44 percent.

In graphic terms,

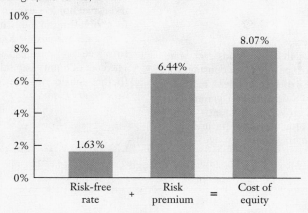

The risk premium for Pearson is the product of the market risk premium for all risky assets, which we estimated to be 6.5 percent at the time of the estimate, multiplied by Pearson's beta coefficient, which is .99 (i.e., .99 × 6.5% = 6.44%).

STEP 2: Decide on a solution strategy

Estimating the cost of common equity for Pearson requires that we arrive at estimates of two market factors and one firm-specific factor. The market factors in Equation (4) consist of the risk-free rate of interest (which we observe to be 1.63 percent at the time of the analysis) and the market risk premium (estimated to be 6.5 percent), and the firm-specific factor is Pearson's beta coefficient (which is estimated to be .99).

STEP 3: Solve

Substituting for the risk-free rate, beta for Pearson, and the risk premium for the market into Equation (4), we calculate an estimate of the cost of common equity for Pearson, that is,

$$k_{cs} = r_f + \beta_{cs}(r_m - r_f) = .0163 + (.99 \times .065) = .0163 + .0644 = .0807 \text{ or } 8.07\%$$

STEP 4: Analyze

Pearson's cost of common equity is estimated to be 8.07 percent, based on our estimates of the risk-free rate of interest of 1.63 percent, the company's equity beta of .99, and an estimated market risk premium of 6.5 percent. This estimate, however, is subject to considerable error because each of the three key factors (risk-free rate, beta, and market risk premium) is a rough estimate. For example, the risk-free rate of interest used here is the 10-year U.S. Treasury bond rate. If the 1-month-to-maturity rate had been used, the risk-free rate estimate would have been 0.01 percent; or, if the 30-year rate were used, it would have been 2.80 percent. The beta coefficient of .99 is also an estimate; in fact, depending upon the time period over which beta is estimated, it can go as low as .8 or as high as 1.2 for Pearson. Finally, the market risk premium of 6.5 percent reflects current estimates of the risk premium, but this premium is ever-changing and has been estimated to be as high as 8 percent or as low as 4 percent. Various combinations of these parameter estimates would lead to widely varying estimates of the cost of common equity. Obviously, the judgment of the analyst making the calculation is critical in arriving at a defensible estimate of the cost of common equity, even when using a model as simple as the CAPM.

STEP 5: Check yourself

Prepare two additional estimates of Pearson's cost of common equity using the CAPM where you use the most extreme values of each of the three factors that drive the CAPM (i.e., the highest and the lowest).

ANSWER: Cost of common equity ranges from 3.33 percent to 12.40 percent.

Your Turn: For more practice, do related **Study Problem** 17 at the end of this chapter.   >> **END Checkpoint 3**

Tools of Financial Analysis—Cost of Common Equity (CAPM)

Name of Tool	Formula	What It Tells You
Cost of Common Equity (Capital Asset Pricing Model) (k_{cs})	$r_f + \beta_{cs}\,(r_m - r_f)$ Definitions: • r_f = the risk-free rate of interest. • g = the expected rate of growth in dividends each year, forever. This growth rate is expected to be constant for all future years such that the expected dividend in Year 1 is equal to the most recent dividend paid (D_0) multiplied by 1 plus the annual rate of growth in dividends. • k_{cs} = the investor's required rate of return for investing in the firm's shares of common stock.	• The rate of return that the firm's common shareholders expect to receive from investing in the firm, which reflects only the systematic risk of the firm's equity • The cost of equity capital to the firm (before considering the cost of raising new equity capital).

Before you move on to 4

Concept Check | 3

1. How can we estimate the cost of new debt financing?
2. How is the cost of new preferred stock estimated?
3. Describe the two approaches that can be taken to estimate the cost of common equity.

Summing Up: Calculating the Firm's WACC

As the final step in our three-step procedure, we calculate the firm's overall cost of capital by taking the weighted average of the firm's financing mix that we evaluated in Steps 1 and 2. When estimating the firm's WACC, we should keep the following issues in mind.

Use Market-Based Weights

First, with regard to the capital structure weights, it is important that the components used to calculate the WACC formula are proportionate with the current importance of each source of financing the firm has used. Typically, this means that the weights should be based on market rather than book values of the firm's securities because market values, unlike book values, represent the relative values placed on the firm's securities at the time of the analysis (rather than the time when the securities were issued).

Use Market-Based Opportunity Costs

Just as was the case with the capital structure weights, the rates of return or opportunity costs of each source of capital should reflect the current required rates of return, rather than historical rates from the time when the capital was raised.

Use Forward-Looking Weights and Opportunity Costs

Firms typically update their estimate of the cost of capital annually, or even quarterly, to reflect changing market conditions. However, in most cases, analysts apply the WACC in a way that assumes that it will be constant for all future periods. This means that they implicitly assume that the weights for each source of financing, the costs of capital for debt and equity, and the corporate tax rate are constant. This assumption is reasonable in most situations; however, there are circumstances in which financial policies will change in predictable ways over the life of the investment. For example, some acquisitions are financed primarily with debt that is rapidly paid down following the acquisition. In this situation the capital structure is expected to change dramatically in the years following the acquisition, which means the weights in the capital structure are expected to change. In these cases, using a WACC that assumes constant weights is not appropriate.

Before you move on to 5

Concept Check | 4

1. Why do we use market values as the basis for calculating the weights used in calculating WACC?
2. Why are current costs and required rates of return used when estimating a firm's WACC instead of historical costs?

5 Estimating Project Costs of Capital

Virtually every firm calculates this number and updates it periodically. The majority of firms use their firm WACC as the discount rate for analyzing whether or not to undertake new investment projects. Using the firm's WACC to evaluate new investment is, in theory, only appropriate if the firm only considers new projects that are identical in risk to the investments it has already made. If the firm has several divisions with different risk levels, the discount rate it should use to evaluate individual investment projects should be different than the WACC.

We should note, however, that a firm's WACC is useful as an estimate of the overall cost of capital to the firm and is useful as the discount rate when we want to value the entire firm. For example, when Starbucks considered the acquisition of Seattle's Best, the appropriate discount rate for the future cash flows of Seattle's Best was the WACC of Seattle's Best.

A recent survey found that more than 50 percent of firms tend to use a single, company-wide discount rate to evaluate all of their investment proposals.[3] This suggests that although there are advantages associated with using specially tailored discount rates for each investment project evaluated by the firm, in practice there are costs of doing so. In the following subsections we discuss those advantages as well as the costs.

The Rationale for Using Multiple Discount Rates

Finance theory suggests that the appropriate discount rate takes into account the opportunity cost of capital, which in turn reflects the risk of the investment. The appropriate opportunity cost can be viewed as the expected rate of return on publicly traded stocks and bonds with equivalent risk. One would not initiate an investment project with expected returns that are less than the returns that can be generated from investments in publicly traded stocks and bonds with equivalent risk, because an investment in the stocks and bonds would clearly dominate the project. Hence, less risky investments, whose cash flows resemble the cash flows of a bond, will have an opportunity cost of capital that is lower than that of more risky investments, whose cash flows resemble the cash flows of a more risky stock.

Figure 4 illustrates the problems that arise when using a single discount rate (such as the firm's WACC) to evaluate projects that have different levels of risk. Specifically, there will be a tendency for the firm to take on too many risky investment projects, such as Project B, which offers an internal rate of return (IRR) that is greater than the firm's WACC but is below the appropriate risk-adjusted WACC. Similarly, where the firm's WACC is used to evaluate investment projects, there will be a tendency to pass up good investment projects that are relatively safe (Project A) and that earn more than the appropriate risk-adjusted cost of capital, but that generate internal rates of return that are less than the firm's WACC. Left unchecked, this bias in favor of high-risk projects will make the firm riskier over time, which will in turn increase its cost of capital.

---

[3]John Graham and Campbell Harvey, "The Theory and Practice of Corporate Finance: Evidence from the Field," *Journal of Financial Economics* 60(2001), 187–243.

Figure 4

Using the Firm's WACC Can Bias Investment Decisions toward Risky Projects

Firms that invest in projects with very different risk characteristics can bias their investment choices if they use the firm's WACC as the discount rate. Using a single WACC for low-risk projects would result in the rejection of low-risk projects such as Project A and the acceptance of high-risk investments such as Project B. Project A, due to its low risk, should be evaluated against a discount rate that is lower than the firm's weighted average cost of capital, and Project B, due to its high risk, should be evaluated against a discount rate that is higher than the firm's weighted average cost of capital.

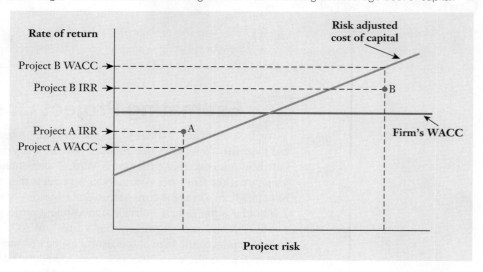

>> END FIGURE 4

Why Don't Firms Typically Use Project Costs of Capital?

There are at least two important reasons for sticking with a single discount rate. First, there are technical issues that can potentially make the use of multiple discount rates more trouble than it is worth. For example, individual investment projects, unless they are very large ones, do not have their own capital structure, nor are the sources of capital for the projects easily identified or their market prices easily observed. Instead, the firm issues equity, and the price of the firm's stock combined with its volatility reflects the average risk of all the firm's investments, not any one particular project.

The second issue that arises with the use of project costs of capital is more subtle and relates to something we will refer to as *influence costs*. These added costs arise as a result of the extra time and effort someone in charge of trying to get a project approved for funding by the firm's upper management spends trying to justify a lower discount rate, as well as the time spent by the firm's managers charged with evaluating the project. In spite of these added costs, some firms do allow for limited flexibility in determining the project cost of capital. We discuss next the primary method for estimating this project cost of capital.

Estimating Divisional WACCs

The approach taken by most firms that undertake investments with very different risk characteristics is to try to isolate their costs of capital for each of their business units or divisions by estimating **divisional WACCs**. The idea here is that the divisions take on investment projects with unique levels of risk, and consequently the WACC used in each division is potentially unique to that division. Generally, divisions are defined either by geographical regions (e.g., the Latin American division) or industry (e.g., exploration and production, pipelines, and refining for a large integrated oil company).

The advantages of using a divisional WACC include the following:

- It provides different discount rates that reflect differences in the systematic risk of the projects evaluated by the different divisions.
- It entails only one cost of capital estimate per division (as opposed to unique discount rates for each project), thereby minimizing the time and effort of estimating the cost of capital.
- The use of a common discount rate throughout the division limits managerial latitude and the attendant influence costs.[4]

Using Pure Play Firms to Estimate Divisional WACCs

One approach that can be taken to deal with differences in the costs of capital for each of the firm's business units involves identifying what we will call "pure play" comparison firms (or "comps") that operate in only one of the individual business areas (where possible). For example, ExxonMobil (XOM) is a fully integrated oil company that engages in everything from the exploration and production of oil to its refining and sale. Specifically, the firm has three different business units:

- **Upstream.** The unit that is involved in searching for oil and gas, drilling exploratory wells, and operating and recovering the oil and gas deposits.
- **Downstream.** Refining of crude oil into a variety of products, including such things as gasoline, jet fuel, and diesel fuel.
- **Chemicals.** The conversion of petroleum into plastics, fertilizers, pesticides, pharmaceuticals, and other by-products.

To estimate the cost of capital for each of these different types of activities, we use the WACCs for comparison firms that are not fully integrated and operate in only one of ExxonMobil's business segments. For example, to estimate the WACC for its Upstream business unit, ExxonMobil might use a WACC estimate for firms that operate in the Oil and Gas Extraction industry class (SIC industry 1300).[5] These firms span a wide variety of sub-industries related to oil and gas exploration, development, and production. Similarly, analysts could use firms in the Petroleum Refining and Related Industries (SIC industry 2900) as comps to estimate the relevant WACC for the Downstream business unit, and they could use firms in Chemicals and Allied Products (SIC industry 2800) as comps to determine the WACC for the Chemicals business unit.

Divisional WACC: Estimation Issues and Limitations

Although the divisional WACC is generally a significant improvement over the single, company-wide WACC, the way that it is often implemented using industry-based comparison firms has a number of potential shortcomings:

- The sample of firms in a given industry may include firms that are not good matches for the firm or one of its divisions. For example, the ExxonMobil company analyst may be able to select a narrower subset of firms whose risk profiles more nearly match the division being analyzed (e.g., in our ExxonMobil example the comparison firms for the Upstream division consisted of the 114 companies in SIC 1300, the Downstream division comparison firms included the 15 firms from SIC 2900, and the comparison firms for the Chemical division included the 293 companies from SIC 2800). The firm's management can easily address this problem by selecting appropriate comparison firms with similar risk profiles from among the many included in these industries.
- The division being analyzed may not have a capital structure that is similar to that of the sample of firms in the industry data. The division may be more or less leveraged than the

---

[4]However, we expect that divisional managers may still expend resources to lobby for lower discount rates for their divisions, so the influence costs associated with allowing managers some discretion over what discount rates to use is not eliminated entirely by the use of a divisional WACC.

[5]SIC is the four-digit Standard Industrial Classification code that is widely used to identify different industries.

firms whose costs of capital are used to proxy for the divisional cost of capital. For example, ExxonMobil raises almost no capital using debt financing, whereas Valero Energy (VLO) has raised 13.75 percent of its capital with debt.[6]

- The firms in the chosen industry that are used to proxy for divisional risk may not be good reflections of project risk. Firms, by definition, are engaged in a variety of activities, and it can be very difficult to identify a group of firms that are predominantly engaged in activities that are truly comparable to those of a given project. Even within divisions, individual projects can have very different risk profiles. This means that even if we are able to match divisional risks very closely, there may still be significant differences in risk across projects undertaken within a division. For example, some projects may entail extensions of existing production capabilities, whereas others involve new product development. Both types of investments take place within a given division, but they have very different risk profiles.

- Good comparison firms for a particular division may be difficult to find. Most publicly traded firms report multiple lines of business, yet each company is classified into a single industry group. In the case of ExxonMobil we found three operating divisions (Upstream, Downstream, and Chemicals) and identified an industry proxy for each.

The preceding discussion suggests that although the use of divisional WACCs to determine project discount rates may represent an improvement over the use of a company-wide WACC, this methodology is far from perfect. However, if the firm has investment opportunities with risks that vary principally with industry-risk characteristics, the use of a divisional WACC has clear advantages over the use of the firm's WACC. It provides a methodology that allows for different discount rates, and it avoids some of the influence costs associated with giving managers complete leeway to select project-specific discount rates. Figure 5 summarizes the cases for using a single-firm WACC and divisional WACCs to evaluate investment opportunities.

Finance in a **Flat World**

Why Do Interest Rates Differ among Countries?

Suppose that you are working for Intel Corporation (ITC), which has investment opportunities all around the world. Assume that when Intel borrows in the United States the borrowing rate is 6 percent; however, when the firm borrows in Brazil to finance its investments there, the borrowing rate is close to 12 percent. Should the firm's cost of capital for its investment projects in Brazil reflect the 6 percent U.S. cost of borrowing or the 12 percent Latin American cost of borrowing?

To answer this question it is important to remember two fundamental maxims in regard to the cost of capital:

- The first is that nominal cash flows must be discounted at nominal interest rates. If nominal cash flows are calculated in the home country's currency, taking into account the home country's inflation rate, then the discount rate should use the local interest rates, which reflect the expected local inflation rates.

- The second maxim is that discount rates should reflect the opportunity cost of capital. Clearly, interest rates in Brazil are a better measure of the opportunity costs of investing in Brazil than are interest rates in the United States.

Your Turn: Study Question 11.

---

[6]This estimate is based on year-end 2005 financial statements, using book values of interest-bearing short- and long-term debt and the market value of the firm's equity on February 16, 2006.

Figure 5

Choosing the Right WACC: Discount Rates and Project Risk

There are good reasons for using a single, company-wide WACC to evaluate the firm's investments even where there are differences in the risks of the projects the firm undertakes. The most common practice among firms that use a variety of discount rates to evaluate new investments in an effort to accommodate risk differences is the divisional WACC. The latter represents something of a compromise that minimizes some of the problems encountered when attempting to estimate both the project-specific costs of capital and the costs that arise where a single discount rate is used that is equal to the firm's WACC.

Method	Description	Advantages	Disadvantages	When to Use
WACC	Estimated WACC for the firm as an entity; used as the discount rate on *all* projects.	• Familiar concept to most business executives. • Minimizes estimation costs, as there is only one cost of capital calculation for the firm. • Reduces the problem of influence cost issues.	• Does not adjust discount rates for differences in project risk. • Does not provide for flexibility in adjusting for differences in project debt in the capital structure.	• Projects are similar in risk to the firm as a whole. • Using multiple discount rates creates significant problems with influence costs.
Divisional WACC	Estimated WACC for individual business units or divisions within the firm; used as the only discount rates within each division.	• Uses division-level risk to adjust discount rates for individual projects. • Reduces influence costs to the competition among division managers to lower their division's cost of capital.	• Does not capture intra-division risk differences in projects. • Does not account for differences in project debt capacities within divisions. • Potential influence costs are associated with the choice of discount rates across divisions. • Difficult to find single-division firms to proxy for divisions.	• Individual projects within each division have similar risks and debt capacities. • Discount rate discretion creates significant influence costs within divisions but not between divisions.

>> END FIGURE 5

Concept Check | 5

1. What is the main problem that firms encounter when using the firm's WACC as the cost of capital for all their investment analyses?
2. What are divisional WACCs, and how do they address the problems encountered in using a single, company-wide WACC?

 Flotation Costs and Project NPV

When firms raise money to finance new investments by selling bonds and stock, they incur **flotation costs**—fees that are paid to an investment banker and costs incurred when securities are sold at a discount to the current market price. When new securities are issued, they are often sold for a price slightly below the prevailing market price as an enticement for new investors to purchase them.

WACC, Flotation Costs, and NPV

Naples Distribution Company is considering an opportunity to expand its distribution business to the southeastern part of the United States. The expansion is expected to generate after-tax cash flows of $5.5 million per year in perpetuity (which means the company expects to earn $5.5 million every year forever—this keeps the calculations simple for our illustration). Naples plans to raise the $50 million needed to finance the investment using 50 percent debt and 50 percent new common stock.

Naples' investment banker estimates that the firm's after-tax cost of debt financing is 4 percent, and its cost of common equity financing is 16 percent. Combining these costs using Equation (1), we calculate the firm's WACC to be 10 percent:

$$WACC = (4\% \times .50) + (16\% \times .50) = 10\%$$

For the moment, let's ignore the flotation costs incurred to raise the $50 million and calculate the NPV for the investment as follows:

$$NPV = \frac{\text{Present Value of}}{\text{the Future Cash Flows}} - \frac{\text{Initial Cost of}}{\text{Making the Investment}}$$

Remember that the present value of a perpetuity is simply the cash flow divided by the discount rate, so

$$NPV = \frac{\$5.5 \text{ million}}{.10} - \$50 \text{ million} = \$5 \text{ million}$$

Based on this analysis, it appears that the planned expansion will be a positive-NPV investment that will create $5 million in value for the firm's shareholders. However, this analysis ignores the fact that Naples will have to pay an investment banker to help raise the $50 million and that these costs are a part of the project's cash outlay.

If the flotation cost of issuing bonds is 4 percent and the flotation costs for equity are 10 percent, then the weighted average of the two costs can be calculated using Equation (5) as follows:

$$\frac{\text{Weighted Average}}{\text{Flotation Cost}} = \left(w_d \times \frac{\text{Flotation Cost}}{\text{of Debt as a Percent}}\right) + \left(w_{cs} \times \frac{\text{Flotation Cost}}{\text{of Equity as a Percent}}\right) \quad \textbf{(5)}$$

Substituting the appropriate values for Naples, we get the following:

$$\frac{\text{Weighted Average}}{\text{Flotation Cost}} = (.50 \times .04) + (.50 \times .10) = .07 \text{ or } 7\%$$

Because Naples must pay 7 percent of any funds raised in flotation costs, the firm will have to issue more than $50 million to get the financing it needs for the planned expansion of its business. Specifically, we can calculate how much total financing the company will need (i.e., the flotation cost adjusted initial outlay) using the following relationship:

$$\frac{\text{Financing}}{\text{Needed}} = \frac{\text{Flotation Cost Adjusted}}{\text{Initial Outlay}} - \left(\frac{\text{Flotation Cost}}{\text{as a Percent}} \times \frac{\text{Flotation Cost Adjusted}}{\text{Initial Outlay}}\right)$$

$$= \frac{\text{Flotation Cost Adjusted}}{\text{Initial Outlay}}\left(1 - \frac{\text{Flotation Cost}}{\text{as a Percent}}\right)$$

Solving for the flotation cost adjusted initial outlay, that is, how much must be raised to cover the initial outlay plus flotation costs, we get

$$\frac{\text{Flotation Cost Adjusted}}{\text{Initial Outlay}} = \frac{\dfrac{\text{Financing}}{\text{Needed}}}{\left(1 - \dfrac{\text{Flotation Cost}}{\text{as a Percent}}\right)} \quad \textbf{(6)}$$

After adjusting for flotation costs, the initial cash outlay for the proposed investment is

$$\frac{\text{Flotation Cost Adjusted}}{\text{Initial Outlay}} = \frac{\$50 \text{ million}}{(1 - .07)} = \$53.76 \text{ million}$$

Thus, to obtain the $50 million it needs to finance the proposed investment, Naples will have to sell $53.76 million worth of bonds and common stock, which includes flotation costs of $3.76 million.

Using the adjusted initial cost of the investment, the NPV of the project is now

$$NPV = \frac{\$5.5 \text{ million}}{.10} - \$53.76 \text{ million} = \$1.24 \text{ million}$$

The NPV of the proposed expansion project is still positive but is a great deal smaller than before. The key learning point here is that flotation costs incurred in raising the funds used to finance the firm's investments are important and must be considered when evaluating the NPV of a new investment.

Checkpoint 4

Incorporating Flotation Costs into the Calculation of NPV

The Tricon Telecom Company is considering a $100 million investment that would allow it to develop fiber-optic high-speed Internet connectivity for its 2 million subscribers. The investment will be financed using the firm's desired mix of debt and equity with 40 percent debt financing and 60 percent common equity financing. The firm's investment banker advised the firm's CFO that the issue costs associated with debt would be 2 percent and the equity issue costs would be 10 percent.

Tricon uses a 10 percent cost of capital to evaluate its telecom investments and has estimated that the new fiber-optic project will yield future cash flows valued at $115 million. However, to this point no consideration has been given to the effect of the costs of raising the financing for the project or flotation costs. Should the firm go forward with the investment in light of the flotation costs?

STEP 1: Picture the problem

The NPV will be equal to the present value of the future cash inflows less the initial outlay and flotation costs.

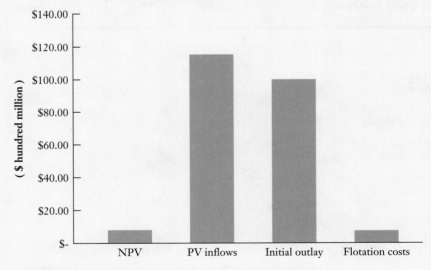

STEP 2: Decide on a solution strategy

To add consideration for flotation costs, Tricon must first estimate the average flotation costs it will incur when raising the funds. This can be done using Equation (5). Next, the "grossed up" investment outlay can be estimated using Equation (6) and subtracted from the present value of the expected future cash flows to determine whether the project has a positive NPV.

(4 CONTINUED >> ON NEXT PAGE)

STEP 3: Solve

We use Equation (5) to estimate the weighted average flotation cost as follows:

$$\begin{array}{c}\text{Weighted Average} \\ \text{Flotation Cost}\end{array} = \left(w_d \times \begin{array}{c}\text{Flotation Cost} \\ \text{of Debt as a Percent}\end{array} + w_{cs} \times \begin{array}{c}\text{Flotation Cost} \\ \text{of Equity as a Percent}\end{array}\right) \tag{5}$$

$$\begin{array}{c}\text{Weighted Average} \\ \text{Flotation Cost}\end{array} = (.40 \times .02) + (.60 \times .10) = .068 \text{ or } 6.8\%$$

The "grossed up" initial outlay for the $100 million project can now be estimated using Equation (6) as follows:

$$\begin{array}{c}\text{Flotation Cost} \\ \text{Adjusted Initial Outlay}\end{array} = \frac{\text{Financing Needed}}{\left(1 - \begin{array}{c}\text{Flotation Cost} \\ \text{as a Percent}\end{array}\right)} \tag{6}$$

$$\begin{array}{c}\text{Flotation Cost} \\ \text{Adjusted Initial Outlay}\end{array} = \frac{\$100 \text{ million}}{(1 - .068)} = \$107.30 \text{ million}$$

The NPV of the investment can now be calculated using the "grossed up" or flotation cost adjusted initial cash outlay, that is,

$$NPV = \$115 \text{ million} - 107.30 \text{ million} = \$7.70 \text{ million}$$

STEP 4: Analyze

After incorporating consideration for flotation costs, the project still appears profitable with a roughly $7.7 million NPV. However, the flotation costs are substantial at over $7.3 million. Ignoring flotation costs can easily result in the acceptance of investment opportunities that destroy shareholder value.

STEP 5: Check yourself

Before Tricon could finalize the financing for the new project, stock market conditions changed such that new stock became more expensive to issue. In fact, flotation costs rose to 15 percent of new equity issued and the cost of debt rose to 3 percent. Is the project still viable (assuming the present value of the future cash flows remain unchanged)?

ANSWER: Flotation costs rise to $11.36 million and NPV is $3.64 million.

Your turn: For more practice, do related **Study Problem** 29 at the end of this chapter.

>> END Checkpoint 4

Before you begin end-of-chapter material

Concept Check | 6

1. What are flotation costs, and how do they affect a firm's cost of raising capital?
2. How can flotation costs be incorporated into project analysis?

Applying the Principles of Finance to This Chapter

P Principle 1: **Money Has a Time Value** In calculating investors' required rates of return, one approach we use is based on the discounted cash flow valuation models developed earlier, which rely on Principle 1.

P Principle 2: **There Is a Risk–Return Tradeoff** The risks associated with investing in common stock versus bonds are reflected in the costs of these sources of funding.

P Principle 3: **Cash Flows Are the Source of Value** In calculating investors' required rates of returns, one approach used relies on the discounted cash flow valuation approach developed earlier when we examined valuation of stocks and bonds. This approach uses cash flows as the measure of value.

P Principle 4: **Market Prices Reflect Information** The costs of individual sources of capital are estimated using observed market prices for a firm's financial claims (debt or equity securities). Principle 4 tells us that these prices provide the best estimates of the underlying intrinsic value of these securities.

P Principle 5: **Individuals Respond to Incentives** It is often in the best interest of a division manager to argue for a low cost of capital for his or her division (compared to other divisions) so that the division can reap a larger portion of the company-wide capital expenditure budget. This poses a problem for the firm's shareholders where the division manager successfully argues that his or her projects are less risky than they are such that the firm's shareholders would not receive an adequate return on some of the projects the division undertakes.

Chapter Summaries

Understand the concepts underlying the firm's overall cost of capital and the purpose for its calculation.

SUMMARY: A firm's cost of capital is equal to a weighted average of the opportunity costs of each source of capital used by the firm, including debt, preferred stock, and common equity. To properly capture the cost of all these sources of capital, the individual costs are based on current market conditions and not historical costs.

KEY TERMS

Cost of capital The discount rate that is used to calculate the firm's overall value.

Cost of common equity (k_{cs}) The rate of return the firm must earn in order to satisfy the requirements of its common stockholders.

Weighted average cost of capital (WACC) A composite of the individual costs of financing incurred by each capital source. A firm's weighted cost of capital is a function of (1) the individual costs of capital, (2) the capital structure mix, and (3) the level of financing necessary to make the investment.

Concept Check | 1

1. How is an investor's required rate of return related to the firm's cost of capital?
2. Why is the firm's cost of capital calculated as a weighted average?
3. List the three-step procedure used to estimate a firm's weighted average cost of capital.

KEY EQUATION

$$
\begin{aligned}
\begin{array}{c} \text{Weighted} \\ \text{Average Cost} \\ \text{of Capital } (WACC) \end{array} = &\left[\left(\begin{array}{c} \text{After-tax Cost} \\ \text{of Debt } (k_d) \end{array} \right) \times \left(\begin{array}{c} \text{Proportion of} \\ \text{Capital Raised} \\ \text{by Debt } (w_d) \end{array} \right) \right] \\
+ &\left[\left(\begin{array}{c} \text{Cost of Common} \\ \text{Stock } (k_{cs}) \end{array} \right) \times \left(\begin{array}{c} \text{Proportion of} \\ \text{Capital Raised} \\ \text{by Common Stock } (w_{cs}) \end{array} \right) \right]
\end{aligned} \tag{1}
$$

Evaluate a firm's capital structure, and determine the relative importance (weight) of each source of financing.

Concept Check | 2

1. Should book or market values be used to determine the weights used in calculating the WACC? Explain.
2. Why are accounts payable not included in the capital structure used to estimate a firm's WACC?

SUMMARY: Firms typically raise funds from banks and investors that provide both debt and equity capital. The firm's weighted average cost of capital is determined by the weight of each financing choice in the firm's capital structure. These weights reflect the relative importance of the source of financing, which are proportional to their market values.

Calculate the after-tax cost of debt, preferred stock, and common equity.

SUMMARY: The after-tax cost of debt is typically estimated as the yield to maturity of the promised principal and interest payments for an outstanding debt agreement. This means that we solve for the rate of interest that makes the present value of the promised interest and principal payments equal to the current market value of the debt security. We then adjust this cost of debt for the effect of taxes by multiplying it by 1 minus the firm's tax rate.

The cost of preferred stock financing is estimated in a manner very similar to that for debt, but with two differences. First, because preferred stock typically does not mature, the present value equation for valuing the preferred stock involves solving for the value of a level perpetuity. Second, because preferred dividends are not tax deductible, there is no adjustment to the cost of preferred stock for taxes.

The cost of common equity is somewhat more difficult to estimate than either debt or preferred stock because the common stockholders do not have a contractually specified return on their investment. Instead, the common stockholders receive the residual earnings of the firm or what's left over after all other claims have been paid.

Two approaches are widely used to estimate the cost of common equity financing. The first is based on the dividend growth model, which is used to solve for the rate that will equate the present value of future dividends with the current price of the firm's shares of stock. The second uses the Capital Asset Pricing Model.

KEY TERMS

Cost of debt The rate that has to be received from an investment in order to achieve the required rate of return for the creditors. This rate must be adjusted for the fact that an increase in interest payments will result in lower taxes. The cost is based on the debtholders' opportunity cost of debt in the capital markets.

Cost of preferred equity The rate of return that must be earned on the preferred stockholders' investment in order to satisfy their required rate of return. The cost is based on the preferred stockholders' opportunity cost of preferred stock in the capital markets.

Risk premium The amount by which the required rate of return exceeds the risk-free rate of interest.

KEY EQUATIONS

$$\text{Preferred Stockholder's Required Rate of Return } (k_{ps}) = \frac{\text{Preferred Dividend } (Div_{ps})}{\text{Preferred Stock Price } (P_{ps})} \qquad \textbf{(2a)}$$

$$\begin{array}{c}\text{Common Equity Required} \\ \text{Rate of Return } (k_{cs})\end{array} = \frac{\text{Common Stock Dividend for Year 1 } (D_1)}{\begin{array}{c}\text{Market Price} \\ \text{of Common Stock } (P_{cs})\end{array}} + \begin{array}{c}\text{Growth Rate in} \\ \text{Dividends } (g)\end{array} \qquad \textbf{(3a)}$$

$$\begin{array}{c}\text{Cost of Common} \\ \text{Equity } (k_{cs})\end{array} = \begin{array}{c}\text{Risk-Free} \\ \text{Rate } (r_f)\end{array} + \overbrace{\begin{array}{c}\text{Equity Beta} \\ \text{Coefficient } (\beta_{cs})\end{array} \underbrace{\left(\begin{array}{c}\text{Expected Return on} \\ \text{the Market Portfolio } (r_m)\end{array} - \begin{array}{c}\text{Risk-Free} \\ \text{Rate } (r_f)\end{array}\right)}_{\text{Market Risk Premium}}}^{\begin{array}{c}\text{Risk Premium for Common Equity} \\ (= \text{Equity Beta} \times \text{Market Risk Premium})\end{array}} \qquad \textbf{(4)}$$

Concept Check | 3

1. How can we estimate the cost of new debt financing?
2. How is the cost of new preferred stock estimated?
3. Describe the two approaches that can be taken to estimate the cost of common equity.

Concept Check | 4

1. Why do we use market values as the basis for calculating the weights used in calculating WACC?
2. Why are current costs and required rates of return used when estimating a firm's WACC instead of historical costs?

Calculate a firm's weighted average cost of capital.

SUMMARY: The firm's WACC is defined as follows:

$$WACC = (k_d \times (1 - T) \times w_d) + (k_{ps} \times w_{ps}) + (k_{cs} \times w_{cs}) \qquad \textbf{(1)}$$

where k_d, k_{ps}, and k_{cs} are the cost of capital for the firm's debt, preferred stock, and common equity, respectively. T is the marginal corporate tax rate and w_d, w_{ps}, and w_{cs} are the fractions of the firm's total financing (weights) that are comprised of debt, preferred stock, and common equity, respectively. The weights used to calculate WACC should theoretically reflect the market values of each capital source as a fraction of the total market value of all capital sources (i.e., the market value of the firm). In some cases, market values are not observed and analysts use book values instead.

Discuss the pros and cons of using multiple, risk-adjusted discount rates. Describe the divisional cost of capital as a viable alternative for firms with multiple divisions.

SUMMARY: Finance theory is very clear about the appropriate rate at which the cash flows of investment projects should be discounted. The appropriate discount rate should reflect the opportunity cost of capital, which in turn reflects the risk of the investment being evaluated.

However, an investment evaluation policy that allows managers to use different discount rates for different investment opportunities may be difficult to implement. First, coming up with discount rates for individual projects can be time consuming and difficult and may simply not be worth the effort. In addition, when firms allow the cost of capital to vary for each project, overzealous managers may waste corporate resources lobbying for a lower discount rate to help ensure the approval of their pet projects.

To reduce these estimation and lobbying costs, most firms have either just one corporate cost of capital or a single cost of capital for each division of the company. Divisional WACCs are generally determined by using information from publicly traded single-segment firms.

KEY TERM

Divisional WACC The cost of capital for a specific business unit or division.

Concept Check | 5

1. What is the main problem that firms encounter when using the firm's WACC as the cost of capital for all their investment analyses?

2. What are divisional WACCs, and how do they address the problems encountered in using a single, company-wide WACC?

 Adjust NPV for the costs of issuing new securities when analyzing new investment opportunities.

SUMMARY: When firms raise money in the financial markets they often obtain the services of an investment banker who helps the firm sell its debt or equity securities and in return receives a commission or fee. The existence of these flotation costs raises the effective cost of new financing to the firm and consequently reduces the value of any investments the firm might undertake. We can account for flotation costs when calculating NPV by adding them to the initial project outlay.

KEY TERM

Flotation costs The transaction costs incurred when a firm raises funds by issuing a particular type of security.

KEY EQUATION

$$\text{Flotation Cost Adjusted Initial Outlay} = \frac{\text{Financing Needed}}{\left(1 - \dfrac{\text{Flotation Cost}}{\text{as a Percent}}\right)} \quad (6)$$

Concept Check | 6

1. What are flotation costs, and how do they affect a firm's cost of raising capital?

2. How can flotation costs be incorporated into project analysis?

Study Questions

1. What is a firm's WACC?

2. Describe the three-step process for estimating WACC.

3. What are the basic sources of financing included in a firm's capital structure? Specifically, what financing sources are excluded from the firm's capital structure when calculating firm WACC?

4. **(Related to Regardless of Your Major: Understanding the Role of the Cost of Capital)** In the *Regardless of Your Major: Understanding the Role of the Cost of Capital* feature, what should be the opportunity cost of funds in valuing the cash flows from the ownership of a McDonald's franchise? How would you respond to your friend after having read the entire chapter? Remember that your friend is a complete novice when it comes to finance, so try to be very clear in your guidance.

5. What are the pros and cons of using risk-adjusted costs of capital for individual investments?

6. Divisional WACCs are the most popular method used in practice to risk-adjust the cost of capital. Describe how you might go about estimating divisional WACCs. What are the pros and cons of using divisional WACCs?

7. Companies that face large investments that they cannot finance internally through the retention of earnings must go to the financial markets to raise the needed funds. When they do this they will incur what are commonly referred to as flotation costs. Discuss how these flotation costs should be incorporated into the firm's analysis of net present value.

8. The financial crisis of 2007–2009 and the ensuing attempts by the Federal Reserve to stave off a deepening recession affected the cost of capital for all firms. Specifically, although very short-term Treasury bill rates were driven to near zero as investors sought the relative safety of government-issued securities, the spread between comparable-maturity Treasury issues and corporate issues soared. How would you describe the impact of these events on the cost of capital for the average U.S. corporation?

9. What are flotation costs, and how should they be incorporated into the analysis of an investment's net present value?

10. In the chapter introduction we discussed the Starbucks (SBUX) acquisition of Seattle's Best Coffee Company in 2003. Discuss the relevance of Seattle's Best's WACC as the opportunity cost of funds that should be used in valuing the acquisition. What if Starbucks planned to finance the entire $72 million acquisition using cash and Starbucks' common stock, thereby using no debt? Does this fact alter your thinking about the appropriate discount rate for valuing Seattle's Best? If so, how?

11. **(Related to Finance in a Flat World: Why Do Interest Rates Differ among Countries?)** Explain the rationale given for differences we observe in interest rates between countries discussed in the *Finance in a Flat World: Why Do Interest Rates Differ among Countries?* feature.

12. **Figure 3 contains average yields to maturity for corporate bonds of differing maturities and default ratings.** The yields are based on spreads to Treasury securities. Using the figure, what is the spread to Treasury for an A-rated corporate bond with a 10-year maturity? Bond spreads are typically stated in basis points. What is a basis point? What is the basis point spread for a BB-rated corporate bond with a 30-year maturity (in basis points)?

Study Problems

Determining the Firm's Capital Structure Weights

1. **(Defining capital structure weights)** Templeton Extended Care Facilities, Inc. is considering the acquisition of a chain of cemeteries for $400 million. Because the primary asset of this business is real estate, Templeton's management has determined that they will be able to borrow the majority of the money needed to buy the business. The current owners have no debt financing but Templeton plans to borrow $300 million and invest only $100 million in equity in the acquisition. What weights should Templeton use in computing the WACC for this acquisition?

2. **(Defining capital structure weights)** In August of 2009 the capital structure of the Emerson Electric Corporation (EMR) (measured in book and market values) appeared as follows:

(Thousands of dollars)	Book Values	Market Values
Short-term debt	$ 1,221,000	$ 1,221,000
Long-term debt	11,927,000	11,927,000
Common equity	9,113,000	26,170,000
Total capital	$22,261,000	$39,318,000

What weights should Emerson use when computing the firm's weighted average cost of capital?

Estimating the Cost of Individual Sources of Capital

3. **(Individual or component costs of capital)** Compute the cost of capital for the firm for the following:

    a. A bond that has a $1,000 par value (face value) and a contract or coupon interest rate of 11 percent. Interest payments are $55.00 and are paid semiannually. The bonds have a current market value of $1,125 and will mature in 10 years. The firm's marginal tax rate is 34 percent.

    b. A new common stock issue that paid a $1.80 dividend last year. The firm's dividends are expected to continue to grow at 7 percent per year, forever. The price of the firm's common stock is now $27.50.

    c. A preferred stock that sells for $125, pays a 9 percent dividend, and has a $100 par value.

    d. A bond selling to yield 12 percent where the firm's tax rate is 34 percent.

4. **(Individual or component costs of capital)** Your firm is considering a new investment proposal and would like to calculate its weighted average cost of capital. To help in this, compute the cost of capital for the firm for the following:

    a. A bond that has a $1,000 par value (face value) and a contract or coupon interest rate of 12 percent that is paid semiannually. The bond is currently selling for a price of $1,125 and will mature in 10 years. The firm's tax rate is 34 percent.

    b. If the firm's bonds are not frequently traded, how would you go about determining a cost of debt for this company?

    c. A new common stock issue that paid a $1.75 dividend last year. The par value of the stock is $15, and the firm's dividends per share have grown at a rate of 8 percent per year. This growth rate is expected to continue into the foreseeable future. The price of this stock is now $28.

    d. A preferred stock paying a 10 percent dividend on a $125 par value. The preferred shares are currently selling for $150.

    e. A bond selling to yield 13 percent for the purchaser of the bond. The borrowing firm faces a tax rate of 34 percent.

5. **(Individual or component costs of capital)** You have just been hired to compute the cost of capital for debt, preferred stock, and common stock for the Mindflex Corporation.

    a. Cost of debt: Because Mindflex's bonds do not trade very frequently, you have decided to use 9 percent as your cost of debt, which is the yield to maturity on a portfolio of bonds with a similar credit rating and maturity as Mindflex's outstanding debt. In addition, Mindflex faces a corporate tax rate of 34 percent.

    b. Cost of common equity: Mindflex's common stock paid a $1.25 dividend last year. In addition, Mindflex's dividends are growing at a rate of 6 percent per year and this growth rate is expected to continue into the foreseeable future. The price of this stock is currently $30.

    c. Cost of debt: Now let's assume that Mindflex's bonds are frequently traded. A Mindflex bond has a $1,000 par value (face value) and a coupon interest rate of 13 percent that is paid semiannually. The bonds are currently selling for $1,125 and will mature in 20 years. Mindflex's corporate tax rate is 34 percent.

    d. Cost of preferred stock: Mindflex's preferred stock pays a 10 percent dividend on a $125 par value. However, the market price at which the preferred shares could be sold is only $90.

6. **(Individual or component costs of capital)** Compute the cost of capital for the firm for the following:

    a. Currently bonds with a similar credit rating and maturity as the firm's outstanding debt are selling to yield 8 percent while the borrowing firm's corporate tax rate is 34 percent.

    b. Common stock for a firm that paid a $2.05 dividend last year. The dividends are expected to grow at a rate of 5 percent per year into the foreseeable future. The price of this stock is now $25.

    c. A bond that has a $1,000 par value and a coupon interest rate of 12 percent with interest paid semiannually. A new issue would sell for $1,150 per bond and mature in 20 years. The firm's tax rate is 34 percent.

    d. A preferred stock paying a 7 percent dividend on a $100 par value. If a new issue is offered, the shares would sell for $85 per share.

7. **(Related to Checkpoint 2)** **(Cost of common equity)** Salte Corporation is issuing new common stock at a market price of $27. Dividends last year were $1.45 and are expected to grow at an annual rate of 6 percent, forever. What is Salte's cost of common equity?

8. **(Cost of common equity)** Falon Corporation is issuing new common stock at a market price of $28. Dividends last year were $1.30 and are expected to grow at an annual rate of 7 percent, forever. What is Falon's cost of common equity capital?

9. **(Cost of debt)** Temple-Midland, Inc. is issuing a $1,000 par value bond that pays 8 percent annual interest and matures in 15 years. Investors are willing to pay $950 for the bond and Temple faces a tax rate of 35 percent. What is Temple's after-tax cost of debt on the bond where interest is paid semiannually?

10. **(Cost of debt)** Belton Distribution Company is issuing a $1,000 par value bond that pays 7 percent annual interest that is paid semiannually and matures in 15 years. Investors are willing to pay $958 for the bond. The company is in the 18 percent marginal tax bracket. What is the firm's after-tax cost of debt on the bond?

11. **(Cost of preferred stock)** The preferred stock of Walter Industries Inc. currently sells for $36 a share and pays $2.50 in dividends annually. What is the firm's cost of capital for the preferred stock?

12. **(Cost of preferred stock)** The preferred stock of Gator Industries sells for $35 and pays $2.75 per year in dividends. What is the cost of preferred stock financing? If Gator were to issue 500,000 more preferred shares just like the ones it currently has outstanding, it could sell them for $35 a share but would incur flotation costs of $3 per share. What are the flotation costs for issuing the preferred shares, and how should these costs be incorporated into the NPV of the project being financed?

13. **(Cost of debt)** The Walgreen Corporation is contemplating a new investment that it plans to finance using one-third debt. The firm can sell new $1,000 par value bonds with a 15-year maturity at a price of $950 that carry a coupon interest rate of 13 percent that is paid semiannually. If the company is in a 34 percent tax bracket, what is the after-tax cost of capital to Walgreen for the bonds?

14. **(Cost of preferred stock)** Your firm is planning to issue preferred stock. The stock is expected to sell for $98 a share and will have a $100 par value on which the firm will pay a 14 percent dividend. What is the cost of capital to the firm for the preferred stock?

15. **(Related to Checkpoint 2)** **(Cost of common equity)** The common stock for Oxford, Inc. is currently selling for $22.50, and the firm paid a dividend last year of $1.80. The dividends and earnings per share are projected to have an annual growth rate of 4 percent into the foreseeable future. What is the cost of common equity for Oxford?

16. **(Cost of common equity)** The common stock for the Bestsold Corporation sells for $58 a share. Last year the firm paid a $4 dividend, which is expected to continue to grow 4 percent per year into the indefinite future. If Bestsold's tax rate is 34 percent, what is the firm's cost of common equity?

17. **(Related to Checkpoint 2 and Checkpoint 3)** **(Cost of common equity)** The common stock for the Hetterbrand Corporation sells for $60, and the last dividend paid was $2.25. Five years ago the firm paid $1.90 per share, and dividends are expected to grow at the same annual rate in the future as they did over the past five years.

   a. What is the estimated cost of common equity to the firm using the dividend growth model?

   b. Hetterbrand's CFO has asked his financial analyst to estimate the firm's cost of common equity using the CAPM as a way of validating the earlier calculations. The risk-free rate of interest is currently 4.5 percent, the market risk premium is estimated to be 5 percent, and Hetterbrand's beta is .80. What is your estimate of the firm's cost of common equity using this method?

18. **(Cost of debt)** Gillian Stationery Corporation needs to raise $600,000 to improve its manufacturing plant. It has decided to issue a $1,000 par value bond with an 8 percent

annual coupon rate (with interest paid semiannually) and a 10-year maturity. Investors require a 10 percent rate of return.

a. Compute the market value of the bonds.
b. How many bonds will the firm have to issue to receive the needed funds?
c. What is the firm's after-tax cost of debt if the firm's tax rate is 34 percent?

19. **(Cost of debt)** Sincere Stationery Corporation needs to raise $500,000 to improve its manufacturing plant. It has decided to issue a $1,000 par value bond with a 10 percent annual coupon rate with interest paid semiannually and a 10-year maturity. The investors require a 9 percent rate of return.

a. Compute the market value of the bonds.
b. How many bonds will the firm have to issue to receive the needed funds?
c. What is the firm's after-tax cost of debt if its tax rate is 34 percent?

20. **(Cost of debt)** Use Figure 3 to estimate the yield to maturity on a firm that plans to issue 30-year bonds and whose debt is rated BB+. What is the spread to Treasury for the debt issue in basis points?

21. **(Cost of debt)** Tellington Inc. recently discussed issuing a 10-year-maturity bond issue with the firm's investment banker. The firm was advised that it would have to pay 8 to 9 percent on the bonds. Using Figure 3, what does this rate suggest to you about the firm's default rating?

Calculating the Firm's WACC

22. **(Related to Checkpoint 1) (Weighted average cost of capital)** The target capital structure for QM Industries is 40 percent common stock, 10 percent preferred stock, and 50 percent debt. If the cost of common equity for the firm is 18 percent, the cost of preferred stock is 10 percent, the before-tax cost of debt is 8 percent, and the firm's tax rate is 35 percent, what is QM's weighted average cost of capital?

23. **(Weighted average cost of capital)** In the spring of last year, Tempe Steel learned that the firm would need to reevaluate the company's weighted average cost of capital following a significant issue of debt. The firm now has financed 45 percent of its assets using debt and 55 percent using equity. Calculate the firm's weighted average cost of capital where the firm's borrowing rate on debt is 8 percent, it faces a 40 percent tax rate, and the common stockholders require a 20 percent rate of return.

24. **(Weighted average cost of capital)** Crypton Electronics has a capital structure consisting of 40 percent common stock and 60 percent debt. A debt issue of $1,000 par value, 6 percent bonds that mature in 15 years and pay annual interest will sell for $975. Common stock of the firm is currently selling for $30 per share and the firm expects to pay a $2.25 dividend next year. Dividends have grown at the rate of 5 percent per year and are expected to continue to do so for the foreseeable future. What is Crypton's cost of capital where the firm's tax rate is 30 percent?

25. **(Weighted average cost of capital)** The target capital structure for Jowers Manufacturing is 50 percent common stock, 15 percent preferred stock, and 35 percent debt. If the cost of common equity for the firm is 20 percent, the cost of preferred stock is 12 percent, and the before-tax cost of debt is 10 percent, what is Jowers' cost of capital? The firm's tax rate is 34 percent.

26. **(Weighted average cost of capital)** Bane Industries has a capital structure consisting of 60 percent common stock and 40 percent debt. The firm's investment banker has advised the firm that debt issued with a $1,000 par value, 8 percent coupon (interest paid semiannually), and maturing in 20 years can be sold today in the bond market for $1,100. Common stock of the firm is currently selling for $80 per share. The firm expects to pay a $2 dividend next year. Dividends have grown at the rate of 8 percent per year and are expected to continue to do so for the foreseeable future. What is Bane's weighted average cost of capital where the firm faces a tax rate of 34 percent?

27. **(Weighted average cost of capital)** As a member of the Finance Department of Ranch Manufacturing, your supervisor has asked you to compute the appropriate discount rate to use when evaluating the purchase of new packaging equipment for the plant. Under

the assumption that the firm's present capital structure reflects the appropriate mix of capital sources for the firm, you have determined the market value of the firm's capital structure as follows:

Source of Capital	Market Values
Bonds	$4,000,000
Preferred stock	$2,000,000
Common stock	$6,000,000

To finance the purchase, Ranch Manufacturing will sell 10-year bonds paying interest at a rate of 7 percent per year (with semiannual payments) at the market price of $1,050. Preferred stock paying a $2.00 dividend can be sold for $25. Common stock for Ranch Manufacturing is currently selling for $55 per share and the firm paid a $3 dividend last year. Dividends are expected to continue growing at a rate of 5 percent per year into the indefinite future. If the firm's tax rate is 30 percent, what discount rate should you use to evaluate the equipment purchase?

28. **(Weighted average cost of capital)** As a consultant to GBH Skiwear, you have been asked to compute the appropriate discount rate to use in the evaluation of the purchase of a new warehouse facility. You have determined the market value of the firm's current capital structure (which the firm considers to be its target mix of financing sources) as follows:

Source of Capital	Market Value
Bonds	$500,000
Preferred stock	$100,000
Common stock	$400,000

To finance the purchase, GBH will sell 20-year bonds with a $1,000 par value paying 8 percent per year (paid semiannually) at the market price of $950. Preferred stock paying a $2.50 dividend can be sold for $35. Common stock for GBH is currently selling for $50 per share. The firm paid a $4 dividend last year and expects dividends to continue growing at a rate of 4 percent per year into the indefinite future. The firm's marginal tax rate is 34 percent. What discount rate should you use to evaluate the warehouse project?

Flotation Costs and Project NPV

29. **(Related to Checkpoint 4) (Flotation costs and NPV analysis)** The Faraway Moving Company is involved in a major plant expansion that involves the expenditure of $200 million in the coming year. The firm plans on financing the expansion through the retention of $150 million in firm earnings and by borrowing the remaining $50 million. In return for helping sell the $50 million in new debt, the firm's investment banker charges a fee of 200 basis points (where one basis point is .01 percent). If Faraway decides to adjust for these flotation costs by adding them to the initial outlay, what will the initial outlay for the project be?

30. **(Flotation costs)** The Pandora Internet Radio Company was started in 2000 to provide a personalized radio listening experience over your computer or iPhone and is privately owned. However, its success could easily lead its owners to take the company public with the sale of common stock to the public. When companies sell common stock for the first time the flotation cost can be very high. If Pandora needs $75 million to finance an acquisition and sells shares to the public, how much stock would it have to sell if flotation costs are expected to be 15 percent?

31. **(Flotation costs)** Two-Foot Tools, Inc. sells and distributes work footwear and other clothing for people who work under extreme cold conditions such as in the Arctic or Antarctica. The company recently borrowed $10 million net of issuance costs equal to 1.5 percent of the total amount of funds borrowed from a consortium of banks and agreed to pay 9 percent interest before considering taxes of 30 percent. The cost of the new distribution facility is $20 million, and the remaining $10 million needed to finance the investment will come from prior years' retained earnings. Given the firm's plans, what should the initial outlay for the plant expansion be if flotation costs are accounted for by adjusting the initial outlay?

Mini-Case

The Nealon Manufacturing Company is in the midst of negotiations to acquire a plant in Fargo, North Dakota. The company CFO, James Nealon, is the son of the founder and CEO of the company and heir-apparent to the CEO position, so he is very concerned about making such a large commitment of money to the new plant. The cost of the purchase is $40 million, which is roughly one-half the size of the company today.

To begin his analysis, James has launched the firm's first-ever cost-of-capital estimation. The company's current balance sheet, restated to reflect market values, has been converted to percentages as follows:

Nealon, Inc., Balance Sheet—2013

Type of Financing	Percentage of Future Financing
Bonds (8%, $1,000 par, 30-year maturity)	38%
Preferred stock (5,000 shares outstanding, $50 par, $1.50 dividend)	15%
Common stock	47%
Total	100%

The company paid dividends to its common stockholders of $2.50 per share last year, and the projected rate of annual growth in dividends is 6 percent per year for the indefinite future. Nealon's common stock trades over the counter and has a current market price of $35 per share. In addition, the firm's bonds have an AA rating. Moreover, AA bonds are currently yielding 7 percent. The preferred stock has a current market price of $19 per share.

a. If the firm is in a 34 percent tax bracket, what is the weighted average cost of capital (i.e., firm WACC)?

b. In the analysis done so far we have not considered the effects of flotation costs. Assume now that Nealon is raising a total of $40 million using the above financing mix. New debt financing will require that the firm pay 50 basis points (i.e., one-half a percent) in issue costs, the sale of preferred stock will require the firm to pay 200 basis points in flotation costs, and the common stock issue will require flotation costs of 500 basis points.

i. What are the total flotation costs the firm will incur to raise the needed $40 million?

ii. How should the flotation costs be incorporated into the analysis of the $40 million investment the firm plans to make?

Photo Credits

Credits are listed in order of appearance.

Star Stock/Alamy; Yuri Arcurs/Fotolia

Capital Structure Policy

From Chapter 15 of *Financial Management: Principles and Applications*, Twelfth Edition. Sheridan Titman, Arthur J. Keown, and John D. Martin.

Capital Structure Policy

Chapter **Outline**

1 A Glance at Capital Structure Choices in Practice ⟶ **Objective 1.** Describe a firm's capital structure.

2 Capital Structure Theory ⟶ **Objective 2.** Explain why firms have different capital structures and how capital structure influences a firm's weighted average cost of capital.

3 Why Do Capital Structures Differ across Industries? ⟶ **Objective 3.** Describe some fundamental differences in industries that drive differences in the way they finance their investments.

4 Making Financing Decisions ⟶ **Objective 4.** Use the basic tools of financial analysis to analyze a firm's financing decisions.

P Principle 2: **There Is a Risk–Return Tradeoff** provides us with insights as to why different firms have different capital structures. Managers are often tempted to take on more debt because it can increase the rate of return earned on the stockholders' investment in the firm. However, this higher expected return comes with a cost—the higher use of debt financing makes the firm's stock riskier, which increases the required rate of return on the stock. In addition, the additional debt makes it more likely that the firm will have difficulties meeting its debt obligations. **P** Principle 3: **Cash Flows Are the Source of Value**, is also important for understanding capital structure. Indeed, one of the main messages from this chapter is that the capital structure choice is important only when it affects the total cash flows that can be distributed to the firm's equity and debt holders. **P** Principle 5: **Individuals Respond to Incentives** becomes important because if managers only own a small fraction of the firm's stock, they may act in their own self-interests rather than in the shareholders' interests. One way to help managers focus on shareholder interests is to increase the firm's debt obligations.

How Do Firms Finance Their Investments?

A firm's capital structure—the mix of the different sources of capital it uses to finance its investments—is a critical determinant of both the rate of return earned from investing in the firm's shares of common stock as well as the riskiness of the investment. The firm's financing decisions are one of the three fundamental decisions that are made by the financial manager.[1] However, different firms tend to make very different financing decisions. Some firms finance their investments primarily with debt, whereas others finance their investments primarily with equity. For example, in 2012 Apple (AAPL) had no bank debt or bonds outstanding, whereas American Electric Power (AEP) borrowed almost $18 billion in short- and long-term debt to help finance its $52 billion of total assets. The question of why different firms make different financing choices forms the basis of our study of capital structure in this chapter.

We open our discussion of capital structure in Section 1 by taking a closer look at the capital structures of a variety of different firms. After observing that different firms can have very different capital structures, we then turn in Section 2 to capital structure theory to help us understand why these differences exist.

Finally, in Section 3 we conclude this chapter by discussing the tools used by financial managers in practice to measure the costs and benefits that determine the optimal mix of debt and equity financing. To achieve this objective, the financial manager must consider several factors, including the tax consequences of debt versus equity financing, the costs of financial distress brought on by having too much debt, the managerial incentives associated with debt financing, and the importance of information differences between company managers and outside investors.

---

[1] The three basic questions addressed in the study of finance are: (i) deciding what long-term investments to undertake, (ii) choosing how the firm should raise the money needed to fund its investments (the subject of this chapter), and (iii) assessing how to best manage the cash flows that arise in the firm's day-to-day operations.

Regardless of Your Major…

"Capital Structure Matters to You!"

When firms borrow money they are obligated by the terms of the loan agreement to repay it, and if they do not meet the terms of the agreement the firm can be forced into bankruptcy.

So when a firm uses more debt than it can afford to service, it places the firm at risk of defaulting on its financial obligations and being forced into bankruptcy. This has very costly implications for the firm's employees, creditors, and stockholders. This is exactly what happened in 2008 to the investment bank Lehman Brothers, which had a debt-to-equity ratio of 33 to 1, and in 2009 to the automaker General Motors, which owed more than $26 billion that it could not repay. If you were an employee of one of these companies you were probably laid off permanently or, at the very least, you were faced with a very uncertain future as the company attempted to work its way out of bankruptcy. Even if you were not an employee, chances are that your 401(k) retirement fund may have been invested in one of these companies and you suffered. If you were a stockholder you probably lost all of your investment, and if you were a bondholder you may have recovered pennies on the dollar. So, regardless of whether you work in sales, operations, or finance, you need to understand some basic facts about the different ways that firms raise capital and how these financing choices affect the firm's earnings and its ability to invest in the future.

Your Turn: See Study Question 1.

 ## A Glance at Capital Structure Choices in Practice

One of the primary duties of a financial manager is to raise capital to finance the firm's investments. For every dollar the firm invests it must come up with a dollar in financing in the form of liabilities or owners' equity. The mix of debt and equity used by the firm is defined as its *capital structure*. In this chapter we will discuss how firms make the financing decisions that determine their capital structure.

The primary objective of capital structure management is to maximize the total value of the firm's outstanding debt and equity. We refer to the resulting mix of financing sources in the capital structure that maximizes this combined value as the **optimal capital structure**.

Defining a Firm's Capital Structure

A firm's capital structure consists of owners' equity and its interest-bearing debt, including short-term bank loans. The firm's capital structure does not include everything listed on the liabilities and owners' equity side of the balance sheet. We define the combination of capital structure *plus* the firm's non-interest-bearing liabilities, such as accounts payable and accrued expenses, to be the firm's **financial structure**.

It is common practice to describe a firm's *financial structure* using the debt ratio, which is the proportion of a firm's assets that has been financed by liabilities, that is,

$$\text{Debt Ratio} = \frac{\text{Total Liabilities}}{\text{Total Assets}} \qquad (1)$$

However, as we pointed out earlier, when analyzing a firm's capital structure we restrict our attention to the firm's interest-bearing debt. In addition, it is customary to describe a firm's capital structure using current market values as opposed to the book values. The ratio of debt to enterprise value satisfies both of these qualifications. The enterprise value of a firm is an alternative measure of firm value that looks at the market value of the firm focusing on what it would cost to buy the company—that is, the market value of the equity after paying off its debts and liquidating any excess or non-operating cash and near-cash (marketable securities) investments. Technically, we would like to use the market value of both debt and equity; however, the debt-to-enterprise-value ratio is typically computed using the book value of the firm's debt obligations because the market value of a firm's debt is difficult to obtain, as debt securities, unlike equity securities, are not as actively traded. Enterprise value is defined as follows:

$$\text{Enterprise Value} = \left(\begin{array}{c}\text{Book Value of} \\ \text{Interest-Bearing Debt}\end{array} - \begin{array}{c}\text{Excess} \\ \text{Cash}\end{array}\right) + \begin{array}{c}\text{Market Value of} \\ \text{Equity}\end{array} \quad (2)$$

Alternatively, where the term **net debt** is used to refer to the term in parenthesis, we define enterprise value as follows:

$$\text{Enterprise Value} = \begin{array}{c}\text{Net} \\ \text{Debt}\end{array} + \begin{array}{c}\text{Market Value of} \\ \text{Equity}\end{array} \quad (2a)$$

By subtracting excess cash from the firm's interest-bearing debt the analyst is simply recognizing that the business could operate without these cash and near-cash investments and could pay down the firm's debt with the excess cash. Therefore, the firm's use of debt financing is actually its net debt.

Note that enterprise value is not the same as the market value of the firm's equity (often referred to as the firm's market capitalization). **Enterprise value** equals the sum of the firm's market capitalization of the firm's equity plus net debt. We can use enterprise value to measure a firm's use of debt financing using the debt-to-enterprise-value ratio, as follows:

$$\text{Debt to Enterprise Value} = \frac{\begin{array}{c}\text{Book Value of} \\ \text{Interest-Bearing Debt}\end{array} - \begin{array}{c}\text{Excess} \\ \text{Cash}\end{array}}{\left(\begin{array}{c}\text{Book Value of} \\ \text{Interest-Bearing Debt}\end{array} - \begin{array}{c}\text{Excess} \\ \text{Cash}\end{array}\right) + \begin{array}{c}\text{Market Value of} \\ \text{Equity}\end{array}} = \frac{\text{Net Debt}}{\text{Enterprise Value}} \quad (3)$$

The book value of a firm's interest-bearing debt includes short-term notes payable (e.g., bank loans), the current portion of the firm's long-term debt (a current liability because this portion of the firm's long-term debt must be repaid within one year or less), and the firm's long-term debt (loans that mature in more than one year plus bonds the firm has issued). Note that in both the numerator and denominator of Equation (3) we net out the firm's excess or non-operating cash and near cash assets. Keep in mind that we are not subtracting out the entire amount of the firm's cash and marketable security holdings, because it would not be feasible to liquidate all cash holdings and still keep the firm running. As a consequence we only subtract excess cash holdings.[2]

Table 1 contains the book-value-based debt ratio and the market-value-based ratios of debt to enterprise value for a sample of large U.S. corporations. Note that the debt ratio is always higher than the debt-to-enterprise-value ratio, and sometimes dramatically higher. Recall that there are two reasons for this: First, the debt ratio is based on book value, and the book value of the firm's equity that is part of the denominator is almost always lower than its market-value counterpart. Second, the net debt used in the numerator of the debt-to-enterprise-value ratio includes only interest-bearing debt and excludes non-interest-bearing debt such as accounts payable and accrued expenses.

If we were to calculate the weighted average cost of capital for Walmart (WMT), we would use the 19.0 percent debt-to-enterprise-value ratio as the weight for debt financing. Because Walmart does not have any preferred stock, the weight assigned to equity financing would be 1 minus 19.0 percent, or 81.0 percent.

In addition to the two debt ratios, Table 1 also includes the times interest earned ratio. This ratio measures the firm's ability to pay the interest on its debt out of operating earnings. Specifically, the ratio is defined as follows:

$$\text{Times Interest Earned Ratio} = \frac{\text{Net Operating Income or EBIT}}{\text{Interest Expense}} \quad (4)$$

---

[2]Although this is technically true, when enterprise value is reported in the financial press it is standard practice to subtract the entire amount of the firm's cash and near-cash assets.

Table 1 Financial and Capital Structures for Selected Firms (Year-End 2012)

The debt ratio equals the ratio of total liabilities divided by the firm's total assets. Total liabilities equal the sum of current and long-term liabilities, including both interest-bearing debt and non-interest-bearing liabilities such as accounts payable and accrued expenses. The debt-to-enterprise-value ratio is the ratio of the firm's net debt less excess cash divided by the firm's enterprise value. The times interest earned ratio is equal to the firm's earnings before interest and taxes (EBIT) divided by interest expense. The first two ratios measure the proportion of the firm's investments financed by borrowing, whereas the latter ratio measures the ability of the firm to make the required interest payments to support its debt.

Ratio Definition	Debt Ratio Total Liabilities Total Assets	Debt-to-Enterprise-Value Ratio Net Debt Enterprise Value*	Times Interest Earned Ratio EBIT Interest Expense
American Electric Power (AEP)	71.9%	46.8%	3.54
Barnes and Noble (BKS)	72.5%	3.8%	Negative
Boeing (BA)	95.6%	17.7%	43.13
Disney (DIS)	46.9%	14.3%	26.12
Ford (F)	91.6%	67.4%	2.96
Johnson & Johnson (JNJ)	5.8%	9.1%	22.65
US Airways (LCC)	97.8%	67.8%	0.13
Safeway (SWY)	75.6%	55.7%	4.24
Walmart (WMT)	62.9%	19.0%	11.51
Average	69.0%	33.5%	14.28
Maximum	97.8%	67.8%	43.13
Minimum	5.8%	3.8%	0.13

*Because of the difficulty in calculating excess cash, we have assumed excess cash to be zero in these calculations.

Note that in Table 1 there is one instance, Barnes & Noble (BKS), in which the times interest earned ratio is actually negative. This occurs due to the fact that the firm was suffering an operating loss.

We now have the financial decision tools to evaluate the firm's capital structure. These tools are as follows:

Tools of Financial Analysis—Capital Structure Ratios

Name of Tool	Formula	What It Tells You
Debt Ratio	$$\frac{Total\ Liabilities}{Total\ Assets}$$	• Measures the extent to which the firm has used borrowed money to finance its assets • A higher ratio indicates a greater reliance on non-owner financing or financial leverage and more financial risk taken on by the firm.
Debt-to-Enterprise-Value Ratio	$$\frac{Book\ Value\ of\ Interest\text{-}Bearing\ Debt - Excess\ Cash}{\left(Book\ Value\ of\ Interest\text{-}Bearing\ Debt - Excess\ Cash\right) + Market\ Value\ of\ Equity}$$ $$= \frac{Net\ Debt}{Enterprise\ Value}$$	• A version of the debt ratio that uses current market values of equity as opposed to book values • The higher the debt-to-enterprise-value ratio, the more financial risk the firm is assuming.
Times Interest Earned Ratio	$$\frac{Net\ Operating\ Income\ or\ EBIT}{Interest\ Expense}$$	• Measures the firm's ability to pay its interest expense from operating income • A higher ratio indicates a greater capability of the firm to pay its interest in a timely manner.

Financial Leverage

The term *financial leverage* is often used to describe a firm's capital structure. This terminology arises from the fact that borrowing a portion of the firm's capital at a fixed rate of interest provides the firm an opportunity to "leverage" the rate of return it earns on its total capital into an even higher rate of return on the firm's equity. We will look into this phenomenon much more closely in the final section; however, it should be noted that if the firm is earning 15 percent on its investments and paying only 9 percent on borrowed money, the 6 percent differential goes to the firm's owners. As a result, the firm's return on equity will be much higher than 15 percent. This is what is known as **favorable financial leverage**. If the firm earns only 9 percent on its investments and must pay 15 percent, then the 6 percent differential here must come out of the owners' share of the investment return and they thus suffer **unfavorable financial leverage**. The key determinant of whether the use of financial leverage is favorable is whether the firm is able to invest the borrowed money at a rate of return that exceeds its cost.

How Do Firms in Different Industries Finance Their Assets?

As we have already seen, firms vary quite a bit in their use of debt financing. We illustrate this in Figure 1, which shows variations in debt-to-enterprise-value ratios across various industries. The average debt-to-enterprise-value ratio for the set of industries shown in the figure is 32 percent. However, the ratio is only 6 percent for E-commerce but 81 percent for Securities brokerage. Why is it that firms choose to finance their investments in very different ways, some using a large amount of debt or financial leverage, and others choosing none? Should the firm's stockholders care about how much debt the firm uses? These are the fundamental issues that we now address in our discussion of capital structure theory.

Figure 1

Debt-to-Enterprise-Value Ratios for Selected Industries

Average debt-to-enterprise-value ratios for firms in selected industries. Net debt includes only the book value of interest-bearing short- and long-term debt of the firm less excess cash. Note that we have assumed excess cash to be zero. We measure the enterprise value of the firm as the sum of the book value of the firm's interest-bearing debt less excess cash plus the market value of its equity.*

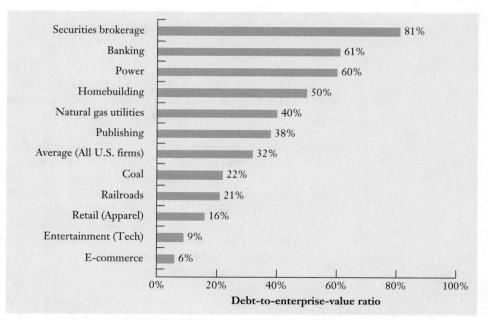

*Because of the difficulty in calculating excess cash, we have assumed excess cash to be zero in these calculations.

>> END FIGURE 1

Concept Check | 1

1. How does the debt ratio differ from the debt-to-enterprise-value ratio?
2. What does the times interest earned ratio measure?
3. What is financial leverage?
4. What determines whether financial leverage is favorable or unfavorable?

2 Capital Structure Theory

We open our discussion of capital structure choices in a hypothetical environment where financing choices do not affect firm value. In this setting the financial manager should not be concerned about capital structure policy. Although the assumptions required for capital structure irrelevance are not realistic, they provide a good starting point for understanding the factors that financial managers should consider when determining their capital structure policy. We will do this by relaxing these unrealistic assumptions and examining how they influence a firm's incentives to use debt and equity financing.

A First Look at the Modigliani and Miller Capital Structure Theorem

Franco Modigliani and Merton Miller's (M&M) analysis of the capital structure choice, which contributed to the Nobel Prizes of each of the authors, provides us with the conditions under which the capital structure decision has no influence on a firm's value and is therefore not a relevant concern for the firm's financial manager. This result is so important to the study of finance that it bears repeating: *M&M showed that, under some idealistic conditions, it does not matter whether a firm uses no debt, a little debt, or a lot of debt in its capital structure.*

Let's look at the basic assumptions that make capital structure irrelevant. It is a bit of a simplification, but M&M's capital structure theory relies upon two fundamental assumptions:

- **Assumption 1.** *The cash flows that a firm generates are not affected by how the firm is financed.* As we will discuss later, this assumption requires that there are no taxes, no costs associated with bankruptcy, and that the firm's debt obligations do not in any way affect its ability to operate its business.

- **Assumption 2.** *Financial markets are perfect.* This means that securities can be traded without cost and individuals can borrow and lend at the same rate as the firm.

Figure 2 illustrates Assumption 1. The pie charts represent the distribution of a firm's $500,000 cash flow based on two alternative capital structures. With Financing Mix A, the firm must repay its debt of $200,000. After repaying the debt obligation, the firm will have $300,000 left that it can distribute to its stockholders. With Financing Mix B, the firm has to repay a debt obligation of only $100,000. So, after repaying the $100,000 debt obligation, the firm has $400,000 it can distribute to its stockholders. Thus, the total amount of cash that the firm distributes to both its debt and equity holders is always equal to the firm's cash flow ($500,000 in our example) regardless of how the firm constructs its capital structure.

Assumption 2, the perfect financial markets assumption, implies that the packaging of cash flows (i.e., whether they are distributed to investors as dividends or interest payments) is not important. Under this assumption, the shareholders can repackage the cash flows provided by the firm in a way that replicates the cash flows they would receive under any possible capital structure.

To understand this, consider two firms that are clones of one another except for how they have financed their investments. In other words, they generate the same total cash flows, but the way those cash flows are divided between the firm's debt holders and equity holders differs. Specifically, Firm No-Debt has no debt, whereas Firm Half-Debt is financed with equal amounts of debt and equity.

Because Firm No-Debt and Firm Half-Debt are clones, their stock prices will be perfectly correlated. That is, when No-Debt's stock price increases, Firm Half-Debt's stock price also

Figure 2

Assumption 1: Cash Distributions to Bondholders and Stockholders Are Not Affected by Financial Leverage

Assumption 1 of the M&M theory states that the total cash flows the firm has available to distribute to its common stockholders and bondholders are not affected by the firm's capital structure decision. Assumption 2 states that the value of the firm is determined by how much cash the firm has to distribute, not by what proportion of it goes to common stockholders or to bondholders. In this example, the firm's investments generate cash flow equal to $500,000 regardless of how the firm is financed.

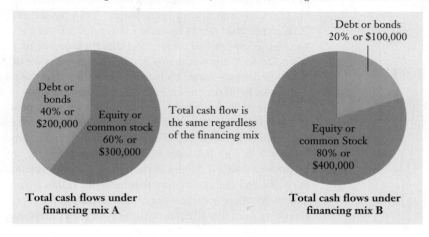

Debt or bonds
20% or $100,000

Debt or
bonds
40% or
$200,000

Equity or
common stock
60% or
$300,000

Equity or
common Stock
80% or
$400,000

Total cash flow is
the same regardless
of the financing mix

**Total cash flows under
financing mix A**

**Total cash flows under
financing mix B**

>> END FIGURE 2

increases. However, this does not mean that the levels of their risks are the same. Firm Half-Debt's stock price will be riskier—both the firm's positive and negative returns will be magnified because of the debt in its capital structure. For example, if Firm No-Debt's stock price increases by 10 percent, Firm Half-Debt's stock price might increase by 15 percent. This is the effect of financial leverage we described earlier. However, a portfolio that appropriately combines stock in Firm Half-Debt with a risk-free bond can have exactly the same risk as the stock in Firm No-Debt. In effect, investing in a risk-free bond (lending) cancels out the effect of Firm Half-Debt's borrowing. For example, if Firm Half-Debt is financed 50 percent with debt and 50 percent with equity, then a portfolio that includes an investment of $10,000 in debt and $10,000 in Firm Half-Debt stock will produce exactly the same returns as a portfolio that is 100 percent invested in Firm No-Debt stock. In other words, investors can undo the effect of the financial leverage in Firm Half-Debt's capital structure by including more bonds in their personal portfolios.

In reality, the relationship between Firm No-Debt and Firm Half-Debt stock just described may not be exact because of transaction costs and other market imperfections. This is why Assumption 2, which assumes that such costs do not exist, is required. If Assumption 2 holds, an investor who likes the returns generated by an investment of $20,000 in the stock of Firm No-Debt will be indifferent between directly purchasing the stock of Firm No-Debt or purchasing $10,000 of Firm Half-Debt's stock along with a $10,000 investment in a bond. Similarly, an investor who likes the returns generated by an investment of $10,000 in the stock of Firm Half-Debt can either directly purchase the stock of Firm Half-Debt or can equivalently purchase $20,000 of Firm No-Debt's stock, financing $10,000 of the purchase by borrowing. The resulting combination of the debt and Firm No-Debt's shares will produce exactly the same returns to the investor as purchasing Firm Half-Debt's shares.

This ability—in perfect markets—to transform the returns from investing in levered firms into unlevered firms, and vice versa, means that no investor would ever pay more or less for a firm's shares simply because the firm either borrowed money or not! We will have more to say about how debt financing affects the risk and returns of a firm's stock, and in the appendix to this chapter we will more explicitly demonstrate that this argument implies that capital structure does not affect how financial markets value a firm's cash flows. If a firm's capital structure choice does not affect the total cash flow it earns from its investments, and if it does not affect how the total cash flow is valued by the financial markets, then there will be no relation between a firm's capital structure and its total value. In effect, if these two assumptions hold, then:

The total market value of the firm's debt and equity is independent of its capital structure decision and the particular mix of debt and equity financing does not matter.

Yogi Berra and the M&M Capital Structure Theory

When asked to summarize the M&M theory in layperson's terms, legendary financial economist Merton Miller referred back to an old Yogi Berra line. When Yogi was asked if he wanted his pizza cut into four or eight pieces, Yogi paused and then decided on four pieces, saying "Cut it into four pieces because I don't think I can eat eight."[3] It doesn't take a Nobel Prize–winning economist to understand that the number of pieces that a pizza is cut into doesn't affect the total amount that is eaten. This is the point of Assumption 1, that the proportion of stocks and bonds issued by the firm does not affect the total amount of cash flows the firm can distribute. In effect, the size of the pizza pie (the value of the firm, which is determined by the cash flows to both creditors and owners) does not depend on the size of the slices (the portions of the firm's cash flow that is distributed to creditors or stockholders, and consequently how much of the firm has been financed with debt and equity). If the size of the pie is not affected by how it is cut, then one might also expect that the joy of eating the pie is also unaffected by how it is sliced. Under Assumption 2, no transactions costs mean that no pizza sticks to the knife and the assumption that individuals can borrow or lend at the same rate as the firm means that there is no additional cost to cutting the pizza into more pieces. Thus, the choice of financing does not affect how those cash flows are valued by the financial markets.

Capital Structure, the Cost of Equity, and the Weighted Average Cost of Capital

Under the Modigliani and Miller theory the value of the firm is not affected by how it is financed. As we briefly mentioned, an important part of Assumption 1 of this theorem is that the firm pays no taxes, which would have an important influence on the cash flows that can be distributed to the firm's investors.

When there are no taxes, the firm's weighted average cost of capital is also unaffected by its capital structure. To illustrate why this must be the case, let's assume that we are valuing a firm whose cash flows are a level perpetuity. The value of the firm then is simply the ratio of the firm's free cash flow divided by its weighted average cost of capital, that is,

$$\text{Firm Value} = \frac{\text{Firm Cash Flow}}{\text{Weighted Average Cost of Capital } (k_{wacc})} \tag{5}$$

where the firm's weighted average cost of capital for the case with no taxes is computed as follows:

$$k_{wacc} = \left[\begin{array}{c} \text{Cost of} \\ \text{Debt } (k_d) \end{array} \times \begin{array}{c} \text{Debt to} \\ \text{Value } (D/V) \end{array} \right] + \left[\begin{array}{c} \text{Cost of} \\ \text{Equity } (k_e) \end{array} \times \begin{array}{c} \text{Equity to} \\ \text{Value } (E/V) \end{array} \right] \tag{6}$$

Because firm value is unaffected by the firm's choice of capital structure and firm cash flows are likewise unaffected by capital structure, this implies that the firm's weighted average cost of capital is also unaffected. If we use the fact that in this case, the firm's k_{wacc} will equal $k_{unlevered}$, which is the cost of capital for an unlevered firm (one that uses no debt financing), with some algebra, it follows that the relationship between the cost of equity and the debt-to-equity ratio is as follows:

$$\begin{array}{c} \text{Cost of} \\ \text{Equity } (k_e) \end{array} = k_{unlevered} + (k_{unlevered} - k_d)\left(\frac{D}{E}\right) \tag{7}$$

To illustrate the relationship between capital structure, cost of equity, and the weighted average cost of capital, consider the case of Elton Enterprises, Inc. Elton can borrow money at 8 percent

---

[3]Yogi Berra played for the Yankees, one of four players to be named the American League's *Most Valuable Player* three times, and one of only six managers to lead both American and National League teams to the World Series. He also was famous for unusual quotes or "Yogiisms," of which two of the most famous were "It ain't over until it's over" and "In theory there are no differences between theory and practice. In practice there is."

and its cost of capital if it uses no financial leverage (its unlevered cost of capital) is 10 percent. If Elton has a debt-to-equity ratio of 1.0 (which means that 50 percent of its capital structure is debt), the cost of debt is 8 percent, and the weighted average cost of capital (WACC) is 10 percent, then the cost of equity, using Equation (7), is equal to 12 percent, that is,

$$\text{Cost of Equity } (k_e) = k_{unlevered} + (k_{unlevered} - k_d)\left(\frac{D}{E}\right) = .10 + (.10 - .08) \times 1.0 = .12 \text{ or } 12\%$$

Note that the cost of equity found in Equation (7) increases with the debt-to-equity ratio (D/E), as we see in Figure 3. However, because there is less weight on the more expensive equity, the firm's WACC—as expressed in Equation (6)—does not change and is always equal to the cost of capital for an unlevered firm.

Figure 3

Cost of Capital and Capital Structure: M&M Theory

Under the M&M theory of capital structure (where there are no taxes), firm value and the firm's weighted average cost of capital are not affected by changes in capital structure. Elton Enterprises has a weighted average cost of capital of 10 percent regardless of how much debt the firm uses. Holding constant the cost of debt financing, this implies an increasing cost of equity as found in Equation (7).

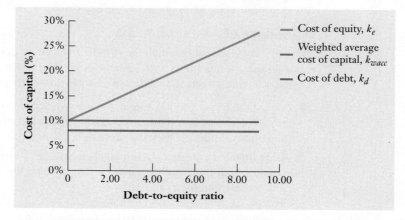

Debt-to-Equity Ratio	Weighted Average Cost of Capital	Cost of Debt	Cost of Equity
0.00	10%	8%	10.00%
0.11	10%	8%	10.22%
0.25	10%	8%	10.50%
0.43	10%	8%	10.86%
0.67	10%	8%	11.33%
1.00	10%	8%	12.00%
1.50	10%	8%	13.00%
2.33	10%	8%	14.67%
4.00	10%	8%	18.00%
9.00	10%	8%	28.00%

Legend:

$$k_{wacc} = \left[\text{Cost of Debt } (k_d) \times \text{Debt to Value } (D/V)\right] + \left[\text{Cost of Equity } (k_e) \times \text{Equity to Value } (E/V)\right]$$

$$\text{Cost of Equity } (k_e) = k_{wacc} + (k_{wacc} - k_d)\left(\frac{D}{E}\right)$$

where D/E is the ratio of debt to equity.

>> END FIGURE 3

Why Capital Structure Matters in Reality

In reality, financial managers care a great deal about how their firms are financed. Indeed, there can be negative consequences for firms that select an inappropriate capital structure, which means that, in reality, at least one of the two M&M assumptions is violated.

Violations of Assumption 2

Assumption 2 is clearly violated in reality. Transaction costs can be important and, because of these costs, the rate at which investors can borrow may differ from the rate at which firms can borrow. When this is the case, firm values may depend on how they are financed because individuals cannot substitute their individual borrowing for corporate borrowing to achieve a desired level of financial leverage. For example, if firms can borrow more cheaply than individuals, it might be better to have firms take on more financial leverage. This would increase both the risk and return of their stocks, and allow individuals who want to take substantial risk in their own portfolios to do so without borrowing. However, these violations of the Modigliani and Miller theorem provide very little in the way of insights regarding why some firms include much more debt in their capital structures than other firms, because the transaction costs that cause differences between the borrowing rates faced by corporations and the rates faced by individuals tend to affect all firms equally.

Violations of Assumption 1 are much more fundamental and provide important insights about why different firms choose different capital structures. As we will discuss, the cash flows generated by firms are in fact influenced by how the firm is financed.

Violations of Assumption 1

Why might the extent to which the firm is financed by debt or equity affect the total after-tax cash flows generated by a firm? As we discuss here, there are three important reasons why capital structure affects the total cash flows available to a firm's debt and equity holders:

1. Under the U.S. tax code, interest is a tax-deductible expense, whereas dividends paid to stockholders are not. Thus, after taxes, firms have more money to distribute to their debt and equity holders if they use more debt financing.[4]

2. Debt financing creates a fixed legal obligation. If the firm defaults on its payments, the creditors can force the firm into bankruptcy and the firm will incur the added costs that this process entails.

3. The threat of bankruptcy can influence the behavior of a firm's executives as well as its employees and customers. On one hand, it can focus managerial attention on improving firm performance. On the other hand, too much debt can lead to changes that make a firm a less desirable employer and supplier.

Corporate Taxes and Capital Structure

In the United States, interest payments are tax deductible, but dividend payments are not. So if the before-tax cash flows are unaffected by how the firm is financed, the after-tax cash flows will be higher if the firm's capital structure includes more debt and less equity.

To illustrate this effect, consider two firms that are identical in every respect except for their capital structure. Firm A uses no financial leverage and has total equity financing of $2,000. Firm B, on the other hand, has borrowed $1,000 on which it pays 5 percent interest and raised the remaining $1,000 with equity. Each firm also has operating income of $200.00. The corporate tax rate on the firm's earnings is 25 percent. In this example, the income statements are as follows:

	Firm A	Firm B
Operating income (EBIT)	$200.00	$200.00
Less interest expense	0.00	(50.00)
Earnings before tax	$200.00	$150.00
Less taxes	(50.00)	(37.50)
Net income	$150.00	$112.50

> Note that Firm B pays $37.50 in taxes, which is $12.50 less than Firm A. This is a result of the fact that the $50 Firm B paid in interest is tax deductible!

---

[4]This is not the case in all countries. The taxing authorities in a number of countries have made changes in their tax laws that reduced or eliminated the tax preference for debt financing.

Because Firm B incurs interest expenses, its after-tax net income is less than that of Firm A. To simplify our analysis, let's assume that both firms pay out 100 percent of their earnings in common stock dividends. By adding the total dividends paid to equity holders to the interest expense paid to the debt holders, we get the following:

	Firm A	Firm B
Equity dividends	$150.00	$112.50
Interest payments	0.00	50.00
Total distributions (to stockholders and bondholders)	$150.00	$162.50

Total distributions to the firm's owners (equity dividends) and to the creditors (interest payments) are only $150 for Firm A, whereas they are $162.50 for Firm B. The reason for the $12.50 difference can be traced directly to the fact that the $50 in interest payments is deductible from Firm B's taxable income and saves the firm $.25 \times \$50 = \$12.50$ in taxes. We refer to the tax savings due to the tax deductibility of interest on the firm's debt as **interest tax savings**. These interest tax savings increase the total distributions Firm B can make to its stockholders without reducing the distribution to the debt holders and so add value to the firm and in particular to its stockholders. If the firm saves $12.50 in taxes every year, then the present value of these tax savings is the extra value added by using debt financing. In effect,

$$\begin{bmatrix} \text{Cash flow to} \\ \text{a firm with} \\ \text{financial leverage} \end{bmatrix} = \begin{bmatrix} \text{Cash flow to} \\ \text{the firm without} \\ \text{leverage} \end{bmatrix} + \begin{bmatrix} \text{Interest} \\ \text{tax} \\ \text{savings} \end{bmatrix} \qquad \textbf{(8)}$$

This tax deductibility of interest expense leads firms to include more debt in their capital structures. In essence, corporate income taxes subsidize the firm's use of debt financing by allowing interest to be deducted before corporate taxes are calculated. So if a firm pays a tax rate of 25 percent, it gets a $0.25 tax refund for every dollar it pays in interest but gets nothing for the dividends it pays to the firm's common stockholders.

Corporate Taxes and the WACC. It is also the case that the tax deductibility of interest payments causes the firm's weighted average cost of capital to decline as it includes more debt in its capital structure. To illustrate this, consider the example found in Figure 4, where the cost of unlevered equity financing is assumed to be 10 percent and the cost of debt is 8 percent before taxes. If we assume a 40 percent tax rate, the after-tax cost of debt is 4.8 percent (i.e., $.08 \times (1 - .4) = .048$). As before, the cost of equity increases with the increased use of debt in the capital structure; however, with tax-deductible interest payments the cost of equity increases less, as shown below:

$$\text{Cost of Equity } (k_e) = k_{Unlevered\ Equity} + \left[(k_{Unlevered\ Equity} - k_d)\left(\frac{D}{E}\right) \times (1 - \text{Tax Rate}) \right] \qquad \textbf{(9)}$$

Once again consider the cost of equity for a capital structure with 50 percent debt and 50 percent equity or a debt-to-equity ratio of 1.0. We calculate the cost of equity (levered equity because the firm is assumed to finance half the value of its assets using debt) as follows:

$$\text{Cost of Equity } (k_e) = .10 + (.10 - .08)(1.0) \times (1 - .40) = .112 \text{ or } 11.2\%$$

Substituting for the cost of equity in the formula for the weighted average cost of capital, we get the following:

$$k_{wacc} = \left[\text{Cost of Debt } (k_d)\left(1 - \text{Tax Rate}\right) \times \text{Debt to Value } (D/V) \right] + \left[\text{Cost of Equity } (k_e) \times \text{Equity to Value } (E/V) \right] \qquad \textbf{(10)}$$

$$k_{wacc} = (.08(1 - .40) \times .50) + (.112 \times .50) = .08 \text{ or } 8\%$$

If we make similar calculations for different debt-to-equity ratios, we see that the firm's weighted average cost of capital declines as the debt ratio rises. For example, in Figure 4 we see that with a debt-to-equity ratio of 4 to 1 the cost of equity rises to 15 percent but the

Figure 4

The Cost of Equity and WACC with Tax-Deductible Interest Expense

Where interest expense is tax deductible there is a cost advantage to the use of debt financing. This, in turn, means that the value of the firm increases with the use of debt financing and correspondingly the firm's weighted average cost of capital declines. In this figure the cost of unlevered equity financing is 10%, and the cost of debt is 8% before taxes and 4.8% after taxes (.08 × (1 − .4) = .048).

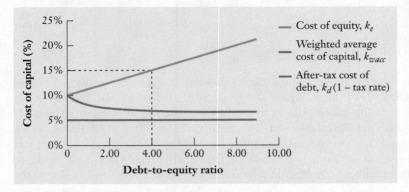

Debt-to-Equity Ratio	After-Tax Cost of Debt	Cost of Equity	Weighted Average Cost of Capital
0.00	4.8%	10%	10.0%
0.11	4.8%	10%	9.6%
0.25	4.8%	10%	9.2%
0.43	4.8%	11%	8.8%
0.67	4.8%	11%	8.4%
1.00	4.8%	11%	8.0%
1.50	4.8%	12%	7.6%
2.33	4.8%	13%	7.2%
4.00	**4.8%**	**15%**	**6.8%**
9.00	4.8%	21%	6.4%

Legend:

$$k_{wacc} = \left[\text{Cost of Debt } (k_d)\left(1 - \text{Tax Rate}\right) \times \text{Debt to Value } (D/V) \right] + \left[\text{Cost of Equity } (k_e) \times \text{Equity to Value } (E/V) \right]$$

$$\text{Cost of Equity } (k_e) = k_{Unlevered\ Equity} + \left[\left(k_{Unlevered\ Equity} - k_d\right)\left(\frac{D}{E}\right)\right]$$

where $k_{Unlevered\ Equity}$ is the cost of equity for a firm that uses no debt and D/E is the ratio of debt-to-equity value.

>> END FIGURE 4

weighted average cost of capital declines to 6.8 percent. Clearly, the implication of the tax deductibility of interest expense for capital structure policy favors the use of debt over equity.[5]

Bankruptcy and Financial Distress Costs

If taxes were the only reason that capital structure affects cash flows, the firm would simply use enough debt financing to generate a tax deduction that is sufficient to eliminate its tax liability. However, the downside of using debt financing quickly becomes apparent when

---

[5]What about personal taxes? In general, personal taxes tend to favor equity financing. The individual tax rate on income that comes in the form of either a dividend or as a capital gain on the stock's appreciation is generally lower than the tax rate individuals pay on interest income. Calculating the total tax benefits associated with debt financing is somewhat difficult because different individuals are subject to different tax rates that depend on the states in which they live as well as their incomes. However, because the majority of the equity for most large U.S. corporations is held by institutions that are not subject to corporate taxes, we can safely assume that at least for these firms the tax code favors debt financing.

the firm's debt obligations exceed its ability to generate cash. When this is the case, the firm will need to work out a deal with its bankers and bondholders to restructure its debt, or the firm might be forced into bankruptcy. In either case, a failure to meet one's debt obligations can generate substantial costs to the firm, costs that we collectively refer to as **financial distress costs**.

For instance, consider what happens to Firm A and Firm B when the economy goes from rapid expansion to deep recession, as illustrated in Table 2. In Panel A we see that even in a deep recession Firm A (which uses no debt financing) will have some, but very modest, earnings. Firm B, on the other hand, will barely meet its debt obligations in a mild recession and will be unable to pay its interest obligations in the event of a deep recession.

In both a mild and deep recession, Firm B will be subject to what economists call *dead-weight costs* that reduce the total amount of the cash flows that the firm can distribute to its debt and equity holders. These costs of financial distress arise because the firm's financial troubles will distract the managers, forcing them to spend their time negotiating with bankers rather than developing new products. They are also likely to generate large legal bills.

Being forced into bankruptcy is obviously costly to the firm, but it is also true that just the threat of bankruptcy, or what we will call *financial distress*, can cause problems for a firm long before the firm finds itself filing for bankruptcy. A firm that is close to bankruptcy is likely to be viewed by its customers and its suppliers as an unreliable business partner. As a result, it is likely to lose sales as customers seek out more reliable suppliers; it may find it difficult to get competitive quotes from its suppliers, who are increasingly worried about being repaid; and it may find it difficult to attract high-quality employees as prospective workers worry more about future layoffs.

Most financial managers will say that another important factor that limits their use of debt financing is that debt financing severely limits their flexibility. For example, if Firms A and B in Table 2 were to find themselves in a mild recession and also in need of funds to finance a new business opportunity, Firm B would find it very difficult to borrow more because it can barely pay the interest it owes on its existing debt. Firm A, on the other hand, has some financial slack in that it has $50 in operating earnings that is not obligated for the payment of interest. In this situation, Firm B's owners may also be unwilling to issue new shares, believing that in this depressed state of the economy their shares are undervalued. As a result, they may have to pass up a profitable investment opportunity. Firm A, on the other hand, will be able to finance the investment. It has more cash flow available to be reinvested (because it is not obligated to pay a dividend) and, because it has no existing debt, it still has the ability to borrow.

The Tradeoff Theory and the Optimal Capital Structure

We have identified two factors that can have a material impact on the role of capital structure in determining firm value:

- **Interest expense is tax deductible.** This fact makes the use of debt financing less costly, and lowers the firm's weighted average cost of capital.

- **Debt makes it more likely that firms will experience financial distress costs.** The contractual interest and principal payments that accompany the use of debt financing increase the likelihood that the firm will go into bankruptcy at some time in the future, which can lead to losses that reduce the cash flows of the firm.

When firms make financing decisions they must trade off these positive and negative factors. On one hand, firms with substantial amounts of taxable income that they can eliminate by taking on debt while facing relatively modest risks of incurring the costs of financial distress will tend to choose relatively high debt ratios. On the other hand, firms that are not generating a lot of taxable income, and that would be subject to substantial costs of financial distress if they have financial difficulties, will want relatively low debt ratios.

Figure 5 contains a saucer-shaped cost of capital curve for a firm that trades off the benefits and costs of using debt. In this illustration the tradeoff of the interest tax savings benefit of using more debt and the increasing expected costs of financial distress result in an optimal capital structure consisting of a debt-to-equity ratio of roughly 1 to 1, or a debt to firm value of 50 percent.

Table 2	Leverage and the Probability of Default

This example illustrates that the use of financial leverage increases the risk of financial distress. Debt financing creates a contractual obligation for the firm to pay interest and principal to the lender in accordance with the terms of the debt agreement (bond indenture). Consequently, the likelihood that the firm will default on its debt obligations increases as the firm increases the proportion of its capital structure that it raises using debt. In this example both firms have invested $2,000 in assets, with Firm A financing 100 percent of its assets using equity and Firm B financing $1,000 with equity and borrowing the remaining $1,000 at 5 percent.

(Panel A)	Firm A (Equity = 100% of Assets or $2,000)				
Probability	5%	20%	50%	20%	5%
Income Statement	**Deep Recession**	**Mild Recession**	**Normal**	**Mild Expansion**	**Rapid Expansion**
Operating Income (EBIT)	$ 10.00	$50.00	$100.00	$200.00	$300.00
Less: Interest Expense	0.00	0.00	0.00	0.00	0.00
Earnings before Tax	$ 10.00	$50.00	$100.00	$200.00	$300.00
Less: Taxes (25%)	(2.50)	(12.50)	(25.00)	(50.00)	(75.00)
Net Income	$ 7.50	$37.50	$ 75.00	$150.00	$225.00
Return on Equity (Net Income/Common Equity)	0.38%	1.88%	3.75%	7.50%	11.25%
Cash Distributions	**Deep Recession**	**Mild Recession**	**Normal**	**Mild Expansion**	**Rapid Expansion**
Equity Dividends	$ 7.50	$37.50	$ 75.00	$150.00	$225.00
Interest Payments	0.00	0.00	0.00	0.00	0.00
Total Distributions	$ 7.50	$37.50	$ 75.00	$150.00	$225.00

(Panel B)	Firm B (Equity = 50% of Assets or $1,000)				
Probability	10%	20%	40%	20%	10%
Income Statement	**Deep Recession**	**Mild Recession**	**Normal**	**Mild Expansion**	**Rapid Expansion**
Operating Income (EBIT)	$ 10.00	$50.00	$100.00	$200.00	$300.00
Less: Interest Expense	(50.00)	(50.00)	(50.00)	(50.00)	(50.00)
Earnings before Tax	$(40.00)	$ 0.00	$ 50.00	$150.00	$250.00
Less Taxes (25%)*	0.00	0.00	(12.50)	(37.50)	(62.50)
Net Income	$(40.00)	$ 0.00	$ 37.50	$112.50	$187.50
Return on Equity	−4.00%	0.00%	3.75%	11.25%	18.75%
Cash Distributions	**Recession**	**Recession**	**Normal**	**Expansion**	**Expansion**
Equity Dividends	$ 0.00	$ 0.00	$ 37.50	$112.50	$187.50
Interest Payments	10.00	50.00	50.00	50.00	50.00
Total Distributions	$ 10.00	$50.00	$ 87.50	$162.50	$237.50

*We simplify the tax treatment of income in this example by ignoring the carry forward/carry back provision of the tax code that would allow a firm that suffered losses to use those losses to reduce taxes paid in a prior period (carry back) or carry the loss forward and reduce its taxes in a future period. For example, in Panel B when the deep recession state is experienced the firm has a ($40.00) taxable loss that can be used to reduce taxable income from a prior period or a future period and save the firm 25% of the loss in taxes, or $10.

Figure 5

The Cost of Capital and the Tradeoff Theory

The tradeoff theory says that the tax savings benefits of debt financing drive down the firm's weighted average cost of capital over reasonable ranges of debt-to-equity ratios. However, as firms issue more and more debt, the expected costs of bankruptcy begin to rise, which in turn increases the costs of debt. This increase in the cost of debt can offset the tax savings benefits of debt, eventually causing the weighted average cost of capital to rise.

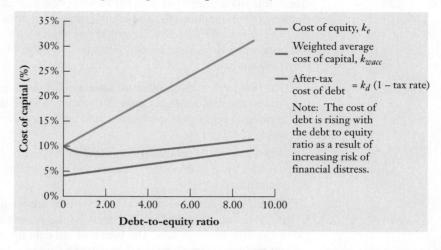

>> END FIGURE 5

Capital Structure Decisions and Agency Costs

Public corporations are managed by professional managers who do not own all the shares of the firms they manage. As learned in **P** Principle 5: **Individuals Response to Incentives**, when the managers who control the firm's operations own only a small fraction of its shares, there will be times when their self-interest is not the same as the interests of the stockholders who own the majority of the firm's shares. When this is the case, the managers may make choices that are not in the shareholders' interests, resulting in what economists call **agency costs**. It is sometimes possible to reduce these agency costs through the use of debt financing. For example, it is often argued that managers of firms that have high levels of cash flow tend to become complacent about controls over spending that cash and may engage in wasteful spending practices such as buying expensive company buildings, airplanes, and so forth. Corporate executives may also invest in new lines of business that provide opportunities for themselves and their employees, but may not be particularly profitable for the firm's stockholders.

One way to limit these choices and to get managers to focus more narrowly on stockholder interests is to increase the firm's debt obligations, thereby reducing the firm's discretionary control over its cash flow. For example, in 2009 a financially distressed Citigroup canceled its planned delivery of a new corporate jet. As we discussed previously, financial distress generally has negative consequences; however, the threat of financial distress can provide a source of discipline that restrains managers who might otherwise make choices that are not in their shareholders' best interests.

Making Financing Choices When Managers Are Better Informed Than Shareholders

Up until now, we have assumed that a firm and its investors agree about the fundamental values of the firm's debt and equity. In reality this may not be the case. Indeed, it is not at all uncommon for managers of companies to believe that their share price is too low, and when this is the case, they may be reluctant to issue new shares. For many closely held smaller companies, this unwillingness to issue what they perceive as underpriced shares is compounded by the fact that issuing shares often means sharing control. For both of these reasons, firms often prefer to raise external capital with debt rather than equity.

This preference for raising external debt is compounded by the fact that investors tend to be skeptical of the motives of firms that issue new shares. As a result, when firms do issue shares it is often greeted as a signal that the firm's stock is overpriced. Indeed, when firms announce their intentions to issue equity, their share price generally falls.

MIT financial economist Stewart Myers suggested that because of the information issues that arise when firms issue equity, firms tend to adhere to the following pecking order when they raise capital:

- The firm first relies on **internal sources of financing**, or the retention of the firm's earnings. If the firm generates more cash than is needed to fund its investments, the cash will be used to repay debt, purchase marketable securities, or repurchase some of the firm's stock.

- When internally generated cash flow falls short of the firm's need for funds, the firm will use its available cash balances and raise additional cash by selling short-term debt securities.

- If the firm's cash and marketable securities are insufficient to meet the firm's financial requirements, then the firm will begin issuing securities beginning with the safest security it can sell, which is debt. The firm will sell debt up until the point where either the costs are prohibitive or where the debt puts the firm at serious risk of default.

- Next, the firm will sell hybrid securities such as convertible bonds, and then, as a last resort, it will sell equity to the public markets.

Managerial Implications

Our brief overview of capital structure theory has revealed the following important learning points:

1. Higher levels of debt in its capital structure can benefit a firm for two reasons: first, interest on the firm's debt is tax deductible, whereas dividends to common stock are not; and second, the use of debt financing can sometimes help align the incentives of managers with those of shareholders.

2. Higher levels of debt in its capital structure will increase the probability that a firm becomes financially distressed or bankrupt. There are costs to the firm from financial distress and bankruptcy that offset the tax and incentives benefits of debt.

The fact that managers tend to be better informed about the value of their firms tends to reduce the frequency of equity issues. This occurs because managers are reluctant to issue equity when they believe that their shares are underpriced. In addition, because investors understand that managers have an incentive to issue stock when it is overpriced, announcements of equity issues generally result in a decline in share prices.

This relationship is presented graphically in Figure 6. Here we see that the tax shield effect is dominant until point A is reached. After point A, the rising costs of the likelihood of firm failure (financial distress) and agency costs cause the market value of the levered firm to decline. The objective for the financial manager here is to find point A by using all of the manager's analytical skills; this effort must also include a good dose of seasoned judgment. At point A, the actual market value of the levered firm is maximized, and the firm's weighted average cost of capital is at a minimum.

Figure 6

Capital Structure and Firm Value with Taxes, Agency Costs, and Financial Distress Costs

This figure considers the value of the firm in three different scenarios, with Scenario III being the most realistic because it incorporates the added value of the interest tax savings as well as the costs of financial distress and agency that go along with the use of debt:

Scenario I: The green horizontal line. In this scenario, the Modigliani and Miller theorem holds, so firm value is not affected by the level of debt.

Scenario II: The blue upward-sloping line. In this scenario, debt payments are tax deductible, but there are no agency and financial distress costs.

Scenario III: The hump-shaped red line. In this scenario, debt influences firm value because of interest tax savings as well as because of agency costs and the cost of financial distress. In this last scenario, the optimal amount of debt for the firm is found where firm value is maximized.

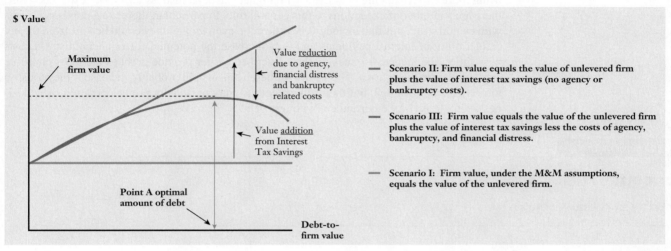

>> END FIGURE 6

Before you move on to 3

Concept Check | 2

1. Who were the financial economists that in 1958 challenged the importance of capital structure management? What is the essence of their theory of capital structure?

2. Discuss the role of the following factors in the firm's capital structure decision: taxes, bankruptcy costs, managerial incentives, and how well informed managers are compared to stockholders.

 # Why Do Capital Structures Differ across Industries?

Recall that in Figure 1 we showed that firms in different industries can have very different capital structures. For example, firms in the computer software industry tend to use very little debt in their capital structures, whereas firms in the casino and gaming industry tend to use much more financial leverage.

To understand these differences we need to think carefully about the costs and benefits associated with including more debt in a firm's capital structure. Let's consider first the importance of corporate taxes, which lower the cost of debt financing relative to equity financing because interest is tax deductible and dividends paid to stockholders are not. Firms in some industries, such as electricity and gas utilities and casinos, tend to generate lots of taxable income, and consequently the likelihood that they will reap the benefit of the tax deductibility of interest payments is very high. However, in industries such as computer software, firms have very little taxable income because of the large expenses associated with developing computer code as well as other research and development expenses. For these firms the tax benefits of financial leverage are less certain, and consequently there will be less to gain from increasing their use of financial leverage.

Financial distress and bankruptcy costs also differ in importance across industries. For a computer and software firm such as Apple, financial distress could be devastating. Customers would be very reluctant to buy an Apple computer with its proprietary operating system if they believed that Apple may not stay in business. For similar reasons, Apple would find it difficult to attract the best programmers if it were financially distressed. It is sometimes said that the "scent of death" can kill a company. Although this applies to software firms, it does not apply to all firms. For example, you probably would not hesitate to enter a casino or stay at a hotel because of concerns about the financial health of the company. These firms can take on lots of debt without jeopardizing the viability of their businesses.

Although we tend to observe firms with lower financial distress costs and higher tax gains using more debt financing than firms with higher financial distress costs and lower tax gains, there are a number of exceptions to this general rule. In particular, there are a number of firms with capital structures that include very little debt, even though they could benefit from the tax deductibility of interest payments and only increase the potential for financial distress costs very little. The incentive issues that we described earlier provide perhaps the most plausible explanation for these firms. The values of these firms would probably increase if they took on more financial leverage, but their top executives may personally prefer operating their businesses in a less risky environment with less debt.

Before you move on to 4

Concept Check | 3

1. What are some reasons for firms in different industries to have different capital structures?

4 Making Financing Decisions

We have just learned that there can be costs and benefits associated with including more debt in a firm's capital structure. To determine the optimal capital structure for the firm, the financial manager must weigh these benefits and costs to come up with an appropriate level of debt. As part of this process, the financial manager will typically compare the firm's capital structure to that of similar firms. In addition, the financial manager will consider the effect of financing alternatives on the level and volatility of the firm's reported earnings per share (EPS), and also the firm's risk of default.

Benchmarking the Firm's Capital Structure

By **benchmarking** a firm's capital structure, we compare the firm's current and proposed capital structures to those of a set of firms that are considered to be in similar lines of business and consequently subject to the same types of risks. For example, we might compare the capital structure of Home Depot to that of Lowe's, but we probably would not compare it to that of Dell Computers.

The objective of benchmarking is not to simply copy what the firm's competitors are doing. Instead, we use benchmarking to determine a starting point for our analysis. For example, consider the situation where the firm being analyzed currently has a debt ratio of 45 percent, and raising additional funds with debt will push the debt ratio to 50 percent. If other firms in similar businesses all have debt ratios less than 30 percent, we would probably want to be extremely cautious about engaging in additional borrowing. In other words, we would want to perform a detailed analysis of the impact of the financing choice on the level and volatility of firm EPS and the risk of default.

Table 3 contains a simple template for the type of benchmarking comparisons the financial analyst will want to make. In the template we include both the debt ratio (total liabilities divided by total assets) and the **interest-bearing debt ratio** as measures of how the firm has financed its assets. The former ratio includes all of the firm's liabilities in the numerator, whereas the latter includes only those liabilities (debts) that are interest bearing. The latter includes such things as bank loans, bonds, and other types of debt on which an explicit interest payment must be made by the borrower to the lender. Specifically excluded are the firm's non-interest-bearing liabilities such as accounts payable and accrued expenses that do not

Table 3   Worksheet for Benchmarking a Capital Structure Decision

Benchmarking is a tool for analyzing financing decisions that compares the effects of the financing alternatives on the firm's financial ratios. The benchmarking process involves calculating a set of financial leverage ratios for the firm under three scenarios: (i) prior to any new financing episode (the firm as it exists today), (ii) with common equity financing, and (iii) with debt financing. The resulting ratios are then compared to these same ratios for similar firms.

Two types of financial ratios are typically used, balance-sheet-based measures of the extent to which debt financing has been used by the firm (i.e., the debt ratio and interest-bearing debt ratio found below) and coverage ratios that indicate the ability of the firm to meet the financial requirements of its debt (i.e., the times interest earned ratio and the EBITDA coverage ratio found below). These financial leverage ratios are then used to compare a firm's capital structure to the financial leverage ratios of similar firms (the final column).

Ratio	Formula	Existing Ratio	Ratio with Common Stock Financing	Ratio with Debt Financing	Comparison Ratios for Similar Firms
Debt ratio	$\dfrac{\text{Total Liabilities}}{\text{Total Assets}}$	____ %	____ %	____ %	____ %
Interest-bearing debt ratio	$\dfrac{\text{Interest-Bearing Debt}}{\text{Total Assets}}$	____ %	____ %	____ %	____ %
Times interest earned ratio	$\dfrac{\text{Earnings before Interest and Taxes}}{\text{Interest Expense}}$	____ times	____ times	____ times	____ times
EBITDA coverage ratio	$\dfrac{\text{Earnings before Interest and Taxes} + \text{Depreciation Expense} + \text{Amortization Expense}}{\text{Interest Expense} + \left(\dfrac{\text{Principal Payments}}{1 - \text{Tax Rate}}\right)}$	____ times	____ times	____ times	____ times

have an explicit interest expense.[6] The only difference in these two ratios is the fact that the latter restricts the definition of debt to debt on which explicit interest payments must be made. Interestingly, Barnes and Noble (BKS) had a debt ratio (total liabilities divided by total assets) of 72.5 percent. However, almost all of the firm's debt was in the form of accounts payable arising out of the sale of gift cards on which the firm paid no interest. When we restrict our attention to interest-bearing debt which is what is used in the Debt-to-Enterprise-Value ratio, Barnes and Noble had a 3.8 percent Debt-to-Enterprise-Value ratio (see Table 1) because of the very small amount of interest-bearing debt outstanding.

Table 3 also includes two measures of the firm's ability to pay the interest and principal on its debt. The first measure is the times interest earned ratio, which is equal to the ratio of the firm's earnings before interest and taxes (EBIT) to interest expense. The second ratio is the **EBITDA coverage ratio**. This latter ratio differs from the times interest earned ratio in both its numerator, which adds non-cash charges such as depreciation and amortization back to EBIT, and in its denominator, which not only includes interest expense but also the principal repayments the firm is obligated to make. Note that the principal payments are "grossed up" to reflect the fact that principal payments are paid using after-tax earnings, whereas interest expense is paid before taxes are paid. Thus, assuming that the firm must make a $100,000 principal payment, it will have to earn $100,000 \div (1 - \text{Tax Rate})$. For example, should the tax rate be 40 percent, then the firm would have to earn $100,000 \div (1 - .40) = \$166,666.67$ before taxes in order to have the needed $100,000 to repay the principal on its debt.

Evaluating the Effect of Financial Leverage on Firm Earnings per Share

The firm's capital structure decisions affect both the level and the volatility of the firm's reported earnings per share (EPS). Firms that use more debt financing, other things remaining the

---

[6]For example, when a firm purchases items for its inventories from one of its suppliers, the credit terms might simply require that the amount of credit extended has to be repaid in 90 days. We would expect that the price of the items purchased would include an implicit charge for the 90-day period for which credit is extended. However, because no explicit rate of interest is stated, we cannot separate out the cost of credit from the pricing of the items purchased.

Benchmarking a Financing Decision

Sister Sarah's Homemade Pies, Inc. is a rapidly growing manufacturer and distributor of frozen pastries and desserts. The company was founded in 1992 by Sarah Goodnight, who used old family recipes and southern home-style cooking to prepare a wide variety of desserts. By 2013 the business had grown to the point that it was expected to produce $50 million in revenues based on total assets of $29.8 million. The firm has outgrown its manufacturing facility and is planning to invest $10 million in a new, modern plant. With the added capacity of the new plant, the firm expects to increase its revenues from $50 million to $60 million per year. In addition, the 20 percent increase in revenues will be accompanied by a 20 percent increase in cost of goods sold and operating expenses. The new equipment will be depreciated over a 10-year life and result in $1 million in additional depreciation expense per year (amortization expenses are zero); assume a 30 percent tax rate.

Two financing alternatives are being considered. The first involves issuing 1.342 million shares of common stock, and the second involves borrowing the entire $10 million ($2 million in additional short-term debt and $8 million in long-term debt). The firm currently owes $6 million in combined short- and long-term debt on which it pays 8 percent interest and pays $1.2 million a year in principal payments. If the debt option is selected, the firm will pay 8 percent interest on the added $10 million in short- plus long-term debt and in addition will pay $2 million per year in principal on the new debt until the note is repaid.

What will the effect be on Sister Sarah's Homemade Pies, Inc.'s financial ratios if the firm uses the equity alternative? What about the debt alternative?

STEP 1: Picture the problem

The firm's 2010 balance sheet that does not reflect the added $10 million, and pro forma balance sheets that do reflect the added financing, are as follows:

Balance Sheet	Pro formas Adjusted for New Financing		
	2013	Equity	Debt
Accounts payable	$ 4,500,000	$ 4,500,000	$ 4,500,000
Short-term debt	$ 1,200,000	$ 1,200,000	$ 3,200,000
Total current liabilities	$ 5,700,000	$ 5,700,000	$ 7,700,000
Long-term debt	4,800,000	4,800,000	12,800,000
Common equity	19,300,000	29,300,000	19,300,000
Total	$29,800,000	$39,800,000	$39,800,000

The firm's income statement for 2013 and pro forma income statements for 2013 that reflect the equity and debt financing options as follows:

Income Statement	Pro formas Adjusted for New Financing		
	2013	Equity	Debt
Revenues	$ 50,000,000	$ 60,000,000	$ 60,000,000
Cost of goods sold	(25,000,000)	(30,000,000)	(30,000,000)
Gross profit	$ 25,000,000	$ 30,000,000	$ 30,000,000
Operating expenses	(10,000,000)	(12,000,000)	(12,000,000)
Depreciation expense	(2,000,000)	(3,000,000)	(3,000,000)
EBIT	$ 13,000,000	$ 15,000,000	$ 15,000,000
Interest expense	(480,000)	(480,000)	(1,280,000)
Earnings before taxes	$ 12,520,000	$ 14,520,000	$ 13,720,000
Taxes	(3,756,000)	(4,356,000)	(4,116,000)
Net income	$ 8,764,000	$ 10,164,000	$ 9,604,000

STEP 2: Decide on a solution strategy

Table 3 provides a useful template for presenting four key financial leverage ratios that can be used to benchmark the firm against others in the industry.

STEP 3: Solve

Calculating the four benchmark financial ratios found in Table 3, we get the following:

Ratios	Formula	Existing Ratio	Ratio with Common Stock Financing	Ratio with Debt Financing
Debt ratio	$\dfrac{\text{Total Liabilities}}{\text{Total Assets}}$	35.2%	26.4%	51.5%
Interest-bearing debt ratio	$\dfrac{\text{Interest-Bearing Debt}}{\text{Total Assets}}$	20.1%	15.1%	40.2%
Times interest earned ratio	$\dfrac{\text{Earnings before Interest and Taxes}}{\text{Interest Expense}}$	27.08	31.25	11.72
EBITDA coverage ratio	$\dfrac{\text{Earnings before Interest and Taxes} + \text{Depreciation Expense} + \text{Amortization Expense}}{\text{Interest Expense} + \left(\dfrac{\text{Principal Payments}}{1 - \text{Tax Rate}}\right)}$	6.84	8.20	3.08

STEP 4: Analyze

Raising the entire $10 million through either an equity offering or by borrowing has a dramatic effect on the firm's capital structure. For example, the debt ratio will either drop from 35.2 percent to 26.4 percent with an equity offering or increase to 51.5 percent if debt is used. The interest-bearing debt ratio changes in a similar manner, dropping from 20.1 percent to 15.1 percent if equity financing is used and rising to 40.2 percent if the debt financing alternative is chosen. The times interest earned ratio will rise slightly from 27.08 to 31.25 if the equity offering is chosen, but drops to only 11.72 with a debt offering. The EBITDA coverage ratio, which incorporates consideration for non-cash expenses (depreciation) in the numerator as well as the repayment of principal in the denominator, increases to 8.20 from 6.84 if equity is used and falls to 3.08 if debt is used.

To complete our benchmark analysis we need to compare the above leverage ratios to the following comparable firm ratios:

Comparable Firm Ratios	
Debt ratio	40%
Interest-bearing debt ratio	30%
Times interest earned ratio	22 times
EBITDA coverage ratio	6 times

Benchmarking Sister Sarah's capital structure against these norms, it is apparent that the debt alternative is a more aggressive use of debt financing than is the norm for the industry. Notice that we are evaluating the impact of the financing decision on the firm only for the year in which the financing is raised. Because the debt will be paid down over time, the current year will be the worst these ratios will look in comparison to the ratio norms. Specifically, the firm will pay down $2 million per year of the new debt in 2014 in addition to $1.2 million of the firm's existing debt. Consequently, we need to think beyond the current year when making the financing decision. Ultimately, the decision of whether or not to use more debt cannot be made based solely on the benchmark comparison to industry norms. For example, Sister Sarah's management may be so confident about the firm's future earnings prospects that they feel they can afford the higher use of debt financing.

STEP 5: Check yourself

Under the debt financing alternative, what will Sister Sarah's financial ratios look like in just two years after the firm has repaid $4 million of the loan (assuming nothing else changes)? (Hint: Subtract $4 million in long-term debt on the balance sheet for the debt financing alternative.)

ANSWER: Debt ratio = 46.1%, interest-bearing debt ratio = 33.5%, times interest earned ratio = 15.63, and EBITDA coverage ratio = 4.10.

Your Turn: For more practice, do related **Study Problems** 1, 3, 5, 9, and 12 at the end of this chapter.

>> END Checkpoint 1

same, will experience greater swings in their earnings per share in response to changes in firm revenues and operating earnings. This is generally referred to as the **financial leverage effect**.

Let's take a look at how financial leverage works. The founders of a newly formed business venture, the House of Toast, Inc., estimate that the firm will need $200,000 to purchase the assets needed to get the business up and running. The company founders are considering the three possible financing plans:

- **Plan A.** No financial leverage is used. Instead, the entire $200,000 is raised by selling 2,000 common shares for $100 each.
- **Plan B.** Moderate financial leverage equal to 25 percent of the assets ($50,000) is borrowed using a debt issue that carries an 8 percent annual interest rate and requires the payment of annual interest. The remaining $150,000 is raised through the sale of 1,500 shares of common stock at a price of $100 per share.
- **Plan C.** Even more financial leverage is used in this plan whereby $80,000 of the $200,000 needed is borrowed (40 percent). The debt issue carries an interest rate of 8 percent and requires the payment of annual interest. The remaining $120,000 is raised by selling 1,200 shares of common stock for $100 per share.

Table 4 contains the balance sheets for the House of Toast, Inc. under each financing plan.

Financial Leverage and the Level of EPS

Financial leverage can sometimes make a firm's earnings per share higher and at other times lower. The key determinant of the effect of financial leverage on the level of earnings per share is the rate of return earned by the firm on its assets. For example, if the firm is borrowing at 8 percent and earns 10 percent on the borrowed money, then the additional 2 percent that the firm earns over the cost of borrowing goes to the common shareholders. This increases both the rate of return earned on the common shareholders' equity and the earnings per share. When this happens the firm is said to benefit from the use of *favorable* financial leverage because the use of debt financing results in higher EPS and an increase in the firm's return on equity.

To illustrate the effect of financial leverage on a firm's earnings per share and the firm's return on equity, consider the three capital structure plans described earlier for the House of Toast, Inc. In this example the firm experiences operating earnings of $10,000 (in what the firm's CFO estimates to be a worst-case scenario), and $40,000 (in what the CFO estimates to be a best-case scenario). As shown in Table 5, in the worst-case scenario the firm earns only 5 percent on its investments, and because it has to pay 8 percent interest on its debt, financial leverage reduces firm earnings per share—if the firm takes either Plans B or C—below what it would achieve if it were all-equity financed (Plan A). However, in the best-case scenario where the firm earns a return on assets of 20 percent (EBIT/Total Assets = $40,000/$200,000), Plans B and C provide higher EPS and higher rates of return on equity than the all-equity plan.

Table 4	Alternative Financial Structures Being Considered by the House of Toast, Inc.		
PLAN A: 0% DEBT			
		Total debt	$ 0
		Common equity	200,000[a]
Total assets	$200,000	Total liabilities and equity	$200,000
PLAN B: 25% DEBT AT 8% INTEREST RATE			
		Total debt	$ 50,000
		Common equity	150,000[b]
Total assets	$200,000	Total liabilities and equity	$200,000
PLAN C: 40% DEBT AT 8% INTEREST RATE			
		Total debt	$ 80,000
		Common equity	120,000[c]
Total assets	$200,000	Total liabilities and equity	$200,000

[a]2,000 common shares outstanding; [b]1,500 common shares outstanding; [c]1,200 common shares outstanding.

| Table 5 | Structure and the Level of EPS for the House of Toast, Inc. |

This example illustrates the effect of the use of financial leverage on a firm's earnings per share and return on common equity. The important thing to note here is that the use of financial leverage has the effect of magnifying increases and decreases in the firm's operating income on EPS and return on common equity.

	Plan A: 0% Debt		Plan B: 25% Debt		Plan C: 40% Debt	
Common shares	2,000		1,500		1,200	
Debt financing	$ 0		$ 50,000		$80,000	
	Worst Case	**Best Case**	**Worst Case**	**Best Case**	**Worst Case**	**Best Case**
Operating return on assets	5%	20%	5%	20%	5%	20%
Operating earnings (EBIT)	$ 10,000	$40,000	$10,000	$40,000	$10,000	$40,000
Less: Interest expense	0	0	(4,000)	(4,000)	(6,400)	(6,400)
Earnings before taxes	$ 10,000	$40,000	$ 6,000	$36,000	$ 3,600	$33,600
Less: Taxes	(5,000)	(20,000)	(3,000)	(18,000)	(1,800)	(16,800)
Net income	$ 5,000	$20,000	$ 3,000	$18,000	$ 1,800	$16,800
Earnings per share (EPS)	$ 2.50	$ 10.00	$ 2.00	$ 12.00	$ 1.50	$ 14.00
Return on equity	2.5%	10.0%	2.0%	12.0%	1.5%	14.0%

Assumptions:		**Legend:**
Total assets	$200,000	Operating return on assets = EBIT/Total assets
Share price	$ 100.00	Return on equity = Net income/Common equity
Borrowing rate	8%	Earnings per share = Net income/Shares outstanding
Corporate tax rate	50%	

Financial Leverage and the Volatility of EPS

Table 5 also illustrates the impact of financial leverage on the volatility of earnings per share. For example, consider the following summary of the effect of increasing EBIT from $10,000 to $40,000 on the EPS of capital structure Plans A, B, and C:

Capital Structure	Worst Case EBIT = $10,000	Best Case EBIT = $40,000	$ Change in EPS	% Change in EPS
Plan A	$2.50	$10.00	$ 7.50	300%
Plan B	2.00	12.00	10.00	500%
Plan C	1.50	14.00	12.50	833%

% Change in EPS for Plan B is calculated as follows:
$$\frac{\$12 - 2}{\$2} = 5 \text{ or } 500\%$$

The $30,000 or 300 percent increase in EBIT from the worst- to best-case scenario results in a 300 percent increase in the EPS of capital structure under Plan A, which has no financial leverage. However, the same increase in EBIT results in a 500 percent increase in the EPS of the firm under Plan B and an 833 percent increase under Plan C. *The key learning point here is that increasing financial leverage, holding everything else the same, leads to greater volatility in EPS!*

What would happen if the direction of the change in EBIT were reversed? In other words, what if EBIT drops from $40,000 to only $10,000? As this example illustrates, financial leverage is a double-edged sword in that it works in both the positive and negative directions—in effect, demonstrating ▣ Principle 2: **There Is a Risk–Return Tradeoff**. When EBIT is high, a more levered firm will realize higher earnings per share. However, if EBIT falls, a firm that uses more financial leverage will suffer a larger drop in earnings per share than a firm that relies less on financial leverage.

Using the EBIT-EPS Chart to Analyze the Effect of Capital Structure on EPS

The **EBIT-EPS chart** (sometimes called the **range of earnings chart**) is the principal tool used to evaluate the effects of capital structure choices on earnings per share. To illustrate how this tool

Checkpoint 2

Evaluating the Effect of Financing Decisions on EPS

The House of Toast, Inc. is considering a new investment that will cost $50,000 and that will increase the firm's annual operating earnings (EBIT) by $10,000 per year from the current level of $20,000 to $30,000. The firm can raise the $50,000 by (1) selling 500 shares of common stock at $100 each, or (2) selling bonds that will net the firm $50,000 and carry an interest rate of 8.5 percent. What is the EPS for the expected level of EBIT equal to $30,000? What is the effect of the financing alternatives on the level and volatility of the firm's EPS if the firm anticipates that its EBIT will fall within the range of $20,000 to $40,000 per year?

STEP 1: Picture the problem

The current and prospective capital structure alternatives can be described using pro forma balance sheets as follows:

Existing Capital Structure		With New Common Stock Financing		With New Debt Financing	
Long-term debt at 8%	$ 50,000	Long-term debt at 8%	$ 50,000	Long-term debt at 8%	$ 50,000
Common stock	150,000	Common stock	200,000	Long-term debt at 8.5%	50,000
				Common stock	150,000
Total liabilities and equity	$200,000	Total liabilities and equity	$250,000	Total liabilities and equity	$250,000
Common shares outstanding	1,500	Common shares outstanding	2,000	Common shares outstanding	1,500

STEP 2: Decide on a solution strategy

A firm's capital structure choice will affect both the level of EPS for a given level of operating earnings (EBIT) and the volatility of changes in EPS corresponding to changes in EBIT. To analyze both of these attributes of the problem, we use pro forma income statements for a range of levels of EBIT that the firm believes is relevant to its future performance.

STEP 3: Solve

Pro forma income statements for the two financing alternatives evaluated at the projected EBIT level of $30,000 reveal that EPS for the common stock and debt alternatives are $6.50 and $7.25, respectively.

	Existing Capital Structure	With New Common Stock Financing	With New Debt Financing
EBIT	$20,000	$30,000	$30,000
Less: Interest expense	(4,000)	(4,000)	(8,250)
Earnings before taxes (EBT)	$16,000	$26,000	$21,750
Less: Taxes at 50%	(8,000)	(13,000)	(10,875)
Net income	$ 8,000	$13,000	$10,875
Less: Preferred dividends	0	0	0
Net income	$ 8,000	$13,000	$10,875
Common shares outstanding	1,500	2,000	1,500
EPS = Net income/Common shares outstanding	$ 5.33	$ 6.50	$ 7.25

Both are considerably above the $5.33 EPS the firm would earn if the new project is rejected and the additional financial capital was not raised. If the firm selects the financing plan that will provide the highest EPS, the debt alternative is clearly favored. However, debt (bond) financing increases the risk of the returns to the equity investors. That is, changes in the firm's EBIT cause bigger changes in the firm's EPS where debt financing is used. To analyze this issue we calculate the EPS that would be earned under the equity financing and debt financing plans over a range of EBIT corresponding to the CFO's estimates of what the firm might actually earn (which are $20,000 to $40,000). We plot these estimates of EPS for each of the capital structures in the EBIT-EPS chart in Figure 7.

Figure 7

EBIT-EPS Chart for the House of Toast, Inc.: Under New Financing

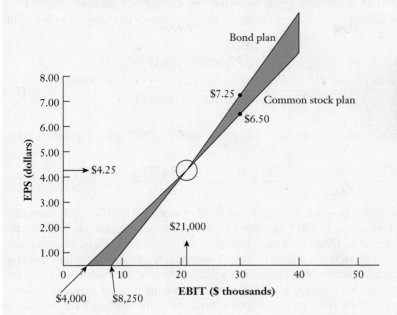

	Earnings per Share	
EBIT	**Common Stock Financing**	**Debt Financing**
$ 4,000	0	(1.42)
8,250	1.06	0
20,000	**4.00**	**3.92**
21,000	4.25	4.25
30,000	6.50	7.25
40,000	**9.00**	**10.58**

>> END FIGURE 7

The EPS for EBIT of $20,000 is $3.92 for the debt alternative and $4.00 for the equity financing alternative. If EBIT is equal to $40,000, however, the debt plan produces $10.58 in EPS compared to only $9.00 for the equity plan. In fact, for EBIT levels above $21,000, the EPS for the debt financing alternative is greater than EPS for equity financing alternative.

STEP 4: Analyze

Within the range $21,000 to $40,000 for EBIT, the House of Toast can expect that the debt plan will provide the same or higher (but more volatile) EPS for the firm. The added volatility in EPS for the debt alternative is evidenced in the steepness of the EBIT-EPS line corresponding to the debt financing plan above. For example, a decrease in EBIT from $40,000 to $20,000 results in a drop in EPS for the debt plan from $10.58 to $3.92 (or –63 percent), whereas the corresponding drop in EPS for the equity plan is from $9.00 to $4.00 (or –56 percent). So, even though the debt plan offers higher EPS for the majority of the anticipated range of EBIT levels ($20,000 to $30,000), it will result in more volatile changes in EPS when EBIT changes from year to year.

STEP 5: Check yourself

House of Toast likes the new investment very much. However, in the weeks since the project was first analyzed the firm has learned that credit tightening in the financial markets has caused the cost of debt financing for the debt financing plan to increase to 10 percent. What level of EBIT produces zero EPS for the new borrowing rate?

ANSWER: EBIT = $9,000.

Your turn: For more practice, do related **Study Problem** 12 at the end of this chapter.   >> END Checkpoint 2

can be used, consider the two financing alternatives faced by the House of Toast, Inc. in Checkpoint 2. The first thing you will want to consider is whether the debt plan produces a higher level of EPS for the most likely range of EBIT values that you expect in the future. The next thing to consider is the possible swings in EPS that might occur under the capital structure alternatives.

Computing EPS Indifference Points for Capital Structure Alternatives

The point of intersection of the two capital structure lines found in Figure 7 is sometimes called the **EBIT-EPS indifference point**. This point identifies the EBIT level at which the EPS will be the same regardless of the financing plan chosen by the firm. This indifference point has major implications for financial planning. At EBIT amounts in excess of the EBIT indifference level, the financing plan with *more* leverage will generate a higher EPS. At EBIT amounts below the EBIT indifference level, the financing plan involving *less* leverage will generate a higher EPS.

We can find the EBIT indifference level graphically, as shown in Figure 7, or by using the following equation:

$$\underbrace{\frac{(\text{EBIT} - \text{Interest Expense}_{\text{Stock Plan}})(1 - \text{Tax Rate})}{\text{Shares Outstanding (Stock Plan)}}}_{\text{EPS for the Stock Plan}} = \underbrace{\frac{(\text{EBIT} - \text{Interest Expense}_{\text{Bond Plan}})(1 - \text{Tax Rate})}{\text{Shares Outstanding (Bond Plan)}}}_{\text{EPS for the Bond Plan}} \quad \textbf{(11)}$$

For the present example, we calculate the indifference level of EBIT using Equation (11) as follows:

$$\frac{(EBIT - \$4{,}000)(1 - .50)}{2{,}000} = \frac{(EBIT - \$8{,}250)(1 - .50)}{1{,}500}$$

When the expression above is solved for EBIT, we see that when EBIT is $21,000, then EPS will be $4.25 under both plans. If EBIT exceeds $21,000, then the debt plan produces higher EPS; if EBIT is lower than $21,000, the equity plan produces the higher EPS of the two plans.

Before concluding this section it should be noted that managers do tend to be very aware of how their capital structure choices affect their firm's EPS. However, our discussion of capital structure theory taught us that earnings per share should not be the primary driver of a firm's capital structure choice. Thus, the type of analysis considered in this section must be used in conjunction with other basic tools in reaching the objective of capital structure management.

Can the Firm Afford More Debt?

In our earlier discussion we described the firm's financial structure as either the relative proportion of debt used to finance the firm's total assets (Equation [1]) or the debt-to-enterprise-value ratio (Equation [3]). These ratios told us something about the relative amount of debt the firm uses, but nothing about the ability of the firm to pay the interest or principal on the debt. In addition, earlier in this chapter we identified the times interest earned ratio as a useful measure of a firm's ability to pay the interest it owes on its debt financing:

$$\frac{\text{Times Interest}}{\text{Earned}} = \frac{\text{Operating Income or EBIT}}{\text{Interest Expense}} \quad \textbf{(3)}$$

For example, in its 2011 income statement Walmart reported earnings before interest and taxes (EBIT) of $26.72 billion and had interest expenses totaling $2.322 billion. Substituting into Equation (3) produces a times interest earned ratio of 10.46 times for the year as follows (all numbers are in thousands of dollars):

$$\frac{\text{Times Interest}}{\text{Earned}} = \frac{\text{Operating Income or EBIT}}{\text{Interest Expense}} = \frac{\$26{,}720{,}000}{\$2{,}322{,}000} = 11.51 \text{ times}$$

This ratio indicates that Walmart can very comfortably afford to pay the interest on its debt (financial leverage), as operating earnings could be reduced to 1/10th of their 2011 level before the firm would have trouble paying its interest expense.

The EBITDA coverage ratio is yet another coverage ratio that refines the times interest earned ratio to incorporate consideration for depreciation and amortization (which are non-cash expenses that are deducted from revenues when calculating EBIT) and also includes consideration for both principal payments that are due during the period as well as interest expense. Specifically, the EBITDA coverage ratio is calculated as follows:

$$\frac{\text{EBITDA}}{\text{Coverage Ratio}} = \frac{\begin{array}{c}\text{Earnings before} \\ \text{Interest and Taxes}\end{array} + \begin{array}{c}\text{Depreciation} \\ \text{Expense}\end{array} + \begin{array}{c}\text{Amortization} \\ \text{Expense}\end{array}}{\text{Interest Expense} + \text{Principal Payments}} = \frac{\text{EBITDA}}{\text{Interest Expense} + \text{Principal Payments}} \quad \textbf{(12)}$$

To illustrate, assume that Walmart's principal payments on its debt in 2011 equaled $5 billion and depreciation expense equals $6.739 billion, and there were no amortization expenses.

The resulting EBITDA coverage ratio for Walmart is calculated as follows (all numbers are in thousands of dollars):

$$\text{EBITDA Coverage Ratio} = \frac{\text{Earnings before Interest and Taxes} + \text{Depreciation Expense} + \text{Amortization Expense}}{\text{Interest Expense} + \text{Principal Payments}} = \frac{\$26{,}720{,}000 + \$6{,}739{,}000}{\$2{,}322{,}000 + \$5{,}000{,}000} = 4.57 \text{ times}$$

This ratio more realistically captures Walmart's ability to service its debt and suggests that EBITDA could drop by over three-fourths of the 2011 level before the firm would be in jeopardy of not being able to pay its interest plus principal out of its 2011 operating earnings.

We now have the financial decision tools to evaluate the firm's capital structure. The latest addition to our decision tools is the EBDITA coverage ratio, shown as follows:

Tools of Financial Analysis—EBITDA Coverage Ratio

Name of Tool	Formula	What It Tells You
EBITDA Coverage Ratio	$\dfrac{EBIT + Depreciation\ Expense + Amortization\ Expense}{Interest\ Expense + Principal\ Payments}$	• An alternative coverage ratio that tells you how many times the firm could pay interest and principal from the cash flow from operations • A higher ratio indicates a lower probability of default.

Survey Evidence: Factors That Influence CFO Debt Policy

John Graham and Campbell Harvey surveyed 392 CFOs and asked them about the importance of potential determinants of their capital structure choices. The CFOs were asked to rate 14 factors using a scale from 0 to 4, with a 0 indicating not important and 4 representing very important. The percentage of respondents that rated a particular factor as either important (3) or very important (4) is reported in Figure 8.

Financial flexibility received the highest rating, with over 59 percent of the respondents rating this factor as either an important or very important factor influencing their decision to use debt financing. Clearly, maintaining the ability to issue either debt or equity by not

Figure 8

CFO Opinions Regarding Factors That Influence Corporate Debt Use

CFOs of 392 firms were asked to rank a list of 14 factors in the order of importance to their firms in making the decision to use debt financing. The percentages of respondents that rated each factor either as important or very important are listed below for the eight highest-rated factors.

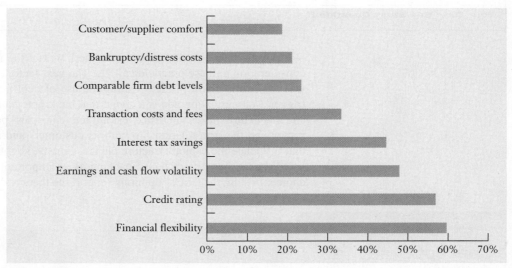

Source: John Graham and Campbell Harvey, "How Do CFOs Make Capital Budgeting and Capital Structure Decisions?", Journal of Applied Corporate Finance, Volume 15, Number 1, (Spring 2002), 14.

>> END FIGURE 8

Finance in a **Flat World**

Capital Structures around the World

Many factors influence the use of debt financing, and one of these factors is the home country of the firm. Consider the following

Country	Leverage Ratio
South Korea	70%
Pakistan	49%
Brazil	47%
Thailand	46%
India	40%
Japan	33%
China	33%
France	28%
Belgium	26%
Mexico	26%
Chile	21%
Germany	17%
United Kingdom	16%
United States	16%
Greece	10%

listing of median leverage ratios (total debt divided by the market value of the firm) by country:*

The highest leverage ratio is observed in South Korea, where the leverage ratio is close to 70 percent, whereas the lowest is only 10 percent, observed in Greece. The median leverage ratio in the United States is only 16 percent, which may seem quite low. However, this is the result of the fact that these ratios are based on the market values of the firms rather than their book value.

What kind of factors might encourage the use of debt in different countries? One factor that researchers found is that firms that operate in countries where the legal systems provide better protection for financial claimants tend to use less total debt, and the debt they use tends to be of a longer-term maturity. In addition, as you might expect, the tax policy of the country that the firm operates within also plays a role in the level of debt that a firm uses.

*The market value of the firm is defined as the market value of common equity plus the book values of preferred stock and total debt.

Source: Joseph P. H. Fan, Sheridan Titman, and Garry J. Twite, "An International Comparison of Capital Structure and Debt Maturity Choices," available at SSRN: http://ssrn.com/abstract=423483.

Your Turn: See Study Question 22.

pushing the firm's capital structure to the limits of the firm's debt capacity is an important consideration to these practicing CFOs. The next factor, in order of importance to the CFOs, was the firm's credit rating. Pushing the use of debt financing past the point where it will trigger a rating downgrade is a signal that bankruptcy and financial distress are more likely, and this in turn makes the firm a less attractive business partner. Indeed, concerns about bankruptcy and the firm relationship with its customers and suppliers were also listed as factors that influence the capital structure choice. Finally, slightly less than 50 percent of the CFOs listed the tax benefits of debt financing as an important influence on their capital structure choice. In sum, the CFOs' opinions support the theory of capital structure policy.

Before you begin end-of-chapter material

Concept Check | 4

1. In what ways does the firm's capital structure affect its earnings per share?
2. What is the EBIT-EPS indifference point, and how is this concept useful in analyzing a capital structure decision?
3. How are various leverage ratios and industry norms used in capital structure management?

P Principle 2: **There Is a Risk–Return Tradeoff** Managers sometimes take on more debt in their capital structures in an attempt to increase the rate of return stockholders receive. However, as we know from Principle 2, the increased return is offset by an increase in risk that results in an increased required rate of return.

P Principle 3: **Cash Flows Are the Source of Value** The relevance of capital structure is determined by whether capital structure choice affects the cash flows that can be distributed to the debt and equity holders.

P Principle 5: **Individuals Respond to Incentives** Added debt and the subsequent need to cover interest payments limits managers' discretionary spending and thereby adds discipline into spending decisions that helps avoid agency problems.

Chapter Summaries

 Describe a firm's capital structure.

SUMMARY: A firm's financial structure is the mix of all items that appear on the right-hand side of its balance sheet. This includes all of the firm's current liabilities as well as long-term debt and owners' equity. For purposes of analyzing a firm's financing decisions, we typically limit our consideration to the firm's capital structure, which includes interest-bearing liabilities such as short- and long-term debt, plus equity (preferred and common). Although it is common practice to evaluate a firm's capital structure using book values, we should use market values when analyzing a firm's capital structure as part of a cost of capital estimation.

KEY TERMS

Enterprise value The sum of the firm's market capitalization plus net debt.

Favorable financial leverage When the firm's investments earn a rate of return (before taxes) that is greater than the cost of borrowing, this results in higher EPS and a higher rate of return on the firm's common equity.

Financial structure The mix of sources of financing used by the firm to finance its assets. Commonly described using the ratio of each source of financing on the right-hand side of the

firm's balance sheet divided by the sum of the firm's total liabilities plus owners' equity.

Net debt The book value of interest-bearing debt less excess cash.

Optimal capital structure The mix of financing sources in the capital structure that maximizes shareholder value.

Unfavorable financial leverage When the firm's investments earn a rate of return (before taxes) that is less than the cost of borrowing, this results in lower EPS and a lower rate of return on the firm's common equity.

KEY EQUATIONS

$$\text{Debt Ratio} = \frac{\text{Total Liabilities}}{\text{Total Assets}} \tag{1}$$

$$\frac{\text{Enterprise}}{\text{Value}} = \left(\frac{\text{Book Value of}}{\text{Interest-Bearing Debt}} - \frac{\text{Excess}}{\text{Cash}} \right) + \frac{\text{Market Value of}}{\text{Equity}} \tag{2}$$

$$\frac{\text{Enterprise}}{\text{Value}} = \frac{\text{Net}}{\text{Debt}} + \frac{\text{Market Value of}}{\text{Equity}} \tag{2a}$$

$$\frac{\text{Debt to Enterprise}}{\text{Value}} = \frac{\dfrac{\text{Book Value of}}{\text{Interest-Bearing Debt}} - \dfrac{\text{Excess}}{\text{Cash}}}{\left(\dfrac{\text{Book Value of}}{\text{Interest-Bearing Debt}} - \dfrac{\text{Excess}}{\text{Cash}} \right) + \dfrac{\text{Market Value of}}{\text{Equity}}} = \frac{\text{Net Debt}}{\text{Enterprise Value}} \tag{3}$$

$$\text{Times Interest Earned Ratio} = \frac{\text{Net Operating Income or EBIT}}{\text{Interest Expense}} \tag{4}$$

Concept Check | 1

1. How does the debt ratio differ from the debt-to-enterprise-value ratio?
2. What does the times interest earned ratio measure?
3. What is financial leverage?
4. What determines whether financial leverage is favorable or unfavorable?

2 Explain why firms have different capital structures and how capital structure influences a firm's weighted average cost of capital.

SUMMARY: Under the Modigliani and Miller (M&M) assumptions, the financing mix or capital structure of the firm does not have any effect on the value of the firm. However, when we relax the M&M assumptions we learn that capital structure can be an important factor in determining the value of the firm. In particular, there are three primary reasons that capital structure can be important. First, because interest payments on the firm's debt are tax deductible but dividend payments on the firm's equity are not, debt financing is favored by the U.S. tax code. Second, interest on debt is a fixed obligation, and firms that default on this obligation can be forced into bankruptcy, which can create numerous costs for the firm. The third factor is that the threat of bankruptcy and more generally financial distress can influence the behavior of a firm's executives and its employees and customers. In particular, the threat of bankruptcy can make the firm a less attractive supplier and employer, but at the same time it can focus the attention of the firm's executives on decisions that contribute to the firm's value, and thereby keep it out of financial trouble.

KEY TERMS

Agency costs The costs incurred by a firm's common stockholders when the firm's management makes decisions that are not in the shareholders' best interest but instead further the interests of the management of the firm.

Financial distress costs The costs incurred by a firm that cannot pay its bills (including principal and interest on debt) in a timely manner.

Interest tax savings The reduction in income tax resulting due to the tax deductibility of interest expense.

Internal sources of financing The retention and reinvestment of firm earnings (i.e., retained earnings) in the firm.

KEY EQUATIONS

$$\text{Firm Value} = \frac{\text{Firm Cash Flow}}{\text{Weighted Average Cost of Capital } (k_{wacc})} \quad (5)$$

$$k_{wacc} = \left[\begin{array}{c}\text{Cost of}\\\text{Debt } (k_d)\end{array} \times \begin{array}{c}\text{Debt to}\\\text{Value } (D/V)\end{array}\right] + \left[\begin{array}{c}\text{Cost of}\\\text{Equity } (k_e)\end{array} \times \begin{array}{c}\text{Equity to}\\\text{Value } (E/V)\end{array}\right] \quad (6)$$

$$\begin{array}{c}\text{Cost of}\\\text{Equity } (k_e)\end{array} = k_{unlevered} + (k_{unlevered} - k_d)\left(\frac{D}{E}\right) \quad (7)$$

$$\left[\begin{array}{c}\text{Cash flow to}\\\text{a firm with}\\\text{financial leverage}\end{array}\right] = \left[\begin{array}{c}\text{Cash flow to}\\\text{the firm without}\\\text{leverage}\end{array}\right] + \left[\begin{array}{c}\text{Interest}\\\text{tax}\\\text{savings}\end{array}\right] \quad (8)$$

$$\begin{array}{c}\text{Cost of}\\\text{Equity } (k_e)\end{array} = k_{Unlevered\,Equity} + \left[(k_{Unlevered\,Equity} - k_d)\left(\frac{D}{E}\right) \times (1 - \text{Tax Rate})\right] \quad (9)$$

$$k_{wacc} = \left[\begin{array}{c}\text{Cost of}\\\text{Debt } (k_d)\end{array}\left(1 - \begin{array}{c}\text{Tax}\\\text{Rate}\end{array}\right) \times \begin{array}{c}\text{Debt to}\\\text{Value } (D/V)\end{array}\right] + \left[\begin{array}{c}\text{Cost of}\\\text{Equity } (k_e)\end{array} \times \begin{array}{c}\text{Equity to}\\\text{Value } (E/V)\end{array}\right] \quad (10)$$

3 Describe some fundamental differences in industries that drive differences in the way they finance their investments.

SUMMARY: Firms that operate in different industries often have very different capital structures. For example, software companies tend to borrow very little, whereas public utilities rely heavily on debt financing. Differences in the capital structure choices of firms in different industries can be traced back to differences in the economic circumstances of the firms in the different industries. The costs and benefits of using debt versus equity vary depending on the inherent business risk of the industry. This difference then affects the likelihood that the firm will experience financial distress, and consequently the firm's willingness to borrow money to finance its investments because borrowing increases the risk of default.

Concept Check | 2

1. Who were the financial economists that in 1958 challenged the importance of capital structure management? What is the essence of their theory of capital structure?

2. Discuss the role of the following factors in the firm's capital structure decision: taxes, bankruptcy costs, managerial incentives, and how well informed managers are compared to stockholders.

Concept Check | 3

1. What are some reasons for firms in different industries to have different capital structures?

4 ## Use the basic tools of financial analysis to analyze a firm's financing decisions.

SUMMARY: The practical analysis of capital structure decisions typically proceeds in two phases. Phase one consists of benchmarking the firm's capital structure against that of one or more competitor firms that are thought to share the same level of overall business risk. In this analysis the firm can assess how the proposed capital structure alternatives will change the capital structure of the firm and provide the basis for comparing this change to similar firms. This will usually involve looking at both capital structure ratios, the debt ratio and interest-bearing debt ratio, as well as an analysis of the expected impact of the alternatives on the level and volatility of the firm's reported earnings per share.

The second phase of the analysis proceeds to a direct assessment of the probability of default to determine whether your firm can afford more or less debt financing than the comparison firms used in the benchmarking exercise. As we described earlier, debt financing brings with it the tax savings from interest expense. However, using excessive amounts of debt will expose the firm to an unacceptable level of risk of financial distress and bankruptcy.

KEY TERMS

Benchmarking Comparing the firm's current and proposed capital structures to those of a set of firms that are considered to be in similar lines of business and consequently subject to the same types of risk.

EBITDA coverage ratio The ratio of the sum of EBIT plus depreciation expense (EBITDA) divided by interest plus annual before-tax principal payments (principal divided by 1 minus the firm's tax rate).

EBIT-EPS chart Graphic representation of the relationship between EPS and the level of firm EBIT.

EBIT-EPS indifference point The level of EBIT that produces the same level of EPS for two different capital structures.

Financial leverage effect The use of debt financing in a firm's capital structure, which increases firm EPS when leverage is favorable and reduces EPS when leverage is unfavorable.

Interest-bearing debt ratio The ratio of interest-bearing debt (short and long term) to total assets.

Range of earnings chart Same as EBIT-EPS chart.

KEY EQUATIONS

EPS for the Stock Plan   EPS for the Bond Plan

$$\frac{(EBIT - \text{Interest Expense}_{\text{Stock Plan}})(1 - \text{Tax Rate})}{\text{Shares Outstanding (Stock Plan)}} = \frac{(EBIT - \text{Interest Expense}_{\text{Bond Plan}})(1 - \text{Tax Rate})}{\text{Shares Outstanding (Bond Plan)}} \quad (11)$$

$$\frac{\text{EBITDA}}{\text{Coverage Ratio}} = \frac{\text{Earnings before Interest and Taxes} + \text{Depreciation Expense} + \text{Amortization Expense}}{\text{Interest Expense} + \text{Principal Payments}} = \frac{\text{EBITDA}}{\text{Interest Expense} + \text{Principal Payments}} \quad (12)$$

Concept Check | **4**

1. In what ways does the firm's capital structure affect its earnings per share?

2. What is the EBIT-EPS indifference point, and how is this concept useful in analyzing a capital structure decision?

3. How are various leverage ratios and industry norms used in capital structure management?

Study Questions

1. **(Related to Regardless of Your Major: Capital Structure Matters to You!)** In the *Regardless of Your Major* feature box we learned about the dangers of using a high proportion of debt financing faced by both General Motors (GM) and Lehman Brothers. How could the failure of these firms possibly matter to you personally or to your parents?

2. How does a firm's *financial structure* differ from its *capital structure*?

3. What are non-interest-bearing liabilities? Give some examples. Why are non-interest-bearing liabilities not included in the firm's capital structure?

4. What is financial leverage? What is meant by the use of the terms *favorable* and *unfavorable* with regard to financial leverage?

5. What is the significance of the notion that a firm's financing decisions are irrelevant? What does this mean to the financial manager?

6. What are the two fundamental assumptions that are used to support the M&M capital structure theory? Describe each in commonsense terms.

7. What does Figure 2 have to say about the impact of a firm's financing decisions on firm cash flow?

8. Under the conditions of the M&M capital structure theory, the firm's financing decisions do not have an impact on firm value. When this theory holds (i.e., is true), how do the firm's financing decisions affect the firm's weighted average cost of capital? Describe how the cost of equity and cost of debt behave as the firm increases its use of debt financing.

9. Describe why capital structure is relevant to the value of the firm. Discuss the potential violations of both of the basic assumptions that support the M&M capital structure theory.

10. What are interest tax savings, and how do they affect the relevance of a firm's financing decisions?

11. What are financial distress costs, and how are they related to the firm's financing decisions?

12. How does the presence of cost of financial distress combined with the tax deductibility of interest (and the resulting interest tax savings) affect a firm's weighted average cost of capital as the firm increases its use of debt financing from no debt to higher and higher levels of debt?

13. What are agency costs, and how do they become a relevant consideration in determining a firm's capital structure?

14. What does the term *benchmarking* mean with respect to making financing decisions?

15. Describe how each of the four financial ratios found in Table 3 is used to help managers make financing decisions.

16. What is EBIT-EPS analysis, and how is it used in helping make financing decisions?

17. The Ballard Corporation is considering adding more debt to its capital structure and has asked you to provide it with some guidance. After looking at future levels of Ballard's EBIT, you feel very confident that in the future it will consistently be above the EBIT-EPS indifference point calculated using Ballard's current capital structure and its proposed capital structure. Based upon this analysis, do you think you would be more inclined to recommend that the company keep its current capital structure or go with the proposed capital structure that will add more debt? Discuss the reasons underlying your recommendation.

18. Explain how industry norms might be used by the financial manager in the design of the company's financing mix.

19. Do you think firms with stable income streams should use higher or lower levels of debt in their capital structures? Why?

20. What is financial flexibility, and why is it an important consideration when evaluating a financing decision?

21. A firm is considering replacing its current production facility with a new robotics production facility. As a result of this move, the firm's fixed costs will increase dramatically. To finance this new project the firm is considering either issuing common stock or issuing debt. Should the firm consider these two decisions (going with the robotics facility and how to finance it) separately? How might the investment decision impact the financing decision?

22. **(Related to Finance in a Flat World: Capital Structures around the World)** In the *Finance in a Flat World* feature box we learned that capital structures differ dramatically in different countries around the world. What are some possible causes for the observed differences?

Study Problems

Capital Structure Policies

1. **(Related to Checkpoint 1) (Calculating debt ratio)** Webb Solutions, Inc. has the following financial structure:

Accounts payable	$ 500,000
Short-term debt	250,000
Current liabilities	$ 750,000
Long-term debt	750,000
Shareholders' equity	500,000
Total	$2,000,000

   a. Compute Webb's debt ratio and interest-bearing debt ratio.
   b. If the market value of Webb's equity is $2,000,000 and the value of the firm's debt is equal to its book value, assuming excess cash is zero, what is the debt-to-enterprise-value ratio for Webb?
   c. If you were a bank loan officer who was analyzing whether or not to loan more money to Webb, which of the ratios calculated in parts a and b is most relevant to your analysis? Why?

2. **(Calculating capital structure weights)** The common stock of Moe's Restaurant is currently selling for $80 per share, has a book value of $60 per share, and there are 1 million shares of common stock outstanding. In addition, the firm also has 100,000 bonds outstanding with a par value of $1,000 that are selling at 110 percent of par. What are the capital structure weights that Moe's should use to analyze its capital structure?

3. **(Related to Checkpoint 1) (Calculating capital structure weights)** Winchell Investment Advisors is evaluating the capital structure of Ojai Foods. Ojai's balance sheet indicates that the firm has $50 million in total liabilities. Ojai has only $40 million in short- and long-term debt on its balance sheet. However, because interest rates have fallen dramatically since the debt was issued, Ojai's short- and long-term debt has a current market price that is 10 percent over its book value or $44 million. The book value of Ojai's common equity is $50 million but the market value of the equity is currently $100 million.

   a. What are Ojai's debt ratio and interest-bearing debt ratio calculated using book values?
   b. What is Ojai's debt-to-enterprise-value ratio calculated using the market values of the firm's debt and equity and assuming excess cash is zero?
   c. If you were trying to describe Ojai's capital structure to a potential lender (i.e., a bank), would you use the book-value-based debt ratio or the market-value-based debt-to-enterprise-value ratio? Why?

4. **(Adjusting a firm's capital structure)** Curley's Fried Chicken Kitchen operates two southern cooking restaurants in St. Louis, Missouri, and has the following financial structure:

Accounts payable	$ 100,000
Short-term debt	400,000
Current liabilities	$ 500,000
Long-term debt	$2,000,000
Owner's equity	1,500,000
Total	$4,000,000

   The firm is considering an expansion that would involve raising an additional $2 million.

   a. What are the firm's debt ratio and interest-bearing debt ratio in its present capital structure?
   b. If the firm wants to have a debt ratio of 50 percent, how much equity does the firm need to raise in order to finance the expansion?

5. **(Related to Checkpoint 1) (Describing a firm's capital structure)** Home Depot, Inc. (HD) operates as a home improvement retailer primarily in the United States, Canada, and Mexico. The balance sheet for Home Depot, Inc. (HD) for February 3, 2008, included the following liabilities and owner's equity:

In Thousands of Dollars	Financial Structure
Liabilities	
Current liabilities	
Accounts payable	$ 9,185,000
Short-term/current debt	2,047,000
Other current liabilities	1,474,000
Total current liabilities	**$12,706,000**
Long-term debt	11,383,000
Other long-term liabilities	2,521,000
Long-term liabilities	**$13,904,000**
Stockholder equity	**$17,714,000**
Total	**$44,324,000**

a. What are Home Depot's debt ratio and interest-bearing debt ratio?
b. If the market value of Home Depot's common equity is $44.90 billion and assuming that Home Depot has no excess cash, what is the firm's debt-to-enterprise-value ratio? (Hint: Assume that the market value of the firm's interest-bearing debt equals its book value.)

6. **(Describing a firm's capital structure)** Lowe's Companies, Inc. (LOW) and its subsidiaries operate as a home improvement retailer in the United States and Canada. As of February 1, 2008, it operated 1,534 stores in 50 states and Canada. The company's balance sheet for February 1, 2008, included the following sources of financing:

In Thousands of Dollars	Financial Structure
Liabilities	
Current liabilities	
Accounts payable	$ 4,137,000
Short-term/current debt	1,104,000
Other current liabilities	2,510,000
Total current liabilities	**$ 7,751,000**
Long-term debt	5,576,000
Other long-term liabilities	670,000
Long-term liabilities	**$ 6,246,000**
Stockholder equity	**$16,098,000**
Total	**$30,095,000**

a. Calculate the values of Lowe's debt ratio and interest-bearing debt ratio.
b. If the market value of Lowe's common equity is $35.86 billion and Lowe's has no excess cash, what is the firm's debt-to-enterprise-value ratio? (Hint: You may assume that the market value of the firm's interest-bearing debt equals its book value.)
c. (Optional) Compare your analysis of Lowe's capital structure to that of Home Depot (HD) in Study Problem 5. Can you assess which of the two firms is more highly levered (i.e., uses the most financial leverage)? If so, what is your assessment of the two firms' capital structure?
d. (Optional) What is the credit rating for Lowe's, and how does it compare to that of Home Depot? (Hint: Look up bond credit ratings online.)

Capital Structure Theory

7. **(Computing interest tax savings)** Dharma Supply has earnings before interest and taxes (EBIT) of $500,000, interest expenses of $300,000, and faces a corporate tax rate of 35 percent.

    a. What is Dharma Supply's net income?

    b. What would Dharma's net income be if it didn't have any debt (and consequently no interest expense)?

    c. What are the firm's interest tax savings?

8. **(Computing interest tax savings)** Presently, H. Swank, Inc. does not use any financial leverage and has total financing equal to $1 million. It is considering refinancing and issuing $500,000 of debt that pays 5 percent interest and using that money to buy back half the firm's common stock. Assume that the debt has a 30-year maturity such that Swank will have no principal payments for 30 years. Swank currently pays all of its net income to common shareholders in the form of cash dividends and intends to continue to do this in the future. The corporate tax rate on the firm's earnings is 35 percent.

Swank's current income statement (before the debt issue) is as follows:

Earnings before interest and taxes (EBIT)	$100,000
Less: Interest expense	0
Equals: Earnings before tax	$100,000
Less: Taxes	(35,000)
Equals: Net income	$ 65,000

    a. If Swank issues the debt and uses it to buy back common stock, how much money can the firm distribute to its stockholders and bondholders next year if the firm's EBIT remains equal to $1 million?

    b. What are Swank's interest tax savings from the issuance of the debt?

    c. Are Swank's stockholders better off after the debt issue? Why or why not?

    d. If there were no corporate taxes on income (and consequently interest expense was not deducted from the firm's taxable income), how would this affect your responses to parts a through c?

Making Financing Decisions

9. **(Related to Checkpoint 1) (Coverage ratio analysis)** The income statements for Home Depot, Inc. (HD) spanning the period 2006–2008 (just before the housing crash, so these are representative years) are as follows:

	2008	2007	2006
Earnings before interest and taxes	$7,316,000	$ 9,700,000	$9,425,000
Interest expense	(696,000)	(392,000)	(143,000)
Income before tax	$6,620,000	$ 9,308,000	$9,282,000
Income tax expense	(2,410,000)	(3,547,000)	(3,444,000)
Net income	$4,210,000	$ 5,761,000	$5,838,000

    a. Calculate the times interest earned ratio for each of the years for which you have data.

    b. What is your assessment of how the firm's ability to service its debt obligations has changed over this period?

10. **(Coverage ratio analysis)** Abbreviated income statements for Lowe's Companies, Inc. (LOW) spanning the period 2006–2008 (just before the housing crash, so these are representative years) are as follows:

	2008	2007	2006
Earnings before interest and taxes	$4,750,000	$5,152,000	$4,654,000
Interest expense	(239,000)	(154,000)	(158,000)
Income before tax	$4,511,000	$4,998,000	$4,496,000
Income tax expense	(1,702,000)	(1,893,000)	(1,731,000)
Net income	$2,809,000	$3,105,000	$2,765,000

a. Calculate the times interest earned ratio for each of the years for which you have data.

b. What is your assessment of how the firm's ability to service its debt obligations has changed over this period?

c. (Optional) How does Lowe's compare to Home Depot (HD) in Study Problem 9? Is it better able to service its debt than Home Depot? Why or why not?

11. **(Leverage and EPS)** You have developed the following pro forma income statement for your corporation. It represents the most recent year's operations, which ended yesterday.

Sales	$45,750,000
Variable costs	(22,800,000)
Revenue before fixed costs	$22,950,000
Fixed costs	(9,200,000)
EBIT	$13,750,000
Interest expense	(1,350,000)
Earnings before taxes	$12,400,000
Taxes (.50)	(6,200,000)
Net income	$ 6,200,000

Your supervisor in the controller's office has just handed you a memorandum asking for written responses to the following questions:

a. If sales should increase by 25 percent, by what percent would earnings before interest and taxes and net income increase?

b. If sales should decrease by 25 percent, by what percent would earnings before interest and taxes and net income decrease?

c. If the firm were to reduce its reliance on debt financing such that interest expense were cut in half, how would this affect your answers to parts a and b?

12. **(Related to Checkpoint 2) (EBIT-EPS analysis)** Abe Forrester and three of his friends from college have interested a group of venture capitalists in backing their business idea. The proposed operation would consist of a series of retail outlets to distribute and service a full line of vacuum cleaners and accessories. These stores would be located in Dallas, Houston, and San Antonio. To finance the new venture two plans have been proposed:

- Plan A is an all-common-equity structure in which $2 million dollars would be raised by selling 80,000 shares of common stock.
- Plan B would involve issuing $1 million in long-term bonds with an effective interest rate of 12 percent plus another $1 million would be raised by selling 40,000 shares of common stock. The debt funds raised under Plan B have no fixed maturity date, in that this amount of financial leverage is considered a permanent part of the firm's capital structure.

Abe and his partners plan to use a 40 percent tax rate in their analysis, and they have hired you on a consulting basis to do the following:

a. Find the EBIT indifference level associated with the two financing plans.

b. Prepare a pro forma income statement for the EBIT level solved for in part a that shows that EPS will be the same regardless whether Plan A or B is chosen.

13. **(EBIT-EPS analysis)** Three recent graduates of the computer science program at the University of Tennessee are forming a company that will write and distribute new application software for the iPhone. Initially, the corporation will operate in the southern region of Tennessee, Georgia, North Carolina, and South Carolina. A small group of private investors in the Atlanta, Georgia, area is interested in financing the start-up company and two financing plans have been put forth for consideration:

- **The first (Plan A) is an all-common-equity capital structure.** Two million dollars would be raised by selling common stock at $20 per common share.
- **Plan B would involve the use of financial leverage.** One million dollars would be raised by selling bonds with an effective interest rate of 11 percent (per annum), and the remaining $1 million would be raised by selling common stock at the $20 price per share. The use of financial leverage is considered to be a permanent part of the firm's capitalization, so no fixed maturity date is needed for the analysis. A 30 percent tax rate is deemed appropriate for the analysis.

a. Find the EBIT indifference level associated with the two financing plans.

b. A detailed financial analysis of the firm's prospects suggests that the long-term EBIT will be above $300,000 annually. Taking this into consideration, which plan will generate the higher EPS?

14. **(EBIT-EPS break-even analysis)** Home Depot, Inc. (HD) had 1.7 billion shares of common stock outstanding in 2008, whereas Lowe's Companies, Inc. (LOW) had 1.46 billion shares outstanding. Given both firms' 2008 earnings levels found in Study Problems 9 and 10, and assuming a 35 percent tax rate for both firms, what is their break-even level of operating income (i.e., the level of EBIT where EPS is the same for both firms)?

Mini-Case

Hewlett-Packard Co. Balance Sheet (October 31, 2007)

On September 27, 2007, Apple Inc. (AAPL) reported the following sources of financing in its balance sheet:

In Thousands of Dollars	Financial Structure
Liabilities	
Current liabilities	
Accounts payable	$ 6,230,000
Short-term/current debt	0
Other current liabilities	3,069,000
Total current liabilities	**$ 9,299,000**
Long-term debt	0
Other long-term liabilities	1,516,000
Long-term liabilities	**$ 1,516,000**
Stockholder equity	**$14,532,000**
Total	**$25,347,000**

Moreover, the firm's 2007 income statement reported earnings of $3.496 billion with no interest expense:

($ thousands)	29-Sep-07	30-Sep-06	24-Sep-05
Earnings before interest and taxes	5,008,000	2,818,000	1,815,000
Interest expense	0	0	0
Income before tax	5,008,000	2,818,000	1,815,000
Income tax expense	(1,512,000)	(829,000)	(480,000)
Net income	3,496,000	1,989,000	1,335,000

If Apple's management were considering the possibility of using debt financing for the first time, it might look at Hewlett-Packard Corporation (HPQ) as a benchmark firm for comparison purposes. Hewlett Packard Corporation (HPQ) used debt financing as shown on the following balance sheet and income statement:

Hewlett-Packard Co. Balance Sheet (October 31, 2007)

In Thousands of Dollars	Financial Structure
Liabilities	
Current liabilities	
Accounts payable	$25,822,000
Short-term/current debt	3,186,000
Other current liabilities	10,252,000
Total current liabilities	**$39,260,000**
Long-term debt	4,997,000
Other long-term liabilities	5,916,000
Long-term liabilities	**$10,913,000**
Stockholder equity	**$38,526,000**
Total	**$88,699,000**

Income Statements (thousands)

Period Ending	31-Oct-07	31-Oct-06	31-Oct-05
Earnings before interest and taxes	9,466,000	7,440,000	3,759,000
Interest expense	(289,000)	(249,000)	(216,000)
Income before tax	9,177,000	7,191,000	3,543,000
Income tax expense	(1,913,000)	(993,000)	(1,145,000)
Net income	7,264,000	6,198,000	2,398,000

a. Describe the capital structure of Hewlett-Packard using both the debt ratio and interest-bearing debt ratio.

b. What is Hewlett-Packard's times interest earned ratio? If HP faces a principal payment equal to $3 billion, what is the firm's EBITDA coverage ratio for 2007? (Hint: HP's tax rate is 20 percent.)

c. Suppose Apple has decided to issue debt financing and use the proceeds to purchase some of its shares of stock from the open market. What fraction of the firm's 2.47 billion shares does the firm need to repurchase so as to make its interest-bearing debt ratio equal to that of Hewlett-Packard? If Apple had carried out the transaction by issuing bonds with an 8 percent rate of interest, what would its earnings per share have been in 2007?

d. Do you think that the proposed change of capital structure makes good financial sense? Why or why not?

Appendix: Demonstrating the Modigliani and Miller Theorem

To illustrate conditions under which the Modigliani and Miller theorem is true, assume there are two firms, Firm A and Firm B, which are identical in every respect except that they are financed differently. Firm A is all-equity financed, whereas Firm B has borrowed a portion of its capital.

Because of the first assumption of the M&M theorem, we know that even though the two firms have different capital structures, they generate identical cash flows, which are uncertain and depend on the overall state of the economy. As we state in Panel A of Figure A.1, the total cash flows of the two firms in a recession equal $50 million, in normal times equal $100 million, and during booming times equal $150 million. To keep the example simple, we assume that these cash flows are generated in exactly one year and that after generating the cash flows, the firm distributes them to its debt and equity holders and then goes out of business. Moreover, we assume that Firm B's debt is risk-free, which means that the firm pays the risk-free interest rate of 5 percent on its debt.

We will assume that Firm A, which is financed completely by equity, is valued at $75 million. Firm B, on the other hand, has a $42 million debt obligation it must repay at the end of one year. Thus, the present value of Firm B's Year 1 debt obligation of $42 million, when discounted at the 5 percent risk-free rate, is $40 million. If the M&M theorem holds, then Firm B must have the same $75 million value as Firm A, which uses no debt financing. Because Firm B's debt is valued at $40 million, the value of Firm B's equity must equal $35 million ($75 million minus $40 million) for the two firms to both be valued at $75 million.

But why does Firm B's equity need to have a value of $35 million? Asked somewhat differently, if the equity value were initially only $30 million, would market forces drive the value up to $35 million? Similarly, if the value of Firm B's equity were $45 million, would market forces drive it back down to $35 million? The answer to both these questions is yes, as we illustrate in Figure A.1 and explain next.

Arbitrage and the Valuation of the Levered and Unlevered Firms

To understand why the total values of Firm A and Firm B must be equal, let's assume that you have $7.5 million to invest and have the opportunity to acquire a 10 percent stake in the equity of either Firm A or Firm B. Which alternative would you prefer? If you invest in Firm A, it will cost you $7.5 million to purchase 10 percent of the firm's equity for $7.5 million (which is 10 percent of its total value of $75 million). In the case found in Panel B, where the shares of Firm B are valued at $35 million, it will take $3.5 million to buy the equity of Firm B (which is 10 percent of the $35 million value of Firm B's equity), leaving you with the remaining $4.0 million ($7.5 million less the $3.5 million invested in Firm B's equity) to invest in risk-free bonds earning the risk-free rate of 5 percent. Panel B of Figure A.1 shows the cash flows you would receive from these two investments. We see that if Firm B's equity is appropriately priced at $35 million, the investor receives exactly the same cash flows from either investment strategy and is therefore indifferent between investing in either Firm A or Firm B.

Panel C of Figure A.1 provides the payoffs in the different states of the economy for the two investments described in the preceding paragraph for the case where Firm B's equity is *underpriced* at $30 million. As you can see, the investment in Firm B's equity, along with the risk-free bonds, generates a greater cash flow in each of the states of the economy. In other words, the Firm B investment dominates the Firm A investment, suggesting that at $30 million, Firm B's equity is underpriced relative to Firm A. If investors were to observe the underpriced shares of Firm B and purchase them, they would drive up its value to $35 million, at which point the shares would be fairly priced.

What if Firm B's equity were *overpriced* at $45 million? In this case, the comparable investment would be $4.5 million in Firm B's equity, which leaves only $3 million to invest in the risk-free bond. As shown in Panel D of Figure A.1, the Firm B investment generates

Figure A.1

Illustrating the M&M Capital Structure Irrelevance Proposition

This example illustrates how the firm's capital structure does not affect the value of the firm (debt plus equity) where the two assumptions underlying the M&M capital structure theorem hold. Specifically,

- Panel A shows how we arrive at the valuation of Firm B's equity given that the unlevered firm (Firm A) has a value of $75 million.
- Panel B illustrates the correct valuation of the levered firm's (Firm B) equity at $35 million.
- Panels C and D identify the arbitrage opportunities that arise where Firm B's equity is under- and overvalued, respectively.

The critical take-away from this figure is that under the conditions assumed by M&M, the values of the unlevered firm (Firm A) and the levered firm (Firm B) must be equal, which means that each firm's capital structure is not important to the value of the firm.

(Panel A) Value of Firm B's Equity Assuming the M&M Proposition Holds

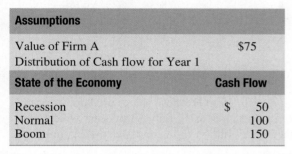

Assumptions	
Value of Firm A	$75
Distribution of Cash flow for Year 1	

State of the Economy	Cash Flow
Recession	$ 50
Normal	100
Boom	150

In this panel we assume that Firms A and B both have values of $75 million. Firm B has a debt obligation of $42 million next year, which means that the current value of Firm B's debt is $40 million and its equity is worth $35 million.

Valuing Firm B's Equity		
Capital Structures	Firm A	Firm B
Debt obligation in year 1	-	42.00
Borrowing rate	-	5%

$42/(1.05)

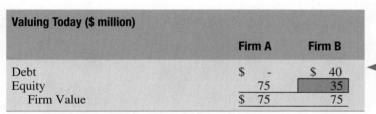

Valuing Today ($ million)		
	Firm A	Firm B
Debt	$ -	$ 40
Equity	75	35
Firm Value	$ 75	75

Assume that an investor has $7.5 million to invest in either Firm A or Firm B and wants to hold 10% of the acquired firm's equity. For Firm B this requires only $3.5 million, so the remaining funds are invested in the risk-free security.

(Panel B) Firm B's Equity Is Valued Correctly at $35 Million

Value of Firm B's equity	$ 35.00 million
Amount invested	7.50 million
Price of 10% of Firm B's shares	3.50 million
Amount invested in risk-free debt	4.00 million

State of the Economy ($ millions)	Cash Flow	Firm A Equity	Debt	+	Firm B Equity	=	Total
Recession	$ 50	$ 5	$ 4.2		$ 0.8		$ 5
Normal	100	$ 10	$ 4.2		$ 5.8		$ 10
Boom	150	$ 15	$ 4.2		$ 10.8		$ 15

After investing the $7.5 million in Firm A's equity the investor will receive $5, $10, or $15 million in cash flows depending on the state of the economy. Similarly, summing the debt plus equity cash flows corresponding to purchasing 10% of Firm B and using the unused funds to purchase risk-free debt, the cash flows are identical to those received from investing in Firm A. Thus, if Firm B's equity is priced at $35 million an investor would be indifferent between buying stock in either of the two firms.

(FIGURE A.1 CONTINUED >> ON NEXT PAGE)

(Panel C) Firm B's Equity Is Underpriced at $30 Million

Value of Firm B's equity	$ 30.00 million
Amount invested	7.50 million
Price of 10% of Firm B's shares	3.00 million
Amount invested in risk-free debt	4.50 million

> Cash flows from investing in Firm B are greater than from investing in Firm A because Firm B's equity is underpriced.

		Firm A			Firm B		
State of the Economy ($ millions)	Cash Flow	Equity	Debt	+	Equity	=	Total
Recession	$ 50	$ 5	$ 4.725		$ 0.8		$ 5.525
Normal	100	$ 10	$ 4.725		$ 5.8		$ 10.525
Boom	150	$ 15	$ 4.725		$ 10.8		$ 15.525

<u>Firm A cash flows to the 10% investor</u>—Same as before.

<u>Firm B cash flows to the 10% investor</u>—The cash flows in this instance are *higher* for Firm B whose shares are "underpriced." Since Firm B's equity is valued at $30 million, we can purchase 10% of the firm's shares using only $3 million, which gives us an additional $500,000 to invest in risk-free debt which earns an additional $0.525 million in interest (i.e., $4.725 million – $4.2 million).

(Panel D) Firm B's Equity Is Overpriced at $45 Million

Value of Firm B's equity	$ 45.00 million
Amount invested	7.50 million
Price of 10% of Firm B's shares	4.50 million
Amount invested in risk-free debt	3.00 million

> Cash flows from investing in Firm B are less than investing in Firm A since Firm B's equity is overpriced.

		Firm A			Firm B		
State of the Economy ($ millions)	Cash Flow	Equity	Dept	+	Equity	=	Total
Recession	$ 50	$ 5	$ 3.15		$ 0.80		$ 3.95
Normal	100	$ 10	$ 3.15		$ 5.80		$ 8.95
Boom	150	$ 15	$ 3.15		$ 10.80		$ 13.95

<u>Firm A cash flows to the 10% investor</u>—Same as before.

<u>Firm B cash flows to the 10% investor</u>—The investor cash flows in this instance are *lower* for the investment in Firm B's "overpriced" equity than from investing in Firm A. Since Firm B's equity is valued at $45 million, 10% of the firm's shares can be purchased for $4.5 million, which leaves only $3 million to invest in risk-free debt. This reduces the investor's interest income by $1.05 million (i.e., $3.15 million – $4.2 million –$1.05 million).

>> END FIGURE A.1

cash flows that are always less than the cash flows from the investment in Firm A. Obviously in this case you would prefer an investment in Firm A over Firm B. In this instance investors would sell Firm B shares, thereby driving down its price to $35 million, at which point there would no longer be a profitable arbitrage opportunity.

SUMMING UP

So what does this mean? Very simply, under the two basic assumptions of the M&M capital structure theory, investors will force the values of otherwise identical firms to be equal even though they have different capital structures. The process by which investors force this to happen is called arbitrage, whereby they buy the shares of the undervalued firm and sell the shares of the overvalued firm.

Photo Credits

558

Dividend Policy

From Chapter 16 of *Financial Management: Principles and Applications*, Twelfth Edition. Sheridan Titman, Arthur J. Keown, and John D. Martin.

Dividend Policy

Chapter **Outline**

1 How Do Firms Distribute Cash to Their Shareholders? ⟶ **Objective 1.** Distinguish between the use of cash dividends and share repurchases.

2 Does Dividend Policy Matter? ⟶ **Objective 2.** Understand the tax treatment of dividends and capital gains, stock dividends, and stock splits, and the conditions under which dividend policy is an important determinant of stock value.

3 Cash Distribution Policies in Practice ⟶ **Objective 3.** Describe corporate dividend policies that are commonly used in practice.

Our discussion of dividend policy pulls from **P** Principle 1: **Money Has a Time Value,** and **P** Principle 3: **Cash Flows Are the Source of Value.** Because the residual cash flows of firms are paid to shareholders in the form of dividends, the value of the firm's equity must equal the discounted value of its future dividends. Given this, it is natural to consider the tradeoff associated with paying fewer dividends today and conserving cash, allowing the firm to pay out more cash in the future. In addition, **P** Principle 4: **Market Prices Reflect Information** comes into play when we examine how stock prices react to the new information conveyed in a dividend change announcement.

Emerson Electric (EMR) Pays Dividends for 53 Consecutive Years

In February of 2010, the Emerson Electric Co. (EMR) announced an increase in its cash dividend for the 53rd consecutive year with a $0.34 per share quarterly dividend. Emerson is one of a shrinking number of firms that can boast such a record. Dividends are losing out to corporate share repurchases as the preferred way to distribute cash to shareholders. In this chapter we look at the cash distribution policies of corporations to learn why these distributions are important and why one method of distribution might be preferred to another.

When a firm generates cash from its operations, the management of the company must decide what to do with it. Specifically, they can do one or some combination of three things with the cash they generate:

- **Alternative #1:** Use the cash to fund new investments.
- **Alternative #2:** Use the cash to pay off some of the firm's debt.
- **Alternative #3:** Distribute the cash back to the firm's shareholders either as cash dividends or as stock repurchases.

Alternative #1 is useful in capital-budgeting decisions. The decision rule usually followed to undertake all investment opportunities that offer a positive net present value (NPV). Alternatives #2 and #3 address the financing decision. The firm can reduce its dependence on debt financing by using its cash to repay all or part of its debt, or it can reduce the equity in its capital structure by distributing cash to the firm's common stockholders.

This chapter is organized around providing answers to three basic questions regarding a firm's dividend policy:

1. What are the pros and cons of the methods the firm can use to distribute cash to its common stockholders?
2. Why should the firm's shareholders care about the firm's dividend policy given that they can generate cash when they need it by selling some of their shares?
3. What cash distribution policies do most firms use in practice?

As we will show, as long as the dividend choice has no effect on the firm's investment and operating choices, and as long the dividend choice has no tax implications, then the actual timing of the dividends has no effect on firm values. What we learn from this is that apart from tax implications, it is the cash flows generated by the firm's investments that determine the firm's value, not the timing and the method of how those cash flows are paid out.

Finally, we discuss the fact that when firms announce dividend increases, their stock prices tend to increase. How do we reconcile this evidence of a positive stock price response to a dividend increase if the timing of dividend payments has no influence on firm values? The positive price reaction to a dividend increase does not necessarily imply that the firm becomes more valuable because it is paying a higher dividend. Rather, the dividend increase conveys favorable information to investors about the firm's ability to generate operating cash flows.

Regardless of Your Major…

"Firms Almost Never Decrease Their Dividend"

The decision to initiate, increase, or decrease a firm's cash dividend is an important decision that is made by the firm's board of directors. The board, in turn, relies on the input of the entire management team in order to make the right decision. When the board is considering an increase in the firm's dividend payout, a prime consideration is whether the dividend payment is sustainable. They do not want to increase dividends today if it is likely that they will have to cut the dividends in the near future. Likewise, they will only cut a dividend payment if it is clear that the higher current payout is no longer sustainable. The latter is most likely to occur in the midst of a recession, as was the case for General Electric (GE) and Dow Chemical (DOW), which both cut their dividends in 2009. Both of these firms faced untenable circumstances, as GE's cut was the first in 71 years and Dow Chemical's last cut was in 1912.

To arrive at the conclusion that the firm should change its dividend payout, the firm's top management will be called upon to advise the board of directors regarding the firm's future prospects. Specifically, because earnings can vary from quarter to quarter, the firm's directors will seek advice from the firm's marketing department to get their views about future sales and from people in operations to get a better understanding of the firm's cost structure going forward. Of course, the financial and accounting staff will combine this information to come up with a dividend policy that should be sustainable, even during mild downturns.

Your Turn: See Study Question 2.

1 Do Firms Distribute Cash to Their Shareholders?

Cash distributions by a firm to its stockholders can take one of two basic forms: a cash dividend or a share repurchase. With a **cash dividend**, cash is paid directly to shareholders. With a **share or stock repurchase**, on the other hand, a company uses its cash to buy back its own shares from the marketplace, thereby reducing the number of outstanding shares. In either case, cash is transferred from the company to the firm's stockholders. Looking at the impact of a cash distribution on the balance sheet, the cash account goes down as the cash is either sent to the shareholders in the form of dividends or used to buy back stock, and on the right-hand side of the balance sheet, there is a corresponding decrease in the equity account. Many firms use a combination of both dividend payments and share repurchases to distribute cash to their shareholders.

Panel A of Figure 1 presents the total corporate earnings, cash dividends, and share repurchases for a broad cross-section of U.S. firms over the period 1972–2000. As shown in Panel B, over this period the total proportion of earnings that firms distributed either as cash

Figure 1

Historical Distributions to Shareholders through Dividends and Share Repurchases
Cash distributions to a firm's shareholders take one of two principal forms: cash dividends and
share repurchases. In recent years two important trends have been observed. First, share repurchases have grown to the point where they are equal to cash distributions through dividends.
Second, the proportion of firm earnings distributed through both approaches has grown from
about 40 percent in the 1970s to near 80 percent by 2000.

(Panel A) Cash Distributions to Shareholders: Dividends
and Repurchases

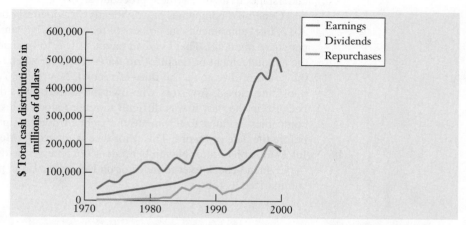

(Panel B) Relative Importance of Dividends and Share Repurchases

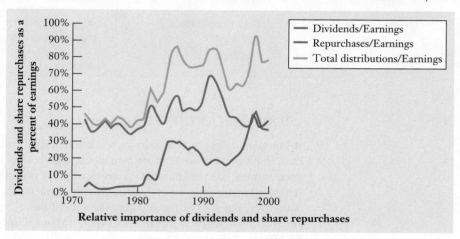

Source: Gustavo Grullon and Roni Michaely, "Dividends, Share Repurchases, and the Substitution Hypothesis,"
Journal of Finance 57, 4 (August 2002), 1649–1684.

>> END FIGURE 1

dividends or share repurchases has grown from about 40 percent at the start of the period to
about 80 percent by the end. As this panel illustrates, the increase in total distributions has
come about because of the very large increase in the distributions from share repurchases.

Cash Dividends

A firm's **dividend policy** determines how much cash it will distribute to its shareholders and
when these distributions will be made. We can characterize a firm's dividend policy in terms
of two fundamental attributes:

1. **The fraction of firm earnings paid in dividends.** This first attribute is typically described in terms of the **dividend payout ratio**, which indicates the amount of dividends

paid relative to the company's earnings. For instance, if the dividend per share is $2 and the earnings per share is $4, the payout ratio is 50 percent ($2 ÷ $4).

2. **The pattern of payments followed by the firm over time.** As will be observed later in the chapter, to the investor, dividend stability may be almost as important as the amount of dividends received.

Dividend Payment Procedures

After the firm's dividend policy has been determined, several procedural details must be arranged. For instance, how frequently are dividend payments made? If a stockholder sells the shares during the year, who is entitled to the dividend? To answer these questions, we need to understand dividend payment procedures.

Generally, companies pay dividends on a quarterly basis. To illustrate, on September 24, 2012, Intel announced that holders of record as of November 7, 2012, would receive a $0.225 per share dividend. The dividend payment was to be made on December 1. September 24 is the announcement or **declaration date**—the date when the dividend is formally declared by the board of directors. The **date of record**, November 7, designates when the stock transfer books are closed. Investors who own the stock on this date receive the dividend. However, because in the past it was difficult to record stock sales on a timely basis, stock brokerage companies decided to terminate the right of ownership to the dividend two working days before the date of record. This prior date is the **ex-dividend date**. Therefore, any acquirer of Intel stock on or after November 5 does not receive the dividend. Finally, the company mails the dividend check to each investor on December 1, the **payment date**. These events may be summarized as follows:

Announcement Date	Ex-Dividend Date	Record Date	Payment Date
September 24	November 5	November 7	December 1
Dividend is declared.	Shares begin trading ex-dividend.	Date on which the company looks at its records to see who receives dividends.	Dividends are distributed to the shareholders of record on the record date.

Stock Repurchases

A company engages in a share or stock repurchase (stock buyback) when it uses the firm's cash to repurchase some of its own stock. This results in a reduction in the firm's cash balance as well as in the number of shares of stock outstanding. We saw in Figure 1 that stock repurchases are now a very popular method for distributing cash to a firm's stockholders. Moreover, the size of the repurchases can be very large. For example, on April 27, 2010, International Business Machines Corp. (IBM) announced that it planned to buy back up to $8 billion of its stock. Moreover, consistent dividend-paying firm Emerson Electric (EMR), which we learned earlier has increased its cash dividend for 53 straight years, also engages in the repurchase of its shares.

How Do Firms Repurchase Their Shares?

Firms use one of three methods to repurchase their shares. The first, and by far the most widely used, is referred to as an **open market repurchase**. Here the firm acquires the stock on the market, often buying a relatively small number of shares every day, at the going market price. This approach may place an upward pressure on the stock price over the period that the stock is acquired. The second method involves the use of a **tender offer**, which is a formal offer by the company to buy a specified number of its shares at a stated price. The tender price is set above the current market price in order to attract sellers. A tender offer is used when the firm wants to repurchase a relatively large number of shares very quickly. The third and final method for repurchasing stock involves purchasing the stock from one or more major stockholders. In this seldom-used method, purchases are made on a negotiated basis.

Personal Tax Considerations: Dividend versus Capital Gains Income

Historically, the tax code has had a built-in preference for capital gains income over dividends. For example, up until recently, dividends were taxed at the ordinary income tax rate. As a result, in the 1960s and 1970s, many individuals paid a 70 percent tax rate on their dividend income. In contrast, capital gains have generally been taxed at a preferred rate that is generally about half the rate on ordinary income. However, one of the important provisions of the 2006 tax act (which continues through 2012) was the extension of the provision of the 2003 tax act that reduced the rate at which corporate dividends and capital gains are taxed.[1] Specifically, the maximum tax rate on dividends and long-term capital gains (on stock held for 366 days or longer) was lowered to 15 percent for most people. In order to qualify for the lower taxes on dividends, you are required to hold the stock on which the dividends are paid for more than 60 days during the 120-day period that begins 60 days before the ex-dividend date. If you do not meet these qualifications the dividends are taxed like ordinary income.

Non-Cash Distributions: Stock Dividends and Stock Splits

A **stock dividend** is a pro-rata distribution of additional shares of stock to the firm's current stockholders. These distributions are generally defined in terms of a fraction paid per share. For example, the firm might pay a stock dividend of .10 shares of stock per share of stock held so that for every 100 shares of stock you own you would receive 10 additional shares. For example, if Aaron Electronics had 1 million shares of stock outstanding and decided to make a 10 percent stock dividend to its shareholders, the total number of shares of stock outstanding would expand by 10 percent to 1.1 million shares. If, prior to the stock dividend, the shares were trading for $100 per share for a total market value of the firm's shares equal to $100 million, then after the stock dividend the share price would decline to $100 million ÷ 1.10 million shares or $90.90. The point here is that the declaration of a stock dividend only increases the number of shares of stock outstanding, such that the total value of the firm's common shares is unchanged. With the increased number of new shares, however, the price per share declines.

Closely related to the stock dividend is the stock split. A **stock split** is essentially a very large stock dividend. For example, a 2-for-1 split would entail issuing two new shares of stock to each shareholder in exchange for each old share they currently hold. Thus the 2-for-1 stock split is equivalent to a 100 percent stock dividend, because both will result in the number of shares outstanding doubling while the share price drops in half.

Accountants consider distributions less than 25 percent to be stock dividends and those greater than 25 percent to be stock splits.[2] The only difference between a stock dividend and a stock split relates to how they are reported on the firm's balance sheet.[3] Despite this difference in accounting treatment, there is no real economic difference between a stock split and a comparable stock dividend.

Rationale for a Stock Dividend or Split

Although stock dividends and splits are less prevalent than cash dividends, a significant number of companies choose to use these share distributions either with or in lieu of cash dividends. Given that these transactions do not involve any cash flow, their popularity is somewhat difficult to understand.

One rationale for splits and stock dividends is that financial executives believe that there is an optimal price range for the firm's stock. Within this range the total market value of the

---

[1]The dividend tax rate through 2012 is 15 percent for qualifying dividends (based on a minimal holding period for the shares) if the individual's marginal tax rate exceeds 15 percent and 0 percent if the marginal tax rate is 15 percent or lower.

[2]The 25 percent standard applies only to corporations listed on the New York Stock Exchange. The American Institute of Certified Public Accountants ruled that a stock dividend greater than 20 or 25 percent of the firm's outstanding shares is a stock split for all practical purposes.

[3]For a stock dividend, an amount equal to the market value of the stock dividend is transferred from retained earnings to the capital stock accounts. With a stock split, only the number of shares changes and the par value of the shares is decreased proportionately.

common stockholders is thought to be maximized. As the price exceeds this range, fewer investors will want to purchase the firm's stock because of the high cost of purchasing the usual round lot (100 shares), thereby restraining the demand for the firm's shares. We can illustrate the problem using an extreme example. The market price for Berkshire Hathaway (BRK-A) class A shares was $133,446 in December 2012.[4] Thus, a 100-share *round lot* of the firm's stock would cost $13.3446 million.[5] It is not hard to believe that a stock split or dividend might improve the demand for these shares—consider, for example, the daily volume on December 26, 2012, was only 787 shares. Several years ago Berkshire Hathaway evidently came to the conclusion that this share price was a bit high when it issued series B shares, often called Baby Berkshires, which were trading for a mere $88.98 a share at the time of this writing. Admittedly, both, these cases are extreme when you look across the prices at which most shares trade. Moreover, it should be noted that the growing prevalence of large institutional investors who can easily purchase even the highest-priced shares has surely diminished concerns that companies may have about having too high of a stock price.

Before you move on to 2

Concept Check | 1

1. What are the two forms of cash distributions that firms typically use?
2. What is the frequency with which cash dividends are typically paid to investors?
3. Identify three motives that might encourage a firm to buy back its common stock shares.
4. What are the three different methods that firms use to repurchase their shares?
5. How is a stock dividend like a stock split, and why do financial managers sometimes use one or the other?

 # Does Dividend Policy Matter?

Franco Modigliani and Merton Miller's (M&M) analysis of capital structure choice, which contributed to the Nobel Prizes of each of the authors, provides us with the conditions under which the capital structure decision has no influence on a firm's value and is therefore not a relevant concern for the firm's financial manager. This result is so important to the study of finance that it bears repeating: *M&M showed that, under some idealistic conditions, it does not matter whether a firm uses no debt, a little debt, or a lot of debt in its capital structure.* A second proposition by these same individuals indicates that, without taxes and transaction costs, cash dividends and share repurchases are equivalent and the timing of the distribution is unimportant. Once we have demonstrated the conditions under which a firm's cash dividend policy does not affect the value of the firm's shares, we then relax these conditions to gain an understanding of why dividend policy is important to shareholders.

The Irrelevance of the Distribution Choice

In this section we will illustrate that the distribution choice is a matter of irrelevance under the following conditions (or assumptions):

1. There are no taxes.
2. No transaction costs are incurred in either buying or selling shares of stock.
3. The firm's operating and investment policies are fixed.

In other words, under the conditions where the Modigliani and Miller capital structure irrelevancy theorem holds, the distribution choice is also irrelevant. This is known as the Modigliani and Miller dividend irrelevancy proposition. We illustrate this proposition in two ways:

1. We first show that the timing of dividend distribution does not affect firm values.
2. Next we show that, in the absence of taxes and transaction costs, a cash dividend is equivalent to a share repurchase.

---

[4]Berkshire Hathaway, Inc. is a publicly owned investment manager that engages in the insurance business through its subsidiaries. The company was founded in 1889 in Omaha, Nebraska, but its primary source of fame today is the fact that it is run by famed investor Warren Buffett (the "Oracle of Omaha"), who is one of the very richest people in the world.

[5]Stock is typically purchased in 100-share blocks referred to as a *round lot*.

After demonstrating the irrelevance of distribution policy to share value, we then show that because of taxes, some investors will prefer to receive a cash distribution in the form of a repurchase rather than a dividend.

The Timing of Dividends Is Irrelevant

To illustrate the irrelevance of the timing of dividend payments, consider the situation faced by Clinton Enterprises, Inc. Clinton is an oil field services company that operates along the Gulf Coast of Louisiana and Texas providing drilling and maintenance services for offshore exploration and production (E&P) companies. The company has no debt, and to keep this simple we assume it can predict its cash flow very accurately over the next two years. One alternative for Clinton (Dividend Policy Alternative #1) would be to take the $35 million it currently has on hand and use it right now to pay a cash dividend, and then pay out an additional $135 million that it expects to have in one year as a dividend one year from now. For simplicity, let's assume that because of changes in technology, Clinton Enterprises will cease to exist at the end of one year, after making its final dividend payment.

The cash flows available for distribution to the firm's shareholders immediately (Year 0) and at the end of the year (Year 1) for Clinton Enterprises are shown in Panel A of Figure 2. If the firm pays out 100 percent of its available cash flow in dividends in Year 0 and Year 1, and Clinton's shareholders require a 15 percent rate of return for their investment in the firm (i.e., $k_{equity} = 15\%$), then the value of Clinton's equity can be calculated as the present value of the dividend payments using Equation (1), that is,

$$\text{Value of Clinton Enterprises' Equity} = \text{Dividend}_{\text{Year 0}} + \frac{\text{Dividend}_{\text{Year 1}}}{(1 + k_{equity})} \qquad \textbf{(1)}$$

Substituting the cash dividends from dividend policy *Alternative #1,* we calculate the value of Clinton's equity as follows:

$$\text{Value of Clinton Enterprises' Equity} = \$35 \text{ million} + \frac{\$135 \text{ million}}{(1 + .15)} = \$35 \text{ million} + \$117.39 \text{ million} = \$152.39 \text{ million}$$

Clinton has 10 million shares of stock outstanding, so the value per share of the firm's stock will be $15.24 ($152.39 million/10 million).

What if Clinton's management decides to pay an amount other than 100 percent of its available cash to the firm's stockholders in Year 0? For example, Panel B contains a second dividend policy alternative (*Dividend Policy Alternative #2*) in which Clinton pays more out in cash dividends in Year 0 than it has on hand. In fact, the firm pays 150 percent of its available cash flow, or $52.5 million, in the Year 0 dividend. Because Clinton has only has $35 million, the added $17.5 million must be raised from outside sources through the issuance of bonds or shares of stock. Because we are exploring the effects of dividend policy we will assume that the firm issues shares of stock so as to not change its "all-equity" capital structure. The new stockholders will demand a 15 percent rate of return on their $17.5 million investment, which means that at the end of Year 1 they will expect to receive $20.125 million (i.e., $17.5 million × [1 + .15] = $20.125 million). This leaves $114.875 million for Clinton's old shareholders out of the firm's Year 1 cash flow of $135 million (i.e., $135 million – 20.125 million = $114.875 million). Note that the value of the original shareholders' common stock is still $152.39 million. Thus, it does not matter whether Clinton pays out 0 percent, 100 percent, or 150 percent of its Year 0 cash in dividends to its shareholders. In all of the cases the value of Clinton's shares remains $15.24 per share!

The Form of Payment (Cash Dividends versus Share Repurchases) Is Irrelevant

To illustrate the irrelevance of the form of the cash distribution, we use an example based on GoFast Enterprises, Inc. GoFast is a distributor of high-performance race car parts primarily for BMW Series 3 and 4 automobiles. Started by Bill and "Little John" Petty, a father and son who share a love of fast cars and racing, the company has grown to become a very successful enterprise over the six years since the company was founded. The firm's management expects GoFast to generate $1,000,000 in cash flow next year that can be distributed to shareholders.[6]

---

[6]Technically, this is equity-free cash flow because it is the cash available for distribution to the firm's stockholders.

Figure 2

Dividend Policy Choices Faced by Clinton Enterprises

Dividend Policy Alternative #1: Clinton Enterprises is an all-equity-financed firm that has $35 million in cash on hand that it can pay out in dividends immediately and another $135 million that it can pay out at the end of the year when the firm ceases operations and liquidates all its assets. The cost of equity for the firm is 15 percent, so any new shares issued will require this rate of return.

Dividend Policy Alternative #2: Clinton Enterprises is an all-equity-financed firm that has $35 million in cash on hand and will have another $135 million at the end of the year when the firm ceases operations and liquidates all its assets. Under this alternative, Clinton will issue $17.5 million through the issuance of shares of stock. The $35 million of cash on hand coupled with the $17.5 million raised through the sale of new stock allows Clinton to pay out $52.5 million in dividends immediately. Because the shareholders require a 15 percent return, after one year it will take $20.125 million (i.e., $17.5 million × [1 + .15] = $20.125 million) to pay off $17.5 million of equity that was raised. This leaves $114.875 million for Clinton's old shareholders out of the firm's Year 1 cash flow of $135 million (i.e., $135 million − 20.125 million = $114.875 million).

(Panel A) *Dividend Policy Alternative #1*: Dividends = 100 percent of Year 0 and Year 1 Cash Flow

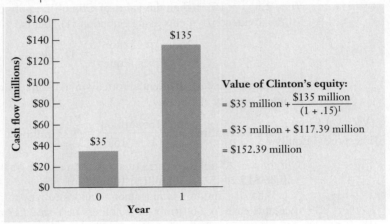

(Panel B) *Dividend Policy Alternative #2*: Dividends = 150 percent of Year 0 Cash Flow and Remainder in Year 1

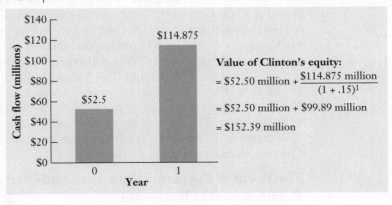

>> END FIGURE 2

Specifically, they are considering two alternatives: (1) pay out the $1 million as a cash dividend or (2) use the cash flow to repurchase shares of company stock.

Individual Investor Wealth Effects: No Personal Taxes

To simplify the analysis, we will initially consider the effect of distributing cash to the firm's shareholders under the assumption that the cash distribution will not impose any transaction costs or tax consequences on the shareholders.

Checkpoint 1

Stock Price and the Timing of Dividend Payments

After operating for more than 50 years, the owners of the Northwest Wire and Cable Company decided that it was time to shut down the firm's business at the end of the year. However, the firm has $4 million in cash available for distribution to its shareholders today and expects to have $30 million at the end of the year to pay as a liquidating dividend. Northwest has 3 million shares outstanding today and is contemplating one of two cash distribution policies. The first (Alternative #1) involves simply paying cash dividends equal to the firm's cash flow both today and at the end of the year. Alternative #2 involves paying a much larger dividend today of $12 million and issuing new shares of stock to raise the $8 million in additional funds needed to fund the dividend. The company's stockholders require a 12 percent rate of return on the firm's shares. What is the value of the firm's equity in total and per share under the two dividend payment plans where the firm has 1 million shares of stock outstanding before issuing any new shares?

STEP 1: Picture the problem

Cash dividends paid under Alternatives #1 and #2 are as follows:

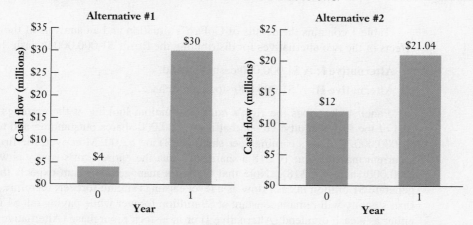

Under Alternative #2 the company will have to raise $8 million from the sale of new common shares. Because the new shareholders will require a 12 percent return on their investment, this will require the firm to pay $8 million × (1.12) = $8.96 million of its $30 million end-of-year cash flow to these new investors. The cash dividend to the existing shareholders at the end of Year 1 will now be only $21.04 million = $30 million – $8.96 million.

STEP 2: Decide on a solution strategy

The value of Northwest Wire and Cable Company's equity is equal to the present value of the firm's expected cash dividends. Because the firm will only distribute a current dividend immediately and one at the end of the year, this means that the value of the firm's equity can be calculated using Equation (1) as follows:

$$\text{Value of Northwest Wire and Cable Company's Equity} = \text{Dividend}_{\text{Year 0}} + \frac{\text{Dividend}_{\text{Year 1}}}{(1 + k_{equity})} \tag{1}$$

STEP 3: Solve

Substituting into the above equation for dividend payment Alternative #1 produces the following estimate of the company's equity value:

$$\text{Value of Northwest Wire and Cable Company's Equity} = \$4 \text{ million} + \frac{\$30 \text{ million}}{(1 + .12)} = \$4 \text{ million} + \$26.79 \text{ million} = \$30.79 \text{ million}$$

The value per share then is $30.79.

For Alternative #2 we perform a similar calculation but substitute the alternative dividends paid to the firm's initial shareholders, that is,

$$\text{Value of Northwest Wire and Cable Company's Equity} = \$12 \text{ million} + \frac{\$21.04 \text{ million}}{(1 + .12)} = \$12 \text{ million} + \$18.79 \text{ million} = \$30.79 \text{ million}$$

Again, the value per share is $30.79.

(1 CONTINUED >> ON NEXT PAGE)

Table 1 contains the details of GoFast's situation and an analysis of the investor wealth effects of the two alternatives for distributing the firm's $1,000,000 in cash flow, that is,

Alternative I: A $1,000,000 cash dividend.

Alternative II: A $1,000,000 stock repurchase.

Panel A describes the firm's current situation, looking at the earnings and the valuation of the firm's equity. Given that it has 500,000 shares outstanding and total earnings of $1,000,000, GoFast's earnings per share (EPS) are $2.00. Moreover, the firm's shares have a current market value of $18 a share such that the entire firm's equity is worth $9 million (500,000 shares × $18).[7] Note that GoFast's management team expects that the firm can generate $1 million in cash flow as a level earnings stream forever; therefore the value of the firm's equity will remain constant at $9 million forever while paying out $1 million per year either as a cash dividend (Alternative I) or in a stock repurchase (Alternative II) and the cost of equity is 11.11 percent.

We analyze the effect of the cash distribution (Alternative I) on the Petty family, which has retained ownership of 10 percent (or 50,000 shares) of GoFast's 500,000 shares outstanding. Note that before any cash distribution is made the 10 percent equity ownership is worth $900,000 (10% × $9 million). Moreover, under Alternative I the Petty family receives a cash dividend of $100,000, which is equal to 10 percent of the $1,000,000 dividend payment. Just prior to the ex-dividend date the shares of GoFast will equal the sum of the present value of the firm's future cash flows, or $9 million plus the accumulated cash used to fund the cash dividend of $1 million, such that the value of the firm's equity will equal $10 million. Given that the firm has 500,000 shares outstanding, this means that the per share price of GoFast's stock will be $20 immediately prior to the payment of the dividend. Once the dividend is paid, the ex-dividend value of the firm's shares will drop by the amount of the per share dividend back to $18 ($20 − $2). Thus, the Petty family would now have 50,000 shares valued at $18 each for a value of $900,000 plus a cash dividend of $100,000 for a total of $1 million.

If Alternative II is taken, GoFast repurchases $1,000,000 worth of its shares at the pre-cash distribution price of $20 per share; hence, the number of shares repurchased equals 50,000 shares (i.e., $1,000,000 ÷ $20). If the Petty family maintains their percentage ownership, they must sell exactly 10 percent of their shares (Alternative II-a). The reduced number of shares outstanding following the repurchase means that EPS will now be $2.22 ($1,000,000 ÷ 450,000 shares), so the value of each share remains at $20, which is the present value of the future dividend stream (100 percent of firm earnings) discounted using the cost of equity of the firm, which is 11.11 percent ($20 = $2.22 ÷ .1111).

Under Alternative II the Petty family receives $100,000 from the sale of 5,000 shares for $20 a share, the same amount of cash they received in Alternative I from the dividend. In

---

[7]Because GoFast is expected to earn a level perpetuity cash flow per share of $2.00 and the stock price is $18.00, this implies a required rate of return on the firm's equity of 11.11 percent, or $2.00/$18.00.

Table 1	Wealth Effects of Cash Distributions: Dividends and Share Repurchases

The following example illustrates that the common stockholder will not care whether the firm pays cash dividends or repurchases shares of stock because the economic consequences of the two cash distribution methods are the same for the stockholder.

Alternative I: A $1,000,000 cash dividend.
Alternative II-a: A $1,000,000 stock repurchase, where the Petty family maintains their percentage ownership of the firm by selling 10 percent of their shares.
Alternative II-b: A $1,000,000 stock repurchase, resulting in the Petty family holdings climbing from 10 percent to 11.11 percent of the shares outstanding.

(Panel A) Firm Setting

			Share Repurchase	
	Current Situation	Alternative I— Pay Dividend	Alternative II-a— Sell Shares	Alternative II-b— Retain Shares
Earnings	$1,000,000			
Shares	500,000	500,000	450,000	450,000
Earnings per Share	$ 2.00	$ 2.00	$ 2.22	$ 2.22
Cost of Equity	11.11%			
Share Price (Pre-distribution)	$ 18.00	$ 20.00	$ 20.00	$ 20.00
Share Price (Post-distribution)		$ 18.00	$ 20.00	$ 20.00
Equity Value (Market Cap)	$9,000,000	$9,000,000	$9,000,000	$9,000,000

(Panel B) Wealth Effects on the Petty Family's 10% Holdings: No Taxes

			Share Repurchase	
Cash Distribution Proceeds		$ 100,000	$ 100,000	$ —
% Share Ownership of Petty Family	10%	10%	10.00%	11.11%
Shares Held by the Petty Family	50,000	50,000	45,000	50,000
Value of Equity Holdings	$ 900,000	$ 900,000	$ 900,000	$1,000,000

			Share Repurchase	
Wealth Effects of the Alternatives		Alternative I— 100% Dividend	Alternative II-a— Sell Shares	Alternative II-b— Retain Shares
Cash Distribution (Dividends or sale of shares)		$ 100,000	$ 100,000	$ —
Total Value of Shares Held by the Petty Family		$ 900,000	$ 900,000	$1,000,000
Total Cash plus Value of Shares		$1,000,000	$1,000,000	$1,000,000

addition, the Petty family retains ownership of 10 percent of the firm's shares (just as in Alternative I), and GoFast equity is still worth $9 million. So the Petty family should be indifferent between these two alternatives.

What would be the wealth effect for the Petty family if they did not sell their shares (Alternative II-b)? Because there are fewer shares of stock outstanding, and the Petty family still owns 50,000 shares, they own a bigger proportion of the company. As a result of the repurchase, the Petty family now owns 11.11 percent of the company (50,000/450,000 = 11.11%) and because the value of the company is $9,000,000, the value of Petty's holdings now $1.0 million ($9,000,000 × 11.11%). Thus, the wealth effect of a stock repurchase where the shares are retained (not sold back) is the same as if GoFast paid a cash dividend or repurchased shares that the Petty family did sell back.

Individual Wealth Effects: Personal Taxes

We have just demonstrated that in the absence of transaction costs and personal taxes the Petty family would be indifferent between the alternative of receiving a cash dividend payment or having the opportunity to sell shares to the firm in a share repurchase. However, this result can change if the tax consequences of the alternatives differ. Before we consider the tax consequences of the alternatives, here are some tax facts concerning dividends and stock repurchases:

Fact #1: 100 percent of the cash dividends received by individuals are taxable in the year in which they are received.

Fact #2: When an individual sells shares of stock, the only part of the cash payment that is taxable is the gain in price over the original price that was paid for the shares (i.e., the original price is the tax basis used to determine whether there has been a gain or loss). So, if you sell shares for $20 that you bought earlier for $18, then you will have to pay tax only on the gain of $2, not the entire $20.

Fact #3: If an individual investor decides not to sell his or her shares back to the company making the stock repurchase, he or she will not incur a taxable gain from the transaction because the investor did not sell. In this instance the investor defers the tax that might eventually have to be paid on his or her gain in the shares.

Post-2003 Tax Treatment: Dividends and Capital Gains Taxed at 15 Percent

To illustrate the effect of differences in tax treatments of dividend payments and share repurchases, we will assume that both dividend income and the gain from the sale of shares of stock are taxed at the same 15 percent rate. Table 2 contains the after-tax cash flow consequences of each of the alternative methods for distributing cash to shareholders that were introduced in Table 1.

In Panel A of Table 2 the tax basis for the Petty shares is zero, so the entire $100,000 cash payment received for the 5,000 shares sold in the stock repurchase is taxable at the 15 percent rate. Note that under Alternative II-b the Petty family continues to own 50,000 shares of Go-Fast and realizes no cash distribution from their investment (and will not realize one until they sell shares in the future). Eventually, when the Petty family sells the shares, they will pay taxes—but there is value in being able to defer those taxes into the future. Remember 🅿 Principle 1: **Money Has a Time Value**, which tells us that pushing a cash expenditure such as taxes further out into the future reduces its present value.

In Panel B of Table 2 we continue to tax dividends and capital gains at the same 15 percent rate. However, in this case we assume that the Petty family initially paid $20 per share (which is their tax basis), which means that when they sell the shares back to GoFast at $20 there is no capital gain to be taxed. In this instance, the Petty family clearly prefers the repurchase plan, regardless of whether they sell the shares (II-a) or retain them (II-b), because they do not incur any taxes, whereas if they received dividends they would have to pay taxes on them.

Pre-2003 Tax Treatment: Dividends Taxed at Higher Rate Than Capital Gains

Prior to the passage of the 2003 tax law, dividends were taxed as ordinary income whereas capital gains were taxed at the capital gains tax rate. In addition, the capital gains tax rate was lower than the ordinary income tax rate for long-term capital gains (gains from the sale of securities held for more than one year). Under this tax scenario, investor preference for share repurchases over cash dividends as a means of distributing corporate cash flow was even stronger. This is a result of the fact that the capital gains tax is based on the gain realized from the sale of shares, not the total value of the cash distribution, and the tax rate on the capital gains was lower than the rate on ordinary income. The tax treatment of capital gains and dividends has changed several times in recent years.

Why Dividend Policy Is Important

We have just demonstrated that tax policy can influence an investor's preference for capital gains income that results from a share repurchase rather than income from cash dividends. However, there are other reasons why a firm might want to continue paying a cash dividend. We review a few of the more important ones in this section.

Table 2 — Dividends versus Share Repurchases with Personal Taxes

This example continues the analysis that began in Table 1 and considers the effect of personal taxes on the Petty family shares in the Go-Fast Corporation. We use a 15 percent personal tax rate for both dividend income and capital gains resulting from the sale of shares for more than the amount originally paid for them (the tax basis). For the share repurchase alternative where the Petty family decides not to sell their shares, we assume they intend to hold them for a period of five years, at which time they will be sold and the taxes on the gain paid.

Alternative I: A $1,000,000 cash dividend.
Alternative II-a: A $1,000,000 stock repurchase, where the Petty family maintains their number of shares by selling 10 percent of their shares.
Alternative II-b: A $1,000,000 stock repurchase, resulting in the Petty family holdings climbing from 10 percent to 11.11 percent of the shares outstanding.

(Panel A) Tax Rates Equal 15% for Dividends and Capital Gains: Basis in Shares Sold Is $0

Tax Basis in Shares	$ 0			
Tax Rate on Dividends and Capital Gains	15%		**Share Repurchase**	
After-Tax Wealth Effects of the Alternatives		**Alternative I—100% Dividend**	**Alternative II-a—Repurchase/Sell Shares**	**Alternative II-b—Repurchase/Retain Shares**
Cash Distribution (Dividends or Sale of Shares)		$100,000	$ 100,000	$ —
Less: Taxes		(15,000)	(15,000)	—
Equals: After-Tax Cash Distribution		$ 85,000	$ 85,000	$ —
Total Value of Shares Held by the Petty Family		900,000	900,000	1,000,000
Total Cash plus Value of Shares		$985,000	$ 985,000	$1,000,000

(Panel B) Tax Rates Equal 15% for Dividends and Capital Gains: Basis in Shares Sold Is $20

Tax Basis in Shares	$ 20.00			
Tax Rate on Dividends and Capital Gains	15%		**Share Repurchase**	
After-Tax Wealth Effects of the Alternatives		**Alternative I—100% Dividend**	**Alternative II-a—Repurchase/Sell Shares**	**Alternative II-b—Repurchase/Retain Shares**
Cash Distribution		$100,000	$ 100,000	$ —
Less: Taxes		(15,000)	—	—
Equals: After-Tax Cash Distribution		$ 85,000	$ 100,000	$ —
Total Value of Shares Held by the Petty Family		900,000	900,000	1,000,000
Total Cash plus Value of Shares		$985,000	$1,000,000	$1,000,000

Transactions Are Costly

Some investors, for example, retired individuals, like to receive cash dividends on a regular basis. Other investors prefer not to receive cash distributions. So, what if an investor wants to invest in a company whose dividend payout policy is not consistent with the investor's own preferences for dividends? As our previous examples illustrate, investors can create their own dividend policy by reinvesting cash dividends if they do not want current income, or by selling some of the shares they own to create cash income if the firm's dividend payout is less than they prefer.

If there were no taxes and investors did not incur transaction costs when they bought and sold shares, they could simply satisfy their personal income preferences by purchasing or selling securities when the dividends received did not satisfy their current needs. However, if taxes are incurred when dividends are paid and if there are costs to buying and selling shares, it is easier for investors to simply select companies to invest in that pay dividends that match up with their particular preferences. Individuals and institutions that need current income would be drawn to companies that have high dividend payouts, whereas individuals with no need for current income would be drawn to companies that pay no dividends.

Because firms with different dividends attract different **dividend clienteles** (groups of investors who prefer the firm's cash distribution policy), it is important that dividend policy remain somewhat stable. For example, a retired individual who bought ExxonMobil (XOM) for its steadily improving dividend might be disappointed if the firm suddenly decided to completely abandon dividends. Likewise, some Google (GOOG) shareholders might be unhappy if Google decided to suddenly start paying high dividends, exposing them to tax liabilities they might not have planned on.

The Information Conveyed by Dividend and Share Repurchase Announcements

Investors and stock market analysts are constantly trying to decipher the information released by firms to better understand what it implies about firm values. This is simply a reflection of P Principle 4: **Market Prices Reflect Information**. As we mentioned in the *Regardless of Your Major* box in the introduction to this chapter, firms tend to increase their dividends only when they believe the higher dividend can be sustained in the future. If this is the case, then a dividend increase is clearly good news. A share repurchase is also viewed very favorably because it shows investors that the firm has generated more money than it currently needs. Of course, the firm's accounting statements also convey information about the firm's recent success. However, accounting statements can be misleading—a cash payout is much easier to interpret.

The timing of large share repurchases also conveys information to shareholders. In a sense, when firms buy back their shares they are making a bet—they would rather repurchase shares when the shares are underpriced versus overpriced. Hence, a share repurchase announcement implies that the firm has plenty of cash and, in addition, that it is a good time to repurchase equity.

The empirical evidence indicates that dividends and share repurchases do in fact convey information to investors. When firms announce that they will increase their dividends, their stock prices do tend to increase. Similarly, when firms announce that they are initiating a repurchase program, their stock prices also tend to rise. In contrast, stock prices tend to decline when firms cut or eliminate their dividends. For instance, in August 2006, Danier Leather (DL.TO) eliminated its annual dividend. As a result, the firm's stock price went from about $7.25 to $6.30—a decrease of about 13 percent.

The Information Conveyed by Stock Dividends and Stock Splits

The announcements of stock dividends and splits also tend to generate positive stock returns. The fact that these announcements convey information to investors is somewhat more difficult to explain, because stock dividends and splits have no effect on the firm's cash flows; and, as we have discussed, it is the cash flows that ultimately determine a firm's value.

There are two theories that have been suggested to explain why stock prices tend to respond favorably to these events. The first explanation relates to the notion that firms have a preferred trading range. There is some empirical support for the idea of a preferred trading range that we can glean from the number of stock splits used by very successful high-growth firms—such as Walmart (WMT), which has split 2 for 1 on 11 different occasions since going public in 1970, and Dell Computer (DELL), which has split 3 for 2 once and 2 for 1 on 6 occasions since going public in 1988. According to this theory, a firm currently priced at $40/share, which has a preferred trading range in the 20s, will be reluctant to instigate a 2-for-1 split if it sees bad news on the horizon. For example, if it sees the possibility of bad news that could drop its share price by 25 percent, from a post-split $20/share to $15/share, it would pass up the opportunity to split its shares. For this reason, investors tend to think that a split implies that there is not likely to be bad news on the horizon.

A second possibility follows from the fact that splits and stock dividends tend to attract attention. If you were the CEO of a company, when would you like to attract the attention of outside analysts and investors? Of course you would not want to attract attention when you have something bad that you would like to hide. This suggests that any corporate-initiated action that attracts attention, even one with no direct effect on cash flows, is likely to convey favorable information.

The Business of Life

The Importance of Dividends

Over the long run, dividends have played a major role in determining the returns to common stock. For large company stocks, around 35 percent of annual returns over the period 1926 through 2005 came from dividends. Is that a big deal? You bet! If you invested $1 in a typical large company stock at the beginning of 1926, from capital appreciation alone it would have grown to $97.85. But if you had reinvested all the dividends and distributions you received, that one dollar would have grown to $2,657.57—proof that dividends are definitely a big deal.

What does all this mean? Simply that if you want to use common stock to accumulate wealth, you must reinvest rather than spend your dividends. Without reinvesting, your accumulation of wealth will be limited to the stock's capital gains. Unfortunately, many dividends may be small enough that you figure you might as well spend them on a pack of Juicy Fruit rather than reinvest them.

One way to avoid buying too much gum and not enough stock is through a dividend reinvestment plan, or DRIP. Under a dividend reinvestment plan, you're allowed to reinvest the dividend in the company's stock automatically without paying any brokerage fees. Most large companies offer such plans, and many stockholders take advantage of them. For example, nearly 40 percent of all PepsiCo (PEP) stockholders participate in dividend reinvestment plans.

A dividend reinvestment plan is a great way to let your savings grow, but it's not without drawbacks. When you sell your stock, you'll have to figure out your income taxes—and that can be overwhelming. Each time you reinvest dividends, you're effectively buying additional shares of stock at a different price. Moreover, even though you don't receive any cash when your dividends are reinvested, you still have to pay income tax as if you actually received those dividends.

A final drawback is the fact that you can't choose where to reinvest your own dividend. What if the company you've invested in is performing moderately well and you'd rather invest in another stock? Unfortunately, you're stuck reinvesting instead of trying something new. Despite these drawbacks, dividend reinvestment plans appeal to many investors. Three sources of companies offering DRIPs are Standard & Poor's *Directory of Dividend Reinvestment Plans* and Evergreen Enterprises' *Directory of Companies Offering Dividend Reinvestment Plans*, both of which may be available at your library; and the Wells Fargo's Investment Plans site https://www.wellsfargo.com/com/shareowner_services/ services_for_shareholders/investment_plans.

Your Turn: See Study Question 8.

Before you move on to 3

Concept Check | 2

1. What are the fundamental conditions or assumptions used by M&M to demonstrate the irrelevance of dividend policy?

2. Describe in simple terms why the timing of a firm's dividend payments that result from its dividend policy should not impact the value of its shares.

3. What is the tax treatment of the investor's dividend income and what is the tax treatment of the income resulting from the firm's stock repurchases?

4. How is it that share repurchases are *tax favored* when compared to a cash dividend, even though the rate of tax paid on dividend income and capital gains income is the same?

 Cash Distribution Policies in Practice

Dividend policies followed in corporate practice are as varied as the companies that use them. However, there are some basic attributes of those policies that can help a firm calibrate its policy with the practices of other firms.

Stable Payout

The responses to a recent survey of corporate CFOs provide us with some insight into how business executives think about dividend policy. The results reported in Panel A of Figure 3 tell whether the survey respondents agreed or strongly agreed with a number of statements

Figure 3

Survey of CFO Opinions Regarding Dividend Policy Issues

(Panel A) Agreement with Dividend Policy Statements

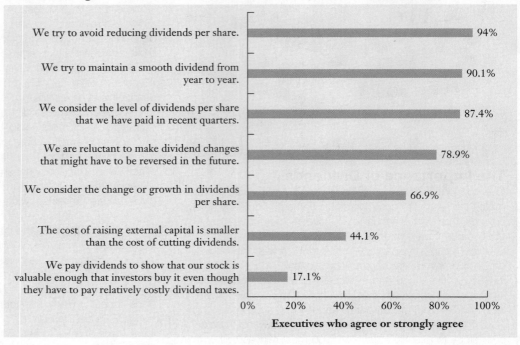

We try to avoid reducing dividends per share. — 94%

We try to maintain a smooth dividend from year to year. — 90.1%

We consider the level of dividends per share that we have paid in recent quarters. — 87.4%

We are reluctant to make dividend changes that might have to be reversed in the future. — 78.9%

We consider the change or growth in dividends per share. — 66.9%

The cost of raising external capital is smaller than the cost of cutting dividends. — 44.1%

We pay dividends to show that our stock is valuable enough that investors buy it even though they have to pay relatively costly dividend taxes. — 17.1%

Executives who agree or strongly agree

(Panel B) Importance of Dividend Policy Statements

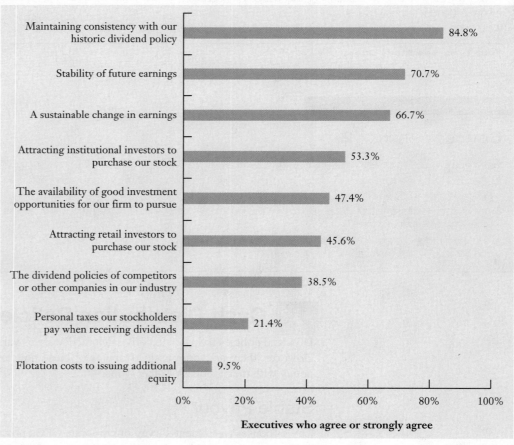

Maintaining consistency with our historic dividend policy — 84.8%

Stability of future earnings — 70.7%

A sustainable change in earnings — 66.7%

Attracting institutional investors to purchase our stock — 53.3%

The availability of good investment opportunities for our firm to pursue — 47.4%

Attracting retail investors to purchase our stock — 45.6%

The dividend policies of competitors or other companies in our industry — 38.5%

Personal taxes our stockholders pay when receiving dividends — 21.4%

Flotation costs to issuing additional equity — 9.5%

Executives who agree or strongly agree

Source: A. Brav, J. R. Graham, C. R. Harvey, and R. Michaely, "Payout Policy in the 21st Century," NBER working paper series, Working paper #9657, April 2003.

>> END FIGURE 3

about dividend policy. The top five policy statements reported in Panel A suggest that executives are very concerned about maintaining a consistent cash payout from year to year.

Panel B of Figure 3 provides a summary of some of the responses to the question "How important are the following factors to your company's dividend decision?" Once again, the importance of maintaining consistency and stability is apparent in the statements that drew the highest rating across the respondents. Therefore, the message from the corporate CFOs is that maintaining a consistent payout is very important.

What about repurchase decisions? Figure 4 looks at the responses of executives to the question "How important are the following factors to your company's repurchase decision?" Table 3 examines the factors that the executives viewed as important in deciding whether to distribute cash to shareholders in the form of dividends versus repurchases. Interestingly, in Figure 4 the top two responses indicate that stock repurchase decisions are driven by the executive's feeling that first, the stock is a good investment relative to its true value, and second, that there is a lack of good investment opportunities to pursue. In addition, among the other reasons given for stock repurchases, one was the tax rate that stockholders pay when they receive repurchases.

Table 3 adds to our understanding of the dividend versus repurchase decision by providing evidence that the flexibility of repurchases appears to be a major factor in the choice of repurchases as opposed to dividends. Not only is the historical level of cash distributions unimportant in repurchase decisions, but also repurchases provide flexibility with no perceived need to match past repurchases. Moreover, reducing repurchases from one year to the next does not seem to have a penalty associated with it; however, the announcement of a repurchase plan is perceived to have a positive impact on stock prices.

The opinions of the corporate CFOs underscore a very important observation about corporate dividend policy in practice that was first documented by John Lintner more than 35 years ago. That is, firms try to maintain a steady cash payout that only increases when firm earnings are thought to be sufficient to support the higher payment with little risk of forcing the company to retreat. Figure 5 illustrates this phenomenon by comparing the percentage changes in dividends and earnings for stocks in the S&P 500 index over the period 1960–2007. Note that the percentage change in dividends from year to year is always well within the bounds of the percentage change in firm earnings. Although dividends are increased and reduced in response to changes in firm earnings, the changes in dividends are always much smaller.

Figure 4

Factors Important to Your Company's Repurchase Decision

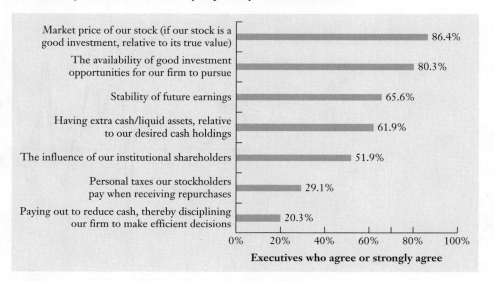

Source: A. Brav, J. R. Graham, C. R. Harvey, and R. Michaely, "Payout Policy in the 21st Century," *Journal of Financial Economics* 77 (September 2005), 483–527.

>> END FIGURE 4

Table 3	Summary of Financial Executives' Views about Payout Policy	
Dividends		**Repurchases**
Very important. Do not cut dividends except in extreme circumstances.	**Historical Level**	Historical level is not important.
Sticky. Inflexible. Smooth through time.	**Flexibility**	Very flexible. No need to smooth out.
Little reward for increasing.	**Consequence If Increased**	Stock price increases when repurchase plan announced.
Big market penalty for reducing or omitting.	**Consequence If Reduced**	Little consequence to reducing from one year to the next, although firms try to complete plans.
Most common target is the level of dividend, followed by payout ratio and growth in dividends. Target is viewed as rather flexible.	**Target**	Most common target is dollar amount of repurchases, a very flexible target.
External funds would be raised before cutting dividends.	**Relation to External Funds**	Repurchases would be reduced before raising external funds.
First maintain historic dividend level; then make incremental investment decisions.	**Relation to Investment**	First make investment decisions; then make repurchase decisions.
Dividend increases tied to permanent, stable earnings.	**Earnings Quality**	Repurchases increase with permanent earnings but also with temporary earnings.

Source: A. Brav, J. R. Graham, C. R. Harvey, and R. Michaely, "Payout Policy in the 21st Century," *Journal of Financial Economics* 77 (September 2005), 483–527.

Figure 5

Changes in Dividends in Response to Changes in Earnings: 1960–2007
The changes in dividends and earnings are averages of the percentage changes in the 500 companies contained in the S&P 500 index.

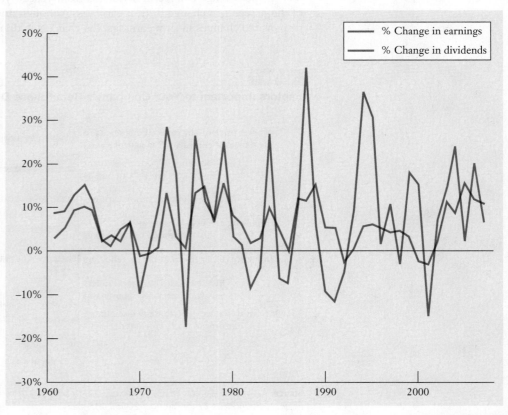

>> END FIGURE 5

Residual Dividend Payout Policy

The stable dividend policy focuses on the stability of the cash dividend payout as a critical determinant of the firm's dividend policy. This focus on the primary importance of the dividend payment is just the opposite of the underlying rationale for the **residual dividend payout policy**. Following the residual payout policy, the firm focuses on the primary importance of financing the firm's investments using its own earnings—which are the lowest-cost source of equity financing—so long as the firm has positive-NPV investment opportunities. Under the residual dividend payout policy, dividends are paid out of the residual earnings that are not needed to finance new investment opportunities.

Although the residual dividend payout policy has some conceptual appeal, it can result in a very volatile stream of dividend payments where the firm's earnings vary from year to year and its positive-NPV investment opportunities also vary over time. The appeal of this policy—which does not entail incurring the costs attendant to the sale of an issue of common shares—is its focus on minimizing the cost of financing new investments by utilizing equity financing from the retention of firm earnings.

Other Factors Playing a Role in How Much to Distribute

In setting a firm's payout policy, financial managers must determine dividend policy in a world that does not fit the simplifying assumptions used to develop theory. So, let us now take a look at some practical considerations that influence a firm's dividend policy.

Liquidity Position

Contrary to common belief, the mere fact that a company shows a large amount of retained earnings on the balance sheet does not indicate that cash is available for the payment of dividends or the repurchase of stock. The firm's current position in liquid assets, including cash, is basically independent of the retained earnings account. Historically, a company with sizable retained earnings has been successful in generating cash from operations, yet these funds are typically either reinvested in the company within a short period or used to pay maturing debt. Thus, a firm may be extremely profitable and still be cash poor. Because dividend payments and stock repurchases are made with cash and not with retained earnings, the firm must have sufficient cash available for payouts to be made. Hence, the firm's liquidity position has a direct bearing on its ability to make payouts.

Lack of Other Sources of Financing

Many small or new companies do not have access to the capital markets, and as a result they must rely upon internally generated funds to fund their investment opportunities. As a consequence, the payout ratio is generally much lower for a small or newly established firm than for a large, publicly owned corporation.

Earnings Predictability

A company's payout ratio depends to some extent on the predictability of a firm's profits over time. If earnings fluctuate significantly, management cannot rely on internally generated funds to meet future needs. When profits are realized, the firm may retain larger amounts to ensure that money is available when needed. Conversely, firms with stable earnings will typically pay out a larger portion of their earnings. These companies have less concern about the availability of profits to meet future capital requirements.

Finance in a **Flat World**

Dividends Abroad

In December 2004, the top story on Wall Street was Microsoft Corp.'s (MSFT) decision to pay out a special dividend of $3 per share. For Microsoft, the total amount of funds being sent to stockholders in this special dividend added up to $32 billion. In fact, Microsoft also announced that it planned to pay out about $75 billion in dividends over the next four years.

Given these numbers, you might venture a guess that the United States leads the way in terms of sending back money to the shareholders in the form of dividends. If so, you would be wrong. Although U.S. companies stand ahead of Japanese companies in terms of paying out dividends, they fall behind European firms. In the United States, the average payout ratio for the S&P 500 stood at 29 percent at the beginning of 2007. In the United States, as in Japan, while dividends have been rising recently, the dividend payout ratio has declined slightly as dividend growth has not kept pace with growth in earnings. In fact, in 2003, the average dividend payout for S&P 500 companies was 34.7 percent—that's a 16.4 percent decline in the average payout ratio in three years.

In Europe, there is a tradition of paying out more of the firm's earnings in the form of dividends. For European firms the average payout ratio runs above 40 percent; but, just as with Japanese and U.S. firms, while dividends have been increasing, the average payout ratio of European firms dropped recently as earnings growth outstripped the growth in dividends.

Your Turn: See Study Question 14.

Before you begin end-of-chapter material

Concept Check | **3**

1. Why is a stable payout policy for cash dividends preferred by so many firms?
2. What are the key factors considered by firms when determining their dividend payout policies?

Principle 1: **Money Has a Time Value** Pushing a cash expenditure such as taxes out into the future has value because of Principle 1. As a result, capital gains, which can result from share repurchase, hold an advantage to investors over dividend payments.

 Principle 3: **Cash Flows Are the Source of Value** Cash flows—regardless of how they are received, either in the form of stock appreciation or dividends—are the source of value of the firm.

 Principle 4: **Market Prices Reflect Information** An increase or decrease in firm's dividend policy can be a source of information to investors, and as such can impact the firm's share price.

Chapter Summaries

1 Distinguish between the use of cash dividends and share repurchases.

SUMMARY: Cash dividends are typically paid quarterly and represent a direct payment of cash to each of the firm's shareholders in direct proportion to the number of shares that she or he owns. Stock repurchases of the firm's shares, on the other hand, are typically made in the open market and result in a cash inflow to the shareholders who sell their shares to the company. The shareholders who do not sell their shares end up with the same number of shares as before but with a higher ownership percentage, as the share repurchase reduces the total number of common shares that are outstanding.

KEY TERMS

Cash dividend Cash paid directly to stockholders.

Date of record The date on which the company looks at its records to see who receives dividends.

Declaration date The date upon which a dividend is formally declared by the board of directors.

Dividend payout ratio The total dollar amount of dividends relative to the company's net income.

Dividend policy The firm's policy that determines how much cash it will distribute to its shareholders and when these distributions will be made.

Ex-dividend date The date upon which stock brokerage companies have uniformly decided to terminate the right of ownership to the dividend, which is two days prior to the date of record.

Open market repurchase A method of repurchasing the firm's stock whereby the firm acquires the stock on the market, often buying a relatively small number of shares every day, at the going market price.

Payment date The date on which the company mails a dividend check to each investor of record.

Share or stock repurchase Also called a stock buyback, the repurchase of common stock by the issuing firm for any of a variety of reasons, resulting in reduction of shares outstanding.

Stock dividend The distribution of shares of up to 25 percent of the number of shares currently outstanding, issued on a pro rata basis to the current stockholders.

Stock split A stock dividend exceeding 25 percent of the number of shares currently outstanding.

Tender offer A formal offer by the company to buy a specified number of shares at a predetermined and stated price. The tender price is set above the current market price in order to attract sellers.

Concept Check | 1

1. What are the two forms of cash distributions that firms typically use?

2. What is the frequency with which cash dividends are typically paid to investors?

3. Identify three motives that might encourage a firm to buy back its common stock shares.

4. What are the three different methods that firms use to repurchase their shares?

5. How is a stock dividend like a stock split, and why do financial managers sometimes use one or the other?

2 Understand the tax treatment of dividends and capital gains, stock dividends, and stock splits, and the conditions under which dividend policy is an important determinant of stock value.

SUMMARY: Historically, the personal tax code has had a built-in preference for capital gains income over dividends. Dividends were taxed at the ordinary income tax rate whereas capital gains (especially long-term) were taxed at preferentially lower taxes. However, one of the important provisions of the 2006 tax act was the extension of the provision of the 2003 tax act that reduced the rate at which corporate dividends and capital gains are taxed. Specifically, the maximum tax rate on dividends and long-term capital gains (on stock held for 366 days or longer) was lowered to 15 percent for most people. In order to qualify for the lower taxes on dividends, you are required to hold the stock on which the dividends are paid for more than 60 days during the 120-day period that begins 60 days before the ex-dividend date. If you did not meet these qualifications, the dividends were taxed like ordinary income.

A stock dividend is just like a cash dividend except that the dividend transfers new shares of the company's stock instead of cash. The net effect of the stock dividend is simply to increase the number of shares of stock the company has outstanding. For example, if the firm were to make a 5 percent stock dividend, this would increase the number of shares outstanding by 5 percent.

A stock split is a tool the firm can use to increase the number of shares outstanding by exchanging a larger number of shares for the existing shares held by each investor. For example, in a 2-for-1 split the company would issue two new shares in exchange for each share currently held. The net result would be a doubling of the number of shares outstanding.

Stock dividends and stock splits have the same effect on the firm in that they both increase the number of shares outstanding and, as a result, the share price declines such that the total value of the firm's common shares is unchanged. For example, a 200 percent stock dividend is equivalent to a 2-for-1 stock split.

The firm's dividend payout decision does not have any effect on the value of the firm in the absence of taxes and when the firm's operating and investment policies are fixed (i.e., are not influenced by the decision to pay, or not to pay, a cash dividend). Specifically, neither the timing of the payment of cash dividends nor the form of the payment (cash dividend or stock repurchase) has an effect on firm value where the above conditions hold.

KEY TERM

Dividend clienteles Groups of investors who prefer the firm's cash distribution policy.

 Describe corporate dividend policies that are commonly used in practice.

SUMMARY: Surveys of corporate executives involved in making dividend payment policies reveal a strong preference for maintaining a stable dividend payout. Given the fact that firm earnings and, consequently, the firm's ability to pay cash dividends fluctuate over time and with the business cycle, it is not surprising that cash dividend payments tend to lag earnings growth. Consequently, the typical practice is for firms to only increase their cash dividend payout where the firm's management feels comfortable that they can sustain the higher dividend payment even under adverse conditions. Other factors that influence the dividend that a firm pays include the firm's liquidity or its access to needed cash, access to sources of cash in the event of an economic downturn, and earnings predictability.

KEY TERM

Residual dividend payout policy A payout policy whereby the company's dividend payment should equal the cash left after financing all the investments that have positive net present values.

Study Questions

1. In the introduction, we pointed out that Emerson Electric Co. (EMR) had paid cash dividends for 53 consecutive years. Look up the company's cash dividend for the most recent year. What is the dividend for that year?

2. **(Related to Regardless of Your Major: Firms Almost Never Decrease Their Dividend)** In the *Regardless of Your Major* feature, we learned that firms try to sustain their dividend payout even in economic downturns. Use the Internet to determine what General Electric (GE) did with respect to its dividend in 2009. Why do you think GE took this action?

3. Explain what a firm's dividend policy is as if you were talking to your grandmother, who has had no formal education in business.

4. A firm's dividend policy is generally characterized in terms of two attributes. Explain each.

5. What is a stock dividend, and how is it similar to a stock split?

6. Your Aunt Mary recently called to ask you about a letter she had just received from her stock broker. She said that the letter notified her that one of the stocks she owns

was paying a 10 percent stock dividend such that her 100 shares would now be 110 shares. Because the stock was trading at $20 a share before the stock dividend, she said that she was thrilled that she now held 110 shares worth $2,200, but wanted to check with you to determine if she was right. Explain to your Aunt Mary what exactly has happened here.

7. Describe the dividend distribution process, including the importance of the declaration date, date of record, and ex-dividend date.

8. **(Related to The Business of Life: The Importance of Dividends)** In *The Business of Life* boxed feature we learned about the importance of dividend reinvestment to creating personal wealth through investing in stocks. Many companies offer what is called dividend reinvestment plans. What are these plans, and how do they work?

9. Cousin Harold runs a pharmacy but likes to dabble in common stock investing as a hobby. One day last week Harold called you to find out what had happened to his portfolio because one of the stocks he owns had announced the decision to purchase 10 percent of the outstanding shares of the company. How will this action affect Cousin Harold's portfolio?

10. Why is a stable dollar dividend policy popular from the viewpoint of the corporation? Is it also popular with investors? Why?

11. Under what conditions is the firm's dividend policy not important to its investors?

12. Your Uncle Bob has no formal education in business or finance but has been investing in the stock market for many years. At a recent family reunion, Uncle Bob told you that he liked to invest in stocks such as Emerson Electric (EMR) because it had a very long history of paying cash dividends. Do you agree with this philosophy? Why or why not?

13. What is the current U.S. tax policy with regard to the taxation of dividend income and capital gains income resulting from a share repurchase? If the individual stockholder could choose whether to receive a cash dividend or have the firm engage in a share repurchase, which should he or she prefer? Explain.

14. **(Related to Finance in a Flat World: Dividends Abroad)** In the *Finance in a Flat World* boxed feature we learned that dividend payout practices differ across the major developed countries of the world. How does the U.S. compare to other countries?

Study Problems

MyFinanceLab How Do Firms Distribute Cash?

Go to www.myfinancelab.com to complete these exercises online and get instant feedback.

1. **(Dividend payout ratio)** Calculate the cash dividend paid per share for each of the firms in the following table using their earnings per share and dividend payout ratio:

Company	Dividend Payout Ratio	Earnings per Share
Emerson Electric Co (EMR)	52%	$2.49
Intel Corporation (INTC)	127%	$0.438
Walmart Stores Inc. (WMT)	30%	$3.41

2. **(Dividend payout ratio)** The Costco Wholesale Corporation (COST) operates membership warehouses that offer a wide variety of branded and private-label products in no-frills, self-service warehouse facilities. In 2008 the company paid total cash dividends of $265,029,000 and had net income of $1,282,725,000.

   a. What was the firm's dividend payout ratio?

   b. If Costco were to earn $1.5 billion in 2009 and maintained the same dividend payout ratio that it paid in 2008, what would the firm's dividends be?

3. **(Ex-dividend stock price)** Paylin Enterprises has declared a $3 dividend for its common stock. On the day before the ex-dividend date the firm's shares are trading for

$28 a share. What do you expect the price of Paylin's shares to be on the day follow-ing the ex-dividend date? Why do you expect the stock price to change?

4. **(Ex-dividend stock price)** Elco Electric Corporation has a stock price of $150 per share and is contemplating the payment of a large one-time cash dividend of $40 per share. The underlying motivation for the large payout comes from management's belief that the firm has more cash than it can profitably reinvest and to keep the cash would adversely affect the incentives of the workforce to strive to create shareholder value. Consequently, the firm's management decided to pay out the large cash divi-dend. What do you think the ex-dividend-date price of the company's shares will be? If the firm's management is right about the stimulating effect of disgorging cash, do you think that the drop in stock price after the ex-dividend date will be smaller than otherwise expected? Why or why not?

5. **(Stock dividend)** The stock price of Alpine Inc. is currently $30 a share. If the firm pays a 10 percent stock dividend, what would you expect the ex-dividend stock price to be? What about a 20 percent stock dividend?

6. **(Stock dividend)** Templeton Care Facilities, Inc. is contemplating a stock dividend. The firm's stock price had risen over the last three years and was trading at $150 per share. The firm's board of directors felt that the trading range should be around $50 to $100, so they wanted to initiate a stock dividend that, other things remaining the same, would result in a $50 share price. What should the stock dividend be so as to result in the desired change in the firm's stock price?

7. **(Stock split)** Reconsider the problem faced by Templeton Care Facilities, Inc. from Study Problem 6. If the firm's board of directors decided to use a stock split rather than a stock dividend, how many new shares should the firm issue for each outstand-ing share?

8. **(Stock splits and stock dividends)** Chaney's Fatburner Gyms, Inc. operates a chain of exercise facilities throughout the Midwest. The firm appeals to middle-aged men who suffer from obesity problems and want to improve their health by entering an exercise program. The firm currently has 8,000,000 shares of stock outstanding that have a current market price of $12. If all else remains constant, what will be the price of Chaney's shares after each of the following?

   a. A 20 percent stock dividend.
   b. A four-for-one stock split.
   c. A 32.5 percent stock dividend.
   d. What would be the total number of shares outstanding after parts a through c?

9. **(Cash dividends)** Marshall Pottery Barn is a privately owned importer of Mexican pottery and garden supplies. The firm plans on paying a $1.50 per share dividend on each of its 5,000 shares of common stock. The firm's most recent balance sheet just before payment of the dividend looks like the following:

Cash	$ 18,000	Accounts payable	$ 22,000
Accounts receivable	22,000	Notes payable	5,000
Inventories	30,000	Current liabilities	$ 27,000
Current assets	$ 70,000	Long-term debt	33,000
Fixed assets	130,000	Equity	140,000
Total assets	$200,000	Total	$200,000

   a. What would happen to the firm's balance sheet after payment of the cash dividend?
   b. If the above balance sheet also represented market values (as well as book val-ues), how would it change following the payment of the cash dividend?

10. **(Stock repurchase and taxes)** The Barryman Drilling Company is planning on repurchasing $1 million worth of the company's 500,000 shares of stock, which is currently trading at a price of $10 per share. Stan Barryman is the founder of the company and still holds 10,000 shares of company stock that he originally purchased for $8 per share. If Stan decides to sell 2,000 of his shares for $10 a share, what will be his after-tax proceeds where capital gains are taxed at 15 percent?

11. **(Cash dividend and taxes)** The Barryman Drilling Company from Study Problem 10 is reconsidering its plan to repurchase $1 million of its common stock and instead plans to pay a $1 million cash dividend, which amounts to $2 per share of common stock. If dividends are taxed at 15 percent, what tax liability does this create for Stan Barryman?

Does Dividend Policy Matter?

12. **(Related to Checkpoint 1) (Dividend irrelevance of the timing of cash dividends)** The Caraway Seed Company sells specialty gardening seeds and products primarily to mail-order and Internet customers. The firm has $200,000 available for distribution as a cash dividend immediately and plans to shut down its business at the end of one year, at which time it will be prepared to pay a liquidating dividend of $1.2 million to the firm's stockholders. The firm's shareholders require a 10 percent rate of return for investing in the all-equity-financed firm.

   a. What do you estimate the value of Caraway's equity to be today if it pays out a $200,000 cash dividend today and plans to pay a $1.2 million liquidating dividend at the end of the year?

   b. If Caraway's board of directors decides to pay a $600,000 dividend today to its existing shareholders using an equity offering selling new shares of common stock to raise the additional $400,000 it needs to make the cash dividend, what will be the value of the existing shares of stock? The new shares?

13. **(Related to Checkpoint 1) (Dividend irrelevance of the timing of cash dividends)** After more than 40 years of operation, the Tyler Brick Mfg. Company has decided it is time to shut down the business. The firm has $125,000 available for distribution as a cash dividend immediately and plans to shut down its business at the end of one year, at which time it will be prepared to pay a liquidating dividend to the firm's stockholders of $14 million. The firm's shareholders require a 15 percent rate of return for investing in the all-equity-financed firm.

   a. What do you estimate the value of Tyler's equity to be today if it pays out a $125,000 cash dividend today and plans to pay out a $14 million liquidating dividend at the end of the year?

   b. If Tyler's board of directors decides to pay a $1,000,000 dividend today to its existing shareholders and uses an equity offering selling new shares of common stock to raise the additional funds that it needs to make the cash dividend, what will be the value of the existing shares of stock? The new shares?

Mini-Case

You've been working for the local newspaper for several years and you've finally got your own column, "Finance Questions: Ask the Expert." Your job is to field readers' questions that deal with finance. This week you are going to address two questions from your readers that have to do with dividends:

Question #1: I own 8 percent of the Standlee Corporation's 30,000 shares of common stock, which most recently traded for a price of $98 per share. The company has since declared its plans to engage in a 2-for-1 stock split.

   a. What will my financial position be after the stock split, compared to my current position? (Hint: Assume the stock price falls proportionately.)

   b. The executive vice president in charge of finance believes the price will not fall in proportion to the size of the split and will only fall 45 percent because she thinks the pre-split price is above the optimal price range. If she is correct, what will be my net gain from the split?

Question #2: I am on the board of directors of the B. Phillips Corporation, and Phillips has announced its plan to pay dividends of $550,000. Presently there are 275,000 shares outstanding, and the earnings per share are $6. It looks to me like the stock should sell for $45 after the ex-dividend date. What if, instead of paying a dividend, the management decided to repurchase stock?

   a. What should be the repurchase price that is equivalent to the proposed dividend (ignoring any tax effects)?

   b. How many shares should the company repurchase?

   c. I want to look out for the small shareholders. If someone owns 100 shares, do you think he would prefer that the company pay the dividend or repurchase stock?

Photo Credits

Financial Forecasting
and Planning

From Chapter 17 of *Financial Management: Principles and Applications*, Twelfth Edition. Sheridan Titman, Arthur J. Keown, and John D. Martin.

Financial Forecasting and Planning

Chapter **Outline**

1 An Overview of Financial Planning

→ **Objective 1.** Understand the goals of financial planning.

2 Developing a Long-Term Financial Plan

→ **Objective 2.** Use the percent-of-sales method to forecast the financing requirements of a firm, including its discretionary financing needs.

3 Developing a Short-Term Financial Plan

→ **Objective 3.** Prepare a cash budget and use it to evaluate the amount and timing of a firm's short-term financing requirements.

Planning is essentially a way for the firm's management to address the basic fact of business life—that the future cannot be known. By planning, however, the firm's management reduces some of the risks that the firm faces by having contingency plans in place that allow them to respond quickly and effectively either to take advantage of opportunities that present themselves or to respond to difficulties in the most cost-effective way. So planning provides a tool for enhancing shareholder returns and reducing risk, which is a natural extension of the application of **P** Principle 2: **There Is a Risk–Return Tradeoff.**

Forecasting Is Difficult (for Everyone)

Forecasting tends to be very difficult. Of course, there are some things that are fairly straightforward to forecast. For example, forecasts of the number of automobiles passing through a toll booth on a particular stretch of freeway can be predicted with a high degree of accuracy. However, forecasting the effects of technological breakthroughs can be extremely difficult. As the following quotes illustrate, even technology mavens have their limitations when it comes to gazing into the technology crystal ball:

"This 'telephone' has too many shortcomings to be seriously considered as a means of communication. The device is inherently of no value to us."

—*Western Union internal memo, 1876*

"There is no reason anyone would want a computer in their home."

—*President, chairman, and founder of Digital Equipment Corp., 1977*

"640K ought to be enough for anybody."

— *Bill Gates, 1981*

Although forecasts are inherently imperfect, one cannot run a business without thinking about the future. Indeed, forecasting can be viewed as the first step in developing a financial plan that allows firms to come up with the required financing for upcoming investment projects as well as to develop contingency plans for when the future does not unfold as expected. Although many CEOs still rely on their "gut feelings," businesses are increasingly using more systematic approaches to forecasting, which has the added benefit of giving executives a more structured approach to planning. Of course, plans based on imperfect forecasts are by definition imperfect. However, with a systematic approach to thinking about what the future *might* be like, firms are better positioned to come up with contingency plans that can be used to improve their ability to respond to adverse events and to take advantage of opportunities as they arise.

In this chapter, we first survey the types of plans that businesses typically use to guide their operations. This includes the strategic plan, the long-range financial plan, and the short-range financial plan. We develop both a long- and short-term financial plan and point out the critical nature of the firm's sales forecast. We also develop the use of the percent-of-sales approach to forecast the firm's future financing requirements using pro forma income statements and balance sheets. Finally, we will learn to prepare a cash budget, a tool that helps us predict the amount and timing of the firm's financing needs and also serves as a benchmark for analyzing the firm's operations over time.

Regardless of Your Major…

"Developing a Financial Plan for the Firm Engages Everyone"

Businesses require planning, and planning requires the cooperation of everyone in the organization. Consider the basic steps involved in developing an annual financial plan for a firm that manufactures a line of dental care products. Step 1: Gather historical data on sales and expenses for each product spanning the last 6 to 12 months. The logical place to start this process is with the firm's accountants, who maintain cost and revenue information by product. Step 2: Analyze the historical data to identify any trends that might be useful in predicting future levels. This analysis would probably fall on the firm's financial analysts, who are developing the financial plan. Step 3: Make adjustments to projections of revenues by product line to reflect the firm's current marketing plans. This analysis logically comes out of the firm's marketing staff, which develops sales plans and forecasts as well as advertising campaigns. The marketing group will also be very familiar with the latest information on competitors and any new product offerings that might impact the sales forecast. Step 4: Revise estimates of per-unit costs and expense estimates to reflect any changes that might be planned for the firm's operations. The firm's operations staff will be the keepers of this information that, when analyzed by the firm's cost accountants, can be used to revise cost-per-unit estimates across all the firm's product lines. Step 5: Forecast the company's after-tax cash flows, which will in turn be used to help the firm decide on its future dividend payment as well as the firm's future financing needs.

Your Turn: See Study Question 1.

An Overview of Financial Planning

In this chapter, we survey the financial planning process. The firm's financial plan is generally divided into two components: a short-term financial plan that spans from several months up to one year, and a long-term financial plan that spans up to five years. The primary objective of both short- and long-range financial planning is the estimation of the firm's future financing needs. Having some idea about what the firm's financing requirements will be before the need arises allows the firm's management to seek out financing with the most advantageous terms possible. However, there is another reason to engage in financial planning: simply engaging in the financial planning process forces managers to think systematically about the future and to develop contingency plans that allow them to quickly respond to the challenges and opportunities that an uncertain future is sure to bring. The point that planning is worthwhile, even in a highly uncertain environment, was forcefully expressed by a former U.S. president and the supreme commander of Allied Forces in Europe during World War II. It was Dwight Eisenhower who said, "In preparing for battle I have always found that plans are useless, but planning is indispensable."

Most firms engage in three types of planning activities that vary in their objectives and degrees of detail. For example, the firm's **strategic plan** defines, in very general terms, how the firm plans to make money in the future. The expenditure to develop the strategic plan can be thought of as a direct application of ▣ Principle 2: **There Is a Risk–Reward Tradeoff**. The strategic plan will answer very general questions about the company, such as the following:

- Who are we and what do we do?
- Who are our customers?
- Who are our competitors and how do we compete (price, quality, features, etc.)?

For the purposes of this chapter, we assume that the firm already has such a plan in place. This strategic plan serves as a guide to the preparation of long- and short-term financial plans.

The **long-term financial plan** generally encompasses a period of three to five years and incorporates estimates of the firm's income statements and balance sheets for each year of the planning horizon. These forecasts of the firm's financial statements are referred to as pro forma financial statements.

The **short-term financial plan** spans a period of one year or less and is a very detailed description of the firm's anticipated cash flows. The format typically used for the short-term financial plan is a cash budget. The **cash budget** is highly disaggregated and contains detailed revenue projections and expenses for the month—or even the week—in which they are expected to occur for each operating unit of the company. The long-term financial plan, by comparison, has less detail, as it aggregates individual operating unit data to the division or firm level.

There are two significant benefits to the firm from developing long- and short-term financial plans. First, the firm has a base plan that is consistent with the firm's long-term goals and strategy. In other words, by preparing a plan, the firm's management can align their day-to-day activities to support the overriding goals and objectives set by the firm's top executives. Second, as former President Eisenhower pointed out so succinctly many years ago, it's the planning process as much as or more than the actual plan that helps the firm prepare for an uncertain future.

Before you move on to 2

Concept Check | 1

1. What are the fundamental benefits of financial planning?
2. Distinguish between a firm's short-term financial plan, long-term financial plan, and strategic plan.

2 | Developing a Long-Term Financial Plan

The long-term financial plan typically spans three to five years and serves as the basis for developing the short-term financial plan. Consequently, we open our discussion of the planning process with a discussion of the development of the three- to five-year long-term financial plan. This process begins with a forecast of firm sales, which then serves as the basis for forecasting the firm's financial position at the end of each year of the planning horizon. The format of the long-term operating financial plan consists of **pro forma income statements** and **pro forma balance sheets**. These pro forma financial statements follow the format of the firm's reported statements, but apply to projected or forecast results for a future period of time. These statements are frequently constructed by first making a forecast of firm revenues and then using the percent-of-sales method to predict balances for each of the entries in both the pro forma income statement and the pro forma balance sheet.

Forecasting a firm's future financing needs using a long-term financial plan can be thought of in terms of three basic steps:

Step 1. Construct a Sales Forecast. The key ingredient in the financial planning process is the sales forecast. This forecast is generally made using (1) information about any past sales trend that is expected to carry over into the period being forecast, and (2) information about the influence of any anticipated events that might materially affect the sales trend.[1] Examples of such events are the start of a major advertising campaign that would provide a boost to future sales, or a change in the firm's pricing policy that could expand the firm's market.

Step 2. Prepare Pro Forma Financial Statements. We can now forecast the firm's asset requirements needed to support the forecast of revenues (Step 1) by preparing pro forma financial statements that include both an income statement and a balance

---

[1]A complete discussion of forecast methodologies is outside the scope of this chapter and is typically found in economics or statistics classes.

sheet. The most common technique for preparing pro forma financial statements is the **percent-of-sales method**. The percent-of-sales method expresses expenses, assets, and liabilities for a future period as percentages of sales. The percentages used to make the forecast can come from the most recent financial statements, from an average computed over several years, from the judgment of the analyst, or from some combination of these methods.

Step 3. **Estimate the Firm's Financing Needs.** Using the pro forma statements, we can extract the cash flow requirements of the firm. The firm's financial statements are not prepared on a cash basis but instead use something called the accrual method. However, we can use the financial statements to estimate the firm's financing needs in cash terms, as we now illustrate with an example.

Financial Forecasting Example: Ziegen, Inc.

We can illustrate our discussion of financial forecasting using Ziegen, Inc., a firm that has been in business for only five years. Ziegen is engaged in the manufacture and marketing of specialty chemicals and its product line includes herbicides and pesticides used in agricultural applications. The company founder, Edward Ziegen, developed a line of organic products that do not require licensed applicators, and Ziegen, Inc. offers its products through farm supply stores and specialty chemical products companies.

Table 1 shows how the percent-of-sales method can be used to construct a pro forma income statement and a pro forma balance sheet for Ziegen, Inc. The company uses the three-step approach to financial planning just outlined. That is, managers make a forecast of the firm's revenues and associated expenses, then estimate the investment in current and fixed assets that is needed to support the projected level of sales, and finally, they estimate what the firm's financing needs will be throughout the planning period.

Step 1. **Forecast Revenues and Expenses.** We see in the pro forma income statement in Table 1 that Ziegen's sales were $10 million and the firm was able to earn net income equal to $500,000 in 2013, which is 5 percent of sales. Ziegen's financial analyst also estimates that the firm will earn 5 percent of the projected $12 million in sales forecast for 2014. Thus, we forecast that in 2014 net income will equal 5 percent of $12 million, or $600,000. Also, Ziegen plans to retain half of its 2014 earnings ($300,000) and reinvest it in the firm while paying out a like amount in dividends.

Step 2. **Prepare Pro Forma Financial Statements.** Ziegen's financial analyst plans to estimate the firm's needs for assets to support firm sales using the percent-of-sales method, where each item in the firm's balance sheet is assumed to vary in accordance with its percent of sales for 2013. Forecasting the firm's pro forma balance sheet for 2014 then involves multiplying the 2013 percentage of sales for current and fixed assets by the $12 million in projected sales for 2014. Thus, according to Table 1, if sales were to rise by $1, fixed assets would rise by $0.40, or 40 percent of the projected increase in sales. Note, however, that if the fixed assets the firm owned at the end of 2013 were sufficient to support the $12 million level of sales projected for 2014, then the fixed assets would not be converted to a percentage of sales because they would have remained unchanged for the period being forecast. If, on the other hand, Ziegen currently operates at full capacity, then an increase in fixed assets will be required to increase sales.

Step 3. **Estimate the Firm's Financing Requirements.** The firm's financing requirements are determined by comparing the projected level of assets needed to support the sales forecast (total assets in the pro forma balance sheet found in Table 1) to the available sources of financing. In essence, we now forecast the liabilities and owner's equity section of the pro forma balance sheet.

Sources of Spontaneous Financing: Accounts Payable and Accrued Expenses

We begin our analysis of the firm's financing sources (liabilities and owner's equity) with accounts payable and accrued expenses, which are the only liabilities that typically vary directly with sales. For this reason, accounts payable and accrued expenses are often referred to as

Table 1 Using the Percent-of-Sales Method to Forecast Ziegen, Inc.'s Financing Requirements for 2014

Preparation of Ziegen's financial forecast for 2014 begins with a forecast of firm sales for the year. This forecast is followed by a projection of assets required to support the projected level of sales. Offsetting the firm's need for discretionary financing is the financing that the firm receives from accounts payable and accrued expenses, which arise automatically (or spontaneously) as a result of the firm's having made a sale. Ziegen's financial analysts forecast $12 million in sales for 2014, which will require that the firm invest a total of $7.2 million in assets. The $1.2 million increase in assets will be financed partially by the $400,000 increase in the levels of accounts payable and accrued expenses (equal to $2.4 million − $2.0 million). In addition, the analysts expect the firm to generate another $300,000 from the firm's retention of one-half the firm's 2014 net income. The firm's discretionary financing need of $500,000 is calculated by subtracting the $400,000 in accounts payable and accrued expenses and the $300,000 increase in retained earnings from the total increase in financing needs of $1.2 million.

Ziegen, Inc. Income Statement for 2013		Calculation	% of 2013 Sales	Ziegen, Inc. Pro Forma Income Statement for 2014	Calculation	
				Sales growth rate =	20%	
Sales	$10,000,000			Sales	$10m × (1 + .20) =	$12,000,000
Net Income	$ 500,000	$.5m/$10m =	5.0%	Net Income	$12m × (.05) =	$ 600,000

Ziegen, Inc. Balance Sheet for 2013		Calculation	% of 2013 Sales	Ziegen, Inc. Pro Forma Balance Sheet for 2014	Calculation	
Current assets	$ 2,000,000	$2m/$10m =	20.0%	Current assets	.20 × 12m =	$ 2,400,000
Net fixed assets	4,000,000	$4m/$10m =	40.0%	Net fixed assets	.40 × 12m =	$ 4,800,000
Total	$ 6,000,000			Total		$ 7,200,000
Accounts payable	$ 1,000,000	$1m/$10m =	10.0%	Accounts payable	.10 × 12m =	$ 1,200,000
Accrued expenses	1,000,000	$1m/$10m =	10.0%	Accrued expenses	.10 × 12m =	1,200,000
Notes payable	500,000		NA[a]	Notes payable	No change	500,000
Current liabilities	$ 2,500,000			Current liabilities		$ 2,900,000
Long-term debt	2,000,000		NA[a]	Long-term debt	No change	$ 2,000,000
Total liabilities	$ 4,500,000			Total liabilities		$ 4,900,000
Common stock (par)	100,000		NA[a]	Common stock (par)	No change	100,000
Paid-in capital	200,000		NA[a]	Paid-in capital	No change	200,000
Retained earnings	1,200,000			Retained earnings	Calculation[b]	1,500,000
Common equity	$ 1,500,000			Common equity		1,800,000
Total	$ 6,000,000			Projected sources of financing		$ 6,700,000
				Discretionary financing needs (Plug figure)[c]		$ 500,000
				Total financing needs = Total assets		$ 7,200,000

[a] Not applicable. These account balances do not vary with sales.

[b] Projected retained earnings for 2014 equals $1,500,000, which is equal to the 2013 level of retained earnings of $1,200,000 plus net income of $600,000 less common dividends equal to 50% of projected net income, or $300,000.

[c] Discretionary financing needs (DFN) for 2014 is a "plug figure" that equals the difference in the firm's projected total financing requirements or total assets equal to $7,200,000 and projected sources of financing, which is $6,700,000. In this scenario DFN is $500,000.

sources of spontaneous financing. The percent-of-sales method can be used to forecast the levels of both these sources of financing. For example, in Table 1 both accounts payable and accrued expenses are 10 percent of sales and total $2.4 million for 2014.

Sources of Discretionary Financing

Raising financing with notes payable, long-term debt, and common stock requires a managerial decision or exercise of managerial discretion. For this reason these sources of financing are termed **discretionary sources of financing**. The retention of some or all of the firm's earnings is also a discretionary source of financing because the retention of earnings is the result of the firm's management having decided not to pay the earnings out in dividends to the firm's stockholders. We estimate that in 2014 Ziegen will retain an additional $300,000. To calculate this change in retained earnings, we first estimate that after-tax profits (projected net income) equal to 5 percent of sales, or $600,000, and then subtract common stock dividends of $300,000.

Summarizing Ziegen's Financial Forecast

We estimate that Ziegen's sales will increase from $10 million in 2013 to $12 million in 2014, which will cause the firm's need for total assets to increase to $7.2 million. These assets represent the firm's total financing needs for 2014 and will be financed by (1) $2.4 million in accounts payable plus accrued expenses (that is, spontaneous liabilities), $2.5 million in short-plus long-term debt, and (2) $1.8 million in common equity, including an additional $300,000 in retained earnings from 2014's net income, leaving (3) $500,000 in additional financing that the firm's management must raise with some combination of borrowing (short- or long-term debt) or the issuance of stock. Because these financing sources are not spontaneously generated by the firm's day-to-day operations, but require a managerial decision, they are commonly referred to as the firm's **discretionary financing needs (DFN)**.

The financial planning process combines estimates of the firm's total financing needs and sources of spontaneous financing to come up with financing requirements that must be met using discretionary sources of financing. We can summarize this calculation as follows:

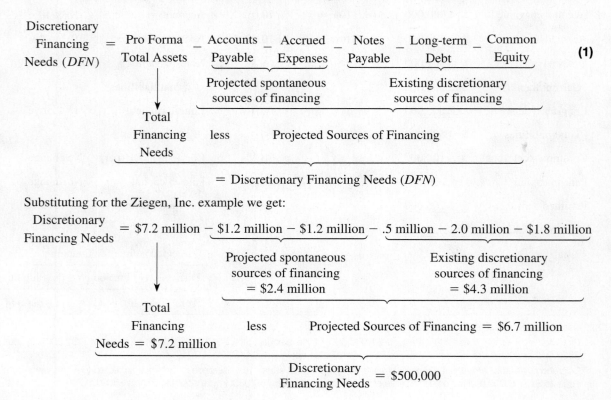

Therefore, Ziegen needs to raise an additional $500,000 in discretionary financing sources such that the firm's $7.2 million in total financing needs will be financed by $2.4 million in spontaneous sources (accounts payable and accrued expenses) and $4.8 million will be financed using discretionary sources. The latter consists of $4.3 million in discretionary sources used by the firm at the end of 2010 plus the $500,000 in added DFN for 2014.

Tools of Financial Analysis—Discretionary Financing Needed

Name of Tool	Formula	What It Tells You
Discretionary Financing Needed (DFN)	Pro Forma Total Assets − Projected Spontaneous Financing − Projected Discretionary Financing Definitions: • Projected Spontaneous Financing = Accounts Payable + Accured Expenses • Projected Discretionary Financing = Notes Payable + Long-term Debt + Common Equity	• The amount of additional financing the firm will need for the planning period • *Discretionary* implies choice or a managerial decision as to the source or sources of financing that the firm will use.

Analyzing the Effects of Profitability and Dividend Policy on the Firm's DFN

After projecting discretionary financing needs, we can quickly and easily evaluate the sensitivity of our projected financing requirements to changes in key variables. For example, using the information from the preceding example, we evaluate the effect of net profit margins (NPMs), which is net income/sales, equal to 1 percent, 5 percent, and 10 percent in combination with dividend payout ratios of 30 percent, 50 percent, and 70 percent, as follows:

Discretionary Financing Needs (DFN) for Various Net Profit Margins and Dividend Payout Ratios

Net Profit Margin	Dividend Payout Ratios = Dividends ÷ Net Income		
	30%	50%	70%
1%	$716,000	$740,000	$764,000
5%	380,000	500,000	620,000
10%	(40,000)	200,000	440,000

If these NPMs are reasonable estimates of the possible ranges of values the firm might experience, and if the firm is considering dividend payouts ranging from 30 percent to 70 percent, then we estimate that the firm's financing requirements will range from ($40,000) (the fact that DFN is negative indicates that the firm has a surplus of $40,000 in financing), to a situation in which it would need to acquire $764,000. Lower NPMs, in turn, mean higher funds requirements. Also, higher dividend payout percentages, other things remaining constant, lead to a need for more discretionary financing. This is a direct result of the fact that a high-dividend-paying firm retains less of its earnings.

Analyzing the Effects of Sales Growth on a Firm's DFN

In Table 1, we analyzed the DFN for Ziegen, Inc., whose sales were expected to grow from $10 million to $12 million during the coming year. Recall that the 20 percent expected increase in sales led to an increase of $500,000 in the firm's need for financing. We referred to this added financing requirement as the firm's DFN because all these funds must be raised from discretionary sources, such as bank borrowing or a new equity issue. These actions require management to exercise its discretion in selecting the source or sources of financing it will use. In this section, we will investigate how a firm's DFN varies with different rates of anticipated growth in sales.

Table 2 contains an expansion of the financial forecast found in Table 1. Specifically, we use the same assumptions and prediction methods that underlie Table 1, but apply them to sales growth rates of 0 percent and 20 percent. We calculate the DFN for these sales growth rates

Table 2   Discretionary Financing Needs (DFN) and the Growth Rate in Sales

Ziegen, Inc. forecasts its financing requirements for 2014 using two different rates of growth in sales: 0 percent and 20 percent. The firm's discretionary financing needs vary dramatically with each of these growth rates, indicating the sensitivity of a firm's financing requirements to the firm's rate of growth in revenues.

Ziegen, Inc. Income Statement for 2013			% of 2013 Sales	Ziegen, Inc. Pro Forma Income Statement for 2014				
				Growth Rates in Sales			0%	20%
Sales	$10,000,000			Sales			$10,000,000	$12,000,000
Net Income	$ 500,000		5.0%	Net Income			$ 500,000	$ 600,000

Ziegen, Inc. Balance Sheet for 2013		Calculation	% of 2013 Sales	Ziegen, Inc. Pro Forma Balance Sheet for 2014	Calculation		0%	20%
Current assets	$ 2,000,000	$2m/$10m =	20.0%	Current assets	.20 × Sales =		$ 2,000,000	$ 2,400,000
Net fixed assets	4,000,000	$4m/$10m =	40.0%	Net fixed assets	.40 × Sales =		$ 4,000,000	$ 4,800,000
Total	$ 6,000,000			Total			$ 6,000,000	$ 7,200,000
Accounts payable	$ 1,000,000	$1m/$10m =	10.0%	Accounts payable	.10 × Sales =		$ 1,000,000	$ 1,200,000
Accrued expenses	1,000,000	$1m/$10m =	10.0%	Accrued expenses	.10 × Sales =		1,000,000	1,200,000
Notes payable	500,000		NAª	Notes payable	No change		500,000	500,000
Current liabilities	$ 2,500,000			Current liabilities			$ 2,500,000	$ 2,900,000
Long-term debt	2,000,000		NAª	Long-term debt	No change		$ 2,000,000	2,000,000
Total liabilities	$ 4,500,000			Total liabilities			$ 4,500,000	$ 4,900,000
Common stock (par)	100,000		NAª	Common stock (par)	No change		$ 100,000	$ 100,000
Paid-in capital	200,000		NAª	Paid-in capital	No change		200,000	200,000
Retained earnings	1,200,000			Retained earnings	Calculation		1,450,000	1,500,000
Common equity	$ 1,500,000			Common equity			$ 1,750,000	$ 1,800,000
Total	$ 6,000,000			Projected sources of financing			$ 6,250,000	$ 6,700,000
				Discretionary financing needs (Plug figure)			$ (250,000)	$ 500,000
				Total financing needs = Total assets			$ 6,000,000	$ 7,200,000

ªNot applicable. These account balances do not vary with sales.

using Equation (1), by which DFN ranges from ($250,000) to $500,000. Note that when DFN is negative (as it is for the 0 percent growth rate case), the firm has more money than it needs to finance the assets used to generate the projected sales. Alternatively, when DFN is positive, the firm must raise additional funds in this amount, by either borrowing or issuing stock.

Figure 1 contains a graphic representation of the relationship between the growth rate in firm sales and DFN found in Table 2. The straight line in the graph depicts the level of DFN for each of the different rates of growth in firm sales. For example, if sales grow by 20 percent, then the firm projects a DFN of $500,000, which must be raised externally by borrowing or with a new equity offering. An important point on the graph is the growth rate in firm sales where DFN equals zero. In the Ziegen example, this occurs where the rate of growth in firm sales equals 6.667 percent. Ziegen's sales can grow at a rate of 6.667 percent in 2014 without the need to seek out additional sources of discretionary financing.

Figure 1

Sales Growth and the Discretionary Financing Needs of the Firm

The more rapidly the firm's revenues (and corresponding needs for assets) are expected to grow, the greater will be its needs for sources of financing above and beyond the profits it retains from its operations. In this example, the firm will have sufficient sources of funds from the retention of 50 percent of its earnings to finance growth rates in sales up to 6.667 percent. However, once the rate of growth in sales exceeds this threshold, the firm will find itself needing to seek out other sources of financing.

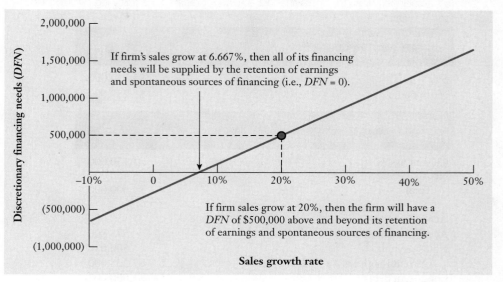

If firm's sales grow at 6.667%, then all of its financing needs will be supplied by the retention of earnings and spontaneous sources of financing (i.e., $DFN = 0$).

If firm sales grow at 20%, then the firm will have a DFN of $500,000 above and beyond its retention of earnings and spontaneous sources of financing.

>> END FIGURE 1

The Business of Life

Your Personal Budget

To many people, the term *budget* brings to mind the idea of *a financial strait jacket*, something that takes all the spontaneity out of life. In reality, a budget is simply a tool that can be used to help you reach your personal goals.

A budget (or cash flow plan) helps you to use restraint, to think about what you spend your money on, to live below your means, and (yes) to be frugal. For example, if you've already spent this month's budgeted amount on eating out at restaurants, the budget indicates that you will be eating at home the rest of the month or you'll have to free up money from another area of your budget. Perhaps you will have to postpone the purchase of the new Kings of Leon CD for one more meal at the City Diner. Unfortunately, self-restraint is tough—especially when you are being bombarded by TV, the Internet, radio, newspapers, and magazine advertisers, all with their sights on your money.

Step 1 involved in developing a personal budget is to document how you are spending your money. To do that, you will want to carefully track your expenses for a month. If you need help, you'll find a number of budgeting worksheets you can download for free on the Internet. An immediate benefit of preparing a budget is that the very act of documenting how you are spending your money will help you identify expenses you can eliminate.

Step 2 in the personal planning process entails the construction of a personal income statement and a balance sheet. These statements provide the basis for evaluating your financial health. Your personal balance sheet, like that of any business, sums up everything you own or owe and allows you to identify your net worth. Your personal income statement shows you where your money comes from, where it goes, and gives you a picture of your spending habits. Once you understand how much you have coming in and how you tend to spend your money, you can figure out how much you can realistically afford to save.

In *Step 3* you will prepare a personal cash budget that becomes the key tool for helping you control your cash inflows and outflows. The cash budget will include projections of your future income and when it will be received, as well as your planned expenditures. Once prepared, the cash budget becomes a tool for controlling your spending habits. By comparing actual expenditures with planned or budgeted expenditures you can gauge how much money you will have left over and what can be saved for future use. Instead of the negative idea of a financial straight jacket, most people find that having a personal cash budget gives them a feeling of control and security.

Your Turn: See Study Question 9.

Checkpoint 1

Estimating Discretionary Financing Needs

The Pendleton Chemical Company manufactures a line of personal-health-care products used in preventing the spread of infectious diseases. The company's principal product is a germ-killing hand sanitizer called "Bacteria-X." In 2013, Pendleton had $5 million in sales, and anticipates an increase of 15 percent in 2014. After performing an analysis of the firm's balance sheet, the firm's financial manager prepared the following pro forma income statement and balance sheet for next year:

Pendleton Chemical Company Pro Forma Income Statement for 2014	15%
Sales	$5,750,000
Net Income	$ 287,500

Pendleton Chemical Company Pro Forma Balance Sheet for 2014	
Current assets	$1,150,000
Net fixed assets	3,450,000
Total	$4,600,000
Accounts payable	1,150,000
Accrued expenses	575,000
Notes payable	500,000
Current liabilities	$2,225,000
Long-term debt	1,000,000
Total liabilities	$3,225,000
Common stock (par)	$ 100,000
Paid-in capital	200,000
Retained earnings	987,500
Common equity	$1,287,500
Projected sources of financing	
Discretionary financing needs (DFN)	
Total financing needs = Total assets	$4,600,000

Based on these estimates, what is the firm's need for discretionary financing for 2014?

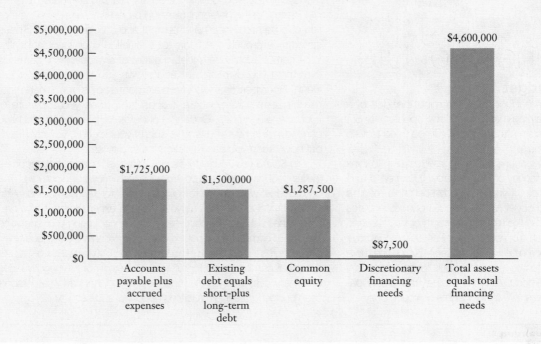

STEP 1: Picture the problem

The firm's discretionary financing needs (DFN) are equal to the financing the firm requires for the year that is not provided by spontaneous sources such as accounts payable and accrued expenses plus retained earnings for the period. In essence we estimate DFN as the "plug figure" that balances the financing side of the firm's pro forma balance sheet.

STEP 2: Decide on a solution strategy

We can calculate DFN using Equation (1) as follows:

$$\begin{matrix} \text{Discretionary} \\ \text{Financing Needs} \end{matrix} = \begin{matrix} \text{Pro Forma} \\ \text{Total Assets} \end{matrix} - \begin{matrix} \text{Accounts} \\ \text{Payable} \end{matrix} - \begin{matrix} \text{Accrued} \\ \text{Expenses} \end{matrix} - \begin{matrix} \text{Notes} \\ \text{Payable} \end{matrix} - \begin{matrix} \text{Long-term} \\ \text{Debt} \end{matrix} - \begin{matrix} \text{Common} \\ \text{Equity} \end{matrix} \qquad (1)$$

Or by simply filling in the blanks in the pro forma balance sheet found above.

STEP 3: Solve

Substituting for the 2011 values estimated for Pendleton into Equation (1), we estimate Pendleton's DFN as follows:

$$\begin{matrix} \text{Discretionary} \\ \text{Financing Needs} \end{matrix} = \$4{,}600{,}000 - 1{,}150{,}000 - 575{,}000 - 500{,}000 - 1{,}000{,}000 - 1{,}287{,}500 = \$87{,}500$$

Or, completing the pro forma balance sheet for Projected Sources of Financing and DFN:

Pendleton Chemical Company
Pro Forma Balance Sheet for 2014

Current assets	$1,150,000
Net fixed assets	3,450,000
Total	$4,600,000
Accounts payable	1,150,000
Accrued expenses	575,000
Notes payable	500,000
Current liabilities	$2,225,000
Long-term debt	1,000,000
Total liabilities	$3,225,000
Common stock (par)	$ 100,000
Paid-in capital	200,000
Retained earnings	987,500
Common equity	$1,287,500
Projected sources of financing	$4,512,500
Discretionary financing needs (DFN)	$ 87,500
Total financing needs = Total assets	$4,600,000

Projected Sources of Financing is the sum of Total Liabilities ($3.225 million) plus Common Equity ($1.2875 million), which equals $4.5125 million. Note that common equity *includes* the $287,500 in net income the firm expects to retain in 2013.

Discretionary Financing Needs (DFN) is equal to Total Financing Needed or pro forma total assets less projected sources of financing. In this case, $4,600,000 − 4,512,500 = $87,500.

STEP 4: Analyze

Pendleton can expect to have to raise $87,500 during the coming year should firm sales grow by 15 percent as anticipated. In actual practice Pendleton's financial manager would consider several scenarios involving different sales growth rates to get some idea as to the possible levels of DFN the firm could face.

STEP 5: Check yourself

Pendleton's management estimates that under the most optimistic circumstances it might experience a 25 percent rate of growth in sales in 2014. Assuming that net income is 5 percent of firm sales, the firm retains 100 percent of its net income, accounts payable and accrued expenses are the same percent of sales as in the 15 percent sales growth forecast, and that both current and fixed assets are equal to a fixed percent of sales (as found in the previous forecast), what do you estimate the firm's DFN to be under these optimistic circumstances?

ANSWER: DFN (40% growth rate in sales) = $650,000. (Remember that short- and long-term debt are assumed to be fixed and that common equity increases by the total amount of net income for the period because no dividends are paid).

Your Turn: For more practice, do related **Study Problems** 7 through 10 at the end of this chapter.   **>> END Checkpoint 1**

Concept Check | 2

1. Why are sales forecasts so important to developing a firm's financial forecast?
2. What is the percent-of-sales method of financial forecasting?
3. Give some examples of spontaneous and discretionary sources of financing.

Developing a Short-Term Financial Plan

There are two basic differences between the short- and long-term operating financial plans. The first is the planning horizon. The short-term plan extends out to one year, whereas the long-term plan goes out three to five years. The second difference relates to the format used to compile and present the two plans. The short-term financial plan is typically presented in the form of a cash budget that contains a great deal of detail concerning the firm's cash receipts and disbursements. The long-term operating financial plan is typically prepared using pro forma income statements and balance sheets, as we have just demonstrated.

Example Cash Budget: Melco Furniture, Inc.

The cash budget represents a detailed plan of future cash flows and is composed of four elements: cash receipts, cash disbursements, net change in cash for the period, and new financing needed. To demonstrate the construction and use of the cash budget, we will use the example of Melco Furniture Company, Inc., a regional distributor of household furniture. Management is in the process of preparing a monthly cash budget for the upcoming six months (January through June 2014). Melco's sales are highly seasonal, peaking in the months of March through May. Roughly 30 percent of Melco's sales are collected one month after the sale, 50 percent two months after the sale, and the remainder during the third month following the sale. Melco attempts to pace its purchases with its forecast of future sales.

Purchases generally equal 75 percent of sales and are made two months in advance of anticipated sales, with payments made in the month following purchases. For example, June sales are estimated at $100,000; thus, April purchases are .75 × $100,000 = $75,000. Correspondingly, payments for purchases equal $75,000 in May. Wages, salaries, rent, and other cash expenses are recorded in Table 3, which provides Melco's cash budget for the six-month period ended in June 2011. Additional expenditures recorded in the cash budget include the purchase of equipment in the amount of $14,000 during February and the repayment of a $12,000 loan in May. In June, Melco will pay $7,500 interest on its $150,000 in long-term debt for the period of January to June 2014. Interest on the $12,000 short-term note (repaid in May for the period January through May) equals $600 and is paid in May.

Melco currently has a cash balance of $20,000 and wants to maintain a minimum balance of $10,000. Additional borrowing necessary to maintain that minimum balance is estimated in the final section of Table 3. Borrowing takes place at the beginning of the month in which the funds are needed. Interest on borrowed funds equals 12 percent per annum, or 1 percent per month, and is paid in the month following the one in which funds are borrowed. Thus, the $364 in interest owed on the $36,350 borrowed in February (1 percent of the outstanding loan balance) will be paid in March.

The financing-needed line in Melco's cash budget determines that the firm's cumulative short-term borrowing will be $36,350 in February, $65,874 in March, $86,633 in April, and $97,599 in May. In June the firm will be able to reduce its borrowing to $79,875. Note that the cash budget indicates not only the amount of financing needed during the period but also when the funds will be needed.

Uses of the Cash Budget

The cash budget serves two very important roles in financial forecasting and planning. The first is as a tool for predicting the amount and timing of the firm's future financing requirements. In the Melco example we learned that Melco required additional financing during February through May

Table 3   Melco Furniture, Inc. Cash Budget for the Six Months Ended June 30, 2014

The cash budget for Melco Furniture, Inc. consists of four components or sections: (1) cash receipts, including cash received from sales made during the month of the budget as well as from sales made in previous months; (2) cash disbursements made during the month for various categories of expenses, such as labor (wages and salaries), rent, and interest and principal on the firm's debt; (3) the calculated change in cash for the month, which is simply cash receipts less cash disbursements; and finally (4) the computation of new financing needed to maintain the firm's desired cash balance.

	October	November	December	January	February	March	April	May	June	July	August
Worksheet											
Sales (forecasted)	55,000	62,000	50,000	60,000	75,000	88,000	100,000	110,000	100,000	80,000	75,000
Purchases (75% of sales in 2 months)			56,250	66,000	75,000	82,500	75,000	60,000	56,250		
Cash receipts											
Collections:											
First month after sale (30%)				15,000	18,000	22,500	26,400	30,000	33,000		
Second month after sale (50%)				31,000	25,000	30,000	37,500	44,000	50,000		
Third month after sale (20%)				11,000	12,400	10,000	12,000	15,000	17,600		
Total cash receipts				57,000	55,400	62,500	75,900	89,000	100,600		
Cash disbursements											
Payments (one-month lag of purchases made the previous month)				56,250	66,000	75,000	82,500	75,000	60,000		
Wages and salaries				3,000	10,000	7,000	8,000	6,000	4,000		
Rent				4,000	4,000	4,000	4,000	4,000	4,000		
Other expenses				1,000	500	1,200	1,500	1,500	1,200		
Interest expense on existing debt[a]								600	7,500		
Taxes						4,460			5,200		
Purchase and equipment					14,000						
Loan repayment[b]								12,000			
Total cash disbursements				64,250	94,500	91,660	96,000	99,100	81,900		
Net change in cash for the period				(7,250)	(39,100)	(29,160)	(20,100)	(10,100)	18,700		
Plus: Beginning cash balance				20,000	12,750	10,000	10,000	10,000	10,000		
Less: Interest on short-term borrowing				0	0	(364)	(659)	(866)	(976)		
Equals: Ending cash balance before short-term borrowing				12,750	(26,350)	(19,524)	(10,759)	(966)	27,724		
New financing needed[c]				0	36,350	29,524	20,759	10,966	(17,724)[d]		
Ending cash balance				12,750	10,000	10,000	10,000	10,000	10,000		
Cumulative borrowing				0	36,350	65,874	86,633	97,599	79,875		

[a]An interest payment of $600 on the $12,000 loan is due in May, and an interest payment of $7,500 on the $150,000 long-term debt is due in June.

[b]The principal amount of the $12,000 loan is also due in May.

[c]The amount of financing that is required to raise the firm's ending cash balance up to its $10,000 desired cash balance.

[d]Negative financing needed simply means the firm has excess cash that can be used to retire a part of its short-term borrowing from prior months.

but had surplus cash in June. Second, the cash budget serves as a tool to monitor and control the firm's operations. The actual cash receipts and disbursements can be compared to budgeted estimates, bringing to light any significant differences. In some cases these differences may simply reflect the fact that the future is uncertain and budgeted figures are estimates. In other cases, differences in what is budgeted and what actually occurs may signal a problem with the firm's collections from its credit customers, or a problem with cost overruns. Thus, the cash budget provides a useful benchmark for analyzing the firm's operations over time.

> **Before you begin end-of-chapter material**

Concept Check | 3

1. What are the basic elements of a cash budget?

2. How is a cash budget used in financial planning?

Applying the Principles of Finance to This Chapter

 Principle 2: **There Is a Risk–Return Tradeoff** arises in the financial planning process because planning provides a process whereby the firm is able to prepare for alternate possible levels of firm sales and correspondingly different financing requirements. By being prepared the firm reduces the risk to its shareholders and increases the value of its common stock.

Chapter Summaries

1 Understand the goals of financial planning.

SUMMARY: The goal of financial planning is the development of a plan that the firm can use as a guide to the future. Such a plan provides the firm with estimates of the firm's financing requirements. However, financial planning offers a second and more subtle goal. The very fact that the firm's management team goes through a careful and thoughtful planning exercise is useful in itself. That is, the very act of thinking systematically about the future helps prepare the firm's management to develop an understanding of what may happen, and this is in itself a valuable exercise.

KEY TERMS

Cash budget A plan for a future period that details the sources of cash a firm anticipates receiving and the amounts and timing of cash it plans to spend.

Long-term financial plan A detailed estimate of a firm's sources and uses of financing for a period that extends three to five years into the future.

Short-term financial plan A forecast of a firm's sources of cash and planned uses of cash spanning the next 12 months.

Strategic plan A general description of the firm, its products and services, and how it plans to compete with other firms in order to sell those products and services.

Concept Check | **1**

1. What are the fundamental benefits of financial planning?
2. Distinguish between a firm's short-term financial plan, long-term financial plan, and strategic plan.

2 Use the percent-of-sales method to forecast the financing requirements of a firm, including its discretionary financing needs.

SUMMARY: The most common technique for forecasting a firm's pro forma financial statements, including both an income statement and balance sheet, is the percent-of-sales method. The percent-of-sales method expresses expenses, assets, and liabilities for a future period as percentages of sales. The percentage used to make the forecast can come from the most recent financial statements, from an average computed over several years, from the judgment of the analyst, or from some combination of these methods.

The primary objective of forecasting a firm's financing needs is to identify the amount of new financing that the firm will need to seek from discretionary sources. By discretionary sources, we mean those sources of financing that require the firm's management to make a conscious decision to use them. These sources contrast with spontaneous sources of financing (such as accounts payable) that arise naturally in the course of doing business. For example, when the firm orders more products to replenish its inventories, the firm's suppliers automatically extend credit to the firm in the form of accounts payable.

KEY TERMS

Discretionary financing needs (DFN) The total amount of financing a firm estimates that it will need for a future period that will not be funded through the retention of earnings or by increases in the firm's accounts payable and accrued expenses.

Discretionary sources of financing Sources of financing that require explicit action by the firm's management. For example, the decision to borrow money from a bank is an example of

discretionary financing, whereas the automatic financing of inventory purchases from an existing supplier that increases a firm's accounts payable is not a discretionary source of financing.

Percent-of-sales method A financial forecasting technique that uses the proportion of the item being forecast (e.g., accounts receivable) to the level of firm sales as the basis for predicting the future level of the item.

Pro forma balance sheet A forecast of each of the elements of a firm's balance sheet.

Pro forma income statement A forecast of each of the elements of a firm's income statement.

Sources of spontaneous financing Sources of financing that arise automatically out of changes in the firm's sales. For example, as firm sales rise the firm may order new items of inventory that are automatically financed with accounts payable based on the terms and conditions negotiated earlier with the firm's suppliers.

KEY EQUATION

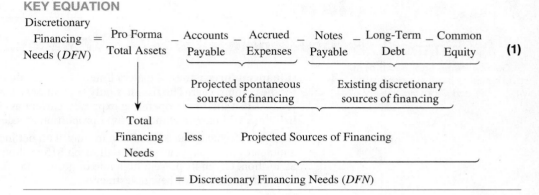

$$
\begin{array}{l}
\text{Discretionary} \\
\text{Financing} \\
\text{Needs } (DFN)
\end{array}
=
\begin{array}{c}
\text{Pro Forma} \\
\text{Total Assets}
\end{array}
-
\underbrace{
\begin{array}{c}
\text{Accounts} \\
\text{Payable}
\end{array}
-
\begin{array}{c}
\text{Accrued} \\
\text{Expenses}
\end{array}
}_{
\begin{array}{c}
\text{Projected spontaneous} \\
\text{sources of financing}
\end{array}
}
-
\underbrace{
\begin{array}{c}
\text{Notes} \\
\text{Payable}
\end{array}
-
\begin{array}{c}
\text{Long-Term} \\
\text{Debt}
\end{array}
-
\begin{array}{c}
\text{Common} \\
\text{Equity}
\end{array}
}_{
\begin{array}{c}
\text{Existing discretionary} \\
\text{sources of financing}
\end{array}
}
\quad (1)
$$

$$
\underbrace{\begin{array}{c}\text{Total} \\ \text{Financing} \\ \text{Needs}\end{array} \quad less \quad \text{Projected Sources of Financing}}
$$

$$= \text{Discretionary Financing Needs } (DFN)$$

Prepare a cash budget and use it to evaluate the amount and timing of a firm's short-term financing requirements.

SUMMARY: The cash budget is the primary tool of financial forecasting and planning. It contains a detailed plan of future cash flow estimates and is comprised of four elements or segments: cash receipts, cash disbursements, net change in cash for the period, and new financing needed. Once prepared, the cash budget also serves as a tool for monitoring and controlling the firm's operations. By comparing actual cash receipts and disbursements to those in the cash budget, the financial manager can gain an understanding of how well the firm is performing. In addition, deviations from the plan serve as an early warning system to signal the onset of financial difficulties ahead.

Study Questions

1. **(Related to Regardless of Your Major: Developing a Financial Plan for the Firm Engages Everyone** In the *Regardless of Your Major* feature, we learned that financial planning engages everyone throughout the organization. How do marketing and accounting specialists contribute to the financial planning process?

2. What is the primary objective of the financial planning process?

3. Forecasting a firm's future sales is the key element in developing a financial plan, yet forecasting can be extremely difficult in some industries. If forecast accuracy is very poor, does this mean that the financial planning process is not worthwhile? Explain your answer.

4. Describe the percent-of-sales method of financial forecasting.

5. Distinguish between the three components of a firm's overall planning process: the short-term operating financial plan, the long-term operating financial plan, and the strategic plan.

6. Compare and contrast discretionary and spontaneous sources of short-term financing.

7. What would be the probable effect of each of the following on a firm's cash position?
   a. A new advertising campaign that results in more rapidly rising sales.
   b. A delay in the payment of the firm's accounts payable.
   c. Offering a more liberal credit policy (to the firm's customers).
   d. Holding larger inventories in an attempt to reduce the probability of being out of stock.

8. A cash budget is usually thought of as a means of planning for future financing needs. Why would a cash budget also be important for a firm that has excess cash on hand?

9. **(Related to The Business of Life: Your Personal Budget** In *The Business of Life* feature box we learned about a three-step process for using budgets to manage our personal finances. Spend a few minutes to think about the three steps of the process and make a first pass at preparing your own budget.

Study Problems

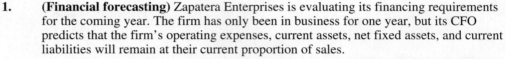

MyFinanceLab

Go to **www.myfinancelab.com** to complete these exercises online and get instant feedback.

Developing a Long-Term Financial Plan

1. **(Financial forecasting)** Zapatera Enterprises is evaluating its financing requirements for the coming year. The firm has only been in business for one year, but its CFO predicts that the firm's operating expenses, current assets, net fixed assets, and current liabilities will remain at their current proportion of sales.

Last year Zapatera had $12 million in sales with net income of $1.2 million. The firm anticipates that next year's sales will reach $15 million with net income rising to $2 million. Given its present high rate of growth, the firm retains all of its earnings to help defray the cost of new investments.

The firm's balance sheet for the year just ended is as follows:

Zapatera Enterprises, Inc.

Balance Sheet	12/31/13	% of Sales
Current assets	$3,000,000	25%
Net fixed assets	6,000,000	50%
Total	$9,000,000	
Liabilities and Owners' Equity		
Accounts payable	$3,000,000	25%
Long-term debt	2,000,000	NA[a]
Total liabilities	$5,000,000	
Common stock	1,000,000	NA[a]
Paid-in capital	1,800,000	NA[a]
Retained earnings	1,200,000	
Common equity	4,000,000	
Total	$9,000,000	

[a]NA. This figure does not vary directly with sales and is assumed to remain constant for purposes of forecasting next year's financing requirements.

Estimate Zapatera's total financing requirements (total assets) and its net funding requirements (discretionary financing needed) for 2014.

2. **(Financial forecasting)** Sambonoza Enterprises projects its sales next year to be $4 million and expects to earn 5 percent of that amount after taxes. The firm is currently in the process of projecting its financing needs and has made the following assumptions (projections):

1. Current assets are equal to 20 percent of sales, and fixed assets remain at their current level of $1 million.

2. Common equity is currently $0.8 million, and the firm pays out half of its after-tax earnings in dividends.

3. The firm has short-term payables and trade credit that normally equal 10 percent of sales, and it has no long-term debt outstanding.

What are Sambonoza's financing needs for the coming year?

3. **(Financial forecasting—percent of sales)** Tulley Appliances, Inc. projects next year's sales to be $20 million. Current sales are at $15 million, based on current assets of $5 million and fixed assets of $5 million. The firm's net profit margin is 5 percent after taxes. Tulley forecasts that current assets will rise in direct proportion to the increase in sales, but fixed assets will increase by only $100,000. Currently, Tulley has $1.5 million in accounts payable (which vary directly with sales), $2 million in long-term debt (due in 10 years), and common equity (including $4 million in retained earnings) totaling $6.5 million. Tulley plans to pay $500,000 in common stock dividends next year.

a. What are Tulley's total financing needs (that is, total assets) for the coming year?
b. Given the firm's projections and dividend payment plans, what are its discretionary financing needs?
c. Based on your projections, and assuming that the $100,000 expansion in fixed assets will occur, what is the largest increase in sales the firm can support without having to resort to the use of discretionary sources of financing?

4. **(Pro forma balance sheet construction)** Use the following industry average ratios to construct a pro forma balance sheet for Carlos Menza, Inc.

Total asset turnover	2 times
Average collection period (assume a 365-day year)	9 days
Fixed asset turnover	5 times
Inventory turnover (based on cost of goods sold)	3 times
Current ratio	2 times
Sales (all on credit)	$4.0 million
Cost of goods sold	75% of sales
Debt ratio	50%

Cash	_____	Current liabilities	_____
Inventory	_____	Long-term debt	_____
Accounts receivable	_____	Common stock plus	_____
Net fixed assets	_____	Retained earnings	_____
Total $	_____	**Total $**	_____

5. **(Financial forecasting)** Which of the following accounts would most likely vary directly with the level of firm sales? Discuss each briefly.

	Yes	No
Cash	_____	_____
Notes payable	_____	_____
Marketable securities	_____	_____
Plant and equipment	_____	_____
Accounts payable	_____	_____
Inventories	_____	_____

6. **(Financial forecasting)** The balance sheet of the Thompson Trucking Company (TTC) follows:

Thompson Trucking Company Balance Sheet, December 31, 2013 ($ millions)

Current assets	$10	Accounts payable	$ 5
Net fixed assets	15	Notes payable	0
Total	$25	Bonds payable	10
		Common equity	10
		Total	$25

TTC had sales for the year ended 12/31/13 of $50 million. The firm follows a policy of paying all net earnings out to its common stockholders in cash dividends. Thus, TTC generates no funds from its earnings that can be used to expand its operations. (Assume that depreciation expense is just equal to the cost of replacing worn-out assets.)

a. If TTC anticipates sales of $80 million during the coming year, develop a pro forma balance sheet for the firm for 12/31/14. Assume that current assets vary as a percent of sales, net fixed assets remain unchanged, and accounts payable vary as a percent of sales. Use notes payable as a balancing entry.

b. How much "new" financing will TTC need next year?

c. What limitations does the percent-of-sales forecast method suffer from? Discuss briefly.

7. **(Related to Checkpoint 1) (Discretionary financing needs and growth)** The most recent balance sheet for the Armadillo Dog Biscuit Co. is shown in the following table. The company is about to embark on an advertising campaign that is expected to raise sales from the current level of $5 million to $7 million by the end of next year. The firm is currently operating at full capacity and will have to increase its investment in both current and fixed assets to support the projected level of new sales. In fact, the firm estimates that both categories of assets will rise in direct proportion to the projected increase in sales.

Armadillo Dog Biscuit Co., Inc. ($ millions)

	Present Level	Percent of Sales	Projected Level
Current assets	$2.0		
Net fixed assets	3.0		
Total	$5.0		
Accounts payable	$0.5		
Accrued expenses	0.5		
Notes payable			
Current liabilities	$1.0		
Long-term debt	$2.0		
Common stock	0.5		
Retained earnings	1.5		
Common equity	$2.0		
Total	$5.0		

The firm's net profits were 6 percent of current year's sales but are expected to rise to 7 percent of next year's sales. To help support its anticipated growth in asset needs next year, the firm has suspended plans to pay cash dividends to its stockholders. In past years, a $1.50 per share dividend was paid annually.

Armadillo's payables and accrued expenses are expected to vary directly with sales. In addition, notes payable will be used to supply the funds that are needed to finance next year's operations that are not forthcoming from other sources.

a. Fill in the table and project the firm's needs for discretionary financing. Use notes payable as the balancing entry for future discretionary financing needs.

b. Compare Armadillo's current ratio and debt ratio (total liabilities/total assets) before the growth in sales and after. What was the effect of the expanded sales on these two dimensions of Armadillo's financial condition?

c. What difference, if any, would have resulted if Armadillo's sales had risen to $6 million in one year and $7 million only after two years? Discuss only; no calculations are required.

8. **(Related to Checkpoint 1) (Discretionary financing needs)** Fishing Charter, Inc. estimates that it invests 30 cents in assets for each dollar of new sales. However, 5 cents in profits are produced by each dollar of additional sales, of which 1 cent can be reinvested in the firm. If sales rise by $500,000 next year from their current level of $5 million, and the ratio of spontaneous liabilities to sales is .15, what will be the firm's need for discretionary financing? (Hint: In this situation you do not know what the firm's existing level of assets is, nor do you know how those assets have been financed. Thus, you must estimate the change in financing needs and match this change with the expected changes in spontaneous liabilities, retained earnings, and other sources of discretionary financing.)

9. **(Related to Checkpoint 1) (Discretionary financing needs)** Harrison Electronics, Inc. operates a chain of electrical lighting and fixture distribution centers throughout northern Arizona. The firm is anticipating expansion of its sales in the coming year as a result of recent population growth trends. The firm's financial analyst has prepared pro forma balance sheets that reflect three different rates of growth in firm sales for the coming year and the corresponding non-discretionary sources of financing the firm expects to have available, as follows:

Harrison Electronics, Inc.

Pro Forma Balance Sheet for 2014		Alternative Growth Rates		
	Calculation	10%	20%	40%
Current assets		$13,200,000	$14,400,000	$16,800,000
Net fixed assets		$19,800,000	$21,600,000	$25,200,000
Total		$33,000,000	$36,000,000	$42,000,000
Accounts payable		$ 2,200,000	$ 2,400,000	$ 2,800,000
Accrued expenses		2,200,000	2,400,000	2,800,000
Notes payable	No change	1,500,000	1,500,000	1,500,000
Current liabilities		$ 5,900,000	$ 6,300,000	$ 7,100,000
Long-term debt	No change	6,500,000	6,500,000	6,500,000
Total liabilities		$12,400,000	$12,800,000	$13,600,000
Common stock (par)	No change	$ 1,000,000	1,000,000	$ 1,000,000
Paid-in capital	No change	2,000,000	2,000,000	2,000,000
Retained earnings		15,550,000	15,600,000	15,700,000
Common equity		$18,550,000	$18,600,000	$18,700,000
Projected sources of financing		$30,950,000	$31,400,000	$32,300,000
Discretionary financing needs				
Total financing needs = Total assets				

a. What are the firm's discretionary financing needs under each of the three growth scenarios?

b. What potential sources of financing are there for Harrison to fulfill its needs for discretionary financing?

10. **(Related to Checkpoint 1) (Discretionary financing needs)** In the spring of 2013 the Caswell Publishing Company established a custom publishing business for its business clients. These clients consisted principally of small- to medium-size companies in Round Rock, Texas. However, the company's plans were disrupted when it landed a large printing contract from Dell Computers Corp. (DELL) that it expected would run for several years. Specifically, the new contract would increase firm revenues by 100 percent. Consequently, Caswell's management knew they would need to make some significant changes in firm capacity, and quickly. The following balance sheet for 2013 and pro forma balance sheet for 2014 reflect the firm's estimates of the financial impact of the 100 percent revenue growth:

Caswell Publishing, Inc. Balance Sheet for 2013		Caswell Publishing, Inc. Pro Forma Balance Sheet for 2014	100%
Current assets	$12,000,000	Current assets	$24,000,000
Net fixed assets	18,000,000	Net fixed assets	$36,000,000
Total	$30,000,000	Total	$60,000,000
Accounts payable	$ 2,000,000	Accounts payable	$ 4,000,000
Accrued expenses	2,000,000	Accrued expenses	$ 4,000,000
Notes payable	1,500,000	Notes payable	1,500,000
Current liabilities	$ 5,500,000	Current liabilities	$ 9,500,000
Long-term debt	6,500,000	Long-term debt	6,500,000
Total liabilities	$12,000,000	Total liabilities	$16,000,000
Common stock (par)	1,000,000	Common stock (par)	$ 1,000,000
Paid-in capital	2,000,000	Paid-in capital	2,000,000
Retained earnings	15,000,000	Retained earnings	15,000,000
Common equity	$18,000,000	Common equity	$18,000,000
Total	$30,000,000	Projected sources of financing	$34,000,000
		Discretionary financing needs	
		Total financing needs = Total assets	

a. How much new discretionary financing will Caswell require based on the above estimates?

b. Given the nature of the new contract and the specific needs for financing that the firm expects, what recommendations might you offer to the firm's CFO as to specific sources of financing the firm should seek to fulfill its DFN?

Developing a Short-Term Financial Plan

11. (**Preparation of a cash budget**) The Sharpe Corporation's projected sales for the first eight months of 2014 are as follows:

January	$ 90,000	May	$300,000
February	120,000	June	270,000
March	135,000	July	225,000
April	240,000	August	150,000

Of Sharpe's sales, 10 percent is for cash, another 60 percent is collected in the month following the sale, and 30 percent is collected in the second month following the sale. November and December sales for 2013 were $220,000 and $175,000, respectively.

Sharpe purchases its raw materials two months in advance of its sales equal to 60 percent of their final sales price. The supplier is paid one month after it makes delivery. For example, purchases for April sales are made in February and payment is made in March.

In addition, Sharpe pays $10,000 per month for rent and $20,000 each month for other expenditures. Tax prepayments of $22,500 are made each quarter, beginning in March.

The company's cash balance on December 31, 2013, was $22,000; a minimum balance of $15,000 must be maintained at all times. Assume that any short-term financing needed to maintain the cash balance is paid off in the month following the month of financing if sufficient funds are available. Interest on short-term loans (12 percent) is paid monthly. Borrowing to meet estimated monthly cash needs takes place at the beginning of the month. Thus, if in the month of April the firm expects to have a need for an additional $60,500, these funds would be borrowed at the beginning of April with interest of $605 (i.e., .12 × 1/12 × $60,500) owed for April being paid at the beginning of May.

a. Prepare a cash budget for Sharpe covering the first seven months of 2014.

b. Sharpe has $200,000 in notes payable due in July that must be repaid or renegotiated for an extension. Will the firm have ample cash to repay the notes?

12. (**Preparation of a cash budget**) Harrison Printing has projected its sales for the first eight months of 2014 as follows:

January	$100,000	May	$275,000
February	120,000	June	200,000
March	150,000	July	200,000
April	300,000	August	180,000

Harrison collects 20 percent of its sales in the month of the sale, 50 percent in the month following the sale, and the remaining 30 percent two months following the sale. During November and December of 2013, Harrison's sales were $220,000 and $175,000, respectively.

Harrison purchases raw materials two months in advance of its sales equal to 65 percent of its final sales price. The supplier is paid one month after delivery. Thus, purchases for April sales are made in February and payment is made in March.

In addition, Harrison pays $10,000 per month for rent and $20,000 each month for other expenditures. Tax prepayments of $22,500 are made each quarter beginning in March. The company's cash balance as of December 31, 2013, was $22,000; a minimum balance of $20,000 must be maintained at all times to satisfy the firm's line-of-credit agreement with its bank. Harrison has arranged with its bank for short-term credit at an interest rate of 12 percent per annum (1 percent per month) to be paid monthly. Borrowing to meet estimated monthly cash needs takes place at the end of the month, and interest is not paid until the end of the following month. Consequently, if the firm were to need to borrow $50,000 during the month of April, then it would pay $500 (= .01 × $50,000) in interest during May. Finally, Harrison follows a policy of repaying its outstanding short-term debt in any month in which its cash balance exceeds the minimum desired balance of $20,000.

a. Harrison needs to know what its cash requirements will be for the next six months so that, if necessary, it can renegotiate the terms of its short-term credit agreement with its bank. To analyze this problem, the firm plans to evaluate the impact of a ±20 percent variation in its monthly sales efforts. Prepare a six-month cash budget for Harrison and use it to evaluate the firm's cash needs.

b. Harrison has a $200,000 note due in June. Will the firm have sufficient cash to repay the loan?

Mini-Case

In November of each year, the CFO of Barker Electronics begins the financial forecasting process to determine the firm's projected needs for new financing during the coming year. Barker is a small electronics manufacturing company located in Moline, Illinois, a city best known as the home of the John Deere Company. The CFO begins the process with the most recent year's income statement, then projects sales growth for the coming year, then estimates net income, and finally then estimates the additional earnings he can expect to retain and reinvest in the firm. The firm's income statement for 2013 follows:

Income Statement ($000)	Year Ended December 31, 2013
Sales	$1,500
Cost of goods sold	(1,050)
Gross profit	$ 450
Operating costs	(225)
Depreciation expense	(50)
Net operating profit	$ 175
Interest expense	(10)
Earnings before taxes	$ 165
Taxes	(58)
Net income	$ 107
Dividends	$ 20
Addition to retained earnings	$ 87

The electronics business has been growing rapidly over the past 18 months as the economy recovers, and the CFO estimates that sales will expand by 20 percent in the next year. Depreciation expense will equal $50,000 and interest expense is estimated to be $10,000. In addition, he estimates the following relationships next year between each of the income statement expense items and sales:

COGS/sales	70%
Operating expenses/sales	15%
Tax rate	35%

Note that for the coming year both depreciation expense and interest expense are projected to remain the same as in 2013.

a. Estimate Barker's net income for 2014 and its addition to retained earnings under the assumption that the firm leaves its dividends paid at the 2013 level.

b. Reevaluate Barker's net income and addition to retained earnings where sales grow at 40 percent over the coming year (assume dividends are the same as in 2013). This scenario requires the addition of new plant and equipment in the amount of $100,000, which increases annual depreciation to $58,000 per year, and interest expense rises to $15,000.

Photo Credits

Credits are listed in order of appearance.

Monart Design/Fotolia; Bertold Werkmann/Shutterstock

Working Capital Management

From Chapter 18 of *Financial Management: Principles and Applications*, Twelfth Edition. Sheridan Titman, Arthur J. Keown, and John D. Martin.

Working Capital Management

Chapter **Outline**

1 Working Capital Management and the Risk–Return Tradeoff

→ **Objective 1.** Describe the risk–return tradeoff involved in managing a firm's working capital.

2 Working Capital Policy

→ **Objective 2.** Explain the principle of self-liquidating debt as a tool for managing firm liquidity.

3 Operating and Cash Conversion Cycles

→ **Objective 3.** Use the cash conversion cycle to measure the efficiency with which a firm manages its working capital.

4 Managing Current Liabilities

→ **Objective 4.** Evaluate the cost of financing as a key determinant of the management of a firm's use of current liabilities.

5 Managing the Firm's Investment in Current Assets

→ **Objective 5.** Understand the factors underlying a firm's investment in cash and marketable securities, accounts receivable, and inventory.

In this chapter we start by considering the risk–return tradeoffs of the balance the firm strikes between current assets and current liabilities. Our analysis of this tradeoff builds upon **P** Principle 2: **There Is a Risk–Return Tradeoff.** Next we examine the principle of self-liquidating debt as a very useful tool for determining the optimal level of working capital. The objective we follow in examining the management of working capital is to find that balance that maximizes shareholder value.

Dell (DELL) Raises the Bar for Working Capital Management

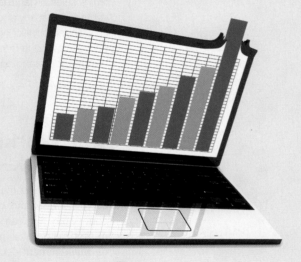

The management at Dell Computer Corporation (DELL) recognized early in the firm's history that it could improve company performance by following a policy of minimizing its investment in net working capital (the difference in the firm's investment in current assets and current liabilities). At the time, Dell's sales were dominated by retail customers who used credit cards to purchase computers. This meant that the firm's investment in accounts receivable was minimal, so the firm focused its attention on reducing inventories and expanding its use of *trade credit,* which is a type of account payable that arises when one firm provides goods or services to a customer with an agreement to bill the customer later.

Dell used a two-pronged attack. First, to reduce inventories, Dell convinced its suppliers to leave truckloads of the items that Dell needed at the back door of Dell's plants. The trucks' contents belonged to the supplier until they were needed by Dell, at which time Dell moved the items from the trailers into its plant. At the same time, Dell's management took full advantage of the trade credit terms by making their payments at the latest possible date. In combination, these actions not only reduced—but actually eliminated—the firm's investment in working capital! Without the drag of working capital on firm performance, the company's profits soared and its stock price rose dramatically.

It's hard to overstate the importance of effectively managing the firm's investment in working capital. Current assets make up about half of the total assets of a typical industrial or retail firm, so it is crucial that managers have a coherent strategy for managing their accounts receivables and payables as well as their cash balances. This was especially true in the recent economic downturn, in which many firms found that having sufficient liquidity to weather the storm proved to be the difference between keeping their doors open or having to close them.

Regardless of Your Major...

"Conflicting Objectives Lead to Problems in Managing a Firm's Working Capital"

The management of working capital involves individuals from across the organization of a firm. For this reason, there are often conflicting points of view about how the firm should manage its working capital. For example, the firm's accounts receivable balance arises from the firm's credit sales and the payment terms that are offered to its customers. The sales force will push for lenient repayment terms as a method for enticing customers to buy the firm's products and services. However, offering more lenient payment terms will mean that the firm will need to make a larger investment in accounts receivables. In addition, inventories are held by the firm to support the firm's production and sales operations. For example, a larger inventory of raw materials makes it easier to smooth out the firm's production process because it allows the production managers to draw down available inventories of raw materials as they are needed for production. Consequently, the firm's operating managers will find it to their advantage to hold large inventories of raw materials. Moreover, holding larger inventories of finished products makes it easier to make sales because customers can be assured that the product will be delivered on a timely basis. For this reason the firm's sales organization will push for larger finished goods inventories. However, holding large inventories is costly and reduces the firm's rate of return on invested capital.

These conflicting points of view within the firm make managing the firm's working capital a difficult task, one that will clearly be easier if the firm's marketing and production managers have a better understanding of the costs and benefits associated with investing in working capital.

Your Turn: See Study Question 2.

 ## Working Capital Management and the Risk–Return Tradeoff

Working capital management encompasses the day-to-day activities of managing the firm's current assets and current liabilities. Because cash, accounts receivable, inventory, and accounts payable can change on a daily and even hourly basis, financial managers may spend more time on working capital management than on any other part of their job. Working capital management decisions include, "How much inventory should we carry?" "Whom should credit be extended to?" "Should the firm purchase items for its inventories on credit or pay cash?" and "If credit is used, when should payment be made?"

Measuring Firm Liquidity

The firm's working capital choices are critical determinants of its ability to pay its bills on time, which we define as the firm's liquidity. The current ratio, which is equal to current assets divided by current liabilities, is a very popular measure of firm liquidity.

The rationale for using the current ratio as a measure of liquidity is as follows: the ability of the firm to pay on time is roughly related to the firm's current assets, which are by definition those assets that will be converted to cash within one year or less. Similarly, the firm's debts that must be repaid over the coming year are included in its current liabilities. Therefore, by comparing the firm's current assets to its current liabilities we get an indication of the firm's liquidity.

The current ratio is closely linked to the firm's net working capital (current assets minus current liabilities). If the current ratio is greater than 1, then net working capital is positive, and vice versa. Consequently, both measures of liquidity provide the same information. However, the current ratio is more widely used because it allows for comparisons across firms of varying sizes. For example, consider the working capital of Firms A and B as follows:

	Firm A	Firm B
Current assets	$50,000	$5,000
Current liabilities	$25,000	$2,500
Net working capital	$25,000	$2,500
Current ratio	2.0	2.0

The net working capital for the two firms is very different owing to the fact that Firm A's current assets and current liabilities are 10 times as large as those of Firm B. However, the current ratios are identical.

Managing Firm Liquidity

To manage liquidity, managers must balance the firm's investments in current assets in relation to its current liabilities. To accomplish this task, the firm's management can minimize the use of current assets by efficiently managing its inventories and accounts receivable, by seeking out the most favorable accounts payable, and by monitoring its use of short-term borrowing.

The current assets a firm has on hand and the current liabilities it faces can vary significantly across different firms. For example, retail giant Walmart (WMT) must carry a huge investment in inventory if it expects to be able to make sales, and it uses trade credit to finance these inventories. To illustrate, at the outset of 2009, Walmart had over $34 billion invested in inventory and had accounts payable of more than $47 billion.

Firms like Walmart can manage their liquidity by holding larger cash and marketable securities balances that can be drawn down in times of need. Alternatively, the firm can increase its liquidity by reducing its short-term borrowing and increasing its use of long-term debt or equity. Once again, the resulting increase in firm liquidity is not free because the cost of long-term debt is generally higher than that of short-term debt, and the opportunity cost of equity funds is higher still.

Risk–Return Tradeoff

The decisions a firm makes that affect its net working capital change the firm's liquidity or ability to pay its bills on time. Thus, working capital decisions involve a risk–return tradeoff. For example, the firm can enhance its profitability by reducing its cash and marketable securities balance because these assets typically earn very low rates of return. However, the increased profitability comes at a price, because the firm is now exposed to a higher risk of not being able to pay its bills on time should an unexpected need for cash arise, because it has lower cash and marketable securities.

Checkpoint 1

Measuring Firm Liquidity

Ford Motor Company (F) suffered along with all the U.S. automakers with the onset of the recession that began in 2007. The following information from the firm's financial statements for 2008 and 2011 provide the information needed to assess the firm's liquidity (Note: all figures below are in $000):

	2008	2011
Cash and cash equivalents	$22,049,000	$35,766,000
Accounts receivable	6,165,000	8,565,000
Inventory	8,618,000	5,901,000
Total current assets	$36,832,000	$50,232,000
Accounts payable	$78,158,000	$60,093,000
Other current liabilities	0	0
Total current liabilities	$78,158,000	$63,093,000

(1 CONTINUED >> ON NEXT PAGE)

Use the net working capital and the current ratio to assess any change in liquidity of the firm over the period spanned by the two sets of financial data.

STEP 1: Picture the problem

Firm liquidity refers to the ability of the firm to pay its bills in a timely fashion. Thus, a rudimentary measure of firm liquidity can be obtained by comparing the assets that the firm has on hand that can be converted to cash within the coming year (current assets) with the bills the firm must pay within the coming year (current liabilities).

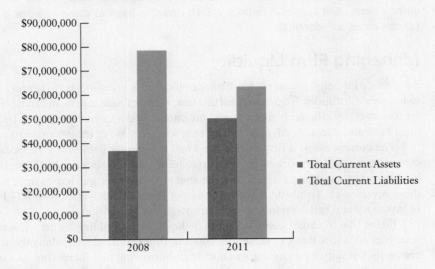

Note, once again, that these figures are in thousands of dollars.

STEP 2: Decide on a solution strategy

Firm liquidity can be measured by a comparison of current assets and current liabilities using the following measures:

$$\frac{\text{Net Working}}{\text{Capital}} = \text{Current Assets} - \text{Current Liabilities}$$

and

$$\frac{\text{Current}}{\text{Ratio}} = \frac{\text{Current Assets}}{\text{Current Liabilities}}$$

STEP 3: Solve

	2008	2011
Net working capital ($000)	$(41,326,000)	$(12,861,000)
Current ratio	0.47	0.80

STEP 4: Analyze

The effects of the recession are clearly visible in the liquidity measures for Ford. This is perhaps most obvious when we compare the current ratios for the two periods. The 2008 ratio is a little more than half that of 2011. Looking more closely at the balance sheet data, we can see one bright spot in that Ford was able to reduce its inventory significantly.

STEP 5: Check yourself

Consider the effect on Ford's liquidity of the firm having the opportunity to enter into a long-term financing arrangement to borrow $2 billion, which could be used to reduce the firm's 2011 accounts payable. What would be the effect of this event on the firm's liquidity measures?

ANSWER: Net working capital = ($10,861,000) and current ratio = .82.

Your Turn: For more practice, do related **Study Problems** 1 and 2 at the end of this chapter.   >> **END Checkpoint 1**

Before you move on to 2

Concept Check | 1

1. How does investing more heavily in current assets, other things remaining the same, increase firm liquidity?
2. How does the use of short-term as opposed to long-term liabilities affect firm liquidity?

Working Capital Policy

Managing the firm's net working capital involves deciding on an investment strategy for financing the firm's current assets and current liabilities. Because each financing source comes with advantages and disadvantages, the financial manager must decide on the sources that are optimal for the firm.

The Principle of Self-Liquidating Debt

A benchmark that is often used for setting working capital policy is the **principle of self-liquidating debt**. This principle states that the maturity of the source of financing should be matched with the length of time that the financing is needed.[1] Following this policy, a seasonal expansion of inventories prior to the Christmas season should be financed with a short-term loan or current liability. The rationale underlying the principle is straightforward. Funds are needed for a limited period of time, and when that time has passed, the cash needed to repay the loan will be generated automatically by the sale of the extra inventory items. Obtaining the needed funds from a long-term source (longer than one year) would mean that the firm would still have the funds after the inventories they helped finance had been sold. In this case the firm would have "excess" liquidity, which it might need to invest in low-yield marketable securities.

Alternatively, if the firm is purchasing new manufacturing equipment that will be used in its factories for many years, then longer-term financing would be better. In this instance, the manufacturing equipment might be financed with a long-term installment loan much like the loan you would use to finance a car or home purchase.

Permanent and Temporary Asset Investments

To implement the principle of self-liquidating debt, or maturity matching, we will find it useful to think about the firm's investments in assets as either temporary or permanent.

Temporary investments in assets, or simply *temporary assets*, are composed of current assets that will be liquidated and not replaced within the current year. These include cash and marketable securities, accounts receivable, and seasonal fluctuation in inventories.

Permanent investments are composed of investments in assets that the firm expects to hold for a period longer than one year. These include the firm's minimum level of current assets, such as accounts receivable and inventories, as well as fixed assets.

Spontaneous, Temporary, and Permanent Sources of Financing

We can categorize the sources of financing used by a firm into one of three subcategories: spontaneous, temporary, and permanent. **Spontaneous sources of financing** arise naturally or spontaneously out of the day-to-day operations of the business and consist of trade credit and other forms of accounts payable. **Trade credit** exists when one firm provides goods or services to a customer with an agreement to bill the customer later. Trade credit, however, is only one form of accounts payable. Other examples include wages and salaries payable that

---

[1]A value-maximizing approach to the management of the firm's liquidity involves assessing the value of the benefits derived from increasing the firm's investment in liquid assets and weighing those benefits against the added costs to the firm's owners resulting from investing in low-yield current assets. Unfortunately, the benefits derived from increased liquidity relate to the expected costs of bankruptcy to the firm's owners, and these costs are very difficult to measure. Thus, a "valuation" approach to liquidity management exists only in the theoretical realm.

arise when the firm pays employees once a month but accrues a liability for wages owed up until the date that payment is actually made. Similarly, interest and taxes are typically paid quarterly but the firm accrues both an interest and a tax liability every day up until the date of the tax payment, thereby creating balances for interest payable and taxes payable.

Temporary sources of financing typically consist of current liabilities the firm incurs on a discretionary basis. Unlike spontaneous sources of financing, the firm's management must make an overt decision to use one of the various sources of temporary financing. Examples include unsecured bank loans, commercial paper (which is simply unsecured promissory notes that firms sell in the money market, with maturities of 1 to 270 days), as well as short-term loans that are secured by the firm's inventories or accounts receivable.

Permanent sources of financing include intermediate-term loans, long-term debt (such as installment loans and bonds), preferred stock, and common equity. These sources are considered permanent because the financing is available for a longer period of time than a current liability. However, permanent and temporary sources of financing are both considered discretionary because neither form of financing arises spontaneously out of the day-to-day operations of the firm and because the use of each source of funds requires an explicit decision by the firm's management.

Figure 1 summarizes the terminology used in implementing the principle of self-liquidating debt to manage firm liquidity. We will refer to this terminology when discussing the working capital policy illustrated in Figure 2.

Figure 1

Terminology Underlying the Principle of Self-Liquidating Debt

(Panel A) Classification of Types of Investments in Assets

Types of Investments in Assets	Definition and Examples
Temporary	Definition—assets that will be liquidated and not replaced within the current year.
	Examples—typically current assets such as inventories and accounts receivable.
Permanent	Definition—assets that the firm expects to hold for a period longer than one year.
	Examples—typically fixed assets such as plant and equipment, although the minimum level of investment in current assets is considered a permanent asset investment as well.

(Panel B) Classification of Types of Sources of Financing

Types of Sources of Financing	Definition and Examples
Spontaneous	Definition—financing sources that arise naturally or spontaneously out of the day-to-day operations of the business.
	Examples—trade credit or accounts payable, accrued expenses related to wages and salaries, as well as interest and taxes.
Temporary	Definition—current liabilities the firm incurs on a discretionary basis. Unlike spontaneous sources of financing, the firm's management must make an overt decision to use one of the various sources of temporary financing.
	Examples—unsecured bank loans and commercial paper, as well as loans secured by the firm's inventories or accounts receivable.
Permanent	Definition—long-term sources of discretionary financing used by the firm.
	Examples—intermediate-term loans, long-term debt (e.g., installment loans and bonds), preferred stock, and common equity.

>> END FIGURE 1

Figure 2

Working Capital Policy: The Principle of Self-Liquidating Debt

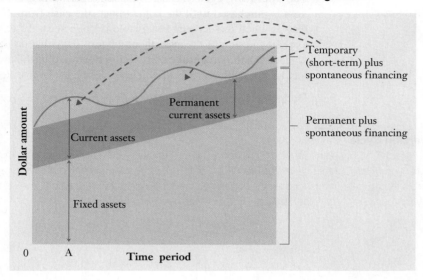

>> END FIGURE 2

A Graphic Illustration of the Principle of Self-Liquidating Debt

Figure 2 illustrates the use of the principle of self-liquidating debt to guide a firm's financing decisions. To interpret the figure, select a point in time to examine the total dollar amount the firm has invested in assets (current plus fixed). For example, at time zero (0) in the figure, the firm's fixed and current assets equal the sum of its permanent plus temporary sources of financing. That is, there is no need for the firm to raise money using temporary financing sources (the financing sources are noted on the right-hand side of the graph). As time progresses, we see that the firm's total assets (as depicted with the dashed line cycling over the top of the graph) rise and fall with temporary expansions in the firm's need for assets; for example, point A might depict a seasonal expansion in the firm's inventories and accounts receivable. During these peak times the firm will use discretionary temporary sources of financing (short-term bank loans, for example) to finance the temporary expansion in asset needs.

The key observation we make from Figure 2 is that the firm's temporary or short-term debt rises and falls with the rise and fall in the firm's temporary investments in current assets. Thus the principle of self-liquidating debt provides the firm's financial manager with a guide to determining whether the firm should use a current liability or longer-term source of financing to fund assets.

Before you move on to 3

Concept Check | 2

1. What is the principle of self-liquidating debt, and how can it be used to help the firm manage its liquidity?
2. What are some examples of permanent and temporary investments in current assets?
3. What makes trade credit a source of spontaneous financing?

Operating and Cash Conversion Cycles

The firm's *operating cycle* and *cash conversion cycle* are two popular measures used to determine how effectively a firm has managed its working capital. The shorter these two cycles are (usually measured in days), the more efficient is the firm's working capital management.

Measuring Working Capital Efficiency

The **operating cycle** measures the time period that elapses from the date that an inventory item is purchased until the firm collects the cash from its sale (if the firm sells on credit, this date is when the account receivable is collected). As can be seen in Figure 3, the operating cycle is the sum of the average number of days that an item is held in inventory before being sold, called the **inventory conversion period**, plus the average number of days it takes to collect an account receivable, which we define as the average collection period.

Operating Cycle = Inventory Conversion Period + Average Collection Period   **(1)**

Figure 3

The Cash Conversion Cycle

A firm's operations typically follow a sequence of milestones: the purchase of items for inventories, the sale of items from inventory for credit, and the collection of accounts receivable. The period of time required for this entire process is called the operating cycle. However, for firms that are able to purchase items for their inventories on credit using accounts payable, the cash conversion cycle is shorter than the operating cycle by the number of days that the firm has to pay its accounts payable.

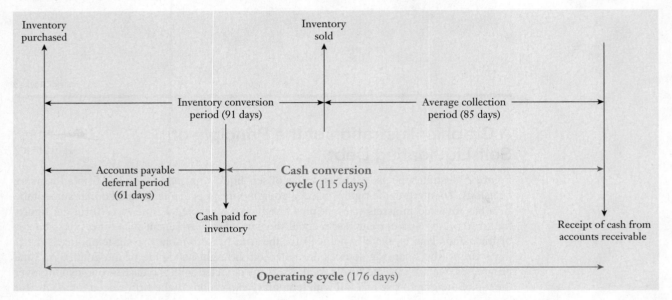

Formulas:

Operating Cycle = Inventory Conversion Period + Average Collection Period   **(1)**

$$\text{Accounts Payable Deferral Period} = \frac{365}{\left(\dfrac{\text{Cost of Goods Sold}} \div {\text{Accounts Payable}}\right)}$$ **(2)**

Cash Conversion Cycle = Operating Cycle − Accounts Payable Deferral Period   **(3)**

$$\text{Inventory Conversion Period} = \frac{365}{\text{Inventory Turnover Ratio}}$$ **(4)**

$$\text{Inventory Turnover Ratio} = \frac{\text{Cost of Goods Sold}}{\text{Inventory}}$$ **(5)**

$$\text{Average Collection Period} = \frac{\text{Accounts Receivable}}{\text{Daily Credit Sales}} = \frac{\text{Accounts Receivable}}{\left(\dfrac{\text{Annual Credit Sales}} \div {365}\right)}$$ **(6)**

>> END FIGURE 3

In the example found in Figure 3, the operating cycle is 176 days, which consists of an inventory conversion period of 91 days plus an average collection period of 85 days.

Note, however, that when the firm is able to purchase items of inventory on credit, it does not have cash tied up for the full length of its operating cycle. In the example found in Figure 3 the firm incurs accounts payable as it purchases items of inventory on credit terms that allow it to pay after 61 days. The formula used to calculate the **accounts payable deferral period** is found in Equation (2):

$$\frac{\text{Accounts Payable}}{\text{Deferral Period}} = \frac{365}{\left(\frac{\text{Cost of}}{\text{Goods Sold}} \div \frac{\text{Accounts}}{\text{Payable}}\right)} \qquad (2)$$

Note that the accounts payable deferral period simply measures how many days, on average, the firm has to pay its suppliers who have provided the firm with trade credit that is the source of accounts payable. Therefore, the **cash conversion cycle** is shorter than the operating cycle as the firm does not have to pay for the items in its inventory for a period equal to the length of the accounts payable deferral period. The cash conversion cycle is defined in Equation (3):

Cash Conversion Cycle = Operating Cycle − Accounts Payable Deferral Period   **(3)**

Managing the firm's working capital impacts its cash conversion cycle in powerful ways. For example, consider the situation faced by computer firm Dell (DELL) in 1989. Dell was a fledgling start-up whose cash conversion cycle was 121.88 days. By 2002, Dell had reduced this number to −37.59 days. How did the company reduce its cash conversion cycle below zero? There are two parts to the answer to this question. The first lies in the fact that Dell reduced the inventory conversion period dramatically, which in turn reduced the operating cycle. Second, Dell was able to stretch out its accounts payables longer than the operating cycle. In other words, the company was able to get credit terms that extended 37.59 days longer than the sum of the time it held inventory plus the days required to collect its accounts receivable!

Dell's strategy entailed ordering the needed parts for its inventories and building a computer only *after* an order was received. Moreover, parts were financed using trade credit. This strategy resulted in virtually no inventory as well as a lengthy accounts payable deferral period such that the cash conversion cycle was actually negative. As Dell's sales grew it actually generated cash flow from the growth in its accounts payable!

Calculating the Operating and Cash Conversion Cycle

The operating and cash conversion cycle numbers found in Figure 3 were calculated using the following example. The example firm has $15 million in annual credit sales and $12 million in cost of goods sold. In addition, the firm maintains an inventory balance of $3 million, has $3.5 million in accounts receivable, and has $2 million in accounts payable outstanding.

To calculate the operating cycle, we need only the inventory conversion period and the accounts receivable collection period. The inventory conversion period can be calculated with a quick manipulation of the inventory turnover ratio,

$$\frac{\text{Inventory}}{\text{Turnover Ratio}} = \frac{\text{Cost of Goods Sold}}{\text{Inventory}} = \frac{\$12,000,000}{\$3,000,000} = 4.0 \qquad (5)$$

This tells us that we run through our average inventory 4.0 times a year, which translates into an inventory conversion period of 91 days,

$$\frac{\text{Inventory}}{\text{Conversion Period}} = \frac{365}{\text{Inventory Turnover Ratio}} = \frac{365}{4.0} = 91 \text{ days} \qquad (4)$$

The inventory conversion period is simply the number of days it takes for the firm to convert its inventory to credit sales. For example, if the firm turns its inventory over 12 times a year, then it takes approximately 30 days to convert inventory to credit sales.

The second half of the operating cycle is the average number of days it takes to convert accounts receivable to cash, or the average collection period. If credit sales are $15 million per year and average accounts receivable is $3.5 million, then

$$\frac{\text{Average Collection}}{\text{Period}} = \frac{\text{Accounts Receivable}}{\text{Daily Credit Sales}} = \frac{\$3,500,000}{\$15,000,000/365} = 85 \text{ days} \tag{6}$$

We calculate the operating cycle, using Equation (1), as the sum of the inventory conversion period (91 days) and the average collection period (85 days), equaling 176 days.

We can calculate the cash conversion cycle using Equation (3), but first we need to calculate the accounts payable deferral period. The accounts payable balance is $2 million, so we can calculate the accounts payable deferral period using Equation (2) as follows:

$$\frac{\text{Accounts Payable}}{\text{Deferral Period}} = \frac{365}{\left(\dfrac{\text{Cost of}}{\text{Goods Sold}} \div \dfrac{\text{Accounts}}{\text{Payable}} \right)} \tag{2}$$

$$\frac{\text{Accounts Payable}}{\text{Deferral Period}} = \frac{365}{\$12,000,000 \div \$2,000,000} = 61 \text{ days}$$

Substituting into Equation (3), we get a cash conversion period of 115 days, as follows:

$$\text{Cash Conversion Cycle} = \text{Operating Cycle} - \text{Accounts Payable Deferral Period} \tag{3}$$

$$\text{Cash Conversion Cycle} = 176 \text{ days} - 61 \text{ days} = 115 \text{ days}$$

Checkpoint 2

Analyzing the Cash Conversion Cycle

Financial information for the Dell Computer Corporation (DELL) and Ford Motor Company (F) is as follows:

$ Thousands	2-Feb-12 Dell	21-Dec-11 Ford
Sales	62,071,000	136,264,000
Cost of Goods Sold	48,260,000	113,345,000
Accounts Receivable	9,803,000	8,565,000
Inventories	1,404,000	5,901,000
Accounts Payable	15,590,000	63,093,000
Current Assets	29,448,000	50,232,000
Current Liabilities	22,001,000	63,093,000

Compute the operating cycle and cash conversion cycle for each of these companies. You may assume for purposes of your analysis that all of the firm sales are credit sales.

STEP 1: Picture the problem

We can visualize the operating and cash conversion cycles using the diagram found in Figure 3 as follows:

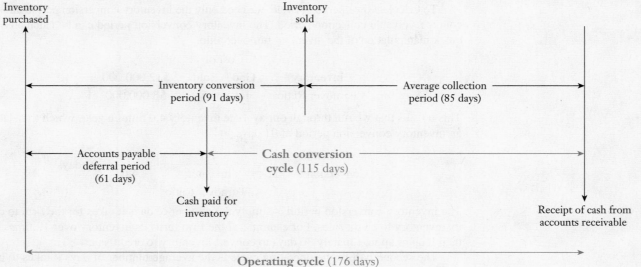

STEP 2: Decide on a solution strategy

The firm's cash conversion cycle and operating cycle are defined as follows:

Operating Cycle = Inventory Conversion Period + Average Collection Period   **(1)**

Cash Conversion Cycle = Operating Cycle − Accounts Payable Deferral Period   **(3)**

To compute these two quantities we need to compute the firm's average collection period, inventory conversion period, and accounts payable deferral period as follows:

$$\frac{\text{Inventory}}{\text{Conversion Period}} = \frac{365}{\text{Inventory Turnover Ratio}} \quad \textbf{(4)}$$

$$\frac{\text{Inventory}}{\text{Turnover Ratio}} = \frac{\text{Cost of Goods Sold}}{\text{Inventory}} \quad \textbf{(5)}$$

$$\frac{\text{Average Collection}}{\text{Period}} = \frac{\text{Accounts Receivable}}{\text{Daily Credit Sales}} = \frac{\text{Accounts Receivable}}{\left(\dfrac{\text{Annual Credit Sales}}{} \div 365\right)} \quad \textbf{(6)}$$

$$\frac{\text{Accounts Payable}}{\text{Deferral Period}} = \frac{365}{\left(\dfrac{\text{Cost of Goods Sold}}{} \div \dfrac{\text{Accounts Payable}}{}\right)} \quad \textbf{(2)}$$

STEP 3: Solve

	Dell	Ford
Average Collection Period	57.65	22.94
Inventory Conversion Period	10.62	19.00
Accounts Payable Deferral Period	117.91	203.18
Operating Cycle	68.26	41.95
Cash Conversion Cycle	(49.65)	(161.23)

STEP 4: Analyze

These results may be somewhat surprising to you. Note that Dell's operating cycle (the sum of the average collection period and inventory conversion period) is somewhat shorter than that of Ford. However, you probably expected Dell's cash conversion cycle to be negative due to its effective use of working capital management practices, but you probably did not expect to see Ford's negative 161.23-day cash conversion cycle. How can this be if Ford is coming out of one of the worst recessions in U.S. automobile history? The answer is found in the very lengthy accounts payable deferral period of 203.18 days. This lengthy period almost surely reflects the fact that Ford is simply not paying some of its bills on time and is extending its payments to conserve liquidity. Alternatively, Ford's management may have negotiated lengthy payment terms for its payables. In either case the firm is benefiting greatly from the use of accounts payable.

STEP 5: Check yourself

If General Motors Corporation (GM) were to have an average collection period of 24.16 days, an inventory conversion period of 39.84 days, and an accounts payable deferral period of 131.42 days, what would its operating and cash conversion cycles be?

ANSWER: 64.01 days and (67.42) days.

Your Turn: For more practice, do related **Study Problems** 5 and 6 at the end of this chapter.   **>> END Checkpoint 2**

Tools of Financial Analysis—Cash Conversion Cycle

Name of Tool	Formula	What It Tells You
Cash Conversion Cycle	*Inventory Conversion Period + Average Collection Period − Accounts Payable Deferral Period* • $\dfrac{\textit{Inventory Conversion}}{\textit{Period}} = \dfrac{365}{\textit{Cost of Goods Sold/Inventory}}$ • $\dfrac{\textit{Average Collection}}{\textit{Period}} = \dfrac{\textit{Accounts Receivable}}{\textit{Daily Credit Sales}}$ • $\dfrac{\textit{Average Payable}}{\textit{Deferral Period}} = \dfrac{365}{\textit{Cost of Goods Sold} \div \textit{Accounts Payable}}$	• The number of days the firm requires to convert cash to inventories to accounts receivable and back to cash net of the effects of trade credit • The shorter the firm's cash conversion cycle, the less money the firm will need to tie up in inventories and accounts receivable.

Before you move on to 4

Concept Check | **3**

1. What is a firm's operating cycle?
2. What is the firm's cash conversion cycle, and how does it differ from the operating cycle?

 ## Managing Current Liabilities

The firm's current liabilities include all of its debt obligations that must be repaid in one year or less. These liabilities include unsecured and secured forms of credit (see Table 1). **Unsecured current liabilities** include trade credit, unsecured bank loans, and commercial paper. These forms of credit are unsecured in that they are backed only by the lender's faith in the ability of the borrower to repay the funds when due.

Secured current liabilities include loans that involve the pledge of specific assets as collateral in the event the borrower defaults in payment of principal or interest. Both accounts receivable and inventories can serve as collateral for short-term loans that are made by a variety of financial institutions, including commercial banks and finance companies. Factoring involves the sale of accounts receivable at a discount to a collections firm called a factor.

Calculating the Cost of Short-Term Financing

When deciding between alternative sources of financing, it is critical that the firm's financial analyst compute the costs incurred when using various sources of short-term financing. The procedure for estimating the cost of short-term credit relies on the basic interest equation:

$$\text{Interest} = \text{Principal} \times \text{Rate} \times \text{Time} \qquad (7)$$

where *interest* is the dollar amount of interest owed based on the principal amount borrowed. *Rate* is the annual rate charged on the loan, and *Time* is the fraction of the year the debt is outstanding. For example, a six-month loan for $1,000 that carries an 8 percent annual rate of interest would require an interest payment of $40:

$$\text{Interest} = \$1000 \times .08 \times \tfrac{1}{2} = \$40$$

We use this basic relationship to calculate the cost of a source of short-term financing, or the annual percentage rate (APR), as follows:

$$\dfrac{\text{Annual Percentage}}{\text{Rate } (APR)} = \dfrac{\text{Interest}}{\text{Principal} \times \text{Time}}$$

or

$$\dfrac{\text{Annual Percentage}}{\text{Rate } (APR)} = \dfrac{\text{Interest}}{\text{Principal}} \times \dfrac{1}{\text{Time}} \qquad (8)$$

Table 1	Sources of Short-Term Credit

(Panel A) Unsecured Sources of Credit:

Trade Credit

Accounts payable arises out of the normal course of business when the firm purchases from its suppliers, who allow the firm to make payment after the delivery of the merchandise or services.

Line of Credit

A **line of credit** is generally an informal agreement or understanding between the borrower and the bank about the maximum amount of credit that the bank will provide the borrower at any one time. Under this type of agreement there is no legal commitment on the part of the bank to provide the stated credit. In a revolving credit agreement, which is a variant of this form of financing, a legal obligation is involved. The line of credit agreement generally covers a period of one year corresponding to the borrower's fiscal year.

Bank Transaction Loans

Bank transaction loans are a form of unsecured short-term bank credit made for a specific purpose. This type of loan is commonly associated with bank credit and is obtained by signing a promissory note.

Commercial Paper

Commercial paper is a short-term debt obligation that is issued by the most creditworthy firms and is bought and sold in the money market. One of the advantages of commercial paper is that it generally carries a lower rate than do bank loans and comparable sources of short-term financing.

(Panel B) Secured Sources of Credit:

Pledging Accounts Receivable (or Inventories)

Under the pledging accounts receivable (or inventories) arrangement, the borrower simply pledges accounts receivable (inventory) as collateral for a loan obtained from either a commercial bank or a finance company. The amount of the loan is stated as a percentage of the face value of the receivables (inventory) pledged. If the firm provides the lender with a general line on its receivables (inventory), then all of the borrower's accounts (inventories) are pledged as security for the loan.

(Panel C) Raising Cash by Selling Accounts Receivables:

Factoring Accounts Receivable

Factoring accounts receivable involves the outright sale of a firm's accounts to a financial institution called a factor. A **factor** is a firm that acquires the receivables of other firms. The factoring institution may be a commercial finance company that engages solely in the factoring of receivables (known as an old-line factor) or it may be a commercial bank. The factor, in turn, bears the risk of collection and, for a fee, services the accounts. The fee is stated as a percentage of the face value of all receivables factored (usually 1 to 3 percent).

For example, the SKC Corporation plans to borrow $1,000 for a 90-day period. At maturity the firm will repay the $1,000 principal amount plus $30 interest. Thus, the rate of interest for the loan can be estimated as follows:

$$APR = \frac{\$30}{\$1,000} \times \frac{1}{90/365} = .03 \times \frac{365}{90} = .1217 \text{ or } 12.17\%$$

Therefore, the annual cost of funds provided by the loan is 12.17 percent.

Evaluating the Cost of Trade Credit

Trade credit provided by a firm's suppliers creates accounts payable. Evaluating the cost of this trade credit requires that we understand the terms under which trade credit is typically given.

Credit Terms and Cash Discounts

Very often the credit terms offered with trade credit involve a cash discount for early payment. For example, a supplier might offer terms of "2/10, net 30," which means that a 2 percent discount is offered for payment within 10 days or the full amount is due in 30 days. Thus, a 2 percent penalty is incurred for not paying within 10 days or for delaying payment from the 10th to the 30th day

Table 2	Annualized Rates of Interest on Selected Trade Credit Terms
Credit Terms	**Annualized Rate**
2/10, net 60	14.90%
2/10, net 90	9.31
3/20, net 60	28.22
6/10, net 90	29.12

(that is, for 20 days). The annual cost of not taking the cash discount can be quite severe. Using a $1 invoice amount, the annualized cost of passing up the discount period using the preceding credit terms and our APR equation found in Equation (8) can be estimated as follows:

$$APR = \frac{\$.02}{\$.98} \times \frac{1}{20/365} = .3724 \text{ or } 37.24\%$$

Note that the 2 percent cash discount is the interest cost of extending the payment period an additional 20 days. Note also that the principal amount of the credit is 98 cents. This amount constitutes the full principal amount as of the 10th day of the credit period because this is the amount that is due if paid by day 10. After the 10th day the cash discount is lost. The annualized cost of passing up the 2 percent discount for 20 days in this instance is 37.24 percent, which is quite expensive when compared to the borrowing rates on short-term bank loans (for most firms). Furthermore, once the discount period has passed, there is no reason to pay before the final due date (the 30th day). Table 2 lists the annualized cost of alternative credit terms. Note that the cost of trade credit varies directly with the size of the cash discount and inversely with the length of time between the end of the discount period and the final due date.

Evaluating the Cost of Bank Loans

We can also apply Equation (8) to the estimation of the cost of bank loans. However, when firms borrow money from a bank they often do so by creating what is called a line of credit. This simply means that the firm has the option to borrow an amount up to the stated amount if it needs to do so. To compensate the bank for providing this line of credit, the borrower is required to maintain a minimum balance in the bank throughout the loan period, called a compensating balance. This required balance (which can be stated as a percent of the line of credit) increases the annualized cost of the loan to the borrower, unless a deposit balance equal to or greater than this balance requirement is ordinarily maintained in the bank.

Checkpoint 3

Calculating the APR for a Line of Credit

M&M Beverage Company has a $300,000 line of credit that requires a compensating balance equal to 10 percent of the loan amount. The rate paid on the loan is 12 percent per annum, $200,000 is borrowed for a six-month period, and the firm does not currently have a deposit with the lending bank. The dollar cost of the loan includes the interest expense as well as the opportunity cost of maintaining an idle cash balance in the compensating balance (which is 10 percent of the loan). To accommodate the cost of the compensating balance requirement, assume that the added funds will have to be borrowed and simply left idle in the firm's checking account. What would the annualized rate on this loan be if there was no compensating balance requirement? What is the annual rate on this loan with the compensating balance requirement?

STEP 1: Picture the problem

In the case where there is a required compensating balance, the amount actually borrowed (B) will be larger than the $200,000 needed. In fact, the needed $200,000 will constitute 90 percent of the total borrowed funds because of the 10 percent compensating balance requirement. Hence, 90(B) = $200,000, such that B, or the amount borrowed, equals $222,222 (B = $200,000/0.90), of which only $200,000 is available for use by the firm. Thus, the interest paid on a $222,222 loan is $13,333.32 (i.e., $222,222 × .12 × 1/2), for the use of $200,000.[2]

---

[2]The same answer would have been obtained by assuming a total loan of $200,000, of which only 90 percent or $180,000 was available for use by the firm; that is, interest is now calculated on the $200,000 loan amount ($12,000 = $200,000 × .12 × 1/2).

Thus, when there is a required compensating balance, we can visualize the problem as receiving $200,000, but paying interest as if $222,222 had been borrowed.

STEP 2: Decide on a solution strategy

To solve for the APR, use Equation (8),

$$APR = \frac{Interest}{Principal} \times \frac{1}{Time}$$

STEP 3: Solve

Without the required compensating balance, M&M will only have to borrow $200,000 to have the use of $200,000; therefore, the annualized cost of credit (assuming a 365-day year) is 12 percent.

$$APR = \frac{\$12,000}{\$200,000} \times \frac{1}{1/2} = 12\%$$

The interest expense on the $200,000 principal amount of the loan for half a year is $12,000 = .12 \times $200,000 \times 1/2. However, in the case where the M&M Beverage Company is required to maintain a compensating balance, it will need to borrow $222,222, and the interest becomes $13,333.32 at the end of the six-month loan period. In this case the cost of credit rises to 13.33 percent because the firm owes $13,333.32 in interest but only gets the use of $200,000:

$$APR = \frac{\$13,333.22}{\$200,000} \times \frac{1}{1/2} = 13.33\%$$

Frequently, bank loans will be made on a "discounted interest" basis. That is, the loan interest will be deducted from the loan amount before the funds are transferred to the borrower. Extending the M&M Beverage Company example to consider discounted interest involves reducing the loan proceeds ($200,000) in the previous example by the amount of interest for the full six months ($13,333.32). The annualized rate of interest on the loan is now:

$$APR = \frac{\$13,333.22}{\$200,000 - \$13,333.32} \times \frac{1}{1/2} = .1429 \text{ or } 14.29\%$$

STEP 4: Analyze

Note that the presence of a compensating balance requirement increases the cost of credit to M&M from 12 percent to 13.33 percent. Adding a requirement that interest be deducted from the loan proceeds (discounted interest) increases the cost of credit from 13.33 percent to 14.29 percent. This results from the fact that the firm pays interest on the same amount of funds as before ($222,222); however, this time it gets the use of $13,333.32 less, or $200,000 − $13,333.32 = $186,666.68.

If M&M needs the use of a full $200,000, then it will have to borrow more than $222,222 so that it can cover both the compensating balance requirement and the discounted interest.

STEP 5: Check yourself

Assume that your firm has a $1,000,000 line of credit that requires a compensating balance equal to 20 percent of the loan amount. The rate paid on the loan is 12 percent per annum, $500,000 is borrowed for a six-month period, and the firm does not currently have a deposit with the lending bank. To accommodate the cost of the compensating balance requirement, assume that the added funds will have to be borrowed and simply left idle in the firm's checking account. What would the annualized rate on this loan be with the compensating balance requirement?

ANSWER: 15 percent.

Your Turn: For more practice, do related **Study Problems** 7 through 14 at the end of this chapter.   **>> END Checkpoint 3**

Tools of Financial Analysis—Annual Percentage Rate (APR)

Name of Tool	Formula	What It Tells You
Annual Percentage Rate (APR)	$$\frac{Interest}{Principal \times Time}$$ • *Interest = Rate × Principal × Time* • *Rate = the stated interest cost per dollar* • *Time = the fraction of a year the loan is outstanding*	• The annual rate of interest for a source of short-term credit • The APR formula does not consider the effects of compound interest.

Concept Check | 4

1. Give some examples of unsecured and secured forms of current liabilities.
2. What does a factor do?
3. What is a bank line of credit?
4. What is the APR equation, and how is it used?

Managing the Firm's Investment in Current Assets

At any point in time, the primary types of current assets that most firms hold are cash and marketable securities, accounts receivable, and inventories. We will first look at cash and marketable securities, then move on to accounts receivable, followed by inventories.

Cash and Marketable Securities

Firms hold cash in their bank accounts and invest in highly liquid investments known as marketable securities. These funds are used to pay the firm's bills on a timely basis, so that when the firm runs short of cash it can easily sell a portion of its marketable securities portfolio to replenish its bank balances. The obvious cost of holding too little cash and marketable securities is the potential for defaulting on one or more of the firm's financial obligations. So, holding sufficient cash and marketable securities is essential. However, holding excessive amounts of these assets is costly because they earn very low rates of return.

Costs of Managing Cash and Marketable Securities

The dilemma faced by the financial manager in managing the firm's cash and marketable securities is a clear application of **P** Principle 2: **There Is a Risk–Return Tradeoff**. To accept the risk of not having sufficient cash on hand, the firm must be compensated with a return on the cash that is invested. Moreover, the greater the risk of the investment in which the cash is placed, the greater the return the firm demands.

What we have established is that firms need cash to pay their bills, and not having sufficient cash when needed can be very costly to the firm. Firms maintain the bulk of their cash invested in a portfolio of relatively safe marketable securities that can be quickly and easily sold and converted to cash in the event the firm needs to replenish its bank account. Consequently, there are two fundamental problems of cash management:

1. Keeping enough cash on hand to meet the firm's cash disbursal requirements on a timely basis.
2. Managing the composition of the firm's marketable securities portfolio.

Problem #1: Maintaining a Sufficient Cash Balance

Maintaining an adequate amount of cash to meet the firm's needs requires an accurate forecast of the firm's cash receipts and disbursements. The firm's cash budget is the principal tool used to accomplish this objective.

Once projections of cash requirements have been made, the firm may want to look into various ways in which it might reduce its need for cash. One method for doing this is by speeding up its cash collections and slowing down its cash disbursements. Let's take a look at this process in more detail.

When a firm pays a bill by writing a check, it takes time for the check to be received by the recipient, for the recipient to process and deposit the check, and for the check to be cleared through the banking system. As a result, the cash balance on the firm's ledger differs from the available balance shown in its bank account. This difference is called **float**. It should be obvious that the payer and the payee have opposite motives when it comes to managing the float involved in the payment process. The paying firm would like to extend the float and retain use of the payment funds as long as possible, whereas the payee firm would like to speed up or shorten float as much as possible so as to gain use of the funds sooner.

Although float management is an important treasury management function, its importance has been dramatically reduced with the advent of electronic funds transfers and changes in check clearing practices within the banking system. In particular, the growing practice of direct, electronic information exchange between businesses, known as electronic data interchange (EDI), effectively eliminates float. Moreover, the October 29, 2003, passage of the Check Clearing Act now allows banks to transmit electronic copies of checks for collection rather than having to deliver the actual check.

Problem #2: Managing the Composition of the Firm's Marketable Securities Portfolio

Firms prefer to hold cash reserves in securities that can be quickly and easily converted to cash with little or no risk of loss. The types of investments used for this purpose are called **money market securities**. Generally, these securities have maturities of less than one year, have virtually no default risk, and can be easily bought and sold. Table 3 describes some of these alternative money market instruments.

Managing Accounts Receivable

Most firms are involved in selling goods or services. Although some of these sales will be for cash, for many firms a large portion of these sales will involve credit. Whenever a sale is made on credit, it increases the firm's accounts receivable balance.

Accounts receivable typically comprises more than 25 percent of a firm's assets. Because cash flows from a sale cannot be invested until the account is collected, control of receivables

Table 3	Features of Selected Money Market Instruments					
Instruments	**Denominations**	**Maturities**	**Basis**	**Liquidity**	**Taxability**
U.S. Treasury bills—direct obligations of the U.S. government	$1,000 and increments of $1,000	28 days, 91 days, and 182 days	Discount	Excellent secondary market	Exempt from state and local income taxes
Federal agency securities—obligations of corporations and agencies created to effect the federal government's lending programs	Wide variation; from $1,000 to $1 million	5 days to more than 10 years	Discount or coupon; usually on coupon	Good for issues of "largest federal" agencies	Generally exempt at local level
Bankers' acceptances—drafts accepted for future payment by commercial banks	No set size; typically range from $25,000 to $1 million	Predominantly from 30 to 180 days	Discount	Good for acceptances of large "money market" banks	Taxed at all levels of government
Negotiable certificates of deposit—marketable receipts for funds deposited in a bank for a fixed time period	$25,000 to $10 million	1 to 18 months	Accrued interest	Fair to good	Taxed at all levels of government
Commercial paper—short-term unsecured promissory notes	$5,000 to $5 million; $1,000 and $5,000 multiples above the initial offering size are sometimes available	3 to 270 days	Discount	Poor; no active secondary market in usual sense	Taxed at all levels of government
Repurchase agreements—legal contracts between a borrower (security seller) and lender (security buyer). The borrower will repurchase at the contract price plus an interest charge	Typical sizes are $500,000 or more	According to terms of contract	Not applicable	Fixed by the agreement; that is, borrower will repurchase	Taxed at all levels of government
Money market mutual funds—holders of diversified portfolios of short-term, high-grade debt instruments	Some require an initial investment as small as $1,000	Shares can be sold at any time	Net asset value	Good; provided by the fund itself	Taxed at all levels of government

takes on added importance; thus efficient collection policies and procedures improve firm profitability and liquidity.

Determinants of the Size of a Firm's Investment in Accounts Receivable

The size of the investment in accounts receivable is determined by several factors. The first is the level of credit sales as a percentage of total sales. The nature of the business tends to determine the blend between credit sales and cash sales. A large grocery store tends to sell exclusively on a cash basis, whereas most construction-lumber supply firms make their sales primarily with credit. Second, the level of sales is also a factor in determining the size of the investment in accounts receivable. Very simply, the more sales, the greater accounts receivable. The third determinant of the level of investment in accounts receivable is credit and collection policies—more specifically, the terms of sale, which include the time allowed until payment is due and any discount for early payment, the quality of the customer who is to receive credit (i.e., the likelihood that he or she will pay you in a timely fashion), and the collection efforts put forth by the firm to collect its delinquent accounts. These factors are summarized in Figure 4.

Terms of Sale

The **terms of sale** identify the possible discount for early payment, the discount period, and the total credit period. They are generally stated in the form "*a/b*, net *c*," indicating that the customer can deduct *a* percent if the account is paid within *b* days; otherwise, the account must be paid within *c* days. Thus, using the example discussed earlier, trade credit terms of 2/10, net 30, indicate that a 2 percent discount can be taken if the account is paid within 10 days; otherwise it must be paid within 30 days. Failure to take the discount represents a cost to the customer. As shown earlier in our discussion of credit term and cash discounts, if the terms are 2/10, net 30, the annualized opportunity cost of passing up this 2 percent discount in order to withhold payment for an additional 20 days is 37.24 percent. This is determined as follows:

$$\text{Annualized Opportunity Cost of Forgoing the Discount} = \frac{a}{1-a} \times \frac{365}{c-b} \tag{9}$$

Figure 4

Determinants of Investment in Accounts Receivable

A firm's accounts receivable balance arises out of its sales on credit. Therefore, the level of accounts receivable the firm has outstanding at any point in time depends on the level of sales, terms of sale offered to customers (i.e., how long they have to repay the firm), the quality of the customers to whom credit is offered (i.e., the likelihood they will repay in a timely manner), and the amount of effort the firm puts into collecting past-due accounts.

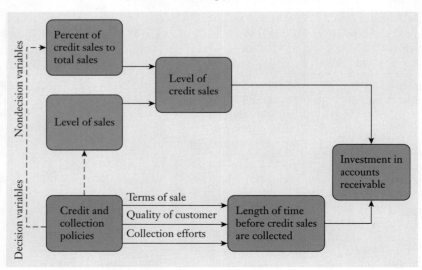

>> END FIGURE 4

As before, substituting the values from the example, we get

$$\frac{.02}{1 - .02} \times \frac{365}{30 - 10} = 37.24\%$$

Typical pre-payment discounts range from .5 percent to 10 percent, and the discount period is typically 10 days, where the total credit period is 30 to 90 days. Although the terms of credit vary radically from industry to industry, they tend to remain relatively uniform within a given industry.

Customer Quality

A second decision variable involves determining the type of customer who qualifies for trade credit. By type we are referring to the quality of the customer's credit history and the likelihood of prompt and timely repayment. Several costs are associated with extending credit to less creditworthy customers. First, as the probability of default increases, it becomes more important that the firm be able to identify which of the possible new customers is high risk. When more time is spent investigating the less creditworthy customer, the costs of credit investigation increase.

Second, default costs also vary directly with the quality of the customer. As the customer's credit rating declines, the chance that the account will not be paid on time, or at all, increases. Thus, taking on less creditworthy customers results in increases in default costs.

Third, collection costs also increase as the quality of the customer declines. More delinquent accounts force the firm to spend more time and money collecting them. Overall, the decline in customer quality results in increased costs of credit investigation, collection, and default.

In determining whether to grant credit to an individual customer, we are primarily interested in the customer's short-run financial well-being. Thus, liquidity ratios, other obligations, and the overall profitability of the customer become the focal point in this analysis. Credit-rating services, such as Dun & Bradstreet, provide information on the financial status, operations, and payment history for most firms. Other possible sources of information would include credit bureaus, trade associations, chambers of commerce, competitors, bank references, public financial statements, and, of course, the firm's past relationship with the customer.

One way in which both individuals and firms are often evaluated as credit risks is through the use of **credit scoring**, the numerical evaluation of each applicant based on the applicant's current debts and history of making payments on a timely basis. This score is then evaluated according to a predetermined standard to determine whether credit should be extended. Credit scoring is efficient and relatively inexpensive for the lender. Its benefit to the borrower is that it reduces the lender's uncertainty; therefore the lender is more often able to make credit available to good-risk customers at lower interest rates.

Collection Efforts

The final credit policy variable we consider relates to collection policies. The key to maintaining control over the collection of accounts receivable is the fact that the probability of default increases with the age of the account. Thus, control of accounts receivable focuses on the control and elimination of past-due receivables. One common way of evaluating the current situation is through ratio analysis. The financial manager can determine whether or not accounts receivable are under control by examining the average collection period, the ratio of receivables to assets, the accounts receivable turnover ratio (the ratio of credit sales to receivables), and the amount of bad debts relative to sales over time. In addition, the manager can perform what is called an *aging of accounts receivable* to provide a breakdown in both dollars and in percentages of the proportion of receivables that are past due. Comparing the current aging of receivables with past data offers even more control. An example of an aging account or schedule appears in Table 5.

The aging schedule provides a listing of how long accounts receivable have been outstanding. Once the delinquent accounts have been identified, the firm's accounts receivable group makes an effort to collect them. For example, a past-due letter, called a dunning letter, is sent if payment is not received on time, followed by an additional dunning letter in a more serious tone if the account becomes three weeks past due, followed after six weeks by a telephone call. Finally, if the account becomes 12 weeks past due, it might be turned over to a collection agency. Again, a direct tradeoff exists between collection expenses and lost goodwill on one hand, and no collection of accounts on the other; this tradeoff is always part of making the decision about when to pressure late-paying accounts.

The Business of Life

Credit Scoring

Your credit score has an enormous effect on your financial life, influencing everything from the rate you pay on your credit cards and the size of your credit line to your insurance rates, your mortgage rate, and the amount of junk mail you receive asking you to take on one more credit card. In short, when it comes to lending money, you'll be evaluated by your credit score. With a strong credit score you'll also be paying a much lower interest rate on any money that you borrow.

Once your credit information has been assembled, it is translated into a three-digit number—your credit score—which measures your creditworthiness.

Figure 5 provides the distribution of the percent of the population with different FICO scores.[3]

What's a good credit score? The national MEDIAN is 723, but the cutoff to get the best rate requires a score of 760 or higher. A score of around 620 is often a cutoff point for receiving credit at any rate. In effect, a good credit score doesn't just mean that you'll get a loan; it also means that you'll be paying less for it. For example, a person with a 760 score will be offered an interest rate of about 9.75 percent less on a loan than a person with a 550 score. Table 4 gives representative rates for different FICO

Table 4	Representative Rates and Monthly Payments for Different FICO Scores on a $25,000, Three-Year Auto Loan in Mid-2009	
FICO Score	**Interest Rate**	**Monthly Payment**
760–850	6.000%	$761
700–759	7.150%	$774
660–699	9.000%	$795
620–659	11.534%	$825
580–619	15.275%	$870
500–579	15.761%	$876

scores along with what the monthly interest payments would be on a $25,000, three-year auto loan.

Now let's look at the five factors that determine your credit score, with Figure 6 illustrating this breakdown.

1. **Your payment history (35 percent of your score).** Because a lender is considering extending credit to you, it only makes sense that the lender wants to know how you've handled your credit payments in the past.

2. **The amount you owe and your available credit (30 percent of your score).** The amounts you owe on your credit cards, your mortgage, your car loans, and any other outstanding debt, along with whether you are close to or at your credit limit, are also factored in.

3. **Length of credit history (15 percent of your score).** The longer your credit accounts have been open and the longer you have had accounts with the same creditors, the higher your credit score will be.

[3]http://www.FICO.com.

Figure 5

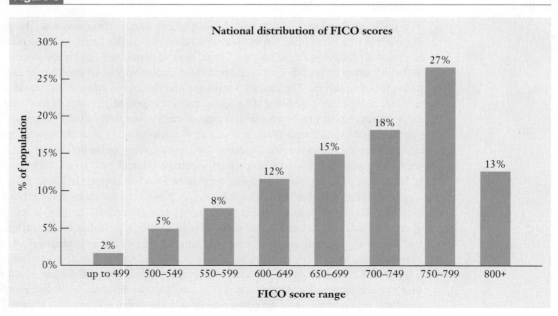

National distribution of FICO scores

FICO score range

>> **END FIGURE 5**

Figure 6

Factors That Determine Your Credit Score

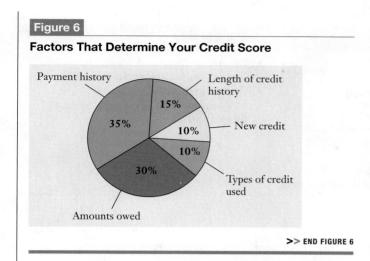

>> END FIGURE 6

5. **New credit (10 percent of your score).** Applying for lots of new credit is generally a bad sign. This is because individuals who are moving toward bankruptcy generally take one last grasp at credit, hoping it will keep them afloat. This will lower your score.

It's important to monitor your credit score. First, you must ensure that there are no errors in your credit report, because that's what is used to calculate your credit score. To do this you'll need to get a copy of it annually. Some experts recommend getting a copy of your credit report every few months to monitor for identity theft. The Fair and Accurate Credit Transactions Act (FACT Act) allows you to request one free copy of your credit report each year from the three major credit bureaus: Experian, Equifax, and Trans Union. If you'd like more information on how to request your report, log on to www.annualcreditreport.com. Take care to ensure that you reach the FACT Act–supported site, as imposter websites are on the rise. Once you have your credit report, you should make sure that the information in it is correct. Look at all the credit accounts listed and make sure both that they are yours and that they are correct.

4. **Types of credit used (10 percent of your score).** If you have several different types of credit outstanding (for example, credit cards, retail accounts, installment loans, auto loans, and a mortgage loan), that is taken as an indicator that you know how to handle your money.

Your Turn: See Study Questions 9 and 13.

Table 5	Aging Accounts Receivable	
Age of Accounts Receivable (Days)	**Dollar Value (00)**	**Percent of Total**
0–30	$2,340	39%
31–60	1,500	25
61–90	1,020	17
91–120	720	12
Over 120	420	7
Total	$6,000	100%

Managing Inventories

Inventory management involves the control of the assets that are produced to be sold in the normal course of the firm's operations. The general categories of inventory include raw-materials inventory, work-in-process inventory, and finished-goods inventory. How much inventory firms carry depends upon the target level of sales and the importance of the inventory. For a typical firm, inventories comprise approximately 5 percent of all assets, but this percentage varies from industry to industry.

Tools of Financial Analysis

Name of Tool	Formula	What It Tells You
Cost of Fore-going a Cash Discount	$$\frac{a}{1-a} \times \frac{365}{c-b}$$ • a = cash discount percent • b = number of days before the cash discount is lost • c = number of days until the full payment must be made • Cash discount terms are typically stated as follows: a/b, net c which means that the buyer gets a cash discount of a if they pay within b days, otherwise the entire invoice is due in c days.	• The cost to the firm of passing up a cash discount for paying within b days • The higher this cost, the greater is the firm's incentive to pay within the cash discount period.

Before you begin end-of-chapter material

Concept Check | 5

1. Describe the relationship between the firm's cash management program and the firm's risk of not being able to pay its bills on time.
2. What are the fundamental decisions that the financial manager must make with respect to cash management?

P Principle 2: **There Is a Risk–Return Tradeoff** An important source of risk to any business relates to the likelihood that the firm will have sufficient cash to pay its bills as they come due. This is known as the risk of illiquidity. However, this risk is largely manageable by the firm's management by monitoring the firm's reserves of cash and other current assets that can easily by converted into cash in comparison to the firm's current liabilities.

Chapter Summaries

Describe the risk–return tradeoff involved in managing a firm's working capital.

SUMMARY: Working capital management involves managing the firm's liquidity, which in turn involves managing (1) the firm's current assets and (2) its current liabilities. Each of these problems involves risk–return tradeoffs. For example, investing in current assets reduces the firm's risk of illiquidity at the expense of lowering its overall rate of return on its investment in assets. Furthermore, reducing the use of short-term sources of financing by using more long-term sources enhances the firm's liquidity but reduces the firm's profitability.

Concept Check | **1**

1. How does investing more heavily in current assets, other things remaining the same, increase firm liquidity?

2. How does the use of short-term as opposed to long-term liabilities affect firm liquidity?

Explain the principle of self-liquidating debt as a tool for managing firm liquidity.

SUMMARY: Self-liquidating debt is a useful principle for guiding the firm's liquidity management decisions. Basically, this principle involves matching the cash flow–generating characteristics of an asset with the maturity of the source of financing used to acquire it. Thus, temporary needs for inventories that will be sold down within a month or two should be financed using very short-term sources of financing that will be repaid when the need for the inventory has passed.

KEY TERMS

Permanent investments Investments in assets that the firm expects to hold for a period longer than one year. These include the firm's minimum level of current assets, such as accounts receivable and inventories, as well as fixed assets.

Permanent sources of financing A source of financing that is expected to be used by the firm for an extended period of time, such as an intermediate-term loan, bonds, or common equity.

Principle of self-liquidating debt A guiding rule of thumb for managing firm liquidity that calls for financing permanent investments in assets with permanent sources of financing, and temporary investments with temporary sources of financing.

Spontaneous sources of financing Financing sources that arise naturally out of the course of doing business and that do not call for an explicit financing decision each time the firm uses them.

Temporary investments in assets Current assets that will be liquidated and not replaced within the current year, including cash and marketable securities, accounts receivable, and seasonal fluctuations in inventories. Also referred to simply as **temporary assets**.

Temporary sources of financing Typically these consist of current liabilities the firm incurs on a discretionary basis. Examples include unsecured bank loans and commercial paper (which is simply unsecured promissory notes with maturities of 1 to 270 days that firms sell in the money market), as well as short-term loans that are secured by the firm's inventories or accounts receivable.

Trade credit A type of account payable that arises when one firm provides goods or services to a customer with an agreement to bill the customer later.

Concept Check | **2**

1. What is the principle of self-liquidating debt, and how can it be used to help the firm manage its liquidity?

2. What are some examples of permanent and temporary investments in current assets?

3. What makes trade credit a source of spontaneous financing?

Use the cash conversion cycle to measure the efficiency with which a firm manages its working capital.

SUMMARY: A key measure of the efficiency with which a firm manages its working capital is the speed with which it cycles cash into inventory, inventory into accounts receivable, and accounts receivable back into cash. This cycle is called the firm's operating cycle. The shorter this cycle time, the less money the firm will have invested in inventories and accounts receivable.

The cash conversion cycle is similar to the operating cycle but nets out of the sum total of the operating cycle the number of days the firm has to pay its accounts payable. For example, if the firm's operating cycle is 100 days but the firm has 60 days to pay for its items of inventory, then the firm has to finance only 40 days' worth of inventory and accounts receivable, not the entire 100 days' worth.

KEY TERMS

Accounts payable deferral period The average period of time the firm uses to repay its trade creditors.

Cash conversion cycle The operating cycle (average collection period plus the inventory conversion period or days of sales in inventories) less the accounts payable deferral period.

Inventory conversion period The number of days a firm uses to convert its inventory into cash or accounts receivable following a sale.

Operating cycle The period of time (usually measured in days) that elapses from the time the firm acquires an item of inventory until that item has been sold and cash has been collected.

KEY EQUATIONS

Operating Cycle = Inventory Conversion Period + Average Collection Period (1)

Cash Conversion Cycle = Operating Cycle − Accounts Payable Deferral Period (3)

Concept Check | 3

1. What is a firm's operating cycle?
2. What is the firm's cash conversion cycle, and how does it differ from the operating cycle?

Evaluate the cost of financing as a key determinant of the management of a firm's use of current liabilities.

SUMMARY: The key consideration in selecting a source of short-term financing is the annualized cost of credit. We use the following formula to solve for the annual percentage rate (APR) when the interest amount, the principal sum, and the time period for financing are known.

$$\text{Annual Percentage Rate }(APR) = \frac{\text{Interest}}{\text{Principal}} \times \frac{1}{\text{Time}} \quad (8)$$

KEY TERMS

Bank transaction loan An unsecured short-term bank credit made for a specific purpose.

Commercial paper A money market security with a maturity of 1 to 270 days, issued (sold) by large banks and corporations, and that is backed by the issuing firm's promise to pay the face amount on the maturity date specified on the note.

Factor A financial institution that purchases accounts receivable from firms.

Line of credit An informal agreement or understanding between the borrower and the bank about the maximum amount of credit that the bank will provide the borrower at any one time.

Secured current liabilities Loans that involve the pledge of specific assets as collateral in the event the borrower defaults in payment of principal or interest.

Unsecured current liabilities Debts of the company that are due and payable within a period of one year and that are secured only by the promise of the firm to repay the debt.

Concept Check | 4

1. Give some examples of unsecured and secured forms of current liabilities.
2. What does a factor do?
3. What is a bank line of credit?
4. What is the APR equation, and how is it used?

Understand the factors underlying a firm's investment in cash and marketable securities, accounts receivable, and inventory.

SUMMARY: The size of a firm's investment in accounts receivable depends on three factors: the percentage of credit sales to total sales, the level of sales, and the credit and collection policies of the firm. The financial manager, however, generally only has control over the terms of the sale, the quality of the customer, and the collection efforts.

Concept Check | 5

1. Describe the relationship between the firm's cash management program and the firm's risk of not being able to pay its bills on time.

2. What are the fundamental decisions that the financial manager must make with respect to cash management?

KEY TERMS

Credit scoring A numerical evaluation of the creditworthiness of an individual borrower based on the borrower's current debts and history of making payments in a timely basis.

Float The amount of the difference between the cash balance shown on a firm's books and the available balance at the firm's bank.

Inventory management The control of the firm's store of assets that are to be sold in the normal course of the firm's operations. The general categories of inventory include raw-materials inventory, work-in-process inventory, and finished-goods inventory.

Money market securities Short-term, low-risk debt instruments that can be sold easily and with very low risk of loss.

Terms of sale The time period until payment must be made, any discount for early payment, the quality of customer who is to receive credit, and the collection efforts put forth by the firm to collect its delinquent accounts.

KEY EQUATION

$$\text{Annualized Opportunity Cost of Forgoing the Discount} = \frac{a}{1-a} \times \frac{365}{c-b} \qquad (9)$$

Study Questions

1. In the chapter introduction we noted that Dell Computers (DELL) is an industry leader in its working capital management practices. Describe how the firm came to have this reputation.

2. **(Related to Regardless of Your Major: Conflicting Objectives Lead to Problems in Managing a Firm's Working Capital)** In the *Regardless of Your Major* feature box we learned that the objectives of a firm's sales force and the goal of maximizing shareholder wealth are not always in sync when it comes to managing the firm's working capital. Describe why the sales force might want to have lax credit terms and how this impacts the firm's investment in working capital.

3. Why is the current ratio used to measure a firm's liquidity?

4. What is the firm's net working capital, and how is it related to the current ratio and a firm's overall liquidity?

5. What is the risk–return tradeoff that arises when a firm manages its working capital?

6. How does a firm's use of short-term debt as opposed to long-term debt subject the firm to a greater risk of illiquidity?

7. What is the principle of self-liquidating debt, and how can it be used to manage a firm's working capital?

8. Define the following terms:
   a. Permanent asset investments
   b. Temporary asset investments
   c. Permanent sources of financing
   d. Temporary sources of financing
   e. Spontaneous sources of financing

9. **(Related to The Business of Life: Credit Scoring)** The boxed feature *The Business of Life: Credit Scoring* describes the credit scoring system used to determine whether credit will be extended. What is a good credit score?

10. How can the basic interest expense formula "interest = principle × rate × time" be used to estimate the annualized cost of short-term credit?

11. Describe verbally the meaning of the following trade credit terms: "2/10, net 30"; "4/20, net 60"; and "3/15, net 45."

12. What factors determine the size of the investment a firm makes in accounts receivable? Which of these factors are under the control of the financial manager?

13. **(Related to The Business of Life: Credit Scoring)** In *The Business of Life: Credit Scoring* boxed feature we learned about the determinants of your credit score. Describe the five components of a credit score and the relative weight or importance of each.

Study Problems

MyFinanceLab

Go to www.myfinancelab.com
to complete these exercises online
and get instant feedback.

Working Capital Management and the Risk–Return Tradeoff

1. **(Related to Checkpoint 1) (Measuring firm liquidity)** The following table contains current asset and current liability balances for Deere and Company (DE):

($ thousands)	2008	2007	2006
Current assets			
Cash and cash equivalents	2,211,400	2,278,600	1,687,500
Short-term investments	0	1,623,300	0
Net receivables	3,944,200	3,680,900	3,508,100
Inventory	3,041,800	2,337,300	1,957,300
Total current assets	**9,197,400**	**9,920,100**	**7,152,900**
Current liabilities			
Accounts payable	6,562,800	3,186,100	4,666,300
Short-term/current long-term debt	8,520,500	9,969,400	8,121,200
Other current liabilities	0	2,766,000	0
Total current liabilities	**15,083,300**	**15,921,500**	**12,787,500**

   a. Measure the liquidity of Deere & Co. for each year using the company's net working capital and current ratio.
   b. Is the trend in Deere's liquidity improving over this period? Why or why not?

2. **(Related to Checkpoint 1) (Measuring firm liquidity)** The following table contains current asset and current liability balances for Microsoft Corporation (MSFT):

	2008	2007	2006
Cash and cash equivalents	10,339,000	6,111,000	6,714,000
Short-term investments	13,323,000	17,300,000	27,447,000
Net receivables	15,606,000	13,237,000	11,256,000
Inventory	985,000	1,127,000	1,478,000
Other current assets	2,989,000	2,393,000	2,115,000
Total current assets	**43,242,000**	**40,168,000**	**49,010,000**
Accounts payable	12,830,000	6,612,000	9,521,000
Short-tem/current long-term debt	0	2,741,000	0
Other current liabilities	17,056,000	14,401,000	12,921,000
Total current liabilities	**29,886,000**	**23,754,000**	**22,442,000**

   a. Assume that you are the lead banker for the syndicate of banks that manages Microsoft Corporation's line of credit. Your boss has asked that you report to him on the current state of Microsoft's liquidity. How would you describe the liquidity of Microsoft in 2008?
   b. Have there been recent changes in Microsoft's liquidity? If so, have the changes been to improve the firm's liquidity? Explain your observations.

Working Capital Policy

3. **(Identifying permanent and temporary asset investments)** Classify each of the investments in assets as either permanent or temporary (explain):
   a. A seasonal increase in a card shop's inventory of Valentine cards.
   b. The acquisition of a new forklift truck that is expected to have a useful life of five years.
   c. An increase in accounts receivable resulting from an expansion in the firm's customer base.

4. **(Identifying spontaneous, temporary, and permanent sources of financing)** Classify each of the following sources of new financing as spontaneous, temporary, or permanent (explain):

a. A manufacturing firm enters into a loan agreement with its bank that calls for annual principal and interest payments spread over the next four years.

b. A retail firm orders new items of inventory that are charged to the firm's trade credit.

c. A trucking firm issues common stock to the public and uses the proceeds to upgrade its tractor fleet.

Operating and Cash Conversion Cycle

5. **(Related to Checkpoint 2) (Calculating the cash conversion cycle)** Network Solutions just introduced a new, fully automated manufacturing plant that produces 2,000 wireless routers per day with materials costs of $50 per router and no other costs. The average number of days a router is held in inventory before being sold is 45 days. In addition, the company generally pays its suppliers in 30 days, while collecting from its customers after 25 days.

a. What is the cash conversion cycle?

b. What would happen to the cash conversion cycle if the company could stretch its payments to suppliers from 30 days to 50 days?

c. How much would working capital financing be reduced if the company stretched its payments to suppliers from 30 days to 50 days?

6. **(Related to Checkpoint 2) (Calculating the operating and cash conversion cycle)** Carraway Seed Company Inc. has for many years cultivated and sold what are known as heritage plants and seeds. For example, the company has sought out older varieties of tomato plants that are no longer grown by commercial vegetable farmers because they either take too long to mature, do not ship well, or do not hold up for long on the store shelf. The company has recently been considering ways to reduce its investment in working capital in order to make itself more profitable. At present the firm has an inventory conversion period of 90 days and offers credit terms of 30 days that the majority of its customers take full advantage of. The company purchases its inventory items on credit terms that allow it 45 days to pay but has always followed a policy of making cash payments for invoices as soon as they are received, so the accounts payable deferral period is typically only five days.

a. What are Carraway's operating and cash conversion cycles?

b. If Carraway were to decide to take full advantage of its credit terms and delay payment until the last possible date, how would this impact its cash conversion cycle?

c. What would be your recommendation to the company with regard to its working capital management practices and why?

Managing Current Liabilities

7. **(Related to Checkpoint 3) (Estimating the cost of bank credit)** Paymaster Enterprises has arranged to finance its seasonal working-capital needs with a short-term bank loan. The loan will carry a rate of 12 percent per annum with interest paid in advance (discounted). In addition, Paymaster must maintain a minimum demand deposit with the bank of 10 percent of the loan balance throughout the term of the loan. If Paymaster plans to borrow $100,000 for a period of three months, what is the annualized cost of the bank loan?

8. **(Related to Checkpoint 3) (Calculating the cost of trade credit)** Calculate the annualized cost of the following trade credit terms, when payment is made on the net due date (assume a 360-day year).

a. 2/10, net 30

b. 3/15, net 30

c. 3/15, net 45

d. 2/15, net 60

9. **(Related to Checkpoint 3) (Calculating the cost of short-term financing)** The R. Morin Construction Company needs to borrow $100,000 to help finance the cost of a new $150,000 hydraulic crane used in the firm's commercial construction business. The crane will pay for itself in one year, and the firm is considering the following alternatives for financing its purchase:

Alternative A—The firm's bank has agreed to lend the $100,000 at a rate of 14 percent. Interest would be discounted, and a 15 percent compensating balance would be required. However, the compensating-balance requirement would not be binding on R. Morin because the firm normally maintains a minimum demand deposit (checking account) balance of $25,000 in the bank.

Alternative B—The equipment dealer has agreed to finance the equipment with a one-year loan. The $100,000 loan would require payment of principal and interest totaling $116,300.

  a. Which alternative should R. Morin select?

  b. If the bank's compensating-balance requirement were to necessitate idle demand deposits equal to 15 percent of the loan, what effect would this have on the cost of the bank loan alternative?

10. **(Related to Checkpoint 3) (Calculating the cost of a short-term bank loan)** On July 1, 2012, the Southwest Forging Corporation arranged for a line of credit with the First National Bank (FNB) of Dallas. The terms of the agreement call for a $100,000 maximum loan with interest set at 1 percent over prime. In addition, the firm has to maintain a 20 percent compensating balance in its demand deposit account throughout the year. The prime rate is currently 4 percent (assume a 360-day year).

  a. If Southwest normally maintains a $20,000 to $30,000 balance in its checking account with FNB of Dallas, what is the annualized cost of credit through the line-of-credit agreement when the maximum loan amount is used for a full year?

  b. Recompute the annualized cost of trade to Southwest if the firm borrows the compensating balance and it borrows the maximum possible under the loan agreement. Again, assume the full amount of the loan is outstanding for a whole year.

11. **(Related to Checkpoint 3) (Calculating the cost of short-term financing)** You plan to borrow $20,000 from the bank to pay for inventories for a gift shop you have just opened. The bank offers to lend you the money at 10 percent annual interest for the six months the funds will be needed (assume a 360-day year).

  a. Calculate the annualized rate of interest on the loan.

  b. In addition, the bank requires you to maintain a 15 percent compensating balance in the bank. Because you are just opening your business, you do not have a demand deposit account at the bank that can be used to meet the compensating-balance requirement. This means that you will have to put 15 percent of the loan amount from your own personal money (which you had planned to use to help finance the business) in a checking account. What is the cost of the loan now?

  c. In addition to the compensating-balance requirement in part b, you are told that interest will be discounted. What is the annualized rate of interest on the loan now?

12. **(Related to Checkpoint 3) (Calculating the cost of a short-term bank loan)** Jimmy Hale is the owner and operator of the grain elevator in Brownfield, Texas, where he has lived for most of his 62 years. The rains during the spring have been the best in a decade and Mr. Hale is expecting a bumper wheat crop. This prompted Mr. Hale to rethink his current financing sources. He now believes he will need an additional $240,000 for the three-month period ending with the close of the harvest season. After meeting with his banker, Mr. Hale is puzzling over what the additional financing will actually cost. The banker quoted him a rate of 1 percent over prime (which is currently 7 percent) and also requested that the firm increase its current bank balance of $4,000 up to 20 percent of the loan.

  a. If interest and principal are all repaid at the end of the three-month loan term, what is the annual percentage rate on the loan offer made by Mr. Hale's bank?

  b. If the bank were to offer to lower the rate to prime if interest is discounted, should Mr. Hale accept this alternative?

13. **(Related to Checkpoint 3) (Evaluating trade credit discounts)** If a firm buys on trade credit terms of 2/10, net 50 and decides to forgo the trade credit discount and pay on the net day, what is the annualized cost of forgoing the discount (assume a 360-day year)?

14. **(Related to Checkpoint 3) (Evaluating trade credit discounts)** Determine the annualized cost of forgoing the trade credit discount on the following terms (assume a 360-day year):

   a. 1/10, net 20
   b. 2/10, net 30
   c. 3/10, net 30
   d. 3/10, net 60
   e. 3/10, net 90
   f. 5/10, net 60

Mini-Case

Your first major assignment after your recent promotion at Ice Nine involves overseeing the management of accounts receivable and inventory. The first item that you must attend to involves a proposed change in credit policy that would involve relaxing credit terms from the existing terms of 1/50, net 70 to 2/60, net 90 in hopes of securing new sales. The management at Ice Nine does not expect bad debt losses on its current customers to change under the new credit policy. The following information should aid you in the analysis of this problem:

New sales level (all credit)	$8,000,000
Original sales level (all credit)	$7,000,000
Contribution margin	25%
Percent bad debt losses on new sales	8%
New average collection period	75 days
Original average collection period	60 days
Additional investment in inventory	$50,000
Pre-tax required rate of return	15%
New percent cash discount	2%
Percent of customers taking the new cash discount	50%
Original percent cash discount	1%
Percent of customers taking the old cash discount	50%

To help in your decision on relaxing credit terms, you have been asked to respond to the following questions:

a. What determines the size of investment Ice Nine makes in accounts receivable?

b. If a firm currently buys from Ice Nine on trade credit with the present terms of 1/50, net 70 and decides to forgo the trade credit discount and pay on the net day, what is the annualized cost to that firm of forgoing the discount?

c. If Ice Nine changes its trade credit terms to 2/60, net 90, what is the annualized cost to a firm that buys on credit from Ice Nine and decides to forgo the trade credit discount and pay on the net day?

d. What is the estimated change in profits resulting from the increased sales less any additional bad debts associated with the proposed change in credit policy?

e. Estimate the cost of additional investment in accounts receivable and inventory associated with this change in credit policy.

f. Estimate the change in the cost of the cash discount if the proposed change in credit policy is enacted.

g. Compare the incremental revenues with the incremental costs. Should the proposed change be enacted?

Photo Credits

Credits are listed in order of appearance.

Yuri Arcurs/Fotolia; Vladru/Shutterstock

International Business Finance

From Chapter 19 of *Financial Management: Principles and Applications*, Twelfth Edition. Sheridan Titman, Arthur J. Keown, and John D. Martin.

International Business Finance

Chapter **Outline**

1 Foreign Exchange Markets and Currency Exchange Rates

→ **Objective 1.** Understand the nature and importance of the foreign exchange market and learn to read currency exchange rate quotes.

2 Interest Rate and Purchasing-Power Parity

→ **Objective 2.** Describe interest rate and purchasing-power parity.

3 Capital Budgeting for Direct Foreign Investment

→ **Objective 3.** Discuss the risks that are unique to the capital budgeting analysis of direct foreign investments.

When reading this chapter, you should keep in mind two of the basic principles of finance: **P** Principle 2: **There Is a Risk–Return Tradeoff**, and **P** Principle 3: **Cash Flows Are the Source of Value**. As you will see, although there may be higher expected rates of return with many foreign investments, many of them also come with increased risk. In addition, when we evaluate international investment projects we will look to the cash flows that are returned to the parent company as the source of value. Look for them as you work through the different discussions.

Investing Internationally: The Case of McDonald's Corporation (MCD)

It is generally easier for firms to expand the market for their products rather than to develop new products, which is why large companies tend to look for new markets from around the world. That's certainly been the direction that McDonald's has taken in recent years. Today, McDonald's operates more than 34,000 restaurants in over 119 countries. The busiest McDonald's restaurant in the world is not in America but thousands of miles away in Pushkin Square in Moscow, Russia. The store serves 40,000 customers a day, even more than it did on its opening day, January 31, 1990. The menu is essentially the same as in the United States, with the addition of cabbage pie among other traditional Russian food items.

Was this an expensive venture? It certainly was. In fact, the food plants that McDonald's built to supply burgers, fries, and everything else sold there cost more than $60 million. In addition to the costs, there are a number of other factors that make opening an outlet outside of the United States both different and challenging. First, in order to keep the quality consistent with what is served at any McDonald's anywhere in the world, McDonald's spent six years putting together a supply chain that would provide the necessary raw materials that McDonald's demands. On top of that, McDonald's faces risks associated with the Russian economy and its currency that are well beyond the scope of the risk exposures of its restaurants in the United States.

These risks all materialized in 1998 when the Russian economy, along with its currency, the ruble, tanked. In the summer of 1998 the Russian economy spun out of control, and in August the entire banking system failed, resulting in a catastrophic decline in the value of the ruble. Because McDonald's sells its Russian burgers for rubles, when it came time to trade the rubles for U.S. dollars, McDonald's Russian outlets were not worth nearly as much as they were the year before.

Despite the disruptions associated with the 1998 crisis, the Moscow McDonald's has been enormously successful. Moreover, by 2013 there were 330 McDonald's restaurants in 85 Russian cities; these outlets serve more than 950,000 Russian customers every day. It all goes to show that not all new investment opportunities require new products—introducing existing products to new international markets can be equally or even more profitable.

In this chapter we focus on the particular financial challenges faced by an international business. A large part of our discussion will focus on the risks associated with doing business in multiple currencies, along with effective strategies for reducing foreign exchange risk. We'll also cover working capital management and capital structure decisions in the international context.

Regardless of Your Major...

"Working in a Flat World"

The world has become an increasingly international place in which to live and work. Thomas Friedman expounds on this theme in his book *The World Is Flat,* which looks closely at how global boundaries have collapsed, flattening the playing field for all firms worldwide. It no longer matters whether you major in accounting, engineering, economics, marketing, management, or finance, you will be competing with individuals with the same training from around the world. As Thomas Friedman explains in his book, the convergence of technology and events has allowed India, China, and many other countries to become part of the global supply chain for services and manufacturing. Let there be no doubt: there is no going back—not in terms of business or your personal life. The playing field you'll be on for the rest of your life will be an international one.

Your Turn: See Study Question 2.

1 Foreign Exchange Markets and Currency Exchange Rates

The **foreign exchange (FX) market** is by far the world's largest financial market, with daily trading volumes of more than $4 trillion. Trading in this market is dominated by a few key currencies, including the U.S. dollar, the British pound sterling, the Japanese yen, and the euro. The FX market is an over-the-counter market with participants (buyers and sellers) located in major commercial and investment banks around the world. Figure 1 lists the top 10 currencies traded in the FX market and their share of total trading volume.

Some of the major participants in foreign exchange trading include the following:

- **Importers and exporters of goods and services.** For example, when a U.S. importer purchases goods from a Japanese manufacturer and pays using Japanese yen, the importer will need to convert dollars to yen in the FX market. Similarly, if an exporter is paid in a foreign firm's domestic currency, it will enter the FX market to convert the payment to its home currency.

- **Investors and portfolio managers who purchase foreign stocks and bonds.** Investors who acquire the shares of foreign companies that are traded on a foreign exchange need foreign currency to complete the transaction.

- **Currency traders who make a market in one or more foreign currencies.** Currency traders buy and sell different currencies, hoping to make money from their trades. Panel B of Figure 1 lists the top traders in foreign currency in the FX market.

Foreign Exchange Rates

An **exchange rate** is simply the price of one currency stated in terms of another. For example, if the exchange rate of U.S. dollars for British pound was 2 to 1, this means that it would take $2.00 to purchase one pound.

Reading Exchange Rate Quotes

Table 1 shows exchange rates, which are available online from reuters.com, money.cnn.com, finance.yahoo.com, bloomberg.com, fxstreet, imf.org, ex.com, wsj.com, and The Financial Times Online, for December 26, 2012. The Financial Times Online even provides a Currencies Macromap that displays a map of the world with a color-coded view of the performance of the different world currencies relative to a currency of your choice. The center

Figure 1

The Market for Foreign Exchange

Most Traded Currencies

Currency	% Daily Share of Total Volume	Rank
United States dollar (USD $)	84.9%	1
Euro EUR (EUR €)	39.1%	2
Japanese yen (JPY ¥)	19.0%	3
Pound sterling (GBP £)	12.9%	4
Swiss franc (CHF Fr)	6.4%	5
Australian dollar (AUD $)	7.6%	6
Canadian dollar (CAD $)	5.3%	7
Hong Kong dollar (HKD $)	2.4%	8
Swedish krona (SEK kr)	2.2%	9–10
Norwegian krone (NOK kr)	2.2%	9–10
New Zealand dollar (NZD $)	1.6%	11
Mexican peso (MXN $)	1.3%	12
Other	18.6%	
Total[a]	200.0%	

[a]The total is 200% because trading volume includes one trade for buying and one for selling on each transaction, such that volume is double counted.

Source: *Triennial Central Bank Survey* (December 2011), Bank for International Settlements.

>> END FIGURE 1

column gives the number of dollars it takes to purchase one unit of foreign currency. Because the exchange rate is expressed in U.S. dollars, it is referred to as a **direct quote**. Given the figures in Table 1, we can see that it took $1.6133 to buy 1 British pound (£1), $1.0917 to buy 1 Swiss franc, and $1.3183 to buy 1 euro. Conversely, an **indirect quote** indicates the number of foreign currency units it takes to purchase one American dollar. The column on the far right shows the indirect exchange rate.

We can further illustrate the use of direct and indirect quotes with a simple example. Suppose you want to compute the indirect quote from the direct quote for pound given in the center column of Table 1. The direct quote for the British pound is $1.6133. The related indirect quotes are calculated as the reciprocal of the direct quote as follows:

$$\text{Indirect Quote} = \frac{1}{\text{Direct Quote}} \tag{1}$$

Thus,

$$\frac{1}{1.6133} = \text{£.6198}$$

Notice that the indirect quote is identical to that shown in the far-right column of Table 1.

Table 1   Foreign Exchange Rates (December 26, 2012)

Country/Currency	In US$	Per US$
Americas		
Brazil real	0.4791	2.0875
Canada dollar	1.0074	0.9927
Chile peso	0.002086	479.35
Colombia peso	0.0005629	1776.50
Mexico peso	0.0770	12.9923
Asia-Pacific		
Australian dollar	1.0362	0.9650
1-mos forward	1.0338	0.9673
3-mos forward	1.0293	0.9715
6-mos forward	1.0228	0.9777
China yuan	0.1604	6.2352
Hong Kong dollar	0.1290	7.7507
India rupee	0.01818	55.01545
Japan yen	0.01179	84.81
1-mos forward	0.01180	84.78
3-mos forward	0.01180	84.74
6-mos forward	0.01181	84.67
New Zealand dollar	0.8215	1.2172
Pakistan rupee	0.01023	97.720
South Korea won	0.0009314	1073.70
Europe		
Euro area euro	1.3183	0.7585
Norway krone	0.1784	5.6045
Russia ruble	0.03269	30.588
Sweden krona	0.1527	6.5483
Switzerland franc	1.0917	0.9160
1-mos forward	1.0928	0.9151
3-mos forward	1.0939	0.9141
6-mos forward	1.0961	0.9123
Turkey lira	0.5574	1.7940
UK pound	1.6133	0.6198
1-mos forward	1.6133	0.6198
3-mos forward	1.6130	0.6200
6-mos forward	1.6128	0.6200
Middle East/Africa		
Egypt pound	0.1620	6.1716
Israel shekel	0.2667	3.7492
Saudi Arabia riyal	0.2666	3.7504
South Africa rand	0.1166	8.5791
UAE dirham	0.2723	3.6730

Source: Reuters, *The Wall Street Journal Online*, imf.org, Bloomberg.com, ft.com, finance.yahoo.com, fxstreet .com, and cnn.money.com, December 27, 2012.

Exchanging Currencies

U.S. firm Claremont Steel ordered parts for a generator that were made by a German firm. Claremont was required to pay 1,000 euros to the German firm on December 26, 2012. How many dollars were required for this transaction?

STEP 1: Picture the problem

The key determinant of the number of dollars required to purchase the 1,000 euros is the rate of exchange between dollars and euros, which in this case is $1.3183 per euro.

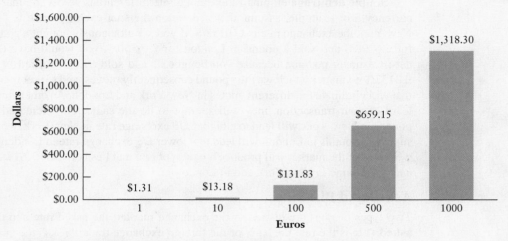

STEP 2: Decide on a solution strategy

To determine the number of dollars needed to purchase the 1,000 euros, we need to know the dollar price of one euro; that is, the direct quote, and multiply it times the 1,000 euros we need.

STEP 3: Solve

The answer, then, is the $/€ exchange rate (the direct quote) times the number of euros we need:

$$\$1.3183 /€ \times €1,000 = \$1,318.30$$

STEP 4: Analyze

In this instance we are able to use the direct quote to get the appropriate exchange rate. If you are concerned about whether to use the direct or indirect quote, simply write down the equation for what you are trying to calculate and make sure that the currency in the denominator of the exchange rate corresponds to the currency you are multiplying it by. For example, in the above example we had the following:

$$\$/€ \times € = \$$$

where $/€ represents a direct quote.

If we were calculating the number of euros that correspond to a particular dollar sum then we would use the indirect quote; that is,

$$€/\$ \times \$ = €$$

where €/$ is an indirect quote.

STEP 5: Check yourself

Suppose an American business had to pay $2,000 to a British resident on December 26, 2012. How many pounds did the British resident receive?

ANSWER: £0.6198 /$ × $2,000 = £1,239.60.

Your Turn: For more practice, do related **Study Problems** 1, 2, 7, and 8 at the end of this chapter.

>> **END Checkpoint 1**

Exchange Rates and Arbitrage

The foreign exchange quotes in two different countries must be consistent with each other. If they are not, then it will be possible to make money by trading on the differences. For example, if the exchange rate quotes between the London and New York spot exchange markets were out of line, then an enterprising trader could make a profit by buying in the market where the currency was cheaper and selling it in the other. Such a buy-and-sell strategy would involve a zero net investment of funds and no risk bearing, yet would provide a sure profit. An individual who profits by doing this is called an arbitrageur, and the process of buying and selling in more than one market to make a riskless profit is called **arbitrage**.

Simple arbitrage eliminates exchange rate differentials across the markets for a single currency. For example, assume that in London the spot exchange rate is £ .6350/$, and in New York the exchange rate is £ .6198/$. If you simultaneously bought a pound in New York for £.6198/$ and sold a pound in London for £ .6350/$, you would have (1) taken a zero-net-investment position because you bought £1 and sold £1, (2) locked in a sure profit of £.0152/$ no matter which way the pound subsequently moves, and (3) set in motion the forces that will eliminate the different quotes in New York and London. As others in the marketplace learn of your transaction, they will attempt to do the same. The increased demand to buy pounds in New York will lead to a higher £/$ exchange rate in New York, while the increased supply of pounds in London will lead to a lower £/$ exchange rate in London. Ultimately, the workings of the market will produce a new spot rate that lies between £ .6198/$ and £ .6250/$ and is the same in New York and in London.

Asked and Bid Rates

Two types of rates are quoted in the exchange market: the asked rate and the bid rate. The **asked rate** is the rate the bank or the foreign exchange trader "asks" the customer to pay in home currency for foreign currency when the bank is selling and the customer is buying. The asked rate is also known as the **selling rate** or the offer rate. The **bid rate** is the rate at which the bank buys the foreign currency from the customer by paying in home currency. The bid rate is also known as the **buying rate**. Note that Table 1 contains only the selling, offer, or asked rate, and not the buying rate.

The bank sells a unit of foreign currency for more than it pays for it. Therefore, the direct asked quote ($/FC) is greater than the direct bid quote. The difference between the asked quote and the bid quote is known as the **bid-asked spread**. When there is a large volume of transactions and the trading is continuous, the spread is small and can be less than 1 percent (.01) for the major currencies. The spread is much higher for infrequently traded currencies. The spread exists to compensate the banks for holding the risky foreign currency and for providing the service of converting currencies.

Cross Rates

A **cross rate** is the exchange rate between two foreign currencies, neither of which is the currency of the domestic country. Cross rates are given in Table 2. Taking the dollar/pound and the euro/dollar rates from columns 3 and 1 of Table 2, let's determine the euro/pound and pound/euro exchange rates. Multiplying the dollar/pound and the euro/dollar exchange rates together, we can see that the dollar will cancel out, leaving the euro/pound exchange rate,

$$(\$/£) \times (€/\$) = (€/£) \tag{2}$$

or

$$1.6133 \times 0.7585 = €1.2237/£$$

Thus, the pound/euro exchange rate is

$$1/1.2237 = £.8172/€$$

You will notice that these rates are the same as those given in Table 2.

Cross-rate computations make it possible to use quotations in New York to compute the exchange rate between pounds, dollars, and euros. Arbitrage conditions hold in cross rates, too.

Table 2	Key Currency Cross Rates (December 26, 2012)

The New York foreign exchange selling rates below apply to trading among banks in amounts of $1 million and more, as quoted at 4 p.m. eastern time by Dow Jones and other sources. Retail transactions provide fewer units of foreign currency per dollar.

	Dollar	Euro	Pound	SFranc	Peso	Yen	CanadnDlr
Canada	0.9927	1.3087	1.6015	1.0837	0.0764	0.0117	. . . .
Japan	84.8066	111.8026	136.8181	92.5856	6.5274	. . . .	85.4312
Mexico	12.9923	17.1281	20.9604	14.1841	. . . .	0.1532	13.0880
Switzerland	0.9160	1.2076	1.4777	. . . .	0.0705	0.0108	0.9227
U.K.	0.6198	0.8172	. . . .	0.6767	0.0477	0.0073	0.6244
Euro	0.7585	. . . .	1.2237	0.8281	0.0584	0.0089	0.7641
U.S.	. . . .	1.3183	1.6133	1.0917	0.0770	0.0118	1.0074

Source: Available from Thomson Reuters, wsj.com, and Bloomberg.com/markets/currencies.

For example, the pound exchange rate in London (the direct quote euros/pound) must be 1.2237 as shown in the example, and the euro exchange rate in London must be £ .8172/€.

Types of Foreign Exchange Transactions

Thus far, the exchange rates and transactions we have discussed are those meant for immediate delivery. This type of exchange rate is called a **spot exchange rate**. Another type of transaction carried out in the foreign exchange markets is known as a **forward exchange rate**, an exchange rate agreed upon today but that calls for delivery of currency at the agreed rate or payment at some future date.

The actual payment of one currency in exchange for the other takes place on a future date called the **delivery date**, and the agreement that captures the terms of both the rate and delivery is called the futures contract or **forward exchange contract**.[1] For example, a forward contract agreed upon on March 1st would specify the exchange rate and might call for delivery on March 31. Note that the forward rate is not necessarily the same as the spot rate that will exist in the future—in fact, no one knows exactly what the exchange rate will be in the future. These contracts can be used to manage a firm's **exchange rate risk** (the risk that tomorrow's exchange rate will differ from today's rate) and are usually quoted for periods of between 30 days and one year. A contract for any intermediate date can be obtained, usually with the payment of a small premium.

Forward rates, like spot rates, are quoted in both direct and indirect form. The direct quotes for the 30-day and 90-day forward contracts on pounds, yen, Australian dollars, and Swiss Francs are given in the center column of Table 1. Like spot rates, the indirect quotes for forward contracts are reciprocals of the direct quotes. The indirect quotes are indicated in the right-hand column of Table 1. The direct quotes are the dollar/foreign currency rate, and the indirect quotes are the foreign currency/dollar rate similar to the spot exchange quotes.

In Table 1, the three-month forward quote for pounds is $1.6130 per pound. This means that the bank is contractually bound to deliver £1 at this price, and the buyer of the contract is legally obligated to buy it at this price. The forward exchange contract obligates the seller to sell pounds at an exchange rate of $1.6130 regardless of the actual spot rate that prevails in three months. If the spot price of the pound is less than $1.6130, then the customer pays more

---

[1]These contracts are very similar, with one major difference being that futures contracts are exchange traded, whereas forward contracts are traded on the over-the-counter market.

than the spot price. If the spot price is greater than \$1.6130, then the customer pays less than the spot price.

The forward rate is often quoted at a premium to or discount from the existing spot rate. A premium would indicate that the foreign currency is more expensive in the forward market and, as such, a dollar buys fewer of the foreign currency in the forward market than in the spot market. If a dollar buys more of the foreign currency in the forward market, then the foreign currency is less expensive in the forward market and it would be selling at a discount. For example, the three-month forward rate for the pound may be quoted as .0003 pound discount (1.6130 forward rate − 1.6133 spot rate). If the British pound's forward price is greater than its spot price, it is said to be selling at a premium relative to the dollar, and the dollar is said to be selling at a discount to the British pound. This premium or discount is also called the **forward-spot differential**.

Notationally, the relationship may be written:

$$F - S = \text{premium } (F > S) \text{ or discount } (S > F)$$

$$F - S = \begin{cases} \text{Premium if } F > S \\ \text{Discount if } F < S \end{cases} \tag{3}$$

where F = the forward rate, direct quote and S = the spot rate, direct quote.

The premium or discount can also be expressed as an annual percentage rate, computed as follows:

$$\frac{F - S}{S} \times \frac{12}{n} \times 100 = \text{annualized percentage} \tag{4}$$

where n = the number of months of the forward contract.

In addition, a positive annualized percentage indicates a premium, whereas a negative annualized percentage indicates a discount.

For example, if you wanted to compute the percent-per-annum discount or premium on the three-month forward pound using the information in Table 1, you would use Equation (4) as follows,

Step 1. Identify F, S, and n.

$$F = 1.6130, S = 1.6133, n = 3 \text{ months}$$

Step 2. Because F is less than S, we compute the annualized percentage discount as follows:

$$\text{Annualized Percentage Discount} = \frac{1.6130 - 1.6133}{1.6133} \times \frac{12 \text{ months}}{3 \text{ months}} \times 100 = -0.0744\%$$

Thus, the percent-per-annum discount (that's why the answer takes on a negative value) on the three-month pound is −0.0744 percent.

Checkpoint 2

Determining the Percent-per-Annum Premium or Discount

You are in need of yen in six months, but before entering a forward contract to buy them, you would like to know their premium or discount from the existing spot rate. Calculate the premium or discount from the existing spot rate for the six-month yen as of December 26, 2012, using the data given in Table 1.

STEP 1: Picture the problem

To determine the premium or discount from the existing spot rate, you first need to know the prices. This can be best visualized through the use of a table, simply presenting the spot and forward rates.

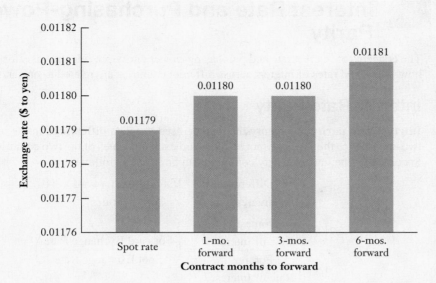

As you can see, the forward rates climb over this period, and the forward rates are above the spot rates, indicating that the forward rate is being quoted at a premium to the existing spot rate.

STEP 2: Decide on a solution strategy

The solution is actually quite simple in this case. We will simply determine the size of the premium and then annualize it using Equation (4).

STEP 3: Solve

Computing the percent-per-annum premium on the six-month yen:

Step 1: Identify F, S, and n.

$$F = 0.01181, S = 0.01179, n = 6 \text{ months}$$

Step 2: Because F is more than S, we compute the annualized percentage premium:

$$= \frac{0.01181 - 0.01179}{0.01179} \times \frac{12 \text{ months}}{6 \text{ months}} \times 100 = 0.339\%$$

STEP 4: Analyze

What determines whether a currency sells at a forward premium or discount? It is market forces, and the relationship between spot and forward exchange rates is described by what we call "interest rate parity"—a concept that we will examine in a moment.

STEP 5: Check yourself

Given the information provided previously, what is the premium on or discount from the existing spot rate on the one-month yen?

ANSWER: Premium of 1.018 percent.

Your Turn: For more practice, do related **Study Problems** 7 and 14 at the end of this chapter.   **>> END Checkpoint 2**

Before you move on to 2

Concept Check | 1

1. What is a spot transaction? What is a direct quote? An indirect quote?
2. What is a forward exchange rate? Why would a company be interested in it?
3. What is the forward spot differential and how is it calculated? Why would a company be interested in it?

2 Interest Rate and Purchasing-Power Parity

The concepts of interest rate and purchasing-power parity provide the basis for understanding how prices and rates of interest across different countries are related to one another.

Interest Rate Parity

Interest rate parity is a theory that can be used to relate differences in the interest rates in two countries to the ratios of spot and forward exchange rates of the two countries' currencies. Specifically, the interest parity condition can be stated as follows:

$$\frac{\text{Difference in}}{\text{interest rates}} = \frac{\text{Ratio of the forward}}{\text{and spot rates}}$$

$$\frac{\left(1 + \dfrac{\text{Domestic}}{\text{Rate of Interest}}\right)}{\left(1 + \dfrac{\text{Foreign}}{\text{Rate of Interest}}\right)} = \left(\frac{\text{Forward Exchange Rate}}{\text{Spot Exchange Rate}}\right) \tag{5}$$

This equation can be rearranged such that,

$$\left(1 + \frac{\text{Domestic}}{\text{Rate of Interest}}\right) = \left(\frac{\text{Forward Exchange Rate}}{\text{Spot Exchange Rate}}\right)\left(1 + \frac{\text{Foreign}}{\text{Rate of Interest}}\right) \tag{5a}$$

To illustrate how this equation is applied, consider the following situation. The six-month risk-free rate of interest in the United States was 2 percent on December 26, 2012. The spot exchange rate between the U.S. dollar and the Japanese yen on this date was 0.01179 and the forward exchange rate for six months hence was 0.01181. According to interest rate parity, what would you expect the six-month risk-free rate of interest to be in Japan? Substituting into Equation (5a) we calculate the following:

$$\left(1 + \frac{\text{U.S. Six-Month Risk-Free}}{\text{Rate of Interest}}\right) = \left(\frac{\text{Forward Exchange Rate}}{\text{Spot Exchange Rate}}\right)\left(1 + \frac{\text{Japanese Six-Month Risk-Free}}{\text{Rate of Interest}}\right)$$

$$(1 + .02) = \left(\frac{0.01181}{0.01179}\right)\left(1 + \frac{\text{Japanese Six-Month Risk-Free}}{\text{Rate of Interest}}\right)$$

$$(1 + .02) = 1.001696\left(1 + \frac{\text{Japanese Six-Month Risk-Free}}{\text{Rate of Interest}}\right)$$

Thus, the Japanese six-month risk-free rate of interest = .018273 or 1.8273%.

What this means is that you get the same total return whether you change your dollars to yen and invest in the risk-free rate in Japan and then convert them back to dollars, or simply invest your dollars in the U.S. risk-free rate of interest. For example, if you started with $100 and converted it to yen at the spot rate of .01179 $/¥, you'd have 8,481.76 yen; if you invested those yen at 1.8273 percent, after six months you'd have ¥8,809.46. Converting this back to dollars at the forward rate, you end up with $102.00, the same amount you would have if you had invested your dollars at the U.S. six-month rate of 2 percent.

Purchasing-Power Parity and the Law of One Price

According to the theory of **purchasing-power parity (PPP)**, exchange rates adjust so that identical goods cost the same amount regardless of where in the world they are purchased. For example, if a 120-GB Apple iPod costs $350 in the United States, and €250 in France, according to the purchasing-power parity theory, the spot exchange rate should be $1.40 per euro ($350/€250). Thus, if you would like to buy a new iPod, you could either buy it for $350 in the United States, or trade in your $350 for €250 and buy your iPod in France—either way it costs you the same amount. Stated formally,

$$\frac{\text{Spot Exchange}}{\text{Rate for Euros}} \times \frac{\text{U.S. Price of}}{\text{an iPod}} = \frac{\text{French Price of}}{\text{an iPod}} \tag{6}$$

More generally, the spot exchange rate for the foreign country (in this case the spot exchange rate for euros) should be equal to the ratio of the price of the good in the home country (P_h) to the price of the same good in the foreign country (P_f), that is,

$$\text{Spot Exchange Rate} = \frac{P_h}{P_f}$$

Thus, as we just showed, the spot exchange rate of \$/€ should be the following:

$$\text{Spot Exchange Rate} = \frac{P_h}{P_f} = \frac{\$350}{€250} = \$1.40/€$$

Therefore, PPP implies that if a new Callaway FT-i golf club cost €300 in France, it should cost €300 × 1.4 = \$420 in the United States where the \$/€ exchange rate is 1.4.

Underlying the PPP relationship is a fundamental economic principle called the **law of one price**. Applied to international trade, this law states that the same goods should sell for the same price in different countries after making adjustment for the exchange rate between the two currencies. The idea is that the worth of a good does not depend on where it is bought or sold. Thus, in the long run, exchange rates should adjust so that the purchasing power of each currency is the same. As a result, exchange rate changes should reflect the international differences in inflation rates, with countries with high rates of inflation experiencing declines in the value of their currencies.

There are enough obvious exceptions to the concept of purchasing-power parity that it may, at first glance, seem difficult to accept. To illustrate differences in purchasing power across countries, we have created a chart showing the worldwide value of a McDonald's Big Mac in local and U.S. currency (Figure 2). As this figure shows, in 2012 a Big Mac cost \$4.33 in the United States; and, given the then-existing exchange rates, it cost an equivalent of \$2.29 in Russia, \$2.13 in Hong Kong, \$6.56 in Switzerland, and \$7.06 in Norway. Why aren't these prices the same? First, tax differences between countries can be one cause. In addition, labor costs and the rental cost of the McDonald's outlets may differ across countries.

So, does this mean that PPP does not hold? Well, it clearly does not hold for what economists call non-traded goods, such as restaurant meals and haircuts. As we all know, for these goods, purchasing-power parity does not hold even within the United States—indeed, a Big Mac does not sell for the same price in Des Moines as it does in Los Angeles. However, for goods that can be very cheaply shipped between countries, such as expensive gold jewelry, we expect PPP to hold relatively closely.

As you can see from Figure 2, a dollar doesn't go very far in Europe and in particular in Denmark, Switzerland, and Norway, but you get a lot for a dollar in Asian countries such as China, Thailand, and Malaysia. Why does this matter? When the world is experiencing economic weakness as it did during 2012, a strong exchange rate like those found in Europe makes it difficult to sell goods abroad and makes foreign goods look less expensive. On the other hand, during periods of economic weakness, a country with a weak exchange rate, such as China, has an easier time selling goods abroad (because they are cheaper). However, the weak exchange rate in 2012 made it more difficult for Chinese consumers to buy pricey imports over cheaper Chinese-produced goods.

The International Fisher Effect

According to the domestic Fisher effect (FE), nominal interest rates reflect the expected inflation rate and a real rate of return. In other words,

$$\begin{matrix} \text{Nominal Rate} \\ \text{of Interest} \end{matrix} = \begin{matrix} \text{Expected Rate} \\ \text{of Inflation} \end{matrix} + \begin{matrix} \text{Real Rate} \\ \text{of Interest} \end{matrix} + \begin{bmatrix} \text{Expected Rate} \\ \text{of Inflation} \end{bmatrix} \begin{bmatrix} \text{Real Rate} \\ \text{of Return} \end{bmatrix} \tag{7}$$

The **International Fisher Effect (IFE)** assumes that real rates of return are the same across the world, so that the differences in nominal returns around the world arise because of different inflation rates. Because the cross product between the expected rate of inflation and the real rate of return is very small, it is often ignored, and the nominal rate is expressed in approximate terms as follows:

$$\begin{matrix} \text{Nominal Rate of} \\ \text{Interest in Country A} \end{matrix} \approx \text{(approximately equals)} \begin{matrix} \text{Expected Rate of} \\ \text{Inflation in Country A} \end{matrix} + \begin{matrix} \text{Real Rate} \\ \text{of Interest} \end{matrix} \tag{8}$$

Figure 2

Purchasing-Power Parity and the Price of a Big Mac

The relative prices of Big Macs are used in a light-hearted attempt to determine the percentage of overvaluation of a currency relative to the U.S. dollar.

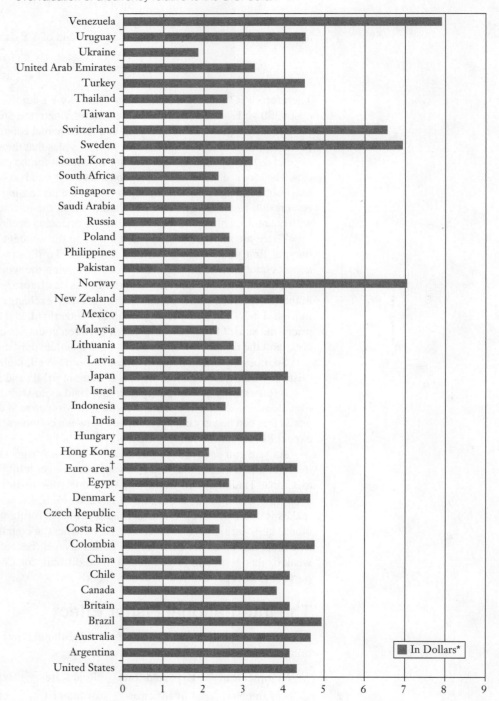

*At current exchange rates (July 25, 2012).

†Average of four cities.

>> END FIGURE 2

As a result,

$$\underset{\text{of Interest}}{\text{Real Rate}} \approx \text{(approximately equals)} \quad \underset{\text{Interest in Country A}}{\text{Nominal Rate of}} - \underset{\text{Inflation in Country A}}{\text{Expected Rate of}} \tag{9}$$

To illustrate this using Equation (7), let's assume that the real rate of interest is 3 percent in all countries. This means that if the expected inflation rate in Great Britain is 10 percent, and the expected inflation rate in Japan is 6 percent, interest rates in Great Britain and Japan (including the cross product) will be (.10 + .03 + .003) or 13.3 percent and (.06 + .03 + .0018) or 9.18 percent, respectively.

Like purchasing-power parity, the International Fisher Effect is just an approximation that will not hold exactly. It is important to understand, though, that if we look at interest rates around the world, we should not necessarily send our money to a bank account in the country with the highest interest rates. That course of action might only result in sending our money to the country with the highest expected rate of inflation. As a result, what we make in terms of higher interest would be offset by what we lose in terms of the value of the currency of the country where the bank is located.

Before you move on to 3

Concept Check | 2

1. What does the term *interest rate parity* mean?
2. What is the law of one price? Give a simple example.
3. What is the International Fisher Effect?

---

3 Capital Budgeting for Direct Foreign Investment

Today, there is no ducking the global markets, and it is common for U.S. firms to open manufacturing and sales operations abroad. In fact, in 2011 Yum! Brands (YUM, the parent company of KFC, Pizza Hut, and Taco Bell) invested over half a billion dollars to purchase the Chinese hot pot chain Little Sheep. **Direct foreign investment** occurs when a company from one country makes a physical investment in other country, for example, building a factory in another country. A **multinational corporation (MNC)** is one that has control over this investment. Examples of such a direct foreign investment include Yum Brands' opening of 656 new restaurants in China in 2011 and Dell Computer Corporation's (DELL) construction of offshore manufacturing facilities.

A major reason for direct foreign investment by U.S. companies is the prospect of higher rates of return from these investments. As you know from Principle 2: **There Is a Risk–Return Tradeoff**, although there may be higher expected rates of return with many foreign investments, many of them also come with increased risk. Many European and Japanese firms, like their American counterparts, have operations abroad as well. During the last decade, these firms have been increasing their sales and setting up production facilities abroad, especially in the United States.

The method used by multinational corporations to evaluate foreign investments is very similar to the method used to evaluate capital budgeting decisions in a domestic context—but with some additional considerations. When corporations invest abroad they generally set up a subsidiary in the country in which they are investing. Funds then are transferred back, or repatriated, to the parent firm in its home country through dividends, royalties, and management fees, with both the dividends and royalties subject to taxation in both the foreign and home countries. Moreover, many countries restrict the flow of funds back to the home country. As a result, there is often a difference between the cash flows that a project produces and the cash flows that can be repatriated to its parent country. To evaluate these investment projects, firms discount *the cash flows that are expected to be repatriated to the parent firm.* As we know from Principle 3: **Cash Flows Are the Source of Value**, we are only interested in the cash

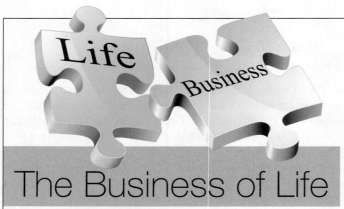

The Business of Life

International Investing

Today, trading in stocks, bonds, and other investments takes place around the clock and around the world. Indeed, there are a number of multinational companies, such as Sony and Toyota, that trade on exchanges in more than one country. So, why would you want to invest internationally? The main advantage, which we illustrate in Figure 3, is that because stock and bond prices in different countries don't always move together, international investments diversify your portfolio.

When the stock or bond market in one country is weak, the market in another country may be strong. For example, in 2011 the U.S. stock markets rebounded and produced average returns of 2 percent, but the stock market in Ireland earned 14 percent. Figure 4 shows the historical range of returns of global investments. These returns show a good deal of risk or volatility of returns, with Pacific stocks ranging from a high of 107.5 percent to a low of −36.2 percent.

By investing exclusively in U.S. markets, you are limiting yourself to half of the available investments. Figure 5 shows this to be the case, with the U.S. stock market accounting for 53 percent of the total world stock market capitalization.

Figure 4

Global Stock Market Returns
Highest and lowest historical annual returns for each region 1970–2011

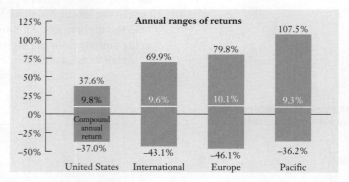

Source: © 2012 Morningstar. All rights reserved. Used with permission.

>> END FIGURE 4

Figure 3

Domestic versus Global Markets

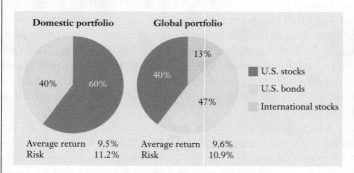

Source: © 2012 Morningstar. All rights reserved. Used with permission.

>> END FIGURE 3

Figure 5

World Stock Market Capitalization

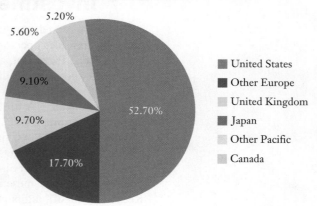

Source: © 2012 Morningstar. All rights reserved. Used with permission.

>> END FIGURE 5

Your Turn: See Study Question 3.

flows that we expect the subsidiary to return to the parent company. In most cases, the timing is crucial. If your project generates cash flows in 2015 that cannot be repatriated until 2018, the cash flows must be discounted from the 2018 date when the cash will be actually received. Once the cash flows are estimated, they must be discounted back to present at the appropriate discount rate or required rate of return, with both the discount rate or required rate of return and the cash flows being measured in the same currency. Thus, if the discount rate is based on dollar-based interest rates, the cash flows must also be measured in dollars.

Looking at an example, let's assume that an American firm is considering investing in a new project that will produce the following cash flows measured in Brazilian reals (BRL) that are expected to be repatriated to the parent company:

Year	Cash Flow (in millions of BRL)
0	−8
1	3
2	4
3	5
4	6

The first task is to determine the appropriate discount rate. Let's assume that the risk-free rate in the home country (the United States) is 4 percent, and that this project is riskier than most. Given the combination of currency risk and other risks associated with doing business in Brazil, the firm has determined that it should require a 10 percent premium over the risk-free rate. Thus, the appropriate discount rate for this project is 14 percent.

Next, the cash flows have to be converted from Brazilian reals into U.S. dollars. The problem we run into is that futures markets (the Chicago Mercantile Exchange) only provide exchange rates for the BRL for about a year forward. However, from Equation (5), we know that forward rates reflect the interest rate differential in the two countries, implying that we can determine forward exchange rates using the following formula:

$$n\text{-Year Forward Exchange Rate} = \left(\frac{\left(1 + \frac{\text{Domestic}}{\text{Rate of Interest}}\right)}{\left(1 + \frac{\text{Foreign}}{\text{Rate of Interest}}\right)}\right)^n \times (\text{Spot Exchange Rate}) \quad \textbf{(10)}$$

Let's assume n is 1, and let's solve for the interest rate differential:

One-Year Forward Exchange Rate $=$ (interest rate differential)^1 $\times$ (Spot Exchange Rate)

Let's assume the one-year forward exchange rate is 0.41BRL/$ and the spot exchange rate is 0.45BRL/$; from that we can determine the interest rate differential to be 0.9111. Thus, we can determine the implied forward exchange rates as follows:

Year	Spot Exchange Rate	×	(Interest Rate Differential)^n	=	Forward Exchange Rate for Year n
0	spot rate			=	0.45BRL/$ or $2.222/BRL
1	0.45BRL/$	×	0.9111	=	0.41BRL/$ or $2.439/BRL
2	0.45BRL/$	×	$(0.9111)^2$	=	0.3735BRL/$ or $2.677/BRL
3	0.45BRL/$	×	$(0.9111)^3$	=	0.3403BRL/$ or $2.939/BRL
4	0.45BRL/$	×	$(0.9111)^4$	=	0.3101BRL/$ or $3.225/BRL

We can now use these forward exchange rates to convert the cash flows measured in Brazilian reals to US$, as follows:

Year	Cash Flow (in millions of BRL)	×	Conversion Factor	=	Cash Flow (in millions of $)
0	−8	×	$2.222/BRL	=	−$17.78
1	3	×	$2.439/BRL	=	7.317
2	4	×	$2.677/BRL	=	10.708
3	5	×	$2.939/BRL	=	14.691
4	6	×	$3.225/BRL	=	19.350

Using the net present value (NPV) equation and discounting these cash flows back to the present at the required rate of return of 14 percent, we get a net present value of $878,620:

$$NPV(\$ \text{ millions}) = -\$17.78 + \frac{\$7.317}{(1 + .14)^1} + \frac{\$10.708}{(1 + .14)^2} + \frac{\$14.691}{(1 + .14)^3} + \frac{\$19.350}{(1 + .14)^4}$$

$$= \$18.25 \text{ million}$$

Thus, the project should be accepted.

Checkpoint 3

International Capital Budgeting

You are working for an American firm that is looking at a new project that will produce the following cash flows, which are expected to be repatriated to the parent company and are measured in South African Rand (SAR):

Year	Cash Flow (in millions of SAR)
0	−8
1	4
2	4
3	5
4	6

In addition, the risk-free rate in the United States is 4 percent and this project is riskier than most; as such, the firm has determined that it should require a 9 percent premium over the risk-free rate. Thus, the appropriate discount rate for this project is 13 percent. In addition, let's assume the current spot exchange rate is .11SAR/$, and the one-year forward exchange rate is .107SAR/$. Calculate the expected cash flows for this project in U.S. dollars, and then use these cash flows to calculate the project's NPV.

STEP 1: Picture the problem

The cash flows, measured in SAR, can be displayed as:

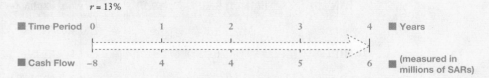

STEP 2: Decide on a solution strategy

To calculate the project's NPV, we must first convert the South African Rand (SAR) into U.S. dollars. Unfortunately, the futures markets (the Chicago Mercantile Exchange) only provide exchange rates for the SAR for about a year forward. However, using Equation (5), we can use the one-year forward rate and the spot rate so that we can calculate the interest rate differential in the two countries.

One-Year Forward Exchange Rate = (interest rate differential)[1] × (Spot Exchange Rate)

We can then use the forward exchange rate to convert the cash flows measured in SARs into U.S. dollars. From there we simply calculate the project's NPV in U.S. dollars using a 13 percent required rate of return.

STEP 3: Solve

In this problem we have a one-year forward rate of 0.107SAR/$ and a spot rate of 0.11SAR/$; from this we can calculate the interest rate differential in the two countries, which is .9727. We can then use the interest rate differential to calculate the forward exchange rate and then convert the cash flows measured in SARs into U.S. dollars. Using the interest rate differential of 0.9727, we then determine the implied forward exchange rates for the project, as follows:

Year	Spot Exchange Rate	×	(Interest Rate Differential)^n	=	Forward Exchange Rate for Year n
0	spot rate			=	0.11SAR/$ or $9.0909/SAR
1	0.11SAR/$	×	0.9727	=	0.107SAR/$ or $9.3458/SAR
2	0.11SAR/$	×	$(0.9727)^2$	=	0.1041SAR/$ or $9.6061/SAR
3	0.11SAR/$	×	$(0.9727)^3$	=	0.1012SAR/$ or $9.8814/SAR
4	0.11SAR/$	×	$(0.9727)^4$	=	0.0985SAR/$ or $10.1523/SAR

We can now use these forward exchange rates to convert the cash flows measured in South African rands to dollars, as follows:

Year	Cash Flow (in millions of SAR)	×	Implied Forward Rate	=	Cash Flow (in millions of $)
0	−8	×	$9.0909/SAR	=	−$72.73
1	4	×	$9.3458/SAR	=	37.38
2	4	×	$9.6061/SAR	=	38.42
3	5	×	$9.8814/SAR	=	49.41
4	6	×	$10.1523/SAR	=	60.91

Using the NPV equation and discounting these cash flows back to the present at the required rate of return of 13 percent, we get a net present value of $538,040:

$$NPV(\$ \text{ millions}) = -\$72.73 + \frac{\$37.38}{(1 + .13)^1} + \frac{\$38.42}{(1 + .13)^2} + \frac{\$49.41}{(1 + .13)^3} + \frac{\$60.91}{(1 + .13)^4}$$
$$= \$62.04$$

Alternatively, solving with a financial calculator,

Data and Key Input	Display
CF; −72.73; ENTER	CF0 = −72.72
↓; 37.38; ENTER	C01 = 37.38
↓; 1; ENTER	F01 = 1.00
↓; 38.42; ENTER	C02 = 38.42
↓; 1; ENTER	F02 = 1.00
↓; 49.41; ENTER	C03 = 49.41
↓; 1; ENTER	F03 = 1.00
↓; 60.91; ENTER	C04 = 60.91
↓; 1; ENTER	F04 = 1.00
NPV; 13; ENTER	
↓CPT	NPV = 62.04

STEP 4: Analyze

It is important to remember that the only cash flows that are relevant are those that are expected to be repatriated back to the home country. In addition, it is important to keep in mind that you use a required rate of return from investing in the same currency that the cash flows are measured in. Here, the required rate of return was in U.S. dollars, so we converted the cash flows into U.S. dollars to maintain consistency between them.

(3 CONTINUED >> ON NEXT PAGE)

STEP 5: Check yourself

You are working for an American firm that is looking at a new project that will produce the following cash flows, which are expected to be repatriated to the parent company and are measured in South African rand (SAR):

Year	Cash Flow (in millions of SAR)
0	−20
1	10
2	10
3	6
4	6

In addition, the risk-free rate in the United States is 4 percent and this project is riskier than most; as such, the firm has determined that it should require a 10 percent premium over the risk-free rate. Thus, the appropriate discount rate for this project is 14 percent. In addition, the current spot exchange rate is .11SAR/$, and the one-year forward exchange rate is .107SAR/$. What is the project's NPV?

ANSWER: $50.16 million.

Your Turn: For more practice, do related **Study Problems** 19 and 20 at the end of this chapter.   **>> END Checkpoint 3**

Foreign Investment Risks

Risk in domestic capital budgeting arises from two sources: (1) business risk related to the specific attributes of the product or service being provided and the uncertainty associated with that market, and (2) financial risk, which is the risk imposed on the investment as a result of how the project is financed. The foreign direct investment opportunity includes both of these sources of risk, plus political risk and exchange rate risk. Let us consider the risks that are unique to international investing.

Political Risk

Political risk can arise if the foreign subsidiary conducts its business in a politically unstable country. A change in a country's political environment frequently brings a change in policies with respect to businesses—and especially with respect to foreign businesses. An extreme change in policy might involve nationalization or even outright expropriation (government seizure) of certain businesses. For example, in 2007 Venezuela nationalized the country's largest telecommunications company, several electrical companies, and four lucrative oil projects that were owned by ExxonMobil Chevron, and ConocoPhillips, and in 2010 it nationalized two U.S.-owned Owens-Illinois glass manufacturing plants. These are the political risks of conducting business abroad. Some examples of political risk are as follows:

1. Expropriation of plants and equipment without compensation.
2. Expropriation with minimal compensation that is below actual market value.
3. Nonconvertibility of the subsidiary's foreign earnings into the parent's currency—the problem of blocked funds.
4. Substantial changes in tax rates.
5. Governmental controls in the foreign country regarding the sale price of certain products, wages and compensation paid to personnel, the hiring of personnel, transfer payments made to the parent, and local borrowing.
6. Requirements regarding the local ownership of the business.

All of these controls and governmental actions put the cash flows of the investment to the parent company at risk. Thus, these risks must be considered before making the foreign investment decision. For example, the MNC might decide against investing in countries with risks of types 1 and 2 in the previous list, whereas other risks can be borne—provided that the returns from the foreign investments are high enough to compensate for them. In fact, insurance against some types of political risks can be purchased from private insurance companies or from the U.S. government's Overseas Private Investment Corporation. It should be noted that although an MNC cannot protect itself against all foreign political risks, political risks are also present in domestic business.

Exchange Rate Risk

Exchange rate risk is the risk that the value of a firm's operations and investments will be adversely affected by changes in exchange rates. For example, if U.S. dollars must be converted into euros before making an investment in Germany, an adverse change in the value of the dollar with respect to the euro will affect the total gain or loss on the investment when the money is converted back to dollars. For example, between May 2011 and July 2011 the value of the euro fell from $1.48/€ to $1.21/€.

Before you begin end-of-chapter material

Concept Check | 3

1. Define the types of risk that are commonly referred to as political risk, and give some examples of them.
2. What is exchange rate risk? Why would a multinational firm be concerned about it?

Applying the Principles of Finance to This Chapter

P Principle 2: **There Is a Risk–Return Tradeoff** Many times there are higher expected rates of return with many foreign investments, but these returns come with increased risk.

P Principle 3: **Cash Flows Are the Source of Value** In capital budgeting for direct foreign investment, it is the cash flows that are returned to the parent company that are the source of value.

Chapter Summaries

Understand the nature and importance of the foreign exchange market and learn to read currency exchange rate quotes.

SUMMARY: The foreign exchange (FX) market is where one currency is traded for another. This is by far the largest financial market in the world, with a daily trading volume of more than $4 trillion. Trading is dominated by a few key currencies, including the U.S. dollar, the British pound sterling, the Japanese yen, and the euro. The FX market is an over-the-counter market rather than a single exchange location like the New York Stock Exchange, where buyers and sellers get together. This means that market participants (buyers and sellers) are located in major commercial and investment banks around the world.

KEY TERMS

Arbitrage The process of buying and selling in more than one market to make riskless profits.

Asked rate The rate a bank or foreign exchange trader "asks" the customer to pay in home currency for foreign currency when the bank is selling and the customer is buying. Also known as the selling rate.

Bid-asked spread The difference between the bid quote and ask price quote.

Bid rate The rate at which the bank buys the foreign currency from the customer by paying in home currency. The bid rate is also known as the buying rate.

Buying rate The rate at which the bank buys the foreign currency from the customer by paying in its home currency. The buying rate is also known as the bid rate.

Cross rate The exchange rate between two foreign currencies, neither of which is the currency of the domestic country.

Delivery date The future date on which the actual payment of one currency in exchange for another takes place in a foreign exchange transaction.

Direct quote The exchange rate that indicates the number of units of the home currency required to buy one unit of a foreign currency.

Exchange rate The price of a foreign currency stated in terms of the domestic or home currency.

Exchange rate risk The risk that tomorrow's exchange rate will differ from today's rate.

Foreign exchange (FX) market The market in which the currencies of various countries are traded.

Forward exchange contract A contract that requires delivery on a specified future date of one currency in return for a specified amount of another currency.

Forward exchange rate The exchange rate agreed upon today for the delivery of currency at a future date.

Forward-spot differential The difference (premium or discount) between the forward and spot currency exchange rates for a country's currency.

Indirect quote The exchange rate that expresses the number of units of foreign currency that can be bought for one unit of home currency.

Selling rate The rate a bank or foreign exchange trader "asks" the customer to pay in home currency for foreign currency when the bank is selling and the customer is buying, also known as the asked rate.

Simple arbitrage Trading to eliminate exchange rate differentials across the markets for a single currency, for example, for the New York and London markets.

Spot exchange rate The ratio of a home currency and foreign currency in which the transaction calls for immediate delivery.

KEY EQUATIONS

$$\text{Indirect Quote} = \frac{1}{\text{Direct Quote}} \tag{1}$$

$$F - S = \text{premium } (F > S) \text{ or discount } (S > F)$$

$$F - S = \begin{cases} \text{Premium if } F > S \\ \text{Discount if } F < S \end{cases} \tag{3}$$

where F = the forward rate, direct quote and S = the spot rate, direct quote.

$$\frac{F - S}{S} \times \frac{12}{n} \times 100 = \text{annualized percentage} \tag{4}$$

where $n = $ the number of months of the forward contract.

Concept Check | **1**

1. What is a spot transaction? What is a direct quote? An indirect quote?
2. What is a forward exchange rate? Why would a company be interested in it?
3. What is the forward spot differential and how is it calculated? Why would a company be interested in it?

2 | Describe interest rate and purchasing-power parity

SUMMARY: The forward exchange market provides a valuable service by quoting rates for the delivery of foreign currencies in the future. The foreign currency is said to sell at a forward premium (discount) from the spot rate when the forward rate is greater (less) than the spot rate, in direct quotation. In addition, the influences of purchasing-power parity (PPP) and the International Fisher Effect (IFE) in determining the exchange rate were discussed.

KEY TERMS

Interest rate parity (IRP) A theory that relates the interest rates in two countries to the exchange rates of their currencies.

International Fisher Effect (IFE) A theory that states that real rates of return are the same across the world, with the difference in returns across the world resulting from different inflation rates.

Law of one price An economic principle that states that a good or service cannot sell for different prices in the same market. Applied to international markets this law states that the same goods should sell for the same price in different countries after making adjustment for the exchange rate between the two currencies.

Purchasing-power parity (PPP) A theory that states that exchange rates adjust so that identical goods cost the same amount regardless of where in the world they are purchased.

KEY EQUATIONS

$$\frac{\left(1 + \dfrac{\text{Domestic}}{\text{Rate of Interest}}\right)}{\left(1 + \dfrac{\text{Foreign}}{\text{Rate of Interest}}\right)} = \left(\frac{\text{Forward Exchange Rate}}{\text{Spot Exchange Rate}}\right) \tag{5}$$

$$\left(1 + \frac{\text{Domestic}}{\text{Rate of Interest}}\right) = \left(\frac{\text{Forward Exchange Rate}}{\text{Spot Exchange Rate}}\right)\left(1 + \frac{\text{Foreign}}{\text{Rate of Interest}}\right) \tag{5a}$$

$$\frac{\text{Nominal Rate}}{\text{of Interest}} = \frac{\text{Expected Rate}}{\text{of Inflation}} + \frac{\text{Real Rate}}{\text{of Interest}} + \left[\frac{\text{Expected Rate}}{\text{of Inflation}}\right]\left[\frac{\text{Real Rate}}{\text{of Return}}\right] \tag{7}$$

$$\frac{\text{Nominal Rate of}}{\text{Interest in Country A}} \approx \text{(approximately equals)} \frac{\text{Expected Rate of}}{\text{Inflation in Country A}} + \frac{\text{Real Rate}}{\text{of Interest}} \tag{8}$$

$$\frac{\text{Real Rate}}{\text{of Interest}} \approx \text{(approximately equals)} \frac{\text{Nominal Rate of}}{\text{Interest in Country A}} - \frac{\text{Expected Rate of}}{\text{Inflation in Country A}} \tag{9}$$

Concept Check | **2**

1. What does the term *interest rate parity* mean?
2. What is the law of one price? Give a simple example.
3. What is the International Fisher Effect?

3 Discuss the risks that are unique to the capital budgeting analysis of direct foreign investments

SUMMARY: The complexities encountered in the direct foreign investment decision include the usual sources of risk—business and financial—faced by domestic investments, plus additional risks associated with political considerations and fluctuating exchange rates. Political risk is due to differences in political climates, institutions, and processes between the home country and abroad. Under these conditions, the estimation of future cash flows and the choice of the proper discount rates are more complicated than for the domestic investment situation.

KEY TERMS

Direct foreign investment When a company from one country makes a physical investment such as building a factory in another country.

Multinational corporation (MNC) A company that has control over direct foreign investments in more than one country.

Political risk The potential for losses that can occur when investing in foreign countries where political decisions can result in losses of property.

KEY EQUATION

$$n\text{-Year Forward Exchange Rate} = \left(\frac{\left(1 + \dfrac{\text{Domestic}}{\text{Rate of Interest}} \right)}{\left(1 + \dfrac{\text{Foreign}}{\text{Rate of Interest}} \right)} \right)^{n} \times (\text{Spot Exchange Rate}) \qquad \textbf{(10)}$$

Concept Check | **3**

1. Define the types of risk that are commonly referred to as political risk, and give some examples of them.
2. What is exchange rate risk? Why would a multinational firm be concerned about it?

Study Questions

1. What additional factors are encountered in international as compared with domestic financial management? Discuss each briefly.

2. **(Related to Regardless of Your Major: Working in a Flat World)** Why do businesses operate internationally, and what different types of businesses tend to operate in the international environment? Why are the techniques and strategies available to these firms different? Why is it important for many businesses to have an international presence?

3. **(Related to The Business of Life: International Investing)** Why is the diversification that international investing provides to individual investors of value?

4. What is meant by arbitrage profits?

5. What are the markets and mechanics involved in engaging in simple arbitrage?

6. How do purchasing-power parity, interest rate parity, and the International Fisher Effect explain the relationships between the current spot rate, the future spot rate, and the forward rate?

7. Define *exchange rate risk* and *political risk*.

8. What steps can a firm take to reduce foreign exchange rate risk? Indicate at least two different techniques.

9. In the New York exchange market, the forward rate for the Indian currency, the rupee, is not quoted. If you were exposed to exchange risk in rupees, how could you cover your position?

10. What risks are associated with direct foreign investment? How do these risks differ from those encountered in domestic investment?

11. How is the direct foreign investment decision made? What are the inputs to this decision process? Are the inputs more complicated than those for the domestic investment decision? Why or why not?

12. A corporation desires to enter a particular foreign market. The direct foreign investment analysis indicates that a direct investment in the plant in the foreign country is not profitable. What other course of action can the company take to enter the foreign market? What are the important considerations?

Study Problems

The data for Study Problems 1 through 6 are given in the following table:

Selling Quotes for Foreign Currencies in New York

Country–Currency	Contract	$/Foreign Currency
Canada–dollar	Spot	.8437
	30-day	.8417
	90-day	.8395
Japan–yen	Spot	.004684
	30-day	.004717
	90-day	.004781
Switzerland–franc	Spot	.5139
	30-day	.5169
	90-day	.5315

Foreign Exchange Markets and Currency Exchange Rates

1. **(Related to Checkpoint 1) (Converting currencies)** An American business needs to pay (a) 10,000 Canadian dollars, (b) 2 million yen, and (c) 50,000 Swiss francs to businesses abroad. What are the dollar payments to the respective countries?

2. **(Related to Checkpoint 1) (Converting currencies)** An American business pays $10,000, $15,000, and $20,000 to suppliers in Japan, Switzerland, and Canada, respectively. How much, in local currencies, do the suppliers receive?

3. **(Indirect quotes)** Compute the indirect quote for the spot and forward Canadian dollar, yen, and Swiss franc contracts.

4. **(Bid, spot, and forward rates)** The spreads on the contracts as a percent of the asked rates are 2 percent for yen, 3 percent for Canadian dollars, and 5 percent for Swiss francs. Show, in a table similar to the preceding one, the bid rates for the different spot and forward rates.

5. **(Foreign exchange arbitrage)** You own $10,000. The dollar rate in Tokyo is 216.6743£. The yen rate in New York is given in the previous table. Are arbitrage profits possible? Set up an arbitrage scheme with your capital. What is the gain in dollars?

6. **(Spot rates)** Compute the Canadian dollar/yen and the yen/Swiss franc spot rate from the data in the preceding table.

7. **(Related to Checkpoint 1 and Checkpoint 2) (Determining the percent-per-annum premium or discount)** You are in need of Australian dollars in six months, but before entering a forward contract to buy them, you would like to know their premium or discount from the existing spot rate. Calculate the premium or discount from the existing spot rate for the six-month Australian dollar as of December 26, 2012, using the data given in Table 1.

The data for Study Problems 8 through 14 are given in the following table:

Selling Quotes for Foreign Currencies in New York

Country–Currency	Contract	$/Foreign Currency
Canada–dollar	Spot	.8439
	30-day	.8410
	90-day	.8390
Japan–yen	Spot	.004680
	30-day	.004720
	90-day	.004787
Switzerland–franc	Spot	.5140
	30-day	.5179
	90-day	.5335

8. **(Related to Checkpoint 1) (Converting currencies)** An American business needs to pay (a) 15,000 Canadian dollars, (b) 1.5 million yen, and (c) 55,000 Swiss francs to businesses abroad. What are the dollar payments to the respective countries?

9. **(Converting currencies)** An American business pays $20,000, $5,000, and $15,000 to suppliers in Japan, Switzerland, and Canada, respectively. How much, in local currencies, do the suppliers receive?

10. **(Indirect quotes)** Compute the indirect quote for the spot and forward Canadian dollar, yen, and Swiss franc contracts using the data found above.

11. **(Bid, ask, and forward rates)** The spreads on the contracts as a percent of the asked rates are 4 percent for yen, 3 percent for Canadian dollars, and 6 percent for Swiss francs. Show, in a table similar to the previous one, the bid rates for the different spot and forward rates.

12. **(Foreign exchange arbitrage)** You own $10,000. The dollar rate in Tokyo is 216.6752£. The yen rate in New York is given in the previous table. Are arbitrage profits possible? Set up an arbitrage scheme with your capital. What is the gain (loss) in dollars?

13. **(Related to Checkpoint 2) (Spot rates)** Compute the Canadian dollar/yen and the yen/Swiss franc spot rate from the data in the preceding table.

 14. **(Related to Checkpoint 2) (Determining the percent-per-annum premium or discount)** You are in need of Swiss (Switzerland) francs in six months, but before entering a forward contract to buy them, you would like to know their premium or discount if the spot rate is 0.9772 and the forward six-month rate is 0.9783.

Interest Rate and Purchasing-Power Parity

15. **(Interest rate parity)** On August 8th the six-month risk-free rate of interest in Switzerland was 4 percent. If the spot exchange rate for dollars for Swiss francs is 0.9252 and the six-month forward exchange rate is 0.9270, what would you expect the U.S. six-month risk-free rate to be?

16. **(Interest rate parity)** On August 8th the three-month risk-free rate of interest in the United States was 3.75 percent and it was 3 percent in Japan. If the spot exchange rate were .009074, what would you expect the forward exchange rate to be?

17. **(Purchasing-power parity)** If a new iMac costs $1,400 and the spot rate for euros is €.76/$, what is the price in euros for the iMac?

18. **(Purchasing-power parity)** If a new Samsung Blu-Ray machine costs ¥4,000 in Japan and the current spot rate is ¥.104/$, how much should this machine cost in the United States?

Capital Budgeting for Direct Foreign Investment

 19. **(Related to Checkpoint 3) (International capital budgeting)** Assume you are working for a firm based in the United States that is considering a new project in the country of Tambivia. This new project will produce the following cash flows measured in TABs (the currency of Tambivia), which are expected to be repatriated to the parent company in the United States.

Year	Cash Flow (in millions of TABs)
0	−12
1	5
2	6
3	7
4	7

In addition, assume the risk-free rate in the United States is 5 percent, and that this project is riskier than most and, as such, the firm has determined that it should require a 12 percent premium over the risk-free rate. Thus, the appropriate discount rate for this project is 17 percent. In addition, the current spot exchange rate is .60TAB/$, and the one-year forward exchange rate is .57TAB/$. What is the project's NPV?

20. **(Related to Checkpoint 3)** **(International capital budgeting)** An American firm is considering a new project in the country of Geeblaistan. This new project will produce the following cash flows measured in BLAs, the currency of Geeblaistan, which are expected to be repatriated to the parent company in the United States.

Year	Cash Flow (in millions of BLA)
0	−20
1	8
2	8
3	7
4	5

In addition, assume the risk-free rate in the United States is 4 percent, and that this project is riskier than most and, as such, the firm has determined that it should require a 14 percent premium over the risk-free rate. Thus, the appropriate discount rate for this project is 18 percent. In addition, the current spot exchange rate is .90BLA/$, and the one-year forward exchange rate is .93BLA/$. What is the project's NPV?

Mini-Case

For your job as the business reporter for a local newspaper, you are given the assignment of putting together a series of articles on multinational finance and the international currency markets for your readers. Much recent local press coverage has been given to losses in the foreign exchange markets by JGAR, a local firm that is the subsidiary of Daedlufetarg, a large German manufacturing firm. Your editor would like you to address several specific questions dealing with multinational finance. Prepare a response to the following memorandum from your editor:

TO: Business Reporter

FROM: Perry White, Editor, *Daily Planet*

RE: Upcoming Series on Multinational Finance

In your upcoming series on multinational finance, I would like to make sure you cover several specific points. In addition, before you begin this assignment, I want to make sure we are all reading from the same script, as accuracy has always been the cornerstone of the *Daily Planet*. I'd like a response to the following questions before we proceed:

1. What new problems and factors are encountered in international as opposed to domestic financial management?

2. What does the term *arbitrage profits* mean?

3. What does interest rate parity refer to?

Use the following data in your response to the remaining questions:

Selling Quotes for Foreign Currencies in New York

Country–Currency	Contract	$/Foreign Currency
Canada–dollar	Spot	.8450
	30-day	.8415
	90-day	.8390
Japan–yen	Spot	.004700
	30-day	.004750
	90-day	.004820
Switzerland–franc	Spot	.5150
	30-day	.5182
	90-day	.5328

4. An American business needs to pay
(a) 15,000 Canadian dollars, (b) 1.5 million yen, and (c) 55,000 Swiss francs to businesses abroad. What are the dollar payments to the respective countries?

5. An American business pays $20,000, $5,000, and $15,000 to suppliers in Japan, Switzerland, and Canada, respectively. How much, in local currencies, do the suppliers receive?

6. Compute the indirect quote for the spot and forward Canadian dollar contract.

7. You own $10,000. The dollar rate in Tokyo is 216.6752. The yen rate in New York is given in the preceding table. Are arbitrage profits possible? Set up an arbitrage scheme with your capital. What is the gain in dollars?

8. Compute the Canadian dollar/yen spot rate from the data in the preceding table.

Photo Credits

Credits are listed in order of appearance.

Adam James/Alamy; Runzelkorn/Shutterstock

Corporate Risk
Management

From Chapter 20 of *Financial Management: Principles and Applications*, Twelfth Edition. Sheridan Titman, Arthur J. Keown, and John D. Martin.

Corporate Risk Management

Chapter **Outline**

1 Five-Step Corporate Risk Management Process

→ **Objective 1.** Define risk management in the context of the five-step risk management process.

2 Managing Risk with Insurance Contracts

→ **Objective 2.** Understand how insurance contracts can be used to manage risk.

3 Managing Risk by Hedging with Forward Contracts

→ **Objective 3.** Use forward contracts to hedge commodity price risk.

4 Managing Risk with Exchange-Traded Financial Derivatives

→ **Objective 4.** Understand the advantages and disadvantages of using exchange-traded futures and option contracts to hedge price risk.

5 Valuing Options and Swaps

→ **Objective 5.** Understand how to value options and how swaps work.

If you think about **P** Principle 1: **Money Has a Time Value** it really deals with the opportunity cost of money. When interest rates are high, there is more value to money, and as a result, strategies that can avoid tying up your money are of value. As we will see, options can do that. Business is inherently risky, as we know from **P** Principle 2: **There Is a** **Risk–Return Tradeoff**. However, in this chapter we learn that a lot of the risks that a firm is exposed to are at least partially controllable. The process of analyzing a firm's risk exposures and determining how best to handle that risk exposure is the focus of a specialized area of finance called risk management.

Some Risk Can (and Should) Be Managed

Corporations are devoting increasing amounts of time and resources to the active management of their risk exposure. They enter into insurance agreements to insure against losses arising from natural disasters and accidents; they use long-term contracts to control the costs associated with outsourcing manufacturing and distribution; and they use financial contracts such as options, forwards and futures, and swap contracts to mitigate potential losses due to adverse changes in foreign exchange rates, interest rates, energy prices, and even bad weather.

Risk management will play a role in your personal life as well as your professional life. For example, in the not-too-distant future you are likely to purchase a house, and to do so you are likely to need a mortgage. About a month prior to closing on your house, you may be offered the opportunity to lock in the mortgage interest rate. For example, you may have the opportunity to choose between locking in the mortgage rate at 4.0 percent today versus waiting to take the going mortgage rate on the day when you actually purchase the home. If you choose to lock in the rate, you will eliminate the risk of having to pay a higher rate of interest should rates increase before you close on the home purchase. If you do this, you will have entered into something called a forward contract with your financial institution—that is, you have agreed upon a price (the rate of interest) for a transaction that will take place on a future date. After purchasing the house, you will continue to make risk management choices. Most notably, you will need to decide on how much insurance to buy to protect against risks that may be associated with natural disasters such as hurricanes, earthquakes, and floods.

While considering financial decision making in the presence of risk, we generally take the risk as something that is a given. In other words, we ignore the possibility that the firm might take actions to alter the risk. In this chapter we consider ways in which the financial manager can alter the risk exposure of the firm through the use of financial contracts. We first demonstrate a five-step process for arriving at a risk management strategy, along with a logical process for carrying it out. Next, we discuss hedging as a strategy designed to minimize a firm's exposure to unwanted risk. We also provide examples of some of the commonly used risk management practices.

Regardless of Your Major...

"Welcome to a Risky World"

The focus of corporate risk management is on managing the factors that determine the risk of a firm's cash flows. Very simply, this risk can be thought of as coming both from forces outside the control of the firm, such as competition from firms selling similar products or the overall health of the economy in general, as well as from factors that are under the control of the firm's management. With respect to the latter, the biggest source of risk comes from uncertainty about the firm's revenues, which are determined to a large extent by the successes and failures of the firm's marketing efforts. Another important contributor to the risk of a firm's cash flows is the firm's production costs. For example, production cost overruns are a major source of risk that can be controlled to some extent through the use of well-designed and well-maintained accounting systems that are used by the firm's operating managers to monitor and control the firm's operations. So, even though you may not be directly involved in the risk management of your firm, your actions contribute to the underlying risk of the firm's cash flows.

Your Turn: See Study Question 1.

1 Five-Step Corporate Risk Management Process[1]

Corporations have spent considerable effort in recent years devising strategies for assessing and managing the risks that they are exposed to in doing business. Any risk management approach generally starts with a procedure for identifying the various risks the firm faces and ends with guidelines for dealing with those risks. The following five-step process illustrates how some of the best-run companies manage risk.

Step 1: Identify and Understand the Firm's Major Risks

As it is not possible to manage risks that have not been identified and understood, the first step in any risk management program is to develop a full understanding of the types of risks the firm faces. These risks relate to the factors that drive the firm's cash flow volatility. The most common sources include the following:

1. **Demand Risk.** Fluctuations in product or service demand driven by competitive forces and the effects of the state of the economy in general. Some of this risk is strictly focused on the firm (e.g., product quality, on-time delivery, and so forth). External competition, as well as the status of the regional and national economy, also influences a firm's demand for its goods and services. For example, the mortgage market crisis of the late 2000s affected the demand for new home construction across the nation. However, the Arizona, California, and Florida markets were hit the hardest for reasons related to their regional economies.

2. **Commodity Risk.** Price fluctuations in commodities that are essential to your business can wreak havoc on the firm's cash flow. For example, the dramatic price increase in the cost of fuel that occurred in 2009–2011 produced huge losses for airline companies as it drove up their cost of operations substantially.

3. **Country or Political Risk.** Where your firm does business can create problems related to maintaining operations in the face of political unrest or unfavorable governmental interference in the firm's operations.

4. **Operational Risk.** Cost overruns related to the firm's operations are another source of volatility in corporate cash flow.

5. **Foreign-exchange Risk.** Unfavorable shifts in the exchange rate between the United States and the foreign countries in which a firm does business can lead to dramatic decreases in corporate cash flow.

---

[1]This discussion is based on Kevin Buehler, Andrew Freeman, and Ron Hulme, "Owning the Right Risks," *Harvard Business Review* (September 2008), 102–110.

Note that four of the five sources of risk just identified are external to the firm. Only operational risk is largely under the direct control of the firm's management. Thus, risk management generally focuses on factors that influence a firm's cash flow volatility that come from outside the firm. This is not to say that operational risks cannot be shifted or managed. They can, for example, be spread out or diffused through outsourcing some of the firm's business functions such as manufacturing, assembly, or information technology.

Step 2: Decide Which Types of Risks to Keep and Which to Transfer

This is perhaps the most critical step in the risk management process. Deciding which risks the firm should retain and which risks the firm should mitigate by passing them along to an outside party is at the very heart of risk management. For example, oil and gas exploration and production (E&P) firms have historically chosen to assume the risk of fluctuations in the price of oil and gas. Because oil and gas price fluctuations are a central part of their business, their investors expect to be exposed to this risk when they buy their stock. However, many E&P firms have recently decided that their real business is oil and gas exploration and production, not energy price speculation. These firms believe that they can operate more efficiently if they mitigate future price fluctuations. One such firm is Chesapeake Energy Corporation (CHK), the second-largest producer of U.S. natural gas, which for years was an active user of derivatives for hedging against the ups and downs of natural gas prices, and between 2006 and 2011 made an estimated $8.7 billion from its gas hedges. However, as natural gas prices dropped to under $4, Chesapeake decided to take a gamble and removed most of its hedges—that move didn't pay off; in fact, Chesapeake lost close to $1 billion from this move as natural gas prices continued to dive to around $2.

Step 3: Decide How Much Risk to Assume

Figure 1 illustrates the concept of a firm's "appetite" for assuming risk, or its **risk profile**. The figure provides three distributions of cash flows that correspond to three different approaches to risk management. The High Risk cash flow distribution represents the scenario where the firm's management does no risk mitigation or transfers. In this case, the firm's cash flows can be as high as $120 million or as low as $15 million, and the expected cash flow is $66.81 million. The Medium Risk scenario involves some risk reductions that pass along risk at the cost of a slight reduction in the expected cash flow to $61 million but with a minimum cash flow of $30 million. Finally, the Low Risk scenario offers an expected cash flow of $58.34 million but has a minimum cash flow of only $50 million. If the firm has principal and interest payments totaling $30 million, dividends of $10 million, plus planned capital expenditures of $8 million, then the risk that the firm's cash flow will not be sufficient to cover all $48 million of the planned expenditures varies from one scenario to another. For example, in the Low Risk scenario, there is a zero probability that the firm's cash flows will be insufficient to cover the planned expenditures, but in the Medium Risk scenario there is an 11.46 percent probability that the firm will not have enough cash to do all that it plans. For the High Risk scenario, the risk increases further such that there is a 16.53 percent probability that the firm will not generate the needed $48 million in cash flow.

In Step 3, management is faced with the question of which risk management scenario they prefer. Unfortunately, there is no formula like the net present value (NPV) formula that we can use to make this decision. Such a choice is more like the capital structure choice, where there is a tradeoff between the cost of financial distress (which is more likely to arise in the higher-risk scenario) and the cost associated with limiting the firm's risk.

Step 4: Incorporate Risk into All the Firm's Decisions and Processes

Once the firm decides on those risks that it will keep and those it will transfer, it is time to implement a system for controlling the firm's risk exposures. This means that every major investment, operating, and financing decision the firm makes must take into consideration the impact on overall firm risk.

For those risks that will be transferred, the firm's management must determine an appropriate means of transferring the risk. In some instances this may involve the purchase

Figure 1

Cash Flow Distributions for Alternative Risk Management Strategies
Each of the three probability distributions corresponds to a different approach to managing firm risk. The High Risk strategy can be interpreted as the "does nothing to transfer risk" strategy. The Medium Risk strategy involves transferring some of the firm's risk to outside parties using the tools of risk management discussed later. Finally, the Low Risk strategy represents the cash flow distribution that results when the firm engages in a risk management strategy whereby it offloads all the risks that it possibly can.

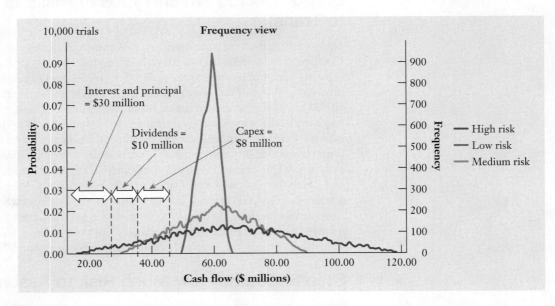

Legend:

Risk Scenario	Expected Cash Flow	Standard Deviation in Cash Flow	Probability of Not Being Able to Meet Capex, Dividend, and Principal and Interest Requirements
Low Risk	$58.34 million	$3.14 million	0.00%
Medium Risk	$61 million	$12.33 million	11.46%
High Risk	$66.81 million	$21.44 million	16.53%

>> END FIGURE 1

of insurance. For example, if the firm is located along the Florida Gulf Coast, it may want to purchase storm damage insurance to reimburse the firm for any storm damage it might incur during hurricane season. The point here is that once the firm has determined that it wants to transfer the risks associated with a facet of its operations, it must then select a cost-effective method for making the transfer. This critical element of the risk management process is our prime focus in this chapter.

Step 5: Monitor and Manage the Risks the Firm Assumes

To assure that the firm's day-to-day decisions are consistent with its chosen risk profile, it is necessary that it put in place an effective monitoring system. Typically, this means that the firm centralizes the responsibility for monitoring the firm's risk exposure with a chief risk officer who reports directly to the company CEO and also presents regularly to the firm's board of directors.

All five steps of the risk management process are essential to implementing and sustaining a risk management program. In the balance of this chapter we will review the alternative approaches that can be taken to managing a firm's risk exposure.

Before you move on to 2

Concept Check | 1

1. What are the five steps in the risk management process?
2. Describe the primary types of risk that a firm might face.

Managing Risk with Insurance Contracts

Insurance is defined as the equitable transfer of the risk of a loss, from one entity to another, in exchange for a premium. Consequently, insurance is a method for transferring risk from the firm to an outside party that is familiar to us all. Essentially, the insured exchanges the risk of a large uncertain, possibly devastating loss to an insurance company in exchange for a guaranteed small loss (the premium).

The decision to purchase insurance transfers the risks covered by the insurance contract to the insurance company. Consequently, insurance offers one method that both companies and individuals can use to manage the risks that they face.

Types of Insurance Contracts

There are as many types of insurance as there are events that someone would like to insure against. The following list of types of risks and corresponding insurance contracts provides an idea of some of the more common types of business insurance contracts that are used to manage some specific risks that firms face.

Type of Risk	Type of Insurance Contract Used to Hedge
Property damage to company facilities due to fire, storm, or vandalism	Property insurance
Loss of business resulting from a temporary shutdown because of fire or other insured peril	Business interruption insurance
Loss of income resulting from the disability or death of an employee in a key position	Key person life insurance
Losses suffered by the officers and directors of the firm due to alleged errors in judgment, breaches of duty, and wrongful acts related to their organizational activities	Director and officer insurance
Losses due to on-the-job injuries suffered by employees	Workers' compensation insurance

Why Purchase Insurance?

When a firm decides to purchase insurance it is typically the result of a cost-benefit type of analysis involving a comparison of the costs of purchasing the insurance contract and the expected costs of retaining the risk that is covered by the insurance. For example, many firms that operate fleets of vehicles will generally insure against the potential losses resulting from accidents in which the company driver is found to be at fault. However, they may not insure the fleet against the costs of damage in case of an accident. Instead they might decide that it is cheaper to self-insure. **Self-insurance** entails setting aside a calculated amount of money to compensate for the potential future loss. Self-insurance, therefore, is a decision to retain a particular risk exposure (property damage in the example used here). The decision to insure against one set of risks and not another reflects the firm's estimates of the potential cost of purchasing the insurance (the size of the premiums) and the benefits that would be derived from having insurance (avoiding the expected losses).

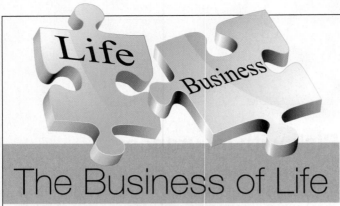

The Business of Life

Do You Need Life Insurance?

Life insurance is an odd thing to purchase—it is not meant to provide a benefit to the purchaser. After all, you are going to be dead when it pays off. So, to understand the proper motive for purchasing life insurance, you need to keep in mind its purpose, which is to provide financial support for your dependents in the event of your death. Life insurance can give you peace of mind by ensuring that your dependents will have the financial resources to pay off your debts, keep their homes, attend college, and be able to live comfortably.

How do you know whether you need life insurance? If you're single and have no dependents, you generally don't need life insurance. However, you still might want to buy life insurance if you're at a higher risk of contracting a terminal illness, such as cancer or AIDS, or an uninsurable condition that could prevent eligibility for later insurance purchases, such as diabetes or heart disease. Furthermore, although insurance policies don't pay off

until you die, if you're terminally ill and need an influx of cash for any reason, it is possible to receive a discounted settlement or to sell your insurance policy at a discount before you die.

So when should you purchase life insurance? Here are some commonsense guidelines that can help you answer this question:

- **You are single and don't have any dependents.** Unless you are concerned that you may not be insurable in the future, purchasing life insurance should probably be a very low priority for you.
- **You are part of a married, double-income couple with no children.** Consider life insurance only if you are concerned that a surviving spouse's lifestyle will suffer should you die today.
- **You are married but are not employed.** Consider life insurance only if you have young children and your spouse would have financial problems with day care and other costs of raising a family should you die today.
- **You are retired.** Consider life insurance only if your spouse could not live on your savings, including Social Security and your pension, should you die today.
- **You have children.** You should have coverage for raising and educating your children until they are financially self-sufficient.
- **You are a married, have a single income, and have no children.** You should have insurance to allow your surviving spouse to maintain his or her lifestyle until he or she can become self-sufficient.
- **You own your own business.** A life insurance policy can allow your family to pay off any business debt should you die today.

Your Turn: See Study Question 6.

Before you move on to 3

Concept Check | 2

1. What is insurance, and how is it used to manage risk?
2. What are some common risks that are transferred through the use of insurance?

 # Managing Risk by Hedging with Forward Contracts

The term **hedging** refers to a strategy designed to offset the exposure to price risk. For example, if you knew that you were going to need to purchase 100,000 barrels of crude oil in one month but were concerned that the price of crude oil might rise over the next 30 days, you might strike an agreement with the crude oil seller to purchase the oil in one month at a price you set today. In this way any increase in the market price of crude will not affect you because you have a prearranged price set today for a future purchase. This contract, by the way, is called a forward contract. Let's see how this works.

A **forward contract** is a contract wherein a price is agreed upon today for an asset to be sold in the future. These contracts are privately negotiated between the buyer and seller. The key feature to a forward contract is the fact that the price determination is made at the time of the contract but the actual purchase and sale do not occur until the maturity of the contract in the future. Forward contracts can be contrasted with something called a spot contract. A **spot contract** is an exchange in which the buyer and seller agree upon a price and complete the exchange immediately. In contrast, a forward contract calls for delivery at a future date but for a price that is agreed upon today.

Whenever you lock in a price today on a transaction that will occur in the future, you have entered into a forward contract. For example, in the introduction we discussed the fact that homebuyers often settle on the interest rate on their mortgage prior to the actual purchase date of their house. Such a transaction is effectively a forward contract.

Because forward contracts allow buyers and sellers to agree upon a price to be paid in the future, these agreements can be used to offset the risk of adverse fluctuations in future prices. Consequently, the risk of such an adverse price movement is transferred to the other party to the forward contract. Let's see how this can work by considering the risk of fluctuating fuel costs and airline fuel costs.

Hedging Commodity Price Risk Using Forward Contracts

Consider the problem faced by Tree-Top Airlines (TTA). In six months the firm will need to purchase jet fuel that is currently selling for $100 per barrel and it does not want to suffer the risks associated with future price fluctuations in the cost of fuel. (For now we will assume that the firm needs just one barrel of fuel. You can multiply the results by any number of barrels to adjust the outcome for TTA's actual fuel needs.)

The firm can enter into a forward contract today with a delivery price equal to the current price of fuel of $100 that will have the payoffs found in Panel A of Figure 2. The firm that owns this position is said to have taken a long position in the forward contract. Note that if the actual price of jet fuel rises to $130, then the forward contract is worth $30 per barrel to TTA. Thus, in six months TTA's cost of fuel remains $100 (i.e., the market price of fuel in six months of $130 less the payoff from the long position in the forward contract, which is $30).

Now let us consider the situation faced by the Pilot Refining Company, which anticipates that it will have jet fuel refined and ready for sale in six months. However, the price it can realize from the sale of the jet fuel is subject to market fluctuations. To eliminate the risk of a drop in the price, Pilot can sell a forward contract (i.e., take a short position) for the delivery in six months at a delivery price of $100. The payoff to this contract is found in Panel B of Figure 2. For example, if the price of jet fuel rises to $130 on the delivery date, then Pilot can sell its jet fuel for this price but the firm suffers a loss of $30 on the forward contract, such that the net price received per barrel is $100.

Hedging Currency Risk Using Forward Contracts

Forward contracts can also be used to hedge currency risk. To illustrate, consider the currency risks faced by The Disney Corporation, which generates revenues from all over the world. One of Disney's biggest sources of income is Tokyo Disney. For illustration purposes assume that Disney expects to receive ¥500 million from its Tokyo operation in three months and another ¥500 million in six months. Disney would like to lock in the exchange rate on these two cash flows and thereby eliminate any risk of an unfavorable move in exchange rates.

To hedge the first cash flow, to be received in three months, Disney uses a forward market hedge arranged with its investment banker. The investment banker indicates that the three-month forward $/¥ rate is 0.009123. To hedge its exchange rate risk Disney uses the following two-step procedure:

Step 1. Enter into a three-month forward contract that requires Disney to sell ¥500 million three months from now at a rate of $0.009123/¥.

Step 2. Three months from now Disney takes its cash flow of ¥500 million and converts it at the contracted rate, providing Disney with $4,561,500 ($0.009123/¥ × ¥500,000,000 = $4,561,500).

The effect of entering into the hedge (selling yen at the forward price of $0.009123) is that Disney locks in this exchange rate with the forward market hedge transaction. No matter what happens to the exchange rate over the next three months, Disney will receive the same dollar amount for the ¥500 million as agreed to in the forward contract.

Figure 2

Delivery Date Profits or Losses (Payoffs) from a Forward Contract

The term **long position** is often used to refer to the ownership of a security, contract, or commodity. That is, if you purchase a share of stock you are said to be "long" on the stock, such that when the price of the stock goes up the holder of the long position benefits or profits. Correspondingly, a **short position** is the opposite of a long position and involves the sale of a security, contract, or commodity. This means that the payoff to a short position is simply the negative of the payoff to a long position. If you would make money with a long position, this means you would lose money with a short position, and vice versa.

(Panel A) Long Position in Forward Contract

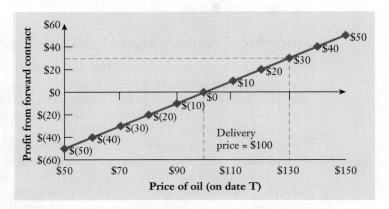

(Panel B) Short Position in Forward Contract

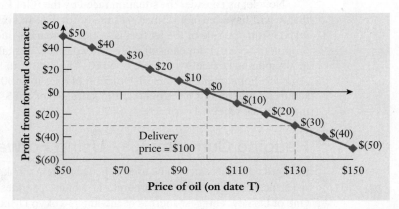

>> END FIGURE 2

Checkpoint 1

Hedging Crude Oil Price Risk Using Forward Contracts

Progressive Refining Inc. operates a specialty refining company that refines crude oil and sells the refined by-products to the cosmetic and plastic industries. The firm is currently planning for its refining needs for one year hence. The firm's analysts estimate that Progressive will need to purchase 1 million barrels of crude oil at the end of the current year to provide the feedstock for its refining needs for the coming year. The 1 million barrels of crude will be converted into by-products at an average cost of $30 per barrel. Progressive will then sell the by-products for $165 per barrel. The current spot price of oil is $125 per barrel, and Progressive has been offered a forward contract by its investment banker to purchase the needed oil for a delivery price in one year of $130 per barrel.

a. Ignoring taxes, if oil prices in one year are as low as $110 or as high as $140, what will be Progressive's profits (assuming the firm does not enter into the forward contract)?

b. If the firm were to enter into the forward contract to purchase oil for $130 per barrel, demonstrate how this would effectively lock in the firm's cost of fuel today, thus hedging the risk that fluctuating crude oil prices pose for the firm's profits for the next year.

STEP 1: Picture the problem

In one year the price of crude oil might be as high as $140 a barrel or as low as $110. Because the cost of 1 million barrels of crude is the firm's primary cost of doing business, the price of crude in one year will have a rather dramatic impact on firm profits if it is not managed or hedged.

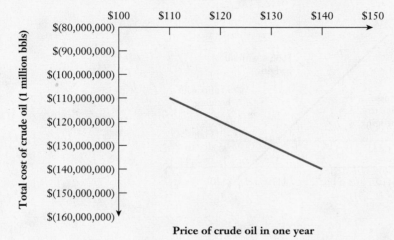

STEP 2: Decide on a solution strategy

Because the firm needs to purchase crude oil in one year, it can hedge this risk by entering into a forward contract whose payoff offsets any increase or decrease in the cost of crude oil (i.e., whose payoff varies in exactly the opposite direction as the price of crude). We learned in Figure 2 that by purchasing a forward contract for crude at a fixed delivery price (in this case $130), the firm can lock in its cost of crude. So, we need to enter into a long position (purchase a forward contract) for the delivery of crude in one year at the price of $130 that covers 1 million barrels (bbls) of oil.

STEP 3: Solve

The following table contains the calculation of firm profits for the case where the price of crude oil is not hedged (column E), the payoff to the forward contract (column F), and firm profits where the price of crude is fully hedged (column G):

Price of Oil/bbl	Total Cost of Oil	Total Revenues	Total Refining Costs	Unhedged Annual Profits	Profit/Loss on Forward Contract	Hedged Annual Profits
A	B $= A \times 1m$	C $= \$165 \times 1m$	D $= \$30 \times 1m$	E $= C + B + D$	F $=(A - \$130) \times 1m$	G $= E + F$
$110	$(110,000,000)	$165,000,000	$(30,000,000)	$25,000,000	$(20,000,000)	$5,000,000
115	(115,000,000)	$165,000,000	(30,000,000)	20,000,000	(15,000,000)	5,000,000
120	(120,000,000)	$165,000,000	(30,000,000)	15,000,000	(10,000,000)	5,000,000
125	(125,000,000)	$165,000,000	(30,000,000)	10,000,000	(5,000,000)	5,000,000
130	(130,000,000)	$165,000,000	(30,000,000)	5,000,000	0	5,000,000
135	(135,000,000)	$165,000,000	(30,000,000)	0	5,000,000	5,000,000
140	(140,000,000)	$165,000,000	(30,000,000)	(5,000,000)	10,000,000	5,000,000
Number of barrels		1,000,000				
Revenues		$165,000,000				
Delivery price		$130.00				

(1 CONTINUED >> ON NEXT PAGE)

STEP 4: Analyze

Where the price of crude is not hedged, firm profits vary from a loss of $5 million up to a profit of $25 million. However, where the cost of crude is fully hedged, firm profits are always $5,000,000. Figure 3 illustrates the gains and losses from hedging.

Figure 3

Gains and Losses from Hedging

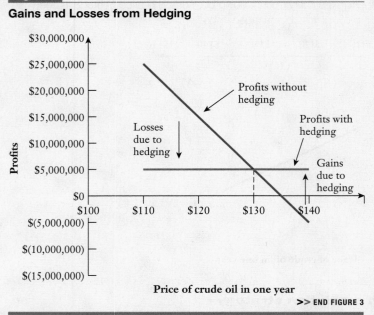

Profits without hedging

Losses due to hedging

Profits with hedging

Gains due to hedging

>> END FIGURE 3

For end-of-year oil prices below $130, the hedging strategy (which calls for a delivery price of $130) actually creates losses for the firm when compared with an open market purchase. However, for prices above $130 the hedging strategy actually reduces the cost of crude to the company and provides gains when compared to simply purchasing in the open market at the end of the year.

This is a simplified view of the power of hedging because we have assumed that the only source of uncertainty regarding future profits is the cost of crude. In fact, Progressive would also face some risk associated with revenues for its product and the cost of refining the crude. The former translates into the risk of varying prices per unit and varying demand for the firm's products, which in turn will determine how much crude oil Progressive will actually need. In other words, the price of crude is not the only source of risk faced by Progressive. Of particular importance is the quantity risk related to how many barrels the firm will actually need to purchase at year end.

STEP 5: Check yourself

Consider the profits that Progressive might earn if it chooses to hedge only 80 percent of its anticipated 1 million barrels of crude oil under the conditions just described.

ANSWER:

Price of Crude A	Profit/Loss on Forward Contract F	80% Hedged Annual Profits G
$110	$(16 million)	$9 million
$140	$8 million	$3 million

Your Turn: For more practice, do related **Study Problem** 3 at the end of this chapter.   >> END Checkpoint 1

The risk of currency fluctuation on the second cash flow of ¥500 million can be similarly eliminated with a six-month forward contract. In this case the six-month forward $/¥ rate is 0.009178, which means that Disney locks in revenues of $4,589,000 ($0.009178/¥ × ¥500,000,000 = $4,589,000).

Suppose now that Toyota is expecting two cash flows in dollars, one in three months of $4,561,500 and one in six months of $4,589,000, from its U.S. operations and wants to lock in the yen value of these cash flows. To do this, Toyota could buy a forward contract to buy yen for dollars in three and six months. This would make the Disney and Toyota contracts mirror images of one another, putting them on opposite sides of the transactions we just described, with Disney selling yen for dollars and Toyota buying yen for dollars. This is essentially what is done with a swap contract, which we discuss later. That is, two parties agree to exchange a specific amount of one currency for another at some specific date in the future.

Limitations of Forward Contracts

Generally, forward contracts are negotiated contracts between the firm managing its risk exposure and a financial intermediary such as an investment bank. The primary advantage of this type of bilateral arrangement is that the contract can be tailored to the specific needs of the firm that is engaging in risk management. However, there are some potentially serious limitations of this approach:

1. **Credit risk exposure.** Both parties to the contract are exposed to **credit** or **default risk**. This is the risk that the other party to the transaction might default on his or her obligation. For example, there were a large number of firms that had entered into various types of risk management or hedging contracts with Enron Corporation that were designed to mitigate the firms' exposure to energy price risk. When Enron failed, these contracts were no longer effective. *The point is that using bilateral negotiated contracts to manage price risk also exposes the firm to credit or default risk of the person or institution on the other side of the transaction.*

2. **Sharing of strategic information.** Because the two parties to a forward contract know who the other party is, they learn about the specific risks that are being hedged. If the parties to the agreement were anonymous (as would be the case if exchange-traded contracts were used), then no such sharing of information would occur.

3. **Market values of negotiated contracts are not easily determined.** Without a market value for the negotiated forward contract, it is difficult to assess the gains and losses the firm has experienced at any point in time.

The limitations noted can be addressed through the use of exchange-traded contracts. Specifically, exchange-traded futures, options, and swap contracts, which we discuss in the next section, provide alternative means for managing corporate risk that do not suffer from the limitations of bilateral negotiated forward contracts.

Before you move on to 4

Concept Check | 3

1. What is a forward contract? Contrast a forward contract with a spot contract.
2. What are the limitations of forward contracts as tools for managing risk?

Managing Risk with Exchange-Traded Financial Derivatives

A **derivative contract** is a security whose value is *derived* from the value of another asset or security (which is referred to as the *underlying asset*). Technically, the forward contracts that were discussed in the previous section are derivative contracts because the value of the forward contract is derived from the value of the underlying asset (e.g., a barrel of oil or one unit of a country's currency). In this section we consider derivative contracts that are traded in the securities markets. Unlike forward contracts that can be customized to meet the specific asset risk and maturity requirements of the hedging firm, financial derivatives traded on organized exchanges are available only for specific assets and for a limited set of maturities. Even so, these derivatives can be effectively used to implement a wide variety of hedging strategies and, as we have just seen, these contracts avoid some important limitations of negotiated forward contracts.

Futures Contracts

A **futures contract** is a contract to buy or sell a stated commodity (such as soybeans or corn) or a financial claim (such as U.S. Treasury bonds) at a specified price at some future specified time. These contracts, like forward contracts, can be used by the financial manager to lock in future prices of raw materials, interest rates, or exchange rates.

There are two basic categories of futures contracts that are traded on futures exchanges or markets: **commodity futures** and **financial futures**. Commodity futures are traded on agricultural products, such as wheat and corn, as well as metals, wood products, and fibers. Financial futures come in a number of different forms, including futures on Treasury bills, notes and bonds, certificates of deposit, Eurodollars, foreign currencies, and stock indices. These financial instruments first appeared in the financial markets in the 1970s, and since then their growth has been phenomenal. Today they dominate the futures markets.

Managing Default Risk in Futures Markets

Futures exchanges use two mechanisms to control credit or default risk. As we noted earlier, credit or default risk is the risk that one of the parties to the futures contract will default on his or her obligation to the other party, thereby negating the value of the hedge. To prevent default, futures exchanges require participants to post collateral called **futures margin**, or just *margin*. This collateral is then used to guarantee that the trader will fulfill his or her obligation under any futures contract the trader enters. The second mechanism used to control for default risk is something called **marking to market**. This means that daily gains or losses from a firm's futures contracts are transferred to or from its margin account.

To illustrate marking to market, let's assume that the Hershey Co. (HSY) is planning its needs for chocolate for the Christmas period and has estimated the amount of chocolate it will need in three months to meet its candy production plans in three months. Because the price of chocolate is subject to fluctuations related to cocoa bean prices, the firm could purchase cocoa bean futures to hedge its price risk exposure. On October 1st Hershey purchases 10 cocoa contracts for November delivery that are trading for $2,578 per contract. Figure 4 shows how Hershey's margin account will be affected by volatility in the price of this contract.

The initial value of the cocoa bean futures contract is $2,578 on October 1st. On October 2nd the contract drops $82 to $2,496. Because Hershey has agreed to pay $2,578, the decline in

Figure 4

Marking to Market on Futures Contracts

Upon initiating a futures contract, the exchange will require the parties to the contract to post an initial margin. In this example the margin is roughly 16 percent of the $25,780 (= $2,578 × 10 contracts) value of the 10 contracts. In addition, the exchange requires that the firm not allow the margin account to drop below a maintenance margin level such that the margin account never goes to zero.

Date	Margin Account Balance on 10 Contracts	Value of 1 Futures Contract	Change in 1 Futures Price	Change in Value of 10 Contracts
1-Oct-12	$4,000	$2,578		
2-Oct-12	3,180	2,496	$(82)	$(820)
3-Oct-12	3,250	2,503	7	70
4-Oct-12	3,880	2,566	63	630

>> END FIGURE 4

value of the contract is deducted from Hershey's margin account for each of the 10 contracts it owns, which reduces the value of the margin account by $820 to $3,180. Following this mark-to-market procedure until the delivery date, we are assured that Hershey and the counterparty to the contract have already posted the gain or loss to the other and the risk of default is thereby negated.

Hedging with Futures

Futures contracts can be used to build financial hedges much like those we discussed using forwards. For example, if Exxon has 2 million barrels of crude to sell at month's end, it can sell (or short) a futures contract for 2 million barrels that matures at month end. This is known as a short hedge. Similarly, if Reynolds Aluminum knows that it will need 2 million tons of ore to feed its smelters next month, it can enter a long hedge by purchasing a futures contract for the requisite ore (i.e., by taking a long position in a futures contract).

In practice, hedging with futures contracts is almost never as neat and tidy as the hypothetical examples we present here. Because futures contracts are only available for a subset of all assets and for a limited set of maturities, it is often not possible to form a perfect hedge.

Restrictions on available futures contracts and maturities give rise to the following practical problems:

1. It may not be possible to find a futures contract on the exact asset that is the source of risk.
2. The hedging firm may not know the exact date when the hedged asset will be bought or sold.
3. The maturity of the futures contract may not match the period for which the underlying asset is to be held or until it must be acquired, in which case the hedge may have to be shut down before the futures contract expiration date.

Failure of the hedge for any of these reasons leads to what is known as **basis risk**. Basis risk arises any time the asset underlying the futures contract is not identical to the asset that underlies the firm's risk exposure. That is, basis risk occurs whenever the price of the asset that underlies the futures contract is not perfectly correlated with the price risk the firm is trying to hedge. As a consequence, where the basis is non-zero, the firm does not have a perfect hedge. In the hypothetical hedges we have described thus far, we have assumed that the asset underlying the futures contract is exactly the same as the one on which the futures contract is written. Where this is the case, the firm can combine its position in the underlying asset with a futures contract of equal value on a similar product, such that the basis risk is zero at the expiration of the contract, and the hedge works.

If futures contracts are not available for every commodity and maturity, then the financial analyst must choose a contract (underlying asset) and a maturity that best fits his or her needs. For example, because there are not active futures contracts for jet fuel, airlines sometimes hedge their jet fuel risk exposure using the NYMEX heating oil futures contracts. The commonsense guide to choosing a contract in this circumstance involves examining the relationship between the price changes of the commodities that are traded and the commodity risk that needs to be hedged. In general, when the correlation is higher, the hedge will be better.

The choice of a contract expiration date would seem rather simple: Select a futures contract that most nearly matches the maturity of the firm's risk exposure. For example, if the firm's risk exposure ends at the end of the month, it seems only reasonable that we hedge its returns using a futures contract that expires as close as possible to the end of the month. In theory this is the appropriate solution to the problem; however, in practice firms often select a futures contract with a slightly longer maturity date. The rationale here is that futures contract prices often behave erratically in the month in which they expire. In addition, if the hedger has a long position in the futures contract and the contract expires before the date when the asset risk exposure is resolved, the hedging firm runs the risk of having to take delivery of the commodity underlying the futures contract.

Options Contracts

There are many situations where firms would like to guarantee a minimum revenue but they do not need to absolutely fix their revenues. For example, an oil company may need to sell oil next year for at least $40/barrel to meet its payroll and interest obligations, but it may still want a share of the upside if oil prices increase substantially. The firm can accomplish this if it hedges with options rather than with forward contracts.

There are two basic types of options: calls and puts. A **call option** gives its owner the right (but not the obligation) to purchase a given number of shares of stock or an asset at a specified price over a given period. Note a key difference between an **option contract** and a futures contract is that the option owner does *not* have to exercise the option. If the price of the underlying common stock or asset on which the option is written goes up, the owner of a call option makes money. You have the option to buy something (for example, shares of common stock) at a set price even though the market price of the stock has risen above the fixed exercise price.

A **put option**, on the other hand, gives its owner the right (but not the obligation) to sell a given number of shares of common stock or an asset at a specified price within a given period. The owner of a put makes money when the price of the underlying common stock or asset on which the put is written drops in value. Just as with a call, a put option gives its owner the *right* to sell the common stock or asset at a set price, but it is not a promise to sell.

Now let's take a look at some of the terminology involved with options.

When an option is purchased, it is nothing more than a contract that *allows* the purchaser to either buy (in the case of a call) or sell (in the case of a put) the underlying stock or asset at a predetermined price. That is, no asset has changed hands, but the price has been set for a future transaction that will occur only if and when the option purchaser exercises the option. We refer to the process of *selling* puts and calls as **option writing**.

The **exercise** or **strike price** for an option is the price at which the stock or asset may be purchased from the option writer in the case of a call, or sold to the option writer in the case of a put. The **option premium** is the price paid for the option. It is generally stated in terms of dollars per share, which for options on common stock cover 100 shares, rather than per option contract. Thus, if a call option premium is $2, then an option contract would cost $200 and would allow the purchase of 100 shares of stock at the exercise price. The **option expiration date** is the date on which the option contract expires. An **American option** contract is one that can be exercised at any time up to the expiration date. A **European option** contract, on the other hand, can be exercised only on the expiration date.

A Graphical Look at Option Pricing Relationships

Perhaps the easiest way to gain an understanding of options is to look at them graphically. Figure 5 presents a profit and loss graph for the purchase of a call on Ford stock with an exercise price of $20 that is bought for a premium of $4. This is termed a "Ford 20 call." In Figure 5 and all other profit and loss graphs, the vertical axis represents the profits or losses realized *on* the option's expiration date, and the horizontal axis represents the corresponding stock price *on* the expiration date. To keep things simple, we will also ignore any transaction costs.

For the Ford call option with a $20 exercise price shown in Figure 5, the call will be worthless at expiration if the value of the stock is less than the exercise or striking price. This is because it would make no sense for an individual to exercise the call option to purchase Ford stock for $20 per share if he or she could buy the same Ford stock from a broker at a price less than $20. Although the option will be worthless at expiration if the stock price is below the exercise price, the most that an investor can lose is the option premium—that is, the amount he or she paid for the option, which in this case was $4. Although this may be the entire investment in the option, it is also generally only a fraction of the stock's price. Once the stock price climbs above the exercise price, the call option takes on a positive value and increases in a linear dollar-for-dollar basis as the stock price increases. Moreover, there is no limit as to how high the profits can climb. In the case of the Ford 20 call, once the price of Ford stock rises above $20, the call becomes valuable. Once the price hits $24, the investor breaks even because he or she has earned enough profits to cover the $4 premium paid for the option in the first place.

To the call writer, the profit and loss graph is the mirror image of the call purchaser's graph. Figure 6 shows the profits and losses at expiration associated with writing a call option. Once again, we will look at the profits and losses at expiration. The maximum profit

Expiration Date Profit or Loss from Purchasing a Call Option

Suppose you purchase a call on Ford Motor Company (F) stock with an exercise price of $20 for a premium of $4. As long as the expiration date price of Ford's common stock is less than the $20 exercise price, the call option will expire worthless. It is said to be "out of the money." If the price of Ford's stock on the expiration date is equal to $20 it is "at the money," and if it is higher than $20 then the call option is "in the money" with a profit equal to the difference between the stock price and the exercise price.

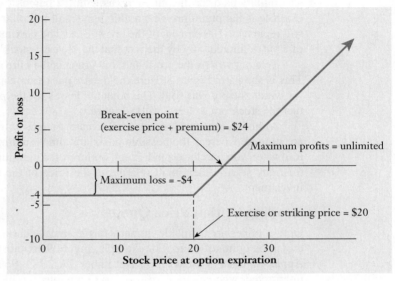

Expiration Date Profit or Loss from Selling (Writing) a Call Option

In this example we assume that you sell or "write" a call option on Ford Motor Company (F) stock with an exercise price of $20 for which you are paid a premium of $4. If the price of Ford's shares ends up below $20 per share, then the call option will expire worthless and the option writer (seller) will not face any financial obligation. However, if the price of Ford's shares rises above $20, the owner of the option gets the difference in the stock price and the exercise price (a profit—see Figure 5) and the option writer faces a loss equal to this same difference.

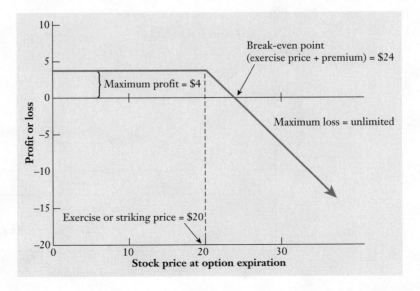

to the call writer is the premium, or how much the writer received when the option was sold, whereas the maximum loss is unlimited.

Looking at the profit and loss graph presented in Figure 7 for the purchase of a Ford 20 put that is bought for $3, we see that the lower the price of the Ford stock, the more the put is worth. Here the put only begins to take on value once the price of the Ford stock drops below the exercise price, which in this case is $20. Then for every dollar that the price of the Ford stock drops, the put increases in value by one dollar. Once the Ford stock drops to $17 per share, the put purchaser breaks even by making $3 on the put, which exactly offsets what he or she initially paid for the put. Here, as with the purchase of a call option, the most an investor can lose is the premium, which although small in dollar value relative to the potential gains, still represents 100 percent of the investment. The maximum gain associated with the purchase of a put is limited only by the fact that the lowest a stock's price can fall to is zero.

To a put writer, the profit and loss graph is the mirror image of the put purchaser's graph. This is shown in Figure 8. Here the most a put writer can earn is the premium, or the amount for which the put was sold. The potential losses for the put writer are limited only by the fact that the stock price cannot fall below zero.

Although the stock price may fluctuate, the possible losses to the purchaser of an option are limited, whereas the possible gains are almost unlimited. That is, the most you can ever lose when you purchase a put or call option is the premium you pay for the contract. Although this may seem rather small relative to the price of the stock, it is still 100 percent of your investment.

Reading Option Price Quotes

Option prices are available in many of the same sources that provide stock prices. However, they look quite different. For example, Figure 9 contains call and put option price quotes for Apple Computers (AAPL) on December 27, 2012. Some of the information can be easily interpreted, whereas some of it is not so obvious. To illustrate, consider the first row of data

---

Figure 7

Expiration Date Profit or Loss on Holding a Put Option

Suppose you purchase a put option on Ford Motor Company (F) stock with an exercise price of $20 and for a premium of $3. As long as the expiration date price of Ford's shares remains above the $20 exercise price, the put is worthless or "out of the money." Should the price of Ford's shares fall below $20 per share on the expiration date, then the put option holder will receive $1 for every dollar the price falls below $20, and once the price falls below $17, he or she will make a profit.

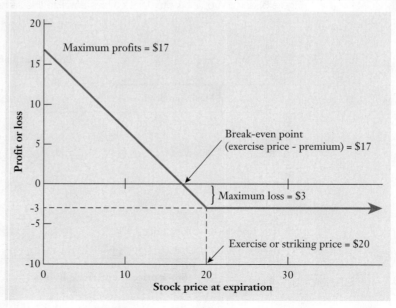

>> END FIGURE 7

Figure 8

Expiration Date Profit or Loss from Selling (Writing) a Put Option

Suppose you write or sell a put option on Ford Motor Company (F) stock with an exercise price of $20 for a premium of $3. Should the price of Ford's shares drop below the $20 exercise price on the put option you have sold, you will then be obligated to pay the difference in the $20 exercise price and the stock price to the holder of the option (see Figure 7).

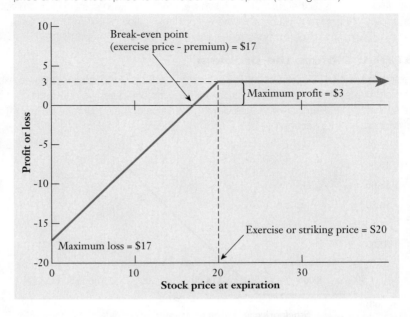

>> END FIGURE 8

Figure 9

Option Price Quotes for Apple Computers (AAPL) on December 27, 2012

Pricing information is provided for both call options, which represent the right to buy the shares of Apple, and put options, which carry with them the right to sell Apple shares. The data included in the graphic include the following: the most recent price of Apple's common stock, "Last Sale" identifies the price of the most recent transaction, "Volume" represents the number of option contracts traded that day, and "Open Int" is the total number of option contracts that have not yet been exercised, expired, or fulfilled by delivery.

AAPL (APPLE INC) Closing price as of 12/27/2012: $515.06

Calls	Last Sale	Vol	Open Int	Puts	Last Sale	Vol	Open Int
13 Jan 510	$20.55	3740	5462	13 Jan 510	$15.45	4034	9364
13 Jan 515	$17.80	3431	3667	13 Jan 515	$17.85	2954	7759
13 Jan 520	$15.50	5714	8395	13 Jan 520	$20.00	2552	16866
13 Jan 525	$13.67	2582	7229	13 Jan 525	$22.55	739	14957
13 Feb 510	$32.20	1326	2737	13 Feb 510	$27.34	646	2832
13 Feb 515	$29.65	829	1485	13 Feb 515	$30.35	543	2681
13 Feb 520	$26.80	1752	3359	13 Feb 520	$32.30	541	2862
13 Feb 525	$24.75	722	2905	13 Feb 525	$35.25	309	3903

Sources: www.cboe.com, www.quote.com, Wall Street Journal online, www.fidelity.com, and OptionsHouse.com

>> END FIGURE 9

Determining the Break-Even Point and Profit or Loss on a Call Option

You are considering purchasing a call option on CROCS, Inc. (CROX) common stock. The exercise price on this call option is $10 and you purchased the option for $3. What is the break-even point on this call option (ignoring any transaction costs but considering the price of purchasing the option—the option premium)? Also, what would be the profit or loss on this option at expiration if the price dropped to $9, if it rose to $11, or if it rose to $25?

STEP 1: Picture the problem

Letting the vertical axis represent the profits or losses realized on the option's expiration date, and letting the horizontal axis represent the stock price on the expiration date, we can visualize the profit or loss on an option, as shown below. Remember we are viewing the value of the option at expiration. To keep things simple, we will also ignore any transaction costs.

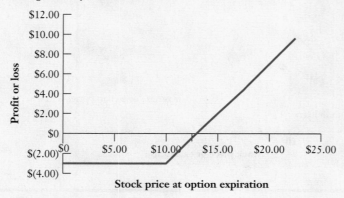

STEP 2: Decide on a solution strategy

The solution is actually quite simple in this case. At the expiration date, the break-even point is equal to exercise price + premium.

STEP 3: Solve

Thus, plugging into the formulas for the break-even point, we get:

Break-even point = exercise price + what you paid for the option

$$= \$10 + \$3 = \$13$$

To calculate the profit or loss on an option at expiration, you merely need to calculate the put or call's value at expiration, then subtract out what you paid for it. When CROCS is selling at $9 and the option was purchased for $3, Profit or Loss = call value − what you paid for the option:

$$= \$0 - \$3 = -\$3.$$

Profit or Loss When CROCS is selling at $11 and the option was purchased for $3, Profit or Loss = call value − what you paid for the option:

$$= \$1 - \$3 = -\$2.$$

When CROCS is selling at $25 and the option was purchased for $3, Profit or Loss = call value − what you paid for the option:

$$= \$15 - \$3 = \$12.$$

STEP 4: Analyze

In this example we have looked at the profit or loss on an option at expiration. However, if we reexamine these relationships at a time before expiration, we would find that options will sell for something slightly different than what is shown in the previous graph. First, an option cannot sell for a negative price; after all, in the worst-case scenario you just let it expire worthless. Second, prior to expiration there is still the possibility that the option may increase in value, and the longer the time to expiration and the more volatile the underlying stock is, the greater the chance that the option will increase in value. This is referred to as the time or speculative value of the option. At expiration, when the chance for future capital gains has been exhausted, the time value is zero.

With a buyer and a seller of an option, you easily see that option trading is a perfect example of a two-sided transaction. Note that this transaction is a zero-sum game—that is, one investor gains at the expense of another investor. Moreover, if commissions are considered, the total becomes negative, and we have a "negative-sum" game. The fact that options are a "negative-sum" game should cause you to approach them with some caution; after all, the person on the other side of the transaction probably has an opposite point of view on that security. It should also make you realize that there aren't any free lunches in options trading—there's always someone on the other side of every trade trying to beat you.

Most people believe that the vast majority of options expire worthless, but that's not the case—only about 30 percent of all options expire worthless. Over 60 percent of all options are traded out, meaning that option buyers sell their options in the market, while option writers buy back options identical to what they originally sold to cancel out their position. The remaining 10 percent of all options are exercised during each monthly cycle, generally in the week prior to expiration.

STEP 5: Check yourself

If you paid $5 for a call option with an exercise price of $25, and the stock is selling for $35 at expiration, what are your profits or losses? What is the break-even point on this call option?

ANSWER: Profits or (losses): $5; break-even point: $30.

Your Turn: For more practice, do related **Study Problem** 5 at the end of this chapter.   >> **END Checkpoint 2**

---

in Figure 9. First we should note that column heading indicates that we are looking at call options and the first call option designated is the "13 Jan 510" option. This identifies the call option that expires on the third Friday in January 2013, where "13 Jan" refers to January 2013 (note that all equity options expire on the third Friday of each month), and "510" indicates a $510.00 strike or exercise price. In the case of a call option, the strike or exercise price identifies the price that the call option allows its holder to purchase the stock for, and in the case of a put, it identifies the price that the put option allows its holder to sell the stock for.

Option contract prices are quoted per share of stock but are sold on 100-share lots. So if you wanted to purchase the February 2013 520 call option on Apple's stock, you would expect to pay the $26.80 asking price multiplied by 100 shares, or $2,680, to purchase the call option contract.

Before you move on to 5

Concept Check | 4

1. What is meant by the term *financial derivative contract*?
2. Define and contrast the following types of financial derivatives: options, futures, and forwards.

 Valuing Options and Swaps

Up until now, we have talked about the value of an option at its maturity date. When the option is in the money (that is, when it has value), the value equals the difference between the price of the underlying asset on which the option is written and the strike price of the option. When the option is out of the money, its value is of course zero. In this section we describe how option prices are determined prior to the maturity date.

The value of a share of stock is determined by the present value of the expected future dividends that the owner of the stock expects to receive. Similarly, the value of an option is the present value of the expected payout when the option matures. However, as we discuss in the next subsection, calculating that present value can be somewhat more complicated.

The Black-Scholes Option Pricing Model

The most popular of the option pricing models is the Black-Scholes option pricing model, developed by Fisher Black and Myron Scholes, two MIT financial economists.[2] Although virtually all options analysts use the Black-Scholes model, what drives the model is not immediately obvious. As such, we will begin by developing a simple understanding of its implications and relationships and, once we understand the implications, we will take a look at the model itself.

The essence of the Black-Scholes options pricing model is in determining the probability that the option will finish in the money—that is, that it will have value when it expires—and what the value of the option will be.

Key Variables in the Black-Scholes Option Pricing Equation

While the Black-Scholes option pricing model can look quite forbidding, it actually boils down to about six input variables on a calculator. Perhaps the easiest way of understanding option pricing is to simply look at those six input variables and see how they influence an option's price. These input variables are as follows:

1. The price of the underlying stock
2. The option's exercise or strike price
3. The length of time left until expiration
4. The expected stock price volatility over the life of the option
5. The risk-free rate of interest
6. The underlying stock's dividend yield

Each of these factors plays a role in determining the probability that the option will finish in the money, and thus in determining the price of the option. Let's take a look at each one of these variables by holding everything constant and varying each one separately.

The Price of the Underlying Stock. A change in the price of the underlying stock leads directly to a change in the value of an option. Just as you'd expect, if you own a call option and the price of the stock increases, the value of your call option will also increase. For example, if the call option allows you to buy a stock for $10 and the price of the stock rises from $12 to $15, you can now purchase shares worth $15 for the $10 exercise price. That's a $3 increase in the value of the option![3]

For put options, the relationship goes in the opposite direction. Because a put allows you to sell the stock for the option's exercise price, a rise in the stock price is a bad thing, and the put option drops in value, as Figure 7 shows. For example, if you own a put option that allows you to sell a share of stock with a current market price of $12 for $20, then the put option is worth $8 to you. However, if the stock price rises from $12 to $15, the put is now only worth $5!

The Option's Exercise or Strike Price. All else being equal, a higher exercise or strike price decreases the value of a call option. That, of course, is because the exercise price of the call option sets the price that the holder of the call must pay to purchase the underlying common stock. The higher the exercise price, other things being the same, the lower will be the value of the call option. However, a higher exercise price for a put option increases the value of the put—it means that the put will allow you to sell the stock for a higher price!

The Length of Time Left until Expiration. When you own either a put or a call option, you're hoping for a "favorable price movement"—an increase in the stock price if you own a call or a decrease in the stock price if you own a put. The longer the time is to expiration, the higher the probability that the stock will experience one of those "favorable price movements" and end up in the money.

---

[2]Myron Scholes and Robert Merton were awarded the Nobel Prize in Economics in 1997 for their work on option pricing. Unfortunately, Fisher Black passed away prior to the award and did not share the prize.

[3]To simplify our discussion of option values, we will assume that the options are being valued on their expiration date. Thus, the value of a call can be found by simply comparing the current market price of the stock on which it is written with the exercise price of the option (similarly for a put). The value of the option prior to the expiration date is higher than this amount because there is still time for the price of the underlying stock on which the option is written to move higher or lower.

As time passes, the length of time until expiration gets shorter and shorter, resulting in a decline in the value of the option. For this reason, options—both puts and calls—are referred to as "wasting assets" that naturally decrease in value over time if all else remains the same.

The Expected Stock Price Volatility over the Life of the Option. You might think that increased stock volatility would make the value of the option drop because the option is now riskier. However, you would be wrong. The greater the expected stock price volatility over the life of the option, the greater the value of either the put or the call option. Why are options worth more when the underlying stock price volatility increases? The reason is that although options provide the holder with an unlimited upside, the holder can lose no more than the price of the option. Therefore, when volatility increases, the potential to make money on the option is greater. But this increase in the upside potential does not change the fact that you can lose no more than the price of the option. For this reason, investors are willing to pay more for options on more volatile stocks.

The Risk-Free Rate of Interest. When you buy a stock, you tie up your money. Although you also tie up some of your money when you buy a call, the amount that's tied up is much less. You can then take the money you've saved by purchasing the option and invest it, earning the risk-free rate of return. So, the higher the risk-free rate, the more valuable a call option is because it ties up less of your money than would be tied up if you had purchased the stock directly.

Now let's hold the price of the stock constant and think about the effect ▣ Principle 1: **Money Has a Time Value** on this relationship. As the risk-free rate of interest increases, perhaps as anticipated inflation increases, the present value of what you would have to pay for the stock if you purchased it at the striking price declines because the discount rate has increased. Thus, holding the price of the stock constant, an increase in the risk-free rate will result in a call option being more valuable.

Conversely, for a put option, as the risk-free rate of interest increases, the present value of what you will receive if you sell the stock at its striking price declines, making the put worth less than if interest rates were lower. Again, because of the time value of money, the present value of selling the stock in the future at a given strike price is less when the risk-free rate of interest is higher. As a result, put options are less attractive, and thus less valuable, when interest rates are higher. Thus, there is a positive relationship between risk-free rate of interest and call prices, and a negative relationship between risk-free rate of interest and put prices.

The Underlying Stock's Dividend Yield. When a firm pays cash dividends to its stockholders we expect the price of its stock to drop by the amount of the cash dividend. However, although the stock price drops, the exercise or striking price of an option on that stock does not change. Thus, the greater the dividends the firm pays out, the less likely it is that the price of its stock will rise above the call's exercise price. This is a result of the fact that the firm's value, and its stock price, fall as a result of the dividend. As a result, the larger the stock's dividend yield, the lower the value of a call option on that stock. Conversely, the more the firm pays out in dividends, the more valuable a put option on that stock is because dividend payments lower the ex-dividend value of the firm, causing the stock price to drop and the value of the put to rise.

The Black-Scholes Option Pricing Equation

Now let's look at the model, the Black-Scholes option pricing model for call options, which can be stated as follows:

$$\text{Call Option Value } (Call) = \left(\begin{array}{c}\text{Stock Price}\\\text{Today } (P_0)\end{array}\right) N(d_1) - \left(\begin{array}{c}\text{Strike}\\\text{Price } (X)\end{array}\right)\left[e^{-\text{ (risk-free rate)} \times \text{(time to expiration)}}\right]N(d_2) \qquad (1)$$

In this formula, the value of the call option is a function of the current stock price (P_0), the strike price of the option (X), the risk-free rate of interest, the time to expiration of the option, plus two remaining terms that need some additional explanation, $N(d_1)$ and $N(d_2)$. Oh, and one more thing—the bracketed term $\left[e^{-\text{(risk-free rate)} \times \text{(time to expiration)}}\right]$ is simply a discount factor where continuous discounting is used and "e" is the base of natural logarithms (approximately 2.7183).

The two remaining terms in Equation (1) are $N(d_1)$ and $N(d_2)$, where $N(d_i)$ is the probability of drawing a value less than d_i from the standard normal distribution. To calculate the Black-Scholes option price, we calculate this probability for two different values, d_1 and d_2, which are defined as follows:

$$d_1 = \frac{ln\left(\dfrac{\text{Stock Price Today}}{\text{Strike Price}}\right) + \left(\text{Risk-Free Rate} + \dfrac{\text{Variance in Stock Returns}}{2}\right) \times \text{Time to Expiration}}{\sqrt{\text{Variance in Stock Returns}} \times \sqrt{\text{Time to Expiration}}} \qquad (2)$$

And

$$d_2 = d_1 - \sqrt{\text{Variance in Stock Returns}} \times \sqrt{\text{Time to Expiration}} \qquad (3)$$

As we have said, to apply this model you need to know the risk-free rate, the current stock price, the strike price, the maturity date, and the variance of the stock returns. Of these variables, the variance must be estimated, but the other variables are directly observable.

Checkpoint 3 provides an example that illustrates how the Black-Scholes formula is used to value a call option. Note that you will need to refer to your statistics book to estimate $N(d_1)$ and $N(d_2)$ or use the Normsdist function found in Excel.

Checkpoint 3

Valuing a Call Option Using the Black-Scholes Model

Consider the following call option:

- the current price of the stock on which the call option is written is $32.00;
- the exercise or strike price of the call option is $30.00;
- the maturity of the option is .25 years;
- the (annualized) variance in the returns of the stock is .16; and
- the risk-free rate of interest is 4 percent.

Use the Black-Scholes option pricing model to estimate the value of the call option.

STEP 1: Picture the problem

The expiration date value for the call option can be visualized as follows:

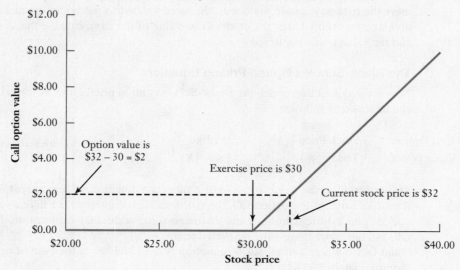

Thus, if the option were expiring today it would be worth $2.00 = $32.00 – $30.00 (i.e., the current stock price minus the strike price). Because the option is not expiring today but has 90 days to expiration, it will be worth more than $2.00, which reflects the prospect that the stock price may rise above the current price of $32.00.

STEP 2: Decide on a solution strategy

The Black-Scholes option pricing model found in Equation (1) provides us with a means of estimating the value of the call option.

STEP 3: Solve

To estimate the value of the call option using Equation (1) we must first solve for d_1 and d_2, as follows:

$$d_1 = \frac{\ln\left(\frac{\$32.00}{\$30.00}\right) + \left(.04 + \frac{.16}{2}\right) \times .25}{\sqrt{.16} \times \sqrt{.25}} = .472693$$

and

$$d_2 = .472693 - \sqrt{.16} \times \sqrt{.25} = .272693$$

Now, using Equation (1) and the table of areas under the standard normal distribution to calculate the $N(di)$ that can be found in any standard statistics book, we calculate the value of the option as follows:[4]

$$\begin{array}{c}\text{Call Option} \\ \text{Value (Call)}\end{array} = \$32(.681784) - \$30\, e^{-.04 \times .25}(.607455) = \$3.77$$

STEP 4: Analyze

Note that the option's value is $3.77 even though the current price is currently just $2.00 greater than the strike price. The reason for this higher value of the call option relates to the potential for an even higher value if the stock price should rise over the next .25 years.

STEP 5: Check yourself

Estimate the value of the previous call option when the exercise price is only $25.

ANSWER: Call option value = $7.51.

Your Turn: For more practice, do related **Study Problems** 10 and 11 at the end of this chapter.   **>> END Checkpoint 3**

Now let's think back to our input variables and see what happens when we make changes in the key parameters of the model. To begin our analysis we lower the strike price of the call option found in Checkpoint 3 from $30 to $25. The value of this option is $7.51 (compared to $3.77), which seems logical. We can now purchase a share of stock for $25 using the call option whereas in the original example we had to pay $30. The value of the option increases as expected.

Next, let us increase the term to maturity on the option to one-half a year. Having a longer period of time over which to exercise the option should, you might expect, make the option more valuable, and indeed it does. Other things being held constant (going back to the $30 strike price), we find that the value of the call option indeed rises to $4.90 (compared to $3.77).

Now let us increase the volatility of the underlying stock on which the option is written from the variance of .16 up to .32 (using the $30 exercise price and .25-year term to maturity). As expected, the increased volatility causes the value of the option to increase to $4.73 (compared to $3.77).

---

[4]We can use the Normsdist (d_i) function in Excel to calculate $N(d_i)$ directly.

Thus, we can use the Black-Scholes options pricing model to value an option. But equally important is the insight it gives us into what variables are important in determining the price of an option:

Tools of Financial Analysis—Option Pricing

Name of Tool	Formula		What It Tells You
Black-Scholes Option Pricing Equation	$= (\textit{Stock Price Today})\, N(d_1) - (\textit{Strike Price})$ $\left(e^{-(\textit{Risk-Free Rate}) \times (\textit{Time to Expiration})}\right) N(d_2)$		• The value of an option—whether it will finish in the money when it expires and what the value of the option will be • This model shows that six variables are important in determining the value of an option: • Price of the underlying stock • Option's exercise or strike price • Length of time until expiration • Expected stock volatility over the life of the option • Risk-free rate of interest • Underlying stock's dividend yield

Swap Contracts

As the name *swap* implies, a **swap contract** involves the swapping or trading of one set of payments for another. Common types of swap contracts involve interest payments or currencies. For example, an **interest rate swap** might involve the trading of fixed interest payments for variable or floating-rate interest payments between two companies. A **currency swap** would involve an exchange of debt obligations in different currencies.

To see how an interest rate swap works, consider the set of swap cash flows found in Figure 10. These cash flows correspond to a five-year fixed-for-floating rate swap (trading payments on a five-year fixed rate loan for the payments on a five-year floating rate loan) with semiannual interest payments and a notional principal of $250 million. The term **notional principal** is used because this is the amount used to calculate payments for the contract, but this amount does not change hands. The floating rate is set to equal the six-month London Interbank Offer Rate, or LIBOR, and the fixed rate is 9.75 percent.

In this illustration, the firm that initiates the swap contract has a floating rate obligation so it must pay the floating-rate payments found in column (D) of Figure 10. However, after entering into the swap the firm now pays the swap counterparty the fixed coupon payments found in column (C) and receives a set of payments equal to the floating-rate payments found in column (D). The floating-rate payments that the firm receives as part of the swap are exactly equal to its floating rate obligations under the terms of its floating-rate loan. Thus, the firm pays the floating rate interest using the proceeds of the swap agreement and then is left with the set of fixed-rate coupon payments. Consequently, the firm has converted its floating-rate loan into a fixed-rate loan.

A swap contract is typically structured as a "zero-cost" security. That is, the fixed rate in the swap contract is set based on the current market conditions and the creditworthiness of the borrower. Note also that the principal amount upon which the swap is based is referred to as the notional principal of the swap because there is no principal that changes hands at the initiation of the swap, nor is one repaid at the end of the agreement. To illustrate how a currency swap agreement can be used to construct a hedge against exchange rate risk, consider an American firm that has a substantial amount of its income generated from sales made in England. To eliminate its exposure to the risk of changing exchange rates, the U.S. firm might enter in a currency swap with an English firm. Consider what would happen if the value of the British pound depreciated from 1.90 dollars to the pound to 1.70 dollars to the pound. In this case each sale made in England would bring fewer dollars back to the parent company in the United States. This could be offset by the effects of the currency swap because it costs the U.S. firm fewer dollars to fulfill the English firm's interest obligations. That is, pounds cost less to purchase, and the interest payments owed are in pounds. The nice thing about a currency swap is that it allows the firm to engage in long-term exchange rate risk hedging because the debt obligation covers a relatively long time period.

Figure 10

Fixed Rate for Floating Interest Rate Swap

The notional principal of the swap is $250 million with coupon interest payments made semiannually. The variable (floating) rate is equal to the six-month LIBOR rate observed at the beginning of each six-month interest period, and the fixed rate is 9.75%.

$$\frac{9.75\%}{2} \times \$250 \text{ million} \qquad \frac{8.5\%}{2} \times \$250 \text{ million}$$

Year (A)	Six-Month LIBOR Rate (B)	Fixed-Rate Coupon (C)	Floating-Rate Coupon (D)	Net Swap Cash Flow Fixed for Floating (E)
0.00	8.5%			
0.50	7.2%	12,187,500	$10,625,000	$(1,562,500)
1.00	10.0%	12,187,500	$ 9,000,000	$(3,187,500)
1.50	9.3%	12,187,500	$12,500,000	$ 312,500
2.00	9.8%	12,187,500	$11,625,000	$ (562,500)
2.50	10.8%	12,187,500	$12,250,000	$ 62,500
3.00	11.3%	12,187,500	$13,500,000	$ 1,312,500
3.50	11.5%	12,187,500	$14,125,000	$ 1,937,500
4.00	10.5%	12,187,500	$14,375,000	$ 2,187,500
4.50	9.5%	12,187,500	$13,125,000	$ 937,500
5.00		12,187,500	$11,875,000	$ (312,500)

>> END FIGURE 10

These look like great ideas—enter into a contract that reduces risk—but just as with the other derivative securities, they are dangerous if used by those who don't understand their risks. For example, in 1994 Procter & Gamble Corporation lost $157 million on swaps that involved interest rate payments made in German marks and U.S. dollars. How did this happen? Exchange rates and interest rates did not go the way Procter & Gamble had anticipated, and the costs were a lot more than the company thought they might ever be. Then in 2012 Philadelphia lost close to $200 million on losses, illustrating the point that if you don't understand the financial instrument, you should not use them.

Credit Default Swaps

Don't confuse credit default swaps with traditional swap contracts. Credit default swaps are more like insurance policies than they are swap contracts. With traditional swap contracts, one set of payments—for example, floating interest rate payments, may be traded for another set of payments, perhaps fixed interest rate payments—but credit default swaps act more like insurance policies in that they pay off if a particular bond or security defaults. For example, if an investor owns a bond, and worries that the bond might default, the investor could purchase a credit default swap on that bond that will pay off if the bond defaults—although this sounds like insurance, it isn't regulated like insurance because it is called a swap. Credit default swaps may sound relatively benign, but they played a central role in the financial market meltdown that led to our recent recession. While the recession began with the collapse of the housing market, it was amplified by problems with credit default swaps.

As banks and financial institutions began issuing mortgage backed securities they found that it was much easier to sell them if they also issued "insurance policies"—credit default swaps—against their default. Unfortunately, things did not stop there and investors realized that credit default swaps were a great way to bet against the housing market, or GM, or the ability of a municipality to pay off its bonds. After all, you don't have to own the underlying security—the mortgage-backed securities, the GM debt, or the risky municipal bonds—and you don't have to suffer a loss to collect, the credit default swap pays off even if you don't own the underlying security. As a result, this market became dominated not by the issuers of the debt, or the owners of the debt, but by third parties simply making a bet that there would or wouldn't be a default.

Think of a Green Bay Packers football game; the Packers have a real stake in the game, if they win, it translates into money for the owner. But there are also many others who don't own the Packers that have a stake in the game—all those who placed bets on the game. They don't own the team, but they benefit depending upon whether the Packers win or lose. That's a side bet, and that's essentially what credit default swaps are. A financial institution might issue credit default swaps on bonds it didn't issue and as long as those bonds don't default, they make money. On the other side of that investment are investors who don't own the bonds, but want to make money if the bonds default so they buy credit default swaps and they will benefit if the bonds default. In effect, buying a credit default swap is like taking out a life insurance policy on someone else, like an unrelated neighbor or even a total stranger. The life insurance policy pays off if that person dies, but that person's family doesn't get the money, you do.

With the collapse of the housing market and the resultant recession, many investors who bought credit default swaps made huge amounts of money—unfortunately, the firms that issued the credit default swaps like Bear Sterns, Lehman Brothers, and the holding company of AIG didn't have enough money behind the credit default swaps to pay off all they owed. Because these were not legally considered a form of insurance, there were no legal requirements to hold an adequate amount of reserves to pay them off. Why did Bear Sterns, Lehman Brothers, and AIG issue all these credit default swaps? They simply felt they would never have to pay them off. How big was the credit default swap market? It is a little hard to say since it was a largely unregulated market, but estimates are that between 2000 and 2008 this market grew from $900 billion to more than $30 trillion with much of this growth associated with mortgage backed securities. The end result of all this was twofold: a freezing up of the credit markets as no one wanted to lend to anyone else for fear they couldn't get their money back if they needed it; and the recession we are just now recovering from.

Before you begin end-of-chapter material

Concept Check | 5

1. What are the six factors that determine the value of an option contract?
2. Define a swap contract and describe how it can be used to manage risk.

Applying the Principles of Finance to This Chapter

 Principle 1: **Money Has a Time Value**, The concept of the time value of money really deals with the opportunity cost of money. When interest rates are high, there is more value to money, and as a result, strategies that can avoid tying up your money are of value. As we will see, options can do that.

 Principle 2: **There Is a Risk–Return Tradeoff** By now you should realize how risky business is and how important it is to reduce that risk. The first step in controlling risk is to understand what the risks are and which

risks you would like to assume and which risks you need to control. From there risk management becomes a process of determining the best way to minimize or hedge away those risks. The analysis of a firm's risk exposure and the determination of how best to handle that risk exposure is the focus of a specialized area of finance called risk management that uses forward, futures, and options contracts along with swaps to manage risk.

Chapter Summaries

1 Define risk management in the context of the five-step risk management process.

SUMMARY: The process of analyzing a firm's exposure to risks of all kinds and determining how best to handle that risk exposure is called risk management. The five-step risk management process includes the following:

Step 1. Identify and Understand the Firm's Major Risks. Typically these will include consideration for demand risk related to the firm's goods and services, commodity price risk related to the commodity inputs the firm uses in its operations, country risk that derives from where the firm's operations are located throughout the world, operational or cost-control risk, and foreign exchange risk.

Step 2. Decide Which Types of Risks to Keep and Which to Transfer. The risks a firm decides to retain are those for which it has some comparative advantage at managing.

Step 3. Decide How Much Risk to Assume. This is a preference issue and will vary from firm to firm. Some management teams are extremely confident in their ability to manage the risks they face, whereas others are much less so.

Step 4. Incorporate Risk into All of the Firm's Decisions and Processes. Once the firm decides on the risks that it will keep and those it will transfer, it is time to implement a system for controlling the firm's risk exposures. This means that every major investment, operating, and financing decision the firm makes must take into consideration the impact of the choices on overall firm risk.

Step 5. Monitor and Manage the Risks the Firm Assumes. To assure that the firm's day-to-day decisions are consistent with its chosen risk profile, it is necessary that it put in place an effective monitoring system. Typically this means that the firm centralizes the responsibility for monitoring the firm's risk exposure with a chief risk officer who reports directly to the company CEO and also presents regularly to the firm's board of directors.

KEY TERM

Risk profile The concept of a firm's "appetite" for assuming risk.

2 Understand how insurance contracts can be used to manage risk.

SUMMARY: The purchase of insurance involves the transfer of the risk of a loss, from one entity to another, in exchange for a payment to the insurance company, is called the contract premium. Essentially, the insured trades the risk of a large, uncertain, possibly devastating loss to an insurance company in exchange for a guaranteed small loss (the premium).

KEY TERMS

Insurance A contract that involves compensation for specific potential future losses in exchange for periodic payments and that provides for the transfer of the risk of a loss, from one entity to another, in exchange for a premium.

Self-insurance A risk management approach where the entity sets aside a sum of money as protection against potential future loss rather than purchasing an insurance policy.

3 | Use forward contracts to hedge commodity price risk.

SUMMARY: A hedge is simply an investment that is undertaken specifically to reduce or cancel the risk of another investment. For example, firms often hedge currency exchange risk and commodity price risk. A forward contract can be used to hedge commodity price risk. For example, if the firm owns a commodity that it expects to sell in the future, it can go ahead and negotiate a selling price for future delivery using a forward contract.

KEY TERMS

Credit or **default risk** The risk of loss as a result of default on a financial obligation, also referred to as default risk.

Forward contract A contract wherein a price is agreed upon today for an asset to be sold in the future. These contracts are privately negotiated between the buyer and seller.

Hedging A strategy designed to minimize exposure to unwanted risk by taking a position in one market that offsets exposure to price fluctuations in an opposite position in another market.

Long position A term used to refer to the ownership of a security, contract, or commodity. When someone owns a security he or she is said to be "long" on the security, such that when the price of the security rises, the individual profits.

Short position A term used to refer to the fact that you have sold a security, contract, or commodity. A short position is exactly the opposite of a long position, such that when the price of the security goes up, the holder of the short position loses money.

Spot contract An exchange in which the buyer agrees to purchase something and the seller agrees to sell it for a specified price, and the exchange is completed at the same time.

Concept Check | 3

1. What is a forward contract? Contrast a forward contract with a spot contract.
2. What are the limitations of forward contracts as tools for managing risk?

4 | Understand the advantages and disadvantages of using exchange-traded futures and option contracts to hedge price risk.

SUMMARY: If the firm uses exchange-traded futures or option contracts to implement a hedge, it may find that the specific types of contracts that are traded do not match up exactly with the characteristics of the investment that the firm is trying to hedge. This mismatch of the specific type of asset and/or the period for which the hedge is being constructed makes the hedge less effective. Even so, many firms regularly use hedges constructed with similar but imperfectly matched options and futures contracts. For example, airlines have used heating oil futures to hedge their jet fuel costs.

KEY TERMS

American option An option that may be exercised at any time up through the contract's expiration date.

Basis risk Risk associated with imperfect hedging that arises because the asset underlying the futures contract is not identical to the asset that underlies the firm's risk exposure.

Call option A contract that gives its holder the right to purchase a given number of shares of stock or some other asset at a specified price over a given time period.

Commodity futures A contract to buy or sell a stated commodity (such as wheat and corn as well as metals, wood products, or fibers) at a specified price and at a specified future date.

Derivative contract A security whose value is *derived* from the value of another asset or security (which is referred to as the *underlying asset*).

European option An option that can only be exercised on its expiration date.

Exercise price The price at which the stock or asset may be purchased from the option writer in the case of a call, or sold to the option writer in the case of a put; also called the strike or striking price.

Financial futures A contract to buy or sell an underlying asset such as Treasury securities, certificates of deposit, Eurodollars, foreign currencies, or stock indices at a specified price at a specified future time.

Futures contract A contract to buy or sell a stated commodity (such as soybeans or corn) or financial claim (such as U.S. Treasury bonds) at a specified price at some future specified time.

Futures margin The amount of money or collateral that must be provided to control credit or default risk on a futures contract; this margin is required to prevent default.

Marking to market Transferring daily gains or losses from a firm's futures contracts to or from its margin account.

Option contract The right, but not the obligation, to buy or sell something (e.g., 100 shares of stock for a stock option) at a specified price and within a specified period of time.

Option expiration date The date on which the option contract expires.

Option premium The price paid for an option.

Option writing The process of *selling* puts and calls.

Put option An option that gives its owner the right (but not the obligation) to sell a given number of shares of common stock or an asset at a specified price within a given period.

Strike price The price at which the stock or asset may be purchased from the option writer in the case of a call, or sold to the option writer in the case of a put; also called the exercise price.

Concept Check | 4

1. What is meant by the term *financial derivative contract*?
2. Define and contrast the following types of financial derivatives: options, futures, and forwards.

KEY EQUATION

$$\frac{\text{Call Option}}{\text{Value } (Call)} = \left(\begin{array}{c} \text{Stock Price} \\ \text{Today } (P_0) \end{array}\right) N(d_1) - \left(\begin{array}{c} \text{Strike} \\ \text{Price } (X) \end{array}\right) \left[e^{-(\text{risk-free rate}) \times (\text{time to expiration})} \right] N(d_2) \qquad \textbf{(1)}$$

5 Understand how to value options and how swaps work.

SUMMARY: To this point in the chapter we have been analyzing the payoff to option contracts on the day that the option contract expires. The value of the option on the expiration date is simply equal to the payoff to the holder of the option. For example, if the price of a stock is $25 and you hold a call option with an exercise price of $20, then on the expiration day your call option is worth $5. Valuing an option prior to the expiration date is a bit more difficult. For example, in the previous situation consider what you might be willing to pay for the same call option if it were 30 days prior to the expiration date. If you exercise immediately you get $5, but you might want to wait because there are still 30 days until the option expires and the price of the underlying stock might rise even higher. Perhaps the best-known model for estimating the value of a call option is the Black-Scholes model. This model provides a way to incorporate consideration for the possibility that the stock price might rise further.

Swap contracts entail the exchange of one set of future payments for another. For example, a very popular swap contract involves the exchange of interest payments on variable interest rate loans for those on a fixed-rate loan (fixed-for-floating rate swap). The exchange of a set of payments denominated in one currency for payments denominated in another currency is a currency swap.

KEY TERMS

Currency swap The exchange or trading of debt obligations whose payments are denominated in different currencies.

Interest rate swap The swapping or trading between two companies of fixed interest payments for variable or floating-rate interest payments.

Notional principal The nominal or face amount on a swap agreement. This is the principal used to calculate payments for swap

contracts, but because this principal does not change hands it is commonly referred to as the "notional" amount of the contract.

Swap contract An agreement in which two parties agree to exchange one set of payments for another. For example, the holder of a stream of fixed interest rate payments on a loan might exchange them for variable-rate payments on a like-size loan.

Concept Check | 5

1. What are the six factors that determine the value of an option contract?
2. Define a swap contract and describe how it can be used to manage risk.

Study Questions

1. **(Related to Regardless of Your Major: Welcome to a Risky World)** In the *Regardless of Your Major* feature, the need to engage in risk management is linked to the day-to-day activities of firm employees from multiple functional areas, including operations, marketing, and accounting. What are the two sources of risk identified in this discussion?

2. Define the term *risk management*.

3. A firm's cash flows are risky for a number of reasons. Identify and discuss five sources of risk or volatility in firm cash flows.

4. What is the risk management policy followed by the Chesapeake Energy Corporation (CHK) with respect to the price of oil and gas it receives for its future production prior to 2011?

5. Firms regularly use insurance as a means of managing their risk exposure. What are some of the types of risks that are typically transferred to insurance companies through the use of insurance contracts?

6. **(Related to The Business of Life: Do You Need Life Insurance?)** *The Business of Life: Do You Need Life Insurance?* box feature discusses factors involved in the decision to purchase life insurance. What are some commonsense guidelines that can be used to answer the question of whether you need life insurance?

7. What is a forward contract, and how does it typically differ from an exchange-traded futures contract?

8. Describe how forward contracts can be used to hedge the risk of fluctuating commodity prices for firms that must purchase them in the future.

9. What are the limitations of the use of forward contracts to construct a hedge against price risk? How does a futures exchange control for these limitations?

10. What is a futures contract?

11. Define a call option and contrast it with a put option.

12. What is a swap contract? How are swap contracts used to hedge interest rate risk?

13. Chemical plants rely upon crude oil as the base material for the manufacture of a whole host of products. How might such a firm hedge the risk of a price increase in the cost of crude oil spanning the next 12 months of its operations?

Study Problems

MyFinanceLab

Go to www.myfinancelab.com to complete these exercises online and get instant feedback.

Managing Risk by Hedging with Forward Contracts

1. **(Forward contract payout)** Construct a delivery date profit or loss graph similar to Figure 2 for a long position in a forward contract with a delivery price of $65. Analyze the profit or loss for values of the underlying asset ranging from $40 to $80.

2. **(Forward contract payout)** Repeat Study Problem 1, but this time draw the profit or loss graph from the perspective of the individual who sold (is short) the forward contract.

3. **(Related to Checkpoint 1) (Hedging with forward contracts)** The Specialty Chemical Company operates a crude oil refinery located in New Iberia, Louisiana. The company refines crude oil and sells the by-products to companies that make plastic bottles and jugs. The firm is currently planning for its refining needs for one year hence. Specifically, the firm's analysts estimate that Specialty will need to purchase 1 million barrels of crude oil at the end of the current year to provide the feed stock for its refining needs for the coming year. The 1 million barrels of crude will be converted into by-products at an average cost of $40 per barrel that Specialty expects to sell for $170 million, or $170 per barrel of crude used. The current spot price of oil is $125 per barrel and Specialty has been offered a forward contract by its investment banker to purchase the needed oil for a delivery price in one year of $130 per barrel.

   a. Ignoring taxes, what will Specialty's profits be if oil prices in one year are as low as $110 or as high as $150, assuming that the firm does not enter into the forward contract?

   b. If the firm were to enter into the forward contract, demonstrate how this would effectively lock in the firm's cost of fuel today, thus hedging the risk of fluctuating crude oil prices on the firm's profits for the next year.

4. **(Margin requirements and marking to market)** Discuss how the exchange requirements that mandate traders to put up collateral in the form of a margin requirement and to use this account to mark their profits or losses for the day serve to eliminate credit or default risk.

Managing Risk with Exchange-Traded Financial Derivatives

5. **(Related to Checkpoint 2) (Call option payouts)** Draw a profit or loss graph (similar to that in Figure 5) for a call contract with an exercise price of $50 for which a $5 premium is paid. You may assume that the option is being evaluated on its expiration date. Identify the break-even point, maximum profits, and maximum losses. Now draw the profit or loss graph assuming an exercise price of $55 and a $6 premium.

6. **(Calculating call option payouts)** Currently a call contract with an exercise price of $10 on a share of List Aerospace's common stock is selling for (that is, its premium is) $2. What would the profit or loss graph (similar to that in Figure 5) look like for this option? In drawing this graph, assume that the option is being evaluated on its expiration date. What are the maximum profits, maximum losses, and the break-even point? How would this graph change if the exercise price was $12 and the price (or premium) of the option was $4?

7. **(Put option payouts)** Draw a profit or loss graph (similar to Figure 7) for a put contract with an exercise price of $45 for which a $5 premium is paid. You may assume that the option is being evaluated on its expiration date. Identify the break-even price of the underlying stock. What are the maximum losses the holder of the option might experience, and what are the maximum gains?

8. **(Calculating put option payouts)** Currently a put contract with an exercise price of $5 on a share of Milybe Aerospace's common stock is selling for (that is, its premium is) $1. What would the profit or loss graph (similar to Figure 7) look like for this option? In drawing this graph, assume that the option is being evaluated on its expiration date. What are the maximum profits, maximum losses, and the break-even point?

9. **(Hedging commodity price risk)** Minelli Enterprises uses large amounts of copper in the manufacture of ceiling fans. The firm has been very concerned about the detrimental impact of rising copper prices on its earnings and has decided to hedge the price risk associated with its next quarterly purchase of copper. The current market price of copper is $3.00 per pound and Minelli's management wants to lock in this price. How can Minelli ensure that it will pay no more than $3 per pound for copper using a forward contract?

Valuing Options and Swaps

10. **(Related to Checkpoint 3) (Call option valuation)** Consider the following call option:
- the current price of the stock on which the call option is written is $20.00;
- the exercise or strike price of the call option is $18.00;
- the maturity of the option is 90 days or .25 year;
- the (annualized) variance in the returns of the stock is .16; and
- the risk-free rate of interest is 4 percent.

a. What is the value of this call option?
b. Value the call option where the exercise price is only $25.
c. Value the call option under the original assumptions stated earlier but with an annualized variance in stock returns of .32. Why did the value of the call option increase when compared to part a?

11. **(Related to Checkpoint 3) (Call option valuation)** You've just been introduced to the Black-Scholes option pricing model and want to give it a try, and would like to use it to calculate the value of a call option on TriHawk stock. Currently, TriHawk's common stock is selling for $25.00 per share, and the call option you are considering has an exercise or strike price of $20.00 with a maturity of 90 days or .25 year. In addition, you have calculated the (annualized) variance in its stock returns to be .09. If the risk-free rate of interest is 4 percent, what would the value of this call option be? How would your answer change if there was only one month left to expiration, but everything else remained the same? Now, what would happen to the value of this call option if the annualized variance in stock returns was .15 rather than .09?

12.   **(Interest rate swap)** Marx and Winter, Inc. operates a chain of retail clothing stores throughout the U.S. Midwest. The firm recently entered into a loan agreement for $20 million that carries a floating rate of interest equal to LIBOR plus 50 basis points (1/2 percent). The loan has a five-year maturity and requires the firm to make semi-annual payments. At the time the loan was being negotiated, Marx and Winter was approached by its banker with a suggestion as to how the firm might lock in the rate of interest on the loan at 6.4 percent using a fixed-for-floating interest rate swap. Under the agreement the company would make a cash payment to the swap counterparty equal to the fixed-rate coupon payment and receive in return a coupon payment reflecting the floating rate.

a. Calculate the swap cash flows over the next five years based on the following set of hypothetical LIBOR rates:

Year (A)	Six-Month LIBOR Rate (B)
0.00	5.44%
0.50	7.20%
1.00	6.40%
1.50	5.92%
2.00	6.24%
2.50	6.88%
3.00	7.20%
3.50	7.36%
4.00	6.72%
4.50	6.08%
5.00	

b. What would motivate a firm's management to enter into a swap contract?

13.   **(Interest rate swap)** The Prince Racket Company manufactures a line of tennis and raquetball equipment. The firm recently entered into a loan agreement for $20 million that carries a floating rate of interest equal to LIBOR plus 100 basis points (1 percent). The loan has a five-year maturity and requires the firm to make semiannual payments. At the time the loan was being negotiated, the company was approached by its banker with a suggestion as to how the firm might lock in the rate of interest on the loan at 8 percent using a fixed-for-floating interest rate swap. Under the agreement the company would make a cash payment to the swap counterparty equal to the fixed-rate coupon payment and receive in return a coupon payment reflecting the floating rate.

a. Calculate the swap cash flows over the next five years based on the following set of hypothetical LIBOR rates:

Year (A)	6-Month LIBOR Rate (B)
0.00	6.80%
0.50	7.20%
1.00	8.00%
1.50	7.40%
2.00	7.80%
2.50	8.60%
3.00	9.00%
3.50	9.20%
4.00	8.40%
4.50	7.60%
5.00	

b. What would motivate a firm's management to enter into such a swap contract?

Mini-Case

For your job as the business reporter for a local newspaper, you are given the task of developing a series of articles on risk management. Much of the recent local press coverage has been given to the losses that some firms have experienced when using financial futures and options. Your editor would like you to address several specific questions in addition to discussing the proper use of these types of contracts in managing corporate risk.

Please prepare your response to the following memorandum from your editor:

TO: Business Reporter

FROM: Perry White, Editor, *Daily Planet*

RE: Upcoming Series on Corporate Risk Management

In your upcoming series on corporate risk management I would like to make sure that you address the following questions:

1. What is corporate risk management?
2. What is the role of insurance in managing the risks that a firm faces?
3. How can forward contracts be used as a risk management tool?
4. What are the advantages and disadvantages of using forwards versus exchange-traded futures contracts in implementing a risk management strategy designed to address the problem of commodity price risk?
5. What are swap contracts, and how are they used in the management of interest rate risk?

Photo Credits

Index

Page references followed by "f" indicate illustrated figures or photographs; followed by "t" indicates a table.

A

abbreviations, 327
Abilities, 86, 434
Abstract, 544
Accountants, 18, 20, 53, 57, 61, 63, 67, 73, 78, 407, 454, 565, 590
Accounting, 1, 4, 13, 16, 19-20, 24-25, 51-54, 57, 61, 67, 73-74, 78-79, 82, 91-92, 99, 106, 110, 113-115, 117, 120-121, 123-126, 169, 189, 239, 307, 339, 357, 362, 375-376, 378, 404, 406, 408, 411, 435, 442, 449, 453-458, 460, 462, 467-468, 472-473, 562, 565, 574, 603, 646, 658, 674, 701
    finance and, 51, 53, 78, 120
Accounting practices, 121, 125
Accounting profit, 20
Accounting rules, 117
Accounting standards, 117, 126
Accounting systems, 82, 376, 674
accounts payable, 1-3, 7, 62-63, 65-66, 70-73, 75, 78, 80, 82, 84, 87, 94, 99, 126, 128-132, 134-135, 138, 406, 408, 411, 413, 416, 421-422, 426-427, 445, 483-484, 486, 505, 518-520, 534-536, 549-550, 553, 584, 592-596, 598-599, 602-607, 614-618, 620-625, 636, 638-639
Accounts receivable, 1, 3, 5-6, 8, 53, 62-66, 70-73, 75, 78-79, 82, 84, 94, 96-101, 105, 108-110, 112, 118, 121, 123-124, 126, 128-135, 138, 280, 406, 408, 410-411, 413, 416, 421-422, 424, 426-427, 584, 602, 605, 612-615, 617-625, 628-631, 633, 635-638, 641
accruals, 135
accuracy, 18-19, 589, 603, 669
Acquisitions, 5, 45, 75-77, 86, 115, 479, 496
addresses, 388
adjustments, 114, 189, 196, 590
ADR, 436
Advances, 171, 420
Advantages, 15, 25, 188, 279, 326, 385, 390, 434, 493, 497, 499-501, 617, 625, 672, 700, 705
Advertising, 13, 115, 359, 425-426, 454, 469, 590-591, 603, 606
    corporate, 13
    evaluating, 469
    local, 425, 469
    online, 469
    product, 425-426, 454, 469, 590
    types of, 13, 359, 590
Advertising campaign, 591, 603, 606
Affect, 4, 15, 20, 70, 108, 153, 165-166, 232, 235-236, 253-255, 259, 263, 277, 286, 295, 313, 339, 348, 351, 353, 387, 404, 406, 413, 421-424, 432, 435, 457, 504, 507, 518, 522-524, 526, 535, 540, 542, 544, 547-548, 551-552, 555, 566, 583-584, 591, 615, 617, 635, 663, 678
Africa, 42, 73, 117, 163, 251, 302, 420, 453, 500, 544, 580, 648, 656
    debt, 73, 117, 302, 500, 544
Age, 163, 171, 188, 205, 207, 267, 631, 633
Agencies, 22, 41, 92, 286-287, 312, 487, 629
Agent, 170, 198-199
Agents, 21
agreement, 1, 4-6, 8, 35, 73, 81, 130, 155, 280, 282-283, 285, 312, 317, 345, 506, 518, 530, 576, 608-609, 613, 617, 625, 629, 635-636, 639-640, 651, 678, 683, 696, 701, 704
Agreements, 53, 130, 629, 673, 679
Agricultural products, 684
AIDS, 678
AIG, 32-33, 698
Aircraft, 33, 404, 433, 453

business, 33, 404
Alabama, 473, 489
American Institute of Certified Public Accountants, 57, 565
American International Group, 32-33
American option, 1, 686, 700
Amortization, 5, 55, 93, 184, 196, 535-537, 542-543, 547
Animals, 397
announcements, 57, 230, 232, 532, 574
    company, 57, 230, 574
Annual percentage rate, 1, 160-161, 163, 166, 624, 627, 636, 640, 652
Apr, 1, 160-161, 163, 166, 624, 627, 636
annual reports, 17, 86, 104, 109
Annuity, 1, 3, 5-6, 174-185, 187-189, 192-202, 205, 207, 292, 365-368, 385, 387-388
    bonus, 207
    deferred, 201
    definition of, 388
    fixed, 1, 6, 175, 198-199
    individual, 3, 5, 178, 181, 188, 192, 195
    life, 5-6, 175, 177, 184, 188-189, 197-198, 200, 365-368, 388
    principle, 5-6, 175-176, 188, 194, 196, 387
    units, 3
    variable, 3, 187
Anomalies, 232
Antarctica, 512
anticipate, 17, 233, 305
Anticipated inflation, 271, 333, 424, 693
appearance, 25, 47, 88, 139, 172, 208, 239, 273, 321, 353, 399, 438, 475, 513, 557, 586, 609, 641, 670, 705
Application, 91, 187, 216, 278, 291, 343, 425, 486, 552, 589-590, 628
Applications, 1, 9, 27, 49, 89, 101, 137, 141, 163, 173, 209, 241, 275, 323, 355, 401, 425, 439, 465, 477, 494, 515, 559, 587, 592, 611, 643, 671
Arbitrage, 1, 7, 554-555, 557, 650, 664, 666-669
Argentina, 42, 73, 117, 163, 251, 302, 420, 453, 500, 544, 580, 656
    debt in, 544
ARM, 284, 316
Asia, 3, 42, 223, 301, 314, 358, 648
Assets, 1-8, 13, 20, 23, 34, 36, 38, 40-42, 44-46, 50, 52-55, 61-74, 77, 79-81, 84, 87, 93-96, 99-113, 115, 117-118, 120-121, 123-136, 138, 211, 232, 244-246, 248, 250, 253-254, 257, 259-260, 263-264, 267, 271, 277, 280, 283, 285, 300-301, 314, 326, 340, 347-348, 399, 406, 411, 413, 415, 417, 422-423, 436, 482, 494-495, 511, 517-521, 527, 530, 534-539, 542, 545, 547, 568, 577, 579, 584, 592-599, 602-607, 612-619, 622, 624, 628-629, 631, 633, 635-638, 684-685, 693
    current, 1-2, 5-8, 40, 45, 53-54, 61-68, 71, 73, 79-81, 84, 87, 94-96, 99-101, 103, 110, 112, 115, 120, 123-136, 138, 232, 267, 285, 301, 406, 482, 494-495, 518-520, 534, 536-537, 545, 547, 579, 584, 592-593, 596, 598-599, 604-607, 612-619, 622, 624, 628, 631, 635-638, 693
    fixed, 1, 4, 6, 8, 23, 38, 40-41, 61-63, 65-67, 77, 80-81, 84, 94, 102, 105, 108-110, 112, 118, 121, 124, 130-134, 136, 280, 283, 340, 348, 411, 413, 415, 521, 584, 592-593, 596, 598-599, 604-607, 617-619, 629, 635
    return on assets, 6, 107-110, 113, 118, 124-126, 128, 131-133, 135-136, 538-539
    total assets turnover ratio, 120
attention, 55-57, 153, 185, 211, 231, 447, 518, 526, 535, 546, 574, 613
Attorneys, 460
Attribute, 424, 563

attributes, 91, 134, 300, 335, 347, 480, 540, 563, 575, 582, 662
AU, 327
Auditors, 22
Australia, 42, 73, 117, 163, 225, 251, 302, 420, 453, 500, 544, 580, 656
    currency, 302, 453, 500, 656
Authority, 46
authorization, 327
Automobile industry, 265
availability, 225, 576-577, 579
Available, 3-4, 7, 38-39, 47, 68-69, 95, 110, 114, 136, 167, 171, 202, 230-232, 235, 255, 346, 362, 397, 407, 451, 466, 484, 488, 490, 494, 523, 526, 529, 532, 544, 567, 569-570, 575, 579, 585, 592, 607-608, 614, 618, 626, 628-629, 631-632, 637, 646, 651, 658, 666, 684-685, 688
avoidance, 398

B

bad news, 230, 243, 574
Balance sheet, 1, 3-4, 6, 8, 24, 50, 52, 54, 56, 61-72, 77, 79-82, 84-85, 93-97, 101-103, 114-115, 121, 123, 126-127, 129-131, 134, 349, 484, 513, 518, 536-537, 545, 549-550, 553, 562, 565, 579, 584, 591-593, 596-599, 602-607, 616
Balance sheets, 61, 70-71, 86-87, 93-94, 104, 131-132, 134-135, 138, 536, 538, 540, 589, 591, 600, 606
Bank deposits, 43
Bank for International Settlements, 647
Banking crisis, 43
Bankruptcy, 2, 13, 18-19, 38, 41, 44, 65, 281, 284, 308, 326, 340, 347, 518, 522, 526, 528-529, 531-534, 543-544, 546-547, 617, 633
    liquidation, 326
    reorganization, 13
Banks, 2, 5, 8, 14, 18, 28, 30-33, 35-36, 40-46, 61, 63, 70, 81, 92, 121, 130, 150, 160, 171, 277-279, 284, 302, 312, 346, 505, 512, 624, 629, 636, 638, 646, 650-651, 664, 697
    balance sheet for, 61, 130
Basic financial statements, 50-52, 54, 79, 82
Basic form, 54
Behavior, 12, 18, 314, 454, 466, 526, 546
Belgium, 544
Benchmarking, 1, 534-537, 547-548
Benefits, 12, 15, 21, 23, 36, 115, 144, 164, 207, 224, 231, 247, 249, 254, 316, 321, 357, 361, 368, 382, 388, 390, 398-399, 405, 416-420, 434, 517, 528-529, 531-534, 544, 546, 591, 602, 614, 617, 677, 680
    extended, 614
    life insurance, 399, 677
    payment of, 36, 368, 529
biases, 232, 235, 442
Bid, 1, 346, 650, 664, 667-668
board of directors, 2, 5, 8, 15-18, 21, 24, 37, 53, 281, 325-328, 347, 562, 564, 581, 584-585, 676, 699
Bond market, 2, 45, 277, 300, 511, 658
Bond prices, 277, 284-285, 296-299, 302, 314, 658
    interest, 277, 284-285, 296-299, 302, 314
Bonds, 1-2, 4-7, 24, 28, 31, 37-38, 40-42, 44-46, 57, 62-64, 81, 134, 156, 167, 170-171, 175-176, 194, 196, 202, 211, 221-223, 230, 232, 236, 276-278, 280-281, 283-287, 289-303, 305-308, 312-316, 318-319, 321, 326, 328, 335, 339-340, 342-343, 346-348, 353, 357, 480, 484, 486-488, 494, 497, 501-503, 505, 508-513, 517, 519, 523-524, 532, 534, 540, 549, 552-554, 567, 605, 618, 635, 646, 658, 684, 697-698, 700
    appeal, 301
    contract, 1-2, 4-7, 44, 81, 290, 348, 509, 684,

697-698, 700
financial institution, 2, 5, 42, 44-45, 278, 698
insurance agent, 170
maintenance, 567, 684
payment, 2, 6-7, 37, 156, 167, 170-171, 176, 202, 221, 281, 284-285, 287, 292, 294, 312-314, 321, 328, 339-340, 534, 553, 567, 605, 618, 646
performance, 7, 24, 221, 328, 335, 339, 540, 567, 646
bookmarking, 47
Borrowing, 4, 8, 13-14, 29, 40, 53, 62, 72, 101, 161, 170-171, 260, 278, 280, 283-284, 286, 301, 341, 406, 421, 480, 485-486, 500, 509, 511-512, 520-521, 523, 526, 530, 534, 536-539, 541, 545-546, 555, 594-596, 600-601, 608-609, 615, 626, 662
brackets, 15, 80, 154, 178, 182, 473
Brand, 57, 325, 359, 424, 434
  packaging, 434
  value proposition, 359
Brand loyalty, 434
Brand names, 57
Brands, 17, 359, 424, 657
  importance of, 424
  manufacturer, 424
  national, 424
  store, 424
Brazil, 31, 42, 73, 117, 163, 251, 302, 420, 453, 500, 544, 580, 648, 656, 659
Breakdown, 5, 184, 196, 631-632
Break-even analysis, 1, 6, 440, 453-458, 462, 467, 472-474, 553
Break-even point, 2, 454-455, 457-458, 460, 462, 467, 472-473, 687-691, 703
Break-even price, 703
Britain, 3, 224, 234, 656-657
British pound, 646-647, 652, 664, 696
Broker, 33-34, 42, 582, 686
Budget, 2, 43, 114, 126, 434, 505, 588-589, 591, 597, 600-604, 608-609, 628
  defined, 2, 126
Budgeting, 1, 12, 17, 23, 167, 356-360, 362, 365, 379, 384-387, 389-390, 398, 402, 413, 432-433, 435, 437, 440, 462, 466, 468, 473-474, 480, 543, 561, 597, 644, 657, 660, 662, 664, 666, 668-669
  capital, 1, 12, 17, 23, 356-360, 362, 365, 379, 384-387, 389-390, 398, 402, 413, 432-433, 435, 437, 440, 462, 466, 468, 473-474, 480, 543, 561, 644, 657, 660, 662, 664, 666, 668-669
Bureau of Labor Statistics, 381
Business cycle, 251, 582
Business interruption insurance, 677
Business operations, 23, 74
Business review, 674
Business risk, 546-547, 662
Business strategy, 358
Buyback, 7, 564, 581
Buyers, 45, 53, 64, 279, 403, 405, 433, 646, 664, 679, 691
  Product, 53, 403, 405, 433

C
Call option, 1, 686-688, 690-695, 700-703
Canada, 550, 648, 651, 656, 658, 667-669
  currency, 648, 651, 656, 667-669
Cannibalization, 405
Capabilities, 359, 500
Capacity, 91, 281, 286, 394, 397, 416, 419, 422, 425, 434, 463, 536, 544, 592, 606-607
Capital, 1-8, 12, 14-17, 23-24, 29-32, 34-35, 37, 39, 41, 43-45, 62-67, 69, 71, 74-78, 80-82, 84-87, 94-96, 101-103, 107, 110, 115, 118, 123, 126, 128-129, 133-134, 138-139, 150, 224-225, 236, 242-243, 253, 258-259, 262-265, 268-270, 272-273, 278-282, 285-286, 297, 317, 331, 333, 346, 353, 356-362, 364-365, 368-369, 376, 379-380, 384-387, 389-390, 398, 402, 406-413, 415-419, 421-428, 430-435, 437, 440, 445-450, 453, 458-459, 462, 466-468, 471, 473-474, 477-513, 515-557, 560-561, 565-567, 572-573, 575-576, 579, 581-584, 593, 596, 598-599, 604, 607, 611-641, 644-645, 657, 660, 662, 664, 666-669, 675, 691
  customer, 1, 7-8, 123, 543, 613, 617, 630-631,

635-638, 664
  definition of, 15, 384, 535
  equity financing and, 540
  fixed, 1, 4, 6, 8, 23, 37, 41, 62-63, 65-67, 77, 80-81, 84, 94, 102, 110, 118, 133-134, 278-280, 297, 317, 364, 398, 407, 409, 411-413, 415, 427, 430-431, 435, 445-450, 453, 458-459, 462, 466-468, 471, 473, 489, 521, 526, 546, 548, 552, 566, 582, 584, 593, 596, 598-599, 604, 607, 617-619, 629, 635
  growth, 2, 17, 74, 85, 115, 225, 272, 331, 333, 346, 353, 409, 422, 490-494, 496, 506, 509-510, 513, 576, 582, 593, 596, 599, 604, 607, 621
  human, 12
  requirements, 2, 6, 280, 346, 406-408, 410-411, 416-417, 421-422, 430-432, 435, 505, 532, 535, 579, 593, 596, 604, 628, 662
  working, 6, 8, 12, 16-17, 23, 64-67, 69, 76-77, 81-82, 84-85, 87, 96, 123, 150, 272, 279-280, 282, 317, 398, 406-413, 415-419, 421-428, 430-432, 434-435, 445-450, 453, 458-459, 467, 471, 474, 500, 576, 611-641, 645, 660, 662, 666, 668
Capital asset pricing model, 1, 7, 242-243, 253, 258-259, 262-265, 268-270, 272-273, 331, 333, 490, 493, 496, 506
Capital budgeting, 1, 12, 17, 23, 356-358, 360, 365, 386-387, 389-390, 402, 413, 432, 440, 462, 473-474, 480, 543, 644, 657, 660, 662, 664, 666, 668-669
Capital equipment, 74, 76, 413, 422, 425
Capital gains, 285, 297, 415, 560, 565, 572-573, 575, 581-584, 691
Capital investment projects, 359-360, 387, 413
Capital structure, 1-2, 4, 6, 8, 12, 17, 23, 95, 101-103, 118, 123, 126, 128-129, 133-134, 138-139, 281, 386, 478, 482-486, 496-499, 501, 505, 507-508, 511-512, 515-557, 561, 566-567, 645, 675
  capitalization, 3, 42, 221, 519, 545, 552, 658
Career, 12-13, 205, 358
Careers, 13, 18, 23
Caribbean, 20, 37, 245
Cash budget, 2, 114, 126, 434, 588-589, 591, 597, 600-604, 608-609, 628
  example of, 600, 602
cash collections, 628
cash disbursements, 600-601, 603, 628
Cash discounts, 135, 625, 630
Cash dividend, 2, 39, 83, 237, 331-332, 339-340, 489, 561-562, 564, 566-573, 575, 579, 581-585, 693
Cash equivalents, 138, 615, 638
Cash flow, 2-5, 7, 16, 20, 23-25, 36, 50-53, 59, 69-70, 72-79, 81-82, 85-87, 142, 144-146, 150, 152-155, 157, 159, 161, 164-166, 174-175, 177, 180-183, 187, 189-194, 197, 201, 203-204, 277, 288, 291-292, 294, 296, 324-325, 328-332, 335, 341, 343, 347, 361-364, 366, 369-372, 374-377, 379-380, 382, 385, 387-389, 391-394, 396-398, 403-429, 432-435, 437, 441-443, 445-446, 448-451, 453-454, 457-459, 463-464, 466, 468-469, 472-473, 484, 490-491, 502, 505, 522-524, 527, 529, 531-532, 543, 546, 548, 554-556, 565, 567-570, 572, 592, 597, 603, 621, 635, 659-662, 668-669, 674-676, 679, 683, 697
Cash flows, 3-8, 11-12, 20, 23-24, 36, 49-88, 91, 96, 123, 142, 144-145, 150, 154-156, 164-165, 175-176, 178, 181-183, 185-198, 201, 203-204, 206, 211, 214, 230, 235, 277, 287-288, 291-292, 294, 312-313, 325, 328-329, 332, 340-341, 343, 347, 357-358, 361-365, 368-380, 382-389, 391-397, 401-438, 440-443, 445-452, 457-460, 462-464, 466-469, 473-475, 479-481, 486, 490, 497, 500, 502-505, 507, 517, 522-524, 526, 528-529, 545, 554-557, 561-562, 567, 570, 574, 581, 590-591, 600, 629, 645, 657, 659-662, 664, 666, 668-669, 674-675, 679, 683, 696, 701, 704
Cash management, 16, 628, 634, 637
Certainty, 297, 464
Channels, 37, 396
Channels of distribution, 396

Checkpoint, 57-58, 66-67, 76, 78, 83-85, 99-100, 103-104, 109-110, 115-116, 127-129, 145, 150, 152, 155, 157, 159, 161, 163, 167-171, 179-180, 182-183, 185-187, 190-191, 193-194, 198-203, 218, 227, 229, 236-238, 246-247, 251-252, 261-262, 266-268, 282-283, 288-289, 292-295, 304-305, 317-320, 332, 337-338, 343, 350-352, 362-364, 366, 368, 370-372, 374-377, 379-380, 390-394, 396, 408-409, 411, 416, 419, 427, 430, 432, 444-445, 447, 449, 451-452, 456-457, 464-465, 469-473, 484, 486, 490, 492-495, 503-504, 510-512, 536-537, 540-541, 549-552, 569-570, 585, 598-599, 606-607, 615-616, 622-623, 626-627, 638-641, 649, 652-653, 660, 662, 667-669, 680, 682, 690-691, 694-695, 702-703
Chicago Mercantile Exchange, 659-660
Chief executive officer, 16, 24
Chief financial officer, 16, 24, 135, 137
  CFO, 16, 24, 137
Chief risk officer, 676, 699
Children, 12, 163, 205, 207, 244, 337, 678
Chile, 225, 544, 648, 656
China, 3, 42, 73, 117, 163, 224, 234, 251, 302, 420, 453, 500, 544, 580, 646, 648, 655-657
  map of, 646
Chinese, 31, 655, 657
Claims, 3-4, 21, 23, 33, 37, 45, 65, 283, 285, 300-301, 326, 340, 347, 479, 505-506
  expenses, 3-4
  record, 3
Classification, 288, 499, 618
Clearing, 367, 629
clothing, 57, 69, 86, 114, 408-409, 411-412, 512, 704
Code of ethics, 18
Collapse, 42, 45, 272, 697-698
Collateral, 2, 4, 7, 280, 300-301, 312, 314, 624-625, 636, 684, 700, 702
Collections, 601, 624, 628
Colombia, 648, 656
Columns, 213, 650
Commercial banks, 28, 30-33, 35-36, 40-41, 43-45, 277, 312, 624, 629
Commercial insurance, 32
Commitment, 279, 513, 625
Commodities, 211, 222-223, 674, 685
Commodity price risk, 672, 679, 699-700, 703, 705
Common market, 325
Common size statements, 90
Communication, 51, 589
Companies, 3-5, 8, 17-18, 29-35, 38, 40, 44-45, 57, 73-74, 92, 103, 113, 116-117, 121, 126, 137, 220-224, 230-231, 237-238, 243, 251, 255, 257, 262, 265-266, 278, 302, 312, 327, 335, 337-338, 342, 346, 360, 398-399, 460, 468, 493, 499, 508, 512, 518, 532, 546, 550-551, 553, 564-567, 573, 575-576, 578-581, 583, 592, 607, 622, 624, 645-646, 657-658, 662-663, 674, 677, 696, 701-702
company policy, 434
Company stock, 215, 568, 575, 584
Comparative advantage, 699
Compensation, 4, 21, 24, 167, 306-307, 662, 677, 699
Compensation plans, 21, 24
Compete, 8, 231, 423, 434, 590, 602
Competition, 359, 390, 403, 420, 434-435, 501, 674
Competitive advantage, 359, 453
Competitors, 56, 92, 95, 104, 137, 359, 404, 425, 435, 534, 576, 590, 631
  identifying, 404
Component parts, 109, 111
compromise, 501
Computer software, 451, 466, 533
Conditions, 7, 95, 125, 135, 214, 281, 296, 311, 351, 390, 425, 442, 444-445, 470, 483, 494, 496, 504-505, 512, 522, 548, 554-555, 560, 566, 575, 581-583, 603, 650, 666, 682, 696
Confidence, 19, 57, 231, 359, 447
Configuration, 449
Conflict, 21, 479
Consideration, 2, 4, 6, 56, 79, 224, 229, 235, 277, 307, 360, 405, 423, 434-435, 442, 467, 503-504, 537, 542, 544-545, 548, 552-553, 562, 636, 675, 699, 701
Consistency, 576-577, 661
Consolidation, 33
Consortium, 512

Constraints, 362, 376
Construction, 51, 54, 57, 79, 127, 192, 270, 394, 444, 473, 597, 600, 605, 630, 639-640, 657, 674
Consumer credit, 40
Consumer Price Index, 221, 223
Consumer products, 396, 432
Consumer protection, 43
Consumers, 33, 43, 251, 655
Consumption, 20, 397, 399
Content, 50, 52, 78-79, 82
Continuity, 15, 23, 364
Contract, 1-8, 18, 22, 44, 81, 206, 279, 290, 341, 344, 348, 394, 463, 465, 468, 509, 607-608, 629, 651-653, 664-665, 667-669, 673, 677-686, 688, 691, 696-704
Contracts, 4-6, 18, 33, 279, 325, 347, 394, 629, 651, 667-668, 672-673, 677-680, 683-686, 689, 696-697, 699-702, 705
  country risk, 699
  leasing, 33
Contribution margin, 2, 455-456, 458, 460, 467, 641
Control, 4-5, 13, 15-16, 23, 53, 57, 105-109, 113-114, 126, 153, 327-328, 386, 531-532, 597, 601, 629, 631, 633, 636-637, 645, 657, 666, 673-675, 684, 699-700, 702
Controlling, 5, 34, 45-46, 79, 107, 597, 603, 675, 699
Conventions, 117, 436
Convergence, 82, 646
conversion, 2, 5, 283, 285-286, 302, 312, 499, 612, 619-624, 636, 639, 660
Convertibility, 300-301
Convertible bonds, 301, 532
Cooperation, 590
Copyright, 1, 9, 27, 49, 89, 141, 173, 209, 241, 275, 323, 355, 401, 439, 477, 515, 559, 587, 611, 643, 671
Corporate bonds, 38, 41, 222, 276, 281, 284-287, 290-292, 300-301, 306, 308, 314, 321, 487-488, 508
Corporate charter, 327, 347
Corporate mergers, 5, 45
Corporate tax rates, 59, 83
Corporate taxes, 50, 59, 83, 526-528, 533, 551
corporation, 1-3, 5-8, 12-18, 23-25, 30, 32, 35-37, 45, 59-60, 80-81, 83, 99-100, 103, 119-120, 128, 133, 136-137, 157, 199, 268-269, 272, 277-278, 281, 285, 301, 312, 314, 318-321, 326, 328, 339, 347-348, 350, 352, 360-361, 428-431, 473, 479-480, 500, 508-511, 548, 552-553, 573, 579, 583-585, 608, 613, 622-623, 625, 638, 640, 645, 657, 663, 666, 675, 679, 683, 697, 701
  advantages of, 15, 625
  definition of, 15, 339
  professional, 12, 23, 25, 328
  stockholders in, 6, 81
Corporations, 1-3, 12, 15, 23, 29, 31-36, 41, 44-45, 59-61, 80, 211, 278, 280-281, 301-302, 307, 328, 359, 384, 437, 519, 526, 528, 531, 561, 565, 629, 636, 657, 673-674
  domestic, 2-3, 15, 34, 211, 657
  foreign, 1-3, 15, 41, 301-302, 657, 673-674
  professional, 12, 23, 328, 531, 673
Corrective action, 445
cost accounting, 16, 442
Cost issues, 501
Cost of goods sold, 2-5, 8, 54-58, 79-80, 83-84, 86, 93, 98-99, 102-103, 106, 108-109, 112-113, 118-119, 124, 127-128, 131-132, 134-136, 408-410, 412-414, 536, 605, 609, 620-624
Costa Rica, 656
  exchange rates, 656
Cost-benefit analysis, 399
Costs, 1-6, 8, 12-13, 20-21, 23, 34, 46, 53, 55, 67, 80-81, 106-108, 111-114, 144, 153, 159, 164, 187, 195, 199, 202, 207, 224, 231, 278-279, 316, 328, 357, 360, 362, 365-369, 371, 374, 377, 381, 385, 387, 391-392, 394, 398-399, 404-407, 409-410, 416-419, 421-425, 427, 430-435, 437, 445-447, 449-451, 453-462, 464, 466-468, 470-473, 475, 478-486, 496-510, 512-513, 517, 522-524, 526, 528-529, 531-534, 543, 546, 548, 552, 566, 568, 572-573, 576, 579, 590, 609, 614, 617, 624, 628, 631, 639, 641, 645, 654-655, 668, 673-674, 677-679, 681, 686, 690, 696-697, 700
  alteration, 468
  conversion, 2, 5, 499, 624, 639

distribution, 3, 6, 8, 46, 55, 279, 360, 391, 407, 450-451, 466, 502, 510, 513, 522, 566, 568, 572-573, 673
  labor costs, 655
  product and, 360, 425, 427
  product lines, 434-435, 590
  sales and, 112, 446, 461, 472, 590, 614
Countries, 3-6, 21, 32-33, 41, 43, 117, 223-225, 234, 302, 420, 500, 508, 526, 544, 548, 583, 645-646, 650, 654-655, 657-662, 664-669, 674
Country risk, 699
  managing, 699
Coupons, 302
Covenants, 279
Creating value, 95
Credit, 1-2, 4-5, 8, 11, 16, 22, 30, 33, 40, 44, 53, 62-63, 68, 70, 75, 79-80, 92, 97, 99, 101, 108, 110, 118, 121-124, 128, 130-136, 161, 163, 167, 202, 221, 278, 280, 289, 300, 307-308, 312-313, 316, 321, 406, 410-411, 416, 422, 487-488, 509, 535, 541, 543-544, 550, 601-605, 608-609, 613-615, 617-633, 635-641, 683-684, 697-698, 700, 702
  debt financing, 4, 101, 124, 488, 535, 541, 543-544
  extension of, 123
  raising funds, 406
Credit cards, 33, 202, 316, 613, 632-633
Credit default swaps, 697-698
credit limit, 632
Credit line, 632
Credit unions, 40
criticism, 382, 389
Cross rate, 2, 650, 664
Currency, 1-4, 7, 16, 300-302, 314, 453, 468, 500, 644-653, 655-657, 659, 661-662, 664-669, 679, 683-684, 696, 700-701
  exchange of, 696, 701
  foreign exchange trading, 646
  managing risk, 683, 700
  net present value, 661
  risk, 1-4, 7, 300-302, 314, 453, 468, 500, 645, 650-651, 657, 659, 662, 664, 666, 668-669, 679, 683-684, 696, 700-701
Currency markets, 669
Currency swap, 2, 696, 701
Current accounts, 128
Current assets, 1-2, 6, 8, 40, 62-67, 71, 73, 80-81, 84, 87, 94, 96, 99-101, 112, 123-124, 126-127, 129-135, 138, 406, 584, 593, 596, 598-599, 604-607, 612-619, 622, 628, 635, 638
Current liabilities, 1-2, 6-8, 62-67, 71, 81, 84, 87, 94, 96, 99-101, 103, 123-124, 126-135, 138, 406, 536, 545, 549-550, 553, 584, 593, 596, 598-599, 604-607, 612-618, 622, 624, 628, 635-636, 638-639
Current ratio, 2, 96-101, 120, 123-124, 127, 129-133, 136, 605-606, 614-616, 637-638
Curves, 308
Customers, 33, 53, 62, 70, 92, 98, 100, 122, 359-360, 396, 399, 403-405, 424, 426, 526, 529, 534, 544, 546, 585, 590, 601, 603, 613-614, 630-631, 639, 641, 645
Czech Republic, 656

D

Damage, 34, 399, 441, 473, 676-677
  property, 399, 473, 677
data, 4, 16, 39, 42, 55, 86, 97, 113, 120-122, 124, 212-213, 221, 224-225, 227, 236-239, 255, 268-269, 287, 289-290, 294, 363, 367, 373, 488, 491, 494, 499, 551-552, 590-591, 616, 629, 631, 652, 661, 667-669, 688-689
data processing, 16
Database, 120
dates, 213, 232, 308
Death, 15, 21, 200, 254, 328, 399, 534, 677-678
Debt, 1-8, 13, 21, 24, 31, 33, 35-37, 39-41, 43, 45-46, 55, 62-68, 71-74, 76-77, 80-81, 84-87, 91, 94, 96, 99, 101-104, 109, 111-112, 117-118, 120, 123-133, 135-136, 138, 166-167, 202, 211, 215, 234, 275-321, 326, 340, 347, 349, 406, 408, 413, 421, 435, 478-489, 496, 500-513, 517-556, 561, 566-567, 579, 584, 593-596, 598-601, 603-607, 609, 612-613, 615, 617-619, 624-625, 629, 632, 635-638, 641, 678, 696-697, 701
  defined, 2, 46, 96, 102, 126, 300, 406, 408, 485, 506, 518-519, 544

Debt capacity, 544
Debt crisis, 43
Debt financing, 3-4, 21, 55, 64, 86, 101, 103-104, 109, 111, 124, 129, 421, 480, 482, 488-489, 496, 500, 502-503, 506, 508, 513, 517, 519, 521, 523-544, 546-548, 552-554, 561
  sources of, 3-4, 64, 86, 480, 482, 517, 532, 546, 553
Debt markets, 276, 278, 312, 316
Debt ratio, 2, 4, 101-102, 104, 111-112, 117-118, 120, 124-125, 128-129, 131-133, 135-136, 518-520, 522, 527, 534-535, 537, 545, 547, 549-550, 553, 605-606
Debt ratios, 519, 529, 534
Debt-to-equity ratio, 518, 524-525, 527-529, 531
Decision criteria, 355-356, 359-377, 379-386, 388-399, 430-431
Decision making, 442, 673
Decision-making, 1, 7, 23, 440, 442, 466-468
  group, 442
Decision-making process, 1, 23, 440, 442, 466, 468
Defined benefit plans, 2, 30, 44
Defined contribution plans, 2, 30, 44
Degree of risk, 40
Demand, 2, 20, 44, 149, 231, 307, 327, 357, 421, 425, 463, 470-471, 485-486, 566-567, 639-640, 650, 674, 682, 699
  change in, 2, 327, 421
  currency, 2, 650
  derived, 425
  increases in, 463
Demand deposits, 2, 44, 640
Denmark, 42, 117, 163, 251, 420, 544, 580, 655-656
Department of Labor, 381
Deposits, 2, 30, 32, 36, 43-44, 168, 176-177, 181, 199-202, 205, 395, 499, 640
Depreciation, 1-5, 55, 58, 61-63, 66-67, 71, 73, 75-77, 79-87, 93-94, 131-132, 134, 136, 407-413, 415-418, 420, 422-423, 425-433, 435-437, 445-451, 453-454, 456-460, 467, 471-475, 535-537, 542-543, 547, 605, 609
Depreciation expense, 2-3, 5, 55, 61, 63, 67, 73, 81, 83-85, 132, 134, 407-411, 413, 416-418, 420, 422-423, 425, 437, 445-451, 453, 456-460, 467, 471-475, 535-537, 542-543, 547, 605, 609
Depression, 39, 43, 45, 265-266
Derivatives, 7, 43, 45, 672, 675, 683-684, 691, 701, 703
design, 24, 172, 321, 398-399, 425-426, 463, 475, 548, 609
  elements of, 24
  principles of, 24
Detailed analysis, 111, 534
Determinant, 102-103, 249, 517, 521, 538, 560, 579, 581, 612, 630, 636, 649
Developed countries, 21, 223-225, 583
Developed country, 3, 224, 234
Dharma, 551
Differentiation, 53, 434
  product, 53, 434
Direct investment, 662, 666
Direct mail, 34
Direct quote, 3, 647, 649, 651-653, 664-665
Direct quotes, 651
Disability, 677
  income, 677
Discipline, 531, 545
Discount rate, 2-3, 6, 154-155, 165, 169, 183, 186, 189, 192-194, 199, 201, 203-204, 206, 287-288, 292, 294-296, 313, 321, 335, 358, 361-366, 368-383, 385, 387-389, 391-398, 406, 412-414, 417, 423, 430-433, 435, 445, 447-448, 464, 474, 479-481, 497-502, 505, 507-508, 511-512, 659-660, 662, 669, 693
Discounts, 135, 383, 625, 630-631, 640-641
Discretionary spending, 545
Disease, 678
Distance, 144
Distribution, 3, 6-8, 38, 42, 46, 55, 79, 110, 120, 212-219, 233-234, 279, 281, 348, 360, 391, 396, 407, 450-452, 466, 469, 502, 510, 513, 522, 527, 555, 560-562, 565-575, 581-583, 585, 606, 632, 673, 675-676, 694-695
  emerging markets, 3, 234
  intermediaries in, 46
  shipping and, 407
Distribution center, 360
Distribution centers, 606

Diversifiable risk, 3, 6, 8, 254, 264
Diversification, 3, 6, 242-252, 254-255, 259, 263-265, 302, 666
Dividend policy, 3, 279, 339, 348, 559-583, 585, 595
Dividends, 2-3, 6-7, 14-15, 24, 37-38, 41, 46, 55-58, 60-61, 64-65, 67, 71-74, 76-77, 79-83, 85, 87, 110, 136, 189, 212-214, 236, 238, 326, 328-336, 338-344, 347-352, 413, 481, 488-493, 496, 506, 509-513, 522, 526-527, 530, 532-533, 540, 551, 560-585, 592-595, 599, 604-606, 609, 657, 675-676, 691, 693
documents, 160, 374
Dollar, 1, 3, 5-7, 19, 23-24, 32, 35, 39, 46, 53-54, 56, 60, 63, 65, 69, 80, 93, 100, 102, 104-108, 110, 113, 115-116, 143-144, 147, 153, 164, 171, 176, 183, 189, 196-197, 201, 213, 219, 302-303, 315, 335-336, 339, 364, 369, 379, 398, 425, 430-432, 435, 453-455, 462, 468, 481, 491, 518, 527, 575, 578, 581, 583, 606, 619, 624, 626-627, 633, 646-652, 654-656, 659, 663-664, 667-669, 679, 686, 688
    cross rates, 650-651
    exchange rates, 7, 453, 646, 648, 650-651, 654-656, 659, 663-664, 667, 679
Dollars, 3, 6, 18, 60, 76, 85, 99-100, 104, 115, 133, 144, 154-155, 164, 188, 193-194, 219, 253, 279, 297, 301-302, 307, 314, 335, 382, 384, 406, 453, 460, 468, 508, 541-543, 550, 552-553, 616, 631, 645-647, 649-651, 654, 656-657, 659-661, 663, 667-669, 683, 686, 696-697
Dominance, 398
Double taxation, 14-15, 23, 60
Dow Jones Industrial Average, 34
Downstream, 499-500
Drugs, 231
Dubai, 192, 351
Duties, 16-17, 24, 408, 518
Duty, 167, 677

E
Earnings, 3, 5-8, 13-15, 18, 21, 23-24, 34, 37, 39, 52-53, 55-62, 64-67, 70-72, 74-75, 78-81, 83-84, 86-87, 93-94, 101-104, 110, 113-118, 120, 124-137, 139, 188, 206, 230-232, 243, 324-326, 328, 333-340, 348, 350-353, 381, 410, 413, 425, 428-429, 435, 457, 473, 481, 489-492, 494, 506, 508, 510, 512-513, 518-520, 526-527, 529-530, 532, 534-544, 546-547, 551-553, 562-565, 570-571, 576-580, 582-583, 585, 592-599, 602, 604-607, 609, 662, 703
    stability of, 576-577, 579
    test, 101, 118, 124, 129, 133, 136
Earnings before interest and taxes, 3, 5, 55-56, 79-80, 93, 102-103, 132, 413, 425, 428-429, 520, 535, 537, 542-543, 547, 551-552
E-commerce, 521
Economics, 20, 253, 359, 442, 497, 577-578, 591, 646, 692
Economy, 3-4, 35, 39, 42-44, 76, 114, 214, 223, 230, 234, 251, 253-254, 259, 266, 271-272, 303, 306, 315, 321, 331, 335, 398, 442-444, 469-470, 529, 554-556, 609, 645, 674
Education, 1, 9, 13, 27, 49, 89, 141, 156, 173, 180, 199, 209, 241, 244, 275, 323, 355, 381, 385, 390, 397, 401, 439, 477, 492, 515, 559, 582-583, 587, 611, 643, 671
Education level, 381
Effective interest rate, 552
Efficiency, 4-5, 8, 21, 23, 25, 79, 95, 102, 105-106, 109, 111-112, 117-118, 124, 128, 133-134, 138-139, 230, 232, 235-236, 397, 423, 612, 620, 636
Egypt, 648, 656
Electronic data, 629
Electronic data interchange, 629
    EDI, 629
Eligibility, 678
E-mail, 398
Emergency fund, 207
Emerging markets, 3, 45, 223-226, 234, 267
    inflation, 223
emphasis, 335, 442
Employees, 29-30, 51-53, 62, 92, 279, 328, 359, 387, 417, 433, 518, 526, 529, 531, 546, 618, 677, 701
    loyalty, 30, 328
Employment, 30, 381

Endowments, 1, 44
England, 42, 73, 117, 163, 251, 302, 420, 453, 500, 544, 580, 696
English, 696
Enron, 18, 57, 122, 683
Entities, 38, 57
Entrepreneur, 442
Entrepreneurs, 15, 442, 468
Environment, 23, 272, 306, 522, 534, 590, 662, 666
Equipment purchases, 374, 417
Equity, 1-8, 14, 23-24, 32-38, 41, 43-46, 52, 61-67, 69, 71-72, 77, 79-81, 84, 87, 94, 101, 103-104, 110-118, 120, 123-126, 128-138, 211, 221-223, 226, 232, 234, 236, 278, 281, 286, 326, 333-334, 339, 348, 350-352, 362, 407, 478-484, 486, 488-496, 498, 500, 502-511, 517-533, 535-546, 548-550, 552-556, 561-562, 567-571, 574, 576, 579, 584-585, 592-596, 598-599, 603-607, 615, 618, 635, 691
    defined, 2, 44, 46, 61, 126, 348, 490, 498, 506, 518-519, 544
    internal, 4-5, 7, 120, 123, 490, 532, 546
    issuing, 2, 4, 6-8, 35-36, 41, 44, 46, 81, 278, 281, 286, 478, 486, 502, 507, 510-511, 532, 536, 548, 552-553, 569, 576, 596
Equity capital, 481-482, 489-491, 496, 505, 510, 552, 555
Equity financing, 64-65, 286, 480, 482, 489, 502-503, 506, 517, 519, 522, 524, 527-528, 533, 535, 537, 540-541, 579
Equity investment, 113
Equity securities, 1, 3, 7, 37, 43, 45-46, 65, 123, 211, 234, 326, 479-480, 484, 505, 507, 519
ETC, 68, 590
ethical dilemmas, 11
Ethical issues, 18
    Enron and, 18
ethical lapses, 18
Ethics, 18-19, 24, 398
    Code of ethics, 18
    Contracts, 18
    Laws, 18-19
EU, 43
Euro, 453, 646-651, 654, 656, 663-664
    currency cross rates, 651
Eurobonds, 300-301, 316
Eurodollars, 4, 684, 700
Europe, 3, 35, 43, 223-224, 301, 314, 580, 590, 648, 655, 658
European option, 3, 686, 700
European Union, 43, 73
    EU, 43
European Union (EU), 43
Evaluation, 2, 272, 286, 358, 382, 398, 404, 406, 421, 435, 439-440, 442-475, 507, 512, 631, 637
evidence, 95, 213, 226, 232, 234, 279, 328, 389, 497, 543, 562, 574, 577
Exchange, 1-8, 31, 33-34, 38, 44-46, 51, 57, 87, 117, 269, 279, 281, 302, 312, 327, 345-346, 349, 453, 565, 582, 629, 644-651, 653-656, 659-669, 672-674, 677, 679, 683-684, 696-697, 699-703, 705
Exchange rate, 2-5, 7, 302, 453, 644, 646-647, 649-651, 653-655, 659-666, 668-669, 674, 679, 696
    depreciation, 2-5, 453
    fixed, 4, 302, 453, 696
Exchange rates, 4, 7, 453, 644, 646, 648, 650-651, 653-656, 659-661, 663-667, 673, 679, 684, 696-697
    Brazil, 453, 648, 656, 659
    Costa Rica, 656
    U.S. dollar and, 654
Exchanges, 3, 6, 34, 38, 44-45, 221, 345-346, 349-350, 658, 677, 684
    security exchanges, 6, 38, 45
Exclusion, 60
Expansion, 3, 15, 31, 36, 130, 266, 272, 351, 359, 391, 394, 397, 402, 414-415, 422-423, 443, 463, 465, 468-469, 502-503, 512-513, 529-530, 549, 595, 605-606, 617, 619, 638
expect, 4, 18-19, 21, 23-24, 35, 37-38, 63, 81, 114, 130, 158, 200, 206, 211, 213-214, 218, 220-221, 227-229, 231-233, 235, 246, 265, 268-271, 304, 316, 320, 329-330, 334, 337, 339, 351, 353, 365, 425, 441, 447, 462, 465, 468, 471, 480-481, 489, 491, 493, 496, 499, 524, 535, 541, 544, 567, 584, 593, 599, 609,

623, 641, 654-655, 659, 668, 675, 691-693, 695
Expectations, 19-20, 37, 51, 243, 263, 309, 311, 333, 336, 409, 423, 447, 462, 468
Expected return, 19-20, 41, 213, 215-220, 233, 237, 244-245, 247-248, 251-252, 258-259, 261-262, 264-272, 291, 312, 329, 341, 350, 358, 480, 493, 506, 517
Expenditures, 16, 31, 62, 69, 75-76, 85-87, 114-115, 157, 163, 374, 395, 407, 411, 413, 417-418, 421-423, 426, 482, 597, 600, 608, 675
    defined, 75
    limitations, 395
Expenses, 1, 3-5, 8, 34, 38, 40, 46, 52-59, 62-63, 69, 71-75, 79-81, 83-84, 86-87, 93-94, 102-103, 105-108, 112-114, 127-132, 134-136, 138, 143, 176, 207, 211, 339, 360, 366, 399, 405, 407-410, 412-413, 415, 418, 421-423, 425, 427, 441, 445-446, 454, 456, 458, 460, 467, 472-473, 475, 483-484, 518-520, 527, 533-534, 536-537, 542, 551, 590-604, 606-607, 609, 618, 631
Experience, 75, 114, 121, 125, 202, 214, 254, 298, 359, 381, 398, 493, 512, 529, 538, 546, 595, 599, 692, 703
expertise, 52, 59, 359
Exporting, 424
Exports, 408
Expropriation, 662
External debt, 532

F
Facebook, 327
Failure, 106, 443, 447, 466, 529, 532, 547, 630, 685
Fair price, 326
Family, 14, 91, 170, 205, 470, 536, 570-573, 583, 678, 698
Fannie Mae, 41
FAST, 157, 384, 480, 567
Favors, 382, 528
Feature, 2, 25, 35, 38, 43-44, 46, 82, 126, 189, 192, 236, 265, 285-286, 312, 316, 340, 349, 390, 415, 417, 423-424, 468, 507-508, 547-548, 582-583, 603-604, 637, 678, 701-702
Federal deficit, 335
Federal government, 41, 221, 629
Federal income tax, 59, 83
Federal Reserve, 19, 32, 43, 508
    structure of, 508
Federal Reserve System, 32
feedback, 83, 126, 167, 198, 236, 266, 317, 350, 390, 424, 469, 508, 549, 583, 604, 638, 667, 702
FICO, 632
Finance, 1, 4, 8, 10-13, 16-19, 21-25, 29-33, 35, 38-42, 44, 46-47, 51, 53, 58, 61, 63-65, 73, 75-76, 78-79, 82, 86, 92, 101-104, 110-111, 117, 120, 123, 126, 128, 130, 135, 139, 143, 145, 163-164, 168-169, 171, 175, 179, 189, 196-197, 200, 202, 205-206, 211-212, 222, 231, 233, 235-236, 239, 251, 255-257, 261-265, 268, 277-278, 280, 282, 284, 287, 302, 312, 316-317, 325-327, 329, 347, 350, 357, 386-387, 404, 406-407, 410, 420-421, 424, 435, 442, 453, 459, 466, 468, 472, 479-480, 490, 492, 494, 497, 500-503, 505, 507-508, 510-513, 516-518, 520-522, 527, 529, 542-546, 548-549, 552, 563, 566, 579-581, 583, 585, 596-597, 602, 606, 615, 617, 619, 624-625, 635-636, 639-640, 643-670, 673, 699
    accounting and, 79, 120, 239, 442, 472
    capital budgeting and, 386, 543
    capital structure, 1, 4, 8, 12, 17, 23, 101-103, 123, 126, 128, 139, 386, 497, 501, 505, 507-508, 511-512, 516-518, 520-522, 527, 529, 542-546, 548-549, 552, 566, 645
    finance function, 16, 24
    summary of, 1, 47
Financial analysis, 53, 69, 76, 78, 89-90, 92-139, 219, 229, 253, 258, 262, 294, 334, 342, 362, 368-369, 374, 377, 380, 384, 413, 460, 462, 482, 489, 491, 496, 516, 520, 543, 547, 553, 595, 624, 627, 634, 696
    applications, 89, 101, 137
Financial assets, 41-42, 46, 211
Financial capital, 362, 540
Financial condition, 8, 53, 57, 79, 84-85, 91, 94, 121, 125-127, 133-134, 606

Financial crises, 43
Financial crisis, 32, 39, 42-43, 45, 232, 271, 508
    banks in, 32, 43
Financial institutions, 17-18, 28, 30, 33-34, 39, 42-44,
    222, 278, 280, 624, 697
Financial instruments, 1-3, 6, 31, 37-41, 44-45, 684
Financial intermediaries, 4, 31-33, 35, 45-46
Financial management, 1, 9-10, 19, 24, 27, 49, 89,
    141, 173, 209, 241, 275, 323, 355, 401, 439,
    477, 515, 559, 587, 611, 643, 666, 669, 671
    capital budgeting, 1, 666, 669
Financial markets, 4, 6, 13, 21-23, 28-31, 33, 35-36,
    39, 42, 44-46, 73, 77-78, 85-86, 212, 220,
    222-223, 230-232, 235, 278, 280, 291, 316,
    326, 414, 423, 507-508, 522-524, 541, 684
Financial panics, 43
Financial plan, 5, 7, 588-591, 600, 602-604, 608
financial reporting, 19, 57, 73-74, 82, 98, 117, 407
Financial reports, 19, 54, 57, 79
    balance sheet, 54, 79
    income statement, 54, 57, 79
    understanding, 54, 57
Financial resources, 678
Financial risk, 117, 225, 520, 662
Financial services, 32-33, 121, 163, 225
Financial statement, 1-2, 4, 50, 52-53, 69, 79-81,
    91-93, 115, 117, 121, 123, 125-126, 131-135
    Balance sheet, 1, 4, 50, 52, 69, 79-81, 93, 115,
        121, 123, 126, 131, 134
    Basic financial statements, 50, 52, 79
Financial Times, 490, 492, 646
Finland, 42, 73, 117, 163, 251, 302, 420, 500, 544,
    580
Fire, 254, 677
    risk of, 254, 677
Firm performance, 74, 90, 102, 335, 413, 481, 526,
    613
Firms, 1, 3-4, 8, 15-19, 22-24, 27-28, 30-40, 42-47, 51,
    53, 57, 59-60, 69, 74-76, 79, 82, 86, 92-101,
    103-104, 106-110, 113, 115, 117, 119-123,
    125, 130-132, 136, 139, 175, 211, 213, 222,
    230-232, 238, 248-249, 254, 261, 265,
    267-268, 277-278, 280, 300, 335-340, 342,
    345-346, 348, 359, 361-362, 364, 369, 374,
    379, 382, 386, 388-390, 407, 413-414, 420,
    424, 436, 453, 462-463, 468, 474, 478, 480,
    487, 491, 496-501, 505, 507-508, 516-518,
    520-523, 526-535, 543-544, 546-548, 550,
    553-555, 557, 560-562, 564, 566, 574-575,
    577-583, 589-590, 602, 613-615, 618, 620,
    625-626, 628-631, 633, 635-636, 645-646,
    657, 666, 674-675, 677, 683, 685, 698, 700,
    702, 705
Fisher Effect, 4-5, 303-305, 315, 655, 657, 665-666
Fixed assets, 1, 4, 6, 23, 61-63, 67, 77, 80-81, 84, 94,
    102, 105, 109-110, 112, 121, 124, 130-132,
    134, 411, 413, 415, 584, 592-593, 596,
    598-599, 604-607, 617-619, 635
Fixed costs, 4, 427, 430-431, 435, 445-447, 450-451,
    453-462, 466-468, 470-473, 475, 548, 552
Fixed expenses, 114
Flexibility, 73, 279, 420, 460, 463, 465, 468, 498, 501,
    529, 543, 548, 577-578
Food, 69, 114, 231, 359, 424, 480, 645
    production, 359
Food and Drug Administration, 231
Forecasting, 6, 53, 330, 402-405, 407-408, 424, 444,
    469, 493, 587-609
    cash disbursements, 600-601, 603
    cash receipts, 600-601, 603
    sales, 6, 53, 403-405, 408, 424, 444, 469, 588-606,
        608-609
Forecasts, 79, 123, 357, 398, 403-404, 407, 414, 424,
    442, 445, 447, 466, 470, 589-591, 596, 600,
    603, 605
Foreign bonds, 302
Foreign competition, 420
Foreign direct investment, 662
Foreign exchange, 1, 3-4, 7, 87, 644-648, 650-651,
    664, 666-669, 673, 699
    cash flows and, 3, 666
Foreign exchange markets, 644, 646, 651, 667, 669
    forward rates, 651, 667
    spot rates, 651, 667
Foreign exchange risk, 645, 699
Foreign subsidiary, 662
Forward contract, 4, 651-653, 665, 667-668, 673,
    678-683, 700, 702-703
Forward contracts, 651, 672, 678-680, 683-684, 686,

700, 702, 705
Forward exchange rate, 4, 651, 653-654, 659-662,
    664-666, 668-669
Forward market, 652, 679
Forward premium, 653, 665
Forward rates, 651-653, 659, 667-668
    fractions, 506
France, 3, 42, 46, 73, 163, 224, 234, 251, 302, 420,
    453, 500, 544, 654-655
    economies of, 251
fraud, 19, 53, 57, 122
fraudulent financial reporting, 74
Freezing, 698
Frequency, 182, 189, 452, 532, 566, 581, 676
Fringe benefits, 416-419
Full line, 552
Fund, 3-6, 12, 17, 30, 33-35, 40, 42, 44-46, 114, 158,
    169, 171, 176-177, 199, 201-202, 205, 207,
    211, 221, 244, 251-252, 266-267, 269-270,
    272-273, 279, 364, 480, 517-518, 532, 561,
    569-570, 579, 619, 629
Futures contract, 1, 4, 651, 684-686, 700, 702
Futures contracts, 5, 651, 684-685, 700, 705

G

GAAP, 57, 59, 61, 73-74, 80, 82, 117, 122, 339
Gambling, 284, 473
General partners, 14
General partnership, 4, 14, 23-24
    limited, 4, 14, 23-24
Generally accepted accounting principles, 57, 115,
    117, 339
    GAAP, 57, 117, 339
Generally accepted accounting principles (GAAP), 339
Generation Xers, 405
Georgia, 552
Germany, 32, 42, 46, 73, 117, 163, 251, 302, 420, 453,
    500, 544, 580, 663
Global supply chain, 646
Globalization, 73, 251
    markets, 73
Goals, 17-18, 114, 361, 405, 588, 591, 597, 602
Going public, 350, 574
Gold, 222, 327, 361, 655
Gold standard, 361
Goods, 2-5, 7-8, 53-58, 62-63, 70, 79-84, 86, 93,
    98-99, 102-103, 106, 108-109, 112-113,
    118-119, 124, 127-128, 131-132, 134-136,
    212-213, 303-306, 315, 406, 408-410,
    412-414, 468, 472, 484, 536, 605, 609,
    613-614, 617, 620-624, 629, 633, 635, 637,
    646, 654-655, 665, 674, 699
    free, 5, 7, 303, 305-306, 315, 408, 410, 412-413,
        633, 654
    intermediate, 635
    normal, 5, 633, 637
    private, 5, 8
    public, 2, 4-5, 57, 63, 81, 213
    substitute, 7
Government, 3, 31, 33, 36, 39, 41, 43, 87, 146, 171,
    211, 215, 221-223, 234, 277, 301-302, 308,
    311, 315, 359-360, 379, 480, 494, 508, 629,
    662-663
    foreign direct investment, 662
    leasing, 33
Government securities, 3, 41, 222, 234, 311, 494
GPS, 14, 51, 57, 66, 86, 396, 470
Graphs, 686
Great Britain, 3, 224, 234, 657
Great Depression, 39, 43, 45
Greece, 43, 544
Gross margin, 120, 137
Gross profit, 4, 55-56, 58, 79, 86, 103, 106, 113, 118,
    124, 126-128, 131-136, 138, 409-410, 412,
    414, 536, 609
Gross profit margin, 4, 56, 79, 86, 106, 113, 118, 124,
    126, 128, 133
Group, 8, 32-35, 96-98, 100-102, 104-108, 110-111,
    113, 115-117, 119, 121-122, 125, 221,
    223-225, 231, 281, 312, 362, 442, 500, 552,
    590, 631
groups, 3, 57, 120, 278, 328, 436, 488, 492, 574, 582
Growth rate, 2, 157, 190-191, 226, 330-334, 336,
    338-339, 347-348, 350-352, 409, 443,
    490-493, 496, 506, 509-510, 593, 596-597,
    599
Guidelines, 121, 244, 265, 360, 403, 405, 407, 421,
    674, 678, 702

H

headlines, 44
Hedge funds, 32, 34, 44, 232
Hedging, 1, 4, 672-673, 675, 678-685, 696, 700,
    702-703
    insurance, 4, 672-673, 678, 702
Hedging strategies, 684
Holding company, 32, 327, 698
Home country, 500, 544, 655, 657, 659, 661, 666
Home currency, 1, 3-4, 7, 646, 650, 664
Hong Kong, 117, 126, 358, 647-648, 655-656
Housing boom, 284
Housing market, 697-698
Housing prices, 43, 284
HTML, 167, 327
HTTP, 32-33, 41-42, 46-47, 78, 139, 163, 290, 327,
    381, 544, 632
humor, 327
Hungary, 656
Hurricanes, 673
hypothesis, 3, 210, 230-233, 235-236, 563

I

Ice, 641
identity theft, 633
III, 38, 77, 82, 133, 168, 359, 444, 469-470, 517, 533,
    535
illustration, 292, 300, 502, 529, 619, 679, 696
Image, 223, 374, 463, 686, 688
IMF, 42, 646, 648
Implementation, 376
Imports, 408, 655
Inc., 1, 9, 11, 17-18, 27, 32-33, 47, 49, 51, 54-57,
    61-64, 66, 71, 73, 75-76, 82-87, 89, 91,
    93-94, 96-98, 101-102, 104-108, 110-116,
    118, 120, 126-131, 134, 137, 141, 173, 209,
    221, 236-237, 239, 241, 243, 257, 261,
    267-270, 272, 275, 297, 318-321, 323, 325,
    327, 350-351, 353, 355, 371, 391, 394,
    396-397, 399, 401, 416, 424-425, 428-429,
    439, 445, 447, 449, 451, 455-457, 469-470,
    473, 477, 483-484, 487, 508, 510-513, 515,
    524, 536, 538-541, 549-551, 553, 559,
    566-567, 583-584, 587, 592-596, 600-601,
    604-607, 611, 639, 643, 671, 680, 690, 704
Incentives, 11, 21-23, 25, 29, 43-44, 51, 57, 79, 91,
    123, 202, 325, 328, 347, 357-358, 387, 403,
    421, 479, 505, 517, 522, 531-533, 545-546,
    584
Income, 1-8, 14-15, 39-40, 50, 52-64, 66-87, 91, 93,
    95, 97, 102-104, 106-118, 123-132, 134-138,
    198, 205-206, 222-224, 234, 283, 285-286,
    306, 321, 326, 334, 339-341, 348, 350, 381,
    407-413, 416, 418-419, 422, 425-427,
    436-437, 446, 448-450, 453-456, 458-460,
    462, 467, 473, 481, 485, 489, 519-520,
    526-530, 533, 536, 539-540, 542, 545-546,
    548, 551-553, 556, 565, 572-573, 575,
    581-583, 589, 591-600, 602-604, 609, 629,
    677-679, 696
    decrease in, 70-73, 78, 82, 409, 581
    differences in, 95, 107, 117, 125-126, 546, 572
    increase in, 2, 4, 6, 63, 70-73, 78, 82, 128-129,
        222, 306, 326, 407-408, 410-412, 416,
        418-419, 422, 446, 448-450, 453,
        458-459, 473, 536, 539, 545, 592-593,
        595, 678
    market, 1-8, 39-40, 54, 61, 63, 67-69, 78-79, 81,
        87, 91, 95, 113-118, 123-126, 129-130,
        136-137, 222-224, 234, 285, 306, 321,
        339, 341, 348, 350, 425, 449, 485,
        519-520, 545, 553, 565, 581, 583, 591,
        629, 678-679, 696
    national, 40, 76, 136-137
    per capita, 223
    permanent, 6, 552
    personal, 14-15, 57, 68-69, 82, 91, 114, 126, 436,
        528, 565, 572-573, 581, 583, 597-598,
        604
Income statement, 1-4, 7, 50, 52-59, 61, 63, 66, 68-72,
    74-75, 77, 79-80, 82-85, 93, 95, 97, 102-103,
    106, 110, 115, 123, 126-131, 135-136,
    409-410, 446, 530, 536, 542, 551-553,
    591-593, 596-598, 602-603, 609
    projected, 591-593, 596, 598, 603, 609
Income tax, 4, 55, 59-60, 83, 87, 446, 546, 551, 553,
    565, 572, 575, 581

Incorporation, 326
Indexes, 225, 335
India, 3, 224, 234, 424, 544, 646, 648, 656
  currency, 3, 646, 648, 656
Indirect quote, 4, 647, 649, 653, 664-665, 667-669
Indirect quotes, 647, 651, 667-668
Individual retirement accounts, 188
  IRAs, 188
  Roth, 188
Indonesia, 656
Industry, 43, 46, 57, 74-76, 98-99, 111, 117-118,
  120-121, 125-126, 131, 133-134, 136, 230,
  254, 265, 335, 385, 403, 420, 436, 473,
  498-500, 533, 536-537, 544, 546-548, 576,
  605, 631, 633, 637
Industry data, 499
Inefficiencies, 232
infer, 486, 494
Inflation, 4-7, 40, 67, 207, 221-223, 255, 271, 276,
  302-310, 315-316, 320, 333, 335, 338, 402,
  413-414, 422-424, 432, 500, 655, 657, 665,
  693
  anticipated, 4, 271, 303-305, 315, 333, 335, 413,
    424, 432, 693
  costs of, 316, 500
Inflation rate, 207, 303, 306, 320, 335, 414, 500, 655,
  657
Information, 3, 7-8, 11, 13, 20-23, 25, 29, 38-39, 44,
  46-47, 51-55, 57, 59, 64, 70, 72, 74, 76-77,
  79-80, 85-86, 90-91, 93, 95, 97, 99-100, 104,
  109, 114-115, 120, 123, 136-137, 139, 207,
  211, 230-233, 235-238, 243, 251, 263,
  266-267, 270, 272-273, 302, 306, 317, 325,
  329, 335, 346-347, 353, 382, 385, 388, 397,
  407, 416, 419, 430-431, 434-435, 445, 447,
  449, 471-472, 474, 479, 486-487, 490, 505,
  507, 517, 532, 561-562, 574, 581, 590-591,
  595, 614-615, 622, 629, 631-633, 641,
  652-653, 675, 683, 688-689
Information systems, 13
Information technology, 675
Infrastructure, 404
  investment in, 404
Inheritance, 15, 167, 171, 199
Initial public offering, 4, 327, 345, 349
  IPO, 4, 345, 349
Initiative, 35
Injury, 399
Innovation, 203, 434
Innovations, 420, 424
  measuring, 420
Insolvency, 8, 285, 314
Insurance, 2, 4, 7, 30-33, 44, 62, 69, 163, 170,
  198-199, 278-279, 281, 399, 454, 473, 566,
  632, 663, 672-673, 676-678, 697-699, 702,
  705
  applications, 163
  contracts, 4, 33, 279, 672-673, 677-678, 697, 699,
    702, 705
  excess, 30-31
  option, 7, 30, 279, 672, 698, 702
  score, 632
  types of, 4, 30, 32-33, 44, 663, 677, 699, 702, 705
Interbank market, 5, 279, 312
Interest, 1-8, 14, 17, 19, 21-25, 31, 36-38, 40-41,
  44-45, 55-60, 65, 79-80, 82-86, 92-93,
  101-104, 110-113, 117-118, 124, 127-129,
  131-136, 138, 142-171, 176-193, 196-206,
  228-229, 235-236, 255, 259, 264, 269, 271,
  273, 275-321, 326, 328, 331, 333, 335,
  338-342, 344, 353, 365-368, 403, 406, 408,
  410, 413-414, 421, 423, 425, 428-429, 435,
  446, 479-481, 483-484, 486-487, 489-490,
  493-496, 500, 505-506, 508-512, 518-522,
  526-540, 542-543, 545-554, 556, 600-601,
  608-609, 618, 624-627, 629, 631-632,
  636-637, 639-640, 644, 653-655, 657,
  659-661, 665-666, 668-669, 673, 675-676,
  679, 684-685, 692-694, 696-697, 699,
  701-705
  credit, 1-2, 4-5, 8, 22, 40, 44, 79-80, 92, 101, 110,
    118, 124, 128, 131-136, 161, 163, 167,
    202, 278, 280, 289, 300, 307-308,
    312-313, 316, 321, 406, 410, 487, 509,
    535, 543, 550, 601, 608-609, 618,
    624-627, 629, 631-632, 636-637,
    639-640, 684, 697, 702
Interest expense, 4, 8, 55, 57-58, 80, 83-84, 93,
  101-104, 110, 112, 117-118, 124, 127-129,

131-132, 134-135, 138, 406, 410, 413, 421,
  425, 446, 481, 519-520, 526-530, 535-537,
  539-540, 542-543, 545-547, 551-553, 601,
  609, 626-627, 637
Interest rate, 1-4, 6-8, 37, 40, 128-129, 143-154,
  156-160, 162, 165-171, 176-179, 181-182,
  184-188, 190-191, 196, 199-204, 206, 279,
  283-285, 287, 293, 296-298, 300, 302-307,
  312, 314-318, 353, 414, 487, 509-510, 538,
  540, 552, 554, 608, 632, 644, 653-654, 657,
  659-661, 665-666, 668-669, 673, 679,
  696-697, 701-702, 704-705
  current, 1-2, 6-8, 40, 128-129, 144, 186, 199,
    201-202, 206, 284-285, 296-298, 312,
    316, 487, 509, 540, 660, 666, 668-669,
    679, 696, 702
  guaranteed, 40, 157, 202
  risk, 1-4, 6-8, 40, 202, 283-284, 287, 293, 297-298,
    300, 302-303, 305-307, 312, 314-318,
    487, 510, 540, 554, 654, 657, 659-660,
    666, 668-669, 673, 679, 696-697,
    701-702, 704-705
Interest rates, 2, 4-5, 7-8, 40-41, 142-143, 151,
  160-161, 166-167, 171, 186-187, 255,
  275-321, 331, 335, 338, 342, 414, 423, 500,
  508, 549, 631, 654-655, 657, 659, 665, 673,
  684, 693, 697, 699
  bond prices and, 297
  determination of, 699
  inflation and, 303, 306, 320, 655
  investment and, 4, 166
  nominal, 4, 7, 160, 166, 303-306, 315, 320, 414,
    423, 500, 655, 657, 665
  real, 4-5, 7, 187, 278, 280, 300-301, 303-310,
    314-315, 320, 335, 338, 414, 423, 508,
    655, 657, 665
Intermediaries, 4, 30-33, 35, 44-46
Internal rate of return, 4-5, 360, 368, 370-371, 377,
  379-380, 384-385, 388-389, 391-394,
  396-397, 430-431, 435, 448, 490, 497
  IRR, 4-5, 360, 370-371, 377, 379-380, 384-385,
    388-389, 392-394, 396-397, 430, 435,
    448, 497
Internal Revenue Service, 16, 437
  IRS, 16, 437
International bonds, 302, 316
International business, 564, 643-663, 665-670
  environment, 662, 666
International capital, 660, 668-669
International comparisons, 117
International Financial Reporting Standards, 73, 117
International Fisher Effect, 5, 655, 657, 665-666
International investment, 645
International markets, 5, 420, 424, 645, 665
International Monetary Fund, 42
International trade, 655
Internet, 38, 85, 120, 167, 256, 396, 404, 423, 492,
  503, 512, 582, 585, 597
Inventories, 1-2, 5-6, 8, 30, 40, 62-66, 70, 72, 75,
  80-81, 94, 96-100, 105, 108-110, 116,
  118-120, 123-124, 126, 130-133, 406, 408,
  410-411, 413, 416, 421-422, 424, 445, 535,
  584, 602-603, 605, 613-615, 617-622,
  624-625, 628, 633, 635-636, 640
Inventory, 2-3, 5-7, 13, 17, 62, 70-72, 75, 84, 87,
  92-94, 96-101, 105, 108-109, 112, 116-121,
  124, 127-136, 138, 280, 346, 406, 411, 416,
  426-429, 445, 602-603, 605, 612, 614-617,
  620-625, 633, 635-639, 641
  management of, 13, 117, 612, 614, 617, 636, 641
Inventory management, 5, 116, 119, 633, 637
Investment, 2-8, 12-13, 15, 17, 19-20, 23-24, 29-37,
  39, 42-46, 52, 61, 63, 65, 67-69, 72, 75, 77,
  80, 92, 94, 98, 101, 103, 105-108, 110-111,
  113-115, 117, 124, 128-130, 135, 145-147,
  150-153, 156-158, 164, 166, 169-171,
  175-176, 179, 181, 183, 192-194, 196,
  198-200, 202-204, 211-229, 231-237, 239,
  242-249, 251-255, 257-259, 261, 263-267,
  269-273, 277-281, 286, 288, 291, 297,
  299-301, 303-305, 312, 315, 326, 329, 331,
  333, 337-340, 347-350, 353, 355-377,
  379-399, 403-417, 419-428, 430-432,
  434-435, 441-443, 445-456, 458-460,
  462-463, 465-471, 474-475, 478-481, 483,
  485-487, 490-491, 493-494, 496-498,
  500-513, 517-518, 521, 523, 529, 540-541,
  548-549, 554, 556-557, 561-562, 566-567,
  569-570, 572, 575-579, 582, 589, 592, 606,

612-615, 617-618, 628-630, 635-637, 639,
  641, 644-646, 650, 657, 662-664, 666, 668,
  675, 679-680, 683, 686, 688, 698-700, 702
  finance and, 12, 255, 326
  government, 3, 31, 33, 36, 39, 43, 146, 171, 211,
    215, 221-223, 234, 277, 301, 315,
    359-360, 379, 480, 494, 508, 629,
    662-663
  gross, 4-5, 34, 63, 94, 103, 106, 113, 124, 128,
    135, 409-410, 412, 414, 432
  interest rates and, 8, 151, 279, 297, 303, 315, 338
  net, 3-8, 33-34, 45, 61, 63, 65, 67-69, 72, 75, 77,
    80, 94, 103, 105-108, 110-111, 113, 115,
    117, 124, 128-130, 135, 339, 350,
    356-358, 360-362, 364, 369-372, 377,
    382, 384-385, 387-394, 396-397, 404,
    406-413, 415-417, 419, 421-422,
    424-428, 430-432, 435, 442, 445-446,
    448-450, 453-456, 458-460, 462,
    466-467, 479-481, 508, 512, 521, 540,
    561, 582, 592, 606, 613-615, 617,
    629-630, 637, 639, 641, 650, 675, 679
  present value and, 176, 356, 387
  private, 5-6, 8, 32, 34-35, 44-46, 231, 235,
    278-280, 312, 381, 663
  stock market and, 46
Investment banker, 279-281, 337, 485-486, 501-503,
  507, 511-512, 679-680, 702
Investment banks, 30-33, 43-44, 46, 646, 664
Investment decisions, 2, 17, 44, 244, 265, 358, 384,
  387, 390, 498, 578
investment proposals, 5, 194, 196, 360, 387, 497
Investment return, 223, 226, 521
Investments, 1, 3, 5-8, 12, 17-19, 21, 23-24, 29-30, 33,
  36, 40, 44-45, 50, 63, 68-69, 77-80, 87, 95,
  103-107, 115, 117, 138, 153, 167, 169, 175,
  179-180, 199, 201, 203-204, 207, 211-212,
  215-216, 220-223, 230-231, 233-235, 239,
  242-255, 257-259, 262-267, 269-270, 272,
  309, 339, 350, 353, 358-362, 364-365, 369,
  371, 375, 378, 385, 387, 392, 394-395, 397,
  402, 404-406, 408, 411, 413, 415, 417,
  422-426, 432-433, 442, 465-466, 468, 474,
  479-480, 482, 493, 497-498, 500-501, 503,
  507-508, 516-523, 532, 538, 545-546, 554,
  561-562, 579, 582, 604, 615, 617-619,
  628-629, 635, 637-638, 644-645, 657-658,
  663-664, 666
  funds of, 5, 45
  returns of, 1, 3, 222, 230, 234, 239, 245, 247-249,
    251, 253-255, 258, 263-265, 480, 523,
    658
  revenues from, 3, 79, 245, 405, 424
Investor relations, 327
Investors, 1, 3-5, 8, 15, 18-21, 23, 25, 29-30, 34-37,
  39-42, 44-46, 52, 56-57, 60, 63, 65, 79-80,
  92-93, 113-117, 123, 139, 169-170, 211, 213,
  220, 222, 226, 230-233, 235-236, 243, 253,
  258, 263-265, 271-272, 277-281, 286, 289,
  301, 306-307, 309, 311-312, 315, 325,
  327-329, 332, 335, 339, 342, 345, 350, 457,
  479-481, 488-489, 501, 505, 508, 510-511,
  517, 522-524, 526, 531-532, 540, 552, 554,
  557, 562, 564, 566-567, 569, 573-576,
  581-583, 646, 666, 675, 693, 697-698
Invoices, 639
IRAs, 188
Ireland, 43, 658
IRR, 4-5, 360, 370-380, 384-386, 388-390, 392-394,
  396-398, 430, 435, 448-450, 458-459, 466,
  497-498
IRS, 16, 437
Israel, 648, 656
Italy, 42-43, 73, 117, 163, 251, 302, 420, 453, 500,
  544, 580
  tax rate, 453

J

Japan, 32, 42, 73, 117, 163, 225, 251, 302, 420, 453,
  468, 500, 544, 580, 648, 651, 654, 656-658,
  667-669
  currency cross rates, 651
  foreign exchange, 648, 651, 667-669
Japanese yen, 646-647, 654, 664
job search, 225
Jobs, 18, 21, 30, 42-43, 328
  movement of, 30
  profitability and, 328
Junk bonds, 300-302, 314, 316

Junk mail, 632
Just-in-time inventory, 100, 121

K

Knowledge, 12-13, 16, 23, 52, 236, 306, 374, 442
Korea, 42, 73, 117, 163, 225, 251, 302, 420, 453, 500,
    544, 580, 648, 656

L

Labor, 381, 394, 433, 601, 655
    investment in, 381
Labor costs, 655
Language, 51-52
Latin America, 42
Latvia, 656
Law of one price, 5, 654-655, 657, 665
Layoffs, 529
Leader, 120, 131, 637
Leadership, 479
Learning, 30, 170, 259, 330, 503, 532, 539
Leasing, 32-33, 434
Ledger, 628
Legal systems, 544
    defined, 544
Legislation, 43, 167
Lehman Brothers, 43, 518, 547, 698
Leverage, 2-4, 6, 8, 102, 104, 111-112, 117, 124, 138,
    460-462, 467, 473, 520-523, 525-527, 530,
    533-539, 542, 544-547, 550-552
Leverage ratio, 544
Leveraged buyout, 5, 34-35, 45
Liabilities, 1-2, 4-8, 23, 45, 52, 54, 61-69, 71, 79-81,
    84, 87, 94, 96, 99-101, 103, 118, 123-124,
    126-135, 138, 406, 518, 520, 534-538, 540,
    545, 547, 549-550, 553, 574, 584, 592-594,
    596, 598-599, 602, 604-607, 612-618, 622,
    624, 628, 635-636, 638-639
    financial statements for, 6, 54, 61, 79, 132-133, 615
Liability, 1, 4-5, 14-15, 23-24, 50, 56, 59-60, 62, 70-71,
    79-80, 83, 87, 169, 349, 407-408, 411, 437,
    446, 519, 528, 585, 617-619, 638
    basis of, 24
    business, 1, 4-5, 14-15, 23-24, 60, 62, 80, 349,
        446, 519, 585, 617-618
    law, 5, 15
    products, 5, 62, 70, 79, 408, 585
LIBOR, 4-5, 279-280, 282-283, 312, 317, 696-697,
    704
    London Interbank Offer Rate, 696
Life insurance, 278, 399, 677-678, 698, 702
    buying, 698
    cost of, 399, 677, 702
    premiums, 677
    private, 278
    term, 678
Lifestyle, 678
Limited liability company, 5, 14-15, 23-24
    definition of, 15
Limited partners, 14
Limited partnership, 4-5, 14, 23-24
Line of credit, 5, 130, 135-136, 280, 625-628, 636,
    638, 640
Liquidation, 6, 46, 326
Liquidity, 1-2, 5-6, 35, 42, 64, 81-82, 95-101, 105, 116,
    118, 123-124, 126-127, 129-130, 133-134,
    138-139, 305-308, 315, 579, 582, 612-619,
    623, 629-631, 635, 637-638
listening, 512
Lithuania, 656
Loading, 119
Loans, 2, 5-8, 14, 24, 30, 32-33, 41-45, 53, 63-64, 68,
    81, 83, 121, 123-124, 143, 151, 160-161,
    167, 171, 176, 184, 199, 222-223, 243, 272,
    278-280, 283-285, 317, 374, 484, 518-519,
    534, 608, 618-619, 624-627, 632-633,
    635-636, 701
Lobbying, 507
Local advertising, 425
Local government, 41
London, 4-5, 7, 31, 279, 312, 490, 650-651, 664, 696
London Interbank Offer Rate, 696
    LIBOR, 696
Long-term assets, 8, 65-66, 72, 87, 411, 482
Long-term debt, 2, 5, 40, 45, 62-63, 65-66, 68, 71-74,
    80-81, 84, 87, 94, 99, 101, 103, 127-128,
    130-132, 135, 138, 234, 277, 300-301, 314,
    349, 484, 508, 517, 519, 521, 536-537, 540,
    545, 549-550, 553, 584, 593-596, 598-601,

604-607, 615, 618, 637-638
    issuance, 87, 594
    notes, 45, 62-63, 65-66, 71-74, 81, 84, 87, 94, 99,
        101, 128, 130-132, 135, 519, 584,
        593-596, 598-599, 605-607, 618
Long-term financing, 616
Long-term liabilities, 65-67, 101, 126, 138, 520, 550,
    553, 617, 635
Loss, 2, 4-7, 15, 19, 21, 33, 41, 46, 54, 56, 63-64, 81,
    138, 166, 169, 212-214, 216, 281, 296-297,
    306-307, 315, 364, 398-399, 411, 415, 446,
    457, 520, 530, 572, 629, 637, 663, 668, 677,
    679, 681-682, 685-690, 697, 699-700,
    702-703
    control, 4-5, 15, 629, 637, 699-700, 702
    direct, 4-5, 399, 629, 668
    distributions, 15, 212-213, 530
    expected, 4-7, 19, 21, 41, 63, 212-214, 216,
        306-307, 315, 398, 411, 446, 668, 677
    forecasting, 6
    income, 2, 4-7, 15, 54, 56, 63-64, 81, 138, 306,
        411, 446, 520, 530, 572, 629, 677, 679
    indirect, 4, 399, 668
    known, 7, 33, 54, 297, 307, 398, 629, 685
    of goods and services, 4, 306, 315
    paying, 166, 315, 572
    ratio, 2, 4-7, 56, 81, 213, 520, 637
    reduction, 4, 7, 64
    reserve, 19
    underwriting, 281

M

Malaysia, 42, 73, 117, 163, 251, 302, 420, 453, 500,
    544, 580, 655-656
Management, 1, 3, 5, 7-8, 9-10, 12-17, 19, 21-25, 27,
    32, 34-35, 37, 49, 52, 54, 57, 72, 76, 79, 83,
    85-86, 89, 95, 102, 105-107, 112-113,
    116-119, 122-123, 127-128, 131-134,
    138-139, 141, 173, 209, 214, 231-232, 241,
    275, 279, 286, 316, 323, 326, 328, 337, 350,
    355, 359, 362, 364, 369, 394-395, 397, 401,
    409, 425-426, 432, 439, 442-443, 446-447,
    449-452, 460, 469-470, 474, 477, 479,
    498-499, 508, 515, 518, 533, 537, 542, 544,
    546-547, 553, 559, 561-562, 567, 570, 579,
    582, 584-585, 587, 589-591, 594-595,
    599-600, 602, 607, 611-641, 643, 645-646,
    657, 666, 669, 671-705
    activities of, 17, 85-86, 614, 701
Management strategies, 676
Managers, 10, 13-14, 17-18, 21, 23-25, 34, 51, 53,
    56-57, 67, 79, 91-92, 95, 105-108, 113, 123,
    127, 164, 279, 281, 284, 289, 325, 328, 339,
    347, 353, 357-359, 362, 364, 368, 375,
    384-387, 403, 421, 442, 444-445, 447, 453,
    457, 462-463, 479, 498-501, 507, 517, 522,
    524, 526, 529, 531-533, 542, 545-546, 548,
    566, 579, 581, 590, 592, 613-615, 646, 674
Manufacturing, 83, 254, 269-270, 360, 364, 371, 391,
    395, 397, 425-426, 445, 451, 454-455, 463,
    510-513, 536, 609, 617, 639, 646, 657, 662,
    669, 673, 675
Margin, 2-6, 56, 79-80, 86, 106-113, 118, 120,
    124-126, 128-129, 131-133, 135-137, 280,
    301, 455-456, 458, 460, 467, 595, 604, 641,
    684-685, 700, 702
Margins, 56, 79, 86, 105-107, 109, 117, 425, 595
Market capitalization, 3, 42, 221, 519, 545, 658
Market economies, 3, 224, 234
Market efficiency, 232, 235-236
Market entry, 390
Market research, 405, 449
Market share, 12, 403, 445
Market size, 445, 466
Market value, 5, 45, 54, 61, 63, 67-69, 81, 95,
    113-118, 124, 129-130, 296-297, 301, 314,
    316, 339, 345, 348, 432, 482-484, 500, 506,
    509, 511-512, 518-521, 524, 532, 544-545,
    549-550, 565, 570, 662, 683
Marketing, 12-13, 16, 86, 92, 281, 359-360, 387, 404,
    425, 434, 442, 452, 562, 590, 592, 603, 614,
    646, 674, 701
    global, 646
    ideas, 359-360, 387
    of value, 387, 404
    people, 12, 562
    place, 425, 590, 646
    value and, 387
Marketplace, 28-31, 35-36, 44, 244, 306, 341, 420,

562, 650
Markets, 2-7, 13, 19, 21-23, 28-31, 33-36, 38-39, 42,
    44-46, 57, 63, 73, 75-78, 81, 85-86, 211-212,
    220, 222-226, 230-236, 252, 259, 267, 276,
    278, 280-281, 286, 291, 307, 312, 316,
    324-326, 329, 345-346, 349-350, 359, 376,
    396, 414, 420, 423-424, 487, 506-508,
    522-524, 532, 541, 579, 644-646, 650-651,
    657-660, 664-667, 669, 674, 684, 698
    development of, 211, 225, 359
Markup, 56, 113
Materials handling, 371
meaning, 31, 235, 237, 246, 248, 250, 284, 340, 345,
    349, 386, 397, 470, 637, 691
    understanding of, 246
Measurement, 220
measurements, 20
mechanics, 154, 482, 666
Media, 121, 492
median, 153, 544, 632
medium, 286, 444, 469-470, 487, 607, 675-676
Memory, 99
Mergers, 5, 45
Mergers and acquisitions, 5, 45
message, 577
    positive, 577
Metrics, 384, 389
Mexico, 42, 73, 117, 163, 225, 251, 302, 395, 408,
    420, 453, 500, 544, 550, 580, 648, 651, 656
    currency cross rates, 651
Middle East, 648
Money, 1-8, 11-16, 18-21, 23-25, 29-31, 33-37, 39-47,
    51-52, 55, 61, 64, 68-69, 77-81, 91-92,
    102-104, 107, 111, 120, 128, 135, 142-172,
    173-208, 211, 222, 225, 231-232, 236,
    243-245, 247-249, 251-252, 257-258,
    266-269, 277-278, 280, 284, 287, 291, 301,
    303, 307, 312, 315, 325-327, 329, 340, 345,
    347, 351, 353, 357, 359-365, 367, 370, 374,
    381-385, 387, 389, 404-408, 413, 421, 423,
    434, 441, 445, 450, 453, 457-458, 466,
    479-480, 485-486, 493, 501, 505, 507-508,
    513, 517-518, 520-521, 523-524, 526, 538,
    546, 549, 551, 561, 572, 574, 579-581, 590,
    596-597, 602, 618-619, 624-626, 629,
    631-633, 635-637, 640, 646, 648, 650, 657,
    663, 673, 677, 680, 686-688, 691-693, 696,
    698-700
    commodity, 2, 4-5, 7, 222, 680, 699-700
    demand for, 149, 231, 307, 327, 357, 421
    M2, 185, 196
    real value of, 307
Money market, 2, 5, 8, 37, 39-40, 45, 618, 625, 629,
    635-637
Mortgage, 5, 12, 33, 40, 42-44, 62, 153, 175, 181,
    184-187, 197, 199-202, 223, 266, 269, 272,
    278, 280, 284, 300-302, 314, 316, 632-633,
    673-674, 679, 697-698
    investment in, 200, 223, 266
Mortgage loans, 43, 223
Motivation, 12, 584
Motorcycles, 405
Multinational corporation, 5, 657, 666
Multinational corporations, 657
Mutual funds, 4, 32-34, 39-41, 44-46, 167, 207, 252,
    280, 629

N

NASDAQ, 5, 38, 45, 327, 345-346, 349
National brands, 424
National markets, 346
Nationalization, 662
Nations, 43
Natural disasters, 673
Negative relationship, 2, 263, 693
Net earnings, 605
Net income, 3, 5-7, 55-59, 64, 71-83, 85-87, 93, 103,
    106-107, 110-113, 115-116, 118, 124-125,
    127-128, 130-132, 134-138, 334, 339, 350,
    410, 425, 481, 526-527, 530, 536, 539-540,
    551-553, 581, 583, 592-596, 598-599, 604,
    609
Net investment, 650
Net present value, 5, 356-358, 360-362, 364, 369-372,
    377, 382, 384-385, 387-394, 396-397, 404,
    412, 430-431, 435, 442, 460, 479-480, 508,
    561, 660-661, 675
    NPV, 5, 360-362, 364, 369-372, 377, 382, 384-385,
        387-394, 396-397, 404, 412, 430, 435,

442, 460, 479-480, 561, 660-661, 675
Net profit, 3, 6, 56, 80, 86, 106-107, 111-113, 118, 120, 124-126, 129, 595, 604
   margin, 3, 6, 56, 80, 86, 106-107, 111-113, 118, 120, 124-126, 129, 595, 604
   to assets, 111
Net working capital, 6, 64-67, 69, 81-82, 84, 96, 406, 427-428, 430-432, 435, 613-617, 637-638
Net worth, 34, 68, 82, 201, 597
Netting, 303
New entrants, 359
New products, 11-12, 211, 359, 434, 468, 529, 645
New York Stock Exchange, 6, 38, 45, 51, 269, 327, 345, 349, 664
New Zealand, 647-648, 656
   currency, 647-648, 656
Newspapers, 597
Nominal interest rate, 166, 303-304, 306, 414
Nominal interest rates, 500, 655
Nondiversifiable risk, 254
Norms, 98, 121, 134, 136, 537, 544, 547-548
North Africa, 42, 73, 117, 163, 251, 302, 420, 453, 500, 544, 580
North America, 35
Norway, 42, 73, 117, 163, 251, 302, 420, 453, 500, 544, 580, 648, 655-656
Norwegian krone, 647
NPV, 5-7, 360-382, 384-398, 404, 412, 419, 425-430, 435, 442-443, 445-452, 458-460, 462, 464-471, 473-475, 478-480, 483, 501-504, 507, 510, 512, 561, 579, 660-662, 669, 675
NYSE, 6, 38-39, 221, 327, 345-346, 349-350

O
Objectives, 29, 67, 590-591, 614, 637
   accounting, 67
Obligation, 2, 6-7, 55, 59, 215, 278, 522, 526, 530, 546, 554-555, 625, 683-684, 686-687, 696, 700-701
Obsolescence, 384
Occurrence, 215, 218
Offer, 5, 8, 29-30, 44, 135, 150, 170, 231, 279, 290, 306, 312, 315, 328, 339, 357, 359, 371, 374, 391, 403-404, 425-426, 432, 441, 468, 488, 561, 564, 575, 581, 583, 608, 625, 640, 650, 696
Offer rate, 650, 696
Offset, 64, 243, 251, 255, 279, 408, 415, 417-419, 531-532, 545, 657, 678-679, 696
Offsets, 4, 108, 117, 410, 416, 681, 688, 700
Offshore manufacturing, 657
Oil, 77, 83, 91, 217-218, 222, 230, 243, 251, 381, 395, 414, 498-499, 567, 662, 675, 678, 680-683, 685-686, 700-702
Operating expenses, 3, 8, 34, 40, 55, 57-58, 79-80, 83-84, 93, 103, 106, 108, 112-113, 127-129, 131-132, 134-135, 138, 408-410, 412-413, 422, 458, 460, 475, 536, 604, 606
Operating income, 1, 3, 5-6, 8, 55-59, 79-80, 82, 86, 93, 102-104, 106-109, 113, 117-118, 124-125, 127-129, 131, 134-135, 138, 407-410, 412-413, 416, 419-422, 426-427, 446, 448-450, 453-456, 458-460, 462, 467, 473, 519-520, 526, 530, 539, 542, 545, 553
Operating leverage, 2, 6, 460-462, 467, 473
Operating margin, 137
Operational risk, 674-675
Operations, 2-3, 5-8, 11-13, 16-17, 23, 36, 44, 52-53, 55-56, 61-62, 64, 71-72, 74-77, 79-81, 83, 85-86, 92, 94, 106, 113, 121, 123-124, 127, 129, 132, 277-278, 359, 365, 385, 387, 391, 406, 408, 413, 415, 422-423, 442, 445, 447, 460, 472-473, 517-518, 531, 543, 552, 561-562, 568, 579, 589-590, 594, 597, 601, 603, 605-606, 614, 617-618, 620, 631, 633, 637, 657, 663, 674, 676, 683, 699, 701-702
Operations management, 13
Opportunities, 7, 18, 29, 44, 108, 175-176, 206, 230, 235-236, 305, 329, 333, 339, 348, 356-359, 361-362, 368-369, 374, 376, 382, 386-389, 395, 398, 420, 423, 463, 468, 478-480, 500, 504, 507, 531, 555, 561, 576-577, 579, 589-590, 645
Opportunity cost, 2, 6, 19, 25, 375, 406, 421, 434, 445, 457, 467, 479-480, 482, 486, 497, 500, 506-508, 615, 626, 630, 637, 673, 699
Opportunity costs, 406-407, 421, 424, 457, 496, 500, 505

Optimism, 442, 466, 469
Option contract, 6, 686, 691, 698, 700-701
Oracle, 346
Organization, 12-13, 16-17, 23-25, 167, 281, 590, 603, 614
Organizational behavior, 12
Organizational structure, 16
Organizations, 10, 13-14
OTC market, 346
   Over-the-counter market, 346
Outlays, 422
Output, 4, 7-8, 452-458, 460, 467-468
   interest rates and, 8
   potential, 4, 7
Outsourcing, 673, 675
overhead, 405, 421, 423-424
Overhead costs, 405, 421
Overseas Private Investment Corporation, 663
Over-the-counter market, 38, 345-346, 349, 646, 651, 664
   OTC market, 346
Ownership, 1-3, 5, 7, 14-15, 21, 23-25, 33-35, 37, 39, 45, 60, 222, 326, 463, 507, 564, 570-571, 581, 662, 680, 700

P
PACE, 78, 580, 600
Packaging, 42, 434, 454, 511, 522
Pakistan, 544, 648, 656
Par value, 1-3, 6, 8, 37, 45, 62-66, 71, 80-81, 94, 110, 284-285, 287, 289, 291-294, 296-302, 312, 314, 316-321, 339-340, 342, 352-353, 489, 509-512, 549, 565
Parameter, 495
Particular risk, 677
Partnership, 4-6, 13-15, 17, 23-24
Patent, 426, 463, 465, 468
payback period, 3, 6, 360, 368, 381-386, 389-390, 394-397
payroll, 685
Per-capita income, 3, 234
Percentage changes, 577-578
Percentage of sales, 592
percentages, 56, 93, 436-437, 513, 543, 592, 595, 602, 631
Performance, 7-8, 20, 22, 24, 34, 51-53, 56, 74-75, 86, 90-92, 102, 113, 116-117, 119, 121, 123, 125, 131-133, 137-139, 221, 228, 239, 243, 266, 272-273, 328, 335, 339, 366, 413, 445, 463, 466-467, 481, 526, 540, 567, 613, 646
   firm performance, 74, 90, 102, 335, 413, 481, 526, 613
Performance measures, 53
Permits, 281
Personal income, 14-15, 68-69, 573, 597
Personal income taxes, 15
Personal property, 68, 436
   business, 68
Philippines, 42, 73, 117, 163, 251, 302, 420, 453, 500, 544, 580, 656
PHP, 290
pie charts, 522
Place, 3, 17-19, 21, 30, 35-37, 44, 100, 115, 125, 169, 198, 205, 231, 248, 252, 300, 304, 332, 423, 425-426, 435, 441, 484, 492, 500, 564, 589-590, 600, 608-609, 646, 651, 658, 664, 673, 676, 686, 699
Planned expenditures, 597, 675
Plans, 1-2, 8, 16, 21, 24, 30, 42, 44, 46, 79, 82-83, 128, 135, 171, 188, 199, 201, 205, 350, 394, 420, 502, 508, 510-513, 538-540, 542, 552-553, 569, 575, 578, 583-585, 589-592, 600, 602, 605-607, 609, 625, 639, 675, 684
   approaches to, 589, 675
   business, 1-2, 16, 24, 46, 82, 188, 201, 502, 508, 538, 552, 569, 575, 583, 585, 589, 592, 602, 607, 609, 625, 675
   reasons for, 44
Pledges, 625
Poland, 656
Policies, 15, 110, 399, 496, 549, 560-561, 566, 569, 575-576, 580, 582, 630-631, 636, 662, 678, 697
   limited, 15, 575
policy statements, 576-577
Political environment, 662
   foreign direct investment, 662
Political risk, 6, 662-663, 666, 674
   management of, 674

   types of, 663, 666, 674
Political risks, 662-663
Population, 3, 163, 223, 234, 483, 606, 632
Portfolio, 1, 3, 5-6, 17, 33-34, 42, 54, 207, 211, 221, 230, 237, 242-255, 257-260, 262-272, 302, 327, 331, 333, 487, 493-494, 506, 509, 523, 583, 628-629, 646, 658
   Model, 1, 242-243, 253, 258-259, 262-265, 268-270, 272, 331, 333, 493-494, 506
Portugal, 43
Pound sterling, 646-647, 664
Power, 6-7, 22, 95, 111, 144, 148-149, 158-159, 166, 257, 262, 301, 303-306, 315, 327-328, 342, 347, 360, 365, 463, 474, 489, 517, 520-521, 644, 654-657, 665-666, 668, 682
PPP, 7, 654-655, 665
Premium, 2-7, 33, 202, 222, 226, 234, 236, 259-262, 264-265, 270-273, 293, 297-300, 304-310, 314-316, 318-319, 327, 333, 361, 479, 493-495, 506, 510, 651-653, 659-660, 662, 664-665, 667-669, 677, 686-690, 699, 701, 703
   forward, 4, 493-494, 651-653, 659-660, 662, 664-665, 667-669, 686, 699, 703
Premiums, 33, 62, 222, 306, 308, 393, 454, 677
   bond, 306, 308
   earned, 222, 306
   gross, 62
   life insurance, 677
   single, 393
Prepayments, 62, 608
Present value, 1, 3, 5-7, 142, 146-147, 149-159, 164-166, 169, 174, 176-177, 181-199, 201, 203-204, 206, 287-288, 292-295, 312-313, 328-332, 334, 336, 340-343, 347-348, 356-358, 360-372, 374, 377, 380-382, 384-385, 387-394, 396-397, 404, 412, 421, 430-431, 435, 442, 460, 464, 466, 473-474, 479-480, 489, 502-504, 506, 508, 527, 554, 561, 567, 569-570, 572, 660-661, 675, 691, 693
   interest rates and, 151
Price, 1-8, 13, 17-19, 21, 33, 36-39, 41, 46-47, 51, 54, 61, 67, 81, 106, 113-118, 120, 124-126, 129-130, 133, 136-137, 139, 157, 170, 198, 201, 211-214, 219, 221, 223, 230, 232-234, 237-239, 243, 251, 281, 284-285, 288-289, 291, 296-307, 312-316, 318-321, 324-333, 335-340, 342, 346, 348, 350-352, 403, 411, 413-415, 418, 425, 428-432, 435, 441, 444-460, 466-467, 469-472, 474-475, 479, 483, 486-487, 489-492, 498, 501, 506, 509-510, 512-513, 522-523, 532, 535, 538-539, 549, 552, 555-557, 562, 564-566, 569-572, 574-575, 577-578, 581-585, 590, 608, 613, 615, 629, 646, 649, 651-652, 654-657, 662, 664-665, 668, 672-675, 678-696, 699-703, 705
   defined, 2, 46, 61, 126, 212, 300, 330, 348, 415, 451, 453, 490, 498, 506, 565, 694
   price changes, 298, 685
Price break, 425
Price changes, 298, 685
Price range, 46, 565, 585
Prices, 1, 3-5, 7-8, 11, 21-23, 25, 29, 38-39, 43-44, 51, 53-54, 62, 79, 91, 115-116, 123, 136, 139, 153, 207, 210-211, 213-214, 222, 230-233, 235, 238-239, 243, 251, 263, 266, 272, 277, 284-285, 296-299, 302-307, 309, 312, 314-315, 321, 325, 329, 331-332, 335, 342, 346-347, 425, 432, 463, 467, 479, 484, 486, 494, 498, 505, 522, 532, 561-562, 566, 574, 577, 581, 652, 654-656, 658, 665, 673, 675, 679-682, 684-686, 688, 691, 693, 702-703
   auction, 325
   break-even, 1, 467, 688, 691, 703
   inflation and, 303, 306, 432, 655
   input, 562
   maximum, 5, 581, 686, 688, 703
   mergers and, 5
   minimum, 532, 675, 685
   retail, 5, 11
   shut-down, 463
Pricing, 1, 7, 11, 137, 231, 242-243, 253, 258-259, 262-265, 268-270, 272-273, 298, 331, 333, 399, 425, 449, 490, 493, 496, 506, 535, 591, 686, 689, 692-696, 703
   elements of, 7
   horizontal, 686

objectives, 591
payment, 7, 331, 535
strategy, 231, 425, 591, 695
value, 1, 7, 11, 137, 231, 243, 268, 270, 298, 331, 425, 449, 490, 506, 535, 686, 692-696, 703
vertical, 259, 686
Prime rate, 640
Principal, 1-8, 17, 30, 35-37, 44-46, 51, 65, 123, 146, 148, 164, 176, 183-184, 196-201, 280-281, 283-285, 287-289, 291-295, 297, 299, 301, 306-307, 312-314, 326, 341-342, 415, 423, 486, 489, 506, 529-530, 535-537, 539, 542-543, 546-547, 551, 553, 563, 598, 601, 624-628, 636, 639-640, 675-676, 696-697, 701
Principal sum, 636
Principles, 1, 9-13, 16, 18-19, 22-25, 27, 29, 44, 49, 51, 53-54, 57, 73, 79, 89, 91, 115, 117, 123, 141, 164, 173, 175, 196, 209, 211, 233, 241, 243, 263, 275, 277, 287, 312, 323, 325, 329, 339, 347, 350, 355, 357, 361, 387, 401, 403, 421, 423, 439, 441-442, 466, 477, 479, 505, 515, 517, 545, 559, 561, 581, 587, 602, 611, 635, 643, 645, 664, 671, 673, 699
Private insurance, 663
Private investors, 552
Private placement, 278-279
Pro forma financial statements, 6, 407, 422, 591-592, 602
Probability, 3, 7, 214-220, 233-234, 237, 245, 266-267, 272, 286, 291, 294, 313, 443-445, 450-452, 464, 466, 469-470, 488, 530, 532, 543, 547, 603, 631, 675-676, 692, 694
objective, 3, 266, 451, 466, 532, 603
subjective, 443
problem solving, 145
product design, 426
Product development, 500
Product differentiation, 434
Product line, 36, 156, 212, 249, 394, 398, 424, 427, 434, 469, 471, 590, 592
Product mix, 7, 468
Product or service, 662, 674
Product quality, 674
Production, 11, 13, 16-17, 327, 359, 381, 395, 397-398, 414, 425, 427-435, 442, 449, 454, 463, 465, 471-472, 498-500, 548, 567, 614, 657, 674-675, 684, 701
national, 327, 398, 674
Production costs, 449, 454, 472, 674
external, 674
Productivity, 12, 399
Products, 2, 5, 8, 11-13, 21, 33, 35, 53-54, 57, 62-63, 70, 79, 81, 92, 116, 129, 137, 211, 214, 244-245, 359, 396, 398, 405, 408, 421, 423-425, 432-435, 447, 468-469, 474, 482, 485, 499, 529, 583, 585, 590, 592, 598, 602, 614, 645, 662, 674, 680, 682, 684, 700, 702
attributes of, 662
consumer products, 396, 432
defined, 2, 408, 485
development of, 211, 359, 602
levels of, 602
packaging, 434
Professionals, 61, 92, 164
Profit, 3-4, 6, 12, 14-15, 17, 20-21, 24-25, 37, 39, 46, 52, 54-56, 58, 63, 68, 79-80, 86, 103, 105-113, 117-118, 120, 124-129, 131-136, 138, 235, 281, 357, 407-410, 412-414, 417-418, 422, 425, 427, 446, 448-450, 453, 458-459, 461, 472, 536, 595, 604, 609, 681-682, 686-690, 702-703
definition of, 15
Profit and loss statement, 54
Profits, 1, 3, 5, 7, 13-14, 20, 24-25, 34, 37, 51, 54-57, 67, 75, 79-80, 82-83, 91, 93, 104, 106-107, 109-110, 118, 123-124, 133, 230-231, 286, 357, 360, 408-409, 425, 432, 435, 437, 445, 455-456, 458, 461-462, 467, 473, 579, 594, 597, 606, 613, 641, 650, 664, 666-669, 680-682, 686-688, 690-691, 700, 702-703
Project cash flows, 361, 364, 368, 372-375, 377-380, 384, 388, 401-402, 404-438, 440-443, 445, 448-449, 451-452, 460, 464, 466, 469, 473
projection, 381, 593
Promotion, 171, 426, 474, 641
Property, 2, 5-6, 15, 65-66, 68, 75, 87, 105, 126, 138, 155, 200, 222, 278, 280, 300-301, 312, 314, 358, 399, 407, 422, 436-437, 454, 473, 666, 677
damage, 399, 473, 677
risks, 312, 666, 677
Property insurance, 677
Property taxes, 454
proposals, 5, 156, 194, 196, 360, 387, 497
producing, 360
types of, 5, 156, 360, 387
Protection, 7, 19, 43, 286, 301, 463, 544, 699
Prototype, 53
Public offering, 4, 278-279, 327, 345, 349
Purchasing, 6-7, 34, 166, 265, 303-306, 315, 377, 392, 394, 397, 418, 449, 473, 523, 555, 564, 566, 573, 617, 644, 654-657, 665-666, 668, 673, 677-678, 681-682, 685, 687, 690, 693, 699
Purchasing power, 6-7, 166, 303-306, 315, 655
purpose, 1, 8, 14, 18, 78, 82, 312, 364, 433-434, 468, 474, 478, 505, 625, 629, 636, 678
general, 8, 14, 625
specific, 1, 8, 312, 625, 636
statement of, 434
Put option, 7, 686, 688-689, 691-693, 701-703

Q

Quality, 7-8, 40, 74-75, 81, 86, 98, 122, 128, 286, 487, 529, 578, 590, 630-631, 636-637, 645, 674
Quick ratio, 96
quotations, 38, 346, 650
quoting, 665

R

Race, 567
Railroads, 521
Rate of return, 1-8, 19, 104, 109, 111, 124, 135, 164, 168-170, 179, 199, 201-202, 211-220, 224, 226-229, 233-239, 242-248, 251-253, 258-267, 269-271, 273, 286, 288, 291, 297, 304-305, 313, 315, 318, 329-334, 336, 338-339, 341-343, 345, 347-353, 360-361, 368, 370-372, 374-380, 384-385, 387-389, 391-394, 396-398, 408-409, 412, 421, 425-431, 435, 448, 457-458, 464, 471, 473-474, 479-483, 485-491, 493-494, 496-498, 505-506, 511, 517, 521, 538, 545, 567-570, 585, 614, 635, 641, 655, 659-661, 665, 693
internal, 4-5, 7, 360, 368, 370-371, 377, 379-380, 384-385, 388-389, 391-394, 396-397, 430-431, 435, 448, 490, 497
Rates, 2-8, 29, 40-41, 44, 59-61, 80, 83, 106, 111, 142-143, 151, 154, 160-161, 166-167, 171, 186-187, 210-224, 226-229, 231, 233-239, 243-246, 248-249, 251-253, 255, 258-259, 261-263, 267-272, 275-321, 331, 333, 335, 338, 342, 353, 372-373, 375-378, 385, 388-392, 397, 404, 414, 423, 443, 453, 466, 470, 478-483, 486, 490-491, 493-494, 496-501, 505-508, 526, 528, 538, 549, 573, 595-597, 599, 606-607, 615, 626, 628, 631-632, 644-646, 648, 650-657, 659-668, 673, 679, 684, 693, 696-697, 699, 704
definition of, 212, 220, 372, 375, 388
excessive, 628
gross, 4-5, 83, 106, 414
reasonable, 106, 236, 286, 291, 306, 486, 491, 494, 496, 595
Rating, 1, 92, 286-287, 290, 300-301, 307-308, 312, 316, 318, 321, 487-488, 509, 511, 513, 543-544, 550, 577, 631
Rating agencies, 92, 286-287, 312, 487
Ratio analysis, 90-91, 111, 118, 121-122, 125, 551, 631
debt ratio, 111, 118, 125
times interest earned ratio, 551
Ratios, 4-5, 8, 38, 74-76, 86, 90-102, 104-108, 110-127, 129-134, 136-139, 232, 325, 335-339, 348, 351-352, 445, 519-521, 527, 529, 531, 534-537, 542, 544, 547-549, 595, 605, 615-616, 631, 654
Raw materials, 5, 62-63, 81, 414, 432, 608, 614, 645, 684
Reach, 153, 159, 179-181, 200, 202, 205, 244, 443, 597, 604, 633
Real estate, 42, 45, 211, 222-223, 269, 272, 280, 357-358, 508
Real interest rate, 303

Real interest rates, 414, 423
Real value, 307
reasonable assurance, 57
Receivables, 40, 70, 97-98, 105, 110, 122, 130, 406, 408, 411, 445, 613-614, 625, 629, 631, 638
and payables, 408, 613
Recession, 39, 42-43, 76, 214, 251, 254, 266, 272, 338, 443-445, 469-470, 508, 529-530, 554-556, 562, 615-616, 697-698
Recessions, 623
recommendations, 281, 608
Records, 2, 57, 564, 581
Reform, 43
Registration statement, 279
Regulation, 18
Regulations, 23, 360
Reinvestment, 5, 224, 379, 546, 575, 583
Relationships, 69, 276, 296, 314, 319-320, 338, 609, 666, 686, 690, 692
Religion, 424
Renovations, 358
Reorganization, 13
Replication, 365
Reporting system, 82
reports, 2, 17, 19, 21, 24, 52, 54, 57, 61, 79, 81, 86, 104, 109, 224, 287, 290, 492, 676, 699
body of, 290
components of, 54, 109
format for, 54
producing, 2, 54, 79
types of, 52, 224, 699
Resale, 61, 281
research, 12, 29, 41, 107, 115, 232, 327, 359, 405, 442, 449, 533
planning, 12
primary, 29
Research and development, 107, 115, 359, 533
cost of, 359, 533
Reserves, 33, 76, 629, 635, 698
initial, 629
loss, 33, 629
policy, 698
Resources, 23, 61, 78, 99, 129, 167, 222, 256, 349, 352, 499, 507, 673, 678
Responsibility, 2, 16, 19, 23-24, 30, 44, 676, 699
Restricted, 5, 24, 32
Restrictions, 15, 279, 414, 685
Retail stores, 11, 396
Retailers, 33
Retailing, 57, 85
Retained earnings, 5, 7-8, 52, 56, 62, 64-67, 70-72, 79-81, 84, 87, 94, 103, 110, 114, 128-129, 132, 134, 136, 350, 513, 546, 565, 579, 593-594, 596, 598-599, 604-607, 609
Retention, 3, 5, 65, 72, 149, 333-334, 350-352, 508, 512, 532, 546, 579, 593-594, 597, 602
Retirement, 1-2, 12, 17, 30, 44, 46-47, 68, 76, 85, 87, 144, 158-159, 169, 171, 188-189, 198-202, 205, 207, 230, 244, 251, 267, 270, 279, 381, 518
Retirement plans, 1, 30, 44, 46
Return on assets, 6, 107-110, 113, 118, 124-126, 128, 131-133, 135-136, 538-539
Return on equity, 3, 7, 110-113, 117-118, 120, 124-126, 128-129, 131-133, 136, 333-334, 348, 350-352, 521, 530, 538-539
ROE, 110, 333-334, 351-352
Return on investment, 111, 215, 218
Reuters, 646, 648, 651
Revenue, 4-5, 16, 52-54, 79-81, 86, 106-107, 137-138, 358-360, 390, 404-405, 409, 414, 425, 437, 444-445, 454, 461, 470, 552, 590-591, 607, 685
marginal, 5, 80
Revenue estimates, 404
Revenue recognition, 53-54, 79
Revenues, 3-4, 6-8, 20, 52-58, 62, 74, 79-80, 83, 85-86, 93, 106-107, 127, 245, 359-360, 365, 403-405, 407-410, 412-415, 419-425, 427, 444-446, 448-451, 453-462, 467, 469, 536, 538, 542, 590-592, 596-597, 607, 641, 674, 679, 681-683, 685
Rewards, 13, 22, 25
Risk, 1-8, 11, 18-20, 22-25, 29, 34, 40-41, 44, 103, 113, 117, 202, 209-239, 241-273, 277, 281, 283-284, 286-288, 290-295, 297-303, 305-321, 325-326, 329, 331, 333-334, 336, 338-340, 342, 344, 347-348, 357-358, 361, 377, 382, 384-390, 399, 439-475, 478-480,

486-489, 491, 493-501, 505-508, 510, 517-518, 520, 523, 526, 530-532, 534, 539-540, 545-547, 554-556, 577, 589-590, 602, 612-615, 625, 628-629, 631, 634-635, 637-638, 645, 650-651, 654, 657-660, 662-664, 666, 668-669, 671-705

asset, 1, 3-5, 7-8, 113, 117, 221-222, 226, 233, 242-245, 248-249, 253, 255, 257-260, 262-265, 268-273, 277, 295, 313, 331, 333, 387, 493, 496, 506, 508, 629, 635, 637-638, 678, 683-686, 691, 700-702

business, 1-7, 11, 18, 20, 23-25, 29, 34, 103, 212, 225, 236, 245, 251, 281, 284, 286, 316, 326, 339, 358, 385-386, 389-390, 399, 442, 446-447, 454, 460, 468, 471-472, 474, 498-501, 507-508, 531, 534, 546-547, 584, 589, 602, 625, 635, 637, 645, 650-651, 654, 657-660, 662-663, 666, 668-669, 673-675, 677-678, 681, 699, 702, 705

classification, 288, 499
commercial, 2, 8, 40-41, 44, 223, 277, 312, 625, 629, 635, 664
commodity price, 672, 679, 699-700, 703, 705
currency exchange rate, 664
definition of, 212, 220, 336, 339, 384, 388
diversifiable, 3, 6, 8, 243, 254, 262, 264
enterprise, 3, 318, 518, 520, 545
financial, 1-8, 11, 18-19, 22-25, 29, 34, 40-41, 44, 103, 113, 117, 209-212, 214, 219-223, 225-232, 234-235, 241, 244, 253, 256, 258, 261-262, 270-271, 277, 281, 284, 286, 291-295, 300, 302-303, 306, 308, 316, 326, 329, 334, 342, 377, 384, 386, 390, 439, 442, 445, 449, 460, 462, 466, 474, 479, 489, 491, 496-497, 500, 505, 507-508, 510, 517-518, 520, 523, 526, 530-532, 534, 539-540, 545-547, 577, 589-590, 602, 614-615, 625, 628, 631, 634, 637, 645, 662, 664, 666, 669, 671-673, 675, 678, 683-685, 687, 691-692, 696-698, 700-701, 703, 705
fire, 254, 677
insurable, 678
interest rate, 1-4, 6-8, 40, 202, 283-284, 287, 293, 297-298, 300, 302-303, 305-307, 312, 314-318, 487, 510, 540, 554, 654, 657, 659-660, 666, 668-669, 673, 679, 696-697, 701-702, 704-705
market, 1-8, 11, 22-23, 25, 29, 34, 40-41, 44, 113, 117, 210-211, 220-225, 230-237, 242-243, 246-247, 251, 253-265, 267-273, 277, 281, 284, 287-288, 290-295, 297-301, 306-307, 312-314, 316-321, 325, 329, 331, 333, 336, 338-339, 342, 344, 347-348, 384, 390, 445, 449, 463, 466, 474, 479, 486-487, 493-498, 500-501, 505-506, 508, 510, 518, 520, 523, 532, 545, 554, 577, 625, 629, 635, 637, 645, 650-651, 658, 662, 664, 666, 674, 678-679, 682-686, 691-692, 696-698, 700, 702-703
nondiversifiable, 254
objective, 3, 29, 44, 210, 242, 244, 266, 281, 440, 442, 448, 451, 466, 468, 478, 517-518, 532, 534, 590, 602, 612-613, 628, 672
operational, 674-675, 699
personal, 11, 18, 23, 25, 225, 244, 265, 358, 390, 466, 471, 523, 577, 673
political, 6, 662-663, 666, 674
property, 2, 5-6, 222, 300-301, 312, 314, 358, 399, 454, 473, 666, 677
pure, 460, 499
speculative, 7, 44, 286, 487, 691
strategic, 8, 589-590, 602, 683
subjective, 443
tolerance for, 225, 236
underwriting, 281
Risk management, 7, 671-705
    decision making, 673
    financial, 7, 671-673, 675, 678, 683-685, 687, 691-692, 696-698, 700-701, 703, 705
    personal, 673
    steps of, 676
Risk of loss, 2, 5, 399, 629, 637, 700
Risks, 22, 25, 29, 43-44, 211, 216, 232-233, 243-245, 254-255, 287, 290, 312, 321, 441-442, 456, 463, 466, 468, 500-501, 505, 523, 529, 534, 589, 631, 644-645, 659, 662-663, 666,

673-679, 683, 697, 699, 702, 705
political risks, 662-663
ROE, 110, 333-334, 336, 338-339, 351-352
Role, 10-11, 14, 22, 24, 29, 36, 153, 156, 182, 253, 280-281, 312, 345, 347, 387, 390, 441-442, 453, 480, 507, 529, 533, 544, 546, 575, 579, 673, 692, 697, 705
    managerial, 533, 546
Roth IRAs, 188
Round lot, 566
routers, 639
Royalties, 657
Russia, 42, 73, 117, 163, 251, 302, 420, 453, 500, 544, 645, 648, 655-656

S

S corporation, 103, 120, 480, 645
Salaries, 55, 381, 416-419, 446, 454, 460, 600-601, 617-618
Salary, 2, 12, 44, 171, 206, 381
Sales, 1-8, 12, 17, 20, 33, 45, 51, 53-57, 63, 70, 72, 74-75, 79-80, 83-84, 86, 92-93, 95, 97-99, 101-109, 111-113, 117-118, 121, 123-125, 127-136, 155, 168, 211, 233, 246-247, 272, 335, 360, 396, 399, 403-406, 408, 410-411, 416, 421, 423-426, 430-432, 434-435, 442, 444, 446-462, 467, 469-473, 475, 518, 529, 552, 562, 564, 588-606, 608-609, 613-615, 620-624, 629-631, 633, 636-637, 641, 657, 696
Sales and marketing, 86, 92
Sales force, 614, 637
    management of, 614
Sarbanes-Oxley Act, 18-19, 24
Saudi Arabia, 648, 656
Saving, 29-30, 47, 68, 114, 153, 167, 176-178, 188-189, 198, 202-203, 205, 225
scope, 3, 57, 59, 415, 422-423, 459, 463, 468, 591, 645
Securities, 1-8, 19, 28-29, 31-46, 54, 57, 61, 65, 100, 117, 123, 126, 129, 133, 135, 166, 211-212, 220-225, 230, 233-236, 248, 251, 253, 255, 258, 266, 270, 272, 277-281, 300-302, 306-312, 315, 326-327, 343, 345-346, 478-480, 484, 493-494, 496, 501, 505, 507-508, 519, 521-522, 532, 572-573, 605, 612, 615, 617, 628-629, 635-637, 684, 697-698, 700
Securities and Exchange Commission, 34, 57, 117, 279, 312, 327
Securitization, 42
Security, 1-8, 22, 35-38, 44-46, 65, 137, 169, 205, 207, 211, 215, 219-220, 226, 230-231, 233, 235, 237, 242, 247, 253, 258-262, 264-265, 268-272, 277, 280-281, 287, 289-290, 306-308, 313-314, 321, 327, 339-341, 345-347, 349, 470, 480, 494, 506-507, 519, 532, 555, 597, 625, 629, 636, 678, 680, 683, 691, 696-697, 700
    investing in, 6-7, 169, 211, 219, 226, 233, 237, 253, 265, 555
Selection, 37, 121, 125
Self-insurance, 7, 677, 699
Self-interest, 22, 25, 531
Sellers, 8, 45, 564, 581, 646, 664, 679
Sensitivity, 7, 264, 440, 443, 445, 447-449, 451-453, 460, 466, 468, 471, 474, 595-596
SEP, 239, 256, 553
September 11, 2001, 309, 311
Services, 2, 4, 7-8, 18, 32-33, 44, 53-54, 70, 79, 82, 98, 121, 163, 167, 225, 279, 286, 289, 303-306, 315, 364, 394, 423, 483-484, 494, 507, 567, 575, 602, 613-614, 617, 625, 629, 631, 635, 646, 674, 699
    attributes of, 575
    defined, 2, 44
    differentiation, 53
    levels of, 602, 629
Shareholder, 2, 5-6, 17, 21, 47, 79, 91, 123, 325, 328, 339, 347-348, 357-358, 362, 369, 384-385, 387, 449, 457, 479, 482, 504, 517, 545, 565, 584, 589, 613, 637
Shareholders, 1, 3, 7-8, 15, 17-19, 21-22, 24, 35, 38, 52, 58, 61, 64, 66, 73, 78-81, 87, 95, 110, 114-115, 123-125, 243, 325-329, 341, 347, 350, 361, 387, 403, 442, 457, 466, 481, 489-491, 496, 502, 505, 517, 522, 531-532, 538, 546, 549, 551, 560-570, 572, 574-575, 577, 580-581, 585, 602

shipping, 362, 407, 416, 418-419, 430-431, 433, 435
Short-term debt, 5, 31, 37, 40, 65-67, 72, 80, 84, 87, 96, 126-127, 130, 234, 484, 508, 532, 536, 549, 609, 615, 619, 625, 637
Short-term financing, 8, 23, 603, 608, 624-625, 636, 639-640
SIMPLE, 7, 19, 23, 64, 72, 146, 148-150, 157, 160-161, 164, 166, 168, 176, 185, 189-190, 226, 229, 231-232, 235, 248-249, 253, 259, 328, 331-333, 337, 341, 343, 358-360, 362, 394, 404-405, 415, 437, 450, 461, 491, 493, 495, 502, 534, 554, 567, 575, 582, 647, 650, 653, 657, 664-666, 685-686, 690, 692
Singapore, 656
Size, 8, 14, 64, 90-91, 93-95, 101, 106, 108, 123, 126-127, 184, 192, 203, 221, 255, 335, 339, 360, 445, 466, 468, 474, 513, 524, 564, 585, 607, 626, 629-630, 632, 636-637, 641, 653, 677, 701
Skills, 474, 532
Slope, 255-256, 259-261, 265, 269, 307
Small business, 15, 23
    definition of, 15
Small business owners, 15
Social Security, 205, 207, 321, 678
    credits, 321
Society, 18
software, 149, 164, 255, 257, 362, 375, 381, 451, 466, 533-534, 546, 552
    evaluation of, 466
Sole proprietorship, 7, 13-14, 17, 23-24
South Africa, 42, 73, 117, 163, 251, 302, 420, 453, 500, 544, 580, 648, 656
South Korea, 42, 73, 117, 163, 251, 302, 420, 453, 500, 544, 580, 648, 656
Spain, 42-43, 73, 117, 163, 251, 302, 420, 453, 500, 544, 580
specific purpose, 1, 8, 312, 625, 636
Speculation, 675
Spot market, 652
Spot rate, 650-654, 659-661, 665-669
Spot rates, 651, 653-654, 667-668
spreadsheets, 149
Standard deviation, 7, 212, 215-219, 222-223, 233-234, 237, 245, 247-255, 263, 265-267, 273, 676
Statement of cash flows, 73-76, 86-87
statistics, 38, 212, 216, 236, 381, 591, 694-695
Status, 15, 68, 82, 631, 674
Stock, 1-8, 15, 17-19, 21-22, 24, 31, 33-34, 36-46, 51-52, 57, 60, 62-67, 71-72, 74, 76, 79-81, 83-85, 87, 91, 94, 98, 103, 110, 113-116, 123-124, 128-130, 132-134, 136-137, 139, 169, 189, 202, 210-218, 220-232, 234-239, 243-244, 246-249, 251, 254-257, 260, 264-272, 281, 285-286, 301-302, 312, 314, 323-353, 396, 406, 413, 478-486, 488-498, 501-506, 508-513, 517, 519, 522-523, 527-528, 532, 535-538, 540-542, 544, 547-549, 551-553, 555, 560-562, 564-579, 581-585, 593-594, 596, 598-599, 602-607, 613, 618, 639, 658, 664, 675, 680, 684, 686-696, 700-703
Stock exchanges, 3, 34, 44
Stock markets, 19, 38, 325, 658
Stock sales, 564
Stockholders, 1-3, 6, 8, 15, 18, 21, 23-24, 38, 51, 55-57, 60, 62-65, 69, 71, 77, 79, 81-84, 91, 94, 104, 110, 113, 117, 123, 129-130, 135-136, 138, 212, 243, 272, 283, 326, 328-329, 331, 338, 340-341, 347, 349, 357-359, 387, 413, 437, 479-480, 482, 485-486, 488-490, 505-506, 511, 513, 517-518, 521-524, 526-527, 531, 533, 545-546, 551, 561-562, 564-567, 569, 575-577, 580-581, 585, 594, 605-606, 693
Store of value, 222
Stories, 47
Strategic planning, 12, 16
    new products, 12
Strategies, 230-232, 286, 645, 666, 673-674, 676, 684, 699
    competitive, 674
    corporate, 232, 286, 674, 676, 684
Strategy, 4, 46, 58, 66, 77, 94, 99, 104, 106, 109, 116, 145, 150, 152, 155, 157, 159, 161, 180, 183, 186, 190-191, 193, 218, 228, 230-232, 246, 248, 251-252, 261, 282, 288, 292, 295, 304-305, 332, 337, 343, 358, 363, 366, 370,

372, 376, 380, 409, 417, 425, 444, 448, 451-452, 456, 464, 479, 485, 492, 495, 503, 536, 540, 554, 569, 591, 599, 613, 616-617, 621, 623, 627, 649-650, 653, 660, 673, 676, 678, 681-682, 690, 695, 700, 705
  combination, 109, 246, 613
  defined, 46, 451, 485, 621, 623
  focus, 77, 358, 417, 673, 676
  push, 332
Stress, 232, 403
Strike price, 8, 686, 691-695, 701, 703
Students, 143, 326, 364
Subprime mortgage crisis, 44
Subprime mortgages, 41-42
Subsidiaries, 550, 566
Substitution, 462, 563
Success, 18, 37, 86, 106-107, 232, 325-326, 359, 404, 420, 443, 445, 447, 466-467, 512, 574
summarizing, 82, 232, 594
Sunk costs, 8, 405-407, 421, 424
Supply, 13, 44, 254, 551, 592, 606, 630, 645-646, 650
  currency, 645-646, 650
  of money, 13
Supply chain, 13, 645-646
Support, 135-136, 236, 280, 300, 351, 360, 397, 404, 434, 447, 471, 474, 483, 520, 544, 548, 574, 577, 591-593, 605-606, 614, 678
Surplus, 31, 595, 601
  total, 595, 601
surveys, 582
Sustainability, 86
Sweden, 42, 73, 117, 163, 251, 302, 420, 453, 500, 544, 580, 648, 656
Swiss franc, 647, 667-668
Switzerland, 648, 651, 655-656, 667-669
system, 32, 43, 63, 73, 82, 100, 117, 125-126, 279, 328, 346, 362, 371, 375-376, 378, 381, 391-392, 394, 407, 425, 436, 447, 534, 603, 628-629, 637, 645, 675-676, 699
Systematic risk, 8, 242, 253-255, 257-260, 264, 268-269, 333, 493-494, 496, 499

T

Tables, 135, 147, 290
Taiwan, 225, 656
Tangible assets, 232
Tariffs, 408
  defined, 408
Tax rates, 59-61, 80, 83, 528, 573, 662
Taxation, 14-15, 23, 60, 583, 657
  double taxation, 14-15, 23, 60
Taxes, 2-5, 8, 14-16, 36, 41, 49-50, 52-88, 93, 102-103, 112-113, 127, 129, 131-132, 134-136, 188, 205, 224, 407-413, 415-418, 422, 425, 427-429, 433, 437, 446, 448-450, 453-454, 458-459, 473, 480-482, 489, 506, 512, 520, 522, 524-528, 530, 533, 535-537, 539-540, 542-543, 545-547, 551-553, 565-568, 571-573, 575-577, 581-582, 584-585, 601, 604-605, 609, 618, 629, 680, 702
  corporate, 2, 5, 14-16, 41, 50, 55, 57, 59-60, 68, 80, 83, 86, 413, 415, 481, 506, 526-528, 533, 539, 543, 551, 565, 572, 575, 577, 581-582, 680, 702
  flat, 73-74, 82, 453
  gift, 535
  income, 2-5, 8, 14-15, 50, 52-64, 66-87, 93, 102-103, 112-113, 127, 129, 131-132, 134-136, 205, 224, 407-413, 416, 418, 422, 425, 427, 437, 446, 448-450, 453-454, 458-459, 473, 481, 489, 520, 526-528, 530, 533, 536, 539-540, 542, 545-546, 551-553, 565, 572-573, 575, 581-582, 604, 609, 629
  property, 2, 5, 15, 65-66, 68, 75, 87, 407, 422, 437, 454, 473
  revenues from, 3, 79, 409, 536
  sales, 2-5, 8, 53-57, 63, 70, 72, 74-75, 79-80, 83-84, 86, 93, 102-103, 112-113, 127, 129, 131-132, 134-136, 408, 410-411, 416, 425, 446, 448-450, 453-454, 458-459, 473, 552, 601, 604-605, 609, 629
teams, 22, 404, 524, 699
  effective, 699
  types of, 699
Technological advances, 420
Technology, 38, 121, 261, 360, 396, 420, 423, 426,

463, 465, 468, 471, 474, 567, 589, 646, 675
  information technology, 675
Telecommunications, 662
telephone, 34, 345, 589, 631
Tenure, 435
Term bonds, 211, 298, 307, 314
Term loan, 6, 143, 617, 635
Termination, 427-432, 435
Terminology, 37, 277, 283, 285, 306, 521, 618, 686
Test marketing, 434
Thailand, 42, 73, 117, 163, 251, 302, 420, 453, 500, 544, 580, 655-656
Theft, 633
  identity, 633
Threats, 420
three-step process, 335, 347, 507, 604
Time value of money, 25, 79, 142-172, 173-174, 176-208, 291, 307, 325, 357, 360, 365, 382-383, 385, 389, 458, 693, 699
Times interest earned ratio, 8, 101-102, 104, 117, 124, 128-129, 519-520, 522, 535, 537, 542, 545, 551-553
Timing, 2, 8, 11, 144, 164, 230, 287, 313, 329, 347, 379, 387, 421, 437, 441, 463, 465, 468, 562, 566-567, 569-570, 574-575, 582, 585, 588-589, 600, 602-603, 659
  forecasting and, 588, 600, 603
tone, 631
  evaluating, 631
Total asset turnover, 3, 8, 102, 104-105, 107-112, 118, 124-125, 129, 131-133, 135-136, 605
Total assets, 2, 4, 6, 8, 53, 61-62, 64-68, 71, 80-81, 87, 93-94, 101-102, 104-105, 107-113, 118, 120, 123-125, 127-135, 138, 517-518, 520, 534-539, 542, 545, 547, 584, 592-596, 598-599, 603-607, 613, 619
Total assets turnover ratio, 120
Total cost, 55, 399, 454-455, 681
Total costs, 112, 454-455, 457, 467
Total market value, 483, 506, 524, 565
Total revenue, 5, 80-81, 86, 138, 444-445, 454
Trade, 1, 5-6, 8, 35, 38, 45-46, 61, 81, 121, 232, 245, 307-309, 336, 345, 349, 410-411, 422, 487, 509, 529, 566, 604, 613, 615, 617-619, 621, 624-626, 630-631, 635-637, 639-641, 645, 647, 654-655, 658, 691
  domestic, 654-655, 658
Trade associations, 631
Trade credit, 8, 410-411, 422, 604, 613, 615, 617-619, 621, 624-626, 630-631, 635, 637, 639-641
Trailers, 613
Training, 76, 84, 239, 428-429, 646
Transactions, 13, 33, 35, 37, 312, 345, 524, 565, 573, 633, 650-651, 683
  consistent, 573, 650
Transfers, 582, 629, 675, 677
Transportation, 69, 114
  costs, 114
treasurer, 16-17, 24
Treasury bills, 40, 215, 221-223, 237, 246-247, 267, 269-270, 272, 306, 315, 494, 629, 684
Treasury bonds, 4, 7, 31, 289, 307-308, 313, 684, 700
Treasury securities, 4, 307-310, 315, 493-494, 508, 700
Treasury stock, 8, 64, 81, 87
trend analysis, 8, 119, 125
Trends, 86, 563, 590, 606
Trucks, 119, 393, 399, 432-433, 613
Trust, 18, 24, 171, 211, 283, 378
Trust Fund, 171, 211
Trustee, 281, 283, 285
Trusts, 222-223
Turkey, 42, 73, 117, 163, 251, 302, 420, 453, 500, 544, 580, 648, 656
  currency, 302, 453, 500, 648, 656
  inflation, 302, 500
Turnover, 1, 3-5, 8, 97-102, 104-105, 107-112, 116-125, 128-129, 131-133, 135-136, 445, 605, 620-621, 623, 631

U

Ukraine, 656
Uncollectible accounts, 97
Underwriter, 281
Underwriting, 35, 279, 281
  field, 281
  risk, 281
Unemployment, 39
  in 2007, 39

Unions, 40
Unit production, 449
United Arab Emirates, 192, 656
United Kingdom, 544, 658
United States, 3, 21, 31-32, 38-39, 42-43, 45, 53, 57, 59, 73, 76, 82, 91, 103, 114, 117, 126, 222, 225, 230, 234, 236, 278, 281, 316, 408, 420, 453, 468, 500, 502, 526, 544, 550, 580, 645, 647, 654-660, 662, 668-669, 674, 696
  foreign direct investment, 662
Upstream, 499-500
Uruguay, 420, 656
U.S, 2-4, 7, 15, 19, 28-31, 34, 39-43, 45-46, 76, 82, 85, 117, 160, 211, 215, 220-225, 236, 246, 251, 277, 289-290, 301-302, 306-308, 310, 313-315, 335, 381, 386, 389, 394, 396, 420, 424-425, 433, 453, 468, 483, 488, 493-495, 500, 508, 519, 521, 526, 528, 546, 562, 580, 583, 590, 615, 623, 629, 645-647, 649, 651, 654-664, 668, 675, 683-684, 696-697, 700, 704
U.S., 2-4, 7, 15, 19, 28-31, 34, 39-43, 45-46, 76, 82, 85, 117, 160, 211, 215, 220-225, 236, 246, 251, 277, 289-290, 301-302, 306-308, 310, 313-315, 335, 381, 386, 389, 394, 396, 420, 424-425, 433, 453, 468, 483, 488, 493-495, 500, 508, 519, 521, 526, 528, 546, 562, 580, 583, 590, 615, 623, 629, 645-647, 649, 651, 654-664, 668, 675, 683-684, 696-697, 700, 704
U.S. Census Bureau, 381
U.S. Department of Labor, 381
U.S. dollar, 302, 453, 468, 646, 654, 656, 664
  euro and, 453
U.S. economy, 43
U.S. Securities and Exchange Commission, 117
U.S. Treasury bills, 40, 246, 315, 629
U.S. Treasury bonds, 4, 31, 307, 684, 700
Utilities, 114, 255, 257, 319, 421, 423, 446, 460, 521, 533, 546
Utility, 255, 262, 327, 342, 405, 421
Utility companies, 262

V

Value, 1-8, 11, 17-21, 23-25, 32-33, 37-39, 42, 45-47, 51-55, 59, 61-69, 71, 79-81, 91, 94-96, 100, 110-111, 113-118, 121, 123-125, 129-130, 136-137, 139, 141-172, 173-208, 214, 218, 221-222, 226-233, 235, 237, 239, 243-244, 248-249, 267-268, 270, 276-277, 282-289, 291-302, 307-308, 312-314, 316-321, 324-326, 328-332, 334-336, 338-345, 347-353, 356-375, 377, 379-385, 387-398, 403-404, 407-409, 411-413, 415-419, 421-422, 425-426, 428-435, 441-443, 445-453, 455-458, 460, 462-469, 471-475, 479-484, 486-487, 489-490, 494, 497, 500, 502-512, 517-525, 527-529, 532-533, 535, 542, 544-546, 548-550, 554-556, 560-562, 565-575, 577, 581-582, 584-585, 589, 602, 613, 617, 625, 629, 633, 645, 652, 655, 657, 660-664, 666, 672-673, 675, 683-686, 688, 690-696, 698-703
  building, 3, 6, 17, 38, 45, 68, 390, 393, 425, 435, 460, 464, 473, 479, 657, 666
  defined, 2, 46, 61, 96, 100, 176, 300, 330, 341, 348, 361, 375, 382, 388-389, 408, 415, 451, 453, 490, 506, 518-519, 544, 565, 694
  market value, 5, 45, 54, 61, 63, 67-69, 81, 95, 113-118, 124, 129-130, 296-297, 301, 314, 316, 339, 345, 348, 432, 482-484, 500, 506, 509, 511-512, 518-521, 524, 532, 544-545, 549-550, 565, 570, 662, 683
  marketing and, 387, 442
Value added, 362, 527
Value creation, 360, 382
Value proposition, 359
Vandalism, 677
Variability, 4, 214, 220, 224, 248-249, 254, 286, 314
Variable costs, 8, 427, 445, 447, 454-458, 460-462, 467, 470-471, 552
Variable expenses, 114, 454
Variables, 153, 156, 246, 331-332, 338-339, 445, 451, 466, 472, 494, 595, 692, 694-696
Variance, 7-8, 212, 215-217, 220, 233-234, 236, 243, 248, 253, 263, 694-695, 703
Venezuela, 656, 662

    foreign direct investment, 662
      political environment, 662
Venture capital, 8, 34-35, 45
Venture capitalists, 552
Violence, 399
Vision, 17
Visualize, 103, 109, 116, 142, 144-145, 159, 161, 164, 186, 251, 304, 622, 627, 690
Volume, 38-39, 106, 230, 345, 454, 472, 543, 566, 646-647, 650, 664, 689
Volumes, 8, 235, 646
Voting rights, 37-38, 327

W

Wages, 53, 62, 129, 454, 600-601, 617-618, 662
    differences in, 601
    minimum, 600, 617-618
Wall Street Journal, 39, 327, 648, 689
War, 254, 590
Warehousing, 396
Warranty, 432
Water, 395, 425, 441
Weaknesses, 4, 124, 132
Wealth, 17-18, 21, 24, 47, 217, 219, 222, 357, 360-362, 369, 385, 449, 568, 570-573, 575, 583, 637
Wealth effect, 571
Web, 82
websites, 17, 349, 633
wireless access, 404
Won, 13, 19, 23-24, 110, 155, 181, 230, 648
Work, 5, 11, 17-18, 20-21, 30, 53, 62, 70, 92, 95, 99, 121, 163, 167, 171, 181, 183, 201-202, 204, 206, 231-232, 281, 351, 359, 398, 404, 406, 421, 435, 470, 481, 512, 518, 529, 583, 633, 637, 645-646, 672, 679, 692, 701
Workers, 171, 205, 381, 397, 428-429, 453, 529, 677
workforce, 29, 381, 584
Working capital, 6, 8, 12, 17, 23, 64-67, 69, 76-77, 81-82, 84-85, 87, 96, 150, 280, 282, 317, 406-413, 415-419, 421-428, 430-432, 434-435, 445-450, 453, 458-459, 467, 471, 474, 611-641, 645
workplace, 79, 91, 123
World, 3, 5, 7, 12-13, 17-19, 25, 31-33, 37, 42-43, 45-46, 73, 82, 103, 117, 126, 149, 163, 192, 201, 217, 223, 234, 251, 254, 285, 302, 309, 316, 330, 337, 345-346, 357, 409, 414, 420, 424, 453, 468, 500, 508, 524, 544, 548, 566, 579-580, 583, 590, 645-646, 654-655, 657-658, 664-666, 674, 679, 699, 701
World War, 590
WWW, 32-34, 38-39, 41-42, 47, 83, 95, 120, 126, 167, 198, 225, 236, 266, 290, 317, 327, 337, 350, 390, 424, 469, 508, 549, 575, 583, 604, 632-633, 638, 667, 689, 702

X

Xers, 405
    Generation Xers, 405

Y

Yankee bonds, 302
Yen, 302, 468, 646-648, 651-654, 664, 667-669, 679, 683
Yuan, 648

Z

Zero-sum game, 691